COGNITIVE PSYCHOLOGY

AN ANTHOLOGY OF THEORIES, APPLICATIONS, AND READINGS

REVISED EDITION

EDITED BY JEFFREY ANASTASI

SAM HOUSTON STATE UNIVERSITY

cognella
San Diego, CA

Bassim Hamadeh, CEO and Publisher
Christopher Foster, General Vice President
Michael Simpson, Vice President of Acquisitions
Jessica Knott, Managing Editor
Kevin Fahey, Cognella Marketing Manager
Jess Busch, Senior Graphic Designer
Jamie Giganti, Project Editor
Brian Fahey, Licensing Associate

First published in the United States of America in 2013 by Cognella, Inc.

Printed in the United States of America

ISBN: 978-1-62131-131-7 (PBK)

www.cognella.com 800.200.3908

CONTENTS

CHAPTER 1
Introduction to Cognitive Psychology and Its History

Cognition

JEFFREY S. ANASTASI

Cognitive psychology is the scientific study of the mental processes that underlie behavior. These mental processes comprise a number of areas, including attention, memory, perception, thinking, reasoning, problem solving, decision making, language, knowledge representation, mental imagery, and motivation and concept formation. This focus on mental processes contrasts with behaviorism, which studied only behaviors that could be directly observed. Cognitive psychology is flourishing at the beginning of the twenty-first century, and its principles have been applied to clinical and counseling psychology, personality theory, developmental psychology, social psychology, comparative psychology, forensics and legal psychology, and education, among other disciplines. Other independent schools of thought have developed from cognitive psychology, including cognitive science and cognitive neuroscience.

HISTORY

Some historians have argued that cognitive psychology represents a shift in the psychological paradigm away from the limits of behaviorism (Gardner 1985; Sperry 1993). Others suggest that cognitive psychology simply represents a return to the same topics that existed prior to the founding of behaviorism (Hergenhahn 1994, p. 555). Extensive evidence indicates that cognitive psychology does not represent the study of a novel topic but a return to a focus on mental events

that behaviorism failed to allow. Throughout the history of psychology, some form of cognitive psychology always existed (Hergenhahn 1997, p. 551). The questions raised by cognitive psychologists also occupied early thinkers. The ancient Greek philosopher Aristotle (384–322 BCE), for example, wrote on various topics in cognitive psychology. However, during the 1930s to 1950s, when radical behaviorism was experiencing its strongest period, it was generally accepted that cognitive events either did not exist or should be ignored by psychologists because they could not be studied objectively (Hergenhahn 1997, p. 551). However, as psychologists became less captivated by behaviorism, they began to shift toward a cognitive approach that was broader in scope than behaviorism.

The Downfall of Behaviorism Several findings led to the downfall of behaviorism and the eventual rise of cognitive psychology. According to strict behaviorism, two things must occur if an organism is to learn: (1) the organism must actually perform the behavior, and (2) the behavior must lead to some type of a consequence (i.e., reinforcement or punishment). The continuation of behaviorism's control of psychology rested on these basic premises. However, three major findings showed these premises to be unnecessary: cognitive maps, latent learning, and observational learning (or modeling).

Cognitive Maps and Latent Learning The American psychologist Edward Chace Tolman (1886–1959) is best known for his research on cognitive maps and latent learning. His work with cognitive maps showed that an organism could possess a mental representation of a physical space that would allow the organism to follow alternate routes to a food reward even if the organism was never reinforced for that route in the past (Tolman et al. 1946). Tolman's work with latent learning showed that rats were able to learn their way through a maze even if they never received reinforcement while they explored the maze (Tolman and Honzik 1930). In Tolman's study, the number of errors made by rats that were regularly rewarded gradually decreased as they learned their way through a maze. Other rats in a no-reward condition received no reinforcement for the first ten days of training but were simply placed in the maze for the same amount of time as the regularly rewarded rats. On the eleventh day, these rats were given a food reward. Much to the behaviorists' surprise, these rats made the same number of errors as the regularly rewarded rats on the twelfth day of training, rather than showing the gradual learning curve predicted by behaviorists. This research showed that the rats learned the maze, even without reinforcement.

Observational Learning and Modeling Psychologist Albert Bandura is probably best known for his work demonstrating observational learning. Bandura showed that organisms can learn by watching another organism receive reinforcement or punishment (Bandura et al. 1966). Thus, it is not necessary that the learner actually perform the behavior, nor must the learner receive reinforcement or punishment in order to learn.

Each of these findings failed to validate the most basic behaviorist premises. Additionally, many psychologists began to become less enchanted with behaviorism because of the limitations concerning what could be studied. For example, behaviorists felt that psychology should study only topics or phenomena that could be studied objectively and directly observed. Although cognitive psychology retained the practice of studying topics in an objective, scientific manner, the inclusion of only those topics that were based on direct observation was eliminated. While many research topics of interest to psychologists (thinking, perception, attention, motivation, emotion, decision processes, problem solving, language, etc.)

stood outside the realm of psychological study under behaviorism, many of these topics became central to the cognitive psychology movement and are still studied today.

The Rise of Cognitive Psychology Richard Robins, Samuel Gosling, and Kenneth Craik (1999) have presented an analysis of the gradual decline in the behaviorist approach and the eventual rise of cognitive psychology. Cognitive psychology became more and more influential as it overtook the behaviorist approach by 1970 based on the number of articles published in the most prominent psychology journals. There were, however, several important earlier publications and studies that led to the resurgence of cognitive psychology.

The German psychologist Hermann Ebbinghaus (1850–1909) demonstrated in 1885 that complex mental processes, such as memory, could be studied using an objective, experimental approach. He studied nonsense syllables (or letter strings that did not make up words, such as YHB) and recorded the number of trials it took to learn the list to perfection. He then measured the savings score (i.e., how much time was saved as one learned the list to perfection again) as a measure of memory.

The Principles of Psychology (1890) by William James (1842–1910) cited numerous studies investigating cognitive phenomena and discussed many topics that currently interest cognitive psychologists, such as attention, perception, memory, and reasoning. James also argued that the human mind does not simply react to stimuli in the environment (a common behaviorist idea) but instead is dynamic and interactive.

Remembering: A Study in Experimental and Social Psychology (1932), by British psychologist Frederic Charles Bartlett (1886–1969), showed that memory was predictable and subject to systematic errors. In particular, Bartlett noted that memory errors were influenced by the rememberer's attitudes, beliefs, schemas, and preconceptions. He proposed that memory is a constructive process such that our own interpretations and biases have a huge impact on what we remember, rather than remembering strictly verbatim information.

American psychologist George A. Miller is probably the one scientist who has had the largest impact in the formation of cognitive psychology as a formal school of thought. In fact, many historians have suggested that his article "The Magical Number Seven, Plus or Minus Two: Some Limits on our Capacity for Processing Information" (1956) was the official beginning of cognitive psychology. This article essentially defined the capacity limits of short-term memory.

Several additional events were also critical for the development of cognitive psychology as a formal school of thought. World War II (1939–1945) led to the development of cognitive psychology and human factors engineering (Proctor and Van Zandt 1994, p. 5). As more complex instruments were developed, the U.S. military became increasingly interested in how humans interacted with such instruments. These questions involved such topics as attention, memory, perception, and decision making. On September 11, 1956, many important researchers attended a symposium at the Massachusetts Institute of Technology and become excited about the direction of this new approach (Matlin 2005, p. 7). So important was this symposium that some historians have argued that this date marks the official beginning of cognitive psychology.

German-born psychologist Ulric Neisser coined the term *cognitive psychology* with the publication of his book *Cognitive Psychology* in 1967. The journal *Cognitive Psychology* was founded in 1969, providing an outlet for researchers specifically interested in cognitive topics. Fifteen additional journals focusing on cognitive psychology were established during the next twenty years, indicating a rise in interest in cognitive topics and the rise of cognitive psychology.

AREAS OF INTEREST IN COGNITIVE PSYCHOLOGY

Attention. This area of research looks at an array of topics that focus on our ability to pay attention to specific stimuli while excluding other stimuli (selective attention) or to pay attention to two stimuli at the same time (divided attention). Topics include pattern recognition, object recognition, selective attention, divided attention, and subliminal perception.

Perception. Perception is the use of previous knowledge to gather and interpret stimuli registered by the senses (Matlin 2005). This process actively organizes and interprets sensory information in order to make it meaningful. Perception is usually discussed in conjunction with sensory

processes with simple stimuli, but it is also studied in terms of how it functions in more complex social situations. For example, if someone bumped into you while walking down the street, your perception of the incident might be dependent upon the characteristics of the other individual. You might interpret it as an accident if an elderly woman bumped into you, but your interpretation might be different if the other person was a member of a group of boisterous teenagers.

Memory. This broad area of research focuses on the encoding, storage, and retrieval processes involved when one remembers information at a later time. Experts generally agree that memories are a result of not only the specific event that is being remembered but also the specific thoughts, emotions, and knowledge that the rememberer possesses. Furthermore, events or thoughts that occur after the encoded event also have an impact on what is remembered.

Language. This area of research focuses on how humans (and nonhumans) acquire and use language. There is also a major focus on the specific language rules (or grammar) that accompany language processing.

Thinking. This broad area of research includes various topics such as problem solving, decision making, mental imagery, and logic. The general focus is on the internal thought processes. Such thought processes may occur prior to overt behavior or during overt behavior, or they may occur as a result of external stimuli. Cognitive neuroscience may use brain-imaging techniques to provide objective measurements of when thinking occurs and which part of the brain is active during specific tasks.

Knowledge Representation. This area of research investigates how information is stored and accessed by the brain. Much of the research in this area focuses on mental models that explain how knowledge is stored in the brain. The two main codes that have been proposed for knowledge representation are based upon analog or propositional codes. Other major areas of research include categorization and how people utilize schemas and scripts in everyday life.

Artificial Intelligence. The information-processing approach to cognitive psychology uses the computer as a model for the human mind. This branch of cognitive psychology led to connectionist frameworks and the parallel distributed processing approach to studying cognition. The analogy that is the basis for the study of artificial intelligence is that computer connections between stored knowledge or idea units are similar to the physical, neural networks present in the brain (McClelland and Rumelhart 1985).

OTHER DISCIPLINES THAT EVOLVED FROM COGNITIVE PSYCHOLOGY

Cognitive Neuroscience. This area combines the basic research techniques and issues from cognitive psychology with various methods (e.g., brain scanning, event-related potential, and single-cell recording) to evaluate the physiological functioning of the brain. Cognitive neuroscience has helped scientists better understand how the brain works and what each part of the brain does, and it provides insight into brain abnormalities or damage.

Cognitive Science. Cognitive science is a multidisciplinary field that studies the workings of the mind by combining the approaches of cognitive psychology, neuroscience, and computer science. It may include other fields, such as philosophy, sociology, linguistics, and anthropology (Sobel 2001). Cognitive science takes a more holistic approach, since it utilizes techniques and theories from many different fields of study.

BIBLIOGRAPHY

Bandura, Albert, Joan E. Grusec, and Frances L. Menlove. 1966. Observational Learning as a Function of Symbolization and Incentive Set. *Child Development* 37: 499–506.

Bartlett, Frederic C. 1932. *Remembering: A Study in Experimental and Social Psychology*. New York: Macmillan.

Ebbinghaus, Hermann. (1885) 1913. *Memory: A Contribution to Experimental Psychology*. Trans. Henry A. Ruger and Clara E. Bussenues. New York: Teachers College, Columbia University.

Gardner, Howard. 1985. *The Mind's New Science: A History of the Cognitive Revolution*. New York: Basic Books.

Hergenhahn, B. R. 1994. *An Introduction to the History of Psychology*. 3rd ed. Pacific Grove, CA: Brooks/Cole. (5th ed. 2005. Belmont, CA: Wadsworth).

James, William. 1890. *The Principles of Psychology*. New York: Holt.

Matlin, Margaret W. 2005. *Cognition*. 6th ed. New York: Wiley.

McClelland, James L., and David E. Rumelhart. 1985. Distributed Memory and the Representation of General and Specific Information. *Journal of Experimental Psychology: General* 114: 159–188.

Miller, George A. 1956. The Magical Number Seven, Plus or Minus Two: Some Limits on our Capacity for Processing Information. *Psychological Review* 63: 81–97.

Neisser, Ulric. 1967. *Cognitive Psychology*. New York: Appleton-Century-Crofts.

Proctor, Robert W., and Trisha Van Zandt. 1994. *Human Factors in Simple and Complex Systems*. Needham Heights, MA: Allyn and Bacon.

Robins, Richard W., Samuel D. Gosling, and Kenneth H. Craik. 1999. An Empirical Analysis of Trends in Psychology. *American Psychologist* 54: 117–128.

Sobel, Carolyn P. 2001. *The Cognitive Sciences: An Interdisciplinary Approach*. Mountain View, CA: Mayfield.

Sperry, Roger W. 1993. The Impact and Promise of the Cognitive Revolution. *American Psychologist* 48: 878–885.

Tolman, Edward C., and Charles H. Honzik. 1930. Introduction and Removal of Reward, and Maze Performance in Rats. *University of California Publications in Psychology* 4: 257–273.

Tolman, Edward C., B. F. Ritchie, and D. Kalish. 1946. Studies in Spatial Learning II: Place Learning vs. Response Learning. *Journal of Experimental Psychology* 36: 221–229.

Psychology as the Behaviorist Views It

JOHN B. WATSON

Psychology as the behaviorist views it is a purely objective experimental branch of natural science. Its theoretical goal is the prediction and control of behavior. Introspection forms no essential part of its methods, nor is the scientific value of its data dependent upon the readiness with which they lend themselves to interpretation in terms of consciousness. The behaviorist, in his efforts to get a unitary scheme of animal response, recognizes no dividing line between man and brute. The behavior of man, with all of its refinement and complexity, forms only a part of the behaviorist's total scheme of investigation.

It has been maintained by its followers generally that psychology is a study of the science of the phenomena of consciousness. It has taken as its problem, on the one hand, the analysis of complex mental states (or processes) into simple elementary constituents, and on the other the construction of complex states when the elementary constituents are given. The world of physical objects (stimuli, including here anything which may excite activity in a receptor), which forms the total phenomena of the natural scientist, is looked upon merely as means to an end. That end is the production of mental states that may be 'inspected' or 'observed.' The psychological object of observation in the case of an emotion, for example, is the mental state itself. The problem in emotion is the determination of the number and kind of elementary constituents present, their loci, intensity, order of appearance, etc. It is agreed that introspection is the method *par excellence* by means of which mental states may be manipulated for purposes of psychology. On this assumption, behavior data (including under this term everything which goes under the name of comparative psychology) have no value *per se*. They possess significance only in so far as they may throw light upon conscious states.[1] Such data must have at least an analogical or indirect reference to belong to the realm of psychology.

Indeed, at times, one finds psychologists who are sceptical of even this analogical reference. Such scepticism is often shown by the question which is put to the student of behavior, "What is the bearing of animal work upon human psychology?" I used to have to study over this question. Indeed it always embarrassed me somewhat. I was interested in my own work and felt that it was important, and yet I could not trace any close connection between it and psychology as my questioner understood psychology. I hope that such a confession will clear the atmosphere to such an extent that we will no longer have to work under false pretences. We must frankly admit that the facts so important to us which we have been able to glean from extended work upon the senses of animals by the behavior method have contributed only in a fragmentary way to the general theory of human sense organ processes, nor have they suggested new points of experimental attack. The enormous number of experiments which we have carried out upon learning have likewise contributed little to human psychology. It seems reasonably clear that some kind of compromise must be effected: either psychology must change its viewpoint so as to take in facts of behavior, whether or not they have bearings upon the problems of 'consciousness'; or else behavior must stand alone as a wholly separate and independent science. Should human psychologists fail to look with favor upon our overtures and refuse to modify their position, the behaviorists will be driven to using human beings as subjects and to employ methods of investigation which are exactly comparable to those now employed in the animal work.

Any other hypothesis than that which admits the independent value of behavior material, regardless of any bearing such material may have upon consciousness, will inevitably force us to the absurd position of attempting to *construct* the conscious content of the animal whose behavior we have been studying. On this view, after having determined our animal's ability to learn, the simplicity or complexity of its methods of learning, the effect of past habit upon present response, the range of stimuli to which it ordinarily responds, the widened range to which it can respond under experimental conditions—in more general terms, its various problems and its various ways of solving them—we should still feel that the task is unfinished and that the results are worthless, until we can interpret them by analogy in the light of consciousness. Although we have solved our problem we feel uneasy and unrestful because of our definition of psychology: we feel forced to say something about the possible mental processes of our animal. We say that, having no eyes, its stream of consciousness cannot contain brightness and color sensations as we know them—having no taste buds this stream can contain no sensations of sweet, sour, salt and bitter. But on the other hand, since it does respond to thermal, tactual and organic stimuli, its conscious content must be made up largely of these sensations; and we usually add, to protect ourselves against the reproach of being anthropomorphic, "if it has any consciousness." Surely this doctrine which calls for an analogical interpretation of all behavior data may be shown to be false: the position that the standing of an observation upon behavior is determined by its fruitfulness in yielding results which are interpretable only in the narrow realm of (really human) consciousness.

This emphasis upon analogy in psychology has led the behaviorist somewhat afield. Not being willing to throw off the yoke of consciousness he feels impelled to make a place in the scheme of behavior where the rise of consciousness can be determined. This point has been a shifting one. A few years ago certain animals were supposed to possess 'associative memory,' while certain others were supposed to lack it. One meets this search for the origin of consciousness under a good many disguises. Some of our texts state that consciousness arises at the moment when reflex and instinctive activities fail properly to conserve the organism. A perfectly adjusted organism would be lacking in consciousness. On the other hand whenever we find the presence of diffuse activity which results in habit formation, we are justified in assuming consciousness. I must confess that these arguments had weight with me when I began the study of behavior. I fear that a good many of us are still viewing behavior problems with something like this in mind. More than one student in behavior has attempted to frame criteria of the psychic—to devise a set of objective, structural and functional criteria which, when applied in the particular instance, will enable us to decide whether such and such responses are positively conscious, *merely* indicative of consciousness, or whether they are purely 'physiological.' Such problems as these can no longer satisfy behavior men. It would be better to give up the province altogether and admit frankly that the study of the behavior of animals has no justification, than to admit that our search is of such a 'will o' the wisp' character. One can assume either the presence or the absence of consciousness anywhere in the phylogenetic scale without affecting the problems of behavior *by* one jot or one tittle; and without influencing in any way the mode of experimental attack upon them. On the other hand, I cannot for one moment assume that the paramecium responds to light; that the rat learns a problem more quickly by working at the task five times a day than once a day, or that the human child exhibits plateaux in his learning curves. These are questions which vitally concern behavior and which must be decided by direct observation under experimental conditions.

This attempt to reason by analogy from human conscious processes to the conscious processes in animals, and *vice versa*: to make consciousness, as the human being knows it, the center of reference of all behavior, forces us into a situation similar to that which existed in biology in Darwin's time. The whole Darwinian movement was judged by the bearing it had upon the origin and development of the human race. Expeditions were undertaken to collect material which would establish the position that the rise of the human race was a perfectly natural phenomenon and not an act of special creation. Variations were carefully sought along with the evidence for the heaping up effect and the weeding out effect of selection; for in these and the other Darwinian mechanisms were to be found factors sufficiently complex to account for the origin and race differentiation of man. The wealth of material collected at this time was considered valuable largely in so far as it tended to develop the concept of evolution in man. It is strange that this situation should have remained the dominant one in biology for so many years. The moment zoology undertook the experimental study of evolution and descent, the situation immediately changed. Man ceased to be the center of reference. I doubt if any experimental biologist today, unless actually engaged in the problem of race differentiation in man, tries to interpret his findings in terms of human evolution, or ever refers to it in his thinking. He gathers his data from the study of many species of plants and animals and tries to work out the laws of inheritance in the particular type upon which he is conducting experiments. Naturally, he follows the progress of the work upon race differentiation in man and in the descent of man, but he looks upon these as special topics, equal in importance with his own yet ones in which his interests will never be vitally engaged. It is not fair to say that all of his work is directed toward human evolution or that it must be interpreted in terms of human evolution. He does not have to dismiss certain of his facts on the inheritance of coat color in mice because, forsooth, they have little bearing upon, the differentiation of the *genus homo* into separate races, or upon the descent of the *genus homo* from some more primitive stock.

In psychology we are still in that stage of development where we feel that we must select our material. We have a general place of discard for processes, which we anathematize so far as their value for psychology is concerned by saying, "this is a reflex"; "that is a purely physiological fact which has nothing to do with psychology." We are not interested (as psychologists) in getting all of the processes of adjustment which the animal as a whole employs, and in finding how these various responses are associated, and how they fall apart, thus working out a systematic scheme for the prediction and control of response in general. Unless our observed facts are indicative of consciousness, we have no use for them, and unless our apparatus and method are designed to throw such facts into relief, they are thought of in just as disparaging a way. I shall always remember the remark one distinguished psychologist made as he looked over the color apparatus designed for testing the responses of animals to monochromatic light in the attic at Johns Hopkins. It was this: "And they call this psychology!"

I do not wish unduly to criticize psychology. It has failed signally, I believe, during the fifty-odd years of its existence as an experimental discipline to make its place in the world as an undisputed natural science. Psychology, as it is generally thought of, has something esoteric in its methods. If you fail to reproduce my findings, it is not due to some fault in your apparatus or in the control of your stimulus, but it is due to the fact that your introspection is untrained.[2] The attack is made upon the observer and not upon the experimental setting. In physics and in chemistry the attack is made upon the experimental conditions. The apparatus was not sensitive enough, impure chemicals were used, etc. In these sciences a better technique will give reproducible results. Psychology is otherwise. If you can't observe 3–9 states of clearness in attention, your introspection is poor. If, on the other hand, a feeling seems reasonably clear to you, your introspection is again faulty. You are seeing too much. Feelings are never clear.

The time seems to have come when psychology must discard all reference to consciousness; when it need no longer delude itself into thinking that it is making mental states the object of observation. We have become so enmeshed in speculative questions concerning the elements of mind, the nature of conscious content (for example, imageless thought, attitudes, and Bewusseinslage, etc.) that I, as an experimental student, feel that something is wrong with our premises and the types of problems which develop from them. There is no longer any guarantee that we all mean the same thing when we use the terms now current in psychology. Take the case of sensation. A sensation is defined in terms of its attributes. One psychologist will state with readiness that the attributes of a visual sensation are *quality, extension, duration,* and *intensity.* Another will add *clearness.* Still another that of *order.* I doubt if any one psychologist can draw up a set of statements describing what he means by sensation which will be agreed to by three other psychologists of different training. Turn for a moment to the question of the number of isolable sensations. Is there an extremely large number of color sensations—or only four red, green, yellow and blue? Again, yellow, while psychologically simple, can be obtained by superimposing red and green spectral rays upon the same diffusing surface! If, on the other hand, we say that every just noticeable difference in the spectrum is a simple sensation, and that every just noticeable increase in the white value of a given color gives simple sensations, we are forced to admit that the number is so large and the conditions for obtaining them so complex that the concept of sensation is unusable, either for the purpose of analysis or that of synthesis. Titchener, who has fought the most valiant fight in this country for a psychology based upon introspection, feels that these differences of opinion as to the number of sensations and their attributes; as to whether there are relations (in the sense of elements) and on the many others which seem to be fundamental in every attempt at analysis, are perfectly natural in the present undeveloped state of psychology. While it is admitted that every growing science is full of unanswered questions, surely only those who are wedded to the system as we now have it, who have fought and suffered for it, can confidently believe that there will ever be any greater uniformity than there is now in the answers we have to such questions. I firmly believe that two hundred years from now, unless the introspective method is discarded, psychology will still be divided on the question as to whether auditory sensations have the quality of 'extension,' whether intensity is an attribute which can be applied to color, whether there is a difference in 'texture' between image and sensation and upon many hundreds of others of like character.

The condition in regard to other mental processes is just as chaotic. Can image type be experimentally tested and verified? Are recondite thought processes dependent mechanically upon imagery at all? Are psychologists agreed upon what feeling is? One states that feelings are attitudes. Another finds them to be groups of organic sensations possessing a certain solidarity. Still another and larger group finds them to be new elements correlative with and ranking equally with sensations.

My psychological quarrel is not with the systematic and structural psychologist alone. The last fifteen years have seen the growth of what is called functional psychology. This type of psychology decries the use of elements in the static sense of the structuralists. It throws emphasis upon the biological significance of conscious processes instead of upon the analysis of conscious states into introspectively isolable elements. I have done my best to understand the difference between functional psychology and structural psychology. Instead of clarity, confusion grows upon me. The terms sensation, perception, affection, emotion, volition are used as much by the functionalist as by the structuralist. The addition of the word 'process' ('mental act as a whole,' and like terms are frequently met) after each serves in some way to remove the corpse of 'content' and to leave 'function' in its stead. Surely if these concepts are elusive when looked at from a content standpoint, they are still more deceptive when viewed from the angle of function, and especially so when function is obtained by the introspection method. It is rather interesting that no functional psychologist has carefully distinguished between 'perception' (and this is true of the other psychological terms as well) as employed by the systematise and 'perceptual process' as used in functional psychology. It seems illogical and hardly fair to criticize the psychology which the systematist gives us, and then to utilize his terms without carefully showing the changes in meaning which are to be attached to them. I was greatly surprised some time ago when I opened Pillsbury's book and saw psychology defined as the 'science of behavior.' A still more recent text states that psychology is the 'science of mental behavior.' When I saw these promising statements I thought, now surely we will have texts based upon different lines. After a few pages the science of behavior is dropped and one finds the conventional treatment of sensation, perception, imagery, etc., along with certain shifts in emphasis and additional facts which serve to give the author's personal imprint.

One of the difficulties in the way of a consistent functional psychology is the parallelistic hypothesis. If the functionalist attempts to express his formulations in terms which make mental states really appear to function, to play some active role in the world of adjustment, he almost inevitably lapses into terms which are connotative of interaction. When taxed with this he replies that it is more convenient to do so and that he does it to avoid the circumlocution and clumsiness which are inherent in any thoroughgoing parallelism.[3] As a matter of fact I believe the functionalist actually thinks in terms of interaction and resorts to parallelism only when forced to give expression to his views. I feel that *behaviorism* is the only consistent and logical functionalism. In it one avoids both the Scylla of parallelism and the Charybdis of interaction. Those time-honored relics of philosophical speculation need trouble the student of behavior as little as they trouble the student of physics. The consideration of the mind-body problem affects neither the type of problem selected nor the formulation of the solution of that problem. I can state my position here no better than by saying that I should like to bring my students up in the same ignorance of such hypotheses as one finds among the students of other branches of science.

This leads me to the point where I should like to make the argument constructive. I believe we can write a psychology, define it as Pillsbury, and never go back upon our definition: never use the terms consciousness, mental states, mind, content, introspectively verifiable, imagery, and the like. I believe that we can do it in a few years without running into the absurd terminology of Beer, Bethe, Von Uexküll, Nuel, and that of the so-called objective schools generally. It can be done in terms of stimulus and response, in terms of habit formation, habit integrations and the like. Furthermore, I believe that it is really worth while to make this attempt now.

The psychology which I should attempt to build up would take as a starting point, first, the observable fact that organisms, man and animal alike, do adjust themselves to their environment by means of hereditary and habit equipments. These adjustments may be very adequate or they may be so inadequate that the organism barely maintains its existence; secondly, that certain stimuli lead the organisms to make the responses. In a system of psychology completely worked out, given the response the stimuli can be predicted; given the stimuli the response can be predicted. Such a set of statements is crass and raw in the extreme, as all such generalizations must be. Yet they are hardly more raw and less realizable than the ones which appear in the psychology texts of the day I possibly might illustrate my point better by choosing an everyday problem which anyone is likely to meet in the course of his work. Some time ago I was called upon to make a study of certain species of birds. Until I went to Tortugas I had never seen these birds alive. When I reached there I found the animals doing certain things: some of the acts seemed to work peculiarly well in such an environment, while others seemed to be unsuited to their type of life. I first studied the responses of the group as a whole and later those of

individuals. In order to understand more thoroughly the relation between what was habit and what was hereditary in these responses, I took the young birds and reared them. In this way I was able to study the order of appearance of hereditary adjustments and their complexity, and later the beginnings of habit formation. My efforts in determining the stimuli which called forth such adjustments were crude indeed. Consequently my attempts to control behavior and to produce responses at will did not meet with much success. Their food and water, sex and other social relations, light and temperature conditions were all beyond control in a field study. I did find it possible to control their reactions in a measure by using the nest and egg (or young) as stimuli. It is not necessary in this paper to develop further how such a study should be carried out and how work of this kind must be supplemented by carefully controlled laboratory experiments. Had I been called upon to examine the natives of some of the Australian tribes, I should have gone about my task in the same way. I should have found the problem more difficult: the types of responses called forth by physical stimuli would have been more varied, and the number of effective stimuli larger. I should have had to determine the social setting of their lives in a far more careful way. These savages would be more influenced by the responses of each other than was the case with the birds. Furthermore, habits would have been more complex and the influences of past habits upon the present responses would have appeared more clearly. Finally, if I had been called upon to work out the psychology of the educated European, my problem would have required several lifetimes. But in the one I have at my disposal I should have followed the same general line of attack. In the main, my desire in all such work is to gain an accurate knowledge of adjustments and the stimuli calling them forth. My final reason for this is to learn general and particular methods by which I may control behavior. My goal is not "the description and explanation of states of consciousness as such," nor that of obtaining such proficiency in mental gymnastics that I can immediately lay hold of a state of consciousness and say, "this, as a whole, consists of gray sensation number 350, of such and such extent, occurring in conjunction with the sensation of cold of a certain intensity; one of pressure of a certain intensity and extent," and so on *ad infinitum*. If psychology would follow the plan I suggest, the educator, the physician, the jurist and the business man could utilize our data in a practical way, as soon as we are able, experimentally, to obtain them. Those who have occasion to apply psychological principles practically would find no need to complain as they do at the present time. Ask any physician or jurist today whether scientific psychology plays a practical part in his daily routine and you will hear him deny that the psychology of the laboratories finds a place in his scheme of work. I think the criticism is extremely just. One of the earliest conditions which made me dissatisfied with psychology was the feeling that there was no realm of application for the principles which were being worked out in content terms.

What gives me hope that the behaviorist's position is a defensible one is the fact that those branches of psychology which have already partially withdrawn from the parent, experimental psychology, and which are consequently less dependent upon introspection are today in a most flourishing condition. Experimental pedagogy, the psychology of drugs, the psychology of advertising, legal psychology, the psychology of tests, and psychopathology are all vigorous growths. These are sometimes wrongly called "practical" or "applied" psychology. Surely there was never a worse misnomer. In the future there may grow up vocational bureaus which really apply psychology. At present these fields are truly scientific and are in search of broad generalizations which will lead to the control of human behavior. For example, we find out by experimentation whether a series of stanzas may be acquired more readily if the whole is learned at once, or whether it is more advantageous to learn each stanza separately and then pass to the succeeding. We do not attempt to apply our findings. The application of this principle is purely voluntary on the part of the teacher. In the psychology of drugs we may show the effect upon behavior of certain doses of caffeine. We may reach the conclusion that caffeine has a good effect upon the speed and accuracy of work. But these are general principles. We leave it to the individual as to whether the results of our tests shall be applied or not. Again, in legal testimony, we test the effects of recency upon the reliability of a witness's report. We test the accuracy of the report with respect to moving objects, stationary objects, color, etc. It depends upon the judicial machinery of the country to decide whether these facts are ever to be applied. For a 'pure' psychologist to say that he is not interested in the questions raised in these divisions of the science because they relate indirectly to the application of psychology shows, in the first place, that he fails to understand the scientific aim in such problems, and secondly, that he is not interested in a psychology which concerns itself with human life. The only fault I have to find with these disciplines is that much of their material is stated in terms of introspection, whereas a statement in terms of objective results would be far more valuable. There is no reason why appeal should ever be made to consciousness in any of them. Or why introspective data should ever be sought during the experimentation, or published in the results. In experimental pedagogy especially, one can see the desirability of keeping all of the results on a purely objective plane. If this is done, work there on the human being will be comparable directly with the work upon animals. For example, at Hopkins, Mr. Ulrich has obtained certain results upon the distribution of effort in learning—using rats as subjects. He is prepared to give comparative results upon the effect of having an animal work at the problem once per day, three times per day, and five times per day. Whether it is advisable to have the animal learn only one problem at a time or to learn three abreast. We need to have similar experiments made upon man, but we care as little about his 'conscious processes' during the conduct of the experiment as we care about such processes in the rats.

I am more interested at the present moment in trying to show the necessity for maintaining uniformity in experimental procedure and in the method of stating results in both human and animal work, than in developing any ideas I may have upon the changes which are certain to come in the scope of human psychology. Let us consider for a moment the subject of the range of stimuli to which animals respond. I shall speak first of the work upon vision in animals. We put our animal in a situation where he will respond (or learn to respond) to one of two monochromatic lights. We feed him at the one (positive) and punish him at the other (negative). In a short time the animal learns to go to the light at which he is fed. At this point questions arise which I may phrase in two ways: I may choose the psychological way and say "does the animal see these two lights as I do, *i.e.,* as two distinct colors, or does he see them as two grays differing in brightness, as does the totally color blind?" Phrased by the behaviorist, it would read as follows: "Is my animal responding upon the basis of the difference in intensity between the two stimuli, or upon the difference in wave-lengths ?" He nowhere thinks of the animal's response in terms of his own experiences of colors and grays. He wishes to establish the fact whether wave-length is a factor in that animal's adjustment.[4] If so, what wave-lengths are effective and what differences in wave-length must be maintained in the different regions to afford bases for differential responses? If wave-length is not a factor in adjustment he wishes to know what difference in intensity will serve as a basis for response, and whether that same difference will suffice throughout the spectrum. Furthermore, he wishes to test whether the animal can respond to wave-lengths which do not affect the human eye. He is as much interested in comparing the rat's spectrum with that of the chick as in comparing it with man's. The point of view when the various sets of comparisons are made does not change in the slightest.

However we phrase the question to ourselves, we take our animal after the association has been formed and then introduce certain control experiments which enable us to return answers to the questions just raised. But there is just as keen a desire on our part to test man under the same conditions, and to state the results in both cases in common terms.

The man and the animal should be placed as nearly as possible under the same experimental conditions. Instead of feeding or punishing the human subject, we should ask him to respond by setting a second apparatus until standard and control offered no basis for a differential response. Do I lay myself open to the charge here that I am using introspection? My reply is not at all; that while I might very well feed my human subject for a right choice and punish him for a wrong one and thus produce the response if the subject could give it, there is no need of going to extremes even on the platform I suggest. But be it understood that I am merely using this second method as an abridged behavior method.[5] We can go just as far and reach just as dependable results by the longer method as by the abridged. In many cases the direct and typically human method cannot be safely used. Suppose for example, that I doubt the accuracy of the setting of the control instrument, in the above experiment, as I am very likely to do if suspect a defect in vision? It is hopeless for me to get his introspective report. He will say: "There is no difference in sensation, both are reds, identical in quality." But suppose I confront him with the standard and the control and so

arrange conditions that he is punished if he responds to the control but not with the standard. I interchange the positions of the standard and the control at will and force him to attempt to differentiate the one from the other. If he can learn to make the adjustment even after a large number of trials it is evident that the two stimuli do afford the basis for a differential response. Such a method may sound nonsensical, but I firmly believe we will have to resort increasingly to just such methods where we have reason to distrust the language method.

There is hardly a problem in human vision which is not also a problem in animal vision: I mention the limits of the spectrum, threshold values, absolute and relative, flicker, Talbot's law, Weber's law, field of vision, the Purkinje phenomenon, etc. Every one is capable of being worked out by behavior methods. Many of them are being worked out at the present time.

I feel that all the work upon the senses can be consistently carried forward along the lines I have suggested here for vision. Our results will, in the end, give an excellent picture of what each organ stands for in the way of function. The anatomist and the physiologist may take our data and show, on the one hand, the structures which are responsible for these responses, and, on the other, the physico-chemical relations which are necessarily involved (physiological chemistry of nerve and muscle) in these and other reactions.

The situation in regard to the study of memory is hardly different. Nearly all of the memory methods in actual use in the laboratory today yield the type of results I am arguing for. A certain series of nonsense syllables or other material is presented to the human subject. What should receive the emphasis are the rapidity of the habit formation, the errors, peculiarities in the form of the curve, the persistence of the habit so formed, the relation of such habits to those formed when more complex material is used, etc. Now such results are taken down with the subject's introspection. The experiments are made for the purpose of discussing the mental machinery[6] involved in learning, in recall, recollection and forgetting, and not for the purpose of seeking the human being's way of shaping his responses to meet the problems in the terribly complex environment into which he is thrown, nor for that of showing the similarities and differences between man's methods and those of other animals.

The situation is somewhat different when we come to a study of the more complex forms of behavior, such as imagination, judgment, reasoning, and conception. At present the only statements we have of them are in content terms.[7]

Our minds have been so warped by the fifty-odd years which have been devoted to the study of states of consciousness that we can envisage these problems only in one way. We should meet the situation squarely and say that we are not able to carry forward investigations along all of these lines by the behavior methods which are in use at the present time. In extenuation I should like to call attention to the paragraph above where I made the point that the introspective method itself has reached a *cul-de-sac* with respect to them. The topics have become so threadbare from much handling that they may well be put away for a time. As our methods become better developed it will be possible to undertake investigations of more and more complex forms of behavior. Problems which are now laid aside will again become imperative, but they can be viewed as they arise from a new angle and in more concrete settings.

Will there be left over in psychology a world of pure psychics, to use Yerkes' term? I confess I do not know. The plans which I most favor for psychology lead practically to the ignoring of consciousness in the sense that that term is used by psychologists today. I have virtually denied that this realm of psychics is open to experimental investigation. I don't wish to go further into the problem at present because it leads inevitably over into metaphysics. If you will grant the behaviorist the right to use consciousness in the same way that other natural scientists employ it—that is, without making consciousness a special object of observation—you have granted all that my thesis requires.

In concluding, I suppose I must confess to a deep bias on these questions. I have devoted nearly twelve years to experimentation on animals. It is natural that such a one should drift into a theoretical position which is in harmony with his experimental work. Possibly I have put up a straw man and have been fighting that. There may be no absolute lack of harmony between the position outlined here and that of functional psychology. I am inclined to think, however, that the two positions cannot be easily harmonized. Certainly the position I advocate is weak enough at present and can be attacked from many standpoints. Yet

when all this is admitted I still feel that the considerations which I have urged should have a wide influence upon the type of psychology which is to be developed in the future. What we need to do is to start work upon psychology, making *behavior,* not *consciousness,* the objective point of our attack. Certainly there are enough problems in the control of behavior to keep us all working many lifetimes without ever allowing us time to think of consciousness *an sich.* Once launched in the undertaking, we will find ourselves in a short time as far divorced from an introspective psychology as the psychology of the present time is divorced from faculty psychology.

SUMMARY

1. Human psychology has failed to make good its claim as a natural science. Due to a mistaken notion that its fields of facts are conscious phenomena and that introspection is the only direct method of ascertaining these facts, it has enmeshed itself in a series of speculative questions which, while fundamental to its present tenets, are not open to experimental treatment. In the pursuit of answers to these questions, it has become further and further divorced from contact with problems which vitally concern human interest.

2. Psychology, as the behaviorist views it, is a purely objective, experimental branch of natural science which needs introspection as little as do the sciences of chemistry and physics. It is granted that the behavior of animals can be investigated without appeal to consciousness. Heretofore the viewpoint has been that such data have value only in so far as they can be interpreted by analogy in terms of consciousness. The position is taken here that the behavior of man and the behavior of animals must be considered on the same plane; as being equally essential to a general understanding of behavior. It can dispense with consciousness in a psychological sense. The separate observation of 'states of consciousness' is, on this assumption, no more a part of the task of the psychologist than of the physicist. We might call this the return to a non-reflective and naive use of consciousness. In this sense consciousness may be said to be the instrument or tool with which all scientists

work. Whether or not the tool is properly used at present by scientists is a problem for philosophy and not for psychology.

3. From the viewpoint here suggested the facts on the behavior of amoebae have value in and for themselves without reference to the behavior of man. In biology studies on race differentiation and inheritance in amoebae form a separate division of study which must be evaluated in terms of the laws found there. The conclusions so reached may not hold in any other form. Regardless of the possible lack of generality, such studies must be made if evolution as a whole is ever to be regulated and controlled. Similarly the laws of behavior in amoebae, the range of responses, and the determination of effective stimuli, of habit formation, persistency of habits, interference and reinforcement of habits, must be determined and evaluated in and for themselves, regardless of their generality, or of their bearing upon such laws in other forms, if the phenomena of behavior are ever to be brought within the sphere of scientific control.

4. This suggested elimination of states of consciousness as proper objects of investigation in themselves will remove the barrier from psychology which exists between it and the other sciences. The findings of psychology become the functional correlates of structure and lend themselves to explanation in physico-chemical terms.

5. Psychology as behavior will, after all, have to neglect but few of the really essential problems with which psychology as an introspective science now concerns itself. In all probability even this residue of problems may be phrased in such a way that refined methods in behavior (which certainly must come) will lead to their solution.

NOTES

1. That is, either directly upon the conscious state of the observer or indirectly upon the conscious state of the experimenter.

2. In this connection I call attention to the controversy now on between the adherents and the opposers of imageless thought. The 'types of reactors' (sensory and motor) were also matters of bitter dispute. The complication experiment was the source of another war of words concerning the accuracy of the opponents' introspection

3. My colleague, Professor H. C. Warren, by whose advice this article was offered to the Review, believes that the parallelist can avoid the interaction terminology completely by exercising a little care.

4. He would have exactly the same attitude as if he were conducting an experiment to show whether an ant would crawl over a pencil laid across the trail or go round it.

5. I should prefer to look upon this abbreviated method, where the human subject is told in words, for example, to equate two stimuli; or to state in words whether a given stimulus is present or absent, etc., as the language method in behaviour. It in no way changes the status of experimentation. The method becomes possible merely by virtue of the fact that in the particular case the experimenter and his animal have systems of abbreviations or shorthand behaviour signs (language), any one of which may stand for a habit belonging to the repertoire both of the experimenter and his subject. To make the data obtained but the language method virtually the whole of behaviour—or to attempt to mould all of the data obtained by other methods in terms of the one which has by all odds the most limited range—is putting the cart before the horse with a vengeance.

6. They are often undertaken apparently for the purpose of making crude pictures of what must or must not go on in the nervous system.

7. There is need of questioning more and more the existence of what psychology calls imagery. Until a few years ago I thought that centrally aroused visual sensations were as clear as those peripherally aroused. I had never accredited myself with any other kind. However, closer examination leads me to deny in my own case the presence of imagery in the Galtonian sense. The whole doctrine of the centrally aroused image is, I believe, at present, on a very insecure foundation. Angell as well as Fernald reach the conclusion that an objective determination of image type is impossible. It would be an interesting confirmation of their experimental work if we should find by degrees that

we have been mistaken in building up this enormous structure of the centrally aroused sensation (or image). The hypothesis that all of the so-called 'higher thought' processes go on in terms of faint reinstatements of the original muscular act (including speech here) and that these are integrated into systems which respond in serial order (associative mechanisms) is, I believe, a tenable one. It makes reflective processes as mechanical as habit. The scheme of habit which James long ago described—where each return or afferent current releases the next appropriate motor discharge—is as true for 'thought processes' as for overt muscular acts. Paucity of 'imagery' would be the rule. In other words, wherever there are thought processes there are faint contractions of the systems of musculature involved in the overt exercise of the customary act, and especially in the still finer systems of musculature involved in speech. If this is true, and I do not see how it can be gainsaid, imagery becomes a mental luxury (even if it really exists) without any functional significance whatever. If experimental procedure justifies this hypothesis, we shall have at hand tangible phenomena which may be studied as behavior material. I should say that the day when we can study reflective processes by such methods is about as far off as the day when we can tell by physico-chemical methods the difference in the structure and arrangement of molecules between living protoplasm and inorganic substances. The solutions of both problems await the advent of methods and apparatus.

After writing this paper I heard the addresses of Professors Thorndike and Angell, at the Cleveland meeting of the American Psychological Association. I hope to have the opportunity to discuss them at another time. I must even here attempt to answer one question raised by Thorndike.

Thorndike casts suspicions upon ideo-motor action. If by ideo-motor action he means just that and would not include sensori-motor action in his general denunciation, I heartily agree with him. I should throw out imagery altogether and attempt to show that practically all natural thought goes on in terms of sensori-motor processes in the larynx (but not in terms of 'imageless thought') which rarely come to consciousness in any person who has not groped for imagery in the psychological laboratory. This easily explains why so many of the well-educated laity know nothing of imagery. I doubt if Thorndike conceives of the matter in this way. He and Woodworth seem to have neglected the speech mechanisms.

It has been shown that improvement in habit comes unconsciously. The first we know of it is when it is achieved—when it becomes an object. I believe that 'consciousness' has just as little to do with improvement in thought processes. Since, according to my view, thought processes are really motor habits in the larynx, improvements, short cuts, changes, etc., in these habits are brought about in the same way that such changes are produced in other motor habits. This view carries with it the implication that there are no reflective processes (centrally initiated processes): The individual is always examining objects, in the one case objects in the now accepted sense, in the other their substitutes, viz., the movements in the speech musculature. From this it follows that there is no theoretical limitation of the behavior method. There remains, to be sure, the practical difficulty, which may never be overcome, of examining speech movements in the way that general bodily behavior may be examined.)

Studies in Spatial Learning

Orientation and the Short-Cut

E.C. TOLMAN, B.F. RITCHIE, AND D. KALISH

A. INTRODUCTION

It is the purpose of the present series of experimental reports, of which this is the first, to develop some of the important implications of the senior author's 'theory of expectancy.' We feel that no altogether clear or precise formulation of this theory has previously been presented, largely because the data relevant for such a formulation were not known. The original formulations were admittedly rough and vague. The presentation of the theory in a rough form was, however, perhaps excusable, since it was hoped that further experimental work would be undertaken which would enable such a first formulation to be replaced by one more precise.

One of the consequences of stating the theory in its original rough fashion has apparently been to make it difficult to distinguish the theory from alternative stimulus-response doctrines. For as the argument has progressed it has appeared that, when analyzed, most of the statements of the expectancy theory turned out to sound little different from statements of the opposed stimulus-response theories. Consider for example the following exposition of the expectancy theory as presented by Hilgard and Marquis:

> According to Tolman, in learning a sequence of acts leading to a goal the subject follows 'signs' which mark out the 'behavior-route' leading to the 'significate' or goal. ... In the presence of the 'signs' the subject 'expects' the goal to appear if it follows the 'behavior-route.' (6, p. 88)

Although this statement of the expectancy theory is relatively justified in terms of some of the past formulations given by the senior author, the present writers now feel that it misses the main intent of the theory of expectancy. To make clear why we believe that this is so, let us analyze the implications of such a statement of the theory.

Editor's Note. This article is a reprint of an original work published in 1946 in the *Journal of Experimental Psychology.* 36, 13–24.

The cost of this investigation was met in part by grants to the Department of Psychology from the Research Board of the University of California.

In terms of the passage quoted, let us consider what would be meant by the further specific statement: "This rat expects food at location *L*." In other words, we wish to know how in such a case the term 'expectation' is to be introduced or defined. Implicit in the usual formulations of the expectancy theory (that is, in such a formulation as that just quoted from Hilgard and Marquis), is a definition of the term 'expectation' that makes it equivalent to 'the tendency of an animal to respond in a particular fashion, when appropriately motivated.' Although the term 'expectation' has not previously been given a precise definition, we now believe that the following formulation expresses what is implicit in such usual and earlier formulations:

> When we assert that a rat expects food at location *L*, what we assert is that *if* (1) the rat has been deprived of food for more than twelve hours, (2) he has been trained on path *P*, and (3) he is now placed on path *P*, *then* he will run down path *P*. When we assert that he does not expect food at location *L*, what we assert is that under the same conditions he will *not* run down path *P*.

Such a definition can be expressed formally by means of a conditioned definition of the form: "$P \supset (Q \equiv R)$."[1] The following then, is a conditioned definition which introduces the matrix "*x* expects food at location *L*":

> DF. 1. If *x* is deprived of food and *x* has been trained on path *P* and *x* is now put on path *P*, *then* (*x* runs down path *P* = *x* expects food at location *L*).[2]

This definition, we claim, was implicit in all or most of the earlier formulations of the expectancy theory. We further believe that this definition does not accord with our real intentions as to how the term should be used.

The reason that Definition I does not conform to our intention is that when 'expectation' is defined in such a fashion there seems to be little difference between the expectancy theory and the stimulus-response theories. The latter theories assert that what is learned in any spatial problem is a response-tendency (i.e., a tendency to take the path on which the animal was trained), whenever the animal is appropriately motivated. In the definition of 'expectation' which we have given above, the expectancy theory also asserts that what is learned is a tendency to make a particular response. Thus, the differences between the stimulus-response and expectancy theories, when 'expectation' is defined in such a fashion, are purely terminological. What we would call 'signs,' they would call 'stimuli,' and what they would call 'response-tendencies' we would call 'expectations.'

As a consequence we wish now to reject Definition I and write a new one which we believe will better express the original intent of the senior author, and will make clear the difference between the complete expectancy theory and its rivals. The following, then, expresses our present decision about what we shall mean by the expression "*x* expects food at location *L*":

> When we assert that a rat expects food at location L, what we assert is that if (1) he is deprived of food, (2) he has been trained on path *P*, (3) he is now put on path *P*, (4) path *P* is now blocked, and (5) there are other paths which lead away from path *P*, one of which points directly to location *L*, *then* he will run down the path which points directly to location *L*.

> When we assert that he does *not* expect food at location *L*, what we assert is that, under the same conditions, he will *not* run down the path which points directly to location *L*.

The following is a formal expression of this decision by means of a conditioned definition:

> DF. II. If *x* is deprived of food and *x* has been trained on path *P* and *x* is now put on path *P* and path *P* is now blocked and there are other paths which lead away from path *P*, one of which points directly to location *L*, then (*x* runs down the path which points directly to location *L* = *x* expects food at location *L*).

What Definition II states is that the truth-value of the matrix "*x* expects food at location *L*" is considered identical to that of the matrix "*x* runs down the path which points directly to location *L*" whenever the conditions stated by the antecedent are fulfilled.

Now although it is nonsense to inquire whether any definition is true or false, since it merely expresses a decision about how we will use words, it is extremely important to determine whether the class defined by any definition has any members. That is, it is extremely important in our case, to know whether there are any rats which do in fact take the shortest path to the goal location, when the original path is blocked. This is obviously an empirical problem and can only be settled by experiment. It is, then, the purpose of the experiment reported in this paper to determine the answer to this question.

B. SUBJECTS

Fifty-six female rats, approximately three months old, were used in this experiment. These rats came from the Tryon stock, and 26 of them were Tryon 'brights' and 30 were Tryon 'dulls' (13). Six days before the beginning of our experiment they concluded an 18 day series of daily trials on the Tryon *automatic* maze. Thus, before the beginning of our experiment these rats were 'maze-wise,' and had been trained to a 24-hour wet-food maintenance schedule. All of the trials on the Tryon maze were run in the afternoon between one and five P.M. In our experiment, on the other hand, all trials were run at night between eight and eleven P.M.

C. APPARATUS

Figs. 1 and 2 present diagrams of the apparatus which were used. In Fig. 1 we see the apparatus used in the preliminary training. It consisted of an unpainted wooden circular table top, which was three feet in diameter, and several unpainted pine elevated paths which were two in. in width. Path *AB* was 24 in. in length and was used as a starting path. Paths *CD, DE,* and *EF* were all 18 in. in length, while path *FG* was 60 in. long. A stand with a sliding food-box was located at the end of path *FG*, and whenever a rat entered one of its stalls the whole box moved in the direction indicated by the arrow, until an empty stall was ready for the next rat. Each stall was 4 in. wide, 10 in. deep, and 6 in. high. Within each stall was placed a white glass bird-bath, and on the rim of this bird-bath was placed a half-teaspoon of wet food. A 5-watt bulb in an ordinary desk lamp was the only illumination in the room. It was located at *H*, six in. behind the sliding food-box. The reflector on this lamp was turned in such a way that the light was primarily directed down path *FG*. Fastened to the sides of path *CD* were two pieces of unpainted plywood, which were 18 in. high and 30 in. in length. These formed an alley which began in the middle of the table-top and ended just at the point where path *CD* turns into path *DE*.

In Fig. 2 we see the apparatus used in the test trial. This consisted of the same starting path, circular table-top, alley

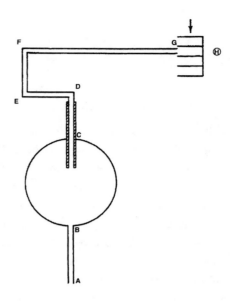

Figure 1. *Apparatus used in preliminary training.*

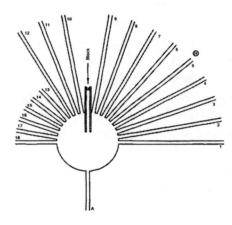

Figure 2. *Apparatus used in the test trial.*

on path *CD*, and lamp at *H*. But the food-box and paths *DE, EF,* and *FG* were removed. At the end of the alley on path *CD*, a block was placed. Then 12 six-foot unpainted pine paths were placed around the circular table-top. These paths began at a point 90 degrees to the right of path *CD* and radiated in a counter-clockwise fashion, each path being placed 10 degrees to the left of its neighbor. These paths were firmly nailed to a supporting structure so that the table-top could be revolved independently of these paths.

The six 24-in. paths to the left of the last six-foot path were shorter because the size of the room in which the experiment was conducted did not permit any greater length.

D. METHOD

Pre-test procedures. Two days before the first run on the apparatus in Fig. 1, the rats were put on a 24-hour wet-food maintenance schedule, being fed every evening at 10:30 P.M.

On Day 1 the rats were given three trials. On the first trial they were put by hand into the food-box and allowed to eat for five min. On the second trial they were put in the middle of path *FG* and allowed to run to *G* and into the food-boxes. On the third trial they were started at *F* and allowed to run into the food-boxes. They were then returned to their home cages and fed their full ration approximately 30 min. later.

On Day 2 they were given three more trials. On the first trial they ran from *F* to the food-boxes. On the second trial they were put by hand into the alley on path *CD* and forced to run from there out onto path *DE* and from there to the food-boxes. This was repeated on the third trial.

On Day 3 they were again given three trials. On the first trial they were forced to run out of the alley on path *CD*. On the second and third trials they were started at *A* and allowed to explore the table-top, run through the tunnel and on to the food-boxes.

On Day 4 they were given three trials starting from *A* in the same manner as on the last two trials on Day 3. Thus, after their training on Day 4, each rat had run five times to the food-boxes at *G,* from the starting place at *A*.

Test procedures. On Day 5 one test trial was given. The apparatus was changed to that represented in Fig. 2. Each rat was started at *A*, allowed to run into the blocked alley on *CD*, to return out of the alley, and to explore the table-top and the various alternative paths which radiated from it. The rat's trial ended as soon as it had chosen one of the paths and had run out to the end of it. If any rat took more than six min. to make such a choice it was removed. This was indicated in the protocol record by the expression 'No choice.' The circular table-top was revolved after each rat had run across it, and before the next one was started. This was done to prevent any possibility of 'tracking.'

E. RESULTS

On the test trial three of the 56 rats were discarded because they made 'No choice' after six min. After having explored all of the paths and the table-top, all three of these rats returned to the center of the table and refused to move from there except to return either to the alley or to the starting place.

Of the remaining 53 rats, 19, or 36 percent, chose path No. 6 which ended at a point four in. to the left of the place where the food-box entrance had been during the pre-test trials. This path No. 6 was, of all the paths offered, the most direct path to the former goal location.

The remaining 34 rats were distributed in a 'random' fashion over the other 11 paths. The distribution of the total group of the 53 rats is represented in the graph in Fig. 3.

The mean choice time for the 53 rats was three min. and 28 sec, while no rat chose a path in less than 85 sec. Their behavior during the time before they made a choice consisted chiefly in (1) returns to the blocked ally and to the starting point, and (2) exploration of the table-top and paths. In exploring these paths they would run out 12 to 18 in. and then return to the table-top. It was also observed that all rats which went out on any path more than 24 in. continued running until they reached the end of the path. No rat made any choice without having first gone around the edge of the table-top at least once, and without having tentatively explored more than one other path.

Two points should be noted about the frequencies of the other paths. (1) The relatively large number of rats, 9, or 17 percent, which chose path No. 1, may have been an artifact of the experimental apparatus. Path No. 1 was the last of the paths offered on the right-hand side. Thus, we might suppose that had there been more paths after No. 1, some of the rats which chose No. 1 would have chosen these others. The fact that there was no such 'piling-up' on path No. 12, can be explained by the fact that this was not the last path on the left-hand side. There were the six additional two-foot paths. These were not included in the graph in Fig. 3 because they were not considered comparable to the longer paths. Their importance, however, was probably negligible, since only eight of the 56 rats chose any of these shorter paths. But, it is important to notice that of these eight rats, four were ones which later chose path No. 1. Thus, almost half of the rats recorded on No. 1

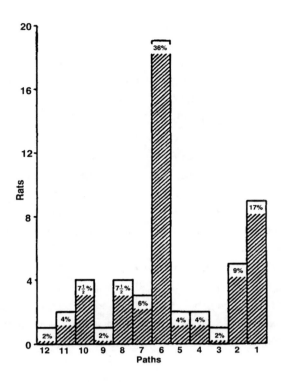

Figure 3. *Numbers of rats which chose each of the paths.*

chose this path only after having chosen one of the shorter paths.

(2) One should also notice the frequencies on paths No. 9 and No. 10. These two paths are the ones that are most similar, or spatially closest to, the original path on which the rats were practiced during the pre-test training. The *combined* frequencies of these two paths is only nine percent.

Finally, of the 19 rats which chose path No. 6, 10 were Tryon 'brights' and nine were Tryon 'dulls.'

F. DISCUSSION

It is evident that at least in our experimental situation practice on a specific route, or response sequence, produces in some rats a disposition to take the shortest Euclidean path to the goal, whenever this path is available and the practiced one is blocked. This is what we set out to discover. In terms of what we said in the introduction, then, the class defined by the matrix *"x* expects food at location *L"* is not null.

This discovery is, of course, not entirely new. Lashley (7) observed rats climb out of the alley of his maze and run directly towards the food-box. Dennis (2) reported

that when the walls of his maze were removed his rats ran directly to the food-box. Helson (4) also observed similar short-cutting to the food-box. These experimenters were not, however, primarily interested in this phenomenon, but were working on other problems. Later workers such as Higginson (5), Valentine (14) and Gilhousen (3) turned their attention directly to the short-cut problem. They were concerned, however, with a different aspect of the phenomenon. They wanted to discover if the rat would choose the short-cut path when both the short-cut and the longer original path were open. Although Higginson reported that some of his rats did choose the shortcut under such conditions, both Valentine and Gilhousen concluded that the tendency was to take the short-cut depended upon the speed at which the rat was moving when he came to the choice point. It is obvious that the problem which they set for the rats was primarily one of noticing the new path. We, on the other hand, were merely concerned with discovering what direction the rats would take when the original path *was blocked*.

A question arises at this point about whether it is correct to say that our rats chose the path pointing towards the goal location. Some critics might prefer to say that they merely ran towards the light, a response which was rewarded during the pre-testing training. Since the location of the light and the former location of the food are nearly identical in our experiment this criticism raises an important point.

In answer to this criticism we should first explain that we are not asserting that rats can exhibit such orientational behavior when there are no cues or landmarks present. We believe that such choices can only be made when there are distinctive stimuli in the environment which enable the rat to judge its own location relative to other places in the environment. The light, we believe, performed such a function and was not a mere conditioned stimulus, as such a criticism would suppose.

The reasons why we believe that the light was not a mere conditioned stimulus are (1) that the original light stimulus and the light stimulus on the test trials were different, and (2) that the original response differed greatly from the correct response on the test trial. The light stimulus in the pre-test training was faced head-on when the rat came down path FG. The light stimulus when running down path No. 6, on the other hand, was not faced head-on, but was received at an angle of 50 degrees. Should the critic suggest that this difference was not great enough to prevent sensory generalization, we should answer that then the generalization should also be effective on the paths adjacent to path No. 6. However, we see that while 19 rats took path No. 6, the total frequency on paths No. 5 and No. 7 was only five rats. This would hardly be expected if the choice of path No. 6 was determined solely by the similarity of the light stimulus on this path to the stimulus on the original path, since the stimuli on paths No. 5 and No. 7 were not very different from the stimulus on path No. 6. The angle at which the light was received on path No. 5 was 40 degrees, while it was 60 degrees for path No. 7.

But not only was the light stimulus different in the test trial from the stimulus in the pre-test training, but the responses to the two situations also differed. The original response was one of running through the alley, turning left (away from the light), turning right (at right angles to the light), and again turning right (directly towards the light). The correct response on the test trial, on the other hand, consisted in avoiding the alley and in choosing path No. 6 from the other 18 paths, and running down this straight path. For all these reasons we believe that is it not correct to say that our rats were merely running towards the light. Rather, we should say that they were running towards the location of the former goal, and that this location was indicated by the position of the light.

Now, how are we going to account for the fact that not all of our rats chose this shortest path? One hypothesis that might be suggested is that these rats differed in some orientational ability. However, the fact that 10 of the short-cut groups were Tryon 'brights' and nine were Tryon 'dulls,' throws some doubt upon this hypothesis. This doubt is based upon the assumption that Tryon's 'brights' and 'dulls' are different because of differences in orientational abilities. A second hypothesis that suggests itself is that the rats which failed to take the short-cut were overtrained on the pre-test training and thus were fixated on the original path. However, the fact that only nine percent of the rats took the two paths that were closest to the original one, makes this hypothesis quite questionable. Finally, we believe that the reason that the remaining rats failed to take the short-cut was that they had not had enough training and thus had not yet learned the location of the food. With a few more days training we should have that only nine percent of the rats took the two paths that were closest to the original one, makes this hypothesis quite questionable. Finally, we

believe that the reason that the remaining rats failed to take the short-cut was that they had not had enough training and thus had not yet learned the location of the food. With a few more days training we should have expected that the remaining rats would have chosen the shortcut.

A further question now arises—why do we give the name 'expectation' to these dispositions? Would not a less anthropomorphic term be more suitable? The reason why we have chosen this word is that we wish to emphasize the difference between the kind of orientational behavior exhibited in the traditional conditioning experiments. In short, we believe that the behavior exhibited by our rats is similar in important respects to human symbolic behavior.

No one would deny that when someone reads, understands, and believes a sign like, "There is bread in the kitchen," he then *expects* bread to be in the kitchen. Difficulties arise, however, when we try to describe this expectation in terms of behavior. In the first place, there is no known simple response which is uniformly associated with an expectation of bread in the kitchen. In fact, when there is no motivation there is no response at all. However, none of us would wish to assert that because there is no response in such circumstances, there is no expectation. For this reason we must reject any explicit definition of 'expectation' in terms of any single response or set of responses. This is the point which the senior writer has stressed in all his discussions of latent learning (9, 10, 11, 12).

Now let us consider those cases in which the person is motivated and some response occurs. Even now there is no single response or set of responses which is uniformly associated with this expectation. A wide variety of responses may be observed in such a situation, and all that they seem to have in common is that they all are functions of the relation between the location of the person who has the expectation and the location of the kitchen. Since this relation may change from one occasion to another, the response to this sign differs on different occasions. All of this illustrates that it is very difficult to describe such expectations in terms of behavior. About all that can be said, as Bertrand Russell (8) has pointed out, is that the hungry bread-lover responds appropriately to the fact that *he* is *here* and the kitchen is *there*.

Of course this statement is not very helpful unless we are able to characterize what is meant by the word 'appropriate.' However, in a situation as simple as the one we are concerned with, we may say that the person's behavior is 'appropriate' to the degree that it approaches the shortest Euclidean path from this location to the kitchen. Now, in order to be able to respond appropriately when in a new situation (one from which he has never been sought bread) it is necessary that the person recognize the abstract location of the kitchen, that is, its spatial relation to other places in the environment. If, on the other hand, the location of the kitchen is merely recognized as the place which is the terminus of all the paths which have been traversed in the past when seeking bread, then this person would be helpless when either all these old paths are blocked, or he is in a new location. Put in other words, if the sign, "There is bread in the kitchen," were a conditioned stimulus for a specific set of alternative response sequences and if the original paths for these response sequences were not available, then the conditioning would have prepared him for no solution to the problem. Thus, if the person is able to solve this problem and pick a new path which is in fact appropriate, then this sign cannot be a mere conditioned stimulus. Further, we must suppose that his knowledge of the location of the kitchen is abstracted from the location of any of the paths, and is a function of the kitchen's spatial relation to the total environment.

We have discussed some of the things that are involved in human behavior when someone expects a goal in a particular location. We have elaborated this human example because few people will deny that humans behave in this fashion, or that it is correct to call such behavior by the word 'expectation.'

However, all that we have said applies equally well, we believe, to the spatial behavior of the rats in our experiment. The problem we set for our rats demanded the same kind of abstract knowledge of the location of the food. If the goal location had been recognized merely as the terminus of the original path, or the place of the terminal response in the original response sequence, then our rats would have been helpless on the test trial. The fact that they selected the shortest path indicates that what was learned during the preliminary training was not a mere response sequence, or an expectation that this particular path led to the goal. They learned, instead, a disposition to orient towards the physical location of the goal. Because of this we have chosen the word 'expectation' as the name for this orientational disposition.

G. SUMMARY

1. The original rough formulation of the expectancy theory is difficult to distinguish from the alternative stimulus-response doctrines. Part of this difficulty results from the fact that implicit in this rough formulation, is a definition of the matrix "x expects a goal at location L," which makes it equivalent to the matrix "x runs down the practiced path," when certain conditions are fulfilled. Because of this difficulty, we have rejected this definition.

2. We have suggested instead a definition of the matrix "x expects a goal at location L" which makes it equivalent to the matrix "x runs down the path which points directly to the location L," when certain conditions are fulfilled.

3. To determine whether rats will run down such a path, whenever the original path is blocked, we have run 56 female rats in a situation which conformed to these conditions.

4. Thirty-six percent of the rats chose the path which pointed directly towards the location of the goal. The remaining rats were distributed over the other paths in a chance fashion.

5. We have concluded (1) that rats do learn to expect goals in specific locations, (2) that there are important similarities between this behavior and human symbolic behavior, and (3) that these similarities justify our using the word 'expectation' as a name for the disposition to short-cut when the original path is blocked.

REFERENCES

CARNAP, R. TESTABILITY AND MEANING. *PHILOS. SCI.,* 1936, 3, 419–471; 1947, 4, 1–40.

DENNIS, W. THE SENSORY CONTROL OF THE WHITE RAT IN THE MAZE HABIT. *J. GENET. PSYCHOL.,* 1929, 36, 626–627.

GILHOUSEN, H. C. AN INVESTIGATION OF INSIGHT' IN RATS. *SCIENCE.* 1931, 73, 711–712.

HELSON, H. INSIGHT IN THE WHITE RAT. *J. EXP. PSYCHOL.,* 1927, 10, 378397.

HIGGINSON, G. D. VISUAL PERCEPTION IN THE WHITE RAT. *J. EXP. PSYCHOL.,* 1926, 9, 337–347.

HILGARD, E. R., & MARQUIS, D. G. *CONDITIONING AND LEARNING.* NEW YORK: APPLETON-CENTURY, 1940.

LASHLEY, K. S. *BRAIN MECHANISMS AND INTELLIGENCE.* CHICAGO: UNIV. CHICAGO PRESS, 1929.

RUSSELL, B. *AN INQUIRY INTO MEANING AND TRUTH.* W. W. NORTON, 1940.

TOLMAN, E. C. *PURPOSIVE BEHAVIOR IN ANIMALS AND MEN.* NEW YORK: APPLETON-CENTURY, 1932.

TOLMAN, E. C. THE LAW OF EFFECT. (SYMPOSIUM). *PSYCHOL. REV.,* 1938, 45, 200–203.

TOLMAN, E. C. THEORIES OF LEARNING. IN: F. A. MOSS, ED., *COMPARATIVE PSYCHOLOGY.* NEW YORK: PRENTICE-HALL, 1934.

TOLMAN, E. C. THE DETERMINERS OF BEHAVIOR AT A CHOICE POINT. *PSYCHOL REV.,* 1938, 45, 1–41.

TRYON, R. C. INDIVIDUAL DIFFERENCES. IN: F. A. MOSS, ED., *COMPARATIVE PSYCHOLOGY.* NEW YORK: PRENTICE-HALL, 1934.

VALENTINE, W. L. VISUAL PERCEPTION IN THE WHITE RAT. *J. COMP. PSYCHOL.,* 1928, 8, 369–375.

NOTES

1. This is what Carnap (1) has called a 'bilateral reduction sentence.' Sentences of this form are, he argues, essential for the introduction or definition of disposition predicates.

2. A matrix is an expression which contains a free variable. When a value is specified for this variable, and the name of this value is substituted for the variable, the matrix becomes a sentence. Note that it is the matrix "x expects food at location L" which is being introduced, and not the matrix "x *is* an expectation." We do not introduce, and need not introduce, the latter matrix. Carnap illustrates this point by showing that in physics we need never introduce the matrix "x *is* an electric charge." All that we need for experimental purposes, he argues, is the matrix "x has an electric charge." In the remaining sections of this paper whenever we refer to our definition of 'expectation' we are elliptically referring to a conditioned definition containing the matrix "x expects food at location L," and not one containing the matrix "x *is* an expectation." Finally, it should be pointed out that what Definition I states is that the truth-value of the matrix "x expects food at location L" is considered identical to that of the matrix "x runs down path P," whenever the conditions stated by the antecedent are fulfilled.

Carr Appointed Editor of the *Journal of Experimental Psychology: Human Perception and Performance*, 1994–1999

The Publications and Communications Board of the American Psychological Association announces the appointment of Thomas H. Carr, PhD, Michigan State University, as editor of the *Journal of Experimental Psychology: Human Perception and Performance* for a 6-year term beginning in 1994. As of December 15, 1992, manuscripts should be directed to

> Thomas H. Carr, PhD
> Department of Psychology
> Michigan State University
> East Lansing, Michigan 48824

Manuscript submission patterns for *JEP: Human Perception and Performance* make the precise date of completion of the 1993 volume uncertain. The current editor, James E. Cutting, PhD, will receive and consider manuscripts until December 14, 1992. Should the 1993 volume be completed before that date, manuscripts will be redirected to Dr. Carr for consideration in the 1994 volume.

Imitation of Film-Mediated Aggressive Models

ALBERT BANDURA, DORTHEA ROSS, AND SHEILA A. ROSS

In a test of the hypothesis that exposure of children to film-mediated aggressive models would increase the probability of Ss' aggression to subsequent frustration, 1 group of experimental Ss observed real-life aggressive models, a 2nd observed these same models portraying aggression on film, while a 3rd group viewed a film depicting an aggressive cartoon character. Following the exposure treatment, Ss were mildly frustrated and tested for the amount of imitative and nonimitative aggression in a different experimental setting. The overall results provide evidence for both the facilitating and the modeling influence of film-mediated aggressive stimulation. In addition, the findings reveal that the effects of such exposure are to some extent a function of the sex of the model, sex of the child, and the reality cues of the model.

Most of the research on the possible effects of film-mediated stimulation upon subsequent aggressive behavior has focused primarily on the drive reducing function of fantasy. While the experimental evidence for the catharsis or drive reduction theory is equivocal (Albert, 1957; Berkowitz, 1962; Emery, 1959; Feshbach, 1955, 1958; Kenny, 1952; Lövaas, 1961; Siegel,

1956), the modeling influence of pictorial stimuli has received little research attention.

A recent incident (*San Francisco Chronicle*, 1961) in which a boy was seriously knifed during a re-enactment of a switchblade knife fight the boys had seen the previous evening on a televised rerun of the James Dean movie, *Rebel Without a Cause,* is a dramatic illustration of the possible imitative influence of film stimulation. Indeed, anecdotal data suggest that portrayal of aggression through pictorial media may be more influential in shaping the form aggression will take when a person is instigated on later occasions, than in altering the level of instigation to aggression.

In an earlier experiment (Bandura & Huston, 1961), it was shown that children readily imitated aggressive behavior exhibited by a model in the presence of the model. A succeeding investigation (Bandura, Ross, & Ross, 1961), demonstrated that children exposed to aggressive models generalized aggressive responses to a new setting in which the model was absent. The present study sought to determine the extent to which film-mediated aggressive models may serve as an important source of imitative behavior.

Aggressive models can be ordered on a reality-fictional stimulus dimension with real-life models located at the reality end of the continuum, nonhuman cartoon characters at the fictional end, and films portraying human models occupying an intermediate position. It was predicted, on the basis of saliency and similarity of cues, that the more

Albert Bandura, Dorothea Ross, and Sheila A. Ross, "Imitation of Film-Mediated Aggressive Models," *Journal of Abnormal and Social Psychology*, vol. 66, no. 1, pp. 3–11. Copyright © 1963 by American Psychological Association. Reprinted with permission.

remote the model was from reality, the weaker would be the tendency for subjects to imitate the behavior of the model.

Of the various interpretations of imitative learning, the sensory feedback theory of imitation recently proposed by Mowrer (1960) is elaborated in greatest detail. According to this theory, if certain responses have been repeatedly positively reinforced, proprioceptive stimuli associated with these responses acquire secondary reinforcing properties and thus the individual is predisposed to perform the behavior for the positive feedback. Similarly, if responses have been negatively reinforced, response correlated stimuli acquire the capacity to arouse anxiety which, in turn, inhibit the occurrence of the negatively valenced behavior. On the basis of these considerations, it was predicted subjects who manifest high aggression anxiety would perform significantly less imitative and nonimitative aggression than subjects who display little anxiety over aggression. Since aggression is generally considered female inappropriate behavior, and therefore likely to be negatively reinforced in girls (Sears, Maccoby, & Levin, 1957), it was also predicted that male subjects would be more imitative of aggression than females.

To the extent that observation of adults displaying aggression conveys a certain degree of permissiveness for aggressive behavior, it may be assumed that such exposure not only facilitates the learning of new aggressive responses but also weakens competing inhibitory responses in subjects and thereby increases the probability of occurrence of previously learned patterns of aggression. It was predicted, therefore, that subjects who observed aggressive models would display significantly more aggression when subsequently frustrated than subjects who were equally frustrated but who had no prior exposure to models exhibiting aggression.

METHOD

Subjects

The subjects were 48 boys and 48 girls enrolled in the Stanford University Nursery School. They ranged in age from 35 to 69 months, with a mean age of 52 months.

Two adults, a male and a female, served in the role of models both in the real-life and the human film-aggression condition, and one female experimenter conducted the study for all 96 children.

General Procedure

Subjects were divided into three experimental groups and one control group of 24 subjects each. One group of experimental subjects observed real-life aggressive models, a second group observed these same models portraying aggression on film, while a third group viewed a film depicting an aggressive cartoon character. The experimental groups were further subdivided into male and female subjects so that half the subjects in the two conditions involving human models were exposed to same-sex models, while the remaining subjects viewed models of the opposite sex.

Following the exposure experience, subjects were tested for the amount of imitative and nonimitative aggression in a different experimental setting in the absence of the models.

The control group subjects had no exposure to the aggressive models and were tested only in the generalization situation.

Subjects in the experimental and control groups were matched individually on the basis of ratings of their aggressive behavior in social interactions in the nursery school. The experimenter and a nursery school teacher rated the subjects on four five-point rating scales which measured the extent to which subjects displayed physical aggression, verbal aggression, aggression toward inanimate objects, and aggression inhibition. The latter scale, which dealt with the subjects' tendency to inhibit aggressive reactions in the face of high instigation, provided the measure of aggression anxiety. Seventy-one percent of the subjects were rated independently by both judges so as to permit an assessment of interrater agreement. The reliability of the composite aggression score, estimated by means of the Pearson product-moment correlation, was .80.

Data for subjects in the real-life aggression condition and in the control group were collected as part of a previous experiment (Bandura et al., 1961). Since the procedure is described in detail in the earlier report, only a brief description of it will be presented here.

Experimental Conditions

Subjects in the Real-Life Aggressive condition were brought individually by the experimenter to the experimental room and the model, who was in the hallway outside the room, was invited by the experimenter to come and join in the game. The subject was then escorted to one corner of the room and seated at a small table which contained potato prints, multicolor picture stickers, and colored paper. After demonstrating how the subject could design pictures with the materials provided, the experimenter escorted the model to the opposite corner of the room which contained a small table and chair, a tinker toy set, a mallet, and a 5-foot inflated Bobo doll. The experimenter explained that this was the model's play area and after the model was seated, the experimenter left the experimental room.

The model began the session by assembling the tinker toys but after approximately a minute had elapsed, the model turned to the Bobo doll and spent the remainder of the period aggressing toward it with highly novel responses which are unlikely to be performed by children independently of the observation of the model's behavior. Thus, in addition to punching the Bobo doll, the model exhibited the following distinctive aggressive acts which were to be scored as imitative responses:

The model sat on the Bobo doll and punched it repeatedly in the nose.

The model then raised the Bobo doll and pommeled it on the head with a mallet.

Following the mallet aggression, the model tossed the doll up in the air aggressively and kicked it about the room. This sequence of physically aggressive acts was repeated approximately three times, interspersed with verbally aggressive responses such as, "Sock him in the nose…," "Hit him down…," "Throw him in the air…," "Kick him…," and "Pow."

Subjects in the Human Film-Aggression condition were brought by the experimenter to the semi-darkened experimental room, introduced to the picture materials, and informed that while the subjects worked on potato prints, a movie would be shown on a screen, positioned approximately 6 feet from the subject's table. The movie projector was located in a distant corner of the room and was screened from the subject's view by large wooden panels.

The color movie and a tape recording of the sound track was begun by a male projectionist as soon as the experimenter left the experimental room and was shown for a duration of 10 minutes. The models in the film presentations were the same adult males and females who participated in the Real-Life condition of the experiment. Similarly, the aggressive behavior they portrayed in the film was identical with their real-life performances.

For subjects in the Cartoon Film-Aggression condition, after seating the subject at the table with the picture construction material, the experimenter walked over to a television console approximately 3 feet in front of the subject's table, remarked, "I guess I'll turn on the color TV," and ostensibly tuned in a cartoon program. The experimenter then left the experimental room. The cartoon was shown on a glass lens screen in the television set by means of a rear projection arrangement screened from the subject's view by large panels.

The sequence of aggressive acts in the cartoon was performed by the female model costumed as a black cat similar to the many cartoon cats. In order to heighten the level of irreality of the cartoon, the floor area was covered with artificial grass and the walls forming the backdrop were adorned with brightly colored trees, birds, and butterflies creating a fantasyland setting. The cartoon began with a close-up of a stage on which the curtains were slowly drawn revealing a picture of a cartoon cat along with the title, *Herman the Cat*. The remainder of the film showed the cat pommeling the Bobo doll on the head with a mallet, sitting on the doll and punching it in the nose, tossing the doll in the air, and kicking it about the room in a manner identical with the performance in the other experimental conditions except that the cat's movements were characteristically feline. To induce further a cartoon set, the program was introduced and concluded with appropriate cartoon music, and the cat's verbal aggression was repeated in a high-pitched, animated voice.

In both film conditions, at the conclusion of the movie the experimenter entered the room and then escorted the subject to the test room.

Aggression Instigation

In order to differentiate clearly the exposure and test situations subjects were tested for the amount of imitative learning in a different experimental room which was set off from the main nursery school building.

The degree to which a child has learned aggressive patterns of behavior through imitation becomes most evident when the child is instigated to aggression on later occasions. Thus, for example, the effects of viewing the movie, *Rebel Without a Cause,* were not evident until the boys were instigated to aggression the following day, at which time they re-enacted the televised switchblade knife fight in considerable detail. For this reason, the children in the experiment, both those in the control group, and those who were exposed to the aggressive models, were mildly frustrated before they were brought to the test room.

Following the exposure experience, the experimenter brought the subject to an anteroom which contained a varied array of highly attractive toys. The experimenter explained that the toys were for the subject to play with, but, as soon as the subject became sufficiently involved with the play material, the experimenter remarked that these were her very best toys, that she did not let just anyone play with them, and that she had decided to reserve these toys for some other children. However, the subject could play with any of the toys in the next room. The experimenter and the subject then entered the adjoining experimental room.

It was necessary for the experimenter to remain in the room during the experimental session; otherwise, a number of the children would either refuse to remain alone or would leave before the termination of the session. In order to minimize any influence her presence might have on the subject's behavior, the experimenter remained as inconspicuous as possible by busying herself with paper work at a desk in the far corner of the room and avoiding any interaction with the child.

Test for Delayed Imitation

The experimental room contained a variety of toys, some of which could be used in imitative or nonimitative aggression, and others which tended to elicit predominantly nonaggressive forms of behavior. The aggressive toys included a 3-foot Bobo doll, a mallet and peg board, two dart guns, and a tether ball with a face painted on it which hung from the ceiling. The nonaggressive toys, on the other hand, included a tea set, crayons and coloring paper, a ball, two dolls, three bears, cars and trucks, and plastic farm animals.

In order to eliminate any variation in behavior due to mere placement of the toys in the room, the play material was arranged in a fixed order for each of the sessions.

The subject spent 20 minutes in the experimental room during which time his behavior was rated in terms of predetermined response categories by judges who observed the session through a one-way mirror in an adjoining observation room. The 20-minute session was divided in 5-second intervals by means of an electric interval timer, thus yielding a total number of 240 response units for each subject.

The male model scored the experimental sessions for all subjects. In order to provide an estimate of interjudge agreement, the performances of 40% of the subjects were scored independently by a second observer. The responses scored involved highly specific concrete classes of behavior, and yielded high interscorer reliabilities, the product-moment coefficients being in the 90s.

Response Measures

The following response measures were obtained:

Imitative aggression. This category included acts of striking the Bobo doll with the mallet, sitting on the doll and punching it in the nose, kicking the doll, tossing it in the air, and the verbally aggressive responses, "Sock him," "Hit him down," "Kick him," "Throw him in the air," and "Pow."

Partially imitative responses. A number of subjects imitated the essential components of the model's behavior but did not perform the complete act, or they directed the imitative aggressive response to some object other than the Bobo doll. Two responses of this type were scored and were interpreted as partially imitative behavior:

Mallet aggression. The subject strikes objects other than the Bobo doll aggressively with the mallet.

Sits on Bobo doll. The subject lays the Bobo doll on its side and sits on it, but does not aggress toward it.

Nonimitative aggression. This category included acts of punching, slapping, or pushing the doll, physically aggressive acts directed toward objects other than the Bobo doll, and any hostile remarks except for those in the verbal imitation category; for example, "Shoot the Bobo," "Cut him," "Stupid ball," "Knock over people," "Horses fighting, biting."

Aggressive gun play. The subject shoots darts or aims the guns and fires imaginary shots at objects in the room.

Ratings were also made of the number of behavior units in which subjects played nonaggressively or sat quietly and did not play with any of the material at all.

RESULTS

Since the distributions of scores departed from normality and the assumption of homogeneity of variance could not be made for most of the measures, the Freidman two-way analysis of variance by ranks was employed for testing the significance of the obtained differences.

Total Aggression

The mean total aggression scores for subjects in the real-life, human film, cartoon film, and the control groups are 83, 92, 99, and 54, respectively. The results of the analysis of variance performed on these scores reveal that the main effect of treatment conditions is significant ($Xr^2 = 9.06$, $p < .05$), confirming the prediction that exposure of subjects to aggressive models increases the probability that subjects will respond aggressively when instigated on later occasions. Further analyses of pairs of scores by means of the Wilcoxon matched-pairs signed-ranks test show that subjects who viewed the real-life models and the film-mediated models do not differ from each other in total aggressiveness but all three experimental groups expressed significantly more aggressive behavior than the control subjects.

Imitative Aggressive Responses

The Freidman analysis reveals that exposure of subjects to aggressive models is also a highly effective method for shaping subjects' aggressive responses ($Xr^2 = 23.88$, $p < .001$). Comparisons of treatment conditions by the Wilcoxon test reveal that subjects who observed the real-life models and the film-mediated models, relative to subjects in the control group, performed considerably more imitative physical and verbal aggression.

The prediction that imitation is positively related to the reality cues of the model was only partially supported. While subjects who observed the real-life aggressive models exhibited significantly more imitative aggression than subjects who viewed the cartoon model, no significant differences were found between the live and film, and the film and cartoon conditions, nor did the three experimental groups differ significantly in total aggression or in the performances of partially imitative behavior. Indeed, the available data suggest that, of the three experimental conditions, exposure to humans on film portraying aggression was the most influential in eliciting and shaping aggressive behavior. Subjects in this condition, in relation to the control subjects, exhibited more total aggression, more imitative aggression, more partially imitative behavior, such as sitting on the Bobo doll and mallet aggression, and they engaged in significantly more aggressive gun play. In addition, they performed significantly more aggressive gun play than did subjects who were exposed to the real-life aggressive models).

Influence of Sex of Model and Sex of Child

In order to determine the influence of sex of model and sex of child on the expression of imitative and nonimitative aggression, the data from the experimental groups were combined and the significance of the differences between groups was assessed by *t* tests for uncorrelated means. In statistical comparisons involving relatively skewed distributions of scores the Mann-Whitney *U* test was employed.

Sex of subjects had a highly significant effect on both the learning and the performance of aggression. Boys, in relation to girls, exhibited significantly more total aggression ($t = 2.69$, $p < .01$), more imitative aggression ($t = 2.82$, $p < .005$), more aggressive gun play ($z = 3.38$, $p < .001$), and more nonimitative aggressive behavior ($t = 2.98$, $p < .005$). Girls, on the other hand, were more inclined than boys to sit on the Bobo doll but refrained from punching it ($z = 3.47$, $p < .001$).

The analyses also disclosed some influences of the sex of the model. Subjects exposed to the male model, as compared to the female model, expressed significantly more aggressive gun play ($z = 2.83$, $p < .005$). The most marked differences in aggressive gun play ($U = 9.5$, $p < .001$), however, were found between girls exposed to the female model ($M = 2.9$) and males who observed the male model ($M = 19.8$). Although the overall model difference in partially imitative behavior, Sits on Bobo, was not significant, Sex $\times$ Model subgroup comparisons yielded some interesting results. Boys who observed the aggressive female model, for example, were more likely to sit on the Bobo doll without punching it than boys who viewed the male model ($U = 33$, $p < .05$). Girls reproduced the nonaggressive component of the male model's aggressive pattern of behavior (i.e., sat on the doll without punching it) with considerably higher frequency than did boys who observed the same model ($U = 21.5$, $p < .02$). The highest incidence of partially imitative responses was yielded by the group of girls who viewed the aggressive female model ($M = 10.4$), and the lowest values by the boys who were exposed to the male model ($M = 0.3$). This difference was significant beyond the .05 significance level. These findings, along with the sex of child and sex of model differences reported in the preceding sections, provide further support for the view that the influence of models in promoting social learning is determined, in part, by the sex appropriateness of the model's behavior (Bandura et al., 1961).

Aggressive Predisposition and Imitation

Since the correlations between ratings of aggression and the measures of imitative and total aggressive behavior, calculated separately for boys and girls in each of the experimental conditions, did not differ significantly, the data were combined. The correlational analyses performed on these pooled data failed to yield any significant relationships between ratings of aggression anxiety, frequency of aggressive behavior, and the experimental aggression measures. In fact, the array means suggested nonlinear regressions although the departures from linearity were not of sufficient magnitude to be statistically significant.

DISCUSSION

The results of the present study provide strong evidence that exposure to filmed aggression heightens aggressive reactions in children. Subjects who viewed the aggressive human and cartoon models on film exhibited nearly twice as much aggression than did subjects in the control group who were not exposed to the aggressive film content.

In the experimental design typically employed for testing the possible cathartic function of vicarious aggression, subjects are first frustrated, then provided with an opportunity to view an aggressive film following which their overt or fantasy aggression is measured. While this procedure yields some information on the immediate influence of film-mediated aggression, the full effects of such exposure may not be revealed until subjects are instigated to aggression on a later occasion. Thus, the present study, and one recently reported by Lövaas (1961), both utilizing a design in which subjects first observed filmed aggression and then were frustrated, clearly reveal that observation of models portraying aggression on film substantially increases rather than decreases the probability of aggressive reactions to subsequent frustrations.

Filmed aggression, not only facilitated the expression of aggression, but also effectively shaped the form of the subjects' aggressive behavior. The finding that children modeled their behavior to some extent after the film characters suggests that pictorial mass media, particularly television, may serve as an important source of social behavior. In fact, a possible generalization of responses originally learned in the television situation to the experimental film may account for the significantly greater amount of aggressive gun play displayed by subjects in the film condition as compared to subjects in the real-life and control groups. It is unfortunate that the qualitative features of the gun behavior were not scored since subjects in the film condition, unlike those in the other two groups, developed interesting elaborations in gun play (for example, stalking the imaginary opponent, quick drawing, and rapid firing), characteristic of the Western gun fighter.

The view that the social learning of aggression through exposure to aggressive film content is confined to deviant children (Schramm, Lyle, & Parker, 1961), finds little support in our data. The children who participated in the experiment are by no means a deviant sample, nevertheless, 88% of the subjects in the Real-Life and in the Human Film condition, and 79% of the subjects in the Cartoon Film condition, exhibited varying degrees of imitative aggression. In assessing the possible influence of televised stimulation on viewers' behavior, however, it is important to distinguish between learning and overt performance. Although the results of the present experiment demonstrate that the vast majority of children *learn* patterns of social behavior through pictorial stimulation, nevertheless, informal observation suggests that children do not, as a rule, *perform* indiscriminately the behavior of televised characters, even those they regard as highly attractive models. The replies of parents whose children participated in the present study to an open-end questionnaire item concerning their handling of imitative behavior suggest that this may be in part a function of negative reinforcement, as most parents were quick to discourage their children's overt imitation of television characters by prohibiting certain programs or by labeling the imitative behavior in a disapproving manner. From our knowledge of the effects of punishment on behavior, the responses in question would be expected to retain their original strength and could reappear on later occasions in the presence of appropriate eliciting stimuli, particularly if instigation is high, the instruments for aggression are available, and the threat of noxious consequences is reduced.

The absence of any relationships between ratings of the children's predisposition to aggression and their aggressive behavior in the experimental setting may simply reflect the inadequacy of the predictor measures. It may be pointed out, however, that the reliability of the ratings was relatively high. While this does not assure validity of the measures, it does at least indicate there was consistency in the raters' estimates of the children's aggressive tendencies.

A second, and perhaps more probable, explanation is that proprioceptive feedback alone is not sufficient to account for response inhibition or facilitation. For example, the proprioceptive cues arising from hitting responses directed toward parents and toward peers may differ little, if any; nevertheless, tendencies to aggress toward parents are apt to be strongly inhibited while peer aggression may be readily expressed (Bandura, 1960; Bandura & Walters, 1959). In most social interaction sequences, proprioceptive cues make up only a small part of the total stimulus complex and, therefore, it is necessary to take into consideration additional stimulus components, for the most part external, which probably serve as important discriminative cues for the expression of aggression. Consequently, prediction of the occurrence or inhibition of specific classes of responses would be expected to depend upon the presence of a certain pattern of proprioceptive or introceptive stimulation together with relevant discriminative external stimuli.

According to this line of reasoning, failure to obtain the expected positive relationships between the measures of aggression may be due primarily to the fact that permissiveness for aggression, conveyed by situational cues in the form of aggressive film content and play material,

was sufficient to override the influence of internal stimuli generated by the commission of aggressive responses. If, in fact, the behavior of young children, as compared to that of adults, is less likely to be under internal stimulus control, one might expect environmental cues to play a relatively important role in eliciting or inhibiting aggressive behavior.

A question may be raised as to whether the aggressive acts studied in the present experiment constitute "genuine" aggressive responses. Aggression is typically defined as behavior, the goal or intent of which is injury to a person, or destruction of an object (Bandura & Walters, 1959; Dollard, Doob, Miller, Mowrer, & Sears, 1939; Sears, Maccoby, & Levin, 1957). Since intentionality is not a property of behavior but primarily an inference concerning antecedent events, the categorization of an act as "aggressive" involves a consideration of both stimulus and mediating or terminal response events.

According to a social learning theory of aggression recently proposed by Bandura and Walters (in press), most of the responses utilized to hurt or to injure others (for example, striking, kicking, and other responses of high magnitude), are probably learned for prosocial purposes under nonfrustration conditions. Since frustration generally elicits responses of high magnitude, the latter classes of responses, once acquired, may be called out in social interactions for the purpose of injuring others. On the basis of this theory it would be predicted that the aggressive responses acquired imitatively, while not necessarily mediating aggressive goals in the experimental situation, would be utilized to serve such purposes in other social settings with higher frequency by children in the experimental conditions than by children in the control group.

The present study involved primarily vicarious or empathic learning (Mowrer, 1960) in that subjects acquired a relatively complex repertoire of aggressive responses by the mere sight of a model's behavior. It has been generally assumed that the necessary conditions for the occurrence of such learning is that the model perform certain responses followed by positive reinforcement to the model (Hill, 1960; Mowrer, 1960). According to this theory, to the extent that the observer experiences the model's reinforcement vicariously, the observer will be prone to reproduce the model's behavior. While there is some evidence from experiments involving both human (Lewis & Duncan,

1958; McBrearty, Marston, & Kanfer, 1961; Sechrest, 1961) and animal subjects (Darby & Riopelle, 1959; Warden, Fjeld, & Koch, 1940), that vicarious reinforcement may in fact increase the probability of the behavior in question, it is apparent from the results of the experiment reported in this paper that a good deal of human imitative learning can occur without any reinforcers delivered either to the model or to the observer. In order to test systematically the influence of vicarious reinforcement on imitation, however, a study is planned in which the degree of imitative learning will be compared in situations in which the model's behavior is paired with reinforcement with those in which the model's responses go unrewarded.

REFERENCES

ALBERT, R. S. THE ROLE OF MASS MEDIA AND THE EFFECT OF AGGRESSIVE FILM CONTENT UPON CHILDREN'S AGGRESSIVE RESPONSES AND IDENTIFICATION CHOICES. *GENET. PSYCHOL. MONOGR.,* 1957, 55, 221–285.

BANDURA, A. RELATIONSHIP OF FAMILY PATTERNS TO CHILD BEHAVIOR DISORDERS. PROGRESS REPORT, 1960, STANFORD UNIVERSITY, PROJECT NO. M–1734, UNITED STATES PUBLIC HEALTH SERVICE.

BANDURA, A., & HUSTON, ALETHA C. IDENTIFICATION AS A PROCESS OF INCIDENTAL LEARNING. *J. ABNORM. SOC. PSYCHOL.,* 1961, 63, 311–318.

BANDURA, A., ROSS, DOROTHEA, & ROSS, SHEILA A. TRANSMISSION OF AGGRESSION THROUGH IMITATION OF AGGRESSIVE MODELS. *J. ABNORM. SOC. PSYCHOL.,* 1961, 63, 575–582.

BANDURA, A., & WALTERS, R. H. *ADOLESCENT AGGRESSION.* NEW YORK: RONALD, 1959.

BANDURA, A., & WALTERS, R. H. *THE SOCIAL LEARNING OF DEVIANT BEHAVIOR: A BEHAVIORISTIC APPROACH TO SOCIALIZATION.* NEW YORK: HOLT, RINEHART, & WINSTON, IN PRESS.

BERKOWITZ, L. *AGGRESSION: A SOCIAL PSYCHOLOGICAL ANALYSIS.* NEW YORK: MCGRAW-HILL, 1962.

DARBY, C. L., & RIOPELLE, A. J. OBSERVATIONAL LEARNING IN THE RHESUS MONKEY. *J. COMP. PHYSIOL. PSYCHOL.,* 1959, 52, 94–98.

DOLLARD, J., DOOB, L. W., MILLER, N. E., MOWRER, O. H., & SEARS, R. R. *FRUSTRATION AND AGGRESSION.* NEW HAVEN: YALE UNIVER. PRESS, 1939.

EMERY, F. E. PSYCHOLOGICAL EFFECTS OF THE WESTERN FILM: A STUDY IN TELEVISION VIEWING: II. THE EXPERIMENTAL STUDY. *HUM. RELAT.,* 1959, 12, 215–232.

FESHBACH, S. THE DRIVE-REDUCING FUNCTION OF FANTASY BEHAVIOR. *J. ABNORM. SOC. PSYCHOL.,* 1955, 50, 3–11.

FESHBACH, S. THE STIMULATING VERSUS CATHARTIC EFFECTS OF A VICARIOUS AGGRESSIVE ACTIVITY. PAPER READ AT THE EASTERN PSYCHOLOGICAL ASSOCIATION, 1958.

HILL, W. F. LEARNING THEORY AND THE ACQUISITION OF VALUES. *PSYCHOL. REV.,* 1960, 67, 317–331.

KENNY, D. T. AN EXPERIMENTAL TEST OF THE CATHARSIS THEORY OF AGGRESSION. UNPUBLISHED DOCTORAL DISSERTATION, UNIVERSITY OF WASHINGTON, 1952.

LEWIS, D. J., & DUNCAN, C. P. VICARIOUS EXPERIENCE AND PARTIAL REINFORCEMENT. *J. ABNORM. SOC. PSYCHOL.,* 1958, 57, 321–326.

LÖVAAS, O. J. EFFECT OF EXPOSURE TO SYMBOLIC AGGRESSION ON AGGRESSIVE BEHAVIOR. *CHILD DEVELOPM.,* 1961, 32, 37–44.

MCBREARTY, J. F., MARSTON, A. R., & KANFER, F. H. CONDITIONING A VERBAL OPERANT IN A GROUP SETTING: DIRECT VS. VICARIOUS REINFORCEMENT. *AMER. PSYCHOLOGIST,* 1961, 16, 425. (ABSTRACT)

MOWRER, O. H. *LEARNING THEORY AND THE SYMBOLIC PROCESSES.* NEW YORK: WILEY, 1960.

SAN FRANCISCO CHRONICLE. "JAMES DEAN" KNIFING IN SOUTH CITY. *SAN FRANCISCO CHRON.,* MARCH 1, 1961, 6.

SCHRAMM, W., LYLE, J., & PARKER, E. B. *TELEVISION IN THE LIVES OF OUR CHILDREN.* STANFORD: STANFORD UNIVER. PRESS, 1961.

SEARS, R. R., MACCOBY, ELEANOR E., & LEVIN, H. *PATTERNS OF CHILD REARING.* EVANSTON: ROW, PETERSON, 1957.

SECHREST, L. VICARIOUS REINFORCEMENT OF RESPONSES. *AMER. PSYCHOLOGIST,* 1961, 16, 356. (ABSTRACT)

SIEGEL, ALBERTA E. FILM-MEDIATED FANTASY AGGRESSION AND STRENGTH OF AGGRESSIVE DRIVE. *CHILD DEVELOPM.,* 1956, 27, 365–378.

WARDEN, C. J., FJELD, H. A., & KOCH, A. M. IMITATIVE BEHAVIOR IN REBUS AND RHESUS MONKEYS. *J. GENET. PSYCHOL.,* 1940, 56, 311–322.

NOTES

1. This investigation was supported in part by Research Grants M-4398 and M-5162 from the National Institute of Health, United States Public Health Service, and the Lewis S. Haas Child Development Research Fund, Stanford University.

    The authors are indebted to David J. Hicks for his generous assistance with the photography and to John Steinbruner who assisted with various phases of this study.

2. This research was carried out while the junior author was the recipient of an American Association of University Women International Fellowship for postdoctoral research.

CHAPTER 2
Cognitive Neuroscience

Introducing Cognitive Neuroscience

JAMIE WARD

Between 1928 and 1947, Wilder Penfield and colleagues carried out a series remarkable experiments on over 400 living human brains (e.g. Penfield & Rasmussen 1950). The patients in question were undergoing brain surgery for epilepsy. To identify and spare regions of the brain involved in movement and sensation, Penfield electrically stimulated regions of the cortex while the patient was still conscious. The procedure was not painful (the surface of the brain does not contain pain receptors) but the patients did report some fascinating experiences. When stimulating the occipital lobe one patient reported "a star came down towards my nose". Upon stimulating a region near the central sulcus, another patient commented "those fingers and my thumb gave a jump". After temporal lobe stimulation, another patient claimed "I heard the music again; it is like the radio". She was later able to recall the tune she heard and was absolutely convinced that there must have been a radio in the operating theatre. Of course, the patients had no idea when the electrical stimulation was being applied. They couldn't physically feel it or see it. As far as they were concerned, an electrical stimulation applied to the brain felt pretty much like a mental/cognitive event.

This book tells the emerging story of how mental processes such as thoughts, memories, and perceptions are organized and implemented by the brain. It is also concerned with how it is possible to study the mind and brain, and how we know what we know. The term **cognition** collectively refers to a variety of higher mental processes such as thinking, perceiving, imagining, speaking, acting and planning. **Cognitive neuroscience** is a bridging discipline between cognitive science and cognitive psychology, on the one hand, and biology and neuroscience, on the other. It has emerged as a distinct enterprise only recently and has been driven by methodological advances that enable the study of the human brain safely in the laboratory. It is perhaps not too surprising that earlier methods, such as direct electrical stimulation of the brain, failed to enter into the mainstream of research.

This chapter begins by placing a number of philosophical and scientific approaches to the mind and brain in an historical perspective. The coverage is selective rather than exhaustive, and students with a particular interest in these issues might want to read more deeply elsewhere (e.g. Gross, 1998). The chapter then provides a basic overview of the current methods used in cognitive neuroscience. A more detailed analysis and comparison of the different methods is provided in Chapters 3 to 5. Finally, the chapter

> ### Key Terms
>
> **Cognition:** A variety of higher mental processes such as thinking, perceiving, imagining, speaking, acting and planning.
>
> **Cognitive neuroscience:** Aims to explain cognitive processes in terms of brain-based mechanisms.

attempts to address some of the criticisms of the cognitive neuroscience approach that have recently been articulated.

COGNITIVE NEUROSCIENCE IN HISTORICAL PERSPECTIVE

Philosophical Approaches to Mind and Brain

Philosophers as well as scientists have long been interested in how the brain could create our mental world. How is it that a physical substance can give rise to our feelings, thoughts and emotions? This has been termed the **mind-body problem**, although it should more properly be called the mind-brain problem because it is now agreed that the brain is the key part of the body for cognition. One position is that the mind and brain are made up of different lands of substance, even though they may interact. This is known as **dualism**, and the most famous proponent of this idea was René Descartes (1596–1650). Descartes believed that the mind was non-physical and immortal whereas the body was physical and mortal. He suggested that they interact in the pineal gland, which lies at the centre of the brain and is now considered part of the endocrine system. According to Descartes, stimulation of the sense organs would cause vibrations in the body/brain that would be picked up in the pineal gland, and this would create a non-physical sense of awareness. There is little hope for cognitive neuroscience if dualism is true because the methods of physical and biological sciences cannot tap into the non-physical domain (if such a thing were to exist).

Even in Descartes' time, there were critics of his position. One can identify a number of broad approaches to the mind-body problem that still have a contemporary resonance. Spinoza (1632–1677) argued that mind and brain were two different levels of explanation for the same thing, but not two different kinds of thing. This has been termed **dual-aspect theory** and it remains popular with some current researchers in the field (e.g. Velmans, 2000). An analogy can be drawn to wave-particle duality in physics in which the same entity (e.g. an electron) can be described both as a wave and as a particle.

An alternative approach to the mind-body problem that is endorsed by many contemporary thinkers is **reductionism** (e.g. Churchland, 1995; Crick, 1994). This position states that although cognitive, mind-based concepts (e.g. emotions, memories, attention) are currently useful for scientific exploration, they will eventually be replaced by purely biological constructs (e.g. patterns of neuronal firings, neurotransmitter release). As such, psychology will eventually reduce to biology as we learn more and more about the brain. Advocates of this approach note that there are many historical precedents in which scientific constructs are abandoned when a better explanation is found. In the seventeenth century, scientists believed that flammable materials contained a substance, called *phlogiston,* which was released when burned. This is similar to classical notions that fire was a basic element along with water, air and earth. Eventually, this construct was replaced by an understanding of how chemicals combine with oxygen. The process of burning became just one example (along with rusting) of this particular chemical reaction. Reductionists believe that mind-based concepts, and conscious experiences in particular, will have the same status as phlogiston in a future theory of the brain. Those who favour dual-aspect theory over reductionism point out that an emotion will still *feel* like an emotion even if we were to fully understand its neural basis and, as such, the usefulness of cognitive, mind-based concepts will never be fully replaced.

Scientific Approaches to Mind and Brain

Our understanding of the brain emerged historically late, largely in the nineteenth century, although some important insights were gained during classical times. Aristotle (384–322 BC) noted that the ratio of brain size to body size was greatest in more intellectually advanced species, such as humans. Unfortunately, he made the error of claiming that cognition was a product of the heart rather than the brain.

> ### Key Terms
>
> **Mind–body problem:** The problem of how a physical substance (the brain) can give rise to our feelings, thoughts and emotions (our mind).
>
> **Dualism:** The belief that mind and brain are made up of different kinds of substance.
>
> **Dual-aspect theory:** The belief that mind and brain are two levels of description of the same thing.

He believed that the brain acted as a coolant system: the higher the intellect, the larger the cooling system needed. In the Roman age, Galen (circa AD 129–199) observed brain injury in gladiators and noted that nerves project to and from the brain. Nonetheless, he believed that mental experiences themselves resided in the ventricles of the brain. This idea went essentially unchallenged for well over 1500 years. For example, when Vesalius (1514–1564), the father of modern anatomy, published his plates of dissected brains, the ventricles were drawn in exacting detail whereas the cortex was drawn crudely and schematically. Others followed in this tradition, often drawing the surface of the brain like the intestines. This situation probably reflected a lack of interest in the cortex rather than a lack of penmanship. It is not until one looks at the drawings of Gall and Spurzheim (1810) that the features of the brain become recognizable to modern eyes.

Gall (1758–1828) and Spurzheim (1776–1832) received a bad press, historically speaking, because of their invention and advocacy of **phrenology**. Phrenology had two key assumptions. First, that different regions of the brain perform different functions and are associated with different behaviours. Second, that the size of these regions produces distortions of the skull and correlates with individual differences in cognition and personality. Taking these two ideas in turn, the notion of **functional specialization** within the brain has effectively endured into modern cognitive neuro-science, having seen off a number of challenges over the years (Flourens, 1824; Lashley, 1929). The observations of Penfield and co-workers on the electrically stimulated brain provide some striking examples of this principle. However, the functional specializations of phrenology were not empirically derived and were not constrained by theories of cognition. For example, Fowler's famous phrenologist's head had regions dedicated to "parental love", "destructiveness" and "firmness". Moreover, skull shape has nothing to do with cognitive function.

Aside from inventing phrenology, Gall and Spurzheim made a number of important anatomical observations, such as delineating between the functions of white and grey matter, and the realization that the brain is folded to conserve space (see Gross, 1998). Their empirical observations and theoretical insights paved the way for future developments in the nineteenth century, the most notable of which are Broca's reports of two brain-damaged patients (Broca, 1861). Broca documented two cases in which acquired brain damage had impaired the ability to speak but left other aspects of cognition relatively intact. He concluded that language could be localized to a particular region of the brain. Subsequent studies argued that language itself was not a single entity but could be further subdivided into speech recognition, speech production and conceptual knowledge (Lichtheim, 1885; Wernicke, 1874). This was motivated by the observation that brain damage can lead either to poor speech comprehension and good production, or good speech comprehension and poor production (see Chapter 10 for full details). This suggests that there are at least two speech faculties in the brain and that each can be independently impaired by brain damage. This body of work was a huge step forward in terms of thinking about mind and brain. First, empirical observations were being used to determine what the building blocks of cognition are (is language a single faculty?) rather than listing them from first principles. Second and related, they were developing models of cognition that did not make direct reference to the brain. That is, one could infer that speech recognition and production were separable without necessarily knowing *where* in the brain they were located, or how the underlying neurons brought these processes about. The approach of using patients with acquired brain damage to inform theories of normal cognition is called **cognitive neuropsychology** and remains highly influential today (Chapter 5 discusses the logic of this method in detail). Cognitive neuropsychology is now effectively subsumed within the term "cognitive neuroscience", where the latter phrase is seen as being less restrictive in terms of methodology.

Whereas discoveries in the neurosciences continued apace throughout the nineteenth and twentieth centuries, the formation of psychology as a discipline at the end of

> **Key Terms**
>
> **Reductionism:** The belief that mind-based concepts will eventually be replaced by neuroscientific concepts.
>
> **Phrenology:** The failed idea that indivdual differences in cognition can be mapped onto differences in skull shape.
>
> **Functional specialization:** Different regions of the brain are specialised for different functions.

the nineteenth century took the study of the mind away from its biological underpinnings. This did not reflect a belief in dualism, it was due, in part, to some pragmatic constraints. Early pioneers of psychology, such as William James and Sigmund Freud, were interested in topics like consciousness, attention, and personality. Neuroscience has had virtually nothing to say about these issues until quite recently. Another reason for the schism between psychology and biology lies in the notion that one can develop coherent and testable theories of cognition that do not make claims about the brain. The modern foundations of cognitive psychology lie in the computer metaphor of the brain and the **information processing** approach, popular from the 1950s onwards. For example, Broadbent (1958) argued that much of cognition consists of a sequence of processing stages. In his simple model, perceptual processes occur, followed by attentional processes that transfer information to short-term memory and thence to long-term memory (see also Atkinson & Shiffrin, 1968). These were often drawn as a series of box-and-arrow diagrams. The implication was that one could understand the cognitive system in the same way as one could understand the series of steps performed by a computer program, and without reference to the brain. The idea of the mind as a computer program has advanced over the years along with advances in computational science. For example, many cognitive models contain some element of interactivity and parallel processing. **Interactivity** refers to the fact that stages in processing may not be strictly separate and that later stages can begin before earlier stages are complete. Moreover, later stages can influence the

outcome of early ones (**top-down processing**).

Parallel processing refers to the fact that lots of different information can be processed simultaneously (serial computers process each piece of information one at a time). Although these computationally explicit models are more sophisticated than earlier box-and-arrow diagrams they, like their predecessors, do not always make contact with the neuroscience literature (Ellis & Humphreys, 1999).

COMPUTATIONAL AND CONNECTIONIST MODELS OF COGNITION

In the 1980s, powerful computers became widely accessible as never before. This enabled cognitive psychologists to develop computationally explicit models of cognition (that literally calculate a set of outputs given a set of inputs) rather than the computationally inspired, but underspecified, box-and-arrow approach. One particular way of implementing computational models has been very influential; namely the **neural network**, connectionist or parallel distributed processing (PDP) approach (McClelland, Rumelhart, & Group 1986). These models are considered in a number of places throughout this book, notably in the chapters dealing with memory, speaking, and literacy.

Connectionist models have a number of architectural features. First, they are composed of arrays of simple information-carrying units called nodes. **Nodes** are information-carrying in the sense that they respond to a particular set of inputs (e.g. certain letters, certain sounds) and produce a restricted set of outputs. The responsiveness of a node depends on now strongly it is connected to other nodes in the network (the "weight" of the connection) and how active the other nodes are. It is possible to calculate, mathematically, what the output of any node would be, given a set of input activations and a set of weights. There are a number of advantages to this type of model. For example, by adjusting the weights over time as a result of experience, the model can develop and learn. The parallel processing enables large amounts of data to be processed simultaneously. A more controversial claim is that they have "neural plausibility". Nodes, activation and weights are in many ways analogous to neurons, firing rates and neural connectivity, respectively. However, these models have been criticized for being too powerful in that they can learn many things that real brains cannot (e.g. Pinker & Prince, 1988). A more moderate view is that connectionist models provide examples of ways in which the brain *might* implement a given cognitive function. Whether or not the brain actually *does* implement cognition in that particular way will ultimately be a question for empirical research in cognitive neuroscience.

The Birth of Cognitive Neuroscience

It was largely advances in imaging technology that provided the driving force for modern-day cognitive neuroscience. Raichle (1998) describes how brain imaging was in a "state of indifference and obscurity in the neuroscience community in the 1970s" and might never have reached prominence if it were not for the involvement of cognitive psychologists in the 1980s. Cognitive psychologists had already established experimental designs and information-processing models that could potentially fit well with these emerging methods. It is important to note that the technological advances in imaging not only led to the development of functional imaging, but also enabled brain lesions to be described precisely in ways that were never possible before (except at post mortem).

Present-day cognitive neuroscience is composed of a broad diversity of methods. These will be discussed in detail in subsequent chapters. At this juncture, it is useful to compare and contrast some of the most prominent methods. The distinction between *recording* methods and *stimulation* methods is crucial in cognitive neuroscience. Electrical stimulation of the brain in humans is now rarely carried out. The modern-day equivalent of these studies uses magnetic, not electric, fields and is called transcranial magnetic stimulation (TMS). These can be applied across the skull rather than directly to the brain. This method will

be considered in Chapter 5, alongside the effect of organic brain lesions. Electrophysiological methods (EEG/ERP and single-cell recordings) and magnetophysiological methods (MEG) record the electrical/magnetic properties of neurons themselves. These methods are considered in Chapter 3. In contrast, functional imaging methods (PET and fMRI) record physiological changes associated with blood supply to the brain which evolve more slowly over time. These are called haemodynamic methods and are considered in Chapter 4.

The methods of cognitive neuroscience can be placed on a number of dimensions:

- The **temporal resolution** refers to the accuracy with which one can measure *when* an event is occurring. The effects of brain damage are permanent and so this has no temporal resolution as such. Methods such as EEG, MEG, TMS and single-cell recording have millisecond resolution. PET and fMRI have temporal resolutions of minutes and seconds, respectively, that reflect the slower haemodynamic response.

The methods of cognitive neuroscience can be placed on a number of dimensions:

- The **spatial resolution** refers to the accuracy with which one can measure *where* an event is occurring. Lesion and functional imaging methods have comparable resolution at the millimetre level, whereas single-cell recordings have spatial resolution at the level of the neuron.
- The *invasiveness* of a method refers to whether or not the equipment is located internally or externally. PET is invasive because it requires an injection of a radio-labelled isotope. Single-cell recordings are performed on the brain itself and are normally only carried out in non-human animals.

DOES COGNITIVE PSYCHOLOGY NEED THE BRAIN?

As already noted, cognitive psychology developed substantially from the 1950s, using information-processing models that do not make direct reference to the brain. If this way of doing things remains successful, then why change? Of course, there is no reason why it should change. The claim is not that cognitive neuroscience is replacing cognitive psychology (although some might endorse this view) but merely that cognitive psychological theories can inform theories and experiments in the neurosciences and vice versa. However, others have argued that this is not possible by virtue of the fact that information-processing models do not make claims about the brain (Coltheart, 2004b; Harley, 2004).

Coltheart (2004b) poses the question: "Has cognitive neuroscience, or if not might it ever (in principle, or even in practice) successfully use data from cognitive neuroimaging to make theoretical decisions entirely at the cognitive level (e.g. to adjudicate between competing information-processing models of some cognitive system)?" (p. 21). Henson (2005) argues that it can in principle and that it does in practice. He argues that data from functional imaging (blood flow, blood oxygen) comprise just another dependent variable that one can measure. For example, there are a number of things that one could measure in a standard forced-choice reaction-time task: reaction time, error rates, sweating (skin conductance response), muscle contraction (electromyograph), scalp electrical recordings (EEG) or haemodynamic changes in the brain (PET, fMRI). Each measure will relate to the task in some way and can be used to inform theories about the task.

To illustrate this point, consider one example. One could ask a simple question such as: "does visual recognition of words and letters involve computing a representation that is independent of case?" For example, does the reading system treat "E" and "e" as equivalent at an early stage in processing or are "E" and "e" treated as different letters until some later stage (e.g. saying them aloud)? A way of investigating this using a reaction-time measure is to present the same word twice in the same or different case (e.g. radio-RADIO, RADIO-RADIO) and compare this with situations in which the word differs (e.g. mouse-RADIO, MOUSE-RADIO). One general finding in reaction-time studies is that it is faster to process a stimulus if the same stimulus has recently been presented. For example, if asked to make a speeded decision about RADIO (e.g. is it animate or inanimate) then performance will be faster if it has been previously encountered. Dehaene et al. (2001) investigated this mechanism by comparing reaction-time measures with functional imaging (fMRI) measures. In his task, the first word in each pair was presented very briefly and was followed by visual noise. This prevents the participants from consciously perceiving it and, hence, one can be sure that they are not saying the word. The second word is consciously seen and requires a response. Dehaene et al. found that reaction times are faster to the second word when it follows the same word, irrespective of case. Importantly, there is a region in the left fusiform cortex that shows the same effect (although in terms of "activation" rather than response time). In this concrete example, it is meaningless to argue that one type of measure is "better" for informing cognitive theory (to return to Coltheart's question) given that both are measuring different aspects of the same thing. One could explore the nature of this effect further by, for instance, presenting the same word in different languages (in bilingual speakers), presenting the words in different locations on the screen and so on. This would provide further insights into the nature of this mechanism (e.g. what aspects of vision does it entail, does it depend on word meaning). However, both reaction-time measures and brain-based measures could be potentially informative. It is not the case that functional imaging is merely telling us *where* cognition is happening and not *how* it is happening.

Another distinction that has been used to contrast cognitive psychology and cognitive neuroscience is that between software and hardware, respectively (Coltheart, 2004b; Harley, 2004). This derives from the familiar computer analogy in which one can, supposedly, learn about information processing (software) without knowing about the brain (hardware). As has been shown, to some extent this is true. But the computer analogy is a little misleading. Computer software is written by computer programmers (who, incidentally, have human brains). However, information processing is not written by some third person and then inscribed into the brain. Rather, the brain provides causal constraints on the nature of information processing. This is not analogous to the computer domain in which the link between software and hardware is arbitrarily determined by a computer programmer. To give a simple example, one model of word recognition suggests that words are recognized by searching words in a mental dictionary one by one until a match is found (Forster, 1976). The weight of evidence from cognitive psychology argues against this serial search, and in favour of words being searched in parallel (i.e. all candidate words are considered at the same time). But why should this be so? Computer programs can be made to recognize words adequately with both serial search and parallel search. The reason why human information processing uses a parallel search and not a serial search probably lies in the relatively slow *neural* response time (acting against serial search). This constraint does not apply to the fast processing of computers. Thus, cognitive psychology may be sufficient to tell us the structure of information processing but it may not answer deeper questions about why information processing should be configured in that particular way.

DOES NEUROSCIENCE NEED COGNITIVE PSYCHOLOGY?

It would be no exaggeration to say that the advent of techniques such as functional imaging have revolutionized the brain sciences. For example, consider some of the newspaper headlines above that have appeared in recent years. Of course, it has been well known since the nineteenth century that pain, mood, intelligence and sexual desire would be largely a product of processes in the brain. The reason why headlines such as these are extraordinary is because now the technology exists to be able to study these processes *in vivo*. Of course, when one looks inside the brain one does not "see" memories, thoughts, perceptions and so on (i.e. the stuff of cognitive psychology). Instead, what one sees is grey matter, white matter, blood vessels and so on (i.e. the stuff of neuroscience). It is the latter, not the former, that one observes when conducting a functional imaging experiment. Developing a framework for linking the two will necessarily entail dealing with the mind-body problem either tacitly or explicitly. This is a daunting challenge.

Is functional imaging going to lead to a more sophisticated understanding of the mind and brain than was achieved by the phrenologists? Some of the newspaper reports in the figure suggest it might not. One reason why phrenology failed is because the method had no real scientific grounding; the same cannot be said of functional imaging. Another reason why phrenology failed was that the psychological concepts used were naïve. It is for this reason that functional imaging and other advances in neuroscience do require the insights from cognitive psychology to frame appropriate research questions and avoid becoming a new phrenology (Uttal, 2001).

The question of whether cognitive, mind-based concepts will eventually become redundant (under a reductionist account) or coexist with neural-based accounts (e.g. as in dual-aspect theory) is for the future to decide. But for now, cognitive, mind-based concepts have an essential role to play in cognitive neuroscience.

IS THE BRAIN MODULAR?

The notion that the brain contains different regions of functional specialization has been around in various guises for 200 years. However, one particular variation on this theme has attracted particular attention and controversy—namely Fodor's (1983, 1998) theory of **modularity**. First, Fodor makes a distinction between two different classes of cognitive process: central systems versus modules. The key difference between them relates to the types of information they can process. Modules are held to be **domain specific** in that they process only one particular type of information (e.g. colour, shape, words, faces), whereas central systems are held to be domain independent in that the type of information processed is non-specific (candidates would be memory, attention, executive functions). According to Fodor, one advantage of modular systems is that, by processing only a limited

Key Terms

Modularity: The notion that certain cognitive processes (or regions of the brain) are restricted in the type of information they process.

type of information, they can operate rapidly, efficiently and in isolation from other cognitive systems. An additional claim is that modules may be innately specified in the genetic code.

Many of these ideas have been criticized on empirical and theoretical grounds. For example, it has been suggested that domain specificity is not innate although the means of acquiring it could be (Karmiloff-Smith, 1992). Moreover, systems like reading appear modular in some respects but cannot be innate because they are recent in evolution. Others have argued that evidence for interactivity suggests that modules are not isolated from other cognitive processes (Farah, 1994).

On balance, the empirical evidence does not strongly favour this version of modularity. However, the extent to which the brain contains regions of functional specialization and domain specificity is still an active area of debate.

> **Key Terms**
>
> **Domain-specificity:** The idea that a cognitive process (or brain region) is dedicated solely to one particular type of information (e.g. colour, faces, words).

SUMMARY AND KEY POINTS OF THE CHAPTER

- The mind–body problem refers to the question of how physical matter (the brain) can produce mental experiences, and this remains an enduring issue in cognitive neuroscience.
- To some extent, the different regions of the brain are specialized for different functions.
- Functional neuroimaging has provided the driving force for much of the development of cognitive-neuroscience, but there is a danger in merely using these methods to localize cognitive functions without understanding how they work.
- Cognitive psychology has developed as a discipline without making explicit references to the brain. However, biological measures can provide an alternative source of evidence to inform cognitive theory and the brain must provide constraining factors on the nature and development of the information processing models of cognitive science.

EXAMPLE ESSAY QUESTIONS

- What is the "mind–body problem" and what frameworks have been put forward to solve it?
- Is cognitive neuroscience the new phrenology?
- Does cognitive psychology need the brain? Does neuroscience need cognitive psychology?

RECOMMENDED FURTHER READING

- Gross, C.G. (1998). *Brain, vision, memory.* Cambridge, MA: MIT Press. Subtitled "Tales in the history of neuroscience", the book does just that and in an engaging way.
- Henson, R. (2005). What can functional neuroimaging tell the experimental psychologist? *Quarterly Journal of Experimental Psychology, 58A,* 193–233. An excellent psychology and a rebuttal of common criticisms.
- Uttal, W.R. (2001). *The new phrenology: The limits of localising cognitive processes in the brain.* Cambridge, MA: MIT Press. An interesting overview of the methods and limitations of cognitive neuroscience.
- Velmans, M. (2000). *Understanding consciousness.* London: Routledge. In-depth coverage of the mind-body problem, drawing on some evidence from cognitive neuroscience.

Routes to Remembering

The Brains Behind Superior Memory

ELEANOR A. MAGUIRE, ELIZABETH R. VALENTINE, JOHN M. WILDING, AND
NARINDER KAPUR

Why do some people have superior memory capabilities? We addressed this age-old question by examining individuals renowned for outstanding memory feats in forums such as the World Memory Championships. Using neuropsychological measures, as well as structural and functional brain imaging, we found that superior memory was not driven by exceptional intellectual ability or structural brain differences. Rather, we found that superior memorizers used a spatial learning strategy, engaging brain regions such as the hippocampus that are critical for memory and for spatial memory in particular. These results illustrate how functional neuroimaging might prove valuable in delineating the neural substrates of mnemonic techniques, which could broaden the scope for memory improvement in the general population and the memory-impaired.

Humans have an enduring fascination with memory. We are moved by the devastating effects of Alzheimer's disease on the one hand, and are often covetous of superior memory on the other. A testament to the latter is the interest throughout history in prodigious individuals renowned for spectacular mnemonic feats[1–3]. Despite its popular appeal, however, exceptional memory is seldom addressed in mainstream research[3–5], a fact which stands in contrast to the voluminous literature on memory loss. Although our understanding of the functional anatomy of human memory in the context of brain damage has certainly grown over the years, there have been far fewer attempts to explore the other end of the cognitive spectrum—those with superior memory.

One reason for the lack of interest may be that individuals with exceptionally good memories are in some way distinct, limiting the inferences that can be made about memory in the general population. However, it is equally possible that individuals with exceptional memory merely make more or better use of memory capabilities that we all possess, or perhaps they employ clever mnemonic devices or learning strategies[3]. Given that the basis of superior memory is still largely unknown, important insights into the structure of human memory may be missed by not exploring better-than-average memorizers as well as those with memory deficits. Moreover, understanding superior memory may also inform our efforts to improve memory in the general population and the memory-impaired. Some clues about the nature of superior memory can and have been gleaned from behavioral testing[3]. However, documenting the neural underpinnings would offer significant insights into the mechanisms of exceptional memory performance.

Expertise within specific knowledge domains (such as chess[6], calculation[7], and cars and birds[8]) has been examined previously with functional neuroimaging, but people with more generalized superior memory abilities have not been studied. Here we report the neural basis of memory in such individuals. Although exceptional individuals have been sporadically documented in the literature, they are more difficult to find than those with memory problems, who often seek advice. However, the World Memory Championships—a unique gathering of individuals performing exceptional memory feats across a range of tasks—is held annually in London[3,9]. We therefore examined eight participants who are or have been placed at the highest levels in the World Memory Championships, as well as two other individuals studied previously for their extraordinary memory accomplishments (see reports of TE and TM in ref. 3). The ten superior memorizers (SMs) were compared with ten matched control subjects who did not report any exceptional memory capabilities.

We set out to address three main questions. First, do SMs differ from control subjects in other intellectual abilities, which could drive the apparent superiority in memory functioning? Second, as there are reports of structural brain differences in groups with specific skills[10,11], are SMs predisposed to superior memory performance by virtue of having structurally different brains compared with control subjects, either innately or by developing their superior memory[10]? And finally, using functional magnetic resonance imaging (fMRI), we investigated if there were differences between SMs and controls in the brain areas engaged while processing incoming information. The present results show that superior memory was not due to exceptional intellect or to structural brain differences. Rather, we found that superior memory was associated with the preferential engagement of three brain regions in particular: medial parietal cortex, retrosplenial cortex and the right posterior hippocampus.

RESULTS
Neuropsychological testing

The superior memorizers were not exceptional in their performance on tests of general cognitive ability; they were in the high-average range in both general verbal and non-verbal skills, comparable to normal controls. As expected, the SMs performed significantly better than control subjects on tests of working and long-term verbal memory, these tasks being similar to those commonly featured in memory competitions. The two groups did not differ on the measure of visual memory, perhaps owing to the fact

that the SMs do not in general practice recall of visual patterns.

Structural brain imaging

Optimized structural MRI images of the brains of SMs and control subjects were compared for differences in gray matter volume using whole-brain voxel-based morphometry (VBM)[12]. For structural brain analysis, VBM has many advantages over region-of-interest (ROI) techniques in that it is automated rather than observer-based, and the whole brain is considered with no *a priori* regions of interest. VBM is sensitive to structural hippocampal changes in clinical[13] as well as non-clinical[10,14] subjects. For example, structural differences between the hippocampi of London taxi drivers and the general population have been reported[10]. Importantly, the MRI scans of the taxi drivers were not only analyzed using VBM, but they were also independently analyzed using the standard ROI approach focusing on the hippocampus. The findings from the two techniques were completely concordant, confirming the appropriateness of using VBM to study the hippocampus in non-clinical samples. Another study using VBM also reports hippocampal differences in a non-clinical context in relation to gender[14].

When the SMs and control subjects were compared, no significant differences were evident (either at a threshold of $P < 0.05$ corrected for multiple comparisons, or at the more liberal $P < 0.005$ uncorrected). Among the SMs, there were no changes in gray matter volume as a function of the number of years engaged in actively challenging their superior memory, or in relation to performance on the standard measures or later experimental measures (see below). Although our samples were quite small, VBM changes have been detected in similar settings[10,13]. This result suggests that superior memory in the SMs is not associated with structural brain differences (that can be detected by VBM).

Functional brain imaging

As neither exceptional intellect nor gross structural brain differences seemed to relate to superior memory, we then used fMRI to index neural activity while subjects were learning new information. During scanning, the SMs and control subjects learned items that were presented visually and the order in which they were presented—tasks at which the SMs excel. Imaging data were recorded during learning, and behavioral performance was measured for order and item recognition memory.

One potential confound with this fMRI protocol, given that SMs tend to perform better than control subjects, is that differences in brain activity may reflect the amount of information being successfully learned rather than the mechanisms underlying the cognitive process. To address this issue, we included three classes of stimuli in the fMRI study. Three-digit numbers, which are items that the SMs particularly excel at learning, were expected to elicit a large performance difference between the two groups. The second stimulus type comprised faces, which are items that the SMs are excellent at learning but that can also be well retained by many individuals in the general population, so less of a difference was expected between the two groups. The final stimulus type was snowflakes[15], which are unusual and difficult to verbalize; thus we expected little or no difference between the two subject groups for this stimulus type. This expected range of performance differences was indeed reflected in the data, with the greatest difference between groups seen for the digit stimuli, then faces and finally snowflakes. Thus we could differentiate brain activity that covaried with performance from activity that was associated with the learning process itself (irrespective of the amount of material being learned).

fMRI analysis showed that several brain regions were active for all contrasts in both groups. To verify which brain regions were active in each subject for each contrast, we did a conjunction analysis (Methods). Briefly, by calculating the contrast for each stimulus type minus its control task, we removed low-level and stimulus-related visuo-perceptual factors. This showed that several brain regions were active in all subjects during the learning of all stimulus types. These included bilateral superior frontal sulcus (Talairach coordinates (x, y, z):−24, 12, 63; 30, 6, 60), left medial superior frontal sulcus (−3, 18, 45), bilateral caudate (−12, 12, 12; 12, 3, 15), left angular gyrus (−30,−72, 36) and bilateral cerebellum (−33,−57,−33; 33,−63,−33). In addition, the left middle occipital gyrus (−21,−90,−12) was active for all subjects for snowflakes only. The left posterior

inferior frontal sulcus (−48, 15, 21) was active for both groups, except during digit learning in the control subjects.

Our main interest was in the difference between the fMRI data of the SMs and control subjects. The two groups were compared directly, and the resulting differences were of two sorts: (i) some brain areas, such as the right cerebellum, were active in both groups for all stimulus types but were more active in the SMs and (ii) more notably, some areas were active only in the SMs and not in the controls at the thresholds used. Several brain regions were active in SMs for all stimulus types, irrespective of performance: left medial superior parietal gyrus, bilateral retro-splenial cortex, and right posterior hippocampus.

In addition to the above differences present for all stimulus types, areas more active in the SMs for digits were the right cingulate cortex, left fusiform cortex and left posterior inferior frontal sulcus. According to the probability map of this region[16], this activation is unlikely (probability 5–25%) to be in Broca's area (pars opercularis). For faces, the area that was more active in SMs was in the vicinity of right pallidum; for snowflakes, the area in the vicinity of left pallidum.

Had the memory performance of SMs and control subjects differed significantly across all tasks, it would be conceivable that the fMRI activation differences might merely reflect this difference in performance. However, our experimental design ensured a range of performance, from the SMs being much better than controls (digits) to both groups performing similarly (snowflakes). The main findings hold, irrespective of performance differences, showing that these regions were involved in the learning process *per se* and not merely in the efficacy of encoding. We did, however, also test for changes in activity associated with level of performance, and compared the SMs and control subjects directly. When performance scores were entered as covariates, the only difference to emerge between the groups was in the order test for digits, where bilateral ventral putamen was more active in the SMs (−21,−3,−3; 21,−3,−6).

DISCUSSION

We conclude that the increased activity in the medial parietal cortex, retrosplenial cortex and right posterior hippocampus of the SMs was not a function of better performance, as these differences pertained even when performance between the SMs and controls was matched, as in the snowflakes task. These brain regions are known to be important for memory, and are implicated in spatial memory and navigation[17–20]. Debriefing of subjects after scanning revealed that all of the SMs used mnemonics during the learning phase. Mnemonics are strategies for encoding information with the sole purpose of making it more memorable[21]. Nine out of the ten SMs used the mnemonic known as the 'method of loci' for some or all of the tasks. The origin of this ancient method, sometimes called the 'journey' or 'mental walk' technique[22], is attributed to the Greek poet Simonides of Ceos in 477 BC[1], who describes using routes and visualizing to-be-remembered items at salient points along the routes, and then mentally retracing those routes during recall. The efficacy of the method of loci is reflected in its continued use over two and a half millennia in virtually unchanged form. It is interesting to note that, although very proficient in the use of this spatial mnemonic, no structural brain changes were detected in the right posterior hippocampus of the SMs, as have been found in London taxi drivers[10]. This may be because taxi drivers store a large and complex spatial representation of London, whereas the SMs use and re-use a more constrained set of routes.

The distinctive activations of SMs may simply reflect differences between the two groups in the engagement of associative memory. However, debriefing of the subjects revealed striking similarities between the two groups in their use of feature selection and association. During the encoding of faces, both SMs and controls reported noting significant features (hair, eyes) or associating each face with a person they knew or with a personality trait. For the snowflakes, the main strategy for both groups was to select significant features and associate them with objects. Only the SMs associated the digit stimuli with images (in one case words and then images) of people, animals or objects. None of the control subjects reported such associations. In all cases, except the control subjects during digit learning, the left posterior inferior frontal sulcus, which is an area previously reported to be involved in learning associations, was active[23,24]. Direct comparison between the two groups confirmed this area to be more active in SMs for digit learning. Along with other activations such as those in the caudate nucleus[23], the posterior inferior frontal area may reflect the associative aspects of these learning tasks.

Crucially, only the SMs proceeded to use their newly-associated stimuli in the route strategy. None of the control subjects reported using any standard mnemonic techniques.

We therefore believe that the parietal, retrosplenial and right posterior hippocampal activations in the SMs reflected the use of the route strategy, either in learning the new items on the routes and/or in retrieving the routes themselves, which were typically real and familiar. There are other possible interpretations; for example, the SMs were well-practiced in using mnemonics (on average, for more than eleven years), and the observed pattern of activations may instead or in addition reflect the duration of use of the method of loci. Alternatively, it may be that the fMRI group differences relate to a special facility on the part of SMs for using this mnemonic. The examination of a control group of subjects newly instructed in the method of loci will be an important element of future studies to further clarify this issue.

Memory superiority has mainly been attributed to mnemonics[3,25]. Mnemonic devices are often regarded as overly complicated, requiring explicit effort to use, and thus limited in their relevance for everyday memory. In some situations, however, such devices are very effective, and it has been argued that mnemonics such as the method of loci do indeed organize information in a manner that is relevant to our daily lives[21]. These strategies may simply be more efficient variations of normal memory functions[26], systematizing the natural process. Mnemonics are reported to be effective in memory remediation in elderly[27] and special needs[28] populations. The value of mnemonics in the context of acquired brain injury and disease is less clear[29,30], although there is little knowledge of the precise brain areas engaged by different mnemonic strategies. The aim of the current study was not to examine mnemonics specifically or the method of loci, but rather to compare SMs and control subjects. Our findings do, however, indicate that fMRI could prove valuable in delineating the neural substrates of mnemonic techniques. This may extend the horizon for effective memory improvement in the general population and facilitate rational and focused rehabilitative interventions in patients.

In summary, we have addressed the long-standing question of why some people have superior memories compared with those of others. We found that those with superior memory use a spatial learning strategy and engage brain regions that are critical for spatial memory. The longevity and success of the method of loci in particular may point to a natural human proclivity to use spatial context—and its instantiation in the right hippocampus—as one of the most effective means to learn and recall information.

METHODS

Subjects. All participants gave informed written consent in accordance with the local research ethics committee. Data from 10 SMs are reported; all were male and one was left-handed. Eight of the SMs are or have been placed at the highest levels in the World Memory Championships. All gave explicit consent for disclosure of this information. The remaining two SMs had both been studied previously, and their extraordinary memory feats are documented elsewhere[3]. Ten control subjects also participated. All were male, and each was matched with a SM according to age and handedness. All participants were healthy at the time of scanning. For one SM, there was a query of dyslexia as a child in the early 1960s, but he has had no difficulties in adulthood; one was reported to have had seizures in childhood that resolved at puberty without recurrence.

Materials and procedure. During the fMRI scan, subjects were asked to learn items that were presented visually and to learn the order (sequence) in which they occurred. There were three types of stimuli: three-digit numbers, faces and snowflakes. Different stimulus types were not mixed within a sequence. There were six items per sequence and five sequences of each stimulus type. The order of stimulus types was pseudorandom. Each item in a sequence was presented alone on the screen for 4 s. After a sequence was presented, the subject then saw pairs of stimuli from that sequence and indicated by key press which of the two items came earlier in the sequence (note that the items could have been from any point in the sequence). There were three such pairs; thus subjects saw each item once more during this order recognition task. Each pair was on screen for 5 s, and the subject had to respond within this time. This retrieval task was included to provide an online assessment of order memory and to encourage subjects to actively engage in the learning tasks; although modeled, it was not the primary interest of the fMRI study.

There was a control task for each stimulus type. As in the learning tasks, stimuli appeared one at a time for 4 s each, but there were only two stimuli for control trials, and they were repeated alternately three times. Thus there was minimal memory load, and subjects paid attention for any change in the appearance of an item. In the case of the faces or snowflakes, this change was in the form of blurring of the image, and a change in the font used for the digits. The changes occurred only very rarely (once for each stimulus type in the scanning session). Subjects responded by key press to a visually presented question as to whether they had noted a change or not after the presentation of the control stimuli in a trial was complete. Thus, the learning and control tasks were comparable with respect to visual and perceptual inputs and (absence of) motor demands. All stimuli were presented on an off-white background and shown centrally.

After scanning, each subject performed forced-choice recognition memory tests for each stimulus type (outside of the scanner). Each test comprised items seen during scanning and an equal number of foils. The subject saw two items at a time on the screen for 4 s and responded by key press to identify which one of each pair was seen during scanning. Subjects then indicated by key press whether or not they were confident in their response. Each subject was debriefed about how he had performed the tasks during scanning and the strategies, if any, he had used. In addition, a number of standard general abilities tests were also administered to assess whether SMs and control subjects were comparable in their basic intellectual, verbal and visual abilities.

Image acquisition and data analysis. Data were acquired using a 2-tesla Magnetom VISION (Siemens GmbH, Erlangen, Germany) MRI system. Contiguous multi-slice T2*-weighted fMRI images were obtained with echo-planar imaging (echo time (TE), 40 ms; whole head: 32 slices, each 3 mm thick, 3 s per volume). For each subject, high-resolution volumetric MR images were acquired using an optimized MPRAGE sequence affording enhanced gray/white matter contrast and segmentation[31]. Functional images were processed and analyzed using Statistical Parametric Mapping (SPM99, Wellcome Department of Imaging Neuroscience, London, UK) in a standard manner as described elsewhere[32], with a smoothing kernel of 8 mm full-width half maximum (FWHM).

The standard boxcar model was used to characterize fMRI activation effects. Each contrast (functional data for each stimulus minus those for its control task) was calculated for each subject and then brought to the second level in the standard manner using SPM99. The findings for each group (SMs and controls) were then calculated using a random effects analysis. Commonalities across all subjects were also calculated in a standard manner with SPM99, using contrasts from each subject. As these were all orthogonal, it was possible to ascertain which areas were commonly active across subjects for a given contrast. The main aim of the experiment was to consider any possible differences between SMs and control subjects. To examine this, the two groups were directly compared in SPM99 at the random effects level. Only those fMRI activations surviving a threshold of $P < 0.05$ corrected for multiple comparisons were considered; this applied throughout, for group effects, conjunction analyses and group differences. For two areas of particular interest specified in advance—the hippocampus and prefrontal cortex—we used a threshold of $P < 0.001$ uncorrected, although the majority of activations in these areas also survived the $P < 0.05$ corrected threshold.

Structural MRI data were analyzed using an optimized method of whole-brain voxel-based morphometry (VBM[12]) implemented in SPM99, using a smoothing kernel of 10 mm FWHM. Regionally specific differences in gray matter density between subject groups were assessed. The significance threshold was set at $P < 0.05$ (corrected).

ACKNOWLEDGMENTS

This work was supported by the Wellcome Trust and the University of London Central Research Fund. We thank D. Passingham, U. Noppeney, C. Good, T. Singer, J. Winston and P. Abbott for assistance and advice. We are also grateful for the interest and participation of all the superior memorizers and control volunteers.

Competing interests statement

The authors declare that they have no competing financial interests.

NOTES

1. Yates, F.A. *The Art of Memory* (Pimlico, London, 1966).
2. Luria, A.R. *The Mind of a Mnemonist* (Penguin, Harmondsworth, UK, 1975).
3. Wilding, J. & Valentine, E. *Superior Memory* (Psychology Press, Hove, UK, 1997).
4. Brown, E. & Deffenbacher, K. Forgotten mnemonists. *J. Hist. Behav. Sci.* 11, 342–349 (1975).
5. Neisser, U. *Memory Observed: Remembering in Natural Contexts* 377–381 (Freeman, San Francisco, 1982).
6. Amidzic, O., Riehle, H.J., Fehr, T., Wienbruch, C. & Elbert, T. Pattern of focal y-bursts in chess players. *Nature* **412**, 603 (2001).
7. Presenti, M. *et al.* Mental calculation in a prodigy is sustained by right prefrontal and medial temporal areas. *Nat. Neurosci.* **4**, 103–107 (2001).
8. Gauthier, I., Skudlarski, P., Gore, J.C. & Anderson, A.W. Expertise for cars and birds recruits brain areas involved in face recognition. *Nat. Neurosci.* **3**, 191–197 (2000).
9. Butcher, J. Dominic O'Brien—master mnemonist. *The Lancet* **356**, 836 (2000).
10. Maguire, E.A. *et al.* Navigation-related structural change in the hippocampi of taxi drivers. *Proc. Natl. Acad. Sci. USA* **97**, 4398–4403 (2000).
11. Schlaug, G., Jancke, L., Huang, Y. & Steinmetz, H. *In vivo* evidence of structural brain asymmetry in musicians. *Science* **267**, 699–701 (1995).
12. Ashburner, J. & Friston, K.J. Voxel-based morphometry—the methods. *Neuroimage* **11**, 805–821 (2000).
13. Gadian, D.G. *et al.* Developmental amnesia associated with early hypoxicischemic injury. *Brain* **123**, 499–507 (2000).
14. Good, C.D. *et al.* Cerebral asymmetry and the effects of sex and handedness on brain structure: a voxel based morphometric analysis of 465 normal adult human brains. *Neuroimage* **14**, 685–700 (2001).
15. Bentley, W.A. & Humphreys, W.J. *Snow Crystals* (Dover, New York, 1962).
16. Tomaiuolo, F. *et al.* Morphology, morphometry and probability mapping of the pars opercularis of the inferior frontal gyrus: an *in vivo* MRI analysis. *Eur. J. Neurosci.* **11**, 3033–3046 (1999).

17. Maguire, E.A. *et al.* Knowing where, and getting there: a human navigation network. *Science* **280**, 921–924 (1998).

18. Burgess, N., Maguire, E.A. & O'Keefe, J. The human hippocampus and spatial and episodic memory. *Neuron* **35**, 625–641 (2002).

19. O'Keefe, J. & Nadel, L. *The Hippocampus as a Cognitive Map* (Oxford Univ. Press, Oxford, 1978).

20. Maguire, E.A. The retrosplenial contribution to human navigation: a review of lesion and neuroimaging findings. *Scand. J. Psychol.* **42**, 225–238 (2001).

21. Bellezza, F.S. Mnemonic devices: classification, characteristics and criteria. *Rev. Educ. Res.* **51**, 247–275 (1981).

22. Bower, G.H. Analysis of a mnemonic device. *Am. Scientist* **58**, 496–510 (1970).

23. Toni, I. & Passingham, R.E. Prefrontal-basal ganglia pathways are involved in the learning of arbitrary visuomotor associations: a PET study. *Exp. Brain Res.* **127**, 19–32 (1999).

24. Dolan, R.J. & Fletcher, P.C. Dissociating prefrontal and hippocampal function in episodic memory encoding. *Nature* **388**, 582–585 (1997).

25. Chase, W.G. & Ericsson, K.A. Skill and working memory. In *The Psychology of Learning and Motivation* Vol. 16 (ed. Bower, G.H.) 1–58 (Academic, New York, 1982).

26. Roediger, H.L. The effectiveness of four mnemonics in ordering recall. *J. Exp. Psych. Hum. Learn. Mem.* **6**, 558–567 (1980).

27. Verhaeghen, P. & Marcoen, A. On the mechanisms of plasticity in young and older adults after instruction in the method of loci: evidence for an amplification model. *Psychol. Aging* **11**, 164–178 (1996).

28. Bender, B.G. & Levin, J.R. Pictures, imagery, and retarded children's prose learning. *J. Educ. Psych.* **70**, 583–588 (1978).

29. Richardson, J.T.E. The efficacy of imagery mnemonics in memory remediation. *Neuropsychologia* **33**, 1345–1357 (1995).

30. Wilson, B.A. Memory rehabilitation. in *Neuropsychology of Memory* 3rd edn. (eds. Squire, L.R. & Schacter, D.L.) 263–272 (Guilford Press, New York, 2002).

31. Deichmann, R., Good, C.D., Josephs, O., Ashburner, J. & Turner, R. Optimization of 3D MP-RAGE sequences for structural brain imaging. *Neuroimage* **12**, 112–127 (2000).

32. Maguire, E.A., Vargha-Khadem, F. & Mishkin, M. The effects of bilateral hippocampal damage on fMRI regional activations and interactions during memory retrieval. *Brain* **124**, 1156–1170 (2001).

33. Oldfield, R.C. The assessment and analysis of handedness: the Edinburgh Inventory. *Neuropsychologia* **9**, 97–113 (1971).

34. Nelson, H.E. & Wilson, J.R. *National Adult Reading Test* (NART) 2nd edn. (Berkshire, Windsor, UK, 1991).

35. *Wechsler Abbreviated Scale of Intelligence* (WASI). (The Psychological Corporation, San Antonio, Texas, 1999).

36. Rey, A. L'examen psychologique dans les cas d'encephalopathy. *Archives de Psychologie* **28**, 286–340 (1942).

37. Osterrieth, P.A. Le test de copie d'une figure complexe. *Archives de Psychologie* **30**, 206–356 (1944).

38. Coughlan, A. & Hollows, S.E. *Adult Memory and Information Processing Battery* (AMIPB). Psychology Department, St. James Hospital, Leeds, UK (1985).

39. *Wechsler Adult Intelligence Scale—Revised* (British Adaptation) (WAIS-R). (The Psychological Corporation, San Antonio, Texas, 1986).

40. Bennett-Levy, J., Polkey, C.E. & Powell, G. Self-report of memory skills after temporal lobectomy: the effect of clinical variables. *Cortex* **16**, 543–557 (1980).

41. McMillan, T.M. Investigation of everyday memory in normal subjects using the Subjective Memory Questionnaire (SMQ). *Cortex* **20**, 333–347 (1984).

Remembering Episodes

A Selective Role for the Hippocampus During Retrieval

LAURA L. ELDRIDGE, BARBARA J. KNOWLTON, CHRISTOPHER S. FURMANSKI,
SUSAN Y. BOOKHEIMER, AND STEPHEN A. ENGEL

Some memories are linked to a specific time and place, allowing one to re-experience the original event, whereas others are accompanied only by a feeling of familiarity. To uncover the distinct neural bases for these two types of memory, we measured brain activity during memory retrieval using event-related functional magnetic resonance imaging. We show that activity in the hippocampus increased only when retrieval was accompanied by conscious recollection of the learning episode. Hippocampal activity did not increase for items recognized based on familiarity or for unrecognized items. These results indicate that the hippocampus selectively supports the retrieval of episodic memories.

Studies of neuropsychological patients have revealed that damage to the medial temporal lobe can produce a deficit in declarative memory, the conscious memory for facts and events[1]. Due to the diffuse nature of many medial temporal lobe lesions (which may include entorhinal, perirhinal and parahippocampal cortices as well as hippocampus), it is difficult to ascertain the role of individual structures. Although some evidence indicates that the hippocampus is particularly important for declarative memory[2–5], other evidence suggests that the hippocampus

only supports memories embedded in a particular spatial and temporal context[6–10], a form of declarative memory known as episodic memory. Thus, controversy currently surrounds whether hippocampal patients exhibit a selective deficit only in their memory for episodes or a more general impairment in conscious memory.

Despite the great wealth of information provided by studies of neuropsychological patients, these investigations may ultimately be unable to resolve the complete role of the hippocampus in memory because they cannot fully distinguish encoding and retrieval deficits. The re-experience of time and place during retrieval differentiates episodic memories from other forms of declarative memory. As a result, it is critical to study how the hippocampus is involved in retrieval processes to understand whether the hippocampus is uniquely involved in episodic memory. Unfortunately, hippocampal patients tend to suffer from a pronounced learning deficit that may obscure the true nature of an additional retrieval deficit[3,9].

Neuroimaging techniques provide a means for measuring patterns of neural activity associated with retrieval processes in normal subjects. This allows for retrieval processes to be isolated from those processes associated with learning. Functional neuroimaging has identified medial temporal lobe regions that are important for establishing memories[11–15]. For instance, activity in parahippocampal cortex during encoding predicts whether memories will later be judged as episodic, based on familiarity, or forgotten[16].

Although neural activity has also been measured during memory retrieval, activity in the hippocampus has rarely been reported[17].

To determine the role of the hippocampus in memory retrieval, we used functional magnetic resonance imaging (fMRI) to measure changes in blood flow associated with neural activity in normal subjects during episodic and non-episodic retrieval. Subjects were told to memorize each word for a subsequent memory test. They were not given any instructions on memorization techniques nor was there a secondary task. Twenty minutes later, as functional images were acquired, we presented the subjects with studied and unstudied items. We asked them first to determine whether they had studied the word, and then to classify their memory for the word as episodic or non-episodic. Thus, on each trial the subject made two button-press responses. If the hippocampus is selectively involved in episodic memory, then it should be particularly active during the retrieval of memories that subjects classify as episodes.

To categorize the type of memory retrieved on each trial, subjects performed the remember-know task[18] during scanning, in which subjects classify their memories as either episodic (remember) or based on familiarity (know). This task has been used extensively to identify episodic recollections under a variety of conditions. Accuracy for remember and know judgments can be dissociated by several manipulations, including dividing attention at study or altering the frequency of studied words[19,20]. As the first step of the task, subjects indicated whether they confidently recognized the item. For recognized items, subjects then made a remember (R) response if they could recollect the moment the item was studied or a know (K) response if they had no such recollection. R responses could, for example, be based on perceptual details subjects noticed or associations they made with the word during study. Know (K) responses indicated that the word was highly familiar but unaccompanied by recollections of the specific moment the word was presented. Encoding conditions were the same for all studied words. However, at retrieval, episodic content was only available for items given an R response. The fMRI data were selectively averaged according to these different types of retrieval events.

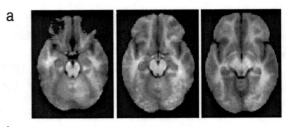

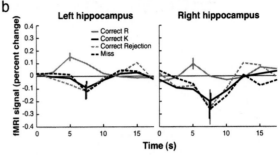

Fig. 1. *Results from anatomically defined hippocampal regions of interest. (**a**) Sections from the anatomical template with the left hippocampal region of interest outlined in red. The right hippocampus was selected using the same anatomical landmarks in the right hemisphere. (**b**) Averaged event-related responses in the hippocampus from 11 subjects. In left hippocampus, correct R response amplitudes were reliably larger than zero ($t_{10} = 4.56, p < 0.001$), indicating a significant increase from baseline. The correct R response amplitudes were also larger than the correct K ($t_{10} = 4.62, p < 0.001$), correct rejection ($t_{10} = 3.76, p < 0.01$), and miss response amplitudes ($t_{10} = 4.29, p < 0.01$). In right hippocampus, correct R response amplitudes were reliably larger than correct K ($t_{10} = 3.10, p < 0.05$) and miss response amplitudes ($t_{10} = 4.47, p < 0.01$). Error bars represent ± one standard error (between subjects) of estimated response amplitudes.*

RESULTS

Typically, subjects are more accurate at discriminating between studied and unstudied items using R responses than K responses[19,20]. When subjects incorrectly recognize an unstudied item, they are more likely to classify the memory as a K response than as an R response because details of the study episode should be absent. Our behavioral results showed this expected pattern; the R false alarm rate was 1%, and the K false alarm rate was 33%. In addition, subjects accurately identified old items when they made an R response (mean hit rate, 42%; d´ = 2.58). Subjects also accurately identified old items using the K response (mean hit rate, 73% under the assumption that all remembered items were also known; d´ = 1.17). Despite some difference in the number of trials in each condition (correct R, mean ± s.d., 45.0 ± 16.6; correct K, 32.9 ± 7.4; correct rejection, 17.7 ± 5.5; miss, 26.0 ± 11.0), each of the included conditions contained sufficient numbers of trials (at least 10 per subject) for analysis.

Analysis of the fMRI data indicated that the hippocampus was active selectively during episodic retrieval. We identified a hippocampal region of interest in each hemisphere, which consisted of the CA fields and dentate gyrus, using only anatomical landmarks. These regions of interest (ROIs) were determined blind to activation patterns in each subject. Event-related responses averaged within these regions of interest are shown in Fig. 1. In the left hippocampus, correct R trials produced significant increases in MR signal relative to the fixation baseline. MR signal associated with correct R responses was also significantly greater than signal associated with correct K responses, correct rejection of new items, and miss responses, in which subjects did not recognize old items. In individual subject analyses, correct R responses resulted in greater MR signal than correct K responses in 10 of the 11 subjects.

Importantly, correct K, correct rejection and miss responses were of equal size, and all differed reliably from

Table 1. *Locations of differential R and K activity.*

| Region | H | Talairach coordinates | | | t-value |
		x	y	z	
R > K					
Middle frontal gyrus	L	−30	32	45	5.89
Posterior cingulate gyrus	R	13	−23	45	4.28
Precentral gyrus	R	51	−9	40	4.17
Inferior parietal gyrus	L	−43	−56	40	5.60
Inferior parietal/angular gyrus	R	53	−58	35	3.64
Inferior frontal gyrus	R	55	7	25	6.61
Inferior parietal gyrus	L	−50	−41	25	5.23
Middle temporal gyrus	L	−44	−63	20	5.84
Posterior cingulate gyrus	R	17	−57	15	4.47
Superior temporal gyrus	L	−58	−39	10	8.32
Caudate nucleus	L	−12	16	5	4.28
Insula	L	−36	−8	0	5.76
Hippocampus	L	−32	−23	−10	5.26
Parahippocampal gyrus★	R	21	−38	−10	4.52
Fusiform gyrus	R	34	−55	−15	6.06
K > R					
Anterior cingulate gyrus★	R	11	16	40	5.14
Anterior cingulate gyrus	L	−12	14	40	3.97
Superior frontal sulcus★	R	23	52	25	5.60

Approximate anatomical locations, hemispheres (H, and coordinates in standard stereotaxic space[33] are given for regions showing significant differential activity between correct R and correct K responses (t_{10} > 3.17, p < 0.01 uncorrected). ★Regions that also showed a significant difference between correct K and correct rejection responses.

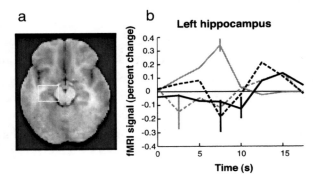

b **Left hippocampus**

Fig. 2. *Results from hippocampal region of interest using a statistical map. (a) Statistical map comparing correct R and correct K response amplitudes. Red voxels represent larger amplitudes for correct R responses. Only voxels with a t-value greater than a threshold of 4.95 are shown. No voxels in this slice showed greater response amplitudes for correct K than for correct R trials. The white square highlights a differentially active region in the left hippocampus (Talairach coordinates, −32,−23,−10). (b) Event-related responses for differentially active voxels within the left hippocampal region. The response amplitude for correct R trials was greater than for correct K trials ($t_{10} = 8.82$, used for pixel selection), correct rejection trials, miss trials, and zero.*

correct R responses. Although functional MRI data cannot determine the absolute level of activity of a structure, our data suggest that the hippocampus was not more active when items were familiar than when they were unfamiliar. Only episodic retrieval produced a pattern of hippocampal activity that was distinguishable from activity produced by unrecognized items.

The pattern of activity in the right hippocampus was similar. Correct R responses were larger than correct K and miss responses, but the difference between correct R and correct rejection responses did not reach statistical significance. The larger effect in left hippocampus may be due to the verbal nature of the stimuli. Studies of memory encoding have also found material-specific lateralization in the medial temporal lobe[11,12].

A second analysis identified regions throughout the brain that showed reliable differences between correct R and correct K response amplitudes (**Table 1**). This analysis localized the differential hippocampal activity to a region within

central portions of the left hippocampus (**Fig. 2**). In addition, greater activation associated with correct R responses than with correct K responses was evident bilaterally in regions of the inferior parietal gyrus and in the left middle frontal gyrus. Several regions also showed greater activity for correct K responses than for correct R responses, including left anterior insula, right superior frontal sulcus and bilateral anterior cingulate. The regions outside the hippocampus overlap with areas commonly activated in memory retrieval tasks[21,22].

A difference in hippocampal activation may exist between correct K and correct rejection responses that was too small to be detected by our study. However, the overall pattern of activity suggests that the absence of a difference between correct K and correct rejection responses in hippocampus was not due to a general lack of sensitivity. In several of the brain regions listed in Table 1, correct K responses were larger than correct rejection responses, indicating that the analyses could detect such differences. The pattern of hippocampal activity cannot simply be explained by the amount of time spent on the task. The two decisions leading to a correct R response (1.7 s) were made faster than those for a correct K (2.2 s; $t_{10} = 12.41$, $p < 0.01$), correct rejection (2.3 s; $t_{10} = 6.56$, $p < 0.01$), or miss response (2.4 s; $t_{10} = 7.86$, $p < 0.01$). Thus, subjects completed the trials that produced the greatest hippocampal responses in the least amount of time, suggesting that hippocampal activity is not the result of general mental effort.

DISCUSSION

The present results may explain why some previous studies have failed to find activation in the hippocampus during retrieval[23,24]. Studies that average hippocampal activity across episodic and non-episodic retrieval are likely to find little activation. Our data predict this outcome because during episodic retrieval MR signal increased in the hippocampus, whereas during non-episodic retrieval it decreased; the same cancellation of signal may also have occurred in the K condition of another study that used the R-K procedure[25]. It is likely that the K condition in this study[25] contained both episodic and non-episodic memories, because it used a version of the R-K task that may not adequately distinguish between episodic and non-episodic forms of memory. The way in which the subject is instructed to perform the R-K task has a profound effect on the classification of memories. If subjects decide in a single step whether an item is an R, a K or new, they will tend to use the R and K labels to indicate strong and weak memory[26], rather than episodic and non-episodic memory. The procedure used in the present study, in which subjects first decide if they recognize an item and subsequently decide for recognized items whether the item corresponds to an R or a K, seems to encourage subjects to apply the R and K labels as episodic and non-episodic memory.

Our results are consistent with theories asserting that the hippocampus is necessary for the retrieval of episodes, but provide no evidence that it is necessary for recognition based on familiarity. The present data do not directly address whether the hippocampus is important for the retrieval of other forms of non-episodic memory, such as memory for facts. Nevertheless, our results suggest that the hippocampus is not important for the retrieval of all forms of declarative memory. In addition, the role of this structure in retrieval must be time-limited, because memories acquired long before hippocampal damage can be retrieved normally[3]. A process of consolidation occurs over time so that eventually the hippocampus is no longer required even for episodic retrieval.

Selective lesions of the hippocampus in animals produce recognition deficits in some tasks[27], but leave performance unimpaired in other tasks[28]. These results parallel the present findings, which suggest that the hippocampus is required only for some forms of recognition. Episodic memory cannot be directly assessed in animals. However, one critical feature of episodic memory is the retrieval of spatio-temporal context, which can be assessed in non-humans using contextual learning protocols. In contextual learning, animals must encode and retrieve the configuration of features that compose the context in order to perform the task. Hippocampal lesions cause specific impairments in these tasks[29]. Lesions restricted to the hippocampus in rats, for example, produce deficits in contextual fear conditioning, though not in conditioning to discrete cues[30].

Episodic memories are the conjunction of features that compose a particular event. The function of the hippocampus during retrieval may be to help reinstate these complex conjunctions of features. The fMRI data presented here may provide a glimpse of the hippocampus as it binds together the disparate elements of a retrieved experience.

METHODS

Subjects. Twelve healthy, right-handed subjects were run in the experiment (age range 22–38). One subject was excluded from all analyses because of excessive motion during scanning. These studies were performed under a protocol approved by the UCLA Office for the Protection of Research Subjects.

Stimuli. Stimuli consisted of 108 target words and 27 lures. Each of the 9 functional scans contained 12 target words and 3 lures in a random order. A design with a relatively low number of lures was chosen to ensure that sufficient numbers of correct K trials were obtained, while maintaining reasonably high levels of accuracy. In each five-second trial, subjects were first prompted to decide whether or not they recognized the item (3 s), and subsequently for recognized items whether they remembered or knew it (2 s). Responses were recorded via button presses. If the item was not recognized, the subject pressed either button at the second prompt. Between trials, subjects maintained fixation for 15 s. Subjects were instructed to disengage from retrieval performance during the fixation period.

fMRI methods. A 3T GE Signa scanner with ANMR echo-planar upgrade was used for all functional imaging. A T2*-weighted gradient echo sequence was used to measure blood-oxygen level dependent contrast (TR, 2.5 s; TE, 45 ms) in 16 horizontal slices (voxel size, $3.125 \times 3.125 \times 5$ mm). Each scan contained 15 trials.

AIR software[30] was used for image realignment, transformation into standard stereotaxic space, and spatial smoothing (6 mm Gaussian kernel) of data used in the group average. We divided each fMRI time series into 20-s blocks corresponding to each trial. We classified the subject's responses as either 'hit' or 'false alarm' for R, K and not recognized trials. We averaged the corresponding 20 s of fMRI data for each response type separately. There were too few R and K false alarms to allow further analysis of those trials. Over half of the subjects had less than 10 R and K false alarms combined. All subsequent analyses considered only correct R, correct K, correct rejection and miss (incorrect not recognized) responses.

Response amplitudes were computed for the average event-related responses by fitting a gamma function to the data[32]. The gamma fitting procedure estimated both a lag and amplitude parameter for each averaged response of each subject.

For all analyses, response amplitudes were compared using a paired *t*-test, implementing a random-effects model. For the hippocampal analysis, response amplitudes were computed for anatomically defined regions of interest (CA fields and dentate gyrus) in each subject. The regions of interest were specified using the group anatomical template and verified in each subject's individual anatomy images. For the full brain analysis, paired *t*-tests were conducted at each voxel. Statistical parametric maps were then displayed for each contrast. The regional differences that are reported consist of at least five contiguous voxels that surpass a threshold of $p < 0.01$ ($t > 3.17$) without correction for multiple comparisons. These regions were localized on the normalized anatomical template and labeled using the nomenclature of Talairach and Tournoux[33].

ACKNOWLEDGMENTS

We thank M. Cohen, M. Fanselow, J. Mazziotta and L. Squire for comments on the manuscript and A. Toga for computational resources. This work was supported by the Brain Mapping Medical Organization, the Ahmanson Foundation, the Pierson-Lovelace Foundation, the Tamkin Foundation and the Jennifer Jones-Simon Foundation. L.L.E. was funded by a National Science Foundation graduate fellowship.

NOTES

1. Squire, L. R. & Knowlton, B. J. in *The New Cognitive Neurosciences* (ed. Gazzaniga, M. S.) 765–779 (MIT Press, Cambridge, Massachusetts, 1999).

2. Zola-Morgan, S., Squire, L. R. & Amaral, D. G. Human amnesia and the medial temporal region: enduring memory impairment following a bilateral lesion limited to field CA1 of the hippocampus. *J. Neurosci.* **6**, 2950–2967 (1986).

3. Rempel-Clower, N. L., Zola, S. M., Squire, L. R. & Amaral, D. G. Three cases of enduring memory impairment after bilateral damage limited to the hippocampal formation. *J. Neurosci.* **16**, 5233–5255 (1996).

4. Ostergaard, A. L. & Squire, L. R. Childhood amnesia and distinctions between forms of memory: A comment on Wood, Brown, and Felton. *Brain Cogn.* **14**, 127–133 (1990).

5. Squire, L. R. & Zola, S. M. Episodic memory, semantic memory, and amnesia. *Hippocampus* **8**, 205–211 (1998).

6. Moscovitch, M. Recovered consciousness: A hypothesis concerning modularity and episodic memory. *J. Clin. Exp. Neuropsychol.* **17**, 276–290 (1995).

7. Aggleton, J. P. & Brown, M. W. Episodic memory, amnesia, and the hippocampal-anterior thalamic axis. *Behav. Brain Sci.* **22**, 425–489 (1999).

8. Tulving, E. & Markowitsch, H. J. Episodic and declarative memory: Role of the hippocampus. *Hippocampus* **8**, 198–204 (1998).

9. Vargha-Khadem, F. *et al.* Differential effects of early hippocampal pathology on episodic and semantic memory. *Science* **277**, 376–380 (1997).

10. Tulving, E., Hayman, G. A. C. & Macdonald, C. A. Long-lasting perceptual priming and semantic learning in amnesia: A case experiment. *J. Exp. Psychol. Learn. Mem. Cogn.* **17**, 595–617 (1991).

11. Kelley, W. M. *et al.* Hemispheric specialization in human dorsal frontal cortex and medial temporal lobe for verbal and nonverbal memory encoding. *Neuron* **20**, 927–936 (1998).

12. Wagner, A. D. *et al.* Building memories: remembering and forgetting of verbal experiences as predicted by brain activity. *Science* **281**, 1188–1191 (1998).

13. Rombouts, S. A. *et al.* Visual association encoding activates the medial temporal lobe: a functional magnetic resonance imaging study. *Hippocampus* **7**, 594–601 (1997).

14. Fernandez, G. *et al.* Successful verbal encoding into episodic memory engages the posterior hippocampus: a parametrically analyzed functional magnetic resonance imaging study. *J. Neurosci.* **18**, 1841–1847 (1998).

15. Dolan, R. J. & Fletcher, P. F. Encoding and retrieval in human medial temporal lobes: an empirical investigation using functional magnetic resonance imaging (fMRI). *Hippocampus* **9**, 25–34 (1999).

16. Brewer, J. B. *et al.* Making memories: Brain activity that predicts how well visual experience will be remembered. *Science* **281**, 1185–1187 (1998).

17. Schacter, D. L. & Wagner, A. D. Medial temporal lobe activations in fMRI and PET studies of episodic encoding and retrieval. *Hippocampus* **9**, 7–24 (1999).

18. Tulving, E. Memory and consciousness. *Can. Psychol.* **26**, 1–12 (1985).

19. Gardiner, J. M. & Parkin, A. J. Attention and recollective experience in recognition memory. *Memory Cogn.* **18**, 579–583 (1990).

20. Knowlton, B. J. The relationship between remembering and knowing: A cognitive neuroscience perspective. *Acta Psychol.* **98**, 253–265 (1998).

21. Buckner, R. L., Koutstaal, W., Schacter, D. L., Wagner, A. D. & Rosen, B. R. Functional-anatomic study of episodic retrieval using fMRI. I. Retrieval effort versus retrieval success. *Neuroimage* **7**, 151–162 (1998).

22. Rugg, M. D. *et al.* Neural correlates of memory retrieval during recognition memory and cued recall. *Neuroimage* **8**, 262–273 (1998).

23. Buckner, R. L. *et al.* Functional-anatomic study of episodic retrieval. II. Selective averaging of event-related fMRI trials to test the retrieval success hypothesis. *Neuroimage* **7**, 163–175 (1998).

24. Saykin, A. J. *et al.* Functional differentiation of medial temporal and frontal regions involved in processing novel and familiar words: an fMRI study. *Brain* **122**, 1963–1971 (1999).

25. Henson, R. N., Rugg, M. D., Shallice, T., Josephs, O. & Dolan, R. J. Recollection and familiarity in recognition memory: an event-related functional magnetic resonance imaging study. *J. Neurosci.* **19**, 3962–3972 (1999).

26. Hicks, J. L. & Marsh, R. L. Remember-know judgments can depend on how memory is tested. *Psychonomic Bull. Rev.* **6**, 117–122 (1999).

27. Zola, S. M., Squire, L. R., Teng, E., Stefanacci, L., Buffalo, E. A. & Clark, R. E. Impaired recognition memory in monkeys after damage limited to the hippocampal region. *J. Neurosci.* **20**, 451–463 (2000).

28. Murray, E. A. & Mishkin, M. Object recognition and location memory in monkeys with excititoxic lesions of the amygdala and hippocampus. *J. Neurosci.* **18**, 6568–6582 (1998).

29. Rudy, J. W. & O'Reilly, R. C. Contextual fear conditioning, conjunctive representations, pattern completion, and the hippocampus. *Behav. Neurosci.* **113**, 867–880 (1999).

30. Kim, J. J. & Fanselow, M. S. Modality-specific retrograde amnesia of fear. *Science* **256**, 675–677 (1992).

31. Woods, R. P. *et al.* Creation and use of a Talairach-compatible atlas for accurate, automated, nonlinear intersubject registration, and analysis of functional imaging data. *Hum. Brain Mapp.* **8**, 73–79 (1999).

32. Boynton, G. M. *et al.* Linear systems analysis of functional magnetic resonance imaging in human V1. *J. Neurosci.* **16**, 4207–4221 (1996).

33. Talairach, J. & Tournoux, P. *Co-Planar Stereotaxic Atlas of the Human Brain* (Thieme Verlag, Stuttgart, 1988).

The Interpretive Cortex

The Stream of Consciousness in the Human Brain Can Be Electrically Reactivated

WILDER PENFIELD

There is an area of the surface of the human brain where local electrical stimulation can call back a sequence of past experience. An epileptic irritation in this area may do the same. It is as though a wire recorder, or a strip of cinematographic film with sound track, had been set in motion within the brain. The sights and sounds, and the thoughts, of a former day pass through the man's mind again.

The purpose of this article is to describe, for readers from various disciplines of science, the area of the cerebral cortex from which this neuron record of the past can be activated and to suggest what normal contribution it may make to cerebral function.

The human brain is the master organ of the human race. It differs from the brains of other mammals particularly in the greater extent of its cerebral cortex. The gray matter, or cortex, that covers the two cerebral hemispheres of the brain of man is so vast in nerve cell population that it could never have been contained within the human skull if it were not folded upon itself, and refolded, so as to form a very large number of fissures and convolutions. The fissures are so deep and so devious that by far the greater portion of this ganglionic carpet (about 65 percent) is hidden in them, below the surface.

It is from these two homologous temporal lobes, and from nowhere else, that electrical stimulation has occasionally produced physical responses which *may* be divided into (i) experiential responses and (ii) interpretive responses.

EXPERIENTIAL RESPONSES

Occasionally during the course of a neurosurgical operation under local anesthesia, gentle electrical stimulation in this temporal area, right or left, has caused the conscious patient to be aware of some previous experience (1). The experience seems to be picked out at random from his own past. But it comes back to him in great detail. He is suddenly aware again of those things to which he paid attention in that distant interval of time. This recollection of an experiential sequence stops suddenly when the electrical current is switched off or when the electrode is removed from contact with the cortex. This phenomenon we have chosen to call an experiential response to stimulation.

Case examples (2). The patient S.Be. observed, when the electrode touched the temporal lobe (right superior temporal convolution), "There was a piano over there and someone playing. I could hear the song you know." When the cortex was stimulated again without warning, at approximately the same point, the patient had a different experience. He said: "Someone speaking to another, and he mentioned a name but I could not understand it ... It was like a dream." Again the point was re-stimulated without his knowledge. He said quietly: "Yes, 'Oh Marie, Oh Marie'! Someone is singing it." When the point was stimulated a fourth time he heard the same song again and said it was the "theme song of a radio program."

The electrode was then applied to a point 4 centimeters farther forward on the first temporal convolution. While the electrode was still in place, S.Be. said: "Something brings back a memory. I can see Seven-Up Bottling Company—Harrison Bakery." He was evidently seeing two of Montreal's large illuminated advertisements.

The surgeon then warned him that he was about to apply the electrode again. Then, after a pause, the surgeon said "Now," but he did not stimulate. (The patient has no means of knowing when the electrode is applied, unless he is told, since the cortex itself is without sensation.) The patient replied promptly, "Nothing."

A woman (D.F.) (3) heard an orchestra playing an air while the electrode was held in place. The music stopped when the electrode was removed. It came again when the electrode was reapplied. On request, she hummed the tune, while the electrode was held in place, accompanying the orchestra. It was a popular song. Over and over again, restimulation at the same spot produced the same song. The music seemed always to begin at the same place and to progress at the normally expected tempo. All efforts to mislead her failed. She believed that a gramaphone was being turned on in the operating room on each occasion, and she asserted her belief stoutly in a conversation some days after the operation.

A boy (R.W.) heard his mother talking to someone on the telephone when an electrode was applied to his right temporal cortex. When the stimulus was repeated without warning, he heard his mother again in the same conversation. When the stimulus was repeated after a lapse of time, he said, "My mother is telling my brother he has got his coat on backwards. I can just hear them."

The surgeon then asked the boy whether he remembered this happening. "Oh yes," he said, "just before I came here." Asked again whether this seemed like a dream, he replied: "No, it is like I go into a daze."

J.T. cried out in astonishment when the electrode was applied to the temporal cortex; "Yes doctor, yes doctor. Now I hear people laughing—my friends in South Africa!"

When asked about this, he explained the reason for his surprise. He seemed to be laughing with his cousins, Bessie and Ann Wheliow, whom he had left behind him on a farm in South Africa, although he knew he was now on the operating table in Montreal.

INTERPRETIVE RESPONSES

On the other hand, similar stimulation in this same general area may produce quite a different response. The patient discovers, on stimulation, that he has somehow changed his own interpretation of what he is seeing at the moment, or hearing or thinking. For example, he may exclaim that his present experience seems familiar, as though he had seen it or heard it or thought it before. He realizes that this must be a false interpretation. Or, on the contrary, these things may seem suddenly strange, absurd. Sights or sounds may seem distant and small, or they may come unexpectedly close and seem loud or large. He may feel suddenly afraid, as though his environment were threatening him, and he is possessed by a nameless dread or panic. Another patient may say he feels lonely or aloof, or as though he were observing himself at a distance.

Under normal circumstances anyone may make such interpretations of the present, and these interpretations serve him as guides to action or reaction. If the interpretations are accurate guides, they must be based upon previous comparable experience. It is conceivable, therefore, that the recall mechanism which is activated by the electrode during an experiential response and the mechanism activated in an interpretive response may be parts of a common inclusive mechanism of reflex recognition or interpretation.

No special function had been previously assigned by neurologists to the area in each temporal lobe that is considered "interpretive," though some clinicians have suggested it might have to do with the recall of music. The term *interpretive cortex*, therefore, is no more than slang to be employed for the purposes of discussion. The terms *motor cortex, sensory cortex,* and *speech cortex* began as slang phrases and have served such a purpose. But such phrases must not be understood to signify independence of action of separated units in the case of any of these areas. Localization of function in the cerebral cortex means no more than specialization of function as compared with other cortical regions, not separation from the integrated action of the brain.

Before considering the interpretive cortex further, we may turn briefly to the motor and sensory areas and the speech areas of the cortex. After considering the effects of electrical stimulation there, we should be better able to understand the results of stimulation in the temporal lobes.

SPECIALIZATION OF FUNCTION IN THE CORTEX

Evidence for some degree of localization within the brain was recognized early in the 19th century by Flourens. He concluded from experiment that functional subdivision of "the organ of the mind" was possible. The forebrain (4), he said (cerebral hemispheres and higher brain stem) had to do with thought and will power, while the cerebellum was involved in the coordination of movement.

In 1861, Paul Broca showed that a man with a relatively small area of destruction in a certain part of the left hemisphere alone might lose only the power of speech. It was soon realized that this was the speech area of man's dominant (left) hemisphere. In 1870, Fritsch and Hitzig applied an electric current to the exposed cortex of one hemisphere of a lightly anesthetized dog and caused the legs of the opposite side to move. Thus, an area of cortex called motor was discovered.

After that, localization of function became a research target for many clinicians and experimentalists. It was soon evident that in the case of man, the pre-central gyrus in each hemisphere was related to voluntary control of the contralateral limbs and that there was an analogous area of motor cortex in the frontal lobes of animals. It appeared also that other separate areas of cortex in each hemisphere were dedicated to sensation (one for visual sensation, others for auditory, olfactory, and discriminative somatic sensation, respectively).

It was demonstrated, too, that from the "motor cortex" there was an efferent bundle of nerve fibers (the pyramidal tract) that ran down through the lower brain stem and the spinal cord to be relayed on out to the muscles. Through this efferent pathway, voluntary control of these muscles was actually carried out. It was evident, too, that there were separate sensory tracts carrying nerve impulses in the other direction, from the principal organs of special sense (eye, ear, nose, and skin and muscle) into separate sensory areas of the cortex.

These areas, motor and sensory, have been called "projection areas." They play a role in the projection of nerve currents to the cortex from the periphery of the body, and from the cortex to the periphery. This makes possible (sensory) awareness of environment and provides the individual with a means of outward (motor) expression. The motor cortex has a specialized use during voluntary action, and each of the several sensory areas has a specialized use, when the individual is seeing, hearing, smelling, or feeling.

TRAVELING POTENTIALS

The action of the living brain depends upon the movement, within it, of "transient electrical potentials traveling the fibers of the nervous system." This was Sherrington's phrase. Within the vast circuits of this master organ, potentials travel, here and there and yonder, like meteors that streak across the sky at night and line the firmament with trails of light. When the meteors pass, the paths of luminescence still glow a little while, then fade and are gone. The changing patterns of these paths of passing energy make possible the changing content of the mind. The patterns are never quite the same, and so it is with the content of the mind.

Specialized areas in the cortex are at times active and again relatively quiet. But, when a man is awake, there is always some central integration and coordination of the traveling potentials. There must be activity within the brain stem and some areas of the cortex. This is centrencephalic integration (5).

SENSORY, MOTOR, AND PSYCHICAL RESPONSES TO CORTICAL STIMULATION

My purpose in writing this article is to discuss in simple words (free of technical terms) the meaning of the "psychical" responses which appear only on stimulation of the so-called interpretive cortex. But before considering these responses let us consider the motor and sensory activity of the cortex for a moment.

When the streams of electrical potentials that pass normally through the various areas of sensory cortex are examined electrically, they do not seem to differ from each other except in pattern and timing. The essential difference is to be found in the *fact that* the visual *stream* passes to the visual cortex and then to one subcortical target and the auditory stream passes through the auditory cortex and then on to another subcortical target.

When the surgeon stimulates the intact sensory cortex he must be sending a current along the next "piece of road" to a subcortical destination. This electrode (delivering, for example, 60 "waves" per second of 2-millisecond duration and 1-volt intensity) produces no more than elementary sight when applied to visual cortex. The patient reports colors, lights, and shadows that move and take on crude outlines. The same electrode, applied to auditory cortex, causes him to hear a ringing or hissing or thumping sound. When applied to postcentral gyrus it produces tingling or a false sense of movement.

Thus, sensation is produced by the passage inward of electrical potentials. And when the electrode is applied to the motor cortex, movement is produced by passage of potentials outward to the muscles. In each case positive response is produced by conduction in the direction of normal physiological flow—that is, by dromic conduction (6).

Responses to electrical stimulation that may be called "psychical," as distinguished from sensory or motor, have been elicited from certain areas of the human cortex. But they have never been produced by stimulation in other areas. There are, of course, other large areas of cortex which are neither sensory nor motor in function. They seem to be employed in other neuron mechanisms that are also associated with psychical processes. But the function of these other areas cannot, it seems, be activated by so simple a stimulus as an electric current applied to the cortex.

DREAMY STATES OF EPILEPSY

"Epilepsy" may be defined, in Jackson's words, as "the name for occasional, sudden, excessive, rapid and local discharges of grey matter." Our aim in the operations under discussion was to remove the gray matter responsible for epileptic attacks if that gray matter could be spared. When the stimulating electrode reproduced the psychical phenomenon that initiated the fit, it provided the guidance sought (7).

During the 19th century clinicians had recognized these phenomena as epileptic. They applied the term *intellectual aura* to such attacks. Jackson substituted the expression *dreamy states* (see 8). These were, he said, "psychical states during the onset of certain epileptic seizures, states which are much more elaborate than crude sensations." And again, he wrote, "These are all voluminous mental states and yet of different kinds; no doubt they ought to be classified, but for my present purpose they may be considered together."

"The state," he said, "is often like that occasionally experienced by healthy people as a feeling of 'reminiscence.'" Or the patient has "dreamy feelings," "dreams mixing up with present thoughts," "double consciousness," a "feeling of being somewhere else," a feeling "as if I went back to all that occurred in my childhood," "silly thoughts."

Jackson never did classify these states, but he did something more important. He localized the area of cortex from which epileptic discharge would produce dreamy states. His localization was in the anterior and deep portions of the temporal lobes.

Case example. Brief reference may be made to a specific case. The patient had seizures, and stimulation produced responses which were first recognized as psychical.

In 1936, a girl of 16 (J.V.) was admitted to the Montreal Neurological Institute complaining of epileptic attacks, each of which was ushered in by the same hallucination. It was a little dream, she said, in which an experience from early childhood was reenacted, always the same train of events. She would then cry out with fear and run to her mother. Occasionally this was followed immediately by a major convulsive seizure.

At operation, under local anesthesia, we tried to set off the dream by a gentle electrical stimulus in the right temporal lobe. The attempt was successful. The dream was produced by the electrode. Stimulation at other points on the temporal cortex produced sudden fear without the dream. At still other points, stimulation caused her to say that she saw "someone coming toward me." At another point, stimulation caused her to say she heard the voices of her mother and her brothers (9).

This suggested a new order of cortical response to electrical stimulation. When the neighboring visual sensory area of the cortex is stimulated, any patient may report seeing stars of light or moving colors or black outlines but never "someone coming toward me." Stimulation of the auditory sensory cortex may cause any patient to report that he hears ringing, buzzing, blowing, or thumping sounds, perhaps, but never voices that speak. Stimulation in the areas of sensory cortex can call forth nothing more than the elements of visual or auditory or tactile sensation, never happenings that might have been previously experienced.

During the 23 years that have followed, although practically all areas of the cerebral cortex have been stimulated and studied in more than 1000 craniotomies, performed under local anesthesia, psychical responses of the experiential or interpretive variety have been produced only from the temporal cortex (10, 11).

CLASSIFICATION

It seems reasonable to subdivide psychical responses and psychical seizures (epileptic dreamy states) in the same way, classifying them as "interpretive" or "experiential." Interpretive psychical responses are those involving interpretations of the present experience, or emotions related to it; experiential psychical responses are reenactments of past experiences. Interpretive seizures are those accompanied by auras and illusions; experiential seizures are those accompanied by auras and hallucinations.

The interpretive responses and seizures may be divided into groups (11) of which the commonest are as follows: (i) recognition, the illusion that things seen and heard and thought are familiar (deja vu phenomenon); (ii) visual illusion, the illusion that things seen are changing—for example, coming nearer, growing larger (macropsia); (iii) auditory illusion, the illusion that things heard are changing—for example, coming near, going away, changing tempo; (iv) illusional emotion, the emotion of fear or, less often, loneliness, sorrow, or disgust.

Experiential phenomena (hallucinations) are an awareness of experiences from the past that come into the mind without complete loss of awareness of the present.

DISCUSSION

What, then, is the function of the interpretive cortex? This is a physiological question that follows the foregoing observations naturally.

An electrode, delivering, for example, 60 electrical pulses per second to the surface of the motor cortex, causes a man to make crude movements. When applied to the various sensory areas of the cortex, it causes him to have crude sensations of sight or sound or body feeling. This indicates only that these areas have something to do with the complicated mechanism of voluntary action or conscious sensation. It does not reveal what contribution the cortex may make, or in what way it may contribute to skill in making voluntary movement or qualify the incoming sensory streams.

In the case of the interpretive cortex, the observations are similar. We may say that the interpretive cortex has something to do with a mechanism that can reactivate the vivid record of the past. It has also something to do with a mechanism that can present to consciousness a reflex interpretation of the present. To conclude that here is the mechanism of memory would be an unjustified assumption. It would be too simple.

What a man remembers when he makes a voluntary effort is apt to be a generalization. If this were not so, he might be hopelessly lost in detail. On the other hand, the experiential responses described above are detailed reenactments of a single experience. Such experiences soon slip beyond the range of voluntary recall. A man may summon to mind a song at will. He hears it then in his mind, not all at once but advancing phrase by phrase. He may sing it or play it too, and one would call this memory.

But if a patient hears music in response to the electrode, he hears it in one particular strip of time. That time runs forward again at the original tempo, and he hears the orchestration, or he sees the player at a piano "over there." These are details he would have thought forgotten.

A vast amount of work remains to be done before the mechanism of memory, and how and where the recording takes place, are understood. This record is not laid down in the interpretive cortex, but it is kept in a part of the brain that is intimately connected with it.

Removal of large areas of interpretive cortex, even when carried out on both sides, may result in mild complaints of memory defect, but it does not abolish the capacity to remember recent events. On the other hand, surgical removals that result in bilateral interference with the underlying hippocampal zone do make the recording of recent events impossible, while distant memory is still preserved (12).

The importance of the hippocampal area for memory was pointed out long ago in a forgotten publication by the Russian neurologist Bechterew (13). The year before publication Bechterew had demonstrated the case before the St. Petersburg Clinic for Nervous and Mental Diseases. The man on whom Bechterew reported had "extraordinary weakness of memory, falsifications of memory and great apathy." These defects were shown at autopsy to be secondary to lesions of the mesial surface of the cortex of both temporal lobes. The English neurologists Glees and Griffith (14) reported similar defects, a half century later, in a patient who had symmetrical lesions of the hippocampus and of hippocampal and fusiform gyri on both sides.

The way in which the interpretive cortex seems to be used may be suggested by an example: After years of absence you meet, by chance, a man whose very existence you had forgotten. On seeing him, you may be struck by a sudden sense of familiarity, even before you have time to "think." A signal seems to flash up in consciousness to tell you that you've seen that man before. You watch him as he smiles and moves and speaks. The sense of familiarity grows stronger. Then you remember him. You may even recall that his name was Jones. The sight and the sound of the man has given you an instant access, through some reflex, to the records of the past in which this man has played some part. The opening of this forgotten file was subconscious. It was not a voluntary act. You would have known him even against your will. Although Jones was a forgotten man a moment before, now you can summon the record in such detail that you remark at once the slowness of his gait or a new line about the mouth.

If Jones had been a source of danger to you, you might have felt fear as well as familiarity before you had time to consider the man. Thus, the signal of fear as well as the signal of familiarity may come to one as the result of subconscious comparison of present with similar past experience.

One more example may be given from common experience. A sudden increase in the size of objects seen and in sounds heard may mean the rapid approach of something that calls for instant avoidance action. These are signals that, because of previous experience, we sometimes act upon with little consideration.

SUMMARY

The interpretive cortex has in it a mechanism for instant reactivation of the detailed record of the past. It has a mechanism also for the production of interpretive signals. Such signals could only be significant if past records are scanned and relevant experiences are selected for comparison with present experience. This is a subconscious process. But it may well be that this scanning of past experience and

selection from it also renders the relevant past available for conscious consideration as well. Thus, the individual may refer to the record as he employs other circuits of the brain.

Access to the record of the past seems to be as readily available from the temporal cortex of one side as from that of the other. Auditory illusions (or interpretations of the distance, loudness, or tempo of sounds) have been produced by stimulation of the temporal cortex of either side. The same is true of illusional emotions, such as fear and disgust.

But, on the contrary, visual illusions (interpretations of the distance, dimension, erectness, and tempo of things seen) are only produced by stimulation of the temporal cortex on the nondominant (normally, right) side of the brain. Illusions of recognition, such as familiarity or strangeness, were also elicited only from the nondominant side, except in one case.

CONCLUSION

"Consciousness," to quote William James (15), "is never quite the same in successive moments of time. It is a stream forever flowing, forever changing." The stream of changing states of mind that James described so well does flow through each man's waking hours until the time when he falls asleep to wake no more. But the stream, unlike a river, leaves a record in the living brain.

Transient electrical potentials move with it through the circuits of the nervous system, leaving a path that can be followed again. The pattern of this pathway, from neuron to neuron along each nerve-cell body and fiber and junction, is the recorded pattern of each man's past. That complicated record is held there in temporal sequence through the principle of durable facilitation of conduction and connection.

A steady stream of electrical pulses applied through an electrode to some point in the interpretive cortex causes a stream of excitation to flow from the cortex to the place where past experience is recorded. This stream of excitation acts as a key to the past. It can enter the pathway of recorded consciousness at any random point, from childhood on through adult life. But having entered, the experience moves forward without interference from other experiences. And when the electrode is withdrawn there is a likelihood, which lasts for seconds or minutes, that the stream of excitation will enter the pathway again at the same moment of past time, even if the electrode is reapplied at neighboring points (16).

Finally, an electric current applied to the surface of what may be called the interpretive cortex of a conscious man (i) may cause the stream of former consciousness to flow again or (ii) may give him an interpretation of the present that is unexpected and involuntary. Therefore, it is concluded that, under normal circumstances, this area of cortex must make some functional contribution to reflex comparison of the present with related past experience. It contributes to reflex interpretation or perception of the present.

The combination and comparison of present experience with similar past experience must call for remarkable scanning of the past and classification of similarities. What contribution this area of the temporal cortex may make to the whole process is not clear. The term *interpretive cortex* will serve for identification until students of human physiology can shed more light on these fascinating findings.

REFERENCES AND NOTES

1. W. Penfield, J. *Mental Sci.* **101**, 451 (1955).
2. These patients, designated by the same initials, have been described in previous publications in much greater detail. An index of patients (designated by initials) may be found in any of my books.
3. This case is reported in detail in W. Penfield and H. Jasper, *Epilepsy and the Functional Anatomy of the Human Brain* (Little, Brown, Boston, 1954) (published in abridged form in Russian (translation by N. P. Graschenkov and G. Smirnov) by the Soviet Academy of Sciences, 1958).
4. The forebrain, or prosencephalon, properly includes the diencephalon and the telencephalon, or higher brain stem, and hemispheres. Flourens probably had cerebral hemispheres in mind as distinguished from cerebellum.
5. "Within the brain, a central transactional core has been identified between the strictly sensory or motor systems of classical neurology. This central reticular mechanism has been found capable of grading the activity of most other parts of the brain."—H. Magoun, *The Waking Brain* (Thomas, Springfield, III., (1958).
6. W. Penfield, *The Excitable Cortex in Conscious Man* (Thomas, Springfield, Ill, 1958).
7. It did more than this; it produced illusions or hallucinations that had never been experienced by the patient during a seizure.
8. J. Taylor, Ed., *Selected Writings of John Hughlings Jackson* (Hodder and Stoughton, London, 1931), vol. 1, *On Epilepsy and Epileptiform Convulsions.*
9. Twenty-one years later this young woman, who is the daughter of a physician, was present at a meeting of the National Academy of Sciences in New York while her case was discussed. She could still recall the operation and the nature of the "dreams" that had preceded her seizures (W. Penfield, *Proc. Natl. Acad. Sci. U.S.* **44**, 51 (1958)).
10. In a recent review of the series my associate, Dr. Phanor Perot, has found and summarized 35 out of 384 temporal lobe cases in which stimulation produced experiential responses. All such responses were elicited in the temporal cortex. In a study of 214 consecutive operations for temporal lobe epilepsy, my associate Sean Mullan found 70 cases in which interpretive illusion occurred in the minor seizures before operation, or in which an interpretive response was produced by stimulation during operation. In most cases it occurred both before and during operation.
11. S. Mullan and W. Penfield, *A.M.A. Arch. Neurol. Psychiat.* **81**, 269 (1959).
12. W. Penfield and B. Milner, *A.M.A. Arch. Neurol. Psychiat.* **79**, 475 (1958).
13. W. V. Bechterew, "Demonstration eines Gehirns mit Zerstörung der vorderen und inneren Theile der Hirnrinde beider Schlafenlappen," *Neurol. Zentralbl. Leipzig* **19**, 990 (1900). My attention was called to this case recently by Dr. Peter Gloor of Montreal.
14. P. Glees and H. B. Griffith, *Monatsschr. Psychiat. Neurol.* **123**, 193 (1952).
15. W. James, *The Principles of Psychology* (Holt, New York, 1910).
16. Thus, it is apparent that the beam of excitation that emanates from the interpretive cortex and seems to scan the record of the past is subject to the principles of transient facilitation already demonstrated for the anthropoid motor cortex (A. S. F. Grünbaum and C. Sherrington, *Proc. Roy. Soc.* (*London*) **72B**, 152 (1901); T. Graham Brown and C. S. Sherrington, *ibid.* **85B**, 250

(1912)). Similarly subject to the principles of facilitation are the motor and the sensory cortex of man (W. Penfield and K. Welch, J. *Physiol.* (*London*) **109**, 358 (1949)). The patient D.F. heard the same orchestra playing the same music in the operating room more than 20 times when the electrode was reapplied to the superior surface of the temporal lobe. Each time the music began in the verse of a popular song. It proceeded to the chorus, if the electrode was kept in place.

17. W. Penfield and L. Roberts, *Speech and Brain Mechanisms* (Princeton Univ. Press, Princeton, N. J., 1959).
18. G. Jelgersma, *Atlas anatomicum cerebri humani* (Scheltenia and Holkema, Amsterdam).

CHAPTER 3
Perceptual Processes

Sensation and Perception

RONALD COMER AND ELIZABETH GOULD

ON AND OFF SENSATION

Have you ever noticed how enticing the aroma of your favorite restaurant is when you first walk through the front door? The smell of foods you enjoy coming from the kitchen make your mouth water. Depending on how long it's been since you last ate a meal, you might develop an urgent craving to order as soon as possible!

After you order, while you wait for your meal to arrive, you may not even notice it, but your awareness of the food odors in the room is probably gradually diminishing. By the time your meal is delivered to your table, you are probably not even noticing the smells that seemed so strong when you first entered the restaurant. When the server places your plate on the table, right under your nose, however, you might suddenly begin to notice the smell of food again—this time your own.

Our sense of smell contributes greatly to our enjoyment of a good meal. In fact, all of our senses become involved when we enjoy a meal. We use vision, our sense of sight, to admire the food on the plate. Hearing lets us listen to the sizzle of a particularly hot dish, or enjoy conversation with our dining companions. Obviously, our sense of taste is involved once we actually take a bite of food, but so are our senses of touch, as we discern the temperature and texture of the food. Without our touch senses, we could not tell a rough, cool salad from a smooth, warm soup.

Psychologists have generally agreed that there are five senses: smell, taste, touch, sound, and sight. Touch is actually a complex of senses collectively referred to as the *cutaneous senses* or the *somatosenses*. These include pressure, vibration, pain, temperature, and position. Although we will discuss each of these five major senses separately in this chapter, in most of our day-to-day experiences, we actually use these sensory systems or *modalities* to experience the world.

We use our senses in two almost inseparable processes. One process is **sensation**, the act of using our sensory systems to detect stimuli present in the environment around us. Once acquired, sensory information must be interpreted in the context of past and present sensory stimuli. This process, which also involves recognition and identification (for example, the realization that you recognize the smell in a restaurant as pizza cooking), is broadly defined as **perception**.

Sensation and perception are both critical for our interpretation of, and interaction with, the environment. Accurate functioning of our sensory systems is critical for survival. Imagine how greatly diminished your chances of survival would be if you could not see a fire, feel its heat, hear others crying "fire," smell the smoke, or interpret any of these sensations appropriately. Aside from the clear adaptive significance of our ability to sense and

> **sensation** the act of using our sensory systems to detect environmental stimuli.

> **perception** recognition and identification of a sensory stimulus

perceive the world, our life experiences are greatly enriched by these processes. Let's explore them in more detail.

COMMON FEATURES OF SENSATION

LEARNING OBJECTIVE 1 Describe characteristics shared by all the senses, including receptor cells, transduction, and thresholds, and differentiate between top-down and bottom-up processes of perception.

Each of our sensory systems is set up to convert the physical stimuli we receive from the world outside our bodies into neural information. Sensation and perception occur differently in each of our sensory modalities, but our senses also share some common processes. Each of the senses has a set of specialized cells called **sensory receptor cells** that convert a specific form of environmental stimuli into neural impulses, the form of communication used in our brains and nervous systems. This conversion is called **sensory transduction**.

Our sensory receptors can be activated by very weak stimuli. A stimulus must, however, reach a certain level of intensity before we can detect it, because the conversion of physical stimuli into neural impulses only occurs when the stimuli reach this level or threshold. The minimal stimulus necessary for detection by an individual is called the **absolute threshold**. Although the absolute threshold varies from person to person, in most cases, it is surprisingly small. For instance, many normal humans are capable of detecting a candle flame a mile away on a clear night (Galanter, 1962). Researchers have also worked to determine the smallest difference that we can detect between two stimuli, called the **difference threshold** or **just noticeable difference**. When sensory systems are working optimally, the difference threshold is also remarkably small.

Our senses are generally organized to detect change. This makes adaptive sense since most stimuli we are exposed to are not important enough to warrant our attention. Imagine how difficult it would be to concentrate on reading this chapter if sensory information about the odors of your breath, the taste of your mouth, the sound of the clock ticking, and the touch of your clothing were all competing with your ability to read! To combat the possibility of being unable to focus on the salient or important cues, our sensory systems respond to the continual presence of the same stimulus with a decreased response to that stimulus, a process called **sensory adaptation**.

Although it's possible that the diminished sense of smell people experience as they sit in a restaurant may be due to blocked sinuses, it's much more likely that this experience occurs as a result of sensory adaptation. Our ability to detect odors gradually fades when we are in their presence for a prolonged period. Sensory adaptation can be overcome by providing a much stronger stimulus, which is what happens when your restaurant meal is delivered to your table. Now that the source of the smell is more concentrated in your vicinity, your ability to smell is renewed. Although the sense of smell is perhaps most prone to this response, all of our sensory systems exhibit some form of adaptation.

Sensation and perception almost always happen together. Researchers, however, have worked to study each process separately and to determine how the two work together. Perception can occur through **bottom–up processing**, which begins with the physical stimuli from the environment, and proceeds through transduction of those stimuli into neural impulses. The signals are passed along to successively more complex brain regions, and ultimately result in the recognition of a visual stimulus. For example, when you look at the face of your grandmother, your eyes convert light energy into neural impulses, which travel into the brain to visual regions. This information forms the basis for sensing the visual stimulus and ultimately its perception. Equally important to perception, however, is **top–down processing**, which involves previously acquired knowledge. When you look at grandma's face, for example, brain regions that store information about what faces

---

sensory receptor cells specialized cells that convert a specific form of environmental stimuli into neural impulses.

sensory transduction the process of converting a specific form of environmental stimuli into neural impulses.

absolute threshold the minimal stimulus necessary for detection by an individual.

---

difference threshold or just noticeable difference the minimal difference between two stimuli necessary for detection of a difference between the two.

---

sensory adaptation the process whereby repeated stimulation of a sensory cell leads to a reduced response.

---

look like, particularly those that are familiar to us, can help you to perceive and recognize the specific visual stimulus.

Typically, perception involves both bottom-up and top-down processing occurring at the same time. The combination lets us rapidly recognize familiar faces and other stimuli. Bottom-up and top-down processing are involved in sensation and perception of all sensory modalities. For example, recognizing familiar songs involves not only information carried from the ear to the brain but also the matching of that information with previously stored information about the music. We also combine bottom-up and top-down processes to help us recognize the smell or taste of a familiar food.

> **bottom-up processing** perception that proceeds by transducing environmental stimuli into neural impulses that move onto successively more complex brain regions.
>
> **top-down processing** perception processes led by cognitive processes, such as memory or expectations.

Before You Go On

What Do You Know?

1. What is sensory transduction?
2. What are absolute and difference thresholds?
3. Compare and contrast bottom-up and top-down processing.

What Do You Think? Describe examples of sensory adaptation that you have experienced in two or more of your sensory modalities.

THE CHEMICAL SENSES: SMELL AND TASTE

When nothing else subsists from the past, after the people are dead, after the things are broken and scattered ... the smell and taste of things remain.
  -*Marcel Proust, novelist*

LEARNING OBJECTIVE 2 Summarize the biological changes that underlie smell and taste.

Smell and taste are usually called the *chemical senses* because they involve responses to particular chemicals. Smell, our **olfactory sense**, and taste, our **gustatory sense**, emerged early in our evolutionary history (Doty, 1986). The sense of smell, in particular, is more sensitive and of greater significance to less complex animals, who use it for social communication as well as finding food and avoiding predators (Yahr, 1997; Mech & Boitani, 2003). This is less so for humans who rely more heavily on vision. However, the contributions of both smell and taste to the safety, social communication, and overall quality of life in humans are often underestimated. The ability to detect dangerous odors, such as smoke or a gas leak, or dangerous flavors, such as tainted food or poison, can be critical to our survival. In addition, some of our greatest pleasures in life come from the ability to smell and taste—to smell a rose or, as we all know, to enjoy a good meal.

In this section, we'll explore the environmental stimuli that create aromas and flavors, the organs we use to sense those stimuli, and how we transform environmental stimuli into brain signals that eventually help us perceive different smells and tastes. We'll also discuss the development of these abilities, some very interesting differences among people in their ability to taste and smell things, and some problems that can go wrong in the olfactory and gustatory systems.

Taste and Smell: How They Work

Sensation in the smell or olfactory system begins when chemicals called **odorants** enter the nose, as shown in "What Happens in the Brain When We Eat Pizza" on the following pages. Odorants are converted to neural signals at sensory receptors located in our nasal mucosa. These sensory receptors are located on the *cilia,* or hairlike structures, of **olfactory receptor neurons** (McEwen, 2008).

When odorants enter the nose, these chemicals bind to specific receptors located on the olfactory receptor neurons in a lock-and-key fashion. Only certain airborne chemicals bind to specific receptors (Buck, 1996). When enough odorant molecules have bound to receptors, the combination sets off an action potential in the olfactory receptor

> **olfactory sense** our sense of smell.
>
> **gustatory sense** our sense of taste.

neuron. As we described in Chapter 4, the action potential *or firing* of a neuron sends a message to other neurons. The firing of olfactory receptor neurons is transmitted to the brain, as we'll see next.

Continuous binding of certain odorants, such as those contained in the main ingredients of a restaurant dinner, will result in fatigue of the olfactory receptor neurons to which they bind. In other words, the cell will stop responding to the odorant unless it's given a chance to recover so it can fire again (Dalton, 2000). If you were to step outside the restaurant to make a phone call, for example, you would probably notice the food smells again when you stepped back into the restaurant, because your olfactory receptor neurons would have gotten a break from constant exposure to the food odorants. When a stimulus is continuously present, however, as when you remain sitting in the restaurant, the only way the olfactory receptor neurons will respond to the odorant would be if the stimulus is increased in magnitude. As we saw, this is the case when the food is brought directly to your table. Many more odorant molecules are now available to your nose and its olfactory receptor neurons.

odorants airborne chemicals that are detected as odors.

olfactory receptor neurons sensory receptor cells that convert chemical signals from odorants into neural impulses that travel to the brain.

In humans, the sense of smell is very closely tied to the sense of taste. Have you ever noticed how dull your sense of taste is when you have a bad cold? This is due, in large part, to mucous blocking the access of odorants to the olfactory receptors located on the cilia. What we normally refer to as *taste* is really *flavor,* a combination of smell and taste.

Taste, the gustatory sense, is itself independent of smell and its major organ is the tongue. Your tongue is covered with bumps, called **papillae**. Papillae contain clumps of **taste buds**, each of which contains sixty to one hundred sensory receptor cells for taste. Taste receptor cells have cilia that contain the actual receptors. These cilia extend through the pores of the taste receptor and are exposed to the contents of your mouth.

There are four major kinds of taste receptors. Each responds to a specific taste in our food: 1) sweet, 2) sour, 3) bitter, and 4) salt (Sugita, 2006). A fifth type of taste receptor has also been discovered—*umami*. Umami is the taste of monosodium glutamate (MSG). It is a chemical additive used in cooking some Asian food and American fast food. Each of these five types of taste receptors uses a slightly different mechanism for transduction of the chemicals in food to neural impulses in the gustatory system. For example, salt activates its taste receptors by sending sodium ions into the channels on the taste receptor cell. Since sodium ions are positively charged, the electrical charge of the taste receptor then becomes more positive. Taste buds are not evenly distributed across the tongue but most tastes can be recognized to a greater or lesser degree on most parts of the tongue.

The overall sensations we experience when we eat food are not just the result of combined interactions between olfactory and gustatory senses. Much of the information we get about food is delivered to us through one of the touch or *tactile* senses. The consistency of a particular food is not relayed to the brain via the taste receptors, but rather by inputs from touch receptors located on the tongue. The role of food consistency in determining preference is much greater than you might imagine. Many adult humans reject certain foods, such as raw oysters or cooked okra, specifically because those foods have a "slimy" texture.

In addition, the sensation we experience when we eat a "hot," as in spicy, meal is related to a component of the tactile system that communicates information about pain. A chemical called *capsaicin,* from chili peppers, activates pain receptors located in the tongue (Numazaki & Tominaga, 2004). These pain impulses, in conjunction with tactile information about the food texture, as well as the flavors (smell and taste) associated with the food, can combine to produce a sensation that is pleasurable to many people.

papillae bumps on the tongue that contain clumps of taste buds.

taste buds clusters of sensory receptor cells that convert chemical signals from food into neural impulses that travel to the brain.

Suppose a food is not spicy, but is hot in the other meaning of the word in that it just came out of the oven. We've all had the experience of burning our mouths, which can damage the taste receptors on the tongue. As the box accompanying this section points out, the sensory receptors of taste are unusual because they regenerate when this happens.

What Happens in the Smell and Taste BRAIN?

Signals from our olfactory receptor neurons travel to the brain via the olfactory nerve. Information carried along the olfactory nerves travels first to a structure called the **olfactory bulb**, located at the base of the front of the brain, beneath the frontal lobes. Olfactory information is then sent to regions of the cerebral cortex that are important for recognizing and discriminating among odors, including the piriform cortex (Wilson, 2001).

The ability of our cortex to recognize patterns of inputs from a variety of olfactory receptors is most likely responsible for our detection of certain odors. Studies have shown that the piriform cortex is *plastic* or changeable in adulthood (Li et al, 2008). That is, the parts of piriform cortex that normally recognize specific odorants can change with experience, actually remapping this brain region. The chemical structures of some pairs of molecules are so similar that untrained humans can't discriminate between them (the two odors are usually below the just noticeable difference).

However, if exposure to one of the chemicals is paired with a painful shock to the leg, humans can be taught to discriminate between the odors (Li et al, 2008). This is a remarkable example of top-down processing. Learning about associations between odors and other experiences (such as a shock) can influence our ability to perceive sensory information in the future. In parallel with the new ability to discriminate the odors of closely related molecules, the areas of the piriform cortex that are activated by each of the previously indistinguishable molecules become more distinct from each other.

The olfactory bulb also sends information to the amygdala, an area important for emotions and fear, as well as indirectly to the hippocampus, an area important for learning and memory. Many people report that certain smells are evocative of past events (Lehrer, 2007). The smell of baking might remind you of visiting your grandmother as a young child, the smell of peanut butter might remind you of your elementary-school cafeteria, and so on. The ability of smells to call up memories is probably related in part to olfactory connections to the hippocampus and amygdala.

Taste receptor cells do not have axons but instead synapse with sensory neurons in the tongue to send information to our brains. Taste information is sent to the *thalamus* and eventually, the cerebral cortex. We'll see throughout this chapter that the thalamus is a relay station for incoming sensory information of many kinds; all of our sensory systems except olfaction have a main pathway through the thalamus.

Taste information is integrated with reward circuits in the brain (Norgren et al., 2006) and rewarding tastes seem to be processed separately

> **olfactory bulb** the first region where olfactory information reaches the brain on its way from the nose.

from aversive tastes. Tastes that are considered to be rewarding, such as salty and sweet, activate overlapping areas in the taste cortex. By contrast, tastes generally considered to be less pleasurable, such as bitter and sour, activate regions that overlap less with rewarding tastes and more with one another in the taste cortex (Accolla et al., 2007). Taste and smell information are processed through separate pathways but there is convergence in the association parts of neocortex, namely in the prefrontal cortex.

In addition to integrating information about taste in general, part of the cortex that receives taste information, called the *insula*, is associated with the emotion of disgust.

Neuroimaging studies have shown that this brain region becomes activated not only when we smell or taste something revolting but also when we view repulsive visual images (Calder et al., 2007; Schienle et al., 2008).

Smell and Taste How We Develop

The sense of smell is relatively well developed at birth. Research suggests that, within hours of birth, a newborn baby is capable of telling his or her own mother from another woman using only the sense of smell. In fact, olfactory functioning seems to be in place even before birth. Newborn infants show a learned preference to the odors of their mother's amniotic fluid. After birth, infants quickly learn to recognize the smell of their own mother's milk. Exposure to odors of their mother's milk has a calming effect on infants when they are experiencing a brief, minor painful stimulus, such as a needle stick in the heel (Nishitani et al., 2009). This effect doesn't appear to be as

Regeneration in the Taste and Smell Systems

If you, like most people, have had the experience of burning your tongue on too-hot food, you've probably noticed that by the next day or so, your ability to taste has returned and your tongue is no longer painful. This is due to the remarkable regenerative characteristics of the taste buds. Taste receptor cells normally turn over—they die and are replaced—in a matter of days. The process happens even faster when they are damaged. Our olfactory receptor neurons are also constantly turning over under normal circumstances (Farbman, 1997).

The capacity to regenerate on such a large scale and so rapidly is probably necessary because the receptor neurons for both taste and smell are exposed to the external environment.

Unlike the sensory receptors of the eye, which are protected by the eyeball, or those of the ear, which are protected by the eardrum, the surface of the tongue and the mucosa of the nose are directly exposed to any number of noxious chemical molecules that may enter our mouths or noses. Because destruction of receptors is likely under such circumstances, we need to constantly regenerate receptor cells just to continue normal functioning of our smell and taste systems.

Neurobiologists study the regenerative capabilities of the taste buds and olfactory receptor neurons in hopes of understanding exactly *how* these cells are constantly rejuvenating. Scientists and medical professionals hope that understanding these mechanisms may someday enable replacement of other types of cells, ones that currently don't seem capable of repair when they are damaged.

specific to the milk as it is to the mother—exposure to other odors that the baby has associated with the mother, such as vanillin, has the same calming effect as mother's milk odor (Goubet et al., 2007).

The ability to taste is also well formed at birth in humans. Newborn humans show an innate preference for sugar and aversion to bitter or sour tastes. Babies move their faces toward a sweet substance and make sucking movements with their mouths, but turn away and grimace when presented with a sour or bitter substance (Rosenstein & Oster, 1988).

Researchers have shown that by about seven years of age, children develop a preference for sour tastes (Liem & Mennella, 2003). This may explain the popularity of candies such as Sour Patch Kids. However, the aversion to bitter tastes typically lasts until adulthood. At this time, bitter foods, such as blue cheese and dark chocolate can emerge as favorites.

Many of these developmental changes are the result of learning. As children grow, they become accustomed to different tastes. However, there is some evidence to suggest that the gustatory system itself changes from infancy to adulthood. We form taste buds before we are even born, and as newborns, have higher concentrations of them on our tongues than we

will as adults. Children also have taste buds on their palates, inside the cheeks, and the back of their mouths (Nilsson, 1979). Although these regions continue to contain taste buds in adults, their numbers decline with time.

The high number of taste buds in children may explain why they are often picky eaters. The tastes of certain foods may seem too strong to children, because their larger number of taste buds produces more neural impulses than adults would generate from the same food. Some researchers suggest that this developmental phenomenon might actually be adaptive in helping us survive. If young children enjoyed ingesting substances with strong or bitter tastes, they might be at higher risk of poisoning.

Children often refuse or eat very little of unfamiliar foods (Koivisto Hursti, 1999). Although neuroimaging studies on developing humans have yet to be done with regard to taste, it's tempting to speculate that as individuals grow and their tastes broaden, areas in the taste cortex represented by certain tastes are modified. It's likely that increased exposure to certain foods, especially when paired with positive social interactions and encouragement from parents, result in a remapping of previously aversive taste information on the gustatory cortex.

Smell and Taste HOW We Differ

Among humans, there is a wide range in the ability to detect certain odors. Some people seem relatively insensitive to even pungent odors, while others are particularly sensitive. Some of these individual differences are related to learning. Childhood exposure to particular odors decreases the reaction to those odors in adulthood.

In addition to these learned differences, research suggests that females are generally more sensitive to smell than males are, and that this sensitivity varies with the stage of the menstrual cycle (Pause et al., 1996). Around the time of ovulation, women are more sensitive to odors than during other stages of the cycle. Women's ability to detect different odors also diminishes after menopause (Hughes et al, 2002). The exact biological mechanisms that underlie these differences are not known, but it is possible that reproductive hormones, such as estrogen, alter the excitability, or the likelihood of firing of olfactory neurons.

There is also considerable individual variability in the ability to taste. Researchers group people into three different categories with respect to taste sensitivity: nontasters (25 percent of people), medium tasters (50 percent), and supertasters (25 percent). These groups are distinguished based on their ability to detect and respond negatively to a specific bitter substance (Bartoshuk et al., 1996). Supertasters are repulsed by the bitter chemical. Nontasters do not even notice the bitter taste although they are capable of detecting other tastes. Medium tasters notice it, but do not find the taste particularly offensive. These functional differences are the result of variations in the concentration of taste buds on the tongue.

Women make up a higher proportion of supertasters than do men (Bartoshuk et al.,1994). This heightened sensitivity of both chemical sensory systems, smell and taste, is likely to have had adaptive significance for women. Since the chemicals in women's diets are passed along to their children when women are pregnant or nursing, the ability to detect and avoid potentially harmful odors and tastes may have contributed to survival of the species by protecting infants from toxic substances.

When Things Go Wrong

Smell and Taste

True taste disorders are rare. In fact, most people who seek medical assistance complaining that they cannot taste are actually suffering from problems with their olfactory, as opposed to gustatory, systems. People with a condition called **anosmia** have lost the ability to smell. They can often still taste sweet, salt, sour, bitter, and umami, but they can no longer detect other flavors, since those require the additional information provided by food odorants.

> **anosmia** inability to smell.

In some rare cases— typically as a result of head trauma or oral surgery—humans lose the ability to taste itself, a condition called **ageusia**. Head trauma is also a leading cause of anosmia (Haxel et al, 2008). Sometimes the nerves that carry olfactory information from the olfactory receptor neurons to the olfactory bulb can be sheared, cutting off the pathway by which information about smell reaches the brain. People with Alzheimer's disease

> **ageusia** inability to taste.

also suffer from a diminished sense of smell that is probably due to a combined degeneration of olfactory receptor neurons and neurons located in olfactory brain regions (Djordjevic et al., 2008).

Although humans can certainly survive without the ability to smell, their quality of life is considerably diminished. Many people with anosmia report feelings of depression. In addition, there are safety and social issues to consider. Since we use our sense of smell to detect dangers, such as smoke or spoiled food, anosmia increases the risk of injury. Moreover, socially acceptable cultural practices of hygiene may become difficult to follow with anosmia, since humans often use olfactory cues to make decisions about bathing, washing clothes, and brushing teeth. People with anosmia can learn to cope effectively with their condition by using other sensory systems to detect danger. They might, for example, use sound cues, such as a blaring smoke detector to notice smoke, or visual cues, such as appearance and freshness dates, to detect spoiled food.

The chemical senses are also involved in the symptoms of some people with migraine headaches or epilepsy.

For instance, a specific odor can initiate the onset of a migraine (Kelman, 2007). Likewise, patients with a certain form of epilepsy, called *reflex epilepsy,* will experience a seizure only after exposure to a specific odor. Although the reasons for this remain unknown, these individuals find it necessary to avoid specific intense odorants. In other patients suffering from migraines or epilepsy, stimuli from the other sensory systems, such as touch, sound, and sight, can initiate the headaches or seizures.

Some people experience hallucinations called *auras* either before or during migraine headaches or epileptic seizures. Auras can involve any of the sensory systems. People with these conditions might have touch, sound, or sight hallucinations, and some experience strong, often unpleasant, smells or tastes. The involvement of different senses indicates which brain circuits are compromised in these conditions. For example, if a person's seizure is preceded by strong olfactory hallucinations, it's likely that his or her olfactory pathways are initiating the seizure, or at least participating in its generation.

Before You Go On

What Do You Know?

4. What five tastes have specific receptors?
5. Which parts of the brain are involved in sensing and perceiving odors?
6. What are supertasters?
7. How are smell and taste involved with migraines and epileptic seizures?

What Do You Think? This section of the chapter listed some ways, such as using smoke detectors, for people with anosmia to compensate for their lack of smell. What other ways can you suggest that people with anosmia might use to replace the safety and pleasures that a sense of smell provides?

THE TACTILE OR CUTANEOUS SENSES: TOUCH, PRESSURE, PAIN, VIBRATION

LEARNING OBJECTIVE 3 Describe how the different senses of touch work and what can happen when things go wrong.

As with the chemical senses, there are rewarding and aversive types of tactile stimuli. The pleasure associated with a relaxing back massage or stroking a baby's cheek stands in stark contrast to the discomfort of getting a scrape or burn. The tactile or somatosensory system is actually a complex sense. Our skin contains a variety of sensory receptors to register different types of physical stimuli (Munger & Ide, 1988).

- **Free nerve endings** are located mostly near the surface of the skin and function to detect touch, pressure, pain, and temperature.
- **Meissner's corpuscles** transduce information about sensitive touch and are found in the hairless regions of the body, such as the fingertips, lips, and palms.
- **Merkel's discs** transduce information about light to moderate pressure against the skin.
- **Rufftni's end-organs** are located deep in the skin. They register heavy pressure and movement of the joints.
- **Pacinian corpuscles** are also buried deep in the skin and respond to vibrations and heavy pressure.

Depression of the skin activates free nerve endings that give us the sense of being touched. As you may have noticed, your skin is not equally sensitive to tactile stimuli over your whole body. Certain parts of your body, for example, the skin on your elbow, are much less sensitive to touch than other areas, such as your face and hands. These differences likely arise as a result of different densities of free nerve endings. Areas that are more sensitive have more free nerve endings.

We can also experience sensory adaptation, resulting in reduced tactile sensation from depression of the skin that continues for a period of time. This happens to you every day when you put on your clothing; shortly after getting dressed, you are no longer aware of the tactile stimulus your clothing provides (unless of course it is too tight).

What Happens in the Tactile Senses BRAIN

Our brains use a variety of related processes to help us perceive general information about a range of nonpainful touch sensations, including pressure, temperature, and general touch. Pain perception is also an important, but not yet fully understood, function.

The Touching Brain When we touch something, or something touches us, our free nerve endings send tactile information into the spinal cord. The signals travel up the spinal cord to the brain. In the brain, touch information is first received in the thalamus, and then routed from there to the somatosensory cortex (located in the parietal lobe). Information about pressure and vibration is generally transmitted to the brain in a similar way, after being converted to neural impulses by the specialized receptors described above.

Our brain processes tactile information *contralaterally,* or on the opposite side of the brain from the side of the body where the touch occurred. So, if you touch something with your left hand, the information is eventually processed by the somatosensory cortex on the right side of your brain.

As we discussed in Chapter 4, the somatosensory cortex does not have an equal representation of all parts of the body (Kakigi et al., 2000). For example, tactile inputs from the hands take up proportionately more space in the somatosensory cortex than those from the back. This seems reasonable, given the fact that our hands are specialized for object manipulation, and we need to process information from them in great detail. As described in the box accompanying this section, other animals have somatosensory systems that are adapted to provide high-resolution tactile information from the parts of their bodies that are especially important to their daily lives. Information about pressure and vibration is generally transmitted to the brain in a similar way after being converted to neural impulses by the specialized receptors described above.

> **free nerve endings** sensory receptors that convert physical stimuli into touch, pressure, or pain impulses.

Pain and the Brain Like general touch information, painful sensations are also transmitted to the brain via free nerve endings. Pain information travels to the brain via two different types of pain fibers. One system, called the *fast pathway,* uses myelinated axons that, as we discussed in Chapter 4, carry signals faster than unmyelinated axons. Messages about sharp, localized pain travel along the fast pathway directly up the spinal cord to the thalamus and to areas of the somatosensory cortex. Pain information received via the fast pathway helps us to respond quickly with a withdrawal reflex, such as pulling a hand away after touching a hot stove. The slower pain pathway uses more unmyelinated axons—these inputs communicate with brain regions involved in processing emotions. Pain we perceive via the slow pathway is more often burning pain than sharp pain.

> **Meissner's corpuscles** sensory receptors that convert physical stimuli about sensory touch on the fingertips, lips, and palms.
>
> **Merkel's discs** sensory receptors that convert information about light to moderate pressure on the skin.
>
> **Ruffini's end-organs** sensory receptors that respond to heavy pressure and joint movement.
>
> **Pacinian corpuscles** sensory receptors that respond to vibrations and heavy pressure.

Like all other sensory systems we've discussed so far, the pain system shows evidence of sensory adaptation. A common example of this can be experienced when eating a spicy meal. Recall that the sensation of eating chili peppers is mostly due to the activation of pain fibers located on the tongue. Oftentimes, when a very "hot" food is first ingested, the pain response seems great. However, as the meal progresses, the response diminishes and we are less likely to experience discomfort. This is due to adaptation of the pain fibers and a subsequent decrease in their activity. However, when pain is associated with actual tissue damage or an abnormality in the pain system, as discussed below, pain can be persistent and debilitating.

The Tactile Senses How We Develop

The tactile senses are generally in place at birth. In fact, studies have shown that fetuses can respond to the touch of a hair at a relatively early stage in prenatal development (Lagercrantz & Changeux, 2009). However, the ability to recognize and respond to different somatosensory stimuli occurs only after birth and involves further brain development as well as learning.

For children, one of the most enjoyable types of somatosensory input is being tickled. Although rough or prolonged tickling can become abusive, when tickled under the right circumstances, children often explode with laughter. The reaction we have to tickling is a result of activation of somatosensory pathways in an uneven, uncontrollable and unexpected manner. Not only are our sensory systems organized to detect change, but they are most tuned to stimuli that are unexpected and surprising. When you move your body and produce tactile sensations, these stimuli are less noticeable to you than are sensations produced by another individual. The sensations of your own legs touching one another when you cross your legs, for example, is generally less noticeable than a similar touch on your leg would be if someone sitting next to you brushed their leg against yours. Likewise, your reaction to your cat jumping onto your lap is likely to be much greater if you have your eyes closed when it happens. This differential response to surprising tactile stimuli appears to be a defense mechanism that has adaptive significance. It is probably also the reason why being tickled by someone else is more effective at producing an emotional reaction than trying to tickle yourself. Our enjoyment of being tickled generally diminishes as we age. This is likely due to the fact that adults are better at anticipating stimuli, and hence are more difficult to surprise, than are children.

Tactile Senses HOW We Differ

Humans differ greatly in their ability to detect physical stimuli on the skin. In addition, they differ in the degree to which they find certain tactile stimulation pleasurable or aversive. For example, some people enjoy an intense back massage while others do not. Of all the somatosensory experiences, the one that has received the most research attention is that of pain. Pain management for surgical procedures and other medical conditions is a critical part of patient care. There are dramatic differences in both the threshold to detect pain and the degree to which pain causes emotional suffering. Some of these differences can be attributed to ethnicity. For example, studies have shown that Japanese people have a lower pain threshold than Caucasians. These differences extend to reports of the detection of nonpainful stimuli as well (Komiyama et al, 2009).

Although learning plays some role, groups of people also differ in the actual sensation and perception of pain as a result of physical differences in their sensory systems. Studies have shown, for example, that women have a lower threshold for detecting pain than do men. They report greater pain intensity than men in response to the same stimulus (Garcia et al., 2007). One interpretation of this sex difference is that women are just less able to cope psychologically with painful stimuli since they haven't been "toughened up." In fact, research suggests that women may have about twice as many pain receptors in their facial skin than men. This suggests a physical cause for at least some of the differences in pain sensitivity. It is not yet known whether this difference exists throughout the body or whether it is specific to the face.

Neuroimaging studies show that people's brains react differently depending on their sensitivity to pain (Dubé et al., 2009). People exposed to a high temperature stimulus in one study exhibited varied responses, for example. Those who reported feeling pain showed changes in activity in their thalamus, somatosensory cortex, and cingulate cortex areas. Those who did not report feeling pain, showed similar activity in the thalamus, but no changes in the cortical regions. Although there may be differences in the two groups' sensory receptors in their skin, these findings suggest that differences in activation of brain circuitry may also underlie varied responses to painful stimuli.

One theory, the **gate control theory of pain** attempts to explain the relationship of brain activity to pain by suggesting that some patterns of neural activity can actually create a "gate" that prevents messages from reaching parts of the brain where they are perceived as pain (Melzack, 1999).

Early versions of this theory hypothesized that pain signals were blocked in the spinal cord, but

> **gate control theory of pain** suggests that certain patterns of neural activity can close a "gate" to keep pain information from traveling to parts of the brain where it is perceived.

later research has focused on neurochemicals or patterns of activity in the brain itself. Individual differences in gating mechanisms may result in the wide range of pain sensitivity across people.

When Things Go Tactile Senses Wrong

As we've seen, sensing and perceiving pain are normal, and important, functions of our tactile senses. Some people, however, experience either too much pain or too little. Sometimes, people even feel pain and other sensations in limbs or other body parts that have actually been removed.

Chronic Pain The most common abnormality associated with the somatosensory system is that of chronic pain, pain that lasts longer than three months. In the United States, a relatively large percentage of the population, about one in six people, suffers from chronic pain. There are multiple causes of chronic pain, although in some cases the cause cannot be identified. In all cases, however, pain management is a critical issue, since prolonged pain sensations can interfere with daily functioning, and may lead to depression or even suicide.

Specialized: Somatosensory Systems: Whiskers and Star-Shaped Noses

Humans have a very high concentration of tactile receptors on our hands, particularly on the fingertips. The many receptors provide us with very detailed, high-resolution tactile information. This level of detail is very adaptive to us, because our hands are our primary tools for making fine movements. Other mammals, particularly those without hands, have concentrated tactile receptors on different parts of their bodies. They rely on these specific body parts for fine touch information, much in the same way we rely on our hands.

Rats and mice, for example, have movable whiskers that they use to detect information in their environments (Feldman & Brecht, 2005). Their whiskers are sensitive to movements of air and physical stimuli. When rats or mice move through small openings or dig tunnels, they use the movement of their whiskers to help them determine the location of the walls of these confined spaces.

The star-nosed mole is named for its specialized nose, shaped like a star, which has 21 appendages. This creature lives mostly underground and is almost completely blind. It navigates throughout its dark environment by using its star-shaped nose as a blind person would use his or her hands, to accomplish such tasks as finding food and exploring its spatial environment (Catania & Remple, 2004).

Just as a good deal of the somatosensory cortex in our brains is used to process information from the hands, a large amount of space in the brains of other animals is devoted to processing information from their specialized somatosensory features. The somatosensory cortex in the brain of a rodent devotes a proportionately large amount of space to processing information from the whiskers, for example, and the nose representation in the star-nosed mole somatosensory cortex is proportionately larger than that devoted to other body parts.

Researchers have identified two groups of chemicals naturally produced by our nervous systems that have pain relieving properties, **endorphins** and **enkephalins**. Endorphins and enkephalins belong to a class of molecules called *opiates*. As we will see in Chapter 6, this class of chemicals also includes pain-killing drugs, such as morphine and heroin. When opiates are present in the nervous system naturally, they are referred to as *endogenous opiates*. These molecules are released by neurons after intense physical exercise, stress, and sexual experience. They are thought to be responsible for the so-called *runner's high* as well as for the ability of some people to perform heroic physical actions under extreme duress.

Medical practitioners use opiate drugs that mimic or stimulate the endogenous opiate system for pain relief. However, this approach has been problematic because people easily become addicted to opiate drugs. Opiate drugs are not only addictive when

endorphins naturally-occurring pain-killing chemicals in the brain.

enkephalins naturally-occurring pain-killing chemicals in the brain.

they are abused illegally, such as heroin, but when they are prescribed medically, as happens with morphine. Repeated use of these drugs to treat chronic pain can produce a physiological dependence that is very difficult to overcome. In addition, these drugs become less effective with continual use, so higher and higher doses are needed to achieve pain relief. Opiates suppress breathing, however, so they can be very dangerous at high doses. Eventually, people with chronic pain can reach a point where the dose of medicine needed to reduce their pain would be enough to stop their breathing and kill them, but lower doses do not provide them with pain relief. Scientists continue to explore new avenues for pain relief that do not produce addictions or unwanted side effects.

In extreme debilitating cases of chronic pain, physicians have turned to neurosurgery. Destroying the pathways that carry information about pain stimuli to the brain can be effective for some people. An extreme form of neurosurgery to relieve intractable chronic pain is a *cingulotomy,* destruction of the cingulate cortex (Cetas et al, 2008).

No Pain Some people are incapable of detecting painful stimuli. While the idea of feeling no pain may sound appealing at first, the fact is that our ability to recognize and respond to discomfort is critical for preventing physical damage to the body. Consider how often you shift position in your chair when you are studying or sitting in a lecture. If you were unable to receive signals of discomfort from your body, you would not move to relieve pressure on your skin. The parts of your skin under continuous pressure would develop sores or bruises. Since many everyday experiences would be damaging to our bodies if we were not able to detect discomfort, a lack of ability to detect pain can be very dangerous.

Some people are born unable to feel pain. A rare genetic condition called *familial dysautonomia* is associated with an inability to detect pain or temperature (Axelrod, 2004). Children with this disorder are at grave risk of life-threatening injuries and must be monitored very carefully. Loss of pain sensation can also be acquired later in life. Some medical conditions, including diabetes, can cause *neuropathies,* or nerve dysfunction, that block pain sensations arising from the person's extremities. People with such neuropathies may not notice if they sustain an injury in an affected area,

such as a toe. Sometimes tissue can get so damaged that it must be amputated.

Phantom Limb Sensations Many individuals with amputated limbs report tactile hallucinations or *phantom* sensations of touch, pressure, vibration, pins and needles, hot, cold, and pain in the body part that no longer exists. Some people even feel the sensation of a ring on the finger or a watch on the wrist of an amputated arm. Similar phantom experiences have been reported in woman who have undergone mastectomy for the treatment of breast cancer (Björkman et al., 2008).

Researchers believe that such phantom sensations are the result of abnormal activity in the somatosensory cortex of the brain. When a body part is removed, the part of somatosensory cortex that previously received its input does not become inactive. Instead, somatosensory inputs from intact body parts expand to occupy those regions of the cortex (Ramachandran, 2005). Since information from the face is represented in an area of the somatosensory cortex located near that of the arm and hand, a person whose arm was amputated is likely to experience an expansion of the somatosensory inputs from his or her face into the arm and hand regions of cortex.

Although researchers do not fully understand how reorganization of somatosensory cortex produces phantom sensations, there is clearly a memory component to the

---

1. List the different types of tactile receptors in the skin and the primary functions of each.
2. Compare and contrast slow and fast pain pathways.
3. Why do children so often enjoy getting tickled?
4. What are some possible explanations for individual differences in pain sensitivity?

What Do You Think? Have you experienced an occasion when your senses have worked together to either enhance or diminish pain or another touch sense? For example, did certain sights or sounds make pain better or worse?

Before You Go On

What Do You Know?

1. List the different types of tactile receptors in the skin and the primary functions of each.
2. Compare and contrast slow and fast pain pathways.

phenomenon. People are more likely to experience phantom sensations that they actually felt previously, as opposed to random sensations. For example, someone who previously wore a ring or a watch is more likely have the sense of wearing one after an amputation than is a person who didn't wear a watch or ring. Similarly, people who previously experienced considerable pain in their now-missing body part are much more likely to feel phantom pain.

THE AUDITORY SENSE: HEARING

LEARNING OBJECTIVE 4 Summarize what happens when we hear.

Hearing, the auditory sense, plays a very important role in social communication as well as in our ability to detect danger. In addition to these clearly adaptive roles, the ability to hear enriches our lives through music and other pleasurable sounds.

The auditory system is designed to convert **sound waves**, vibrations of the air, into neural impulses. Sound waves have two major qualities that produce our perceptions of different sounds:

*   *Frequency.* The *frequency* of a sound wave refers to the number of cycles the wave completes in a certain amount of time. Frequency of a sound wave is measured in units called *Hertz* (Hz) which represent cycles per second. The frequency of a sound wave is responsible for producing the *pitch* of a sound. The voice of Mickey Mouse is a high-frequency sound wave that produces

PRACTICALLY SPEAKING: Quick Ways to Reduce Acute Pain

As we discuss in this chapter, medical practitioners are constantly seeking ways to provide relief to patients in chronic, or continuing, pain. But what about acute pain, the short-term pain you feel when you bump your leg on a table, for example?

Gate control theory suggests that touch sensations, which frequently travel along fast fibers, can help prevent some pain sensations traveling on the slow pathways from reaching areas of your brain where they are perceived. According to this theory, the brain only processes so much input, so touch can help to set up a "gate" that stops pain. This explains why we have a tendency to rub the skin of areas of our body that have been injured. For example, if you walk into a piece of furniture, you might rub your leg to dampen the pain.

Focusing on your breathing may also help. We often tend to gasp and then hold our breath when we injure ourselves, such as bumping a leg. Formal methods of pain control, such as the Lamaze method for childbirth, work in part by altering this natural tendency, by teaching people to breathe in short, panting gasps (Leventhal et al, 1989).

Distraction can also help, whereas anxiously focusing on pain can make it worse (al Absi & Rokke, 1991). Some studies have suggested that simply looking at a pleasant view, can affect pain tolerance (Ulrich, 1984). Other evidence suggests that in order for a distraction to be effective, the experience must be active. Studies have shown that playing an interesting videogame can dampen pain detection, whereas passive watching of a TV show has little effect. Stress and sexual experience also decrease the perception of pain. So, if you bump your leg on the way into a big job interview or on a hot date, perhaps you would not notice the pain as much as you would under other circumstances!

a high-pitched sound. Although the range of hu-

sound waves vibrations of the air in the frequency of hearing.	

man hearing is quite large, we hear sounds best within the range of 2,000–5,000 Hz, which encompasses the frequencies of most sounds that humans actually make, such as babies crying and people talking.

- *Amplitude.* The *amplitude* of a sound wave refers to the strength of a given cycle. Waves with higher peaks and lower bottoms are higher amplitude than those that do not reach such extremes. The amplitude of a sound wave is responsible for our detection of *loudness.* Waves with high amplitudes produce loud sounds, while those with low amplitudes sound soft. Loudness is measured in units called *decibels* (dB).

Our detection of sound begins, of course, in the ear. Sound waves are converted to neural impulses in the ear through several steps.

1. First, sound waves enter the outer ear and at its deepest part, deflect the ear drum or **tympanic membrane**.

   tympanic membrane the ear drum.

2. Vibrations of the tympanic membrane set in motion a series of three tiny bones or **ossicles**, called the *hammer, anvil,* and *stirrup.* The stirrup, which is the last bone in the chain, hits the **oval window**, a membrane separating the ossicles and the inner ear.

3. Deflection of the oval window causes a wave to form in the fluid-filled **cochlea** of the inner ear. When fluid moves in the cochlea, it deflects the **basilar membrane** that runs down the middle of the cochlea. The basilar membrane is covered with rows of **hair cells**, the auditory sensory receptors. Movement of the basilar membrane bends the hair cells that transduce the "fluid sound wave" into electrical activity.

4. The hair cells communicate with nerves in the cochlea that, in turn, send the neural impulses to the brain.

There are two major theories about how the auditory system converts sound waves into all the various sounds we can perceive. The first, called *frequency theory,* suggests that different sound frequencies are converted into different rates of action potentials or firing in our auditory nerves. According to this theory, high-frequency sounds produce a more rapid firing than do low-frequency sounds. Although there may

ossicles tiny bones in the ear called the *hammer, anvil,* and *stirrup.*

oval window a membrane separating the ossicles and the inner ear, deflection of which causes a wave to form in the cochlea.

be some truth to frequency theory—different firing rates contribute to sound perception of low tones—researchers agree that this theory cannot fully explain sound perception.

The second theory, called *place theory,* seems to account for a greater degree of auditory perception. Place theory holds that differences in sound frequency activate different regions on the basilar membrane. Regions along the basilar membrane send inputs to the brain that are encoded according to the place along the membrane where the inputs originated.

As with the other sensory systems we've discussed, adaptation also occurs in the auditory system when we are continuously exposed to sounds. We can adapt to sounds in several ways. First, our ears respond to very loud sounds by contracting muscles around the ear's opening so that less of the sound wave can enter the ear. This also happens when you talk, so that the sound of your own voice, which is so close to your ear, is not deafening. Second, the hair cells of the ear also become less sensitive to continuous noises. Unfortunately, if the noise is loud enough, it can actually damage the hair cells (Petrescu, 2008). Unlike receptors for the chemical senses, our sensory receptors in the ear are not readily replaced, so such damage to the hair cells makes the ear permanently less sensitive. To protect your own hair cells from such permanent damage, which is associated with hearing loss, avoid prolonged exposure to loud noises—including the music coming through your iPod!

Finally, the brain can filter out many sounds that are not important,

cochlea fluid-filled structure in the inner ear, contains the hair cells.

basilar membrane structure in the cochlea where the hair cells are located.

hair cells sensory receptors that convert sound waves into neural impulses.

even if they are relatively loud. This ability enables you to carry on a conversation with your friends at a noisy party. This phenomenon, often referred to as the *cocktail party effect,* is another example of top-down processing. The brain is able to attend to, and pick up on, relevant sounds even in a very noisy environment. These relevant sounds, such as your name or the names of people who interest you, grab your attention and focus your auditory perception because you have previously learned their importance. So background noise, even if it's also the sounds of people talking, interferes minimally with hearing a conversation, as long as the conversation is of interest to us.

To determine the importance of a particular sound, it's necessary to localize it in space, to figure out where it is coming from. For example, if you're driving in a car and you hear the sound of an ambulance siren, you need to determine whether the ambulance is far away or close up in order to decide whether or not to pull over to the side of the road to let the ambulance pass. You also need to determine from which direction the sound is approaching you. The auditory system uses several cues to help localize sound:

- *General loudness* We learn from many early experiences that loud sounds are usually closer to us than are quiet sounds, so that eventually we automatically use the loudness of a sound to assess the distance between ourselves and the source of the sound.
- *Loudness in each ear* Because of the distance between our ears and the presence of the head between our ears, there are slight differences between each ear in the loudness of the same sound wave. The ear closer to the sound hears a louder noise than the ear farther from the sound. This difference is particularly useful in detecting the location of high-frequency sounds.
- *Timing* Another cue used to localize sound is differences in the time at which sound waves hit each ear. Sound waves will reach the ear closer to the source of the sound before they reach the ear farther away. Since the ears are separated in space, a sound wave will also hit each ear at a slightly different part of its wave cycle, creating a phase difference. This cue is particularly useful to us in localizing sounds with low frequencies.

We also adjust our heads and bodies to assess the location of sounds. These movements allow us to hear how the sound changes while we're in different positions and to use those changes to help make a reasonable approximation of its location. Finally, the use of other sensory systems, such as vision, may come into play. For instance, you might confirm the location of the ambulance when you look into your rearview mirror and see it approaching.

What Happens in the Hearing BRAIN?

After auditory information is transduced from sound waves by the hair cells in the basilar membrane of the cochlea, it travels as signals from nerves in the cochlea to the brainstem, the thalamus, and then the auditory cortex, which is located in the temporal lobe. Part of the primary auditory cortex is organized in a **tonotopic map.** That is, information transmitted from different parts of the cochlea (sound waves of different frequency and, hence, sounds of different pitch) is projected to specific parts of the auditory cortex, so that our cortex maps the different pitches of sounds we hear. Auditory information from one ear is sent to the auditory cortex areas on both sides of the brain. This enables us to integrate auditory information from both sides of the head and helps us to locate the sources of sounds.

From the primary auditory cortex, auditory information moves on to the auditory *association areas* in the cortex. As we described in Chapter 4, association areas of the brain's cortex are involved in higher-order mental processes. Association areas help to link the sounds we hear with parts of the brain involved in language comprehension.

Association areas also integrate, or coordinate auditory information with signals from other sensory modalities. Have you ever noticed how distracting it is to watch a movie that has an audio slightly out of synchrony with the video image? This is because the brain is set up to integrate information from multiple sensory systems. Over time, we learn to have expectations about the coincidence of certain visual stimuli with specific sounds. When the sounds in a movie do not match the visual images the way they would in real life, our expectations

> **tonotopic map** representation in the auditory cortex of different sound frequencies.

are violated and our attention is drawn to this discrepancy from the norm.

In some people, the integration of sensory systems in the brain can sometimes lead to abnormal crossover of different modalities. As described in the box accompanying this section, people who experience a condition known as *synesthesia,* perceive sensations in a different modality from that of the original stimulus. Synesthesia is not a debilitating abnormality; in fact it has sometimes been described as enriching, particularly when it occurs in artistic or musical individuals.

Hearing How We *Develop*

Our ears are formed and capable of transducing sound waves before we are even born. In fact, human fetuses have been shown to respond to noises long before birth. Research has shown that fetuses respond to loud noises with a startle reflex and that after birth, they are capable of recognizing some sounds they heard while in utero. However, the ability to recognize and respond appropriately to a wide variety of sound stimuli is acquired over many years of postnatal life. Sounds associated with language, for example, become recognizable over postnatal development, as do those associated with music. We describe language development in more detail in Chapter 9.

Sensitive periods exist for the development of both language and music learning (Knudson, 2004). As we described in Chapter 3, we acquire certain abilities during sensitive periods of development much more easily that we do after the sensitive period has ended. The tonotopic map in the primary auditory cortex of the brain is organized during such a sensitive period of development (de Villers-Sidani et al., 2007). Studies in experimental animals have shown that exposing animals to pure tones during a certain time in development, leads to a larger representations of those sounds in the auditory cortex. The same exposure after the sensitive period in development is over has no such effect. If a sound is made important to the animal, however, by pairing it either with a reward, such as water, or a punishment, such as an electric shock, the primary auditory cortex can be reorganized so that more of it responds to the relevant tone (Bakin et al., 1996). Such top-down processing of tones indicates that this region of the brain still shows plasticity after the sensitive period is over. It is not as easy, however, to remap the brain after a sensitive

period as it is during one. The stimuli needed to produce changes in older animals must be very strong and important, compared to those needed for younger animals (Kuboshima & Sawaguchi, 2007). In humans, the auditory brain is set up to acquire information about speaking and music most readily relatively early in life, during the preschool years. It is more difficult, but by no means impossible, for us to learn additional languages or certain music skills after we mature.

Hearing HOW We Differ

We differ greatly in our ability to detect specific sounds. People show particular differences in their ability to identify certain notes in a scale. **Absolute pitch** refers to the ability to recognize an individual note in isolation. This is very difficult for most people. Only about 1 in 10,000 people in Western countries has absolute pitch. This ability seems to originate in childhood, between the ages of three and six years, through musical training, and it is associated with differences in brain anatomy (Zatorre, 2003). Research has shown that portions of the cortex are actually thinner in individuals with absolute pitch (Bermudez et al, 2009). Although it's not clear whether people with absolute pitch start out with a thinner cortex or whether they develop it through training, it's possible that synaptic pruning contributes to this structural difference.

> **absolute pitch** the ability to recognize or produce any note on a musical scale.

Studies have shown, however, that people who speak tonal languages, or languages in which differences in tone convey meaning, such as Vietnamese and Mandarin Chinese, are more likely to develop absolute pitch than those speaking Western languages. This again suggests the possibility that early learning of auditory information related to tones can have a permanent effect on the functioning of this sensory system.

Just as some people exhibit absolute pitch, others are tone deaf, or unable to discern differences in pitch. Although tone deafness or *amusia* is sometimes the result of damage to the auditory system, it can be present from birth, and researchers believe it may be related to genetics (Peretz et al., 2007). Tone deafness affects up to 4 percent of the population and mostly results in a diminished appreciation for music. Although music appreciation is an important enriching ability, people with tone deafness are able to enjoy all other aspects of life. This condition only presents serious social problems when it occurs in cultures where the language is tonal.

When Things Go Hearing Wrong

There are many conditions that lead to abnormalities in the auditory system. Some cause either partial or total **deafness**, the loss of hearing. Abnormalities in the auditory system can also add unwanted auditory perceptions.

Deafness Deafness has a variety of causes. It can be genetic or caused by infection, physical trauma or exposure to toxins, including overdose of common medications such as aspirin.

Since speech is an important mode of communication for humans, deafness can have dramatic consequences for socialization. This is particularly a concern for children, because young children need auditory stimulation in order to develop normal spoken language skills. For this reason, physicians try to identify auditory deficits at an early life stage. Parents can then make choices among different options to help their children with

> **deafness** loss or lack of hearing.

Specialized: Somatonsensory System Synesthesia

Can you see noise or taste words? Some people can. This condition is called *synesthesia*. The name comes from two Greek words: *syn,* meaning together, and *aesthesis,* meaning perception, and therefore refers to "joined perception." People who have synesthesia experience a stimulus that normally would be perceived by one sense in a different sensory modality. They may actually see colors or images when they hear music.

The most common form of synesthesia is called *colored letters or numbers.* A person who has this form always sees a color in response to a specific letter or number. There are also synesthetes who smell particular odors in response to touch, who hear noises in response to smell, or who feel a tactile stimulus in response to sight. There are even some individuals who possess synesthesia involving three or more senses, but this is especially unusual.

People who experience synesthesia are not simply imagining their unusual sensations. Neuroimaging studies have shown that sensory areas normally not affected by particular stimuli are activated if that sense is involved in the synesthetic experience (Nunn el al., 2002). For example, the auditory cortex of sight-sound synesthetes, as well as the visual cortex, becomes active in response to particular visual stimuli that cause synesthesia. The brain of a person who can hear a picture or color really does respond as though the stimulus were producing sound waves, as well as reflecting light waves.

---

deafness. Some deaf individuals learn to use sign language and other methods of communication that rely on the senses other than hearing. Research over the past years has made progress in the construction of cochlear implants that help individuals with deafness to hear sounds (Sharma et al., 2009). Although this work is developing at a rapid pace, there remain many deaf people who are not helped by cochlear implants, however. (Battmer et al., 2009). This is one reason that many individuals and families choose to avoid them. Some in the deaf community also believe that hearing is not necessary in order to lead a productive and fulfilling life. For them, the potential benefits of implants may not outweigh the potential risks of surgery required to place them in the cochlea (Hyde & Power, 2006).

Hearing Unwanted Sounds About one of every 200 people is affected by *tinnitus,* or ringing in the ear. Tinnitus has multiple causes, some of which are related to abnormalities in the ear itself (Lanting et al, 2009). Most people are able to cope with the noise, but some find it too loud and distracting to ignore.

> "I have unwittingly helped to invent and refine a type of music that makes its principal exponents deaf. Hearing loss is a terrible thing because it cannot be repaired."
>
> —*Pete Townshend, rock musician of the band The Who*

Patients with epilepsy in the temporal cortex have reported the perception of hearing complex auditory stimuli, such as a musical tune (Wieser, 2003). This symptom, which can be completely distracting and disturbing to the patient, is the result of abnormal electrical activity in brain circuits that store complex auditory memories. Treatment for epilepsy sometimes involves neurosurgery to remove the part of the brain that is responsible for starting the seizures. Brain surgery in the temporal lobes, where auditory information is processed is particularly dangerous, however, because the temporal lobe also houses Wernicke's area, which is critical for language comprehension.

Before You Go On

What Do You Know?

12. What happens in the ear to transduce sound waves into neural signals?
13. What is a tonotopic map?
14. What are sensitive periods and how are they important for hearing?
15. What is tinnitus?

What Do You Think? What would you suggest including in an ideal early school curriculum, to develop children's auditory systems to their maximum capabilities?

THE VISUAL SENSE: SIGHT

LEARNING OBJECTIVE 5 Describe key processes in visual sensation and perception.

The ability to see and make sense of the visual world around us plays a very important role in human life. We use our vision in virtually all of our activities. Most of our social experiences have a visual component, for example. Vision is important for communication: facial expressions and "body language" or nonverbal communication help to convey information that is often lost in spoken language. No doubt related to its importance to us, the visual sense is particularly well developed in humans. Some estimates suggest that about half of the cerebral cortex of our brains is devoted to processing some type of visual stimuli.

The stimulus for vision is light. Light is made up of particles called *photons*. The light that we can see is part of the electromagnetic spectrum of energy that also includes many forms we cannot see, such as X-rays and radio waves. Like sound, light travels in waves. The visible spectrum of light ranges from about 400 to 700 nanometers in wavelength (a nanometer is a billionth of a meter). Different wave-lengths within our visible spectrum appear to us as different colors. Objects in the world absorb and reflect light in varying levels and patterns—those that reflect more light are perceived as brighter.

Seeing the Light

Vision begins when light enters the eye. Muscles in the iris—the colored part of the eye that you can see—adjust the size of our pupils to let in more or less of the light reflected from objects around us. These muscles also adjust the shape of the lens, focusing the light that enters the eye onto a specialized sheet of nerve cells in the back of the eye, called the **retina**. The retina is where we transduce light waves into neural impulses that the brain can process. Two major classes of visual receptors or **photoreceptors** exist in the retina, the **rods** and the **cones**. The rods predominate. There are over 100 million rods in the human retina. Rods are important for detecting light; they are highly sensitive to small amounts of light and are critical for night vision.

The cones are much fewer in number, with only about 6 million per human retina. Cones respond to light of different wave-lengths, which is how we detect color.

When light reaches the photoreceptors, a series of chemical reactions take place. The rods and cones stimulate the bipolar cells that, in turn, cause ganglion cells to then

retina a specialized sheet of nerve cells in the back of the eye containing the sensory receptors for vision.

photoreceptors the sensory receptor cells for vision, located in the retina.

rods photoreceptors most responsive to levels of light and dark.

cones photoreceptors responsive to colors.

optic nerve the bundle of axons of ganglion cells that carries visual information from the eye to the brain.

fovea center of the retina, containing only cones, where vision is most clear.

fire. The axons of the ganglion cells are bundled together to form the **optic nerve**. Signals from the ganglion cells travel along the optic nerve out of the eye and into the brain.

Rods and cones are not evenly distributed throughout the retina. Cones are concentrated more in the center than the periphery of the retina. The **fovea**, the region of the retina where our vision is at its sharpest, is entirely made up of cones. Rods are distributed throughout the rest of the retina and, unlike cones, are concentrated at the peripheral edges of the retina. Have you ever noticed that your peripheral vision is not particularly acute? It mostly enables you to detect movement, but not necessarily details. This is due to that fact that rods dominate the peripheral parts of the retina. The retina also contains a region that is completely lacking in rods and cones. This area produces a blind spot in your visual field. The *blind spot* is the location where your optic nerve leaves your retina. Because the visual parts of the brain are very good at filling in incomplete images, the blind spot is not noticeable under normal circumstances. With some manipulation of your visual inputs, however, you can experience your blind spot.

Like the other sensory systems we previously discussed, the visual system undergoes sensory adaptation. Dilation and constriction of the pupil, the opening in the center of the iris, is one way that the visual system adapts to the light. When you go from inside your home to outside on a bright, sunny day, you may immediately feel the need to squint, and shade your eyes. Your eyes quickly adapt to light, however, in part by constriction of the pupil that decreases the amount of light entering the eye. Conversely, to allow vision to occur in dark places, the pupil will open further to let in more light.

Seeing in Color

As we noted earlier, cones enable us to see color. The color of a visual stimulus can be described along three dimensions: hue, saturation, and brightness. The variety of colors we can perceive is related to the different combinations of these three characteristics.

- *Hue* refers to the wave-length of light that the visual stimulus produces. This is the most basic aspect of color, whether the stimulus is red, blue, yellow, or some other color.

- *Saturation* refers to how pure and deep the color appears—in other words, how much white is mixed into the color.
- *Brightness* of a color refers to how much light emanates or is reflected from the visual stimulus.

No single theory yet entirely explains how we perceive color. Two theories of color vision in combination help to explain a good deal, however. One theory, called the *trichromatic theory* of color vision, maintains that there are three different sensors for color and that each type of sensor responds to a different range of wave-lengths of light (Balaraman, 1962). We can certainly see more than just three colors, however. The rich variations we can detect in color arise from combinations in relative activation of these three types of sensors. This theory is largely correct, in that people with normal color vision have three different kinds of cones. One type responds to light in the yellowish-red wave-lengths, another to the green wave-lengths, and the third to light in the bluish-purple wave-lengths. Typically, at least two of the cone types will respond to a certain wave-length of visible light, but in varying increments. The combination of the signals produced by cones is what enables the brain to respond to a multitude of colors.

An alternative theory about color vision is called the *opponent process theory* (Buchsbaum & Gottschalk, 1983). This theory maintains that color pairs work to inhibit one another in the perception of color. For example, red inhibits the perception of green, yellow inhibits the perception of blue, and black inhibits the perception of white. There is also some truth to this theory because we cannot mix certain combinations of colors. For example, we cannot see reddish green or bluish yellow; instead we see brown or green, respectively. Opponent processing may be the result of activity in a region of the thalamus that receives visual information, called the *lateral geniculate nucleus*. Inputs to this nucleus from one color of an opposing pair inhibit those from the other color in the pair. So inputs carrying red information prevent the firing of neurons that convey green information, and so on for the other opponent pairs.

You can observe opponent processing at work by staring at a white dot in the middle of a green and black flag. After about 30 seconds, if you stare at a white sheet of paper, you will see an *afterimage* that is red and white. This also works with other colors in the opponent pairs. A white-on-black image will produce a black-on-white afterimage, and a yellow image will produce a blue afterimage. Afterimages happen when one color in an opponent pair inhibits the other. When we release this inhibition by looking away from the first color, the previously inhibited color overcompensates and creates an image in the opponent color.

The two theories can be used together to explain color blindness. Very few people are actually unable to see any colors at all. Most people who have what is called *color blindness* are really just unable to distinguish certain colors. Most common is red-green color blindness, which is tested with images. Studies suggest that people with this problem have a shortage of cones that respond to either the greenish or reddish wave-lengths. Therefore, the lateral geniculate nucleus of their thalamus does not receive sufficient inputs that enable it to inhibit either red or green colors, making people unable to distinguish between the two colors (Weale, 1983; Wertenbaker, 1981).

What Happens in the Sight BRAIN?

Visual information leaving the retina travels via the optic nerve to the brainstem. After synapsing with neurons in the *superior colliculus,* visual information then communicates with the thalamus. From the thalamus, visual input travels to the primary visual cortex, located in the occipital lobe.

Basic visual information is transmitted throughout the brain via a partially crossed set of axons. Visual information from the middle part of your visual field, closest to your nose, is sent, via axons that cross to the other side of your brain, to the opposite side of your visual cortex. Visual information from the lateral part of your visual field, closest to your temples, travels to the same side of the visual cortex.

Once visual information reaches the primary visual cortex, it is processed to enable the detection of very simple features, such as lines and edges (Hubel & Wiesel, 1959). However, we don't see the world as a collection of lines and edges. Instead, we see a rich set of complex visual stimuli that change as we and the world around us move. Detection of complex visual stimuli occurs as a result of circuitry that involves association areas of visual cortex. Recall from our discussion of hearing that association areas are involved with higher-order processes of perception: thinking and memory.

The pathways that process information about complex visual stimuli can be roughly divided into the *"what"* and the *"where"* pathways. That is, the regions that process visual information to help us determine *what* is the identity of an object (is it an apple, a car, or a house) are different from those where we process the visual information to figure out *where* in space the object is located (is the apple on the table, under the table, or behind the table). The "what" pathway involves axons that travel from the occipital cortex to the temporal cortex. The "where" pathway involves axons that travel from the occipital cortex to the parietal cortex.

How do researchers know about the brain regions that serve these complex functions? Recall from Chapter 4 that one way scientists have determined the function of certain brain regions is by examining the deficits displayed by people who have sustained damage in particular areas of their brains, usually as a result of stroke, disease, or head trauma. Patients with damage to the parts of the temporal cortex, which houses the "what" pathway, exhibit a condition called *visual agnosia*. Although their vision remains intact, they cannot recognize objects visually. When shown a rose, they can describe it, but they cannot name it. If they are allowed to touch or smell the rose, however, they can immediately identify it as a rose. A more specified form of visual agnosia that happens to people with damage to a certain part of the "what" pathway is called *prosopagnosia*. Individuals with prosopagnosia cannot recognize faces (Farah et al., 1995). Sometimes these patients can recognize familiar individuals by concentrating on some visual characteristic that is not directly related to facial features, such as the person's hairstyle or eyeglasses, but their ability to recognize the face itself is lost (Sacks, 1985).

Patients with damage to the "where" pathway also have normal vision, but they have lost the ability to locate objects in space. For example, when given the task of pouring water from a pitcher into a glass, they will invariably miss and pour the water onto the table or floor. A very interesting form of damage to the "where" pathway results in a condition called *hemi-neglect* (Mesulam, 1981). Patients with hemi-neglect completely ignore one side of their visual field. Because nerves that carry visual information cross to the opposite sides of the brain, people with damage to the left side of their "where" pathways neglect the right side, and vice versa. When asked to copy a drawing, people with hemi-neglect will leave out one half of it. Women with this condition have been known to apply makeup and do their hair only on one side.

In addition to the information researchers have gained from studying patients with brain damage, neuroimaging studies of people without brain damage have confirmed the presence of the "what" and "where" pathways. Indeed, these types of studies have shown that brain activity changes in specific parts of the "what" pathways when the participants are viewing objects (Reddy & Kanwisher, 2006).

So far we have discussed vision from a bottom-up perspective. Light comes in through the eye and the neural impulses generated are passed to successively more complex brain regions that ultimately result in the perception of a visual stimulus. Equally important to visual perception, however, is top-down processing, which involves previously acquired knowledge. Like perception involving the other sensory systems, visual perception involves both bottom-up and top-down processing occurring at the same time. Brain regions that store information about what objects look like can help us to perceive visual stimuli that are partially hidden or of different size from when we originally encountered them.

Putting Together the Parts: Gestalt Principles We don't see images as a series of small patches of color or a series of simple features. Instead, our visual system assembles this information into coherent objects and scenes. Even when we see a small part of an object or scene partially obscured by another object, we are able to perceive it as a whole, given limited visual information. Our brains are organized to fill in the missing parts so that we perceive and recognize meaningful stimuli. As we described earlier, part of our ability to perceive images comes from our use of cognitive processes, such as memory and learning, to help us recall from prior experience images that match the stimuli we are sensing.

The area of study focused on understanding principles by which we perceive and recognize visual stimuli in their entirety despite limited information is called *Gestalt* psychology. As mentioned in Chapter 1, Gestalt psychologists believe that perception helps us to add meaning to visual information, so that "the whole is greater than the sum of the parts" of what we see. Gestalt psychologists

have identified several laws by which visual information is organized into coherent images:

- *Proximity* The law of proximity indicates that visual stimuli near to one another tend to be grouped together. For example, AA AA AA is seen as three groups while AAA AAA is seen as two groups despite the fact that each set has six As.
- *Similarity* The law of similarity indicates that stimuli resembling one another tend to be grouped together. So AAaa is viewed as two groups because of the dissimilar appearance of upper and lowercase letters.
- *Continuity* The law of continuity indicates that stimuli falling along the same plane tend to be grouped together. ᴬᴬᴬ would be organized into two perceptual groups because they are not on the same line.
- *Good form* The law of good form indicates that stimuli forming a shape tend to be grouped together while those that do not remain ungrouped. Compare ☺ to O:) The former are perceived as a smiley face while the latter are perceived as three separate symbols.
- *Closure* The law of closure indicates that we tend to fill in small gaps in objects so that they are still perceived as whole objects.

These laws of visual organization work to create meaningful information out of the vast array of photons our eyes typically encounter when we look at something.

Sometimes, however, our brains tendency to impose order can lead us to perceive sights that are, in fact, illusions. Only careful examination reveals that the drawings depict physically impossible situations.

Getting in Deep When you look at the items on the table in a restaurant, how do you know which items are closer to you and which are farther away? We use a number of methods for depth perception, determining the distance of objects away from us and in relation to one another.

Because our eyes are set a slight distance apart, we do not see exactly the same thing with each eye. This **retinal disparity**, the slightly different stimuli recorded by the retina of each eye, provide us with a *binocular* cue of depth. Our brains use the discrepancies between the visual information received from our two eyes to help us judge the distance of objects from us. You can observe your own

retinal disparity the slight difference in images processed by the retinas of each eye.

retinal disparity by holding up a finger at arm's length away from your face. Close first one eye, then the other, and note how the position of your finger seems to change relative to objects in the background beyond the finger.

Another binocular cue to depth is actually tactile. We feel the changes in the muscles around our eyes as we shift them to look at objects at various distances. Closer objects require more **convergence**, turning our eyes inward toward our noses. Use your finger again to demonstrate convergence. Start with the finger at arm's length from you and watch it as you bring it closer and closer to your face. Note the sensations you feel as you do so.

We also use a number of other cues to determine depth. The following are sometimes called **monocular cues**, because, if needed, they can help us judge depth based on information from only one eye.

convergence inward movement of the eyes to view objects close to oneself.

monocular cues visual clues about depth and distance that can be perceived using information from only one eye.

- *Interposition* When one object blocks part of another from our view, we see the blocked object as farther away.
- *Elevation* We see objects that are higher in our visual plane as farther away than those that are lower.
- *Texture gradient* We can see more details of textured surfaces, such as the wood grain on a restaurant table, that are closer to us.
- *Linear perspective* Parallel lines seem to converge in the distance.
- *Shading* We are accustomed to light, such as sunlight, coming from above us. We use differences in the shading of light from the top to the bottom of our field of view to judge size and distance of objects.
- *Familiar size* Once we have learned the sizes of objects, such as people or restaurant plates, we assume that they stay the same size, so objects that look smaller than usual must be farther away than usual.

- *Relative size* When we look at two objects we know are about the same size, if one seems smaller than the other, we see it as farther away than the other.

Although some studies show that we can perceive depth at very early ages, and may even be born with some depth perception abilities, top-down processing also plays a part in depth processing (Banks & Salapatek, 1983). We use our memories of the sizes of objects around us, for example, to help judge depth.

Artists use monocular depth cues to help us "see" depth in their two-dimensional representations. In essence, they create an illusion of depth. Because visual perception happens nearly automatically, we are quite susceptible to such visual illusions. For example, people from cultures that have a lot of architecture and structures featuring straight edges, such as the United States, are easily fooled by the Ponzo illusion and Müller-Lyer illusion, which both take advantage of our tendency to use linear perspective to judge distance (Berry et al, 1992; Brislin & Keating, 1976).

Seeing What We Expect to See: Perceptual Constancies Top-down processing also contributes to **perceptual constancies,** our tendencies to view objects as unchanging in some ways, even though the actual visual sensations we receive are constantly shifting. We tend to see the food on our plate as the same colors, for example, even when a restaurant owner dims the lights for the evening and the actual light waves we are receiving change in intensity, a phenomenon known as color *constancy* (Schiffman, 1996). Once we have learned the shape of an object, we also experience shape constancy (Gazzaniga, 1995). We may get visual input of only the edge of a plate as server sets it on a restaurant table in front of us, but we perceive the plate as a round disk.

Another consistency, size consistency, helps us in depth perception, as noted above. Once we have learned the size of an object, we expect it to stay the same. Top-down processing, based on our memory of the object's size, leads us to assume that if it looks smaller than usual, it is probably far away, instead

perceptual constancies our top-down tendency to view objects as unchanging, despite shifts in the environmental stimuli we receive.

of thinking that the object has somehow shrunk. As with our other perceptual processes, perceptual constancies, while usually very useful in helping us understand the world, can sometimes lead us to "see" illusions. A common size illusion, for example, is the moon illusion. The moon stays the same size all the time, but when we view it close to a horizon it appears much bigger than when we see it farther from the horizon (Kaufman & Rock, 1989).

Sight How We Develop

Newborn infants are capable of seeing, but their visual acuity is much less than it will be after a few months. For a short time after birth, human babies focus mostly on contrasts. For example, a baby will stare at the hairline of his or her caregiver, instead of the face.

By the time we are about two months old, visual acuity has improved and infants seem to focus intently on faces. Their focal range is limited, though. They see objects best that are within a foot away. Perhaps not coincidentally, this is about the distance people tend to place their faces when interacting with babies. Over the next several months, our visual acuity improves so that by the end of the eighth month, vision in babies is quite similar to that of normal adults. These early life changes in vision are due to the postnatal development of the visual nervous system. As we'll see next, proper development of the visual system requires visual experience during a specific part of early life.

When Things Go Sight Wrong

Many common vision problems can be corrected today. Increasingly common laser surgeries or the lenses in glasses or contacts can help people cope with nearsightedness, or difficulty seeing things clearly far away, and farsightedness, problems seeing near objects clearly, for example. Eye-care practitioners help with a variety of other problems as well. Sometimes, however, there is no treatment available, or treatment is begun too late to prevent people from losing vision in one or both eyes.

Amblyopia To see the world as a whole, both eyes must work together to produce not two separate images, but one comprehensive image. To do this, motor control of both eyes is important. Newborn infants often do not move their eyes in tandem. It is not uncommon for parents to report concern that their young infants sometimes appear to have crossed eyes. This is a normal characteristic that typically resolves itself within a few months after birth as the eye muscles and the motor system that controls them mature.

Some people, however, do not naturally develop coordinated movement of both eyes. This condition is called *strabismus* and affects about 2 percent of the population. To avoid seeing double images, children with strabismus will rely on the visual information from one eye while ignoring information from other. Strabismus is commonly treated by having the child wear a patch over the stronger eye, thus forcing the child to use the weaker one, or by surgery. If children are treated during early life, their normal binocular vision can be preserved.

If strabismus remains uncorrected past the age of about six years, however, it will eventually lead to a loss of visual abilities in the weaker eye, or *amblyopia*. Amblyopia can be a permanent condition that results from abnormal development of the brain's visual cortex. As we discussed in Chapter 3, many development psychologists suggest that there are not only sensitive periods, when we can develop certain skills with greater ease than at other time in our lives, but also "critical periods," which are the *only* times during which certain developments can take place. Amblyopia develops if we do not receive visual stimulation from both eyes during the critical period of development for the normal maturation of the visual brain. After about the age of six, the brains of children with strabismus seem to lose the ability to use information from both eyes and instead process inputs only from one eye.

Blindness About 12 million people in the United States suffer from visual impairments that are either total or so severe and uncorrectable that these individuals are characterized as blind. There are many potential causes of blindness. Some are congenital, or present at birth, while others are acquired later in life. Diseases that can produce blindness include diabetes, glaucoma, and macular degeneration.

Since humans rely so heavily on visual information, living without adequate visual input is very challenging. A number of devices have been created to help blind people live independently. Braille, a system of reading that involves touch, has significantly improved quality of life for the blind. Braille uses various combinations of raised dots to replace traditional printed letters and numbers.

Visually impaired individuals can become so proficient at reading Braille that they can actually read faster than people with normal vision typically read printed material. Researchers have found that blind individuals who become experts at reading Braille are actually using parts of their "visual" brain to process the sophisticated tactile information. Neuroimaging studies have shown that parts of the occipital and temporal cortices that normally process visual information are activated in blind individuals while they read Braille. It is also noteworthy that the individuals with congenital blindness use more of their visual brains to read Braille than did those who became blind later in life. This may be another example of a critical period at work. The acquisition of Braille reading skills as a child may allow for the reorganization of the visual system to serve some new function. Learning Braille later in life may lead to less dramatic reorganization because those parts of the visual brain have already become "hard-wired," or less plastic and open to change.

Before You Go On

What Do You Know?

1. What are rods and cones?
2. What are the two theories of color vision and how do they work together?
3. What do the "what" and "where" pathways in the brain do?
4. What are the two major types of depth perception cues and what is the difference between them?
5. What is strabismus, how is it treated, and what can happen if it is not treated promptly?

What Do You Think? Is the cliche, "Seeing is believing," really true? Why or why not?

SUMMARY

- Sensation is the process of converting physical stimuli from our environment into neural impulses that the brain can process. Perception is the process of interpreting the neural signals to understand the information we receive.

Common Features of Sensation and Perception

LEARNING OBJECTIVE 1 Describe characteristics shared by all the senses, including receptor cells, transduction, and thresholds, and differentiate between top-down and bottom-up processes of perception.

- Our sensory systems convert physical stimuli into neural information with specialized cells called *sensory receptor cells* that convert a specific form of environmental stimuli into neural impulse by a process called *sensory transduction.*
- The conversion of physical stimuli into neural impulses only occurs when the stimuli reach a certain level, or threshold. The absolute threshold is the minimum level of a stimulus we can detect. The difference threshold is the smallest difference we can detect between two similar stimuli.
- Our sensory systems are set up to detect change. With continuous exposure to a stimulus, adaptation occurs.

The Chemical Senses: Smell and Taste

LEARNING OBJECTIVE 2 Summarize what happens when we smell and taste.

- Smell, our olfactory sense, converts chemical odorants into neural signals that the brain can use. Taste, our gustatory sense, is closely intertwined with smell. Most flavors are a combination of scents with the five basic tastes we can discern: sweet, salty, sour, bitter, and umami.
- Our tactile sense combines with taste and smell, to help us appreciate, or dislike the textures of foods and to experience temperature and "hot" sensations from capsaicin in spicy foods.

- Taste buds in papillae on the tongue convert chemicals in our food to neural signals the brain can use. Taste receptors and smell receptors are routinely replaced, since they are more vulnerable to damage than other sensory receptors. Information about smell goes directly from the olfactory bulb to the olfactory cortex. Areas of the brain that process smells and tastes are plastic, or changeable. Processing of smells also sometimes overlaps with emotions and memories.
- Our preferred tastes change as we mature from childhood to adulthood, probably from a combination of learning and physical changes in the mouth.
- True disorders of taste are rare; people more frequently lose part or all of their sense of smell. Anosmia can present safety risks and diminish pleasure in life.

The Tactile or Cutaneous Senses: Touch, Pressure, Pain, Vibration

LEARNING OBJECTIVE 3 Describe how the different senses of touch work and what can happen when things go wrong.

- A variety of sensory receptors throughout our bodies convert touch, pressure, or temperature stimuli into neural impulses that our brains can perceive.
- The sensory cortex of the brain maps touch sensations. Especially sensitive or important body parts receive disproportionately large representation in the cortex.
- Pain travels to the brain via both a fast pathway and a slow pathway.
- People differ greatly in the perception of pain. Some of the differences are related to culture and gender. Others are individual.
- The gate control theory of pain suggests that certain patterns of neural activity can close a "gate" so that pain information does not reach parts of the brain where it is perceived.
- Medical professionals continue to search for ways to relieve people's chronic pain. Opiate drugs that simulate natural pain-killing endorphins or enkephalins are addictive. Sometimes practitioners resort to neurosurgery, which stops a patient from receiving all touch signals.
- The inability to feel pain can put people at high risk for injuries.

- People who have lost body parts surgically or through accidents often feel phantom sensations in the missing body part. These may be related to reorganization of the somatosensory cortex after an amputation.

The Auditory Sense: Hearing

LEARNING OBJECTIVE 4 Summarize what happens when we hear.

- The frequency and amplitude of sound waves produce our perceptions of pitch and loudness of sounds.
- When sounds enter the ear, they move the ear drum, which sets in motion the ossicles. The last of these, the stirrup, vibrates the oval window, setting into motion fluid in the cochlea. Hair cells on the basilar membrane in the cochlea transduce movements along the basilar membrane into neural signals the brain can interpret.
- Frequency theory suggests that patterns in the firing rates of the neurons are perceived as different sounds. Place theory suggests that information from different locations along the basilar membrane is related to different qualities of sound.
- Top-down processing lets us use the general loudness of sounds, as well as differences in the signals received from each ear, to determine location of a sound.
- Different pitches are represented in a tonotopic map in the auditory cortex of the brain. Association areas of the cortex help us recognize familiar sounds, including speech.
- The brain integrates information from multiple sensory systems to enable the appropriate recognition and response to stimuli. Some people experience an overlap of sensory systems known as synesthesia.
- As young children, we experience a sensitive period during which it is especially easy for us to learn auditory information, including language and music. Some people, particularly those exposed to pure tones during this sensitive period, develop absolute pitch.
- Common hearing problems include hearing loss and deafness, as well as hearing unwanted sounds, such as tinnitus.

The Visual Sense: Sight

LEARNING OBJECTIVE 5 Describe key processes in visual sensation and perception.

- Vision is very important to humans, and a great deal of our brain is involved in processing-visual information.
- Rods and cones in the retina at the back of the eye change light into neural impulses. Cones provide detailed vision and help us perceive color, while rods provide information about intensity of light.
- Two different theories in combination—trichomatic theory and opponent process theory—explain a good deal of how we perceive color.
- The fovea at the center of the retina contains only cones and provides our sharpest vision. We have a blind spot where the optic nerve leaves the retina to carry information to the brain.
- In the brain, visual information is processed through the "what" and "where" pathways.
- Damage to the brain can produce deficits in sensation, as well as abnormal sensory experiences.
- Top-down processing is involved in much visual perception. Gestalt theorists have identified several principles by which we recognize stimuli even when visual inputs are limited. We use binocular and monocular cues for depth perception. Perceptual constancies, based on learning from previous experiences, help us to see things as stable despite constant shifts in our visual inputs. These top-down processes can be "fooled" by visual illusions.
- Without adequate visual stimulation through both eyes during a critical period of life, we may not develop binocular vision, a condition known as amblyopia.
- Blind individuals can use other sensory modalities to compensation for the loss of visual information. Learning Braille with touch involves the use of brain areas normally used for vision.

KEY TERMS

sensation
perception
sensory receptor cells
sensory transduction
absolute threshold
difference threshold or just noticeable difference
sensory adaptation
bottom-up processing
top-down processing
olfactory sense
gustatory sense
odorants
olfactory receptor neurons
papillae
taste buds
olfactory bulb
anosmia
ageusia
free nerve endings
Meissner's corpuscles
Merkel's discs
Ruffini's end-organs
Pacinian corpuscles
gate control theory of pain
endorphins
enkephalins
sound waves
tympanic membrane
ossicles
oval window
cochlea
basilar membrane
hair cells
tonotopic map
absolute pitch
deafness
retina
photoreceptors
rods
cones
optic nerve
fovea
retinal disparity
convergence
monocular cue
perceptual constancies

The Machinery of Colour Vision

SAMUEL G. SOLOMON AND PETER LENNIE

Some fundamental principles of colour vision, deduced from perceptual studies, have been understood for a long time. Physiological studies have confirmed the existence of three classes of cone photoreceptors, and of colour-opponent neurons that compare the signals from cones, but modern work has drawn attention to unexpected complexities of early organization: the proportions of cones of different types vary widely among individuals, without great effect on colour vision; the arrangement of different types of cones in the mosaic seems to be random, making it hard to optimize the connections to colour-opponent mechanisms; and new forms of colour-opponent mechanisms have recently been discovered. At a higher level, in the primary visual cortex, recent studies have revealed a simpler organization than had earlier been supposed, and in some respects have made it easier to reconcile physiological and perceptual findings.

Two hundred years ago, Young[1] suggested that colour vision depends on the excitation of three fundamental mechanisms with different but overlapping spectral sensitivities. More than a hundred years ago, Hering[2] suggested that the appearance of colours depends on mechanisms that bring together in opposition (for example,

red versus green) the signals that are elicited by lights from different parts of the spectrum. These perceptual observations have guided physiological investigations, which over the past 40 years have confirmed the existence of three fundamental mechanisms whose signals are later brought together in opposition. This seemingly simple hierarchical organization indicates that specific visual tasks might be readily assigned to neural mechanisms at each stage of the pathway (BOX 1). However, recent work has revealed an unexpected richness of physiological organization that is invisible to the perceptual scientist.

We review here the machinery through which the brain might provide for colour vision, proceeding from the photoreceptors to the cerebral cortex (BOX 1). We focus on the mechanisms of primate colour vision, in humans and in our closest animal model, the macaque monkey. We describe, in the retina and in the lateral geniculate nucleus, many more pathways for colour signals than seemed possible only 15 years ago. We then show that signal transformations within the primary visual cortex (V1) accomplish much of what needs to be done to accommodate findings from perceptual studies. New work has also provided much clearer evidence than we have had until now about which cells in the cortex convey information about colour, and has sharpened our understanding of the relationship between colour vision and binocular vision.

Box 1 The dominant visual pathway in primates

The left panel shows a schematic drawing of the pathway from the retina to the primary visual cortex (V1) through the dorsal lateral geniculate nucleus (LGN) of the thalamus. The right panels highlight the important anatomical structures. Light entering the eye passes through the ganglion cells and is imaged on the photoreceptor layer (rod photoreceptors, which are not active in colour vision, are found between the cones). Signals from photoreceptors pass through bipolar cells to ganglion cells, the axons of which form the optic nerve, which projects principally to the LGN. The horizontal and amacrine cell pathways within the retina allow spatial comparisons of cone signals. Ganglion cells from the temporal retina project to the ipsilateral LGN (red lines) and those from the nasal retina project to the contralateral LGN (green lines). Within the LGN, the projections from the two eyes are aligned, so the same topographic map (of the contralateral half of the visual field) is found in all layers. The axons of LGN neurons project almost exclusively to V1, where they terminate primarily in layer 4 and form ocular dominance columns (a small fraction of LGN cells project to extrastriate areas: see REF. 163 and the references therein). The termination site within layer 4 depends on the layer in which the LGN neuron is found: parvocellular (P) cells project mainly to layer 4Cβ

magnocellular (M) to layer 4Cα, and koniocellular (K) cells to layer 4A and lower layer 3. The shading depicts the distinct pattern that emerges when slices through V1 are stained for cytochrome oxidase activity. Reactivity is particularly high in layer 4 and in patches that dot the superficial layers 2 and 3.

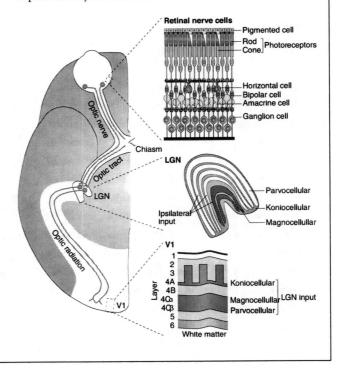

THE BUILDING BLOCKS OF COLOUR VISION

Photoreception. The spectrum of light that is visible to humans and most other mammals spans wave-lengths of ~400–700 nm. Humans with normal colour vision can distinguish many thousands of colours[3]. To accomplish this we use the signals from three types of cone photoreceptor, whose greatest sensitivities are to short (S, ~430 nm), medium (M, ~530 nm) and long (L, ~560 nm) wave-lengths, but whose tuning is broad enough that each responds to light throughout much of the visible spectrum (FIG. 1). The spectral sensitivity of a photoreceptor is best understood as a measure of the probability that the receptor will absorb a photon of a particular wave-length. Once absorbed, the identity of the photon is lost, so no single photoreceptor can distinguish a change in the wave-length of light from a change in its intensity. This is the principle of univariance[4].

Colour vision, the ability to distinguish lights of different spectral composition, regardless of intensity, depends on the comparison of signals from photoreceptors with different spectral sensitivities. The presence of three types of cone photoreceptor makes human colour vision 'trichromatic'. It is dichromatic when there are two types, as is the case in some humans, most New World primates, and most other mammals. Some nocturnal mammals, including owl monkeys[5], have only one type of cone photoreceptor.

The spectral sensitivity of a mammalian photo-receptor is determined by the **opsin** it expresses, which in the outer segment is covalently bound to a **chromophore**[6]. The spectral sensitivity of this compound is determined by the sequence of amino acids that make up the opsin protein. Small changes in the opsin sequence can shift the most effective wave-length: for example, differences in two of the ~350 amino acids in the L-and M-opsins of the human retina account for most of the 30 nm difference in their peak wave-lengths[7,8], and differences at a further 5 sites can introduce more subtle variants. Although animals of other phyla can express four different opsins in the cone photoreceptors, mammals seem to have lost all but two (one sensitive to short wave-lengths and another sensitive to long wave-lengths). Subsequently in evolution, primates seem to have regained a third opsin (for a review, see REF. 9), providing two opsins (M-and L-) that cover the middle- and long-wave-length parts of the spectrum. The genes that code for the L-and M-opsins are found in an array on the X-chromosome, with the L-opsin gene being closest to the region that controls gene expression, with one or more M-opsin genes downstream of it, although only the first seems to be expressed[10,11]. The genes are vulnerable to alteration or loss, resulting (much more often in men than in women) in loss or impairment of the capacity to distinguish colours in the middle- and long-wave-length parts of the spectrum. The close similarity and concatenation of the L-and M-genes in Old World primates makes it likely that the ancestor of macaques and humans possessed a single L-opsin gene on the X-chromosome, and that this gene then duplicated and mutated into the gene for the M-opsin.

If one of the L-or M-opsin genes is deleted or fatally mutated and not expressed, dichromacy is inevitable (although see REF. 12). In Old World primates, there are two potential dichromatic phenotypes: all the non-S-cone photoreceptors might express the same opsin, or the photoreceptors that would otherwise have expressed the dysfunctional opsin express no opsin at all. These are not mutually exclusive—the phenotype should depend on the type of mutation—and there is evidence for both[13,14].

> **Opsin**
> A G protein membrane-bound receptor usually found in rod and cone photoreceptors that initiates phototransduction. Its spectral sensitivity depends on the sequence of amino acids.

> **Chromophore**
> A molecule, or part of one, that changes conformation upon absorbing light, inducing a conformational change in the opsin bound to it and thereby triggering phototransduction.

Other variations in the properties of photoreceptors should affect trichromatic vision. First, the peak sensitivity of the opsins can be changed by non-fatal mutations, through **crossing over**. Such shifts in spectral sensitivity give rise to characteristic anomalies of colour vision (almost exclusively in men), depending on the opsin that is affected: **deuternomaly** arises when the spectral sensitivity of the M-opsin shifts, and **protanomaly** when that of the L-opsin shifts. Genetic screening has shown that there are many anomalous opsins among the human population[15,16], but only large shifts seem to cause noticeable deficits in colour vision. Second, the ratio of L-to M-cones in the photoreceptor mosaic varies widely, from approximately 0.4 to more than 10 (REFS17–19). This might be expected to influence colour vision, but does not; for example, the wave-length that individuals describe as uniquely yellow does not depend on the proportion of L-cones in the mosaic[19].

One to three percent of ganglion cells in most mammalian retinas are intrinsically photosensitive: they express the photo-pigment melanopsin, a G-protein-coupled receptor. The light response of this pigment is much slower than that of cones or rods, so it probably does not contribute to colour vision as it is normally studied (although it is important for the control of circadian rhythms[20], and probably for the pupillary light reflex[21]). Nevertheless, these ganglion cells project to the dorsal lateral geniculate nucleus (LGN) of the thalamus, the main pathway for vision, so they might contribute directly to perception[22]. Their intrinsic photosensitivity does not adapt to the ambient light, and so they could provide a signal for absolute brightness[22]. Were the signal from melanopsin important for the perception of brightness, its distinctive spectral sensitivity should allow this to be revealed (FIG. 1): the prediction being that **ganzfelds** illuminated by different monochromatic lights that equally excite

> **Crossing over**
> During meiosis, two like-chromosomes can both break; each can reconnect with the fragment from the other, exchanging genes or parts of genes in the process.

> **Deuteranomaly**
> Small deviations of colour vision from the normal observer (often only revealed in tasks requiring fine discriminations) brought about by mutations that shift the spectral sensitivity of the M-cone opsin.

melanopsin should be judged as equally bright.

The photoreceptor mosaic. Colour vision depends on the comparison of activity in different photoreceptors, but these photoreceptors lie in a two-dimensional sheet, with only a single photoreceptor at any one position. So, for colour vision we must make comparisons across space. For the best spatial resolution of colour variations, we might want photoreceptors to be arranged in a triangular lattice (much like a shadow-mask television tube). Indeed, we might expect the mechanisms that determine which opsin is expressed in each photoreceptor to also confer spatial order on the cone mosaic (such that, for example, neighbouring photoreceptors act mutually to suppress the expression of the same opsin). The S-cones in primates are histologically distinctive, and their proportion (5–10% of all cones) and quasi-regular distribution in the retina have been known for some time[18,23–25]. Until recently, it was assumed that L-and M-cones (which are not easy to distinguish) were arranged in a regular lattice. However, modern measurements[26,27], culminating in the extraordinary images of the living primate retina provided by recent studies[18,28,29], one of which is shown in FIG. 1, have now refuted this assumption.

Rather than lying in a triangular lattice, the L-and M-cones are distributed as if the type (L or M) of each cone is determined randomly[8]. Little is known about the developmental mechanisms of cone differentiation and migration, and the apparently random mosaic might arise from the interplay of non-stochastic processes[18]. The ratio of L-:M-cones seems to depend on the cones' location in the retina, generally increasing in the far periphery, and this does not easily fit the random hypothesis[18,30–33]. Across large areas and for purely chromatic L-M modulation[18], a random mosaic will produce the same spatial frequency resolution as a crystalline one. Nevertheless, the

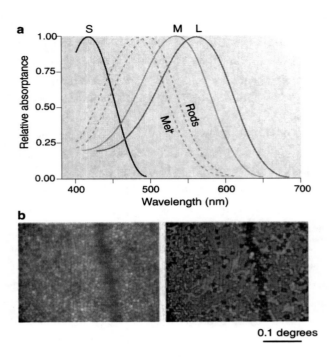

Figure 1 Spectral sensitivities of L-cones, M-cones and S-cones. a | *Shown for comparison are the spectral sensitivities of rods and intrinsically photosensitive ganglion cells (which express melanopsin, Mel+ from REF. 22).* **b** | *Spatial arrangement of the different types of cones in the photoreceptor mosaic in the human retina 18. The images are the mosaic of a single individual, JP, 0.8 degrees from the fovea in the temporal retina. The greyscale image shows the arrangement of photoreceptors. Three additional images are then obtained, each after exposure to intense lights of different wave-lengths, and compared to this reference. Each intense light bleaches photopigment in some cone types more than others, so the type—S, M or L—of cone can be recovered by comparing changes in absorptance induced by each of the three conditions. On the right, false colouring shows the type of cone—red for L-cones, green for M and blue for S. In this mosaic, the L-cones outnumber the M-cones by a ratio of ~2.3:1. The S-cones are much less numerous, roughly 4% of all cones here. The L-and M-cones are distributed randomly, so there are frequent clumps of cones of one type.*

clusters of cones of one type that develop in these mosaics have significant implications for colour vision: they make the achievable spatial resolution of colour vision different in each local region of the retina, and will cause a physically identical stimulus to evoke different patterns of activity depending on its location on the mosaic. In perception this might have its corollary in the various colour sensations that can be elicited by the same small light[34,35]. The upshot is that, in a mosaic containing clusters of cones of a single type, the area of the retina that must be sampled to form a neural representation of hue that does not depend on retinal location is larger than it would be were the mosaic crystalline. This must limit the acuity of colour vision.

ORGANIZATION OF SUBCORTICAL PATHWAYS

Because a single photoreceptor cannot distinguish between a change in the wave-length of light and a change in its intensity, the analysis of colour requires the comparison of signals from different types of cones. Early perceptual observations[2,36] indicated that the representation of hue is organized along two fundamental dimensions—red-green variation and blue-yellow variation (BOX 2).

Early neurophysiological investigations of post-receptor colour mechanisms looked at neurons in the primate LGN. Neurons in this relay station, which have **receptive fields** that are largely indistinguishable from those of the retinal ganglion cells that drive them (BOX 1), have chromatic properties that at first sight seemed strikingly like those suggested by perceptual work[37,38]. Later work firmly established two distinct groups of neurons and characterized them quantitatively[39-41]. Neurons in one group oppose the signals of L-and M-cones: these are the midget ganglion cells and their targets are in the parvocellular (P) layers of the LGN. Neurons in the other group receive strong signals from S-cones, opposed to some combination of signals from L-and M-cones (FIG. 2): these are usually found in zones bordering the principal layers of the LGN. As we have learned more about these groups, it has become increasingly clear that they have no simple connections with the fundamental perceptual dimensions.

Receptive fields

The region of visual space (or, equivalently, an area on the retinal surface) where presentation of an appropriate pattern of light causes changes in the activity of a neuron.

The receptive fields of P-cells. P-cells receive inputs from only L-and M-cones, and these inputs generally have opposite signs (FIG. 2), which indicates that P-cells are important for red-green colour vision (for an alternative view, see REFS 42,43). However, there seem to be many more P-cells than are necessary to support colour vision, and no other pathway provides the sampling density that is needed to support fine spatial resolution, indicating that the P-pathway is essential for spatial vision. It was recognized early on that cone-opponency in P-cell receptive fields might be provided by their centre-surround spatial structure (with, for example, L-cones providing the main input to the centre, and M-cones providing the main input to the surround), so the capacity to support red-green colour vision might have exploited mechanisms that were developed for spatial vision[44-48].

The complexity of supporting these two roles is highlighted by the recent discovery[28,29] that the apparently random distribution of L-and M-cones can lead to large clusters of one type, making it hard to construct receptive fields that have both precise spatial and precise chromatic properties. To understand how this is accomplished we need to know two things. First, does colour vision require receptive fields where the inputs from different types of cone are tightly specified? Second, do cone inputs to the receptive fields of P-cells differ from what we would expect from indiscriminate sampling of the cone mosaic? The answer to the first question is probably 'no': models without selective wiring of cone inputs in retinal receptive fields can account for many aspects of human colour vision[49,50]. Moreover, individuals with different L:M-cone ratios have similar colour vision[18,19]. It seems unlikely that, in these individuals, retinal receptive fields have managed to assign fixed weights to each cone type without loss of spatial acuity. The second question has proved much more difficult to answer.

Cone-specific inputs to the centre and surround will confer on a P-cell receptive field the highest possible sensitivity to chromatic signals. But chromatic opponency can also arise through the antagonistic interactions of two mechanisms that have substantial spectral overlap, as would be the case if the centre and surround drew inputs randomly from the photoreceptor mosaic. There is no known anatomical mechanism through which the centre and surround select inputs from specific types of cone[51-53], but we know almost nothing of the chromatic properties of amacrine and bipolar cells in the primate retina[54,55] (BOX 1), so it has been hard to discern the pathways through which cones provide input to ganglion cell receptive fields.

In the central retina, P-cells probably derive their principal excitatory input from only one cone[56,57]; physiological investigations of the cone specificity of inputs to P-cell surrounds in the central retina have generally been inconclusive[41,58–62]. This is not surprising, because the functional difference between cone-selective and indiscriminate connections is small. Given this, and the absence of selective connections to M-or L-cones in the outer retina, there seems no reason to suppose that the opponent mechanisms in P-cell receptive fields are cone-selective.

Outside the central retina, the receptive field centres of P-cells draw on several cones, so indiscriminate sampling of the cone mosaic would cause the colour-opponent organization to become more variable. Nevertheless, although opponency is weaker on average in the peripheral retina than in the central retina, it is not absent[61,63]. The surrounds of P-cells are also larger in the peripheral retina and may draw on hundreds of cones, so without selective wiring most of them should have the same spectral sensitivity (that of the average of L-and M-cones in the photoreceptor mosaic), and there is some evidence for this[61]. Chromatic opponency in peripheral P-cells must arise through dominance of the centre mechanism by cones of a particular class, but to understand whether this arises through chance will require a quantitative model of the impact of clusters of cones of one type[64].

Pathways that carry signals from S-cones. Subcortical receptive fields are commonly described by the sign, 'ON' or 'OFF', of the centre mechanism. This sign is determined by the response of the neuron to uniform illumination by white light: ON when activity increases with increasing illumination, OFF when activity increases with decreasing illumination. In the same way, increased activity accompanying increasing S-cone activation means that the sign of the majority of S-cone input to the receptive field is ON. We usually think of ON and OFF pathways as providing complimentary representations of the retinal image, but recent work indicates that for S-cone signals this is not the case.

It has long been known that a specialized bipolar cell provides ON S-cone signals ('S-ON', often called 'blue-ON') to later visual processes[65,66]. It now seems clear that this S-cone pathway, which is preserved in diurnal primates[67] and found in other mammals[68], is phylogenetically

Box 2 Colour space and isoluminance

Panel **a** show a three-dimensional colour space, the axes of which are the activation level of each cone type (L, M and S). Within this space is a series of parallel surfaces; in each of these the activity of L-and M-cones varies so that their sum remains constant (L ≈−2M). These surfaces are called isoluminant, where lights differ in hue and saturation but not in luminance; one surface is shown in the figure. S-cones do not usually contribute to the sensation of luminance, so in the space formed by the cone activations the surface forms a plane parallel to the axis of S-cone activation. A physiologically relevant transformation of this space[39,164] is shown in panel **b**, where the same surface is redrawn. Two axes now define it as a plane. One axis represents the level of S-cone activation (S), the other is the difference between L-and M-cone activation (L -M). The plane formed by these two axes is isoluminant because throughout it the sum of L-and M-cone activity is constant. When stimuli are defined by excursions from the centre of this plane (the white point), the angle within the plane defines the level of cone activation and hue, as is shown in panel **c**. Here, 0 degrees is an excursion from the white point to +L -M (increased L-cone activity and decreased M-cone activity) and 270 degrees is increased S-cone activity. Normal to this plane is an achromatic axis along which the signals of all cones vary.

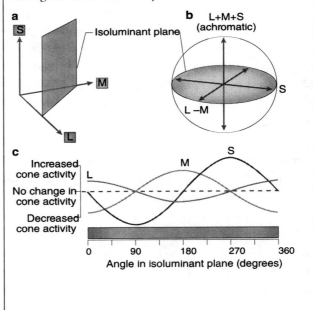

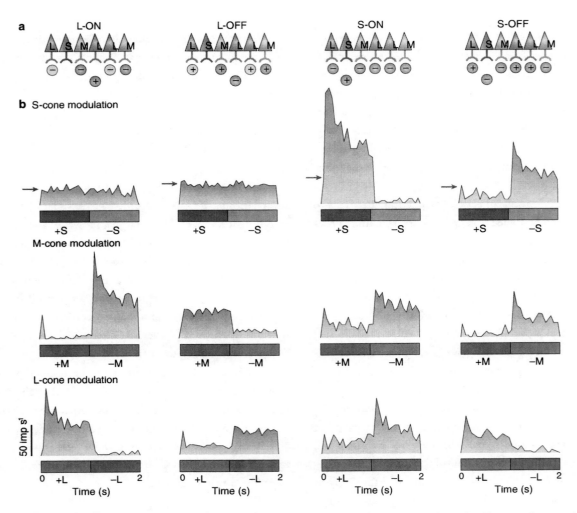

Figure 2 Cone inputs to four different types of neuron in the macaque lateral geniculate nucleus. a | *Which cones contribute inputs to the receptive field are shown—the plus sign indicates cones for which increases in activation lead to increased firing of the neuron, the minus indicates the cones where decreases in activation lead to increased firing. Cones that probably provide input to the surround are shown in the upper level, and to the centre in the lower level. Lighter shading of the circles indicates that the contribution of that class of cone to the opponent mechanism is uncertain.* **b** | *The average firing rates during selective modulation of cone activity (upper, modulation of the S-cones only; middle, M-cones; lower, L-cones). Two P-cells (L-cone ON, L-cone OFF) receive input only from L-and M-cones; two K-cells (S-ON, S-OFF) also receive input from S-cones. Two other neuron types important in colour vision—M-ON and M-OFF—are not shown, and their responses would be the mirror image of L-ON and L-OFF cells. Arrows in the top panels show the spontaneous discharge rate. imp s^{-1}, impulses per second.*

ancient. S-cones are sparsely distributed, so they cannot support high visual acuity. It is therefore likely that the S-cone pathway evolved to provide colour vision in a common (dichromatic) ancestor of these mammals[69].

We have learned much about some S-cone pathways through in vitro intracellular recordings of primate retinal ganglion cells, which are then stained to identify their morphology[22,70,71]. Early recordings showed that the ganglion cells that give S-ON responses have a distinctive

bistratified morphology and form part of a pathway that is separate from the long-established midget-parvocellular system. S-ON neurons are generally found in the koniocellular (K) layers of the LGN[38,72,73] (BOX 1). In macaques in which the activity of cortical neurons has been silenced by application of muscimol (an agonist of GABA$_A$ (γ-aminobutyric acid A) receptors) to reveal the activity of LGN afferents to different cortical layers, S-ON responses are found only in the superficial layers 3 and 4A[74], to which the neurons in the LGN K-layers project[75,76]. The receptive fields of S-ON cells in the retina and LGN are larger than those of P-cells, consistent with the large dendritic tree of the small-bistratified retinal ganglion cell[54,61,77,78]. Their receptive fields are also distinctive in other ways: they are often sensitive to the direction of motion of an achromatic drifting grating[79,80], a property that is not usually thought to be present in the retino-geniculate pathway to the visual cortex.

Recent work, using injections of a retrograde dye into the LGN and microelectrode recording from the subsequently labelled ganglion cells[22,71,81], has identified three further morphologically distinct types of ganglion cell that carry signals from S-cones. One type receives excitatory input from S-cones and two receive inhibitory input from S-cones—one of these is the intrinsically photosensitive (melanopsin-expressing) ganglion cell described earlier. The source of OFF S-cone signals in ganglion cells remains unclear—a recent description of an OFF S-cone bipolar cell has proved controversial[82,83].

Some recent observations have helped to identify the possible roles of some of the different types of ganglion cell that carry S-cone signals. We have re-examined the cone inputs to the receptive fields of macaque LGN neurons[79,84]. As expected, most receptive fields in the P-layers are L-M opponent with little or no input from S-cones; some magnocellular cells might respond to S-cone modulation, but they are always much more sensitive to modulation of the L-or M-cones[58,85–87]. In addition to these cells, we found many neurons that responded strongly to modulation of the S-cones in and around the koniocellular zones separating the P-layers. S-cone input to these neurons was as likely to be 'OFF' as it was 'ON' (FIG. 2). The colour preferences of S-ON cells were reasonably homogenous, with excitatory S-cone input usually opposed to the summed activity of L-and M-cones; thus, they gave little response to isoluminant red-green (L–M) modulation[39,41,88] (BOX 2). The colour preference of S-OFF cells was more heterogeneous[89], but usually intermediate between that of S-ON cells and red-green opponent P-cells. This arises because in many S-OFF cells the input from M-cones has the same sign as that of the S-cones, and both are opposed to the input from L-cones (FIG. 2). S-OFF cells in the LGN also differ reliably from S-ON cells in preferring higher rates of drift and having lower contrast sensitivity.

All this indicates that functionally distinct pathways signal increments and decrements in S-cone activity, consistent with the morphological differences in the retinal ganglion cells from which they originate.

EARLY SIGNAL TRANSFORMATIONS IN THE CORTEX

Signals that are important for colour vision are provided by several groups of LGN neurons, the axons of which project to different layers of V1 (REF. 74). However, the receptive field properties of neurons in V1 are rarely like those of the LGN: few cortical neurons respond to spatially uniform stimulation and most are selective for the orientation of edges; most respond well to achromatic modulation and less well or not at all to chromatic modulation (a powerful stimulus to most LGN cells). There remains substantial disagreement about the role of these neurons in colour vision. About 5–10% of neurons in V1 respond robustly to purely chromatic modulation and little, if at all, to achromatic modulation: these are most obviously important for colour vision. Among them, colour preferences are widely distributed, with only a slight bias towards those that predominate in LGN, but how these preferences are formed is a matter of debate.

Colour preferences of receptive fields. One of the most remarkable properties of V1 is that, despite being at least four (and often more) synapses away from the photoreceptors, the receptive fields of many neurons can be well characterized by supposing a linear combination of cone signals[88,90–94]. Other neurons have more complex receptive field properties, but even in these the linear models can be very informative[84,90,95,96]. This has allowed us to interpret the chromatic responses of cortical receptive fields in terms of the cone signals that provide their input.

The L-and M-cone inputs to cortical receptive fields have been extensively studied. In many neurons these inputs are of the same sign, so the receptive field is generally insensitive to chromatic modulation. This organization resembles that found in LGN magno-cellular cells[97], although it does not imply that those cells provide the input: the receptive fields of cortical cells are much larger than those in the LGN, so they must get input from many LGN cells[98]. As would be the case for a retinal receptive field drawing indiscriminately from many photoreceptors, a cortical receptive field that draws indiscriminately from many P-cells will also tend to be non-opponent[99]. Other V1 receptive fields show weakly opponent interactions between L-and M-cone signals, and respond well to both chromatic and achromatic modulation[84,90,96,100–102]. We cannot rule out the possibility that cone-opponency in many of these cells has arisen by chance (as has been argued for the receptive fields of P-cells), but some of their other properties are important and we discuss them in more detail below. Finally, roughly 10% of neurons show well-balanced, strongly opponent L-and M-cone inputs.

In most cortical receptive fields the S-cones provide much less input than the L-and M-cones[88,90,96]. Nevertheless, a substantial fraction of V1 neurons, larger than that in the LGN, receive at least some input from S-cones[84,88,96]. The prevalence of weak S-cone signals in V1 neurons indicates that these signals spread rapidly after entering the cortex, but it is not clear what function this might have[93,103,104]. As in the LGN, receptive fields with a strong S-cone input are encountered rarely, even among the subset of cells that respond best to isoluminant modulation, and are presumed to be important for colour vision[84,96]. Among these the arrangement of cone inputs to the receptive field varies and includes every possible type, but the most common chromatic signature is that found in the S-OFF cells of the LGN (with L-cone signals opposed to those of S-and M-cones[84,91]).

The variety of colour preferences shown by neurons in all layers of V1 indicates that signals from the LGN are recombined early in the cortex. Some direct evidence for this comes from recent work that has exploited **contrast adaptation** to reveal 'fundamental' chromatic mechanisms. Contrast adaptation has proved to be a powerful tool in the study of human colour vision[105,106], and we know that the contrast sensitivity of most cortical neurons is reduced by prolonged modulation of their preferred stimulus[107]. Those that respond well to isoluminant modulation are also desensitized by contrast adaptation[108], despite the fact that the P-cells which drive them are not[109]. Adaptation also deforms the chromatic tuning of these neurons, in complex ways: it usually reduces sensitivity, especially to the adapted colour direction, but responses to other colour directions can increase during adaptation; adaptation to either the L-M or S direction generally leaves responses to

the other unaffected. This rich range of behaviours can be readily explained by supposing that cortical neurons and the inhibitory mechanisms that regulate their sensitivity are both[84] driven by a sum of inputs from two fatigable mechanisms in the input layers: one driven by opposed inputs from L-and M-cones, the other driven by inputs from S-cones[108]. The chromatic signature of the S-mechanism is like that of LGN cells that receive strong S-cone input, but the chromatic signature of the L-M mechanism is unlike that of P-cells—it is not sensitive to achromatic modulation.

Spatial properties of receptive fields. Perceptual studies have revealed much about the properties of mechanisms that might allow us to distinguish the spatial forms of patterns defined solely by variations in hue[110–114]. To encode both the spatial and chromatic contrast in a local spatial region, a neuron requires a receptive field in which the spatially antagonistic regions are chromatically opponent. The 'double-opponent' receptive field exemplifies one form of this (BOX 3). The arrangement of this field's subregions causes a neuron to respond well to a small chromatic stimulus, or one containing spatial colour contrast, but much less well to a larger uniform one and not at all to an achromatic stimulus of any spatial structure. Neurons with this kind of receptive field have been found in the goldfish retina[115] but not in the primate retina; they have been sought in the monkey visual cortex[116–121], but clear-cut examples have rarely been found[94]. Some reports of V1 neurons thought to possess this kind of receptive field[91,92,116,122] have been challenged on methodological grounds[123,124]. The relatively few V1 neurons that clearly prefer a chromatic stimulus to an achromatic one are usually insensitive to the precise spatial form (orientation, width) of that stimulus, so the receptive fields are spatially homogeneous[90,100,101] (BOX 4).

If V1 neurons that are strongly chromatically opponent show little evidence of spatial opponency, how is the spatial structure of chromatic patterns to be discerned? One possibility for which there is a little evidence is that neurons with double-opponent receptive fields emerge in V2 or beyond[101,118,120,121,125–129]. Another possibility is that the capacity to encode the spatial structure of chromatic patterns depends on V1 neurons that respond to both colour contrast and brightness contrast. The receptive fields of these neurons are often selective for the width

Box 3 Two types of receptive field that might be important for colour vision

Each panel shows a schematic of the one-dimensional spatial profile of sensitivity, with L-and M-cone inputs of opposite sign; the preferred colour stimulus is shown below. The left panel shows a receptive field in which the opposed inputs from different cone types are largely overlapping in space, so the neuron gives strong responses to uniform coloured fields (but not to white ones). Such receptive fields are sometimes called single-opponent, because there is cone-opponency but not spatial opponency. The right panel shows a double-opponent receptive field, which can be conceived as two single-opponent receptive fields, of opposite sign, placed side-by-side. The resultant receptive field has balanced, spatially displaced, excitatory and inhibitory inputs from each cone type. It therefore does not respond to uniform fields of any colour, or to white light. It does respond well to purely chromatic edges.

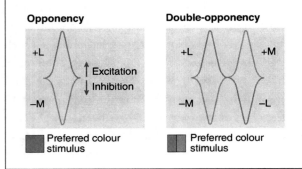

and orientation of edges, defined either by colour or by brightness[90,96,100–102,130,131].

Most neurons in the visual cortex have receptive fields in both eyes, but early physiological studies indicated that those carrying chromatic signals were distinctively monocular[116,122,132]. Indirect support for this came from findings that colour-preferring cells were localized in the 'blobs' of dense cytochrome oxidase reactivity that characterize the upper layers of V1 (REFS 116,124), and lie in the centres of ocular dominance columns[133,134]. Later work found little relationship between blobs and the colour-preference of receptive fields[90,131], and recent optical imaging confirms that the relationship is weaker than first reported[135,136]. But why should we expect the machinery of colour vision to be monocular? Although **stereopsis** is poor when stimuli are isoluminant[137–139], there

have been frequent findings of binocular interactions in human colour vision even for the most basic of tasks[140,141]. Consistent with this, colour-preferring neurons in V1 are at least as likely to be binocular as any other type of neuron[136,142].

Moreover, as is the case for other early cortical neurons[143], the colour-preferring neurons combine fairly linearly the inputs from the two eyes (FIG. 3). The receptive fields of colour-preferring neurons seem well equipped to support binocular single vision and the perception of surface colour, but because they generally lack spatial structure they are not well suited to coding fine stereoscopic detail.

Specialized cortical pathways for colour vision?
Distinct populations of neurons carry the signals for colour vision to V1; within V1 there are functionally distinct classes of chromatically selective neurons. The signals about colour that leave V1 provide the capacity to isolate changes in colour from changes in brightness, to specify hue, and to combine information from the two eyes; these representations are substantially invariant to changes in spatial structure and contrast. Assuming these signals reach perception (which might not always be the case[144–146]), what further analysis of colour remains to be done? We usually think of the cortical areas that ascend from V1 to the inferotemporal cortex as supporting 'mid-level' visual tasks, such as constructing contour and texture representations and segregating surfaces in depth, or as generating object-centred representations. For colour vision this presumably means the 'colouring-in' of surfaces, and the identification of regions that belong together.

In areas beyond V1, the functional properties of neurons depend increasingly on extraretinal signals, so it is harder to study them in anaesthetized animals; we know correspondingly less about the chromatic properties of receptive fields and about the distinctiveness of chromatic pathways. Nevertheless, we have some information about how colour signals are propagated and transformed.

In area V2 there are colour-preferring neurons, the colour sensitivity of which depends on the surrounding context[101]. This attribute has often been considered a distinctive property of neurons in the macaque V4 (REFS 118,120,121,129), a visual area that is the gateway to the temporal lobe and is broadly important for the representation of object structure[147,148]. V4 and its presumed homologue in humans have attracted attention as regions that might have a special significance for colour vision. Some humans with lesions to the ventromedial occipital cortex have impaired colour vision, although this is often accompanied by other deficits[149–152]. Functional imaging of this region provides more equivocal evidence on a special role in colour vision[153–155]: chromatic stimuli induce activity, but so do various kinds of achromatic visual stimuli. This is perhaps not unexpected, as colour experience embraces both the hue and the brightness of surfaces, but it points to the difficulty of establishing the function of a cortical area on the basis of its responses to a limited number of rather simple and constrained stimuli.

Bearing in mind these cautions, the most promising functional imaging studies might be those that seek to define the visual areas involved in colour vision by determining how their chromatic sensitivities change with parametric variation of, for example, temporal frequency of the visual stimulus or adaptation state[156–158].

These manipulations have well-characterized effects on human vision, and understanding how they influence signals in different cortical regions could help us to identify likely and unlikely chromatic pathways.

FUTURE DIRECTIONS

This brief review of recent work demonstrates that we have made major advances. Nevertheless, there remain substantial gaps in our knowledge of all stages of colour vision. In the retina we still know little about the pathways from cones to ganglion cells, or why human colour vision seems to be hardly affected by variation in the proportions of cones of different types. Introducing genes for novel pigments into animals with reduced colour vision[159,160] could help us to understand how these early networks are constructed and how

---

Stereopsis

The capacity to determine the distance to a surface through the comparison of the disparate images formed in the two eyes.

---

plastic they can be. In primates, retinal ganglion cells of types that are not yet well characterized might also be important in colour vision: without knowledge of these, it is difficult to constrain models of receptive field properties at later stages. In the cortex, the problems are different, and stem principally from our not having a clear idea of the properties to be expected of neurons that are responsible for colour perception. We have suggested[84] that one requirement of neurons involved in the analysis of colour is that their chromatic properties be stable in the face of changes in other properties of a stimulus (such as orientation, size and contrast). Relatively few neurons in V1 meet this requirement, and those that do are ill-equipped to represent the spatial attributes of surfaces. Given the great differences between the attributes of neurons that are most obviously relevant to colour vision and those most obviously relevant to spatial vision, perhaps the most interesting challenge will be to understand how the chromatic properties of objects are perceptually bound to their spatial properties. Functional imaging might be helpful here, but to understand the roles of individual neurons will probably require the recording or stimulation of candidate neurons, or groups of neurons, during tasks that rely on the analysis of colour[161,162].

NOTES

1. Young, T. On theory of light and colours. *Phil. Trans. R. Soc.* **92**, 12–48 (1802).

2. Hering, E. *Outlines of a Theory of the Light Sense* (Harvard Univ. Press, Cambridge, Massachusetts, 1874/1964).

3. Krauskopf, J. & Gegenfurtner, K. R. Color discrimination and adaptation. *Vision Res.* **32**, 2165–2175 (1992).

4. Rushton, W. A. H. Pigments and signals in colour vision. *J. Physiol.* **220**, 1–31 (1972).

5. Jacobs, G. H., Deegan, J. F., Neitz, J., Crognale, M. A. & Neitz, M. Photopigments and color vision in the nocturnal monkey, *Aotus. Vision Res.* **33**, 1773–1783 (1993).

6. Wald, G. The receptors of human color vision. *Science* **145**, 1007–1016 (1964).

7. Neitz, M., Neitz, J. & Jacobs, G. H. Spectral tuning of pigments underlying red-green color vision. *Science* **252**, 971–973 (1991).

Box 4 Spatial and chromatic structure of receptive fields in V1

The left panels show schematics of the most common types of spatial frequency tuning curves obtained from neurons in the macaque primary visual cortex (V1)[90,96,100–102]. Tuning curves for achromatic gratings are shown by the black lines, and for isoluminant L-M gratings by the red lines. The right panels show the spatial and chromatic structure of the receptive fields that might give rise to these tuning curves. In each case the L-cones (red) provide the principal excitatory input. The top panels show a type I cell[116], where L-cones provide input to an excitatory mechanism; an inhibitory mechanism, which accumulates signals over a different spatial region, draws mainly from M-cones. For achromatic gratings the signals of L-and M-cones are opposed to each other (reflecting the signs of their inputs), but for isoluminant gratings their signals sum (because as L-cone activity increases, M-cone activity decreases). Thus, the spatial frequency tuning curves are band-pass for achromatic gratings but not for isoluminant gratings. The middle panels show a type II receptive field. Here, the mechanisms that accumulate M-cone signals and L-cone signals are the same size, so there is no spatial tuning for either achromatic or isoluminant gratings. Because the M-cone input is slightly weaker than the L-cone input, the cell responds weakly to achromatic modulation. The bottom panels show bandpass spatial frequency tuning curves for both isoluminant and achromatic gratings. This might arise if the receptive field had two subregions, each of which

resembled the receptive field of a type II cell[123], but with cone-inputs that were not well balanced. The spatial structure would attenuate responses to low spatial frequencies for both achromatic and isoluminant gratings. Band-pass spatial tuning could also arise if in some type I cells (top panels) there was an extra component (depicted by the yellow shading) to the receptive field: a suppressive region sensitive to all colours[101,124], and more sensitive to low spatial frequencies than to high frequencies[165].

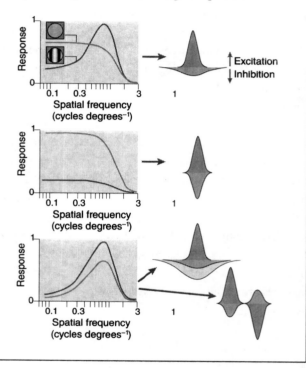

8. Nathans, J. The evolution and physiology of human color vision: insights from molecular genetic studies of visual pigments. *Neuron* **24**, 299–312 (1999).

9. Jacobs, G. H. & Rowe, M. P. Evolution of vertebrate colour vision. *Clin. Exp. Optom.* **87**, 206–216 (2004).

10. Hayashi, T., Motulsky, A. G. & Deeb, S. S. Position of a 'green-red' hybrid gene in the visual pigment array determines colour-vision phenotype. *Nature Genet.* **22**, 90–93 (1999).

11. Nathans, J., Thomas, D. & Hogness, D. S. Molecular genetics of human color vision: the genes encoding blue, green, and red pigments. *Science* **232**, 193–202 (1986).

   A genetic analysis of human photopigments that underpins our knowledge of the evolution of colour vision.

12. Neitz, J., Neitz, M., He, J. C. & Shevell, S. K. Trichromatic color vision with only two spectrally distinct photopigments. *Nature Neurosci.* **2**, 884–888 (1999).

13. Carroll, J., Neitz, M., Hofer, H., Neitz, J. & Williams, D. R. Functional photoreceptor loss revealed with

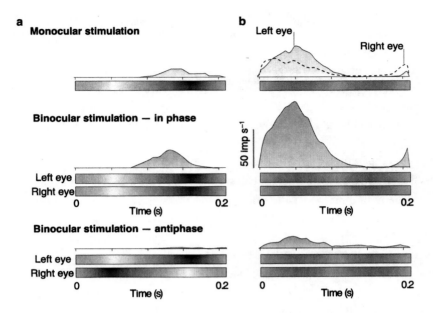

Figure 3 Binocular responses of a colour-preferring neuron in the visual cortex of a macaque. a | *Responses to achromatic drifting gratings presented to each eye alone (top panel), to both eyes, in the same phase (middle panel) and to both eyes, but in antiphase (lower panel). When the gratings in the two eyes have the same phase, both receptive fields are stimulated together and the response is greater than for stimulation of either eye alone. In antiphase, the left eye sees white at the same time as the right eye sees black, and vice versa. The signals from the two eyes' receptive fields therefore interfere, and there is little response from the neuron.* **b** | *Same, for isoluminant L-M gratings. In this case, antiphase stimulation means that the left eye receptive field sees red while the right sees green, and vice versa. The responses shown here and in FIG. 2 were obtained from extracellular recordings in anaesthetized macaques.*

adaptive optics: an alternate cause of color blindness. *Proc. Natl Acad. Sci. USA* **101**, 8461–8466 (2004).

14. Kremers, J., Usui, T., Scholl, H. P. & Sharpe, L. T. Cone signal contributions to electroretinograms (correction of electrograms) in dichromats and trichromats. *Invest. Ophthalmol. Vis. Sci.* **40**, 920–930 (1999).

15. Jagla, W. M., Jagle, H., Hayashi, T., Sharpe, L. T. & Deeb, S. S. The molecular basis of dichromatic color vision in males with multiple red and green visual pigment genes. *Hum. Mol. Genet.* **11**, 23–32 (2002).

16. Neitz, M. *et al.* Variety of genotypes in males diagnosed as dichromatic on a conventional clinical anomaloscope. *Vis. Neurosci.* **21**, 205–216 (2004).

17. Carroll, J., Neitz, J. & Neitz, M. Estimates of L:M cone ratio from ERG flicker photometry and genetics. *J. Vis.* **2**, 531–542 (2002).

18. Hofer, H., Carroll, J., Neitz, J., Neitz, M. & Williams, D. R. Organization of the human trichromatic cone mosaic. *J. Neurosci.* **25**, 9669–9679 (2005).

19. Neitz, J., Carroll, J., Yamauchi, Y., Neitz, M. & Williams, D. R. Color perception is mediated by a plastic neural mechanism that is adjustable in adults. *Neuron* **35**, 783–792 (2002).
An elegant experiment showing the dependence of colour sensation on experience, and its independence from the proportions of different classes of receptors in the cone mosaic.

20. Berson, D. M. Strange vision: ganglion cells as circadian photoreceptors. *Trends Neurosci.* **26**, 314–320 (2003).

21. Gooley, J. J., Lu, J., Fischer, D. & Saper, C. B. A broad role for melanopsin in nonvisual photoreception. *J. Neurosci.* **23**, 7093–7106 (2003).

22. Dacey, D. M. *et al.* Melanopsin–expressing ganglion cells in primate retina signal colour and irradiance and project to the LGN. *Nature* **433**, 749–754 (2005).

23. Curcio, C. A. *et al.* Distribution and morphology of human cone photoreceptors stained with anti-blue opsin. *J. Comp. Neurol.* **312**, 610–624 (1991).

24. de Monasterio, F. M., Schein, S. J. & McCrane, E. P. Staining of blue-sensitive cones of the macaque retina by a fluorescent dye. *Science* **213**, 1278–1281 (1981).

25. Martin, P. R. & Grunert, U. Analysis of the short wavelength-sensitive ('blue') cone mosaic in the primate retina: comparison of New World and Old World monkeys. *J. Comp. Neurol.* **406**, 1–14 (1999).

26. Mollon, J. D. & Bowmaker, J. K. The spatial arrangement of cones in the primate fovea. *Nature* **360**, 677–679 (1992).

27. Packer, O. S., Williams, D. R. & Bensinger, D. G. Photopigment transmittance imaging of the primate photoreceptor mosaic. *J. Neurosci.* **16**, 2251–2260 (1996).

28. Roorda, A. & Williams, D. R. The arrangement of the three cone classes in the living human eye. *Nature* **397**, 520–522 (1999).

An important technical innovation—adaptive optics—allows for ultra-high resolution in vivo imaging of the photoreceptor mosaic.

29. Roorda, A., Metha, A. B., Lennie, P. & Williams, D. R. Packing arrangement of the three cone classes in primate retina. *Vision Res.* **41**, 1291–1306 (2001).

30. Bowmaker, J. K., Parry, J. W. L. & Mollon, J. D. in *Normal and Defective Colour Vision* (eds Mollon, J. D., Pokorny, J. & Knoblauch, K.) 39–50 (Oxford Univ. Press, New York, 2003).

31. Deeb, S. S., Diller, L. C., Williams, D. R. & Dacey, D. M. Interindividual and topographical variation of L:M cone ratios in monkey retinas. *J. Opt. Soc. Am. A* **17**, 538–544 (2000).

32. Hagstrom, S. A., Neitz, J. & Neitz, M. Variations in cone populations for red-green color vision examined by analysis of mRNA. *Neuroreport* **9**, 1963–1967 (1998).

33. Neitz, M., Balding, S. D., McMahon, C., Sjoberg, S. A. & Neitz, J. Topography of long-and middle-wave-length sensitive cone opsin gene expression in human and Old World monkey retina. *Vis. Neurosci* **23**, 379–385 (2006).

34. Hofer, H., Singer, B. & Williams, D. R. Different sensations from cones with the same photopigment. *J. Vis.* **5**, 444–454 (2005).

35. Krauskopf, J. Color appearance of small stimuli and the spatial distribution of color receptors. *J. Opt. Soc. Am.* **54**, 1171–1178 (1964).

36. Hurvich, L. M. & Jameson, D. An opponent-process theory of color vision. *Psychol. Rev.* **64**, 384–404 (1957).

37. De Valois, R. L., Abramov, I. & Jacobs, G. H. Analysis of response patterns of LGN cells. *J. Opt. Soc. Am.* **56**, 966–977 (1966).

The first physiological study of colour opponency in neurons of the macaque LGN highlights mechanisms of the kind postulated by Hering.

38. Hubel, D. H. & Wiesel, T. N. Effects of varying stimulus size and color on single lateral geniculate cells in Rhesus monkeys. Proc. *Natl Acad. Sci. USA* **55**, 1345–1346 (1966).

39. Derrington, A. M., Krauskopf, J. & Lennie, P. Chromatic mechanisms in lateral geniculate nucleus of macaque. *J. Physiol.* **357**, 241–265 (1984).

A quantitative analysis of responses of LGN neurons to chromatic modulation shows two distinct chromatically opponent groups.

40. Lankheet, M. J., Lennie, P. & Krauskopf, J. Distinctive characteristics of subclasses of red-green P-cells in LGN of macaque. *Vis. Neurosci.* **15**, 37–46 (1998).

41. Smith, V. C., Lee, B. B., Pokorny, J., Martin, P. R. & Valberg, A. Responses of macaque ganglion cells to the relative phase of heterochromatically modulated lights. *J. Physiol.* **458**, 191–221 (1992).

42. Rodieck, R. W. in *Comparative Primate Biology Volume 4: Neurosciences* (eds Steklis, H. D. & Erwin, J.) 203–278 (Alan R. Liss, New York, 1988).

43. Calkins, D. J. & Sterling, P. Evidence that circuits for spatial and color vision segregate at the first retinal synapse. *Neuron* **24**, 313–321 (1999).

44. Lennie, P. Parallel visual pathways: a review. *Vision Res.* **20**, 561–594 (1980).

45. Paulus, W. & Kroger-Paulus, A. A new concept of retinal colour coding. *Vision Res.* **23**, 529–540 (1983).

46. Shapley, R. M. & Perry, V. H. Cat and monkey retinal ganglion cells and their visual functional roles. *Trends Neurosci.* **9**, 229–235 (1986).

47. Ingling, C. R. Jr & Martinez-Uriegas, E. The relationship between spectral sensitivity and spatial sensitivity for the primate r-g X-channel. *Vision Res.* **23**, 1495–1500 (1983).

48. Dreher, B., Fukada, Y. & Rodieck, R. W. Identification, classification and anatomical segregation of cells with X-like and Y-like properties in the lateral geniculate nucleus of Old World primates. *J. Physiol.* **258**, 433–452 (1976).

49. Mullen, K. T. & Kingdom, F. A. A. Losses in peripheral colour sensitivity predicted from 'hit and miss' post-receptoral cone connections. *Vision Res.* **36**, 1995–2000 (1996).

50. Mullen, K. T. & Kingdom, F. A. Differential distributions of red-green and blue-yellow cone opponency across the visual field. *Vis. Neurosci.* **19**, 109–118 (2002).

51. Calkins, D. J. & Sterling, P. Absence of spectrally specific lateral inputs to midget ganglion cells in primate retina. *Nature* **381**, 613–615 (1996).

52. Dacey, D. M., Lee, B. B., Stafford, D. K., Pokorny, J. & Smith, V. C. Horizontal cells of the primate retina: cone specificity without spectral opponency. *Science* **271**, 656–659 (1996).

53. Jusuf, P. R., Martin, P. R. & Grunert, U. Synaptic connectivity in the midget-parvocellular pathway of primate central retina. *J. Comp. Neurol.* **494**, 260–274 (2006).

54. Dacey, D. M. Parallel pathways for spectral coding in primate retina. *Ann. Rev. Neurosci.* **23**, 743–775 (2000).

55. Dacey, D. M. et al. Center-surround receptive field structure of cone bipolar cells in primate retina. *Vision Res.* **40**, 1801–1811 (2000).

56. McMahon, M. J., Lankheet, M. J., Lennie, P. & Williams, D. R. Fine structure of parvocellular receptive fields in the primate fovea revealed by laser interferometry. *J. Neurosci.* **20**, 2043–2053 (2000).

57. Polyak, S. L. *The Retina* (Univ. Chicago Press, Chicago, 1941).

58. Reid, R. C. & Shapley, R. M. Space and time maps of cone photoreceptor signals in macaque lateral geniculate nucleus. *J. Neurosci.* **22**, 6158–6175 (2002).

59. Lankheet, M. J., Lennie, P. & Krauskopf, J. Temporal-chromatic interactions in LGN P-cells. *Vis. Neurosci.* **15**, 47–54 (1998).

60. Lee, B. B. & Yeh, T. Receptive fields of primate retinal ganglion cells studied with a novel technique. *Vis. Neurosci.* **15**, 161–175 (1998).

61. Solomon, S. G., Lee, B. B., White, A. J., Ruttiger, L. & Martin, P. R. Chromatic organization of ganglion cell receptive fields in the peripheral retina. *J. Neurosci.* **25**, 4527–4539 (2005).

62. Buzas, P., Blessing, E. M., Szmajda, B. A. & Martin, P. R. Specificity of M and L cone inputs to receptive fields in the parvocellular pathway: random wiring with functional bias. *J. Neurosci.* **26**, 111 48–111 61 (2006).

63. Diller, L. et al. L and M cone contributions to the midget and parasol ganglion cell receptive fields of macaque monkey retina. *J. Neurosci.* **24**, 1079–1088 (2004).

64. Martin, P. R., Lee, B. B., White, A. J., Solomon, S. G. & Ruttiger, L. Chromatic sensitivity of ganglion cells in the peripheral primate retina. *Nature* **410**, 933–936 (2001).

65. Kouyama, N. & Marshak, D. W. Bipolar cells specific for blue cones in the macaque retina. *J. Neurosci.* **12**, 1233–1252 (1992).

66. Mariani, A. P. Bipolar cells in monkey retina selective for the cones likely to be blue-sensitive. *Nature* **308**, 184–186 (1984).

67. Ghosh, K. K., Martin, P. R. & Grunert, U. Morphological analysis of the blue cone pathway in the retina of a New World monkey, the marmoset Callithrix jacchus. *J. Comp. Neurol.* 379, 211–225 (1997).

68. Haverkamp, S. et al. The primordial, blue-cone color system of the mouse retina. *J. Neurosci.* **25**, 5438–5445 (2005).

69. Mollon, J. D. "Tho' she kneel'd in that place where they grew …" The uses and origins of primate color vision. *J. Exp. Biol* **146**, 21–38 (1989).

70. Dacey, D. M. & Lee, B. B. The 'blue-on' opponent pathway in primate retina originates from a distinct bistratified ganglion cell type. *Nature* **367**, 731–735 (1994).

The first intracellular recordings from macaque retinal ganglion cells showed that different morphological types have different chromatic properties.

71. Dacey, D. M., Peterson, B. B., Robinson, F. R. & Gamlin, P. D. Fireworks in the primate retina: in vitro

photodynamics reveals diverse LGN-projecting ganglion cell types. *Neuron* **37**, 15–27 (2003).

72. Hendry, S. H. C. & Reid, R. C. The koniocellular pathway in primate vision. *Ann. Rev. Neurosci.* **23**, 127–153 (2000).

73. Martin, P. R., White, A. J. R., Goodchild, A. K., Wilder, H. D. & Sefton, A. E. Evidence that blue-on cells are part of the third geniculocortical pathway in primates. *Eur. J. Neurosci.* **9**, 1536–1541 (1997).

74. Chatterjee, S. & Callaway, E. M. Parallel colour-opponent pathways to primary visual cortex. *Nature* **426**, 668–671 (2003).

Afferents from the LGN are recorded in V1, revealing a strict segregation of chromatic properties in the inputs to each layer.

75. Solomon, S. G. Striate cortex in dichromatic and trichromatic marmosets: neurochemical compartmentalization and geniculate input. *J. Comp. Neurol.* **450**, 366–381 (2002).

76. Hendry, S. H. C. & Yoshioka, T. A neurochemically distinct third channel in the macaque dorsal lateral geniculate nucleus. *Science* **264**, 575577 (1994).

77. Derrington, A. M. & Lennie, P. Spatial and temporal contrast sensitivities of neurones in lateral geniculate nucleus of macaque. *J. Physiol.* **357**, 219–240 (1984).

78. Chichilnisky, E. J. & Baylor, D. A. Receptive-field microstructure of blue-yellow ganglion cells in primate retina. *Nature Neurosci.* **2**, 889–893 (1999).

79. Tailby, C., Solomon, S. G. & Lennie, P. Multiple S-cone pathways in the macaque visual system. *COSYNE*, 20 (2006).

80. Forte, J. D., Hashemi-Nezhad, M., Dobbie, W. J., Dreher, B. & Martin, P. R. Spatial coding and response redundancy in parallel visual pathways of the marmoset *Callithrix jacchus. Vis. Neurosci.* **22**, 479–491 (2005).

81. Dacey, D. M. & Packer, O. S. Colour coding in the primate retina: diverse cell types and cone-specific circuitry. *Curr. Opin. Neurobiol.* **13**, 421–427 (2003).

82. Klug, K., Herr, S., Ngo, I. T., Sterling, P. & Schein, S. Macaque retina contains an S-cone OFF midget pathway. *J. Neurosci.* **23**, 9881–9887 (2003).

83. Lee, S. C., Telkes, I. & Grunert, U. S-cones do not contribute to the OFF-midget pathway in the retina of the marmoset, *Callithrix jacchus. Eur. J. Neurosci.* **22**, 437–447 (2005).

84. Solomon, S. G. & Lennie, P. Chromatic gain controls in visual cortical neurons. *J. Neurosci.* **25**, 4779–4792 (2005).

85. Chatterjee, S. & Callaway, E. M. S cone contributions to the magnocellular visual pathway in macaque monkey. *Neuron* **35**, 1135–1146 (2002).

86. Sun, H., Smithson, H. E., Zaidi, Q. & Lee, B. B. Specificity of cone inputs to macaque retinal ganglion cells. *J. Neurophysiol.* **95**, 837–849 (2006).

87. Sun, H., Smithson, H. E., Zaidi, Q. & Lee, B. B. Do magnocellular and parvocellular ganglion cells avoid short-wave-length cone input? *Vis. Neurosci.* **23**, 441–446 (2006).

88. De Valois, R. L., Cottaris, N. P., Elfar, S. D., Mahon, L. E. & Wilson, J. A. Some transformations of color information from lateral geniculate nucleus to striate cortex. Proc. *Natl Acad. Sci. USA* **97**, 4997–5002 (2000).

89. Valberg, A., Lee, B. B. & Tigwell, D. A. Neurones with strong inhibitory S-cone inputs in the macaque lateral geniculate nucleus. *Vision Res.* **26**, 1061–1064 (1986).

90. Lennie, P., Krauskopf, J. & Sclar, G. Chromatic mechanisms in striate cortex of macaque. *J. Neurosci.* **10**, 649–669 (1990).

A comparison of chromatic properties of V1 neurons with those in the LGN, showing how colour signals are transformed.

91. Conway, B. R. Spatial structure of cone inputs to color cells in alert macaque primary visual cortex (V-1). *J. Neurosci.* **21**, 2768–2783 (2001).

92. Conway, B. R., Hubel, D. H. & Livingstone, M. S. Color contrast in macaque V1. *Cereb. Cortex* **12**, 915–925 (2002).

93. Cottaris, N. P. & De Valois, R. L. Temporal dynamics of chromatic tuning in macaque primary visual cortex. *Nature* **395**, 896–900 (1998).

94. Conway, B. R. & Livingstone, M. S. Spatial and temporal properties of cone signals in alert macaque primary visual cortex. *J. Neurosci.* **26**, 10826–10846 (2006).

95. Horwitz, G. D., Chichilnisky, E. J. & Albright, T. D. Blue-yellow signals are enhanced by spatiotemporal luminance contrast in macaque V1. *J. Neurophysiol.* **93**, 2263–2278 (2005).

96. Johnson, E. N., Hawken, M. J. & Shapley, R. Cone inputs in macaque primary visual cortex. *J. Neurophysiol.* **91**, 2501–2514 (2004).

97. Vidyasagar, T. R., Kulikowski, J. J., Lipnicki, D. M. & Dreher, B. Convergence of parvocellular and magnocellular information channels in the primary visual cortex of the macaque. *Eur. J. Neurosci.* **16**, 945–956 (2002).

98. Angelucci, A. & Sainsbury, K. Contribution of feedforward thalamic afferents and corticogeniculate feedback to the spatial summation area of macaque V1 and LGN. *J. Comp. Neurol.* **498**, 330–351 (2006).

99. Lennie, P. & D'Zmura, M. Mechanisms of color vision. *Crit. Rev. Neurobiol.* **3**, 333–400 (1988).

100. Johnson, E. N., Hawken, M. J. & Shapley, R. The spatial transformation of color in the primary visual cortex of the macaque monkey. *Nature Neurosci.* **4**, 409–416 (2001).
    An analysis of the spatial and chromatic properties of different types of receptive fields in V1.

101. Solomon, S. G., Peirce, J. W. & Lennie, P. The impact of suppressive surrounds on chromatic properties of cortical neurons. *J. Neurosci.* **24**, 148–160 (2004).

102. Thorell, L. G., De Valois, R. L. & Albrecht, D. G. Spatial mapping of monkey V1 cells with pure color and luminance stimuli. *Vision Res.* **24**, 751–769 (1984).

103. De Valois, R. L. & De Valois, K. K. A multi-stage color model. *Vision Res.* **33**, 1053–1065 (1993).
    Reviews the discrepancies between known physiology and colour perception, and presents a plausible model to reconcile them.

104. De Valois, R. L., De Valois, K. K. & Mahon, L. E. Contribution of S opponent cells to color appearance. *Proc. Natl Acad. Sci. USA* **97**, 512–517 (2000).

105. Krauskopf, J., Williams, D. R. & Heeley, D. W. Cardinal directions of color space. *Vision Res.* **22**, 1123–1131 (1982).
    A seminal study that reveals through habituation three mechanisms that have a fundamental input to colour vision; the subsequent paper shows that these three mechanisms must be complemented by other, less fundamental ones.

106. Krauskopf, J., Williams, D. R., Mandler, M. B. & Brown, A. M. Higher order color mechanisms. *Vision Res.* **26**, 23–32 (1986).

107. Carandini, M., Movshon, J. A. & Ferster, D. Pattern adaptation and cross-orientation interactions in the primary visual cortex. *Neuropharmacology* **37**, 501–511 (1998).

108. Tailby, C., Solomon, S. G., Dhruv, N. T., Majaj, N. J. & Lennie, P. Habituation reveals cardinal chromatic mechanisms in striate cortex of macaque. *J. Vis.* **5**, 80a (2005).

109. Solomon, S. G., Peirce, J. W., Dhruv, N. T. & Lennie, P. Profound contrast adaptation early in the visual pathway. *Neuron* **42**, 155–162 (2004).

110. Cardinal, K. S. & Kiper, D. C. The detection of colored Glass patterns. *J. Vis.* **3**, 199–208 (2003).

111. Mandelli, M. J. & Kiper, D. C. The local and global processing of chromatic Glass patterns. *J. Vis* **5**, 405–416 (2005).

112. Bradley, A., Switkes, E. & De Valois, K. Orientation and spatial frequency selectivity of adaptation to color and luminance gratings. *Vision Res.* **28**, 841–856 (1988).

113. Clifford, C. W., Spehar, B., Solomon, S. G., Martin, P. R. & Zaidi, Q. Interactions between color and luminance in the perception of orientation. *J. Vis* **3**, 106–115 (2003).

114. Forte, J. D. & Clifford, C. W. Inter-ocular transfer of the tilt illusion shows that monocular orientation mechanisms are colour selective. *Vision Res.* **45**, 2715–2721 (2005).

115. Daw, N. W. Goldfish retina: organization for simultaneous color contrast. *Science* **158**, 942–944 (1967).

116. Livingstone, M. S. & Hubel, D. H. Anatomy and physiology of a color system in the primate visual cortex. *J. Neurosci.* **4**, 309–356 (1984).

117. Desimone, R., Schein, S. J., Moran, J. & Ungerleider, L. G. Contour, color and shape analysis beyond the striate cortex. *Vision Res.* **25**, 441–452 (1985).

118. Schein, S. J. & Desimone, R. Spectral properties of V4 neurons in the macaque. *J. Neurosci.* **10**, 3369–3389 (1990).

119. Wachtler, T., Sejnowski, T. J. & Albright, T. D. Representation of color stimuli in awake macaque primary visual cortex. *Neuron* **37**, 681–691 (2003).

120. Zeki, S. M. Colour coding in the cerebral cortex: the reaction of cells in monkey visual cortex to wavelengths and colours. *Neuroscience* **9**, 741–765 (1983).

121. Zeki, S. M. Colour coding in the cerebral cortex: the responses of wave-length-selective and colour-coded cells in monkey visual cortex to changes in wavelength composition. *Neuroscience* **9**, 767–781 (1983).

122. Livingstone, M. & Hubel, D. Segregation of form, color, movement, and depth: anatomy, physiology, and perception. *Science* **240**, 740–749 (1988).

123. Shapley, R. & Hawken, M. Neural mechanisms for color perception in the primary visual cortex. *Curr. Opin. Neurobiol.* **12**, 426–432 (2002).

124. Ts'o, D. Y. & Gilbert, C. D. The organization of chromatic and spatial interactions in the primate striate cortex. *J. Neurosci.* **8**, 1712–1727 (1988).

125. Gegenfurtner, K. R., Kiper, D. C. & Fenstemaker, S. B. Processing of color, form, and motion in macaque area V2. *Vis. Neurosci* **13**, 161–172 (1996).

126. Gegenfurtner, K. R., Kiper, D. C. & Levitt, J. B. Functional properties of neurons in macaque area V3. *J. Neurophysiol.* **77**, 1906–1923 (1997).

127. Kiper, D. C., Fenstemaker, S. B. & Gegenfurtner, K. R. Chromatic properties of neurons in macaque area V2. *Vis. Neurosci.* **14**, 1061–1072 (1997).

128. Moutoussis, K. & Zeki, S. Responses of spectrally selective cells in macaque area V2 to wave-lengths and colors. *J. Neurophysiol.* **87**, 2104–2112 (2002).

129. Kusunoki, M., Moutoussis, K. & Zeki, S. Effect of background colors on the tuning of color-selective cells in monkey area V4. *J. Neurophysiol.* **95**, 3047–3059 (2006).

130. Friedman, H. S., Zhou, H. & Von Der Heydt, R. The coding of uniform colour figures in monkey visual cortex. *J. Physiol.* **548**, 593–613 (2003).

131. Leventhal, A. G., Thompson, K. G., Liu, D., Zhou, Y. & Ault, S. J. Concomitant sensitivity to orientation, direction, and color of cells in layers 2, 3, and 4 of monkey striate cortex. *J. Neurosci.* **15**, 1808–1818 (1995).

132. Hubel, D. H. & Livingstone, M. S. Segregation of form, color, and stereopsis in primate area 18. *J. Neurosci.* **7**, 3378–3415 (1987).

133. Horton, J. C. & Hubel, D. H. Regular patchy distribution of cytochrome oxidase staining in primary visual cortex of macaque monkey. *Nature* **292**, 762–764 (1981).

134. Livingstone, M. & Hubel, D. H. Thalamic inputs to cytochrome oxidase-rich regions in monkey visual cortex. *Proc. Natl Acad. Sci. USA* **79**, 6098–6101 (1982).

135. Landisman, C. E. & Ts'o, D. Y. Color processing in macaque striate cortex: relationships to ocular dominance, cytochrome oxidase, and orientation. *J. Neurophysiol.* **87**, 3126–3137 (2002).

136. Landisman, C. E. & Ts'o, D. Y. Color processing in macaque striate cortex: electrophysiological properties. *J. Neurophysiol.* **87**, 3138–3151 (2002).

137. Kingdom, F. A. & Simmons, D. R. Stereoacuity and colour contrast. *Vision Res.* **36**, 1311–1319 (1996).

138. Krauskopf, J. & Forte, J. D. Influence of chromaticity on vernier and stereo acuity. *J. Vis.* **2**, 645–652 (2002).

139. Livingstone, M. S. & Hubel, D. H. Psychophysical evidence for separate channels for the perception of form, color, movement, and depth. *J. Neurosci.* **7**, 3416–3468 (1987).

Outlines the strong hypothesis of vision as a serial, parallel and hierarchical process.

140. Ikeda, M. & Nakashima, Y. Wave-length difference limit for binocular color fusion. *Vision Res.* **20**, 693–697 (1980).

141. Simmons, D. R. The binocular combination of chromatic contrast. *Perception* **34**, 1035–1042 (2005).

142. Peirce, J. W., Solomon, S. G., Forte, J., Krauskopf, J. & Lennie, P. Chromatic tuning of binocular neurons in early visual cortex. *J. Vis.* **3**, 24a (2003).

143. Cumming, B. G. & DeAngelis, G. C. The physiology of stereopsis. *Ann. Rev. Neurosci.* **24**, 203–238 (2001).

144. Gur, M. & Snodderly, D. M. A dissociation between brain activity and perception: chromatically opponent cortical neurons signal chromatic flicker that is not perceived. *Vision Res.* **37**, 377–382 (1997).

145. Shady, S. & MacLeod, D. I. Color from invisible patterns. *Nature Neurosci.* **5**, 729–730 (2002).

146. Shady, S., MacLeod, D. I. & Fisher, H. S. Adaptation from invisible flicker. *Proc. Natl Acad. Sci. USA* **101**, 5170–5173 (2004).

147. Gallant, J. L., Braun, J. & Van Essen, D. C. Selectivity for polar, hyperbolic, and Cartesian gratings in macaque visual cortex. *Science* **259**, 100–103 (1993).

148. Tootell, R. B., Nelissen, K., Vanduffel, W. & Orban, G. A. Search for color 'center(s)' in macaque visual cortex. *Cereb. Cortex* **14**, 353–363 (2004).

149. Bouvier, S. E. & Engel, S. A. Behavioral deficits and cortical damage loci in cerebral achromatopsia. *Cereb. Cortex* **16**, 183–191 (2006).

150. Damasio, A., Yamada, T., Damasio, H., Corbett, J. & McKee, J. Central achromatopsia: behavioral, anatomic, and physiologic aspects. *Neurology* **30**, 1064–1071 (1980).

151. Ruttiger, L. et al. Selective color constancy deficits after circumscribed unilateral brain lesions. *J. Neurosci.* **19**, 3094–3106 (1999).

152. Zeki, S. A century of cerebral achromatopsia. *Brain* **113**, 1721–1777 (1990).

153. Brewer, A. A., Liu, J., Wade, A. R. & Wandell, B. A. Visual field maps and stimulus selectivity in human ventral occipital cortex. *Nature Neurosci.* **8**, 1102–1109 (2005).

A convincing analysis of the functional specialization of early extrastriate cortical areas.

154. Hadjikhani, N., Liu, A. K., Dale, A. M., Cavanagh, P. & Tootell, R. B. Retinotopy and color sensitivity in human visual cortical area V8. *Nature Neurosci.* **1**, 235–241 (1998).

155. McKeefry, D. J. & Zeki, S. The position and topography of the human colour centre as revealed by functional magnetic resonance imaging. *Brain* **120**, 2229–2242 (1997).

156. Engel, S. A. & Furmanski, C. S. Selective adaptation to color contrast in human primary visual cortex. *J. Neurosci.* **21**, 3949–3954 (2001).

157. Engel, S. A. Adaptation of oriented and unoriented color-selective neurons in human visual areas. *Neuron* **45**, 613–623 (2005).

158. Liu, J. & Wandell, B. A. Specializations for chromatic and temporal signals in human visual cortex. *J. Neurosci.* **25**, 3459–3468 (2005).

159. Smallwood, P. M., Wang, Y. & Nathans, J. Role of a locus control region in the mutually exclusive expression of human red and green cone pigment genes. *Proc. Natl Acad. Sci. USA* **99**, 1008–1011 (2002).

160. Smallwood, P. M. et al. Genetically engineered mice with an additional class of cone photoreceptors: implications for the evolution of color vision. *Proc. Natl Acad. Sci. USA* **100**, 11706–11711 (2003).

161. Newsome, W. T., Britten, K. H. & Movshon, J. A. Neuronal correlates of a perceptual decision. *Nature* **341**, 52–54 (1989).

162. Salzman, C. D., Britten, K. H. & Newsome, W. T. Cortical microstimulation influences perceptual judgements of motion direction. *Nature* **346**, 174–177 (1990).

163. Sincich, L. C., Park, K. F., Wohlgemuth, M. J. & Horton, J. C. Bypassing V1: a direct geniculate input to area MT. *Nature Neurosci.* **7**, 1123–1128 (2004).

164. MacLeod, D. I. & Boynton, R. M. Chromaticity diagram showing cone excitation by stimuli of equal luminance. *J. Opt. Soc. Am.* **69**, 1183–1186 (1979).

Describes a simple colour space, which has become standard, where hue is defined in a plane formed by two axes—one of S-cone activation and another of differential L-and M-cone activation.

165. Webb, B. S., Dhruv, N. T., Solomon, S. G., Tailby, C. & Lennie, P. Early and late mechanisms of surround suppression in striate cortex of macaque. *J. Neurosci.* **25**, 11666–11675 (2005).

ACKNOWLEDGMENTS

We thank N. Dhruv, J. Forte, J. Krauskopf, J. Peirce and C. Tailby for help in experiments and analysis, and for many discussions, over several years, at the Center for Neural Science, New York University, USA. We are grateful to H. Hofer and D. Williams for providing the mosaics of Figure 1; N. Gilroy, E. Weston and A. White also commented on the figures. Supporting grants were made to S.G.S. from the National Institutes of Health, and the Australian National Health and Medical Research Council.

Competing interests statement
The authors declare no competing financial interests.

FURTHER INFORMATION
Soloman's laboratory:
http://www.physiol.usyd.edu.au/span/samuels/
Access to this links box is available online.

Gorillas in Our Midst

Sustained Inattentional Blindness for Dynamic Events

DANIEL J. SIMONS AND CHRISTOPHER F. CHABRIS

ABSTRACT

With each eye fixation, we experience a richly detailed visual world. Yet recent work on visual integration and change detection reveals that we are surprisingly unaware of the details of our environment from one view to the next: we often do not detect large changes to objects and scenes ('change blindness'). Furthermore, without attention, we may not even perceive objects ('inattentional blindness'). Taken together, these findings suggest that we perceive and remember only those objects and details that receive focused attention. In this paper, we briefly review and discuss evidence for these cognitive forms of 'blindness'. We then present a new study that builds on classic studies of divided visual attention to examine inattentional blindness for complex objects and events in dynamic scenes. Our results suggest that the likelihood of noticing an unexpected object depends on the similarity of that object to other objects in the display and on how difficult the priming monitoring task is. Interestingly, spatial proximity of the critical unattended object to attended locations does not appear to affect detection, suggesting that observers attend to objects and events, not spatial positions. We discuss the implications of these results for visual representations and awareness of our visual environment.

1 INTRODUCTION

"It is a well-known phenomenon that we do not notice anything happening in our surroundings while being absorbed in the inspection of something; focusing our attention on a certain object may happen to such an extent that we cannot perceive other objects placed in the peripheral parts of our visual field, although the light rays they emit arrive completely at the visual sphere of the cerebral cortex."

Rezso Balint 1907 (translated in Husain and Stein 1988, page 91)

Perhaps you have had the following experience: you are searching for an open seat in a crowded movie theater. After scanning for several minutes, you eventually spot one and sit down. The next day, your friends ask why you ignored them at the theater. They were waving at you, and you looked right at them but did not see them. Just as we sometimes overlook our friends in a crowded room, we occasionally fail to notice changes to the appearance of those around us. We have all had the embarrassing experience of failing to notice when a friend or colleague shaves off a beard, gets a haircut, or starts wearing contact lenses. We feel that we perceive and remember everything around us, and we take the occasional blindness to visual details to be an unusual exception. The richness of our visual experience leads us to believe that our visual representations will

Daniel J. Simmons and Christopher F. Chabris, "Gorillas in Our Midst: Sustained Inattentional Blindness for Dynamic Events," *Perception*, vol. 28, no. 9, pp. 1059-1074. Copyright © 1999 by Pion Ltd. Reprinted with permission.

include and preserve the same amount of detail (Levin et al 2000).

The disparity between the richness of our experience and the details of our representation, though 'well known' to Balint in 1907, has been studied only sporadically in the psychological literature since then, and many of the most striking results appear to have been neglected by contemporary researchers. Although the past 20 years have seen increasing interest in the issue of the precision of visual representations, a series of studies from the 1970s and 1980s using dynamic visual displays provides some of the most dramatic demonstrations of the importance of attention in perception (see Neisser 1979 for an overview). In these studies, observers engage in a continuous task that requires them to focus on one aspect of a dynamic scene while ignoring others.

At some point during the task an unexpected event occurs, but the majority of observers do not report seeing it even though it is clearly visible to observers not engaged in the concurrent task (Becklen and Cervone 1983; Littman and Becklen 1976; Neisser 1979; Neisser and Becklen 1975; Rooney et al 1981; Stoffregen et al 1993; Stoffregen and Becklen 1989). Although these studies have profound implications for our understanding of perception with and without attention, and despite their obvious connection to more recent work on visual attention (e.g. change blindness, attentional blink, repetition blindness, inattentional blindness), the empirical approach has fallen into disuse. One goal of our research is to revive the approach used in these original studies of 'selective looking' in the context of more recent work on visual attention.

Over the past few years, several researchers have demonstrated that conscious perception seems to require attention. When attention is diverted to another object or task, observers often fail to perceive an unexpected object, even if it appears at fixation—a phenomenon termed 'inattentional blindness' (e.g. Mack and Rock 1998).[1] These findings are reminiscent of another set of findings falling under the rubric of 'change blindness'. Observers often fail to notice large changes to objects or scenes from one view to the next, particularly if those objects are not the center of interest in the scene (Rensink et al 1997). For example, observers often do not notice when two people in a photograph exchange heads, provided that the change occurs during an eye movement (Grimes 1996; see Simons and Levin 1997 for a review).

Such studies suggest that attention is necessary for change detection (see also Scholl 2000), but not sufficient, as even changes to attended objects are often not noticed (Levin and Simons 1997; Simons and Levin 1997, 1998; Williams and Simons 2000). For example, observers who were giving directions to an experimenter often did not notice that the experimenter was replaced by a different person during an interruption caused by a door being carried between them (Simons and Levin 1998).

Both areas of research focus on two fundamental questions. (i) To what degree are the details of our visual world perceived and represented? (ii) What role does attention play in this process? We will review recent evidence for inattentional blindness to provide a current context for a discussion of earlier research on the perception of unexpected events. We then present a new study examining the variables that affect inattentional blindness in naturalistic, dynamic events, and consider the results within the broader framework or recent attention research, including change blindness.

1.1 Inattentional blindness

Studies of change blindness assume that, with attention, features can be encoded (abstractly or otherwise) and retained in memory. That is, all of the information in the visual environment is potentially available for attentive processing. Yet, without attention, not much of this information is retained across views. Studies of inattentional blindness have made an even stronger claim: that, without attention, visual features of our environment are not perceived at all (or at least not consciously perceived)—observers may fail not just at change detection, but at perception as well.

Recent work on the role of attention in perception has explored what happens to unattended parts of simple visual displays (Mack and Rock 1998; Mack et al 1992; Moore and Egeth 1997; Newby and Rock 1998; Rock et al 1992; Rubin and Hua 1998; Silverman and Mack 1997). In traditional models of visual search, features are often assumed to be processed preattentively if search speeds are unaffected by the number of distracter items in the display (ie the feature 'pops out' effortlessly). Preattentive processing of some features would allow for rapid perception of more complex objects that are built by combining such sensory primitives. However, visual search tasks may not truly assess the processing of unattended stimuli because observers have the expectation that a target may appear—observers know that they will have to search the display for a particular stimulus. Hence, they may expect to perceive these features, which would allow their visual/cognitive system to anticipate the features. The inattentional-blindness paradigm developed by Mack, Rock, and colleagues avoids this potential confound of knowledge of the task (e.g. Mack and Rock 1998), allowing a more direct assessment of the perception of unattended stimuli. In a typical version of their task, observers judge which of two arms of a briefly displayed large cross is longer. On the fourth trial of this task, an unexpected object appears at the same time as the cross. After this trial, observers are asked to report if they saw anything other than the cross. After answering this question, observers view another trial, now with the suggestion that something might appear. This allows an assessment of perception under conditions of divided attention. Last, subjects complete a final, full-attention trial in which they look for and report the critical object but ignore the cross. Performance on the critical, unattended trial is compared with that on the divided-attention and full-attention trials to estimate the degree to which attention influences perception. The difference in the proportion of subjects noticing on the full-attention and critical trials is the amount of inattentional blindness.

Several clear patterns emerge from this body of research (see Mack and Rock 1998 for an overview). (i) About 25% of subjects are inattentionally blind when the cross is presented at fixation and the unexpected object is presented parafoveally (subjects typically detect the critical stimulus on divided attention and full-attention trials). (ii) About 75% of subjects are inattentionally blind when the cross is presented parafoveally and the unexpected object is presented at fixation, suggesting an effortful shift of attention away from fixation to the cross and possible inhibition of processing at the ignored fixation location. (iii) These levels of detection are no different for features thought to be preattentively processed (e.g. color, orientation, motion) and those thought to require effort. (iv) Although objects composed of simple visual features are not easily detected, some meaningful stimuli are. Observers typically notice their own name or a smiley face even when they did not expect it. Note, however, they do not tend to notice their own name if one letter is changed (see also Rubin and Hua

1998). Observers do not consciously perceive the visual features, but they do perceive the meaning. (v) Observers seem to focus attention on particular locations on the screen. Objects that appear inside this zone of attention are more likely to be detected than those appearing outside (Mack and Rock 1998; Newby and Rock 1998), suggesting that attention is focused not on the object or event itself, but on the area around that object.

1.2 'Selective looking'

These recent studies of inattentional blindness used simple, brief visual displays under precisely controlled timing conditions, in the vein of work on visual search and related attention paradigms that were largely designed to examine how we select and process features and objects. The paradigm was designed to be a visual analogue of dichotic-listening studies conducted during the 1950s and 1960s (Cherry 1953; Moray 1959; Treisman 1964), and largely succeeded in replicating the classic auditory effects with visual stimuli. Although relatively little unattended information reaches awareness, some particularly meaningful stimuli do. Despite the similarity of these theoretical conclusions, they are fundamentally different in an important way. Almost by necessity, dichotic-listening tasks involve dynamic rather than static events. Listening studies reveal a degree of 'inattentional deafness' that extends over time and over changes in the unattended stimulus.

In that sense, the computer-based inattention paradigm is not a true analogue of dichotic-listening tasks. Although the theoretical conclusions match our experience of not seeing friends in a crowded theater (and hearing our own name spoken at a noisy party), the experimental paradigm may not fully capture all aspects of that natural situation (see Neumann et al (1986) for a discussion of the difficulties of equating auditory and visual divided-attention tasks). However, an earlier series of studies by Neisser and his colleagues did use dynamic events to address many of the same questions.

In an initial study (Neisser and Becklen 1975), observers viewed a display which presented two overlapping, simultaneous events. (The superimposition was achieved by showing both of the separately recorded events on an angled, half-silvered mirror.) One of the events was a hand-slapping game in which one player extended his hands with palms up and the other player placed his hands on his opponents hands with palms down. The player with palms up tries to slap the back of the other player's hands, and the other player tries to avoid the slap. The second event depicted three people moving in irregular patterns and passing a basketball. Subjects were asked to closely monitor one of the two events. If they monitored the hand game, they pressed a button with each attempted slap. If they monitored the ball game, they pressed the button for each pass. Each subject viewed a total of ten trials. The first two trials showed each of the games alone. On the 3rd and 4th trials, both events were presented simultaneously, but subjects were asked to follow only one of them. On the 5th and 6th trials, subjects attempted to respond to both events, using one hand to respond to each (only twenty actions per minute rather than forty occurred in these two and subsequent trials). On the last four trials, subjects responded to only one of the events, but an additional unexpected event occurred as well. In trial 7, the two hand-game players stopped and shook hands. On trial 8, one of the ball-game players threw the ball out of the game and the players continued to pretend to be passing the ball. The ball was returned after 20 s of fake throws. On trial 9, the hand-game players briefly stopped their game and passed a small ball back and forth. On trial 10, each of the ball-game players stepped off camera and was replaced by a woman and, after 20 s, the original men returned in the same fashion.

The results of this study are largely consistent with the findings of computer-based inattention studies. In the initial trials, subjects could easily follow one event while ignoring another event occupying the same spatial position. (This was true even when subjects were not allowed to move their eyes; see Littman and Becklen (1976).) Not surprisingly, they had much greater difficulty simultaneously monitoring both events. More importantly, in the initial trial with an unexpected event, only one of twenty-four people spontaneously reported the hand shake, and three others mentioned it in post-experiment questioning. None of the subjects spontaneously reported the disappearance of the ball, three spontaneously reported the ball pass in the hand game, and three reported the exchange of women for men on the final trial. Subjects who noticed one of the unusual events were more likely to notice subsequent unusual events, much as subjects in the

divided-attention conditions in inattentional blindness studies typically reported the presence of the previously 'unexpected' object (Mack and Rock 1998). In total, 50% of Neisser and Becklen's (1975) subjects showed no indication of having seen any of the unexpected events, and even subjects who did notice typically could not accurately report the details of them.

In a more recent version of this sort of divided-visual-attention task, observers viewed superimposed videotapes of two of the ball games described above (Becklen, Neisser, and Littman, discussed in Neisser 1979).[2] The players in one game wore black shirts and the players in the other game wore white shirts. This change made the attended and ignored events more similar, and therefore more difficult to discriminate. Nevertheless, observers could successfully follow one game while ignoring the other even when both teams wore the same clothing (in fact, the same three players appeared in each video stream).

In subsequent studies of selective looking, Neisser and his colleagues used this 'basketball-game' task (see Neisser (1979) for a description of several different versions). In the most famous demonstration, observers attend to one team of players, pressing a key whenever one of them makes a pass, while ignoring the actions of the other team. After about 30 s, a woman carrying an open umbrella walks across the screen (this video was also superimposed on the others so all three events were partially transparent). She is visible for approximately 4 s before walking off the far end of the screen. The games then continue for another 25 s before the tape is stopped. Of twenty-eight naive observers, only six reported the presence of the umbrella woman, even when questioned directly after the task (Neisser and Dube, cited in Neisser 1979). Interestingly, when subjects had practice performing the task on two similar trials before the trial with the unexpected umbrella woman, 48% noticed her. When subjects just watched the screen and did not perform any task, they always noticed the umbrella woman, a result consistent with the inattentional-blindness findings reviewed earlier (and with work on saccade-contingent changes; see Grimes 1996; McConkie and Zola 1979).

Interestingly, Neisser (1979) mentioned an additional study in which the umbrella woman wore the same-color shirt as either the attended or the unattended team. Apparently, this feature-similarity manipulation caused little difference in the rate of noticing. Also, when the unexpected character was a small boy rather than the umbrella woman, fewer subjects noticed him, and when the umbrella woman stopped her motion and performed a little dance, more subjects noticed. These latter two findings suggest that properties of an unattended stimulus can capture attention, even though similarity to attended stimuli seemed to make little difference. However, these findings must be evaluated tentatively, because the details of the experimental paradigm were not presented by Neisser (1979).

In one of the few published empirical reports with this paradigm, Becklen and Cervone (1983) examined the effect of eliminating the delay between the umbrella-woman's appearance and the questioning of subjects. They found no difference in noticing rates when the entire video was shown (35%) and when the video ended immediately after the umbrella woman left the scene (33%). Furthermore, performance was substantially worse when the video ended as the umbrella woman was halfway across the court (7%), even though that meant that the last image subjects saw included the umbrella woman. These subjects provided accurate descriptions of the scene, including details of the player locations, but did not mention an umbrella woman. Neisser and Rooney (cited in Becklen and Cervone 1983) addressed the same question by interrupting the action as the umbrella woman was two-thirds of the way across the screen. Immediately after the interruption, a split screen appeared with the umbrella woman on one side and a boy holding a soda can on the other; subjects were asked to pick which they had seen. When the results were corrected for guessing, only 30% of observers had noticed the umbrella woman, a level comparable to that shown in postexperiment interviews.

These findings provide important evidence against the notion of 'inattentional amnesia', an alternative account of findings of inattentional blindness and change blindness. According to this view (Wolfe 1999), the unexpected event is consciously perceived, but immediately forgotten. Hence, the failure to report its appearance reflects a failure of memory rather than of perception. In this case, however, even though subjects are tested immediately after the event, they are no better at detecting it. Furthermore, when people notice the unexpected event in this task, they sometimes smile or laugh; nonnoticers show no outward signs of detection. The forgetting would have to be so rapid as to be inseparable from the act of perception to allow any sort of amnesia to explain these findings.

This early work on selective looking raised a number of questions needing further study. What role does similarity between the unexpected and attended events play in detection? Are particularly unusual events more or less likely to be detected? Does task difficulty increase or decrease detection? Perhaps the most important question left unanswered in this early work is what role the unusual superimposition of the events played in causing inattentional blindness. Most cognitive psychologists we have talked to found these results interesting, but were somewhat less convinced of the importance of the failures to notice unexpected events. After all, the video superimposition gives the displays an odd appearance, one not typically experienced in the real world and one in which the players and the umbrella woman are not as easy to see as they would be without superimposition.

One more recent study has looked at performance when all of the actors and the umbrella woman are shot from a single video camera, with no superimposition (Stoffregen et al 1993). Under these conditions, the players and umbrella woman occluded each other and the balls. If failures to notice the umbrella woman in earlier studies resulted from the unnatural appearance of the superimposed version of the display, performance might be much better with a 'live' version. Subjects performed the task for approximately 30 s before the umbrella woman appeared and walked across the screen. The camera angle used for this film was much wider than in earlier studies—it showed an entire regulation basketball court. Consequently, the umbrella woman was visible for a longer time (12 s) and the players and the umbrella woman were substantially smaller on screen than in earlier studies. Another notable difference is that only twelve passes occurred during the 60-s video (rather than 20–40 as in earlier studies). Even in this live version of the study, only three of twenty normal subjects tested reported the presence of the umbrella woman. Although this finding does suggest that visual superimposition was not the cause of failures of noticing, it did not match the stimulus conditions of the other studies and did not directly compare performance with and without superimposition. The difference in camera angle (and consequent character size) alone may well have affected detection rates, so this study is not a well-controlled test of the generalizability of inattentional-blindness phenomena to more natural stimulus conditions.

Despite the importance of all the unanswered questions raised by these studies, to our knowledge the findings reviewed above are the only published reports using dynamic, naturalistic events to study the detection of unexpected objects.[3] Taken together, these studies lead to a number of striking conclusions, some consistent and others inconsistent with findings with simple displays. Unlike the computer-based studies (e.g. Mack and Rock 1998; Newby and Rock 1998), the video studies demonstrate that inattentional blindness does not result from attention being focused elsewhere in the display. In the superimposed version of the display, the umbrella woman occupied exactly the same spatial position as the attended players and balls. In fact, the balls even passed through the umbrella woman. This finding is inconsistent with the computer-based result that detection was better when the unexpected object appeared within the region defined by the attended object (Mack and Rock 1998). Several factors might account for this difference. First, there were simply more objects to attend to in the video displays, so attention may not have stayed on any one location for long. Second, the dynamic display may have captured and held attention more effectively than the cross task. Third, the video task may simply have been harder, leaving fewer attentional resources available to process unanticipated events. These video studies do show that a form of inattentional blindness can last much longer than the brief exposure times used in recent static-display studies. Subjects missed ongoing events that lasted for more than 4 s.

Although these differences between the computer-based and video studies are important, the general similarity of the conclusions is striking. In both cases, observers often do not see unanticipated objects and events. The video studies suggest that these findings can help explain real-world phenomena such as our inability to see our friends in a crowded movie theater or airplanes on an approaching runway when our attention is focused on a different goal. Both change blindness and inattentional blindness show that attention plays a critical role in perception and in representation. Without attention, we often do not see unanticipated events, and even with attention, we cannot encode and retain all the details of what we see.

Although these video studies of inattentional blindness help to generalize findings from simple displays to more complex situations, the original reports do not fully examine all of the critical questions. For example, there is a hint that the visual similarity of the unexpected object to the attended ones makes no difference, but the details of that study were never published. Furthermore, the experiments did not systematically consider the role of task difficulty in detection. Perhaps most importantly, no direct comparisons were made between performance with the superimposed version of the display and with the 'live' version. In the studies reported here, we attempt to examine each of these factors. We also consider the nature of the unusual event. To combine all of these factors orthogonally within a single consistent paradigm, we filmed several video segments with the same set of actors in the same location on the same day. We then asked a large number of naive observers to watch the video recordings and later answer questions about the unexpected events.

2 METHOD

2.1 Observers

Two-hundred twenty-eight observers, almost all undergraduate students, participated in the experiment. Each observer either volunteered to participate without compensation, received a large candy bar for participating, or was paid a single fee for participating in a larger testing session including another, unrelated experiment.

2.2 Materials

Four videotapes, each 75 s in duration, were created. Each tape showed two teams of three players, one team wearing white shirts and the other wearing black shirts, who moved around in a relatively random fashion in an open area (approximately 3 m deep x 5.2 m wide) in front of a bank of three elevator doors. The members of each team passed a standard orange basketball to one another in a regular order: player 1 would pass to player 2, who would pass to player 3, who would pass to player 1, and so on. The passes were either bounce passes or aerial passes; players would also dribble the ball, wave their arms, and make other movements consistent with their overall pattern of action, only incidentally looking directly at the camera.

After 44–48 s of this action, either of two unexpected events occurred: in the Umbrella–Woman condition, a tall woman holding an open umbrella walked from off camera on one side of the action to the other, left to right. The actions of the players, and this unexpected event, were designed to mimic the stimuli used by Neisser and colleagues. In the Gorilla condition, a shorter woman wearing a gorilla costume that fully covered her body walked through the action in the same way. In either case, the unexpected event lasted 5 s, and the players continued their actions during and after the event.

There were two styles of video: in the Transparent condition, the white team, black team, and unexpected event were all filmed separately, and the three video streams were rendered partially transparent and then superimposed by using digital video-editing software. (Neisser and colleagues achieved similar effects using analog equipment or a physical apparatus that superimposed separate displays by means of mirrors.) In the Opaque condition, all seven actors were filmed simultaneously and could thus occlude one another and the basketballs; this required some rehearsal to eliminate collisions and other accidents, and to achieve natural-looking patterns of movement. All videos were filmed with an SVHS video camera (Panasonic AG456U) and were digitized and edited by using a nonlinear digital-editing system (Media 100LX and Adobe Aftereffects, running on Power Computing hardware). All editing of the videos was accomplished after digitization, so the degree of signal loss due to multiple generations of editing was minimized and also equated across conditions. Stimuli were created by mastering the digitally edited sequences to VHS format tapes. Thus, videos were created with the following four display types: Transparent/Umbrella Woman, Transparent/Gorilla, Opaque/Umbrella Woman, and Opaque/Gorilla. The first of these was most similar to the conditions tested by Neisser and colleagues.

2.3 Procedures

All observers were tested individually and gave informed consent in advance. Before viewing the videotape, observers were told that they would be watching two teams of three players passing basketballs and that they should pay attention to either the team in white (the White condition) or the team in black (the Black condition). They were told that they should keep either a silent mental count of the total number of passes made by the attended team (the Easy condition) or separate silent mental counts of the number of bounce passes and aerial passes made by the attended team (the Hard condition). Thus, for each of the four displays, there were four task conditions—White/Easy, White/Hard, Black/Easy, and Black/Hard—for a total of sixteen individual conditions. Each observer participated in only one condition.

After viewing the videotape and performing the monitoring task, observers were immediately asked to write down their count(s) on paper.[4] They were then asked to provide answers to a surprise series of additional questions. (i) While you were doing the counting, did you notice anything unusual on the video? (ii) Did you notice anything other than the six players? (iii) Did you see anyone else (besides the six players) appear on the video? (iv) Did you see a gorilla (woman carrying an umbrella) walk across the screen? After any "yes" response, observers were asked to provide details of what they noticed. If at any point an observer mentioned the unexpected event, the remaining questions were skipped. After the questioning, observers were asked whether they had ever previously participated in an experiment similar to this or had ever heard of such an experiment or the general phenomenon. (Observers who answered "yes" were replaced and their data were discarded.) Last, the observer was debriefed; this included replaying the videotape on request. Each testing session lasted 5–10 min.

Twenty-one experimenters tested the observers. To ensure uniformity of procedures, we developed a written protocol in advance and reviewed it with the experimenters before they began to collect data. This document specified what the experimenters would say to each observer, when they would say it, how and when they would show the videotape, how they would collect and record the data, and how they would debrief observers. Experimenters used a variety of television monitors, ranging from 13 to 36 inches (diagonal) in screen size to present the videotapes.

3 RESULTS

Data from thirty-six observers were discarded for a variety of reasons: either (i) the observer already knew about the phenomenon and/or experimental paradigm (n

$= 14$), (ii) the observer reported losing count of the passes ($n = 9$), (iii) passes were incompletely or inaccurately recorded ($n = 7$), (iv) the observer's answer could not be clearly interpreted ($n = 5$), or (v) the observer's total pass count was more than three standard deviations away from the mean of the other observers in that condition ($n = 1$). The remaining 192 observers were distributed equally across the sixteen conditions of the 2 x 2 x 2 x 2 design (twelve per condition).

Although we asked a series of questions escalating in specificity to determine whether observers had noticed the unexpected event, only one observer who failed to report the event in response to the first question ("did you notice anything unusual?") reported the event in response to any of the next three questions (which culminated in "did you see a ... walk across the screen?"). Thus, since the responses were nearly always consistent across all four questions, we will present the results in terms of overall rates of noticing.

Out of all 192 observers across all conditions, 54% noticed the unexpected event and 46% failed to notice the unexpected event, revealing a substantial level of sustained inattentional blindness for a dynamic event and confirming the basic results of Neisser and colleagues. More observers noticed the unexpected event in the Opaque condition (67%) than in the Transparent condition (42%); $\chi^2_{(1)} = 12.084$, $p < 0.001$; $n = 96$ per condition. However, even in the Opaque case, a substantial proportion of observers (33%) failed to report the event, despite its visibility and the repeated questions about it.

More observers noticed the unexpected event in the Easy (64%) than in the Hard (45%) condition $\chi^2_{(1)} = 6.797$, $p < 0.009$; $n = 96$ per condition). To confirm that these monitoring tasks differed in difficulty, we calculated the SD of the total pass counts reported by observers in each condition; the average SD was 2.71 in the eight Easy conditions and 6.77 in the eight Hard conditions, indicating that the Hard monitoring task was indeed more difficult. Accordingly, the correlation across conditions between the frequency of noticing and the SD of the total pass count was $r = -0.56$. The effect of task difficulty was greater in the Transparent conditions (Easy 56%, Hard 27%; $\chi^2_{(1)} = 8.400$, $p < 0.004$; $n = 48$ per condition) than in the Opaque conditions (Easy 71%, Hard 62%; $\chi^2_{(1)}) = 0.7\ 50$, $p < 0.386$; $n = 48$ per condition), suggesting a multiplicative effect on residual attention capacity of tracking difficult-to-see stimuli and keeping two running counts in working memory.

Next we examined differences in the detection of the two unexpected events. The Umbrella Woman was noticed more often than the Gorilla overall (65% versus 44%; $\chi^2_{(1)} = 8.392$, $p < 0.004$; $n = 96$ per condition). This relation held regardless of the video type, monitoring task, or attended team, suggesting that the Umbrella Woman was either a more visually salient event than the Gorilla,[5] more consistent with observers' expectations about situations involving basketballs, more semantically similar to the attended events, or all three. However, when observers attended to the actions of the Black team, they noticed the Gorilla much more often than when they attended to the actions of the White team (Black 58%, White 27%; $\chi^2_{(1)} = 9\ 579$, $p < 0.002$; $n = 48$ per condition). By contrast, attending the Black team versus the White team made little difference in noticing the Umbrella Woman (Black 62%, White 69%; $\chi^2_{(1)} = 0.416$, $p < 0.519$; $n = 48$ per condition). The Gorilla was black, whereas the Umbrella Woman wore pale colors that differed from both the Black and the White team. Thus, contrary to the suggestion of Neisser (1979), it appears that observers are more likely to notice an unexpected event that shares basic visual features in this case, color—with the events they are attending to. In a sense, this effect is the opposite of the traditional 'pop-out' phenomenon in visual search tasks, which occurs when an item that differs in basic visual features from the rest of the display is easier to notice and identify.

It is possible that subjects who lost count of the passes would be most likely to notice the unexpected event. This is unlikely, however, for two reasons. First, subjects who reported losing count were replaced prior to data analysis. Second, we calculated the point-biserial correlation r between noticing (coded as I for reporting and 0 for not reporting the event) and the subject's absolute deviation from an accurate pass count (measured as the number of passes above or below the correct range) for each condition except the Opaque/Umbrella-Woman/White/Easy condition, which engendered 100% noticing. Across these fifteen conditions the correlations averaged to $r = 0.15$, suggesting that noticing was not strongly associated with counting poorly or inattentively.

4 DISCUSSION

Our findings have replicated, generalized, and extended the surprising result first reported by Neisser and colleagues (Bahrick et al 1981; Becklen and Cervone 1983; Littman and Becklen 1976; Neisser 1979; Neisser and Becklen 1975; Rooney et al 1981; Stoffregen et al 1993; Stoffregen and Becklen 1989), and have demonstrated a robust phenomenon of sustained inattentional blindness for dynamic events. In particular, we have shown the following.

(i) Approximately half of observers fail to notice an ongoing and highly salient but unexpected event while they are engaged in a primary monitoring task. This extends the phenomenon of inattentional blindness (e.g. Mack and Rock 1998) by at least an order of magnitude in the duration of the event that can be missed. To stretch this limit further, we tested a longer and more salient unexpected event in an additional condition not reported above. In a separate Opaque-style video recording, the Gorilla walked from right to left into the live basketball-passing event, stopped in the middle of the players as the action continued all around it, turned to face the camera, thumped its chest, and then resumed walking across the screen (this action began after 35 s and lasted 9 s in a stimulus tape 62 s long).

Twelve new observers[6] watched this video while attending to the White team and engaging in the Easy monitoring task; only 50% noticed the event. This is roughly the same as the percentage that noticed the normal Opaque/Gorilla-walking event (42%) under the same task conditions.

(ii) This sustained inattentional blindness occurs more frequently if the display is transparent, with actors seeming to move through each other (as used in earlier studies), but observers often miss even fully visible objects appearing in live-action opaque displays. This latter finding is contrary to the intuitions of researchers who believed that the original effect was due to the unusual nature of the transparent video, and provides further evidence that inattentional blindness is a ubiquitous perceptual phenomenon rather than an artifact of particular display conditions.

(iii) The level of inattentional blindness depends on the difficulty of the primary task; in principle, inattentional blindness in this paradigm could be continuously varied by appropriately manipulating the difficulty of the monitoring task.

(iv) Observers are more likely to notice unexpected events if these events are visually similar to the events they are paying attention to. (On the basis of our results it is logically possible that dissimilarity to the ignored events is instead the crucial factor.)

(v) Objects can pass through the spatial extent of attentional focus (and the fovea) and still not be 'seen' if they are not specifically being attended. This conclusion is consistent with Mack and Rock's (1998) finding that observers often fail to notice a bar or square moving stroboscopically across fixation during a 200 ms display. In each of our videotapes, the unexpected object more than once crossed the path of the basketball and/or a player throwing or catching the ball, the observers would have had to pay attention to both of those elements of the display to perform the monitoring task.

In most respects, the results of this study are consistent with computer-based studies of inattentional blindness. Observers fail to report unexpected, suprathreshold objects when they are engaged in another task. Both sets of findings are consistent with the claim that there is no conscious perception without attention. The consistency of the theoretical conclusions that can be drawn from these two radically different paradigms is reassuring. Whether the unexpected object is flashed for 200 ms in an otherwise empty display or it moves dynamically across a natural scene for 5 s, observers are unlikely to notice it if attention is otherwise engaged. This consistency suggests that the results of computer-based studies of inattentional blindness can and do generalize to situations closer to our real-world experiences.

The results of our experiments also call to mind recent findings from research on change blindness. Many studies of change blindness focus on simple displays of letters or dots to determine how little information is preserved from one view to the next. More recently, change-blindness research has moved from using simple displays of letters, dots, and words (e.g. Pashler 1988; Phillips 1974) to more complex, naturalistic displays for which more information is available for selection (see Simons and Levin 1997 for a review). Given the simplicity and relative meaninglessness of the simple displays, the generalizability of the results to more naturalistic viewing conditions was not certain (see Simons 2000, for discussion). The recent thrust of work on change blindness has been to examine whether the inferences drawn from work with simple displays will hold for more natural displays. One dramatic demonstration was at least partly responsible for this move toward increased naturalism. When viewing photographs of natural scenes in preparation for a memory test, people missed large, meaningful changes that occurred during eye movements (Grimes 1996). For example, observers often failed to notice when two people in a photograph exchanged hats or even when they exchanged heads. These findings have been replicated in subsequent work on saccade-contingent changes (Currie et al 1995; Henderson and Hollingworth, in press; McConkie and Currie 1996).

This change blindness for natural scenes has been extended to a number of other paradigms. For example, when an original and modified image are presented in rapid alternation with a blank screen interposed between them, observers have great difficulty detecting changes (Rensink et al 1997). This 'flicker' technique shows that change blindness is not limited to saccade-contingent changes. In the case of saccade-contingent changes, the blur on the retina caused by the eye movement itself leads to suppression of visual processing during the change, thereby preventing detection of any local transients. The blank screen in the flicker study has essentially the same effect, producing a global change signal that prevents detection of the local one caused by the change. Similar change blindness has been shown for changes across cuts or pans in motion pictures (Levin and Simons 1997; Simons 1996), eye blinks (O'Regan et al 2000), and 'mud splashes' (O'Regan et al 1999). As noted earlier, even when one conversation partner is replaced by a different person during a brief interruption, observers often fail to notice the change (Simons and Levin 1998).

As in studies of inattentional blindness, the likelihood of change detection depends on the focus of attention. In studies of inattentional blindness, when observers are attending to another object or event, they are less likely to notice the unexpected event. In studies of change detection, people are better able to report changes to attended than unattended objects. For example, people are faster to detect changes in the flicker paradigm when the changed object is of central interest in the scene (Rensink et al 1997). Central objects are more likely to garner attentional resources, and if we have a limited capacity for holding information across views, changes to objects that receive

more effortful processing are more likely to be detected (see Rensink 2000; Scholl 2000). Just as we often fail to perceive unexpected events, we often fail to notice unexpected changes to the visual details of our environment—in both cases, this applies even when attention is focused on the area of the event or change.

Although the theoretical conclusions drawn from real-world studies are not altogether different from those derived from work with simple displays, they do show that change blindness is a general property of the visual system and that it applies to almost all aspects of visual processing. We apparently do not retain a detailed visual representation of our surroundings from one view to the next, even for displays with all the richness of natural scenes. Similarly, studies of sustained inattentional blindness suggest that we fail to perceive unexpected objects even under naturalistic viewing conditions.

The results of our studies of sustained inattentional blindness, however, do contrast in an interesting way with those of one recent change-blindness study (Simons et al, in preparation). In that experiment, a female experimenter dressed in athletic clothing and carrying a basketball approaches a passerby in public and asks directions to a gym. During this interaction, a crowd of confederates walked between the two and surreptitiously took the basketball away. When asked if they noticed anything changed or anything different about her appearance, a minority of observers reported noticing that the basketball was gone. But when asked a follow-up question specifically referring to the basketball, most of the remaining observers 'remembered' the basketball and were able to describe its unusual coloring. Thus, a visual change can be encoded but not explicitly reported until a specific retrieval cue is provided. In the experiment reported here, however, not one of the eighty-eight nonnoticers 'remembered' the Gorilla or Umbrella-Woman events when specifically asked about it, and several did not believe that the event had happened until the videotape was replayed for them.

While there are several important differences between these paradigms that could account for this difference in behavior, they share the feature that a condition of inattention was created (by the conversation in the basketball disappearance study or by the monitoring task here) that apparently prevented many observers from becoming aware of a salient visual change. Perhaps the crucial difference is that whereas the conversation simply reduced the observer's attention by drawing it away from the critical object, the monitoring task in this study required observers to attend to one event while ignoring another that was happening in the same region of space. This 'directed ignoring' could inhibit perception of not just the ignored event but of all unattended events, thereby preventing the formation of an explicit memory trace. Whether inattentional blindness occurs because the target is similar to the intentionally ignored items or different from the attended items is an open question that would be relatively difficult to explore by using video-based displays but could be explored by using more controlled computer-based tasks.

One alternative interpretation of our findings is that subjects did consciously perceive the unexpected object, however briefly, but immediately forgot they had seen it (Wolfe 1999). Although this inattentional-amnesia explanation can in principle account for our findings, it seems less plausible that the inattentional-blindness account for a number of reasons. First, detecting unusual objects or events would be a useful function for a visual system to have; immediately forgetting them would defeat this purpose. This is especially true for a prolonged, dynamic event. Given that the unexpected object in our experiments was available for further examination (something that was less true of earlier studies with briefly flashed objects), we might expect observers to try to verify their percept in these studies, thereby leading to a preserved representation. Furthermore, if observers did consciously perceive and then forget the gorilla, they presumably would not be particularly surprised when asked if there had been a gorilla in the display. Yet, observers in our study were consistently surprised when they viewed the display a second time, some even exclaiming, "I missed that?!" It seems more parsimonious to assume that observers were never aware of the unexpected object than to assume that they saw a gorilla, then forgot about it, and then were shocked to see it when told to look for it. Last, as noted earlier, Becklen and Cervone (1983) found no improvement in noticing when the video was stopped immediately after the unexpected event rather than several seconds later. However, finding a direct test to distinguish between never perceiving an object and immediately forgetting it will be difficult because the inattentional-amnesia proponents could always argue that the memory test came too late. Thus, it may not be possible to distinguish empirically between the amnesia and the blindness explanations.

Although our findings suggest that unexpected events are often overlooked, the question of whether they leave an implicit trace remains open. Unnoticed stimuli in the static-inattentional-blindness paradigm can lead to priming effects (Mack and Rock 1998). However, those experiments did not require subjects to ignore anything. Neisser and colleagues found that subjects under the conditions we have described as directed ignoring were no more likely to select the unexpected object in a two-alternative forced-choice recognition test than were other subjects when asked to report it directly (Neisser and Rooney 1982, as cited in Becklen and Cervone 1983). However, forced choice may not be as sensitive as other implicit memory tests. Future research should explore the issues of preserved representations and directed ignoring within the sustained-inattentional-blindness paradigm we have reintroduced here.

ACKNOWLEDGMENTS

Many thanks to all of the people who helped with filming the videos or collecting the data for this study: Jennifer Shephard (Umbrella Woman), Elisa Cheng (Gorilla), Judith Danovitch, Steve Most, Alex Wong (White team), Amy Delpolyi, Jason Jay, Megan White (Black team), Dan Ellard, Samantha Glass, Jeremy Gray, Sara Greene, Annya Hernandez, Orville Jackson, Latanya James, David Marx, Steve Mitroff, Carolyn Racine, Kathy Richards, Chris Russell Laurie Santos, Steve Stose, Ojas Tejani, Dan Tristan, Amy Wiseman, Leah Wittenberg, and Amir Zarrinpar (data collection, in alphabetical order). Thanks also to M J Wraga for suggesting the first part of the title of this article, to Brian Scholl for discovering the Balint quotation, to Dick Neisser for inspiration, to Larry Taylor for helping to avoid collisions during the filming of the videos, and especially to Jerry Kagan for lending us his gorilla suit. Additional thanks to Steve Most, Brian Scholl, two anonymous reviewers, and everyone else who commented on earlier versions of this manuscript and presentations of these results.

Miniaturized and abbreviated versions of the videos used in this study are available, in QuickTime format, via the Internet at: http://coglab.wjh.harvard.edu/gorilla/

index.html. No animals were harmed during the making of the videos.

REFERENCES

Bahrick L E, Walker A S, Neisser U, 1981 "Selective looking by infants" Cognitive Psychology 13 377–390

Becklen R, Cervone D, 1983 "Selective looking and the noticing of unexpected events" Memory and Cognition 11 601–608

Cherry E C, 1953 "Some experiments upon the recognition of speech, with one and with two ears" Journal of the Acoustical Society of America 25 975–979

Chun M M, Jiang Y, 1998 "Contextual cueing: Implicit learning and memory of visual context guides spatial attention" Cognitive Psychology 36 28–71

Currie C, McConkie G W, Carlson-Radvansky L A, Irwin D E, 1995 "Maintaining visual stability across saccades: Role of the saccade target object" technical report UIUC-BI-HPP-95–01, Beckman Institute, University of Illinois

Grimes J, 1996 "On the failure to detect changes in scenes across saccades", in Perception (Vancouver Studies in Cognitive Science) Ed. K Akins, volume 2 (New York: Oxford University Press) pp 89–110

Haines R F, 1989 "A breakdown in simultaneous information processing", in Presbyopia Research: From Molecular Biology to Visual Adaptation Eds G Obrecht, L W Stark (New York: Plenum) pp 171–175

Henderson J M, Hollingworth A, in press "The role of fixation position in detecting scene changes across saccades" Psychological Science Husain M, Stein J, 1988 "Rezso Balint and his most celebrated case" Archives of Neurology 45 89–93

Levin D T, Momen N, Drivdahl S B, Simons D J, 2000 "Change blindness blindness: The metacognitive error of overestimating change-detection ability" Visual Cognition (in press)

Levin D T, Simons D J, 1997 "Failure to detect changes to attended objects in motion pictures" Psychonomic Bulletin and Review 4 501–506

Littman D, Becklen R, 1976 "Selective looking with minimal eye movements" Perception & Psychophysics 20 77–79

Mack A, Rock I, 1998 Inattentional Blindness (Cambridge, MA: MIT Press)

Mack A, Tang B, Tuma R, Kahn S, 1992 "Perceptual organization and attention" Cognitive Psychology 24 475–501

McConkie G W, Currie C B, 1996 "Visual stability across saccades while viewing complex pictures" Journal of Experimental Psychology: Human Perception and Performance 22 563–581

McConkie G W, Zola D, 1979 "Is visual information integrated across successive fixations in reading?" Perception & Psychophysics 25 221–224

Moore C M, Egeth H, 1997 "Perception without attention: Evidence of grouping under conditions of inattention" Journal of Experimental Psychology: Human Perception and Performance 23 339–352

Moray N, 1959 "Attention in dichotic listening: Affective cues and the influence of instructions" Quarterly Journal of Experimental Psychology 11 56–60

Neisser U, 1979 "The control of information pickup in selective looking", in Perception and its Development. A Tribute to Eleanor J Gibson Ed. A D Pick (Hillsdale, NJ: Lawrence Erlbaum Associates) pp 201–219

Neisser U, Becklen R, 1975 "Selective looking: Attending to visually specified events" Cognitive Psychology 7 480–494

Neumann O, Heijden A H C van der, Allport D A, 1986 "Visual selective attention: Introductory remarks" Psychological Research 48 185–188

Newby E A, Rock I, 1998 "Inattentional blindness as a function of proximity to the focus of attention" Perception 27 1025–1040

O'Regan J K, Deubel H, Clark J J, Rensink R A, 2000 "Picture changes during blinks: Looking without seeing and seeing without looking" Visual Cognition (in press)

O'Regan J K, Rensink R A, Clark J J, 1999 "Change-blindness as a result of 'mudsplashes'" Nature (London) 398 34

Pashler H, 1988 "Familiarity and visual change detection" Perception & Psychophysics 44 369–378

Phillips W A, 1974 "On the distinction between sensory storage and short-term visual memory" Perception & Psychophysics 16 283–290

RENSINK R A, 2000 "VISUAL SEARCH FOR CHANGE: A PROBE INTO THE NATURE OF ATTENTIONAL PROCESSING" *VISUAL COGNITION* (IN PRESS)

RENSINK R A, O'REGAN J K, CLARK J J, 1997 "TO SEE OR NOT TO SEE: THE NEED FOR ATTENTION TO PERCEIVE CHANGES IN SCENES" *PSYCHOLOGICAL SCIENCE* **8** 368–373

ROCK I, LINNETT C M, GRANT P, MACK A, 1992 "PERCEPTION WITHOUT ATTENTION: RESULTS OF A NEW METHOD" *COGNITIVE PSYCHOLOGY* **24** 502–534

ROONEY P, BOYCE C, NEISSER U, 1981 "A DEVELOPMENTAL STUDY OF NOTICING UNEXPECTED EVENTS" UNPUBLISHED MANUSCRIPT

RUBIN N, HUA L,1998 "PERCEIVING OCCLUDED OBJECTS UNDER CONDITIONS OF INATTENTION" *INVESTIGATIVE OPHTHALMOLOGY & VISUAL SCIENCE* **39**(4) S1113

SCHOLL B J, 2000 "ATTENUATED CHANGE BLINDNESS FOR EXOGENOUSLY ATTENDED ITEMS IN A FLICKER PARADIGM" *VISUAL COGNITION* (IN PRESS) SILVERMAN M, MACK A, 1997 "PRIMING BY ICONIC IMAGES" *INVESTIGATIVE OPHTHALMOLOGY & VISUAL SCIENCE* **38**(4) S963

SIMONS D J, 1996 "IN SIGHT, OUT OF MIND: WHEN OBJECT REPRESENTATIONS FAIL" *PSYCHOLOGICAL SCIENCE* **7** 301–305

SIMONS D J, 2000 "CURRENT APPROACHES TO CHANGE BLINDNESS" *VISUAL COGNITION* (IN PRESS)

SIMONS D J, CHABRIS C F, LEVIN D T, (IN PREPARATION) "CHANGE BLINDNESS IS NOT CAUSED BY LATER EVENTS OVERWRITING EARLIER ONES IN VISUAL SHORT TERM MEMORY"

SIMONS D J, LEVIN D T, 1997 "CHANGE BLINDNESS" *TRENDS IN COGNITIVE SCIENCES* **1** 261–267

SIMONS D J, LEVIN D T, 1998 "FAILURE TO DETECT CHANGES TO PEOPLE IN A REAL-WORLD INTERACTION" *PSYCHONOMIC BULLETIN AND REVIEW* **5** 644–649

STOFFREGEN T A, BALDWIN C A, FLYNN S B, 1993 "NOTICING OF UNEXPECTED EVENTS BY ADULTS WITH AND WITHOUT MENTAL RETARDATION" *AMERICAN JOURNAL ON MENTAL RETARDATION* **98** 273–284

STOFFREGEN T A, BECKLEN R C, 1989 "DUAL ATTENTION TO DYNAMICALLY STRUCTURED NATURALISTIC EVENTS" *PERCEPTUAL AND MOTOR SKILLS* **69** 1187–1201

TREISMAN A, 1964 "MONITORING AND STORAGE OF IRRELEVANT MESSAGES IN SELECTIVE ATTENTION" *JOURNAL OF VERBAL LEARNING AND VERBAL BEHAVIOR* **3** 449–459

WILLIAMS P, SIMONS D J, 2000 "DETECTING CHANGES IN NOVEL, COMPLEX THREE-DIMENSIONAL OBJECTS" *VISUAL COGNITION* (IN PRESS)

WOLFE J M, 1999 "INATTENTIONAL AMNESIA", IN *FLEETING MEMORIES. COGNITION OF BRIEF VISUAL STIMULI* ED. V COLTHEART (CAMBRIDGE, MA: MIT PRESS) PP 71–94

NOTES

1. Mack and Rock (1998) draw a distinction between conscious perception and implicit perception. Consistently with this distinction, when we use the term 'perceive' (or 'notice' or 'see') in this paper, we mean that observers have at some point had a conscious experience of an object or event. However, it is important to note that even when observers do not perceive an object, it may still have an implicit influence on their subsequent decisions and performance (e.g. Chun and Jiang 1998; Moore and Egeth 1997).

2. Many of the 'selective-looking' studies conducted by Neisser and his colleagues were never published in complete empirical reports. In such cases, as here, we have cited unpublished or in-preparation manuscripts on the basis of their descriptions in other, published materials.

3. Haines (1989) did address this topic as part of a larger human-interface study. Pilots attempted to land a plane in a flight simulator while using a head-up display of critical flight information superimposed on the 'windshield'. Under these conditions, some pilots failed to notice that a plane on the ground was blocking their path. In addition, Mack and Rock (1998) report several studies in which the unexpected object moved stroboscopically across part of the display, often without being detected during the 200 ms viewing period.

4. Note that in all the Transparent conditions, the correct counts were identical because the same passing sequences were used to create both of the Transparent display tapes (Umbrella Woman and Gorilla). In the Opaque conditions, the correct counts varied because the passing sequences were filmed separately for each of the unexpected events.

5. Visual salience, here, could refer to the relative distinctiveness of the unexpected objects in relation to the other players or to the background of the scene. Furthermore, the Umbrella Woman may have been spatially more distinctive in that her umbrella

extended above the heads of the other players whereas the Gorilla was the same height as the other players.

6. Data from two additional observers were discarded, one because he already knew about the effect, the other because his answer could not be clearly interpreted.

Change Blindness

DANIEL J. SIMONS AND DANIEL T. LEVIN

Although at any instant we experience a rich, detailed visual world, we do not use such visual details to form a stable representation across views. Over the past five years, researchers have focused increasingly on 'change blindness' (the inability to detect changes to an object or scene) as a means to examine the nature of our representations. Experiments using a diverse range of methods and displays have produced strikingly similar results: unless a change to a visual scene produces a localizable change or transient at a specific position on the retina, generally, people will not detect it. We review theory and research motivating work on change blindness and discuss recent evidence that people are blind to changes occurring in photographs, in motion pictures and even in real-world interactions. These findings suggest that relatively little visual information is preserved from one view to the next, and question a fundamental assumption that has underlain perception research for centuries: namely, that we need to store a detailed visual representation in the mind/brain from one view to the next.

Since antiquity, scholars have assumed the need for precise, veridical representations of our visual world[1]. Modern researchers recognize that the two-dimensional retinal image cannot fully and unambiguously represent a three-dimensional world, and since Descartes, they have posited adjustments to the retinal image to compensate for distortions and ambiguities. In order to form an accurate, stable representation, we must somehow extract the invariant structure of the world from our ever-changing sensory experience. For example, as we view scenes in the real world, we move our eyes (saccade) three to four times each second. Across fixations, objects in the world are projected onto different parts of the retina. Somehow, we integrate information across these fixations to achieve a stable representation; we must recognize that two consecutive views are, in fact, of the same scene even when the viewpoint or viewing angle differs. Recently, research on how we integrate visual information across fixations has spawned a new series of studies focusing on our ability to detect changes from one view of a scene to the next. These studies have produced a set of results that, consistent with earlier evidence for memory distortions, suggest a high degree of 'change blindness'; observers do not appear to retain many visual details from one view to the next. These recent findings and their implications for how we represent our visual world are the primary focus of this review.

EVIDENCE FOR CHANGE BLINDNESS

Although change detection has only recently become a topic of intense inquiry, research spanning many areas of cognitive psychology has hinted at current findings. At times, research on visual integration of information across eye movements has revealed striking examples of our inability to detect changes (see Box 1). Research on recognition memory for large numbers of photographs also suggested the possibility of change blindness. The primary purpose of such studies was to demonstrate an impressive capacity to remember photographs from a single presentation, but they also revealed a lack of specificity in representations (see Box 2). Perhaps the most intriguing precursor to contemporary studies of change blindness comes from the informal observations of film makers and editors (see Box 3; several recent studies are described in the text).

Over the past ten years, a number of studies have begun to address our inability to detect changes to objects and scenes from one view to the next (see Box 4). Some experiments changed images during saccades. Others made changes during blinks or during a blank interval between two pictures. Still others made changes to scenes while observers viewed a motion picture cut or a real-world occlusion event. What is striking about this diversity of approaches is the similarity of the results. In all of these experiments, observers fail to notice dramatic changes to displays. We will now turn to evidence for and mechanisms underlying change blindness across saccades.

Saccade-contingent changes

Imagine viewing a set of photographs for an upcoming recognition test. As you study the photographs, you shift your attention among the objects in the image and you scan the image with your eyes. Periodically, while your eyes are moving rapidly from one object to the next, something in the scene is changed. The experimenters mention that the scenes may change at times and that you should let them know if you see something change. Sounds easy, right? You are studying the photographs intently for a test, so you should have a fairly complete representation.

Box 1. Visual integration across eye movements

During the 1970s, evidence for visual masking and for the integration of visual information at a single retinal location[a,b], together with the general acceptance of the construct of iconic memory (a short-term sensory memory that retains a detailed picture-like representation of a scene)[c], inspired a model for achieving a continuous experience[d]. This model suggested that visual images from consecutive views are combined in a visual buffer, much as two overhead transparencies can be superimposed.

Although this model seems plausible, it cannot account for continuity under natural viewing conditions. Somehow, visual integration in the real world must accommodate changes to our eye, head and body positions. In order for the visually integrative buffer model to work, stimuli presented on two different fixations or at two different retinal locations must be integrated visually. That is, our visual system must determine that an object is the same even when it stimulates different areas of the retina on consecutive fixations. In one test of this hypothesis, subjects fixated a point in the center of a display and a 12-dot pattern was presented briefly to parafoveal vision. Shortly thereafter, subjects moved their eyes to the parafoveal location and a second 12-dot pattern was presented. When the two patterns were combined, one dot was missing, and subjects were asked to determine the location of the missing dot. Although initial studies supported the notion of a visually integrative buffer[e], later studies controlling for methodological and display artifacts have failed to replicate the initial finding[f,k] (for recent reviews, see Refs 1 and m). Therefore, this research fails to support the hypothesis that we form an accurate representation by storing and integrating precise visual information from one fixation to the next.

Additional evidence for the absence of integrated visual representation across eye movements comes from the study of preview effects in reading. One particularly dramatic example comes from the study of preview effects in reading. One particularly dramatic example comes from a task in which observers read lines of text that alternated case with each letter (e.g. AlTeRnAtEd CaSe)[n]. During some saccades, every letter in the sentence changed case, so that the visual form of every word was different. Surprisingly, when the changes occurred during an eye movement, subjects almost never noticed. That is, subjects not only failed to integrate the visual form of the letters from one instant to the next, they could not even tell that the visual form was changing. Apparently, the information integrated across fixations during reading is not contingent on the precise visual form of the word. More recently, studies of reading have inspired a series of studies of integration of pictorial information across eye movements. These studies have focused on the benefits of a parafoveal preview on processing during a subsequent fixation[m,o,p,q]. One recent study showed that when the complementary sets of contours from an object were shown before and after an eye movement, in general, observers were unable to detect the change and the contour change had no effect on naming latencies[o]. The visual form was not sufficiently represented to allow detection of the change.

In a sense, studies of visual integration and studies of change detection address the same issues using complementary methodologies. Studies of visual integration focus on the ability to combine two distinct images, essentially adding their contents. Studies of change detection focus on the ability to subtract one image from another, thereby finding the difference. Both approaches allow an exploration of the specificity of scene representations.

References

A DI LOLLO, V. (1980) TEMPORAL INTEGRATION IN VISUAL MEMORY *J. EXP. PSYCHOL. GEN.* 109, 75–97

B KAHNEMAN, D. (1968) METHOD, FINDINGS, AND THEORY IN STUDIES OF VISUAL MASKING *PSYCHOL. BULL.* 70, 404–425

C NEISSER, U. (1967) *COGNITIVE PSYCHOLOGY*, APPLETON-CENTURY-CROFTS

D MCCONKIE, G.W. AND RAYNER, K. (1976) IDENTIFYING THE SPAN OF THE EFFECTIVE STIMULUS IN READING: LITERATURE REVIEW AND THEORIES OF READING, IN *THEORETICAL MODELS AND PROCESSES OF READING* (2ND EDN) (SINGER, H. AND RUDDELL, R.B., EDS), PP. 137–162, INTERNATIONAL READING ASSOCIATION

E JONIDES, J., IRWIN, D.E. AND YANTIS, S. (1982) INTEGRATING VISUAL INFORMATION FROM SUCCESSIVE FIXATIONS *SCIENCE*, 215, 192–194

F BRIDGEMAN, B. AND MAYER, M. (1983) FAILURE TO INTEGRATE VISUAL INFORMATION FROM SUCCESSIVE FIXATIONS *BULL. PSYCHONOMIC SOC.* 21, 285–286

G IRWIN, D.E., BROWN, J.S. AND SUN, J-S. (1988) VISUAL MASKING AND VISUAL INTEGRATION ACROSS SACCADIC EYE MOVEMENTS *J. EXP. PSYCHOL. GEN.* 117, 276–287

H IRWIN, D.E., YANTIS, S. AND JONIDES, J. (1983) EVIDENCE AGAINST VISUAL INTEGRATION ACROSS SACCADIC EYE MOVEMENTS *PERCEPT. PSYCHOPHYSIOL.* 34, 49–57

I JONIDES, J., IRWIN, D.E. AND YANTIS, S. (1983) FAILURE TO INTEGRATE INFORMATION FROM SUCCESSIVE FIXATIONS *SCIENCE* 222, 188

J RAYNER, K. AND POLLATSEK, A. (1983) IS VISUAL INFORMATION INTEGRATED ACROSS SACCADES? *PERCEPT. PSYCHOPHYSIOL.* 34, 39–48

K SUN, J-S. AND IRWIN, D.E. (1987) RETINAL MASKING DURING PURSUIT EYE MOVEMENTS: IMPLICATIONS FOR *J. EXP. PSYCHOL. HUM. PERCEPT. PERFORM.* 13, 140–145

L IRWIN, D.E. (1991) INFORMATION INTEGRATION ACROSS SACCADIC EYE MOVEMENTS *COGNIT. PSYCHOL.* 23, 420–456

M POLLATSEK, A. AND RAYNER, K. (1992) WHAT IS INTEGRATED ACROSS FIXATIONS? IN *EYE MOVEMENTS AND VISUAL COGNITION: SCENE PERCEPTION AND READING* (RAYNER, K., ED.), PP. 166–191, SPRINGER-VERLAG

N MCCONKIE, G.W. AND ZOLA, D. (1979) IS VISUAL INFORMATION INTEGRATED ACROSS SUCCESSIVE FIXATIONS IN READING? *PERCEPT. PSYCHOPHYSIOL.* 25, 221–224

O HENDERSON, J.M. (1997) TRANSSACCADIC MEMORY AND INTEGRATION DURING REAL-WORLD OBJECT PERCEPTION *PSYCHOL. SCI.* 8, 51–55

P POLLATSEK, A., RAYNER, K. AND COLLINS, W.E. (1984) INTEGRATING PICTORIAL INFORMATION ACROSS EYE MOVEMENTS *J. EXP. PSYCHOL. GEN.* 113, 426–442

Q POLLATSEK, A., RAYNER, K. AND HENDERSON, J.M. (1990) ROLE OF SPATIAL LOCATION IN INTEGRATION OF PICTORIAL INFORMATION ACROSS SACCADES *J. EXP. PSYCHOL. HUM. PERCEPT PERFORM.* 16, 199–210

Surprisingly, observers failed to notice when two men in a photograph exchanged different colored hats and only 50% noticed when two people exchanged heads[2]. In all, subjects missed nearly 70% of the changes that occurred during an eye movement. Subsequent studies[3,4] have confirmed the basic pattern described by Grimes. During an eye movement, we apparently lose, or at least lose access to, many of the visual details of the previous view. But is change blindness limited to cases in which information must be integrated across eye movements? These dramatic findings, accompanied by theoretical predictions of sparse visual representations[5-7], spurred a flurry of investigations into the mechanisms underlying change blindness.

Change blindness across simulated saccades

One aspect of eye movements that might account for change blindness is the existence of motion transients across the retina. In a sense, the target change cannot be identified because the eye is processing change signals from every location. If global transients effectively mask the ability to localize an individual transient or change, then any display that creates global transients should make change detection difficult. In order to examine this possibility, several laboratories ndependently developed a technique designed to mimic eye movements without changing the fixation location[8,9].

Experiments using the flicker paradigm found that almost none of the changes were detected during the first cycle of alternation, and many changes were not detected even after nearly one minute of alternation[9]. When the blank screen was removed, eliminating the disruption caused by the global transient, the changes were detected easily[9,10]. The change blindness caused by a flashed blank screen suggests the possibility that other forms of global transient should be equally successful in hiding changes. In fact, another recent study has demonstrated comparable results when changes are made contingent on blinks[11].

All of these findings illustrate the absence of a precise visual representation that survives global transients, yet they all suffer from one potential criticism. In all of these experiments, the global transient effectively covers the location of the change. Perhaps the blank screen, eye movement or blink actually serves as a mask, interrupting processing at that location. Another recent series of studies eliminates the masking explanation using the same alternating images used in the flicker studies. Rather than interspersing a blank screen, experimenters flashed a set of dot patterns at arbitrary positions on the image simultaneously with the image change[12]. These dots created several additional local transients, giving the appearance of a mud splash hitting the windscreen of a car. However, they did not mask the image change. Even so, these additional local transients had an effect similar to an eye movement or a flashed blank screen: observers could not detect changes immediately, even though the changes produced local retinal transients. Although the degree of change blindness was somewhat attenuated relative to performance in the flicker paradigm (R.A. Rensink, pers. commun.), change detection still required substantial time and effort.

The role of attention and expectations

The relatively long detection latencies in these studies of change blindness suggest that change detection is an active searching process in which individual objects are encoded and compared sequentially across views. Although the data do not speak directly to the nature of the search for changes, one particular result reinforces this possibility. Changes to objects in the 'center of interest' of a scene (according to independent ratings) are detected more readily, even when the physical magnitude of the change is comparable to that of a non-central change[9,10]. This finding suggests that attention is focused on central objects either more rapidly or more often, thereby allowing faster change detection. The notion of a center of interest has important implications for how we encode our environment. Given the results of the mud splash and flicker experiments, we know that changes will not be encoded automatically and that some effort is needed to detect changes even with a localized transient. Apparently the center of interest benefit derives not from the automatic representation of a precise visual image but from the abstraction of a scene's contents.

If abstraction plays a central role in our representation of scenes from one view to the next, then broad expectations about a scene may influence how we encode objects in that scene and, consequently, how we represent those objects. Interestingly, some of the early work on scene context and expectations found similar change blindness and center of interest effects[13,14]. For example, in one experiment, observers viewed scenes that included both

Box 2. Recognition memory for photographs

In typical studies of scene memory, observers viewed hundreds and sometimes thousands of photographs of natural scenes. Later, they tried to identify which photographs they had studied and which they had never viewed before[a,b,c,d]. Although the larger conclusion of these studies was that observers can recognize previously viewed photographs at surprisingly high rates (sometimes exceeding 95% recognition after extended delays), several studies noted that memory for the images was not tied to the precise visual form of the image[c,e]. When previously viewed photographs were mirror-reversed during a test, observers did not detect the change and reported them as previously viewed[c]. These findings suggest not only that we fail to detect changes to the exact visual form of a scene but, also, that we can extract the gist or meaning of a scene and use it for recognition[a].

References

A NICKERSON, R.S. (1965) SHORT-TERM MEMORY FOR COMPLEX MEANINGFUL VISUAL CONFIGURATIONS: A DEMONSTRATION OF CAPACITY *CAN. J. PSYCHOL.* 19, 155–160

B SHEPARD, R.N. (1967) RECOGNITION MEMORY FOR WORDS, SENTENCES, AND PICTURES *J. VERB. LEARN. VERB. BEHAV.* 6, 156–163

C STANDING, L, CONEZIO, J. AND HABER, R.N. (1970) PERCEPTION AND MEMORY FOR PICTURES: SINGLE-TRIAL LEARNING OF 2500 VISUAL STIMULI *PSYCHONOMIC SCI.* 19, 73–74

D STANDING, L. (1973) LEARNING 10,000 PICTURES. *Q. J. EXP. PSYCHOL.* 25, 207–222

E PEDZEK, K. ET AL. (1988) PICTURE MEMORY: RECOGNIZING ADDED AND DELETED DETAILS *J. EXP. PSYCHOL. LEARN. MEM. COGNIT.* 14, 468–476

changed. Observers were more likely to notice changes to the schema-inconsistent objects than the schema-consistent ones (also see Ref. 15). Unexpected objects are more likely to garner attentional resources, and attended objects are more likely to be retained from one view to the next. More recently, superior recognition of inconsistent objects has been shown in recognition of objects from real rooms[16] (but see Ref. 13 for evidence that schema-consistent objects ate better retained). Friedman anticipated many current claims of change blindness when she noted that for expected objects: 'local visual details of objects …are thus not generally encoded'[14]. She also made the prediction that any change not altering the abstract description of a scene substantially is unlikely to be detected.

If scene schemas help determine which changes will be noticed, then models proposing precise representations of the visual details of our environment may still prevail. Perhaps change blindness only applies to peripheral and unattended objects. Even if the visual details of peripheral objects are not represented precisely, the details of centrally attended objects may be. Several laboratories have tested this possibility.

Changes to attended objects

One test of the detectability of changes to attended objects comes from a task in which participants duplicate a pattern of colored blocks[17]. Participants were observing the display carefully, in order to perform an action, so the model must be considered the center of interest of the scene. Yet, they failed to notice a change to the model pattern when it occurred during an eye movement.

In another series of studies[18], observers viewed an array of five objects on a computer monitor. After two seconds, the array was replaced with a blank screen, followed shortly by another array of five objects. The second array was either identical to the first or was different in one of three ways: (a) one of the objects was moved to a previously empty location, (b) one object was replaced by an object that was not in the original array, or (c) two objects in the original array switched places. Observers were asked to determine whether or not any change had occurred (see Refs 19 and 20 for earlier work using a similar method). As in the flicker paradigm, observers missed changes when an object was replaced with a different object or when

consistent and inconsistent objects in preparation for an upcoming recognition task[14]. During the testing phase, observers were asked to discriminate previously viewed images from similar images in which an object had been

Box 3. Insights from film makers

In the movie *Ace Ventura: When Nature Calls*, the pieces on a chess board disappear completely from one shot to the next. In *Goodfellas*, a child is playing with blocks that appear and disappear across shots. One inevitable consequence of film production is the need to shoot scenes out of order, and often to shoot components of the same scene at different times. As a result, unintentionally, many details within a scene may change from one view to the next. Although film makers go to considerable effort to eliminate such errors, almost every movie—in fact, almost every cut—has some continuity mistake. Yet, most of the time, people are blind to these changes. (Film makers are, of course, justified in trying to eliminate glaring errors given the potential costs of some audience members noticing the change. If just one viewer notices such a change, the popular media and the Internet community will publicize the change and inspire people to look for the editing mistake rather than focusing on the movie.)

Film makers have long had the intuition that changes to the visual details of a scene across cuts are not detected by audiences, particularly when editing allows for smooth transitions[a]. For example, the film maker Lev Kuleshov[b] notes that: 'convincing montage makes the audience overlook … minor defects (for example when the actors costume changes between shots), though I repeat that this is only possible if the scene is edited correctly (in case of bad montage the blunder will leap to the eye).' Dmytryk[a] notes that change blindness is evident when mistakes occur: 'far from the viewer's center of interest. If he is watching the actor's eyes, a mismatch of an arm or hand will be ignored nine times out of ten.' Such intuitions underlie Hochberg's more recent speculations about the 'sketchiness' of visual memory[c] and clearly predict the center of interest effects described in the text.

The craft of film editing constitutes a rich body of knowledge about vision. Film makers must do explicitly what our visual system does automatically: they must combine a series of partial views (individual shots) into a coherent whole (a continuous scene) without audiences noticing the transitions. Some editors even suggest ways to cause audiences to move their eyes or blink, thereby allowing a cut to go unnoticed[a]. This process of constructing a continuous visual scene has taught film makers that the visual details are not central to our understanding of a scene, but it has also given them intuitions about what is central. For example, film makers track the gaze direction of actors in each shot and are careful not to violate the relative spatial locations of gaze targets. Ongoing empirical studies of the importance of cues such as gaze direction and motion in motion pictures may provide a better understanding of how we perceive the layout of scenes in the real world.

References

A DMYTRYK, E. (1984) *ON FILM EDITING: AN INTRODUCTION TO THE ART OF FILM CONSTRUCTION*, FOCAL PRESS.

B KULESHOV, L. (1987) *SELECTED WORKS: FIFTY YEARS IN FILMS* (AGRACHEV, D. AND BELENKAYA, N., TRANSLATORS), RADUGA PUBLISHERS.

C HOCHBERG, J. (1986) REPRESENTATION OF MOTION AND SPACE IN VIDEO AND CINEMATIC DISPLAYS, IN *HANDBOOK OF PERCEPTION AND HUMAN PERFORMANCE* (VOL. 1) (BOFF, K.R., KAUFMAN, L.K. AND THOMAS, J.P., EDS), PP. 22.1–22.64, JOHN WILEY AND SONS.

two objects switched places. As in the block-copying task, observers clearly focused attention on the objects in each display. The primary goal of the task was change detection, so they knew that they should encode the objects. In recent pilot studies using the same paradigm coupled with eye tracking (D.J. Simons and M. Spivey-Knowlton, unpublished), we found that, typically, observers look at all of the objects in the display. Thus, change blindness does not appear to result from a failure to focus attention on the target object during the trial.

Although these two studies using different methods converge on the conclusion that even attended objects may not be encoded sufficiently to allow change detection, both involved displays in which the observer's attention shifts from object to object during encoding. Perhaps our visual system can only tolerate one central object at a time. Successful change detection may only occur when

Box 4. What is in a view

The word 'view' has a number of distinct meanings in perception research. A view can refer to a single fixation, a single viewing position or angle, or even a photograph of a scene. Here we take a view to be an unchanging image, essentially a snapshot of a scene. For studies of visual integration across eye movements (see Box 1), views are equivalent to fixations; observers fixate a single image and after they move their eyes, the scene has been changed, producing a different view. In studies of change detection across simulated saccades, each time the image changes observers experience a different view. In motion pictures, each change in camera angle produces a new view of the scene even though the content of the scene itself may be unchanged. Across a cut, a view change occurs between the final frame of the first shot and the initial frame of the second shot. Using this definition, all of the work we discuss involves changes across views, even when the changes occur across long delay intervals.

the target object is the central object immediately before and after the change. To examine this possibility, we used motion pictures to change an object that remained central throughout the scene[21] (see Box 3). In these films, a single character performed a simple action such as rising from a chair and answering a telephone or entering through a doorway and sitting in a chair. During the action sequence, we cut from one camera angle to another, and during that cut, the original actor in the scene was replaced by a different person who then completed the action. The changes in camera angle followed conventional editing techniques by cutting in the middle of the action[22]. Even though the character was clearly the central object in the scene, 67% of observers failed to detect the change from one actor to another. Despite their change blindness, observers could describe the action sequence accurately and sometimes described properties of one or both actors. The actors were clearly dis-criminable; when given a set of films, half of which had changes to the actor and half of which did not, observers who had been instructed to look for changes had little trouble detecting them (see Box 3).

Outstanding questions

• Evidence reviewed in the text suggests that scene-inconsistent objects are coded more thoroughly than scene-consistent objects[14,16,29]. How do we form expectations for a scene and to what extent do they influence our coding of objects and our ability to detect changes? If expectations influence what we attend to in a scene, then an instructional manipulation might lead to a radical difference in change blindness. Specifically, we would predict that a single change occurring in an ambiguous scene might be noticed for one interpretation but not another. More specifically, would changes only be detected when they violate expectations about a scene?

• When observers are not searching actively for a change, in general, they do not detect changes, even to the central object in a scene. When our behavioral goal is not change detection, we tend to encode the gist of a scene without explicitly coding the details that would allow change detection. In such cases, we are attending to objects and scenes, but we do not appear to encode the details necessary for change detection. What then does it mean to 'attend to' an object? Are there different kinds of attention that might influence change detection? How does the attention that leads to successful change detection differ from the kind of attention that makes an object the center of interest?

• What sorts of changes are likely to be noticed and what differentiates those from unnoticed ones? We have some evidence that changes to spatial layout are detected more readily than changes to object properties[18], but a simple thought experiment shows that some property changes should be easy to notice. For example, if one of the actors in a video were replaced with a skunk, people would certainly notice the change. What aspect of this change would make it noticed more easily?

• Does change blindness indicate the absence of representations? Although this conclusion may be appealing, the possibility remains that more sensitive measures than change detection would reveal some underlying representation. Recent work on inattentional blindness shows that background objects in the visual field can influence judgments even if observers are unaware of their existence[30]. If so, what is the nature of these representations (for example, how precise and detailed are they) and in what ways do they influence our behavior? If such 'implicit' representations are precise and detailed, why do they not allow us to detect changes?

- How can we reconcile evidence for form-specific visual memory in priming studies[31,32] with change blindness?

Although these findings demonstrate that changes to objects in the center of interest are not necessarily noticed, they support the claim that attention and abstract encoding are necessary for change detection. When observers search for and encode the features that individuate people, they can detect the change. Yet, under natural viewing conditions, they are unlikely to do so. Instead, they encode the gist of the scene (in this case, the specific action and a few characteristics of the actor) and ignore the visual details. As long as the gist remains the same, change detection is unlikely because observers have not expended the effort to encode more details. This encoding strategy makes sense given the innumerable perceptual features in a natural scene or event, but it also illustrates the degree to which we lack a detailed representation of our world.

Although these findings of change blindness, taken together, support the conclusion that we lack a precise representation of our visual world from one view to the next, none of them focused on the representation of real objects in our environment. All of them presented scenes and objects on computer monitors and television displays which clearly lack many of the properties of real objects. One final series of studies examined the possibility that computer displays and motion pictures do not reflect how we process objects in the real world. In these studies, we extended the person change video studies[21] to the real world. Imagine that a person approaches you and asks for directions. Kindly, you oblige and begin describing the route. While you are talking, two people interrupt you rudely by carrying a door right between you and the person you were talking to. Surely you would notice if the person you were talking to was then replaced by a completely different person. When we actually conducted this study, only 50% of observers noticed the change (D.J. Simons and D.T. Levin, unpublished). The two experimenters wore different clothing, were different heights and builds, had different haircuts and had noticeably different voices.

Interestingly, those who did notice the change were students of roughly the same age as the experimenters and those who failed to notice it were older than the experimenters. We theorized that this age difference may reflect a difference in how people abstracted the gist of the scene. Older participants would be more likely to encode the event as 'some student asking directions'; younger participants would be more likely to individuate the features of a person in their own social group and, thereby, would be more likely to encode those features that would discriminate the two experimenters[23]. To examine this possibility, we replicated the door event with the same two experimenters dressed as construction workers (again with different clothing) under the assumption that these costumes would place the experimenters in a social group distinct from the students. Under these conditions, fewer than half of the students noticed the change. These studies demonstrate convincingly that paying attention to an object by no means guarantees change detection. The central object in a scene and the focus of a social interaction changed without observers noticing. As in studies of recognition memory for objects in photographs and rooms[14,16], observers were unlikely to notice changes that did not violate the gist of the scene. In this case, as long as the rough description of the scene was the same before and after the change, observers did not notice.

SUMMARY AND FUTURE DIRECTIONS

Taken as a whole, these findings provide a striking picture of our ability to perceive and represent scenes. Although the ability to discriminate and recognize photographs of scenes can be exceptionally good[24–28], memory for the properties and features of objects in scenes is surprisingly transitory. Findings from research on perception for action, change detection, motion picture perception and real world interactions all suggest that the visual details of object properties are not retained automatically from one view to the next. We fail to notice changes to scenes when they do not produce a motion on our retina that attracts attention. Although changes to central objects are more likely to be detected, they are not detected automatically.

Therefore, attention is necessary, but not sufficient, for change detection.

Given failures of change detection, we must question the assumption that we have a detailed representation of our visual world. And, given our success in interacting and behaving in our environment, we must ask whether such detailed representations are even necessary. Although change blindness might appear to contradict our phenomenal experience of a stable, continuous world it may actually account for this impression. During any fixation we have a rich visual experience. From that visual experience, we abstract the meaning or gist of a scene. During the next visual fixation, we again have a rich visual experience, and if the gist is the same, our perceptual system assumes the details are the same. Consider, for example, a busy city street. In this kind of scene, a variety of property changes occur during the normal course of events. People are occluded by walking behind barriers, cars move, revealing previously hidden objects on the sidewalk, and people may shift a bag to the other arm or take out a handkerchief. All of these changes are rapid and might occur during saccades or between successive glances. A system that is too precise in tracking visual details would, in the words of William James, present a 'blooming, buzzing confusion'. In contrast, a system that gives a rich perceptual experience at any instant, but only integrates the gist (and perhaps the layout and movement direction) from one view to the next would give the impression of stability rather than chaos. This system would be successful at ignoring unreliable object property information, focusing instead on the information that the perceiver needs to know. Thus, change blindness supports the phenomenal experience of continuity by not preserving too much information from one view to the next.

ACKNOWLEDGMENTS

The author thanks John Henderson and Ron Rensink for their comments and suggestions on an earlier draft of this manuscript.

REFERENCES

LINDBERG, D.C. (1976) THEORIES OF VISION FROM AL-KINDI TO KEPLER, UNIVERSITY OF CHICAGO PRESS

GRIMES, J. (1996) ON THE FAILURE TO DETECT CHANGES IN SCENES ACROSS SACCADES, IN PERCEPTION (VANCOUVER STUDIES IN COGNITIVE SCIENCE) (VOL. 2) (AKINS, K, ED.), PP. 89–110, OXFORD UNIVERSITY PRESS

CURRIE, C. ET AL. (1995) MAINTAINING VISUAL STABILITY ACROSS SACCADES: ROLE OF THE SACCADE TARGET OBJECT. TECHNICAL REPORT UIUC-BI-HPP-95–01, BECKMAN INSTITUTE, UNIVERSITY OF ILLINOIS

McCONKIE, G.W. AND CURRIE, C.B. (1996) VISUAL STABILITY ACROSS SACCADES WHILE VIEWING COMPLEX PICTURES J. EXP. PSYCHOL. HUM. PERCEPT. PERFORM. 22, 563–581

DENNETT, D.C. (1991) CONSCIOUSNESS EXPLAINED, LITTLE, BROWN AND COMPANY

O'REGAN, J.K. (1992) SOLVING THE 'REAL' MYSTERIES OF VISUAL PERCEPTION: THE WORLD AS AN OUTSIDE MEMORY CAN. J. PSYCHOL. 46, 461–488

STROUD, J.M. (1955) THE FINE STRUCTURE OF PSYCHOLOGICAL TIME. IN INFORMATION THEORY IN PSYCHOLOGY: PROBLEMS AND METHODS (QUASTLER, H., ED.), PP. 174–207, FREE PRESS

BLACKMORE, S.J. ET AL. (1995) IS THE RICHNESS OF OUR VISUAL WORLD AN ILLUSION? TRANSSACCADIC MEMORY FOR COMPLEX SCENES PERCEPTION 24, 1075–1081

RENSINK, R.A., O'REGAN, J.K. AND CLARK, J.J. (1997) TO SEE OR NOT TO SEE: THE NEED FOR ATTENTION TO PERCEIVE CHANGES IN SCENES PSYCHOL. SCI. 8, 368–373

TARR, M.J. AND AGINSKY, V. (1996) FROM OBJECTS TO SCENES: SPECULATIONS ON SIMILARITIES AND DIFFERENCES. PAPER PRESENTED AT THE SCENE RECOGNITION WORKSHOP, MAX-PLANK-INSTITUT FÜR BIOLOGISCHE KYBERNETIK, TÜBINGEN, GERMANY.

O'REGAN, J.K. ET AL. (1997) PICTURE CHANGES DURING BLINKS: NOT SEEING WHERE YOU LOOK AND SEEING WHERE YOU DON'T LOOK INVEST. OPHTHALMOL. VIS. SCI. 38, S707

O'REGAN, J.K., RENSINK, R.A. AND CLARK, J.J. (1996) "MUD SPLASHES" RENDER PICTURE CHANGES INVISIBLE INVEST. OPHTHALMOL. VIS. SCI. 37, S213

BREWER, W.F. AND TREYENS, J.C. (1981) ROLE OF SCHEMATA IN MEMORY FOR PLACES COGNIT. PSYCHOL. 13, 207–230

FRIEDMAN, A. (1979) FRAMING PICTURES: THE ROLE OF KNOWLEDGE IN AUTOMATIZED ENCODING AND MEMORY FOR GIST J. EXP. PSYCHOL. GEN. 108, 316–355

HENDERSON, J.M., HOLLINGWORTH, A. AND WEEKS, P.A.J. (1996) THE INFLUENCE OF SCENE CONTEXT ON OBJECT PERCEPTION. PAPER PRESENTED AT THE SCENE RECOGNITION

Workshop, Max-Plank-Institut für Biologische Kybernetik, Tübingen, Germany

Pedzek, K. *et al.* (1989) Memory for real-world scenes: The role of consistency with schema expectation *J. Exp. Psychol. Learn. Mem. Cognit.* 15, 587–595

Ballard, D.H., Hayhoe, M.M. and Pelz, J.B. (1995) Memory representations in natural tasks *J. Cogn. Neurosci.* 7, 66–80

Simons, D.J. (1996) In sight, out of mind: When object representations fail *Psychol. Sci.* 7, 301–305

Pashler, H. (1988) Familiarity and visual change detection *Percept. Psychophysiol.* 44, 369–378

Phillips, W.A. (1974) On the distinction between sensory storage and short-term visual memory *Percept. Psychophysiol.* 16, 283–290

Levin, D.T. and Simons, D.J. Failure to detect changes to attended objects in motion pictures *Psychonomic Bull. Rev.* (In press)

Dmytryk, E. (1984) *On Film Editing: An Introduction to the Art of Film Construction*, Focal Press

Rothbart, M. and John, O.P. (1985) Social categorization and behavioral episodes: A cognitive analysis of the effects of intergroup contact *J. Social Issues* 41, 81–104

Intraub, H. (1981) Rapid conceptual identification of sequentially presented pictures *J. Exp. Psychol. Hum. Percept. Perform.* 7, 604–610

Nickerson, R.S. (1965) Short-term memory for complex meaningful visual configurations: A demonstration of capacity *Can. J. Psychol.* 19, 155–160

Potter, M.C. (1976) Short-term conceptual memory for pictures. *J. Exp. Psychol. Hum. Learn. Mem.* 2, 509–522

Shepard, R.N. (1967) Recognition memory for words, sentences, and pictures *J. Verb. Learn. Verb. Behav.* 6, 156–163

Standing, L., Conezio, J. and Haber, R.N. (1970) Perception and memory for pictures: Single-trial learning of 2500 visual stimuli *Psychonomic Sci.* 19, 73–74

Henderson, J.M. (1997) Transsaccadic memory and integration during real-world object perception *Psychol. Sci.* 8, 51–55

Moore, C.M. and Egeth, H. (1997) Perception without attention: Evidence of grouping under conditions of Inattention *J. Exp. Psychol. Hum. Percept. Perform.* 23, 339–352

DeSchepper, B. and Treisman, A. (1996) Visual memory for novel shapes: Implicit coding without attention *J. Exp. Psychol. Learn. Mem. Cognit.* 22, 27–47

Graf, P. and Ryan, L. (1990) Transfer-appropriate processing for implicit and explicit memory *J. Exp. Psychol. Learn. Mem. Cognit.* 16, 978–992

CHAPTER 4
Attention and Consciousness

Paying Attention

DANIEL REISBERG

Consider your circumstances right now. You are paying attention to this page, reading these words. However, there are thousands of other inputs available to you, things you could pay attention to if you chose. For example, you're paying attention to the meanings of these words, but you could choose instead to look at the shapes of the letters, rather than the words themselves. You could, if you chose, contemplate the color of the paper, or its texture. If you wanted to, you could look up from the page and look at any of the people or objects in the room with you. And these are just the *visual* inputs. There are also many sounds in the room. Perhaps the radio is on, or perhaps you can hear someone at the next desk turning pages. Perhaps the room is silent, but even so, you could focus on the silence, much as a sentry listens carefully to detect intruders.

This list could easily be extended, but by now the point should be clear: The stimulus you're attending to is only one of many that are available to you, and this fact invites two crucial observations. First, it seems clear that you could choose to pay attention to any of the things just mentioned, and if you did, you would be virtually oblivious to the other things on the list. Indeed, until you read the previous paragraph, you probably were oblivious to the other stimuli we mentioned! How do you do this? How do you manage to avoid the distractors and focus your attention in just the manner you wish, selecting only one input of many? Second, there seems to be one thing you cannot do: you cannot pay attention to all of these things at once. If you start musing about your weekend, you are likely to lose track of what's on the page; if you start planning your term paper, you won't finish the reading assignment. Of course, it is possible in some circumstances to divide your attention, to deal with two different inputs at once. You can, if you choose, hum a melody while reading these words; most people can walk and chew gum at the same time; and so on. But where are the limits? When can you do two (or more) things at the same time, and when can't you?

SELECTIVE LISTENING

Many early studies of attention employed a task called **shadowing**. In this task, participants hear a tape recording of someone speaking and must echo this speech back, word for word, while they are listening to it. Shadowing is initially challenging, but it becomes relatively easy after a minute of practice. (You might try it, shadowing a voice on the radio or TV.)

In most experiments, the message to be shadowed, the **attended channel**, is presented through stereo headphones, so that participants hear the attended channel through, say, the right earphone. A different message—the **unattended channel**—is presented in the left earphone, and participants are instructed simply to ignore this message. This overall setup is referred to as **dichotic listening**.

PREVIEW OF CHAPTER THEMES

- In this chapter, we argue that multiple mechanisms are involved in the seemingly simple act of paying attention. In particular, people must take many different steps to facilitate the processing of desired inputs; in the absence of these steps, our ability to pick up information from the world is dramatically reduced.

- Many of the steps we take in order to perceive have a "cost" attached to them: They require the commitment of mental resources. These resources are limited in availability, and this is part of the reason why we cannot pay attention to two inputs at once: This would require more resources than we have.

- Divided attention (the attempt to do two things at once) can also be understood in terms of resources:

We can perform two activities at the same time, provided that the activities do not require more resources than we have available.

- Some of the mental resources we use are specialized, and so they are required only for tasks of a certain sort. Other resources are more general, needed for a wide range of tasks. The resource demand of a task can, however, be diminished through practice.

- We emphasize that attention is best understood not as a process or mechanism, but as an achievement. Like most achievements, paying attention involves many different elements, all of which help us to be aware of the stimuli we're interested in, and not pulled off track by irrelevant distractors.

Under these circumstances, participants easily follow one message, and their shadowing performance is generally near perfect. At the same time, however, they hear remarkably little from the unattended channel. If we ask them, after a minute or so of shadowing, to report what the unattended message was about, they cannot (Cherry, 1953). They cannot even tell if the unattended channel contained a coherent message or just random words. In fact, in one study, participants shadowed coherent prose in the attended channel, while in the unattended channel they heard a text in Czech, read with English pronunciation. Thus, the individual sounds (the vowels, the consonants) resembled English, but the message itself was (for an English speaker) gibberish. After a minute of shadowing, only 4 of 30 participants detected the peculiar character of the unattended message (Treisman, 1964).

More recent studies have documented a similar pattern with *visual* inputs. Participants in one study watched a TV screen that showed a team of players in white shirts passing a ball back and forth; the participants had to signal each time the ball changed hands. Interwoven with these players (and visible on the same TV screen) was another team, wearing black shirts, also passing a ball back and forth; participants were instructed to ignore these. Participants easily did this selective task, and they were so intent on the white team that they didn't see other, rather salient, events that appeared on the screen, right in front of their eyes. For example, they entirely failed to notice when another player wearing a gorilla costume walked through the middle of

the game, pausing briefly to thump his chest before exiting! (Neisser & Becklen 1975; Simons & Chabris, 1999; for a similar result in which participants fail to perceive unattended faces, see Jenkins, Lavie, & Driver, 2005).

However, people are not altogether oblivious to the unattended channel: In selective listening experiments, they easily and accurately report whether the unattended channel contained human speech, musical instruments, or silence. If the unattended channel contains human speech, they can report whether the speaker was male or female, had a high or low voice, was speaking loudly or softly. (For reviews of this early work, see Broadbent, 1958; Kahneman, 1973.) It seems, then, that physical attributes of the unattended channel are heard, even though participants seem oblivious to the unattended channel's semantic content.

Some Unattended Inputs Are Detected

However, some results do not fit this pattern. Some bits of the unattended input seem to "leak" through and get noticed. In one study, people were asked to shadow one passage while ignoring a second passage. Embedded within the unattended channel, though, was a series of names, including the participant's own name. Overall, participants heard very little of the unattended message, in keeping with the other studies mentioned. Nonetheless, about a third of them did hear their own name (Moray, 1959). As we commonly say, the name seemed to "catch" their attention.

Other contents will also catch your attention, if you are suitably primed for them: Mention of a movie you just saw, or mention of your favorite restaurant, will often be noticed in the unattended channel. More generally, words with some personal importance will also be noticed (A. R. A. Conway, Cowan, & Bunting, 2001; Wood & Cowan, 1995).

These results are often referred to under the banner of the **cocktail party effect**. There you are at a party, engaged in conversation. Many other conversations are taking place in the room, but somehow you're able to "tune them out." You are aware that other people in the room are talking, but you don't have a clue what they're saying. All you hear is the single conversation you're attending, plus a buzz of background noise. But now imagine that someone a few steps away from you mentions the name of a close friend of yours. Your attention is immediately caught by this, and you find yourself listening to that other conversation and (momentarily) oblivious to the conversation you had been engaged in. This experience, easily observed outside the laboratory, is precisely parallel to the pattern of experimental data.

How can we put all of these results together? How can we explain both our general insensitivity to the unattended channel and also the cases in which the unattended channel "leaks through"?

Perceiving and the Limits on Cognitive Capacity

At the very start, we have two broad options for how we might think about attention. One option focuses on what we do with the *unattended* input. Specifically, the proposal is that we somehow block processing of the inputs we're not interested in, much as a sentry blocks the path of unwanted guests but simply stands back and allows legitimate guests to pass. This sort of proposal was central for early theories of attention, which suggested that we erect a filter that shields us from potential distractors. Desired information (the attended channel) is not filtered out and so goes on to receive further processing (Broadbent, 1958).

Evidence suggests we can shut out distractors in this way, but this "shutting out" seems to work on a distractor-by-distractor basis. In other words, we can inhibit our response to *this* distractor and do the same for *that* distractor, and these

efforts can be quite successful. However, the same efforts are of little value if some new distractor comes along; in that case, we need to develop a new skill aimed specifically at blocking the new intruder (Fenske, Raymond, Kessler, Westoby, & Tipper, 2005; Jacoby, Lindsay, & Hessels, 2003; Milliken, Joordens, Merikle, & Seiffert, 1998; Milliken & Tipper, 1998; Reisberg, Baron, & Kemler. 1980; Tsushima, Sasaki, & Watanabe, 2006).

In addition, further evidence indicates that this is only a small part of the story. That's because not only do we block the processing of distractors, but we are also able to *promote* the processing of *desired* stimuli.

Inattentional Blindness

As we saw in Chapter 3, perception involves a considerable amount of activity—as you organize and interpret the incoming stimulus information. One might think that this activity would require some initiative and some resources from you, and the evidence suggests that it does.

In one experiment, participants were told that they would see large "+" shapes on a computer screen, presented for 200 milliseconds, followed by a pattern mask. If the horizontal bar of the "+" was longer than the vertical, the participants were supposed to press one button; if the vertical was longer, they had to press a different button. As a complication, participants weren't allowed to look directly at the "+" Instead, they fixated (pointed their eyes at) a mark in the center of the computer screen—a **fixation target**—and the "+" shapes were shown just off to one side.

For the first three trials of the procedure, events proceeded just as the participants expected, and the task was relatively easy. On Trial 3, for example, participants made the correct response 78% of the time. On Trial 4, though, things were slightly different: While the target "+" was on the screen, the fixation target disappeared and was replaced by one of three shapes—a triangle, a rectangle, or a cross. Then the entire configuration (the "+" target and this new shape) was replaced by a pattern mask.

Immediately after the trial, participants were asked: Was there anything different on this trial? Was anything present, or anything changed, that wasn't there on previous trials? Remarkably, 89% of the participants reported that there was no change; they had apparently failed to see anything other than the (attended) "+." To probe the participants further, the researchers then told them (correctly) that during the previous trial the fixation target had momentarily disappeared and had been replaced by a shape. The participants were then asked what that shape had been and were explicitly given the choices of a triangle, a rectangle, or a cross. The responses to this question were essentially random. Even when probed in this fashion, participants seemed not to have seen the shape that had been directly in front of their eyes (Mack & Rock, 1998; also see Mack, 2003).

What's going on in this study? Some researchers have proposed that the participants in this experiment did see the target shapes but, a moment later, couldn't *remember* what they had just seen (Wolfe, 1999). Mack and Rock, however, offer a stronger claim: They note that the participants were not expecting any shapes to appear and were not in any way prepared for these shapes. As a consequence, Mack and Rock claim, the participants literally failed to see the shapes, even though they were staring straight at them. This failure to see, caused by inattention, has been dubbed **inattentional blindness** (Mack & Rock, 1998; also see Mack, 2003).

Which of these accounts is correct? Did participants fail to see the input? Or did they see it but, just a few milliseconds later, forget what they'd seen? For purposes of theory, this distinction is crucial, but for the moment let's emphasize what the two proposals have in common: By either account, our normal ability to see what's around us, and to make use of what we see, is dramatically diminished in the absence of attention.

Conscious Perception, Unconscious Perception

Mack and Rock, the investigators who documented the inattentional blindness phenomenon, draw a strong claim from these data: There is no perception, they claim, without attention. However, this claim needs an important refinement, and so, more precisely, Mack and Rock argue there is no *conscious* perception without attention (Mack & Rock, 1998. p. 14).

To see why this refinement is needed, consider the following experiment (Moore & Egeth, 1997; for other data pertinent to this claim, see Mack, 2003; Mack & Rock, 1998). Participants were shown a series of images on a

computer screen; each image contained two horizontal lines surrounded by a pattern of black and white dots, and the participants' task was to decide which of the two lines was longer, the top one or the bottom. For the first three trials of this procedure, the background dots on the computer screen were arranged randomly. On Trial 4, however, and with no warning to participants, the pattern of dots shown creates a stimulus configuration that reproduces a standard geometric illusion, the Müller-Lyer illusion. Focusing their attention on the two horizontal lines, however, the participants didn't perceive this pattern. When they were asked immediately after the trial whether they had noticed any pattern in the dots, none reported seeing the pattern. They were then told directly that there had been a pattern and were asked to choose it (out of four choices available); 90% selected one of the incorrect patterns. Plainly, then, this experiment reproduces the finding of inattentional blindness.

Nonetheless, the participants were influenced by the dot pattern. In the standard Müller-Lyer display, the "fins" make the top horizontal line appear longer than the bottom horizontal line, even though both lines are exactly the same length. The dot pattern in the Moore and Egeth displays did the same, and 95% of the participants reported that the top line was longer than the bottom one, even though, in the display, both were the same length.

Notice, then, that the participants were completely unaware of the fins, but were still influenced by them. No participant reported seeing the fins, but virtually all responded in the length judgment in a fashion consistent with the fins. (For related data, see Russell & Driver, 2005.) The obvious conclusion, then, is that participants did perceive the fins in some way, but did not consciously perceive them. We will return to issues of conscious and unconscious perception in Chapter 15; for now, it seems attention may be needed for *conscious* perception, but perhaps you can unconsciously detect (and be influenced by) patterns in the world even in the absence of attention.

Change Blindness

Similar conclusions emerge from studies of **change blindness**—observers' inability to detect changes in scenes they are looking directly at. In some experiments, participants are shown pairs of pictures separated by a brief blank interval (e.g., Rensink, O'Regan, & Clark, 1997). The pictures in the pair are identical except for some single aspect: an "extra" engine shown on the airplane in one picture and not in the other; a man not wearing a hat in one picture but wearing one in the other; and so on. Participants know from the start that their task is to detect these changes, but even with this clear understanding of the task, the task is quite difficult. If the change involves something central to the scene, observers may need as many as a dozen alternations between the pictures before they detect the change. If the change involves some peripheral aspect of the scene, then as many as 25 alternations may be required.

A related pattern emerges when participants watch movies. In one study, observers watched a movie of two women having a conversation. During the film, the camera first focused on one woman, then on the other, just as it would in an ordinary TV show or movie. The crucial element of this experiment, though, was that aspects of the scene changed every time the camera angle changed. For example, when the camera was pointing at Woman A, you could plainly see the red plates on the table between the women. When the camera was shifted to point at Woman B, just a fraction of a second later, the plates had miraculously turned white. Most observers, however, noticed none of these changes. In one experiment, a film containing a toral of nine changes was shown to ten participants. Only one participant claimed to notice the changes, and when pressed, this participant merely said there was a difference in "the way people were sitting." When allowed to watch the film again and told explicitly to look out for changes, observers noticed (on average) only two of the nine changes (D. T. Levin & Simons, 1997; Shore & Klein, 2000; Simons, 2000).

Incredibly, the same result pattern can be documented with live (not filmed) events. In a remarkable study, an investigator (let's call him "Bo") approached pedestrians on a college campus and asked for directions to a certain building. During the conversation, two men carrying a door approached and deliberately walked *between* Bo and the research participant. As a result, Bo was momentarily hidden (by the door) from the participant's view, and in that moment Bo traded places with one of the men carrying the door. A second later, therefore, Bo was able to walk away, unseen, while the new fellow (who had been carrying the door) stayed behind and continued the conversation with the participant.

Roughly half of the participants failed to notice this switch. They continued the conversation as though nothing had happened—despite the fact that Bo and his replacement were wearing different clothes, had easily distinguishable voices, and so on. When asked directly whether anything odd had happened in this event, many participants commented only that it was rude that the guys carrying the door had walked right through their conversation (Simons & Ambinder, 2005; for other studies of change blindness, see Most et al., 2001, and Rensink, 2002; for similar effects with auditory stimuli, see Gregg & Samuel, 2008; Vitevitch, 2003; for studies of why some unattended stimuli nonetheless "catch" our attention, see Most, Scholl, Clifford, & Simons, 2005).

Early Versus Late Selection

In several paradigms, then, people seem oblivious to stimuli that are directly in front of their eyes—whether the stimuli are simple displays on a computer screen, or photographs, or movies, or real-life events. As we noted earlier, though, there are two ways we might think about these results: These studies may reveal genuine limits on *perception*, so that participants literally don't see these stimuli; or these studies may reveal limits on *memory*, so that people do see the stimuli but immediately forget what they have just seen.

Which proposal is correct? One approach to this question hinges on when the perceiver selects the desired input, and (correspondingly) when the perceiver ceases the processing of the unattended input. According to the **early selection** hypothesis, the attended input is identified and privileged from the start, so that the unattended input receives little analysis (and so is never perceived). According to the **late selection** hypothesis, however, all inputs receive relatively complete analysis. But it is only the attended input that reaches consciousness, or (as a related idea) it is only the attended input that is remembered.

It turns out that each hypothesis captures part of the truth. On the one side, we have already considered a case in which people seem genuinely unaware of the distractors but are nevertheless influenced by them (pp. 102–103). This seems to be a case of *late selection*, in which the distractors were perceived, but the perception—even if influential—was not conscious. But, on the other side, we can also find evidence for *early selection*, with distractor stimuli receiving little analysis, and indeed falling out of the stream of processing at a very early stage. Relevant evidence comes, for example, from studies that record the electrical activity of the brain in the milliseconds after a stimulus has arrived. These studies confirm that the brain activity for attended inputs is distinguishable from that for unattended inputs just 60 or 70 ms after the stimulus presentation—a time interval in which the earliest sensory processing is still under way (Hillyard, Vogel, & Luck, 1998). Apparently, in these cases, the attended input is privileged from the very start.

Other data also provide evidence for early selection. For example, recording from neurons in Area V4 of the visual cortex shows that the neurons are more responsive to attended inputs than to unattended ones, almost as if attention made the light areas seem brighter and dim areas seem darker (Carrasco, Ling, & Read, 2004; Carrasco, Penpeci-Talgar, & Eckstein, 2000; Reynolds, Pasternak, & Desimone, 2000). Other studies suggest that attention may modulate neural events even earlier in the stream of visual processing—perhaps as early as the lateral geniculate nucleus (O'Connor, Fukui, Pinsk, & Kastner, 2002; also see Yantis, 2008). These results argue powerfully that attention doesn't just change what we remember or what we're aware of. Attention can also literally change what we perceive.

But what accounts for this mixed pattern? Why do the data sometimes indicate late selection, and sometimes early? The answer depends in part on the nature of the attended input. If this input is particularly complex, then the processing of this input will demand a lot of effort and a lot of cognitive resources. (We will have more to say about these "resources" later in the chapter.) In this case, little effort will be left over for other stimuli, with the consequence that the other stimuli receive less processing, leading to a data pattern consistent with early selection. In contrast, if the attended input is relatively simple, processing will demand few resources, leaving more available for the unattended inputs. Here the unattended inputs will probably receive more analysis, and so we'll see the pattern of late selection (after Lavie, 1997, 2001, 2005; Macdonald & Lavie, 2008; for some challenges to this claim, though, see Mack, 2003).

Selective Priming

Whether selection is early or late, however, it's clear that looking directly at an input isn't by itself enough to allow conscious perception. But, in that case, what else is needed? Likewise, we've noted that people seem to hear little from the unattended channel during dichotic listening, but are reasonably likely to detect some inputs—such as their own name. How should we think about these facts? And, with this, we've also now suggested that "resources" are needed for perceiving, but what are those resources? Let's tackle these questions.

In Chapter 3, we proposed that recognition requires a network of detectors, and we argued that these detectors fire most readily, and most quickly, if they are suitably primed. But what does that priming involve? In some cases, priming is produced by one's visual experience—specifically, whether each detector has been used recently or frequently in the past. But as we suggested at the end of Chapter 3, priming can also come from another source: your expectations about what the stimulus will be.

The proposal, then, is that people can literally prepare themselves for perceiving by priming the suitable detectors. Let's hypothesize in addition that this priming isn't free. Instead, you must spend some effort or allocate some resources in order to do the priming, and let's suppose that these resources are in limited supply.

This simple idea helps explain several findings we've already met. Why don't participants notice the shapes in the inattentional blindness studies? It may be that they don't expect any stimulus, so they have no reason to prepare for any stimulus. As a result, the stimulus, when it's presented, falls on unprepared (thus, unresponsive) detectors.

What about selective listening? In this case, one does not want to hear the distractor, so devoting resources to the distractor would be, at best, a waste of these resources. Therefore, the detectors needed for the distractor receive no resources and so are unprimed, literally making it more difficult to hear the distractor. But why, on this account, does attention sometimes "leak," so that we do hear some aspects of the unattended input? Think about what will happen if your name is uttered on the unattended channel. The detectors for this stimulus are already primed, but this is not because you are, at that moment, expecting to hear your name. Instead, the detectors are primed simply because this is a stimulus you have often encountered in the past. Thanks to this prior exposure, the activation level of these detectors is already high; you don't need to prime them further. So these detectors will fire even if your attention is elsewhere.

Two Types of Priming

The idea, in short, is that resources are needed to prime detectors, and that those resources are in limited supply. These proposals certainly seem promising, but can we find evidence to confirm these claims directly? In a classic series of studies, Posner and Snyder (1975) gave people a straightforward task: A pair of letters was shown on a computer screen, and participants had to decide, as swiftly as they could, whether the letters were the same or different. So someone might see "A A" and answer "same," or might see "A B" and answer "different."

Before each pair, participants saw a warning signal. In the neutral condition, the warning signal was a plus sign ("+"). This signal notified participants that the stimuli were about to arrive but provided no other information. In a different condition, the warning signal was itself a letter and actually matched the stimuli to come. So someone might see the warning signal "C" followed by the pair "C C." In this case, the warning signal actually served to prime the participants for the stimuli. In a third condition, though, the warning signal was misleading. The warning signal was again a letter, but it was a letter different from the stimuli to come. Participants might see "C" followed by the pair "F F." Let's call these three conditions *neutral*, *primed*, and *misled*.

In this simple task, accuracy rates are very high. But the *speed* of responding varies from condition to condition, and we can use these speeds as a way of exploring what's going on in the participants' minds. Specifically, in each condition, Posner and Snyder recorded how quickly people responded. By comparing these response times (or RTs) in the *primed* and *neutral* conditions, we can ask what benefit there is from the prime. Likewise, by comparing RTs in the *misled* and *neutral* conditions, we can ask what cost there is, if any, from being misled.

Before we turn to the results, though, we need one further complication: Posner and Snyder ran this procedure in two different versions. In one version, the warning signal was an excellent predictor of the upcoming stimuli: For example, if the warning signal was an *A*, there was an 80% chance that the upcoming stimulus pair would contain As. In Posner and Snyder's terms, the warning signal provided a "high validity" prime. In a different version of the procedure, the warning signal was a poor predictor of the upcoming stimuli: If the warning signal was an *A*, there was only a 20% chance that the upcoming pair would contain As. This is the "low validity" condition.

Let's consider the low-validity condition first, and let's focus on those rare occasions in which the prime did match the subsequent stimuli. That is, we are focusing on 20% of the trials and ignoring the other 80%. In this condition, the participant can't use the prime as a basis for predicting the stimuli because, after all, the prime is a poor indicator of things to come. Therefore, the prime should not lead to any specific expectations. Nonetheless, we do expect faster RTs in the *primed* condition than in the *neutral* condition: Thanks to the prime, the relevant detectors have just fired, and so the detectors should still be warmed up. When the target stimuli arrive, therefore, the detectors should fire more readily, allowing a faster response. This is, in effect, a case of repetition priming, as described in Chapter 3.

The results bear this out, RTs were reliably faster (by roughly 30 ms) in the *primed* condition than in the *neutral* condition. Apparently, then, detectors can be primed by mere exposure to a stimulus. Or, to put it differently, priming is observed even in the absence of expectations. This priming seems truly stimulus-based.

What about the *misled* condition? With a low-validity prime, misleading participants had no effect: Performance in the *misled* condition was the same as performance in the *neutral* condition. Priming the "wrong" detector, it seems, takes nothing away from the other detectors—including the detectors actually needed for that trial. This fits with our discussion in Chapter 3: Each of the various detectors works independently of the others. Thus, priming one detector obviously influences the functioning of that specific detector, but neither helps nor hinders the other detectors.

Let's look next at the high-validity primes. In this condition, people might see, for example, a "J" as the warning signal, and then the stimulus pair "J J." Presentation of the prime itself will fire the J-detectors, and this should, once again, "warm up" these detectors, just as the low-validity primes did. Thus, we expect a stimulus-driven benefit from the prime. However, the high-validity primes may also have another influence: High-validity primes are excellent predictors of the stimulus to come. Participants are told this at the outset, and they have lots of opportunity to see that it is true. High-validity primes will therefore produce a warm-up effect and also an expectation effect, whereas low-validity primes produce only the warm-up. We should therefore expect the high-validity primes to help participants more than low-validity primes—and that's exactly what the data show. The combination of warm-up and expectations, in other words, leads to faster responses than warm-up alone. From the participants' point of view, it pays to know what the upcoming stimulus might be.

Just as important, though, is what happened in the *misled* condition: With high-validity primes, responses in the *misled* condition were *slower* than responses in the *neutral* condition. That is, misleading participants actually hurt performance. As a concrete example, *F*-detection was slower if G was primed, compared to *F*-detection when the prime was simply the neutral warning signal ("+").

Explaining the Costs and Benefits

The message of these data is clear: There are two types of primes. One type is stimulus-based—produced merely by presentation of the priming stimulus, with no role for expectations. The other type of priming is expectation-based, and is created only when the participant believes the prime allows a prediction of what's to come.

These types of primes can be distinguished in several ways. First, expectation-based priming is larger in magnitude than the stimulus-based priming, leading to a greater benefit in the RT data. Second, expectation-based priming takes longer to kick in: Stimulus-based priming can be observed immediately after the prime; priming based on expectations takes roughly a half second to develop (Neely, 1977).

Third, the two types of priming can also be distinguished in terms of their "cost." Stimulus-based priming appears to be "free," and so we can prime one detector without taking anything away from the other detectors. We see this in the low-validity condition, in the fact that the *misled* trials lead to responses just as fast as those in the *neutral* trials. Expectation-based priming, however, does have a cost, as we see in the high-validity condition. Here priming the "wrong" detector does take something away from the other detectors, and so

participants are worse off when they're misled than when they received no prime at all.

What produces this cost? As an analogy, think about being on a limited budget. Imagine that you have just $50 to spend on groceries. You can spend more on ice cream if you wish, but if you do, you'll have that much less to spend on other foods. Any increase in the ice cream allotment must be covered by a decrease somewhere else. This trade-off arises, though, only because of the limited budget. If you had unlimited funds, you could spend more on ice cream and still have enough money for everything else.

Expectation-based priming shows the same pattern. If the Q-detector is primed, this takes something away from the other detectors. Getting prepared for one target seems to make people less prepared for other targets. But we just said that this sort of pattern implies a limited "budget." If an unlimited supply of activation were available, one could prime the Q-detector and leave the other detectors just as they were. And that is the point: Expectation-based priming, by virtue of revealing costs when misled, reveals the presence of a **limited-capacity system**.

We can now put the pieces together. Ultimately, we need to explain the facts of **selective attention**, including the fact that while listening to one message you hear little content from other messages. To explain this, we have proposed that perceiving involves some work, and this work requires some limited mental resources. That is why you can't listen to two messages at the same time; doing so would demand more resources than you have. And now, finally, we are seeing evidence for those limited resources; The Posner and Snyder research (and many other results) reveals the workings of a limited-capacity system, just as our hypothesis demands.

Chronometric Studies and Spatial Attention

The Posner and Snyder study shows us how a person's expectations about an upcoming stimulus can influence the processing of that stimulus. But what exactly is the nature of these expectations? How precise, or how vague, are they? To see the point, imagine that participants are told, "The next stimulus will be a *T*," In this case, they know exactly what to get ready for. But now imagine that participants are told, "The next stimulus will be a letter" or

"The next stimulus will be on the left side of the screen," Will these cues allow people to prepare themselves?

These issues have been examined in studies of **spatial attention**—that is, our ability to focus on a particular position in space, and thus to be better prepared for any stimulus that appears in that position, In an early study, Posner, Snyder, and Davidson (1980) required their participants simply to detect letter presentations; the task was just to press a button as soon as a letter appeared. Participants kept their eyes pointed at a central fixation mark, and letters could appear either to the left or to the right of this mark.

For some trials, a neutral warning signal was presented, so that participants knew a trial was about to start but had no information about stimulus location. For other trials, an arrow was used as the warning signal. Sometimes the arrow pointed left, sometimes right; and the arrow was generally an accurate predictor of the location of the stimulus-to-come: If the arrow pointed right, the stimulus would be on the right side of the computer screen. (In the terms we used earlier, this is a high-validity cue.) On 20% of the trials, however, the arrow misled participants about location.

The results show a familiar pattern (Posner et al., 1980, Exp. 2): With high-validity priming, the data show a benefit from cues that correctly signal where the upcoming target will appear. Concretely, with a neutral warning signal, people took 266 ms to detect the signal. With a correct prime, they were faster: 249 ms. This isn't a huge difference, but keep the task in mind: All participants had to do was detect the input. Even with the simplest of tasks, therefore, it pays to be prepared.

What about the trials in which participants were misled? RTs in this condition averaged 297 ms, 31 ms (about 12%) slower than the neutral condition. Once again, therefore, we're seeing evidence of a limited-capacity system: In order to devote more attention to (say) the left position, one has to devote *less* attention to the right. If the stimulus then shows up on the right, one is less prepared for it—hence the cost of being misled.

Attention as a Searchlight

Studies of spatial attention suggest to some psychologists that visual attention can profitably be compared to a searchlight beam that can "shine" anywhere in the visual field. The "beam" marks the region of space for which one is prepared, so inputs within the beam are processed more efficiently and more swiftly. The beam can be wide or narrowly focused, and it can be moved about at will as one explores (attends to) one aspect of the visual field or another.

Let's emphasize, though, that the searchlight idea is referring to movements of *attention*, and not movements of the eyes. Of course, eye movements do play an important role in our selection of information from the world: If we want to learn more about something, we look at it. (For more on how we move our eyes to explore a scene, see Rayner, Smith, Malcolm, & Henderson, 2009.) But even so, movements of the eyes can be separated from movements of attention, and it's attention that's moving around in the Posner et al. study. We know this because of the timing of the effects: Eye movements are surprisingly slow, requiring 180 to 200 ms. But the benefits of primes can be detected within the first 150 ms after the priming stimulus is presented. Thus, the benefits of attention occur prior to any eye movement, and so they cannot be a consequence of eye movements.

But what exactly does the "searchlight" accomplish? What is different, in our processing of an input, when the light is "shining" on that input? The answer, we've said, is priming: When we say that the searchlight of attention is shining on a stimulus, this is just another way of saying that a person is priming the relevant detectors for that stimulus. This priming allows the detectors to work more swiftly and more efficiently, promoting our perception of the input. Without this priming, the detectors would be less responsive, and this helps explain why we are much less likely to perceive unattended inputs.

Attending to Objects, of Attending to Positions

There are, however, also important differences between attention and a searchlight beam. (For a broad overview of spatial attention and the searchlight notion, see Wright & Ward, 2008.) Think about how an actual searchlight works. If, for example, a searchlight shines on a donut, then part of the beam will fall on the donut's hole and so illuminate the plate underneath the donut. Similarly, if the searchlight isn't aimed quite accurately, it may also illuminate the plate just to the left of the donut. The region illuminated by the beam, in other words, is defined purely in spatial terms: a circle of light at a particular position. That position may or may not line up with the boundaries of the object you're shining the beam on.

Is this how attention works—so that we pay attention to whatever it is that falls in a certain region of space? In this case, we might on some occasions end up paying attention to part of this object, part of that. An alternative is that we pay attention to objects, rather than to *positions in space*. To continue the example, the target of our attention might be the donut itself, rather than the donut's location. In that case, the plate just to the left, and the bit of plate visible through the donut's hole, might be close to our focus, but they aren't part of the attended object and so aren't attended.

Which is the correct view of attention? Do we pay attention to regions in space, whatever the objects (or parts of objects) are that fall in that region? Or do we pay attention to objects? It turns out that each view captures part of the truth.

One line of evidence comes from the study of people who have suffered forms of brain damage (typically in the parietal cortex) that produce extraordinary problems in paying attention. For example, patients with **unilateral neglect syndrome** seem to ignore all inputs coming from one side of the body. A patient with neglect syndrome will eat food from only one side of the plate, will wash only half of his or her face, and will fail to locate sought-for objects if they are on the neglected side (Heilman, Watson, & Valenstein, 1985; Sieroff, Pollatsek, & Posner, 1988). This syndrome usually results from damage to the *right* parietal lobe, and so the neglect is for the *left* side of space. (Remember the brain's contralateral organization; see Chapter 2.) Thus, in the laboratory, neglect patients will read only the right half of words shown to them; that is, they will read "pigpen" as "pen," "parties" as "ties," and so on. If asked to cross out all the *E*s on a page, the patient will cross out the *E*s on only the right side of the page.

Taken at face value, these symptoms seem to support a space-based account of attention: The afflicted patient seems insensitive to all objects within a spatially defined region—namely, everything to the left of his current focus. If an object falls half within the region and half outside of it, then it's the spatially defined region that matters, not the object's boundaries. This is evident, for example, in how these patients read words—responding only to the word's right half, apparently oblivious to the word's overall boundaries.

Other evidence, however, demands further theory. In one study, patients with neglect syndrome had to respond to targets that appeared within a barbell-shaped frame. Not surprisingly, they were much more sensitive to the targets appearing within the red circle (on the right) and missed many of the targets appearing in the blue circle (on the left); this result simply confirms the patients' diagnosis. What is crucial, though, is what happened next: While the patients watched, the barbell frame was slowly spun around, so that the red circle, previously on the right, was now on the left, and the blue circle, previously on the left, was now on the right.

What should we expect in this situation? If the patients consistently neglect a region of space, they should now be more sensitive to the right-side blue circle. A different possibility is more complicated: Perhaps these patients have a powerful bias to attend to the right side, and so initially they attend to the red circle. Once they have "locked in" to this circle, however, it is the object, and not the position in space, that defines their focus of attention. According to this view, if the barbell form rotates, they will continue attending to the red circle (this is, after all, the focus of their attention), even though it now appears on their "neglected" side. This prediction turns out to be correct: When the barbell rotates, the patients' focus of attention seems to rotate with it (Behrmann & Tipper, 1999).

To describe these patients, therefore, we need a two-part account. First, the symptoms of neglect syndrome plainly reveal a spatially defined bias: These patients neglect half of space. But, second, once attention is directed toward a target, it is the target itself that defines the focus of attention; if the target moves, the focus moves with it. In this way, the focus of attention is object-based, not space-based. (For more on these issues, and on some of the intriguing complications in neglect syndrome, see Awh, Dhaliwal, Christensen, & Matsukura, 2001; Chen & Cave, 2006; Logie & Della Salla, 2005; Richard, Lee, & Vecera, 2008; Scholl, 2001.)

Could it be that this complex pattern appears only in neglect patients, so that the pattern is somehow a by-product of their brain damage? The answer to this is clearly no. Normal participants, too, show a mix of space-based and object-based attention. We have already seen evidence for the spatial base: The Posner et al.(1980) study and many results like it show that participants can focus on a particular region of space in preparation for a stimulus. In this situation, the stimulus has not yet appeared; there is no object to focus on. Therefore, the attention must be spatially defined.

In other cases, though, attention is heavily influenced by object boundaries. For example, in several studies participants have been shown displays with visually superimposed stimuli, as if a single television set were showing two channels at the same time (Neisser & Becklen 1975; Simons & Chabris. 1999). Participants can easily pay attention to one of these stimuli and ignore the other. This selection cannot be space-based (because both stimuli are in the same place) and so must be object-based.

Similarly, Egly, Driver, and Rafal (1994) had their participants look at a computer screen that showed two rectangles, one on the left side of the screen and one on the right. The participants' task was to respond as soon as they saw a target at one end (top or bottom) of one of the rectangles. In the majority of trials, a cue signaled in advance where the target would appear—in which rectangle, and at which end of the rectangle. In other trials, though, the cue was misleading: It signaled a location, but the target appeared elsewhere. Sometimes the target appeared in the same rectangle as the cue, but at the rectangle's opposite end; sometimes the target appeared in the other rectangle.

Not surprisingly, participants were fastest when the cue accurately signaled where the target would be; this observation echoes other results we have already discussed. What's crucial, though, is the comparison between misleading cues that at least signaled the proper rectangle, and misleading cues that signaled the *wrong* rectangle. According to a space-based account, there should be no difference between these two cases, because the display had been arranged so that both of the targets were the same distance from the misleading cue. According to an object-based account, though, these two cases will be different. Let's say that the cue draws attention to the top of the left-hand rectangle, and the target then appears in the bottom of that rectangle. In that case, the cue at least led participants to focus on the proper rectangle, and so attention will (on an object-based account) include that rectangle. As a result, responses will be quicker in this condition than they would be if the cue signaled the wrong rectangle altogether.

The latter prediction turns out to be correct. The cues in this study didn't just draw attention to a *location*. They also drew attention to the *object* that was in that location. Hence, in this way, our description of attention needs to be object-based as well as space-based.

Perceiving and the Limits on Cognitive Capacity: An Interim Summary

Our account is growing complex, so let's pause to take stock of where we are. At the broadest level, we have suggested that two different mechanisms are involved in selective attention. One mechanism serves to *inhibit,* or block out, the processing of *unwanted* inputs; this is, in effect, a mechanism for "ignoring" inputs in which we have no interest. A second mechanism *facilitates* the processing of *desired* inputs. This is a mechanism for "paying attention."

We've also seen, though, that the mechanism for paying attention has several parts. In other words, we take many different steps to promote the processing of inputs we're interested in. If we know the target's identity in advance, we can prime the relevant detectors. If we know only *where* the target will appear, we can prime detectors for the appropriate region of space; then, once we locate the object in that region, we prime detectors for that object.

Moreover, we have suggested that there is some flexibility in *when* the selection takes place. In some circumstances, the perceiver makes an early selection of the desired input, so that the unattended input receives relatively little processing. In other circumstances, the unattended input receives a fuller analysis—even if that input never penetrates into the perceiver's conscious awareness.

In light of all these points, the term "attention" seems not to label a particular process or a particular mechanism. Instead, we probably need to think of paying attention as an *achievement*, something that you are able to do. Like many other achievements (e.g., doing well in school, staying healthy, earning a good salary), paying attention involves many elements. The exact set of elements varies from occasion to occasion. Sometimes a strong distractor is on the scene, making it essential that you inhibit your response to that distractor. Sometimes no distractors are in view, so inhibition plays a smaller role. Sometimes you know in advance what the stimulus will be, so you can prime just the right detectors. Sometimes stimuli are less predictable, so your priming must be more diffuse. In all cases, though, multiple steps are needed to ensure that you end up aware of (and able to remember) the stimuli you're interested in, and not pulled off track by irrelevant inputs.

DIVIDED ATTENTION

So far in this chapter, we have been emphasizing situations in which you want to focus on a single input. If other tasks and other stimuli are on the scene, they are mere distractors. Our concern, therefore, has been on how you manage to select just the desired information, while avoiding irrelevant distraction.

There are circumstances, however, in which you want to do multiple things at once, in which you want to divide your attention among various tasks or various inputs. In some cases you can do this, but your ability to perform concurrent tasks is clearly limited. Almost anyone can walk and talk simultaneously, but it is far harder to solve calculus problems while reading a history text. Why are some task combinations difficult, while others are easy?

Our first step toward answering this question is, however, already in view. We have proposed that perceiving requires resources that are in short supply; the same is presumably true for other mental tasks—remembering, reasoning, problem-solving. They, too, require resources, and without these resources, these processes cannot go forward. All of this provides a straightforward account of **divided attention**: One can perform concurrent tasks only if the sum of the tasks' demands is within the "cognitive budget." Thus, for example, solving calculus problems requires some mental resources, and so does reading a text. You have enough resources to do either one of these tasks by itself, but not enough for both; if you try to do both at the same time, you will fail.

But what are these hypothesized mental resources? Do all tasks, no matter what they involve, draw on the same mental resources? Or are mental resources somehow specialized, so that the resources required by a task depend on the exact nature of the task?

The Specificity of Resources

Some mental resources do seem relatively specialized and so are drawn on only by certain sorts of tasks. This is why

it is more difficult to combine two verbal tasks than it is to combine a verbal task with a spatial task. To make this idea concrete, imagine that you are trying to read a list of words while simultaneously listening to someone give a speech. Both of these tasks draw on resources specialized for verbal tasks, and it's likely that listening to the speech will exhaust these resources. As a result, reading while listening will be impossible: The reading requires resources that aren't available. But now imagine that you are trying to look at pictures while listening to the speech. This will be much easier because picture-viewing doesn't require verbal resources, and so it won't matter if those resources have been exhausted by some other task.

This pattern—greater interference among more similar tasks—is easily demonstrated. In an early study by Allport, Antonis, and Reynolds (1972), participants heard a list of words presented through headphones into one ear, and their task was to shadow these words. At the same time, they were also presented with a second list. No immediate response was required to this second list, but later on, memory was tested for these items. In one condition, these memory items consisted of words presented into the other ear, so the participants were hearing (and shadowing) a list of words in one ear while simultaneously hearing the memory list in the other. In a second condition, the memory items were presented visually. That is, while the participants were shadowing one list of words, they were also seeing, on a screen before them, a different list of words. Finally, in a third condition, the memory items consisted of pictures, also presented on a screen.

These three conditions have similar requirements—namely, shadowing one list while memorizing another. But the first condition (hear words + hear words) involves very similar tasks; the second condition (hear words + see words) involves less similar tasks; the third condition (hear words + see pictures), even less similar tasks. If performance is limited by task-specific resources, then it seems most likely that the first pair of tasks will compete with each other for resources, and least likely that the last pair will. Thus, in terms of task-specific resources, we would expect the most interference in the first condition, the least in the third. And that is what the data show. (For further evidence, see Brooks, 1968; Hirst, 1986; Hirst & Kalmar, 1987.)

Plainly, therefore, the likelihood of interference increases when tasks are similar. Even so, we can still demonstrate interference between tasks that are completely different from each other. Evidence comes from many sources, including one often-discussed case: talking on a cell phone while driving. The conversation requires an auditory input and speech as output; the material being attended to is verbal. Driving, on the other hand, involves a visual input and hand and foot motion as output; the material being attended to is spatial. One might therefore think that there is little or no overlap in the resources required for these two tasks, and so little chance that the tasks will compete for resources.

It turns out, however, that driving and cell-phone use do interfere with each other; this is reflected, for example, in the fact that phone use has been implicated in many automobile accidents (Lamble, Kauranen, Laakso, & Summala, 1999). The interference can be observed even if the phones are of the hands-free type so that the driver's hands can remain on the steering wheel. Even with a hands-free phone, drivers engaged in cell-phone conversations are more likely to be involved in accidents, more likely to overlook traffic signals, and slower to hit the brakes when they need to (Kunar, Carter, Cohen, & Horowitz, 2008; Levy & Pashler, 2008; Strayer, Drews, & Johnston, 2003; Strayer & Drews, 2007; also see Spence & Read, 2003).

Identifying General Resources

Apparently, tasks as different as driving and talking compete with each other for some mental resource; otherwise, we have no explanation of the interference. This resource, therefore, must be fairly general in its application—so that it applies to verbal tasks and spatial ones, tasks with visual inputs and tasks with auditory inputs. But what is this general resource?

Researchers have offered various answers to this question, and it is likely that all the answers are correct. In other words, there are likely to be *several* task-general resources, with each contributing to the limits on how (or whether) we can divide attention between tasks. Some authors, for example, liken mental resources to an energy supply or a bank account, drawn on by all tasks, and we have used this analogy in much of our discussion. For example, Kahneman (1973) hypothesized that mental tasks require the expenditure of mental effort (also see Eysenck, 1982).

The term "effort" was meant rather literally here, so that mental tasks require effort in about the same fashion that physical tasks do.

Other authors have offered different views, conceiving of these resources more as "mental tools" rather than as some sort of mental "energy supply" (A. Allport, 1989; Baddeley, 1986; Bourke & Duncan, 2005; Dehaene, Sergent & Changeux, 2003; Johnson-Laird, 1988; Just, Carpenter, & Hemphill, 1996; Norman & Shallice, 1986). For example, Pashler and Johnston have proposed a mental mechanism that is required for *selecting* and *initiating* responses, including both physical responses and mental ones (such as the beginning of a memory search or the making of a decision; McCann & Johnston, 1992; Pashler, 1991, 1992, 1996; Pashler & Johnston, 1989; but also see Tombu & Jolicoeur, 2003). This **response selector** presumably plays a key role in coordinating the timing of our various activities, and so it serves as a mental traffic cop, controlling which processes go forward at any moment in time.

The response selector can initiate only one response at a time, and so, on this proposal, divided attention often involves a system of "turn-taking." Thus, if you are trying to divide your attention between Task A and Task B, you might first select and launch some action that is part of Task A; while that is happening, Task B must be put on hold for a moment. Then, while that first step of Task A is being carried out, you can use the response selector to launch the first step for Task B. Then, while that step is being executed, you can use the selector to launch the next step of A, and so on. This back-and-forth sequence allows both tasks to go forward—but often in a slower, less efficient manner than if either was being performed on its own.

Executive Control as a Limited Resource

The response selector is concerned with the moment-by-moment timing of our various responses. A different type of general resource, required for many tasks, involves more global processes—including the processes needed for *planning* our various activities. In particular, many theorists have highlighted the role of the mind's "central executive"—a mechanism that sets goals and priorities, chooses strategies, and, in general, directs the function of many cognitive processes (Baddeley, 1986, 1996; A. R. A. Conway, Kane, &

Engle, 2003; for some possible complications, see Logan, 2003).

Several proposals about the "executive" have been proposed; let's look at one in particular (Engle & Kane, 2004; Unsworth & Engle, 2007): Engle and his associates have suggested that much of our day-to-day functioning is guided by habit and prior associations. After all, most of the situations we find ourselves in resemble those we've encountered in the past, and so we don't need to start from scratch in figuring out how to behave. Instead, we can rely on the responses or strategies we've used previously.

In some cases, though, we want to behave in a fashion that's different from how we've behaved in the past—perhaps because our goals have changed, or perhaps because the situation has changed in some way that makes prior habits no longer useful. In such cases, we need to over-rule the action or strategy supplied by memory. To do this, Engle proposes, we need to take steps to keep our current goal in mind, so that this goal, and not habit, will guide our actions. As a related problem, some settings contain triggers that powerfully evoke certain responses. If we wish to make some *other* response, we need to take steps to avoid the obvious trap.

Within this context, Engle's proposal is that **executive control** is a task-general mental resource needed whenever someone wants to avoid interference from previous habit. This control provides two essential functions: It works to *maintain* the desired goal in mind; simultaneously, it serves to *inhibit* automatic or habitual responses.

Engle has proposed that people differ in how effective their executive control is—with some people literally having more control over their own thought processes. We can measure someone's degree of executive control with measures of their *working-memory capacity* (WMC), and it turns out that people with a larger WMC have an advantage in many tasks, including those that involve resisting distraction and those that involve resisting habit or reflex. (We'll describe in Chapter 5 how this capacity is measured.)

In one study, participants were initially required to fix their eyes on a target (Kane, Bleckley, Conway, & Engle, 2001). When a cue arrived, participants in one condition were asked to move their eyes *toward* the cue. This was easy, because this requirement is in line with ordinary habit: Whenever a stimulus appears suddenly in our view, we tend to move our eyes toward the stimulus to inspect it, just as this

condition requires. In another condition, however, participants were asked to do something more difficult: They were asked to override habit and, as soon as the cue arrived, make an eye movement in the opposite direction, *away from* the cue.

The first condition in this experiment should not require executive control; there is no need to override the habitual response. Consistent with this prediction, individuals with smaller WMC were just as fast and just as accurate in making the desired response as individuals with a larger WMC. The second condition, though, is different and should require executive control, overriding habit. And, consistent with the theory, individuals with larger WMC were uniformly more successful in the task—faster and less likely to fall into the trap of moving their eyes (contrary to instructions) toward the cue.

This eye-movement task fits well with the hypotheses we are discussing, but the task is not deeply interesting for its own sake. It is important, therefore, that measures of WMC are also correlated with a range of other tasks. Thus, individuals with a greater working-memory capacity are better at resisting distraction, and staying "on task," whenever they are working on something that is at all challenging (Kane et al., 2007). People with a larger WMC are also likely to score higher on the verbal SAT, to be better in reading comprehension and the following of directions, better at reasoning tasks and computer-language learning, and so on (Engle & Kane, 2004; Salthouse & Pink, 2008). All of this makes sense if we assume that each of these various tasks requires, as one component, an ability to maintain goals in mind and to resist various forms of interference.

Researchers have also made headway in identifying the neural underpinnings of WMC, and at least two areas of the brain appear to be involved. First, the prefrontal cortex (roughly, the brain area right behind the eyes) seems to play a crucial role in "goal maintenance"—the process of keeping one's current goal in mind. This is reflected, for example, in the finding that people who have suffered damage to the prefrontal cortex often show a pattern of "goal neglect"—falling into habit and failing to work toward their assigned goals in a particular task, even though they understand the current goals perfectly well (Duncan, Burgess, & Emslie, 1995; Duncan et al., 1996). Other evidence comes from a study in which participants had to perform a Stroop task (described later in this chapter), which requires a response *different from* the one provided by habit. Data from fMRI scans showed that activation in the prefrontal cortex increased in the seconds leading up to each trial, and the greater the activation, the lower the chance of error—that is, the *greater* the chance that participants would be able to resist the force of habit (Braver & Cohen, 2001; MacDonald, Cohen, Stenger, & Carter, 2000; for more on the prefrontal cortex, and its role as an "executive," see Aron, 2008; Stuss & Knight, 2002).

Second, different evidence suggests that other brain structures—including the anterior cingulate—may play a role in detecting situations that call for two conflicting responses. In such situations, this structure seems to trigger increased activation in other areas, including the prefrontal cortex, which then work to overcome the conflict (Botvinick, Cohen, & Carter, 2004; also see Egner, 2008).

These two brain functions—goal maintenance (supported by the prefrontal cortex) and conflict detection (supported by the anterior cingulate)—fit well with the claims that Engle and others have made about executive control. More generally, these neuroscience findings add support to the claim that there are certain processes, certain mechanisms, that will be needed for a wide range of tasks and, therefore, are the task-general mental resources described by our theories.

Divided Attention: An Interim Summary

Again, let's pause to take stock of where we are. Our consideration of *selective* attention drove us toward a several-part account, with one mechanism apparently serving to block out unwanted distractors, and then a number of other mechanisms all serving to promote the processing of interesting stimuli. Now, in our discussion of *divided* attention, we again seem to require several elements in our theory. Interference between tasks is plainly increased if the tasks are similar to each other, presumably because similar tasks overlap in their processing requirements and so make competing demands on mental resources that are specialized for that sort of task. It is on this basis, then, that our overall account of divided attention needs to take task-specific resources into account.

At the same time, interference can also be demonstrated with tasks that are entirely different from each other—driving and talking on a cell phone, for example. Thus, our account also needs to include resources general enough in their use that they're drawn on by almost any task. We've argued that there are likely to be several of these general resources: an energy supply needed for mental tasks; a response selector needed whenever a task involves the launching of successive steps; executive control, needed whenever a task requires "rising above" prior habits and tendencies; and probably others as well. No matter what the resource, though, the key principle will be the same: Tasks will interfere with each other if their combined demand for a resource is greater than the amount available—that is, if the demand exceeds the supply.

PRACTICE

We still need to add a complication to our account—namely, the effect of *practice*. To introduce the issue, let's return to the example of talking on a cell phone while driving. For a skilled driver, this task combination is easy *if* the driving is straightforward and the conversation is relatively simple. Indeed, many drivers manage this pair of simultaneous tasks every day, without causing traffic accident after traffic accident. Things fall apart, though, the moment the conversation becomes complex or the driving becomes challenging (e.g., because the driver has to merge into traffic or negotiate a complex turn). That's when the two tasks visibly interfere with each other: Engaged in deep conversation, the driver misses a turn; while maneuvering through the intersection, the driver suddenly stops talking.

These facts can easily be fit into our framework: It seems likely that there's a close relationship between how complicated a task is and how resource-demanding it is. Concretely, driving in ordinary circumstances makes only a light demand on executive control and only occasional demands on the response selector. Driving in a challenging situation makes a much heavier demand on these resources. The same is true for conversation: A casual chat with a friend requires few resources; a profound interview requires more. It's no wonder, then, that you can combine these tasks (driving and talking) when they're easy, but not when they're hard: Difficult driving requires a lot of resources, and so does difficult conversation. Together, they'll demand more resources than you have available.[1]

The Effects of Practice

What we've just said is true only for a skilled driver. For a *novice* driver, the task of driving is difficult all by itself, even on a straight road with no traffic. If, therefore, we ask the novice to do anything else at the same time—whether it's talking on a cell phone or even listening to the radio—we put the driver (and other cars) at substantial risk.

Why are things so different after practice than before? The main proposal should be obvious: We have already said, first of all, that mental tasks require resources, with the particular resources required, and the *amount* of those resources required, dependent on the nature of the task. Let's now add the claim that as a task becomes more practiced it requires *fewer* resources. Why should this be? Why does practice diminish a task's resource demand? Actually, the answer to these questions flows naturally from the way we've defined some of the resources. For example, the executive control that's measured by working-memory capacity (WMC) is needed whenever one has to rise above habit and do things in a new way. Early in practice, though, there are no habits to fall back on, because the task is brand-new. As a result, executive control is needed all the time. With practice, the person acquires a repertoire of habits, associations, and procedures, and so can rely more and more on these routine thoughts and actions. Thus, the demand for executive control decreases.

The same is true for the response selector. Early in practice, you have to decide what the first step of your performance should be, and then launch that step. Then you have to choose the second step and launch it, and so on. Thus, the response selector is needed a lot—for the selection and launching of each individual step. After practice, though, you can handle things differently. Because you know in advance what the steps of the task will be, you can approach the task with the entire sequence in mind and so use the response selector just once: to launch the whole sequence. Thus, there's no need for a series of choices ("What do I do next?") and, with that, no need for a series of launches, one for each of the task's steps. Instead, you simply do a single memory lookup ("What was the sequence of steps I used last time?"), and the response selector is needed to launch this overall routine. Once that's done, you can just run off the routine with no further need for the selector.

It is not surprising, therefore, that with practice, tasks make smaller demands on mental resources. These resources, it seems, are intimately tied up with the *control* of our mental performance—making plans for what to do, launching each step, and so on. Once a routine is established, there is less need for this control and, with that, less need for the resources.

Why Does Practice Improve Performance?

We have so far discussed why practice makes a task less resource-demanding. But what about the other obvious effect of practice—namely, the fact that it makes performance *better*? After all, there is no question that a pianist plays more beautifully after rehearsing a piece for a while, or that athletes play more skillfully after practice. Similar observations can be made for mental skills, such as solving problems, reading, or doing calculations. These, too, are more successful after practice than before. What produces this improvement?

The answer to this question has several parts, but one part hinges on the points we have already discussed, as well as the broad idea of resource availability. To understand this point, let's start with the fact that most tasks that you do have multiple components, and you will succeed in the tasks only if you can handle all the components. To continue our example of driving, a skilled driver needs to keep track of her steering *and* how fast she is going *and* how far she is from the car in front of her, and so on. If the driver neglects any of these elements, the result could be disastrous.

Cast in these terms, it appears that complex tasks, all by themselves, can create problems in divided attention: To do the task, you need to be able to divide your attention among the task's parts, and that's where practice comes in. Early in practice, the various parts of a task will each require resources, and that makes it impossible to think about all the tasks' parts at once. Thus, the novice tennis player getting ready to serve the ball will focus all his resources on how he tosses the ball upward. As a result, the player won't have any resources left over for other aspects of the serve—like choosing where to aim.

With practice, however, the elements of a task each become easier, thereby freeing up resources for dealing with other elements of the same task. This is what allows the driver (or the tennis player) to deal with multiple elements simultaneously, which is precisely what skilled performance requires.

In addition, this shift in resource demand also makes it possible to think about *new* elements of a task—elements that are beyond the reach of any novice. As an example, a skilled chess player is, of course, sensitive to the locations of the various pieces on the board and is alert to how these pieces might move in the next few steps of the game. But for the expert, these elements are so obvious, and thinking about them is so automatic, that resources are left over for other, more abstract aspects of the game: What long-term strategy does the player want to develop? Are there hints in the opponent's moves so far that might signal her long-term strategy? The novice has no resources for these "higher-order" elements, and this lack of resources places powerful limits on the quality of the novices play.

Automaticity

In all these ways, then, practice can make tasks *easier* and also *better*. Both of these improvements are made possible by the fact that practice decreases resource demands; this decrease, in turn, comes from the fact that practice diminishes the need for moment-by-moment *control* of a task.

All of this has an important implication: If, after practice, a task is no longer drawing on mechanisms that provide control, then the task is, in a sense, *uncontrolled*. Consistent with this suggestion, many psychologists distinguish **controlled tasks** and **automatic tasks**. Controlled tasks are typically novel tasks or tasks that require considerable flexibility in one's approach. Automatic tasks, in contrast, are typically highly familiar and do not require great flexibility. The person approaches these tasks with a well-learned routine—a sequence of responses (often triggered by specific stimuli) that have gotten the job done in the past. Usually this routine has been learned through practice, but it can also be learned from some good advice or a skilled teacher. In any case, once the routine is acquired, the automatic task doesn't need to be supervised or controlled, and so it requires few resources.

We have been discussing the advantages of this **automaticity**: An automatic task is usually easy and can be readily combined with other tasks. But automaticity also has a downside: Since automatic tasks are *not* controlled,

in some circumstances they can act as if they were "mental reflexes."

A striking example of this lack of control involves an effect known as **Stroop interference**. In the classic demonstration of this effect, study participants were shown a series of words and asked to name aloud the color of the ink used for each word. The trick, though, was that the words themselves were color names. So people might see the word "BLUE" printed in green ink and would have to say "green" out loud, and so on (Stroop, 1935).

This task turns out to be enormously difficult. There is a strong tendency to read the printed words themselves rather than naming the ink color, and people make many mistakes in this task. Presumably, this reflects the fact that word recognition, especially for college-age adults, is enormously well practiced and, as a consequence, can proceed automatically. This is a condition, therefore, in which mental control should be minimal, and that is certainly consistent with the errors that we observe. (There is, however, debate over the exact mechanisms that produce this interference; for some of that debate, see Besner & Stolz, 1999a, 1999b; Durgin, 2000; Engle & Kane, 2004; Jacoby et al., 2003; Kane & Engle, 2003. For some discussion of how automatic actions may be shaped by circumstances, see Bargh, 1989; Bargh & Chartrand, 1999.)

Where Are the Limits?

We are nearing the end of our discussion of attention, and so it again may be useful to summarize where we are. Two simple ideas lie at the heart of our account: First, tasks require resources, and second, you cannot "spend" more resources than you have. These claims are central for almost everything we have said about selective and divided attention.

We need to complicate this account, however, in two regards: First, there seem to be different types of resources, and second, the exact resource demand of a task depends on several different factors. What are those factors? The nature of the task matters, of course, so that the resources required by a verbal task (e.g., reading) are different from those required by a spatial task (e.g., remembering a shape). The novelty of the task and how much flexibility the task requires also matter. Connected to this, *practice* matters, with well-practiced tasks requiring fewer resources.

What, then, sets the limits on divided attention? When can you do two tasks at the same time, and when not? The answer varies, case by case. If two tasks make competing demands on task-specific resources, the result will be interference. If two tasks make competing demands on task-general resources (such as the response selector, or executive control), again the result will be interference. In addition, it will be especially difficult to combine tasks that involve similar stimuli—combining two tasks that both involve printed text, for example, or that both involve speech. This is because similar stimuli can sometimes "blur together," with a danger that you'll lose track of which elements belong in which input ("Was it the man who said 'yes,' or the woman?"; "Was the red dog in the top picture or the bottom?"). This sort of "crosstalk" (leakage of bits of one input into the other input) can itself compromise performance.

In short, it looks like we need a multipart theory of attention, with performance limited by different factors on different occasions. This draws us once more to a claim we made earlier in the chapter: Attention cannot be thought of as a skill, or a mechanism, or a capacity. Instead, attention is an *achievement*—an achievement of performing multiple activities simultaneously, or an achievement of successfully avoiding distraction when you wish to focus on a single task. And, as we have seen, this achievement rests on an intricate base, so that many skills, mechanisms, and capacities contribute to our ability to attend.

Finally, one last point. We have discussed various limits on human performance—that is, limits on how much you can do at any one time. How rigid are these limits? We have discussed the improvements in divided attention that are made possible by practice, but are there boundaries on what practice can accomplish? Can one perhaps gain new mental resources or, more plausibly, find new ways to accomplish a task in order to avoid the bottleneck created by some limited resource? At least some evidence indicates that the answer to these questions may be yes; if so, many of the claims made in this chapter must be understood as being claims about what is *usual,* and not claims about what is *possible* (Hirst, Spelke, Reaves, Caharack, & Neisser, 1980; Spelke, Hirst, & Neisser, 1976). With this, many traditions in the world—Buddhist meditation traditions, for example—claim it is possible to *train* attention so that one has better control over one's mental life; how do these claims fit into the framework we

have developed in this chapter? These are issues in need of further exploration, and in truth, what is at stake here is a question about the boundaries on human potential, making these issues of deep interest for future researchers to pursue.

CHAPTER SUMMARY

- People are often quite oblivious to unattended inputs; they are unable to tell if an unattended auditory input is coherent prose or random words, and they often fail altogether to detect unattended visual inputs, even though such inputs are right in front of the viewer's eyes. However, some aspects of the unattended inputs are detected. For example, people can report on the pitch of the unattended sound and whether it contained human speech or some other sort of noise. Sometimes they can also detect stimuli that are especially meaningful; some people, for example, hear their own name if it is spoken on the unattended channel.

- These results suggest that perception may require the commitment of mental resources, with some of these resources helping to prime the detectors needed for perception. This proposal is supported by studies of inattentional blindness, studies showing that perception is markedly impaired if the perceiver commits no resources to the incoming stimulus information. The proposal is also supported by results showing that we perceive more efficiently when we can anticipate the upcoming stimulus (and so can prime the relevant detectors). In many cases, this anticipation is spatial—if, for example, we know that a stimulus is about to arrive at a particular location. This priming, however, seems to draw on a limited-capacity system, and so priming one stimulus or one position takes away resources that might be spent on priming some other stimulus.

- Our ability to pay attention to certain regions of space has encouraged many researchers to compare attention to a searchlight beam, with the idea that stimuli falling "within the beam" are processed more efficiently. However, this searchlight analogy is potentially misleading. In many circumstances, we do seem to devote attention to identifiable regions of space, no matter what falls within those regions. In other circumstances, though, attention seems to be object-based, not space-based, and so we pay attention to specific objects, not specific positions.

- Perceiving, it seems, requires the commitment of resources, and so do most other mental activities. This provides a ready account of divided attention: It is possible to perform two tasks simultaneously only if the two tasks do not in combination demand more resources than are available. Some of the relevant mental resources are task-general, and so are called on by a wide variety of mental activities. These include the response selector, mental effort, and working-memory capacity. Other mental resources are task-specific, required only for tasks of a certain type.

- Divided attention is clearly influenced by practice, and so it is often easier to divide attention between familiar tasks than between unfamiliar tasks. In the extreme, practice may produce automaticity, in which a task seems to require virtually no mental resources but is also difficult to control. One proposal is that automaticity results from the fact that decisions are no longer needed for a well-practiced routine; instead, one can simply run off the entire routine, doing on this occasion just what one did on prior occasions.

NOTES

1. As a practical note, let's emphasize that challenges like a sudden increase in the demands of driving, or a sudden shift in the conversation's complexity, can arise without warning. As a result, you never know when the conversation and driving will demand more resources than you've got (and so cause interference), and this is why most psychologists would recommend that you never talk on the cell phone while driving. If you follow that advice, then there's no risk that interference might unexpectedly arise. Whether drivers (including the psychologists themselves) heed this advice, however, is a separate matter.

Double-Blind Tests of Subliminal Self-Help Audiotapes

ANTHONY G. GREENWALD, ERIC R. SPANGENBERG, ANTHONY R. PRATKANIS, AND JAY ESKENAZI

ABSTRACT

Three replications of a double-blind experiment tested subliminal audiotape products that were claimed to improve memory or to increase self-esteem. Conditions of use adhered to manufacturers' recommendations, and subjects (N = 237) were limited to persons who desired the effects offered by the tapes. Actual content and labeled content of tapes were independently varied, so that some subjects who believed they were using memory tapes were actually using self-esteem tapes, and vice versa. After a month of use, neither the memory nor the self-esteem tapes produced their claimed effects. Nevertheless, a general improvement for all subjects in both memory and self-esteem (a nonspecific placebo effect) was observed, and more than a third of the subjects had the illusion of improvement specific to the domain named on the tape's label.

Subliminal self-help (SSH) audiotapes are widely advertised as being able to produce many desirable effects, including weight loss, smoking cessation, anxiety reduction, and improvement of sexual function. In ordinary use, purchasers of SSH tapes know and desire the target effect, which is clearly marked on the tape label and in accompanying literature. However, in listening (perhaps daily) to the tape, the user may hear nothing relevant to the target effect. The audible content of the tape typically consists of relaxing material, often music or recorded nature sounds.

There are numerous reports of claimed therapeutic effects of subliminal audiotapes, but no such report has appeared in a competitively refereed psychology journal. Further, many of these reports have been produced by researchers associated with manufacturers of the tapes (Becker & Charbonnet, 1980; Borgeat & Chaloult, 1985; Doche-Budzynski & Budzynski, 1989; Taylor, 1988; VandenBoogert, 1984; see review by Eich, in press).

The present research was conducted to provide a rigorous assessment of therapeutic effectiveness of selected SSH audiotapes. Four aspects of procedure were essential to the experimental protocol. First, a double-blind method was used in order to separate effects of subliminal content from possible placebo effects. Second, conditions closely resembled the conditions of ordinary use of SSH tapes, in order not to omit contextual aspects of the ordinary procedure that might be necessary to claimed effects. Third, the research used subjects who were motivated to achieve the goals claimed by the tapes, because such motivation is plausibly a precondition for occurrence of claimed effects and is a condition that applies generally in the marketplace. And, fourth, the research used both pretest and posttest measures of status relative to the target goals, in order to obtain the increased sensitivity afforded by analyses of covariance with pretests used as covariates.

Among the target goals for which SSH tapes were available from several manufacturers, improving memory and increasing self-esteem were selected both because it was

Anthony G. Greenwald, Eric R. Spangenberg, Anthony R. Pratanis, and Jay Eskenazi, "Double-blind Tests of Subliminal Self-help Audiotapes," *Psychological Science*, vol. 2, no. 2, pp. 119–122. Copyright © 1991 by Sage Publications. Reprinted with permission.

easy to locate subjects who desired these goals, and because several well-established measures that could be used in a pretest-posttest design were available. Some manufacturers generously provided multiple copies of their tapes for the research; with manufacturers' permission, we also duplicated mail-ordered tapes for use in the research. Audible identifications of contents (at the beginnings of some of the tapes) were carefully and selectively erased by an audio laboratory prior to giving any tapes to subjects.[1]

METHOD

The research was conducted in three similar replications.[2] Subjects were recruited from the student and adult populations of university communities; posters and newspaper advertisements sought the participation of volunteers who were interested in participating in a study of memory and self–esteem subliminal audiotapes. Of 288 volunteers (186 female, 102 male) who completed pretests, 237 (82%; 149 female, 88 male) returned to complete posttests at the end of one month of SSH tape use. Tapes provided by three manufacturers were used in the course of the research; their audible content consisted of classical music, popular music, or recorded nature (surf of woodlands) sounds. (A preliminary analysis tested for differences among the tapes provided by the three manufacturers; no differences were found, and the results below are reported for a design that did not include manufacturer as a variable.)

The research used a within-subjects double-blind procedure that is possible when two for more treatments that have different target effects are perceptually indistinguishable. After completing both memory and self-esteem pretests, each subject was given a tape to which a memory or self-esteem label had been randomly assigned. As a consequence of this procedure, for example, subjects who received a self-esteem-labeled memory tape served simultaneously as treatment subjects for the memory tape and as placebo subjects for the self-esteem tape. (In the informed consent procedure, subjects had indicated interest in receiving either tape and had agreed to be randomly assigned to a tape, but were not explicitly informed that they might receive a mislabeled tape.)

Although the specific measures that were used varied across replications, each replication included three measures of self-esteem (e.g., Coopersmith, 1967; Rosenberg, 1965)

and three or four measures of memory (e.g., Wechsler, 1945). After the pretest administration of these measures, tapes were randomly assigned to subjects, who were asked to listen to the tape every day for one month, which is a period indicated by most SSH tape vendors as sufficient to produce advertised effects. Subjects returned within 5 weeks to the laboratory for the posttest session, which included self-esteem and memory tests parallel to the pretest. (Memory test materials were varied between pretests and posttests, with order counterbalanced across subjects, in order to avoid specific practice effects.) The posttest session also included single items to assess self-perceived improvement in memory ability and in self-esteem (e.g., "Do you feel that the tape has improved your memory?" (answered "yes" or "no".))

RESULTS

As expected, each memory and self-esteem test was strongly correlated with other tests of the same construct, whereas memory and self-esteem were uncorrelated (overall $r = -.06$ for combined memory and self-esteem scores at pretest). Each replication's data were prepared for analysis by converting each pretest self-esteem and memory scale to standard-score form (zero mean, unit variance, standardizing across subjects who completed posttests). The multiple pretest measures for self-esteem were then averaged into a single pretest self-esteem measure, and similarly for memory. Next, the parallel posttest scales were standardized and combined. The posttest scales were standardized using the mean and standard deviation for the corresponding pretest scale, in order to preserve both the scale unit and the direction of posttest change relative to pretest. The major tests of significance were then conducted as analyses of covariance in the 2 (subliminal content; self-esteem vs. memory) x 2 (tape label: self-esteem vs. memory) design of each experiment, using the combined posttest measure as criterion and the combined pretest measure as covariate.[3] Analyses were conducted separately for the self-esteem and memory measures. A 2-tailed $a = .05$ criterion was used for significance tests.

The main results are shown in Figure 1. If the claimed subliminal content effects had materialized, there should have been higher posttest memory scores for subjects receiving subliminal memory content than for those receiving self-esteem content, and higher posttest self-esteem scores for those who received subliminal self-esteem content than for those who received memory content. The results tended to be opposite to these expectations. For memory (see Fig. 1B), the findings were nonsignificant ($F(1, 224) < 1$), but for self-esteem (see Fig. 1A), the data were unexpectedly significant in the direction opposite to the claimed effect ($F(1, 224) = 9.12$). It is clear that the claimed effects did not materialize.

Figure 1 shows that posttest means tended to be greater in the domain corresponding to the label on the assigned tape than in the domain not named on the label. This effect, however, was weak and not statistically significant (for self-esteem, $F(1, 224) < 1$; for memory, $F(1, 224) = 2.19$, ns).

Figure 1 also shows that all posttest means were substantially above zero, indicating that both self-esteem and memory scores generally increased above their pretest levels (which were standardized at a mean of zero). These increases were strong effects, as can be seen by comparing them to the standard errors of means shown in Figure 1. (For self-esteem, $F(1, 224) = 116.73, p < .001$; for memory, $F(1,224) = 52.91, p < .001$) This result may be a nonspecific placebo effect—an improvement of subjects memory

and self-esteem by virtue of being in the experiment, independent of condition assignment. It is also possibly a practice effect, especially in the case of the memory measures, for which the use of similar items at pretest and posttest might have led to some general improvement.

Figure 2 gives the findings for measures of self-perceived improvement. There were no effects of subliminal content on these measures ($Fs < 1$ for both memory and self-esteem). At the same time, the data showed clearly that subjects tended to believe that they had improved in the domain corresponding to the label on their assigned tape. Overall, approximately 50% of subjects believed that they had improved in the domain corresponding to the label they received, compared to only about 15% believing they had improved in the domain corresponding to the label not received. For the effect of tape label on self-perceived improvement in memory, $F(1, 211) = 28.20. p < .001$; for self-esteem, $F(1, 125) = 24.40, p < .001$ (degrees of freedom are lower for self-esteem because the measure for self-esteem was not included in one replication).

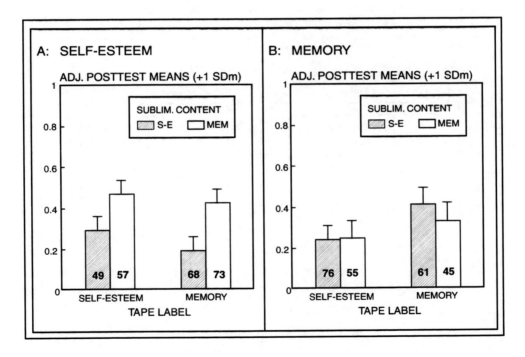

Fig. 1. *Adjusted posttest means as a function of audiotape subliminal content and tape label. The dependent variable is the average of standardized scores on multiple self-esteem or memory scales; zero is at the mean of pretest scores.*

DISCUSSION

The double-blind design permitted separation of subliminal content effects from placebo (or label) effects. The results established that there was no trace of a subliminal content effect corresponding to manufacturers' claims. There was a suggestion of a placebo effect associated with subjects' belief about which tape they had received, but this was not statistically significant despite the design's substantial power to detect a relatively small effect.[4]

The strong effect of tape label on measures of self-perceived improvement, coupled with its lack of significant effect on the multiscale measures of the target effects, indicates that the effect of tape label on perceived improvement is not mediated by any effect of tape label on actual changes in self-esteem and memory (see Baron & Kenny, 1986). The effect of tape label on perceived improvement can therefore be described as an *illusory* placebo effect. Other such illusions—i.e., that a treatment produced its expected effect—have recently been demonstrated in several other domains (Conway & Ross, 1984; Ross, 1989).

The significant reverse-direction effect of the SSH tapes that were designed to increase self-esteem is not explainable from any theoretical perspective of which we are aware. On the one hand, these unexpected findings allow an even stronger conclusion than simple nonconfirmation of the claimed product effect; they allow statistical rejection of any hypothesis of an effect in the claimed direction. On the other hand, it might be argued that any effect of subliminal content, even one opposite from expectation, indicates some unconsciously mediated effect. This is a variant on the argument offered by researchers on extrasensory perception (ESP or psi) that reverse effects are expected from skeptical subjects ("goats"), and thus confirm the validity of psi (see Alcock, 1987; Rao & Palmer, 1987). However, this explanation should not be applied to the present research, because our subjects were not skeptics. Rather, our subjects volunteered in the hope of experiencing improvement, and at the end of the experiment many believed that the tapes had been effective.

Our research demonstrated no effects corresponding to the subliminal content effects claimed by manufacturers, but did demonstrate two substantial placebo effects. One was a nonspecific placebo effect—an across-the-board increase in memory and self-esteem that was independent of condition assignment. This result has many potential explanations that cannot be selected among on the basis of our design. Perhaps the least interesting of these is that the result might be due to practice provided by the pretest.

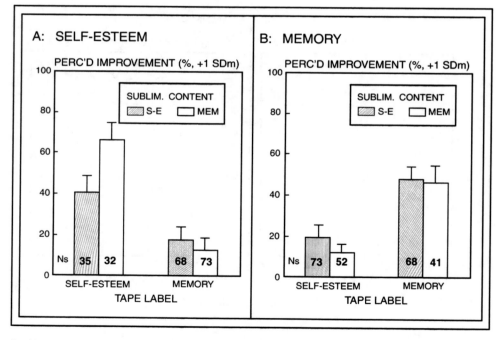

Fig. 2. *Percent of subjects perceiving improvement in self-esteem and memory as a function of audiotape subliminal content and tape label.*

That explanation can easily be tested by using a Solomon (1949) four-group design, in which half of the subjects receive a tape treatment and half do not, and within each of those groups half of the subjects receive posttests without having been previously pretested. The second placebo effect was confined to measures of self-perceived improvement, and was specific to the dimension for which subjects believed their tape had been designed. Although this effect of tape label on self-perceived improvement was illusory (in the sense of not being determined by gains on the multiscale measures of the target dimensions), nevertheless it may be worthy of further exploration. That is, such an illusory placebo effect may have the potential to become an actual effect by mechanisms of expectancy or self-fulfilling prophecy (Darley & Fazio. 1980; Orne, 1969: Rosenthal, 1969; Ross & Olson, 1981).

CONCLUSION

The experiments described in this reponse are the most extensive double-blind tests yet conducted of claimed therapeutic effects of audiotapes having subliminal verbal content. The findings showed clearly that subliminal audiotapes designed to improve memory and to increase self-esteem did not produce effects associated with subliminal content. Pending further double-blind research, it seems most prudent to regard the general class of claims for therapeutic efficacy of subliminal audio content as lacking in empirical foundation.

Acknowledgments—This research was supported in part by a research grant from the National Institute of Mental Health (MH41328), The authors thank Jonathon D. Brown and Timothy E. Moore for comments on a preliminary draft. The research was conducted while Eric R. Spangenberg was at the University of Washington, and Jay Eskenazi at the University of California, Santa Cruz.

REFERENCES

ALCOCK, J.E. (1987). PARAPSYCHOLOGY: SCIENCE OF THE ANOMALOUS OR SEARCH FOR THE SOUL? *BEHAVIORAL AND BRAIN SCIENCES, 10.* 553–643.

BARON, R.M., & KENNY. D.A. (1986). THE MODERATOR-MEDIATOR VARIABLE DISTINCTION IN SOCIAL PSYCHOLOGICAL RESEARCH: CONCEPTUAL, STRATEGIC, AND STATISTICAL CONSIDERATIONS. *JOURNAL OF PERSONALITY AND SOCIAL PSYCHOLOGY, 51.* 1173–1182.

BECKER, H.C. & CHARBONNET, K.D. (1980, MARCH). APPLICATIONS OF SUBLIMINAL VIDEO AND AUDIO STIMULI IN THERAPEUTIC, EDUCATIONAL, INDUSTRIAL, AND COMMERCIAL SETTINGS. PRESENTED AT MEETINGS OF NORTHEAST BIOENGINEERING CONFERENCE, CAMBRIDGE, MA.

BORGEAT, F. & CHALOULT, L. (1985). A RELAXATION EXPERIMENT USING RADIO BROADCASTS. *CANADA'S MENTAL HEALTH, 33.* 11–13.

COHEN, J. (1977). *STATISTICAL POWER ANALYSIS FOR THE BEHAVIORAL SCIENCES* (REV. ED.). NEW YORK: ACADEMIC PRESS.

COHEN. J., & COHEN, P. (1983). *APPLIED MULTIPLE REGRESSION/CORRELATION ANALYSIS FOR THE BEHAVIORAL SCIENCES* (2ND ED.). HILLSDALE, NJ: ERLBAUM.

CONWAY, M., & ROSS, M. (1984). GETTING WHAT YOU WANT BY REVISING WHAT YOU HAD. *JOURNAL OF PERSONALITY AND SOCIAL PSYCHOLOGY, 47.* 738–748.

COOPERSMITH, S, (1967). *THE ANTECEDENTS OF SELF-ESTEEM.* SAN FRANCISCO: FREEMAN.

DARLEY, J.M., & FAZIO, R. H. (1980). EXPECTANCY CONFIRMATION PROCESSES ARISING IN THE SOCIAL INTERACTION SEQUENCE. *AMERICAN PSYCHOLOGIST, 35,* 867–881.

DOCHE-BUDZYNSKI, L., & BUDZYNSKI, T.H. (1989). SUBLIMINAL SELF-ESTEEM ENHANCEMENT IN ADULT TYPE A MALES. *EDUCATION. 110,* 50–56.

EICH, E. (IN PRESS). SUBLIMINAL SELF-HELP. IN R.A. BJORK & D. DRUCKMAN (EDS.), *IN THE MIND'S EYE: UNDERSTANDING THE BASIS OF HUMAN PERFORMANCE.* WASHINGTON, DC: NATIONAL ACADEMY PRESS.

ORNE, M.T. (1969). DEMAND CHARACTERISTICS AND THE CONCEPT OF QUASI-CONTROLS. IN R. ROSENTHAL & R.L. ROSNOW (EDS.), *ARTIFACT IN BEHAVIORAL RESEARCH* (PP. 143–179). NEW YORK: ACADEMIC PRESS.

PRATKANIS, A.R., ESKENAZI, J., & GREENWALD, A.G. (1990). WHAT YOU EXPECT IS WHAT YOU BELIEVE (BUT NOT NECESSARILY WHAT YOU GET): ON THE INEFFECTIVENESS OF SUBLIMINAL SELF-HELP AUDIOTAPES. UNPUBLISHED MANUSCRIPT. UNIVERSITY OF CALIFORNIA, SANTA CRUZ.

RAO, K.R., & PALMER. J. (1987). THE ANOMALY CALLED PSI: RECENT RESEARCH AND CRITICISM. *BEHAVIORAL AND BRAIN SCIENCES, 10,* 539–643.

ROSENBERG, M. (1965). *SOCIETY AND THE ADOLESCENT SELF-IMAGE.* PRINCETON, NJ: PRINCETON UNIVERSITY PRESS.

Rosenthal, R. (1969). Interpersonal expectations: Effect of the experimenter's hypothesis. In R. Rosenthal & R.L. Rosnow (Eds.), *Artifact in behavioral research* (pp. 181–277). New York: Academic Press.

Ross, M. (1989). Relation of implicit theories to the construction of personal histories. *Psychological Review, 96.* 341–357.

Ross, M., & Olson, J.M. (1981). An expectancy-attribution model of the effects of placebos. *Psychological Review. 88.* 408–437.

Solomon, R.L. (1949). An extension of control group design. *Psychological Bulletin, 46,* 137150.

Spangenberg, E.R. (1990). An empirical test of subliminal self-help audiotapes: Are expectancies the active ingredient? Unpublished doctoral dissertation, University of Washington.

Taylor, E. (1988). *Subliminal learning: An eclectic approach.* Salt Lake City: Just Another Reality Publishing.

VandenBoogert, C. (1984). A study of Potentials Unlimited subliminal persuasion/self-hypnosis tapes. Grand Rapids, MI: Potentials Unlimited, Inc.

Wechsler, D. (1945). A standardized memory scale for clinical use. *Journal of Psychology. 19,* 8795.

NOTES

1. In obtaining tapes for the research, we proposed that no manufacturers' names would be included in reports of this research. This removed the possibility of conflict of interest on the part of researchers, and also eliminated any possibility that the results might be interpreted as either an endorsement or criticism of specific brands.

2. One replication was conducted in Santa Cruz, California, and two were conducted in Seattle, Washington. The Santa Cruz and the second Seattle replication were identical indesign; the first Seattle replication differed by adding weight loss as an additional studied goal. No effects of any kind were found for weight loss. In the combined analysis reported here, subjects who received weight-loss tape products or labels are grouped with those who received memory tapes or labels, as appropriate, in analyses of the self-esteem results, and with those who received self-esteem tapes or labels, as appropriate, in analyses of the memory results. Analyses showed no significant interaction effects involving replication as a design factor, as a consequence of which we omit report of the replication factor in presenting results (see Pratkanis, Eskenazi. & Greenwald, 1990, and Spangenberg, 1990, for detailed reports of the individual studies).

3. As a check on the appropriateness of our use of analysis covariance, the data were first examined to assess homogeneity of within-group regression slopes of posttest measures on their associated pretests (see Cohen & Cohen, 1983. p. 319). These slopes were homogeneous for all of the post test measures (F ratios < 2), indicating that covariance analyses were valid. Next, we looked for pretest differences between treatments. One such difference was found, consisting of lower pretest self-esteem among subjects who received tapes with self-esteem labels than among those who received tapes with memory labels. This difference could reduce the accuracy of the test of tape label on self-esteem, but does not affect the focal test for effects of actual subliminal content.

4. The sample size of 237 provided power(probability of detecting an effect at the 2-tailed $\alpha = .05$ level) of .90 for a main-effect difference between treatment means of .166 on the combined posttest self-esteem measure of Figure 1; for memory, there was power of .90 to detect a treatment difference of .206. For comparison, Cohens (1977) standard "small" effect corresponds to mean differences of .164 in self-esteem and .182 in post-test memory: our design had power, respectively, of .897 and .871 to detect these small effects.

Influence of Subliminal Visual Images on the Experience of Anxiety

ROXANA ROBLES, RICHARD SMITH, CHARLES S. CARVER, AND A. RODNEY WELLENS

Can affect-generating cues be processed outside awareness? A study is reported that examined the effect on subjective affect caused by stimuli presented subliminally. Threatening images, neutral images, and humorous images were embedded in three (separate) videotapes, which were shown to subjects at exposure times that precluded recognition of the images. Self-rated state anxiety assessed immediately afterward (via two separate measures) was highest among subjects exposed to the threatening images, lower in the group exposed to the neutral images, and lowest in the group exposed to the humorous images. In contrast, but consistent with expectations, the subliminal stimuli had no effect on a measure of trail anxiety.

Research on the effects of stimuli that are presented subliminally (outside awareness) has provoked interest and controversy for decades (see, e.g., Dixon, 1971; Erdelyi, 1974; Erinksen, 1960; Goldiamond, 1958; McConnell, Culler, & McNeil, 1958; for a more recent review, see Dixon, 1981). Interest in the effects of such stimulation has recently been reawakened among personality and social psychologists (e.g., Bargh & Pietromonaco. 1982) due in part to evolving conceptualizations of cognitive processes and the role of these processes in social perception (e.g., Wyer A. Srull, 1984). Most recent research on subliminal stimulation has focused on how social perception is influenced by subliminal activation of evaluative-interpretive information

in memory. The study reported here, in contrast, derives from the question of whether subliminal stimuli can influence subjective mood. A number of theorists have argued that the information leading to emotions is processed outside consciousness and with greater speed than other information (e.g., Nielson & Sarason. 1981). It would seem reasonable to hypothesize, then, that the experience of mood may be influenced by stimuli that are presented outside awareness.

A variety of evidence from previous research is relevant to this question, but most of it is indirect. For example, Silverman and his colleagues have conducted a large number of studies of subliminal effects, which were designed from a psychodynamic perspective (see, e.g., Silverman, 1976). The studies focused on subject groups that in theory should have specific kinds of unconscious conflicts. The stimulus material was intended to stir up the conflict that was relevant to a given group. This, in turn, should (and typically did) exacerbate a theoretically expected symptom.

Though one might argue that these effects were measures by anxiety (caused by the unconscious conflict) the dependent measures typically were not measures of affect per se. When the research did focus on measures of affect, the measures were a step removed from the subliminal stimulus itself—for example, depression being measured after presenting aggressive-wish stimuli. In two studies directly measuring the affect most closely related to the stimuli, no effect was found (Rutstein & Goldberger, 1973; Varga, 1973). There is ambiguity about he meaning of this null finding, however, because both studies used highly restrictive subject groups (Silverman, 1976).

Another source of indirect evidence on the hypothesis is the literature of perceptual defense. These studies (e.g., McGinnies, 1949) appear to imply that negative affect can be generated through unconscious processing. That is, taboo words are often found to have higher recognition thresholds than neutral words, presumably because they create anxiety (prior to recognition) that interferes with processing in some way (see Erdelyi 1974, for a discussion of several possibilities). This evidence on the question we are posing is indirect, however, in that the dependent measures involve recognition of words (and sometimes autonomic indices such as GSR), rather than subjective feeling states.

Two studies that bear more directly on the issue of interest here were reported recently by Tycer, Lewis and Lee (1978). In the first study they presented anxiety-related words subliminally while presenting neutral words at a consciously perceptible level. This procedure led to increases in self-reports of anxiety. Unfortunately, however, the study lacked a necessary control group to which anxiety-related words were *not* presented. Thus any conclusions drawn from this study must be regarded as suggestive at best.

In a second study, Tyrer et al. used films as a vehicle to present either neutral images or anxiety-inducing images. The anxiety stimulus consisted of a view taken from inside a moving car, which was projected at five times normal speed. Tyrer et al. provided specific justification for the use of this film as a stimulus, but our inference is that the high speed of presentation was expected to generate anxiety through the "looming" effect of objects being passed by the car. Subjects in a control condition were shown a soothing film—a swan floating serenely on a lake. In each case, the presentation was rendered subliminal by sharply restricting the amount of light passing from the projector and by increasing ambient illumination around the projection screen.

The anxiety film in this study produced ratings of higher anxiety than occurred in response to the soothing film. However, once again a true control group was lacking, which makes it unclear whether to attribute the difference to the anxiety film, the soothing film, or both. Moreover, the authors subsequently were unable to replicate the effect when they attempted to better control the content of the film on several dimensions unrelated to the target dimension (Lee & Tyrer. 1981). This failure further clouds the answer to the question with which they began.

Thus there is little *direct* information to indicate whether subliminal stimuli can directly influence subjectively experienced affect.[1] The study reported here was an attempt to test the hypothesis. In this study, we presented subjects with a visual stimulus that was fully perceptible, in the form of a TV image. Embedded in this stimulus were visual images that were chosen as having affect-influencing properties. These images were presented at exposure durations that should have left the below-recognition threshold. After exposure to this set of stimuli, subjects completed self-report measures of the feeling quality that was relevant to the subliminal stimuli.

METHOD

Pilot Study

A pilot study (undertaken prior to the main study) allowed an initial test of the hypothesis and, at the same time, raised some methodological issues. Subjects in the pilot study watched either an anxiety-inducing or a neural videotape, completed the anxiety portion of the Multiple Affect Adjective Checklist (MAACL) Today Form (Zuckerman & Lubin, 1965) and then completed a questionnaire in which they had an opportunity to indicate any awareness of the subliminal stimuli, and their impressions of the experiment's purpose.

The videotape sequence, made especially for this study, displayed a 2-min segment of a young woman walking leisurely through a forest. The tape was used unmodified in the control condition. In the experimental condition seven frames containing images with negative emotional content were inserted into the tape at seven different points. Each of the seven single frames was intended to be displayed for 1/30th of a second, though limitations of the equipment used did not allow complete control over the edit length. Unfortunately, with this exposure time a substantial minority of subjects in the experimental condition reported having seen elements that were actually part of the inserted frames-elements such as faces, eyes, and so on.

Though greater anxiety was reported among experimental than control subjects (after deleting those who had reported seeing inserts), $p < .01$, several problems suggest the need for caution in drawing conclusions from these data. These problems were addressed in designing and conducting the main experiment. The most obvious problem, of course, was that several subjects reported seeing what were intended to be subliminal frames in the videotape. For this reason, the exposure time in the main experiment was further reduced by showing the videotape at twice its normal speed, thus decreasing by half the exposure time for each image displayed.

A second issue was raised by the substance of the videotape (supraliminal stimulus) used in the pilot study. Anecdotal evidence suggested that the scenes of a young female model walking in a forest may have had sexually arousing (thus emotion-inducing) qualities for male subjects. This evidence suggested the importance of using a tape with more neutral content. A third problem was that the control tape contained no inserts of *any* kind. It is possible that the mere presence of inserts (whatever their content) has an effect on mood. To circumvent this problem, the control condition in the main study included inserts of nonemotional material.

Finally, the pilot study used only negative emotional stimuli. There is no theoretical reason, however, to expect the effect of subliminal exposure to be united to negative stimuli A better test of the hypothesis thus would involve manipulating mood bidirectionally, that is toward negative for some, toward positive for others. For this reason, the main study included both positive and negative stimulus conditions.

Subjects and Procedure

The participants in the main study were 130 undergraduates (54 females and 76 males) from the University of Miami. Subjects were randomly assigned to one of the three conditions, with 45 (23 men and 22 women) in the positive group, 42 (21 of each sex) in the neutral (control) group, and 43 (22 men and 21 women) in the negative group. Each individual tested was met by the experimenter and taken to a cubicle, where he or she was seated approximately 6 ft away from a TV monitor. Each was asked to watch a 2-min videotape of a set of computer-generated graphics, with an indication that he or she would be asked questions about it later on. Each subject watched one of three videotapes in an otherwise darkened room.

Immediately after viewing the video sequence, subjects were asked to write down any reactions they had regarding the video and to indicate what they thought had been the experiment's purpose. This measure allowed the subject to indicate any awareness of what were intended to be subliminal stimuli. After responding to these instructions, subjects completed the anxiety portion of the MAACL and both portions of the State-Trait Anxiety Inventory (STAI-A-State and STAI-A-Trait; Spielberger, Gorsuch, & Lushene, 1970). All subjects then were questioned more explicitly and were debriefed concerning the general nature of the experiment.

As noted above, subjects were given ample opportunity to indicate any awareness of the subliminal inserts. Only one subject's response gave any evidence of such awareness. This subject (who had been in the negative condition) reacted to the debriefing statement by saying that she thought she had seen a particular image that had not, in fact, been in the tape. When further questioned, this subject was not able to name correctly any of the stimuli actually inserted into the tape. Nonetheless, data from this subject were withheld from data analysis. Most subjects in the study reacted with surprise to the information (conveyed during eventual debriefing) that they had viewed a tape with subliminal splices.

Stimuli

Supraliminal. The supraliminal video sequence was shown on a 13-in. Panasonic Quintrix II solid state color television monitor and was played back on an RCA Selecta Vision video VHS cassette recorder. The video sequence displayed to each subject consisted of the first 2 min of the silent demonstration program from "Atari World" by United Software of America. This sequence includes a computer graphics program in which apparent three-dimensional color images are produced (i.e., an xyz coordinate plane, a scene of a kitchen, and an office room) rotating vertically and horizontally, thereby showing a view of the image from all angles.

Subliminal. Editing of subliminal splices consisted of electronically transferring a single frame of video (positive, neutral, and negative frames, in the respective tapes) from a source tape to a destination tape (i.e., into the previously recorded computer graphics sequence). Insertions were made on a Panasonic video editor. Thirteen frames were chosen for each experimental condition. Individual frames were inserted into the computer graphics sequence after successive 7-sec interval of time. The edited sequence was then re-recorded twice at two times its normal speed. Thus no subliminal insert was exposed for longer than 1/60th of a second (one video field) in the final version of the tapes (by contrast, in the Bargh & Pietromonaco, 1982, research the exposure time was constant at 1/10 of a second). Unfortunately, owing to technical limitations, several of the intended inserts failed to be recorded onto the final (double-speed) version. The tapes as finally constituted had 19 images in the negative condition and 15 images in the positive condition, whereas all 26 inserts survived the editing process for the neutral condition.

The content of the inserts was as follows. Positive inserts came from a popular animated cartoon program. Cartoon images were chosen on the basis of our subjective impression that cartoon characters are associated in most people's minds with cuteness, humor, and an absence of threat. Care was taken to choose only images that depicted cartoon characters (Bugs Bunny, Tom and Jerry, Mighty Mouse, Daffy Duck, and the Road Runner) in smiling poses. Negative inserts came from two movies: *An American Werewolf in London* and *Ghost Story*. The scenes chosen depicted threatening and violent stimuli such as bloodied and agonized faces, monsters, devils, and so on. For the neutral (control) condition, a series of gray featureless images were inserted into the supraliminal tape. Blank gray edits were chosen because they simulate the approximate average illumination of the positive and negative mood-inducing frames.

RESULTS

The design of this study was a 2 × 3 factorial, with three levels of treatment (positive, neutral, and negative subliminal stimuli) crossed by sex of subject. The major hypothesis was that exposure to negative stimuli would result in higher levels of state anxiety and that exposure to positive stimuli would result in lower levels of state anxiety, compared with the neutral condition. An additional prediction was that

exposure to the subliminal stimuli would have no effect on trait anxiety. To test these predictions, a 2 × 3 analysis of variance was carried out on each of the three dependent measures: MAACL, STAI-A-State. and STAI-A-Trait.

Analysis of the MAACL yielded only a significant main effect for experimental condition, $F(2,123)= 18.31, p <.001$. Group contrasts showed that mean anxiety scores among subjects in the positive condition were reliably lower than those in the neutral control condition, $t (123) = 3.28, p < .01$, which in turn were reliably lower than those in the negative condition, $t (123) = 2.69, p < .01$.

Analysis of the STAI-A-State measure also yielded a significant main effect for condition, $F(2,123)= 12.72, p < .001$, along with a main effect for sex. $F(1,123) = 6.46, p < .02$. (There was no significant interaction between sex and condition.) Contrasts revealed that state anxiety scores among subjects in the positive condition were significantly lower than those in the neutral condition, $t (123) = 2.57, p <.02$, which in turn were significantly lower than those in the negative condition, $t (123) = 2.40, p < .03$. The main effect obtained for sex reflects the fact that mean anxiety scores for males combined across condition ($M = 33.68$), were lower than the scores of females combined across condition ($M= 37.19$).

Analysis of the STAI-A-Trait measure yielded no significant main effect or interaction. This finding can be interpreted in either of two ways. First, the subject groups apparently did not differ in anxiety proneness. Therefore the effects found across treatment conditions can safely be attributed to the experimental manipulations. Second, the manipulation apparently had no influence on self-reports of trait anxiety. This is perfectly consistent with our expectations. The experimental manipulation should *not* have had such an influence, and it is reassuring to find that it did not.

DISCUSSION

The results of this study are consistent with the hypothesis that information presented outside conscious awareness can exert an influence on subjective emotional experience. Our procedures incorporated controls for the amount and nature of visible stimulation and for the presence of subliminal inserts across all conditions of the study. Subjects exposed to threatening pictorial stimuli subsequently reported higher levels of state anxiety, compared with the anxiety baseline reported in the control group (thereby replicating findings from a pilot study). Subjects exposed to humorous stimuli reported lower levels of state anxiety than did the same control group. This latter finding suggests that subliminal effects on feelings can be bidirectional. Finally, it is important to note that these effects were specific to *state* anxiety, with no such difference emerging in self-ratings of trait anxiety.

Relation to Other Research

The effects reported here complement the findings of other recent research. For example, in one recent project, Bargh and Pietromonaco (1982) presented subliminally words pertaining to aggressiveness and hostility. This exposure influenced subsequent perceptions of an ambiguously portrayed stimulus person—that is, made evaluations of that person more negative. This finding conceptually replicated earlier results of Bach and Klein (1957), Smith, Spence, and Klein (1959), Allison (1963), Somekh and Wilding (1973), and Sackeim, Packer, and Gur (1977).

This group of findings can be interpreted in either of two related ways. Both interpretations assume models of memory in which nodes of information vary in level of activation from moment to moment, with activation above some threshold corresponding to awareness (Collins & Loftus, 1975; see also Andersor & Bower, 1973). Partial activation renders a node more easily brought to full awareness by subsequent processing of node-related information. One possbility is that low-level processing yielded partial activation of a category of meaning (e.g. hostility, in the case of Bargh & Pietromonaco) that then was preferentially used in construing the target figure, requiring only that the use be plausible (cf. Higgins, R. Holes, & Jones, 1977). Another possibility (suggested by Bargh & Pietromonaco, 1982) is that their subjects may have extracted the *emotional tone* conveyed by the subliminally presented words which then influenced the evaluative responses made to the target figure. This latter possibility it consistent with the idea that emotional qualities are stored in memory in much the same way as is other information (Bower & Cohen, 1982). Indeed, these two explanations are not mutually exclusive—a negative emotional tone may be an element that is intrinsic to the mental representation of the category of hostility.

These previous effects all differ from the present finding, however, in one important way. In the previous studies, the dependent variable was an *evaluative judgment about some external stimulus*. Those earlier effects clearly imply the activation of meaning in memory by the subliminal stimuli (even if the "meaning" activated was an emotional quality), but they do not imply that the stimuli had an effect on the subject's mood state. The outcome variable of the study reported here, in contrast, was precisely that—the subject's self-reported mood.

Assessment of Subliminality

Though the findings of this study are consistent with our hypothesis, we should acknowledge one limitation on our conclusions. Specifically, we did not include groups in this study whose sole purpose was to verify that the insertions were subliminal. How to go about ensuring that material intended to be outside awareness really is outside awareness is not an easy problem to resolve (for a discussion of this and related issues see Holender, 1986, the 27 commentaries that follow his article, and his response to those commentaries). One approach (used by Bargh & Pietromonaco, 1982) is to incorporate a condition into the study in which subjects are exposed to the alleged subliminal stimuli and are asked immediately afterward to specify what stimuli had been presented, from a larger set of possibilities. If subjects identify the stimuli at a level no better than chance, one is relatively confident that the stimuli did not reach awareness.

Even procedures such as this are not without their ambiguities, however. Being unable to identify what one has seen may or may not reflect an absence of awareness at the instant of initial exposure. Though the line that passes between exposure and presentation of the multiple choice question is brief, it is arguable that a real (if only momentary) awareness decays sufficiently in that interval to reduce recognition to the level of chance. A subject may still be aware of having been aware of the stimulus at the earlier moment, but that current awareness (and the fact that it negates the claim of subliminality) would not be reflected in the measure that is being taken (correct identification of the stimuli).

A different kind of ambiguity emerges if subjects guess the stimuli at a level better than chance. In this case, the conclusion is likely to be drawn that the stimuli were processed consciously.[2] Is this conclusion warranted? Recall the assumption that presentation outside awareness produces partial activation of memory traces and that partial activation renders that information more accessible for later use (Collins & Loftus, 1975). If this were so, then a subsequent presentation of the same stimulus might well lead to better than chance identifications even when the initial stimulus was processed outside awareness, provided the initial activation on were sufficiently intense. Indeed, this argument relies on precisely the same conceptual mechanism as is usually used to account for findings such as those of Bargh and Pietromonaeo (1982).

It should be apparent from this discussion that there are a number of complex issues hiding behind the deceptively simple question of how to make sure that a stimulus has been presented subliminally. In the study reported here, we are limited to the following conclusion: At the point of being questioned, our subjects were unaware of having been aware of the subliminal inserts to which they were exposed earlier in the session.

Implications

The findings reported here seem to us to open up a variety of additional questions concerning the processing of affect-related information at a level outside consciousness. One might ask, for example, whether subjective emotional tone is influenced by the processing (at levels that fail to reach awareness) of information *already stored in memory*. This question is particularly interesting when taken in combination with a second body of research and theory, bearing on the idea that the self or self-concept constitutes a broad and elaborate schematic memory structure (e.g., Greenwald & Pratkanis, 1984; Kuiper, MacDonald & Deny, 1983; Markus, 1977; Rogers, Kuiper, & Kirker, 1977). It is implicit in this point of view that one or another segment of the self-schema is virtually always activated during wakefulness, because of the fact that people tend to process their life experiences by reference to themselves (but see Higgins, King, & Mavin, 1982, for an alternative view). It is only a small extrapolation from this idea to assume that very large portions of the self-schema are chronically in

a condition of *partial* activation (see Higgins et al., 1982, for evidence that certain interpretive schemas are indeed chronically in such states).

The self-schema presumably incorporates a good deal of affect-relevant information. More important, people doubtlessly differ from each other in what sort of affect is embedded in the self-schema. For example, the self-images of depressed persons incorporate substantial negative content, information, implying inadequacies of one sort or another (Kuiper et al., 1983). Presumably this descriptive information is also linked to information specifying negative feelings. If the self-schema of such a person were partially activated—that is, if the information were being processed at a low level, outside conscious awareness—the result might well be the generation of negative feelings. Note, however, that such an influence of low-level processing on subjective mood state would not lead to conscious recognition of the *source* of the affect.

Beck (1967) has argued that self-critical cognition arises relatively spontaneously in persons who are depressed and that the depressive mood is attributable to this self-critical cognition. Indeed, the idea that self-critical "self-talk" is a major determinant of dysfunctional emotional states that become a prominent theme in the cognitive-behavioral approach to understanding disorder. What we are suggesting here, however, is something different. We are suggesting that depressed feelings can be induced *without* conscious rumination about negatively evaluated qualities of self.

Indeed, this hypothesis—which in conceptualization derives rather directly from the present data—seems to reopen the entire question of whether "automatic thoughts" determine affective tone, or vice versa. A similar line of argument is easily used to discuss "free-floating" anxiety. Perhaps the experience of anxiety stems from processing of anxiety-related memory content, but processing at levels so low that the content of the material and the source of the anxiety remain unrecognized. Though it is not entirely clear how these possibilities might be tested empirically, we regard them as intriguing and potentially important.

NOTES

1. At least two studies other than those reviewed here have addressed a related, but distinct, question: the degree to

which subliminal stimuli can influence subjective *motive* states (Byrne, 1959; Hawkins, 1970).

2. An open question is whether this conclusion would be drawn even if subjects were to report not having seen the stimuli.

REFERENCES

ALLISON, J. (1963). COGNITIVE STRUCTURE AND RECEPTIVITY TO LOW INTENSITY STIMULATION. *JOURNAL OF ABNORMAL AND SOCIAL PSYCHOLOGY.* 67.133–138.

ANDERSON, J. R., & BOWER, G. H.(1973). *HUMAN ASSOCIATIVE MEMORY.* WASHINGTON. DC: V. H. WINSTON.

BACH, S., & KLEIN, G. S. (1957). CONSCIOUS EFFECTS OF PROLONGED SUBLIMINAL EXPOSURE OF WORDS. *AMERICAN PSYCHOLOGIST,* 12, 397.

BARGH, J. A., & PIETROMONAEO, P. (1982). AUTOMATIC INFORMATION PROCESSING AND SOCIAL PERCEPTION: THE INFLUENCE OF TRAIL INFORMATION PRESENTED OUTSIDE OF CONSCIOUS AWARENESS ON IMPRESSION FORMATION. *JOURNAL OF PERSONAL AND SOCIAL PSYCHOLOGY.* 43, 437–449.

BECK. A. T. (1967). *DEPRESSION-CLINICAL, EXPERIMENTAL AND THEORETICAL ASPECTS.* NEW YORK: HARPER & ROW.

BOWER, G. H., & COHEN, P. R. (1982). EMOTIONAL INFLUENCES IN MEMORY AND THINKING: DATA AND THEORY. IN M S. CLARK & S. T. FISKE (EDS.) *AFFECT END COGNITION* (PP. 291–331). HILLSDALE. NJ: LAWRENCE ERLBAUM.

BYRNE, D. (1959). THE EFFECTS OF A SUBLIMINAL FOOD STIMULUS ON VERBAL RESPONSES. *JOURNAL OF APPLIED PSYCHOLOGY.* 43, 249–252.

COLLINS. A.M.A., LOFTUS. E. F. (1975). A SPREADING-ACTIVATION THEORY OF SEMANTIC PROCESSING. *PSYCHOLOGICAL REVIEW,* 82, 407–428.

DIXON, N. F. (1971) SUBLIMINAL PERCEPTION: *THE NATURE OF A CONTROVERSY,* LONDON McGRAW-HILL.

DIXON. N. F. (1981). *PRECONSCIOUS PROCESSING.* NEW YORK: JOHN WILEY.

ERDELYI, M. H. (1974). A NEW LOOK AT TIE NEW LOOK: PERCEPTUAL DEFENSE AND VIGILANCE. *PSYCHOLOGICAL REVIEW,* 81, 1–25.

ERIKSEN, C. W. (1960). DISCRIMINATION AND LEARNING WITHOUT AWARENESS: A METHODOLOGICAL SURVEY AND EVALUATION. *PSYCHOLOGICAL REVIEW.* 67, 279–300.

GOLDIAMOND, I. (1958). INDICATORS OF PERCEPTION: I. SUBLIMINAL PERCEPTION, SUBCEPTION, UNCONSCIOUS PERCEPTION: AN ANALYSIS IN TERMS OF PSYCHOPHYSICAL INDICATOR METHODOLOGY *PSYCHOLOGICAL BULLETIN.* 55, 373–411.

GREENWALD, A.G., & PRATKANIS. A. R. (1984). THE SELF. IN R. S. WYER. JR., & T. K. SRULL (EDS.). *HANDBOOK OF SOCIAL COGNITION* (VOL. 3, PP. 129–178). HILLSDALE, NJ: LAWRENCE ERLBAUM.

HAWKINS, D. (1970) THE EFFECTS OF SUBLIMINAL STIMULATION ON DRIVE LEVEL AND BRAND PREFERENCE. *JOURNAL OF MARKETING RESEARCH,* 7, 322–326.

HIGGINS, E. T. KING, G.A. & MAVIN. G. H.(1982). INDIVIDUAL CONSTRUCT ACCESSIBILITY AND SUBJECTIVE IMPRESSIONS AND RECALL. *JOURNAL OF PERSONALITY AND SOCIAL PSYCHOLOGY.* 43, 35–47.

HIGGINS, E. T., R. HOLES, W.S., & JONES, C. R. (1977). CATEGORY ACCESSIBILITY AND IMPRESSION FORMATION, *JOURNAL OF EXPERIMENTAL SOCIAL PSYCHOLOGY.* 13. 141–154.

HOLENDER, D. (1986). SEMANTIC ACTIVATION WITHOUT CONSCIOUS IDENTIFICATION IN DICHOTIC LISTENING. PARAFOVEAL VISION, AND VISUAL MASKING: A SURVEY AND APPRAISAL. *THE BEHAVIORAL, AND BRAIN SCIENCE,* 9,1–23.

KUIPER, N. A., MacDONALD, M. R., & DERRY, P. A. (1983). PARAMETERS OF A DEPRESSION SELF-SCHEMA. IN J. SULS & A. G. GREENWALD (EDS.), *PSYCHOLOGICAL PERSPECTIVES ON THE SELF* (VOL.2, PP. 191–217). HILLSDALE, NJ: LAWRENCE ERLBAUM.

LEE, I., & TYRER, P. (1981). SELF-REPORT AND PHYSICOLOGICAL RESPONSES TO SUBLIMINAL AND SUPRALIMINAL MOTION PICTURES. *JOURNAL OF NERVOUS AND MENTAL DISEASE.* 169, 294–298.

MARKUS, H. (1977). SELF-SCHEMATA AND PROCESSING OF INFORMATION ABOUT THE SELF. *JOURNAL OF PERSONALITY AND SOCIAL PSYCHOLOGY.* 35, 63–78.

McGINNIES, E. (1949) EMOTIONALITY AND PERCEPTUAL DEFENSE. *PSYCHOLOGICAL REVIEW.* 56, 244–251.

McCONNELL, J. V. CUTLER. R. L. & McNEIL, E. B. (1958). SUBLIMINAL STIMULATION: AN OVERVIEW. *AMERICAN PSYCHOLGIST.* 13, 229–239.

NIELSON, S. L., & SARASON, I. G. (1981) EMOTION, PERSONALITY, AND SELECTIVE ATTENTION. *JOURNAL OF PERSONALITY AND SOCIAL PSYCHOLOGY.* 41, 945–960.

ROGERS, T. B., KUIPER, N. A., & KIRKER, W. S. (1977). SELF-REFERENCE AND THE ENCODING OF PERSONAL INFORMATION. *JOURNAL OF PERSONALITY AND SOCIAL PSYCHOLOGY.* 35, 677–688.

RUTSTEIN, E. H., & GOLDBERGER, L. (1973). THE EFFECTS OF AGGRESSIVE STIMULATION ON SUICIDAL PATIENTS: AN EXPERIMENTAL STUDY OF THE PSYCHOANALYTIC THEORY OF SUICIDE. IN B. RUBINSTEIN (ED), *PSYCHOANALYSIS AND CONTEMPORARY SCIENCE* (VOL. 2). NEW YORK: MACMILLAN.

SACKEIM, H. A. PACKER, I. K., & GUR. R. C. (1977). HEMISPHERICITY, COGNITIVE SET, AND SUSCEPTIBILITY TO SUBLIMINAL PERCEPTION. *JOURNAL OF ABNORMAL PSYCHOLOGY*. 86, 624–630.

SILVERMAN, L. H. (1976). PSYCHOANALYTIC THEORY: THE REPORTS OF MY DEATH ARE GREATLY EXAGGERATED. *AMERICAN PSYCHOLOGIST*, *31*, 621–637.

SMITH, G. J., SPENCE, D. P., & KLEIN. G. S. (1959). SUBLIMINAL EFFECTS OF VERBAL STIMULI. *JOURNAL OF ABNORMAL AND SOCIAL PSYCHOLOGY*. 59, 167–176.

SOMEKH, D. E., & WILDING, J. M. (1973). PERCEPTION WITHOUT AWARENESS IN A DICHOTIC VIEWING SITUATION. *BRITISH JOURNAL OF PSYCHOLOGY*, 64, 339–349.

SPIELBERGER, C. D., GORSUCH, R. L. & LUSHENE. R. E. (1970). MANUAL FOR THE STATE-TRAIT ANXIETY INVENTORY (*SELF EVALUATION QUESTIONNAIRE*). PALO ALTO, CA: CONSULTING PSYCHOLOGISTS PRESS.

TYRER, P., LEWIS, P., & LEE, I. (1978). EFFECTS OF SUBLIMINAL AND SUPRALIMINAL STRESS ON SYMPTOMS OF ANXIETY. *JOURNAL OF NERVOUS AND MENTAL DISEASE*. 166, 88–95.

VARGA, M. (1973). *AN EXPERIMENTAL STUDY OF ASPECTS OF THE PSYCHOANALYTIC STUDY OF ELATION*. UNPUBLISHED DOCTORAL DISSERTATION. NEW YORK UNIVERSITY.

WYER. R. S., JR., & SRULL, T. K. (EDS.) (1984). *HANDBOOK OF SOCIAL COGNITION*. HILLSDALE, NJ: LAWRENCE ERLBAUM.

ZAJONC, R. B. (1980). FEELING AND THINKING: PREFERENCES NEED NO INFERENCES. *AMERICAN PSYCHOLOGIST*. 35, 151–175.

ZUCKERMAN, M., & LUBIN, B. (1965). *MANUAL FOR THE MULTIPLE AFFECT ADJECTIVE CHECKLIST*. SAN DIEGO, CA: EDUCATIONAL AND INDUSTRIAL TESTING SERVICE.

Memory for Events Occurring Under Anesthesia

ELIZABETH F. LOFTUS, JONATHAN W. SCHOOLER, GEOFFREY R. LOFTUS, AND DENNIS T. GLAUBER

A number of anecdotal reports suggest that people have memories for incidents that happened while they were anesthetized. The present study investigated this possibility by studying an anesthetized patient's later memory for a word list. During an abdominal myomectomy, the patient was read a list of 100 unrelated words. Three subsequent memory tests were given, at 28, 53 and 82 hours after exposure. Recognition was at chance level. The results cast doubt on the suggestion that anesthetized patients have memory for events occurring while unconscious.

Several years ago, a California anesthesiologist, Dr. M., was accused of lewd and lascivious conduct for allegedly committing sodomy on female patients during surgery. Many civil suits were filed against Dr. M. by women who generally could not remember anything about the surgery but feared they had been victims. Some of those patients were subsequently hypnotized to "unlock" their unconscious memories of what occurred during surgery. One patient who initially remembered nothing after surgery claimed later, after hypnosis "refreshed" her memory, that she remembered a penis entering her mouth. In response to this incident, one physician interviewed by a reporter for the *Sacramento Union* said that there is evidence that anesthetized patients can recall minute details after surgery. Specifically, the physician said that patients can sometimes allegedly remember entire conversations and physical actions of operating room personnel, even though they were in a deep state of unconsciousness.

Can people recall events that occurred while they were anesthetized during surgery? A few anecdotal reports and quasi-experiments suggest that it may be possible for a patient to remember sounds and words that were spoken. For example, in one case, a female patient who had positive feelings toward her surgeon before surgery, did not afterwards. After her surgery, she recalled hearing her surgeon utter these specific words during the operation: "Well, that will take care of this old bag!" In another instance, one more closely resembling a true experiment, ten patients participated (Levinson 1967). At a specified point in time, when each patient was deeply anesthetized, the anesthetist said something like: "Just a moment. I don't like the patient's color. The lips are too blue, very blue. More oxygen please ... Good everything is fine now."

One month later, the patients were told to reexperience the operation while under hypnosis. Four of the ten were able to "repeat practically verbatim the traumatic words used by the anesthetist. A further four patients displayed a severe degree of anxiety while reliving the operation ... The remaining two ...denied hearing anything." (Levinson 1967: 23)

Collectively, these reports hint that it may be possible for a patient to recall sounds or words spoken during surgery. However, methodological problems in the prior work render the findings problematic. For example, in many instances the person conducting the test of memory was aware of the material presented during surgery and thus might inadvertently have influenced the reported recollection. In other instances, there could have been a temporary decrease in the depth of anesthesia. Such a situation can occur where muscle relaxants are used which permit surgery to be performed with lower drug concentrations than would be possible without such relaxants (Adam 1976; Trustman et al. 1977).

We here report the results of a rigorous experimental test conducted on a patient who was undergoing an abdominal myomectomy under general anesthesia. The patient was an experimental psychologist with a keen interest in human memory in general (Loftus 1979, 1980; Loftus and Loftus 1976) and in the possibility of memory for events occurring during anesthesia; thus informed consent was freely granted. The second author (J. Schooler) created a list of 100 words to be read to the patient by the anesthesiologist (D. Glauber) during surgery. The words were taken from a standard source (Kucera and Francis 1976) frequently utilized in research on human memory. Seventy-five minutes after oral premedication of diazepam 10 mg, anesthesia was induced with thiopental 200 mg. Following endotracheal intubation, anesthesia was maintained with nitrous oxide 60% in oxygen, together with Isoflurane in inspired concentrations of 1–3%. Surgery commenced 30 minutes after induction and a further 30 minutes later the words were read at the rate of one word every two seconds. The subject-patient was undoubtedly anesthetized throughout to a depth suitable for surgery.

Testing was initiated 28 hours after surgery. Immediately prior to formal testing, the subject attempted to recall freely any words that may have been heard. She "recalled" 20 items, none of which were on the original list.

Three formal memory tests were then administered by the third author (G. Loftus) who was blind to the correct answers. The three tests were identical and used the standard two-alternative forced-choice procedure. During the test, the experimenter read pairs of words, 100 pairs in all, and for each pair the subject indicated which word seemed familiar. Her instructions were to respond with a 1 or 2 on each trial to indicate the first or second word, and to guess when necessary. The words were tested in the same order in which they were initially given. The three tests were given at 28, 53, and 82 hours after initial exposure.

On the first recognition test, the subject correctly identified the study item 53% of the time. Her performance on the second and third tests was 53% and 45%, respectively. None of these figures is significantly different from chance performance of 50%.

A potential problem with the use of three identical tests of all items should probably be acknowledged. On the second (and third) test trials, a subject may have difficulty discriminating weakly represented "studied" items from distractors that occurred on the first (and second) test. Although this potential problem cannot account for the poor performance observed on the first test, future research may wish to employ a procedure in which a subset of the target items is tested only once on each of several tests.

It should be noted that generally recognition memory for lists of words of this type is quite good (although not usually perfect) when subjects are exposed in a waking state. In one study, subjects who were exposed to over 500 different words and tested shortly thereafter using the same procedure correctly identified the study item in 88% of the test pairs (Shepard 1967). To test the hypothesis that the particular subject-patient used in the current research would have performed poorly whether anesthetized or not, the subject was exposed to an identical learning and testing procedure one month after her operation. A different set of words was used, taken from the same source. On tests given 28 and 55 hours after initial learning, performance was 94% and 92% respectively, well above chance.

Standard memory testing with waking subjects generally yields typical serial position functions (Zechmeister and Nyberg 1982). The serial position effect is the finding that words at the beginning and end of a list are remembered better than words in the middle of the list. There were no such serial position effects apparent in this study. For example, on the first test administered 28 hours after exposure, the subject's performance for each successive fifth of the list was: 50%, 60%, 65%, 65%, and 30%, respectively. Only one of the first three and one of the last three words were correctly recognized.

For purposes of providing some baseline performance with which to compare our results, we considered several possibilities. One was to use the generally good recognition memory for words observed in previous work, and to assume that memory for the current list would similarly be reasonably high if exposure and testing occurred during normal waking consciousness. Another was to assume simply that any significant departure from chance performance would be suggestive of some information processing during anaesthesia. As noted, this result did not obtain. Another was to test the subject at a later time, when initial learning and subsequent recall could be tested under normal waking conditions. As noted, this procedure produced reasonably good performance. As an afterthought, we tested one of the physicians who participated in the surgery, a first-year resident with some experience in abdominal myomectomies. The test was conducted 82 hours after exposure, at the same time that the patient-subject received her third test. The physician-subject and the patient-subject were shielded from the responses of each other. The physician-subject correctly identified only 50% of the words that had been spoken during surgery—exactly chance performance—and volunteered that she only felt confident about two words. She claimed to be very absorbed in the operation during the presentation of the words. What can be inferred from the physician's failure to remember? One of our colleagues suggested, facetiously, that the failure showed that even proximity to anesthesia can produce impairments in memory storage. More seriously, we suggest that the physician's failure, if replicable, may extend the present results beyond anesthesia situations towards non-awareness studies in general. Such a conclusion awaits the outcome of future experiments conducted with a variety of tests that may be more sensitive.

It could be argued that had hypnosis been used with the patient better memory for the words would have been revealed. However, controlled laboratory studies have consistently failed to demonstrate improvement of memory under hypnosis, a conclusion reached quite explicitly in a recent and thorough review of the literature (Smith 1983). Moreover, one needs to worry, with hypnosis, about the potential for hypnotically created memory (Laurence and Perry 1983).

Although only one subject was used in the present study, the results raise a doubt as to the viability of claims that persons can be made to recall events that occurred during surgery. In instances where this has been claimed, one must consider the possibilities that the so-called memories are simple constructions or confabulations in the minds of patients, that anesthetization was not complete, or that inadvertent "coaching" on the part of the experimenter contributed to the finding.

Despite the doubt we have about memory for items that occurred while a person was anesthetized, our results do apply only to deliberate or intentional memory, that is cases in which a person is aware that he or she is remembering a particular past event. These results still leave open the possibility that information presented under anesthesia leaves some lasting impression that cannot be revealed in tests of retention that require remembering to be deliberate or intentional (Eich 1984). In a shadowing study involving the recognition and spelling of previously unattended homophones, Eich (1984) showed that information in the nonshadowed channel could bias the spelling of a homophone, even when subjects could not explicitly recognize having been exposed to that homophone. In discussing his results Eich (1984) left open the question of whether the same pattern of recognition and spelling performance would be revealed in the context of general anesthesia. However, since we used a test that demands awareness of memory, Eich would probably say our experiment was doomed before it began.

Other complaints are also possible. For example, suppose we had used a test that does not demand awareness of remembering, and still found poor performance. We could then anticipate the criticism that the material may not have been sufficiently emotional for it to be subject to some degree of deep, semantic analysis.

Despite the fact that our study leaves many questions unanswered, our inability to observe memory for events occurring under anesthesia is of particular importance considering the various potential artifacts in previous studies. Because of the general practice of not presenting null effects, all too often published results based upon experimental artifacts or chance fluctuations may go unchallenged. We welcome the opportunity to publish in a regular journal this single-subject experiment that favors a null hypothesis; we hope our study contributes to greater skepticism regarding the notion of memory under anesthesia.

REFERENCES

ADAM, N., 1976. 'DISRUPTION OF MEMORY FUNCTIONS ASSOCIATED WITH GENERAL ANESTHETICS'. IN: J.F. KIHLSTROM AND F.J. EVANS (EDS.). *FUNCTIONAL DISORDERS OF MEMORY.* HILLSDALE, NJ: ERLBAUM.

EICH, E., 1984. 'MEMORY FOR UNATTENDED EVENTS: REMEMBERING WITH AND WITHOUT AWARENESS.' *MEMORY AND COGNITION* 12. 105–111.

KUCERA, H. AND W. N. FRANCIS, 1976. *COMPUTATIONAL ANALYSIS OF PRESENT-DAY AMERICAN ENGLISH.* PROVIDENCE, RI: BROWN UNIVERSITY PRESS.

LAURENCE, J. AND C. PERRY. 1983. 'HYPNOTICALLY CREATED MEMORY AMONG HIGHLY HYPNOTIZABLE SUBJECTS.' *SCIENCE* 222. 523–524.

LEVINSON, B.W., 1967. 'STATES OF AWARENESS DURING GENERAL ANESTHESIA'. IN: J.W. LASSNER (ED.). *HYPNOSIS AND PSYCHOSOMATIC MEDICINE.* NEW YORK: SPRINGER.

LOFTUS, E.F., 1979. *EYEWITNESS TESTIMONY.* CAMBRIDGE, MA: HARVARD UNIVERSITY PRESS.

LOFTUS, E.F., 1980. 'MEMORY.' *READING,* MA: ADDISON-WESLEY.

LOFTUS, G.R. AND E.F. LOFTUS, 1976. *HUMAN MEMORY.* HILLSDALE, NJ: ERLBAUM.

SHEPARD, R.N., 1967. 'RECOGNITION MEMORY FOR WORDS, SENTENCES AND PICTURES.' *JOURNAL OF VERBAL LEARNING AND VERBAL BEHAVIOR* 6. 156–163.

SMITH. M.C., 1983. 'HYPNOTIC MEMORY ENHANCEMENT OF WITNESSES: DOES IT WORK?' *PSYCHOLOGICAL BULLETIN* 94, 387–407.

TRUSTMAN. R., S. DUBROVSKY AND R. TITLEY, 1977. 'AUDITORY PERCEPTION DURING GENERAL ANESTHESIA—MYTH OR FACT?' *INTERNATIONAL JOURNAL OF CLINICAL AND EXPERIMENTAL HYPNOSIS* 25. 88–105.

ZECHMEISTER. E.B. AND S.E. NYBERG. 1982. *HUMAN MEMORY.* MONTEREY, CA: BROOKS/COLE.

CHAPTER 5
Short-Term Memory

Learning, Memory and Forgetting

MICHAEL W. EYSENCK AND MARK T. KEANE

INTRODUCTION

This chapter and the next two are concerned with human memory. All three chapters deal with intact human memory, but Chapter 7 also considers amnesic patients. Traditional laboratory-based research is the focus of this chapter, with more naturalistic research being discussed in Chapter 8. As we will see, there are important links among these different types of research. Many theoretical issues are relevant to brain-damaged and healthy individuals whether tested in the laboratory or in the field.

Theories of memory generally consider both the architecture of the memory system and the processes operating within that structure. Architecture refers to the way in which the memory system is organised and processes refer to the activities occurring within the memory system.

Learning and memory involve a series of stages. Processes occurring during the presentation of the learning material are known as "encoding" and involve many of the processes involved in perception. This is the first stage. As a result of encoding, some information is stored within the memory system. Thus, storage is the second stage. The third (and final) stage is retrieval, which involves recovering or extracting stored information from the memory system.

We have emphasised the distinctions between architecture and process and among encoding, storage, and retrieval. However, we cannot have architecture without process, or retrieval without previous encoding and storage.

ARCHITECTURE OF MEMORY

Throughout most of the history of memory research, it has been assumed that there is an important distinction between short-term memory and long-term memory. It seems reasonable that the processes involved in briefly remembering a telephone number are very different from those involved in long-term memory for theories and research in psychology. This traditional view is at the heart of multi-store models, which are discussed initially. In recent times, however, some theorists have argued in favour of unitary-store models in which the distinction between short-term and long-term memory is much less clear-cut than in the traditional approach. We will consider unitary-store models shortly.

Multi-store model

Several memory theorists (e.g., Atkinson & Shiffrin, 1968) have described the basic architecture of the memory system. We can identify a multi-store approach based on the common features of their theories. Three types of memory-store were proposed:

- Sensory stores, each holding information very briefly and being modality specific (limited to one sensory modality).
- Short-term store of very limited capacity.

- Long-term store of essentially unlimited capacity holding information over very long periods of time.

The basic multi-store model is shown in Figure 6.1. Environmental stimulation is initially received by the sensory stores. These stores are modality-specific (e.g., vision, hearing). Information is held very briefly in the sensory stores, with some being attended to and processed further by the short-term store. Some information processed in the short-term store is transferred to the long-term store. Long-term storage of information often depends on rehearsal. There is a direct relationship between the amount of rehearsal in the short-term store and the strength of the stored memory trace. There is much overlap between the areas of attention and memory. Broadbent's (1958) theory of attention (see Chapter 5) was the main influence on the multi-store approach to memory. For example, Broadbent's buffer store resembles the notion of a sensory store.

Sensory stores

The visual store is often known as the iconic store. In Sperling's (1960) classic work on this store, he presented a visual array containing three rows of four letters each for 50 ms. Participants could usually report only 4–5 letters, but claimed to have seen many more. Sperling assumed this happened because visual information had faded before most of it could be reported. He tested this by asking participants to recall only *part* of the information presented. Sperling's results supported his assumption, with part recall being good provided that the information to be recalled was cued very soon after the offset of the visual display.

Sperling's (1960) findings suggested that information in iconic memory decays within about 0.5 seconds, but this may well be an underestimate. Landman, Spekreijse, and Lamme (2003) pointed out that the requirement to verbally identify and recall items in the part-recall condition may have interfered with performance. They imposed simpler response demands on participants (i.e., is a second stimulus the same as the first one?) and found that iconic memory lasted for up to about 1600 ms.

Iconic storage is very useful for two reasons. First, the mechanisms responsible for visual perception always operate on the icon rather than directly on the visual environment. Second, information remains in iconic memory for upwards of 500 ms, and we can shift our attention to aspects of the information within iconic memory in approximately 55 ms (Lachter, Forster, & Ruthruff, 2004). This helps to ensure we attend to important information.

The transient auditory store is known as the echoic store. In everyday life, you may sometimes have been asked a question while your mind was on something else. Perhaps you replied, "What did you say?", just before realising that you do know what had been said. This "playback" facility depends on the echoic store. Estimates of the duration of information in the echoic store are typically within the range of 2–4 seconds (Treisman, 1964).

KEY TERM

echoic store: a sensory store in which auditory information is briefly held.

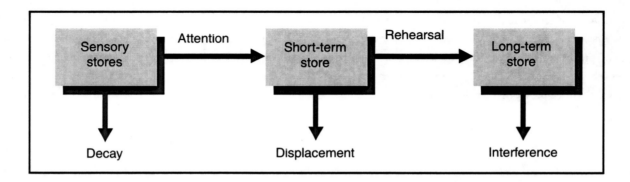

Figure 6.1 The multi-store model of memory.

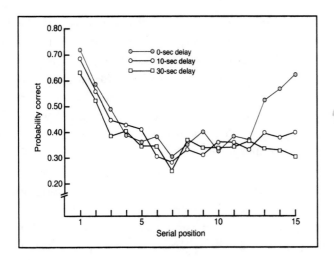

Figure 6.2 Free recall as a function of serial position and duration of the interpolated task. *Adapted from Glanzer and Cunitz (1966).*

Short- and long-term stores

The capacity of short-term memory is very limited. Consider digit span: participants listen to a random series of digits and then repeat them back immediately in the correct order. Other span measures are letter span and word span. The maximum number of units (e.g., digits) recalled without error is usually "seven plus or minus two" (Miller, 1956). However, there are two qualifications concerning that finding. First, Miller (1956) argued that the capacity of short-term memory should be assessed by the number of chunks (integrated pieces or units of information). For example, "IBM" is one chunk for those familiar with the company name International Business Machines but three chunks for everyone else. The capacity of short-term memory is often seven chunks rather than seven items. However, Simon (1974) found that the span in chunks was less with larger chunks (e.g., eight-word phrases) than with smaller chunks (e.g., one-syllable words).

Second, Cowan (2000, p. 88) argued that estimates of short-term memory capacity are often inflated because participants' performance depends in part on rehearsal and on long-term memory. When these additional factors are largely eliminated, the capacity of short-term memory is typically only about four chunks. For example, Cowan et al. (2005) used the running memory task—a series of digits ended at an unpredictable point, with the participants' task being to recall the items from the end of the list. The digits

were presented very rapidly to prevent rehearsal, and the mean number of items recalled was 3.87.

The recency effect in free recall (recalling the items in any order) refers to the finding that the last few items in a list are usually much better remembered in immediate recall than those from the middle of the list. Counting backwards for 10 seconds between the end of list presentation and start of recall mainly affects the recency effect (Glanzer & Cunitz, 1966; see Figure 6.2). The two or three words susceptible to the recency effect may be in the short-term store at the end of list presentation and so especially vulnerable. However, Bjork and Whitten (1974) found that there was still a recency effect when participants counted backwards for 12 seconds after each item in the list was presented. According to Atkinson and Shiffrin (1968), this should have eliminated the recency effect.

KEY TERM

---

chunk: a stored unit formed from integrating smaller pieces of information.
recency effect: the finding that the last few items in a list are much better remembered than other items in immediate free recall.

The above findings can be explained by analogy to looking along a row of telephone poles. The closer poles are more distinct than the ones farther away, just as the most recent list words are more discriminable than the others (Glenberg, 1987).

Peterson and Peterson (1959) studied the duration of short-term memory by using the task of remembering a three-letter stimulus while counting backwards by threes followed by recall in the correct order. Memory performance reduced to about 50% after 6 seconds and forgetting was almost complete after 18 seconds (see Figure 6.3), presumably because unrehearsed information disappears rapidly from short-term memory through decay (see Nairne, 2002, for a review). In contrast, it is often argued that forgetting from long-term memory involves different mechanisms. In particular, there is much cue-dependent forgetting, in which the memory traces are still in the memory system but are inaccessible (see later discussion).

Nairne, Whiteman, and Kelley (1999) argued that the rate of forgetting observed by Peterson and Peterson (1959) was

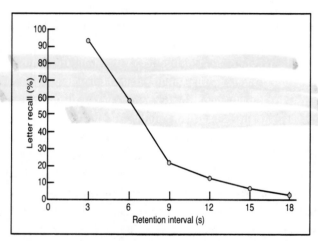

Figure 6.3 Forgetting over time in short-term memory. *Data from Peterson and Peterson (1959).*

especially rapid for two reasons. First, they used all the letters of the alphabet repeatedly, which may have caused considerable interference. Second, the memory task was difficult in that participants had to remember the items themselves and the presentation order. Nairne et al. presented different words on each trial to reduce interference, and tested memory only for order information and not for the words themselves. Even though there was a rehearsal-prevention task (reading aloud digits presented on a screen) during the retention interval, there was remarkably little forgetting even over 96 seconds (see Figure 6.4).

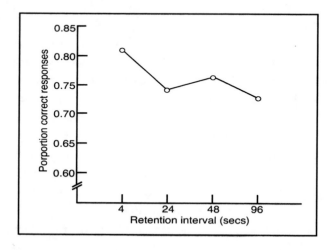

Figure 6.4 Proportion of correct responses as a function of retention interval. *Data from Nairne et al. (1999).*

This finding casts doubt on the notion that decay causes forgetting in short-term memory. However, reading digits aloud may not have totally prevented rehearsal.

Finally, we turn to the strongest evidence that short-term and long-term memory are distinct. If short-term and long-term memory are separate, we might expect to find some patients with impaired long-term memory but intact short-term memory and others showing the opposite pattern. This would produce a double dissociation. The findings are generally supportive. Patients with amnesia (discussed in Chapter 7) have severe impairments of many aspects of long-term memory, but typically have no problem with short-term memory (Spiers, Maguire, & Burgess, 2001). Amnesic patients have damage to the medial temporal lobe, including the hippocampus (see Chapter 7), which primarily disrupts long-term memory (see Chapter 7).

A few brain-damaged patients have severely impaired short-term memory but intact long-term memory. For example, KF had no problems with long-term learning and recall but had a very small digit span (Shallice & Warrington, 1970). Subsequent research indicated that his short-term memory problems focused mainly on recall of letters, words, or digits rather than meaningful sounds or visual stimuli (e.g., Shallice & Warrington, 1974). Such patients typically have damage to the parietal and temporal lobes (Vallar & Papagno, 2002).

Evaluation

The multi-store approach has various strengths. The conceptual distinction between three kinds of memory store (sensory store, short-term store, and long-term store) makes sense. These memory stores differ in several ways:

- temporal duration
- storage capacity
- forgetting mechanism(s)
- effects of brain damage

Finally, many subsequent theories of human memory have built on the foundations of the multi-store model, as we will see later in this chapter.

However, the multi-store model possesses several serious limitations. First, it is very oversimplified. It was assumed that the short-term and long-term stores are both *unitary*, i.e., each store always operates in a single, uniform way. As we will see shortly, Baddeley and Hitch (1974) proposed replacing the concept of a single short-term store with a working memory system consisting of *three* different components. That is a more realistic approach. In similar fashion, there are several long-term memory systems (see Chapter 7).

Second, it is assumed that the short-term store acts as a gateway between the sensory stores and long-term memory (see Figure 6.1). However, the information processed in the short-term store has already made contact with information stored in long-term memory (Logie, 1999). For example, consider the phonological similarity effect: immediate recall of visually presented words in the correct order is worse when they are phonologically similar (sounding similar) (e.g., Larsen, Baddeley, & Andrade, 2000). Thus, information about the sounds of words stored in long-term memory affects processing in short-term memory.

Third, Atkinson and Shiffrin (1968) assumed that information in short-term memory represents the "contents of consciousness". This implies that only information processed consciously can be stored in long-term memory. However, learning without conscious awareness of what has been learned (implicit learning) appears to exist (see later in the chapter).

Fourth, multi-store theorists assumed that most information is transferred to long-term memory via rehearsal. However, the role of rehearsal in our everyday lives is very limited. More generally, multi-store theorists focused too much on structural aspects of memory rather than on memory processes.

Unitary-store models

In recent years, various theorists have argued that the entire multi-store approach is misguided and should be replaced by a unitary-store model (see Jonides, Lewis, Nee, Lustig, Berman, & Moore, 2008, for a review). Unitary-store models assume that, "STM (short-term memory) consists of temporary activations of LTM (long-term memory) representations or of representations of items that were recently perceived" (Jonides et al., 2008, p. 198). Such activations will often occur when certain representations are the focus of attention.

Unitary-store models would seem to have great difficulty in explaining the consistent finding that amnesic patients have essentially intact short-term memory in spite of having severe problems with long-term memory. Jonides et al. (2008) argued that amnesic patients have special problems in forming novel relations (e.g., between items and their context) in both short-term and long-term memory. Amnesic patients apparently have no problems with short-term memory because short-term memory tasks typically do not require relational memory. This leads to a key prediction: amnesic patients should have impaired short-term memory performance on tasks requiring relational memory.

According to Jonides et al. (2008), the hippocampus and surrounding medial temporal lobes (typically damaged in amnesic patients) play a crucial role in forming novel relations (sometimes called binding) (see Chapter 7). Multi-store theorists assume that these structures are much more involved in long-term memory than in short-term memory. However, it follows from unitary-store models that the hippocampus and medial temporal lobes would be involved if a short-term memory task required forming novel relations.

Evidence

Evidence supporting the unitary-store approach was reported by Hannula, Tranel, and Cohen (2006). They studied patients who had become amnesic as the result of an anoxic episode (involving deficient oxygen supply). In one experiment, scenes were presented for 20 seconds. Some scenes were repeated exactly, whereas others were repeated with one object having been moved spatially. Participants decided whether each scene had been seen previously. It was assumed that short-term memory was involved when a given scene was repeated in its original or slightly modified form immediately after its initial presentation (Lag 1) but that long-term memory was involved at longer lags.

The findings are shown in Figure 6.5. Amnesic patients performed much worse than healthy controls in short-term memory (Lag 1) and the performance difference between the two groups was even larger in long-term memory. The crucial issue is whether performance at Lag 1 was *only* due to short-term memory. The finding that amnesics' performance fell to chance level at longer lags

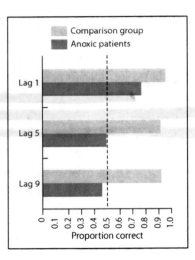

Figure 6.5 Proportion of correct responses for healthy controls (comparison group) and amnesics (anoxic patients). *The dashed line represents chance performance. From Hannula et al. (2006).*

suggests that they may well have relied almost exclusively on short-term memory at Lag 1. However, the finding that controls' performance changed little over lags suggests that they formed strong long-term relational memories, and these long-term memories may well account for their superior performance at Lag 1.

Further support for the unitary-store approach was reported by Hannula and Ranganath (2008). They presented four objects in various locations and instructed participants to rotate the display mentally. Participants were then presented with a second display, and decided whether the second display matched or failed to match their mental representation of the rotated display. This task involved relational memory. The key finding was that the amount of activation in the anterior and posterior regions of the left hippocampus predicted relational memory performance.

Shrager, Levy, Hopkins, and Squire (2008) pointed out that a crucial issue is whether memory performance at short retention intervals actually depends on short-term memory rather than long-term memory. They argued that a distinguishing feature of short-term memory is that it involves active maintenance of information throughout the retention interval. Tasks that mostly depend on short-term memory are vulnerable to distraction during the retention

interval because distraction disrupts active maintenance. Shrager et al. divided their memory tasks into those susceptible to distraction in healthy controls and those that were not. Amnesic patients with medial temporal lobe lesions had essentially normal levels of performance on distraction-sensitive memory tasks but were significantly impaired on distraction-insensitive memory tasks. Shrager et al. concluded that short-term memory processes are intact in amnesic patients. Amnesic patients only show impaired performance on so-called "short-term memory tasks" when those tasks actually depend substantially on long-term memory.

Evaluation

The unitary-store approach has made memory researchers think deeply about the relationship between short-term and long-term memory. There are good reasons for accepting the notion that activation of part of long-term memory plays an important role in short-term memory. According to the unitary-store approach (but not the multi-store approach), amnesic patients can exhibit impaired short-term memory under some circumstances. Some recent evidence (e.g., Hannula et al., 2006) supports the prediction of the unitary-store approach. Functional neuroimaging evidence (e.g., Hannula & Ranganath, 2008) also provides limited support for the unitary-store approach.

What are the limitations of the unitary-store approach? First, it is oversimplified to argue that short-term memory is *only* activated by long-term memory. We can manipulate activated long-term memory in flexible ways and such manipulations go well beyond simply activating some fraction of long-term memory. Two examples of ways in which we can manipulate information in short-term memory are backward digit recall (recalling digits in the opposite order to the presentation order) and generating novel visual images (Logie & van der Meulen, 2009). Second, there is no convincing evidence that amnesic patients have impaired performance on relational memory tasks dependent primarily on short-term memory. It seems likely that amnesic patients only perform poorly on "short-term memory" tasks that depend to a large extent on long-term memory (Shrager et al., 2008). Third, there is no other evidence that decisively favours the unitary-store approach over the multiple-store approach. However, the search for such evidence only recently started in earnest.

WORKING MEMORY

Baddeley and Hitch (1974) and Baddeley (1986) replaced the concept of the short-term store with that of working memory. Since then, the conceptualisation of the working memory system has become increasingly complex. According to Baddeley (2001) and Repovš and Baddeley (2006), the working memory system has four components (see Figure 6.6):

- A modality-free central executive resembling attention.
- A phonological loop holding information in a phonological (speech-based) form.
- A visuo-spatial sketchpad specialised for spatial and visual coding.
- An episodic buffer, which is a temporary storage system that can hold and integrate information from the phonological loop, the visuo-spatial sketchpad, and long-term memory. This component (added 25 years after the others) is discussed later.

The most important component is the central executive. It has limited capacity, resembles attention, and deals with any cognitively demanding task. The phonological loop and the visuo-spatial sketchpad are slave systems used by the central executive for specific purposes. The phonological loop preserves the order in which words are presented, and the visuo-spatial sketchpad stores and manipulates spatial and visual information. All three components have limited capacity and are relatively independent of each other. Two assumptions follow:

(1) If two tasks use the same component, they cannot be performed successfully together.
(2) If two tasks use different components, it should be possible to perform them as well together as separately.

Numerous dual-task studies have been carried out on the basis of these assumptions. For example, Robbins et al. (1996) considered the involvement of the three original components of working memory in the selection of chess moves by weaker and stronger players. The players selected continuation moves from various chess positions while also performing one of the following tasks:

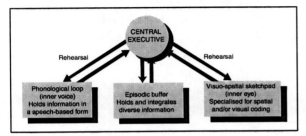

Figure 6.6 The major components of Baddeley's working memory system. *Figure adapted from Baddeley (2001).*

According to Robbins et al, (1996), selecting good chess moves requires use of the central executive and the visuo-spatial sketchpad, but not of the phonological loop.

- *Repetitive tapping:* this was the control condition.
- *Random number generation:* this involved the central executive.
- *Pressing keys on a keypad in a clockwise fashion:* this used the visuo-spatial sketchpad.
- *Rapid repetition of the word "see-saw":* this is articulatory suppression and uses the phonological loop.

Robbins et al. (*1996*) found that selecting chess moves involved the central executive and the visuo-spatial sketchpad but not the phonological loop (see Figure 6.7). The effects of the various additional tasks were similar on stronger and weaker players, suggesting that both groups used the working memory system in the same way.

KEY TERMS

visuo-spatial sketchpad: a component of working memory that is involved in visual and spatial processing of information.

episodic buffer: a component of working memory that is used to integrate and to store briefly information from the phonological loop, the visuo-spatial sketchpad, and long-term memory.

articulatory suppression: rapid repetition of some simple sound (e.g., "the, the, the"), which

uses the articulatory control process of the phonological loop.

Phonological loop

Most early research on the phonological loop focused on the notion that verbal rehearsal (i.e., saying words over and over to oneself) is of central importance. Two phenomena providing support for this view are the phonological similarity effect and the word-length effect. The phonological similarity effect is found when a short list of visually presented words is recalled immediately in the correct order. Recall performance is worse when the words are phonologically similar (i.e., having similar sounds) than when they are phonologically dissimilar. For example, FEE, HE, KNEE, LEE, ME, and SHE form a list of phonologically similar words, whereas BAY, HOE, IT, ODD, SHY, and UP form a list of phonologically dissimilar words. Larsen, Baddeley, and Andrade (2000) used those word lists, finding that recall of the words in order was 25% worse with the phonologically similar list. This phonological similarity effect occurred because participants used speech-based rehearsal processes within the phonological loop.

The word-length effect is based on memory span (the number of words or other items recalled immediately in the correct order). It is defined by the finding that memory span is lower for words taking a long time to say than for those taking less time. Baddeley, Thomson, and Buchanan (1975) found that participants recalled as many words presented visually as they could read out loud in 2 seconds. This suggested that the capacity of the phonological loop is determined by temporal duration like a tape loop. Service (2000) argued that these findings depend on phonological complexity rather than on temporal duration. Reassuringly, Mueller, Seymour, Kieras, and Meyer (2003) found with very carefully chosen words that memory span depended on the articulatory duration of words rather than their phonological complexity.

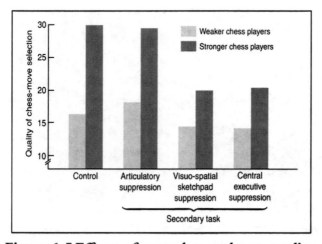

Figure 6.7 Effects of secondary tasks on quality of chess-move selection in stronger and weaker players. *Adapted from Robbins et al. (1996).*

KEY TERMS

phonological similarity effects: the finding that serial recall of visually presented words is worse when the words are phonologically similar rather than phonologically dissimilar.

word-length effect: the finding that word span is greater for short words than for long words.

In another experiment, Baddeley et al. (1975) obtained more direct evidence that the word-length effect depends on the phonological loop. The number of visually presented words (out of five) that could be recalled was assessed. Some participants were given the articulatory suppression task of repeating the digits 1 to 8 while performing the main task. The argument was that the articulatory suppression task would involve the phonological loop and so prevent it being used on the word-span task. As predicted, articulatory suppression eliminated the word-length effect (see Figure 6.8), suggesting it depends on the phonological loop.

As so often in psychology, reality is more complex than was originally thought. Note that the research discussed so far involved the *visual* presentation of words. Baddeley et al. (1975) obtained the usual word-length effect when there was auditory presentation of word lists. Puzzlingly, however, there was still a word-length effect with auditorily

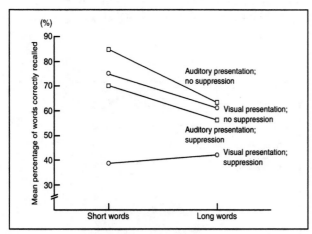

Figure 6.8 Immediate word recall as a function of modality of presentation (visual vs. auditory), *presence versus absence of articulatory suppression, and word length. Adapted from Baddeley et al. (1975).*

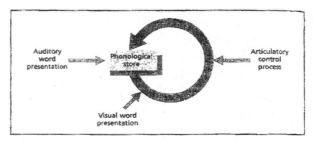

Figure 6.9 Phonological loop system as envisaged by Baddeley (1990).

presented words even when articulatory suppression was used (see Figure 6.8). This led Baddeley (1986, 1990; see Figure 6.9) to argue that the phonological loop has two components:

- A passive phonological store directly concerned with speech perception.
- An articulatory process linked to speech production that gives access to the phonological store.

According to this account, words presented auditorily are processed differently from those presented visually. Auditory presentation of words produces *direct* access to the phonological store regardless of whether the articulatory control process is used. In contrast, visual presentation of words only permits *indirect* access to the phonological store through sub-vocal articulation.

The above account makes sense of many findings. Suppose the word-length effect observed by Baddeley et al. (1975) depends on the rate of articulatory rehearsal (see Figure 6.8). Articulatory suppression eliminates the word-length effect with visual presentation because access to the phonological store is prevented. However, it does *not* affect the word-length effect with auditory presentation because information about the words enters the phonological store directly.

Progress has been made in identifying the brain areas associated with the two components of the phonological loop. Some brain-damaged patients have very poor memory for auditory-verbal material but essentially normal speech production, indicating they have a damaged phonological store but an intact articulatory control process. These patients typically have damage to the left inferior parietal cortex (Vallar & Papagno, 1995). Other brain-damaged patients have an intact phonological store but a damaged articulatory control process shown by a lack of evidence for rehearsal. Such patients generally have damage to the left inferior frontal cortex.

Similar brain areas have been identified in functional neuroimaging studies on healthy volunteers. Henson, Burgess, and Frith (2000) found that a left inferior parietal area was associated with the phonological store, whereas left prefrontal cortex was associated with rehearsal. Logie, Venneri, Delia Sala, Redpath, and Marshall (2003) gave their participants the task of recalling letter sequences presented auditorily in the correct order. All participants were instructed to use subvocal rehearsal to ensure the involvement of the rehearsal component of the phonological loop. The left inferior parietal gyrus and the inferior and middle frontal gyri were activated.

Evaluation

Baddeley's theory accounts for the word-length effects and for the effects of articulatory suppression. In addition, evidence from brain-damaged patients and from functional neuroimaging studies with healthy participants indicates the existence of a phonological store and an articulatory control process located in different brain regions. Our understanding of the phonological loop is greater than that for the other components of the working memory system.

What is the value of the phonological loop? According to Baddeley, Gathercole, and Papagno (1998, p. 158), "The function of the phonological loop is not to remember familiar words but to learn new words." Supporting evidence was reported by Papagno, Valentine, and Baddeley (1991). Native Italian speakers learned pairs of Italian words and pairs of Italian-Russian words. Articulatory suppression (which reduces use of the phonological loop) greatly slowed the learning of foreign vocabulary but had little effect on the learning of pairs of Italian words.

Several studies have considered the relationship between children's vocabulary development and their performance on verbal short-term memory tasks involving the phonological loop. The capacity of the phonological loop generally predicts vocabulary size (e.g., Majerus, Poncelet, Elsen, & van der Linden, 2006). Such evidence is consistent with the notion that the phonological loop plays a role in the learning of vocabulary. However, much of the evidence is correlational—it is also possible that having a large vocabulary increases the effective capacity of the phonological loop.

Trojano and Grossi (1995) studied SC, a patient with extremely poor phonological functioning. SC showed reasonable learning ability in most situations but was unable to learn auditorily presented word-nonword pairs. Presumably SC's poorly functioning phonological loop prevented the learning of the phonologically unfamiliar nonwords.

Visuo-spatial sketchpad

The visuo-spatial sketchpad is used for the temporary storage and manipulation of visual patterns and spatial movement. It is used in many situations in everyday life (e.g., finding the route when walking; playing computer games). Logie, Baddeley, Mane, Donchin, and Sheptak (1989) studied performance on a complex computer game called Space Fortress, which involves manoeuvring a space ship around a computer screen. Early in training, performance on Space Fortress was severely impaired when participants had to perform a secondary visuo-spatial task. After 25 hours' training, the adverse effects on the computer game of carrying out a visuo-spatial task at the same time were greatly reduced, being limited to those aspects directly involving perceptuo-motor control. Thus, the visuo-spatial sketchpad was used throughout training on Space Fortress, but its involvement decreased with practice.

The most important issue is whether there is a *single* system combining visual and spatial processing or whether

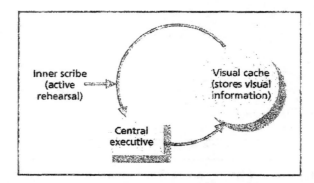

Figure 6.10 The visuo-spatial sketchpad or working memory as envisaged by Logie.
Adopted from Logie (1995), Baddeley, Mane, Donchin, and Sheptak.

there are partially or completely *separate* visual and spatial systems. According to Logie (1995; see Figure 6.10), the visuo-spatial sketchpad consists of two components:

- **Visual cache:** This stores information about visual form and colour.
- **Inner scribe:** This processes spatial and movement information. It is involved in the rehearsal of information in the visual cache and transfers information from the visual cache to the central executive.

Recent developments in theory and research on the visuo-spatial sketchpad are discussed by Logie and van der Meulen (2009).

Klauer and Zhao (2004) explored the issue of whether there are separate visual and spatial systems. They used two main tasks—a spatial task (memory for dot locations) and a visual task (memory for Chinese ideographs). There were also three secondary task conditions:

- A movement discrimination task (spatial interference).
- A colour discrimination task (visual interference).
- A control condition (no secondary task).

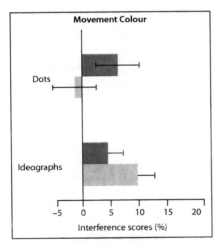

Figure 6.11 Amount of interference on a spatial task (dots) and a visual task (ideographs) as a function of secondary task (spatial: movement vs. visual: colour discrimination). *From Klauer and Zhao (2004).*

What would we expect if there are somewhat separate visual and spatial systems? First, the spatial interference task should disrupt performance more on the spatial main task than on the visual main task. Second, the visual interference task should disrupt performance more on the visual main task than on the spatial main task. Both predictions were supported (see Figure 6.11).

Additional evidence supporting the notion of separate visual and spatial systems was reported by Smith and Jonides (1997) in an ingenious study. Two visual stimuli were presented together, followed by a probe stimulus.

Participants decided whether the probe was in the same location as one of the initial stimuli (spatial task) or had the same form (visual task). Even though the stimuli were identical in the two tasks, there were clear differences in patterns of brain activation. There was more activity in the right hemisphere during the spatial task than the visual task, but more activity in the left hemisphere during the visual task than the spatial task.

Several other studies have indicated that different brain regions are activated during visual and spatial working-memory tasks (see Sala, Rämä, & Courtney, 2003, for a review). The ventral prefrontal cortex (e.g., the inferior and middle frontal gyri) is generally activated more during visual working-memory tasks than spatial ones. In contrast, more dorsal prefrontal cortex (especially an area of the superior prefrontal sulcus) tends to be more activated during spatial working-memory tasks than visual ones. This separation between visual and spatial processing is consistent with evidence that rather separate pathways are involved in visual and spatial perceptual processing (see Chapter 2).

Evaluation

Various kinds of evidence support the view that the visuo-spatial sketchpad consists of somewhat separate visual (visual cache) and spatial (inner scribe) components. First, there is often little interference between visual and spatial tasks performed at the same time (e.g., Klauer & Zhao, 2004). Second, functional neuroimaging data suggest that the two components of the visuo-spatial sketchpad are located in different brain regions (e.g., Sala et al., 2003; Smith & Jonides, 1997). Third, some brain-damaged patients have damage to the visual component but not to the spatial component. For example, NL found it very hard to describe details from the left side of scenes in visual imagery even though his visual perceptual system was essentially intact (Beschin, Cocchini, Della Sala, & Logie, 1997).

Many tasks require both components of the visuo-spatial sketchpad to be used in combination. It remains for the future to understand more fully how processing and information from the two components are combined and integrated on such tasks. In addition, much remains unknown about interactions between the workings of the visuo-spatial sketchpad and the episodic buffer (Baddeley, 2007).

Central executive

The central executive (which resembles an attentional system) is the most important and versatile component of the working memory system. Every time we engage in any complex cognitive activity (e.g., reading a text; solving a problem; carrying out two tasks at the same time), we make considerable use of the central executive. It is generally assumed that the prefrontal cortex is the part of the brain most involved in the functions of the central executive. Mottaghy (2006) reviewed studies using repetitive tran-scranial magnetic stimulation (rTMS; see Glossary) to disrupt activity within the dorsolateral prefrontal cortex. Performance on many complex cognitive tasks was impaired by this manipulation, indicating that dorsolateral prefrontal cortex is of importance in central executive functions. However, we need to be careful about associating the central executive too directly with prefrontal cortex. As Andrés (2003) pointed out, patients with damage to prefrontal cortex do not always show executive deficits, and some patients with no damage to prefrontal cortex nevertheless have executive deficits.

One way of trying to understand the importance of the central executive in our everyday functioning is to study brain-damaged individuals whose central executive is impaired. Such individuals suffer from dysexecutive syndrome (Baddeley, 1996), which involves problems with planning, organising, monitoring behaviour, and initiating behaviour. Patients with dysexecutive syndrome typically have damage within the frontal lobes at the front of the brain (adverse effects of damage to the prefrontal cortex on problem solving are discussed in Chapter 12). However, some patients seem to have damage to posterior (mainly parietal) rather than to frontal regions (e.g., Andrés, 2003). Brain-damaged patients are often tested with the Behavioural Assessment of the Dysexecutive Syndrome (BADS; Wilson, Alderman, Burgess, Emslie, & Evans, 1996). This consists of various tests assessing the ability to shift rules, to devise and implement a solution to a practical problem, to divide time effectively among various tasks, and so on. Individuals with dysexecutive syndrome as assessed by the BADS typically have great problems in holding down a job and functioning adequately in everyday life (Chamberlain, 2003).

The conceptualisation of the central executive has changed over time. As Repovš and Baddeley (2006, p. 12) admitted, it was originally "a convenient ragbag for unanswered questions related to the control of working memory and its two slave subsystems." In the original model, the central executive was *unitary*, meaning that it functioned as a single unit. In recent years, theorists have increasingly argued that the central executive is more complex. Baddeley (1996) suggested that four of the functions of the central executive were as follows: switching of retrieval plans; timesharing in dual-task studies; selective attention to certain stimuli while ignoring others; and temporary activation of long-term memory. These are examples of executive processes, which are processes that serve to organise and co-ordinate the functioning of the cognitive system to achieve current goals.

Miyake et al. (2000) identified three executive processes or functions overlapping partially with those of Baddeley (1996). They assumed these functions were related but separable:

- *Inhibition function:* This refers to "one's ability to deliberately inhibit dominant, automatic, or prepotent responses when necessary" (p. 55). Friedman and Miyake (2004) extended the inhibition function to include resisting distractor interference. For example, consider the Stroop task, on which participants have to name the colours in which words are printed. In the most difficult condition, the words are conflicting colour words (e.g., the word BLUE printed in red). In this condition, performance is slowed down and there are often many errors. The inhibition function is needed to minimise the distraction effect created by the conflicting colour word. It is useful in preventing us from thinking and behaving in habitual ways when such ways are inappropriate.

- *Shifting function:* This refers to "shifting back and forth between multiple tasks, operations, or mental sets" (p. 55). It is used when you switch attention from one task to another. Suppose, for example, you are presented with a series of trials, on each of which two numbers are presented. In one condition, there is task switching: on some trials you have to multiply the two numbers and on other trials you have to divide one *by* the other. In the other condition, there are long blocks of trials on which you always multiply the two numbers and there are other long blocks of trials on which you always divide one number by the other. Performance is slower in the task-switching condition, because attention has to be switched backwards and forwards between the two tasks. Task switching involves the shifting function, which allows us to shift attention rapidly from one task to another. This is a very useful ability in today's 24/7 world.

- *Updating function:* This refers to "updating and monitoring of working memory representations" (p. 55). It is used when you update the information you need to remember. For example, the updating function is required when participants are presented with members of various categories and have to keep track of the most recently presented member of each category. Updating is useful if you are preparing a meal consisting of several dishes or, more generally, if you are trying to cope with changing circumstances.

Evidence

Various kinds of evidence support Miyake et al.'s (2000) identification of three executive functions. First, there are the findings from their own research. They argued that most cognitive tasks involve various processes, which makes it difficult to obtain clear evidence for any single process. Miyake et al. administered several tasks to their participants and then used latent-variable analysis. This form of analysis focuses on positive correlations among tasks as the basis for identifying the common process or function involved. Thus, for example, three tasks might all involve a common process (e.g., the shifting function) but each task might also involve additional specific processes. Latent variable analysis provides a useful way of identifying the common process. Miyake et al. found evidence for three separable executive functions of inhibition, shifting, and monitoring, but also discovered that these functions were positively correlated with each other.

Second, Collette et al. (2005) administered several tasks designed to assess the same three executive processes, and used positron emission tomography (PET; see Glossary) to compare brain activation associated with each process. There were two main findings. First, each executive process or function was associated with activation in a different region within the prefrontal cortex. Second, all the tasks produced activation in the right intraparietal sulcus, the left superior parietal sulcus, and the left lateral prefrontal cortex. Collette et al. suggested that the right intraparietal sulcus is involved in selective attention to relevant stimuli plus the suppression of irrelevant information; the left superior parietal sulcus is involved in switching and integration processes; and the lateral prefrontal cortex is involved in monitoring and temporal organisation.

Are there executive processes or functions not included within Miyake et al.'s (2000) theory? According to Baddeley (1996), one strong contender relates to the dual-task situation, in which people have to perform two different tasks at the same time. Executive processes are often needed to co-ordinate processing on the two tasks. Functional neuroimaging studies focusing on dual-task situations have produced somewhat variable findings (see Chapter 5). However, there is sometimes much activation in prefrontal areas (e.g., dorsolateral prefrontal cortex) when people perform two tasks at the same time but not when they perform only one of the tasks on its own (e.g., Collette et al., 2005; Johnson & Zatorre, 2006). Such findings suggest that co-ordination of two tasks can involve an executive process based mainly in the prefrontal cortex.

Further support for the notion that there is an executive process involved specifically in dual-task processing was reported by Logie, Cocchini, Della Sala, and Baddeley (2004). Patients with Alzheimer's disease were compared with healthy younger and older people on digit recall and tracking tasks, the latter of which involved keeping a pen on a red oval that moved randomly. The Alzheimer's patients were much more sensitive than the healthy groups to dual-task demands, but did not differ in their ability to cope with single-task demands. These findings suggest that Alzheimer's patients have damage to a part of the brain involved in dual-task co-ordination. MacPherson, Della Sala, Logie, and Wilcock (2007) reported very similar findings using verbal memory and visuo-spatial memory tasks.

Dysexecutive syndrome

Stuss and Alexander (2007) argued that the notion of a dysexecutive syndrome is flawed because it implies that brain damage to the frontal lobes typically damages *all* central executive functions of the central executive. They accepted that patients with widespread damage to the frontal lobes have a global dysexecutive syndrome. However, they claimed there are three executive processes based in different parts of the frontal lobes:

- *Task setting:* This involves planning and was defined as "the ability to set a stimulus-response relationship ... necessary in the early stages of learning to drive a car or planning a wedding (p. 906).

- *Monitoring:* This was defined as "the process of checking the task over time for 'quality control' and the adjustment of behaviour (p. 909).

- *Energisation:* This involves sustained attention or concentration and was defined as "the process of initiation and sustaining of any response ....Without energisation ... maintaining performance over prolonged periods will waver" (pp. 903–904).

All three executive processes are very general in that they are used across an enormous range of tasks. They are not really independent, because they are typically all used when you deal with a complex task. For example, if you have to give a speech in public, you would first plan roughly what

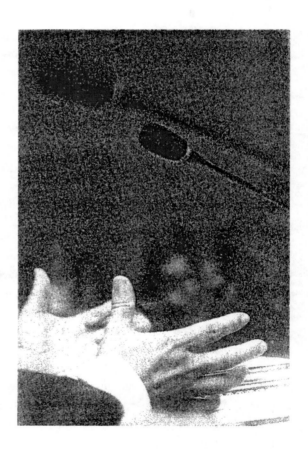

Public speaking involves all three of Stuss and Alexander's (2007) executive functions: planning what you are going to say (task setting); concentrating on delivery (energisation); and checking that what you say is as intended (monitoring).

you are going to say (task setting), concentrate through the delivery of the speech (energisation), and check that what you are saying is what you intended (monitoring).

Stuss and Alexander (2007) tested their theory of executive functions on patients having fairly specific lesions within the frontal lobes. In view of the possibility that there may be reorganisation of cognitive structures and processes following brain damage, the patients were tested within a few months of suffering brain damage. A wide range of cognitive tasks was administered to different patient groups to try to ensure that the findings would generalise.

Stuss and Alexander found evidence for the three hypothesised processes of energisation, task setting, and monitoring. They also discovered that each process was associated with a different region within the frontal cortex. Energisation involves the superior medial region of the frontal cortex, task setting involves the left lateral frontal region, and monitoring involves the right lateral frontal region. Thus, for example, patients with damage to the right lateral frontal region generally fail to detect the errors they make while performing a task and so do not adjust their performance.

Why do the processes identified by Stuss and Alexander (2007) differ from those identified by Miyake et al. (2000)? The starting point in trying to answer that question is to remember that Stuss and Alexander based their conclusions on studies with brain-damaged patients, whereas Miyake et al. studied only healthy individuals. Nearly all executive tasks involve common processes (e.g., energisation, task setting, monitoring). These common processes are positively correlated in healthy individuals and so do not emerge clearly as separate processes. However, the differences among energisation, task setting, and monitoring become much clearer when we consider patients with very specific frontal lesions. It remains for future research to show in more detail how the views of Stuss and Alexander and of Miyake et al. can be reconciled.

Evaluation

There has been real progress in understanding the workings of the central executive. The central executive consists of various related but separable executive processes. There is accumulating evidence that inhibition, updating, shifting, and dual-task co-ordination may be four major executive processes. It has become clear that the notion of a dysexecutive syndrome is misleading in that it suggests there is a *single* pattern of impairment. Various executive processes associated with different parts of frontal cortex are involved.

Two issues require more research. First, the executive processes suggested by behavioural and functional neuro-imaging studies on healthy individuals do not correspond precisely with those suggested by studies on patients with damage to the frontal cortex. We have speculated on the reasons for this, but solid evidence is needed. Second, while we have emphasised the differences among the major executive processes or functions, there is plentiful evidence suggesting that these processes are fairly closely related to each other. The reasons for this remain somewhat unclear.

Episodic buffer

Baddeley (2000) added a fourth component to the working memory model. This is the episodic buffer, in which information from various sources (the phonological loop, the visuo-spatial sketchpad, and long-term memory) can be integrated and stored briefly. According to Repovš and Baddeley (2006, p. 15), the episodic buffer, "is episodic by virtue of holding information that is integrated from a range of systems including other working memory components and long-term memory into coherent complex structures: scenes or episodes. It is a buffer in that it serves as an intermediary between subsystems with different codes, which it combines into multi-dimensional representations."

In view of the likely processing demands involved in integrating information from different modalities, Baddeley (2000, 2007) suggested that there would be close links between the episodic buffer and the central executive. If so, we would expect to find prefrontal activation on tasks involving the episodic buffer, because there are associations between use of the central executive and prefrontal cortex.

KEY TERM

episodic buffer: a component of working memory that is used to integrate and to store briefly information from the phonological loop, the-visuo-spatial sketch pad, and long-term memory.

Why did Baddeley add the episodic buffer to the working memory model? The original version of the model was limited because its various components were too separate in their functioning. For example, Chincotta, Underwood, Abd Ghani, Papadopoulou, and Wresinki (*1999*) studied memory span for Arabic numerals and digit words, finding that participants used both verbal and visual encoding while performing the task. This suggests that participants combined information from the phonological loop *and* the visuo-spatial sketchpad. Since these two stores are separate, this combination and integration process must take place elsewhere, and the episodic buffer fits the bill.

Another finding hard to explain within the original working memory model is that, in immediate recall, people can recall about five unrelated words but up to 16 words presented in sentences (Baddeley, Vallar, & Wilson, 1987). The notion of an episodic buffer is useful, because this is where information from long-term memory could be integrated with information from the phonological loop and the visuo-spatial sketchpad.

Evidence

Zhang et al. (2004) obtained evidence consistent with the notion that the episodic buffer is often used in conjunction with the central executive. Their participants had to recall a mixture of digits and visual locations, a task assumed to require the episodic buffer. As predicted, there was greater right prefrontal activation in this condition than one in which digits and visual locations were not mixed during presentation.

Baddeley and Wilson (2002) provided support for the notion of an episodic buffer. They pointed out that it had generally been assumed that good immediate prose recall involves the ability to store some of the relevant information in long-term memory. According to this view, amnesic patients with very impaired long-term memory should have very poor immediate prose recall. In contrast, Baddeley and Wilson argued that the ability to exhibit good immediate prose recall depends on two factors: (1) the capacity of the episodic buffer; and (2) an efficiently functioning central executive creating and maintaining information

in the buffer. According to this argument, even severely amnesic patients with practically no delayed recall of prose should have good immediate prose recall provided they have an efficient central executive. As predicted, immediate prose recall was much better in amnesics having little deficit in executive functioning than in those with a severe executive deficit.

Other studies suggest that the episodic buffer can operate independently of the central executive. Gooding, Isaac, and Mayes (2005) failed to replicate Baddeley and Wilson's (2002) findings in a similar study. Among their amnesic patients (who were less intelligent than those studied by Baddeley and Wilson), there was a non-significant correlation between immediate prose recall and measures of executive functioning. It is possible that using the central executive to maintain reasonable immediate prose recall requires high levels of intelligence. Berlingeri et al. (2008) found in patients with Alzheimer's disease that 60% of those having almost intact performance on tasks requiring the central executive nevertheless had no immediate prose recall. This finding also casts doubt on the importance of the central executive on tasks involving the episodic buffer.

Rudner, Fransson, Ingvar, Nyberg, and Ronnberg (2007) used a task involving combining representations based on sign language and on speech. This episodic buffer task was not associated with prefrontal activation, but was associated with activation in the left hippocampus. This is potentially important because the hippocampus plays a key role in binding together different kinds of information in memory (see Chapter 7). An association between use of the episodic buffer and the hippocampus was also reported by Berlingeri et al. (2008). They found among patients with Alzheimer's disease that those with most atrophy of the anterior part of the hippocampus did worst on immediate prose recall.

Evaluation

The addition of the episodic buffer to the working memory model has proved of value. The original three components of the model were too separate from each other and from long-term memory to account for our ability to combine different kinds of information (e.g., visual, verbal) on short-term memory tasks. The episodic buffer helps to provide the "glue" to integrate information within working memory.

Some progress has been made in tracking down the brain areas associated with the episodic buffer. The hippocampus is of central importance in binding and integrating information during learning, and so it is unsurprising that it is associated with use of the episodic buffer. The evidence suggests that use of the episodic buffer is sometimes associated with the central executive, but we do not know as yet what determines whether there is an association.

It is harder to carry out research on the episodic buffer than on the phonological loop or the visuo-spatial sketchpad. We have to use complex tasks to study the episodic buffer because it involves the complicated integration of information. In contrast, it is possible to devise relatively simple tasks to study the phonological loop or the visuo-spatial sketchpad. In addition, there are often close connections between the episodic buffer and the other components of the working memory system. That often makes it difficult to distinguish clearly between the episodic buffer and the other components.

Overall evaluation

The working memory model has several advantages over the short-term memory store proposed by Atkinson and Shiffrin (1968). First, the working memory system is concerned with both active processing and transient storage of information, and so is involved in all complex cognitive tasks, such as language comprehension (see Chapter 10) and reasoning (see Chapter 14).

Second, the working memory model explains the partial deficits of short-term memory observed in brain-damaged patients. If brain damage affects only one of the three components of working memory, then selective deficits on short-term memory tasks would be expected.

Third, the working memory model incorporates verbal rehearsal as an optional process within the phonological loop. This is more realistic than the enormous significance of rehearsal within the multi-store model of Atkinson and Shiffrin (1968).

What are the limitations of the working memory model? First, it has proved difficult to identify the number and nature of the main executive processes associated with the central executive. For example, disagreements on the nature of executive functions have emerged from approaches based on latent-variable analyses of executive tasks (Miyake et al., 2000) and on data from brain-damaged patients (Stuss & Alexander, 2007). One reason for the lack of clarity is that most complex tasks involve the use of more than one executive process, making it hard to establish the contribution that each has made.

Second, we need more research on the relationship between the episodic buffer and the other components of the working memory system. As yet, we lack a detailed account of how the episodic buffer integrates information from the other components and from long-term memory.

LEVELS OF PROCESSING

What determines how well we remember information over the long term? According to Craik and Lockhart (1972), what is crucial is how we process that information during learning. They argued in their levels-of-processing approach that attentional and perceptual processes at learning determine what information is stored in long-term memory. There are various levels of processing, ranging from shallow or physical analysis of a stimulus (e.g., detecting specific letters in words) to deep or semantic analysis; the greater the extent to which meaning is processed, the deeper the level of processing. They implied that processing nearly always proceeds in a serial fashion from shallow sensory levels to deeper semantic ones. However, they subsequently (Lockhart & Craik, 1990) admitted that that was an oversimplification and that processing is often parallel.

Craik and Lockhart's (1972) main theoretical assumptions were as follows:

- The level or depth of processing of a stimulus has a large effect on its memorability.
- Deeper levels of analysis produce more elaborate, longer lasting and stronger memory traces than do shallow levels of analysis.

Craik and Lockhart (1972) disagreed with Atkinson and Shiffrin's (1968) assumption that rehearsal *always* improves long-term memory. They argued that rehearsal involving simply repeating previous analyses (maintenance rehearsal) does not enhance long-term memory. In fact, however, maintenance rehearsal typically has a rather small (but beneficial) effect on long-term memory (Glenberg, Smith, & Green, 1977).

Evidence

Numerous studies support the main assumptions of the levels-of-processing approach. For example, Craik and Tulving (1975) compared recognition performance as a function of the task performed at learning:

- *Shallow graphemic task:* decide whether each word is in uppercase or lowercase letters.
- *intermediate phonemic task:* decide whether each word rhymes with a target word.
- *Deep semantic task:* decide whether each word fits a sentence containing a blank.

Depth of processing had impressive effects on memory performance, with performance more than three times higher with deep than with shallow processing. In addition, performance was generally much better for words associated with "Yes" responses on the processing task than those associated with "No" responses. Craik and Tulving used incidental learning—the participants did not realise at the time of learning that there would be a memory test. They argued that the nature of task processing rather than the intention to learn is crucial.

Craik and Tulving (1975) assumed that the semantic task involved deep processing and the uppercase/lowercase task involved shallow processing. However, it would be preferable to assess depth. One approach is to use brain-imaging to identify the brain regions involved in different kinds of processing. For example Wagner, Maril, Bjork, and Schacter (2001) found there was more activation in the left inferior frontal lobe and the left lateral and medial temporal lobe during semantic than perceptual processing. However, the findings have been somewhat inconsistent. Park and Rugg (2008b) presented word pairs and asked participants to rate the extent to which they shared a semantic theme (deep processing) or sounded similar (shallow processing). Memory was better following semantic processing than phonological processing. However, successful memory performance was associated with activation in the left ventrolateral prefrontal cortex regardless of the encoding task. This finding suggests that there is no simple relationship between processing task and patterns of brain activation.

Craik and Tulving (1975) argued that elaboration of processing (i.e., the amount of processing of a particular kind) is important as well as depth of processing. Participants were presented on each trial with a word and a sentence containing a blank, and decided whether the word fitted into the blank space. Elaboration was manipulated by using simple (e.g., "She cooked the _____") and complex "The great bird swooped down and carried off the struggling _____") sentence frames. Cued recall was twice as high for words accompanying complex sentences.

Long-term memory depends on the *kind* of elaboration as well as the *amount*. Bransford, Franks, Morris, and Stein (1979) presented either minimally elaborated similes (e.g., "A mosquito is like a doctor because they both draw blood") or multiply elaborated similes (e.g., "A mosquito is like a raccoon because they both have heads, legs, jaws"). Recall was much better for the minimally elaborated similes than the multiply elaborated ones, indicating that the nature of semantic elaborations needs to be considered.

KEY TERM

maintenance rehearsal: processing that involves simply repeating analyses which have already been carried out.

Eysenck (1979) argued that distinctive or unique memory traces are easier to retrieve than those resembling other memory traces. Eysenck and Eysenck (1980) tested this notion using nouns having irregular grapheme-phoneme correspondence (i.e., words not pronounced in line with pronunciation rules, such as "comb" with its silent "b"). In one condition, participants pronounced these nouns as if they had regular grapheme-phoneme correspondence, thus producing distinctive memory traces. Other nouns were simply pronounced normally, thus producing nondistinctive memory traces. Recognition memory was much better in the former condition, indicating the importance of distinctiveness.

Morris, Bransford, and Franks (1977) argued that stored information is remembered only if it is of *relevance* to the memory test. Participants answered semantic or shallow (rhyme) questions for lists of words. Memory was tested by a standard recognition test, in which list and non-list words were presented, or by a rhyming recognition test. On this

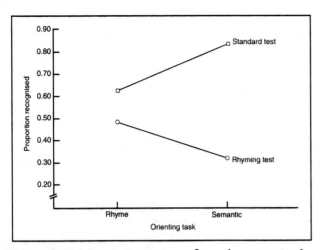

Figure 6.12 Mean proportion of words recognised as a function of orienting task (semantic or rhyme) and of the type of recognition task (standard or rhyming). *Data are from Morris et al. (1977), and are from positive trials only.*

latter test, participants selected words that rhymed with list words: the words themselves were *not* presented. With the standard recognition test, the predicted superiority of deep over shallow processing was obtained (see Figure 6.12). However, the *opposite* result was reported with the rhyme test, which disproves the notion that deep processing always enhances long-term memory.

Morris et al. (1977) argued that their findings supported transfer-appropriate processing theory. According to this theory, different kinds of learning lead learners to acquire different kinds of information about a stimulus. Whether the stored information leads to subsequent retention depends on the *relevance* of that information to the memory test. For example, storing semantic information is essentially irrelevant when the memory test requires the identification of words rhyming with list words. What is required for this kind of test is shallow rhyme information. Further evidence supporting transfer-appropriate theory is discussed later in the chapter.

Nearly all the early research on levels-of-processing theory used standard memory tests (e.g., recall, recognition) involving explicit memory (conscious recollection). It is also important to consider the effects of level of processing on implicit memory (memory not involving conscious recollection; see Chapter 7). Challis, Velichkovsky, and Craik (1996) asked participants to learn word lists under various conditions: judging whether the word

was related to them (self-judgement); simple intentional learning; judging whether it referred to a living thing (living judgement); counting the number of syllables (syllable task); or counting the number of letters of a certain type (letter type). The order of these tasks reflects decreasing depth of processing. There were four explicit memory tests (recognition, free recall, semantic cued recall involving a word related in meaning to a list word, and graphemic cued recall involving a word with similar spelling to a list word), and two implicit memory tests. One of these tests involved answering general knowledge questions in which the answers corresponded to list words, and the other involved completing word fragments (e.g., c _ pp _ _).

For the four explicit memory tests, there was an overall tendency for performance to increase with increasing depth of processing, but there are some hard-to-interpret differences as well (see Figure 6.13). We turn now to the implicit memory tests. The word-fragment test failed to show any levels-of-processing effect, whereas level of processing had a significant effect on the general knowledge memory test. The general knowledge memory test is a conceptual

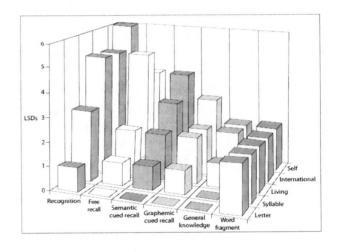

Figure 6.13 Memory performance as a function of encoding conditions and retrieval conditions. *The findings are presented in units of least significant differences (LSDs) relative to baseline performance, meaning that columns of differing heights are significantly different. Reprinted from Roediger (2008), based on data in Challis et al. (1996), Copyright © 1996, with permission from Elsevier.*

implicit memory test based on meaning. As a result, it seems reasonable that it would be affected by level of processing, even though the effects were much smaller than with explicit memory tests. In contrast, the word-fragment test is a perceptual implicit memory test not based on meaning, which helps to explain why there was no levels-of-processing effect with this test.

In sum, levels-of-processing effects were generally greater in explicit memory than implicit memory. In addition, there is some support for the predictions of levels-of-processing theory with all memory tests other than the word-fragment test. Overall, the findings are too complex to be explained readily by levels-of-processing theory.

Evaluation

Craik and Lockhart (1972) argued correctly that processes during learning have a major impact on subsequent long-term memory. This may sound obvious, but surprisingly little research before 1972 focused on learning processes and their effects on memory. Another strength is the central assumption that perception, attention, and memory are all closely interconnected, and that learning and remembering are by-products of perception, attention, and comprehension. In addition, the approach led to the identification of elaboration and distinctiveness of processing as important factors in learning and memory.

The levels-of-processing approach possesses several limitations. First, it is generally difficult to assess processing depth. Second, Craik and Lockhart (1972) greatly underestimated the importance of the retrieval environment in determining memory performance. As Morris et al. (1977) showed, the typical levels effect can be reversed if stored semantic information is irrelevant to the requirements of the memory test. Third, long-term memory is influenced by depth of processing, elaboration of processing, and distinctiveness of processing. However, the relative importance of these factors (and how they are interrelated) remains unclear. Fourth, findings from amnesic patients (see Chapter 7) cannot be explained by the levels-of-processing approach. Most amnesic patients have good semantic or deep processing skills, but their long-term memory is extremely poor, probably because they have major problems with consolidation (fixing of newly learned information in long-term memory) (Craik, 2002; see Chapter 7). Fifth,

Craik and Lockhart (1972) did not explain precisely *why* deep processing is so effective, and it is not clear why there is a much smaller levels-of-processing effect in implicit than in explicit memory.

IMPLICIT LEARNING

Do you think you could learn something without being aware of what you have learned? It sounds improbable. Even if we do acquire information without any conscious awareness, it might seem somewhat pointless and wasteful—if we do not realise we have learned something, it seems unlikely that we are going to make much use of it. What we are considering here is implicit learning, which is, "learning without conscious awareness of having learned" (French & Cleeremans, 2002, p. xvii). Implicit learning has been contrasted with explicit learning, which involves conscious awareness of what has been learned.

Cleeremans and Jiménez (2002, p. 20) provided a fuller definition of implicit learning: "Implicit learning is the process through which we become sensitive to certain regularities in the environment (1) in the absence of intention to learn about these regularities, (2) in the absence of awareness that one is learning, and (3) in such a way that the resulting knowledge is difficult to express." You probably possess skills that are hard to express in words. For example, it is notoriously difficult to express what we know about riding a bicycle.

KEY TERM

implicit learning: learning complex information without the ability to provide conscious recollection of what has been learned.

Implicit learning is "learning without conscious awareness of having learned". Bike riding is an example of implicit learning in which there is no clear conscious awareness of what has been learned.

There are clear similarities between implicit learning and implicit memory, which is memory not depending on conscious recollection. You may wonder why implicit learning and implicit memory are not discussed together. There are three reasons. First, there are some differences between implicit learning and implicit memory. As Buchner and Wippich (1998) pointed out, implicit learning refers to "the (incidental) acquisition of knowledge about the structural properties of the relations between (usually more than two) objects or events." In contrast, implicit memory refers to "situations in which effects of prior experiences can be observed despite the fact that the participants are not instructed to relate their current performance to a learning episode" (Buchner & Wippich, 1998). Second, studies of implicit learning have typically used relatively complex, novel stimulus materials, whereas most studies of implicit memory have used simple, familiar stimulus materials. Third, relatively few researchers have considered the relations between implicit learning and implicit memory.

How do the systems involved in implicit learning differ from those involved in explicit learning and memory? Reber (1993) proposed five such characteristics (none has been established definitively):

- *Robustness:* Implicit systems are relatively unaffected by disorders (e.g., amnesia) affecting explicit systems.
- *Age independence:* Implicit learning is little influenced by age or developmental level.
- *Low variability:* There are smaller individual differences in implicit learning and memory than in explicit learning and memory.
- *IQ independence:* Performance on implicit tasks is relatively unaffected by IQ.
- *Commonality of process:* Implicit systems are common to most species.

We can identify three main types of research on implicit learning. First, there are studies to see whether healthy participants can learn fairly complex material in the absence of conscious awareness of what they have learned. According to Reber (1993), individual differences in such learning should depend relatively little on IQ. It is often assumed that implicit learning makes minimal demands on attentional resources. If so, the requirement to perform an additional attentionally-demanding task at the same time should not impair implicit learning.

Second, there are brain-imaging studies. If implicit learning depends on different cognitive processes to explicit learning, the brain areas associated with implicit learning should differ from those associated with explicit learning. More specifically, brain areas associated with conscious experience and attentional control (e.g., parts of the prefrontal cortex) should be much less activated during implicit learning than explicit learning.

Third, there are studies on brain-damaged patients, mostly involving amnesic patients having severe problems with long-term memory. Amnesic patients typically have relatively intact implicit memory even though their explicit memory is greatly impaired (see Chapter 7). If amnesic patients have intact implicit learning but impaired explicit learning, this would provide evidence that the two types of learning are very different.

You might imagine it would be relatively easy to decide whether implicit learning has occurred—we simply ask participants to perform a complex task without instructing them to engage in deliberate learning. Afterwards, they indicate their conscious awareness of what they have learned. Implicit learning has been demonstrated if learning occurs in the absence of conscious awareness of the nature of that learning. Alas, there are several reasons why participants fail to report conscious awareness of what they have learned. For example, there is the "retrospective problem" (Shanks & St. John, 1994): participants may be consciously aware of what they are learning at the time, but have forgotten it when questioned at the end of the experiment. Shanks and St. John proposed two criteria for implicit learning to be demonstrated:

- *Information criterion:* The information participants are asked to provide on the awareness test must be the information responsible for the improved level of performance.
- *Sensitivity criterion:* "We must be able to show that our test of awareness is sensitive to all of the relevant

knowledge" (p. 374). People may be consciously aware of more task-relevant knowledge than appears on an insensitive awareness test, leading us to underestimate their consciously accessible knowledge.

Complex learning

Much early research on implicit learning involved artificial grammar learning. On this task, participants initially memorise meaningless letter strings (e.g., PVPXVPS; T5XXTW). After that, they are told that the memorised letter strings all follow the rules of an artificial grammar, but are not told the nature of these rules. Next, the participants classify *novel* strings as grammatical or ungrammatical. Finally, they describe the rules or the artificial grammar. Participants typically perform significantly above chance level on the classification task, but cannot describe the grammatical rules (e.g., Reber, 1967). Such findings are less impressive than they appear. As several researchers have found (e.g., Channon, Shanks, Johnstone, Vakili, Chin, & Sinclair, 2002), participants' decisions on the grammaticality of letter strings do *not* depend on knowledge of grammatical rules. Instead, participants classify letter strings as grammatical when they share letter pairs with the letter strings memorised initially and as ungrammatical when they do not. Thus, above-chance performance depends on conscious awareness of two-letter fragments, and provides little or no evidence of implicit learning.

The most commonly used implicit learning task involves serial reaction time. On each trial, a stimulus appears at one out of several locations on a computer screen, and participants respond rapidly with the response key corresponding to its location. There is typically a complex, repeating sequence over trials in the various stimulus locations, but participants are not told this. Towards the end of the experiment, there is typically a block of trials conforming to a novel sequence, but this information is not given to participants. Participants speed up during the course of the experiment but respond much slower during the novel sequence (see Shanks, 2005, for a review). When questioned at the end of the experiment, participants usually show no conscious awareness that there was a repeating sequence or pattern in the stimuli presented to them.

One strength of the serial reaction time task is that the repeating sequence (which is crucial to the demonstration

of implicit learning) is incidental to the explicit task of responding to the stimuli as rapidly as possible. However, we need to satisfy the information and sensitivity criteria (described above) with this task. It seems reasonable to make the awareness test very similar to the learning task, as was done by Howard and Howard (1992). An asterisk appeared in one of four locations on a screen, under each of which was a key. The task was to press the key corresponding to the position of the asterisk as rapidly as possible. Participants showed clear evidence of learning the underlying sequence by responding faster and faster to the asterisk. However, when given the awareness test of predicting where the asterisk would appear next, their performance was at chance level. These findings suggest there was implicit learning—learning occurred in the absence of conscious awareness of what had been learned.

Contrary evidence that participants have some conscious awareness of what they have learned on a serial reaction time task was reported by Wilkinson and Shanks (2004). Participants were given either 1500 trials (15 blocks) or 4500 trials (45 blocks) on the task and showed strong evidence of sequence learning. Then they were told there was a repeated sequence in the stimuli, following which they were presented on each of 12 trials with part of the sequence under one of two conditions. In the *inclusion* condition, they guessed the next location in the sequence. In the *exclusion* condition, they were told they should avoid guessing the next location in the sequence. If sequence knowledge is wholly implicit, then performance should not differ between the inclusion and exclusion conditions because participants would be unable to control how they used their sequence knowledge. In contrast, if it is partly explicit, then participants should be able to exert intentional control over their sequence knowledge. If so, the guesses generated in the inclusion condition should be more likely to conform to the repeated sequence than those in the exclusion condition. The findings indicated that explicit knowledge was acquired on the serial reaction time task.

Similar findings were reported by Destrebecqz et al. (2005) in another study using the serial reaction time task. The interval of time between the participant's response to one stimulus and the presentation of the next one was either 0 ms or 250 ms, it being assumed that explicit learning would be more likely with the longer interval.

Participants responded progressively faster over trials with both response-to-stimulus intervals. As Wilkinson and Shanks (2004) had done, they used inclusion and exclusion conditions. Participants' responses were significantly closer to the training sequence in the inclusion condition than in the exclusion condition, suggesting that some explicit learning occurred, especially when the response-to-stimulus interval was long. In addition, as discussed below, brain-imaging findings from this study suggested that explicit learning occurred.

If the serial reaction time task genuinely involves implicit learning, performance on that task might well be unaffected by the requirement to perform a second, attentionally-demanding task at the same time. This prediction was tested by Shanks, Rowland, and Ranger (2005). Four different target stimuli were presented across trials, and the main task was to respond rapidly to the location at which a target was presented. Half the participants performed only this task, and the remainder also carried out the attentionally-demanding task of counting targets. Participants with the additional task performed much more slowly than those with no additional task, and also showed significantly inferior sequence learning. Thus, attentional resources were needed for effective learning or the sequence on the serial reaction time task, which casts doubt on the notion that such learning is implicit. In addition, both groups of participants had significantly more accurate performance under inclusion than exclusion instructions, further suggesting the presence of explicit learning.

As mentioned above, Reber (1993) assumed that individual differences in intelligence have less effect on implicit learning than on explicit learning. Gebauer and Mackintosh (2007) carried our a thorough study using various implicit learning tasks (e.g., artificial grammar learning; serial reaction time). These tasks were given under standard implicit instructions or with explicit rule discovery instructions (i.e., indicating explicitly that there were rules to be discovered). The mean correlation between implicit task performance and intelligence was only +0.03, whereas it was +0.16 between explicit task performance and intelligence. This supports the hypothesis. It is especially important that intelligence (which is positively associated with performance on the great majority of cognitive tasks) failed to predict implicit learning performance.

Brain-imaging studies

Different areas of the brain should be activated during implicit and explicit learning if they are genuinely different. Conscious awareness is associated with activation in many brain regions, but the main ones are the anterior cingulate and the dorsolateral prefrontal cortex (Dehaene & Naccache, 2001; see Chapter 16). Accordingly, these areas should be more active during explicit than implicit learning. In contrast, it has often been assumed that the striatum is associated with implicit learning (Destrebecqz et al., 2005). The striatum is part of the basal ganglia; it is located in the interior areas of the cerebral hemispheres and the upper region of the brainstem.

Functional neuroimaging studies have provided limited support for the above predictions. Grafton, Hazeltine, and Ivry (1995) found that explicit learning was associated with activation in the anterior cingulate, regions in the parietal cortex involved in working memory, and areas in the parietal cortex concerned with voluntary attention. Aizenstein et al. (2004) found that there was greater activation in the prefrontal cortex and anterior cingulate during explicit rather than implicit learning. However, they did not find any clear evidence that the striatum was more activated during implicit than explicit learning.

Destrebecqz et al. (2005) pointed out that most so-called explicit or implicit learning tasks probably involve a mixture of explicit and implicit learning. As mentioned before, they used inclusion and exclusion conditions with the serial reaction time task to distinguish clearly between the explicit and implicit components of learning. Activation in the striatum was associated with the implicit component of learning, and the mesial prefrontal cortex and anterior cingulate were associated with the explicit component.

In sum, failure to discover clear differences in patterns of brain activation between explicit and implicit learning can occur because the tasks used are not pure measures of these two forms of learning. It is no coincidence that the study distinguishing most clearly between explicit and implicit learning (Destrebecqz et al., 2005) is also the one producing the greatest support for the hypothesised associations of prefrontal cortex with explicit learning and the striatum with implicit learning.

Brain-damaged patients

As discussed in Chapter 7, amnesic patients typically perform very poorly on tests of explicit memory (involving conscious recollection) but often perform as well as healthy individuals on tests of implicit memory (on which conscious recollection is not needed). The notion that separate learning systems underlie implicit learning and explicit learning would be supported if amnesic patients showed intact levels of implicit learning combined with impaired explicit learning. Explicit learning in amnesics is often severely impaired, but amnesics' performance on tasks allegedly involving implicit learning is variable (see Vandenberghe, Schmidt, Fery, & Cleeremans, 2006, for a review). For example, Knowlton, Ramus, and Squire (1992) found that amnesics performed as well as healthy controls on an implicit test on which participants distinguished between grammatical and ungrammatical letter strings (63% versus 67% correct, respectively). However, they performed significantly worse than the controls on an explicit test (62% versus 72%, respectively).

KEY TERM

striatum: it forms part of the basal ganglia of the brain and is located in the upper part of the brainstem and the inferior part of the cerebral hemispheres.

Meulemans and Van der Linden (2003) pointed out that amnesics' performance on Knowlton et al.'s (1992) implicit test may have depended on explicit fragment knowledge (e.g., pairs of letters found together). Accordingly, they used an artificial grammar learning task in which fragment knowledge could not influence performance on the test of implicit learning. They also used a test of explicit learning in which participants wrote down ten letter strings they regarded as grammatical. The amnesic patients performed as well as the healthy controls on implicit learning. However, their performance was much worse than that of the controls on explicit learning.

There is evidence of implicit learning in amnesic patients in studies on the serial reaction time task. The most thorough such study was carried out by Vandenberghe et al. (2006). Amnesic patients and healthy controls were given two versions of the task: (1) deterministic sequence (fixed

repeating sequence); and (2) probabilistic sequence (repeating sequence with some deviations). The healthy controls showed clear evidence of learning with both sequences. The use of inclusion and exclusion instructions indicated that healthy controls showed explicit learning with the deterministic sequence but not with the probabilistic one. The amnesic patients showed limited learning of the deterministic sequence but not of the probabilistic sequence. Their performance was comparable with inclusion and exclusion instructions, indicating that this learning was implicit.

Earlier we discussed the hypothesis that the striatum is of major importance in implicit learning. Patients with Parkinson's disease (the symptoms of which include limb tremor and muscle rigidity) have damage to the striatum and so we could predict that they would have impaired implicit learning. The evidence generally supports that prediction (see Chapter 7 for a fuller discussion). Siegert, Taylor, Weatherall, and Abernethy (2006) carried out a meta-analysis of six studies investigating the performance of patients with Parkinson's disease on the serial reaction time task. Skill learning on this task was consistently impaired in the patients relative to healthy controls. Wilkinson and Jahanshahi (2007) obtained similar findings with patients having Parkinson's disease using a different version of the serial reaction time task. In addition, they reported convincing evidence that patients' learning was implicit (i.e., lacked conscious awareness). The patients performed at chance level when trying to recognise old sequences. In addition, their knowledge was not under intentional control, as was shown by their inability to suppress the expression of what they had learned when instructed to do so.

We have seen that there is some evidence that amnesic patients have poor explicit learning combined with reasonably intact implicit learning. We would have evidence of a double dissociation (see Glossary) if patients with Parkinson's disease had poor implicit learning combined with intact explicit learning. This pattern has occasionally been reported with patients in the early stages of the disease (e.g., Saint-Cyr, Taylor, & Lang, 1988). However, Parkinson's patients generally have impaired explicit learning, especially when the learning task is fairly complex and involves organisation of the to-be-learned information (see Vingernhoets, Vermeule, & Santens, 2005, for a review).

Evaluation

There has been a considerable amount of recent research on implicit learning involving three different approaches: behavioural studies on healthy participants; functional neuroimaging studies on healthy participants; and studies on amnesic patients. Much of that research suggests that implicit learning should be distinguished from explicit learning. Some of the most convincing evidence has come from studies on braindamaged patients. For example, Vanderberghe et al. (2006) found, using the serial reaction time task, that amnesic patients' learning seemed to be almost entirely at the implicit level. Other convincing evidence has come from functional neuro-imaging studies. There is accumulating evidence that explicit learning is associated with the prefrontal cortex and the anterior cingulate, whereas implicit learning is associated with the striatum.

What are the limitations of research on implicit learning? First, it has proved hard to devise tests of awareness that can detect *all* the task-relevant knowledge of which people have conscious awareness. Second, some explicit learning is typically involved on the artificial grammar learning task and the serial reaction time task (e.g., Destrebecqz et al., 2005; Shanks et al., 2005; Wilkinson & Shanks, 2004). Third, the brain areas underlying what are claimed to be explicit and implicit learning are not always clearly different (e.g., Schendan, Searl, Melrose, & Stern, 2003).

What conclusions can we draw about implicit learning? It is too often assumed that finding that explicit learning plays some part in explaining performance on a given task means that *no* implicit learning occurred. It is very likely that the extent to which learners are consciously aware of what they are learning varies from individual to individual and from task to task. One possibility is that we have greatest conscious awareness when the representations of what we have learned are stable, distinctive, and strong, and least when those representations are unstable, non-distinctive, and weak (Kelly, 2003). All kinds of intermediate position are also possible.

Sun, Zhang, and Mathews (2009) argued that learning nearly always involves implicit and explicit aspects, and that the balance between these two types of learning changes over time. On some tasks, there is initial implicit learning based on the performance of successful actions owed by explicit learning of the rules apparently explaining why those actions are successful. On other tasks, learners start with explicit rules and then engage in implicit learning based on observing their actions directed by those rules.

THEORIES OF FORGETTING

Forgetting was first studied in detail by Hermann Ebbinghaus (1885/1913). He carried out numerous studies with himself as the only participant (not a recommended approach!). Ebbinghaus initially learned a list of nonsense syllables lacking meaning. At various intervals of time, he recalled the nonsense syllables. He then re-learned the list. His basic measure of forgetting was the savings method, which involved seeing the reduction in the number of trials during re-learning compared to original learning. Forgetting was very rapid over the first hour after learning but slowed down considerably after that (see Figure 6.15). These findings suggest that the forgetting function is approximately logarithmic.

Rubin and Wenzel (1996) analysed the forgetting functions taken from 210 data sets involving numerous memory tests. They found (in line with Ebbinghaus (1885/1913) that a logarithmic function most consistently described the rate of forgetting (for alternative possibilities, see Wixted, 2004). The major exception was autobiographical memory, which showed slower forgetting. One of the possible consequences of a logarithmic

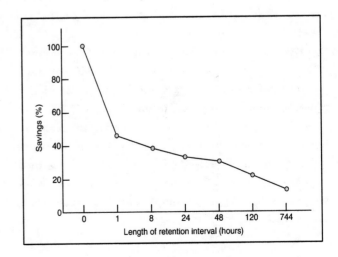

Figure 6.15 Forgetting over time as indexed by reduced savings. *Data from Ebbinghaus (1885/1913).*

Proactive interference			
Group	Learn	Learn	Test
Experimental	A-B (e.g. Cat-Tree)	A-B (e.g. Cat-Dirt)	A-C (e.g. Cat-Dirt)
Control	–	A-C (e.g. Cat-Dirt)	A-C (e.g. Cat-Dirt)

Retroactive interference			
Group	Learn	Learn	Test
Experimental	A-C (e.g. Cat-Dirt)	A-C (e.g. Cat-Dirt)	A-C (e.g. Cat-Dirt)
Control	A-C (e.g. Cat-Dirt)	–	A-C (e.g. Cat-Dirt)

Note: for both proactive and retroactive interference, the experimental group exhibits interference. On the test, only the first word is supplied, and the participants must provide the second word.

Figure 6.16 Methods of testing for proactive and retroactive interference.

forgetting function is Jost's (1897) law: if two memory traces differ in age but are of equal strength, the older one will decay more slowly over any given time period.

Most studies of forgetting have focused on declarative or explicit memory (see Chapter 7), which involves conscious recollection of previously learned information. Comparisons of forgetting rates in explicit and implicit memory (in which conscious recollection is not required) suggest that forgetting is slower in implicit memory. Tulving, Schacter, and Stark (1982) carried out a study in which participants initially learned a list of relatively rare words (e.g., "toboggan"). One hour or one week later, they received a test of explicit memory (recognition memory) or a word-fragment completion test of implicit memory. Word fragments (e.g., _ O _ O _ GA _) were presented and participants filled in the blanks to form a word without being told that any of the words came from the list studied previously. Recognition memory was much worse after one week than one hour, whereas word-fragment completion performance was unchanged.

KEY TERM

savings method: a measure or forgetting introduced by Ebbinghaus, in which the number of trials for re-learning is compared against the number for original learning.

Dramatic evidence of long-lasting implicit memories was reported by Mitchell (2006). His participants tried to identify pictures from fragments having seen some of them before in a laboratory experiment 17 years previously. They did significantly better with the pictures seen before; thus providing strong evidence for implicit memory after all those years! In contrast, there was rather little explicit memory for the experiment 17 years earlier. A 36-year-old male participant confessed, "I'm sorry—I don't really remember this experiment at all."

In what follows, we will be discussing the major theories of forgetting in turn. As you read about these theories, bear in mind that they are not mutually exclusive. Thus, it is entirely possible that all the theories discussed identify some of the factors responsible for forgetting.

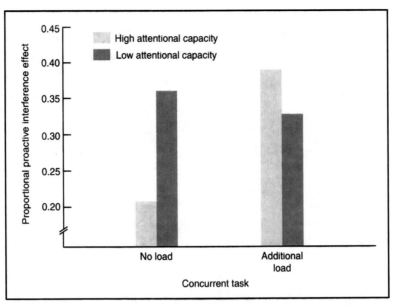

Figure 6.17 Amount of proactive interference as a function of attentional capacity (low vs. high) and concurrent task (no vs. additional load). *Data from Kane and Engle (2000).*

Interference theory

The dominant approach to forgetting during much of the twentieth century was interference theory. According to this theory, our ability to remember what we are currently learning can be disrupted (interfered with) by previous learning (proactive interference) or by future learning (retroactive interference) (see Figure 6.16).

Interference theory dates back to Hugo Munsterberg in the nineteenth century. For many years, he kept his pocket-watch in one particular pocket. When he moved it to a different pocket, he often fumbled about in confusion when asked for the time. He had learned an association between the stimulus, "What time is it, Hugo?", and the response of removing the watch from his pocket. Later on, the stimulus remained the same. However, a different response was now associated with it, thus causing proactive interference.

Research using methods such as those shown in Figure 6.16 revealed that proactive and retroactive interference are both maximal when two different responses are associated with the same stimulus and minimal when two different stimuli are involved (Underwood & Postman, 1960). Strong evidence of retroactive interference has been obtained in studies of eyewitness testimony in

which memory of an event is interfered with by post-event information (see Chapter 8).

Proactive interference

Proactive interference can be very useful when circumstances change. For example, if you have re-arranged everything in your room, it is a real advantage to forget where your belongings used to be.

Most research on proactive interference has involved declarative or explicit memory. An exception was a study by Lustig and Hasher (2001). They used a word-fragment completion task (e.g., A _ L _ _ GY), on which participants wrote down the first appropriate word coming to mind. Participants previously exposed to words almost fitting the fragments (e.g., ANALOGY) showed evidence of proactive interference.

Jacoby, Debner, and Hay (2001) argued that proactive interference might occur for two reasons. First, it might be due to problems in retrieving the correct response (discriminability). Second, it might be due to the great strength of the incorrect response learned initially (bias or habit). Thus, we might show proactive interference because the correct response is very weak or because the incorrect response is very strong. Jacoby et al. found consistently that proactive interference was due more to strength of the incorrect first response than to discriminability.

At one time, it was assumed that individuals *passively* allow themselves to suffer from interference. Suppose you learn something but find your ability to remember it is impaired by proactive interference from something learned previously. It would make sense to adopt active strategies to minimise any interference effect. Kane and Engle (2000) argued that individuals with high working-memory capacity (correlated with intelligence) would be better able to resist proactive interference than those with low capacity. However, even they would be unable to resist proactive interference if performing an attentionally demanding task at the same time as the learning task. As predicted, the high-capacity participants with no additional task showed the least proactive interference (see Figure 6.17).

The notion that people use active control processes to reduce proactive interference has been tested in several studies using the Recent Probes task. A small set of items (target set) is presented, followed by a recognition probe. The task is to decide whether the probe is a member of the target set. On critical trials, the probe is *not* a member of the current target set but was a member of the target set used on the previous trial. There is clear evidence of proactive interference on these trials in the form of lengthened reaction times and increased error rates.

Which brain areas are of most importance on proactive interference trials with the Recent Probes task? Nee, Jonides, and Bennau (2007) found that the left ventrolateral prefrontal cortex was activated on such trials. The same brain area was also activated on a directed forgetting version of the Recent Probes task (i.e., participants were told to forget some of the target set items). This suggests that left ventrolateral prefrontal cortex may play an important role in suppressing unwanted information.

Nee et al.'s (2007) study could not show that left ventrolateral prefrontal cortex actually controls the effects of proactive interference. More direct evidence was reported by Feredoes, Tononi, and Postle (2006). They administered transcranial magnetic stimulation (TMS; see Glossary) to left ventrolateral prefrontal cortex. This produced a significant increase in the error rate on proactive interference trials, suggesting that this brain area is directly involved in attempts to control proactive interference.

Retroactive interference

Numerous laboratory studies using artificial tasks such as paired-associate learning (see Figure 6.16) have produced large retroactive interference effects. Such findings do not necessarily mean that retroactive interference is important in everyday life. However, Isurin and McDonald (2001) argued that retroactive interference explains why people forget some of their first language when acquiring a second one. Bilingual participants fluent in two languages were first presented with various pictures and the corresponding words in Russian or Hebrew. Some were then presented with the same pictures and the corresponding words in the other language. Finally, they were tested for recall of the words in the first language. There was substantial retroactive interference—recall of the first-language words became progressively worse the more learning trials there were with the second-language words.

Retroactive interference is generally greatest when the new learning resembles previous learning. However, Dewar, Cowan, and Delia Sala (2007) found retroactive interference even when no new learning occurred during the retention interval. In their experiment, participants learned a list of words and were then exposed to various tasks during the retention interval before list memory was assessed. There was significant retroactive interference even when the intervening task involved detecting differences between pictures or detecting tones. Dewar et al. concluded that retroactive interference can occur in two ways: (1) expenditure of mental effort during the retention interval; or (2) learning of material similar to the original learning material. The first cause of retroactive interference probably occurs more often than the second in everyday life.

Lustig, Konkel, and Jacoby (2004) identified two possible explanations for retroactive interference in paired-associate learning. First, there may be problems with controlled processes (active searching for the correct response). Second, there may be problems with automatic processes (high accessibility of the incorrect response). They identified the roles of these two kinds of processes by assessing retroactive interference in two different ways. One way involved direct instructions (i.e., deliberately retrieve the correct responses) and the other way involved indirect instructions (i.e., rapidly produce the first response coming to mind when presented with the cue). Lustig et al. assumed that direct instructions would lead to the use of controlled and automatic processes, whereas indirect instructions would primarily lead to the use of automatic processes.

What did Lustig et al. (2004) find? First, use of direct instructions was associated with significant retroactive interference on an immediate memory test (cued recall) but not one day later. Second, the interference effect found on the immediate test depended mainly on relatively automatic processes (i.e., accessibility of the incorrect response). Third, the disappearance of retroactive interference on the test after one day was mostly due to reduced accessibility of the incorrect responses. Thus, relatively automatic processes are of major importance in retroactive interference.

Evaluation

There is strong evidence for both proactive and retroactive interference. There has been substantial progress in understanding interference effects in recent years, mostly involving an increased focus on underlying processes. For example, automatic processes make incorrect responses accessible, and people use active control processes to minimise interference effects.

What are the limitations of interference theory? First, the emphasis has been on interference effects in declarative or explicit memory, and detailed information about interference effects in implicit memory is lacking. Second, interference theory explains why forgetting occurs but not directly why the rate of forgetting decreases over time. Third, more needs to be done to understand the brain mechanisms involved in interference and attempts to reduce interference.

Repression

One of the best-known theories of forgetting owes its origins to the bearded Austrian psychologist Sigmund Freud (1856–1939). He claimed that very threatening or traumatic memories are often unable to gain access to conscious awareness, using the term repression to refer to this phenomenon. According to Freud (1915/1963, p. 86), "The essence of repression lies simply in the function of rejecting and keeping something out of consciousness." However, Freud sometimes used the concept to refer merely to the inhibition of the capacity for emotional experience (Madison, 1956). Even though it is often believed

that Freud regarded repression as unconscious, Erdelyi (2001) showed convincingly that Freud accepted that repression is sometimes an active and intentional process. It is harder to test the notion of repression if it can be either unconscious or conscious.

KEY TERM

repression: motivated forgetting of traumatic or other threatening events.

Most evidence relating to repression is based on adult patients who have apparently recovered repressed memories of childhood sexual and/or physical abuse in adulthood. As we will see, there has been fierce controversy as to whether these recovered memories are genuine or false. Note that the controversy centres on *recovered* memories—most experts accept that continuous memories (i.e., ones constantly accessible over the years) are very likely to be genuine.

Evidence

Clancy, Schacter, McNally, and Pitman (2000) used the Deese-Roediger-McDermott paradigm, which is known to produce false memories. Participants are given lists of semantically related words and are then found to falsely "recognise" other semantically related words not actually presented. Clancy et al. compared women with recovered memories of childhood sexual abuse with women who believed they had been sexually abused but could not recall the abuse, women who had always remembered being abused, and female controls. Women reporting recovered memories showed higher levels of false recognition than any other group (see Figure 6.18), suggesting that these women might be susceptible to developing false memories.

Lief and Fetkewicz (1995) found that 80% of adult patients who admitted reporting false recovered memories had therapists who made direct suggestions that they had been the victims of childhood sexual abuse. This suggests that recovered memories recalled *inside* therapy may be more likely to be false than those recalled *outside* therapy (see box).

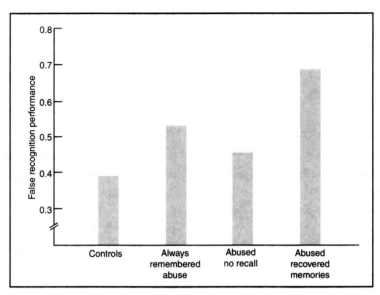

Figure 6.18 False recognition of words not presented in four groups of women with lists containing eight associates. *Data from Clancy et al. (2000).*

Motivated forgetting

Freud, in his repression theory, focused on some aspects of motivated forgetting. However, his approach was rather narrow, with its emphasis on repression of traumatic and other distressing memories and his failure to consider the cognitive processes involved. In recent years, a broader approach to motivated forgetting has been adopted.

Motivated forgetting of traumatic or other upsetting memories could clearly fulfil a useful function. In addition, much of the information we have stored in long-term memory is outdated or irrelevant, making it useless for present purposes. For example, if you are looking for your car in a car park, there is no point in remembering where you have parked the car previously. Thus, motivated or intentional forgetting can be adaptive (e.g., by reducing proactive interference).

Memories of abuse recovered inside and outside therapy

Geraerts, Schooler, Merckeibach, Jelicic, Haner, and Ambadar (2007) carried out an important study to test whether the genuineness of recovered memories depends on the context in which they were recovered. They divided adults who had suffered childhood sexual abuse into three groups: (1) those whose recovered memories had

been recalled inside therapy; (2) those whose recovered memories had been recalled outside therapy; and (3) those who had continuous memories. Geraerts et al. discovered how many of these memories had corroborating evidence (e.g., someone else had also reported being abused by the same person; the perpetrator had confessed) to provide an approximate assessment of validity.

What did Geraerts et al.(2007) find? There was corroborating evidence, for 45% of the individuals in the continuous memory for 37% of those who had recalled memories therapy, and for 0% of those who had recalled memories inside therapy. These findings suggest that recovered memories recalled outside therapy are much more likely to be genuine than those recalled inside therapy. In addition, those individuals whose memories were recalled outside therapy reported being much more surprised the existence of these memories than did those whose memories were recalled inside therapy. Presumably those whose recovered memories emerged inside therapy were unsurprised at these memories because they had previously been led to expect them by their therapist.

Geraerts et al. (2008) asked various groups of adults who claimed memories of childhood sexual abuse to recall the most positive and the most anxiety-provoking event they had experienced during the past two years. The participants were then told to try to suppress thoughts relating to these events, and to keep a diary record of any such thoughts over the following week. Adults who had recovered memories outside therapy were much better at this than control participants, those who had recovered memories inside therapy, and those who had continuous memories.

In sum, it appears that many of the traumatic memories recovered by women outside therapy are genuine. The finding that such women are especially good at suppresing-emotional memories under laboratory conditions helps to explain why they were unaware of their traumatic memories for long periods of time prior to recovery.

Directed forgetting

Directed forgetting is a phenomenon involving impaired long-term memory caused by an instruction to forget some information presented for learning (see Geraerts & McNally, 2008, for a review). Directed forgetting has been studied in two ways. First, there is the item method. Several words are presented, each followed immediately by an instruction to remember or to forget it. After all the words have been presented, participants are tested for their recall or recognition of *all* the words. Memory performance on recall and recognition tests is typically worse for the to-be-forgotten words than for the to-be-remembered words.

Second, there is the list method. Here, participants receive two lists of words. After the first list has been presented, participants are told to remember or forget the words. Then the second list is presented. After that, memory is tested for the words from both lists. Recall of the words from the first list is typically impaired when participants have been told to forget those words compared to when they have been told to remember them. However, there is typically no effect when a recognition memory test is used.

Why does directed forgetting occur? Directed forgetting with the item method is found with both recall and recognition, suggesting that the forget instruction has its effects during learning. For example, it has often been suggested that participants may selectively rehearse remember items at the expense of forget items (Geraerts & McNally, 2008). This explanation is less applicable to the list method, because participants have had a substantial opportunity to rehearse the to-be-forgotten list items before being instructed to forget them. The finding that directed

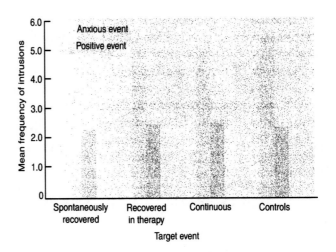

Figure 6.19 Mean numbers of intrusions of anxious and positive events over seven days for patients who had recovered traumatic memories outside therapy (spontaneously recovered). *Inside therapy (recovered in therapy), or who had had continuous traumatic memories (continuous), and non-traumatised controls. Based on data in Geraerts et al.(2008)*

forgetting with the list method is not found in recognition memory suggests that directed forgetting in recall involve retrieval inhibition or interference (Geraert & McNally, 2008).

Inhibition: executive deficit hypothesis

A limitation with much of the research is that the precise reasons *why* directed forgetting has occurred are unclear. For example, consider directed forgetting in the item-method paradigm. This could occur because to-be-forgotten items receive much less rehearsal than to-be-remembered items. However, it could also occur because of an active process designed to inhibit the storage of words in long-term memory. Wylie, Foxe, and Taylor (2007) used fMRI with the item-method paradigm to test these rival hypotheses. In crude terms, we might expect *less* brain activity for to-be-forgotten items than to-be-remembered ones if the former simply attract less processing. In contrast, we might expect *more* brain activity for to-be-forgotten items if active processes are involved. In fact, intentional forgetting when compared with intentional remembering was associated with *increased* activity in several areas (e.g., medial frontal gyrus (BA10) and cingulated gyrus (BA31)) known to be involved in executive control.

Anderson and Green (2001) developed a variant of the item method known as the think no–think paradigm. Participants first learn a list of cue–target word pairs (e.g., Ordeal–Roach). Then they are presented with cues studied earlier (e.g., Ordeal) and instructed to think of the associated word (Roach) (respond condition) or to prevent it coming to mind (suppress condition). Some of the cues were not presented at this stage (baseline condition).

Finally, all the cues are presented and participants provide the correct target words. Levy and Anderson (2008) carried out a meta-analysis of studies using the think/no–think paradigm. There was clear evidence of directed forgetting (see Figure 6.20). The additional finding that recall was worse in the suppress condition than in the baseline condition indicates that inhibitory processes were involved in producing directed forgetting in this paradigm.

What strategies do participants use in the suppress condition? They report using numerous strategies, including forming mental images, thinking of an alternative word or thought, or repeating the cue word (Levy & Anderson, 2008). Bergstrom, de Fockert, and Richardson-Klavehn (2009) manipulated the strategy used. Direct suppression of the to-be-forgotten words was more effective than producing alternative thoughts.

Anderson et al. (2004) focused on individual differences in memory performance using the think/no–think paradigm. Their study was designed to test the executive deficit hypothesis, according to which the ability to suppress memories depends on individual differences in executive control abilities. Recall for word pairs was worse in the suppress condition than in the respond and baseline conditions. Of special importance, those individuals having the greatest activation in bilateral dorsolateral and ventro-lateral prefrontal cortex were most successful at memory inhibition. Memory inhibition was also associated with reduced hippocampal activation—this is revealing because

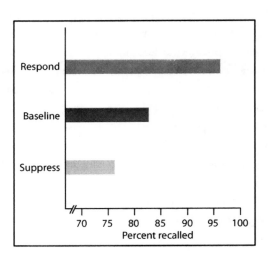

Figure 6.20 Meta–analysis of final recall performance in the think/no–think procedure as a function of whether participants had earlier tried to recall the item (respond), suppress the item (suppress), or had had no previous reminder (baseline). *Reprinted from Levy and Anderson (2008), Copyright © 2008, with permission from Elsevier.*

the hippocampus plays a key role in episodic memory (see Chapter 7). These findings suggest that successful intentional forgetting involves an executive control process in the prefrontal cortex that disengages hippocampal processing.

Additional support for the executive deficit hypothesis was reported by Bell and Anderson (in preparation). They compared individuals high and low in working memory capacity (see Chapter 10), a dimension of individual differences strongly related to executive control and intelligence. As predicted, memory suppression in the think/no–think paradigm was significantly greater in the high capacity group.

Is research using the think/no–think paradigm relevant to repression? There are encouraging signs that it is. First, Depue, Banich, and Curran (2006, 2007) had participants learn to pair unfamiliar faces with unpleasant photographs (e.g., a badly deformed infant; a car accident) using the paradigm. The findings were very similar to those of Anderson et al. (2004). There was clear evidence for suppression of unwanted memories and suppression was associated with increased activation of the lateral prefrontal cortex and reduced hippocampal activity. Second, Anderson and Kuhl (in preparation) found that individuals who had experienced several traumatic events showed superior memory inhibition abilities than those who had experienced few or none. This suggests that the ability to inhibit or suppress memories improves with practice.

Evaluation

Directed forgetting is an important phenomenon. The hypothesis that it involves executive control processes within the frontal lobes has received much empirical support. The extension of this hypothesis to account for individual differences in directed forgetting has also been well supported. In addition, the notion that research on directed forgetting may be of genuine relevance to an understanding of repression is important. A major implication of directed forgetting research is that suppression or repression occurs because of deliberate attempts to control awareness rather than occurring unconsciously and automatically, as suggested by Freud.

Directed forgetting is clearly one way in which forgetting occurs. However, most forgetting occurs in spite of our best efforts to remember, and so the directed forgetting approach is not of general applicability. The suppression effect in the think/no-think paradigm (baseline-suppression conditions) averages out at only 6% (see Figure 6.20), suggesting it is rather weak. However, participants spent an average of only 64 seconds trying to suppress each item, which is presumably massively less than the amount of time many individuals devote to suppressing traumatic memories. Most research on directed forgetting has used neutral and artificial learning materials, and this limits our ability to relate the findings to Freud's ideas about repression.

Cue-dependent forgetting

Forgetting often occurs because we lack the appropriate cues (cue-dependent forgetting). For example, suppose you are struggling to think of the name of the street on which a friend of yours lives. If someone gave you a short list of possible street names, you might have no difficulty in recognising the correct one.

Tulving and Psotka (1971) showed the importance of cues. They presented between one and six word lists, with four words in six different categories in each list. After each list, participants free recalled as many words as possible (original learning). After all the lists had been presented, participants free recalled the words from all the lists (total free recall). Finally, all the category names were presented and the participants tried again to recall all the words from all the lists (free cued recall).

There was strong evidence for retroactive interference in total free recall, since word recall from any given list decreased as the number of other lists intervening between learning and recall increased. However, there was essentially *no* retroactive interference or forgetting when the category names were available to the participants. Thus, the forgetting observed in total free recall was basically cue-dependent forgetting (due to a lack of appropriate cues).

Tulving (1979) developed the notion of cue-dependent forgetting in his encoding specificity principle: "The probability of successful retrieval of the target item is a monotonically increasing function of *informational overlap* between the information present at retrieval and the information stored in memory" (p. 408; emphasis added). If you are bewildered by that sentence, note that "monotonically increasing function" refers to a generally rising function that does not decrease at any point. Tulving also assumed that the memory trace for an item generally consists of the item itself plus information about context (e.g., the setting; current mood state). It follows that memory-performance should be best when the context at test is the same as that at the time of learning.

The encoding specificity principle resembles the notion of transfer-appropriate processing (Morris et al., 1977; see earlier in chapter). The central idea behind transfer-appropriate processing is that long-term memory is best when the processing performed at the time of test closely resembles that at the time of learning. The main difference between these two notions is that transfer-appropriate processing focuses more directly on the processes involved.

KEY TERM

encoding specificity principles: the notion that retrieval depends on the overlap between the information available at retrieval and the information in the memory trace.

Many attempts to test the encoding specificity principle involve two learning conditions and two retrieval conditions. This allows the researcher to show that memory depends on the information in the memory trace *and* the information available in the retrieval environment. Thomson and Tulving (1970) presented pairs of words in which the first was the cue and the second was the to-be-remembered word. The cues were weakly associated with the list words (e.g., "Train-BLACK") or strongly associated (e.g., "White-BLACK"). Some of the to-be-remembered items were tested by weak cues (e.g., "Train-?"), and others were tested by strong cues (e.g., "White-?").

Thomson and Tulving's (1970) findings are shown in Figure 6.21. As predicted, recall performance was best when the cues provided at recall *matched* those provided at learning. Any change in the cues reduced recall, even when the shift was from weak cues at input to strong cues at recall. Why were strong cues associated with relatively poor memory performance when learning had involved weak cues? Tulving assumed that participants found it easy to generate the to-be-remembered words to strong cues, but failed to recognise them as appropriate. However, that

is not the whole story. Higham and Tam (2006) found that participants given strong cues at test after weak cues at learning found it harder to generate the target words than other participants given strong cues at test who had not previously engaged in any learning?. This happened because participants given weak cues at learning had formed a mental set to generate mainly weak associates to cues.

Mood-state dependent memory refers to the enhanced ease in recalling events that have an emotional tone similar to our current mood. If we're feeling happy and content, we are more likely to recall pleasant memories; when depressed we are likely to retrieve unpleasant ones.

Context is important in determining forgetting. For example, information about current mood state is often stored in the memory trace, and there is more forgetting if the mood state at the time of retrieval is different. The notion that there should be less forgetting when the mood state at learning and retrieval is the same is known as mood-state-dependent memory. There is reasonable evidence for mood-state-dependent memory (see Chapter 15). However, the effect is stronger when participants are in a positive rather than negative mood because they are motivated to alter negative moods.

Other kinds of context are also important. Marian and Neisser (2000) studied the effects of linguistic context. Russian-English bilinguals recalled personal memories when prompted with cues presented in the Russian or English language. The participants generated Russian memories (based on experiences in a Russian-speaking

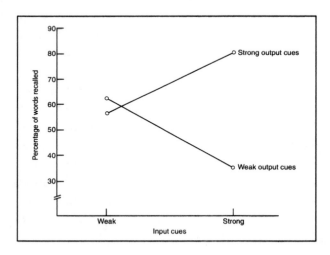

Figure 6.21 Mean word recall as a function of input cues (strong or weak) and output cues (strong or weak). *Data from Thomson and Tulving (1970).*

context) to 64% of the cues in Russian compared to only 35% when the cues were in English.

The effects of context are often stronger in recall than recognition memory. Godden and Baddeley (1975) asked participants to learn a list of words on land or 20 feet underwater, followed by a test of free recall on land or under water. Those who had learned on land recalled more on land and those who learned underwater did better when tested underwater. Overall, recall was about 50% higher when learning and recall took place in the same environment. However, there was no effect of context when. Godden and Baddeley (1980) repeated the experiment using recognition memory rather than recall.

We all know that recognition is generally better than recall. For example, we may be unable to recall the name of an acquaintance but if someone mentions their name we instantly recognise it. One of the most dramatic predictions from the encoding specificity principle is that recall should sometimes be better than recognition. This should happen when the information in the recall cue overlaps more than the information in the recognition cue with the information stored in the memory trace. Muter (1978) presented participants with people's names (e.g., DOYLE, THOMAS) and asked them to circle those they "recognised as a person who was famous before 1950". They were then given recall cues in the form of brief descriptions plus first names of the famous people whose surnames had appeared on the recognition test (e.g., author of the Sherlock Holmes stories: Sir Arthur Conan _____; Welsh poet: Dylan _____). Participants recognised only 29% of the names but recalled 42% of them.

Brain-imaging evidence supporting the encoding specificity principle and transfer-appropriate processing was reported by Park and Rugg (2008a). Participants were presented with pictures and words and then on a subsequent recognition test. Each item was tested with a congruent cue (word-word and picture-picture conditions) or an incongruent cue (word-picture and picture-word conditions). As predicted by the encoding specificity principle, memory performance was better in the congruent than in the incongruent conditions.

Park and Rugg (2008) carried out a further analysis based on brain activity at learning for items subsequently recognised. According to transfer-appropriate processing, it is more important for successful recognition for words

to be processed at learning in a "word-like" way if they are tested by picture cues than by word cues. In similar fashion, successful recognition of pictures should depend more on "picture-like" processing at study if they are tested by pictures cues than by word cues. Both predictions were supported, suggesting that long-term memory is best when the processing at the time of learning is similar to that at the time of retrieval.

Rugg, Johnson, Park, and Uncapher (2008) reported similar findings supporting transferappropriate processing. However, they pointed out that the similarity in patterns of brain activation at learning and retrieval was never very great. This probably happened because only some of the processing at the time of learning directly influenced what information was stored. In addition, only some of the processing at retrieval directly determined what was retrieved.

Evaluation

The overlap between the information stored in the memory trace and that available at the time of retrieval often plays an important role in determining whether retrieval occurs. Recent neuroimaging evidence supports both the encoding specificity principle and transfer-appropriate processing. The emphasis placed on the role of contextual information in retrieval is also valuable. As we have seen, several different kinds of context (e.g., external cues; internal mood states; linguistic context) influence memory performance.

What are the limitations of Tulving's approach? First, it is most directly applicable to relatively simple memory tasks. Tulving assumed that the information at the time of test is compared in a simple and direct way with the information stored in memory to assess informational overlap. That is probably often the case, as when we effortlessly recall autobiographical memories when in the same place as the original event (Bernisen & Hall, 2004). However, if you tried to answer the question, "What did you do six days ago?", you would probably use complex problem-solving strategies not included within the encoding specificity principle.

Second, the encoding specificity principle is based on the assumption that retrieval occurs fairly automatically. However, that is not always the case. Herron and Wilding (2006) found that active processes can be involved in retrieval. People found it easier to recollect episodic memories relating to when and where an event occurred when they adopted the appropriate mental set or frame of mind before-hand. Adopting this mental set was associated with increased brain activity in the right frontal cortex.

Third, there is a danger of circularity (Eysenck, 1978). Memory is said to depend on "informational overlap", but this is rarely measured. It is tempting to infer the amount of informational overlap from the level of memory performance, which is circular reasoning.

Fourth, as Eysenck (1979) pointed out, what matters is not only the informational overlap between retrieval information and stored information but also the extent to which retrieval information allows us to *discriminate* the correct responses from the incorrect ones. Consider the following thought experiment (Nairne, 2002b). Participants read aloud the following list of words: write, right, rite, rite, write, right. They are then asked to recall the word in the third serial position. We increase the informational overlap for some participants by providing them with the sound of the item in the third position. This increased informational overlap is totally unhelpful because it does not allow participants to discriminate the correct spelling of the sound from the wrong ones.

Fifth, Tulving assumed that context influences recall and recognition in the same way. However, the effects of context are often greater on recall than on recognition memory (e.g., Godden & Baddeley, 1975, 1980).

Consolidation

None of the theories considered so far provides a wholly convincing account of forgetting over time. They identify factors causing forgetting, but do not indicate clearly why forgetting is greater shortly after learning than later on. Wixted (2004a, 2005) argued that the secret of forgetting may lie in consolidation theory. Consolidation is a process lasting for a long time (possibly years) that fixes information in long-term memory. More specifically, it is assumed that the hippocampus plays a vital role in the consolidation of memories (especially daily episodic memories for specific events and episodes), with many memories being stored ultimately in various parts of the neocortex, including the temporal lobes. A key assumption is that recently formed memories still being consolidated are especially vulnerable

to interference and forgetting. Thus, "New memories are clear but fragile and old ones are faded but robust" (Wixted, 2004a, p. 265).

According to some versions of consolidation theory (e.g., Eichenbaum, 2001), the process of consolidation involves two major phases. The first phase occurs over a period of hours and centres on the hippocampus. The second phase takes place over a period of time ranging from days to years and involves interactions between the hippocampal region, adjacent entorhinal cortex and the neocortex. This second phase only applies to episodic memories and semantic memories (stored knowledge about the world). It is assumed that such memories are stored in the lateral neocortex of the temporal and other lobes.

Consolidation theory is relevant to two of the oldest laws of forgetting (Wixted, 2004b). First, there is Jost's (1897) law (mentioned earlier), according to which the older of two memories of the same strength will decay slower. According to the theory, the explanation is that the older memory has undergone more consolidation and so is less vulnerable. Second, there is Ribot's (1882) law, according to which the adverse effects of brain injury on memory are greater on newly formed memories than older ones. This is temporally graded retrograde amnesia. It can be explained on the basis that newly formed memories are most vulnerable to disruption because they are at an early stage of consolidation.

Evidence

Several lines of evidence support consolidation theory. First, consider the form of the forgetting curve. A decreasing rate of forgetting over time since learning follows from the notion that cent memories are vulnerable due to an ongoing process of consolidation. Consolidation theory also provides an explanation of Jost's law.

Second, there is research on Ribot's law which claims that brain damage adversely affects recently-formed memories more than older ones. Such research focuses on patients with retrograde amnesia, which involves impaired memory for events occurring before the onset of the amnesia. Many of these patients have suffered damage to the hippocampus as the result of an accident, and this may have a permanently adverse effect on consolidation processes. As predicted by consolidation theory, numerous patients with retrograde amnesia show greatest forgetting for those memories formed very shortly before the onset of amnesia (Manns, Hopkins, & Squire, 2003). However, retrograde amnesia can in extreme cases extend for periods of up to 40 years (Cipolotti et al., 2001).

Third, consolidation theory predicts that newly-formed memories are more susceptible to retroactive interference than are older memories. On the face of it, the evidence is inconsistent. The amount of retroactive interference generally does not depend on whether the interfering material is presented early or late in the retention interval (see Wixted, 2005, for a review). However, the great majority of studies have only considered specific retroactive interference (i.e., two responses associated with the same stimulus). Consolidation theory actually claims that newly-formed memories are more susceptible to interference from *any* subsequent learning. When the interfering material is dissimilar, there is often more retroactive interference when it is presented early in the retention interval (Wixted, 2004a).

KEY TERM

retrograde amnesia: impaired memory for events occurring before the onset of amnesia.

Fourth, consider the effects of alcohol on memory. People who drink excessive amounts of alcohol sometimes suffer from "blackout", an almost total loss of memory for all events occurring while they were conscious but very drunk. These blackouts probably indicate a failure to consolidate memories formed while intoxicated. An interesting (and somewhat surprising) finding is that memories formed shortly *before* alcohol consumption are often better remembered than those formed by individuals who do not subsequently drink alcohol (Bruce & Pihl, 1997). Alcohol probably prevents the formation of new memories that would interfere with the consolidation process of the memories formed just before alcohol consumption.

Thus, alcohol protects previously formed memories from disruption.

Fifth, Haist, Gore, and Mao (2001) obtained support for the assumption that consolidation consists of two phases. Participants identified faces of people famous in the 1980s or 1990s. Selective activation of the hippocampus for famous faces relative to non-famous ones was only found for those famous in the 1990s. In contrast (and also as predicted), there was greater activation in the entorhinal cortex connected to widespread cortical areas for famous faces from the 1980s than from the 1990s.

Evaluation

Consolidation theory has various successes to its credit. First, it explains *why* the rate of forgetting decreases over time. Second, consolidation theory successfully predicts that retrograde amnesia is greater for recently formed memories and that retroactive interference effects are greatest shortly after learning. Third, consolidation theory identifies the brain areas most associated with the two phases of consolidation.

What are the limitations of consolidation theory? First, we lack strong evidence that consolidation processes are responsible for all the effects attributed to them. For example, there are various possible reasons why newly formed memories are more easily disrupted than older ones. Second, consolidation theory indicates in a *general* way why newly formed memory traces are especially susceptible to interference effects, but not the more *specific* finding that retroactive interference is greatest when two different responses are associated with the same stimulus. Third, forgetting can involve several factors other than consolidation. For example, forgetting is greater when there is little informational overlap between the memory trace and the retrieval environment (i.e., encoding specificity principle), but this finding cannot be explained within consolidation theory. Fourth, consolidation theory ignores cognitive processes influencing forgetting. For example, as we have seen, the extent to which forgetting due to proactive interference occurs depends on individual differences in the ability to inhibit or suppress the interfering information.

CHAPTER SUMMARY

- ### Architecture of memory
  According to the multi-store model, there are separate sensory, short-term, and long-term stores. Much evidence (e.g., from amnesic patients) provides general support for the model, but it is clearly oversimplified. According to the unitary-store model, short-term memory is the temporarily activated part of long-term memory. There is support for this model in the finding that amnesics' performance on some "short-term memory" tasks is impaired. However, it is likely that long-term memory plays an important role in determining performance on such tasks.

- ### Working memory
  Baddeley replaced the unitary short-term store with a working memory system consisting of an attention-like central executive, a phonological loop holding speech-based information, and a visuo-spatial sketchpad specialised for spatial and visual coding. More recently Baddeley has added a fourth component (episodic buffer) that integrates and holds information from various sources. The phonological loop and visuo-spatial sketchpad are both two-component systems, one for storage and one for processing. The central executive has various functions, including inhibition, shifting, updating, and dual-task co-ordination. Some brain-damaged patients are said to suffer from dysexecutive syndrome, but detailed analysis indicates that different brain regions are associated with the functions of task setting, monitoring, and energisation.

- ### Levels of processing
  Craik and Lockhart (1972) focused on learning processes in their levels-of-processing theory. They identified depth of processing (the extent to which meaning is processed), elaboration of processing, and distinctiveness of processing as key determinants of long-term memory. Insufficient attention was paid to the relationship between processes at learning and those at retrieval. In addition, the theory isn't explanatory, it is hard to assess processing depth, and shallow processing can lead to very good long-term memory.

- ### Implicit learning
  Much evidence supports the distinction between implicit and explicit learning, and amnesic patients often show intact implicit learning but impaired explicit learning. In addition, the brain areas activated during explicit learning (e.g., pre-frontal cortex) differ from those activated during implicit learning (e.g., striatum). However, it has proved hard to show that claimed demonstrations of implicit learning satisfy the information and sensitivity criteria. It is likely that the distinction between implicit and explicit learning is over-simplified, and that more complex theoretical formulations are required.

- ### Theories of forgetting
  Strong proactive and retroactive interference effects have been found inside and outside the laboratory. People use active control processes to minimise proactive interference. Much retroactive interference depends on automatic processes making the incorrect responses accessible. Most evidence on Freud's repression theory is based on adults claiming recovered memories of childhood abuse. Such memories when recalled outside therapy are more likely to be genuine than those recalled inside therapy. There is convincing evidence for directed forgetting, with executive control processes within the prefrontal cortex playing a major role. Forgetting is often cue-dependent, and the cues can be external or internal. However, decreased forgetting over time is hard to explain in cue-dependent terms. Consolidation theory provides an explanation for the form of the forgetting curve, and for reduced forgetting rates when learning is followed by alcohol.

FURTHER READING

- Baddeley, A.D. (2007). *Working memory: Thought and action*. Oxford: Oxford University Press. Alan Baddeley, who has made massive contributions to our understanding of working memory, has written an excellent overview of current knowledge in the area.

- Baddeley, A.D., Eysenck, M.W., & Anderson, M.C. (2009). *Memory.* Hove, UK: Psychology Press. Several chapters in this book provide additional coverage of the topics discussed in this chapter (especially forgetting).

- Jonides, J., Lewis, R.L., Nee, D.E., Lustig, C.A., Berman, M.G., & Moore, K.S. (2008). The mind and brain of short-term memory. *Annual Review of Psychology, 59,* 193–224.

- This chapter discusses short-term memory at length, and includes a discussion of the multi-store and unitary-store models.

- Repovš, G., & Baddeley, A. (2006). The multi-component model of working memory: Explorations in experimental cognitive psychology. *Neuroscience, 139,* 5–21. This article provides a very useful overview of the working memory model, including a discussion of some of the most important experiment findings.

- Roediger, H.L. (2008). Relativity of remembering: Why the laws of memory vanished. *Annual Review of Psychology, 59,* 225–254. This chapter shows very clearly that learning and memory are more complex and involve more factors than is generally assumed to be the case.

- Shanks, D.R. (2005). Implicit learning. In K. Lamberts & R. Goldstone (eds.), *Handbook of Cognition.* London: Sage. David Shanks puts forward a strong case for being critical of most of the evidence allegedly demonstrating the existence of implicit learning.

- Wixted, J.T. (2004). The psychology and neuroscience of forgetting. *Annual Review of Psychology, 55,* 235–269. A convincing case is made that neuroscience has much to contribute to our understanding of forgetting.

Short-Term and Working Memory

ALAN D. BADDELEY

The study of short-term memory, the retention of small amounts of information over brief time intervals, formed a major component of the development of cognitive psychology during the 1960s. It had a strong theoretical component, derived from the increasingly influential computer metaphor, combined in Britain at least with a concern for application to problems such as those of air traffic communication (Broadbent, 1958) and of coding in telephony and postal systems (Conrad, 1964). The attempt to develop information-processing models of short-term memory (STM) led to some major controversies (see below). Unfortunately, resolving these issues unequivocally proved beyond the capability of the methods available at the time, resulting in a decline of interest in STM during the 1970s, and subsequently even to a declaration of its demise (Crowder, 1982).

However, as the old concept of STM was losing favor, it became incorporated within a more complex framework, *working memory* (WM), which proposed that the older concept of a unitary store be replaced by a multicomponent system that utilized storage as part of its function of facilitating complex cognitive activities such as learning, comprehending, and reasoning (Baddeley & Hitch, 1974). Interest in WM continued to develop through the 1980s, though with somewhat different emphases on different sides of the Atlantic. During the 1990s, the whole area has received a further boost from the development of functional imaging techniques, with the components of

working memory offering an appropriate level of complexity for the developing techniques of brain scanning. This development was facilitated by the very fruitful relationship between cognitive psychology and the neuropsychology of working memory, which provided hypotheses as to which areas of the brain might be most likely to be involved in particular tasks, together with concepts that facilitate the linking of the neuroanatomy to a coherent cognitive framework. Finally, and coincidentally, some of the old applied problems are now beginning to resurface. In both the United States and Britain, for example, there is currently considerable concern about the best way to extend the ever-expanding series of telephone codes so as to optimize capacity without unduly increasing length, while new areas such as pharmaceutical prescribing errors are beginning to highlight the need for an understanding of the processes involved and to draw upon the empirical work of the 1960s (Lambert, 1997).

As a result of these various developments, there is a growing interest in the field of STM and WM from scientists whose principal training has been in other areas, but who wish to incorporate measures of short-term and working memory into their work. Finally, the area continues to attract good young researchers who see the study of working memory as an important interface between research on memory, perception, and attention.

While there are many overviews of the area, ranging from the relatively brief (Baddeley, 1992) to the chapter length (Baddeley, 1996) and the book length (Gathercole, 1996; Miyake & Shah, in press), neither these nor journal articles tend to include the sort of practical detail that is so important if one wishes to carry out or evaluate experiments. The present chapter aims to go some way toward filling this gap, while bearing in mind that the only way to fully understand a technique is to use it. Here STM and WM are treated separately, since the relevant techniques, driven by the specific theoretical issues of the time, tend to be somewhat different. However, it is important to bear in mind that they do form part of the same tradition, and that it is increasingly common for 1960s techniques and methods to find new uses in the 1990s. It may be useful, however, to begin with some terminology.

TERMINOLOGY

The division of memory into two or more systems was proposed by William James (1890), who distinguished between *primary memory,* which he regarded as closely associated with conscious awareness, and *secondary memory,* which referred to more durable memories. When the interest in fractionating memory revived in the late 1950s, the term STM was used to refer to tasks in which small amounts of material were retained over brief intervals, in contrast to LTM, which involved retention over more than a few seconds. It subsequently became clear that performance on STM tasks was not a pure reflection of the hypothetical underlying system, but was also influenced by LTM. To avoid confusion, some investigators used different terms to refer to the hypothetical underlying theoretical memory systems, such as *short-term* and *long-term store* (STS and LTS: Atkinson & Shiffrin, 1968), or reverting to *primary* and *secondary memory* (Waugh & Norman, 1965).

In recent years, the term *working memory* proposed by Miller, Galanter, and Pribram (1960) has been developed to emphasize the functional role of STM as part of an integrated system for holding and manipulating information during the performance of complex cognitive tasks (Baddeley & Hitch, 1974). Unfortunately, the same term has been used independently within the animal learning literature, where it refers to situations in which the animal needs to retain information across several trials during the same day (Olto Walker, & Gage, 1978), almost certainly involving different mechanisms from those involved in the typical human WM task. Finally the production system approach to computational modeling proposed by Newell and Simon (1972) postulates a working memory unlimited capacity, although this is not assumed to be related to the limited capacity STM system proposed by experimentalis such as Baddeley and Hitch (1974). Fortunately, the context is usually sufficient avoid too much confusion between the various users of the term.

SHORT-TERM MEMORY

Methods and Techniques

Before going on to discuss recent theoretical developments in the area, it may be useful to describe some of the rich armament of methods and techniques that have been developed to study verbal and visual STM.

Verbal STM

Memory Span

Subjects are presented with a sequence of items, which they attempt to reproduce in the presented order. Typically, digits, consonants or words are used. Presentation may be visual or auditory, with auditory presentation tending to give a slight advantage, particularly over the last one or two items, the so-called *modality effect.* Rates of presentation typically range from 0.5s to 2s per item, with 1s probably being the commonest. Presentation rate is not a major variable within this range, but faster rates run the risk of errors owing to failure to perceive, while slower rates give sufficient time for subjects to engage in complete and often highly variable rehearsal strategies.

Recall may be spoken or written. It is usual to require the subject to recall in the order of presentation, and to monitor that this is the case. Performance is typically measured in terms of the maximum level achieved, with span formally being the point at which the subject recalls the ordered sequence of items on 50% of occasions. This is not easy to determine directly, and hence a number of approximations are used. One simple method is to take the mean of the length of the three longest sequences correctly recalled, so a subject being correct on three out of four 7-item sequences, and one at length eight, would have a score of 7.33.

Memory span has the disadvantage that many of the data collected come from sequence lengths at which performance is perfect, hence providing little information. More information may be gained from using a procedure in which all sequences are presented at the same length, which should be at or slightly beyond span. Performance can then be scored either in terms of number of *sequences* completely correct or of number of *items* recalled in the correct serial position.

In his classic paper *The magic number seven*, George Miller (1956) speculated that in the area of absolute perceptual judgments, subjects could typically distinguish about 7 separate categories, while a typical digit span was about 7 items. He went on to emphasise that this latter conclusion was a gross oversimplification since it was possible to increase this substantially by *chunking*, a process whereby several items are aggregated into a larger super item. Perhaps the clearest demonstration of this is in immediate memory for prose material; memory span for unrelated words is about 5 or 6, whereas with meaningful sentences, spans of 16 words or more are not unusual (Baddeley, Vallar, & Wilson, 1987). Syntax and meaning make prose highly redundant, and an early paper by Miller and Selfridge (1950) showed that the more closely a string of words approximates to English prose, the longer the memory span. However, although absolute number of words increases with approximation to English, Tulving and Patkau (1962) showed that the number of chunks remains constant.

Free Recall

This simple task involves presenting the subject with a list, typically of words, that subjects attempt to recall in any order they wish. The classic serial position curve shows excellent recall of the last few items (the *recency effect*), somewhat better recall of the first one or two items (the *primacy effect*), and a relatively flat function between.

A brief filled delay will wipe out the recency effect while having little effect on earlier items. Virtually any variable that will influence long-term learning (e.g., rate of presentation, familiarity of material, the presence of a secondary task, or the age of the subject) will influence earlier items but have little or no impact on the recency effect (Glanzer, 1972). The recency effect reflects a strategy of first recalling the earlier items, and is abolished if subjects are dissuaded from this. It appears to be a very basic and robust strategy that is found in young children, amnesic patients, and even patients suffering from Alzheimer's disease (Glanzer, 1972; Baddeley & Hitch, 1993).

The primacy effect is less marked and less robust. It may reflect a number of variables, but in particular the tendency to give more attention and possibly more rehearsal to the initial item (Hockey, 1973).

While the typical serial position function operates across a wide range of lengths and presentation rates, most experimenters avoid sequences of less than 10 items, since there is a tendency for subjects to attempt to recall short sequences in serial order. Presentation rate is typically slower than in memory span, since this increases the amount of recall from the earlier long-term part of the curve, with 2s per item being the most common presentation rate. It is also not uncommon to use semantically categorized material, since this again increases performance and also gives some indication as to whether the subject is able to take advantage of meaning (Tulving & Pearlstone, 1966).

Short-Term Forgetting

The classic paradigm here was developed by Peterson and Peterson (1959); their subjects were presented with three consonants and required to retain them over a delay ranging from 0–18s, during which they counted backwards in threes. Performance reflects an STM component that declines over about 5 seconds (Baddeley & Scott, 1971), and an LTM component reflecting the extent to which items can be discriminated from prior items, the result of *proactive interference* (PI; Keppel & Underwood; 1962). PI can be prevented by changing the type of material to be remembered—for example, switching from animals to flowers (Wickens, 1970) or by inserting a delay between successive trials (Loess & Waugh, 1967), resulting in a recovery of performance (*release from PI*), followed by a further buildup of PI.

Memory Probe Techniques

The act of recalling an item can itself produce forgetting, either because the time taken to recall allows farther trace decay or because the recall process disrupts the memory trace. One way of avoiding both of these is through probe techniques, whereby only part of the remembered material is sampled. For example, Sperling (1963) presented subjects with 3 rows of 4 letters. At recall, one of the 3 rows is cued by a tone. Since the subject does not know in advance which row, one can legitimately multiply that score by the number of rows to estimate the capacity of the memory system, which is typically greater than that obtained using more standard total recall methods. In a variant of this, Waugh and Norman (1965) presented their subjects with a series of digit strings varying in length. The experimenter then provided one item from the string and required the subject to produce the next in sequence. Recall performance showed a very clear recency effect, which was minimally affected by rate of presentation, suggesting that forgetting was principally due to the limited capacity of the short-term store rather than to temporal trace decay.

A variant of the memory probe technique was developed by Sternberg (1966), who used speed of response as a means of investigating the storage of items within the memory span. A digit list ranging in length from 1 to 6 was presented, followed by a probe digit. The task was to decide whether the probe digit had been part of the previously presented sequence. Reaction time increased linearly with the length of the presented sequence. This occurred not only for positive probes but also for negative probes, where the item had not been in the list. Sternberg proposed a model based on the analogy of a computer serially scanning its memory store, with the slope of the function relating RT to number items in store providing a measure of hypothetical scanning rate, typically about 40 ms per item. The fact that slopes for "yes" and "no" responses were the same prompted Sternberg to suggest that the search was exhaustive. If subjects could respond as soon as they detected a match with—the probe, then the "yes" response slope should be shallower than the "no." This led to intensive experimental work that uncovered phenomena inconsistent with the scanning model, such as effects of recency (Corballis, Kirby, & Miller, 1972) and repetition effects (Baddeley & Ecob, 1973), leading to the proposal of alternative models (Anderson, 1973; Theios,

1973). With the growth in number of models and a lack of crucial experimental evidence, the technique became unfashionable, although it is still quite extensively used as a measure of cognitive deficit following drugs or stressors, for which it provides a neat and reasonably sensitive measure. In the absence of any broadly accepted theoretical interpretation, it continues to offer a theoretical challenge.

Nonverbal STM

Research on STM was dominated by verbal tasks, probably because the material is so easy to manipulate and record. However, analogous effects have been shown for visual memory. Dale (1973) required subjects to remember the location of a single point on an open field over a delay filled by verbal counting, finding that accuracy declined steadily over time. Phillips (1974) presented subjects with a matrix of which half the cells were filled, presenting a second matrix for recognition after a filled delay varying in length. Performance remained high over the delay for simple 2 x 2 matrices, with forgetting becoming steeper as the complexity of the matrix increased. In a subsequent study, Phillips and Christie (1977) presented subjects with a sequence of matrix patterns, observing that only the last pattern showed evidence of excellent initial performance followed by rapid decay, while earlier matrices showed a low level of performance. This pattern of results, therefore, suggests a short-term visual memory store that is limited to one pattern, with performance on that pattern being a function of its complexity. This has been used to develop a measure of pattern span in which the subject is shown a pattern and attempts to reproduce it on a matrix. The test begins with a 2 x 2 matrix with half the cells filled, increasing to a point at which the subject is no longer able to accurately reproduce the pattern, which for a normal adult is typically around 16 cells (Delia Sala, Gray, Baddeley, & Wilson, 1997).

An alternative measure of visuo-spatial span is the Corsi block tapping task (Milner, 1968), in which the subject is faced with an array of 9 quasi-randomly arranged blocks. The experimenter taps a particular sequence of blocks and asks the subject to imitate, starting with just 2 and building up to a point at which performance breaks down, typically around 5 taps. This task has a sequential and motor component missing from the pattern span, and appears to measure a different aspect of visuo-spatial memory, since patients can be impaired on one but not the other; furthermore, spatial activity interferes with Corsi span, while intervening abstract pictures differentially interferes with pattern span (Delia Sala, Gray, Baddeley, Allamano, & Wilson, in press).

Memory for location using a technique somewhat similar to that developed by Dale suggests that visual and verbal STM involve different brain regions (Smith & Jonides, 1995) and also that the maintenance of even a single item involves an active process involving the frontal lobes (Goldman-Rakic, 1996; Haxby, Ungerleider, Horwitz, Rapoport, & Grady, 1995).

Research on other nonverbal retention is less well developed, but studies of memory for kinaesthetic stimuli (Adams & Dijkstra, 1966) and tactile stimuli (Gilson & Baddeley, 1969) show rapid forgetting over a short delay, whereas memory for odors (Engen, Kuisma, & Eimas, 1973) does not.

Theoretical Issues

Despite earlier suggestions that there might be more than one kind of memory (Hebb, 1949; James, 1890), the issue was largely ignored until the discovery of the short-term forgetting of small amounts of information over filled intervals by Brown (1958) and Peterson and Peterson (1959), which led the investigators to propose separate LTM and STM memory systems, with short-term forgetting reflecting the spontaneous decay of the memory trace. This view was resisted, notably by Melton (1963), who argued strongly for a unitary memory system in which forgetting reflected associative interference between the items retained, rather than trace decay. The importance of PI in the STM paradigm (Keppel & Underwood, 1962) suggested that interference effects certainly occur in STM, although these in turn could be interpreted as reflecting limited capacity, rather than classic associative interference (Waugh & Norman, 1965). The issue of whether short-term-forgetting-reflects-decay-or—interference-remains unresolved.

During the mid-1960s proponents of a dichotomy between STM and LTM generated evidence from a range of sources, including:

Two Component Tasks: Tasks such as free recall appear to have separate components, with the recency effect reflecting STM, while earlier items appear to depend upon LTM (Glanzer, 1972).

Acoustic and Semantic Coding: Conrad (1962) showed that errors in recalling visually presented consonants tended to be similar in sound to the correct items (e.g., *B* is remembered as *V*), suggesting that recall is based on an acoustic code. Baddeley (1966a, 1966b) showed that immediate recall sequences of 5 unrelated words was highly susceptible to acoustic similarity but insensitive to semantic similarity, while delayed recall of 10-word lists showed exactly the opposite pattern. Using a probe technique, Kintsch and Buschke (1969) showed that the recency part of the function reflected acoustic similarity effects, while performance on earlier items reflected semantic coding. These studies, therefore, appeared to suggest a predilection for acoustic coding in STM and semantic coding in LTM.

Neuropsychological Evidence: Amnesic patients such as the classic case HM (Milner, 1966) showed grossly impaired LTM, together with preserved span. Such patients also showed preserved recency, and if intellectually otherwise intact, normal performance on the Peterson Short-Term Forgetting Task (Baddeley & Warrington, 1970). In contrast, a second class of patient appeared to show the opposite pattern with digit spans of 1 or 2 items, very poor Peterson performance, and little or no recency, coupled with apparently normal LTM (Shallice & Warrington, 1970). This double dissociation strongly supported a separation of LTM and STM.

By the late 1960s, a range of models began to appear in which STM and LTM were conceptualized as separate systems. The most influential of these was the Atkinson and Shiffrin (1968) model, which became known as the *modal model*. As shown in figure 5.1, it assumes that information comes in from the environment through a parallel series of sensory memory systems into a limited-capacity short-term store, which forms a crucial bottle-neck between perception and LTM. The STS was also assumed to be necessary for recall, and to act as a limited-capacity working memory.

In the early 1970s, the modal model encountered two major problems. The first concerned its assumptions regarding long-term learning, while the second involved its capacity to explain the neuropsychological evidence.

The modal model assumed that the longer an item was held in STS, the greater the chance of its being transferred to the LTS. This assumption was challenged (e.g., Craik & Watkins, 1973), leading Craik and Lockhart (1972) to propose their levels of processing hypothesis. This proposes that the durability of memory increases with depth of processing, hence processing a word in terms of its visual appearance leads to little learning. Phonological processing in terms of sound is somewhat better, whereas deeper semantic processing leads to the best retention. While the detailed application of this model can be criticized (Baddeley, 1978), there is no doubt that it represents a good

account of a considerable amount of data, and that the underdevelopment of its treatment of coding represents a limitation of the modal model.

The second problem with the modal model stems from its apparent prediction that patients with a grossly impaired STS should encounter associated problems in long-term learning. Furthermore, since the STS was assumed to act as working memory, allowing complex information processing to proceed, then such patients should also have major general information-processing deficits. However, the few relatively pure cases studied appeared to have normal long-term memory and to lead largely normal lives (Shallice & Warrington, 1970; Vallar & Shallice, 1990).

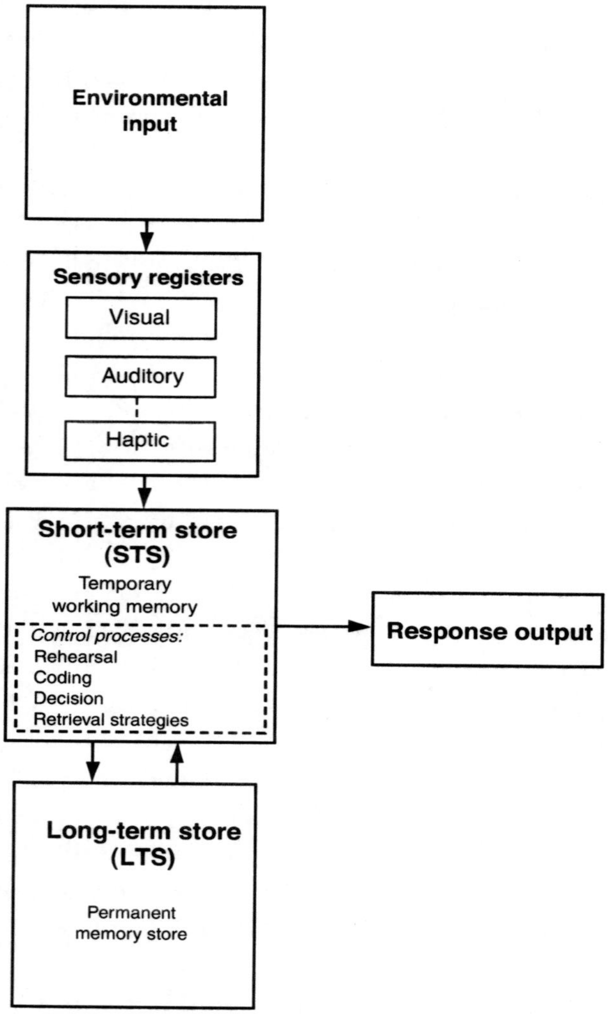

WORKING MEMORY

In order to tackle this problem, Baddeley and Hitch (1974) proposed that the concept of a single unitary STM be replaced by a multi-component system, focusing on three subsystems. These comprised two slave systems; one, the *phonological loop* was concerned with storing acoustic and verbal information, while the second, the *visuo-spatial sketchpad,* was its visual equivalent (see figure 5.2). The overall system was assumed to be controlled by a limited-capacity attentional system, the *central executive.* While the details of this model and its terminology are by no means universally accepted, the last 20 years have seen an increasing tendency for the term *working memory* to be used, together with a broad general acceptance of the usefulness of postulating a system that combines executive control with more specialized storage systems that show important differences between visual and verbal material (Miyake & Shah, 1999). For that reason, the tripartite structure will be used as a basis for the review, while accepting that there may be a subsequent need to postulate other components.

Verbal Working Memory

This system, labeled by Baddeley and Hitch the *articulatory* or *phonological loop,* is closest in character to the original concept of a short-term store. It is assumed to be defective in the type of patient studied by Shallice and Warrington (1970). The general cognitive disruption implied by the modal model does not occur because the central executive

Figure 5.1 Atkinson & Shiffrin's (1968) influential model of STM.

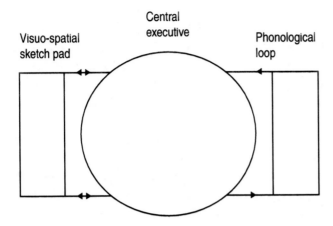

Figure 5.2 The Working Memory model proposed by Baddeley & Hitch (1974).

Visuo-spatial sketch pad

Central executive

Phonological loop

is intact in such patients. The phonological loop is assumed to comprise two components, a store in which an acoustic or phonological memory trace is held. The trace is assumed to decay within about two seconds unless performance is maintained by the second component, the process of subvocal articulatory rehearsal. This process is not only able to refresh the memory trace but can also register visually presented but nameable material in the phonological store by means of articulation. The principal evidence for phonological coding is the previously described acoustic similarity effect, while the role of the articulatory process is supported by the *word length effect,* whereby the immediate memory span for words is a direct function of the length of the constituent items. A simple rule of thumb is that subjects can remember as many items as they can say in two seconds (Baddeley, Thompson, & Buchanan, 1975). Baddeley and Hitch explained this phenomenon in terms of trace decay, proposing that subvocal maintenance rehearsal occurs in real time, hence long words take longer to rehearse, allowing more forgetting through trace decay. Cowan et al. (1992) suggest that the word length effect principally is a function of forgetting during the process of recall, with longer words taking longer to produce, hence allowing more decay. As the effect can also be found, though to a lesser extent, with probed recall, it seems likely that both rehearsal rate and output time contribute to the word-length effect (Avons, Wright, & Pammer, 1994).

Articulatory suppression is a procedure whereby the subject is required to utter some repeated redundant sound

such as the word "the" while performing another task such as memory span. Murray (1968) showed that suppression reduces performance and also eliminates the phonological similarity effect, with visual, though not with auditory, presentation. This is assumed to occur because suppression prevents the subject from converting the visual stimulus into a verbal code that is suitable for registering in the phonological store. With auditory presentation, access to the store is assumed to be automatic (Baddeley, 1986). The effect of suppression on the word-length effect is assumed to be somewhat different. Since the word-length effect is a direct function of rehearsal, suppression will remove the effect, regardless of whether presentation is auditory or visual, as indeed is the case (Baddeley, Lewis, & Vallar, 1984).

Another area of considerable activity and controversy in connection with the word-length effect relates to individual differences. If trace decay is responsible for the word-length effect, then subjects who rehearse more slowly should show poorer performance. This was indeed found by Baddeley et al. (1975). Nicolson (1981) observed that developmental changes in children's memory span were associated with changes in speed of articulation, suggesting that faster rehearsal might be responsible for the increase in span with age. The effect was replicated by subsequent studies (e.g., Hitch, Halliday, Dodd, & Littler, 1989), while research on serial recall of pictured objects suggested that verbal coding was a strategy that children begin to adopt between the ages of 7 and 10, as reflected by the influence on performance of the acoustic similarity of the names in the set and of their spoken length (Hitch, Halliday, Schaafstad, & Hefferman, 1991). Younger children appear to use some form of visual code, and hence perform more poorly when the items depicted are similar in shape—for example, a spoon, a pen, and a twig.

When material is presented auditorily, phonological similarity and word-length effects appear at a much earlier age, a result which was initially taken to suggest that rehearsal begins at this early stage. However, opinion is now shifting toward the assumption that this very early rehearsal reflects a different and relatively automatic process—more like a spontaneous internal echoing of the stimulus than a coherent cumulative rehearsal strategy such as is found in older children and adults (Gathercole & Hitch, 1993).

Finally, there has been considerable interest in recent years in the possible evolutionary function of the phonological loop; if patients can show gross impairment in memory span with little impact on everyday functioning, can the loop be of much biological significance? Initial work focused on the possible role of the loop in language comprehension (Vallar & Baddeley, 1984). Although there are some differences among patients, the general consensus is that most have difficulty only when syntactic structures require the literal maintenance of the first part of the sentence until it is disambiguated at the end, as for example in the case of self-embedded sentences (see Vallar & Shallice, 1990, for a review).

A much stronger case for the importance of the phonological loop can be made in the case of new phonological learning. For example, PV, a patient with a very pure STM deficit, showed no difficulty in learning to associate pairs of words in her own language, but was grossly impaired in capacity to learn the vocabulary of an unfamiliar language, Russian (Baddeley, Papagno, & Vallar, 1988). In a subsequent study, Gathercole and Baddeley (1990) found that children with a specific language disability were particularly impaired in their capacity to hear and repeat back unfamiliar sound sequences. This deficit was more pronounced than their language impairment and did not appear to be attributable to either perceptual or speech production problems. This work led to the development of a non-word repetition test in which the subject attempts to repeat spoken nonwords ranging in length from 2 syllables (e.g., *ballop*) to 5 (e.g., *voltularity*). Nonword repetition performance proved to correlate with level of vocabulary development across a wide range of ages; over the 4-to 5-year range, cross-lagged correlation suggested that nonword repetition was causally related to the subsequent development of vocabulary, rather than the reverse (see Baddeley, Gathercole, & Papagno, 1998, for a review). Finally, the phonological short-term store appears to be related to the capacity for second-language acquisition in both children (Service, 1992) and adults (Papagno, Valentine, & Baddeley, 1991), with variables such as articulatory suppression, phonological similarity, and word length all influencing the acquisition of novel word forms but not affecting the capacity to associate pairs of already familiar words, a process that is assumed to depend principally on semantic coding (Papagno & Vallar, 1992).

Neurobiological Evidence

Neuropsychological studies of STM patients suggested an impaired phonological store (Vallar & Baddeley, 1984; Vallar & Shallice, 1990). The capacity to articulate overtly is not necessary for rehearsal since dysarthric patients with a peripheral disruption to speech production appear to have normal rehearsal capacities (Baddeley & Wilson, 1985). However, dyspraxia, a disruption of the basic capacity to program speech output, does interfere with memory performance (Waters, Rochon, & Caplan, 1992).

More recently, functional imagery studies using PET and fMRI have produced clear evidence for a phonological short-term store located in the perisylvian region of the left hemisphere, together with a separate rehearsal component associated with Broca's area (Paulesu, Frith, & Frackowiak, 1993; Awh et al., 1996).

Visuo-Spatial Working Memory

As described earlier, evidence for the storage of visual information has been available for many years. The use of visuo-spatial coding for verbal material was demonstrated particularly neatly by Brooks (1967), using a technique in which subjects were induced to store a sequence of sentences by recoding them in terms of a path through a visually presented matrix. Using this paradigm, Baddeley, Grant, Wight, and Thomson (1973) showed that visuo-spatial tracking, but not verbal coding, interfered with visual-imagery-based performance in contrast to a broadly equivalent verbally coded task. Further work suggested that the coding was specifically *spatial* (Baddeley & Lieberman, 1980). However, using a somewhat different memory paradigm involving the use of visual imagery in paired-associate learning, Logie (1986) showed that performance could be disrupted by the simple requirement to observe patterns or patches of color, a *visual* rather than a spatial task.

Most disrupting tasks tend to involve both visual and spatial processing, and may also tend to have an executive component (see Logie, 1995, for a review). The technique recently developed by Quinn and McConnell (1996) appears to minimize disruption to anything other than the visual component of the working memory system. Their disrupting task simply requires the subject to fixate on a screen on which a large matrix of cells is continuously flickering on and off. They find that this influences performance when subjects are learning paired associates using an imagery mnemonic, while having no effect on rote learning performance, in contrast to the effects of irrelevant speech, which produces the opposite pattern.

Further evidence for separating visual and spatial aspects of STM come from the observation that pattern span, in which subjects have to reproduce a pattern of filled and unfilled cells in a matrix, is disrupted by the subsequent requirement to look at a series of abstract pictures, but not by a spatial tapping task, in contrast to the more spatial and serial Corsi Block Tapping Task, which shows exactly the opposite pattern (Delia Sala et al., in press).

Neurobiological Evidence

Evidence for separate visual and spatial components of the STM system come from neuropsychological studies, with separate patients capable of performing the Corsi Block but not the pattern span task and vice versa (Delia Sala et al., in press). Finally, neuroradiological evidence indicates the separability of visual and verbal memory (Smith, Jonides, & Koeppe, 1996), and within that, a distinction between spatial and object-based components (Smith et al., 1995). This area continues to develop, and further fractionation seems probable (Baddeley, 1998b).

EXECUTIVE PROCESSES

Individual Difference in Working Memory Span

While work utilizing the Baddeley and Hitch model has tended to concentrate on the slave systems, postponing a more detailed analysis of the central executive, North American research on working memory has tended to follow the opposite pattern, though with notable exceptions. Furthermore, while neuropsychological evidence has played a particularly important role in European research on working memory, North American research has been more strongly influenced by the psychometric-tradition with its concern for individual differences within the normal population. The two approaches are complementary and will be considered in turn.

In a classic paper, Daneman and Carpenter (1980) operationally defined working memory as the system responsible for the simultaneous storage and manipulation of information. They developed a measure, *working memory-span,* in which subjects were required to read out a series of sentences and then recall the final word of each. The maximum number of sentences for which all the final words can be correctly recalled is the working memory span, which for normal subjects ranges between 2 and 5. Daneman and Carpenter then demonstrated that span correlated highly with reading comprehension in a sample of student subjects. This finding has been replicated many times (see Daneman & Merikle, 1996, for a review). A series of follow-up studies contrasted subjects who were high and low in span, demonstrating, for example, that there were qualitative differences in the way in which prose is processed by the two groups; for example, high-span subjects are more able to resolve textual ambiguities and to carry information across from one sentence to another in order to do so (Daneman & Carpenter, 1983).

Views differ as to whether the measure was concerned with a language-specific system as proposed, for example, by Daneman and Tardif (1987) or reflects a more general executive processing capacity, as suggested by Turner and Engle (1989), who showed that a measure they call *operation span,* based on arithmetic, predicts reading comprehension virtually as well as the original-sentence span.

Further support for the working memory span measure comes from Kyllonen and Christal (1990), who demonstrate that performance on a cluster of working memory span tasks correlates highly with more traditional measures of fluid intelligence while being less subject to the influence of prior knowledge and providing better prediction of success in acquiring practical skills such as programming than more traditional measures.

However, despite the apparent success of the working memory span measures, they have recently come under criticism, notably from Waters and Caplan (1996a, 1996b), who question the interpretation of earlier results and also report data from neuropsychological patients of various types that inconsistent with the theoretical interpretation offered by Carpenter and Just (1992). The criticism is relatively recent and the issue still unresolved (see Just, Carpenter, & Keller, 1996). It seems likely that working memory span probably involves the interaction of several cognitive subsystems. This highlights the importance of understanding the task if this approach is to continue to be fruitful.

Analysis of the WM span task has been one of the major problems tackled by Engle and his group. Engle (1996) showed that high-span subjects are better at generating items from semantic categories but, paradoxically, are more impaired than low-span subjects by the requirement to perform a concurrent task. This is interpreted as reflecting the successful use of attentional resources by the high-span subjects to minimize disruption from already generated items, a strategy that is disrupted by the concurrent load. Low-span subjects are unaffected by load because they are incapable or perhaps unwilling to use the inhibitory strategy, and are unaffected by a concurrent attentional demand. A similar intriguing pattern of results is obtained in studying performance on the Sternberg scanning task, for which there is again evidence for a qualitative difference in performance between high-and low-span subjects that is attributed to the capacity to maintain a memory representation against the disruption of potentially interfering items (Conway & Engle, 1994).

While Engle's work is highly creative in linking individual difference measures and more traditional memory measures such as category fluency and the Sternberg task, it appears to demonstrate qualitative differences in performance between high-and low-span subjects. These would seem to be at least as likely to result from differences in strategy as from a qualitative difference in the way in which the memory system works. In either case, the discontinuity casts doubt on using working memory span as a continuous measure. Even more seriously, these results suggest that many of the findings in this area, which are typically based on young students who are presumably of above-average intelligence for the population, may not generalize to samples of older subjects from a wider intellectual range. The success of Kyllonen in using the measures suggests that there is an important core to the work, but the measures are not yet well understood. At the very least, it would be useful to have work that separates out the role of the slave systems from that of executive processes. The necessity for such a separation is supported both by further psychometric research in the working memory span tradition (Shah & Miyake, 1996) and by the growing amount of evidence from functional imagery studies (Smith & Jonides, 1995).

Analysing the Central Executive

Work from a multicomponent approach to working memory has tended to use secondary task techniques, contrasting low processing load tasks such as articulatory suppression and spatial tapping that are targeted at the slave systems, with more demanding tasks, such as random generation of digits or key presses. Baddeley (1986) suggested that the capacity to produce a random stream of items such as digits or letters was constrained by the capacity of the central executive to break away from well-learned stereotypes such as the alphabet by continuously switching to new retrieval plans. Random generation does indeed dramatically impair complex tasks such as choosing the appropriate move in chess, in contrast to the simple suppression effect of reciting the alphabet (Robbins et al., 1996). Similarly, a concurrent digit span task can be shown to interfere with manual generation, with randomness decreasing linearly with digit load (Baddeley, Emslie, Kolodny, & Duncan, 1998).

The initial model of the central executive (Baddeley, 1986) was strongly influenced by Norman and Shallice's (1986) Supervisory Attentional System (SAS), and like the SAS was assumed to depend on the operation of the frontal lobes. However, a clear distinction was made between the question of anatomical localization and that of the functional analysis of the system assumed to reflect the operation of the central executive. It was suggested that the use of the term frontal syndrome should be avoided; the term *dysexecutive syndrome* was proposed as an alternative (Baddeley & Wilson, 1988).

One danger with the concept of a central executive is that of postulating a homunculus that is simply assumed to have whatever capacities are necessary to account for the data (Parkin, 1998). One response to this charge (Baddeley, 1998a) is to argue for the value of homunculi as a means of allowing the investigator to set aside some of the more intractable problems. The danger occurs when the theorist treats the homunculus as a solution rather than as a problem to be solved.

The question of how to analyze the central executive remains a difficult one. One approach is, of course, that based on individual differences described above. A second is to attempt to understand the breakdown of executive processes following brain damage in frontal lobe patients (e.g., Shallice & Burgess, 1996) or in patients suffering from Alzheimer's disease (Baddeley, Bressi, Delia Sala, Logie, &

Spinnler, 1991). Both these approaches have proposed a number of separable executive subprocesses, such as the capacity to focus and switch attention and to divide it among a number of sources. Division of attention appears to be particularly impaired in Alzheimer's disease, for example, while being relatively preserved in normal elderly subjects (Baddeley et al., 1991). Given the richness and complexity of executive processes, fractionation is likely to be a long and complex task. There is evidence to suggest, however, that it will benefit substantially from the development of functional imagery studies, which are already giving a very clear indication that different areas of the frontal lobes may be specialized for different executive functions (for an overview, see the papers included in Roberts, Robbins, & Weiskrantz, 1998).

Suppose that we are successful in identifying a finite array of executive processes, will we then have solved the central executive problem? Clearly not, since a crucial issue is the way in which the constituent processes interact. At present we have little evidence to constrain the possibilities, which range from a hierarchical structure with one dominant function, to an array of executive processes of approximately equal status, with a set of rules of interaction from which consensus emerges. If the former, then what is the process that dominates and, if the latter, what are the mechanisms that allow consensus to be reached? The same question arises within the more specialized subsidiary systems accessed. We know that verbal memory span is strongly influenced by phonological factors, but is in addition somewhat sensitive to visual similarity and can, of course, be strongly influenced by semantic and linguistic factors when sentences are retained. As a recent survey of current models of working memory illustrates (Miyake & Shah, 1999), the question of how information from different sources is integrated lies at the heart of many approaches to working memory and is likely to offer one of the most important and challenging problems facing the study of working memory in the years to come.

Acknowledgment The support provided by grant G9423916 from the Medical Research Council is gratefully acknowledged.

REFERENCES

Adams, J. A., & Dijkstra, S. (1966). Short-term memory for motor responses. *Journal of Experimental Psychology, 71,* 314–318.

Anderson, J. A. (1973). A theory for the recognition of items from short memorized lists. *Psychological Review, 80,* 417–438.

Atkinson, R. C, & Shiffrin, R. M. (1968). Human memory: A proposed system and its control processes. In K. W. Spence (Ed.), *The psychology of learning and motivation: Advances in research and theory* (pp. 89–195). New York: Academic Press.

Avons, S. E., Wright, K. L., & Pammer, K. (1994). The word-length effect in probed and serial recall. *Quarterly Journal of Experimental Psychology, 47A,* 207–231.

Awh, E., Jonides, J., Smith, E. E., Schumacher, E. H., Koeppe, R. A., & Katz, S. (1996). Dissociation of storage and retrieval in verbal working memory: Evidence from positron emission tomography. *Psychological Science, 7,* 25–31.

Baddeley, A. D. (1966a). Short-term memory for word sequences as a function of acoustic, semantic and formal similarity. *Quarterly Journal of Experimental Psychology, 18,* 362–365.

Baddeley, A. D. (1966b). The influence of acoustic and semantic similarity on long-term memory for word sequences. *Quarterly Journal of Experimental Psychology, 18,* 302–309.

Baddeley, A. D: (1978). The trouble with levels: A re-examination of Craik and Lockhart framework for memory research. *Psychological Review, 85,* 139–152.

Baddeley, A. D. (1986). *Working memory.* Oxford: Oxford University Press.

Baddeley, A. D. (1992). Working memory. *Science, 255,* 556–559.

Baddeley, A. D. (1996). The concept of working memory. In S. E. Gathercole (Ed.), *Models of short-term memory* (pp. 1–27). Hove, England: Psychology Press.

Baddeley, A. D. (1998a). The central executive: A concept and some misconceptions. *Journal of the International Neuropsychology Society, 4,* 523–526.

Baddeley, A. D. (1998b). Recent developments in working memory. *Current Opinion in Neurobiology, 8,* 234–238.

Baddeley, A. D., Bressi, S., Delia Sala, S., Logie, R., & Spinnler, H. (1991). The decline of working memory

IN ALZHEIMER'S DISEASE: A LONGITUDINAL STUDY. *BRAIN, 114*, 2521–2542.

BADDELEY, A. D., & ECOB, J. R. (1973). REACTION TIME AND SHORT-TERM MEMORY. IMPLICATIONS OF REPETITION EFFECTS FOR THE HIGH-SPEED EXHAUSTIVE SCAN HYPOTHESIS. *QUARTERLY JOURNAL OF EXPERIMENTAL PSYCHOLOGY, 25*, 229–240.

BADDELEY, A. D., EMSLIE, H., KOLODNY, J., & DUNCAN, J., (1998). RANDOM GENERATION AND THE EXECUTIVE CONTROL OF WORKING MEMORY. *QUARTERLY JOURNAL OF EXPERIMENTAL PSYCHOLOGY, 51A*, 819–852.

BADDELEY, A., GATHERCOLE, S., & PAPAGNO, C. (1998). THE PHONOLOGICAL LOOP AS A LANGUAGE LEARNING DEVICE. *PSYCHOLOGICAL REVIEW, 105*, 158–173.

BADDELEY, A. D., GRANT, S., WIGHT, E., & THOMSON, N. (1973). IMAGERY AND VISUAL WORKING MEMORY. IN P. M. A. RABBITT & S. DORNIC (EDS.), *ATTENTION AND PERFORMANCE V* (PP. 205–217). LONDON: ACADEMIC PRESS.

BADDELEY, A. D., & FLITCH, G. J. (1974). WORKING MEMORY. IN G. A. BOWER (ED.), *THE PSYCHOLOGY OF LEARNING AND MOTIVATION* (PP. 47–89). NEW YORK: ACADEMIC PRESS.

BADDELEY, A. D., & HITCH, G. J. (1993). THE RECENCY EFFECT: IMPLICIT LEARNING WITH EXPLICIT RETRIEVAL? *MEMORY AND COGNITION, 21*, 146–155.

BADDELEY, A. D., LEWIS, V. J., & VALLAR, G. (1984). EXPLORING THE ARTICULATORY LOOP. *QUARTERLY JOURNAL OF EXPERIMENTAL PSYCHOLOGY, 36*, 233–252.

BADDELEY, A. D., & LIEBERMAN, K. (1980). SPATIAL WORKING MEMORY. IN R. S. NICKERSON (ED.), *ATTENTION AND PERFORMANCE VIII* (PP. 521–539). HILLSDALE, NJ: ERLBAUM.

BADDELEY, A. D., PAPAGNO, C, & VALLAR, G. (1988). WHEN LONG-TERM LEARNING DEPENDS ON SHORT-TERM STORAGE. *JOURNAL OF MEMORY AND LANGUAGE, 27*, 586–595.

BADDELEY, A. D., & SCOTT, D. (1971). SHORT-TERM FORGETTING IN THE ABSENCE OF PROACTIVE INTERFERENCE. *QUARTERLY JOURNAL OF EXPERIMENTAL PSYCHOLOGY, 23*, 275–283.

BADDELEY, A. D., THOMSON, N., & BUCHANAN, M. (1975). WORD LENGTH AND THE STRUCTURE OF SHORT-TERM MEMORY. *JOURNAL OF VERBAL LEARNING AND VERBAL BEHAVIOUR, 14*, 575–589.

BADDELEY, A. D., VALLAR, G., & WILSON, B. A. (1987). SENTENCE COMPREHENSION AND PHONOLOGICAL MEMORY: SOME NEUROPSYCHOLOGICAL EVIDENCE. IN M. COLTHEART (ED.), *ATTENTION AND PERFORMANCE XII: THE PSYCHOLOGY OF READING* (PP. 509–529). LONDON: ERLBAUM.

BADDELEY, A. D., & WARRINGTON, E. K. (1970). AMNESIA AND THE DISTINCTION BETWEEN LONG- AND SHORT-TERM MEMORY. *JOURNAL OF VERBAL LEARNING AND VERBAL BEHAVIOR, 9*, 176–189.

BADDELEY, A. D., & WILSON, B. (1985). PHONOLOGICAL CODING AND SHORT-TERM MEMORY IN PATIENTS WITHOUT SPEECH. *JOURNAL OF MEMORY AND LANGUAGE, 24*, 490–502.

BADDELEY, A. D., & WILSON, B. (1988). FRONTAL AMNESIA AND THE DYSEXECUTIVE SYNDROME. *BRAIN & COGNITION, 7*(2), 212–230.

BROADBENT, D. E. (1958). *PERCEPTION AND COMMUNICATION.* LONDON: PERGAMON PRESS.

BROOKS, L. R. (1967). THE SUPPRESSION OF VISUALIZATION BY READING. *QUARTERLY JOURNAL OF EXPERIMENTAL PSYCHOLOGY, 19*, 289–299.

BROWN, J. (1958). SOME TESTS OF THE DECAY THEORY OF IMMEDIATE MEMORY. *QUARTERLY JOURNAL OF EXPERIMENTAL PSYCHOLOGY, 10*, 12–21.

CONRAD, R. (1962). AN ASSOCIATION BETWEEN MEMORY ERRORS AND ERRORS DUE TO ACOUSTIC MASKING OF SPEECH. *NATURE, 193*, 1314–1315.

CONRAD, R. (1964). ACOUSTIC CONFUSION IN IMMEDIATE MEMORY. *BRITISH JOURNAL OF PSYCHOLOGY, 55*, 75–84.

CONWAY, A. R. A., & ENGLE, R. W. (1994). WORKING MEMORY AND RETRIEVAL: A RESOURCE-DEPENDENT INHIBITION MODEL, *JOURNAL OF EXPERIMENTAL PSYCHOLOGY: GENERAL, 123*, 354–373.

CORBALLIS, M. C., KIRBY, J., & MILLER, A. (1972). ACCESS TO ELEMENTS OF A MEMORISED LIST. *JOURNAL OF EXPERIMENTAL PSYCHOLOGY, 94*, 185–190.

COWAN, N., DAY, L., SAULTS, J. S., KELLER, T. A., JOHNSON, T., & FLORES, L. (1992). THE ROLE OF VERBAL OUTPUT TIME AND THE EFFECTS OF WORD LENGTH ON IMMEDIATE MEMORY. *JOURNAL OF MEMORY AND LANGUAGE, 31*, 1–17.

CRAIK, F. I. M., & LOCKHART, R. S. (1972). LEVELS OF PROCESSING: A FRAMEWORK FOR MEMORY RESEARCH. *JOURNAL OF VERBAL LEARNING AND VERBAL BEHAVIOR, 11*, 671–684.

CRAIK, F. I. M., & WATKINS, M. J. (1973). THE ROLE OF REHEARSAL IN SHORT-TERM MEMORY. *JOURNAL OF VERBAL LEARNING AND VERBAL BEHAVIOR, 11*, 671–684.

CROWDER, R. G. (1982). THE DEMISE OF SHORT-TERM MEMORY. *ACTA PSYCHOLOGICA, 50*, 291–323.

DALE, H. C. A. (1973). SHORT-TERM MEMORY FOR VISUAL INFORMATION. *BRITISH JOURNAL OF PSYCHOLOGY, 64*, 1–8.

DANEMAN, M., & CARPENTER, P. A. (1980). INDIVIDUAL DIFFERENCES IN WORKING MEMORY AND READING. *JOURNAL OF VERBAL LEARNING AND VERBAL BEHAVIOUR, 19*, 450–466.

Daneman, M., & Carpenter, P. A. (1983). Individual difference in integrating information between and within sentences. *Journal of Experimental Psychology: Learning, Memory and Cognition, 9*, 561–584.

Daneman, M., & Merikle, P. M. (1996). Working memory and language comprehension: A meta-analysis. *Psychonomic Bulletin & Review, 3*, 422–433.

Daneman, M., & Tardif, T. (1987). Working memory and reading skill re-examined, In M. Coltheart (Ed.), *Attention and performance* (pp. 491–508). Hove, England: Erlbaum.

Della Sala, S., Gray, C., Baddeley, A.D., Allamano, N., & Wilson, L. (in press). Pattern span: A means of unwelding visuo-spatial memory. *Neuropsychologia.*

Della Sala, S., Gray, C., Baddeley, A. D., & Wilson, L. (1997). *The visual patterns test: A test of short-term visual recall.* Flempton Bury & Edomonds, England: Thames Valley Test Company.

Engen, T., Kuisma, J. E., & Eimas, P. D. (1973). Short-term memory of odors. *Journal of Experimental Psychology 99,* 222–225.

Engle, R. W. (1996). Working memory and retrieval: An inhibition-resource approach. In J. T. E. Richardson, R. W. Engle, L. Hasher, R. H. Logie, E. R. Stoltfus, & R. T. Zacks (Eds.), *Working memory and human cognition* (pp. 89–119). New York: Oxford University Press.

Gathercole, S. E. (1996). *Models of short-term memory.* Hove, England: Psychology Press.

Gathercole, S. E., & Baddeley, A. D. (1990). Phonological memory deficits in language-disordered children: Is there a causal connection? *Journal of Memory and Language, 29,* 336–360.

Gathercole, S. E., & Hitch, G. J. (1993). Developmental changes in short-term memory: A revised working memory perspective. In A. Collins, S. E. Gathercole, M. A. Conway, & P. E. Morris (Eds.), *Theories of memory.* Hove, England: Erlbaum.

Gilson, A. D., & Baddeley, A. D. (1969). Tactile short-term memory. *Quarterly Journal of Experimental Psychology, 21,* 180–184.

Glanzer, M. (1972). Storage mechanisms in recall. In G. H. Bower (Ed.), *The psychology of learning and motivation: Advances in research and theory.* New York: Academic Press.

Goldman-Rakic, P. S. (1996). The prefrontal landscape: Implications of functional architecture for understanding human mentation and the central executive. *Philosophical Transactions of the Royal Society (Biological Sciences), 351,* 1445–1453.

Haxby, J. V., Ungerleider, L. G., Horwitz, B., Rapoport, S. I., & Grady, C. L. (1995). Hemispheric differences in neural systems for face working memory: a PET-rCBF study. *Human Brain Mapping, 3,* 68–82.

Hebb, D. O. (1949). *Organization of behavior.* New York: John Wiley.

Hitch, G. J., Halliday, M. S., Dodd, A., & Littler, J. E. (1989). Development of rehearsal in short-term memory: Differences between pictorial and spoken stimuli. *British Journal of Developmental Psychology, 7,* 347–362.

Hitch, G. J., Halliday, M. S., Schaafstal, A. M., & Heffernan, T. M. (1991). Speech, "inner speech" and the development of short-term memory: Effects of picture labelling on recall. *Journal of Experimental Child Psychology 51,* 220–234.

Hockey, G. R. J. (1973). Rate of presentation in running memory and direct manipulation of input processing strategies. *Quarterly Journal of Experimental Psychology, 25,* 104–111.

James, W. (1890). *The principles of psychology.* New York: Holt, Rinehart & Winston.

Just, M. A., Carpenter, P. A., & Keller, T. A. (1996). The capacity theory of comprehension: New frontiers of evidence and arguments. *Psychological Review, 103,* 773–780.

Keppel, G., & Underwood, B. J. (1962). Proactive inhibition in short-term retention of single items. *Journal of Verbal Learning and Verbal Behavior, 1,* 153–161.

Kintsch, W., & Buschke, H. (1969). Homophones and synonyms in short-term memory. *Journal of Experimental Psychology, 80,* 403–407. Kyllonen, P. C., & Christal, R. E. (1990). Reasoning ability is (little more than) working memory capacity. *Intelligence, 14,* 389–433.

Lambert, B. L. (1997). Predicting look-alike and sound-alike medication errors. *American Journal of Health-system Pharmacy, 54,* 1161–1171.

Loess, H., & Waugh, N. C. (1967). Short-term memory and inter-trial interval. *Journal of Verbal Learning and Verbal Behaviour, 6,* 445–460.

Logie, R. H. (1986). Visuo-spatial processing in working memory. *Quarterly Journal of Experimental Psychology, 38A,* 229–247.

Logie, R. H. (1995). *Visuo-spatial working memory.* Hove, England: Erlbaum.

Melton, A. W. (1963). Implications of short-term memory for a general theory of memory. *Journal of Verbal Learning and Verbal Behavior, 2,* 1–21.

Miller, G. A. (1956). The magical number seven, plus or minus two: Some limits on our capacity for processing information. *Psychological Review, 63,* 81–97.

Miller, G. A., Galanter, E., & Pribram, K. H. (1960). *Plans and the Structure of Behavior.* New York: Holt, Reinhart & Winston.

Miller, G. A., & Selfridge, J. A. (1950). Verbal context and the recall of meaningful material. *American Journal of Psychology, 63,* 176–185.

Milner, B. (1966). Amnesia following operation on the temporal lobes. In C. W. M. Whitty & O. L. Zangwill (Eds.), *Amnesia* (pp. 109–133). London: Butterworths.

Milner, B. (1968). Visual recognition and recall after right temporal-lobe excision in man. *Neuropsychologia, 6,* 191–209.

Miyake, A., & Shah, P. (Eds.). (1999). *Models of Working Memory: Mechanisms of active maintenance and executive control.* New York: Cambridge University Press.

Murray, D. J. (1968). Articulation and acoustic confusability in short-term memory. *Journal of Experimental Psychology, 78,* 679–684.

Newell, A., & Simon, H. A. (1972). *Human problem solving.* Englewood Cliffs, NJ: Prentice-Hall.

Nicolson, R. (19–81), The relationship between memory span and processing speed. In M. Friedman, J. P. Das, & N. O'Connor (Eds.), *Intelligence and learning* (pp. 179–184). New York: Plenum Press.

Norman, D. A., & Shallice, T. (1986). Attention to action: Willed and automatic control of behaviour. In R. J. Davidson, G. E. Schwarts, & D. Shapiro (Eds.), *Consciousness and self-regulation. Advances in research and theory* (pp. 1–18). New York: Plenum Press.

Olton, D. S., Walker, J. A., & Gage, F. H. (1978). Hippocampal connections and spatial discrimination. *Brain Research, 139,* 295–308.

Papagno, C., Valentine, T., & Baddeley, A. D. (1991). Phonological short-term memory and foreign language vocabulary learning. *Journal of Memory and Language, 30,* 331–347.

Papagno, C., & Vallar, G. (1992). Phonological short-term memory and the learning of novel words: The effect of phonological similarity and item length. *Quarterly Journal of Experimental Psychology, 44A,* 47–67.

Parkin, A. J. (1998). The central executive does not exist. *Journal of the International Neuropsychology Society, 4,* 518–522.

Paulesu, E., Frith, C. D., & Frackowiak, R. S. J. (1993). The neural correlates of the verbal component of working memory. *Nature, 362,* 342–345.

Peterson, L. R., & Peterson, M. J. (1959). Short-term, retention of individual verbal items. *Journal of Experimental Psychology, 58,* 193–198.

Phillips, W. A. (1974). On the distinction between sensory storage and short-term visual memory. *Perception and Psychophysics, 16,* 283–290.

Phillips, W. A., & Christie, D. F. M. (1977). Components of visual memory. *Quarterly Journal of Experimental Psychology, 29,* 117–133.

Quinn, G., & McConnell, J. (1996). Irrelevant pictures in visual working memory. *Quarterly Journal of Experimental Psychology, 49A,* 200–215.

Robbins, T., Anderson, E., Barker, D., Bradley, A., Fearneyhough, C., Henson, R., Hudson, S., & Baddeley, A. D. (1996). Working memory in chess. *Memory and Cognition, 24*(1), 83–93.

Roberts, A. C., Robbins, T. W., & Weiskrantz, L. (1998). *The pre-frontal cortex: Executive and cognitive functions.* Oxford: Oxford University Press.

Service, E. (1992). Phonology, working memory and foreign-language learning. *Quarterly Journal of Experimental Psychology, 45A,* 21–50. Shah, P., & Miyake, A. (1996). The separability of working memory resources for spatial thinking and language processing. *Journal of Experimental Psychology: General, 125,* 4–27.

Shallice, T., & Burgess, P. (1996). The domain of supervisory processes and temporal organization of behaviour. *Philosophical Transactions of the Royal Society of London Series B—Biological Sciences, 352*(1346), 1405–1411.

Shallice, T., & Warrington, E. K. (1970). Independent funtioning of verbal memory stores: A neuropsychological study. *Quarterly Journal of Experimental Psychology, 22,* 261–273.

Smith, E. E., & Jonides, J. (1995). Working memory in humans: Neuropsychological Evidence. In M. Gazzaniga (Ed.), *The cognitive neurosciences* (pp. 109–1020). Cambridge, MA: MIT Press.

SMITH, E., JONIDES, J., & KOEPPE, R. A. (1996). DISSOCIATING VERBAL AND SPATIAL WORKING MEMORY USING PET. *CEREBRAL CORTEX, 6,* 11–20.

SMITH, E. E., JONIDES, J., KOEPPE, R. A., AWH, E., SCHUMACHER, E., & MINOSHIMA, S. (1995). SPATIAL VERSUS OBJECT WORKING MEMORY: PET INVESTIGATIONS. *JOURNAL OF COGNITIVE NEUROSCIENCE, 7,* 337–358.

SPERLING, G. (1963). A MODEL FOR VISUAL MEMORY TASKS. *HUMAN FACTORS, 5,* 19–31.

STERNBERG, S. (1966). HIGH-SPEED SCANNING IN HUMAN MEMORY. *SCIENCE, 153,* 652–654.

THEIOS, J. (1973). REACTION TIME MEASUREMENTS IN THE STUDY OF MEMORY PROCESS: THEORY AND DATA. IN G. H. BOWER (ED.), *THE PSYCHOLOGY OF LEARNING & MOTIVATION.* VOL. 7. (PP. 43–85). NEW YORK: ACADEMIC PRESS.

TULVING, E., & PATKAU, J. E. (1962). CONCURRENT EFFECTS OF CONTEXTUAL CONSTRAINT AND WORD FREQUENCY ON IMMEDIATE RECALL AND LEARNING OF VERBAL MATERIAL. *CANADIAN JOURNAL OF PSYCHOLOGY, 16,* 83–95.

TULVING, E., & PEARLSTONE, Z. (1966). AVAILABILITY VERSUS ACCESSIBILITY OF INFORMATION IN MEMORY FOR WORDS. *JOURNAL OF VERBAL LEARNING AND VERBAL BEHAVIOR, 5,* 381–391.

TURNER, M. L., & ENGEL, R. W. (1989). IS WORKING MEMORY CAPACITY TASK-DEPENDENT? *JOURNAL OF MEMORY AND LANGUAGE, 28,* 127–154.

VALLAR, G., & BADDELEY, A. D. (1984). FRACTIONATION OF WORKING MEMORY. NEUROPSYCHOLOGICAL EVIDENCE FOR A PHONOLOGICAL SHORT-TERM STORE. *JOURNAL OF VERBAL LEARNING AND VERBAL BEHAVIOUR, 23,* 151–161.

VALLAR, G., & SHALLICE, T. (EDS.). (1990). *NEUROPSYCHOLOGICAL IMPAIRMENTS OF SHORT-TERM MEMORY.* CAMBRIDGE: CAMBRIDGE UNIVERSITY PRESS.

WATERS, G. S., & CAPLAN, D. (1996A). THE MEASUREMENT OF VERBAL WORKING MEMORY CAPACITY AND ITS RELATION TO READING COMPREHENSION. *QUARTERLY JOURNAL OF EXPERIMENTAL PSYCHOLOGY, 49A,* 51–79.

WATERS, G. S., & CAPLAN, D. (1996B). THE CAPACITY THEORY OF SENTENCE COMPREHENSION: CRITIQUE OF JUST & CARPENTER (1992). *PSYCHOLOGICAL REVIEW, 103,* 761–772.

WATERS, G.S., ROCHON, E., & CAPLAN, D. (1992). THE ROLE OF HIGH-LEVEL SPEECH PLANNING IN REHEARSAL: EVIDENCE FROM PATIENTS WITH APRAXIA OF SPEECH. *JOURNAL OF MEMORY AND LANGUAGE, 31,* 54–73. WAUGH, N. C, & NORMAN, D. A. (1965). PRIMARY MEMORY. *PSYCHOLOGICAL REVIEW, 72,* 89–104.

WICKENS, D. D. (1970). ENCODING CATEGORIES OF WORDS: AN EMPIRICAL APPROACH TO MEANING. *PSYCHOLOGICAL REVIEW, 77,* 1–15.

Suppressing Unwanted Memories by Executive Control

MICHAEL C. ANDERSON AND COLLIN GREEN

Freud proposed that unwanted memories can be forgotten by pushing them into the unconscious, a process called repression[1]. The existence of repression has remained controversial for more than a century, in part because of its strong coupling with trauma, and the ethical and practical difficulties of studying such processes in controlled experiments. However, behavioural and neurobiological research on memory and attention shows that people have executive control processes directed at minimizing perceptual distraction[2,3], overcoming interference during short and long-term memory tasks[3–7] and stopping strong habitual responses to stimuli[8–13]. Here we show that these mechanisms can be recruited to prevent unwanted declarative memories from entering awareness, and that this cognitive act has enduring consequences for the rejected memories. When people encounter cues that remind them of an unwanted memory and they consistently try to prevent awareness of it, the later recall of the rejected memory becomes more difficult. The forgetting increases with the number of times the memory is avoided, resists incentives for accurate recall and is caused by processes that suppress the memory itself. These results show that executive control processes not uniquely tied to trauma may provide a viable model for repression.

Executive control processes studied in behavioural[6,9,14] and neurobiological[2,4,10–13,15–17] research on cognition may provide a mechanism for the voluntary form of repression (suppression) proposed by Freud[1]. To test this hypothesis, we adapted the go/no-go paradigm used to study executive control over motor actions in primates[18] and humans[15–17] for use in a memory retrieval task. First, we trained subjects on 40 unrelated word pairs (for example, ordeal-roach) so that they could recall the right-hand member of each pair when provided with the left-hand member. Next, subjects performed a critical task requiring them to exert executive control over the retrieval process. On each trial of this think/no-think task, a cue from one of the pairs appeared on the computer screen. Depending on which cue appeared, subjects were told either to recall and say (think about) the associated response word (respond pairs), or not to think about the response (suppression pairs). For the latter pairs, we emphasized that subjects should not allow the associated memory to enter consciousness at all. If subjects accidentally responded to a suppression pair, they heard a beep signalling an error. To increase the need to recruit inhibitory control mechanisms, we required subjects to fixate on the cue word for the entire time (4 s) that it appeared on the screen, discouraging perceptual avoidance and generating a constant threat that the associated memory might intrude into consciousness. Thus, suppression trials required the stopping of both a prepotent motor response and the entrance of an unwanted memory into awareness. Before this phase, we told subjects which cues would require suppression so that they would recognize these words on sight. Subjects performed suppression and respond trials on different pairs that were intermixed. On each trial, no visual marking indicated which cue words were suppression items, forcing

Michael Anderson and Collin Green, "Suppressing Unwanted Memories by Executive Control," *Nature*, vol. 410, no. 6826, pp. 366-369.

subjects to identify each cue to know whether to recall or suppress the associated memory.

The objective of the think/no-think task was to determine whether attempting to prevent awareness of an unwanted memory would hinder its later retrieval. To evaluate whether this occurred, the next phase required subjects

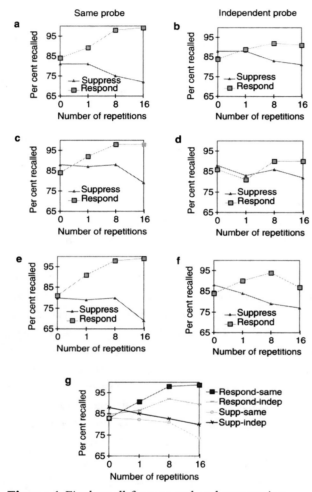

Figure 1 Final recall for respond and suppression items as a function of the number of repetitions for the same-probe (SP) and independent-probe (IP) tests. *a, b, Experiment 1; c, d, experiment 2; e, f, experiment 3; g, averaged across experiments. Note the negative slope for recall of the suppressed item, indicating increasing inhibition. Inhibition (0 vs 16 suppressions) was significant (P< 0.01) in all experiments, and did not interact with type of test cue (F < 1 in all cases; analysis of variance). Inhibition was significant (P < 0.05) in every SP and IP test for every experiment (a–f).*

to recall the response for each of the cue words. We emphasized that the previous goal of avoiding the associated items was no longer relevant and that a response should be recalled for every cue. If trying to prevent a memory from entering awareness recruits inhibitory control processes that impair that memory's retrievability, recall for suppression items should be worse than for baseline pairs on this test. In all experiments reported here, baseline items were studied pairs that did not appear as either respond or suppression items during the think/no-think phase.

In experiment 1, we varied the number of suppression or respond trials given for each pair. Subjects received 0,1,8 or 16 trials for each suppression and each respond item. If excluding unwanted memories from awareness recruits inhibitory control, recall should be worse after 16 suppression attempts than after 0 attempts (baseline). As shown in Fig. 1a, final recall of suppressed items was worse than of baseline items, and impairment increased linearly with suppression practice. In contrast, recall improved across repetitions for respond items, demonstrating the established benefits of retrieving memories on their later recall. These diverging patterns show that controlling awareness not only terminated the powerful facilitative effects of retrieval, but also impaired the recall of suppressed items to below their baseline level (0 suppression attempts). The increasing inhibition with repetition further indicates that unwanted memories might be especially vulnerable in settings requiring protracted avoidance, unlike the modest time (1 min over 16 suppressions) afforded by our task.

Impaired memory for suppression items indicates that there may be an executive control process that suppresses (reduces activation of) the unwanted memory itself (for example, roach in Fig. 2). However, mechanisms other than inhibition may be at work[6]. For instance, one strategy for avoiding an unwanted memory would be to generate diversionary thoughts to environmental stimuli that remind us of it. New associations between these stimuli and the diversionary thoughts may interfere during later attempts to recall the memory. Alternatively, terminating retrieval may degrade the association between the cue and the response. Neither of these alternatives requires us to assume that the unwanted memory itself is inhibited and thus they do not require the postulation of an executive inhibition process. To isolate the contribution of inhibition, we used the independent probe method[6]. If inhibition impairs the unwanted memory itself, recall should be worse regardless of whether that item is tested with the cue used to train suppression or with a novel cue (Fig. 2). However, associative interference and unlearning predict that forgetting should be limited to the originally trained cue. To distinguish between these models, we retested subjects from experiment 1 with cues not previously encountered in the experiment ('independent probes'). For each item, we cued subjects with a semantic category and the initial letter of the response word (for example, for ordeal-roach, subjects received 'insect r_____') and asked them to recall the studied word that fit the cues. On this new independent probe (IP) test, recall of suppressed items was again worse than baseline (Fig. 1b), and the impairment was higher when recall had been avoided more. The amount of forgetting did not differ reliably from when the originally trained cue was used in the test (for example, ordeal in the same probe (SP) test condition, Fig. 1a). This finding rules out associative interference and unlearning and shows that impairment is localized to the unwanted memory itself. This strongly supports the existence of an inhibitory control mechanism[6].

It was necessary to show that subjects did not recall and then withhold suppression items on the final test. They might have done so out of confusion, given our emphasis on withholding responses during the think/no-think phase. To address this, we expanded our test instructions to emphasize that subjects should recall an item to every cue regardless of earlier instructions, even if they were guessing. To further encourage responding, we offered a monetary reward for correct answers. These incentives had little impact on the inhibition effect (Fig. 1c, d). Impairment was significant overall, increased with repetition, and did not vary with the type of test cue, again supporting the inhibitory control view. Although the instructions to guess enhanced recall of suppression and baseline items when the studied cue was given (P < 0.01), the linear trend for inhibition did not differ reliably across experiments (F< 1).

Subjects might have guessed the hypothesis of the experiment and tried to conform to the expectation of impaired memory by withholding items. To address this, we altered the final test instructions to make subjects believe that we expected improved memory for suppression items. We told subjects that research suggests that when people try not to think about something, they ironically

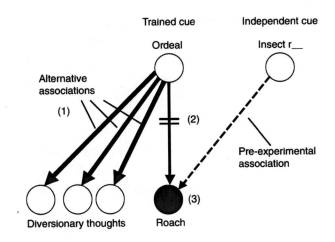

Figure 2 Three mechanisms that can explain impaired recall in the same-probe condition, the cue–target connection (2). *The suppression hypothesis states that suppression illustrated with a stimulus pair. Associative interference posits that suppression training inhibits the target (3). Note that testing the target with an independent cue leads subjects to generate diversionary thoughts (1) to the trained cue that interfere during circumvents interference (1) and unlearning (2). Any impairment found with this test may later attempts to recall the target. Unlearning assumes that suppression training weakens can be attributed to effects localized to the target.*

think about it more, as when people try not to think about falling asleep at night and then experience insomnia[19]. We noted that this research predicts that memory for suppression items should improve because the avoided memories should intrude during suppression trials. Post-experimental questionnaires indicated that subjects believed that this was our rationale (average rating of 4.2 on a 5-point belief scale) and most endorsed the theory on the basis of experience. These new test instructions had little effect on the inhibition pattern (Fig. 1e, f).

Success in our think/no-think task is defined by participants' subjective awareness of the unwanted memory during suppression trials, a state which cannot be measured. Efforts to control this state nevertheless left their mark on memory. However, the apparent memory deficit may reflect suppression of the overt motor response associated with the unwanted memory. To test this, we removed the instruction to suppress awareness of the memory during the think/no-think phase. We instead asked subjects to recall the memory, but not say it aloud, rendering this an episodic go/no-go task. Recall did not decline with the number of verbal suppressions, and this pattern did not vary with the cue used to test items (Fig. 3a, b). In contrast, when experiments 1–3 are combined, the linear trend for inhibition was reliable for the SP and IP test conditions (P< 0.001, Fig. 1g) and these effects did not vary reliably across experiments. Importantly, the linear inhibition effect was statistically larger in the think/no-think task (experiments 1–3) than in the go/no-go task (experiment 4). These findings isolate impaired recall of unwanted memories to cognitive operations directed at keeping them out of awareness.

Our results imply that a process exists that impairs the retention of memories when they are deliberately kept out of consciousness. When people encounter a stimulus that is known to cue an unwanted memory, this process can be recruited to prevent awareness of the memory. The regulation of consciousness is accomplished by an inhibitory control mechanism that suppresses the unwanted memory itself (as shown by our independent probe data), and not merely by the momentary filling of working memory with diversionary thoughts. Delayed recall of the unwanted memory is worse than a baseline condition in which no reminders of the memory were presented in the interim. This paradoxical pattern arises because repeated exposure to reminders makes it necessary for people to adapt their patterns of thought internally with executive control processes. Thus, frequent encounters with reminders should make an unwanted memory less accessible, a finding noted in some clinical studies of psychogenic amnesia[20].

Our results clarify the nature and scope of inhibitory processes previously shown to impair episodic recall, and link those processes to behavioural and neurobiological research on executive control. Work on retrieval-induced forgetting[6] has shown that memories that interfere with the retrieval of other targets are inhibited, but it has not previously been established whether inhibition is under strategic control. Research into directed forgetting[7,21,22] suggests a controllable inhibition process, but one limited in scope to an immediately preceding temporal interval. The present findings show a controllable inhibition process that can be flexibly targeted to a specific prepotent memory after intervening memories have been acquired. These

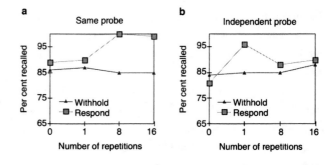

Figure 3 *Final recall of withhold and respond items as a function of the number of repetitions. **a**, Performance in the same test probe (SP) condition, **b**. Performance in the Independent probe condition (IP). In both conditions, withhold item performance does not decrease with repetition. None of the inhibition effects were significant (F< 1 in all cases). There was reliably more inhibition in experiments 1–3 than in experiment 4 (P< 0.05), and a reliably greater linear trend for inhibition (P< 0.05). Neither of these tendencies interacted with type of test cue (F< 1).*

findings do not support the popular idea that attempting to suppress an unwanted thought makes it hyperaccessible, at least as this idea applies to suppressing episodic memories[19].

The need to terminate retrieval in the think/no-think paradigm can be viewed as one instance of the need to override prepotent or habitual responses when they are inappropriate, a function presumed to require executive control[4,8–10,12,13,23,24]. Related tasks such as the go/no-go procedure are widely used to study this executive function and have been shown to recruit dorsolateral prefrontal cortex (DLPFC) and anterior cingulate cortex (ACC with ventral PFC)[15–17]. Other studies show a specific role of DLPFC in overcoming interference from competing representations in working memory[4], in selecting one item in working memory as the basis for responding[26] and in on-line manipulation of information[27]. The sustained regulation of awareness required by our procedure is likely to use such processes. This suggests that the think/no-think task recruited DLPFC and ACC, perhaps with medial temporal regions, to control awareness of the memory[28,29]. If this is true, the present memory deficits provide a behavioural marker of the action of this network on rejected memories and suggest that this network exerts control through inhibition[4,6,11,12,25].

Whatever their neural basis, our results establish a direct link between internal operations that control phenomenal awareness of a memory and its later accessibility. These findings thus support a suppression mechanism that pushes unwanted memories out of awareness, as posited by Freud. Research on retrieval-induced forgetting shows that suppression can have a lasting impact on a memory's accessibility[6]. Suppression in the current paradigm may be similarly enduring. Furthermore, if retrieving diversionary thoughts becomes habitual, inhibition may be sustained without any intention of avoiding the unwanted memory[30]. Together, these factors provide a viable model of repression, and its potential evolution from an intentional to an unintentional process. If so, repression may not be tied uniquely to psychological defence, but may rather reflect the action of a general executive control process, directed at declarative memories of past experience.

METHODS

Thirty-two neurologically normal college students participated in each experiment, except experiment 4, in which there were sixteen. Each participant was trained on 40 critical and 10 filler word pairs. The stimulus and response members of each pair had a weak pre-experimental relationship, and were unrelated to words in other pairs. The response members were chosen so that each was a member of its own category (for example, insects), to permit later testing of that item with an extralist category cue. The word pairs were exposed individually for 5 s in the centre of a computer screen with the response printed to the right of the stimulus. Test-feedback cycles followed in which subjects were presented with the stimulus member and asked to say the response aloud as quickly as possible. The correct answer was given visually if the response was omitted. Test-feedback cycles on all the pairs continued until a minimum of 50% of the pairs were correctly recalled.

After initial study, subjects were given the think/no-think phase instructions, and were then presented with the 15 stimulus members from the to-be-suppressed pairs without their responses. Subjects familiarized themselves with the stimuli so that they could identify them during suppression trials and prevent the associated memory item from coming to mind. After a brief practice session on the think/no-think task using filler items, subjects were given 377 trials in which respond and suppression stimuli were randomly intermixed. On each trial, a fixation cross appeared for 200 ms, followed by a stimulus member in the centre of the screen. For respond trials, the stimulus was presented for up to 4 s, or until the subject responded, and subjects had to report the response as quickly as possible. For suppression trials, the stimulus remained on the screen for 4 s. If a subject responded, a loud error beep sounded. Trials were separated by a 400-ms intertrial interval. Suppression and respond trials were conducted on different word pairs, with five pairs participating in each of the 0 (baseline), 1, 8 and 16-repetition conditions for both the respond and suppression conditions. Respond trials on filler pairs were also included so that 67% of the trials in the think/no-think phase required a response, encouraging a strong mental set to respond that had to be overridden, as in go/no-go tasks.

After the think/no-think phase, we tested the subjects' memory for all of the word pairs in two ways. In both tests, a cue for each word pair was presented in the centre of the screen for up to 4 s, or until subjects spoke the response. Pairs for the different respond and suppress conditions were intermixed pseudo-randomly, with the constraint that the average test position for each condition was equated. In the same-probe test, subjects' recall for each pair was cued with the stimulus member that was paired with the response throughout the experiment. In the independent probe test, subjects were cued with the category name for each exemplar along with its first letter. In each case, subjects were asked to recall the studied item that fit the cues and not to withhold any items. Half of the subjects in each experiment got the same-probe test first, and half were given the independent probe test first.

Subjects in experiment 2 were given 25 cents for each correct answer, up to a maximum of $4. Subjects in experiment 3 were given a questionnaire after the experiment in which they were asked about their impressions of our (false) hypothesis that memory would improve with attempts to suppress an item.

NOTES

1. Freud, S. in *The Standard Edition of the Complete Psychological Works of Sigmund Freud 1* (ed. J. Strachey) 117–128 (Hogarth, London, 1966).

2. Chao, L. L. & Knight, R. T. Human prefrontal lesions increase distractibility to irrelevant sensory inputs. *Cog. Neurosci. Neuropsychol.* **6**, 1605–1610 (1995).

3. Dagenbach, D. & Carr, T. H. (eds) *Inhibitory Processes in Attention, Memory, and Language* (Academic, San Diego, 1994).

4. Smith, E. E. & Jonides, J. Storage and executive processes in the frontal lobes. *Science* **283**, 1657–1661 (1999).

5. Hasher, L. & Zacks, R. T. Working memory, comprehension and aging: A review and a new view. *Psychol. Learn. Motiv.* **22**, 193–225 (1988).

6. Anderson, M. C. & Spellman, B. A. On the status of inhibitory mechanisms in cognition: Memory retrieval as a model case. *Psychol. Rev.* **102**, 68–100 (1995).

7. Bjork, R.A. in *Varieties of Memory and Consciousness: Essays in Honour of Endel Tulving* (eds Roediger, H. L. & Craik, F. I. M.) 309–330 (Lawrence Erlbaum Associates, Hillsdale, 1989).

8. Luria, A.R. *Higher Cortical Function in Man* (Basic Books, New York, 1966).

9. Logan, G. D. & Cowan, W. B. On the ability to inhibit thought and action: A theory of an act of control. *Psychol. Rev.* **91**, 295–327 (1984).

10. Posner, M. I. & Peterson, S. E. The attention system of the human brain. *Annu. Rev. Neurosci.* **13**, 25–42 (1990).

11. Knight, R. T., Staines, W. R., Swick, D. & Chao, L. L. Prefrontal cortex regulates inhibition and excitation in distributed neural networks. *Acta Psychol.* **101**, 159–178 (1999).

12. Cohen, J. D. & Servan-Schreiber, D. Context, cortex, and dopamine: A connectionist approach to behavior and biology in schizophrenia. *Psychol. Rev.* **99**, 45–77 (1992).

13. Carter, C. S., Botvinick, M. M. & Cohen, J. D. The contribution of the anterior cingulate cortex to executive processes in cognition. *Rev. Neurosci.* **10**, 49–57 (1999).

14. Mayr, U. & Keele, S. W. Changing internal constraints on action: The role of backward inhibition. *J. Exp. Psychol. Gen.* **129**, 4–26 (2000).

15. Casey, B. J. *et al.* A developmental functional MRI study of prefrontal activation during performance of a go-no-go task. *J. Cogn. Neurosci.* **9**, 835–847 (1997).

16. Garavan, H., Ross, T. J. & Stein, E. A. Right hemispheric dominance of inhibitory control: An event-related functional MRI study. *Proc. Natl Acad. Sci. USA* **96**, 8301–8306 (1999).

17. de Zubicaray, G. I. *et al.* Motor response suppression and the prepotent tendency to respond: A parametric fMRI study. *Neuropsychologia* **38**, 1280–1291 (2000).

18. Sakagami, M. & Niki, H. Spatial selectivity of go/no-go neurons in the monkey prefrontal cortex. *Exp. Brain Res.* **100**, 165–169 (1994).

19. Wegner, D. M. Ironic processes of mental control. *Psychol. Rev.* **101**, 34–52 (1994).

20. Freyd, J. J. *Betrayal Trauma: The Logic of Forgetting Childhood Abuse* (Harvard Univ. Press, Cambridge, MA, 1996).

21. Geiselman, R. E., Bjork, R. A. & Fishman, E. L. Disrupted retrieval in directed forgetting: A link with posthypnotic amnesia. *J. Exp. Psychol. Gen.* **112**, 58–72 (1983).

22. Conway, M. A, Harries, K., Noyes, J., Racsmany, M. & Frankish, C. R. The disruption and dissolution of directed forgetting: Inhibitory control of memory. *J. Mem. Lang.* **43**, 409–430 (2000).

23. Norman, D. A. & Shallice, T. in *Consciousness and Self-Regulation: Advances in Research and Theory* (eds Davison, R. J., Schwardz, G. E. & Shapiro, D.) 1–18 (Plenum, New York, 1986).

24. MacDonald, A. W., Cohen, J. D., Andrew-Stenger, V. & Carter, C. S. Dissociating the role of the dorsolateral prefrontal and anterior cingulate cortex in cognitive control. *Science* **288**, 1835–1838 (2000).

25. Shimamura, A. P. The role of the prefrontal cortex in dynamic filtering. *Psychobiology* **28**, 207–218 (2000).

26. Rowe, J. B. *et al.* The prefrontal cortex: Response selection or maintenance within working memory. *Science* **288**, 1656–1660 (2000).

27. D'Esposito, M. *et al.* Functional MRI studies of spatial and nonspatial working memory. *Cogn. Brain Res.* **7**, 1–13 (1998).

28. Schacter, D. L. & Wagner, A. D. Medial temporal lobe activations in fMRI and PET studies of episodic encoding and retrieval. *Hippocampus* **9**, 7–24 (1999).

29. Schacter, D. L. Memory and awareness. *Science* **280**, 59–60 (1998).

30. Anderson, M. C. Active Forgetting: Evidence for functional inhibition as a source of memory failure. *J. Aggression Maltreatment Trauma* (in the press).

ACKNOWLEDGMENTS

The research reported here was supported by a grant from the US National Institute of Mental Health.

Correspondence and requests for materials should be addressed to M.C.A. (e-mail: mcanders@darkwing.uoregon.edu).

CHAPTER 6
Long-Term Memory

Long-Term Memory

MARGARET W. MATLIN

PREVIEW

Chapter 5 focuses on long-term memory, in other words, the memories that you've gathered throughout your lifetime. This chapter first examines factors that are relevant when you acquire new information. For example, the research on depth of processing shows that memory is typically more accurate if you process information in terms of its meaning, rather than more superficial characteristics. If you have ever returned to a once-familiar location and experienced a flood of long-lost memories, you know the importance of another factor, called encoding specificity. In addition, emotional factors influence your memory in several ways. For example, if you have been watching a violent show on television, your memory will be relatively poor for the advertisements appearing during that show. We'll also discuss how personality characteristics can influence the way you recall the components of a story.

The next section of the chapter, on the retrieval of memories, demonstrates that memory accuracy can also be influenced by the way memory retrieval is measured. For instance, individuals with amnesia earn low scores on traditional recall tests, but they perform quite well on some nontraditional memory tests. This section also looks at the memory abilities of individuals with expertise in a particular subject area.

Autobiographical memory, the topic of the last section in this chapter, refers to your memory for the everyday events in your life. Your memory is influenced by your general knowledge about objects and events; this general knowledge is usually helpful, but it may create memory errors. This section also examines source monitoring, a process you use when you try to determine whether you really performed an action or merely imagined it. This discussion points out that so-called flashbulb memories are typically not very accurate. Finally, the chapter looks at eyewitness testimony, which shows that misleading information can sometimes alter your memory.

INTRODUCTION

Take a minute to think about the contents of your own long-term memory. For example, can you remember some of the details about the first day that you attended the class for which you are using this textbook? Now try to recall the names of your high school science teachers. Can you remember some of the characteristics of your closest friends during fifth grade? Memory is one of our most important cognitive activities. Consistent with Theme 4 of this book, it is closely connected with numerous other cognitive processes (Einstein & McDaniel, 2004).

Chapter 4 emphasized the fragility of working memory. As that chapter illustrated, information that we want to retain can disappear from memory after less than a minute. In contrast, Chapter 5 demonstrates that your long-term memory can retain material for many decades.

Before we examine long-term memory, let's review some familiar terminology and introduce some important new distinctions. As we noted in earlier chapters, psychologists often divide memory into two basic categories called working memory (the brief, immediate memory for material we are currently processing) and long-term memory. Long-term memory has a large capacity; it contains our memory for experiences and information that we have accumulated over a lifetime.

Like many psychologists, I'm not firmly convinced that working memory and long-term memory are two distinctly different kinds of memory. However, I do believe that the division is a convenient way to partition the enormous amount of research about our memory processes.

Psychologists often subdivide long-term memory into more specific categories. Once again, this subdivision reflects convenience, rather than a conviction that the subdivisions represent distinctly different kinds of memory. One popular system subdivides long-term memory into episodic memory, semantic memory, and procedural memory (Herrmann, Yoder, Gruneberg, & Payne, 2006; Hoerl, 2001; Tulving, 2002).

Episodic memory focuses on your memories for events that happened to you; it allows you to travel backward in subjective time to reminisce about earlier episodes in your life. Episodic memory includes your memory for an event that occurred ten years ago, as well as a conversation you had 10 minutes ago. Episodic memory is the major focus of this chapter.

In contrast, semantic memory describes your organized knowledge about the world, including your knowledge about words and other factual information. For example, you know that the word semantic is related to the word meaning, and you know that Ottawa is the capital of Canada. Chapter 8 of this textbook focuses on semantic memory and our general knowledge about the world.

Finally, procedural memory refers to your knowledge about how to do something. For instance, you know how to ride a bicycle, and you know how to send an e-mail message to a friend. We will mention some aspects of procedural memory in this chapter, in connection with implicit memory (pp. 136–140), and also in Chapter 6, in connection with prospective memory (pp. 177–180).

In the current chapter, we'll look at three aspects of long-term memory. We'll begin with encoding, which

refers to your initial acquisition of information; during encoding, information is embedded in your memory (Einstein & McDaniel, 2004). Then we'll explore retrieval, which refers to locating information in storage and accessing that information. Our final section examines autobiographical memory. Autobiographical memory1 refers to memory for events and topics related to your own everyday life. Incidentally, we'll continue to examine long-term memory in Chapter 6, which emphasizes memory-improvement strategies.

ENCODING IN LONG-TERM MEMORY

In this section, we'll look at four important questions about encoding in long-term memory:

1. Are we more likely to remember items that we processed in a deep, meaningful fashion, rather than items processed in a shallow, superficial fashion?
2. Are we more likely to remember items if the context at the time of encoding matches the context at the time of retrieval?
3. How do emotional factors influence memory accuracy?
4. How do people's goals about social relationships influence memory accuracy?

Before you read further, though, be sure to try Demonstration 5.1 on this page.

Levels of Processing

In 1972, Fergus Craik and Robert Lockhart wrote an article about the depth-of-processing approach. This article became one of the most influential publications in

---

1 Many psychologists consider episodic memory and autobiographical memory to be highly similar. However, others argue that the research on episodic memory emphasizes accuracy, whereas the research on autobiographical memory emphasizes the qualitative "match" between the event and the memory for the event (Koriat et al., 2000). Some psychologists also argue that autobiographical memory may include some semantic information. For example, you know the date on which you were born, even if you have no recall for that life event (Roediger & Marsh, 2003).

DEMONSTRATION 5.1
Levels of Processing

Read each of the following questions and answer "yes" or "no" with respect to the word that follows.

1. Is the word in capital letters?   BOOK
2. Would the word fit this sentence:
   "I saw a in a pond"?   duck
3. Does the word rhyme with BLUE?   safe
4. Would the word fit this sentence:
   "The girl walked down the _____"?   house
5. Does the word rhyme with FREIGHT?   WEIGHT
6. Is the word in small letters?   snow
7. Would the word fit this sentence:
   "The_____was reading a book"?   STUDENT
8. Does the word rhyme with TYPE?   color
9. Is the word in capital letters?   flower
10. Would the word fit this sentence:
    "Last spring we saw a _____"?   robin
11. Does the word rhyme with BALL?   HALL
12. Is the word in small letters?   TREE
13. Would the word fit this sentence:
    "My _____is 6 feet tall"?   TEXTBOOK
14. Does the word rhyme with SAY?   Day
15. Is the word in capital letters?   FOX

Now, without looking back over the words, try to remember as many of them as you can. Calculate the percentage of items you recalled correctly for each of the three kinds of tasks: physical appearance, rhyming, and meaning.

---

the history of research on memory (Roediger, Gallo, & Geraci, 2002). The **levels of processing approach** argues that deep, meaningful kinds of information processing lead to more permanent retention than shallow, sensory kinds of processing. (This theory is also called the **depth-of-processing approach**.)

The levels-of-processing approach predicts that your recall will be relatively accurate when you use a deep level of processing. In Demonstration 5.1, for instance, you used deep processing when you considered a word's meaning (e.g., whether it would fit in a sentence). The levels-of-processing approach predicts that your recall will be relatively poor when you use a shallow level of processing. For example, you will be less likely to recall a word when you considered its physical appearance (e.g., whether it is typed in capital letters) or its sound (e.g., whether it rhymes with another word).

In general, then, people achieve a deeper level of processing when they extract more meaning from a stimulus. When you analyze for meaning, you may think of other associations, images, and past experiences related to the stimulus. You are especially likely to remember a stimulus that you analyzed at a very deep level (Roediger, Gallo, & Geraci, 2002). As we'll see in Chapter 6, most memory-improvement strategies emphasize deep, meaningful processing.

Let's examine some of the research on the levels-of-processing approach. We'll first consider general material, and then we'll consider an especially deep level of processing called *self-reference*.

Levels of Processing and Memory for General Material. The major hypothesis emerging from Craik and Lockhart's (1972) paper was that deeper levels of processing should produce better recall. For example, in an experiment similar to Demonstration 5.1, Craik and Tulving (1975) found that people were about three times as likely to recall a word if they had originally answered questions about its meaning rather than if they had originally answered questions about the word's physical appearance. Numerous reviews of the research conclude that deep processing of verbal material generally produces better recall than shallow processing (Craik, 1999, 2006; Lockhart, 2001; Roediger & Gallo, 2001).

Deep levels of processing encourage recall because of two factors: distinctiveness and elaboration. **Distinctiveness** means that a stimulus is different from other memory-traces. Suppose that you are interviewing for a job. You've just learned that one man is especially important in deciding whether you will be hired, and you want to be sure to remember his name. You'll need to use deep processing and spend extra time processing his name. You'll try to figure out something unusual about his name that makes it different from other names you've heard in this interview context (Hunt, 2006). Furthermore, when you provide a distinctive encoding for a person's name, it will be less vulnerable to interference from other names (Craik, 2006; Schacter & Wiseman, 2006; Tulving & Rosenbaum, 2006).

The second factor that operates with deep levels of processing is **elaboration**, which requires rich processing in terms of meaning and interconnected concepts (Craik, 1999, 2006; Smith, 2006). For example, if you want to understand the term *levels of processing*, you'll need to appreciate how this concept is related to both distinctiveness and elaboration. Think about the way you processed the word *duck* in Demonstration 5.1, for example. Perhaps you thought about the fact that you had indeed seen ducks on ponds and that a restaurant menu had listed duck with an orange sauce. This kind of semantic encoding encouraged rich processing. In contrast, if the instructions for that item had asked whether the word *duck* was printed in capital letters, you would simply have answered "yes" or "no." You would not need to spend time on extensive elaboration.

Let's consider research on the importance of elaboration. Craik and Tulving (1975) asked participants to read sentences and decide whether the words that followed were appropriate to the sentences. Some of the sentence frames were simple, such as "She cooked the_____." Other sentence frames were elaborate, such as "The great bird swooped down and carried off the struggling_____." The word that followed these sentences was either appropriate (for example, *rabbit*) or inappropriate (for example, *rock*). You'll notice that both kinds of sentences required deep or semantic processing. However, the more elaborate, more detailed sentence frame produced far more accurate recall.

Other research demonstrates that deep processing also enhances our memory for faces. For instance, people recognize more photos of faces if they had previously judged whether the person looked honest, rather than judging a more superficial characteristic, such as the width of the person's nose (Bloom & Mudd, 1991; Sporer, 1991). People also recall faces better if drey have been instructed to pay attention to the distinctions between faces (Mäntylä, 1997).

Levels of Processing and the Self-Reference Effect. According to the **self-reference effect**, you will remember more information if you try to relate that information to yourself (Burns, 2006; Gillihan & Farah, 2005; Rogers et al., 1977; Schmidt, 2006). Self-reference tasks tend to encourage especially deep processing. Let's look at some representative research on the self-reference effect and then consider a problem with participants who do not follow instructions. Then we'll discuss several factors that help to explain the self-reference effect.

1. *Representative research.* In the classic demonstration of the self-reference effect, T. B. Rogers and his coauthors (1977) asked participants to process lists of words according to three kinds of instructions usually studied in levels-of-processing research. These three instructions included: (1) the words' visual characteristics, (2) their acoustic (sound) characteristics, or (3) their semantic (meaning) characteristics. Another group processed the words in terms of self-reference: (4) the participants were told to decide whether a particular word could be applied to themselves.

The results showed that recall was poor for the two tasks that used shallow processing—that is, processing in terms of visual characteristics or acoustic characteristics. The recall was much better when people had processed in terms of semantic characteristics. However, the self-reference task produced much better recall than all other tasks.

Apparently, when we think about a word in connection with ourselves, we develop a particularly memorable coding for that word. For example, suppose that you are trying to decide whether the word *generous* applies to yourself. You might remember how you loaned your notes to a friend who had missed class, and you shared a box of candy with your friends—yes, *generous* does apply. The self-reference task requires organization and elaboration. These mental processes increase the probability of recalling an item.

The research on the self-reference effect also demonstrates one of the themes of this book. As Theme 3 proposes, our cognitive system handles positive instances more effectively than negative instances. In the self-reference studies, people are more likely to recall a word that *does* apply to themselves rather than a word that *does not* apply (Bellezza, 1992; Ganellen & Carver, 1985; Roediger & Gallo, 2001). For example, the participants in Bellezza's (1992) study recalled 46% of the adjectives that applied to themselves, compared with 34% of the adjectives that did not apply.

Research shows that the self-reference effect improves recall for participants from different age groups, using a variety of instructions and stimuli (e.g., Thompson et al., 1996). Furthermore, Symons and Johnson (1997) gathered the results of 129 different studies that had been conducted on the self-reference effect, and they performed a meta-analysis. The **meta-analysis technique** is a statistical method for synthesizing numerous studies on a single topic. A meta-analysis computes a statistical index that tells us whether a variable has a statistically significant effect. Symons and Johnson's meta-analysis confirmed the pattern we have described: People recall significantly more items when they use the self-reference technique, rather than semantic processing or any other processing method.

2. *Participants' failure to follow instructions.* The self-reference effect is definitely robust. However, Mary Ann Foley and her coauthors (1999) have demonstrated that the research may actually *underestimate* the power of self-reference. Specifically, these investigators speculated that research participants might sometimes "cheat" when they have been instructed to use relatively shallow processing for stimuli. In fact, the participants might actually use the self-reference technique instead.

In one of their studies, Foley and her coauthors (1999) instructed students to listen to a list of familiar, concrete nouns. However, before hearing each word, they were told about the kind of mental image they should form. Let's consider two of the conditions, in which the students were instructed (1) to "visualize the object," or (2) to "imagine yourself using the object."

For the first analysis of the data, Foley and her colleagues classified the results according to the instructions supplied by the experimenter, prior to each word. Notice that this first analysis produced identical recall for the two conditions.

That is, students recalled 42% of the words, whether they had been instructed to use relatively shallow processing or deep, self-reference processing.

Fortunately, however, Foley and her colleagues had also asked the students to describe their visual image for each word during the learning task. As the researchers had suspected, people in the "visualize the object" condition often inserted themselves into the mental image, so that they had actually used self-reference processing. In a second analysis, the researchers sorted the words according to the processing methods that the students had actually used, rather than the instructions they had received. As you can see, the second analysis revealed that the recall was more than three times as high for the self-reference condition as for the visualized-object condition.

The research by Foley and her colleagues (1999) has important implications beyond this particular study. The research shows that our cognitive processes are active (Theme 1). People do not just passively follow instructions and do what they are told. Researchers need to keep in mind that participants are likely to transform the instructions, and this transformation can influence the results of the study.

3. *Factors responsible for the self-reference effect.* Let's now turn our attention to another issue: Why should we recall information especially well when we apply it to ourselves? As Tulving and Rosenbaum (2006) emphasize, a cognitive phenomenon typically requires more than just one explanation. Let's consider three factors that contribute to the self-reference effect.

One factor is that the self produces an especially rich set of cues. You can easily link these cues with new information that you are trying to learn. These cues are also distinctive; they seem very different from one another. For example, your trait of honesty seems different from your trait of intelligence (Bellezza, 1984; Bellezza & Hoyt, 1992).

A second factor is that self-reference instructions encourage people to consider how their personal traits are related to one another. As a result, retrieval will be easier and more effective (Burns, 2006; Klein & Kihlstrom, 1986; Thompson et al., 1996).

A third factor is that you rehearse material more frequently if it is associated with yourself. You're also more likely to use rich, complex rehearsal when you associate material with yourself (Thompson et al., 1996). These rehearsal strategies facilitate later recall.

In short, several major factors work together to help you recall material related to yourself. Several years ago, some research also suggested neurological correlates for the self-reference effect (e.g., Craik et al., 1999; Kircher et al., 2000; Macrae et al., 2004).

Unfortunately, however, a careful analysis of the research uncovered inconsistencies in the findings (Gillihan & Farah, 2005). Specifically, when people think about themselves, the instructions do not automatically activate one specific region of the brain. The self-reference effect is well established. Unfortunately, the biological explanation for this effect remains elusive.

The Effects of Context: Encoding Specificity

Does this scenario sound familiar? You are in the bedroom and realize that you need something from the kitchen. Once you arrive in the kitchen, however, you have no idea why you made the trip. Without the context in which you encoded the item you wanted, you cannot retrieve this memory. You return to the bedroom, which is rich with contextual cues, and you immediately remember what you wanted. Similarly, an isolated question on an exam may look completely unfamiliar, although you could probably remember the answer in the appropriate context.

These examples illustrate the **encoding specificity principle**, which states that recall is better if the retrieval context is similar to the encoding context (Brown & Craik, 2000; Nairne, 2005; Tulving & Rosenbaum, 2006). In contrast, forgetting often occurs when the two contexts do not match. Three other, similar terms for the encoding specificity principle are context-dependent memory, transfer-appropriate processing, and reinstatement of

context (Craik, 2006; Roediger & Guynn, 1996). Let's now consider this topic of encoding specificity in more detail. We'll begin with some representative research, and then we'll see how the research forces us to modify our earlier conclusions about levels of processing.

Research on Encoding Specificity. In a representative study, Viorica Marian and Caitlin Fausey (2006) tested people living in Chile who were fluent in both English and Spanish. The participants listened to four stories about topics such as chemistry and history. They heard two stories in English and two in Spanish.

After a short delay, the participants listened to questions about each story. Half of the questions were asked in the language that matched the language of the original story (e.g., Spanish-Spanish), and half had a mismatch between the language of the story and the language of the questions (e.g., Spanish-English). The participants were instructed to answer in the same language that was used for the questions.

For example, people were relatively accurate if they had heard the story in Spanish, and they also answered the questions in Spanish. They were less accurate if they heard the story in Spanish and answered the questions in English. (Incidentally, we will examine bilingualism in more detail in Chapter 10.)

In an earlier, conceptually similar study, participants were relatively accurate when the gender of the voice during encoding matched the gender of the voice during retrieval (Geiselman & Glenny, 1977). They were less accurate when the gender of the voices did not match.

Everyone reading this book can readily recall real-life examples of the encoding specificity principle. Psychologists have also explained why context effects help us to function competently in our daily lives. Basically, we often forget material associated with contexts other than our present context. After all, we don't need to remember numerous details that might have been important in a previous setting but are no longer relevant at the present time (Bjork & Bjork, 1988). For instance, you don't want your memory to be cluttered with details about the math textbook you used in fifth grade or the senior trip you took in high school.

Context effects are easy to demonstrate in real life. However, context effects are often inconsistent in the laboratory (e.g., Baddeley, 2004; Nairne, 2005; Roediger & Guynn, 1996). For example, why should context effects be important in one experiment (e.g., Smith et al., 1978), and yet have absolutely no influence in a highly similar replication experiment (e.g., Bjork & Richardson-Klavehn, 1987)? Let's consider two potential explanations.

1. *Different kinds of memory tasks.* One explanation for the discrepancy between real life and the laboratory is that the two situations typically test different kinds of memory (Roediger & Guynn, 1996). To explore this point, we need to introduce two important terms: *recall* and *recognition*. When memory researchers test recall, the participants must reproduce the items they learned earlier. (For example, can you recall the definition for *elaboration*?) In contrast, when memory researchers test recognition, the participants must identify whether they saw a particular item at an earlier time. (For example, did the word *morphology* appear earlier in this chapter?)

Let's return to encoding specificity. Our real-life examples often describe a situation in which we *recall* an earlier experience, and that experience occurred many years earlier (Roediger & Guynn, 1996). Encoding specificity is typically strong in these real-life, long-delay situations. For example, when I smell a particular flower called verbena, I am instantly transported back to a childhood scene in my grandmother's garden. I specifically recall walking through the garden with my cousins, an experience that happened decades ago. In contrast, the laboratory research focuses on *recognition*, rather than *recall*: "Did this word appear on the list you saw earlier?" Furthermore, that list was typically presented less than an hour earlier. Encoding specificity is typically weak in these laboratory, short-delay situations.

In summary, then, the encoding-specificity effect is most likely to occur in memory tasks that (a) assess your recall, (b) use real-life incidents, and (c) examine events that happened long ago.

2. *Physical versus mental context.* In their studies on encoding specificity, researchers often manipulate the physical context in which material is encoded and retrieved. However, physical context may not be as important as *mental* context. It is possible that physical details—such as the characteristics of the room—are relatively trivial in determining whether the encoding context matches the retrieval context. Instead, as Eich (1995) points out, "How well information transfers from one environment to another depends on how similar the environments feel, rather than on how similar they look" (p. 293).

Eich's comment should remind you of the study by Foley and her colleagues (1999), in which participants' mental activities often did not match the researchers' specific instructions. Researchers need to look beyond the variables that they believe they are manipulating and pay attention to the processes going on inside the participants' heads. This importance of mental activities is also crucial to the next topic, which brings us back to the level-of-processing issue.

Levels of Processing and Encoding Specificity. Craik and Lockhans (1972) original description of the levels-of-processing approach emphasized *encoding*, or how items are placed into memory. It did not mention details about *retrieval*, or how items are recovered from memory. However, people recall more material if the retrieval conditions match the encoding conditions (Moscovitch & Craik, 1976). Thus, encoding specificity can override level of processing. In fact, shallow processing can be more effective than deep processing when the retrieval task emphasizes superficial information. Notice that this point is *not* consistent with the original formulation of the levels-of-processing approach.

Let's consider a study that demonstrates the importance of the similarity between encoding and retrieval conditions (Bransford et al., 1979). Suppose that you performed the various encoding tasks in Demonstration 5.1. Imagine, however, that you were then tested in terms of rhyming patterns, rather than in terms of recalling the words on that list. For example, you might be asked, "Was there a word on the list that rhymed with *toy*?" People usually perform better on this rhyming test if they had originally performed the shallow-encoding task (rhyming), rather than the deep-encoding task (meaning). This area of research demonstrates that deep, semantic processing is effective only if the retrieval conditions also emphasize these deeper, more meaningful features (Roediger & Guynn, 1996).

Theme 4 of this textbook points out that our cognitive processes are often interrelated. The research on encoding specificity emphasizes that memory often requires problem solving: To determine how to store some information, you'll need to figure out the characteristics of the retrieval task (Phillips, 1995). For example, how would you study the material in this chapter if you knew you would be tested on your *recall* (e.g., by answering essay questions like those at the end of each chapter)? Would your study techniques be different if you were tested on your *recognition* (e.g., by having to answer multiple-choice questions)?

In summary, then, memory is sometimes—but not always—enhanced when the retrieval context resembles the encoding context (Nairne, 2005). However, the benefits of encoding specificity are more likely when items are tested by recall (rather than recognition), when the stimuli are real-life events, and when the items have been in memory for a long time. In addition, encoding specificity depends on mental context more than physical context. Furthermore, we've seen that encoding specificity can modify the level-of-processing effect; in some cases, the match between encoding and retrieval is even more important than deep processing. As you'll see next, context is also relevant when we examine how emotions and mood can influence memory.

Emotions, Mood, and Memory

During the last decade, the amount of psychological research on emotions, mood, and memory has increased dramatically (Uttl, Siegenthaler, & Ohta, 2006). In everyday speech, we often use the terms emotion and mood interchangeably, and the terms are somewhat similar. However, psychologists define emotion as a reaction to a specific stimulus. In contrast, mood refers to a more general, long-lasting experience (Bower & Forgas, 2000). For example, you may have a negative emotional reaction to the unpleasant fragrance you just smelled in a locker room, whereas you may be in a relatively positive mood today. Before you read further, try Demonstration 5.2.

Cognitive psychologists acknowledge that emotion and mood can influence our cognitive processes. Let's consider two ways in which emotion and mood can affect our memory:

1. We typically remember pleasant stimuli more accurately than other stimuli;
2. We typically recall material more accurately if our mood matches the emotional nature of the material, an effect called *mood congruence*.

Memory for Items Differing in Emotion. In 1978, my co-author and I proposed that the people's enhanced recall of pleasant items is part of a more *general Pollyanna Principle*

(Matlin & Stang, 1978). **The Pollyanna Principle** states that pleasant items are usually processed more efficiently and more accurately than less pleasant items. The principle holds true for a wide variety of phenomena in perception, language, and decision making (Matlin, 2004). However, our focus in this chapter is on long-term memory. Let's consider several ways in which the emotional nature of the stimuli can influence memory.

1. *More accurate recall for pleasant items.* For nearly a century, psychologists have been interested in the way that emotional tone can influence memory (e.g., Balch, 2006b; Hollingworth, 1910; Thompson et al., 1996). In a typical study, people learn lists of words that are pleasant, neutral, or unpleasant. Then their recall is tested after a delay of several minutes to several months. In a review of the literature, we found that pleasant items are often recalled better than negative items, particularly if the delay is long (Matlin, 2004; Matlin & Stang, 1978). For example, in 39 of the 52 studies that we located on long-term memory, pleasant items were recalled significantly more accurately than unpleasant items. Incidentally, neutral items are usually recalled least accurately of all, suggesting that the intensity of an item's emotional tone is also important (Bohanek et al., 2005; Talarico et al., 2004).

Demonstration 5.2 is a simplified version of a study conducted by William Balch (2006b). Check back and count how many pleasant words you recalled from this list: 1, 3, 4, 7, 8, 10, 12, 14, 15, 18, 21, 23. Then count how many words you recalled from this list of unpleasant words: 2, 5, 6, 9, 11, 13, 16, 17, 19, 20, 22, 23. Was your recall more accurate for the pleasant words than for the unpleasant words? When Balch tested introductory psychology students, he found that they recalled significantly more of the positive words.

Furthermore, people generally recall pleasant events more accurately than unpleasant events (Mather, 2006; Walker et al., 1997). One potential explanation is that people's memory for pleasant events is more vivid and clear than for unpleasant events (D'Argembeau et al, 2003; Levine & Bluck, 2004). A related finding is that drivers quickly forget their near-accidents; in fact, they remember only 20% of these accidents just two weeks later (Chapman & Underwood, 2000).

2. *More accurate recall for neutral stimuli associated with pleasant stimuli.* Media violence is an important issue in

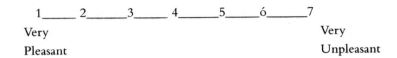

DEMONSTRATION 5.2

Remembering English Words

1_____	2_____	3_____	4_____	5____	6_____	7

Very
Pleasant

Very
Unpleasant

On a sheet of paper, write each of the words. Then rate each word, using the above scale.

1. Hope	9. Loss	17. Insult
2. Fool	10. Trust	18. Praise
3. Style	11. Theft	19. Panic
4. Interest	12. Liberty	20. Grudge
5. Quarrel	13. Decay	21. Travel
6. Hunger	14. Comfort	22. Fraud
7. Cure	15. Benefit	23. Wisdom
8. Beauty	16. Trouble	24. Rumble

Now cover up this list for the remainder of the demonstration. Take a break for a few minutes. Then write down as many words as you can recall. Count how many of the following words you remembered correctly: Hope, Style, Interest, Cure, Beauty, Trust, Liberty, Comfort, Benefit, Praise, Travel, Wisdom.

Then count how many of the following words you remembered correctly: Fool, Quarrel, Hunger, Loss, Theft, Decay, Trouble, Insult, Panic, Grudge, Fraud, Rumble.

Did you recall more from the first category or the second category?

Source: Balch, 2006b.

North American culture. Surveys suggest that about 60% of television programs depict violence. Furthermore, numerous studies have concluded that media violence has an impact on children's aggression (Bushman, 2003; Bushman & Huesmann, 2001; Kirsh, 2006).

However, we'll consider a different component of media violence: Do people remember commercials less accurately when they are associated with violent material? To answer this question, Bushman (1998) recorded 15-minute segments of two videos. One video, *Karate Kid III*, showed violent fighting and destruction of property. The other video, *Gorillas in the Mist*, was judged equally exciting by undergraduate students, but it contained no violence. Bushman then inserted two 30-second advertisements for neutral items into each of the two video clips.

College students watched either the violent or the nonviolent film clip. Then they were asked to recall the two brand names that had been featured in the commercials and to list everything they could recall about the commercials. The results showed significantly better recall—on both measures—for commercials that had appeared in the nonviolent film. Additional research demonstrates that anger and violence typically reduce memory accuracy (Bushman, 1998, 2003, 2005; Gunter et al., 2005; Levine & Burgess, 1997).

Individuals who are concerned about societal violence should be interested in Bushman's research, because they can use this research in persuading advertisers to place their ads during nonviolent programs. Advertisers obviously want viewers to remember their product's name, as well as information about the product. In light of this research, advertisers should be hesitant to sponsor violent programs.

3. *Over time, unpleasant memories fade faster.* Richard Walker and his coauthors (1997) asked undergraduate students to record one personal event each day for about fourteen weeks and to rate both the pleasantness and the intensity of the event. Three months later, the participants returned, one at a time, for a second session. A researcher read off each event from the previous list, and the student was instructed to rate the current pleasantness of that event. In the analysis of the results, the rating did not change for those events that were originally considered to be neutral. However, the events originally considered to be pleasant were now considered to be slightly less pleasant. In contrast, the events originally considered to be unpleasant were now considered to be much more pleasant. Consistent with the Pollyanna Principle, people tend to rate past events more positively with the passage of time, a phenomenon called the **positivity effect**.

Additional research shows that elderly people are especially likely to show this positivity effect (Kennedy et al., 2004; Mather, 2006). Furthermore, Walker and his colleagues (2003) studied two groups of students; one group consisted of students who did not have tendencies toward depression, and one group had depressive tendencies. Those who did not have depressive tendencies showed the usual positivity effect. In contrast, the students with depressive tendencies showed equal fading for unpleasant and pleasant events. In other words, when people at risk for depression look back on their lives, the unpleasant events still remain unpleasant! As you can imagine, this research has important implications for clinical psychologists. Therapists must address a depressed client's interpretation of past events, as well as the current situation.

So far, we have considered how the pleasantness of the stimuli influences memory. As we've seen, pleasant stimuli usually fare better than less pleasant ones: (1) We often remember them more accurately; (2) we tend to forget information when it is associated with violent, unpleasant stimuli; and (3) over time, pleasant memories fade less than unpleasant memories. Let's now see how memory is influenced by the match between your mood and the emotional tone of the stimuli.

Mood Congruence. A second major category of studies about mood and memory is called mood congruence. *Mood congruence* means that you recall material more accurately if it is congruent with your current mood (Fiedler et al., 2003; Joorman &

Siemer, 2004; Schwarz, 2001). For example, a person who is in a pleasant mood should remember pleasant material better than unpleasant material, whereas a person in an unpleasant mood should remember unpleasant material better.[2]

Consider a study by Laura Murray and her colleagues (1999). Like Walker and his colleagues (2003), these researchers tested one group of students who did not have tendencies toward depression, and one group with depressive tendencies. The participants were instructed to look at a series of 20 positive- and 20 negative-trait words. Later, the participants recalled as many words as possible from the original list.

Murray and her colleagues found results that were consistent with earlier research, as well as the research on depression and working memory we considered in Chapter 4. Specifically, the nondepressed individuals recalled a greater overall percentage of the words than did the depression-prone individuals. In addition, the nondepressed students recalled a significantly greater percentage of positive words than negative words. In contrast, the depression-prone students recalled a slightly greater percentage of negative words than positive words.

In these studies about mood congruence, nondepressed people typically recall more positive than negative material. In contrast, depression-prone people tend to recall more negative material (Fiedler et al., 2003; Mather, 2006; Parrott & Spackman, 2000; Schwarz, 2001). Like the results of the research by Walker and his colleagues (2003), these findings are important for clinical psychologists. If depressed people tend to forget the positive experiences they have had, their depression could increase still further (Schacter, 1999).

Individual Differences: Social Goals and Memory

So far, the Individual Differences features in this book have focused on psychological disorders. In Chapter 2, you saw that people with schizophrenia have difficulty perceiving

---

2 A similar-sounding phenomenon is called mood-dependent memory in which you may remember more material if your mood at the time of retrieval matches your mood at the time of encoding. Mood-dependent memory is one example of the encoding specificity principle, and the research shows that this effect is often weak or nonexistent (Forgas, 2001; Ryan & Eich, 2000).

human faces. Chapter 3 showed that individuals with obsessive-compulsive disorder have more trouble than other people when they try to push a specific thought out of their consciousness. Chapter 4 pointed out that people with major depression typically have deficits in several components of working memory.

In this chapter—and many others in this textbook—our Individual Differences feature will not focus on a psychological problem that might interest clinical psychologists. In this chapter, for example, we will explore a personality characteristic that varies in the general population. In connection with long-term memory, let's consider a dimension called social goals (Strachman & Gable, 2006). **Social goals** refers to your style of interacting with other people, in terms of friendships and other interpersonal relationships.

If you have a high score in **approach social goals**, you tend to emphasize close relationships with other people. On a standardized questionnaire assessing social goals, you would supply a high rating to questions such as "I will be trying to deepen my relationships with my friends this quarter" and "I will be trying to enhance the bonding and intimacy in my close relationships" (Strachman & Gable, 2006, p. 1449). If you have a high score in **avoidance social goals**—as the name suggests—you tend to avoid close relationships with other people. On a questionnaire, you would supply a high rating to questions such as "I will be trying to avoid getting embarrassed, betrayed, or hurt by my friends" and "I will be trying to make sure that nothing bad happens to my close relationships" (p. 1449).

Amy Strachman and Shelly Gable (2006) asked college students to read a story that focused on interpersonal relationships. This story included a variety of statements from all three emotional categories, positive, neutral, and negative. After completing the story, the students were instructed to recall the essay as accurately as possible.

The results of this study showed that social goals were not related to the actual number of items that students recalled correctly. However, the students who were high in approach social goals tended to recall the neutral statements as being more positive than they actually were in the story. In contrast, students who were high in avoidance social goals tended to recall the neutral and positive statements as being more negative than they actually were in the story. This group also remembered more of the negative statements and fewer of the positive statements, compared to those who were high in approach social goals. The research also showed that the differences in recall could not be explained by the participants' mood—the topic we discussed.

In summary, people's personal characteristics help to explain their memory patterns. Specifically, their social goals influence which items they will remember. These social goals also influence whether they remember items as being more positive or more negative than they actually were.

SECTION SUMMARY: ENCODING IN LONG-TERM MEMORY

1. Long-term memory can be subdivided into three categories: episodic memory, semantic memory, and procedural memory; episodic memory is most relevant for the current chapter.

2. The research on levels of processing shows that stimuli are remembered better with deep, meaningful processing, rather than with shallow, sensory processing.

3. Deep processing encourages recall because of distinctiveness and elaboration.

4. Research on the self-reference effect demonstrates that memory is greatly improved by relating stimuli to your own personal experience; to obtain a valid assessment of the self-reference effect, the stimuli must be classified in terms of the participant's actual mental activities, rather than in terms of the experimenter's instructions.

5. The self-reference effect works because the self is a rich source of memory ideas, and because self-reference instructions encourage people to think about how their own characteristics are interrelated. Furthermore, self-reference increases elaborative rehearsal.

6. The encoding-specificity effect is most likely to operate when memory is tested by recall, when real-life events are studied, when the original event happened long ago, and when mental context is emphasized. In addition, encoding specificity can modify the depth-of-processing effect.

7. Research on the influence of emotions and mood on memory shows that (a) people generally recall pleasant stimuli more accurately than unpleasant stimuli; (b) people recall less information if they see the material during a violent television program; (c) unpleasant memories grow more neutral over time, compared to pleasant memories.

8. Memory is more accurate when the material to be learned is congruent with a person's current mood (mood congruence).

9. Students with high scores in "approach social goals" tend to recall stories with neutral statements as being relatively positive. In contrast, students with high scores on "avoidance social goals" tend to recall neutral and positive statements as being relatively negative.

RETRIEVAL IN LONG-TERM MEMORY

So far in this chapter, we have emphasized encoding processes. We examined how your long-term memory could be influenced by the level of processing that you used in encoding the material, by the context at the time of encoding, by emotional and mood-related factors during encoding, and by your social goals.

Naturally, we cannot discuss encoding without also mentioning retrieval. After all, psychologists need to test how accurately you can *retrieve* information in order to examine how effectively you encoded the information. Furthermore, many memory errors can be traced to inadequate retrieval strategies (Einstein & McDaniel, 2004).

However, retrieval was relatively unimportant in the preceding section of this chapter. Now we'll move retrieval to the center stage. Let's first consider the distinction between two types of retrieval tasks, called explicit and implicit memory tasks. Then we'll focus on the two extremes of memory ability by exploring the topics of amnesia and memory expertise.

Throughout this section, keep Theme 1 in mind: Our cognitive processes are active, rather than passive. Yes, sometimes we retrieve material from memory in an effortless fashion; you see a friend, and her name seems to spontaneously appear in your memory. Other times, retrieval requires hard work! For example, you might try to recover someone's name by strategically re-creating the context in

which you met this person (Koriat, 2000; Roediger, 2000). Who else was present, how long ago was it, and where did this event take place?

Explicit Versus Implicit Memory Tasks

Imagine this scene: A young woman is walking aimlessly down the street, and she is eventually picked up by the police. She seems to be suffering from an extreme form of amnesia, because she has lost all memory of who she is. Unfortunately, she is carrying no identification. Then the police have a breakthrough idea: They ask her to begin dialing phone numbers. As it turns out, she dials her mother's number, even though she is not aware whose number she is dialing.

Daniel Schacter tells this story to illustrate the difference between explicit and implicit measures of memory (as cited in Adler, 1991). This difference can be demonstrated for people with normal memory as well as for those who have amnesia. Let us clarify the basic concepts of this distinction and then look at some research.

Definitions and Examples. Demonstration 5.3 provides two examples of explicit memory tasks and two examples of implicit memory tasks. Try these examples before you read further.

So far, we have focused on **explicit memory tasks**. On an explicit memory task, the researcher directly instructs participants to remember information; the participants are conscious that their memory is being tested, and the test requires them to intentionally retrieve some information they previously learned (Roediger & Amir, 2005).

Almost all the research we have discussed in Chapters 4 and 5 has used explicit memory tests. The most common explicit memory test is *recall*. As we discussed in the preceding section, a recall test requires the participant to reproduce items that were learned earlier. Another explicit memory test is *recognition*, in which the participant must identify which items on a list had been presented at an earlier time.

In contrast, an implicit memory task assesses memory indirectly. On an **implicit memory task**, people see the material (usually a series of words or pictures); later, during the test phase, people are instructed to complete a cognitive task that does not directly ask for either recall or recognition (Lockhart, 2000; Roediger & Amir, 2005). For example, in Part B1 of Demonstration 5.3, you filled in the blanks in several words. Previous experience with the material—in this case, the words at the beginning of the demonstration—facilitated your performance on the task (Roediger & Amir, 2005).

On an implicit memory task, the researchers avoid using words such as *remember* or *recall*. For example, in Schacter's anecdote about the woman with amnesia, dialing a phone number was a test of implicit memory. Implicit memory shows the effects of previous experience that creep out in our ongoing behavior, when we are not making a conscious effort to remember the past (Kihlstrom et al., 2007; Roediger & Amir, 2005).

Researchers have devised numerous measures of implicit memory (Amir & Selvig, 2005; Roediger & Amir, 2005; Wiers & Stacy, 2006). You tried two of these in Demonstration 5.3. For example, in Task B1, if you stored the words in the original list in your memory, you would be able to complete those words (for example, *commerce* and *village*) faster than the words in Task B1 that had not been on the list (for example, *letter* and *plastic*).

Task B2 illustrates a second measure of implicit memory, called a **repetition priming task**. In a repetition priming task, recent exposure to a word increases the likelihood that you'll think of this particular word, when you are given a cue that could evoke many different words. For example, on Task B2, you were likely to supply the words *kitchen*, *horse*, and *bookstore*—words you had seen at the beginning of the demonstration. In contrast, you were less likely to supply words you had not seen, such as *dining room*, *cow*, and *drugstore*.

During the last twenty five years, implicit memory has become a popular topic in research on memory (Roediger & Amir, 2005). For example, we'll see in Chapter 8 that researchers can use implicit memory tasks to assess people's unconscious attitudes about gender, ethnicity, and other social categories (Nosek et al., 2007).

Research with Normal Adults. A variety of studies demonstrate that normal adults often cannot remember stimuli when they are tested on an explicit memory task. However, they do remember the stimuli when tested on an implicit memory task.

One intriguing finding focuses on normal adults who have received anesthesia during surgery. These people often show no evidence of memory for information transmitted under anesthesia (for example, a conversation between the surgeon and the anesthesiologist) when memory is assessed with explicit memory tests. However, in most of the research studies, these people do remember a substantial amount of information when memory is assessed with implicit memory tests (Kihlstrom & Cork, 2007).

Some of the studies on explicit and implicit memory illustrate a pattern that researchers call a dissociation. A **dissociation** occurs when a variable has large effects on Test A, but little or no effects on Test B; a dissociation also occurs when a variable has one kind of effect if measured by Test A, and exactly the opposite effect if measured by Test B. The term *dissociation* is similar to the concept of a statistical interaction, a term that might sound familiar if you've taken a course in statistics.

Let's consider an illustration of a dissociation based on the research on the level-of-processing effect. As you know from the first section of this chapter, people typically recall more words if they have used deep levels of processing to encode them. For example, participants recall more items on an explicit memory test if they had originally used semantic encoding rather than encoding physical appearance. However, on an *implicit* memory test, semantic and perceptual encoding may produce similar memory scores, or people may even score lower if they had used semantic encoding (e.g., Jones, 1999; Richardson-Klavehn & Gardiner, 1998). Notice that these results fit the definition of a dissociation because depth of processing has a large positive effect on memory scores on Test A (an explicit memory task), but depth of processing has no effect or even a negative effect on memory scores on Test B (an implicit memory task).

We need to emphasize, however, that some variables have the same effect on both explicit and implicit memory. For example, in Chapter 4 we discussed proactive interference. **Proactive interference** means that people have trouble learning new material because previously learned material keeps interfering with new learning. According to the research, proactive interference operates on both explicit and implicit memory tasks (Lustig & Hasher, 2001a, 2001b). In both cases, memory for new material is less accurate because the earlier material keeps interfering.

The research on implicit memory illustrates that people often know more than they can reveal in actual recall. As a result, this research has potential implications for applied

---

DEMONSTRATION 5.3
Explicit and Implicit Memory Tasks

Take out a piece of paper. Then read the following list of words:

picture commerce motion village vessel
window number horse custom amount
fellow advice dozen flower kitchen bookstore

Now cover up that list for the remainder of the demonstration. Take a break for a few minutes and then try the following tasks:

A. *Explicit Memory Tasks*

1. *Recall*: On the piece of paper, write down as many of those words as you can recall.
2. *Recognition*: From the list below, circle the words that appeared on the original list:

woodpile fellow leaflet fitness number butter
motion table people dozen napkin
picture kitchen bookstore horse advice

B. *Implicit Memory Tasks*

1. *Word completion*: From the word fragments below, provide an appropriate, complete word. You may choose any word you wish.

v_s_e_ l_t_e_ v_l_a_e p_a_t_c m_t_o_ m_n_a
n_t_b_o_ c_m_e_c_ a_v_c_ t_b_e_ f_o_e_ c_r_o_
h_m_w_r_ b_o_s_o_e

2. *Repetition priming*: Perform the following tasks:

* Name three rooms in a typical house.
* Name three different kinds of animals.
* Name three different kinds of stores.

---

areas such as education, clinical psychology, and advertising (Jones, 1999).

Individuals with Amnesia

In this section and the next, we'll consider individuals who have unusual memory abilities. We'll first discuss people with **amnesia**, who have severe deficits in their episodic memory (Kalat, 2007). Then we'll examine the impressive performance of memory experts.

One form of amnesia is **retrograde amnesia**, or loss of memory for events that occurred *prior* to brain damage; the deficit is especially severe for events that occurred during the years just before the damage (Brown, 2002; Meeter et al., 2006; Meeter & Murre, 2004). For example, one woman known by the initials L.T. cannot recall events in her life that happened prior to an accident that injured her brain. However, her memory is normal for events after the injury (Conway & Fthenaki, 2000; Riccio et al., 2003).

The other form of amnesia is **anterograde amnesia**, or loss of memory for events that have occurred *after* brain damage (Kalat, 2007). For several decades, researchers have studied a man with anterograde amnesia who is known only by his initials, H.M. (James & MacKay, 2001; Milner, 1966). H.M. had such serious epilepsy that neurosurgeons operated on his brain in 1953. Specifically, they removed a portion of his temporal lobe region, as well as his **hippocampus,** a structure underneath the cortex that is important in many learning and memory tasks (Thompson, 2005).

The operation successfully cured H.M.'s epilepsy, but it left him with a severe kind of memory loss. H.M. has normal semantic memory, and he can accurately recall events that occurred before his surgery. However, he cannot learn or retain new information. For example, in 1980, he moved to a nursing home. Four years later, he still could not describe where he lived. For many years after the operation, he persisted in reporting that the year was 1953 (Corkin, 1984).

The research demonstrates that people with anterograde amnesia often recall almost nothing on tests of explicit memory such as recall or recognition. That is, they do poorly when asked to *consciously* remember an event that happened after they developed amnesia. Interestingly, however, they perform fairly accurately on tests of implicit memory (Schacter & Badgaiyan, 2001; Weiskrantz, 2000).

Let's consider the pioneering work conducted by Elizabeth Warrington and Lawrence Weiskrantz (1970). These researchers presented some English words to individuals with anterograde amnesia. Then the researchers administered several recall and recognition tasks. Compared to normal control-group participants, the individuals with amnesia performed much more poorly on both kinds of explicit memory tasks. So far, then, the results are not surprising.

However, Warrington and Weiskrantz (1970) also administered implicit memory tasks. The tasks were presented as word-guessing games, though they actually assessed memory for the words shown earlier. For example, they showed the previously presented English words in a mutilated form that was difficult to read. The participants were told to guess which word was represented. Amazingly, the implicit memory scores of the participants with amnesia and the control-group participants were virtually identical. Both groups correctly supplied the words from the previous list for about 45% of the mutilated stimuli. These results have been replicated many times since the original research, using both visual and auditory tasks (e.g., Bower, 1998; Roediger & Amir, 2005; Schacter et al., 1994).

Notice that the research by Warrington and Weiskrantz (1970) is an excellent example of a dissociation. As we noted, a dissociation occurs when a variable has a large effect on one kind of test, but little or no effect on another kind of test. In this case, the dissociation was evident because the variable of memory status (amnesic versus control) had a major effect when measured by explicit memory tests, but this same variable had no effect when measured by implicit memory tests.

The research on individuals with amnesia reminds us that memory is an extremely complex cognitive process. Specifically, people who apparently remember nothing when their memory is tested on a recall task can actually perform quite well when memory is measured in a different fashion.

Expertise

Whereas people with amnesia experience severe memory deficits, people with expertise demonstrate impressive memory abilities. A person with **expertise** shows consistently exceptional performance on representative tasks in a particular area (Ericsson, 2003a, 2003b, 2006). K. Anders Ericsson is the psychologist who currently has the greatest "expertise" in the area of expertise. As Ericsson emphasizes (cited in Schraw, 2005), practice is more important than inborn skill. In fact, expertise in a particular domain requires intensive, practice on a daily basis (Ericsson, 2003a; Ericsson et al., 2004).

Our first topic in this discussion illustrates that people's expertise is context specific. Next, we'll examine some of the ways in which memory experts and novices differ. Our final topic—indirectly related to expertise—explores how people can identify individuals from their own ethnic background more accurately than individuals from another ethnic group.

The Context-Specific Nature of Expertise. Researchers have studied memory experts in numerous areas, such as chess, sports, ballet, maps, musical notation, and memorizing extremely long sequences of numbers. In general, researchers have found a strong positive correlation between knowledge about an area and memory performance in that area (Schraw, 2005; Vicente & Wang, 1998). Experts remember material significantly more accurately than nonexperts, in terms of both recognition and recall (Brandt et al., 2005). Furthermore, experts' memory is more accurate immediately after the material is presented, and also after a long delay (Noice & Noice, 2002).

Interestingly, however, people who are expert in one area seldom display outstanding *general* memory skills (Kimball & Holyoak, 2000; Wilding & Valentine, 1997). For instance, chess masters are outstanding in their memory for chess positions, but they do not differ from nonexperts in their basic cognitive and perceptual abilities (Cranberg & Albert, 1988).

Furthermore, memory experts typically do not receive exceptional scores on tests of intelligence (Wilding & Valentine, 1997). For example, men who are experts in remembering information at the horse races do not score especially high on standard IQ tests. In fact, one horse race expert had an eighth-grade education and an IQ of 92 (Ceci & Liker, 1986). Incidentally, in Chapter 11, we'll see that memory expertise for specific areas of knowledge also helps people solve problems in these areas.

How Do Experts and Novices Differ? From the information we've discussed—as well as from other resources—we know that memory experts have several advantages over nonexperts (Ericsson & Kintsch, 1995; Ericsson & Lehmann, 1996; Herrmann, Gruneberg, et al., 2006; Herrmann, Yoder, et al., 2006; Kimball & Holyoak, 2000; McCormick, 2003; Noice & Noice, 1997; Roediger, Marsh, & Lee, 2002; Schraw, 2005; Simon & Gobet, 2000; Van Overscheide et al., 2005; Wilding & Valentine, 1997). Let's consider these advantages:

1. Experts possess a well-organized, carefully learned knowledge structure, which assists them during both encoding and retrieval. For instance, chess players store a number of common patterns that they can quickly access.

2. Experts are more likely to reorganize the new material they must recall, forming meaningful chunks in which related material is grouped together.

3. Experts typically have more vivid visual images for the items they must recall.

4. Experts work hard to emphasize the distinctiveness of each stimulus during encoding. As we saw, distinctiveness is essential for accurate memory.

5. Experts rehearse in a different fashion. For example, an actor may rehearse his or her lines by focusing on words that are likely to trigger recall.

6. Experts are better at reconstructing missing portions of information from material that they partially remember.

7. Experts are more skilled at predicting the difficulty of a task and at monitoring their progress on this task.

Throughout this book, we have emphasized that our cognitive processes are active, efficient, and accurate (Themes 1 and 2). These cognitive processes also employ both top-down and bottom-up strategies (Theme 5). As we can see from the previous list, these characteristics are especially well developed for someone with memory expertise in a given area.

Own-Race Bias. The information on expertise has interesting implications for face recognition. Specifically, people are generally more accurate in identifying members of their own ethnic group than members of another ethnic group, a phenomenon called **own-race bias** (Brigham et al., 2007; Meissner et al., 2005; Walker & Hewstone, 2006). This effect is also known as the *other-race effect* or the *cross-race effect*.

Research in the United States typically shows that both Black and European American individuals are more accurate in recognizing faces of people from their own ethnic group (MacLin & Malpass, 2001; Meissner et al., 2005; Wright et al., 2003). Similar findings are reported for face recognition with European American and Asian individuals (Brigham et al., 2007; Ng & Lindsay, 1994).

One explanation for the own-race bias is that people develop expertise for the facial features of the ethnic group with whom they frequently interact. As a result, faces representing their own ethnic group acquire distinctiveness. As you know from previous discussions in this chapter, memory is most accurate when the stimuli are distinctive. Consistent with this research, Van Wallendael and Kuhn (1997) found that Black students rated Black faces as more distinctive than European American faces. In contrast,

European American students rated European American faces as more distinctive than Black faces.

In the United States, Blacks represent about 13% of the population, and Latinas/os represent about 14% of the population (U.S. Census Bureau, 2006). In contrast, the largest non-White population in Great Britain is South Asian, a group with origins in countries such as India, Pakistan, and Bangladesh. South Asians represent only about 4% of the British population (Walker & Hewstone, 2006). As a result, White people would have relatively little experience in interacting with South Asian people. In contrast, South Asian people would have relatively extensive experience interacting with White people.

Pamela Walker and Miles Hewstone (2006) studied facial recognition in British high school students who were either White or South Asian. Each student looked at photographs of faces that had been altered. Within each gender category, the faces differed along a continuum. On one end of the continuum, the faces looked clearly South Asian; at the other end, the faces looked clearly White. Other faces represented intermediate combinations of the two sets of facial features. In each case, the student saw photos of two faces—one after the other—and then judged whether the faces were the same or different.

British White students made more accurate judgments for White faces than for South Asian faces. In contrast, the British South Asian students were equally accurate for both kinds of faces. It would be interesting to see whether British White students also demonstrate more of the own-race bias in long-term memory for faces, compared to South Asian students.

We would expect to find that own-race bias decreases when people have greater contact with members of other ethnic groups. (In fact, the research by Walker and Hewstone suggests this outcome.) The research generally shows some support for the contact hypothesis, although the evidence is not strong (Brigham et ah, 2007; Meissner & Brigham, 2001; Wright et al., 2003).

Some researchers have explored expertise in social categories other than ethnicity. For example, Anastasi and Rhodes (2003) studied younger-adult and older-adult participants. They found that participants from these two age groups were most accurate in identifying people in their own group. In the next section, we will explore several additional factors that influence accuracy in identifying faces.

SECTION SUMMARY: RETRIEVAL IN LONG-TERM MEMORY

1. Explicit memory tasks instruct participants to recall or recognize information, In contrast, implicit memory tasks require participants to perform a cognitive task, such as completing a word that has missing letters.

2. When people hear information while they are anesthetized, they may recall much more of that information on an implicit task than on an explicit task. Research also indicates that depth of processing has no impact on an implicit memory task, even though it has a major effect on an explicit memory task.

3. Individuals with retrograde amnesia have difficulty recalling events that occurred prior to brain damage.

4. Individuals with anterograde amnesia have difficulty recalling events that occurred after brain damage. They may recall almost nothing on tests of explicit memory; however, on tests of implicit memory, they can perform as accurately as people without brain damage.

5. Expertise has an important effect on long-term memory, although expertise is context-specific. Compared to novices, experts have cognitive advantages such as well-organized knowledge structures and vivid visual images.

6. According to the research on own-race bias, people have more expertise in recognizing faces from their own ethnic group, in part because their expertise makes these faces more distinctive.

AUTOBIOGRAPHICAL MEMORY

As we noted at the beginning of the chapter, autobiographical memory is memory for events and issues related to yourself. Autobiographical memory usually includes a verbal narrative; it may also include imagery about the events, emotional reactions, and procedural information (Roediger, Marsh, & Lee, 2002). In general, the research in this area examines recall for naturally occurring events that happen outside the laboratory. Your autobiographical memory is a vital part of your identity, shaping your personal history and your self-concept (Lampinen et al., 2004; Lieberman, 2007; McAdams, 2004).

The previous two sections in this chapter focused on encoding and retrieval in long-term memory, and they primarily examined laboratory research. In general, the dependent variable in these studies is the number of items correctly recalled—a *quantity*-oriented approach to memory (Koriat et al., 2000). In contrast, in autobiographical memory, the dependent variable is memory *accuracy*; does your recall match the actual events that happened, or does it distort the events? Therefore, autobiographical memory usually focuses on the correspondence between an actual event and an individual's memory for that event.

The studies of autobiographical memory are typically high in ecological validity (Bahrick, 2005; Esgate & Groome, 2005; Lampinen et al., 2004). As we noted in Chapter 1, a study has ecological validity if the conditions in which the research is conducted are similar to the natural setting to which the results will be applied.

Interest in autobiographical memory has grown rapidly during the last thirty years. Here are some representative topics:

1. Immigrant Latinas/os recalling their life stories in both English and Spanish (Schrauf& Rubin, 2001).
2. Older adults describing themes in their life stories (Bluck & Habermas, 2001; Pasupathi, 2001).
3. Memory failures that people experience in their everyday life (Gennaro et al., 2005; Herrmann & Graneberg, 2006).
4. "Earwitness testimony," or accuracy in identifying someone's voice (Kerstholt et al., 2006; Yarmey, 2007).
5. Brain-imaging studies of autobiographical memory (Conway, 2001 ; Lieberman, 2007).

This discussion of autobiographical memory first looks at schemas. Schemas can shape your memory for previous event, so that this memory becomes more consistent with your current viewpoint. Next, we'll examine source monitoring, which shows that you can make mistakes when you try to remember where and when you learned certain information. Then an in-depth section on the so-called "flashbulb memory" examines some especially vivid memories. Our final topic is eyewitness testimony, an area of research that has obvious applications in the courtroom.

This discussion of autobiographical memory illustrates several important characteristics of our memory for life events:

1. Although we sometimes make errors, our memory is often accurate for a variety of information (Theme 2). For example, adults can recall the names of streets near their childhood home and material from their elementary school textbooks (Read & Connolly, 2007).
2. When people do make mistakes, they generally concern peripheral details and specific information about commonplace events, rather than central information about important events (Goldsmith et al., 2005; Sutherland & Hayne, 2001; Tuckey & Brewer, 2003). In fact, it's usually helpful not to remember numerous small details that would interfere with memory for more important information (Bjork et al., 2005).
3. Our memories often blend together information; we actively construct a memory at the time of retrieval (Davis & Loftus, 2007; Kelley & Jacoby, 2000; Koriat, 2000). Notice that this constructive process is consistent with Theme 1: Our cognitive processes are typically active, rather than passive.

Schemas and Autobiographical Memory

This discussion of schemas emphasizes how you remember common, ordinary events. A **schema** consists of your general knowledge or expectation, which is distilled from your past experiences with an event or a person (Davis & Loftus, 2007; Koriat et al., 2000). For example, you have probably developed a schema for "eating lunch." You tend to sit in a particular area with the same group of people. Your conversation topics may also be reasonably standardized. You have also developed a schema for the events that occur during the first day of a class and for purchasing items in a grocery store. You have even developed a schema for yourself.

We use schemas to guide our recall. As time passes, we still remember the gist of an event, although we may forget the schema-irrelevant information (Davis & Loftus, 2007; Goldsmith et al., 2005; Tuckey & Brewer, 2003). Chapter 8 explores in more detail how schemas influence a variety of cognitive processes. However, in the present chapter, we'll examine a topic that is especially relevant to autobiographical memory, called the consistency bias.

During recall, we often reveal a **consistency bias**; that is, we tend to exaggerate the consistency between our past feelings and beliefs and our current viewpoint (Davis & Loftus, 2007; Schacter, 1999, 2001). As a consequence, our memory of the past may be distorted. For example, suppose that a researcher asks you today to recall how you felt about feminism when you were a high school student. You would tend to construct your previous emotions so that they would be consistent with your current emotions. We generally see ourselves as being consistent and stable (Greenwald et al., 2002). As a result, we underestimate how we have changed throughout our lives. For example, we recall that our previous political views and activities are highly similar to our current perspective. As Schacter (2001) summarizes the consistency bias, "The way we were depends on the way we are" (p. 139).

The consistency bias suggests that we tell our life stories so that they are consistent with our current schemas about ourselves (Ceballo, 1999). For example, Honig (1997), a historian, interviewed Chicana garment workers who had participated in a strike at a garment manufacturing company in El Paso, Texas. Shortly after the strike, these women viewed the strike as a life-transforming experience that had changed them from timid factory workers into fearless, self-confident activists.

When Honig returned to interview these same women several years later, they recalled that they had *always* been assertive and nonconforming—even prior to the strike. It's possible that they selectively recalled assertive episodes from their pre-strike lives—episodes consistent with their current self-schemas. As Honig argues, these Chicana garment workers are "not inventing nonexistent past experiences, but they are retelling them with the language, perceptions, and mandates of their present" (1997, p. 154). Notice the interdisciplinary nature of research on the consistency bias: It explores the interface of cognitive psychology, personality/social psychology, and history.

We have seen that schemas can influence our memories of the past, so that they seem more similar to our present feelings, beliefs, and actions. Now let's move away from schemas to consider another component of autobiographical memory, called source monitoring.

Source Monitoring

Something like this has certainly happened to you: You borrowed a book from a friend, and you distinctly remember returning it. However, the next day, you find that the book is still on your desk. Apparently, you simply *imagined* returning the book. Or perhaps you are trying to recall where you learned some background information about a movie you saw. Did a friend tell you this information, or did you learn it from a review of the movie? This process of trying to identify the origin of memories and beliefs is called **source monitoring** (Johnson, 1997, 2002; Pansky et al., 2005).

According to Marcia Johnson and Carol Raye (2000), we often try to sort out the source of information in our memory. We include cues such as our schemas and expectations, as well as the nature of the details. Unfortunately, our source monitoring sometimes produces mistakes.

For example, suppose that you are working on a project with a classmate, and you are trying to anticipate what suggestions your classmate will supply. Later on, you are likely to remember that your friend actually *did* provide these suggestions (Foley et al., 2006).

In a related study, Marsh and his colleagues (1997) asked two groups of college students to discuss an open-ended question on a topic such as methods for improving their university. One week later, the participants in both groups returned for a second session. One group took a recognition test. Specifically, the participants identified whether each item on a list had been their own idea or someone else's idea. The participants in this group seldom made source-monitoring mistakes; that is, they seldom claimed that an idea generated by another person had really been their own idea.

When the other group returned for the second session, they were given the original open-ended topic. The experimenter asked them to write down new answers to the question—answers that no one had supplied before. Interestingly, this group of individuals frequently committed source-monitoring errors. That is, they frequently wrote down answers that another person had supplied one week earlier. Apparently, a recognition test forces us to adopt stricter criteria with respect to source monitoring. In contrast, our criteria are more relaxed when we generate ideas.

Source-monitoring errors are puzzling. Can't we even remember what we ourselves said, as opposed to what another person said? According to Defeldre (2005), people may also plagiarize inadvertently. For example, one student believed that he had composed a truly new song. However, in reality, the melody of the song was based on a melody composed by another songwriter.

Earlier in the chapter, we saw that our memory has a positive bias; we tend to remember pleasant events, and negative events become more positive as time passes. Similarly, we seem to have a "wishful thinking bias," which leads us to make errors in source monitoring. For example, suppose you consulted a number of sources before you bought a new PDA made by the Handy Dandy company. A friend asks you what information you consulted before making the decision. You'll tend to recall that the extremely positive review for the Handy Dandy model came from a trustworthy source, such as *Consumer Reports*, rather than a less reliable source, such as an e-mail from a friend (Gordon et al., 2005).

In some cases, the mistakes in source monitoring can have much more serious consequences. For many years, Marcia Johnson (1996, 1998, 2002) has emphasized that source-monitoring errors occur at a societal level, not just at the individual level. Our government, the media, and corporations must engage in vigorous source monitoring in order to determine which events really happened and which are fictional. Unfortunately, individuals are seldom aware of source monitoring until they make a source-monitoring error. Similarly, society is seldom aware of source monitoring until we discover that this monitoring has failed.

A representative source-monitoring failure occurred in 2003, when President George W. Bush was trying to provide justifications for starting the Iraq War. In his State of the Union address in early 2003, Bush discussed one important reason to justify invading Iraq. Specifically, he announced that Iraq was negotiating with an African country to buy uranium (an ingredient used in making nuclear weapons).

Six months later, the public learned that this claim was based on clearly falsified documents from Niger, a country in west-central Africa. Also, the Central Intelligence Agency claimed that their agents had tried to warn the president that the information from Niger was false. Furthermore, the president maintained that his State of the Union address had been cleared by the CIA (Isikoff & Lipper, 2003). Unfortunately, several different errors in source monitoring on "the uranium question" probably helped to push the United States into an expensive, destructive war.

Marcia Johnson (2002) emphasizes that government agencies, the media, and corporation executives need to be meticulous about checking the accuracy of their information. Their goal should be to limit both the frequency and the size of source-monitoring errors.

So far, our discussion of autobiographical memory has explored memory schemas and source monitoring. Now let's consider the related topic of "flashbulb memories," which are memories that seem especially vivid. As you'll see, people commit errors when they try to recall the circumstances in which they learned about an important event—just as they commit errors in recalling the circumstances during source monitoring.

IN DEPTH

Flashbulb Memories

At some point in the near future, try Demonstration 5.4. This demonstration illustrates the so-called flashbulb-memory effect. **Flashbulb memory** refers to your memory for the circumstances in which you first learned about a very surprising and emotionally arousing event. Many people believe that they can accurately recall trivial details about what they were doing at the time of this event (Brown & Kulik, 1977; Esgate & Groome, 2005).

One of my clearest flashbulb memories, like many of my generation, is of learning that President John Kennedy had been shot. I was a sophomore at Stanford University, just ready for a midday class in German. As I recall, I had entered the classroom from the right, and I was just about to sit down at a long table on the right-hand side of the room. The sun was streaming in from the left. Only one other person was seated in the classroom, a blond fellow named Dewey. He turned around and said, "Did you hear that President Kennedy has been shot?" I also recall my reaction and the reactions of others as they entered the room.

President Kennedy was shot more than forty years ago, yet trivial details of that news still seem stunningly clear to many people (Neisser & Libby, 2000). You can probably think of personal events in your own life that triggered flashbulb memories, such as the death of a relative, a political tragedy, or an amazing surprise.

People also report extremely vivid memories for highly positive events, as well as tragedies. For example, an Indian friend of mine recalls in detail the circumstances in which he heard Mohandas Gandhi—the nonviolent political leader—speaking to a crowd of people in Gauhati, India. My friend was only 5 years old at the time, yet he vividly recalls that Gandhi was wearing a white outfit, and he was accompanied by two women. He can recall that his aunt, who was with him, was wearing a white sari with a gold and red border. He can also distinctly remember how the heat of the day had made him very thirsty.

Let's first consider the classic study by Brown and Kulik (1977) which introduced the term "flashbulb memory." Then we'll discuss the research that focuses on memory for the events of September 11, 2001.

The Classic Study. Roger Brown and James Kulik (1977) were the first researchers to study whether various important political events triggered contextually rich memories. They found that people tended to describe details such as their location when they heard the news and the person who gave them the news. Notice whether your friends included this information in their responses to Demonstration 5.4.

Brown and Kulik (1977) suggested that people's flashbulb memories are more accurate than memories of less surprising events. However, many later studies suggested that people made numerous errors in recalling details of national events, even though they claimed that their memories for these events were very vivid (Roediger, Marsh, & Lee, 2002; Schooler & Eich, 2000).

Memories about September 11, 2001. Several researchers have studied recall of a tragedy that is especially vivid for most U.S. students—the terrorist attacks of September 11, 2001. Let's look at an especially thorough study by Jennifer Talarico and David Rubin (2003), and then we'll discuss additional observations about people's memory for that event.

On September 12, the day after the attacks, Talarico and Rubin asked students at a North Carolina university to report specific details about how they had learned about the attacks. The students also provided similar information for an ordinary event that had occurred at about the same time. This ordinary event served as a control condition that could be contrasted with the "flashbulb memory" of the attack.

After the initial session, the students were randomly assigned to one of three recall-testing sessions. Some returned to be tested one week later, others returned six weeks later, and still others returned thirty-two weeks later. At these recall-testing sessions, Talarico and Rubin asked the students a variety of questions, including the details of their memory for the attack and for the everyday event. These details were checked against the details that had been supplied on September 12, and the researchers counted the number of consistent and inconsistent details.

The number of details provided on September 12 provides the baseline for the number of consistent details. As you can see, the consistency drops over time for each of the three testing sessions. However, the drop was similar for the terrorist-attack memory and for the everyday memory. The number of inconsistent details could not be assessed until the one-week recall-testing session. The number of inconsistent details increases slightly over time for both kinds of memories. Interestingly, however, the students in all conditions reported that they were highly confident that their recall of the terrorist attacks had been accurate.

A related study by Kathy Pezdek (2003b) examined whether students' proximity to New York City influenced their memories about September 11, 2001. She found that students at a college in New York City recalled significantly more factual details about the tragedy than students at colleges in California and Hawaii. This finding makes sense because the New York City students were an average of only 7 blocks from the World Trade Center at the time they learned about the attack. Also, they were much more likely than the other students to have family members and friends whose lives were impacted by the event. In contrast, the New York City students were less likely than others to provide details about how they learned about the event.

Pezdek suggests that the New York students focused on rehearsing and remembering the detailed events of the tragedy, because these objective details could impact the lives of people they knew. In contrast, most of the students from California and Hawaii did not need to know these details, so they could focus on their own personal memories that focused on how they first learned about the tragedy. So, what can we conclude from all this information about flashbulb memories? It's likely that we do not need to invent any special mechanism to explain them. Yes, these memories can sometimes be more accurate than our memories for ordinary events. However, these enhanced memories can usually be explained by standard mechanisms such as rehearsal frequency, distinctiveness, and elaboration (Koriat et al., 2000; Neisser, 2003; Read & Connolly, 2007). Furthermore, both flashbulb memories and "ordinary memories" grow less accurate with the passage of time (Kvavilashvili et al., 2003; Read & Connolly, 2007; Schmolck et al., 2000).

Eyewitness Testimony

So far, our discussion of autobiographical memory has explored memory schemas, source monitoring, and flashbulb memories. Now let's consider eyewitness testimony, the most extensively researched topic within the domain of autobiographical memory. Memory schemas can alter a witness's testimony. You'll also see that some of the errors in eyewitness testimony can be traced to faulty source monitoring. People believe they really witnessed something that had actually been suggested to them in a different situation (Mitchell & Johnson, 2000).

We have seen throughout this chapter that people's long-term memory is reasonably accurate, especially if we consider memory for the gist of a message. However, eyewitness testimony requires people to remember specific details about people and events. In these cases, mistakes are more likely (Castelli et al., 2006; Wells & Olson, 2003).

When eyewitness testimony is inaccurate, the wrong person may go to jail or in the worst cases—be put to death.

Consider the case of Gary Graham, who was a suspect in the murder of Bobby Lambert. In truth, there was no convincing evidence for Graham's guilt—nothing like DNA or fingerprint evidence. When Graham came to trial, jury members were informed that Graham had a pistol *similar* to one that had shot Lambert. They were not told that the Houston police had concluded that it was not the *same* pistol.

Furthermore, eight eyewitnesses had seen the killer near the store, but seven of them were unable to identify Graham as the killer. His fate—the death penalty—was sealed by one woman's eyewitness testimony, even though she testified that she had seen his face at night for about 3 seconds, from a distance of about 30 feet. In addition, the court never heard the testimony of two eyewitnesses whose information contradicted the testimony of that one woman. Graham's case was never reviewed. Was Gary Graham genuinely guilty? We'll never know, because he was executed on June 22, 2000 (Alter, 2000).

Reports like this one have led psychologists to question the validity of eyewitness testimony. In many criminal cases, the only evidence available for identifying the culprit is the eyewitness testimony provided by people who were present at the crime scene.

Fortunately, DNA testing became more common during the late 1990s, and it was used for some individuals who had been convicted before the tests were available (Herrmann, Gruneberg, et al., 2006). Researchers analyzed samples of imprisoned people whose DNA did not match the biological sample from the scene of the crime. More than 75% of these people had been pronounced guilty

---

DEMONSTRATION 5.4
Flashbulb Memory

Ask several acquaintances whether they can identify any memories of a very surprising event. Tell them, for example, that many people believe that they can recall—in vivid detail—the circumstances in which they learned about the death of President Kennedy, or the September 11, 2001, terrorist attacks.

Also tell them that other vivid memories focus on more personal important events. Ask them to tell you about one or more memories, particularly noting any small details that they recall.

because of erroneous eyewitness testimony (Castelli et al., 2006; Wells & Olson, 2003).

In our discussion of eyewitness testimony, let's first consider how inaccuracies can arise when people are given misleading information after the event that they had witnessed. Next, we'll summarize several factors that can influence the accuracy of eyewitness testimony. Then we'll see whether witnesses who are *confident* about their eyewitness testimony are also more *accurate* about their judgments. Our final topic in this discussion is the recovered memory/false memory debate.

The Post-Event Misinformation Effect. Errors in eyewitness testimony can often be traced to incorrect information. In the **post-event misinformation effect**, people first view an event, and then afterward they are given misleading information about the event; later on, they mistakenly recall the misleading information, rather than the event they actually saw (Davis & Loftus, 2007; Pansky et al., 2005; Pickrell et al., 2004).

Earlier in the chapter, we discussed proactive interference, which means that people have trouble recalling new material because previously learned, old material keeps interfering with new memories. The misinformation effect resembles another kind of interference called retroactive interference. In **retroactive interference**, people have trouble recalling old material because some recently learned, new material keeps interfering with old memories. For example, suppose that an eyewitness saw a crime, and then a lawyer supplied some misinformation while asking a question. Later on, the eyewitness may have trouble remembering the events that actually occurred at the scene of the crime, because the new misinformation is interfering.

In the classic experiment on the misinformation effect, Elizabeth Loftus and her coauthors (1976) showed participants a series of slides. In this sequence, a sports car stopped at an intersection, and then it turned and hit a pedestrian. Half the participants saw a slide with a yield sign at the intersection; the other half saw a stop sign.

Twenty minutes to a week after the participants saw the slides, they answered a questionnaire about the details of the accident. A critical question contained information that was either consistent with a detail in the original slide series, inconsistent with that detail, or neutral (i.e., did not mention the detail). For example, some people who had seen the yield sign were asked, "Did another car pass the red Datsun while it was stopped at the yield sign?" (consistent). Other people were asked, "Did another car pass the red Datsun while it was stopped at the stop sign?" (inconsistent). For still other people, the question did not mention the sign (neutral). To answer this question, all participants saw two slides, one with a stop sign and one with a yield sign. They were asked to select which slide they had previously seen.

People who saw the inconsistent information were much less accurate than people in the other two conditions. They selected a sign, based on the information in the questionnaire, rather than the original slide. Many studies have replicated the detrimental effects of misleading post-event information (e.g., Pickrell et al., 2004; Roediger & McDermott, 2000; Schacter, 2001; Wade et al., 2002).

The misinformation effect can be at least partly traced to faulty source monitoring (Davis & Loftus, 2007; Schacter et al., 1998). For example, in the study by Loftus and her colleagues (1978), the post-event information in the inconsistent-information condition encouraged people to create a mental image of a stop sign. During testing, they had trouble deciding which of the two images—the stop sign or the yield sign—they had actually seen in the original slide series.

The research on the misinformation effect emphasizes the active, constructive nature of memory. As Theme 1 points out, cognitive processes are active, rather than passive. The constructivist approach to memory argues that we construct knowledge by integrating what we know, so that our understanding of an event or a topic is coherent, and it makes sense (Davis & Loftus, 2007; Mayer, 2003; Pansky et al., 2.005). In the case of the study by Loftus and her colleagues (1978), the people in the inconsistent condition made sense of the event by concluding that the car had paused at the stop sign.

Notice, then, that the consistency bias is one component of the constructivist approach. In short, memory does not consist of a list of facts, all stored in intact form and ready to be replayed like a videotape. Instead, we construct a memory by blending information from a variety of sources (Davis & Loftus, 2007; Hyman & Kleinknecht, 1999).

Factors Affecting the Accuracy of Eyewitness Testimony. As you can imagine, a variety of factors influence whether eyewitness testimony is accurate. We have already mentioned three potential problems in eyewitness testimony: (1) People may create memories that are consistent with their schemas; (2) people may make errors in source monitoring; and (3) post-event misinformation may distort people's recall. Here are several other important variables:

1. *Errors are more likely when there is a long delay between the original event and the time of the testimony.* As time passes, recall accuracy decreases for most of our ordinary memories. A long delay in eyewitness testimony also allows more opportunities for "contamination" from post-event misinformation (Dysart & Lindsay, 2007; Esgate & Groome, 2005; Read & Connolly, 2007).

2. *Errors are more likely if the misinformation is plausible.* For instance, in the classic study by Loftus and her colleagues (1978), a stop sign is just as plausible as a yield sign, so participants in that study often made errors. People are also likely to say that an event occurred in their own life (when it really did not) if the event seems consistent with other similar experiences (Castelli et al., 2006; Davis & Loftus, 2007; Hyman & Loftus, 2002).

3. *Errors are more likely if there is social pressure* (Roebers & Schneider, 2000; Roediger & McDermott, 2000; Smith et al., 2003). People make many errors in eyewitness testimony if they have been pressured to provide a specific answer (for example, "Exactly when did you first see the suspect?"). In contrast, the testimony is more accurate when people are allowed to report in their own words, when they are given sufficient time, and when they are allowed to say, "I don't know" (Koriat et al., 2000; Weils et al., 2000).

4. *Errors are more likely if eyewitnesses have been given positive feedback.* Eyewitnesses are much more certain about the accuracy of their decision if they had previously been given positive feedback—even a simple "Okay" (Douglass & Steblay, 2006; Semmler & Brewer, 2006; Wells & Bradfield, 1999). Unfortunately, in real-life lineups, the eyewitnesses often hear this kind of encouragement (Wells & Olson, 2003). Now try Demonstration 5.5, below.

The Relationship Between Memory Confidence and Memory Accuracy. In some studies, researchers ask participants to judge how confident they are about the accuracy of their eyewitness testimony. Interestingly, in many situations, participants are almost as confident about their misinformation-based memories as they are about their genuinely correct memories (Koriat et al., 2000; Penrod & Cutler, 1999; Perfect, 2004; Wells & Olson, 2003). In other words, people's confidence about their eyewitness testimony is not strongly correlated with the accuracy of their testimony. In fact, the correlations are typically between +.30 and +.503 (Leippe & Eisenstadt, 2007).

This research has a practical application for the legal system. Jury members are much more likely to believe a confident eyewitness than an uncertain one (Brewer et al., 2005; Koriat et al., 2000; Penrod & Cutler, 1999). Unfortunately, however, the research shows that a *confident* eyewitness is not necessarily an *accurate* eyewitness.

The Recovered Memory/False Memory Controversy. If you scan popular magazines such as *Newsweek* or *People*, you seldom come across articles on working memory, the encoding-specificity principle, or source monitoring. However, between about 1995 and 2005, one topic from cognitive psychology attracted media attention: the controversy about recovered memory versus false memory (e.g., Eisen et al., 2002; Freyd & DePrince, 2001; Gallo, 2006; Goodman et al., 2007; Lynn & McConkey, 1998; Williams & Banyard, 1999). During this period, cognitive psychologists, therapists, and lawyers published more than 800 books and articles about this topic (Smith & Gleaves, 2007).

A complete discussion of this controversy is beyond the scope of a cognitive psychology textbook. Furthermore, the so-called "memory wars" have not been resolved, though most professionals now seem to favor a compromise position. We will summarize five important components of this issue. Before you read further, however, be sure that you have tried Demonstration 5.5.

1. *The two contrasting positions in the controversy.* Most of the discussion about false memory focuses on childhood sexual abuse. One group of researchers argues that memories can be forgotten and then recovered. According

---

3   A correlation is a statical measure of the relationship between two variables, in which .00 represents no relationship and +1.00 represents a strong positive relationship.

to this recovered-memory perspective, some individuals who experienced sexual abuse during childhood managed to forget that memory for many years. At a later time, often prompted by a specific event or by encouragement from a therapist, this presumably forgotten memory comes flooding back into consciousness (Smith & Gleaves, 2007; Schacter, 2001).

A second group of researchers interprets phenomena like this in a different light. We must emphasize that this second group agrees that childhood sexual abuse is a genuine problem that needs to be addressed. However, these people deny the accuracy of many reports about the sudden recovery of early memories. Specifically, the false-memory perspective proposes that many of these recovered memories are actually incorrect memories; that is, they are constructed stories about events that never occurred (Davis & Loftus, 2007; Gerrie et al., 2005; Hyman St Loftus, 2002; Loftus & Guyer, 2002a, 2002b; Reyna et al., 2007).

2. *The potential for memory errors.* Our discussion throughout this section on autobiographical memory should convince you that memory is less than perfect. For example, people are often guided by schemas, rather than their actual recall of an event. Also, the research on source monitoring shows that people cannot recall with absolute accuracy whether they performed an action or merely imagined performing it. We also saw that eyewitness testimony can be flawed, especially when witnesses receive misinformation (Hyman & Loftus, 2002).

Similar problems arise in recalling memories from childhood. For instance, some psychotherapists suggest to clients that they had been sexually abused during childhood. This suggestion could easily be blended with reality to create a false memory (Kihlstrom, 1998). These statements encourage clients to invent a false memory, especially because we noted earlier that people make more errors when they have experienced social pressure (Smith et al., 2003).

We cannot easily determine whether a memory of childhood abuse is correct. After all, the situation is far from controlled, and other, independent witnesses are rarely available (Berliner & Briere, 1999; Koriat et al., 2000). Furthermore, PET scans and other techniques cannot reliably distinguish between correct and incorrect recall of abuse (McNally, 2003; Schacter, 2001).

However, psychologists have conducted research and created theories that are designed to address the recovered memory/false memory issue. Let's first consider laboratory research that demonstrates false memory. Then we'll discuss why the situation of sexual abuse during childhood may sometimes require a different kind of explanation, rather than one that can explain false memory for emotionally neutral material.

3. *Laboratory evidence of false memory.* Research in the psychology laboratory clearly demonstrates that people often "recall" seeing a word that was never actually presented. In contrast to the real-life recall of sexual abuse, the laboratory research is very straightforward and unemotional. Researchers simply ask participants to remember a list of words they had seen earlier, and their accuracy can be objectively measured. For example, Demonstration 5.5 asked you to memorize and recall two lists of words, and then you checked your accuracy. Take a moment now to check something else. On List 1, did you write down the word *sleep*? Did you write *river* on List 2?

If you check the original lists, you'll discover that neither *sleep* nor *river* was listed, In research with lists of words like these, Roediger and McDermott (1995) found a false-recall rate of 55%. People made intrusion errors by listing words that did not appear on the lists. Intrusions are common on this task because each word that *does* appear on a list is commonly associated with a missing word, in this case either *sleep* or *river*. This experiment has been replicated numerous times, using different stimuli and different testing conditions (e.g., Foley et al., 2006; Neuschatz et al., 2007; Roediger & Gallo, 2004). These researchers argue that similar intrusions could occur with respect to childhood memories. People may "recall" events that are related to their actual experiences, but these events never actually occurred.

Other studies have demonstrated that laboratory-research participants can construct raised memories for events during childhood that never actually happened. These false memories include being attacked by a small dog, being lost in a shopping mall, seeing someone possessed by demons, and becoming ill after eating hard-boiled eggs (e.g., Bernstein et ab, 2005; Gerrie et al, 2005; Hyman & Kleinknecht, 1999; Pickrell et al., 2004).

However, we need to emphasize that only a fraction of participants actually claim to remember an event that did not occur. For example, researchers tried to implant a false memory that the research participant had attended a wedding at the age of 6. According to this fake story, the 6-year-old had accidentally bumped into a table containing a punch bowl, spilling punch on a parent of the bride. Interestingly, 25% of the participants eventually recalled this false memory—an entire event that did not actually occur (Hyman et al., 1995; Hyman & Loftus, 2002). Notice, however, that 75% of the students refused to "remember" the specific event.

4. *Arguments for recovered memory.* One problem is that these laboratory studies have little ecological validity with respect to memory for childhood sexual abuse (Freyd & Quina, 2000). Consider the studies on recalling word lists. There's not much similarity between "remembering" a word that never appeared on a list and a false memory of childhood sexual abuse. In addition, the events—such as spilling the contents of a punch bowl—are somewhat embarrassing. However, these events have no sexual content, and they could be discussed in public. In contrast, students cannot be convinced to create false memories for more embarrassing events, such as having had an enema as a child (Pezdek et al., 1997).

Many people who have been sexually abused as children have continually remembered the incidents, even decades later. However, some people may genuinely not recall the abuse. For example, researchers have studied individuals who had been treated in hospital emergency rooms for childhood sexual abuse, or individuals whose sexual abuse had been documented by the legal system. Still, some of them fail to recall the episode when interviewed as adults (Goodman et al., 2003; Pezdek & Taylor, 2002; Schooler,

---

DEMONSTRATION 5.5

Remembering Lists of Words

For this demonstration, you must learn and recall two lists of words. Before beginning, take out two pieces of paper. Next, read List 1, then close the book and try to write down as many of the words as possible. Then do the same for List 2. After you have recalled both sets of words, check your accuracy. How many items did you correctly recall?

List 1	List 2
bed	water
rest	stream
awake	lake
tired	Mississippi
dream	boat
wake	tide
snooze	swim
blanket	flow
doze	run
slumber	barge
snore	creek
nap	brook
peace	fish
yawn	bridge
drowsy	winding

2001). Indeed, some people can forget about the incident for many years, but they suddenly recall it decades later.

Jennifer Freyd and Anne DePrince propose an explanation for these cases of recovered memory (DePrince & Freyd, 2004; Freyd, 1996, 1998). They emphasize that childhood sexual abuse is genuinely different from relatively innocent episodes such as spilled wedding punch. In particular, they propose the term **betrayal trauma** to describe how a child may respond adaptively when a trusted parent or caretaker betrays him or her by sexual abuse. The child depends on this adult and must actively inhibit memories of abuse in order to maintain an attachment to the adult (Anderson, 2001).

5. *Both perspectives are partially correct.* In reality, we must conclude that both the recovered-memory perspective and the false-memory perspective are at least partially correct (Castelli et al., 2006; Herrmann et al., 2006). Indeed, some people have truly experienced childhood sexual abuse, and they may forget about the abuse for many decades until a critical event triggers their recall. Furthermore, other people may never have experienced childhood sexual abuse, but a suggestion about abuse creates a false memory of childhood experiences that never really occurred. In still other cases, people can provide accurate testimony about how they have been abused, even years afterwards (Brainerd & Reyna, 2005; Castelli et al., 2006; Goodman & Paz-Alonso, 2006).

We have seen throughout this chapter that human memory is both flexible and complex. This memory process can account for temporarily forgetting events, it can account for the construction of events that never actually happened, and it can also account for accurate memory—even when the events are horrifying.

SECTION SUMMARY: AUTOBIOGRAPHICAL MEMORY

1. Research on autobiographical memory typically has high ecological validity; this research shows that our memories are usually accurate, although we may make errors on some details, and we may blend together information from different events.

2. Memory schemas encourage us to make errors in recalling events; in addition, we may reveal a consistency bias by exaggerating the similarity between our current self-schema and our previous characteristics.

3. The research on source monitoring shows that we may have difficulty deciding whether something really happened, instead of imagining it, and we may have difficulty deciding where we learned some information.

4. Flashbulb memories are rich with information, and we are often confident that they are accurate; however, even memories for tragedies—such as the September 11, 2001 tragedy—are typically no more accurate than memories for important personal events.

5. In eyewitness testimony, the post-event misinformation effect can occur if misleading information is introduced after a witness has seen an event. The research is consistent with the constructivist approach to memory.

6. Errors in eyewitness memory are more likely if the witness observed an event long ago, if the misinformation is plausible, if social pressure was applied, or if positive feedback was supplied.

7. An eyewitness's self-confidence is not strongly correlated with his or her memory accuracy.

8. Both sides of the recovered memory/false memory controversy are at least partially correct. Some people may indeed forget about a painful childhood memory, recalling it years later. Other people apparently construct a memory of abuse that never really occurred, and still other people continue to have accurate memory for abuse, long afterwards.

CHAPTER REVIEW QUESTIONS

1. Suppose that you are in charge of creating a public service announcement for television. Choose an issue that is important to you, and describe at least five tips from this chapter that would help you make an especially memorable advertisement. Be sure to include depth of processing as one of the tips.

2. What is encoding specificity? Think of a recent example where encoding specificity explained why you temporarily forgot something. How strong are the effects of encoding specificity?

3. Give several examples of explicit and implicit memory tasks you have performed in the past few

days. What is dissociation, and how is it relevant in the research that has been conducted with both normal adults and people with amnesia?

4. According to one saying, "The more you know, the easier it is to learn." What evidence do we have for this statement, based on the material discussed in this chapter? Be sure to include information on expertise and schemas as part of your answer.

5. Although this textbook focuses on cognitive psychology, several topics discussed in this chapter are relevant to other areas, such as social psychology, personality psychology, and abnormal psychology. Summarize this research, discussing topics such as the self-reference effect, emotions and memory, and the consistency bias.

6. Define the term "autobiographical memory," and mention several topics that have been studied in this area. How does research in this area differ from more traditional laboratory research? List the advantages and disadvantages of each approach. Point out how Roediger and McDermott's (1995) study on false memory for English words highlights both the advantages and disadvantages of the laboratory approach.

7. Describe how schemas could lead to a distortion in the recall of a flashbulb memory. How might misleading post-event information also influence this recall? In answering the two parts of this question, use the terms proactive inhibition and retroactive inhibition.

8. The constructivist approach to memory emphasizes that we actively revise our memories in the light of new concerns and new information. How would this approach be relevant if a woman were to develop a false memory about her childhood, and she also shows a strong consistency bias? How would this approach be relevant for other topics in the section about autobiographical memory?

9. Chapter 6 emphasizes methods for improving your memory. However, the present chapter also contains some relevant information and hints about memory improvement. Review Chapter 5, and make a list of suggestions about memory improvement that you could use when you study for the next examination in cognitive psychology.

10. Researcher Daniel Schacter (2001) wrote a book describing several kinds of memory errors. He argues, however, that these errors are actually byproducts of a memory system that usually functions quite well. What textbook theme is related to his argument? Review this chapter and list some of the memory errors people may commit. Explain why each error is a byproduct of a memory system that works well in most everyday experiences.

Context-Dependent Memory in Two Natural Environments

On Land and Underwater

D.R. GODDEN AND A.D. BADDELEY

In a free recall experiment, divers learnt lists of words in two natural environments: on dry land and underwater, and recalled the words in either the environment of original learning, or in the alternative environment. Lists learnt underwater were best recalled underwater, and vice versa. A subsequent experiment shows that the disruption of moving from one environment to the other was unlikely to be responsible for context-dependent memory.

The philosopher John Locke cites the case of a young man who learned to dance in a room containing an old trunk. Unfortunately, however, 'the idea of this remarkable piece of household stuff had so mixed itself with the turns and steps of all his dances, that though in that chamber he could dance excellently well, yet it was only while that trunk was there; nor could he perform well in any other place unless that or some other trunk had its due place in the room' (Locke, cited in Dennis, 1948, p. 68).

The belief that what is learnt in a given environment is best recalled in that environment has of course been a useful standby for detective story writers from Wilkie Collins onwards, although the empirical evidence for such a belief is somewhat equivocal. Farnsworth (1934) and Pessin (1932) were both unable to obtain a context-dependent memory effect. A later study by Jensen *et al.* (1971) was more successful, but a recent unpublished study

by Hitch (personal communication) failed to observe any effect. An alternative approach to the context-dependent phenomenon utilizes a retroactive interference (RI) design in which material learned in one environment is followed by a second set of material presented in either the same or a different environment, which in turn is followed by a recall test on the original material. This final test itself may be in the initial environment or in the interpolated environment. Using this design, Bilodeau & Schlosberg (1951) found that an interpolated list caused only half as much RI when it was learned in a room differing markedly from that in which original learning took place. Comparable results were obtained by Greenspoon & Ranyard (1957), and by Zentall (1970). However, Strand (1970) has presented evidence suggesting that the inferior retention observed when the recall environment is different results not from the different context *per se*, but from the disruption that occurs when the subject moves from one environment to the other. She required the subjects in her control conditions, in which learning and recall were in the same environment, to leave the room and have a drink of water from a drinking fountain before beginning the recall phase of the experiment. Under these conditions she found no reliable difference between subjects who learned the interfering material in the same and those who learned in a different environment.

The evidence for context-dependent memory is therefore far from convincing. Furthermore, a number of the studies which have obtained effects have used extremely artificial environments, suggesting that any effect observed may not generalize beyond the conditions under which the experiment was run. Dallett & Wilcox (1968), in one of their conditions, required their subjects to stand with their heads inside an oddly shaped box containing flashing lights of different colours (two subjects had to be excused due to nausea), while in a further study Rand & Wapner (1967) strapped their subjects to a board which was then rotated so as to keep the subject either supine or erect. As Brunswik (1956) has pointed out, it is important for the psychologist to check the 'ecological validity' of his results by ensuring that they are applicable to the real world, and are not limited to the artificial conditions of the psychological laboratory. The experiments to be described are therefore concerned with investigating the phenomenon of context-dependent memory in two natural environments. Egstrom et al. (1972) observed that divers had considerable difficulty in recalling material learnt under water, and since recognition memory was not impaired in this way, they suggested that the defect was probably due to a context-dependent memory effect rather than to differential learning underwater. Unfortunately, since the appropriate controls were not included, such a conclusion was purely speculative. However, the underwater environment does present a particularly good example of a natural environment which differs dramatically from that on the surface. The diver underwater is weightless, has restricted vision, and subjectively is in an environment which is as different from the surface as any he is ever likely to experience. Divers were therefore asked to learn word lists both on land and underwater and subsequently recalled either on land (Dry) or underwater (Wet). Each diver performed under all four possible conditions: DD (Learn Dry, Recall Dry); DW (Learn Dry, Recall Wet); WW and WD. Should the phenomenon of context-dependent memory exist under these conditions, performance when learning and recall took place in the same environment (DD and WW) should be significantly better than when recall took place in a different environment to that of learning (DW and WD).

EXPERIMENT I
Method
Subjects

Eighteen subjects were tested, comprising 13 male and five female members of a university diving club.

Apparatus

Five lists of words, each consisting of 36 unrelated, different, two-and three-syllable words chosen at random from the Toronto word bank, were constructed and subsequently recorded on tape (see *Procedure*).

Two Diver Underwater Communication (DUC) sets were used. A DUC set consists of a surface-to-diver telephone cable, terminating in a bone transducer, which, placed on the diver's mastoid, enables both surface-to-diver and diver-to-surface communication. The two DUC sets were slightly amended such that taped material, monitored by the surface operator, could be presented directly to the subject using a cassette tape-recorder. Twin transducers on each set allowed two separate pairs of subjects to be tested during the same period. Weighted formica boards, sealed with fablon, enabled subjects to record responses in pencil both above and underwater. Subjects used standard SCUBA breathing apparatus and diving equipment of various designs dictated by personal preference.

Procedure

All instructions and stimuli for each experimental session were recorded on tape. Efficient auditory perception of stimuli by a submerged diver using SCUBA apparatus is seriously impaired by the noise of his breathing. The presentation of the material was therefore grouped, so as to allow the diver to adopt a comfortable breathing rate which did not interfere with his auditory perception. Thus, each list was presented in blocks of three words. Within each block, the words were spaced at 2 sec. intervals. Between each block, a 4 sec. interval enabled subjects to exhale, inhale and hold their breath in readiness for the presentation of the next block, and so on.

Each tape began with an explanation of this breathing procedure, followed by a 'breathing pattern' section, to ensure that subjects were breathing correctly and in rhythm before the first word of the list appeared. This section consisted of nine spoken presentations of the letter *z*, in three blocks of three, and with identical spacings to those of the words in the list itself. Immediately after each block of *z*'s, subjects heard the command 'breathe'. The presentation of the word list followed on naturally in rhythm, and the command to breathe was then dropped.

On each tape (one for each of the 16 condition/list combinations), the relevant list was presented twice. Between the first and second presentations, a gap of 10 sec. allowed subjects a short rest with unconstrained breathing. The second presentation was again preceded by the breathing pattern section.

To eliminate possible primary memory effects, the second presentation of each list was followed by 15 digits which subjects were required to copy at a rate of two seconds per digit. This was followed by the next instruction (e.g. 'Ascend to the shore station'), and a 4 min. delay. This recurred in all conditions and was necessary to enable subjects to comply safely with the relevant instruction. They were then instructed to write down in any order as many of the words from the list as they could remember. Two minutes were allowed for this, after which the session was terminated.

The original 16 subjects were split at random into four groups of four. Prior to the first experimental session, all subjects underwent a practice session, comfortably seated around a table. During this, they first practised the breathing technique, then the task itself, using a practice list.

Pairings of the remaining four lists $L_1...L_4$ with the four conditions, and the temporal orderings of the conditions for each of the four groups, were arranged according to a Graeco-Latin square design. Subjects experienced one condition per diving session, and the sessions were separated by approximately 24 hr. The design was such that each group experienced conditions and lists in different orders, that a given condition/list pair was never administered to more than one group, and that lists and conditions had equal representation on each experimental session.

Testing took place at open water sites near Oban, Scotland, in most cases as soon as subjects returned from their scheduled dive for the day. The latter consideration helped to ensure that subjects began each session in roughly the same state, that is, wet and cold. They were tested in pairs which remained the same across all sessions.

Subjects in environment D (Dry) sat by the edge of the water, masks tipped back, breathing tubes removed, and receivers in place. In environment W (Wet), subjects dived to approximately 20 ft., taking with them their formica board and two pencils, and with their receivers in position. Heavy weighting enabled them to sit on the bottom, and the session began after a verbal signal to the surface operator signified their readiness.

Due to a series of technical difficulties, two subjects were eventually dropped from the programme. They were subsequently replaced by another pair who were tested at a freshwater site.

Results

Mean recall scores and standard deviations: An analysis of variance showed there to be no significant main effect on recall performance due to either the environment of learning or that of recall. The interaction between the effect of learning and recall environment was, however, highly significant ($F = 22\cdot0$; d.f. = 1, 12; $P = < 0\cdot001$). Thus the effect on recall of the environment of recall depended on the environment of original learning. No other interactions proved significant. Finally, to look in more specific detail at the data, a Wilcoxon matched-pairs, signed-ranks test showed that, for learning in environment D, recall in environment D was better than recall in environment W ($P < 0\cdot005$) while for learning in environment W, recall in W was better than recall in D ($P < 0\cdot025$). There was no significant difference in recall between conditions DD and WW, nor between conditions DW and WD.

Discussion

The results of Expt. I are clearly in line with the context-dependent memory hypothesis: what was learned under water was best recalled under water and vice versa. Before accepting a context-dependent interpretation, however, some possible shortcomings of the experiment should be considered. The divers were on a pleasure-diving holiday at the time of the experiment, and it is entirely due to their good will in agreeing to participate, and tolerance in accepting the subsequent demands of the experiment that the latter was completed at all. Nevertheless, since the divers were in no way committed to the experiment, some limitations on what could reasonably be done were experienced. Thus, there was no control over the time of day at which subjects were tested. In addition the experiment had to be run each day at the diving site chosen by the subjects, rather than at a constant location. Diving expeditions are notoriously difficult to organize and run smoothly. In an equipment-intensive operation which depends strongly on such local conditions as weather, fitness, etc., something will usually disrupt planned routine. Some divers may not, for medical reasons, dive each day. A dive may have to be aborted due to equipment failure, and so on. These problems were experienced to some degree, as was the unexpected. One diver was nearly run over during an underwater experimental session by an ex-army, amphibious DUKW. Thus it proved impossible to complete the session in four successive days, and the time between sessions varied both within and between subjects. None the less, under realistic open water conditions, and even subject to the above problems, a highly significant interaction between the environment of learning and that of recall emerged.

Before concluding that this result reflects the effect of context-dependent memory three alternative explanations should be considered. The first of these assumes differential cheating between the four conditions, with subjects in the WW group copying items down before the recall signal. Unfortunately, since it was not practicable to combine monitoring of both the subject and the shore station, this is a logical possibility. It is, however, unlikely for the following reasons; (1) had this been the case, higher level of WW performance might have been expected unless subjects were cheating in a particularly restrained manner; (2) it would be difficult to cheat without the awareness and connivance of one's diving partner; and (3) this particular group of subjects had virtually all had previous involvement in an underwater research project of their own, several were in fact research scientists, and social pressures against cheating would be considerable. Nevertheless, differential, restrained collaborative cheating remains a possible explanation. The second alternative explanation assumes that subjects rehearse during the unfilled interval between presentation and test, the degree of rehearsal being greater in the WW and DD conditions than in WD and DW, where subjects might be expected to be distracted by the procedure of getting into or out of the water. Thirdly, there has been a

suggestion (Strand, 1970) that context-dependent effects may not be due to environmental change *per se*, but instead to disruption caused by taking the subject from one environment to the other in the context-change conditions. Thus further discussion of the apparent context-dependent effect found here will be postponed until after the report of the next experiment.

EXPERIMENT II

This tests both the differential rehearsal and disruption hypotheses by comparing the standard DD condition used in Expt. I with a modified DD condition in which subjects are required to enter the water and dive during the 4 min. delay between presentation and the subsequent dry test. Both the differential rehearsal and disruption hypotheses should predict poorer retention in this condition, whereas a context-dependent hypothesis would not predict a decrement, since both learning and recall occur in the same environment.

Method
Subjects

Sixteen members of the Scottish Sub-Aqua Club served as voluntary subjects.

Apparatus

Subjects when in the water breathed using a snorkel tube, since this was administratively more convenient than SCUBA equipment. For the limited diving involved the two types of equipment may be regarded as equivalent. All other apparatus including word lists was the same as for Expt. I.

Procedure

As before, stimuli and instructions were all presented via tape. In condition *n* (non-disrupted), tapes employing the relevant lists under condition DD for Expt. I were used. For condition d, (disrupted), the disruption instruction (to enter the water, swim a short distance, dive to approximately 20 ft., and return to the original position) was dubbed on to copies of the above tapes.

Subjects were assigned randomly to four groups as they volunteered. Prior to the experimental session, subjects practised the task and were then tested at an open water diving site near Oban, Scotland, immediately on their return from their scheduled day's dive.

A within-subject design was adopted. Groups 1 and 2 experienced condition *n* on the first session while groups 3 and 4 were presented first with condition d. List *A* occurred on the first session and List *B* on the second, for groups 1 and 3; List *B* was used on the first session and List *A* on the second, for groups 2 and 4. The two sessions were separated by approximately 24 hr.

Insufficient volunteers were found at Oban to complete the design. Consequently, a further three subjects from Stirling University were tested on a subsequent occasion at a freshwater site.

Results

In condition *n*, the mean number of words recalled was 8·44 (σ = 4·1), while condition *d* produced a mean recall score of 8·69 (σ = 3·2). The marginal difference, in the opposite direction to that predicted by the disruption hypothesis, did not approach significance.

DISCUSSION

Scores obtained in Expt. II were lower than those obtained during the comparable DD conditions of Expt. I. Two possible reasons for this arise. Considerable background noise from other nearby diving groups persisted at a relatively constant rate throughout the experiment; this was not generally the case in Expt. I. Furthermore, most of the volunteers, unlike Expt. I subjects (largely medical students), were unfamiliar with testing situations and experimental procedures. Whatever the reason, the criticism might arise that possible effects of disruption might be masked by a floor effect. However, the two mean scores, both between 8 and 9, represent about 25 per cent recall, a reasonable level at which one might expect an effect to be measurable if it exists. Secondly, if 'high scorers' are identified as those subjects who scored higher than the mean under either condition, it is found that this sub-group recalled a mean of 10·1 words in condition *n* and 10·4 in condition *d*, suggesting that the absence of a disruption effect characterizes

both high and low scores. Thus it can be concluded that under open water conditions similar to those for Expt. I, disruption was not a significant factor.

CONCLUSIONS

The effect of the environment or context of recall on performance depends upon the environment of learning. Recall is better if the environment of original learning is reinstated. This is unlikely to be due to disruption, and one can be reasonably confident that it is a truly context-dependent phenomenon. The results were obtained under real conditions, away from the laboratory, and using natural environments. The open water setting for the project limited the design such that two separate experiments were needed. However, within the limitations thus imposed, it appears that the phenomenon of context-dependent memory not only exists, but is robust enough to affect normal behaviour and performance away from the laboratory.

We acknowledge the invaluable help rendered by the Clydebank, East Kilbride, and Stirling University Sub-Aqua Clubs. In particular we would like to thank the United London Hospitals Diving Group. The experiment was supported by a grant from the Medical Research Council.

REFERENCES

BILODEAU, I. M. & SCHLOSBERG, H. (1951). SIMILARITY IN STIMULATING CONDITIONS AS A VARIABLE IN RETROACTIVE INHIBITION. *J. EXP. PSYCHOL.* **41**, 119–204.

BRUNSWIK, E. (1956). *PERCEPTION AND THE REPRESENTATIVE DESIGN OF PSYCHOLOGICAL EXPERIMENTS.* BERKELEY: UNIVERSITY OF CALIFORNIA PRESS.

DALLETT, K. & WILCOX, S. G. (1968). CONTEXTUAL STIMULI AND PROACTIVE INHIBITION. *J. EXP. PSYCHOL.* **78**, 475–480.

DENNIS, W. (ED.) (1948). READINGS IN THE HISTORY OF PSYCHOLOGY. NEW YORK: APPLETON-CENTURY-CROFTS.

EGSTROM, G. H., WELTMAN, G., BADDELEY, A. D., CUCCARO, W. J. & WILLIS, M. A. (1972). UNDERWATER WORK PERFORMANCE AND WORK TOLERANCE. REPORT NO. 51, BIO-TECHNOLOGY LABORATORY, UNIVERSITY OF CALIFORNIA, LOS ANGELES.

FARNSWORTH, P. R. (1934). EXAMINATIONS IN FAMILIAR AND UNFAMILIAR SURROUNDINGS. *J. SOC. PSYCHOL.* **5**, 128–129.

GREENSPOON, J. & RANYARD, R. (1957). STIMULUS CONDITIONS AND RETROACTIVE INHIBITION. *J. EXP. PSYCHOL.* **53**, 55–59.

JENSEN, L. C. HARRIS, K. & ANDERSON, D. C. (1971). RETENTION FOLLOWING A CHANGE IN AMBIENT CONTEXTUAL STIMULI FOR SIX AGE GROUPS. *DEV. PSYCHOL.* **4**, 394–399.

PESSIN, J. (1932). THE EFFECT OF SIMILAR AND DISSIMILAR CONDITIONS UPON LEARNING AND RELEARNING. *J. EXP. PSYCHOL.* **15**, 427–435.

RAND, G. & WAPNER, S. (1967). POSTURAL STATUS AS A FACTOR IN MEMORY. *J. VERB. LEARN, VERB. BEHAV.* **6**, 268–271.

STRAND, B. Z. (1970). CHANGE OF CONTEXT AND RETROACTIVE INHIBITION. *J. VERB. LEARN, VERB. BEHAV.* **9**, 202–206.

ZENTALL, T. R. (1970). EFFECTS OF CONTEXT CHANGE ON FORGETTING IN RATS. *J. EXP. PSYCHOL.* **86**, 440–448.

Confidence, not Consistency, Characterizes Flashbulb Memories

J.M. TALARICO AND D.C. RUBIN

Abstract—*On September 12, 2001, 54 Duke students recorded their memory of first hearing about the terrorist attacks of September 11 and of a recent everyday event. They were tested again either 1, 6, or 32 weeks later. Consistency for the flashbulb and everyday memories did not differ in both cases declining over time. However, ratings of vividness, recollection, and belief in the accuracy of memory declined only for everyday memories. Initial visceral emotion ratings correlated with later belief in accuracy, but not consistency, for flashbulb memories. Initial visceral emotion ratings predicted later posttraumatic stress disorder symptoms. Flashbulb memories are not special in their accuracy, as previously claimed, but only in their perceived accuracy.*

Flashbulb memories are extremely vivid, long-lasting memories for unexpected, emotionally laden, and consequential events. Historical events that have led to flashbulb memories include the assassinations of Abraham Lincoln (Colgrove, 1899), John F. Kennedy (Brown & Kulik, 1977), Martin Luther King, Jr. (Brown & Kulik, 1977), and Olof Palme (Christianson, 1989); the resignation of Margaret Thatcher (Conway et al., 1994); the space-shuttle *Challenger* explosion (Neisser & Harsch, 1992); and the O.J. Simpson murder-trial verdict (Schmolck, Buffalo, & Squire, 2000). The terrorist attacks on the United States on September 11, 2001, the focus of this study, are the latest events to evoke flashbulb memories. The properties of flashbulb memories, what causes their occurrence, the accuracy of the memories, and the influence of emotion on them have all come into question (Winograd & Neisser, 1992).

We chose the following as the most important and tractable questions we could ask about the phenomenon of flashbulb memory. Compared with everyday memories from the same time, are flashbulb memories more consistent? Do participants have a greater sense of recollection and vividness of flashbulb memories, as well as greater belief in their accuracy? What effect does the emotional impact have on the differences observed? In what ways do the properties of flashbulb and everyday memories differ?

One critical issue is the assumption that "people remember these sorts of public negative emotional events better than ordinary events that occurred equally long ago" (Christianson, 1992, p. 194). In a symposium on flashbulb memories organized by Winograd and Neisser (1992), the need to empirically test this assumption was identified by both Rubin (1992) and Brewer (1992), who both noted that many conclusions drawn by previous research were limited by the omission of such a control. Therefore, to obtain a fair representation of nonflashbulb autobiographical memories from the same time period as the flashbulb memories of the September 11 attacks, we asked participants to identify and report an everyday event from the days preceding the attacks to serve as a control memory. A range of days was necessary to ensure that participants could select a sufficiently

Jennifer M. Talarico and David C. Rubin, "Confidence, Not Consistency, Characterizes Flashbulb Memories," *Psychological Science*, vol. 14, no. 5, pp. 455-461. Copyright © 2003 by Sage Publications. Reprinted with permission.

memorable event; we decided on a maximum difference of 3 days between the everyday event and the flashbulb events, as we considered this difference to be inconsequential compared with the length of the retention intervals. These intervals varied across participants, but each individual was tested immediately after the attacks and once later. It is difficult to assess the objective accuracy of autobiographical memory; however, consistency is measurable and is a necessary (though not sufficient) condition for accuracy. Inconsistencies imply that at least one report is inaccurate.

There are also distinct properties associated with flashbulb memories, such as increased recollection, exceptional vividness, greater belief in their accuracy, and enhanced rehearsal (Rubin & Kozin, 1984). We therefore assessed recollection, vividness, belief in accuracy, and rehearsal for both flashbulb and everyday memories using rating-scale questions. Of particular interest is the role of emotion in flashbulb memories. Christianson (1992), Gold (1992), and Reisberg and Heuer (1992) all argued that emotion's effect on memory can account for most of the flashbulb memory phenomenon. Therefore, we had participants rate visceral and emotional reactions during both recall sessions and complete a measure of posttraumatic stress disorder (PTSD) symptoms at the second session (Weathers, Litz, Huska, & Keane, 1994).

METHOD

Participants

On September 12, 2001, Duke students were contacted and tested for their memory of hearing about the terrorist attacks on the United States the previous morning. They were then randomly assigned to one of three follow-up sessions scheduled within the limits of the academic calendar to produce roughly equal steps on a logarithmic scale (Rubin & Wenzel, 1996). The first group of 18 participants (4 of whom were male; $M = 18.67$ years) was tested 7 days (1 week) later, the second group of 18 (6 of whom were male; $M = 17.78$ years) was tested 42 days (6 weeks) after the initial event, and the last group of 18 (4 of whom were male; $M = 19.11$ years) was tested 224 days (32 weeks) after the event. Participants were compensated with class credit or $10.

Open-Ended Questionnaires

At each experimental session, participants were asked a series of open-ended questions. The first set of questions asked specifically about how the participant heard of the terrorist attacks on the United States on Tuesday, September 11, 2001, and the second set asked about an everyday event from the participant's life in the days prior to the attacks. For the September 11 memories, we asked: "Who or what first told you the information?" "When did you first hear the news?" "Where were you when you first heard the news?" "Were there others present, and if so, who?" "What were you doing immediately before you first heard the news?" and "Are there any other distinctive details from when you first heard the news?" For everyday memories, we asked: "What was the event?" "When did this event occur?" "Where were you, physically?" "Were there others present, and if so, who?" "What were you, personally, doing?" and "Are there any other distinctive details from the event?" Three blank lines followed each question. For the everyday event, the participant was also asked to provide a two-to three-word description that could serve as a cue for that unique event in the future. The types of events listed for the everyday memory were typical for the life of an average college student (e.g., parties, sporting events, and studying).

Autobiographical Memory Questionnaire

In addition, for each of these events, participants were asked to complete the Autobiographical Memory Questionnaire, a rating-scale measure that was designed to assess various properties of autobiographical memory (Sheen, Kemp, & Rubin, 2001).

Key properties

Recollection of the event and belief that the event occurred as remembered are the definitive properties of autobiographical memory according to Brewer (1986, 1995), Conway (1995), and Rubin (1995), among others. We created a *recollection* measure by collapsing responses to questions about how much "I feel as though I am reliving" the experience (from 1, *not at all*, to 7, *as clearly as if it were happening now*) and "while remembering the event now,

I feel that I travel back to the time it happened" (from 1, *not at all*, to 7, *completely*). A composite measure of *belief* was obtained by averaging responses to questions asking whether the participants "believe the event in my memory really occurred in the way I remember it" (from 1, *100% imaginary*, to 7, *100% real*) and whether they could be persuaded that their memory of the event "was wrong" (from 1, *not at all*, to 7, *completely*; reverse scored). Participants rated how much they could "see it in my mind," "hear it in my mind," and "know the setting where it occurred" (from 1, *not at all*, to 7, *as clearly as if it were happening now*). Following the flashbulb memory literature (Brown & Kulik, 1977; Rubin & Kozin, 1984), we averaged these responses into one *vividness* measure. We also asked participants whether they "actually remember it rather than just knowing it happened" (from 1, *not at all*, to 7, *completely*); this was our *remember/know* measure.

Language and narrative

The participants were asked if the memory came "in words or pictures as a coherent *story* or episode and not as an isolated fact, observation, or scene"; *"in pieces* with missing bits"; and *"in words"*; and whether it was "based on details *specific* to my life, not on general knowledge that I would expect most people to have" (all rated from 1, *not at all*, to 7, *completely*).

Emotion

Because emotion is considered by some researchers to be the "special mechanism" that explains the flashbulb memory phenomenon, we looked at various emotional aspects of the participants' memories. One question asked participants to rate the current emotional *intensity* of the memory (from 1, *not at all*, to 7, *extremely*). We also asked participants if they felt the emotions "as strongly as I did then" (*same intensity*: from 1, *not at all*, to 7, *as clearly as if it were happening now*). Similarly, we asked participants if they felt "the same particular emotions I felt at the time of the event" (*same emotion*: from 1, *completely different*, to 7, *identically the same*). There were also four questions that asked about current visceral responses to the memory: "I feel my heart pound or race," "I feel tense all over," "I feel sweaty or clammy," and "I feel knots, cramps, or butterflies in my

stomach" (all rated from 1, *not at all*, to 7, *more than for any other memory*). Responses to these last four questions were averaged to form a global *visceral-response* measure. Finally, current *valence* of the memory was assessed by averaging responses to a scale of positive emotional tone and reverse-scored responses to a scale of negative emotional tone (both originally scored from 1, *not at all*, to 7, *entirely*).

Other features

Finally, we examined ways of remembering. Because participants often poorly judge the objective frequency of occurrence of past behaviors (Fiedler & Armbruster, 1994; Parducci, 1968), we had them use relative rating scales to measure rehearsal rates, rather than estimate the number of past rehearsals. Participants rated how often they "thought about" and "talked about" the event and how often it came to them "out of the blue, without my trying to think about it" (from 1, *not at all*, to 7, *more than for any other memory*). These ratings were then collapsed into a total *rehearsal* measure. *Field versus observer* modes of remembering were assessed with one question asking participants if they saw the event "out of my own eyes rather than those of an outside observer" (from 1, *not at all*, to 7, *completely*).

Second Session

The second session was identical to the first except that the everyday event was cued with the brief description individuals provided at the initial session, whereas the flashbulb event was cued with the same phrase as at the initial session ("how you first heard about the news of the attacks on America on Tuesday, September 11, 2001"). Also, all participants were asked to complete the PTSD Checklist for a Specific Experience (PCL-S), a short survey designed to assess PTSD symptoms (Weathers et al., 1994).

Data Scoring

The recall data were scored by two independent raters who counted the number of details provided. A detail was generally any noun, verb phrase, or unique modifier. Consistency scores for the free-recall portion of the experiment were based on coding guidelines developed from earlier, independent coding attempts. In general, coders marked details as *consistent* if participants used the same or similar words to describe the same real-world entity. For example, if a participant initially said "a friend" was with him and later said "Sue" was with him, these details would have been marked consistent. Those details that were directly contradictory (the majority of the inconsistent cases) or that could not refer to the same real-world entity were marked as *inconsistent*. For example, it would be inconsistent for a participant to say initially that "Mike" was with him and say later that "Sue" was with him. Saying that "Mike" was present initially and "Mike and Sue" were present later would be scored as one consistent and one inconsistent detail. Disagreements in coding were resolved by discussion. Reliability between the two coders for the number of details recorded was 96% for the flashbulb memories and 97% for the everyday memories, based on a subset of 22 reports.

RESULTS

The measures of recall consistency showed no difference between flashbulb and everyday memories as a function of the passage of time and the lack of interactions between memory type (flashbulb vs. everyday) and the passage of time (session, group, and their interaction). The two kinds of memory did differ in their phenomenological properties, however. Furthermore, the interactions between memory type and the passage of time were nearly zero for the recall questions, but were significant for several of the rated properties of the memories. Language-narrative and emotions (with the exception of a floor effect in ratings of visceral emotions for the everyday event) showed only a main effect of memory type, with flashbulb memories higher in narrative coherence, less fragmented, of greater emotional intensity, and of more negative valence.

Consistency

The primary question of interest was whether flashbulb memories are more consistent over time than everyday memories. The mean numbers of consistent and inconsistent details were similar for flashbulb and everyday memories and followed the same pattern over time. A repeated measures analysis of variance (ANOVA) analyzed

the effects of three factors on the number of consistent and inconsistent details: memory type (flashbulb vs. everyday), session (first vs. second, collapsing all three delay periods), and group (second session 7 vs. 42 vs. 224 days after the first session).

For total number of inconsistent details, the effect of session was omitted because there could not be an inconsistent detail at the first session. Memory decayed over time, as shown by both decreasing number of consistent details and by increasing number of inconsistent details; this was true for both flashbulb memories and memories of everyday events. For both kinds of memories, at most 25% of the consistent details at any time period came from the same individual recall question, so these results were not driven by any one category of response. For each of the seven recall questions, there was a significant effect of session for consistent responses and no interaction with memory type. In contrast, responses to the question asking about "distinctive details" contributed 42% of the inconsistent details across all time periods for both flashbulb and everyday memories. Brown and Kulik (1977) emphasized the persistence of seemingly irrelevant details in flashbulb memories, whereas we more often found that individuals listed different details at different times.

Flashbulb memories are not immune to forgetting, nor are they uncommonly consistent over time. This seems to be strong evidence for the absence of a special mechanism for the consistency of flashbulb memories. Instead, exaggerated belief in memory's accuracy at long delays, belief that is unrelated to true memory consistency, is what may have led to the conviction, even among some researchers, that flashbulb memories are more accurate than everyday memories.

Key Properties

Levels of recollection, belief, remember/know, and vividness remained high and constant for flashbulb memories, but decreased over time for everyday memories. Using ANOVAs of the same design as for recall, we examined ratings of various properties of the memories. There were main effects of session and memory type for recollection, belief, remember/know, and vividness; each of these measures also showed a memory-type-by-session interaction, and for belief there was an additional three-way interaction. Thus, participants (erroneously, but reliably) believed that their memories for September 11 were more consistent than everyday memories, a belief that may have been supported by similar patterns of judgments of recollection, remember/know, and vividness.

Language and Narrative

Memory type, session, and group also affected the language and narrative aspects of the memories. Flashbulb memories came as more coherent stories than everyday memories ($M = 4.68$ vs. $M = 3.61$) and were less likely to come in pieces ($M = 3.29$ vs. $M = 4.53$), counter to what would be expected for traumatic memories (Berntsen, Willert, & Rubin, in press).

Other Features

Results for rehearsal were consistent with assumptions in the early studies of flashbulb memory (e.g., Brown & Kulik, 1977): Participants rehearsed flashbulb events more than everyday memories ($M = 5.23$ vs. $M = 2.46$), and the ratings of rehearsal for both kinds of memories combined decreased with time, from 4.23 initially to 3.93, 3.58, and 2.85, at the three delays.

There was a memory-type-by-session interaction for mode of remembering. As in previous research, the feeling of seeing a memory through the eyes of an outside observer increased over time for everyday memories (Nigro & Neisser, 1983); for flashbulb memories, participants' feeling of seeing a memory through their own eyes remained the same over time. Though the likelihood that participants saw the memory through their own eyes was slightly higher for everyday memories than flashbulb memories initially, over time, participants were much more likely to see the everyday memory through the eyes of an outside observer than to see the flashbulb memory from an observer's perspective.

Emotion

The most salient characteristic of emotion is valence, and, not surprisingly, participants rated the flashbulb memories as more negative in valence ($M = -1.89$) than the everyday

memories ($M = 0.61$). There was a main effect of memory type, but no other effects of session or of group, nor any interactions. This difference should not have affected our subsequent analyses on emotional contributions to memory phenomena, however, as Scott and Ponsoda (1996) studied flashbulb memories for negative and positive events and found no differences between them. Therefore, differences in intensity or emotional consistency should be independent from valence differences.

All other emotional variables had main effects of memory type and session, with means lower for everyday memories than for flashbulb memories and lower for delayed memories than for more immediate memories, except that there was no main effect of memory type for whether the same emotions were felt at recall as at the time of the event. There was an interaction between memory type and session for visceral and intensity ratings. Everyday memories ($M = 1.55$ for visceral, $M = 2.64$ for intensity) were initially rated as much lower than flashbulb memories ($M = 3.58$ for visceral, $M = 5.31$ for intensity) and so had less room to drop. But although there were differences between overall emotional investment for flashbulb and everyday memories, the emotional intensity, as measured by both direct intensity ratings and indirect visceral ratings, decreased over time for both.

Correlations Between Sessions

Last, we examined the effects of various characteristics at the time of the September 12 test on the key properties of memories at the second session. Although strong claims of causality cannot be drawn from this initial-measures-predict-delayed-measures analysis, it can provide insight into possible causal mechanisms. We report all significant correlations between the delayed measures of consistency, inconsistency, belief, and PTSD symptoms and the initial measures (other than belief). In order to remove the effects of differential delay on consistency, we made the means for all groups the same by adding 1.78 and 1.93, for flashbulb and everyday memories, respectively, to all participants' consistency measures in the 6-week group; we added 2.67 and 3.15, respectively, to all participants' consistency measures in the 32-week group. For inconsistency, the effects of delay were removed by adding –0.44, 0, –1.38, and –1.67, respectively.

For the everyday memories, the results are simple: Belief ratings at the delayed test correlated with whether the memory came in pieces on the initial test ($r = -.30, p < .05$). For the flashbulb memories, there were several effects. Number of inconsistencies was correlated with whether the memory came initially as a coherent story and whether the memory came initially in pieces ($r = -.32, p < .05$, and $r = .36, p < .01$, respectively); these results are consistent with the intuition that with less initial coherence and more initial fragmentation, one finds greater inconsistencies later. Contrary to what the literature suggests should be the case (Christianson, 1992; Pillemer, 1984, 1992; Reisberg, Heuer, McLean, & O'Shaughnessy, 1988), no initial ratings, including measures of emotion, correlated with later consistency. Belief at the delayed test was correlated with initial measures of visceral ratings ($r = -.31, p < .05$) and with whether the memory came in pieces ($r = -.35, p < .05$), was remembered versus known ($r = .45, p < .001$), was specific to the participant's own life ($r = .33, p < .05$), and was often rehearsed ($r = .29, p < .05$). Initial visceral response to the flashbulb event was significantly correlated with higher ratings on the PCL-S ($r = .48, p < .001$), the measure of PTSD symptoms we used. Initial valence rating for flashbulb memories was also significantly correlated with PCL-S scores ($r = -.28, p < .05$). Taken together, these results indicate that the more negative the initial reaction, and the more that reaction is felt viscerally, the more PTSD symptoms one will display later.

DISCUSSION

Our design enabled us to draw new conclusions about flashbulb memories because we began testing within 1 day of the flashbulb memory event and then tested each group only once after that, spacing the intervals for the different groups to determine the time course for forgetting. The relative immediacy of the initial report allowed us to see the emergence of inconsistent reports in a way that initial reports obtained well after the event may not (Winningham, Hyman, & Dinnel, 2000). We found a roughly logarithmic decline in consistent details over time for both flashbulb and everyday memories. Our design also eliminated most of the concerns associated with retesting because the 1-week, 6-week, and 32-week groups were independent, so those participants at the

longest retention interval did not benefit from forced rehearsal due to repeated testing.

Brown and Kulik (1977) introspected, "What else can one remember from 1963?" (p. 74), and assumed that their participants' memories were accurate. They then focused on explaining this increased accuracy, not on empirically testing whether their assumption was accurate. We were not the first to attempt to verify this assumption. However, earlier studies did not time-match the everyday event with the flashbulb event (Christianson, 1989; Larsen, 1992), did not comparably cue the everyday and flashbulb events (Christianson, 1989), did not obtain an initial report soon after the flashbulb event occurred (Christianson, 1989), did not compare the flashbulb memory with another autobiographical memory (Bohannon, 1988; Bohannon & Symons, 1992), compared the flashbulb memory with memory for an everyday event that participants were instructed to encode especially well (Weaver, 1993), or used only the researcher as a subject (Larsen, 1992). Weaver (1993) compared consistency and confidence in accuracy for a flashbulb memory and memory for a specially encoded everyday event, and reported results similar to ours.

Another property of flashbulb memories often considered crucial is emotion. In the present study, neither visceral nor emotional ratings related to consistency, as one would have expected from previous literature. However, of all the emotion variables, only visceral ratings correlated with later belief in the accuracy of the flashbulb memories. Presumably, on-line physiological measures would be the best predictors of later belief in the accuracy of flashbulb memories, but even self-ratings of visceral responses were more predictive than were straightforward evaluations of intensity for flashbulb memories. Because this was the first flashbulb memory study we know of to ask about visceral reactions, including other measures of visceral reaction would be a useful addition for future experiments.

We have no evidence that any of our participants suffered PTSD as a result of the events of September 11. Nonetheless, our results may be relevant to the literature on PTSD. First, we found that of the measures taken 1 day after the event, ratings of visceral reactions best predicted PTSD symptoms at the delayed session, suggesting that a fear reaction may be crucial to developing PTSD symptoms. Second, we found that the stressful event was rated as more coherent than the everyday event through all intervals, counter to what most people would expect for a potentially traumatic event (Berntsen et al., in press).

The dissociation between belief in the accuracy of memory and consistency of memory that we found in flashbulb memory reports is not uncommon. McCloskey, Wible, and Cohen (1988); Neisser (1982); Neisser and Harsch (1992); Weaver (1993); Wright (1993); and Schmolck et al. (2000), among others, have all discussed the inconsistencies and errors in flashbulb memory reports. Nor is the association of vividness with belief uncommon. Neisser and Harsch (1992) found that although confidence and accuracy were not related, confidence and imagery were. Johnson and Raye (1981) theorized that individuals rely on the presence of perceptual details to make metamemory judgments accurately. Bell and Loftus (1989) found that including even a small number of seemingly insignificant details will increase the perceived accuracy of a verbal report. Brown and Kulik's (1977) approach provides an example of the frequent confusion of confidently reported stories that include lots of details with objectively accurate memories. The phenomenon they wanted to investigate was the seeming "live quality that is almost perceptual" (p. 74) that is instantly and permanently stored in memory. They assumed accuracy and did not test for consistency.

Our most consistent finding is that a flashbulb event reliably enhances memory characteristics such as vividness and confidence. The true "mystery," then, is not why flashbulb memories are so accurate for so long, as Brown and Kulik (1977) thought, but why people are so confident for so long in the accuracy of their flashbulb memories.

Acknowledgments—This study was funded by a National Defense Science and Engineering Graduate Fellowship awarded to the first author. We are grateful to the Duke University Institutional Review Board for their immediate attention to our request for testing; to Amy Needham and Ruth S. Day for allowing us to come into their classes on September 12, 2002, to recruit participants; and to Ray Tan, David Nguyen, and our other research assistants for helping to code the data. We would also like to thank Simon T. Tonev, Dorthe Berntsen, Robert W. Schrauf, Kevin S. LaBar, Ulric Neisser, Eugene Winograd, and Neil Bohannon for their comments.

REFERENCES

Bell, B.E., & Loftus, E.F. (1989). Trivial persuasion in the courtroom: The power of (a few) minor details. *Journal of Personality and Social Psychology, 56,* 669–679.

Berntsen, D., Willert, M., & Rubin, D.C. (in press). Splintered memories or vivid landmarks? Reliving and coherence of traumatic memories in PTSD. *Applied Cognitive Psychology.*

Bohannon, J.N. (1988). Flashbulb memories of the space shuttle disaster: A tale of two theories. *Cognition, 29,* 179–196.

Bohannon, J.N., & Symons, V.L. (1992). Flashbulb memories: Confidence, consistency, and quantity. In E. Winograd & U. Neisser (Eds.), *Affect and accuracy in recall: Studies of "flashbulb" memories* (Vol. 4, pp. 65–91). New York: Cambridge University Press.

Brewer, W.F. (1986). What is autobiographical memory? In D.C. Rubin (Ed.), *Autobiographical memory* (pp. 25–49). New York: Cambridge University Press.

Brewer, W.F. (1992). The theoretical and empirical status of the flashbulb memory hypothesis. In E. Winograd & U. Neisser (Eds.), *Affect and accuracy in recall: Studies of "flashbulb" memories* (Vol. 4, pp. 274–305). New York: Cambridge University Press.

Brewer, W.F. (1995). What is recollective memory? In D.C. Rubin (Ed.), *Remembering our past: Studies in autobiographical memory* (pp. 19–66). New York: Cambridge University Press.

Brown, R., & Kulik, J. (1977). Flashbulb memories. *Cognition, 5,* 73–99.

Christianson, S.A. (1989). Flashbulb memories: Special, but not so special. *Memory & Cognition, 17,* 435–443.

Christianson, S.A. (1992). Do flashbulb memories differ from other types of emotional memories? In E. Winograd & U. Neisser (Eds.), *Affect and accuracy in recall: Studies of "flashbulb" memories* (Vol. 4, pp. 191–211). New York: Cambridge University Press.

Colgrove, F. (1899). Individual memories. *American Psychologist, 10,* 228–255.

Conway, M.A. (1995). Autobiographical knowledge and autobiographical memories. In D.C. Rubin (Ed.), *Remembering our past: Studies in autobiographical memory* (pp. 67–93). New York: Cambridge University Press.

Conway, M.A., Anderson, S.J., Larsen, S.F., Donnelly, C.M., McDaniel, M.A., McClelland, A.G.R., Rawles,

R.E., & LOGIE, R.H. (1994). THE FORMATION OF FLASH-BULB MEMORIES. *MEMORY & COGNITION, 22*, 326–343.

FIEDLER, K., & ARMBRUSTER, T. (1994). TWO HALFS MAY BE MORE THAN ONE WHOLE: CATEGORY-SPLIT EFFECTS ON FREQUENCY ILLUSIONS. *JOURNAL OF PERSONALITY AND SOCIAL PSYCHOLOGY, 66*, 24–36.

GOLD, P.E. (1992). A PROPOSED NEUROBIOLOGICAL BASIS FOR REGULATING MEMORY STORAGE FOR SIGNIFICANT EVENTS. IN E. WINOGRAD & U. NEISSER (EDS.), *AFFECT AND ACCURACY IN RECALL: STUDIES OF "FLASHBULB" MEMORIES* (VOL. 4, PP. 141–161). NEW YORK: CAMBRIDGE UNIVERSITY PRESS.

JOHNSON, M.K., & RAYE, C.L. (1981). REALITY MONITORING. *PSYCHOLOGICAL REVIEW, 88*, 67–85.

LARSEN, S.F. (1992). POTENTIAL FLASHBULBS: MEMORIES OF ORDINARY NEWS AS THE BASELINE. IN E. WINOGRAD & U. NEISSER (EDS.), *AFFECT AND ACCURACY IN RECALL: STUDIES OF "FLASHBULB" MEMORIES* (VOL. 4, PP. 32–64). NEW YORK: CAMBRIDGE UNIVERSITY PRESS.

MCCLOSKEY, M., WIBLE, C.G., & COHEN, N.J. (1988). IS THERE A SPECIAL FLASHBULB-MEMORY MECHANISM? *JOURNAL OF EXPERIMENTAL PSYCHOLOGY: GENERAL, 117*, 171–181.

NEISSER, U. (1982). SNAPSHOTS OR BENCHMARKS? IN U. NEISSER & I.E. HYMAN (EDS.), *MEMORY OBSERVED: REMEMBERING IN NATURAL CONTEXTS* (PP. 68–74). SAN FRANCISCO: WORTH PUBLISHERS.

NEISSER, U., & HARSCH, N. (1992). PHANTOM FLASHBULBS: FALSE RECOLLECTIONS OF HEARING THE NEWS ABOUT CHALLENGER. IN E. WINOGRAD & U. NEISSER (EDS.), *AFFECT AND ACCURACY IN RECALL: STUDIES OF "FLASHBULB" MEMORIES* (VOL. 4, PP. 9–31). NEW YORK: CAMBRIDGE UNIVERSITY PRESS.

NIGRO, G., & NEISSER, U. (1983). POINT OF VIEW IN PERSONAL MEMORIES. *COGNITIVE PSYCHOLOGY, 15*, 467–482.

PARDUCCI, A. (1968). THE RELATIVISM OF ABSOLUTE JUDGMENTS. *SCIENTIFIC AMERICAN, 219*, 84–90.

PILLEMER, D.B. (1984). FLASHBULB MEMORIES OF THE ASSASSINATION ATTEMPT ON PRESIDENT REAGAN. *COGNITION, 16*, 63–80.

PILLEMER, D.B. (1992). REMEMBERING PERSONAL CIRCUMSTANCES: A FUNCTIONAL ANALYSIS. IN E. WINOGRAD & U. NEISSER (EDS.), *AFFECT AND ACCURACY IN RECALL: STUDIES OF "FLASHBULB" MEMORIES* (VOL. 4, PP. 236–264). NEW YORK: CAMBRIDGE UNIVERSITY PRESS.

REISBERG, D., & HEUER, F. (1992). REMEMBERING THE DETAILS OF EMOTIONAL EVENTS. IN E. WINOGRAD & U. NEISSER (EDS.), *AFFECT AND ACCURACY IN RECALL: STUDIES OF "FLASHBULB"*

MEMORIES (VOL. 4, PP. 162–190). NEW YORK: CAMBRIDGE UNIVERSITY PRESS.

REISBERG, D., HEUER, F., MCLEAN, J., & O'SHAUGHNESSY, M. (1988). THE QUANTITY, NOT THE QUALITY, OF AFFECT PREDICTS MEMORY VIVIDNESS. *BULLETIN OF THE PSYCHONOMIC SOCIETY, 26*, 100–103.

RUBIN, D.C. (1992). CONSTRAINTS ON MEMORY. IN E. WINOGRAD & U. NEISSER (ED.), *AFFECT AND ACCURACY IN RECALL: STUDIES OF "FLASHBULB" MEMORIES* (VOL. 4, PP. 265–273). NEW YORK: CAMBRIDGE UNIVERSITY PRESS.

RUBIN, D.C. (1995). INTRODUCTION. IN D.C. RUBIN (ED.), *REMEMBERING OUR PAST: STUDIES IN AUTOBIOGRAPHICAL MEMORY* (PP. 1–15). NEW YORK: CAMBRIDGE UNIVERSITY PRESS.

RUBIN, D.C., & KOZIN, M. (1984). VIVID MEMORIES. *COGNITION, 16*, 81–95.

RUBIN, D.C., & WENZEL, A.E. (1996). ONE HUNDRED YEARS OF FORGETTING: A QUANTITATIVE DESCRIPTION OF RETENTION. *PSYCHOLOGICAL REVIEW, 103*, 734–760.

SCHMOLCK, H., BUFFALO, E.A., & SQUIRE, L.R. (2000). MEMORY DISTORTIONS DEVELOP OVER TIME: RECOLLECTIONS OF THE O.J. SIMPSON TRIAL VERDICT AFTER 15 AND 32 MONTHS. *PSYCHOLOGICAL SCIENCE, 11*, 39–45.

SCOTT, D., & PONSODA, V. (1996). THE ROLE OF POSITIVE AND NEGATIVE AFFECT IN FLASHBULB MEMORY. *PSYCHOLOGICAL REPORTS, 79*, 467–473.

SHEEN, M., KEMP, S., & RUBIN, D. (2001). TWINS DISPUTE MEMORY OWNERSHIP: A NEW FALSE MEMORY PHENOMENON. *MEMORY & COGNITION, 29*, 779–788.

WEATHERS, F.W., LITZ, B.T., HUSKA, J.A., & KEANE, T.M. (1994). *THE PTSD CHECKLIST (PCL).* (AVAILABLE FROM THE NATIONAL CENTER FOR PTSD, VA MEDICAL CENTER, 215 NORTH MAIN ST., WHITE RIVER JUNCTION, VT 05009–0001)

WEAVER, C.A., III. (1993). DO YOU NEED A "FLASH" TO FORM A FLASHBULB MEMORY? *JOURNAL OF EXPERIMENTAL PSYCHOLOGY: GENERAL, 122*, 39–46.

WINNINGHAM, R.G., HYMAN, I.E., JR., & DINNEL, D.L. (2000). FLASHBULB MEMORIES? THE EFFECTS OF WHEN THE INITIAL MEMORY REPORT WAS OBTAINED. *MEMORY, 8*, 209–216.

WINOGRAD, E., & NEISSER, U. (EDS.). (1992). *AFFECT AND ACCURACY IN RECALL: STUDIES OF "FLASHBULB" MEMORIES* (VOL. 4). NEW YORK: CAMBRIDGE UNIVERSITY PRESS.

WRIGHT, D.B. (1993). RECALL OF THE HILLSBOROUGH DISASTER OVER TIME: SYSTEMATIC BIASES OF "FLASHBULB" MEMORIES. *APPLIED COGNITIVE PSYCHOLOGY, 7*, 129–138.

CHAPTER 7
Memory Applications: Eyewitness Memory

Crime Investigation

Witnesses

EDIE GREENE, KIRK HEILBRUN, WILLIAM H. FORTUNE, AND MICHAEL T. NIETZEL

ORIENTING QUESTIONS

1. *What psychological factors contribute to the risk of mistaken identifications in the legal system?*

2. *How do courts regard the use of hypnotically refreshed memory? What procedures should he followed when hypnosis is used in a forensic setting?*

3. *How do jurors evaluate the testimony of eyewitnesses, and can psychologists help jurors understand the potential problems of eyewitness testimony?*

4. *Can memories for trauma he repressed, and if so, can these memories be recovered accurately?*

The tasks facing the police include investigating crimes and accumulating evidence so that suspects can be identified and arrested. Particularly at the early stages of an investigation, eyewitnesses to those crimes provide important information to police. In fact, sometimes they provide the only solid leads. According to a report from the National institute of justice (Department of Justice, 1999), approximately 75,000 defendants are implicated by eyewitnesses in the United States every year.

But in their attempts to solve crimes—and especially in their reliance on eyewitness observers—police and prosecutors face a number of challenges. Witnesses sometimes make mistakes in their reports to police. The police may pressure them to point the finger at a suspect; sometimes the desire to get a case "nailed down" overshadows the goal of discovering the truth. Hence, the reports of eyewitnesses can lead the police down blind alleys or cause them to arrest the wrong suspect, and the testimony of mistaken observers can lead to wrong verdicts by judges and juries.

The extent to which eyewitness errors create problems for the justice system (and for the people mistakenly identified!) has become increasingly apparent. Of the first 150 people who were exonerated on the basis of analysis of DNA found at the crime scene, approximately 70% had been identified incorrectly by seemingly honest, but mistaken eyewitnesses (Innocence Project, 2005). (The introduction of DNA testing procedures in the 1980s made it possible to take a new look at previously decided cases in which DNA-rich evidence such as blood and semen had been preserved. Unfortunately, only a small fraction of crimes have physical evidence left behind by perpetrators, and even when present, it often is not tested or is destroyed. Furthermore, on occasion, prosecutors have failed to release people from prison even when DNA tests confirmed that they were innocent.) Inaccurate eyewitness identifications account for more wrongful convictions than do false confessions, problems with snitches, and defective or fraudulent science combined (Innocence Project, 2005).

Concern about eyewitnesses' accuracy is not restricted to criminal cases or to the identification of persons (Wells & Loftus, 1984). The results of civil lawsuits are also often affected by the reports of eyewitnesses, and law enforcement officials know that eyewitness descriptions of unusual events cannot always be trusted. The potential unreliability of eyewitness accounts was a major reason why the FBI discounted the theory that the July 1996 explosion of TWA Flight 800 was caused by a missile fired from the ground. Agents doubted the accuracy of at least 20 eyewitness reports of a streak of light shooting skyward seconds before the plane exploded into pieces over the Atlantic Ocean, killing all 230 passengers. In similar fashion, investigators from the National Transportation Safety Board discounted eyewitness reports on the crash of American Airlines Flight 587 over Rockaway Beach, New York, a few months after 9/11 because those reports clashed with the results of the Board's investigation.

Many crimes have only one eyewitness. A rape, for example, is usually witnessed only by the victim, and the same is true for the sexual abuse of children. But eyewitness testimony, even from one person, can still be very convincing to a judge or jury. In fact, eyewitness testimony may be the least reliable but most persuasive form of evidence presented in court (Wells, Small, Penrod, Malpass, Fulero, & Brimacombe, 1998).

EXAMPLES OF MISTAKEN EYEWITNESS IDENTIFICATION

Cases of proven wrongful convictions based on faulty eyewitness testimony abound. The ordeal of Calvin C. Johnson, Jr., is a good example. Johnson, a college graduate with a degree in communications, a job with Delta Air Lines, and some petty crimes under his belt, spent 16 years behind bars for a rape he did not commit. And he is not alone. In fact, Johnson was the 61st person in the United States to be exonerated through the use of DNA testing. Tests in Johnson's case proved definitively that he could not have been the man who raped and sodomized a College Park, Georgia, woman in 1983. Yet the victim had picked Johnson out of a photographic lineup two weeks after her attack and identified him as the rapist at trial. The all-white jury convicted Johnson, who is black, despite the fact that forensic tests excluded him as the source of a pubic hair recovered from the victim's bed, and serology tests conducted on blood found at the scene were inconclusive. The jury also apparently chose to disregard the testimony of four alibi witnesses, including Johnson's fiancée, the fiancée's mother, his employer, and his mother, who claimed that Johnson was home asleep at the time. One of the jurors later stated that the victim's eyewitness testimony had been the most compelling evidence in the case.

One reason why such mistakes are so common is that when eyewitnesses make a tentative identification, police often stop investigating other leads and seek out further evidence that implicates the chosen suspect. This is an example of **confirmation bias**, whereby people look for, interpret, and create information that verifies an existing belief. In terms of eyewitness identification, the goal of finding the truth is submerged, often unintentionally, in the rush to find the cause of a crime. In Johnson's case, police pushed ahead with the case even after the victim picked someone else at a live lineup (conducted after the photographic lineup). She testified at trial that she had picked the wrong person at the lineup because looking at Johnson was too much for her: "I just pushed my eyes away and picked someone else," she reported (Boyer, 2000). (Calvin Johnson's book—entitled *Exit to Freedom*—chronicling his wrongful arrest, conviction, imprisonment, and eventual exoneration, was published by the University of Georgia Press in 2003.)

The Johnson case illustrates one type of eyewitness error—choosing the wrong person from a photographic lineup—but other sources of error also exist. Richard M. Nance (notice the middle initial *M*) was arrested in Los Angeles. His was not a very serious charge, but he was found guilty and sentenced to a brief jail term. In the midst of his ten-day sentence, a nationwide computerized crime network spat out the information that a Richard Lee Nance was being sought in Sonoma County, in northern California, on a burglary charge.

The Sonoma County Sheriff's Department warrant for Richard Lee Nance said he was born on July 3, 1946, was 5 feet 10 inches tall, and had brown hair and brown eyes. The L.A. prisoner's middle name was Marion, not Lee; he was born on July 6, 1946, not July 3; and his eyes were blue, not brown. Yet he was flown to Sonoma County and put in jail, with bail set at $5000. During the pretrial hearing, the burglary victim even pointed to Richard M. Nance and identified him as the man who had stolen a valuable ring and $100 from his farmhouse. Because Richard M. Nance was at the hearing, labeled as the defendant, the victim was quick to assume that Nance was the robber, even though his fingerprints differed from those left at the scene of the crime. As Nance said later, "I can laugh about it now

Thomas Lee Goldstein emerged from the black hell of the California Department of Corrections in April 2004 as a homeless, white-haired man of 55, clad only in a jail jumpsuit and cheap slippers, without a cent to his name. He had spent the previous 24 years in prison for a murder he did not commit, sent there through the false testimony of a supposed eyewitness to a 1979 murder in Long Beach and by a jury convinced of his guilt.

Over the years he was imprisoned, Goldstein slowly lost his sense of disbelief, bitterness, and even revenge fantasies until all he was left with was a sense of numbness (Broder, 2004). Sadly, even his exit from prison was numbing: His first stop was a Veteran's Administration office where he hoped to get a few clothes, some money, and a place to live. But the office computers were down, and officials could locate no record of his three years of service as a Marine. He drove away with his attorney, still homeless and penniless. When asked the next day how he spent his first night of freedom after nearly a quarter-century, Goldstein replied that he "called up an old girlfriend hoping for a day of wild sex. Of course, she wasn't home so I went to the law library instead."

Indeed, Goldstein had become quite a legal scholar in the years he spent behind bars, filing many petitions for his release and eventually earning a paralegal certificate. Those petitions caught the attention of a federal judge in 1996, and in 2002 a federal magistrate determined that Goldstein had been wrongly convicted and ordered him released. He now spends his days as a paralegal in a small Pasadena law firm, working with his attorney on a claim of wrongful imprisonment. In pondering the size of the claim, his attorney, Ronald Kaye, asks, "How do you really evaluate in financial, terms what 24 years of life are worth? He was locked up from age 30–55. He didn't get a chance to find a wife, have children, build a career I ask you, is $25 million enough? Is $50 million enough?" As for Goldstein, his "sustaining fantasy" is of a farm in Kansas: "I dream of owning a large plot of land in the Midwest with a house and a dog and a huge field of flowers and a grassy area. I want to just sit back there and look at the fields and fields of nothing, the antiprison" (Broder, 2004).

but can you believe me sitting there in the bright orange jail jumpsuit. Who else is the guy going to point to? The judge?" Despite the inconsistencies in name, appearance, and fingerprints, it took an investigator from the public defender's office almost a month to unravel the case and get Nance released from jail.

Nance asked rhetorically, "Who else is the witness going to point to?" but witnesses *have* sometimes pointed to the wrong person. In a trial in Washington, D.C., two different U.S. park police officers, on the witness stand, pointed to the defense attorney rather than the defendant when asked to identify the protester charged with assaulting a police officer. After the first witness erred, the defense attorney moved his note pad and papers in front of his client, who began to scribble furiously, thus contributing to the impression that the defendant was the attorney, and vice

versa. After the second misidentification, the government dropped the charges (Strasser, 1989).

You might suppose that people like Calvin Johnson and Richard M. Nance, who had been mistakenly identified and wrongly imprisoned, would have some recourse—that they could get something back for the time they lost in prison. (One wrongly convicted man, James Newsome, was awarded $15 million by a Chicago jury in 2001, $1 million for each of the 15 years Newsome was imprisoned for a 1979 slaying that he did not commit.) But Calvin Johnson received nothing for his years behind bars; Georgia does not have a law providing compensation for people who are wrongly imprisoned. In fact, the majority of people who are wrongly incarcerated get either nothing or a token sum from state compensation funds. One commentator has suggested that the new crime is how little these lost lives are worth (Higgins, 1999). The case of Thomas Lee Goldstein is illustrative (see Box 5.1)

POINTS AT WHICH A MISTAKEN EYEWITNESS IDENTIFICATION CAN OCCUR

Jurors in a criminal trial see a victim take the witness stand and confidently identify the defendant as his or her attacker. Not only may the jurors assume that this identification is accurate, but they are also likely to believe that the victim was just as confident about the initial description or identification. These assumptions fail to recognize the many problems that can undermine the accuracy of a criminal identification (Wells & Olson, 2003).

Mistakes in the process of identification can occur the moment the crime is committed. It may be too dark, events may move too swiftly; or the encounter may be too brief for the victim to perceive the incident accurately. Yet when they are questioned by police, victims are forced to rely on their impressions about the criminal's height, hair color, voice, and other identifying features. These impressions are sometimes translated into sketches of suspects, usually drawn by police artists.

Mistakes can also occur during the investigation of a crime. In cases that involve eyewitnesses, police often ask these witnesses to examine a series of photos (called a photo spread) or a physical lineup of suspects and decide whether the perpetrator is present. During this process, the police may coax reactions from eyewitnesses. At this point, eyewitnesses want to help the police solve the crime; they may feel implicit pressure to identify someone, even if the police do not explicitly encourage them to do so.

The study of eyewitness identification grew out of our understanding of the basic principles involved in perception and memory. All of us, as observers, are prone to making errors in perceiving and remembering events that we experience. But because eyewitnesses must remember experiences that are typically brief, complicated, and sometimes very frightening, they are especially prone to error. To illustrate these errors, we next consider the steps involved in acquiring information from the outside world and recalling it; the very steps that an eyewitness must take to record a moment in time.

BASIS INFORMATION PROCESSING PERCEPTION AND MEMORY

We have all had the experience of greeting someone we recognize, only to realize that we are mistaken—that the person is actually a stranger. Similar mistakes can be made when crime is observed. To process information about a crime, we must first perceive a stimulus and then retain it in our minds at least momentarily. Failures and errors can emerge at any step along the way.

Perception

Although our perceptual abilities are impressive (Penrod, Loftus, & Winkler, 1982), we do make errors. We tend to overestimate the height of criminals. We also overestimate the duration of brief events, although we underestimate the duration of prolonged incidents. When watching a short film, we notice more about the actions than about the persons doing the acting. Studies of change blindness suggest that our mental representations of visual scenes are sparse or incomplete and that people often fail to notice large changes in their visual worlds. For example, 50% of observers failed to notice when the person they were talking to was surreptitiously replaced by a different person as a doorframe was carried between them (Grimes, 1996; Simons & Ambinder, 2005).

Many factors affect our perceptual abilities. For example, if a weapon is present when a crime is committed, we may devote more attention to it than to the facial features or other physical aspects of the person who has the weapon. This **weapon focus effect** has been demonstrated even when people watch a film of a crime (Tooley, Brigham, Maass, & Bothwell, 1987). It appears to be caused not so much by emotional arousal as by the fact that witnesses narrow their attention to the weapon. This limits the amount of attention they can pay to other aspects of the situation, such as physical features of the perpetrator (Shaw & Skolnick, 1999). The weapon focus effect is particularly likely to occur in situations in which, the weapon is surprising and unexpected (Pickel, 1999).

The presence of a weapon can do more than interfere with the perception of visual information; it can affect the processing of auditory information, as well. Kerri Pickel and colleagues showed a film that depicted a man holding either a weapon (e.g., a gun, a switchblade knife) or a neutral object (e.g., a soda pop bottle; a retractable ballpoint pen) and speaking to a woman in such a way that his words were either easy or difficult to understand (Pickel, French, & Betts, 2003). Witnesses had difficulty understanding the man's speech in the latter condition, and the presence of a weapon worsened their comprehension. A reasonable explanation is that their focus on the weapon and their attempt at language comprehension competed for limited perceptual processing time. They had a hard time doing both things at once.

Memory

Experimental psychologists subdivide the building of a memory into three processes: encoding, storage, and retrieval. We describe the memory of eyewitnesses in each of these three stages.

Encoding

Encoding refers to the acquisition of information. Many aspects of a stimulus can affect how it is encoded; stimuli that are only briefly seen or heard cannot be encoded fully, of course. The complexity of a stimulus also affects its encoding, but the relationship is not a straightforward one. As the complexity of an event increases (consider an earthquake, explosion, or tsunami), some aspects of the event probably will be misremembered, while others will be accurately recalled.

Contrary to what many people believe, a stressful situation does not necessarily enhance the encoding of events. Although mild stress or arousal may indeed heighten alertness and interest in the task at hand, extreme stress usually causes the person to encode the information incompletely or inaccurately. Thus if a person is facing an excessively stressful situation, perception is narrowed, encoding is impaired, and less learning occurs than under mild levels of stress. Performance on many tasks is best when the level of arousal is sufficient to ensure adequate attention but not so high as to disrupt accuracy.

Although a number of studies have investigated what people remember about traumatic events, the studies are often criticized for their lack of intensity and real-world applicability. But a recent metaanalysis examined only those studies that involved actual differences in stress level as a function of the experimental manipulations

(Deffenbacher, Bornstein, Penrod, & McGorty 2004). This study combined the results of 27 tests of the effects of heightened stress on eyewitness identification and found support for the idea that high levels of stress negatively affect eyewitnesses' accuracy.

A recent study on the accuracy of eyewitness memory in highly stressful military survival school interrogations provides good evidence of the effects of stress on memory (Morgan et al., 2004). Survival school interrogations are one of the greatest training challenges that active duty military personnel ever experience. (These interrogations are intended to test one's ability to withstand exploitation by the enemy, and to train people to hold up under the physical and mental stresses of capture.)

Participants in this study were 500 soldiers, sailors, and pilots who were placed in mock POW camps and deprived of food and sleep for approximately 48 hours prior to interrogation. During 40 minutes of intense questioning, half of them were physically threatened and all participants were presented with the challenge of being tricked into giving away information. One day later, they were asked to identify their interrogators from an 8-picture photo spread (chance accuracy is therefore 1/8, or 12.5%). The results were startling. Among soldiers who experienced low stress (without the threat of physical injury), 76% were correct in identifying the target from among the photographs shown. By contrast, only 34% of participants who experienced the high stress of a physically threatening situation were correct; the majority incorrectly chose another person.

Characteristics of the witness also affect encoding. We all differ in visual acuity and hearing ability. When we have more experience perceiving a given kind of stimulus, we usually notice its details better than when perceiving it is a novel experience. This is why experienced judges notice flaws in a gymnast's performance that the rest of us can detect only in a slow-motion replay. Different expectancies about upcoming events also influence how they are subsequently perceived; in general, we have a tendency to see what we expect to see.

Storage

The second step in building a memory is the storage of stimulus information. How well do we retain what we encode? Many years ago, the experimental psychologist

Hermann Ebbinghaus showed that early memory loss is rapid. Lipton (1977) illustrated this phenomenon in a setting relevant to the concerns of this chapter. Participants were shown a film of an armed robbery and shooting without any prior knowledge that they would be serving as eyewitnesses. Those who were questioned after one week dredged up 18% less memory information than those who were questioned immediately after viewing the film.

A second phenomenon—a surprising and potentially disturbing one—also occurs during the storage phase. Activities that eyewitnesses carry out or information they learn after they observe an event, which is termed postevent inforaiatioia, can alter their memory of the event. For example, viewing mug shots or photographs of suspects can alter an eyewitness's capacity to recognize faces that he or she viewed before seeing the mug shots (Memon, Hope, Bartlett, & Bull, 2002). Attempting to reconstruct a perpetrator's face using a computer face-composite program (these programs permit eyewitnesses to select various facial features and combine them into an intact face) can also affect a witness' ability to later identify that perpetrator from a lineup (Wells, Charman, & Olson, 2005). In both of these examples, the new activity interferes with memory of the old. In similar fashion, simply providing an eyewitness with information about what other witnesses have already said influences the first witness's recollection (Shaw, Garven, & Wood, 1997).

A similar conclusion derives from the now-classic studies of Elizabeth Loftus (1975, 1979; reviewed in Loftus, 1992, 1993). In one of her projects, participants viewed a one-minute film of an automobile accident and were later asked a series of questions about it. The first question asked either how fast the car was going "when it ran the stop sign" or how fast it was going "when it turned right." Then, on the last question, all subjects were asked whether they had seen a stop sign in the film. In the first group, which had earlier been asked about the speed of the car "when it ran the stop sign," 53% said they had seen a stop sign, whereas only 35% of the second group said they had seen the sign. The effect of the initial question was to "prompt," or refresh, the memory for this part of the film. In a second study, Loftus included a misleading follow-up question that mentioned a nonexistent bam. When questioned one week later, 17% of the subjects reported seeing the barn in the original film! In essence, the new information that was conveyed simply as part of a question was added to the same memory store as the original stimulus.

Retrieval

The third and final step in establishing memory is the **retrieval** of information. This process is not as straightforward as you might think. For example, we all have experienced the "tip of the tongue" phenomenon, when we know an answer or a movie title or a person's name but can't dredge it out of our memory store. Once again, the wording of questions can influence output at the retrieval phase (Wells, Wright, & Bradfield, 1999). For example, consider the question "What was the man with the mustache doing with the young boy?" Assume that the man in question had no mustache. This form of the question may not affect the eyewitness's report of the man's actions, but it may influence memory of the man's appearance. Later, if asked to describe the man, eyewitnesses may incorporate the detail (in this case, the mustache) that was embedded in the original question (Loftus & Greene, 1980).

In recalling information from our memory store, we often generate memories that are, in a sense, accurate but are not relevant to the task at hand. For instance, victims sometimes pick from a lineup or a photo spread the face of a person whom they have seen before but who is not the actual criminal. For example, a clerk at a convenience store who is the victim of a late-night robbery may mistakenly identify an innocent shopper who frequents the store. In an actual case, a Los Angeles judge who was kidnapped and attacked while she was jogging picked a suspect's picture from the police mug book after the attack, and on that basis, he was charged with the crimes. She later stated that she had not remembered at first that he had appeared before her in court four years earlier, for similar offenses, and that she had sentenced him to unsupervised probation (Associated Press, 1988).

This phenomenon, called unconscious transference, was demonstrated experimentally by David Ross and his colleagues, who showed two versions of a filmed robbery to college student witnesses (Ross, Ceci, Dunning, & Toglia, 1994). Half of the witnesses saw the film with an innocent bystander in the background, and the other half saw the same film without the bystander. When witnesses were asked whether they could identify the robber from a lineup (in this particular lineup, the bystander was present but the assailant was missing), eyewitnesses in the first group were three times more likely to misidentify the bystander than eyewitnesses in the latter group. The majority of people who selected the bystander thought that the assailant and the bystander were the same person. This is one means by which innocent persons are sometimes charged with a crime and eventually convicted.

In summary, as Hall, Loftus, and Tousignant (1984) conclude, testing one's memory for an original event can alter the memory for that event; indeed, "the witness reacts as if original memory and post event information had been inextricably integrated" (p. 127).

DISTINGUISHING SYSTEM AND ESTIMATOR VARIABLES

Expanding from this research on basic information processing, psychologists have identified several other variables that can influence the validity of identifications. Professor Gary Wells, a prolific researcher in the area of eyewitness identification, introduced a useful dichotomy to categorize these variables (Wells, 1978). He coined the term system variable to refer to those factors that are under the control of the criminal justice system (for example, the instructions given to eyewitnesses when they consider a lineup or photo spread, and the composition of that lineup or photo spread). The term estimator variable refers to factors that are beyond the control of the justice system and whose impact on the reliability of the eyewitness can only be estimated (examples include the lighting conditions at the time of the crime and whether the culprit was wearing a disguise). Because system variables hold more promise for preventing errors in eyewitness identification (they are, after all, controllable), many psychologists have focused their research efforts on those variables. But research on estimator variables is important, too; it can help us understand the situations in which eyewitnesses may experience problems in perception and memory.

Assessing the Impact of Estimator Variables on Eyewitness Accuracy

We have already described in detail two estimator variables—the witness's stress level at the time of the crime and the presence of a weapon. We will discuss a few other factors here.

Race of the eyewitness

Eyewitnesses are usually better at recognizing and identifying members of their own race or ethnic group than members of another race or ethnic group. In fact, the chances of a mistaken identification are 1.56 times greater when the witness and suspect are of different races than when they are of the same race (Meissner & Brigham, 2001). This phenomenon, which is termed the **other-race effect**, has been examined extensively in laboratory studies, and analysis of DNA exoneration cases show that it is a significant problem in actual cases, as well. In their analysis of 77 known cases of mistaken identification, Scheck, Neufeld, and Dwyer (2000) reported that 35% of these cases involved white victims or witnesses who misidentified black suspects, whereas only 28% of cases involved white victims or witnesses who misidentified white suspects. These figures are even more troubling when one considers that most criminal victimizations happen *within* race (that is, whites are more likely to be victimized by other whites, and blacks are more likely to be victimized by other blacks). Because white-victim/white-perpetrator crimes happen more often than white-victim/black-perpetrator crimes, we would expect that white victims would make more mistakes with white suspects than with black suspects (Wells & Olson, 2001). But that's not what happens.

Understanding the reasons for the other-race effect has vexed psychologists for some time. Racial attitudes are apparently not related to this phenomenon (people with prejudicial attitudes are not more likely to fall victim to the other-race effect than are people with unbiased attitudes). Recent explanations of the other-race effect have tended to involve both cognitive and social processes.

Cognitive interpretations hold that there are differences between faces of one race and faces of another race in terms of the variability in those features, something psychologists refer to as **physiognomic variability**. Faces of one race differ from faces of another race in terms of the *type* of physiognomic variability. For example, white faces show more variability in hair color, and black faces show more variability in skin tone. For eyewitnesses to correctly identify members of other races, they must focus on the characteristics that distinguish that person from other people of the same race. Thus, black eyewitnesses would be better off noticing and encoding a white perpetrator's hair color than her or his skin tone, whereas white eyewitnesses could more profitably pay more attention to a black assailant's skin tone. But because most of us have more experience with members of our own race, our natural instinct is to focus on the features that distinguish members of *our own group*; we have less practice distinguishing one member of another race from other people of that race.

Social psychologists have also tried to explain the other race effect. One reasonable hypothesis is based on social perception and **in-group/out-group differences** (Sporer, 2001). When we encounter the face of a person from another race or ethnic group (the out-group), our first job is to categorize the face as a member of that group (e.g., "That person is Asian"). Attentional resources that are directed toward categorization come at the expense of attention to facial features that would distinguish that person from other members of the out-group. On the other hand, when we encounter the face of a person from our in-group, the categorization step is eliminated, and we immediately devote our attention to distinguishing that person from other members of the in-group. In the end, because identifying people of other races involves both a cognitive and a social process, both explanations may well be right; there probably will never be one all-encompassing theory to explain why it is difficult to do (Wells & Olson, 2001).

Age and gender of the eyewitness

The age and gender of an eyewitness are also estimator variables; we can't control their influence on the justice system, but we can estimate them. Less attention has been focused on understanding the effects of age and gender than on understanding the effects of race. But we can ask whether males make better eyewitnesses than females and whether young people make better eyewitnesses than older people.

The evidence for gender effects is not overwhelming; a meta-analysis of several studies (Shapiro & Penrod, 1986) showed that although women are slightly more likely to make accurate identifications, they also make slightly more

errors than men (because they are more likely to choose someone from a lineup or photo spread). Thus, there is no clear evidence that one gender is superior to the other in ability to identify people from lineups.

There is stronger evidence that the age of the eyewitness matters: Older eyewitnesses and young children make more errors than younger and middle-aged adults (Brimacombe, Jung, Garrioch, & Allison, 2003; Pozzulo & Lindsay; 1998). In addition, the errors of older adults and young children are fairly predictable: They are more likely to choose someone from a lineup in which the culprit is absent and, hence, make more mistaken identifications than young and middle-aged adults (Memon, Bartlett, Rose, & Gray, 2003). But when the lineup contains the culprit, young children and elderly people perform as well as younger adults. (We describe the issues associated with children as witnesses in Chapter 14.)

Speed of identification

One other estimator variable—the speed with which an eyewitness makes an identification from a lineup—has intrigued psychologists recently. Witnesses who make accurate identifications generally take less time to look at a lineup than witnesses who make mistaken identifications, although there is some controversy about what time frame can differentiate accurate from inaccurate identifications (Dunning & Perretta, 2002; Weber, Brewer, Wells, Semmler, & Keast, 2004). Is it 5 seconds, 10 seconds, or 30 seconds? Unfortunately, we don't yet know the answer. Even if we did, the speed of identification could never be a foolproof method of assessing accuracy, but it may hold some promise as an estimator.

Controlling the Impact of System Variables on Eyewitness Accuracy

System variables are those factors in an identification over which the justice system has some control. In general, system variables tend to come into play after the crime or accident, usually during the investigation. In the criminal justice realm, they tend to be associated with how the lineup or photo spread is put together and shown to the eyewitness. We have already touched on two system variables: the influence of postevent information on witnesses' memory, and the effects of questions posed to eyewitnesses.

In the next section, we describe other system variables and the important role they have played in suggesting changes to procedures that investigators use with eyewitnesses.

But first, it may be helpful to draw an analogy between the procedures employed in criminal investigations and the steps used by researchers when doing an experiment (Wells & Luus, 1990). Like scientists, crime investigators begin with a hypothesis (that the suspect actually committed the crime), test the hypothesis (by placing the suspect in a lineup and instructing the eyewitness about what to do when looking at the lineup), observe and record the eyewitness's decision, and draw conclusions from the results (e.g., that the suspect was the assailant).

There are certain principles that are essential to good experimental design (e.g., that observers should be unbiased), and violation of those principles affects the usefulness of the experiment's findings. In similar fashion, violating the principles of good criminal investigation affects the results of the investigation. For example, if the instructions to the eyewitness are biased, if the suspect appears to be different from the other people in the lineup in some obvious way, or if the person conducting the lineup conveys his or her suspicions to the eyewitness, then the results of that identification procedure can be misleading. Applying the analogy of an experiment to criminal investigations enables us to evaluate critically the steps involved in these investigations.

RECOMMENDATIONS FOR REFORMING IDENTIFICATION PROCEDURES

One important aspect of a system variable is that because it is controllable, it can be modified. For example, we know that instructions given to eyewitnesses at a lineup affect the likelihood of correct identifications. Thus, we can suggest that people conducting lineups use only unbiased instructions.

As psychological research findings have accumulated and been disseminated to prosecutors and police officers, some departments have changed the procedures they use with eyewitnesses. In fact, studies showing the impact of system variables on eyewitness accuracy formed the basis for a set of guidelines issued by the U.S. Department of Justice in 1999 on recommended procedures for collecting eyewitness evidence. In her introduction to these

guidelines, then-Attorney General Janet Reno wrote, "Eyewitnesses frequently play a vital role in uncovering the truth about a crime. The evidence they provide can be critical in identifying, charging, and ultimately convicting suspected criminals. That is why it is absolutely essential that eyewitness evidence be accurate and reliable. One way of ensuring we, as investigators, obtain the most accurate and reliable evidence from eyewitnesses is to follow sound protocols in our investigations" (U.S. Department of Justice, 1999, p. iii). Reno also cited the "growing body of research in the field of eyewitness identification" as support for the guidelines.

The guidelines issued by the Justice Department are recommended for use in conducting lineups and photo spreads. These guidelines have two important goals: to maximize accurate identifications and minimize the rate of eyewitness errors. Because police officers want to catch the real culprits and avoid mistaken identifications, we expect that police departments will eventually incorporate many of these recommendations as routine procedure. Already, police in New Jersey, Boston, Madison, the District of Columbia, Chicago, Minneapolis, and most of North Carolina have embraced these principles, and others are being trained in their use (Turtle & Steblay, 2005).

In this section, we describe what is known about four system variables: instructions to eyewitnesses, selection of filler photos, the lineup presentation method, and the influence of feedback. On the basis of this research, psychologists have made suggestions about how these variables should be factored into identification procedures so that those procedures will be fair and unbiased. Many of their recommendations are included in the federal guidelines.

Instructions to the Eyewitness

There is ample research showing that the investigator conducting the photo spread or lineup should instruct the witness that the offender *may or may not be* present in the spread or lineup (Malpass & Devine, 1981). Without this instruction, eyewitnesses may assume that their task is to pick *someone,* so they choose the person who looks most like the perpetrator. Based on her analysis of all the studies that examined the presence of a "might or might not be present" instruction, Professor Nancy Steblay found that use of this instruction reduced the rate of mistaken identifications (i.e., saying that the offender was present in the lineup when he was not) by 42% and did not significantly reduce the rate or correct identifications (i.e., choosing the offender from a lineup in which he was present) (Steblay, 1997).

Selection of Fillers

If the suspect stands out from other people in the lineup or photo spread (the fillers), then he or she can be easily picked out, even by people who did not witness the crime. For example, if the victim of a robbery recalled that the robber had acne and the photo spread or lineup showed only one person (namely, the suspect) with acne, a nonwitness who was simply given the description of the culprit would be able to pick out the suspect. Suspects can stand out from other people in the lineup in a number of different ways: They might be the only person in the lineup with a prominent facial feature; their pictures might be a different size than the others or use a different background; or the suspect might be shown in jail clothes whereas the fillers might appear in street clothes. Defense attorneys who suspect that their clients would stand out from the fillers can now perform a do-it-yourself test on the fairness of a lineup or photo spread. On-line instructions are provided by Professor Roy Malpass from the Eyewitness Identification Research Laboratory at the University of Texas at El Paso (http://eyewitness.utep.edu/diy.html).

Police departments differ in the care they give to creating photo spreads and lineups. To their credit, most police officers try to have all members of a lineup look fairly similar. But others may place the suspect in a lineup of people who differ from that suspect in height, weight, physique, hair style, and other significant features mentioned in the witness's description of the offender. Here are some examples:

> In one case ... the defendant had been picked out of a line-up of six men, of which he was the only Oriental. In other cases, a black-haired suspect was placed among a group of light-haired persons, tall suspects have been made to stand with short suspects, and, in a case where the perpetrator of the crime was known to be a youth, a suspect under twenty was placed in

a line-up with five other persons, all of whom were forty or over. (*United States v. Wade,* 1967)

As the recommended procedures become more widely used, we hope that these miscues will diminish.

Lineup Presentation Method

In a typical lineup or photo spread, the eyewitness sees the suspect and the foils simultaneously. (In a photo spread, six photos are typically arrayed on a single page. In a live lineup, the suspect and foils are shown together, standing in a line.) This procedure is termed **simultaneous presentation**. An alternative procedure is to show suspects and foils sequentially—one at a time (Lindsay & Wells, 1985)—in a procedure called **sequential presentation**. The manner in which a lineup or photo spread is presented can affect the accuracy of identification. For example, Cutler and Penrod (1988) showed a one-minute videotape of a staged liquor store robbery and varied the way in which the lineup was constructed. When the six members of the lineup were shown simultaneously, witnesses falsely accused an innocent person 39% of the time. However, when suspects were shown sequentially, witnesses picked the wrong individual only 19% of the time.

A compilation of 25 studies that compared simultaneous and sequential presentation showed that the chances of mistaken identifications were reduced by nearly half when presentations were sequential (Steblay, Dysart, Fulero, & Lindsay, 2001). However, that good news must be balanced against another concern: whether the identification of actual perpetrators is *also* reduced when lineups and photo spreads are shown sequentially. According to Professor Nancy Steblay and her colleagues, under real-world conditions involving crimes with only one perpetrator and cautionary instructions to the eyewitness, there will be few differences in witnesses' ability to correctly identify a perpetrator as a function of presentation format. Thus, we can be reasonably confident that in most situations, sequential presentation is preferable.

Why are there more mistaken identifications in the traditional lineup (i.e., with simultaneous presentation)? In the simultaneous presentation of individuals in a lineup or photo spread, eyewitnesses tend to identify the person who, in their opinion, looks most like the culprit *relative to* other members of the group. In other words, they make a **relative judgment**. But what happens when the actual culprit is not shown? Under this condition, the relative-judgment process will still yield a positive identification because someone in the group will always look *most* like the culprit (Wells et al., 1998).

Contrast this situation with a lineup or photo spread in which the members are presented sequentially, one at a time. Here, the eyewitness compares each member in turn to his or her memory of the perpetrator and, on that basis, decides whether any person in the lineup is the individual who committed the crime. In other words, they make an **absolute judgment**. The value of sequential presentation is that it decreases the likelihood that an eyewitness will make a relative judgment in choosing someone from the lineup or photo spread.

Professor Gary Wells, a vocal advocate of reforming eyewitness evidence procedures, cleverly demonstrated the use of relative-judgment processes in his "removal without replacement" study (Wells, 1993). In this procedure, all eyewitnesses watched a staged crime. Some were shown a photo spread that included the actual culprit and five foils; their identifications were recorded. Another group saw the same photo spread with one exception: The culprit's photo was removed and was not replaced with another photo. If identifications of the culprit by the culprit-present group are based solely on their recognition of him, then the percentage of people in that group who identified him *plus* the percentage who said "not there" should be exactly the same as the percentage in the culprit-absent group who said "not there." Wells tested this idea by showing 200 eyewitnesses to a staged crime either a culprit-present lineup or a lineup in which the culprit was absent but was not replaced by anyone else. When the culprit was present in the lineup, 54% of eyewitnesses selected him, and 21% said "not there." Did 75% of eyewitnesses in the "target-absent" lineup say "not there"? Unfortunately, no. The "not there" response was given by only 32% of people in that group; the others all mistakenly identified someone else from the lineup. Why? Through a process of relative judgment, eyewitnesses apparently select whoever looks most like the perpetrator.

The Influence of Feedback

Recall our analogy between a criminal investigation and a scientific experiment. One of the cardinal rules of a good experiment is that the person conducting the experiment should not influence the results, a situation referred to as **experimenter bias**. To avoid this problem, experimenters should know little about the study's hypotheses and less about which experimental condition any participant is in. Nearly all clinical drug trials adhere to these rules in that neither the patient taking the pills nor the doctor assessing the patient's health knows whether the pills are actually a new drug or a placebo. These so-called **double-blind testing procedures**, commonplace in medicine and other scientific fields, have gone largely unheeded in criminal investigations (although some jurisdictions are now beginning to adopt them (Post, 2005)).

What happens if the officer conducting the lineup knows who the suspect is? Does that knowledge affect the eyewitness in any way? The answer, based on several recent studies, is yes. A lineup administrator's knowledge of the suspect can affect both the likelihood that an eyewitness will choose someone from the lineup (Phillips, McAuliff, Kovera, & Cutler, 1999) and the confidence that the eyewitness attaches to that choice (Garrioch & Brimacombe, 2001; Semmler, Brewer, & Wells, 2004). Furthermore, eyewitnesses who have a lot of contact with the administrator—either because they are in close physical contact or because they have extensive interactions—are likely to make decisions consistent with the administrator's expectations (Haw & Fisher, 2004). An obvious solution to this situation is to have the lineup administered by someone who does not know which person in the lineup or photo spread is the suspect.

As we have seen, eyewitnesses sometimes express increased certainty in their identifications as a result of events that happen after they choose someone from the lineup. For example, if eyewitnesses get confirming feedback from the lineup administrator ("Good, you identified the suspect"), they inflate the certainty they had in their initial identifications, compared to eyewitnesses who received no such feedback. This inflation of confidence is actually greater for eyewitnesses who are mistaken in their identifications than for eyewitnesses who are correct (Bradfield, Wells, & Olson, 2002). Remarkably, confirming feedback also bolsters eyewitnesses' retrospective confidence in how good a view they had of the perpetrator, how well they could make out details of his face, and how readily they made the identification (Wells, Olson, & Charman, 2003). Even *without* confirming feedback, eyewitnesses infer from the facts of an ongoing investigation and eventual prosecution that they must have picked the suspect from the lineup.

Hence, their confidence increases. This enhanced confidence is troubling because of the repeated finding that the confidence expressed by eyewitnesses during their trial testimony is one of the most compelling reasons why jurors believe such identifications are accurate (Brewer & Burke, 2002).

The problem with witness confidence and its great influence on juries is that many studies have shown that witness confidence is not a very strong predictor of whether the witness's identification is accurate (Sporer, Penrod, Read, & Cutler, 1995). Another problem with eyewitnesses' confidence is its apparent malleability: After making a false-identification from a photo spread, witnesses who were told that another witness identified the same person became highly confident in their false identifications (Luus & Wells, 1994). One result of feedback from the lineup administrator—whether it subtly conveys to the witness that he or she picked the suspect or tells the witness that another person picked the same suspect—is a sense of false confidence.

Can the development of false confidence be prevented? Wells and Bradfield (1998) hypothesized that confidence inflation occurs because at the time that feedback is delivered by the investigator, the eyewitness has not yet formed an independent opinion about his or her confidence. Therefore, asking witnesses to provide a statement of their degree of certainty before giving any feedback can be an effective way to eliminate the problem of false confidence. This recommendation, along with suggestions to use unbiased instructions, similar-looking fillers, and sequential lineups, is included in the Justice Department guidelines.

USE OF HYPNOSIS WITH EYEWITNESSES

Most eyewitnesses cannot remember everything that happened during the crime; their memories are often fragmented and vague. Are there ways to enhance the memories of eyewitnesses—to help them accurately remember facts and details?

Law enforcement officials are eager to use techniques that will increase the detail, accuracy, and usefulness of recollections by victims and other witnesses. Hypnosis has been investigated as an aid to memory and has been credited with helping solve some notorious crimes. Hypnosis was used in the Sam Sheppard murder case, the trial of the Boston Strangler, and the investigation of the assassination of Robert Kennedy. Probably the most notorious example of its use was the 1976 Chowchilla, California, kidnapping case, in which a bus load of 26 schoolchildren and their driver were abducted by three masked kidnappers and buried underground in a large tomb, from which they later escaped. The driver had seen the license plate on one of the kidnappers' vans and had tried to memorize the numbers. However, he was unable to recall the numbers until he was hypnotized. At one point during the hypnotic session, he suddenly called out a license plate number he remembered seeing. The number was correct except for one digit, and this information expedited the capture of the three culprits, who were later convicted and sentenced to life in prison.

What Is Hypnosis?

Everyone is aware of hypnosis, and perhaps you have been hypnotized yourself. During the past two centuries, hypnotism has been used to treat a range of psychological and physical disorders, including obesity, smoking, addictions, pain, fears, asthma, and stress disorders (Flammer & Bongartz, 2003; Montgomery, DuHamel, & Redd, 2000). Many different explanations exist for what occurs during a hypnotized state, as well as for the essential ingredients of hypnosis.

Explanations of hypnosis fall into one of two categories. Some investigators think of hypnosis as a procedure delivered by a skilled practitioner who induces in subjects a special mental state known as a *trance,* which endows them with unique mental abilities. The second perspective focuses on subjects' *suggestibility,* which is maximized during hypnotic inductions. We define hypnosis as a state of *extreme suggestibility,* in which the hypnotized subject is very relaxed, attentive to incoming stimuli, and responsive to suggestions from the hypnotist. In effect, the subject agrees to reduce logical judgment and yield to the hypnotist's instruction. Hypnosis often heightens subjects' attention and imagination, but it also sometimes leads to confusion between imagined memories and memories of real events.

In the past, hypnosis was used extensively by law enforcement officials and government agencies for two main purposes: (1) generating investigative leads that can then be pursued through other means and (2) refreshing the memories of witnesses, victims, or defendants who have forgotten important details of events about which they might testify in court. The methods used to reach these two goals are basically identical, but their legal and professional status is different, as we describe below.

Effects of Hypnosis on Memory: Memory Aid or Altered Memory?

Few professionals find fault with forensic hypnosis when it is restricted to its first purpose: generating new leads for the police. However, the situation is different when hypnosis is used to help a witness recall details that may later be included in court testimony or to help witnesses choose between conflicting versions of events that they have provided on different occasions. In these situations, many observers contend, the technique is fraught with so many problems that it raises risks for criminal defendants and should be allowed only under the strictest of safeguards or banned altogether (e.g., Newman, 2001; Webert, 2003). As a result of these concerns, many U.S. jurisdictions have, in the past decade, abandoned their use of hypnosis, although police in other countries continue to use hypnosis for memory enhancement purposes (Wagstaff, 1999).

What are the dangers of hypnotically enhanced memory? Critics point to five concerns, all consistent with the commonly held theory that memories are malleable and reconstructed, rather than facsimile recordings of prior experiences. The concerns are as follows:

1. Subjects often remember more material when hypnotized than when they are in a nonhypnotized state, an effect known as **hyperamnesia**. This additional material consists of a mixture of accurate and inaccurate recollections (Dywan & Bowers, 1983). False "recollections" can be implanted through suggestions from the hypnotist, or they can originate in other ways that are not yet completely understood. The addition of false information to accurate recollections

is called **confabulation**. For example, an Illinois man was charged with first-degree murder after an eyewitness, under hypnosis, described his license plate. The witness claimed to have seen the car from 230 feet away, at night, with lights shining directly in his eyes. The charges were dropped, however, after an ophthalmologist testified that a person could not see more than 30 feet under such conditions. The net conclusion appears to be that hypnotized subjects do not show a reliable increase in accurate recall compared to nonhypnotized subjects (Steblay & Bothwell, 1994).

2. One reason why confabulation occurs under hypnosis is that subjects relax their standards for reporting information. They become less critical and accept approximations of memory as "accurate enough." These approximations are then added to accurate memories to yield a version of events that is part fact and part fabrication. A second factor that contributes to confabulation is that hypnotized subjects are extremely suggestible and want to please the hypnotist by giving as full a report as possible. This motive encourages subjects to fill in the gaps in their memory with plausible details or with information they believe the hypnotist is expecting.

3. The greatest danger of confabulation is that persons who have been hypnotized find it difficult to separate actual memories from those generated under hypnosis. This problem can be compared to that of the basketball fan who watches a controversial play at an arena and then later watches TV replays of the same play. This fan develops a clear "picture" of the play in memory but is unable to tell which parts of the picture are from the actual game and which come from the TV replay.

4. Not only do hypnotized witnesses find it difficult to distinguish their original memories from those brought out under hypnosis, but they also tend to become more confident about their recall despite the fact that it might contain false recollections (Scoboria, Mazzoni, Kirsch, & Milling, 2002). This confidence can persist long after the hypnosis session has ended. Hypnosis thus translates beliefs or expectations into "memories," a process called **memory hardening**.

5. Several studies have shown that hypnotized subjects are more responsive to the biasing influence of leading questions. For example, Scoboria et al. (2002) played an audiotape story for research participants who then recalled as much as they could about the narrative. At this point, half the participants were hypnotized, and the researchers then asked questions of all participants; some were misleading questions (e.g., "Did the woman have one child or two?") and others were neutral (e.g., "Did the woman have any children?"). Misleading questions produced significantly more memory errors than hypnosis, but the two effects compounded each other, so the combination of misleading questions and hypnosis produced significantly more errors than either manipulation alone. What's interesting about this finding is that leading questions are allowed (and expected) in court, despite the effect that they seem to have on the accuracy of the respondent's memory. However, as you will learn in the next section, witnesses are often not allowed to testify about memories that are enhanced through hypnosis.

Legal Status of Hypnosis

What if, as a result of being hypnotized, a victim claims to be able to identify her attacker—for example, by remembering his name or the license plate of his car? Can such information be introduced at a trial? Courts sharply differ in their responses to the question of whether hypnotically refreshed testimony can be admitted at trial. The decisions cluster into one of three camps.

Up until about 1980, the majority view was that hypnotically assisted testimony was admissible (Diamond, 1980). Today, only five states allow the admission of hypnotically assisted testimony in all circumstances (Webert, 2003). According to this position, identified with the Maryland case of *Harding v State* (1968), the fact that a witness has been hypnotized has a bearing on how much weight a jury should give that person's testimony, but not on whether the testimony is admissible at trial. Courts that allow hypnotically enhanced testimony reason that cross-examination of the eyewitness and testimony of an expert witness can assist jurors and judges in deciding whether hypnotically refreshed testimony is credible.

The second camp takes the position that the admissibility of hypnotically refreshed testimony depends on the circumstances of the case. Some states have adopted the view that such testimony is admissible only if certain safeguards were taken during the hypnosis session. The lead opinion in this category is *State v. Hurd* (1981), decided by the New Jersey Supreme Court, which set out the following guidelines: (1) The hypnosis should be conducted by a specially trained psychiatrist or psychologist. (2) The hypnotist should be independent of the prosecution, the police, and the defense. (3) Information learned prior to the hypnosis should be written and retained so that it can be examined by other parties in the case. (4) The entire hypnosis session should be recorded, preferably on videotape. (5) Only the hypnotist and the subject should be present during any phase of the hypnosis, including the posthypnosis interview. (6) All of the subject's prehypnosis memories for the events in question should be recorded and preserved. Other states and most federal courts consider procedural safeguards only one factor to consider in determining the admissibility of this evidence (Webert, 2003). They follow a more flexible approach, often involving a pretrial hearing, to assess whether, given the circumstances of the case, the testimony is sufficiently reliable and useful to the jury.

The third camp takes a position diametrically opposed to the first. Their position, adopted by the majority of states, is that hypnotically enhanced testimony is inadmissible in court. Many states prohibit a witness who has been hypnotized from testifying about either posthypnotic or prehypnotic recollections in the prosecution of that case. (The rationale is that witnesses will be unable to distinguish memories they recalled prior to hypnosis from those that may have been implanted during the hypnotic interview.) This view became increasingly popular in the 1980s, beginning with the case of *State of Minnesota v Mack* (1980), in which the Supreme Court of Minnesota ruled that hypnosis had not been generally accepted by the scientific community as a reliable method for enhancing accurate recall and that hypnotically refreshed recall was to be excluded from the trial.

This topic was revisited in the 1987 U.S. Supreme Court decision of *Rock v Arkansas* (see Box 5.2 for a summary of the facts of this case), in which the Court held that an automatic ban against hypnotically refreshed testimony violated previously hypnotized defendants' rights to testify on their own behalf. By deciding that hypnotically aided testimony cannot be automatically excluded, the *Rock* court reached a conclusion that is similar to the *Hurd* approach, in which each case is examined on the merits of how the hypnosis is conducted.

Law enforcement officials and victims of crime argue that it is unfair to permit defendants to have their memories refreshed by hypnosis but to deny this opportunity to prosecution witnesses. At the same time, the evidence about the potentially biasing effects of hypnosis is becoming more and more persuasive, so we would not expect a large swing in the direction of relaxing the admissibility standards for hypnotically aided testimony.

In summary, although it generates additional information that the police can check out, hypnosis also increases the risks of inaccurate recall. Given the inconsistent court rulings, what can we say about the wisdom of relying on hypnotically aided memory?

The best use of hypnosis is during the early stages of a criminal investigation. Hypnosis can help witnesses provide clues: a license number, a piece of clothing, a description of a gun. These leads, even if they don't pan out, are better than no clues at all. Inaccurate "facts" are not as damaging at the first stage of a criminal investigation as they are at a trial.

Less desirable is the use of hypnosis by the police to *verify* previously obtained information, especially if such verification involves leading questions. It is even riskier—in fact, undesirable—to hypnotize a witness who has given several different stories in order to learn the "true" story. This step will simply fix in the witness's mind one particular version of the testimony, which he or she then will faithfully produce on demand. The American Medical Association has expressed the opinion that hypnotically induced memories are not accurate enough to be allowed on the witness stand. This seems a wise conclusion.

A potential substitute for hypnosis is the cognitive interview (Fisher & Geiselman, 1992), which uses some of the techniques of hypnosis, including rapport building, instructions to "report everything," and focused attention. Instead of a standard interview ("Tell me what happened"), witnesses participating in a cognitive interview are encouraged to recreate the scene mentally and report everything they can remember. (This process is sometimes referred to as context reinstatement.) The interviewer may ask them to think about the surroundings, the smells and sound, the temperature, the location of the furniture, or anything else that may elicit new memories. The interviewer may suggest that they recall events in reverse order or that they try to reexperience the moods they originally felt. All these activities help reinstate the context in which the crime occurred in the hope that additional memories will appear spontaneously.

Most of the evidence suggests that the cognitive interview has the potential to enhance recall. Furthermore, this enhancement comes without the problems of susceptibility to leading questions and exaggerated confidence that are associated with hypnosis (Geiselman, Fisher, MacKinnon, & Holland, 1985; Kebbell & Wagstaff, 1998).

THE EYEWITNESS IN THE COURTROOM

Despite limitations on the reliability of their identifications, eyewitnesses are one of the prosecution's most influential resources to convict defendants in criminal trials. Jurors put a great deal of weight on testimony from an eyewitness. In a study showing this influence, Loftus(1974) gave subjects a description of an armed robbery that had resulted in two deaths. Of mock jurors who heard a version of the case that contained only circumstantial evidence against the defendant, 18% convicted him. But when an eyewitness's identification of the defendant was presented as well, 72% of the mock jurors convicted him. It is hard to overestimate the power of confident eyewitnesses to convince a jury of the correctness of their testimony.

Psychological research shows that jurors overestimate the accuracy of eyewitnesses. In one study Wells, Lindsay, and Ferguson (1979) staged a "theft" under viewing conditions that were good, moderate, or poor for witnesses. As you might expect, eyewitnesses did a better job when the viewing conditions were good: 74% of them were accurate, compared with 50% in the moderate viewing conditions and 33% in the poor viewing conditions. Then some mock jurors watched these eyewitnesses being cross-examined, after which the jurors indicated whether they believed the eyewitnesses. Belief rates for the good, the moderate, and the poor witnessing conditions were, respectively, 69%, 57%, and 58%. Thus, when the viewing conditions are only so-so or poor, jurors tend to overestimate the witnesses' accuracy.

Jurors overestimate the validity of eyewitnesses' testimony because they appear to be unaware of several of the factors that compromise eyewitness accuracy. For example:

- Jurors have little awareness of the factors that interfere with accurate retention, such as weapon focus, amount of violence in a criminal event, effects of prior exposures (Cutler, Penrod, & Dexter, 1990), and the other-race effect (Abshire & Bornstein, 2003).
- Jurors show a lack of sophistication about the problems inherent in typical lineups and photo spreads used by the police to test witness recognition (Cutler et al., 1990; Loftus & Wagenaar, 1990).
- Jurors are usually not told about those eyewitnesses who could not identify a suspect; even the defendant's attorney may not be aware of these misses (Wells & Lindsay, 1980).

We also know that jurors pay attention to factors that may not help them distinguish accurate from inaccurate eyewitness testimony. One of these factors is the confidence with which an eyewitness testifies. We have already shown that confident testimony can distort jurors' perceptions of other testimony-relevant criteria, such as the eyewitness's opportunity to view the crime. In a study of the effects of eyewitness confidence on mock jurors' verdicts, Brewer and Burke (2002) found that witness confidence had a strong effect on jurors' judgments, regardless of whether the witness gave consistent testimony (i.e., similar responses to questions from prosecutor and defense attorney) or inconsistent testimony (i.e., different responses to prosecutor and defense attorney). This creates a dangerous situation for an innocent defendant because it means that a confident eyewitness can be persuasive to jurors, even when he or she is wrong (Wells, Olson, & Charman, 2002).

SAFEGUARDS AGAINST MISTAKEN IDENTIFICATION

Much, of the eyewitness research is motivated by a desire to increase the accuracy of eyewitnesses. If the validity of eyewitness testimony can be improved (careful adherence to the Department of Justice guidelines would certainly help), then there would be no need to caution jurors and judges about the potential fallibility of eyewitnesses (Seelau & Wells, 1995). Until that time, though, it would seem that

truth would be better served if there were a means by which jurors and judges could be alerted to and educated about some of the problems inherent in eyewitness reports. There are three ways in which this might be done.

Evaluating the Effectiveness of Cross-Examination

First, eyewitnesses can be cross-examined in an attempt to reveal factors that might compromise their identification. But cross-examination may not be especially effective in increasing juror sensitivity to the factors that can affect eyewitness performance (Devenport, Stinson, Cutler, & Kravitz, 2002). For cross-examination to be effective, the following conditions must all be met:

1. Attorneys must have access to the information necessary to cross-examine the eyewitness effectively, including the conditions under which the crime was committed. Unfortunately, like everyone else, attorneys are forced to rely on the witness's memory of the crime, the perpetrator, and the conditions under which the crime was committed. The quality of the information available to attorneys depends on the witness's memory and willingness to cooperate (Penrod & Cutler, 1999).
2. Attorneys must have knowledge of the factors that potentially influence eyewitnesses' performance. Do they have this knowledge? One study has shown that attorneys are generally insensitive to factors that influence the suggestiveness of lineups and are not aware that jurors overestimate the accuracy of eyewitnesses (Stinson, Devenport, Cutler, & Kravitz, 1996). If attorneys lack knowledge of these issues, they may simply ask the wrong questions.
3. Judges must also be aware of the factors that influence the accuracy of an eyewitness's memory because they decide to what extent cross-examination (and other remedies) can be used to guard against erroneous eyewitness testimony. Are judges knowledgeable about concerns related to eyewitness evidence? A recent survey of 160 U.S. judges showed that they were correct on some issues (e.g., that eyewitness testimony about an event often reflects not only what a witness actually saw but also information

obtained later from other sources, and that an eyewitness's perception and memory may be affected by attitudes and expectations) but lack knowledge that eyewitness confidence is not a good indicator of accuracy and that jurors are often unable to distinguish accurate from inaccurate eyewitnesses (Wise & Safer, 2004). Judges also decide whether jurors will receive guidance in order to be better informed about the factors that influence eyewitness performance, so there is serious concern that they may be making these decisions on the basis of biased expectations of eyewitnesses and jurors alike.

How, then, can jurors become better informed about the factors that influence eyewitness performance? Two further remedies have been proposed. One solution would be to allow psychologists who are knowledgeable about the relevant research on perception and memory to testify to juries about their findings. As a second remedy, judges could instruct juries about the potential weaknesses of

BOX 5.2
THE CASE OF
Vicki Rock: Hypnosis and defendants

All the court decisions and changes in state laws described in the text refer to the hypnosis of witnesses, usually victims of a crime. What if a defendant who is charged with a crime claims that he or she cannot remember what happened at a crucial time? Then, if the defendant is hypnotized before the trial and "remembers" facts that would help prove his or her innocence, should this testimony be admitted into evidence?

The U.S. Supreme Court faced this question in the case of *Rock vArkansas* (1987). Vicki Lorene Rock had been convicted of manslaughter in the shooting of her husband, Frank, in 1983 and was sentenced to ten years in prison. After the shooting, she could remember that she and her husband had been arguing, that he pushed her against a wall, and that she wanted to leave the house but he wouldn't let her. She recalled clutching the gun because she thought it would keep him from hitting her again. She also recalled phoning the police, who arrived to find Frank lying on the floor, a bullet in his chest.

Only after Mrs. Rock had been hypnotized was she able to recall that she had not put her finger on the guns trigger, that her husband had grabbed her from behind, that they struggled, and that the gun went off by accident. As a result of this new information, Rock's attorney hired a gun expert to examine the handgun. This investigation revealed that the weapon was defective and prone to fire when hit, even without the trigger being pulled.

The judge at Mrs. Rock's trial, following the law in Arkansas, refused to let jurors hear anything the defendant remembered as a result of being hypnotized. In her appeal, Mrs. Rock contended that this ruling denied her the opportunity to present evidence crucial to her defense.

Note the dilemma facing the U.S. Supreme Court: On the one hand, hypnosis "is not generally regarded by the scientific community as reliable" (to quote the Arkansas attorney general), and recent rulings had restricted its application. On the other hand, a defendant has a Fourteenth Amendment constitutional right to due process; in this case, the defendant's defense depended on the recollection of events that she could not remember before she was hypnotized.

The Supreme Court ruled 5–4 in favor of Mrs. Rock and struck down the Arkansas law prohibiting all hypnotically refreshed testimony. Mrs. Rock was granted a new trial. In the majority opinion, justice Harry Blackmun acknowledged that hypnosis may produce "incorrect recollections" but said that the Arkansas court decision excluding all hypnotically refreshed testimony per se was "arbitrary." However, the decision did not open the door to all types of hypnotically enhanced testimony. Blackmun wrote, "We express no opinion on the admissibility of previously hypnotized witnesses other than criminal defendants."

eyewitness identifications and suggest how to interpret this testimony. (Of course, both solutions require judges to be aware of the vagaries of eyewitness testimony and of jurors' need for instruction!) We describe these two alternatives next.

Evaluating the Expert Testimony of Psychologists

Psychologists could have much to say to jurors about experimental research on eyewitness testimony: that eyewitnesses are sometimes inaccurate, that extreme stress usually inhibits accurate and complete encoding, that feedback from a lineup administrator can increase an eyewitness's confidence, that extremely confident eyewitnesses are not necessarily accurate, and that differences in the way lineups are constructed and presented to witnesses affect eyewitness accuracy. Note that the expert witness does not tell the jury what to believe about a particular eyewitness or whether the eyewitness is accurate. Even the eyewitness cannot always know this with certainty. Rather, the expert's task is to provide the jury with a scientifically based frame of reference within which to evaluate the eyewitness's evidence.

But psychologists are sometimes not allowed to testify about these matters, and appellate courts have generally upheld such decisions. In most states, the decision about whether an expert psychologist can testify is left to the presiding judge—an example of the breadth of discretion that the legal system grants to judges. Recently, federal courts have become more receptive to expert testimony about eyewitness identification. For example, the courts are more likely to allow such testimony when a prosecutor's case against a defendant relies almost entirely on an eyewitness's identification (*United States v. Jordan,* 1996).

Why have judges sometimes been reluctant to let psychological experts testify? First, some judges believe that scientific research on eyewitness identification is not sufficiently established to yield valid research findings. In the past, a few psychologists have agreed with this opinion (e.g., Egeth, 1995; Elliott, 1993; Konecni & Ebbesen, 1986), but most psychologists disagree (Tubb, Kassin, Memon, & Hosch, 2000). Second, judges may believe that such expert testimony would not provide facts that are beyond the common knowledge of most jury members and would

therefore invade the province of the jury as finders and triers of fact. Third, judges fear that admitting such expert testimony would open the gates to conflicting expert testimony, setting the scene for a confusing and uninformative "battle of the experts." (Such battles have occurred in some highly publicized trials involving a criminal defendant's claim of insanity; see Chapter 8.) Finally, judges worry that this type of testimony might lead jurors to give insufficient weight to eyewitness evidence, making them too skeptical of all eyewitnesses (Woocher, 1986), even those who witnessed a crime or accident under good viewing conditions and who were not subjected to suggestive identification procedures. Indeed, expert testimony would be most useful if it could sensitize jurors to variations in witnessing and identification procedures that might threaten the reliability of the identifications. But can it serve this limited function, or does it instead make jurors generally skeptical of all eyewitnesses? Research studies have addressed that question.

Some early studies (e.g., Fox & Walters, 1986; Hosch, Beck, & McIntyre, 1980) manipulated the presence of expert testimony about eyewitnesses in a simulated jury study. Participants in those studies heard testimony from an eyewitness, and some also heard from a defense expert witness about the potential unreliability of eyewitness memory. What effect did the expert have? Generally, the expert testimony resulted in reduced belief in the eyewitness. Unfortunately, because of the design of those early studies, it is hard to know whether the expert sensitized jurors to the factors that might impair the witness's ability to make a correct identification or caused them to become skeptical of all eyewitnesses. Because these studies did not *independently* vary the presence of expert testimony, evidence about the witness's viewing conditions, and identification procedures, sensitivity, and skepticism were confounded. The question remained: Would jurors who heard an expert become distrustful of *all* witnesses (indicating general skepticism) or of only those witnesses whose viewing and identification conditions were poor (indicating sensitivity to the importance of these factors)?

Brian Cutler and his colleagues were eventually able to answer that question (Cutler, Penrod, and Dexter, 1989; Devenport et al., 2002). They showed subjects realistic videotaped trials that focused on the accuracy of an eyewitness's identification from a lineup. Some subjects heard an expert testify about the effects of identification conditions on accuracy, whereas other jurors heard no expert testimony on these matters. In addition, some mock jurors heard evidence that the identification conditions were good (e.g., that the lineup was presented in an unbiased manner), and others heard that they were poor. In other words, the researchers varied the presence of expert testimony and evidence about identification factors *independently*. What do the results say about sensitivity and skepticism? They suggest that the effect of expert testimony was to generally sensitize jurors to the importance of witnessing and identification conditions. There was no evidence that mock jurors became more skeptical about the eyewitness when they heard an expert.

A report of one actual crime also lends anecdotal support to the conclusion that the testimony of an expert witness has impact. Loftus (1984) described the trial of two Arizona brothers charged with the torture of three Mexicans. Two juries were in the courtroom at the same time, one deciding the verdict for Patrick Hanigan, the other deciding the fate of his brother, Thomas. Most of the evidence was from eyewitnesses, and it was virtually identical for the two defendants. However, expert testimony about the inaccuracy of eyewitnesses was introduced in Thomas's trial only. (The jury hearing Patrick Hanigan's case waited in the jury room while this evidence was presented.) Patrick Hanigan was convicted by one jury; his brother was acquitted by the other. This is as close to a "natural experiment" as the legal system has happened to offer for assessing the influence of a psychologist in the courtroom.

To summarize, the bulk of research examining the effects of expert testimony about eyewitness identifications suggests that mock jurors who are exposed to expert testimony about the vagaries of eyewitness identifications do not reject all or even most such identifications, but they do tend to view them a bit more critically. Unfortunately, even when allowed, expert testimony is an expensive safeguard that is available in only a small fraction of the cases that come to trial each year (Wells et al., 1998). Are there other, more readily available remedies?

Evaluating the Effectiveness of Cautionary Jury Instructions

The other major alternative for alerting jurors to the limitations of eyewitnesses is through a judge's instructions.

Since the 1970s, both the federal courts and many state courts have encouraged trial judges to alert jurors to the possible mistakes and misinterpretations of eyewitnesses. In *Neil vBiggers* (1972), the U.S. Supreme Court specified five conditions that jurors should consider in evaluating identification evidence:

1. The opportunity for witnesses to view the criminal at the time of the crime
2. The length of time between the crime and the later identification
3. The level of certainty shown by the witnesses at the identification
4. The witnesses' degree of attention during the crime
5. The accuracy of the witnesses' prior description of the criminal.

The Court reasoned that satisfactory reports on these conditions would suggest that an eyewitness's report was accurate. These conditions were restated and reaffirmed five years later in *Manson V. Braithwaite* (1977).

Although psychologists were pleased to see the Supreme Court take this action, they did not agree with all its strictures. Research supports consideration of the first two guidelines and the fourth and fifth conditions are plausible. It is recommendation 3—to take into account the witnesses' level of certainty—that is most questionable as a factor in evaluating identification evidence. We have already mentioned two problems related to witness confidence: It is not a strong predictor of accuracy, and it is malleable in the face of feedback. Therefore, advising jurors to assess a witness's level of certainty may be misleading. As some consolation, a study that examined how people combine these five criteria in an overall judgment of a witness's accuracy showed that certainty does not carry more weight than the other criteria (Bradfield & Wells, 2000). Instead, people used all five criteria to assess identification accuracy.

Many states have followed the Supreme Court's lead in using a cautionary instruction similar to that from *Neil v Biggers*. The instructions typically mention the eyewitness's degree of certainty as one of the factors that jurors should use to assess accuracy.

But even these less-than-perfect cautionary instructions have not been universally accepted in the courts. Some individual judges are reluctant to use such instructions. The defense typically requests that the instruction be given, but judges sometimes refuse. One reason is their concern that these instructions intrude on the jury's task. When asked whether they would use a cautionary instruction on eyewitness reliability in their courts, 78% of the judges polled said that it was improper to give such an instruction to the jury; only 12% approved (Greene, 1988).

What effects do cautionary instructions have on jurors' beliefs about eyewitness accuracy? One study compared the effectiveness of the so-called *Teljaire* instruction, a frequently used instruction based on the case of *U.S. v. Teljaire* (1972), and a set of instructions modeled after typical expert testimony regarding eyewitness reliability (Ramirez, Zemba, & Geiselman, 1996). The researchers were interested in the "sensitivity versus skepticism" concerns that we mentioned with regard to expert psychological testimony. The *Teljaire* instruction reduced mock jurors' sensitivity to eyewitness evidence (probably because that instruction mentions only vague directives and gives little indication how jurors should evaluate the evidence) and produced either skepticism or overbelief in the eyewitness, depending on the timing of the instruction. However, an instruction that incorporated information likely to be delivered by an expert preserved jurors' sensitivity to the factors that influence eyewitness reliability.

One might think that judges should be willing to issue an instruction that apparently increases sensitivity to witnessing conditions and that does not simultaneously cause jurors to question the truthfulness of *all* eyewitnesses. In general, though, judges will not deliver an instruction that provides the kind of detail that is inherent in expert testimony on eyewitness reliability. In a recent survey, judges were asked whether they would deliver jury instructions on issues for which jurors may lack knowledge (e.g., confidence malleability, weapon focus, and lineup presentation format). Only approximately one-quarter of the judges said that they would (Wise & Safer, 2004). As a result, most jurors are not informed about the possibility of suggestive lineup procedures, the debilitating effects of stress on eyewitness memory, and a host of other factors that reduce the accuracy of eyewitness reports.

REPRESSED AND RECOVERED MEMORIES

Although the retrieval of memories over short time periods is a complex task, these complications pale in comparison to those involved in retrieving memories that have been forgotten over long time periods. Two basic processes need to be distinguished in discussing and understanding long-lost memories. The first is natural forgetting, which tends to occur when people simply do not think about events that happened years earlier. Just as you might have trouble remembering the names of your third-and fourth-grade teachers (or at least remembering which teacher taught which grade), witnesses to crimes, accidents, and business transactions are likely to forget the details of these events, if not the entire event, after the passage of months or years. Such forgetting or misremembering is even more likely when the target event is confused with prior or subsequent events that bear some resemblance to it.

No one disputes the reality of natural forgetting. However, much more controversy exists about a second type of lost memory: memories that are presumed to have been repressed over long time periods. These scenarios involve events that are thought to be so traumatizing that after they are experienced, individuals bury them deeply in their unconscious through a process of emotionally motivated forgetting called repression. For example, soldiers exposed to the brutal horrors of combat and citizens who experienced a natural disaster such as an earthquake are sometimes unable to remember the traumas they obviously suffered. In such cases, repression is thought to serve a protective function by sparing the individual from having to remember and relive horrifying scenes. Furthermore, it is often reported that these repressed memories stay unconscious, and hence forgotten, unless and until they either are spontaneously recalled or are retriggered by exposure to some aspect of the original experience. (The smell of gasoline might remind a soldier of the battlefield, or the sight of an unusual cloud formation might remind an earthquake victim of the sky's appearance on the day of the disaster.)

A related unconscious process is dissociation, in which victims of abuse or other traumas are thought to escape the full impact of an event by psychologically detaching themselves from it. This process is thought to be particularly strong in children, who, because they are still forming integrated personalities, find it easier to escape from the pain of abuse by fantasizing about made-up individuals and imagining that the abuse is happening to those others. Many clinical psychologists believe that such early episodes of dissociation, involving unique ideas, feelings, and behavior, form the beginning of the altered personalities that are found in dissociative identity disorder (formerly called multiple personality disorder).

Repressed Memories and Memory Recovery Therapy

In legal circles, the memory issue that has received the most attention involves a set of claims by adults that they (1) suffered sexual/physical abuse as children (often at the hands of parents or other trusted adults), (2) repressed or dissociated any memory of these horrors for many years as a form of unconscious protection, and (3) eventually recovered their long-lost memories of the abuse. Some of the allegations of priest abuse that came to light and plagued the Roman Catholic Church in the 1990s and early 2000s, including the case of Father Paul Shanley, followed this pattern (Box 5.3).

Sometimes, repressed memories are recovered only after a person participates in "memory-focused" psychotherapy that applies techniques such as hypnosis, age regression, sodium amytal ("truth serum"), guided visualization, diary writing, or therapist instructions to help clients remember past abuse (Lindsay & Read, 1995). Such "derepression" techniques have been advocated by popular books on incest (e.g., Bass & Davis, 1988) and by therapists who believe that unless severe childhood traumas are recalled, confronted, and defused, they will cause mental problems (Blume, 1990). Some therapists who suspect clients of harboring repressed memories of abuse may ask the clients highly suggestive questions, such as "You sound like you might have been abused; what can you tell me about that?" or "You show many of the signs of childhood sexual abuse; can you tell me some of the things you think might have happened to you when you were a very young child?" One book explicitly encouraged women to believe that they were abused as infants by several perpetrators: "How old do you think you were when you were first abused? Write down the very first number that pops into your head, no matter how improbable it seems to you. ... Does it seem too young to be true? I assure you it is not"

(Fredrickson, 1992, pp. 59–66). In addition to being asked to dredge up memories of traumatic incidents, clients are often encouraged by therapists to join special support groups, such as Survivors of Incest Anonymous, that urge their members to search aggressively for buried memories of abuse.

Many researchers and therapists question the empirical and clinical validity of repressed-memory techniques, especially when apparent memories of trauma resurface many years after the alleged incidents and then only after the individual has been in therapy that first presumes and then finds such memories (Gerrie, Garry, & Loftus, 2005; Holmes, 1995). These skeptics point out that most people who suffer severe trauma do not forget the event; in fact, many of them suffer intrusive recollections of it for years afterward. Skepticism is also fueled by the fact that some alleged victims claim to have recalled traumas that happened when they were less than 1 year old, a feat that nearly all research on childhood memory and amnesia shows is not possible, for reasons related to neurological development.

One of the most widely cited studies on this topic confirms that it is possible for people to forget horrible events that happened to them in childhood, but it does not answer the question of how this forgetting occurs or how memories are usually recovered. Linda Williams (1994) interviewed 129 women who had experienced well-documented cases of childhood sexual abuse. She asked these women detailed questions about their childhood abuse histories, which had occurred an average of 17 years earlier. More than one-third of the women did not report the abuse they had experienced in childhood. But this figure does not prove that the forgetting was due to repression. It is possible that when the abuse occurred, the women were too young to be fully aware of it; in addition, some of the women might have been unwilling to report sexual abuse to an interviewer, who was a relative stranger, even if they did remember it.

However, what should we make of the sudden recall of events that a person claims to have repressed for years? If recollections of past abuse do not stem from actual traumatic events, where else could they originate? Several sources are possible, including fantasies, distorted recollections, and even the unintentional planting of memories by therapists who try (perhaps too hard) to find reasons for clients' psychological problems.

The possibility that therapy clients can recover memories of childhood abuse that have been long repressed has led many states to pass legislation that allows victims of childhood sexual abuse to bring suit against their attackers long after the alleged abuse occurred. (Typically, all lawsuits must be filed within a prescribed "limitations period" dating from the occurrence of the act that caused harm. The defendant can bar a plaintiff's claim if the complaint was filed too late.) These **delayed-reporting statutes** suspend the statute of limitations and grant abuse survivors who claim to have repressed their memory of abuse, and were therefore unaware that it occurred, the right to bring a lawsuit within three years from the date of *recovering* the memory.

The fundamental questions are these: Are recovered memories true memories, consisting of vivid, albeit delayed, recall of past horrors? Or are they pseudomemories, created by needy and suggestible clients responding to overzealous therapists who are trying to find a convincing explanation for their clients' current problems? Even psychologists are deeply divided on these questions. In fact, the Working Group on Investigation of Memories of Childhood Abuse, appointed by the American Psychological Association, was so deeply divided that the group was forced to issue two reports. One report, written by clinical psychologists (Alpert, Brown, & Courtois, 1998), suggests that intolerable emotional and physical arousal can lead a child victim to use numbing and/or dissociative coping strategies; that these strategies may interfere with or impair encoding, storage, and retrieval of memories; and that numbing responses may lead to delayed recall. A second report, authored by experimental research psychologists (Ornstein, Ceci, & Loftus, 1998), pointed out that suggestibility, memory distortions, and misleading information can work to degrade memory performance; that memory for traumatic experiences can be highly malleable; and that it is relatively easy to create pseudomemories for events that never occurred.

We are not, of course, suggesting that child abuse does not occur. Not only does it occur, but it is a serious problem both in the United States and throughout the world. It appears that children who were abused are at increased risk to suffer mental disorders in adulthood. The real question is whether allegations of childhood abuse that first surface only after intensive searching for them in therapy are

trustworthy (Bottoms, Shaver, & Goodman, 1996; Loftus, 1997b).

Can we really be sure that these alleged abuses took place? Is it possible that some memories, especially those that appear to have been repressed for years, only then to be recovered through aggressive "memory work" therapy, are imagined or made up? Although it is always difficult to assess the authenticity of any one individual's memories, evidence is accumulating that false memories can be implanted, that people can be led through suggestion and misinformation to believe such memories are real, and that third parties such as therapists may find it difficult to distinguish authentic from unauthentic recollections (Lindsay, Hagen, Read, Wade, & Garry, 2004; Porter, Yuille, & Lehman, 1999). One wonders, for example, about the authenticity of Paul Ingram's memories (see Box 5.4).

Creating Pseudomemories

In recent years, many psychologists have studied claims of repressed memories and the techniques used to retrieve them. They have used laboratory research and real-life cases to document how memories can be built from the suggestions of others.

One way that psychologists have been able to implant false memories is by enlisting the help of family members, who suggest to adult research participants that these relatives recall a fabricated event. For example, with help from participants' relatives, Loftus and Pickrell (1995) constructed a false story that the participant had been lost during a shopping trip at the age of 5, was found crying by an elderly person, and was eventually reunited with family members. After reading this story, participants wrote what they remembered about the event. Nearly 30% of participants either partially or fully remembered the made-up event, and 25% claimed in subsequent interviews that they remembered the fictitious situation. Other efforts to implant childhood memories have produced similar results, leading subjects to believe such fictitious experiences as being attacked by a vicious animal, being saved from drowning by a lifeguard, and attending a wedding reception and accidentally spilling punch on the parents of the bride (Heaps & Nash, 2001; Hyman, Husband, & Billings, 1995; Porter et al., 1999). People with higher dissociative capacity and hypnotizability are apparently more susceptible to these suggestions than others (Loftus, 1997a).

Still other experimental procedures have been used to examine the malleable nature of **autobiographical memory** (memory for one's past experiences). These include guided memory techniques to plant "impossible" memories about experiences that occurred shortly after birth (Spanos, Burgess, Burgess, Samuels, & Blois, 1999) and interpretation of participants' dreams to suggest that they had experienced a critical childhood event such as being harassed by a bully before the age of 3 (Mazzoni, Loftus, Seitz, & Lynn, 1999). Simply imagining an event from one's past can affect the belief that it actually occurred (Mazzoni & Memon, 2003), even when the event is completely implausible—for example, shaking hands with Bugs Bunny at a Disney theme park (Braun, Ellis, & Loftus, 2002). (The Bugs Bunny character was created by Warner Brothers, not Disney.)

How can we account for this "imagination inflation" effect? One possibility stems from the notion of **source contusion**. The act of imagining may make the event seem more familiar, but that familiarity is mistakenly related to childhood memories rather than to the act of imagination itself. Other studies suggest that the frequency of imagining is important: The more times participants imagine a nonexistent event, the more likely they are to report having experienced it (Thomas, Bulevich, & Loftus, 2003). The creation of false memories is most likely to occur when people who are having trouble remembering are explicitly encouraged to imagine events and discouraged from thinking about whether their constructions are real.

Recent neuroscientific data have shown that there are changes in brain activity as a result of visual imaging (Gonsalves, Reber, Gitelman, Parrish, Mesulam, & Palier, 2004). This may help explain how imagination can lead to false remembering. But bear in mind that even though false childhood memories can be implanted in some people, the memories that result from suggestions are not always false. Unfortunately, without corroboration, it is very hard to know which distant memories are true and which were implanted via suggestion.

False Memories in Court

Evidence that false memories are a significant problem for the law comes in two basic forms. First, several accusers have ultimately retracted their claims of repressed memories for abuse. One of the most highly publicized retractions involved another case of alleged priest abuse—this one filed in 1993 by Stephen Cook, who claimed that he had been sexually abused as a teenager 17 years earlier by the late Joseph Bernardin, when Bernardin had been archbishop of the Catholic archdiocese in Cincinnati. Cook reported that he had repressed these memories for years, only to recover them while hypnotized as part of therapy. The allegations were forcefully denied by Cardinal Bernardin, who at the time of the lawsuit was the head of Chicago's archdiocese and the senior-ranking Roman Catholic official in the United States. Ironically, Bernardin was well known nationally for his work helping children who had been sexually abused by priests. Cook ultimately dropped the lawsuit after admitting that his charges were based on false memories. He and Bernardin reconciled shortly before Cook died of AIDS in 1995.

A second source of information about false memories comes from court cases in which parents sue therapists who have used aggressive memory recovery techniques to help the adult children of these parents recover supposedly repressed memories of childhood sexual abuse. The claims in these malpractice lawsuits usually take the following form: (1) the abuse never occurred, (2) the therapists created and implanted false memories of abuse through their uncritical use of memory retrieval techniques, and (3) the clients ultimately came to believe the false memories and accused their parents of the abuse, sometimes suing them under delayed-reporting statutes or even filing criminal charges against them. These cases have sometimes resulted in large financial settlements to those who were falsely accused, including Gary Ramona (see Box 5.5).

SUMMARY

1. *What psychological factors contribute to the risk of mistaken identifications in the legal system?* Evidence produced by eyewitnesses often makes the difference between an unsolved crime and a conviction. In the early stages of a crime investigation, eyewitness

BOX 5.3 Recovered memories and the case against Father Paul Stanley

On February 11, 2002, Paul Busa, the man who would eventually accuse Father Paul Shanley—a controversial and ... charismatic Roman Catholic priest—of child sexual abuse years before, was working as an Air Force police officer in Colorado. That day, he received a phone call from his girlfriend in Boston, telling him of a newspaper article citing accusations against Mr. Shanley by a childhood friend of Busa's. The sex abuse scandal that rocked the Roman Catholic Church had just broken, and allegations against Father Shanley and other priests were coming to light. In this context, Busa began to recall his own abuse at the hands of Father Shanley, although these memories had apparently been repressed for years. The accuser then began to speak openly about his abuse. Busa eventually received $500,000 from the Boston archdiocese to settle a civil lawsuit against Shanley, and he agreed to proceed to trial in the criminal case against the now-defrocked former priest. Father Shanley, 74, was accused of molesting Busa, who was between the ages of 6 and 12, by pulling him out of Sunday school classes and orally and digitally raping him.

At the trial, the alleged victim, now a barrel-chested firefighter who lives in Massachusetts, gave emotional—even teary—testimony about the multiple incidents of abuse in the church bathroom, the pews, the rectory, and even the confession booth. Busa testified that he was so traumatized by the memories that surfaced years later that he was unable to continue to function in the Air Force. "I felt like my world was coming to an end," he said (Belluck, 2005). Despite some inconsistencies in his recollections and testimony from a defense expert witness who explained how false memories can be created in susceptible minds, the jury was apparently convinced by Busa's seemingly heartfelt testimony. They convicted Father Shanley on two counts of rape and two counts of indecent assault on a child. He was sentenced to 12 to 15 years in prison.

accounts can provide important clues and permit suspects to be identified. But witnesses often make mistakes, and mistaken identifications have led to the conviction of numerous innocent people. Errors can occur at the moment the crime is committed or at any of the three phases of the memory process: encoding, storage, and retrieval. Furthermore, subsequent questioning and new experiences can alter what has been remembered from the past. In describing the factors that affect the reliability of eyewitness memory, psychologists distinguish estimator variables—variables whose impact on an identification can only be estimated and not controlled—from system variables—variables that are under the control of the justice system. Much recent research has focused on a particular set of system variables related to the way lineups are conducted.

2. *How do courts regard the use of hypnotically refreshed memory? What procedures should he followed when hypnosis is used in a forensic setting?* The courts have taken different positions on the admissibility of hypnotically induced testimony. Three cautions seem paramount: (1)

The hypnosis should be carried out by a psychiatrist or a psychologist who is unaware of the facts of the case, not by a police officer, (2) the procedures should be recorded so that they can be scrutinized by others, and (3) the products of such hypnosis during the investigation of a crime either should not be used as evidence during the trial or should be admitted only under exceptional circumstances. A context reinstatement technique has recently been suggested as a substitute for forensic hypnosis.

3. *How do jurors evaluate the testimony of eyewitnesses, and can psychologists help jurors understand the potential problems of eyewitness testimony?* Psychological tests of eyewitnesses' accuracy conclude that eyewitnesses can be mistaken, although rates of accuracy depend on many factors—some environmental, some personal, and some related to the interval between the crime and the recall. Despite these limitations, jurors are heavily influenced by the testimony of eyewitnesses, and they tend to overestimate the accuracy of such witnesses, relying to a great extent on the confidence of the eyewitness. To

alert jurors to these problems, two types of special interventions have been tried (in addition to the routine use of cross-examination of witnesses). Some trial judges permit psychologists to testify as expert witnesses about the problems in being an accurate eyewitness. Laboratory evaluations of mock juries find that such testimony generally sensitizes jurors to factors that affect an eyewitness's reliability. The other intervention, encouraged by the U.S. Supreme Court and several state courts, is for the judge to give the jurors a "cautionary instruction," sensitizing them to aspects of the testimony of eyewitnesses that they should especially consider.

4. *Can memories for trauma be repressed, and if so, can these memories be recovered accurately?* The problems that threaten accurate memories are compounded in cases in which an individual claims to have recovered memories for traumatic childhood events that have been repressed or dissociated for long periods. The accuracy of repressed and then recovered memories is particularly suspect when the recollections occur in the context of therapies that use suggestive memory retrieval techniques such as hypnosis. Recent research shows that people can "remember" events that never happened, sometimes simply by imagining them. Litigation involving the recovery of repressed memories involves lawsuits brought by victims claiming that therapists led them to believe that they were abused in the past and lawsuits brought by the accused claiming that therapists promoting such false recollections are guilty of malpractice.

KEY TERMS

absolute judgment

autobiographical memory

change blindness

cognitive interview

confabulation

confirmation bias

context reinstatement

delayed-reporting statutes

dissociation

double-blind testing procedure

encoding

estimator variable

experimenter bias

hyperamnesia

in-group/out-group differences

memory hardening

other-race effect

physiognomic variability

postevent information

relative judgment

repression

retrieval

sequential presentation

simultaneous presentation

source confusion

storage

system variable

unconscious transference

weapon focus effect

BOX 5.4
THE CASE OF
Paul Ingram: Real memories or fabricated memories?

The case of Paul Ingram provides one chilling example of how false memories might be created (Ofshe, 1992). Ingram, a sheriff's deputy in Olympia, Washington, was arrested for child abuse in 1988. He steadfastly denied the allegations, but the police continued to question and pressure him over the next five months, despite the lack of much evidence to support the allegations of sexual abuse that two of Ingram's children had lodged against him. To spur Ingram's memory, a psychologist or a detective would repeatedly describe to him an act of abuse, such as Ingram and other men raping his daughter. At first, Ingram would have no memory for such incidents, but after concerted effort, including praying and being hypnotized to strengthen his memory, he started "recalling" some details. Ultimately, Paul Ingram confessed not just to the charges of incest but also to rapes, assaults, and participation in a satanic cult that was believed to have killed 25 babies (Wright, 1994).

To check the accuracy of Ingram's memory, sociologist Richard Ofshe, hired as a consultant to the prosecution, asked Ingram to recall an event that Ofshe totally fabricated—that Ingram had forced his son and daughter to have sex with each other in front of him. Just as with the police interrogation, Ingram could not remember anything at first, but after thinking and praying about it, he gradually formed images of the event and, within a matter of hours, endorsed a three-page confession to the events Ofshe fabricated. Ofshe concluded that Paul Ingram was not a sex offender or satanic cult member, but a vulnerable man with a strong heed to please authorities and a highly suggestible nature that made him fall easily into a trance.

Ultimately, Paul Ingram decided to plead guilty to six: counts of third-degree rape. Throughout many years of incarceration, he insisted that he never abused his children, and he was eventually released, in April 2003. He was required to register as a sex offender in Washington State. Was Paul Ingram duped into confessing on the basis of false memories, or was he a guilt-ridden abuser who finally admitted his guilt? Questions such as these are at the heart of the controversy over whether therapists should aggressively try to help clients recover memories of abuse that they suspect have been repressed.

BOX 5.5
THE CASE OF
Gary Ramona, his daughter's false memories, and the therapists who suggested them

The first case in which a parent successfully sued a therapist for implanting a false memory of abuse was brought by Gary Ramona, once a highly paid executive at a large winery in Napa County, California. Ramona accused family counselor Marche Isabella and psychiatrist Richard Rose of planting false memories of trauma in his daughter, Holly, while she was their 19-year-old patient. In his suit, Ramona claimed that the therapists told Holly that her bulimia and depression were caused by having been repeatedly raped by her father when she was a child. They also told her, he claimed, that the memory of this molestation was so traumatic that she had repressed it for years. According to Ramona, Dr. Rose, then gave Holly sodium amytal to confirm the validity of her "recovered memory." Finally, Isabella was said to have told Holly's mother that up to 80% of all bulimics had been sexually abused (a statistic for which no scientific support exists).

At their trial, the therapists claimed that Holly suffered flashbacks of what seemed to be real sexual abuse. She also became increasingly depressed and bulimic after reporting these frightening images. In addition, Holly's mother, Stephanie, who had divorced her husband after Holly's allegations came to light, testified that she suspected her husband might have abused Holly. She listed several pieces of supposedly corroborating evidence: that Holly had complained of vaginal pains during childhood, that she always feared gynecological exams and disliked her father touching her; and that Gary had seemed overly eager to baby-sit Holly and their two other daughters when they were young. She also recalled once coming home to find young Holly wandering around the house wearing no underwear; she said she found the underwear, along with bed sheets, in the clothes dryer. During his testimony, Gary Ramona emotionally denied ever sexually abusing his daughter.

The scientific experts who testified on Ramona's behalf criticized the therapists for using risky and dangerous techniques. Elizabeth Loftus (1993), an expert called by Gary Ramona and a leading critic of therapists

who aggressively pursue the recovery of long-buried traumatic memories, charged that these therapists often either suggest the idea of trauma to their clients or are too uncritical in accepting clients' reports of trauma. Another defense witness, Martin Ome, a renowned authority on hypnosis, condemned the use of sodium amytal interviews as "inherently untrustworthy and unreliable" and concluded that Holly's memory had been so distorted by her therapists that she no longer knew what the truth was.

The jury decided that Holly's therapists had indeed acted improperly and, in May 1994, awarded Gary Ramona damages in the amount of $500,000. Since then, there has been other false memory litigation against therapists. In its first two years of operation, the False Memory Syndrome Foundation received more than 13,000 reports from people who said they were victims of false accusations; most were parents whose grown children had charged them with long-past abuse. This organization has also received reports from scores of former therapy patients who admit that their original charges of abuse were false and resulted from therapists encouraging them to "remember" events that never happened.

The threat of false-memory lawsuits adds to the already difficult challenges faced by therapists trying to help adult clients cope with a traumatic childhood. It is obvious that recovered-memory therapy has led to very real damage to some clients and their families (Ofshe & Watters, 1994). It is also clear that the trauma of child abuse does occur and can leave deep and long-lasting emotional scars. Accordingly, therapists must be sympathetic listeners for clients who remember the real horrors of their childhood. At the same time, therapists must be careful to avoid suggesting that clients' problems come from traumas that may never have been inflicted. In they words of Gary Ramona's attorney, Richard Harrington, "if (therapists) use nonsensical theories about so-called repressed memories to destroy people's lives, they will be held accountable."

Reconstruction of Automobile Destruction

An Example of the Interaction Between Language and Memory

ELIZABETH F. LOFTUS AND JOHN C. PALMER

Two experiments are reported in which subjects viewed films of automobile accidents and then answered questions about events occurring in the films. The question, "About how fast were the cars going when they smashed into each other?" elicited higher estimates of speed than questions which used the verbs *collided, bumped, contacted,* or *hit* in place of *smashed.* On a retest one week later, those subjects who received the verb *smashed* were more likely to say "yes" to the question, "Did you see any broken glass?", even though broken glass was not present in the film. These results are consistent with the view that the questions asked subsequent to an event can cause a reconstruction in one's memory of that event.

How accurately do we remember the details of a complex event, like a traffic accident, that has happened in our presence? More specifically,

[1] This research was supported by the Urban Mass Transportation Administration, Department of Transportation, Grant No. WA-11-0004. Thanks go to Geoffrey Loftus, Edward E. Smith, and Stephen Woods for many important and helpful comments. Reprint requests should be sent to Elizabeth F. Loftus. Department of Psychology, University of Washington, Seattle, Washington 98195.

how well do we do when asked to estimate some numerical quantity such as how long the accident took, how fast the cars were traveling, or how much time elapsed between the sounding of a horn and the moment of collision?

It is well documented that most people are markedly inaccurate in reporting such numerical details as time, speed, and distance (Bird, 1927; Whipple, 1909). For example, most people have difficulty estimating the duration of an event, with some research indicating that the tendency is to overestimate the duration of events which are complex (Block, 1974; Marshall, 1969; Ornstein, 1969). The judgment of speed is especially difficult, and practically every automobile accident results in huge variations from one witness to another as to how fast a vehicle was actually traveling (Gardner, 1933). In one test administered to Air Force personnel who knew in advance that they would be questioned about the speed of a moving automobile, estimates ranged from 10 to 50 mph. The car they watched was actually going only 12 mph (Marshall, 1969, p. 23).

Given the inaccuracies in estimates of speed, it seems likely that there are variables which are potentially powerful in terms of influencing these estimates. The present research was conducted to investigate one such variable, namely, the phrasing of the question used to elicit the speed judgment. Some questions are clearly more suggestive than others. This fact of life has resulted in the legal concept of a leading question and in legal rules indicating when leading questions are allowed (*Supreme Court Reporter,* 1973). A leading question is simply one that, either by its form or content, suggests to the witness what answer is desired or leads him to the desired answer.

In the present study, subjects were shown films of traffic accidents and then they answered questions about the accident. The subjects were interrogated about the speed of the vehicles in one of several ways. For example, some subjects were asked, "About how fast were the cars going when they hit each other?" while others were asked, "About how fast were the cars going when they smashed into each other?" As Fillmore (1971) and Bransford and McCarrell (in press) have noted, *hit* and *smashed* may involve specification of differential rates of movement. Furthermore, the two verbs may also involve differential specification of the likely consequences of the events to which they are referring. The impact of the accident is apparently gentler for *hit* than for *smashed*.

EXPERIMENT I
Method

Forty-five students participated in groups of various sizes. Seven films were shown, each depicting a traffic accident. These films were segments from longer driver's education films borrowed from the Evergreen Safety Council and the Seattle Police Department. The length of the film segments ranged from 5 to 30 sec. Following each film, the subjects received a questionnaire asking them first to, "give an account of the accident you have just seen," and then to answer a series of specific questions about the accident. The critical question was the one that interrogated the subject about the speed of the vehicles involved in the collision. Nine subjects were asked, "About how fast were the cars going when they hit each other?" Equal numbers of the remaining subjects were interrogated with the verbs *smashed, collided, bumped,* and *contacted* in place of *hit*. The entire experiment lasted about an hour and a half. A different ordering of the films was presented to each group of subjects.

Results

Following the procedures outlined by Clark (1973), an analysis of variance was performed with verbs as a fixed effect, and subjects and films as random effects, yielding a significant quasi F ratio, $F'(5,55) = 4.65, p < .005$.

Some information about the accuracy of subjects' estimates can be obtained from our data. Four of the seven films were staged crashes; the original purpose of these films was to illustrate what can happen to human beings when cars collide at various speeds. One collision took place at 20 mph, one at 30, and two at 40. The mean estimates of speed for these four films were: 37.7, 36.2, 39.7, and 36.1 mph, respectively. In agreement with previous work, people are not very good at judging how fast a vehicle was actually traveling.

Discussion

The results of this experiment indicate that the form of a question (in this case, changes in a single word) can markedly and systematically affect a witness's answer to that question. The actual speed of the vehicles controlled little variance in subject reporting, while the phrasing of the question controlled considerable variance.

Two interpretations of this finding are possible. First, it is possible that the differential speed estimates result merely from response-bias factors. A subject is uncertain whether to say 30 mph or 40 mph, for example, and the verb *smashed* biases his response towards the higher estimate. A second interpretation is that the question form causes a change in the subject's memory representation of the accident. The verb *smashed* may change a subject's memory such that he "sees" the accident as being more severe than it actually was. If this is the case, we might expect subjects to "remember" other details that did not actually occur, but are commensurate with an accident occurring at higher speeds. The second experiment was designed to provide additional insights into the origin of the differential speed estimates.

EXPERIMENT II
Method

One hundred and fifty students participated in this experiment, in groups of various sizes. A film depicting a multiple car accident was shown, followed by a questionnaire. The film lasted less than 1 min; the accident in the film lasted 4 sec. At the end of the film, the subjects received a questionnaire asking them first to describe the accident in their own words, and then to answer a series of questions about the accident. The critical question was the one that interrogated the subject about the speed of the vehicles. Fifty subjects were asked, "About how fast were the cars going when they smashed into each other?" Fifty subjects were asked, "About how fast were the cars going when they hit each other?" Fifty subjects were not interrogated about vehicular speed.

One week later, the subjects returned and without viewing the film again they answered a series of questions about the accident. The critical question here was, "Did you see any broken glass?" which the subjects answered by checking "yes" or "no." This question was embedded in a list totalling 10 questions, and it appeared in a random position in the list. There was no broken glass in the accident, but, since broken glass is commensurate with accidents occurring at high speed, we expected that the subjects who had been asked the smashed question might more often say "yes" to this critical question.

Results

The mean estimate of speed for subjects interrogated with *smashed* was 10.46 mph; with *hit* the estimate was 8.00 mph. These means are significantly different, $t(98) = 2.00$, $p < .05$.

An independence chi-square test on these responses was significant beyond the .025 level, $\chi^2(2) = 7.76$. The important result is that the probability of saying "yes," P(Y), to the question about broken glass is .32 when the verb *smashed* is used, and .14 with *hit*. Thus *smashed* leads both to more "yes" responses and to higher speed estimates. It appears to be the case that the effect of the verb is mediated at least in part by the speed estimate. The question now arises: Is *smashed* doing anything else besides increasing the estimate of speed? To answer this, the function relating P(Y) to speed estimate was calculated separately for *smashed* and *hit*. If the speed estimate is the only way in which effect of verb is mediated, then for a given speed estimate, P(Y) should be independent of verb. P(Y) is lower for *hit* than for *smashed*; the difference between the two verbs ranges from .03 for estimates of 1–5 mph to .18 for estimates of 6–10 mph. The average difference between the two curves is about .12. Whereas the unconditional difference of .18 between the *smashed* and *hit* conditions is attenuated, it is by no means eliminated when estimate of speed is controlled for. It thus appears that the verb *smashed* has other effects

besides that of simply increasing the estimate of speed. One possibility will be discussed in the next section.

DISCUSSION

To reiterate, we have first of all provided an additional demonstration of something that has been known for some time, namely, that the way a question is asked can enormously influence the answer that is given. In this instance, the question, "About how fast were the cars going when they smashed into each other?" led to higher estimates of speed than the same question asked with the verb *smashed* replaced by *hit*. Furthermore, this seemingly small change had consequences for how questions are answered a week after the original event occurred.

As a framework for discussing these results, we would like to propose that two kinds of information go into one's memory for some complex occurrence. The first is information gleaned during the perception of the original event; the second is external information supplied after the fact. Over time, information from these two sources may be integrated in such a way that we are unable to tell from which source some specific detail is recalled. All we have is one "memory."

Discussing the present experiments in these terms, we propose that the subject first forms some representation of the accident he has witnessed. The experimenter then, while asking, "About how fast were the cars going when they smashed into each other?" supplies a piece of external information, namely, that the cars did indeed smash into each other. When these two pieces of information are integrated, the subject has a memory of an accident that was more severe than in fact it was. Since broken glass is commensurate with a severe accident, the subject is more likely to think that broken glass was present.

There is some connection between the present work and earlier work on the influence of verbal labels on memory for visually presented form stimuli. A classic study in psychology showed that when subjects are asked to reproduce a visually presented form, their drawings tend to err in the direction of a more familiar object suggested by a verbal label initially associated with the to-be-remembered form (Carmichael, Hogan, & Walter, 1932). More recently, Daniel (1972) showed that recognition memory, as well as reproductive memory, was similarly affected by verbal labels, and he concluded that the verbal label causes a shift in the memory strength of forms which are better representatives of the label.

When the experimenter asks the subject, "About how fast were the cars going when they smashed into each other?", he is effectively labeling the accident a smash. Extrapolating the conclusions of Daniel to this situation, it is natural to conclude that the label, smash, causes a shift in the memory representation of the accident in the direction of being more similar to a representation suggested by the verbal label.

References

BIRD, C. THE INFLUENCE OF THE PRESS UPON THE ACCURACY OF REPORT. *JOURNAL OF ABNORMAL AND SOCIAL PSYCHOLOGY*, 1927, **22**, 123–129.

BLOCK, R. A. MEMORY AND THE EXPERIENCE OF DURATION IN RETROSPECT. *MEMORY & COGNITION*, 1974, **2**, 153–160.

BRANSFORD, J. D., & McCARRELL, N. S. A SKETCH OF A COGNITIVE APPROACH TO COMPREHENSION : SOME THOUGHTS ABOUT UNDERSTANDING WHAT IT MEANS TO COMPREHEND. IN D. PALERMO & W. WEIMER (EDS.), *COGNITION AND THE SYMBOLIC PROCESSES*. WASHINGTON, DC.: V.H. WINSTON & CO., IN PRESS.

CAHMICHAIL, L., HOGAN, H. P., & WAI H.R., A. A. AU EXPERIMENTAL STUDY OF THE EFFECT OF LANGUAGE ON THE REPRODUCTION OF VISUALLY PERCEIVED FORM. *JOURNAL OF EXPERIMENTAL PSYCHOLOGY*, 1932, **15**, 73–86.

CLARK, H. H. THE LANGUAGE-AS-FIXED-EFFECT FALLACY: A CRITIQUE OF LANGUAGE STATISTICS IN PSYCHOLOGICAL RESEARCH. *JOURNAL OF VERBAL LEARNING AND VERBAL BEHAVIOR*, 1973, **12**, 335–359.

DANIEL, T. C. NATURE OF THE EFFECT OF VERBAL LABELS ON RECOGNITION MEMORY FOR FORM. *JOURNAL OF EXPERIMENTAL PSYCHOLOGY*, 1972, **96**, 152–157.

FILLMORE, C. J. TYPES OF LEXICAL INFORMATION. IN D. D. STEINBERG AND L. A. JAKOBOVITS (EDS.), *SEMANTICS: AN INTERDISCIPLINARY READER IN PHILOSOPHY, LINGNISTICS, AND PSYCHOLOGY*. CAMBRIDGE: CAMBRIDGE UNIVERSITY PRESS, 1971.

GARDNER, D. S. THE PERCEPTION AND MEMORY OF WITNESSES. *CORNELL LAW QUARTERLY*, 1933, **8**, 391–409.

MARSHALL, J. *LAW AND PSYCHOLOGY IN CONFLICT*. NEW YORK: ANCHOR BOOKS, 1969.

ORNSTEIN, R. E. ON *THE EXPERIENCE OF TIME*. HARMONDSWORTH. MIDDLESEX. ENGLAND: PENGUIN, 1969.

WHIPPLE, G. M. THE OBSERVER AS REPORTER: A SURVEY OF THE PSYCHOLOGY OF TESTIMONY. *PSYCHOLOGICAL BULLETIN*, 1909, **6**, 153–170.

SUPREME COURT REPORTER, 1973, 3: RULES OF EVIDENCE FOR UNITED STATE COURTS AND MAGISTRATES.

Our Changeable Memories

Legal and Practical Implications

ELIZABTH F. LOFTUS

The malleability of memory is becoming increasingly clear. Many influences can cause memories to change or even be created anew, including our imaginations and the leading questions or different recollections of others. The knowledge that we cannot rely on our memories, however compelling they might be, leads to questions about the validity of criminal convictions that are based largely on the testimony of victims or witnesses. Our scientific understanding of memory should be used to help the legal system to navigate this minefield.

Memories are precious. They give us identity. They create a shared past that bonds us with family and friends. They seem fixed, like concrete, so that if you 'stepped' on them they would still be there as they always were.

But memories are not fixed. Everyday experience tells us that they can be lost, but they can also be drastically changed or even created. Inaccurate memories can sometimes be as compelling and 'real' as an accurate memory. In this article, I discuss the ways in which memories can be reshaped and their implications for the legal system. If we cannot believe our own memories, how can we know whether the memories of a victim or a witness are accurate?

REMAKING MEMORIES

We are all familiar with temporary memory problems. "I can't remember the right word," says a colleague at a cocktail party. "Is it senility?" I reply: "Can you remember the word later?" And the usual answer will be yes, proving that the information was not lost, but only temporarily unavailable. Retrieval problems are common.

However, there are also problems with storing something new. This usually occurs simply because the person concerned is not paying attention. But some people are unable to store new information even if they are paying attention and have the opportunity to repeat the new information over and over again—several hours later, it is gone. Such people, including patients with Alzheimer's disease, might not even complain about 'losing their memory' because they do not realize that anything is missing[1].

More insidiously, memories can become scrambled, sometimes in the process of attempting to retrieve something. You might relate a story to a friend but unwittingly include some mistaken details. Later, as you attempt to recall the episode, you might come across your memory of the scrambled recall attempt instead of your original memory. Memory is malleable. It is not, as is commonly thought, like a museum piece sitting in a display case. "Memory is," as the Uruguayan novelist Eduardo Galeano once said, "born every day, springing from the past, and set against it."[2]

Usually the scrambled memory does not matter very much. But if you are an eyewitness to a crime, your scrambled recall could send someone to prison. And, rather than feeling hesitant, you might feel perfectly sure of the truth of your memory. The history of the United States justice system, like those of other countries, is littered with wrongful convictions made on the basis of mistaken memories[3]. Huff recently estimated[4] that about 7,500 people arrested for serious crimes were wrongly convicted in the United States in 1999. He further noted that the rate is thought to be much lower in Great Britain, Canada, Australia, New Zealand and many other nations, especially those that have established procedures for reviewing cases involving the potential of wrongful conviction.

Ronald Cotton, a North Carolina prisoner who was convicted in 1986 of raping a 22-year-old college student, Jennifer Thompson, puts a human face on these cases. Thompson stood up on the stand, put her hand on the Bible and swore to tell the truth. On the basis of her testimony, Cotton was sentenced to prison for life. Eventually, DNA testing—which began 11 years after Thompson had first identified Cotton—proved his innocence. Another man, Bobby Poole, pleaded guilty to the crime[3].

Faulty memory is not just about picking the wrong person. Memory problems were also evident during the sniper attacks that killed ten people in the Washington DC area in 2002 (see for example, REF. 5). Witnesses reported seeing a white truck or van fleeing several of the crime scenes. It seems that a white vehicle might have been near one of the first shootings and media repetition of this information contaminated the memories of witnesses to later attacks, making them more likely to remember white trucks. When caught, the sniper suspects were driving a blue car. Were we observing unwitting memory contamination on a nationwide scale?

Witnesses can be wrong for several reasons. A key reason is that they pick up information from other sources; they combine bits of memory from different experiences. A growing body of research shows that memory more closely resembles a synthesis of experiences than a replay of a videotape[6]. Three decades ago, a method of studying memory distortions was introduced. People watched a simulated crime or accident. Later they were given erroneous information about the details of the event, such as the false detail that a man had curly rather than straight hair. Many of these people later claimed that they had seen a curly-haired person[7]. Studies such as this showed how leading questions or other forms of misinformation could contaminate the memories of witnesses about events that they had recently experienced[8].

In the past decade, the challenges have become greater. Newer studies showed that you could do more than change a detail here and there in someone's memory. You could actually make people believe that a childhood experience had occurred when in fact it never happened. Examples include being lost in a shopping mall for an extended period of time, being rescued by a lifeguard, or surviving a vicious animal attack[9–12]. How is this possible? In our studies, we enlist family members to help us to persuade their relatives that the events occurred. This method has led about a quarter of our subjects to believe that they were lost in a shopping mall for an extended period of time, and were ultimately rescued by an elderly person and reunited with their families. In other studies, we engaged people in guided imagination exercises. We asked people to imagine for a minute that as a child they had tripped and broken a window with their hand. Later, many of them became confident that the event had occurred. In other studies, we encouraged people to read stories and testimonials about witnessing demonic possession, and even these raised confidence that this rather implausible event had happened.

One recurring issue for memory distortion research is the question of whether the events being reported after such a manipulation might have actually happened. Perhaps the subject did break a window but had forgotten about it—the imagination exercise might have triggered a true memory rather than planting a false one. To prove that false memories can be insinuated into memory by these suggestive techniques, researchers have tried to plant memories that would be highly implausible or impossible. For example, one set of studies asked people to evaluate advertising copy. They were shown a fake print advertisement that described a visit to Disneyland and how they met and shook hands with Bugs Bunny. Later, 16% of these subjects said that they remembered meeting and shaking hands with Bugs Bunny[13]. In follow-up research carried out by Grinley in my laboratory, several presentations of fake advertisements involving Bugs Bunny at Disneyland resulted in 25–35% of subjects claiming to have met Bugs Bunny[14]. Moreover, when these subjects were subsequently asked to report precisely what they remembered about their encounter with Bugs Bunny, 62% remembered shaking his hand and 46% remembered hugging him. A few people remembered touching his ears or tail. One person remembered that he was holding a carrot. The scenes described in the advertisement never occurred, because Bugs Bunny is a Warner Bros. cartoon character and would not be featured at a Disney property.

"One of the cleverest and most powerful techniques for planting highly implausible false memories involves the use of fake photographs.

Other 'impossible' memories have been recently planted in British students[15]. The false event was "having a nurse remove a skin sample from my little finger." This medical procedure was not one that was carried out in the United Kingdom, according to extensive investigation of health policy records. After guided imagination, many subjects came to remember the non-existent procedure occurring in their childhood. Some embellished their reported memory with significant detail such as, "There was a nurse and the place smelled horrible."

One of the cleverest and most powerful techniques for planting highly implausible false memories involves the use of fake photographs[16]. Subjects were shown a falsified photograph that was made up of a real photograph of the subject and a relative pasted into a prototype photograph of a hot-air balloon. Family members confirmed that the event had never occurred. Subjects were shown the fake photograph and asked to tell "everything you can remember without leaving anything out, no matter how trivial it may seem." There were two further interviews, and by the end of the series 50% of the subjects had recalled, partially or clearly, the fictitious hot-air balloon ride. Some embellished their reports with sensory details of a hot-air balloon ride during childhood that had never occurred. For example, one subject said "I'm still pretty certain it occurred when I was in sixth grade at, um, the local school there … I'm pretty certain that mum is down on the ground taking a photo."[16]

These studies, and many more like them, show that people can develop beliefs and memories for events that definitely did not happen to them. They can do this when fed strong suggestions—such as "your family told us about this event" or "look at this photograph of you from childhood". They can even do this when induced to imagine the experiences. Large changes in autobiography can be achieved quickly. Attempts to distinguish the false memories from true ones have occasionally shown statistical differences, such as differences in confidence, vividness or amount of detail[17], or differences in lateralized brain potentials[18,19]. For example, in the hot-air balloon study[16] the real memories were expressed with much more confidence than the fake ones. In most studies, any differences between true and false memories are observed only when comparing large groups of true and false memories, and these differences are typically too small to be useful for classifying a single autobiographical memory report as true or false. Psychological science has not yet developed a reliable way to classify memories as true or false. Moreover, it should be kept in mind that many false memories have been expressed with great confidence.

IMPLICATIONS FOR SOCIETY

While researchers continue to investigate false memories, it is evident that there are already lessons to be learned. The fact that the memories of victims and witnesses can be false or inaccurate even though they believe them to be true has important implications for the legal system and for those who counsel or treat victims of crimes.

Some psychotherapists use techniques that are suggestive (along the lines of, "you don't remember sexual abuse, but you have the symptoms, so let's just imagine who might have done it"). These can lead patients to false beliefs and memories, causing great damage to the patients themselves and to those who are accused. In one Illinois case, psychiatrist Bennett Braun was accused by his patient, Patricia Burgus, of using drugs and hypnosis to convince her that she possessed 300 personalities, ate meat loaf made of human flesh and was a high priestess in a satanic cult[20]. By some estimates, thousands of people have been harmed in similar ways by well-meaning providers who apply a 'cure' that ends up being worse than the disease[21]. Law enforcement interrogations that are suggestive can lead witnesses to mistaken memories, even ones that are detailed and expressed with confidence. Hundreds of people have been harmed by witnesses who made a mistake that could have been avoided[22,23]. Of course, even before the police arrive on the scene, witnesses talk to one another and cross contamination can occur. I personally witnessed this when I entered a shop in Cambridge, Massachusetts, moments after a robbery had occurred and before the police arrived. In the immediate aftermath, customers and employees shared their recollections, providing fuel for influencing the thoughts of one another. This is why, during the Washington DC area sniper attacks in 2002, law enforcement officials advised members of the public who might witness the 'next attack' to write down what they saw immediately, even using their hand if they did not have paper. Good advice, but I would suggest having paper handy because the best course of action is to write down everything that can be remembered before witnesses are interrogated or talk to one another. This activity strengthens the memory and protects it to some extent from later contamination[24].

It is often argued that a few false accusations are just the cost of doing business. But this cost includes the potential for the actual perpetrator to commit more crimes, and for the taxpayer to have to pay sizable sums of money in compensation when wrongful convictions are exposed (which probably happens in only a fraction of cases). Although the defendants in most wrongful prosecution cases are government officials or organizations, in one recent case the witness with mistaken memory was successfully sued[25]. Donna Parmeter, a former prison guard, was charged with kidnapping, robbery and torture. She had been identified by the victim, Peter Kretzu, who was tied up, blindfolded and tortured by two masked robbers. Although the attackers wore ski masks, Kretzu claimed that he recognized Donna (from her voice and eyes) and her husband Joseph (from his breathing, laugh, body shape and 'chicken soup' body odour). Kretzu was 100% certain. Donna was eventually exonerated when investigators substantiated her alibi. But she had spent a month in jail, and she later sued, eventually winning a US$100,000 civil judgement against Kretzu. In the past, mistaken witnesses simply went their own ways, although there are a few known instances in which they have made profound apologies to those whom they had falsely accused. Will we now see more cases in which mistaken witnesses end up paying financially for their mistakes?

Although much of the research has focused on wrongful convictions, there is another side to the criminal justice coin. Memory distortions can also contribute to failures to convict a guilty person, not because an innocent person is convicted in their place, but because accurate witness testimony can be undermined. If witnesses misremember some detail, or they are told that their stories conflict with other evidence, they might discount their testimony and be less persuasive than perhaps they should be, or the jury might consider their entire testimony to be unreliable.

Scientific research into memory has the potential to minimize these kinds of problem. Information from psychological scientists (and perhaps neuroscientists) could help to keep the people in power from making decisions on the basis of myths or misconceptions about memory. Scientific knowledge could be shared with relevant individuals in many ways: through workshops for mental health professionals, training for police, seminars for lawyers and judges, judicial instructions or expert testimony for jurors. In one example, Jacob Beard of West Virginia was wrongly convicted of murdering two women and spent many years in prison. He managed to win a second trial. Expert testimony on suggestion and false memory was presented in that second trial, and helped to secure his acquittal. Beard later filed a civil lawsuit, and eventually received a settlement of nearly US$2 million in his case against state and county police[26].

This list of potential venues for education about the nature of memory represents just one proposal for a possible programme for action. Some legislative remedies might also be called for, especially in the most serious cases that can result in a sentence of death. Recently, the Innocence Protection Act was introduced in the United States Congress. It has two useful elements: access to DNA testing for convicted people and improvement in the quality of lawyers who try death penalty cases. Better lawyers might be better acquainted with the problems of memory and how to educate judges and jurors about these problems. Congress will be considering this legislation again in 2003 (REF. 27).

The American Judicature Society proposed the creation of an 'innocence commission' that would study why the legal system has failed in known cases of wrongful conviction. After all, look what the National Transportation Safety Board does when a plane crashes. Few expenses are spared as every aspect of the crash is examined. Not long ago, I proposed an analogous 'National Memory Safety Board' that might concentrate specifically on memory problems that have led to injustice[28]. If the travesties of the past few decades were thoroughly examined side-by-side with scientific knowledge on memory, we would all benefit. It would be too late for the family of Steve Titus, who died of a heart attack at the age of 35 after being falsely convicted of rape. It would be too late for the many death row prisoners who have recently been exonerated by DNA evidence. It would be too late for the scores of innocent defendants who have had to face civil litigation over false claims of satanic ritual abuse and other dubious charges. But it might be in time to keep us from searching for that next white van that does not exist because someone inadvertently planted a false memory.

To reiterate the main points: memory is more prone to error than many people realize. Our memory system can be infused with compelling illusory memories of important events. These grand memory errors have contributed to injustices that could have been avoided or minimized. As a start, I suggest that we all remember an important truth about the mind—paraphrasing Galeano: memory is born anew every day.

1. Duke, L. M., Seltzer, B., Seltzer, J. E. & Vasterling, J. J. Cognitive components of deficit awareness in Alzheimer's disease. *Neuropsychology* **16**, 359–369 (2002).

2. Galeano, E. H. translated by Belfrage, C. (with Schafer, M.) in *The Book of Embraces* 124–125 (Norton & Co., New York, 1991).

3. Connors, E., Lundregan, T., Miller, N. & McEwan, T. *Convicted by Juries, Exonerated by Science: Case Studies in the Use of DNA Evidence to Establish innocence After Trial* (National Institute of Justice, Alexandria, Virginia, 1996).

4. Huff, C. R. What can we learn from other nations about the problem of wrongful conviction? *Judicature* **86**, 91–97 (2002).

5. Kennedy, H. Beltway sniper notches no. 8. Kills man gassing car in Va., dodges dragnet. *NY Daily News* (online), (cited 12 October 2002), http://www.nydailynews.com/news/crime_file/story/26305p-24892c.html (2002).

6. Schacter, D. L. *Searching for Memory* (Basic Books, New York, 1996).

7. Loftus, E. F. & Greene, E. Warning: even memory for faces may be contagious. *Law Hum. Behav.* 4, 323–334 (1980).

8. Loftus, E. F. & Hoffman, H. G. Misinformation and memory: the creation of memory. *J. Exp. Psychol. Gen.* *118*, 100–104 (1989).

9. Heaps, C. M. & Nash, M. Comparing recollective experience in true and false autobiographical memories. *J. Exp. Psychol. Learn. Mem. Cogn.* **27**, 920–930 (2001).

10. Loftus, E. F. & Pickrell, J. E. The formation of false memories. *Psychiatr. Ann.* **25**, 720–725 (1995).

11. Loftus, E. F. Creating false memories. *Sci. Am.* **277**, 70–75 (1997).

12. Porter, S., Birt, A., Yuille, J. C. & Lehman, D. R. Negotiating false memories: interviewer and rememberer characteristics relate to memory distortion. *Psychol. Sci.* **11**, 507–510 (2000).

13. Braun, K. A., Ellis, R. E. & Loftus, E. F. Make my memory: how advertising can change our memories of the past. *Psychol. Mark.* **19**, 1–23 (2002).

14. Grinley, M. J. Effects of Advertising on Semantic and Episodic Memory. Thesis, Univ. Washington (2002).

15. Mazzoni, G. & Memon, A. Imagination can create false autobiographical memories. *Psychol. Sci.* (in the press).

16. Wade, K. A., Garry, M., Read, J. D. & Lindsay, S. A picture is worth a thousand lies. *Psychon. Bull. Rev.* 9, 597–603 (2002).

17. Porter, S., Yuille, J. C. & Lehman, D. R. The nature of real, implanted, and fabricated memories for emotional childhood events. *Law Hum. Behav.* **23**, 517–537 (1999).

18. Fabiani, M., Stadler, M. A. & Wessels, P. M. True but not false memories produce a sensory signature in human lateralized brain potentials. *J. Cogn. Neurosci.* **12**, 941–949 (2000).

19. Gonsalves, B. & Paller, K. A. Neural events that underlie remembering something that never happened. *Nature Neurosci.* **3**, 1316–1320 (2000).

20. Bloomberg, D. Bennett Braun case update: trials set for May, July. *Skeptical inquirer* **23**, 12–13 (1999).

21. Pendergrast, M. *Victims of Memory* 2nd edn (Upper Access, Hinesburg, Vermont, 1996).

22. Huff, C. R., Rattner, A. & Sagarin, E. *Convicted but innocent: Wrongful Conviction and Public Policy* (Sage Publications, Thousand Oaks, California, 1996).

23. Radelet, M. L. Wrongful convictions of the innocent. *Judicature* **86**, 67–68 (2002).

24. Loftus, E. F. *Eyewitness Testimony* (Harvard Univ. Press, Cambridge, Massachusetts, 1996).

25. Pemberton, P. S. Woman falsely accused wins $100,000 judgment. *San Luis Obispo Tribune* B1 (7 December, 2002).

26. Richards, Z. Rainbow case is settled. *Charleston Daily Mail* A1 (4 January 2003).

27. Loge, P. The Innocence Protection Act. *Judicature* **86**, 121 (2002).

28. Loftus, E. F. Memory faults and fixes. *Issues Sci. Technol.* **18**, 41–50 (2002).

ACKNOWLEDGMENT

I thank the neurophysiologist W. Calvin, for provocative discussions about these issues and general guidance.

An Own-Age Bias in Face Recognition in Children and the Elderly

JEFFREY S. ANASTASI AND MATTHEW G. RHODES

In the present study, we examined whether children and older adults exhibit an own-age face recognition bias. Participants studied photographs of children, younger adults, middle-aged adults, and older adults and were administered a recognition test. Results showed that both children and older adults more accurately recognized own-age faces than other-age faces. These data suggest that individuals may acquire expertise for identifying faces from their own age group and are discussed in terms of Sporer's (2001) in-group/out-group model of face recognition.

A number of studies have demonstrated that older adults and children exhibit poorer memory for faces than do younger adults (e.g., Adams-Price, 1992; Chance & Goldstein, 1984; Fulton & Bartlett, 1991; List, 1986; Searcy, Bartlett, & Memon, 2000; Searcy, Bartlett, Memon, & Swanson, 2001). However, this difference may, in part, result from the stimuli typically used in face recognition studies. Specifically, the majority of studies have asked college-aged participants to remember the faces of similar-aged targets. Thus, much of the prior work on age differences in face recognition has ignored whether participants may demonstrate superior recognition of faces from their own age group (i.e., an own-age bias; Wright & Stroud, 2002).

Several investigators have examined this issue by manipulating the age of the photographed individuals studied by participants (e.g., Bäckman, 1991; Bartlett & Leslie, 1986; Fulton & Bartlett, 1991; List, 1986; Mason, 1986; Perfect & Harris, 2003; Wright & Stroud, 2002; Yarmey, 1993; see Perfect & Moon, 2005, for a review). For example, Wright and Stroud presented younger (18- to 25-year-old) and middle-aged (35- to 55-year-old) adults with videos depicting a theft by a younger or a middle-aged perpetrator. Results showed that younger participants were more likely to correctly identify the perpetrator in a lineup when the culprit was also young. Middle-aged participants, in contrast, did not exhibit a significant own-age bias. Fulton and Bartlett reported a similar pattern, since younger adults in their study exhibited better recognition of younger than of older adult faces, whereas older adults demonstrated equivalent levels of accuracy for younger and older faces. On the basis of these data, Fulton and Bartlett suggested that an own-age bias exists for younger adults but is less reliable for older adults.

Contrary to Fulton and Bartlett (1991), an own-age bias has been demonstrated in several cases for older adults (Bäckman, 1991; Perfect & Harris, 2003). For example, Bäckman found that face recognition accuracy was enhanced when older adults were presented with older faces. In addition, Perfect and Harris reported that older adults were nearly three times more likely to correctly identify an older adult than to identify a younger adult from a lineup.

Far fewer studies have examined whether children exhibit a similar own-age bias (Chung, 1997; see also

Jeffrey S. Anastasi and Matthew G. Rhodes, "An Own-age Bias in Face Recognition in Children and the Elderly," *Psychonomic Bulletin & Review*, vol. 12, no. 6, pp. 1043-1047. Copyright © 2005 by Springer Science+Business Media. Reprinted with permission.

Lindholm, 2005; List, 1986). Chung conducted the only face recognition study that, to our knowledge, has investigated the own-age bias in children. Specifically, Chung presented children (7–12 years of age) and adults with photographs from those two age groups. Results showed that, in addition to demonstrating superior recognition of faces than did children, adults also exhibited an own-age bias. No such bias was reported for children.

Thus, it appears that an own-age bias is not consistently evident for older adults and is nonexistent for children. However, none of the previous research has tested both children and older adults in the same study. This is important, since the specific manipulations used in previous studies have varied considerably, making comparisons across studies difficult. Given the paucity of studies for both groups, particularly those with children, further research is needed. Thus, the primary purpose of the present study was to investigate the own-age bias in children and older adults, using a single experiment with the same procedures for both groups. Specifically, both groups of participants attempted to recognize photographs of children, young adults, middle-aged adults, and older adults. If an own-age bias exists, participants should be most accurate when identifying individuals from their own age group and less accurate when identifying individuals from different age groups.

METHOD

Participants

The participants were 70 individuals from two age groups: 40 children, 5–8 years of age ($M = 6.9$, $SD = 0.91$) and 30 older adults, 55–89 years of age ($M = 71.6$, $SD = 10.4$). The children were tested at local elementary schools and at facilities offering after-school programs in the Phoenix area and received small toys or stickers for their participation. Older adults were recruited from retirement communities and activity centers in the Phoenix area and received $5 for their participation. All participants were active and healthy and reported no physical or mental health problems. The participants were tested individually or in groups of up to 4 individuals. Data from 1 child and 1 older adult were excluded because they did not follow instructions.

Materials

The materials consisted of 128 digital photographs of 64 individuals, taken in the Phoenix metropolitan area.[1] Photographs were taken of each individual in two poses (smiling and not smiling) with the same white background and consisted of only their heads and shoulders. The photographs were split into four groups of 32 photographs. Each group consisted of 8 photographs from each age range (5–8, 18–25, 35–45, and 55–75 years), divided equally among males and females. Half of the photographs from each age range were of individuals smiling, and half were of individuals not smiling. The approximate size of the photographic image on the computer monitor for both the study and the test phases was 7.5 × 6 in.

The recognition test consisted of 64 photographs. Following the recommendation of Sporer (2001), alternate-pose photographs were employed so as to test face recognition, rather than picture identification (e.g., recognizing an idiosyncratic feature in a picture of a target, rather than the target itself). Thus, 32 of the photographs (8 from each age range, with an equal number of males and females) were the alternate-pose photographs of individuals viewed during the encoding phase, whereas the remaining 32 photographs (8 from each age range, with an equal number of males and females) had not been studied. All photographs were counterbalanced with respect to old/new status and pose (i.e., smiling or not smiling) and were presented in random order on the recognition test.

Procedure

In the first phase of the experiment, the participants were presented with 32 photographs of both males and females of various ages at a 10-sec rate, using Microsoft PowerPoint. The participants were instructed to categorize the individual in each photograph into one of four age ranges (5–8, 18–25, 35–45, or 55–75 years) by circling the appropriate age range on a form provided. They were not informed about an upcoming memory test.

After completing the photograph ratings, the participants were given a 5-min picture search task (i.e., circling hidden objects in a complex picture). The filler task was selected so that the children would be able to perform the same task as the older adults during the retention interval. Following the filler task, the recognition task was administered. The participants were informed that they would be presented with 64 photographs at a 10-sec rate. They were told that some individuals had been presented earlier, whereas others had not been seen previously. The participants were instructed to indicate whether each individual was presented earlier by circling either *yes* or *no* on a form provided.

RESULTS

All the data reported were first analyzed using a 2 (participant age: children or older adults) $\times$ 4 (photograph age: children, young adults, middle-aged adults, or older adults) mixed-factor ANOVA. Given our a priori predictions, these data were then analyzed separately for each age group. Effect sizes are reported using Cohen's (1988) *d*, where a value of $d = .20$ is considered small, a value of $d = .50$ is considered medium, and a value of $d = .80$ is considered large. The alpha level for all statistical tests was set to .05.

Recognition Data

These data indicate that an own-age bias was present, since the participants demonstrated superior recognition of photographs from their own age group. Analyses of corrected recognition scores (i.e., hits minus false alarms) revealed a significant main effect of photograph age ($F(3,198) = 3.81$, $MS_e = 0.05$) but no main effect of participant age, since recognition did not differ between the two age groups ($F(1,66) = 2.03$, $MS_e = 0.18$, $p = .16$). More important, a significant photograph age $\times$ participant age interaction was present ($F(3,198) = 7.47$, $MS_e = 0.05$), indicative of an own-age bias. Planned comparisons on children's corrected recognition scores showed that recognition of photographs of children ($M = .46$) was significantly higher than recognition of photographs of younger adults ($M = .36$; $t(38) = 1.99$, $p = .05$; $d = .37$) and middle-aged adults ($M = .34$; $t(38) = 2.56$; $d = .50$). Children were marginally more accurate for photographs of children than for photographs of older adults ($M = .37$; $t(38) = 1.78$, $p = .08$; $d = .36$). Older adults' corrected recognition scores were significantly higher for photographs of older adults ($M = .61$) than for photographs of children ($M = .36$; $t(38) = 5.33$; $d = .88$), younger adults ($M = .47$; $t(38) = 2.65$; $d = .51$), and middle-aged adults ($M = .39$; $t(38) = 3.79$; $d = .71$).

Taken together, these data indicate that older adults exhibited a mirror effect (Glanzer & Adams, 1985, 1990), since high levels of hits were accompanied by low levels of false alarms for own-age faces. In contrast, recognition differences for children resulted primarily from higher levels of hits for same-age faces, with false alarms largely equivalent across levels of photograph age. Differences between older adults and children are best characterized in terms of discriminability and response bias, which will be examined next.

Discriminability and Response Bias Data: Chronological Age

The own-age bias observed may reflect differences in sensitivity to own and different-aged faces or may reflect a different decision criterion based on face age. In order to examine this, a signal detection analysis of these data was performed using *d* as an estimate of the ability to discriminate between old and new items and *C* as an estimate of criterion (i.e., response bias). A neutral response bias produces a value of 0 for *C*, a conservative response bias results in positive values, and negative values of *C* are indicative of a liberal response bias. Following Snodgrass and Corwin (1988), all hit and false alarm rates were first adjusted by adding 0.5 to each frequency and dividing by $N + 1$, where N is the number of trials for a particular type of photograph.

Analyses of discriminability (*d*) indicated that discriminability did not differ between children ($M = 1.09$) and older adults ($M = 1.24$; $F < 1$) but did differ on the basis of photograph age ($F(3, 198) = 4.00$, $MS_e = 0.38$). A significant photograph age $\times$ participant age interaction was also present ($F(3, 198) = 7.88$, $MS_e = 0.38$). Follow-up analyses indicated that children's discriminability was marginally better for photographs of children than for photographs of younger adults ($t(38) = 1.74$, $p < .10$; $d = .30$) and middle-aged adults ($t(38) = 1.70$, $p < .10$; $d = .35$). There was no difference in children's discriminability for photographs of children versus those of older adults ($t(38) = 1.51$, $p = .14$; $d = .32$). In contrast to the results for children, discriminability differed considerably across levels of photograph age for older adults. Specifically, older adults' discriminability was significantly better for photographs of older adults than for photographs of children

$(t(28) = 5.37; d = .90)$, younger adults $(t(28) = 2.51; d = .50)$, and middle-aged adults $(/(28) = 3.99; d = .75)$. Thus, older adults demonstrated enhanced discriminability of photographs from their own age group, whereas this effect was weaker for children.

Results from analyses of response bias (C) data showed that children ($M = .38$) were significantly more conservative in their responding than were older adults ($M = .02$; $F(1,66) = 16.34$, $MS_e = 0.50$) and that response bias varied on the basis of photograph age ($F(3,198) = 6.27$, $MS_e = 0.11$). However, a photograph age × participant age interaction was not present ($F(3,198) = 1.07$, $MS_e = 0.11$, $p = .36$). Follow-up tests indicated that children were significantly less conservative in their responses to photographs of children than in their responses to photographs of young adults ($t(38) = 2.32$; $d = .36$), middle-aged adults ($t(38) = 5.04$; $d = .68$), and older adults ($t(38) = 2.33$; $d = .36$). Conversely, older adults' response bias did not differ on the basis of photograph age ($F < 1$; $ds < .19$). Thus, only children were significantly less conservative in their responses to photographs from their own age group than in their responses to photographs from other age ranges.

DISCUSSION

Overall, the data from the present study are consistent with an own-age bias for older adults and children. Specifically, both age groups exhibited higher levels of recognition accuracy for individuals from their own age group than for individuals from other age groups. Thus, the present study adds to a limited body of work demonstrating an own-age bias for older adults (e.g., Bäckman, 1991; Perfect & Harris, 2003) and, to our knowledge, is the only study that has demonstrated an own-age bias in face recognition for children. Such data also suggest that age-related deficits in face recognition may be exaggerated when participants study faces of individuals from other age groups (cf. Wright & Stroud, 2002).

The own-age bias observed here is similar to the better documented own-race bias (i.e., the finding that participants are more likely to remember individuals from their own race than individuals of another, less familiar race; see Meissner & Brigham, 2001, for a review). One explanation of the own-race bias proposes that memory for individuals from a particular race is positively related to the amount of contact one has with individuals from that race (e.g., Brigham & Malpass, 1985; Slone, Brigham, & Meissner, 2000). In a similar manner, individuals may acquire greater expertise at processing more frequently encountered own-race faces, resulting in better memory for such faces (e.g., Levin, 2000; Valentine, 1991). The own-age bias reported in the present study may result from participants' more frequent exposure to individuals from similar age groups, thus leading to greater expertise in identifying own-age faces. Older adults recruited for the present study came from retirement communities, and children were from after-school programs or daycare centers. Both settings would provide ample exposure and, perhaps, greater familiarity with individuals from the same age group, leading to an own-age bias.

However, such familiarity-based explanations have received mixed support within the own-race literature. For example, Meissner and Brigham's (2001) meta-analysis of 39 studies of the own-race bias concluded that contact with members of other races accounted for approximately 2% of the variability in the own-race bias across participants (see also Furl, Phillips, & O'Toole, 2002, for problems in computational models). In addition, a familiarity-based explanation appears to be particularly difficult to apply with respect to age. For example, older adults have been members of other age groups at different points in their lifetime and should have acquired sufficient levels of familiarity with other age groups to make identifications. Thus, it is unclear how older adults would develop a recognition advantage for older faces on the basis of familiarity alone. One possibility is that the own-age bias is not the product of familiarity per se but reflects different processing strategies for in-group versus out-group faces. Such a premise is behind Sporer's (2001) in-group/out-group model (IOM) of face processing. Sporer proposed that in-group faces are processed automatically with configural coding that reflects perceptual expertise for such faces. In contrast, out-group faces are first categorized for out-group status, with the possibility that processing does not extend beyond initial categorization (cf. Rodin, 1987). If additional processing does occur, these processes give "attentional weight to distinguishing out-group from in-group members ... at the expense of dimensions that may be more suitable to differentiate members of a particular out-group" (Sporer, 2001, pp. 83–84). As Sporer noted, the IOM model predicts recognition differences for individuals within several out-groups, including those based on age.

Thus, the own-age bias reported in the present study may result from different processing strategies applied to in-group and out-group faces. In fact, in-group/out-group distinctions may have been encouraged by the encoding instruction to estimate the age of the individual in each photograph, with the attendant processing differences outlined in Sporer's (2001) IOM model. Furthermore, this suggests that the own-age bias may be eliminated or weakened when encoding instructions do not engender a focus on age. Several studies contradict this assumption. For example, own-age biases have been reported following encoding tasks that require judgments of pleasantness (Bartlett & Leslie, 1986; Fulton & Bartlett, 1991) or attractiveness (Anastasi & Rhodes, 2006) or simply instruct participants to remember faces for a later memory test (Mason, 1986; Wright & Stroud, 2002). These data, showing an own-age bias for several encoding tasks, would seem to be predicted by the IOM model. That is, the IOM model suggests that face processing is preceded by an obligatory judgment of whether a face belongs to an in-or an out-group, which in turn dictates the nature of face processing. Therefore, the specific encoding task may not be as important as the initial judgment that a face belongs to an in-or an out-group. Evidence from research in which the own-age bias was compared directly across different encoding tasks and age groups is presently lacking, so this assumption must be regarded as tentative.

Several caveats must be noted with regard to the data reported in the present study. First, children's recognition of photographs of children was significantly better than their recognition of photographs of younger and middle-aged adults. However, their recognition of children was only marginally better than their recognition of older adults. In contrast, older adults consistently demonstrated superior recognition of photographs of older adults, suggesting that the own-age bias may be less robust for children than for older adults. Effect size estimates confirm this conclusion, since across photograph age conditions, older adults exhibited a stronger own-age bias ($d = .69$) than did children ($d = .41$). Second, children demonstrated moderate differences in discriminability between own-age and different-age faces but did exhibit a significantly less conservative response bias for photographs of children.

Older adults exhibited the opposite pattern, showing enhanced discriminability of own-age faces but no difference in response bias.[2] The fact that the own-age bias reflects an effect on discriminability for older adults and on response criterion for children suggests that the nature of the own-age bias may differ between the two age groups. The present study cannot resolve this issue, and further investigation is certainly warranted.

Regardless of the specific mechanisms for the own-age bias, the present study provides important information. Knowledge of the own-race bias has been crucial in the legal system (e.g., Brigham & Malpass, 1985; Meissner & Brigham, 2001; Sporer, 2001), where identification errors have serious consequences. The present study supports a similar memory bias and suggests that accuracy may be diminished when children or older adults must identify individuals of a different age. Thus, both the age of the witness and the age of the perpetrator are crucial factors when an individual's ability to remember previously seen faces is evaluated.

REFERENCES

ADAMS-PRICE, C. (1992). EYEWITNESS MEMORY AND AGING: PREDICTORS OF ACCURACY IN RECALL AND PERSON RECOGNITION. *PSYCHOLOGY & AGING, 7*, 602–608.

ANASTASI, J. S., & RHODES, M. G. (2006). EVIDENCE FOR AN OWN-AGE BIAS IN FACE RECOGNITION. *NORTH AMERICAN JOURNAL OF PSYCHOLOGY, 8*, 237–253.

BACKMAN, L. (1991). RECOGNITION MEMORY ACROSS THE ADULT LIFE SPAN: THE ROLE OF PRIOR KNOWLEDGE. *MEMORY & COGNITION, 19*, 63–71.

BARTLETT, J. C., & LESLIE, J. E. (1986). AGING AND MEMORY FOR FACES VERSUS SINGLE VIEWS OF FACES. *MEMORY & COGNITION, 14*, 371–381.

BRIGHAM, J. C., & MALPASS, R. S. (1985). THE ROLE OF EXPERIENCE AND CONTACT IN THE RECOGNITION OF FACES OF OWN-AND OTHER-RACE PERSONS. *JOURNAL OF SOCIAL ISSUES, 41*, 139–155.

CHANCE, J. E., & GOLDSTEIN, A. G. (1984). FACE-RECOGNITION MEMORY: IMPLICATIONS FOR CHILDREN'S EYEWITNESS TESTIMONY. *JOURNAL OF SOCIAL ISSUES, 40*, 69–85.

CHUNG, M. S. (1997). FACE RECOGNITION: EFFECTS OF AGE OF SUBJECTS AND AGE OF STIMULUS FACES. *KOREAN JOURNAL OF DEVELOPMENTAL PSYCHOLOGY, 10*, 167–176.

Cohen, J. (1988). *Statistical power analysis for the behavioral sciences.* New York: Academic Press.

Fulton, A., & Bartlett, J. C. (1991). Young and old faces in young and old heads: The factor of age in face recognition. *Psychology & Aging, 6,* 623–630.

Furl, N., Phillips, P. J., & O'Toole, A. J. (2002). Face recognition algorithms and the other-race effect: Computational mechanisms for a developmental contact hypothesis. *Cognitive Science, 26,* 797–815.

Glanzer, M., & Adams, J. K. (1985). The mirror effect in recognition memory. *Memory & Cognition, 13,* 8–20.

Glanzer, M., & Adams, J. K. (1990). The mirror effect in recognition memory: Data and theory. *Journal of Experimental Psychology: Learning, Memory, & Cognition, 16,* 5–16.

Levin, D. T. (2000). Race as a visual feature: Using visual search and perceptual discrimination tasks to understand face categories and the cross-race recognition deficit. *Journal of Experimental Psychology: General, 129,* 559–574.

Lindholm, T. (2005). Own-age biases in verbal person memory. *Memory, 13,* 21–30.

List, J. (1986). Age and schematic differences in the reliability of eyewitness testimony. *Developmental Psychology, 22,* 50–57.

Mason, S. E. (1986). Age and gender as factors in facial recognition and identification. *Experimental Aging Research, 12,* 151–154.

Meissner, C. A., & Brigham, J. C. (2001). Thirty years of investigating the own-race bias in memory for faces: A meta-analytic review. *Psychology, Public Policy, & Law, 7,* 3–35.

Perfect, T. J., & Harris, L. J. (2003). Adult age differences in unconscious transference: Source confusion or identity blending? *Memory & Cognition, 31,* 570–580.

Perfect, T. J., & Moon, H. (2005). The own-age effect in face recognition. In J. Duncan, L. Phillips, & P. McLeod (Eds.), *Measuring the mind: Speed, control, and age* (pp. 317–340). Oxford: Oxford University Press.

Rodin, M. J. (1987). Who is memorable to whom: A study of cognitive disregard. *Social Cognition, 5,* 144–165.

Searcy, J. (H.), Bartlett, J. C., & Memon, A. (2000). Influence of post-event narratives, line-up conditions and individual differences on false identification by young and older eyewitnesses. *Legal & Criminological Psychology, 5,* 219–235.

Searcy, J. H., Bartlett, J. C., Memon, A., & Swanson, K. (2001). Aging and lineup performance at long retention intervals: Effects of metamemory and context reinstatement. *Journal of Applied Psychology, 86,* 207–214.

Slone, A. E., Brigham, J. C., & Meissner, C. A. (2000). Social and cognitive factors affecting the own-race bias in Whites. *Basic & Applied Social Psychology, 22,* 71–84.

Snodgrass, J. G., & Corwin, J. (1988). Pragmatics of measuring recognition memory: Applications to dementia and amnesia. *Journal of Experimental Psychology: General, 117,* 34–50.

Sporer, S. L. (2001). Recognizing faces of other ethnic groups: An integration of theories. *Psychology, Public Policy, & Law, 7,* 36–97.

Valentine, T. (1991). A unified account of the effects of distinctiveness, inversion, and race in face recognition. *Quarterly Journal of Experimental Psychology, 43A,* 161–204.

Wright, D. B., & Stroud, J. S. (2002). Age differences in lineup identification accuracy: People are better with their own age. *Law & Human Behavior, 26,* 641–654.

Yarmey, A. D. (1993). Adult age and gender differences in eyewitness recall in field settings. *Journal of Applied Social Psychology, 23,* 1921–1932.

NOTES

1. None of the participants reported knowing any of the individuals depicted in the photographs when they were asked at the conclusion of the experiment.

2. These data contrast with those showing a small effect, reported in the own-race bias literature, in which in-group faces were accompanied by a more conservative criterion than were out-group faces (Meissner & Brigham, 2001).

CHAPTER 8
Memory Applications: Repressed/False Memories

The History and Zeitgeist of the Repressed-False-Memory Debate

Scientific and Sociological Perspectives on Suggestibility and Childhood Memory

RHONDA DOUGLAS BROWN, ELEANOR GOLDSTEIN, AND DAVID F. BJORKLUND

The history of the interface between the psychology of childhood memories and legal cases is a notorious one. Perhaps the phenomena that left the deepest historical scar regarding this issue are the 17th-century witch trials that took place in Europe and America (see Ceci & Bruck, 1993, 1998, for reviews). In Sweden between 1668 and 1676, as a result of children's statements elicited by village priests concerning the alleged sorcery of community members, more than 40 adults were either burned at the stake or beheaded (Ceci & Bruck, 1995). Most notable in U.S. history were the Salem witch trials, in which a group of children called the "circle girls" testified to witnessing community members flying on broomsticks and commanding insects to fly into their mouths to drop bent nails and pins into their stomachs. As a result, 20 defendants were convicted of witch-craft and executed. In the wake of the executions, some of the children publicly recanted their statements, admitting that they had produced false testimonies.

More recently, a less extreme but eerily similar case emerged in Wenatchee, Washington. In 1996, 28 adults from this small town were charged with rape and molestation, and more than 40 children were removed from their homes because of investigators' claims of a widespread child-sex ring. Of those charged, 19 adults were sentenced to prison (14 pleaded guilty and 5 were convicted), and the remainder were either acquitted or their cases were dismissed. As in the 17th-century witch trials, two young sisters, called

M. E. and D. E., provided the substantial testimony in these cases, which included allegations against their own parents. Despite the fact that M. E., D. E., and their brother each originally denied any parental sexual abuse, their mother, who was classified as mentally retarded, was sentenced to 4 years in prison after agreeing to testify against their father, who was sentenced to 23 years in prison. M. E. later recanted her testimony, claiming that she fabricated her reports of ritualistic abuse under pressure from the girls' foster father, Wenatchee Police Detective Robert Perez, who led the investigation. Civil suits totaling at least $100 million were filed by residents of Wenatchee for wrongful prosecution (Tizon, 1996).

Ceci and Bruck (1995) reviewed a number of related cases involving child witnesses that occurred during the mid-1980s to early 1990s, such as the Country Wilk day care case. The rapid emergence of such cases in recent history has led groups such as Concerned Citizens for Legal Accountability to request that U.S. Attorney General Janet Reno open an investigation into matters of wrongful prosecution. Reno, who incidentally was involved as a prosecutor in the Country Walk case, denied the group's appeal.

These cases were primarily concerned with the effects of suggestibility on children's reliability as witnesses. Yet, during this same period, a different but related breed of cases emerged in which the reliability of adults' memories of their childhood experiences was questioned. First, there was a rapid increase in cases in which adults were suing their parents, relatives, or religious leaders for sexual abuse that allegedly occurred during childhood. The prosecution was based on the notion that the memories for abuse were "repressed" before adulthood or therapeutic treatment. Second, as a result of increased public awareness of suggestive therapeutic techniques and the mechanisms of childhood memories, the number of repressed memory cases declined, and reactionary cases, in which clients sued their therapists for false-memory implantation, increased. For example, Patricia Burgus alleged that two psychiatrists at Rush-Presbyterian-St. Luke's hospital in Chicago persuaded her, through the use of hypnosis and other therapeutic techniques, to believe that she was a member of a satanic cult, that she was sexually abused by multiple men, and that she engaged in cannibalism and abused her own children. In 1997, Ms. Burgus reached the largest settlement to that date in a false-memory lawsuit—$10.6 million, although the defendants failed to admit wrongdoing (Belluck, 1997).

In this chapter, we reflect on the Zeitgeist or spirit of the times in which the cases just described emerged, climaxed, and waned. First, we examine the impact of early research on current investigations relevant to the cases concerning children's reliability as witnesses. We also examine theoretical and empirical considerations of mechanisms of memory important to the repressed-false-memory debate that surrounds the cases involving accusations based on "recovered" memories of childhood sexual abuse, which usually emerge during the course of therapy. Finally, we delineate how various social movements and changes in the legal system have led to the upsurge in childhood memory cases during the past two decades, and we present the current state of the childhood memory debate.

RESEARCH ON CHILDHOOD MEMORY

The Salem witch trials had a dramatic impact on the U.S. legal system and on psychologists' willingness, or lack thereof, to investigate suggestibility and childhood memory. There was little need for such studies because children did not typically testify during the period after the witch trials. However, early in the 20th century, several European psychologists conducted research investigating children's suggestibility (see Ceci & Bruck, 1993, 1995, 1998, for reviews), and Freud considered the nature of traumatic childhood memories. After these early investigations, however, the

topic was not examined in any depth again until the late 1970s, when changes in the legal system and social movements led to a resurgence of interest. Here, we examine the roots of early research on suggestibility and childhood memory to provide a historical context for current views of these issues.

Children as Eyewitnesses

Perhaps the earliest and most influential research on children's suggestibility and memory was conducted by Alfred Binet, a French developmental psychologist and father of the IQ test, along with Simon. Binet (1900) outlined two major sources of suggestibility: (a) *autosuggestion,* which arises from a child's internal sources; and (b) *external suggestibility,* which arises from others influencing the child's recollections.

In one demonstration of autosuggestibility, Binet showed children five lines of increasing length and then a series of "target" lines that were the same length as the longest line of the original series, which he asked the children to draw on paper. Binet found that children's drawings of the target line were systematically too long, leading him to conclude that internal suggestions influenced children to deduce that each target line was longer than the line that had come before it.

Reyna (1994) investigated autosuggestibility more directly and attributes developmental differences in internal suggestions to interference effects, with younger children showing more interference sensitivity than older children. Other researchers describe young children's event memory as relying heavily on generalized knowledge of typical events, or *scripts,* which are used as a context for interpreting novel information (Nelson, 1996). This general knowledge may interfere with young children's ability to reconstruct what they witnessed in a specific event to a greater extent than it does for older children (Ceci & Bruck, 1993). In Binet's study, children's prior knowledge of the line series clearly influenced their reconstruction of the target lines.

Although current research has invoked Binet's concept of autosuggestibility, his greatest contribution to the childhood memory literature resulted from his investigations of external suggestibility. In one experiment, Binet examined the effects of an interviewer's suggestions on children's responses by asking them to study five objects (e.g., a button glued onto a poster board) for 10 seconds. He then assessed memory using free recall, direct questions (e.g., "How is the button attached to the board?"), leading questions (e.g., "Wasn't the button attached by a thread?"), or misleading questions (e.g., "What was the color of the thread that attached the button to the board?"). Binet's findings were highly similar to those of current research: (a) Free recall yielded the highest levels of accuracy, whereas misleading questions produced the most inaccurate statements; and (b) children expressed confidence in their responses, regardless of accuracy. Binet concluded that children responded inaccurately because they did not remember the information but felt pressured to answer the questions posed by the interviewer. On the basis of his finding that children rarely corrected inaccurate answers to misleading questions, Binet suggested that the inaccurate information becomes incorporated into memory. He also studied these effects at the group level by asking children in groups of three to respond to misleading questions as quickly as possible. He found that children who responded later were more likely to provide the same answer as the first respondent, even when the response was incorrect—a classic demonstration of small-group conformity.

Binet's study that compared the responses of children ages 7 through 14 to free recall and types of leading questions anticipated modern suggestibility research. For example, Cassel and Bjorklund (1995) examined children's responses to free recall, unbiased questions (similar to Binet's direct questions), positive-leading questions (suggesting a correct answer), and misleading questions (suggesting an incorrect answer) about a witnessed event. Their findings were consistent with Binet's concerning the effects of question type on memory accuracy: near zero levels of incorrect responses to free recall in contrast to the more directive and suggestive questions (unbiased: 17% incorrect; positive leading: 16% incorrect; and misleading: 60% incorrect). Similar to Binet, Cassel and Bjorklund noted that although the amount of information young children produce in free recall is typically low, it is highly accurate (Goodman, Aman, & Hirschman, 1987; Poole & White, 1995). Furthermore, even unbiased questions, despite yielding more information, led to the production of inaccurate information (e.g., Bjorklund, Bjorklund, Brown, & Cassel, 1998; Cassel, Roebers, & Bjorklund, 1996).

In addition to providing empirical evidence of suggestibility effects, Binet's conclusion that misinformation becomes incorporated into children's memories foreshadowed a major theoretical and empirical question: When children assent to leading questions, are they just agreeing with an authoritative interviewer or do they actually come to believe that the misinformation is the truth? Some researchers have explained children's responses to leading questions as acquiescence effects or products of the social demand characteristics present in the forensic interviewing context that do not necessarily lead to changes in memory representations (e.g., Zaragoza, 1991). Other researchers have suggested, like Binet, that misinformation becomes incorporated into memory either through an "overwriting" process, in which misinformation replaces original information, or through integration, in which old information is combined with suggested information (e.g., Hyman, Husband, & Billings, 1995; Loftus, 1979). The current consensus acknowledges that suggestibility effects are complex phenomena that cannot be explained by a single mechanism. Thus, it is likely that acquiescence and changes in memory representation interact to produce the phenomena. For example, a child may initially comply with misinformation, and in reconstructing the event, he or she may begin to question the experience, which may lead to changes in memory representation.

Although Binet provided evidence that misleading questions lead to memory inaccuracy, German psychologist William Stern (1910) offered more applied and ecologically valid demonstrations of suggestibility effects, developing two paradigms that are used in current research. In the first paradigm, participants viewed a picture and were asked to study it for a short period of time, after which free recall was assessed. Then, participants answered questions requesting information that was actually represented in the picture as well as misleading questions that requested information that was not represented in the picture. In one study that tested 7-to 18-year-olds, free recall produced the fewest errors, whereas misleading questions produced the most errors (Stern, 1910). Consistent with modern findings, Stern's results revealed developmental differences, with the youngest children showing the highest levels of susceptibility to misleading questions.

Stern's second paradigm, called the *reality experiment,* in which unsuspecting participants observed staged events, established a more ecologically valid design for investigating the effects of suggestive questioning on eye-witness memory. For example, in one typical experiment, unsuspecting university students observed as an argument broke out between two students in a classroom that escalated to the point of one student drawing a gun on the other. The students in the class who witnessed the incident were questioned afterwards. In drawing conclusions from such reality experiments, Stern cautioned against repeatedly questioning witnesses about the same event because participants may remember their answers to the questions (which may be erroneous) better than the actual event that they witnessed. He also suggested that children might interpret suggestive misleading questions delivered firmly by an authority figure as imperatives; therefore, Stern pinned responsibility for unreliable testimony on the interviewer who poses questions in this manner.

Although technology has somewhat changed the reality experiment from live staged scenes to video presentations of events, it is alive and well in research today. For example, Bjorklund et al. (1998) showed 5-and 7-year-olds a brief video depicting a theft and interviewed them over a 6-week period using free recall, unbiased or misleading questions, and recognition memory assessments. They found that correct free recall and recognition memory declined significantly across the 6-week period, confirming Stern's cautions against repeatedly questioning witnesses about the same event. The results from this study suggest that multiple interviews with suggestive questions lead children, especially 5-year-olds, to not only change their answers but also their memories.

Stern's conclusions imply that results such as these may occur because children remember their answers to questions during an interview better than the actual witnessed event. Modern theorists have provided support for this hypothesis. For example, according to fuzzy-trace theory, information can be represented by verbatim traces, which are more susceptible to forgetting, or gistlike traces, which preserve meaning over details (Reyna & Brainerd, 1995). Brainerd, Reyna, and their colleagues provided evidence illustrating that memory for distractors or misinformation can be more persistent than memory for target or witnessed information depending on whether memories are supported by verbatim or gist traces (Brainerd & Poole, 1997; Brainerd & Reyna, 1998; Brainerd, Reyna,

& Brandse, 1995; Brainerd, Reyna, & Poole, chap. 5, this volume).

As indicated by the modern research just discussed, explanations of suggestibility effects have progressed significantly in proposing possible cognitive mechanisms responsible for the false-memory phenomenon. Historically, it was German psychologist Lipmann (1911) who emphasized how children's cognitive abilities impact their effectiveness as eyewitnesses. He hypothesized that attentional factors influence developmental differences in children's eyewitness memories. More specifically, Lipmann reasoned that children attend to and encode different characteristics of stimuli than adults, making their memories qualitatively different. Typically in interrogative contexts, the questions posed to children focus on attributes of a crime relevant to proving a case; however, children do not necessarily attend to these adult-defined attributes. Lipmann proposed that when children are confronted with questions posed by authoritative adults, they report any information that readily comes to mind, fact or fiction, in order to provide a response, which in turn leads to reconstruction of memories to maintain consistency.

Ultimately, Lipmann's contribution was in emphasizing how children's attentional characteristics and their inability to distinguish fantasy from reality influence their reliability as witnesses, issues that have also been addressed by modern researchers. For example, modern researchers have provided evidence that young children have difficulty in reality monitoring, in other words, separating information that is imagined from information that is actually perceived (e.g., Foley, Santini, & Sopasakis, 1989; Johnson, Hashtroudi, & Lindsay, 1993). Moreover, many of the memory errors children make may be attributed to their difficulty in attributing the source of their knowledge (e.g., Mazzoni, 1998). Contemporary researchers have investigated a host of other cognitive and social factors that influence children's increased susceptibility to suggestion. These factors include a limited knowledge of the event they experienced or witnessed (e.g., Goodman, Quas, Batterman-Faunce, Riddlesberger, & Kuhn, 1997; Ornstein, Shapiro, Clubb, Follmer, & Baker-Ward, 1997), the parent-child relationship (Goodman, Quas, Batterman-Faunce, Riddlesberger, & Kuhn, 1994; Goodman et al., 1997), their beliefs that their memory is invulnerable to suggestion (O'Sullivan, Howe, & Marche, 1996), age differences in the representation of experiences (e.g., Brainerd & Poole, 1997;

Reyna & Brainerd, 1995), responsivity to social-demand characteristics (e.g., Cassel & Bjorklund, 1995; McCloskey & Zaragoza, 1985), and how the interview is conducted (see Ceci & Bruck 1995; Qin, Quas, Redlich, & Goodman, 1997), among others. The general conclusion from over a decade of contemporary research often echoes the interpretation of researchers from the beginning of the 20th century: For a host of cognitive and social reasons, young children's memory is more susceptible to the influences of suggestion than the memories of older children and adults, and care and caution must be taken when interviewing children about important events they have witnessed or experienced, lest the interpretation of the interviewer become the "memory" (or memory report) of the child.

Adult's Memories of Childhood Experiences

The history that is most relevant to the repressed-false-memory cases reviewed earlier concerns two interrelated concepts of Sigmund Freud's (1915/1957) psychoanalytic theory. First, through his clinical interviews with neurotic patients, Freud came to the conclusion that many of his female patients were sexually abused as young children, an idea that is referred to as his *seduction theory*. Second, Freud also theorized that these memories of childhood sexual abuse were repressed, or forced out of the conscious level of awareness, to protect the ego from the traumatic information. However, repression was viewed as incompletely dominating traumatic memories, in that indicators of childhood sexual abuse may seep into consciousness indirectly through dreams, behaviors, neuroses, and other psychological maladies. According to Freud (1940/1963),

Analytic experience has convinced us of the complete truth of the assertion so often to be heard that the child is psychologically father to the adult and the events of his first years are of paramount importance for his later life. It will thus be of special interest to us if there is something that may be described as the central experience of this period of childhood. Our attention is first attracted by the effects of certain influences which do not apply to all children though they are common enough—such as the sexual abuse of children by adults, their

seduction by other children slightly their senior, and what we should not expect, their being deeply stirred by seeing or hearing at first hand sexual behavior between adults (their parents) mostly at a time at which one would not have thought they could either be interested in or understand any such impressions, or be capable of remembering them later. Since these impressions are subjected to repression either at once or as soon as they seek to return as memories, they constitute the determinant for the neurotic compulsion which will subsequently make it impossible for the ego to control the sexual function and will probably cause it to turn away from that function permanently. (pp. 68–69)

In these statements, Freud set forth several defining features of his psychoanalytic theory that would later influence public perceptions of childhood sexual abuse (see later discussion on feminist perspectives): (a) early childhood experiences determine adult personality; (b) childhood sexual abuse by relatives is fairly common; (c) memories of childhood abuse are repressed; and (d) neuroses serve as indicators of repressed abuse memories. (Freud later recanted his seduction theory, realizing that his patients' stories of childhood sexual abuse were all similar because of the suggestive methods, including hypnosis, dream analysis, and trance induction, he used to retrieve memories that were supposedly buried in the unconscious mind.[1])

Despite Freud's rejection of his own seduction theory, his conceptualizations of the relationship between stress and memory have prevailed. In describing the defense mechanism of repression, Freud held that traumatic stress has qualitatively different effects on memory than moderate levels of stress (see also van der Kolk & Fisler, 1995). His defense mechanism inherently predicted a negative relationship between stress and memory, with traumatic events being accessible to memory only within highly supportive contexts, such as the therapeutic atmosphere.

Ethical concerns obviously limit experimental investigations of the relationship between trauma and memory. Consequently, such research has led to conflicting results and constraints on generalizability. Some research has demonstrated a negative relationship between trauma and memory, consistent with Freud's general view (e.g.,

Bugental, Blue, Cortez, Fleck, & Rodriguez, 1992; Merritt, Ornstein, & Spicker, 1994; Peters, 1991); other research has revealed positive effects, supporting the idea that representations of highly charged emotional events exhibit a photographic quality, preserving vivid, detailed information in long-term memory over substantial delays (e.g., Goodman, Hirschman, Hepps, & Rudy, 1991, Experiment 3; Loftus, Polonsky, & Fullilove, 1994; Oates & Shrimpton, 1991); and still other studies have found no significant effects of stress on memory (e.g., Eisen, Goodman, & Qin, 1995; Goodman et al., 1991, Experiment 1; Howe, Courage, & Peterson, 1995; Steward, 1989).

Concerning the recovery of memories, evidence is even more scant. Most studies have involved short-term amnesia recovery from traumatic episodes, thus limiting generalizability (Christianson & Nilsson, 1989). Indeed, memory experts have recently expressed concern regarding claims that memories recovered during the course of therapy were previously repressed and suggest that these memories may be false, products of suggestive techniques as indicated by Freud's rejection of his seduction theory (e.g., Lindsay & Read, 1994; Loftus, 1993; Ofshe & Watters, 1994). Several researchers have attempted to demonstrate that children and adults can create memories of entire events. In the typical false-memory paradigm, participants are asked to remember both true and false events presented in the same manner across multiple interviews. Descriptions of true events are developed from information provided by family members, and experimenters create false events. The false-memory paradigm is designed to assess whether participants will create a personal memory based on a description of a fictitious event.

Research using the false-memory paradigm reveals that children and adults can create false memories of complete, emotional, and self-involving events. In a series of studies, Ceci and his colleagues tested the hypothesis that asking preschoolers to repeatedly think about and create mental images of fictitious events would result in source misattributions and the creation of false memories. In an initial experiment (Ceci, Crotteau-Huffman, Smith, & Loftus, 1994), 58% of preschoolers generated elaborate descriptions, including contextual and affective information, of at least one of the fictitious events (e.g., getting his or her finger caught in a mousetrap and going to the emergency room to have it removed), and 25% generated descriptions

for the majority of the fictitious events. A second study (Ceci, Loftus, Leichtman, & Bruck, 1994) investigated whether children really create memories of the fictitious events or whether they merely comply with an authoritative interviewer. After 11 consecutive weekly interviews, a different interviewer informed each preschooler that the previous interviewer had made mistakes by telling him or her things had happened that did not really happen. Then, the experimenter asked each child which events had really happened. It was predicted that if the children were responding to social demands in previous interviews, then the different interviewer would provide them with the opportunity to correctly reject the false events, demonstrating acquiescence effects. Conversely, if the preschoolers actually believed that the fictitious events happened to them, then they would continue to incorrectly accept the occurrence of fictitious events. Results revealed that most of the children who agreed to the occurrence of fictitious events in previous interviews continued to do so with a different interviewer, providing evidence for memory effects.

The creation of false memories is a phenomenon that is not unique to childhood. Several researchers have shown that even adults demonstrate susceptibility to suggestion. For example, Loftus and Pickrell (1995) demonstrated that 25% of adults provided full or partial accounts of getting lost in a shopping mall during childhood. Similarly, Hyman et al. (1995) found the same percentage of adults reporting false memories using a variety of events (e.g., spilling punch at a wedding reception). Pezdek and Hodge (1999) also replicated Loftus and Pickrell's (1995) findings for getting lost in a mall but provided evidence that it is difficult to implant memories in children for an event that more closely approximates sexual abuse (e.g., a childhood enema). Nevertheless, this line of research clearly indicates that suggestive techniques can lead to a variety of memory distortions. Hyman et al. (1995) observed that their susceptible adults incorporated false information into their autobiographical memories by relying on their stored knowledge of true events. Thus, as Goodman, Emery, and Haugaard (1998) pointed out, some false memories may be based in reality; that is, true memories with false details and false memories with true details may be products of suggestive techniques.

How Are Early Memories Represented?

A major issue relevant to adults' memory of childhood involves the nature of such representations. The primary question concerns whether adults can remember early childhood experiences. Despite research, such as that of Rovee-Collier using conditioning techniques (see Rovee-Collier, 1995; Rovee-Collier & Gerhardstein, 1997, for reviews) and research showing deferred imitation of novel behaviors (see Bauer, 1996; Meltzoff, 1995, for reviews) demonstrating that infants can remember over long delays, the modern consensus maintains that such representations are not likely accessible in later childhood and adulthood; that is, early infancy and childhood memories do not show remarkable stability. Freud referred to the inability to recall early infancy and childhood experiences as *infantile amnesia*. In their review, Pillemer and White (1989) provided support for Freud's insights, reporting that memories of experiences before age 3 are not available to adult consciousness (average age of earliest memory was 3 years) and that memories of experiences between ages 3 and 6 show highly limited accessibility (see Nelson, 1996).

Freud's conception of infantile amnesia was linked to his seduction theory and to repression as a defense mechanism, in that he theorized that adults' memories for early childhood experiences are repressed because of the traumatic nature of sexual overtones present in early infant-parent interactions. Modern explanations of infantile amnesia rely on considerations of the nature of representation, the development of self-concept, information-processing abilities, and language, rather than on universal experiences of infant sexuality (see Bjorklund, 2000). For example, several authors have suggested that for long-term autobiographical memories to be accessible, the "auto" or "self," which develops gradually over early childhood, must be present to provide an anchor for representations of events (Fivush, 1988; Howe & Courage, 1993; Welch-Ross, 1995). Alternatively, Leichtman and Ceci (1993) used fuzzy-trace theory (Brainerd & Reyna, 1990; see earlier discussion on persistence of misinformation) to explain how developmental shifts in information processing (from reliance on verbatim traces to gistlike traces) affect children's event representations. From this perspective, memories from infancy and early childhood are most susceptible to forgetting because they are encoded primarily in the form of verbatim traces; memories from later childhood are increasingly encoded

in the form of fuzzy traces, which are less susceptible to forgetting. Leichtman and Ceci also acknowledge the role of increasing language abilities in contributing to children's representational systems.

What do these modern theories of infantile amnesia lend to the understanding of adults' memories for childhood experiences? They lead to a cautious approach to interpreting reported memories of very early childhood sexual abuse, such as U.S. actress Rosanne's claim that she was molested by her mother at 6 months of age. Research reveals that social-demand characteristics can lead up to 30% of adults to report memories from the first year of life, with some adults reporting memories from the first week of life (Malinoski et al., 1995). Considering what scientists know about transitions between early and later representational systems, it is unlikely that these reports represent veridical autobiographical memories.

The historical perspective offered above established major theoretical and empirical considerations of behavioral science research relevant to children's reliability as witnesses and the nature of adults' memories for childhood experiences. Overall, we can conclude from this research that young children and even adults are susceptible to misleading questions, that the effects of trauma on memory are unclear, and that it is quite difficult for adults to remember very early childhood experiences. Granted that many of the milestones within this area of research have occurred in reaction to the upsurge in childhood memory cases, this historical perspective still allows us to pose the question: Given what has been and is currently known scientifically about memory and considering even the contradictions within the literature, why have countless cases emerged in which children were subjected to misleading questions (as in the Wenatchee, Washington situation) and adults' memories were distorted through suggestive therapeutic techniques (as in the Burgus case)? Next we present a sociological analysis of the Zeitgeist that led to the crescendo of such cases during the past two decades.

A SOCIOLOGICAL PERSPECTIVE

Salem's Legacy

Returning to the 17th-century witch-hunt that occurred in Salem, it is clear that the cultural atmosphere permitted the phenomenon. Ceci, Toglia, and Ross (1990) argued that the social and cultural forces that influenced Salem's children are present to some degree in the current times. The Zeitgeist that led to the witch trials in Salem can be described as an emotionally laden hysteria concerning the practice of witchcraft. The community's shared belief in witchcraft led adults to seek out "evidence" from children, who they believed would always tell the truth, by posing leading questions and encouraging statements confirming their beliefs (Ceci & Bruck, 1993).

From the mid-1980s through the mid-1990s, Americans have witnessed a modern witch-hunt of sorts, with childhood sexual abuse as the target crime rather than witchcraft, as evidenced by the virtual floodgate of sensationalized stories reporting cases of children testifying to widespread sexual abuse in day-care centers and adults suing their parents, relatives, and religious leaders for sexual abuse that allegedly occurred during childhood. In this section, we reflect on this decade and consider the spirit of the times and shared belief systems that provided the social milieu for such cases to flourish. Here, we summarize and expand on arguments made by Goldstein concerning the social movements that preceded and led to a climax of childhood-memory cases during the past two decades (Goldstein, 1997; Goldstein & Farmer, 1993). More specifically, we outline how the radical feminist and recovery movements collaborated in voicing the following shared beliefs concerning childhood sexual abuse:

1. The prevalence of childhood sexual abuse greatly surpasses society's imagination.
2. What constitutes abuse is defined by the victim and can include any inappropriate behavior.
3. Memories for childhood sexual abuse are often repressed or dissociated.
4. Indicators of childhood sexual abuse include numerous physical and emotional maladies, such as headaches, eating disorders, and low self-esteem.
5. Psychotherapy, and group therapy more specifically, are recommended as treatment for recovery from the emotional trauma of childhood sexual abuse (see Forward & Buck, 1978).

We also discuss how the New Age movement influenced individuals' willingness to subject themselves to suggestive

techniques and how this movement may have exacerbated the possibility of false-memory creation by addressing doubts with a reliance on antiscientific attitudes.

Radical Feminism and the Recovery Movement

How can one reconcile the glaring lack of evidence for repressed memories and organized satanic cult activity with the public's beliefs that these phenomena are pervasive in our society? Dawes (1992) explained that beliefs that contradict evidence are developed and sustained by the presence of a group of "authorities" who establish a social consensus to support their beliefs. In the case of repressed memories, representatives from two major social movements, the feminist and recovery movements, comprised the group of "authorities" who carried broad ranges of credentials, from self-proclaimed experts to psychiatrists. These "authorities" actively promoted the theory that women who seek therapy and exhibit fairly general symptoms were repressing memories of childhood sexual abuse. Although we credit the feminist movement for their positive contribution of raising the public's awareness of childhood sexual abuse and the recovery movement for making support accessible to virtually anyone, we believe that these movements contributed to the hysteria that underlies recent cases. Here, we address more specifically how these two movements developed a social consensus that childhood sexual abuse is common and that memories for such abuse are repressed.

How Frequent Is Childhood Sexual Abuse? One goal of the feminist and recovery movements was to establish that the frequency of sexual abuse in society greatly surpassed the public's awareness. Representing the feminist perspective, Forward and Buck (1978) claimed, without referencing the source of their information, that between 10 and 20 million Americans are victims of abuse. Radical feminist social worker Florence Rush (1980) stated that childhood sexual abuse is not "an occasional deviant act, but a devastating commonplace fact of everyday life" (p. xii).

To bolster the impression that childhood sexual abuse is rampant, feminist authors labeled society as "patriarchal" and argued that incest has been used systematically, historically, and universally, as a means of female oppression perpetrated by adult males, and furthermore, that anyone could be guilty of such acts. Rush (1980) attempted to establish a social history of universal acceptance of childhood sexual abuse by men, citing references such as the Talmud, the Bible, ancient Greek writings, traditional fairy tales, and modern films. Herman (1981) attributed society's increased awareness of childhood sexual abuse to the women's liberation movement, proclaimed that the feminist perspective offered the best explanation of the data, and articulated this perspective by stating, "Female children are regularly subjected to sexual assaults by adult males who are part of their intimate social world. The aggressors are not outcasts and strangers; they are neighbors, family friends, uncles, cousins, stepfathers, and fathers" (p. 7).

Thus, the major result of the feminist interpretation of childhood sexual abuse during the 1970s was to establish, by reiteration rather than by evidence, that incest is commonplace in American families. Indeed, Masson (1992) credited the feminist literature of the 1970s with breaking the silence concerning the prevalence of incest. Yet, the National Committee for the Prevention of Child Abuse (1996) reported the following:

> While many estimates have been made, the national incidence rate of sexual abuse remains unknown. The estimate that one in four girls and one in ten boys are abused prior to age 18 became widely known statistically simply from being repeated. Retrospective surveys reveal great variation with 6% to 62%. (p. 1)

Defining Abuse. Another factor that contributed to bolstering the public's impression of the high prevalence of childhood sexual abuse was the expansion of the definition of what constitutes abuse. Herman (1981) effectively expanded the pool of possible incest victims by conceptualizing abuse as occurring along a continuum from the most extreme exaggeration of patriarchal norms, overt incest, to *covert incest*, the term that she used to describe women who had seductive but not incestuous fathers. According to Herman, victims of covert incest were larger in number and experienced similar consequences as victims of overt incest. Forward (1989) continued this loosening of the term *incest* by stating, "Victims of psychological incest may not have been actually touched or assaulted sexually, but

they have experienced an invasion of their sense of privacy or safety" (p. 139).

The recovery movement exaggerated society's perception of victimization by promoting the notion that most of us grew up in or live within the context of a dysfunctional family. On his public television "infomercials" and in his various books, John Bradshaw has claimed that 100% of families are dysfunctional, which implies that everyone needs to recover from something. Bradshaw used the term *emotional incest* as the recovery movement's parallel to Herman's concept of covert incest. Blume (1990) described this emotional incest more explicitly by claiming the following:

> It can be the way a father stares at his daughter's developing body, and the comments he makes. … It can be forced exposure to the sounds or sights of one or both parents' sexual acts … or it can be a father's jealous possessiveness and suspicion of the boys his daughter associates with, his inquisitorial insistence on knowing the details of her sexual encounters. … Horribly, increasingly, it can occur as part of a cult ritual activity engaged in by a network of adults and involving many children—violence and abuse of animals as well." (pp. 8–9)

In response to these claims, Kaminer (1992) stated, "If child abuse is every form of inadequate nurturance, then being raped by your father is in the same class as being ignored or not getting help with your homework. When everything is child abuse, nothing is" (p. 27). Thus, these perpetual reconceptualizations of abuse had the effect of making child abuse seem even more prevalent, increasing the numbers of the incest survivor movement.

Repression of Abuse Memories: Freud's Seduction Theory Revisited. As noted previously, because several of his female patients shared similar stories of early sexual experiences, Freud speculated that many of the psychological maladies exhibited by these patients originated from and served as indicators of repressed memories of childhood sexual abuse. Despite Freud's own rejection of this seduction theory, feminist authors, such as Herman and Forward, resurrected and steadfastly maintained Freud's original ideas.

Herman asserted that Freud rejected his seduction theory as a means of protecting patriarchy and that psychiatrists have conspired to represent women's reports of sexual abuse as fantasies. In the conclusion to one of her studies, she claimed that her findings validate the theory. In 1987, Herman and Schatzow wrote,

> The presumption that most patients' reports of childhood sexual abuse can be ascribed to fantasy no longer appears tenable. ... No positive evidence was adduced that would indicate that any of the patients' reports of sexual abuse were fantasies. In the light of these findings, it would seem warranted to return to the insights offered by Freud's original statement of the etiology of hysteria, and to resume a line of investigation that mental health professionals prematurely abandoned 90 years ago. (p. 11)

Without delineating the mechanisms of memory repression and recovery, Masson (1992), a psychoanalyst and former director of the Freud Archives, supported the feminist perspective's adoption of Freud's seduction theory. Masson referred to Freud's rejection of his seduction theory as a personal failure of courage and abandonment of truth, and believes, as Freud initially did, that adult neuroses are indicators of traumatic memories of sexual abuse that are buried in the unconscious mind.

Representing the recovery movement, Blume (1990) claimed, "Indeed, so few incest survivors in my experience have identified themselves as abused in the beginning of therapy that I have concluded that perhaps half of all incest survivors do not remember that the abuse occurred" (p. 81). She developed The Incest Survivors' Aftereffects Checklist to aid readers in considering whether they have repressed memories of abuse. Some of Blume's symptoms of child abuse from this list of approximately 100 items include nightmares, gastrointestinal problems, arthritis, wearing baby clothes, eating disorders, drug or alcohol abuse, depression, constant anger, high risk-taking, low risk-taking, fear of losing control, low self-esteem, high appreciation of small favors, feeling crazy, feeling different, being compulsively seductive or asexual, avoidance of mirrors, and wanting to change one's name. Blume states, "Among women who had not been aware of childhood sexual abuse but who recognize characteristics in themselves on the checklist, a surprising number began to uncover previously repressed incest" (p. xxiv; for a similar interpretation, see Fredrickson, 1992). This inclusion of individuals who do not remember abuse or exhibit "indicators" elevated the prevalence of childhood sexual abuse once again.

Psychotherapy Unburies Repressed Memories. The majority of feminist authors sanctioned psychotherapy for the recovery of lost memories of abuse and extended advice to therapists concerning inquiries of abuse. Herman (1981) recommended that every patient be questioned about the possibility of childhood sexual abuse:

> Questions about sexual abuse should be incorporated into any clinician's ordinary history-taking. The prevalence of child sexual abuse even in the general population is great enough to warrant routine questioning. ... The burden of responsibility for obtaining a history of incest should lie with the therapist. (p. vii)

Furthermore, she asserted that recovery of repressed memories can alleviate the symptoms discussed previously as indicators of childhood sexual abuse (Herman & Schatzow, 1987). Forward (1989) supported Herman's opinion by stating "many victims still won't mention the incest without prodding from the therapist" (p. 152).

This position was adopted by many psychotherapists. Courtois (1992) expressed her belief that patients should be "educated" (or indoctrinated) by therapists about post-traumatic stress disorder and therapeutic and memorial processes. She stated,

> Education precedes formal recall strategies to insure the survivor a cognitive framework within which to process emotions which accompany recall. ... At times, it may be necessary for the therapist to put the pieces together and speculate about the emerging picture and its significance. (pp. 25–26)

Courtois recommended group therapy as a memory retrieval cue. She claimed, "Groups are very powerful in eliciting memories since survivors associate or 'chain' to each others' recollections and feelings" (pp. 28–29).

Given what the research literature informs us about people's susceptibility to suggestion from authority figures, one would not be surprised if many of the memories recovered under such interviewing techniques were false. These arguments apply to the group-therapy context as well. The process of "chaining" to other group members' recollections described by Courtois appears dangerously close to Binet's findings of suggestibility at the group level. Current conceptualizations of source monitoring suggest that clients in group settings may misattribute others' memories as their own (e.g., Johnson et al., 1993).

In concluding our discussion of the impact of feminist and recovery movement "authorities" in forming a social consensus that childhood sexual abuse is rampant and that memories for such abuse are repressed, we cite a clear example of how politics often overrides science on this issue. In her book, *Revolution From Within: A Book of Self-Esteem* (1992), Gloria Steinem addressed the prevalence of childhood sexual abuse and its indicators and advocated theories of repression and dissociation of sexual abuse memories by making this statement:

> Perhaps, the memory has been pushed out of our consciousness completely. But those images and feelings remain alive in our unconscious—and they can be uncovered. Even abuse so long-term and severe that a child survived only by dissociating from it while it was happening still leaves markers above its burial ground. (p. 72)

Later in the same book, she asserted the following:

> There are telltale signs of such buried trauma … fear of expressing anger at all; substantial childhood periods of which you have no memory of emotions or events …depression … severe eating disorders.… Trust these clues—there is statistical as well as personal evidence that the conditions they point to are widespread. Perhaps a third of the children in the United States have been subjected to sexual and other kinds of severe abuse or neglect. … Frequently, such memories are so painful that they don't surface fully until years after the events occurred. The more extreme and erratic these events, the

younger we were when we experienced them, and the more dependent we were on the people who inflicted them, the more repressed they are likely to be. (pp. 162–163)

Go Where Your Mind Takes You: The New Age Movement, Suggestive Therapeutic Techniques, and Antiscience

The impact of the New Age movement on society's thinking has been underestimated, yet a venture into many bookstores reveals numerous books on past-life channeling and fortune-telling that often outnumber books in the science section. Society has embraced the notion of exploring mind-altering techniques, which obviously have some benefits that contribute to the movement's popularity. For example, relaxation techniques, such as meditation, yoga, and visualization, can yield healing and health maintenance effects. However, such mind-altering techniques can also render unexpected deleterious effects. Here, we discuss the role such techniques have played in contributing to false-memory cases, such as Patricia Burgus', and how the New Age movement has promoted anti-scientific attitudes.

The reach of New Age techniques has extended beyond bookstores and into therapeutic practices. As noted previously, representatives of the feminist and recovery movements offered psychotherapy as the prescription for retrieving lost memories of abuse. Coincidentally (or perhaps not), many of the prominent players in the feminist and recovery movements have offered weekend seminars training therapists in the use of New Age techniques to retrieve memories. Courtois (1992), a clinical psychologist, endorsed a host of "experiential/expressive-cathartic techniques" to aid in the retrieval of lost memories, including hypnosis, imagery, guided movement, body work, and psychodrama. Considering the adverse effects of one such technique, hypnosis, research clearly demonstrates that although hypnosis increases how much a person remembers, much of the information gained is erroneous (e.g., Lynn, Lock, Myers, & Payne, 1997); furthermore, hypnosis increases an individual's confidence in correct and incorrect information. The general consensus among memory researchers concerning the accuracy of information produced by such New Age techniques is that less is more in these cases (Ornstein, Ceci, & Loftus, 1996).

Perhaps the most disturbing product of the New Age movement is the penetration of antiscientific attitudes into public consciousness. New Age abandons science by relying on intuition rather than evidence. Kaminer (1992) expressed her concern with this rejection of scientific findings by stating,

> New Age is an attitude. To demand precision and specificity (what some would call meaning) in a discussion of consciousness paradigms or transpersonal energy vibrations is to reveal yourself as only 'half-minded,' a sorry left-brained creature trapped in rationalism, foolishly focused on the external world. It is to absent yourself from the postbiological, postverbal phase of human evolution and to dwell spiritually in nonlivingness. New Age is aggressively anti-intellectual, proudly nonrational. It's not supposed to make sense. (p. 102)

Representatives of the recovery movement are particularly guilty of disseminating antiscientific attitudes into the public domain. Although Bass and Davis noted in the preface of their book *The Courage to Heal* (1988) that "none of what is presented here is based on psychological theories" (p. 14), they made assertive statements that may sound like scientific fact to readers, such as the following: "Forgetting is one of the most common and effective ways children deal with sexual abuse. ... The human mind has tremendous powers of repression" (p. 42). They also posited, "There are many women who show signs of having been abused without having any memories" (p. 71). Furthermore, Bass and Davis (1988) encouraged intuition over evidence by stating, "If you think you were abused and your life shows the symptoms, then you were. ... To say 'I was abused,' you don't need the kind of recall that would stand up in a court of law" (p. 22). Davis (1991) further promoted the antiscientific notion that memory is not required in realizations of abuse by instructing potential victims to tell themselves, "I'm going to accept the fact that I was abused and make a commitment to heal, even if I never remember the specifics" (p. 118).

In general, the New Age belief in intuitive, nonrational explanations and the disdain for conventional scientific, evidence-based explanations influenced some therapists' practices, particularly when it came to the recovery of repressed childhood memories. The result was an environment that encouraged recollections of events that may never have happened but that were consistent with the prevailing theory of a patient's therapist or of the recollections of one's group members.

The discussion to this point has focused on the role of "authorities" in developing a social consensus that perpetuated false beliefs concerning the nature of childhood memory and how social movements have created a climate that made false-memory cases possible. Next, we address how changes in the judicial system itself have increased the frequency of such cases.

Changes in the Legal System

Although Ceci and Bruck (1993) outlined a number of changes in the legal system since the Salem witch trials, here we focus on two primary issues: (a) changes related to children's testimony and (b) changes in the statute of limitations for crimes that allegedly occurred during childhood.

In response to an increased awareness of childhood sexual abuse, which can partly be attributed to the feminist movement's concerted effort to expose such abuse, the legal system changed their procedures for handling child witnesses. Most jurisdictions abandoned the requirement for corroboration in sexual abuse cases, and many states, after centuries of skepticism, began to permit child testimony, allowing the jury to determine the credibility of children's assertions. Eventually, this loosening of rules resulted in hearsay exceptions, which allowed the admissibility of statements by therapists, pediatricians, and others concerning statements made by children. These changes in the legal system were adopted with the intent of increasing accurate testimony (Harvard Law Review Notes, 1985; Montoya, 1992); however, given the research reviewed at the outset of this chapter, children's ability to accurately testify depends on a number of factors, including their age and the type of questions used for interrogation.

Some researchers have doubted the applicability of current findings to cases of childhood sexual abuse. For example, Goodman and Clarke-Stewart (1991) pointed out that most research investigating children as eyewitnesses tests situations that are qualitatively different from personally experienced sexual abuse. However, although ethical limitations prohibit specific tests of children's eyewitness memory for sexual abuse, research indicates that children are suggestible and can even be persuaded to report that a complete, emotionally laden event involving physical contact happened to them when it really did not as demonstrated in the case that took place in Wenatchee, Washington.

Cases in which adults are suing others for abuse that occurred in childhood have been more drastically influenced by politics. The National Organization for Women (NOW) published a Legal Resource Kit on Incest and Child Sexual Abuse (NOW Legal Defense and Education Fund, 1992) that advocated the view that victims of childhood sexual abuse repress their memories of the trauma and that such memories may be uncovered through therapeutic processes. Furthermore, they argued that women who are victims of such abuse but who do not uncover their lost memories of abuse until later in life experience a violation of rights because they cannot sue the perpetrator because of statute of limitations restrictions. To remedy this situation, the NOW Legal Defense and Education Fund proclaimed,

> We have developed a sophisticated legal argument that proves that the statute of limitations for civil incest cases should begin to run not when acts of incest end, and not at the age of majority, but rather when the victim discovers the injuries she has suffered and their cause. (p. 2)

NOW filed amicus curiae (friend of the court) briefs on this issue and successfully lobbied 20 state legislatures to increase the statute of limitations in cases that involve memories of childhood sexual abuse recovered in therapy. The result of these politically motivated changes in the legal system is that nonabusers (often parents) may be convicted of or pay civil fines for crimes they may not have committed because the judicial system itself, however indirectly, is advocating a theory for which there is little evidence.

False accusations by children (usually groups of children in a single daycare center) of sexual abuse by their caretakers (usually uncovered by persistent questioning by therapists or police officers) and court cases of recovered childhood sexual abuse brought mostly by adult women against a relative or former family friend (again, usually recovered in therapy) peaked by the mid-1990s and are now in decline. By the late 1990s, there were as many or more cases of women suing their therapists for misguided therapy, purporting that memories of abuse were planted by the therapist when in fact no abuse had occurred. What was responsible for this change?

The movements that supported the suggestive interviewing of children and the belief in the recovery of repressed memory did not just run out of steam. Rather, the scientific research that was generated in large part by the social phenomena under discussion here revealed problems that were not easy to ignore. Children are highly suggestible and, although repression may in fact occur, there was no scientific evidence that it occurred to the extent proposed by practitioners of the recovery movement, and memories of abuse from infancy were highly unlikely if not impossible.

But papers published in scientific journals rarely influence potent social movements or belief systems. What turned the tide was scientists becoming involved in the social discussion. They served as expert witnesses in many court cases, and filed amicus curiae statements in appeals of several prominent abuse cases, which resulted in convictions being overturned and wrongly accused people freed. For example, Maggie Bruck and Stephen Ceci (1995) led a group of social scientists in filing an amicus brief in the Kelly Michaels case. Kelly Michaels was a nursery school teacher in Maplewood, New Jersey, who was accused of multiple charges of sexual abuse of the children in her care. Despite the lack of physical evidence, the often bizarre statements made by the children (e.g., she licked peanut butter off children's genitals, played the piano in the nude), and the highly suggestive questioning of the children, Kelly Michaels was convicted and sentenced to 47 years in prison. On the grounds of faulty interview techniques, the Appeals Court of New Jersey reversed her conviction in 1993. Following is a paragraph from the amicus brief authored by Bruck and Ceci and signed by 45 social scientists. It turned the tables on those prosecuting sexual child abuse, and made it clear that it is not a issue of "child advocates" versus "cold-hearted scientists":

> The authors of this brief also wish to convey their deep concern over the children in this case. Our concern is that if there were incidents of sexual abuse, the faulty interviewing procedures make it impossible to ever know who the perpetrators were and how the abuse occurred. Thus, poor interviewing procedures make it difficult to detect real abuse. But we have further concerns. And these involve the interviewing techniques which we view as abusive in themselves. After reading a number of these interviews, it is difficult to believe that adults charged with the care and protection of young children would be allowed to use the vocabulary that they used in these interviews, that they would be allowed to interact with children in such sexually explicit ways, or that they would be allowed to bully and frighten their child witnesses in such a shocking manner. No amount of evidence that sexual abuse had actually occurred could ever justify the use of these techniques especially with three-and four-year-old children. Above and beyond the great stress, intimidation, and embarrassment that many of the children obviously suffered during the interviews, we are deeply concerned about the long-lasting harmful effects of persuading children that they have been horribly sexually and physically abused when in fact there may have been no abuse until the interviews began. The authors of this brief will be permanently disturbed that children were interviewed in such abusive circumstances regardless of the ultimate innocence or guilt of the accused. (cited in Ceci & Bruck, 1995, pp. 292–293)

The reversals of this and other high-profile cases, supported by research scientists, made the evening news and brought another perspective on these and related cases to the public. Prominent scientists such as Elizabeth Loftus and Stephen Ceci appeared on national television news

programs, presented their research, and discussed the undesired consequences of some of the interviewing techniques used both with children and adults in recovering memories of abuse. And although books on New Age and the recovery movement still outnumber books based on scientific evidence on the bookshelves of major book retailers, popular books began to appear written by scientists on the issues of recovered memories (e.g., Loftus & Ketchum, 1994, *The Myth of Repressed Memory*; Ofshe & Watters, 1994, *Making Monsters: False Memories, Psychotherapy, and Sexual Hysteria*) and the credibility of children's testimony following extensive and suggestive interviewing (Ceci & Bruck, 1995, *Jeopardy in the Courtroom: A Scientific Analysis of Children's Testimony*). Gradually, the weight of science, along with the energies of attorneys representing accused parents, began to chip away at claims made by advocates of the recovery movement. The result today, we believe, is a climate in which the horrors of child abuse are not overlooked or minimized but in which society no longer believes that every adult emotional malady is a result of long-forgotten abuse.

CONCLUSION

> "It was the best of times, it was the worst of times. ..."

With apologies to Charles Dickens, we find it likely that future historians of our discipline will characterize current research on the development of memory and cognition in this bipolar manner" (Baker-Ward, Ornstein, & Gordon, 1993, p. 13).

Although Baker-Ward et al. (1993) used this quotation to refer to the distinction between basic and applied research, the sentiment is appropriate when considering the field's positions on the nature of childhood memory for traumatic events. On the one hand, some practitioners advocate repression theories, and on the other, some memory researchers maintain that repression contradicts everything that is known about memory. In response to this debate, the American Psychological Association formed a working group of three clinical psychologists (Alpert, Brown, and Courtois) and three memory researchers (Ceci, Loftus, and Ornstein) to investigate memories of childhood abuse. The final conclusions of the report (Alpert et al., 1996) indicated that the two factions agree that childhood sexual abuse is a pervasive societal problem, that most victims of abuse remember their experiences (although forgetting is possible), and that false-memory creation is possible. However, the clinicians and the scientists candidly admitted that they disagreed on the mechanisms that underlie memory, the privileged status afforded to memories of traumatic events, the relevance of research to understanding memory for traumatic events, the pervasiveness of false-memory creation, and the degree to which true memories can be distinguished from false memories. Although the social environment has changed considerably over the past 5 years or so, the critical issues have not been settled. It is our hope that in the future therapists and scientists can more easily share their ideas and data in an environment that is free from the polarizing polemics that characterized the previous decade.

NOTES

1. Later in his career, Freud wrote,

    Under the influence of the technical procedure which I used at that time, the majority of my patients reproduced from their childhood scenes in which they were sexually seduced by some grown-up persons. With female patients the part of seducer was almost always assigned to their father. I believed these stories, and consequently supposed that I had discovered the roots of the subsequent neurosis in these experiences of sexual seduction in childhood. ... If the reader feels inclined to shake his head at my credulity, I cannot altogether blame him. When, however, I was at last obliged to recognize that these scenes of seduction had never taken place, and that they were only phantasies which my patients had made up or which I myself had perhaps forced on them, I was for sometime completely at a loss. (as cited in Masson, 1992, p. 198)

REFERENCES

ALPERT, J. L., BROWN, L. S., CECI, S. J., COURTOIS, C. A., LOFTUS, E. F., & ORNSTEIN, P. A. (1996). *WORKING GROUP ON INVESTIGATION OF MEMORIES OF CHILDHOOD ABUSE: FINAL REPORT.* WASHINGTON, DC: AMERICAN PSYCHOLOGICAL ASSOCIATION.

BAKER-WARD, L., ORNSTEIN, P. A., & GORDON, B. N. (1993). A TALE OF TWO SETTINGS: YOUNG CHILDREN'S MEMORY PERFORMANCE IN THE LABORATORY AND THE FIELD. IN G. M. DAVIES & R. H. LOGIE (EDS.), *MEMORY IN EVERYDAY LIFE* (PP. 13–41). AMSTERDAM: NORTH-HOLLAND/ELSEVIER.

BASS, E., & DAVIS, L. (1988). *THE COURAGE TO HEAL.* NEW YORK: HARPER & ROW.

BAUER, P. J. (1996). WHAT DO INFANTS RECALL OF THEIR LIVES? MEMORY FOR SPECIFIC EVENTS BY 1-TO 2-YEAR-OLDS. *AMERICAN PSYCHOLOGIST, 51,* 29–41.

BELLUCK, P. (1997, NOVEMBER 6). "MEMORY" THERAPY LEADS TO A LAWSUIT AND BIG SETTLEMENT. *THE NEW YORK TIMES,* PP. A1, A10.

BINET, A. (1900). *LA SUGGESTIBILITÉ.* PARIS: SCHLEICHER FRÈRES.

BJORKLUND, D. F. (2000). *CHILDREN'S THINKING: DEVELOPMENTAL FUNCTION AND INDIVIDUAL DIFFERENCES* (3RD ED.). BELMONT, CA: WADSWORTH.

BJORKLUND, D. E., BJORKLUND, B. R., BROWN, R. D., & CASSEL, W. S. (1998). CHILDREN'S SUSCEPTIBILITY TO REPEATED QUESTIONS: HOW MISINFORMATION CHANGES CHILDREN'S ANSWERS AND THEIR MINDS. *APPLIED DEVELOPMENTAL SCIENCE, 2,* 99–111.

BLUME, E. S. (1990). *SECRET SURVIVORS.* NEW YORK: BALLANTINE.

BRAINERD, C. J., & POOLE, D. A. (1997). LONG-TERM SURVIVAL OF CHILDREN'S FALSE MEMORIES: A REVIEW. *LEARNING AND INDIVIDUAL DIFFERENCES, 9,* 125–152.

BRAINERD, C. J., & REYNA, V. F. (1990). GIST IS THE GRIST: FUZZY-TRACE THEORY AND THE NEW INTUITIONISM. *DEVELOPMENTAL REVIEW, 10,* 3–47.

BRAINERD, C. J., & REYNA, V. F. (1998). FUZZY-TRACE THEORY AND CHILDREN'S FALSE MEMORIES. *JOURNAL OF EXPERIMENTAL CHILD PSYCHOLOGY, 71,* 81–129.

BRAINERD, C. J., REYNA, V E., & BRANDSE, E. (1995). ARE CHILDREN'S FALSE MEMORIES MORE PERSISTENT THAN THEIR TRUE MEMORIES? *PSYCHOLOGICAL SCIENCE, 4,* 141–148.

BRUCK, M., & CECI, S.J. (1995). AMICUS BRIEF FOR THE CASE OF STATE OF NEW JERSEY V. MICHAELS PRESENTED BY COMMITTEE OF CONCERNED SOCIAL SCIENTISTS. *PSYCHOLOGY, PUBLIC POLICY, AND LAW, 1,* 272–322.

BUGENTAL, D. B., BLUE, J., CORTEZ, V, FLECK, K., & RODRIGUEZ, A. (1992). THE INFLUENCE OF WITNESSED AFFECT ON INFORMATION PROCESSING IN CHILDREN. *CHILD DEVELOPMENT, 63,* 774–86.

CASSEL, W. S., & BJORKLUND, D. F. (1995). DEVELOPMENTAL PATTERNS OF EYEWITNESS MEMORY AND SUGGESTIBILITY: AN

ECOLOGICALLY BASED SHORT-TERM LONGITUDINAL STUDY. *LAW AND HUMAN BEHAVIOR, 19,* 507–532.

CASSEL, W. S., ROEBERS, C., & BJORKLUND, D. F. (1996). DEVELOPMENTAL PATTERNS OF EYEWITNESS RESPONSES TO REPEATED AND INCREASINGLY SUGGESTIVE QUESTIONS *JOURNAL OF EXPERIMENTAL CHILD PSYCHOLOGY, 61,* 116–133.

CECI, S. J., & BRUCK, M. (1993). SUGGESTIBILITY OF THE CHILD WITNESS: A HISTORICAL REVIEW AND SYNTHESIS. PSYCHOLOGICAL BULLETIN, 113, 403–439.

CECI, S. J., & BRUCK, M. (1995). *JEOPARDY IN THE COURTROOM: A SCIENTIFIC ANALYSIS OF CHILDREN'S TESTIMONY.* WASHINGTON, DC: AMERICAN PSYCHOLOGICAL ASSOCIATION.

CECI, S. J., & BRUCK, M. (1998). CHILDREN'S TESTIMONY: APPLIED AND BASIC ISSUES. IN W. DAMON (SERIES ED.) & I. E. SIGEL & K. A. RENNINGER (VOL. EDS.), *HANDBOOK OF CHILD PSYCHOLOGY: VOL. 4. CHILD PSYCHOLOGY IN PRACTICE* (5TH ED., PP. 713–774). NEW YORK: WILEY.

CECI, S. J., CROTTEAU-HUFFMAN, M., SMITH, E., & LOFTUS, E. F. (1994). REPEATEDLY THINKING ABOUT NON-EVENTS. *CONSCIOUSNESS AND COGNITION, 3,* 388–407.

CECI, S. J., LOFTUS, E. F., LEICHTMAN, M. D., & BRUCK, M. (1994). THE ROLE OF SOURCE MISATTRIBUTIONS IN THE CREATION OF FALSE BELIEFS AMONG PRESCHOOLERS. *INTERNATIONAL JOURNAL OF CLINICAL AND EXPERIMENTAL HYPNOSIS, 62,* 304–320.

CECI, S. J., TOGLIA, M. P., & ROSS, D. F. (1990). THE SUGGESTIBILITY OF PRESCHOOLERS' RECOLLECTIONS: HISTORICAL PERSPECTIVES ON CURRENT PROBLEMS. IN R. FIVUSH & J. HUDSON (EDS.), *KNOWING AND REMEMBERING IN YOUNG CHILDREN* (PP. 285–300). NEW YORK: CAMBRIDGE UNIVERSITY PRESS.

CHRISTIANSON, S. A., & NILSSON, L. (1989). HYSTERICAL AMNESIA: A CASE OF AVERSIVELY MOTIVATED ISOLATION OF MEMORY. IN T. ARCHER & L. NILSSON (EDS.), *AVERSION, AVOIDANCE, AND ANXIETY: PERSPECTIVES ON AVERSIVELY MOTIVATED BEHAVIOR* (PP. 289–310). HILLSDALE, NJ: LAWRENCE ERLBAUM ASSOCIATES.

COURTOIS, C. (1992). THE MEMORY RETRIEVAL PROCESS IN INCEST SURVIVOR THERAPY. *JOURNAL OF CHILD SEXUAL ABUSE, 1,* 15–29.

DAVIS, L. (1991). *ALLIES IN HEALING.* NEW YORK: HARPERCOLLINS.

DAWES, R. (1992). WHY BELIEVE THAT FOR WHICH THERE IS NO GOOD EVIDENCE? *ISSUES IN CHILD ABUSE ACCUSATIONS, FALL,* 214–218.

EISEN, M. L., GOODMAN, G. S., & QIN, J.J. (1995, APRIL). *EYEWITNESS TESTIMONY IN VICTIMS OF CHILD MALTREATMENT: STRESS,*

MEMORY, AND SUGGESTIBILITY. PAPER PRESENTED AT THE SYMPOSIUM OF THE SOCIETY FOR APPLIED RESEARCH ON MEMORY AND COGNITION, VANCOUVER, CANADA.

FIVUSH, R. (1988). THE FUNCTIONS OF EVENT MEMORY: SOME COMMENTS ON NELSON AND BARSALOU. IN U. NEISSER & E. WINOGRAD (EDS.), *REMEMBERING RECONSIDERED: ECOLOGICAL AND TRADITIONAL APPROACHES TO THE STUDY OF MEMORY* (PP. 277–282). NEW YORK: CAMBRIDGE UNIVERSITY PRESS.

FOLEY, M. A., SANTINI, C, & SOPASAKIS, M. (1989). DISCRIMINATING BETWEEN MEMORIES: EVIDENCE FOR CHILDREN'S SPONTANEOUS ELABORATIONS. *JOURNAL OF EXPERIMENTAL CHILD PSYCHOLOGY, 48,* 146–169.

FORWARD, S. (1989). *TOXIC PARENTS.* NEW YORK: BANTAM.

FORWARD, S., & BUCK, C. (1978). *BETRAYAL OF INNOCENCE: INCEST AND ITS DEVASTATION.* NEW YORK: PENGUIN.

FREDRICKSON, R. (1992). *REPRESSED MEMORIES: A JOURNEY TO RECOVERY FROM SEXUAL ABUSE.* NEW YORK: SIMON & SCHUSTER.

FREUD, S. (1957). REPRESSION. IN J. STRACHEY (ED. AND TRANS.), *THE STANDARD EDITION OF THE COMPLETE PSYCHOLOGICAL WORKS OF SIGMUND FREUD* (VOL. 14, PP. 66–89). LONDON: HOGARTH PRESS. (ORIGINAL WORK PUBLISHED 1915)

FREUD, S. (1963). *AN OUTLINE OF PSYCHO-ANALYSIS.* NEW YORK: NORTON. (ORIGINAL WORK PUBLISHED 1940)

FREYD, P. (1997, FEBRUARY). (LETTER). *FALSE MEMORY SYNDROME NEWSLETTER, 6*(2), 1.

GOLDSTEIN, E. (1997). FALSE MEMORY SYNDROME: WHY WOULD THEY BELIEVE SUCH TERRIBLE THINGS IF THEY WEREN'T TRUE? *THE AMERICAN JOURNAL OF FAMILY THERAPY, 25,* 307–317.

GOLDSTEIN, E., & FARMER, K. (1993). *TRUE STORIES OF FALSE MEMORIES.* BOCA RATON, FL: UPTON.

GOODMAN, G. S., AMAN, C., & HIRSCHMAN, J. E. (1987). CHILD SEXUAL AND PHYSICAL ABUSE: CHILDREN'S TESTIMONY. IN S. J. CECI, M. P. TOGLIA, & D. F. ROSS (EDS.), *CHILDREN'S EYEWITNESS MEMORY* (PP. 1–23). NEW YORK: SPRINGER-VERLAG.

GOODMAN, G. S., & CLARKE-STEWART, A. (1991). SUGGESTIBILITY IN CHILDREN'S TESTIMONY: IMPLICATIONS FOR CHILD SEXUAL ABUSE INVESTIGATIONS. IN J. L. DORIS (ED.), *THE SUGGESTIBILITY OF CHILDREN'S RECOLLECTIONS* (PP. 92–105). WASHINGTON, DC: AMERICAN PSYCHOLOGICAL ASSOCIATION.

GOODMAN, G. S., EMERY, R. E., & HAUGAARD, J. J. (1998). DEVELOPMENTAL PSYCHOLOGY AND LAW: DIVORCE, CHILD MALTREATMENT, FOSTER CARE, AND ADOPTION. IN W. DAMON (SERIES ED.) & I. E. SIGEL & K. A. RENNINGER (VOL.

Eds.), *Handbook of child psychology: Vol. 4. Child psychology in practice* (5th ed., pp. 775–874). New York: Wiley.

Goodman, G. S., Hirschman, J. E., Hepps, D., & Rudy, L. (1991). Children's memory for stressful events. *Merrill-Palmer Quarterly, 37,* 109–158.

Goodman, G. S., Quas, J. A., Batterman-Faunce, J. M., Riddlesberger, M. M., & Kuhn, J. (1994). Predictors of accurate and inaccurate memories of traumatic events experienced in childhood. *Consciousness and Cognition, 3,* 269–294.

Goodman, G. S., Quas, J. A., Batterman-Faunce, J. M, Riddlesberger, M. M., & Kuhn, J. (1997). Children's reactions to and memory for a stressful event: Influences of age, anatomical dolls, knowledge, and parental attachment. *Applied Developmental Science, J,* 54–75.

Harvard Law Review Notes. (1985). The testimony of child sex abuse victims in sex abuse prosecutions: Two legislative innovations. *Harvard Law Review, 98,* 806–827.

Herman, J. L. (1981). *Father-daughter incest.* Cambridge, MA: Harvard University Press.

Herman, J. L., & Schatzow, E. (1987). Recovery and verification of memories of childhood sexual trauma. *Psychoanalytic Psychology, 4,* 1–14.

Howe, M. L., & Courage, M. L. (1993). On resolving the enigma of infantile amnesia. *Psychological Bulletin, 13,* 305–326.

Howe, M. L., Courage, M. L., & Peterson, C. (1995). Intrusions in preschoolers' recall of traumatic childhood events. *Psychonomic Bulletin and Review, 2,* 130–134.

Hyman, I. E., Husband, T. H., & Billings, F. J. (1995). False memories of childhood experiences. *Applied Cognitive Psychology, 9,* 181–197. Johnson, M. K., Hashtroudi, S., & Lindsay, D. S. (1993). Source monitoring. *Psychological Bulletin, 114,* 3–28.

Kaminer, W. (1992). *I'm dysfunctional, you're dysfunctional.* Reading, MA: Addison-Wesley.

Leichtman, M. D., & Ceci, S. J. (1993). The problem of infantile amnesia: Lessons from fuzzy-trace theory. In M. L. Howe & R. Pasnak (Eds.), *Emerging themes in cognitive development: Vol. 1. Foundations* (pp. 195–213). New York: Springer-Verlag.

Lindsay, D. S., & Read, J. D. (1994). Psychotherapy and memories of childhood sexual abuse: A cognitive perspective. *Applied Cognitive Psychology, 8,* 281–338.

Lipmann, O. (1911). Pedagogical psychology of report. *Journal of Educational Psychology, 2,* 253–260.

Loftus, E. F. (1979). The malleability of memory. *American Scientist, 67,* 312–320.

Loftus, E. F. (1993). The reality of repressed memories. *American Psychologist, 48,* 518–537. Loftus, E. F., & Ketchum, K. (1994). *The myth of repressed memory.* New York: St. Martin's Press.

Loftus, E. F., & Pickrell, J. E. (1995). The formation of false memories. *Psychiatric Annals, 25,* 720–725.

Loftus, E. F., Polonsky, S., & Fullilove, M. T. (1994). Memories of childhood sexual abuse: Remembering and repressing. *Psychology of Women Quarterly, 18,* 67–84.

Lynn, S. J., Lock, T. G., Myers, B., & Payne, D. G. (1997). Recalling the unrecallable: Should hypnosis be used to recover memories in psychotherapy? *Current Directions in Psychological Science, 6,* 79–83.

Malinoski, P., Lynn, S. J., Martin, D., Aronoff, A., Neufeld, J., & Gedeon, S. (1995, August), Individual differences in early memory reports: An empirical investigation. Paper presented at the 103rd Annual Convention of the American Psychological Association, New York.

Masson, J. M. (1992). *The assault on truth: Freud's suppression of the seduction theory.* New York: HarperCollins.

Mazzoni, G. (1998). Memory suggestibility and metacognition in child eyewitness testimony: The roles of source monitoring and self-efficacy. *European Journal of Psychology of Education, 13,* 43–60.

McCloskey, M., & Zaragoza, M. (1985). Misleading postevent information and memory for events: Arguments and evidence against the memory impairment hypothesis. *Journal of Experimental Psychology: General, 114,* 1–16.

Meltzoff, A. N. (1995). What infant memory tells us about infantile amnesia: Long-term recall and deferred imitation. *Journal of Experimental Child Psychology, 59,* 497–515.

Merritt, K. A., Ornstein, P. A., & Spicker, B. (1994). Children's memory for a salient medical procedure: Implications for testimony. *Pediatrics, 94,* 17–23.

Montoya, J. (1992). On truth and shielding in child abuse trials. *Hastings Law Journal, 43,* 1259–1319.

National Committee for the Prevention of Child Abuse. (1996, December). *Child sexual abuse* (No. 19) (Brochure). Chicago: Author.

Nelson, K. (1996). *Language in cognitive development: The emergence of the mediated mind.* New York: Cambridge University Press.

NOW Legal Defense and Education Fund. (1992). *Legal remedies for adult survivors of incest and child sexual abuse* (Legal Resource Kit: Incest and Child Sexual Abuse). New York: Author.

Oates, K., & Shrimpton, S. (1991). Children's memories for stressful and nonstressful events. *Journal of Science, Medicine and the Law, 31,* 4–10.

Ofshe, R., & Watters, E. (1994). Making *monsters: False memories, psychotherapy, and sexual hysteria.* New York: Scribner's.

Ornstein, P. A., Ceci, S. J., & Loftus, E. F. (1996). Reply to the Alpert, Brown, and Courtois document: The science of memory and the practice of psychotherapy. In J. L. Alpert, L. S. Brown, S. J. Ceci, C. A. Courtois, E. F. Loftus, & P. A. Ornstein, *Working Group on Investigation of Memories of Childhood Abuse: Final report* (pp. 106–130). Washington, DC: American Psychological Association.

Ornstein, P. A., Shapiro, L. R., Clubb, P. A., Follmer, A., & Baker-Ward, L. (1997). The influence of prior knowledge on children's memory for salient medical experiences. In N. Stein, P. A. Ornstein, B. Tversky, & C. J. Brainerd (Eds.), *Memory for everyday and emotional events* (pp. 83–112.). Mahwah, NJ: Lawrence Erlbaum Associates.

O'Sullivan, J. T., Howe, M. L., & Marche, T. A. (1996). Children's beliefs about long-term retention. *Child Development, 67,* 2989–3009.

Peters, D. P. (1991). The influence of stress and arousal on the child witness. In J. Doris (Ed.), *The suggestibility of children's recollections: Implications for eyewitness testimony* (pp. 60–76). Washington, DC: American Psychological Association.

Pezdek, K., & Hodge, D. (1999). Planting false childhood memories: The role of event plausibility. *Child Development, 70,* 887–895.

Pillemer, D. B., & White, S. H. (1989). Childhood events recalled by children and adults. In H. W. Reese (Ed.), *Advances in child development and behavior* (Vol. 21, pp. 297–340). San Diego, CA: Academic Press.

Poole, D. A., & White, L. T. (1995). Tell me again and again: Stability and change in the repeated testimonies of children and adults. In M. S. Zaragoza, J. R. Graham, G. C. N. Hall, R. Hirschman, & Y. S. Ben-Porath (Eds.), *Memory and testimony in the child witness* (pp. 24–43). Thousand Oaks, CA: Sage.

Qin, J. J., Quas, J. A., Redlich, A. D., & Goodman, G. S. (1997). Children's eyewitness testimony: Memory development in the legal context. In N. Cowan (Ed.), *The development of memory in childhood* (pp. 301–341). Hove East Sussex, UK: Psychology Press.

Reyna, V. F. (1994). Interference effects in memory and reasoning: A fuzzy-trace theory analysis. In F. N. Dempster & C. J. Brainerd (Eds.), *New perspectives on interference and inhibition processes in cognition* (pp. 29–59). San Diego, CA: Academic Press.

Reyna, V. F., & Brainerd, C. J. (1995). Fuzzy-trace theory: An interim synthesis. *Learning and Individual Differences, 7,* 1–75.

Rovee-Collier, C. (1995). Time windows in cognitive development. *Developmental Psychology, 31,* 147–169.

Rovee-Collier, C., & Gerhardstein, P. (1997). Studies in developmental psychology. In N. Cowan (Ed.), *The development of memory in childhood* (pp. 5–39). Hove East Sussex, UK: Psychology Press.

Rush, F. (1980). *The best kept secret: Sexual abuse of children.* Englewood Cliffs, NJ: Prentice-Hall.

Steinem, G. (1992). *Revolution from within: A book of self-esteem.* Boston: Little, Brown.

Stern, W. (1910). Abstracts of lectures on the psychology of testimony and on the study of individuality. *American Journal of Psychology, 21,* 270–282.

Steward, M. (1989). *The development of a model interview for young child victims of sexual abuse* (Tech. Rep. No. 90CA1332). Washington, DC: U.S. Department of Health and Human Services.

Tizon, A. (1996, June 28). Wenatchee braces for sex-ring lawsuits. The *Seattle Times,* p. A1.

van der Kolk, B. A., & Fisler, R. E. (1995). Dissociation and the fragmentary nature of traumatic memories: Overview and exploratory study. *Journal of Traumatic Stress, 8,* 505–525.

Welch-Ross, M. K. (1995). An integrative model of the development of autobiographical memory. *Developmental Review, 15,* 338–365.

Zaragoza, M. (1991). Preschool children's susceptibility to memory impairment. In J. L. Doris (Ed.), *The suggestibility of children's recollections* (pp. 27–39). Washington, DC: American Psychological Association.

True Photographs and False Memories

D. STEPHEN LINDSAY, LISA HAGEN, J. DON READ, KIMBERLEY A. WADE, AND MARYANNE GARRY

ABSTRACT—*Some trauma-memory-oriented psychotherapists advise clients to review old family photo albums to cue suspected "repressed" memories of childhood sexual abuse. Old photos might cue long-forgotten memories, but when combined with other suggestive influences they might also contribute to false memories. We asked 45 undergraduates to work at remembering three school-related childhood events (two true events provided by parents and one pseudoevent). By random assignment, 23 subjects were also given their school classes' group photos from the years of the to-be-recalled events as memory cues. As predicted, the rate of false-memory reports was dramatically higher in the photo condition than in the no-photo condition. Indeed, the rate of false-memory reports in the photo condition was substantially higher than the rate in any previously published study.*

Psychologists have long been interested in memory illusions and distortions, because such errors can inform theories of how memory works (e.g., Bartlett, 1932; Schacter, 2001). In the 1990s, controversy regarding trauma-memory-oriented psychotherapies sharpened that interest in false memories, and led cognitive psychologists to test the hypothesis that suggestive influences can lead adults to "remember" childhood pseudoevents. Loftus and Pickrell (1995) introduced a procedure in which adult research subjects are given brief narrative descriptions of childhood events and asked to work on remembering those events. Subjects are told that all of the narratives were provided by their family members, but one of the narratives describes a pseudoevent that familial informants report subjects did not experience during childhood.

Across eight studies (published in six refereed journal articles) that used variants of this familial-informant false-narrative procedure, 116 of 374 subjects (31%) were scored as having false memories, with rates in individual conditions ranging from 0% to 56% (Hyman & Billings, 1998; Hyman, Husband, & Billings, 1995; Hyman & Pentland, 1996; Loftus & Pickrell, 1995; Pezdek, Finger, & Hodge, 1997; Porter, Yuille, & Lehman, 1999). Some of these studies differentiated between "partial" and "complete" false memories: Although the operationalizations of these categories (and the terms used to label them) varied across studies, the gist of the distinction is that subjects classified as having complete false memories provided more evidence that they genuinely believed they were remembering the pseudoevent, as opposed to merely accepting that it occurred or speculating about it. Across studies making this distinction, 36 of 208 subjects (17%) were classified as having partial false memories and 41 (20%) were classified as having complete false memories. The highest rate of complete false memories in an individual study was 26% (Porter et al.).

In a previous study (Wade, Garry, Read, & Lindsay, 2002), we developed a new procedure in which subjects are given photographs of themselves as children and asked to remember the event depicted in each photo (see Koutstaal, Schacter, Johnson, & Galluccio, 1999, and Schacter, Koutstaal, Johnson, Gross, & Angell, 1997, for studies of the effects of interpolated photos on memory for staged events). Most of the photos (obtained from familial informants) were of events subjects experienced during childhood, but one photo was created by digitally inserting a childhood image of the subject into the basket of a hot-air balloon (an event that familial informants indicated subjects had not experienced). Of 20 subjects, 10 (50%) were classified as reporting memories of the hot-air balloon ride (30% partial, 20% complete).

It is not altogether surprising that doctored photographs like those we used are powerfully suggestive. After all, people perceive photographs as compelling evidence that the depicted events really occurred, and photos provide a rich source of information regarding the perceptual details of suggested events. These characteristics make the false-photo procedure a very useful method for studying false-memory phenomena.

Despite these strengths, the false-photo procedure suffers an obvious limitation in ecological validity and generalizability: People rarely encounter doctored photos of themselves doing things they have never really done. People do, however, sometimes review old family photo albums. Moreover, some trauma-memory-oriented psychotherapists and self-help books have recommended that adults who think they may have been abused in childhood but do not recall such abuse should review family photo albums (e.g., Dolan, 1991; cf. Poole, Lindsay, Memon, & Bull, 1995). The idea is that viewing photos of oneself and others in the childhood environment may cue long-forgotten memories of trauma. That may sometimes occur, but (when combined with other suggestive influences) reviewing childhood photos could also contribute to the formation of false memories. That is, if a person believes that certain kinds of events occurred in his or her childhood, and is motivated to recall such events, childhood photos constitute a source of detailed and vivid perceptual images that may be combined with products of imagination to yield compelling pseudomemories. The current research tested this hypothesis.

METHOD

Subjects

The subjects were 45 undergraduates (36 women and 9 men) who volunteered to participate and were rewarded with optional bonus points in an introductory psychology course.

Procedure

Each subjects' parents provided brief narratives describing two unique, school-related events experienced by their child, one event experienced in Grade 5 or 6 and the other in Grade 3 or 4. Parents were asked to avoid events that were oft-told family stories in favor of events that they thought their child might have some difficulty remembering. All parents reported that their child never experienced our target pseudoevent (putting Slime, a brightly colored gelatinous compound manufactured by Mattel as a toy, in the teacher's desk in Grade 1 or 2). Parents also provided their child's class photo (see Fig. 1) for each of the school years corresponding to target events, and the name and gender of their child's Grade 1 or 2 teacher.

In an initial one-on-one interview, the experimenter read each narrative aloud and asked the subject to recall it, starting with the Grade 5 or 6 event and working back in time to the Grade 1 or 2 pseudoevent. By random assignment, 23 of the subjects (18 women and 5 men) were given a photocopy of their school class's group photo for each year before the corresponding narrative was read to them (the photo and its copy were in color for all but 1 subject). The interviewer encouraged each subject to recall as much as possible about each event, using mental context reinstatement and guided-imagery exercises. The subject then rated (a) the extent to which the memory experience resembled reliving the event (from 1, *not at all*, to 7, *as clearly as if it were happening right now*) (b) the extent to which the subject felt he or she was remembering the event (same scale as for the reliving question), and (c) his or her confidence that the event had occurred as described in the narrative (from 1, *0% confident*, to 7, *100% confident*). The pseudoevent narrative was customized to use the subject's name and his or her teacher's name, as in the following example:

> I remember when Jane was in Grade 1, and like all kids back then, Jane had one of those revolting Slime toys that kids used to play with.

I remember her telling me one day that she had taken the Slime to school and slid it into the teacher's desk before she arrived. Jane claimed it wasn't her idea and that her friend decided they should do it. I think the teacher, Mrs. Smollett, wasn't very happy and made Jane and the friend sit with their arms folded and legs crossed, facing a wall for the next half hour.

At the end of Session 1, subjects were told that for the rest of the experiment they were to focus their efforts on recalling the oldest of the events (i.e., the pseudoevent). They were asked to spend some time each day over the next week working at remembering more about that event, and were given a printed copy of the narrative (and, for subjects in the photo condition, a copy of the class photo) to use as a memory cue. Subjects were asked not to talk to others about the event. Four days later, the interviewer telephoned each subject to check on progress and encourage additional effort, again reading the narrative of the

pseudoevent and fostering "recall" with mental context reinstatement and guided imagery. One week after the initial interview, subjects returned to the lab and were again encouraged to remember as much as possible about the pseudoevent, after which they rated their memories of it on the same scales used in Session 1. Subjects' spoken memory reports were tape-recorded during both sessions.

Two trained judges (blind to the photo/no-photo manipulation) independently reviewed typed transcripts of subjects' spoken reports of their memories of the pseudoevent and judged whether each subject experienced (a) no images or memories, (b) images but not memories, or (c) memories of putting Slime in the teacher's desk. The images-but-no-memories category corresponded to what other researchers have termed partial false memories, and applied to cases in which the subject described images associated with the suggested event but did not appear to experience those images as memories of the event per se. Judges were to classify a report as memories only if the subject appeared to believe that he or she was remembering the

Fig. 1. *Example of the sort of school-class group photos used in the experiment. Note that this example, being the photo of the first author's Grade 2 class, is of somewhat older vintage than those used in the experiment, and that the original of the example and the photos used in the study were in color.*

suggested event. For the Session 1 reports, judges agreed in their categorizations for 42 (93%) of the subjects, and for Session 2 they concurred for 44 (98%) of the subjects. Disagreements were settled by discussion. Judges rated their mean confidence in each categorization, on a scale ranging from 1 (low) to 3 (high); for Session 1 the mean was 2.83 (SD = 0.38), and for Session 2 the mean was 2.80 (SD = 0.27).

RESULTS

Means of subjects' Session 1 memory ratings of the true events from Grades 5 or 6 and 3 or 4 are shown in Table 1. A mixed-model analysis of variance (ANOVA) of the effects of condition (photo vs. no photo) and event (Grade 5–6 vs. 3–4) on these measures indicated a non-reliable tendency for ratings to be slightly higher for the more recent event, $F(1, 43) = 3.57$, $MSE = 6.64$, $p = .07$, $\eta^2 = .08$. In five of the six comparisons, the mean rating was directionally higher in the photo than the no-photo condition, but this effect did not approach significance ($F < 1$). There were no interactions (all $Fs < 1$).

Figure 2 depicts judges' categorizations of subjects' memory reports regarding the pseudoevent. The no-photo condition of our experiment is analogous to the familial-informant false-narrative paradigm, and the results in this condition are consistent with those of studies using that paradigm: In Session 1, 13.6% of the subjects in the no-photo condition were judged to have memories of the pseudoevent, and an additional 31.8% were classified as having images but no memories. The results were also consistent with prior research in that these values increased somewhat in Session 2, with 22.7% of the subjects in the no-photo condition judged as having memories of the pseudo-event, and an additional 22.7% classified as having images but not memories. Most prior publications have collapsed results across partial and complete false memories. By that standard, 45.5% of the subjects in our nvo-photo condition would be said to have developed false memories of the Slime event by Session 2.

We hypothesized that false reports would be even more common in the photo condition. The data pattern from Session 1 fit that prediction, but the tendency for Session 1 false-memory reports to be more common in the photo than no-photo condition did not approach statistical significance, $\eta^2 (1, N = 45) = 1.84$, Fisher's exact $p = .28$, $\phi = .20$, when

measured with the relatively strict memories criterion, and $\chi^2(1, N = 45) = 1.78$, $p = .18$, $\phi = .20$, when either memories or images were classified as false memories. In Session 2, however, 65.2% of the subjects in the photo condition were judged to have memories of the pseudoevent, and an additional 13% were scored as having images but not memories, for a total of 78.2%. False reports in Session 2 were significantly more common in the photo than the no-photo condition, both when measured with the relatively strict memories criterion, $\chi^2(1, N = 45) = 6.50$, $p < .02$, $\phi = .38$, and when measured with the less strict criterion combining reports classified as memories and as images but not memories, $\chi^2(1, N = 45) = 5.15$, $p < .03$, $\phi = .34$.

Subjects rated their memories of the suggested event using the same scales with which they rated their memories of the true events (see Table 2). The key finding is that ratings were significantly higher in the photo than the no-photo condition, $F(1, 43) = 5.31$, $MSE = 8.97$, $p = .03$, $\eta^2 = .11$. Also, ratings increased across sessions, $F(1, 43) = 19.83$, $MSE = 1.99$, $p < .001$, $\eta2 = .30$, and there was a nonsignificant tendency for that increase to be slightly greater in the photo than the no-photo condition, $F(1, 43) = 2.65$, $p = .11$, $\eta2 = .04$.

Even in the photo condition, Session 2 ratings for the suggested event were lower than Session 2 ratings for the true events (especially the Grade 5 or 6 event). Of course, one would expect memory ratings of a *true* Grade 1 or 2 event to tend to be lower than memory ratings of events in later grades. Moreover, the means in Table 2 were calculated using the ratings of all subjects, whether they were or were not judged to have false memories of the suggested event. Figure 3 depicts subjects' mean memory ratings as a function of judges' categorization of subjects' reports, collapsed across the photo and no-photo conditions. Three things are worth emphasizing about these data. First, there was strong convergence between the judges' categorizations and subjects' self-ratings (e.g., subjects who were judged to have neither images nor memories indeed selected ratings near the bottom of the scale on each measure). Second, ratings of memories of the pseudo-event by subjects categorized as having false memories were equivalent to (and sometimes directionally greater than) ratings of memories of the true events. This indicates that these subjects' false memories were as compelling as memories of the true events, at least on these dimensions.

TABLE 1 *Subjects' Mean Ratings of Their Memory Experiences for the True Events as a Function of Condition*

	Grade 5 or 6		Grade 3 or 4	
Measure	No photo	Photo	No photo	Photo
Reliving	4.14 (1.64)	4.26 (0.96)	3.55 (1.90)	3.70 (1.55)
Remembering	4.86 (1.58)	4.91 (1.41)	4.23 (1.59)	4.17 (1.59)
Confidence	6.00 (1.63)	6.35 (0.98)	5.46 (1.82)	5.87 (1.79)

Note. Standard deviations are in parentheses. Rating scales ranged from 1 (low) to 7 (high).

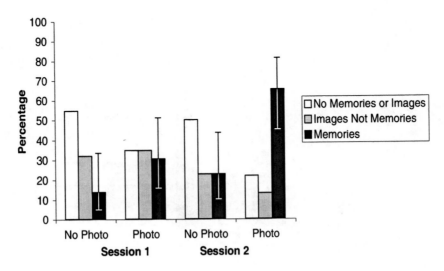

Fig. 2. *Percentage of subjects classified as having no memories or images, images but not memories, and memories of the pseudoevent, as a function of experimental condition and session. The error bars represent 95% confidence intervals around the proportion of subjects classified as having memories of the suggested event, calculated using VassarStats (Lowry, 2003).*

Third, ratings of subjects classified as reporting images but not memories were more similar to ratings of subjects classified as having neither memories nor images than they were to ratings of subjects classified as having memories. This suggests that the images-but-no-memories category should not be considered tantamount to false memories.

During debriefing, subjects were informed that one of the three events they had been asked to remember in the experiment was a made-up false event, and asked which event they thought was the false one. All but 3 subjects (1 in the photo condition and 2 in the no-photo condition) correctly identified the Grade 1 or 2 event as the pseudoevent. When subjects were informed that one of the events was false, it may have been obvious to them that this was the Grade 1 or 2 event because most of the experiment

had focused on that event and they typically had to work at "remembering" anything about it. That these sorts of analytic bases may have contributed to selection of the Grade 1 or 2 event as the false event is supported by several subjects' spontaneous expressions of surprise during debriefing. That is, even subjects who chose the Slime event as the false event often expressed surprise when the experimenter confirmed that it had not really occurred (e.g., "I had no idea"; "I can't believe that. ... I can remember parts of it"; "You mean that didn't happen to me?" "Oh, really? Holy!" "No way! I remember it! That is so weird!" "It was? Oh, really?" "If you didn't tell me it was a false event, I would have left here thinking I did this.").

TABLE 2 *Subjects' Mean Ratings of Their Memory Experiences for the Suggested Event as a Function of Session and Condition*

	Session 1			Session 2	
Measure	No photo	Photo		No photo	Photo
Reliving	1.41$_a$ (0.73)	2.09$_b$ (1.35)		2.00$_b$ (1.31)	3.22$_c$ (1.54)
Remembering	1.50$_a$ (1.01)	1.96$_a$ (1.26)		1.91$_{ab}$ (1.48)	2.83$_b$ (1.61)
Confidence	1.91$_a$ (1.19)	2.46$_a$ (1.51)		2.36$_a$ (1.81)	3.59$_b$ (1.99)

Note. Standard deviations are in parentheses. Rating scales ranged from 1 (low) to 7 (high). Means in the same row that do not share subscripts differ at the $p < .05$ level.

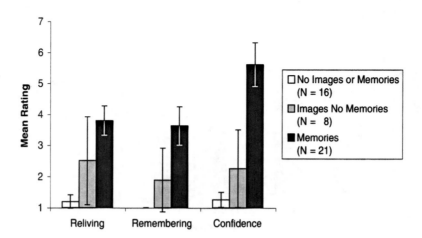

Fig. 3. *Subjects' mean ratings as a function of judges' categorization of subjects' memory reports of the pseudoevent. The error bars show 95% confidence intervals, which were calculated around the individual cell means and so are not specific to particular comparisons.*

DISCUSSION

The results from our no-photo condition converge with prior evidence that combining a plausible narrative attributed to a family member with social pressure, demand characteristics, and sustained memory-recovery techniques can lead a substantial percentage of undergraduate subjects to report memories of a childhood pseudoevent. Additional research is needed to assess the relative contributions of the various components of these suggestive influences in fostering false-memory reports.

Our central finding is that supplementing the other suggestive influences with a photo associated with (but not depicting) the suggested pseudoevent doubled the rate of false-memory reports, yielding a substantially higher rate of false-memory reports than any prior study. Even when

we used a relatively strict criterion for judging whether subjects experienced memories of the suggested event, two thirds of the subjects in the photo condition were classified as having developed false memories (more than twice the previous high, reported by Porter et al., 1999, of 26%). These findings are particularly dramatic in that subjects judged as having false memories gave quite high ratings of the extent to which they felt they were remembering the event, of the extent to which remembering the event was like reliving it, and of their confidence that the event had actually occurred. Indeed, these subjects' ratings of their memories of the pseudoevent were comparable to their ratings of memories of the later-childhood true events. Of course, this finding does not mean that our subjects' false memories were in all ways indistinguishable from accurate autobiographical recollections, but it does suggest that the pseudomemories were often experienced as quite compelling.

What explains the dramatic effect of the true-photo manipulation? One possibility (suggested by M.K. Johnson, personal communication, July 19, 2002) is that having the photos encouraged subjects in the photo condition to spend more time at the remembering task between Sessions 1 and 2 (e.g., because seeing the photo around one's residence might act as a prompt to work on the task or because having the photo might make the task more engaging). At the end of Session 2, subjects were asked how many times they had worked on the remembering task between Sessions 1 and 2. The photo ($M = 6.00$, $SD = 3.58$) and no-photo ($M = 5.68$, $SD = 2.59$) conditions did not differ on this measure, $F < 1$. This self-report measure is of unknown validity, but these findings do not support the idea that subjects in the photo condition spent more time working at remembering the pseudoevent.

We speculate that three different mechanisms may have contributed to the dramatic effect of the photo. First, it may be that the photo added to the authoritativeness of the suggestive narrative. That is, even though the photo did not depict the Slime prank, its presentation may have added to subjects' confidence that the suggested event really happened (cf. Paddock & Terranova, 2001). Second, the photo may have enabled subjects to speculate about details of the pseudoevent (e.g., "Who would my collaborator in the Slime prank have been?"). Hyman and Billings (1998) reported that subjects who freely speculated about a suggested pseudoevent during an initial interview were more likely than other subjects to later be scored as reporting false memories. Subjects in our no-photo condition may have had difficulty entering into such speculations because of inability to recall relevant details, such as the appearances of their classmates and teacher in Grade 1 or 2. Finally, memories of perceptual details from the photo (e.g., the teacher's appearance) may have subsequently been blended with products of imagination to produce vivid images of the pseudoevent, thereby contributing to subjectively compelling false memories (as per the source-monitoring framework of Johnson and her coauthors, e.g., Johnson, Hashtroudi, & Lindsay, 1993).

Articles reporting false-memory-induction studies (and citations of such studies in secondary sources) sometimes collapse across partial and complete false-memory reports, either by not distinguishing the two categories at all or by emphasizing the sum of both when summarizing the false-memory rate. Our findings suggest that this may not be appropriate, because the self-ratings of subjects classified as having images but not memories (analogous to what others have termed partial false memories) more closely resembled the self-ratings of subjects judged to have neither memories nor images than they resembled the ratings of subjects judged to have false memories. Casual inspection of the transcripts reveals that subjects categorized as experiencing images but not memories often appeared to be speculating about, rather than remembering, the suggested event (e.g., they said things along the lines of, "Well, it probably would have been … ." or "I probably would have felt … ."). Such speculations may be an important step toward developing pseudomemories (as per Hyman & Billings, 1998), but given the low ratings such subjects reported on measures of remembering, reliving, and confidence, mere images do not appear to warrant being called false memories.

The pseudoevent in our study was designed to be a distinctive, memorable, one-off event with a modicum of emotional "zing," and to be neither entirely implausible nor likely actually to have occurred. Extant research indicates that the likelihood of false memories is moderated by numerous variables, including the nature of the suggested event (see Lindsay & Read, 2001). Our Slime event differs dramatically and in numerous ways from childhood sexual abuse, so the absolute rate of false memories in our study cannot be used to predict the probability of false memories of childhood sexual abuse. Indeed, it cannot even be assumed that the true-photo effect obtained with the particular event and photos used in this study will generalize to other relatively innocuous childhood pseudoevents. Nonetheless, there is little reason to doubt that the mechanisms involved in our effect can contribute to other sorts of false memories, and therefore our results warrant concern about the riskiness of encouraging clients to review old photo albums during attempts to "recover" suspected but nonremembered histories of childhood sexual abuse.

ACKNOWLEDGMENTS

This research was supported by Natural Science and Engineering Research Council of Canada (NSERC) Grant OGP7920–1997 to J. Don Read, by NSERC Grant OGP0121516–95 to D. Stephen Lindsay, and by a Victoria University of Wellington Strategic Development Fund travel grant and a Targeted Ph.D. scholarship to Kimberley A. Wade. We thank the parents of our subjects for their contributions to this experiment, and Marcia K. Johnson, Colleen M. Kelly, Henry L. Roediger, III, and an anonymous reviewer for helpful comments on prior drafts. Thanks also go to Michael E.J. Masson for statistical advice.

REFERENCES

Bartlett, F.C. (1932). *Remembering: A study in experimental and social psychology*. Cambridge, England: Cambridge University Press.

Dolan, Y.M. (1991). *Resolving sexual abuse: Solution-focused therapy and Ericksonian hypnosis for adult survivors*. New York: Norton.

Hyman, I.E., Jr., & Billings, F.J. (1998). Individual differences and the creation of false childhood memories. *Memory, 6*, 1–20.

Hyman, I.E., Jr., Husband, T.H., & Billings, F.J. (1995). False memories of childhood experiences. *Applied Cognitive Psychology, 9*, 181–197.

Hyman, I.E., Jr., & Pentland, J. (1996). The role of mental imagery in the creation of false childhood memories. *Journal of Memory and Language, 35*, 101–117.

Johnson, M.K., Hashtroudi, S., & Lindsay, D.S. (1993). Source monitoring. *Psychological Bulletin, 114*, 3–28.

Koutstaal, W., Schacter, D.L., Johnson, M.K., & Galluccio, L. (1999). Facilitation and impairment of event memory produced by photograph review. *Memory & Cognition, 27*, 478–493.

Lindsay, D.S., & Read, J.D. (2001). The recovered memories controversy: Where do we go from here? In G. Davies & T. Dalgleish (Eds.), *Recovered memories: Seeking the middle ground* (pp. 71–94). London: Wiley.

Loftus, E.F., & Pickrell, J.E. (1995). The formation of false memories. *Psychiatric Annals, 25*, 720–725.

Lowry, R. (2003). *VassarStats*. Retrieved March 20, 2003, from http://faculty.vassar.edu/lowry/VassarStats.html

Paddock, J.R., & Terranova, S. (2001). Guided visualization and suggestibility: Effect of perceived authority on recall of autobiographical memories. *Journal of Genetic Psychology, 162*, 347–356.

Pezdek, K., Finger, K., & Hodge, D. (1997). Planting false childhood memories: The role of event plausibility. *Psychological Science, 8*, 437–441.

Poole, D.A., Lindsay, D.S., Memon, A., & Bull, R. (1995). Psychotherapy and the recovery of memories of childhood sexual abuse: U.S. and British practitioners' opinions, practices, and experiences. *Journal of Clinical and Consulting Psychology, 63*, 426–437.

Porter, S., Yuille, J.C., & Lehman, D.R. (1999). The nature of real, implanted, and fabricated memories for emotional childhood events: Implications for the recovered memory debate. *Law and Human Behavior, 23*, 517–537.

Schacter, D.L. (2001). *The seven sins of memory: How the mind forgets and remembers*. Boston: Houghton Mifflin.

Schacter, D.L., Koutstaal, W., Johnson, M.K., Gross, M.S., & Angell, K.E. (1997). False recollection induced by photographs: A comparison of older and younger adults. *Psychology & Aging, 12*, 203–215.

Wade, K.A., Garry, M., Read, J.D., & Lindsay, D.S. (2002). A picture is worth a thousand lies: Using false photographs to create false childhood memories. *Psychonomic Bulletin & Review, 9*, 597–603.

Repressed Memories and World War II

Lest We Forget!

BERTRAM P. KARON AND ANMARIE J. WIDENER

The war neuroses of World War II (WWII) provide ample evidence that repression does indeed occur, and that the recovery of these traumatic memories and their related affects led to remission of symptoms. Moreover, these recovered memories were of events that had occured. An illustrative case history from WWII is described. This well-documented body of data, well-known at the time, seems to have been forgotten in current discussions concerning repressed memories.

It is astounding that so many authoritative statements by con-temporary psychologists and psychiatrists refer to repression and repressed memories as a myth (e.g., Holmes, 1992; Ofshe & Watters, 1994; Steele, 1994; Wakefield & Underwager, 1992). They state that repressed memory is an arcane idea for which no clear empirical evidence exists. If there are so-called recovered memories, they are held to be the result of dubious, pseudo- psychotherapeutic interventions.

Laboratory experiments from the 1930s (Diven, 1937; Haggard, 1943) to the present (e.g., Mathews & Wertheimer, 1958; Shevrin, 1978; Shevrin, Williams, Marshall, & Hertel, 1992) have shown evidence for repression, but today's skeptics are either unfamiliar with this research or possibly find it unconvincing. Behavioral therapists and many cognitive therapists have never seen clear evidence of repressed memories because the types of psychotherapy they practice do not routinely reveal such evidence. Of course, the new generation of exclusively biological psychiatrists work in a way that does not require obtaining such evidence. However, psychodynamic psychologists feel that they are constantly exposed in their clinical work to clear evidence of repressed memories. That is, patients typically say they do not remember things that, as the treatment progresses, they do remember. As these memories occur, related symptoms remit.

According to Gardner (1993), "better trained, older psychiatrists" (p. 374) do not believe that there is any evidence for amnesia other than on an organic basis (i.e., concussion or other brain damage syndromes). It is often pointed out that children who have observed the murder of their parents clearly retain the memory, which seems to imply that psychologically painful experiences do not get repressed. Lenor Terr, however, has reported that repeated traumas are more often repressed than a single traumatic event (Terr, 1991). Linda Williams (1994) studied women who had been sexually abused in childhood, where the event was clearly documented at the time of the trauma. She found that 38% of the women had no memory of the event 17 years later.

WORLD WAR II REPRESSION

There is a mass of convincing empirical data on repression that is relatively easily available but seems to have been forgotten. In World War II (WWII), there were literally hundreds of documented battlefield neuroses that involved the repression of traumatic combat experiences (e.g., Grinker & Spiegel, 1945; White, 1964). Professionals who worked in the Veterans Administration (VA) after WWII frequently saw such patients. Charles Fisher (1945) reported treating 20 cases of amnesia caused by repressed battlefield trauma. Each case of traumatic recovered memory could be corroborated by people other than the patient. Kardiner and Spiegel (1947) reported cases of men who, after years of incapacitation, recovered memories that had been forgotten and then recovered from their incapacitating symptoms. One important reason that this mass of data does not immediately come to mind is that there are very few living clinical psychologists who were working as therapists in the VA in the 1940s. Another reason may be that the data itself have been repressed.

Today, these WWII patients would be diagnosed with post-traumatic stress disorder (PTSD). These patients would have no memory of the traumatic battlefield event but would have symptoms, typically of conversion hysteria. Usually, there were other WWII servicemen there who described the traumatic combat experience. The only one who could not remember the experience was the patient with PTSD. When, in psychodynamic therapy, the traumatic experiences—including the patient's affect during the trauma—were reexperienced consciously (i.e., were no longer repressed), the hysterical symptoms disappeared. In order to speed up therapy, there were experimental uses of hypnosis and of sodium pentathol interviews to undo the repression and recover the memories in brief therapy. It was reported that using such procedures allowed the rapid recovery of the patient to pretraumatic functioning. The heightened suggestibility of the patient under hypnosis or pentathol was not considered a problem because the therapist frequently knew many of the realistic details of the combat trauma from other people. Hence, the problem of creating false memories was never a serious issue.

CLINICAL EXAMPLE

The following clinical example illustrates a typical combat hysterical neurosis of WWII involving repression of the combat trauma:

Several years after the end of WWII, a veteran who had been treated by the neurology service of a VA hospital for a paralyzed arm was referred to the VA's psychology service. The neurologists concluded the paralysis was not organic but hysterical. A psychoanalytic psychologist, Edward Karon, treated the patient in psychoanalytic psychotherapy twice a week. After approximately 6 months of treatment, the patient mentioned, "You know, I once got a medal."

The next session, the patient brought in a newspaper clipping and began to talk about a WWII airplane crash reported in that paper. The following session, the patient began to describe the crash. He was the tailgunner in a two-man bomber. Because of the cramped quarters in the tail turret of two-man bombers, tailgunners were chosen to be small in size. The pilot, his friend, was over 6 feet tall and over 200 pounds. After a bombing mission, the plane crashed on its return to the landing field in England. The first three planes from this squadron crashed when landing; then this plane crashed; and the next two planes in that squadron also crashed. Reasonably enough, it was suspected that the planes had been sabotaged.

Because there were three wrecks already on the landing field, the pilot did not attempt to land on the runway. Instead, he attempted to land in a farmer's field. When the plane crashed, the tailgunner broke an arm but was conscious. The plane was on fire; when the fire hit the gas tank, it would explode.

The tailgunner freed himself from the wreckage and yelled for help from the several farmworkers who witnessed the crash. But they would not help because they knew the plane was going to blow up. His friend, the pilot, was unconscious and had broken both his legs. The tailgunner tried to free his friend, but he could not because of the size and weight of the unconscious man. He yelled again for help, but no one came. He knew the plane was going to blow up, but the farmworkers could have rescued the two of them in minutes. He tried again to rescue his friend. He wanted to run, but he did not. With his one good arm, bit by bit, he moved the larger and heavier man out of the plane. He yelled again for help, but no one moved. Bit by bit, he pulled his friend with great difficulty, yelling for help. Eventually, an ambulance came, and he thought the ambulance crew would rush in and quickly move them to safety. But the ambulance crew knew the plane was going to blow up and circled the plane at a distance of 50 feet. When, inch by inch, he had pulled his friend 25 feet from the plane, the ambulance crew ran in and rescued them.

The tailgunner was awarded a medal for his bravery. The pilot, who had been unconscious during the whole event, eventually regained the use of both legs and was able to return to combat. The tailgunner's broken arm completely healed. However, his other arm was paralyzed from then on, even after the war was over. Furthermore, he had no conscious memory of the crash or of saving his friend. He had repressed it.

During this psychotherapy session, he had remembered the details of his experience, including his heroic efforts and conscious terror. At the end of the session, his clothes were wringing wet with perspiration. But for the first time since that event, he had partial movement in his arm.

The hysterical paralysis psychodynamically represented a defense against ever experiencing the horror of that plane crash again. Like all of us would be, he was terrified and wanted to run from the plane to save himself. But his conscience could not let him abandon his friend, no matter how terrified he was or how dangerous the situation. His unconscious was protecting him: If he had broken both arms, he would have had no choice. There would have been no way to save his friend, and, therefore, it would have been all right to run for his life.

However, the unconscious is not realistic. This symptom protected him only from an exact repetition of the trauma, a future danger that would never occur. The war was over. Even if the war had continued and there was another crash, his paralyzed arm would only save his life if his nonparalyzed arm was again broken. Because the memory was repressed, it could not be corrected by accurate information about the present.

He did not gain full use of his arm, however, until the secondary gain of his symptom was also dealt with. As Sigmund Freud first pointed out, once a patient develops a symptom, it will be used for neurotic purposes in addition to those that led to its origin. This patient found it impossible to work at his occupation with a paralyzed arm. Being unable to work involuntarily was a way of expressing hostility to his wife. (In the 1940s and 50s, the traditional American family head-of-household and chief wage earner was the husband; being unable to work was a good way of expressing hostility to his wife.) One year of psychoanalytic psychotherapy sufficed not only to remove this symptom, but also to enable him to function effectively at work and at home.

In short, the war neuroses of WWII provide ample evidence that repression does indeed occur, and that the recovery of these traumatic memories and their related affects led to remission of symptoms. Moreover, these recovered memories were of events that had unquestionably occurred. Current controversies concerning repressed memories are always discussed without reference to this well-documented body of data, which was well-known at the time but seems to have been forgotten. The mental health professions, just as much as individual patients, need to remember their past in order to be effective in the real world.

REFERENCES

DIVEN, K. (1937). CERTAIN DETERMINANTS IN THE CONDITIONING OF ANXIETY REACTIONS. JOURNAL OF PSYCHOLOGY, 3, 291-308.

FISHER, C. (1945). AMNESTIC STATES IN WAR NEUROSIS: THE PSYCHOGENESIS OF FUGUES. THE PSYCHOANALYTIC QUARTERLY, 14, 437-468.

GARDNER, M. (1993). THE FALSE MEMORY SYNDROME. SKEPTICAL INQUIRER, 17, 370-375.

GRINKER, R. R., & SPIEGEL, J. R (1945). MEN UNDER STRESS. NEW YORK: MCGRAW-HILL.

HAGGARD, E. A. (1943). SOME CONDITIONS DETERMINING ADJUSTMENT DURING AND READJUSTMENT FOLLOWING EXPERIMENTALLY INDUCED STRESS. IN S. S. TOMKINS (ED.), CONTEMPORARY PSYCHOPATHOLOGY (PP. 529-544). CAMBRIDGE, MA: HARVARD UNIVERSITY PRESS.

HOLMES, D. S. (1992). THE EVIDENCE FOR REPRESSION: AN EXAMINATION OF SIXTY YEARS OF RESEARCH. IN J. L. SINGER (ED.), REPRESSION AND DISSOCIATION (PP. 85-102). CHICAGO: UNIVERSITY OF CHICAGO PRESS.

KARDINER, A., & SPIEGEL, H. (1947). WAR STRESS AND NEUROTIC ILLNESS. NEW YORK: HOEBER.

MATHEWS, A., & WERTHEIMER, M. (1958). A "PURE" MEASURE OF PERCEPTUAL DEFENSE UNCONTAMINATED BY RESPONSE

SUPPRESSION. *Journal of Abnormal and Social Psychology*, 57, 373-375.

Ofshe, R., & Watters, E. (1994). *Making monsters: False memories, psychotherapy, and sexual hysteria*. New York: Charles Scribner's Sons.

Shevrin, H. (1978). Evoked potential evidence for unconscious mental processes. A review of the literature. In A. S. Prangishvili, A. S., Sherozia, & F. V. Bassin (Eds.), *The unconscious: Nature, functions, methods of study* (pp. 610-625). Tbilisi, U.S.S.R.: Metsnierba.

Shevrin, H,, Williams, W. J., Marshall, R. E,, & Hertel, R. K. (1992). Event-related potential indicators of the dynamic unconscious. *Consciousness & Cognition: An International Journal*, 1, 340-366.

Steele, D. R. (1994). Partial recall. *Liberty*, 7(3), 37-47.

Terr, L. C. (1991). Childhood traumas: An outline and overview. *American Journal of Psychiatry*, 148, 10-20.

Wakefield, H., & Underwager, R. (1992). Recovered memories of sexual abuse: Lawsuits against parents. *Behavioral Sciences and the Law*, 10, 483-507.

White, R. W. (1964). *The abnormal personality*. New York: Ronald Press.

Williams, L. M. (1994). Recall of childhood trauma: A prospective study of women's memories of child sexual abuse. *Journal of Consulting & Clinical Psychology*, 62, 1167-1176.

The Reality of Repressed Memories

ELIZABETH F. LOFTUS

Repression is one of the most haunting concepts in psychology. Something shocking happens, and the mind pushes it into some inaccessible corner of the unconscious. Later, the memory may emerge into consciousness. Repression is one of the foundation stones on which the structure of psychoanalysis rests. Recently there has been a rise in reported memories of childhood sexual abuse that were allegedly repressed for many years. With recent changes in legislation, people with recently unearthed memories are suing alleged perpetrators for events that happened 20, 30, even 40 or more years earlier. These new developments give rise to a number of questions: (a) How common is it for memories of child abuse to be repressed? (b) How are jurors and judges likely to react to these repressed memory claims? (c) When the memories surface, what are they like? and (d) How authentic are the memories?

In 1990, a landmark case went to trial in Redwood City, California. The defendant, George Franklin, Sr., 51 years old, stood trial for a murder that had occurred more than 20 years earlier. The victim, 8-year-old Susan Kay Nason, was murdered on September 22, 1969. Franklin's daughter, Eileen, only 8 years old herself at the time of the murder, provided the major evidence against her father. What was unusual about the case is that Eileen's memory

of witnessing the murder had been repressed for more than 20 years.

Eileen's memory report was believed by her therapist, by several members of her family, and by the San Mateo County district attorney's office, which chose to prosecute her father. It was also believed by the jury, which convicted George Franklin, Sr., of murder. The jury began its deliberations on November 29, 1990, and returned a verdict the next day. Impressed by Eileen's detailed and confident memory, they found her father guilty of murder in the first degree.

Eileen's memory did not come back all at once. She claimed that her first flashback came one afternoon in January 1989 when she was playing with her two-year-old son, Aaron, and her five-year-old daughter, Jessica. At one moment, Jessica looked up and asked her mother a question like "Isn't that right, Mommy?" A memory of Susan Nason suddenly came back. Eileen recalled the look of betrayal in Susie's eyes just before the murder. Later, more fragments would return, until Eileen had a rich and detailed memory. She remembered her father sexually assaulting Susie in the back of a van. She remembered that Susie was struggling as she said "No don't" and "Stop." She remembered her father saying "Now Susie," and she even mimicked his precise intonation. Next, her memory took the three of them outside the van, where she saw her father with his hands raised above his head with a rock in them. She remembered screaming. She remembered walking back to

Elizabeth F. Loftus, "The Reality of Repressed Memories," *American Psychologist*, vol. 48, no. 5, pp. 518–537. Copyright © 1993 by American Psychological Association. Reprinted with permission.

where Susie lay, covered with blood, the silver ring on her finger smashed.

Eileen's detailed and confident memory impressed a number of people. But is her memory authentic? Did she really witness the murder of her best friend 20 years earlier? The idea of repression of early traumatic memories is a concept that many psychotherapists readily accept (Bruhn, 1990). In fact, it has been said that repression is the foundation on which psychoanalysis rests (Bower, 1990). According to the theory, something happens that is so shocking that the mind grabs hold of the memory and pushes it underground, into some inaccessible corner of the unconscious. There it sleeps for years, or even decades, or even forever—isolated from the rest of mental life. Then, one day, it may rise up and emerge into consciousness. Numerous clinical examples fitting this model can be readily found. Many of these examples involve not memory of murder but rather memory of other sorts of childhood trauma, such as sexual abuse, that allegedly has been repressed for decades until recovered in therapy. Rieker and Carmen (1986) described a woman who entered psychotherapy for sexual dysfunction and recovered memories of incest committed by her father. Schuker (1979) described a woman who entered psychotherapy for chronic insomnia, low self-esteem, and other problems and recovered memories of her father sexually assaulting her. M. Williams (1987) described a man who entered therapy for depression and sleep disturbances and recovered memories of a servant molesting him. These anecdotal reports constitute the clinical evidence that clients do indeed manage later to remember some earlier inaccessible painful experience (Erdelyi, 1985). The reports constitute evidence for the core ideas inherent in the theory of repression. Several respected scholars once made the point that, from a clinical standpoint, "the evidence for repression is overwhelming and obvious" (Erdelyi & Goldberg, 1979, p. 384).

On the other hand, the clinical anecdotes and the loose theory used to explain them remain unconvincing to some psychotherapists and to many laboratory researchers. One psychiatrist who has seen more than 200 severely dissociative patients explicitly referred to such anecdotes as "empirical observations lacking in scientific underpinnings" (Ganaway, 1992, p. 203). One researcher described them as "impressionistic case studies" and claimed that they could not be counted as "anything more than unconfirmed clinical speculations" (Holmes, 1990, p. 97). After reviewing 60 years of research and finding no controlled laboratory support for the concept of repression, Holmes suggested, only half jokingly, that any use of the concept be preceded by a warning: "Warning. The concept of repression has not been validated with experimental research and its use may be hazardous to the accurate interpretation of clinical behavior" (p. 97).

Even if Holmes (1990) was right that there is virtually no scientific evidence to demonstrate the authenticity of repressed memories that return, Eileen's memory could still be authentic. Even if Holmes is proved wrong and there does develop solid scientific evidence to support the authenticity of some repressed memories that return, that would not prove that Eileen's memory is authentic. If Eileen's memory is not authentic, where else might all those details come from? Media reports from 20 years before—December 1969, when the body was found—were filled with some of these same details. The facts that the murdered girl's skull was fractured on the right side and that a silver Indian ring was found on the body were reported prominently on the front page of the San Francisco Chronicle ("Susan Nason Body Found," 1969). The fact that she apparently held her hand up to protect herself, inferred from the crushed ring, was also well-known (e.g., San Jose Mercury, "Nason Girl Fought," 1969). Most of the details that fill the rich network of her memory, however, are unfalsifiable or uncheckable—such as her memory for the door of the van that her father got out of after he raped Susie. One additional feature of Eileen's memory, worth noting, is that it changed across various tellings. For example, when she gave a statement to the police in November 1989, she told the police that her father was driving her and her sister Janice to school when they first saw Susie and that he made Janice get out of the van when Susie got in. However, months later at the preliminary hearing, she did not report Janice being in the van. In the statement to the police, the trip happened on the way to school in the morning or on the way back from lunch. During the preliminary hearing, after she presumably was reminded that Susie had not been missing until after school was out, she said it was in the late afternoon because the sun was low. Eileen's memory changed over the tellings, and there were alternative possible sources for details that made the memory seem so rich. This proves that at least some portions of these distant memories are wrong, although other parts could, in theory, still be authentic.

When George Franklin, Jr., was convicted on the basis of little more that the return of a repressed memory, *Newsweek* magazine called it an "incredible" story ("Forgetting to Remember," 1991). It was apparently the first time that an American citizen had been tried and convicted of murder on the basis of a freshly unearthed repressed memory.

MORE REPRESSED MEMORIES

Soon after the Franklin case, a string of others involving newly emerged distant memories appeared in the media. People accused by the holders of repressed memories wrote letters asking for help. Lawyers found themselves being asked to represent parties in legal cases involving repressed memories.

Popular Articles

Long-repressed memories that return after decades, often while a person is in therapy, have become highly publicized through popular articles. In 1991, actress Roseanne Barr Arnold's story was on the cover of *People* magazine. Memories of her mother abusing her from the time she was an infant until she was 6 or 7 years old had returned in therapy ("A Star Cries Incest," 1991; Darnton, 1991). Barr Arnold's was not the first such case to capture the cover of *People* magazine that year. Just three months earlier, *People* had also reported a story about former Miss America Marilyn Van Derbur, who had repressed any knowledge of sexual violation by her father until she was 24 years old and told the world about it after her father died ("The Darkest Secret," 1991; Darnton, 1991). Highly publicized cases involving memories that recently sprang into consciousness were told repeatedly in numerous popular articles in such publications as the *Washington Post* (Oldenberg, 1991), the *Los Angeles Times* (Ritter, 1991), *Seventeen* (Dormen, 1991), *Glamour* (Edmiston, 1990), *Newsweek* (Kantrowitz, 1991), and *Time* (Toufexis, 1991).

Letters

Scores of spontaneously written letters from strangers also describe the emergence of memories. I have received letters written by people who had been accused of abuse by their children. A 75-year-old physician from Florida wrote, desperate to understand why his 49-year-old daughter was suddenly claiming that he had abused her during her early childhood and teen years. A woman from Canada wrote about the nightmare of being "falsely accused of sexual abuse by our 30-year-old daughter." A woman from Michigan wrote about her 38-year-old daughter who, "after a year of counseling now accuses us of abuse ... very much like Roseanne Barr and the former Miss America, Marilyn Van Derbur." A couple from Texas wrote to tell about their youngest son, who had accused them of abusing him long ago. One letter from a mother in California well expresses the pain:

One week before my husband died after an 8-month battle against lung cancer, our youngest daughter (age 38) confronted me with the accusation that he had molested her and I had not protected her. We know who her "therapist" was: a strange young woman ... In the weeks, months that followed, the nature of the charges altered, eventually involving the accusation that my husband and I had molested our grandson, for whom we had sometimes cared while our daughter worked at her painting. This has broken my heart; it is so utterly untrue. This daughter has broken off all relationship with her four siblings. She came greatly under the influence of a book, *The Courage to Heal* (by Bass & Davis, 1988).

The letters articulately convey the living nightmares and broken hearts experienced by those accused by their adult children who suddenly remembered past abuse (see also Doe, 1991). The parents vehemently deny the abuse. Who is right and who is wrong? Is the adult child mis-remembering, or perhaps lying? Are the parents mis-remembering when they deny abuse, or are they deliberately lying?

Legal Cases

Another development after the Franklin conviction was that lawyers started calling psychologists to obtain assistance with a puzzling new type of legal case. For example, one case involved a 27-year-old San Diego woman (KL) who began to have recollections of molestation by her father

(DL), that were repressed but then were later brought out through "counseling and therapeutic intervention" (*Lofft v. Lofft*, 1989). The daughter claimed that her father had routinely and continuously molested and sexually abused her, performing "lewd and lascivious acts, including but not limited to touching and fondling the genital areas, fornication and oral copulation." Her earliest memories were of her father fondling her in the master bedroom when she was three years old. Most of her memories appeared to date back to between the ages of three and eight. She sued her father for damages for emotional and physical distress, medical expenses, and lost earnings. She claimed that because of the trauma of the experience, she had no recollection or knowledge of the sexual abuse until her repression was lifted, shortly before she filed suit.

A few years ago, plaintiffs like KL who claimed to be survivors of childhood sexual abuse would have been barred from suing by statutes of limitations. Statutes of limitations, which force plaintiffs to initiate claims promptly, exist for good reason: They protect people from having to defend themselves against stale claims. They exist in recognition that with the passage of time, memories fade and evidence becomes more difficult to obtain. Succinctly and articulately put, the primary purpose of statutes of limitation is to prevent "surprises through the revival of claims that have been allowed to slumber until evidence has been lost, memories have faded, and witnesses have disappeared" (*Telegraphers v. Railway Express Agency*, 1944, pp. 348–349). When much time has passed, defendants find it hard to mount an effective defense. Although a statute of limitations on child sexual abuse might be suspended until a victim reaches the age of majority or a few years beyond, it previously would not typically have been extended to the age of 27, for example, when KL first recalled her abuse.

In 1989, things changed for plaintiffs in the state of Washington. Legislation went into effect that permitted people to sue for recovery of damages for injury suffered as a result of childhood sexual abuse at any time within three years of the time they *remembered* the abuse (Washington, 1989; see also *Petersen v. Bruen*, 1990). The legislature invoked a novel application of the *delayed discovery doctrine*, which essentially says that the statute of limitations does not begin to run until the plaintiff has discovered the facts that are essential to the cause of action. Traditionally, the delayed discovery doctrine has been used in the area of medical malpractice. For example, a patient who discovered during a physical examination that his abdominal discomfort was caused by a surgical instrument left after an appendectomy performed 20 years earlier could sue because he could not have discovered the facts essential to his harm until he had the examination. Analogizing to the surgical instrument that was hidden from the patient until an exam made its presence known, so the memory for abuse was hidden away until it too is discovered and the plaintiff possesses the facts that are essential to the cause of action.

Within three years of enactment of the Washington statute, 18 other states enacted similar legislation allowing for the tolling of the statue of limitations.[1] Many other states introduced bills in the 1991–1992 legislative sessions that would achieve the same result, or they have begun studying similar legislation. As a consequence, repressed memories now form the basis for a growing number of civil law suits. As one writer put it, "Such wholesale forgetting—or more precisely, the eventual remembering—is forcing society to grapple in unaccustomed ways with the old problem of child molestation" (Davis, 1991, p. 81). Increasing numbers of women, and also some men, are coming out of therapy with freshly retrieved memories of abuse. They sue for damages rather than file criminal complaints, because criminal charges are often too difficult to prove (Davis, 1991). In a few states (e.g., Wyoming), they can also bring criminal charges, and moves are afoot to change laws in more states to permit criminal prosecutions to go forward. As a consequence, juries are now hearing cases in which plaintiffs are suing their parents, relatives, neighbors, teachers, church members, and others for acts of childhood sexual abuse that allegedly occurred 10, 20, 30, even 40 years earlier. Juries and judges are learning about repression of memory and about newly emerged memories of molestation not only in the United States but also in Canada, Great Britain, and other parts of the world.[2]

Many interesting questions leap to mind about repressed memories. Chief among them are, How common are claims of repressed memory? How do people in general and jurors in particular react to claims of recently unburied repressed memories? What are the memories like? How authentic are they?

HOW COMMON ARE CLAIMS OF REPRESSED MEMORY?

There is little doubt that actual childhood sexual abuse is tragically common. Even those who claim that the statistics are exaggerated still agree that child abuse constitutes a serious social problem (Kutchinsky, 1992). I do not question the commonness of childhood sexual abuse itself but ask here about how the abuse is recalled in the minds of adults. Specifically, how common is it to repress memories of childhood sexual abuse? Claims about the commonness of repressed memories are freely made: It is typical to read estimates such as "most incest survivors have limited recall about their abuse" or "half of all incest survivors do not remember that the abuse occurred" (Blume, 1990, p. 81). One psychotherapist with 18 years of experience has claimed that "millions of people have blocked out frightening episodes of abuse, years of their life, or their entire childhood" (Fredrickson, 1992, p. 15). Later, she reported that "sexual abuse is particularly susceptible to memory repression" (p. 23).

Beliefs about the commonness of repressed memories are expressed not only by those in the therapeutic community but also by legal scholars who have used these beliefs to argue for changes in legislation. For example, Lamm (1991) argued in favor of legislation that would ease access to the courts for victims of childhood sexual abuse. She applauded legislation, such as that enacted in California in 1991, that allows victims, no matter how old they are, to sue within three years after discovering their injuries or eight years after reaching majority, whichever date occurs later. As part of her argument that victims should have more time to file claims against their abusers, she expressed a view that "total repression of memories of abuse is common" (p. 2198).

Despite the confidence with which these assertions are made, there are few studies that provide evidence of the extent to which repression occurs. One study (Briere & Conte, in press) sampled 450 adult clinical clients who had reported sexual abuse histories. Therapists approached their individual clients or group clients with this question: "During the period of time between when the first forced sexual experience happened and your 18th birthday was there ever a time when you could not remember the forced sexual experience?" The main result obtained in this largely female (93%) largely White (90%) sample

was that 59% said yes. A yes response was more likely in cases involving violent abuse (physical injury, multiple perpetrators, and fears of death if abuse was disclosed) than nonviolent abuse. Reported amnesia was more likely with early molestation onset, longer abuse, and greater current symptomatology. The authors concluded that amnesia for abuse was a common phenomenon (see also Briere, 1992).

Briere and Conte's (in press) result has been taken by others as evidence for the widespread extent of repression. For example, Summit (1992) interpreted the 59% yes rate as evidence that this proportion of people "went through periods of amnesia when they were not aware of their prior abuse" (p. 22). He used the finding to support the commonness of childhood dissociation.

One problem with Briere and Conte's (in press) estimate is that it obviously depends on how the respondent interprets the eliciting question. A yes response to the question could be interpreted in a variety of ways other than "I repressed my memory for abuse." For example, it could mean "Sometimes I found it too unpleasant to remember, so I tried not to"; or "There were times when I could not remember without feeling terrible"; or "There were times I could not bring myself to remember the abuse because I would rather not think about it." Although no question is free of the possibility of multiple interpretations, the great potential for idiosyncratic interpretation by respondents to the particular wording used by Briere and Conte warrants a further examination of the issue with a different eliciting question.

A further problem with Briere and Conte's (in press) study is that the respondents were all in therapy. If some of their clinicians were under the belief that repression of memory is common, they may have communicated this belief to their clients. Clients could readily infer that, if repression of memory is so common, it is likely to have happened to them, thus the answer to the question is probably yes. This would, of course, inflate the estimates of the prevalence of repression.

Other studies have given much lower estimates for the existence of repression. Herman and Schatzow (1987) gathered data from 53 women in therapy groups for incest survivors in the Boston area. Of the 53 cases, 15 (28%) reported severe memory deficits (including women who could recall very little from childhood and women who showed a recently unearthed repressed memory). Severe memory problems were most likely in cases of abuse that began early in childhood and ended before adolescence. Cases of violent or sadistic abuse were most likely to be associated with "massive repression as a defense" (p. 5).[3]

An even lower estimate was obtained in a study of 100 women in outpatient treatment for substance abuse in a New York City hospital (Loftus, Polonsky, & Fullilove, 1993). More than one half of the women in this sample reported memories of childhood sexual abuse. The vast majority of them remembered the abuse their whole lives. Only 18% claimed that they forgot the abuse for a period of time and later regained the memory. Whether the women remembered the abuse their whole lives or forgot it for a period was completely unrelated to the violence of the abuse.

Of course, the data obtained from the New York sample may include an underestimation factor because there could have been many more women in the sample who were sexually abused, repressed the memory, and had not yet regained it. In support of this hypothesis, one could point to the research of L. M. Williams (1992), who interviewed 100 women, mostly African American, known to have been abused 17 years earlier in their lives. Of these, 38% were amnestic for the abuse or chose not to report it. Perhaps there were women in the New York sample who denied sexual abuse but who were still repressing it. Possibly there are women who were actually abused but do not remember it; however, it is misleading to assume that simple failure to remember means that repression has occurred. If an event happened so early in life, before the offset of childhood amnesia, then a woman would not be expected to remember it as an adult, whether it was abuse or something else. This would not imply the mechanism of repression. Moreover, ordinary forgetting of all sorts of events is a fact of life but is not thought to involve some special repression mechanism. For example, studies have shown that people routinely fail to remember significant life events even a year after they have occurred. One study consisted of interviews with 590 persons known to have been in injury-producing motor vehicle accidents during the previous year. Approximately 14% did not remember the accident a year later. Another study consisted of interviews with 1,500 people who had been discharged from a hospital within the previous year. More than one fourth

did not remember the hospitalization a year later (U.S. government studies, cited in Loftus, 1982).

How common are repressed memories of childhood abuse? There is no absolute answer available. There are few satisfying ways to discover the answer, because we are in the odd position of asking people about a memory for forgetting a memory. For the moment, figures range from 18% to 59%. The range is disturbingly great, suggesting that serious scholarly exploration is warranted to learn how to interpret claims about the commonness of repression and what abuse characteristics the repression might be related to.

JURORS' REACTIONS TO REPRESSED MEMORY CASES

How do people in general and jurors in particular react to repressed memory cases? Are memories that were once previously repressed as credible as memories that were never repressed? Understanding laypeople's reactions and credibility judgments is important not only for theoretical reasons but for practical ones as well. Theoretically speaking, laypeople's implicit or intuitive theories about repressed memories guide society's thinking on this topic.[4] Such implicit theories can also illuminate how therapists' theories of repression are formed; in part they derive from a therapist's own implicit theories.

On a more practical level, understanding implicit theories of repression is important. Plaintiffs' lawyers who are deciding whether to file repressed memory cases are eager to know their likelihood of a successful outcome. Defense lawyers also care, because such subjective probabilities affect their decisions about whether to proceed to trial or to settle a case early. Perhaps most importantly, the plaintiffs should care. Plaintiffs bring lawsuits for myriad reasons. Some therapists encourage their clients to sue as "hope for emotional justice" (Forward & Buck, 1988). One therapist who had treated more than 1,500 incest victims argued that the lawsuit, although grueling, is "a very important step towards devictimization," "a further source of validation," and that "the personal satisfaction can be significant" (Forward & Buck, p. 159). If the lawsuit is good for a plaintiff's mental health, what happens to mental health if a jury does not find the notion of repressed memories tenable and the plaintiff, consequently, does not prevail?

Actual Cases

I start by examining actual cases that have gone to trial in recent years, with a wide range of outcomes. Some trials ended in defense verdicts (e.g., *Lofft* v. *Lofft,* 1989, in San Diego; *Collier v. Collier,* 1991, in Santa Clara County). Others ended in plaintiff verdicts. For example, a 39-year-old woman sued her father in Los Angeles, and the jury awarded $500,000 (McMillan, 1992). A 33-year-old woman sued her uncle in Akron, Ohio, and the jury awarded $5.15 million ($150,000 in compensatory damages and $5 million in punitive damages; Fields, 1992). Because the laws are new and most cases have settled, there are too few actual trials from which to gather data about reactions to repressed memory claims. Until more cases are tried to verdict, it may be necessary to rely on simulated jury research to gather information on this issue.

Simulations

Several juror simulation studies have explored how people are likely to react to repressed memory cases (Loftus, Weingardt, & Hoffman, 1992). In these studies, mock jurors learned about a legal case that arose out of allegations of sexual assault. Subjects considered the case of a daughter (Roberta) and her father (Jim), a case modeled loosely after an actual case tried in the state of Washington in 1991. Roberta, they learned, accused her father of raping her on several occasions when she was approximately 10 years old. She claimed she repressed all memory for these incidents. At about age 20, Roberta's memory returned while she was in therapy. She filed charges against her father a year after her memory came back. Roberta and her therapist blamed her current problems of depression, anxiety, and sexual dysfunction on the sexual abuse that happened when she was 10. Jim denied the allegations, claiming that Roberta was influenced by her therapist's suggestive questioning and that she was looking for someone or something to blame for her troubles.

How did people react to Roberta's claim? Did their reactions differ from reactions to a case that was identical except for the repression of memory? A different set of subjects reacted to a modified scenario involving a different woman (Nancy) whose memory was not repressed. Nancy's factual situation was identical to Roberta's except, subjects were told, Nancy never told anyone until age 20, when she went into therapy and told her therapist. Who is believed more, Roberta or Nancy? Several consistent findings emerged from these studies. First, people tended to be slightly more skeptical about Roberta's case (the repressed memory) than they were about Nancy's case (the nonrepressed memory). Both male and female subjects reacted this way, with males overall being more skeptical.

When subjects disbelieved the claims, they were more likely to think that the false claims were due to an honest mistake than a deliberate lie. One small difference emerged—repressed and nonrepressed memory cases appear to bring slightly different thoughts to mind. When subjects considered Nancy's case, thoughts of lying were slightly more likely to be evoked than when they considered Roberta's case. One of the clearest results was that, in general, the majority of subjects believed that the claims of both Roberta and Nancy were true and accurate.

WHAT ARE THE MEMORIES LIKE?

The quality of the memories that filter back vary tremendously. They are sometimes detailed and vivid and sometimes very vague. Sometimes they pertain to events that allegedly happened in early childhood and sometimes in adolescence. Sometimes they pertain to events that allegedly happened 5 years ago and sometimes 40 years ago. Sometimes they include fondling, sometimes rape, and sometimes ritualism of an unimaginable sort.

Highly detailed memories have been reported even for events that allegedly happened more than 25 years earlier and during the first year of life. One father-daughter case recently tried in Santa Clara County, California, illustrates this pattern (*Collier v. Collier,* 1991). The daughter, DC, a college graduate who worked as a technical writer, claimed that her father sexually abused her from the time she was six months old until she was 18. She repressed the memories until the age of approximately 26, when she was in individual and group therapy.

Other cases involve richly detailed allegations of a more bizarre, ritualistic type, as in a case reported by Rogers (1992a). The plaintiff, Bonnie, in her late 40s at the time of trial, accused her parents of physically, sexually, and emotionally abusing her from birth to approximately age 25. A sister, Patti, in her mid-30s at the time of trial, said she was abused from infancy to age 15. The allegations involved torture by drugs, electric shock, rape, sodomy, forced oral sex, and ritualistic killing of babies born to or aborted by the daughters. The events were first recalled when the plaintiffs went into therapy in the late 1980s.

In short, reports of memories after years of repression are as varied as they can be. One important way that they differ is in terms of the age at which the events being remembered allegedly happened. In many instances, repressed memory claims refer to events that occurred when the child was one year old or less. This observation invites an examination of the literature on childhood amnesia. It is well known that humans experience a poverty of recollections of their first several years in life. Freud (1905/1953) identified the phenomenon is some of his earliest writings: "What I have in mind is the peculiar amnesia which ... hides the earliest beginnings of the childhood up to their sixth or eighth year" (p. 174). Contemporary cognitive psychologists place the offset of childhood amnesia at a somewhat earlier age: "past the age of ten, or thereabouts, most of us find it impossible to recall anything that happened before the age of four or five" (Morton, 1990, p. 3). Most empirical studies of childhood amnesia suggest that people's earliest recollection does not date back before the age of about three or four (Kihlstrom & Harackiewicz, 1982; Howe & Courage, 1993; Pillemer & White, 1989). One study showed that few subjects who were younger than three recalled any information about where they were when they heard about the assassination of President Kennedy, although most subjects who were more than eight at the time had some recall (Winograd & Killinger, 1983). Although one recent study suggests that some people might have a memory for a hospitalization or the birth of a sibling that occurred at age two (Usher & Neisser, in press), these data do not completely rule out the possibility that the memories are not true memories but remembrances of things told by others (Loftus, in press). Still, the literature on childhood amnesia ought to figure in some way into our thinking about recollections of child molestation that supposedly occurred in infancy.

ARE THE MEMORIES AUTHENTIC?

Therapists Beliefs About Authenticity

Many therapists believe in the authenticity of the recovered memories that they hear from their clients. Two empirical studies reveal this high degree of faith. Bottoms, Shaver, and Goodman (1991) conducted a large-scale survey of clinicians who had come across, in their practice, ritualistic and religion-related abuse cases. Satanic ritualistic abuse (SRA) cases involve allegations of highly bizarre and heinous criminal ritual abuse in the context of an alleged vast, covert network of highly organized, transgenerational satanic cults (Braun & Sachs, 1988; Ganaway, 1989, 1991). Clients with SRA memories have reported vividly detailed memories of cannibalistic revels and such experiences as being used by cults during adolescence as serial baby breeders to provide untraceable infants for ritual sacrifices (Ganaway, 1989; Rogers, 1992b). If therapists believe these types of claims, it seems likely that they would be even more likely to believe the less aggravated claims involving ordinary childhood sexual abuse. Bottoms et al.'s (1991) analysis revealed that 30% of responding clinicians had seen at least one case of child sexual abuse. A detailed analysis of 200 clinicians' experiences revealed that a substantial number of cases involved amnesic periods (44% of adult survivor cases). Overall, 93% of clinicians believed the alleged harm was actually done and that the ritualistic aspects were actually experienced by the clients. The conclusion was, in the investigators' own words, "The clinical psychologists in our sample believe their clients' claims" (p. 10).

A different approach to the issue of therapist belief was taken by Loftus and Herzog (1991). This study involved in-depth interviews with 16 clinicians who had seen at least one repressed memory case. In this small, nonrandom sample, 13 (81%) said they invariably believed their clients. One therapist said, "if a woman said it happened, it happened." Another said, "I have no reason not to believe them." The most common basis for belief was symptomatology (low self-esteem, sexual dysfunction, self-destructive behavior), or body memories (voice frozen at young age, rash on body matching inflicted injury). More than two thirds of the clinicians reacted emotionally to any use of the term *authentic,* feeling that determining what is authentic and what is not authentic is not the job of a therapist. The conclusion from this small study was that therapists believe their clients and often use symptomatology as evidence.

These and other data suggest that therapists believe in their clients' memories. They point to symptomatology as their evidence. They are impressed with the emotional pain that accompanies the expression of the memories. Dawes (1992) has argued that this "epidemic" of belief is based in large part on authority and social consensus (p. 214).

Are the Memories Accurate?

There are those with extreme positions who would like to deny the authenticity of all repressed memories and those who would accept them all as true. As Van Benschoten (1990) has pointed out, these extreme positions will exacerbate our problems: "Denial fosters overdetermination, and overdetermination invites denial" (p. 25).

If we assume, then, that some of the memories might be authentic and some might not be, we can then raise this question: If a memory is recovered that is not authentic, where would it come from? Ganaway (1989) proposed several hypotheses to explain SRA memories, and these same ideas are relevant to memories of a repressed past. If not authentic, the memories could be due to fantasy, illusion, or hallucination-mediated screen memories, internally derived as a defense mechanism. Further paraphrasing Ganaway, the SRA memories combine a mixture of borrowed ideas, characters, myths, and accounts from exogenous sources with idiosyncratic internal beliefs. Once activated, the manufactured memories are indistinguishable from factual memories. Inauthentic memories could also be externally derived as a result of unintentional implantation of suggestion by a therapist or other perceived authority figure with whom the client desires a special relationship, interest, or approval.

The Memories Are Authentic

There is no doubt that childhood sexual abuse is tragically common (Daro, 1988). Surveys reveal a large range in the estimated rates (10%–50%), but as Freyd (1991) has argued, even the most conservative of them are high enough to support the enormity of child abuse. A sizeable number of people who enter therapy were abused as children and have always remembered their abuse. Even when they have severe emotional problems, they can provide rich recollections of abuse, often with many unique, peripheral details (Rogers, 1992a). Occasionally the abuse is corroborated, sometimes with very cogent corroboration, such as pornographic photographs. If confirmed abuse is prevalent, many instances of repressed memory abuse cases also could be authentic. Unfortunately, in the repressed memory cases, particularly when memories do not return for 20 or 30 years, there is little in the way of documented corroboration. This, of course, does not mean that they are false.

Claims of corroborated repressed memories occasionally appear in the published literature. For example, Mack (1980) reported on a 1955 case involving a 27-year-old borderline man who, during therapy, recovered memories of witnessing his mother attempting to kill herself by hanging. The man's father later confirmed that the mother had attempted suicide several times and that the son had witnessed one attempt when he was 3 years old. The father's confirmation apparently led to a relief of symptoms in the son. It is hard to know what to make of examples such as these. Did the son really remember back to age 3, or did he hear discussions of his mother's suicide attempts later in life? The memories could be real, that is, genuine instances of repressed memories that accurately returned much later. If true, this would only prove that some memory reports are authentic but obviously not that all reports are authentic. Analogously, examples of repressed memories that were later retracted, later proved to be false, or later proved to be the result of suggestion would only prove that some memory reports are not authentic but obviously not that all such reports are illusory.

Some who question the authenticity of the memories of abuse do so in part because of the intensity and sincerity of the accused persons who deny the abuse. Many of the thousands of people who have been accused flatly deny the allegations, and the cry of "witch hunt" is often heard (Baker, 1992, p. 48; Gardner, 1991). *Witch hunt* is, of course, a term that has been loosely used by virtually anyone faced by a pack of accusers (Watson, 1992). Analogies have been drawn between the current allegations and the witch craze of the 16th and 17th centuries, when an estimated half million people were convicted of witchcraft and burned to death in Europe alone (Harris, 1974; Trott, 1991b). Although the denials during the witch craze are now seen as authentic in the light of hindsight, the current denials of those accused of sexual abuse are not proof that the allegations are false. Research with known rapists, pedophiles, and incest offenders has illustrated that they often exhibit a *cognitive distortion*—a tendency to justify, minimize, or rationalize their behavior (Gudjonsson, 1992). Because accused persons are motivated to verbally and even mentally deny an abusive past, simple denials cannot constitute cogent evidence that the victim's memories are not authentic.

The Memories *Are Not Authentic*

To say that memory might be false does not mean that the person is deliberately lying. Although lying is always possible, even psychotherapists who question the authenticity of reports have been impressed with the honesty and intensity of the terror, rage, guilt, depression, and overall behavioral dysfunction accompanying the awareness of abuse (Ganaway, 1989, p. 211).

There are at least two ways that false memories could come about. Honestly believed, but false, memories could come about, according to Ganaway (1989), because of internal or external sources. The internal drive to manufacture an abuse memory may come about as a way to provide a screen for perhaps more prosaic but, ironically, less tolerable, painful experiences of childhood. Creating a fantasy of abuse with its relatively clear-cut distinction between good and evil may provide the needed logical explanation for confusing experiences and feelings. The core material for the false memories can be borrowed from the accounts of others who are either known personally or encountered in literature, movies, and television.[5]

SOURCES OF DETAILS THAT COULD AFFECT MEMORY

There are at least two important sources that could potentially feed into the construction of false memories. These include popular writings and therapists' suggestions.

Popular Writings

All roads on the search for popular writings inevitably lead to one, *The Courage to Heal* (Bass & Davis, 1988), often referred to as the "bible" of the incest book industry. *The Courage*

to Heal advertises itself as a guide for women survivors of child sexual abuse. Although the book is undoubtedly a great comfort to the sexual abuse survivors who have been living with their private and painful memories, one cannot help but wonder about its effects on those who have no such memories. Readers who are wondering whether they might be victims of child sexual abuse are provided with a list of possible activities ranging from the relatively benign (e.g., being held in a way that made them uncomfortable) to the unequivocally abusive (e.g., being raped or otherwise penetrated). Readers are then told "If you are unable to remember any specific instances like the ones mentioned above but still have a feeling that something abusive happened to you, it probably did" (p. 21). On the next page, the reader is told

You may think you don't have memories, but often as you begin to talk about what you do remember, there emerges a constellation of feelings, reactions and recollections that add up to substantial information. To say, "I was abused," you don't need the kind of recall that would stand up in a court of law. Often the knowledge that you were abused starts with a tiny feeling, an intuition. ... Assume your feelings are valid. So far, no one we've talked to thought she might have been abused, and then later discovered that she hadn't been. The progression always goes the other way, from suspicion to confirmation. If you think you were abused and your life shows the symptoms, then you were. (p. 22)

What symptoms? The authors list low self-esteem, suicidal or self-destructive thoughts, depression, and sexual dysfunction, among others.[6]

Others have worried about the role played by *The Courage to Heal*. A recent survey of several hundred families accused by derepressed memories revealed that the book was implicated "in almost all cases" (Wakefield & Underwager, 1992, p. 486). Complaints about the book range from its repeated suggestion that abuse probably happened even if one has no memories of it and that demands for corroboration are not reasonable, to its overt encouragement of "revenge, anger, fantasies of murder or castration, and deathbed confrontations" (Wakefield & Underwager, 1992, p. 485). In all fairness, however, it should be mentioned that the book is long (495 pages), and sentences taken out of context may distort their intended meaning. Nonetheless, readers without any abuse memories of their own cannot escape the message that there is a strong likelihood that abuse occurred even in the absence of such memories.

The recent incest book industry has published not only stories of abuse but also suggestions to readers that they were likely abused even if there are no memories, that repressed memories of abuse undoubtedly underlie one's troubles, or that benefits derive from uncovering repressed memories and believing them.[7] One popular book about incest is the paperback by E. Sue Blume (1990), the book jacket of which itemizes one of the author's chief credentials as the "Creator of the Incest Survivors' Aftereffects Checklist."[8] Blume, a private practice therapist, tells readers that she has "found that most incest survivors have limited recall about their abuse" (p. 81). She goes on to say that "Indeed, so few incest survivors in my experience have identified themselves as abused in the beginning of therapy that I have concluded that perhaps half of all incest survivors do not remember that the abuse occurred" (p. 81).

Some of the volumes provide exercises to help readers lift the repression. Farmer (1989), for example, tells readers to try one particular exercise "whether or not you have any conscious recollection of the abuse you suffered" (p. 91). The reader is to sit down, relax, and mentally return to childhood. The next step is to choose a particular memory, whether fuzzy or clear, and "bring that memory to your full attention" (p. 91). Details about what to do with the memory are provided, along with an example from the life of "Danielle," who thought about how verbally abusive her father had been, and "Hazel," who remembered anger at her mother's treating her like a rag doll. This exercise allegedly helped to "lift the lid of repression" and unbury the "Hurting Child."

Do these examples lift the lid of repression? Perhaps. But another equally viable hypothesis is that the examples influence the creation of memories or, at the very least, direct the search through memory that the reader will ultimately take.[9]

Therapists' Suggestions

Blume's (1990) observation that so many individuals enter therapy without memories of abuse but acquire memories during therapy naturally makes one wonder about what might be happening in therapy. According to Ganaway (1989), honestly believed but false memories could come about in another way, through unintentional suggestion from therapists. Ganaway noted a growing trend toward the facile acceptance and expressed validation of uncorroborated trauma memories, perhaps in part due to sensitization from years of accusations that the memories are purely fantasy. Herman (1992, p. 180) made a similar point: Whereas an earlier generation of therapists might have been discounting or minimizing their patients' traumatic experiences, the recent rediscovery of psychological trauma has let to errors of the opposite kind. Some contemporary therapists have been known to tell patients, merely on the basis of a suggestive history or symptom profile, that they definitely had a traumatic experience. Even if there is no memory, but merely some vague symptoms, certain therapists will inform a patient after a single session that he or she was very likely the victim of a satanic cult. Once the "diagnosis" is made, the therapist urges the patient to pursue the recalcitrant memories. Although some therapists recommend against persistent, intrusive probing to uncover early traumatic memories (e.g., Bruhn, 1990), others enthusiastically engage in these therapeutic strategies. Evidence for this claim comes in a variety of forms: (a) therapist accounts of what is appropriate to do with clients, (b) client accounts of what happened during therapy, (c) sworn statements of clients and therapists during litigation, and (d) taped interviews of therapy sessions.

Therapist accounts. One therapist, who has treated more than 1,500 incest victims, openly discussed her method of approaching clients (Forward & Buck, 1988). "You know, in my experience, a lot of people who are struggling with many of the same problems you are, have often had some kind of really painful things happen to them as kids—maybe they were beaten or molested. And I wonder if anything like that ever happened to you?" (p. 161). Other clinicians claim to know of therapists who say "Your symptoms sound like you've been abused when you were a child. What can you tell me about that?" (Trott, 1991a, p. 18); or worse, "You sound to me like the sort of person who must have been sexually abused. Tell me what that bastard did to you" (Davis, 1991, p. 82).

At least one clinician advocated "It is crucial ... that clinicians ask about sexual abuse during every intake" (Frawley, 1990). The rationale for this prescription is that a clinician who asks conveys to the client that the client will be believed and that the clinician will join with the client in working through the memories and emotions linked with childhood sexual abuse. Asking about sexual abuse along with a list of other past life events makes sense given the high instance of actual abuse, but the concern is how the issue is raised and what therapists do when clients initially deny an abusive past.

Evidence exists that some therapists do not take no for an answer. One therapist (who otherwise seemed sensitive to problems of memory tampering) still recommended "When the client does not remember what happened to her, the therapist's encouragement to 'guess' or 'tell a story' will help the survivor regain access to the lost material" (Olio, 1989, p. 6). She went on to provide the example of a client who suspected sexual abuse but had no memories. The client had become extremely anxious at a social gathering in the presence of a three-year-old girl. She had no idea why she was upset except that she wanted the little girl to keep her dress down. When encouraged in therapy to tell a story about what was going to happen to the little girl, the client ultimately related with tears and trembling one of the first memories of her own abuse. She used the story to "bypass her cognitive inhibitions and express the content of the memory" (p. 6). Later she "integrated the awareness that she was indeed the little girl in the story" (p. 6). One cannot help but wonder about these mental fantasy exercises in light of known research showing that the simple act of imagination makes an event subjectively more likely (e.g., Sherman, Cialdini, Schwartzman, & Reynolds, 1985).

Even if the therapist does not encourage the client to guess or tell a story, stories sometimes get told in the form of client dreams. If discussions of incest go on during the day, and day residue gets into the dreams at night, it would not be surprising to see that dreams of incest might result. Poston and Lison (1990) described a woman with "repressed memories" of incest who reported a dream about watching a little girl ice skate on a frozen river. In her dream, the woman tried desperately to warn the child that monsters and snakes were making their way through the ice to devour her. Although frightened, the woman was powerless and could not warn the innocent child. A few days later, the client began remembering incest from her childhood. Knowing she had "a trusted relationship with a therapist and a survivor's group that would understand and accept her" (p. 197), the memories began to flow.

Examples of therapists interpreting dreams as signs of memory of abuse can be found throughout the literature. One clinician described with pride how she communicated to her male patient the basis for her suspicions that he had been abused: "On many occasions, I explained that these dreams had preserved experiences and impressions of an indelible nature" (M. Williams, 1987, p. 152).

Frederickson (1992), who has worked with many incest survivors, has also described in detail her methods of getting patients to remember. She recommended that the therapist guide the patient "to expand on or explore images that have broken through to the conscious mind, allowing related images of the abuse to surface. The process lets the survivor complete the picture of what happened, using a current image or flash as a jumping-off point" (p. 97). She also suggested that the therapist help the patient expand on the images and sensations evoked by dreams "to shed light on or recover our repressed memories" (p. 98). She extolled the virtues of hypnosis to "retrieve buried memories" (p. 98) and recommended that patients "jot down suspected memories of abuse you would like to explore. Include your own felt sense of how you think you were abused" (p. 102).

Even if clinicians are not the first to bring up sexual abuse, they will often reinforce what begins as a mere suspicion. One client developed the idea that she might have been sexually abused, tried hypnosis to help her recover memories, and obsessed for years. Only after her therapist stated that she believed sexual assault was "indeed possible" and cited nightmares, phobia of men, and other symptoms as evidence did the client come up with some specific memories (Schuker, 1979, p. 569).

Before leaving the examples of therapist accounts of what goes on in therapy, it is important to add a word of caution. Sherrill Mulhern, a psychiatric anthropologist, has documented the alarming discrepancies that often exist between therapists' accounts of what they have done in therapy and what is revealed in video-or audiotapes of those same sessions (Mulhern, 1991).

If memories are uncovered—whether after repeated probing, after telling stories, after dreams, or seemingly spontaneously—or even if the memories remain buried, therapists often send their clients to support groups. In one study of clients who had, in the course of therapy, verbalized their victimization through ritualistic abuse, the majority reported that they had participated in these types of groups (Shaffer & Cozolino, 1992). One group, Survivors of Incest Anonymous (SIA), publishes extensive reading materials intended to aid the recovery of incest survivors. (SIA merged with Sexual Abuse Anonymous in 1987.) The criteria for admission make it clear that entry is fine for those with no memories of sexual abuse: "Do you have blocks of your childhood you can't remember? Do you have a sense that 'something happened'?" (SIA, 1985). These and other questions (e.g., Do you have problems with self-confidence and self esteem? Do you feel easily intimidated by authority figures?) are among the set of 20 questions that help a potential survivor decide whether SIA can be of assistance. SIA emphasizes that it is OK not to remember at first, because "Many survivors have 'repressed' actual abuse memories in order to survive." However, the goal is to remember: "Participating in SIA helps us to remember what happened to us so we can stop being controlled by incest" (SIA, 1990, p. 1).

Although support groups are undoubtedly invaluable for genuine survivors of sexual abuse, as they are for other survivors of extreme situations, such as combat and political persecution (Herman, 1992, p. 215), concerns about the incest survivor groups have been expressed. Do these groups foster the development of constructed memories? An investigative journalist attending a four-day workshop watched the construction of memory at work (Nathan, 1992). With members recounting graphic details of SRA abuse, how long will they listen to the person who can only say "I think I was abused, but I don't have any memories." Others have worried in the literature that such groups may induce *proto-extension*—that is, they actually encourage a troubled person to remember details from other survivor stories as having happened to them as well (Ellis, 1992).

Client accounts. Another source for suggestions in therapy can be found in client accounts of what happened to them. Recently, clients have been reporting that a therapist has suggested that childhood abuse was the cause of their current distress. However, these clients have no memories of such abuse. One woman from Oregon entered therapy to deal with depression and anxiety, and within a few months her therapist suggested that the cause could be childhood sexual abuse. She wrote asking for help in remembering:

Since that time, he has become more and more certain of his diagnosis ... I have no direct memories of this abuse. ... The question I can't get past is how something so terrible could have happened to me without me remembering anything. For the past two years I have done little else but try to remember. I've tried self-hypnosis and light trance work with my therapist. And I even travelled to childhood homes ... in an attempt to trigger memories.

One client revealed the suggestive nature of his therapist's questioning on ABC's *Primetime Live* (ABC News, 1992). Attorney Greg Zimmerman went to a psychotherapist in Boulder, Colorado, to deal with his father's suicide. He told ABC, "I would try to talk to her about the things that were very painful in my life and she kept saying that there was something else" (p. 1) . Zimmerman grew more and more depressed as the mystery of that "something else" would not unravel, and then, during a therapy session, his therapist stunned him with her diagnosis: "I don't know how to tell you this, but you display the same kinds of characteristics as some of my patients who are victims of Satanic ritualistic abuse" (p. 1). Zimmerman had said nothing whatsoever to her to provoke this diagnosis, apparently her standard.

It is easy to find published accounts that describe the emergence of memories in therapy and the techniques that therapists have used to uncover those memories (e.g., Bass & Thornton, 1991). One account, written under the pseudonym of Jill Morgan, told of a series of positively horrifying memories of abuse by her father. He raped her when she was 4 years old, again at age 9, once again at age 13, for seven straight days and nights at age 15, and for the final time at age 18. For the next several years, all misery was withheld from conscious memory, and then, at age 29, she was helped to remember in therapy: "Through hypnosis and age regression, a skilled therapist gave me back my memory" (p. 111). The involvement of hypnosis and age regression prompts the natural inquiry into whether these techniques produce authentic memories. Unfortunately, the evidence is discouraging: There is an extensive literature seriously questioning the reliability of hypnotically enhanced memory in general (Smith, 1983), and hypnotic age regression in particular (Nash, 1987). Hypnotic attempts to improve memory increase the confidence in what is recalled more than the accuracy

(Bowers, 1992). Even more worrisome is the impossibility of reversing the process; the hypnotically induced memory becomes the person's reality (Orne, 1979). With hypnotic regression, men and women have been known to recall being abducted by aliens aboard exotic spacecraft and other forgotten events (Gordon, 1991).

A more detailed client account is that of Betsy Petersen (1991), as described in an autobiographical account, *Dancing With Daddy.* Petersen, a Harvard graduate and accomplished writer, revealed in her first book that she repressed memory of sexual abuse by her father until she was 45 years old. She now remembers sexual abuse from the time she was 3½ until she was 18. Betsy entered therapy (with "Kris") for problems relating to her children, and almost a year after starting therapy she started worrying, "I'm afraid my father did something to me." She tried hard to recall, putting "together a scenario of what might have happened" (p. 65). When she told her therapist about this, she said "I don't know if I made it up or if it's real." Kris replied, "It feels like a story to you, because when something like that happens, everybody acts like it didn't." Betsy: "You mean it might really have happened!" Kris told her there was a good chance it had happened. Kris told her, in Betsy's words, "It was consistent with what I remembered about my father and my relationship with him, and with the dreams I had been having, and with the difficulties I had being close to my children, and also, she said, with the feelings I had during and after sex with my husband" (p. 65). Betsy worked hard to retrieve incest memories: "I had no memory of what my father had done to me, so I tried to reconstruct it. I put all my skill—as a reporter, novelist, scholar—to work making that reconstruction as accurate and vivid as possible. I used the memories I had to get to the memories I didn't have" (p. 66).[10] If accurate, this account tells us something about one therapist's approach. The therapist convinces the patient with no memories that abuse is likely, and the patient obligingly uses reconstructive strategies to generate memories that would support that conviction. These techniques can be found in numerous autobiographical accounts (see also Smith & Pazder, 1980).

In addition to the first-person accounts, more formal studies of incest survivors provide clues to what might be happening in therapy. One study (Shaffer & Cozolino, 1992) of 20 adults who uncovered ritualistic abuse memories stemming from childhood revealed that the majority sought psychotherapy because of symptoms (e.g., depression and anxiety). The primary focus of their therapy was "the uncovering of memories" (p. 189). The majority participated in 12-step programs (e.g., Incest Survivors Anonymous) as "necessary adjuncts to their psychotherapy" (p. 190). These groups provided substitute families for the clients who had severed ties with their families of origin. Other similar studies of ritualistic abuse rememberers have revealed that most of the victims have no memory of the abuse before therapy (e.g., Driscoll & Wright, 1991) but that techniques such as hypnosis (Driscoll & Wright, 1991) or dreams and artwork (e.g., Young, Sachs, Braun, & Watkins, 1991) were used by therapists to unlock those recalcitrant memories.

Litigation accounts. Information gathered during litigation is another source of knowledge about the emergence of memories in therapy. Take the case of Patti Barton against her father, John Peters, a successful businessman.[11] Depositions taken in the case of *Barton v. Peters* (1990) reveal that Patti Barton began therapy with a Dr. CD, a doctor of divinity, in July 1986. Dr. CD's notes indicate that, during the 32nd session of therapy, Patti expressed "fear her father has sexually tampered with her" (Deposition of CD, April 21, 1991, *Barton V Peters,* 1990, p. 39). This was the first time that anything like that had come up in any of the sessions. Shortly thereafter, Patti related a dream that a man was after her.[12] Dr. CD apparently then used the technique of visualization wherein Patti would try to visualize her past. He got her to remember eye surgery at the age of 7 months. As for the abuse, one of the earliest acts of abuse he managed to dredge up with this method occurred when Patti was 15 months old. "I visualized that my father stuck his tongue in my mouth."

After he stuck his tongue in my mouth—Well, it seemed to last for hours and hours even though I know it didn't. But it was awful to me and an event that seemed to last for hours. I started crying, and I crawled over to the wall. And I started banging my head on the wall. And my mother came into the room, and she picked me up. And I tried to tell her in baby talk what had happened. I said "Ma, ma, ma, ma," and I said, "Da Da, Da, Da" and I said, "Me-e-e-." And that's all that I can remember. (Deposition of PB, May 1991, Barton v. Peters, 1990, p. 193)

Later, Patti would remember that her father touched her in her crotch and put his penis in her mouth when she was three years old, and that she stroked his penis over and over at age four. Rape would come later. Patti's father eventually agreed to give his daughter the deed to a piece of land he owned, but he continued to deny the charges. Her brother, a Baptist minister in Alaska, claimed that Satan's wicked spirits planted untruths in Patti's head (Laker, 1992). Did it take 30-some sessions for the therapist to uncover actual memories of abuse, or 30-some sessions for false memories of abuse to begin to be visualized and constructed?

Taped interviews. Often, confidentiality considerations prevent access to interactions between therapists and clients. However, when cases get into litigation, special interviewing is frequently done, and occasionally it is recorded. Recordings were done in a case implicating a man named Paul Ingram from Olympia, Washington (Watters, 1991). Ingram was arrested for child abuse in 1988, amid expressions of shock from his community. At the time he was chair of the county Republican committee and was chief civil deputy in the sheriff's office. He had worked in law enforcement for more than a decade.

The Ingram case began at a time when waves of rumor and media hype over satanic ritualistic abuse were rampant. At first Ingram denied everything, and detectives told him he was in denial. With the help of a psychologist who exerted enormous pressure over endless hours of interrogation, Ingram's memories of abusing his daughter began to appear. Then the psychologist, with the help of a detective, "interviewed" Ingram's son. In that interview, the son reported on his dreams, and the therapist and detective convinced him that the dreams were real.[13]

In another case, a father (Mr. K) hired a private investigator after his 26-year-old daughter reported a recently uncovered repressed memory and accused him of incest. The investigator, acting under cover, went to see the daughter's therapist complaining that she had nightmares and had trouble sleeping. On the third visit, the therapist told undercover agent that she was an incest survivor. According to the investigator's report (Monesi, 1992), the therapist said this to her pseudopatient: "She then told me that she was certain I was experiencing body memory from a trauma, earlier in life, that I could not remember. I could not remember because my brain had blocked the memory

that was too painful to deal with." When the patient said she didn't remember any trauma, the therapist told her "that is the case and many people at far later times in their lives go through this when the memory starts to surface." The therapist told her that many people go through this experience, such as "Viet Nam Vets, Earthquake Survivors and Incest Survivors." When the patient said that she had never been in Vietnam or in an earthquake, the therapist nodded her head and said "Yes, I know." The therapist then said she should read *Courage to Heal*, a book she recommends to all abuse survivors. After that there was the *Courage to Heal Workbook,* which tells survivors how to cope with the fears and memories. She pulled *Secret Survivors* by E. S. Blume (1990) from the shelf, opened the cover, and read the list of symptoms of incest survivors. With two thirds of the symptoms, she would look at the pseudopatient and shake her head yes as if this was confirmation of her diagnosis. She recommended incest survivor groups. In the fourth session, the diagnosis of probable incest victim was confirmed on the basis of the "classic symptoms" of body memory and sleep disorders. When the patient insisted that she had no memory of such events, the therapist assured her this was often the case.

Why Would Therapists Suggest Things to Their Patients?

The core of treatment, it is widely believed, is to help clients reclaim their "traumatic past" (Rieker & Carmen, 1986, p. 369). Therapists routinely dig deliberately into the ugly underbelly of mental life. They dig for memories purposefully because they believe that in order to get well, to become survivors rather than victims, their clients must overcome the protective denial that was used to tolerate the abuse during childhood (Sgroi, 1989, p. 112). Memory blocks can be protective in many ways, but they come at a cost; they cut off the survivors from a significant part of their past histories and leave them without good explanations for their negative self-image, low self-esteem, and other mental problems. These memories must be brought into consciousness, not as an end in itself but only insofar as it helps the survivors acknowledge reality and overcome denial processes that are now dysfunctional (p. 115).

Another reason therapists may be unwittingly suggesting ideas to their clients is that they have fallen prey to a bias that affects all of us, known as the "confirmatory bias" (Baron, Beattie, & Hershey, 1988). People in general, therapists included, have a tendency to search for evidence that confirms their hunches rather than search for evidence that disconfirms. It is not easy to discard long-held or cherished beliefs, in part because we are eager to verify those beliefs and are not inclined to seek evidence that might disprove them.

The notion that the beliefs that individuals hold can create their own social reality is the essence of the self-fulfilling prophecy (Snyder, 1984). How does "reality" get constructed? One way this can happen is through interview strategies. Interviewers are known to choose questions that inquire about behaviors and experiences thought to be characteristic, rather than those thought to be uncharacteristic, of some particular classification. If therapists ask questions that tend to elicit behaviors and experiences thought to be characteristic of someone who had been a victim of childhood trauma, might they too be creating this social reality?

Whatever the good intentions of therapists, the documented examples of rampant suggestion should force us to at least ponder whether some therapists might be suggesting illusory memories to their clients rather than unlocking authentic distant memories. Or, paraphrasing Gardner (1992), what is considered to be present in the client's unconscious mind might actually be present solely in the therapist's conscious mind (p. 689). Ganaway (1989) worried that, once seeded by the therapist, false memories could develop that replace previously unsatisfactory internal explanations for intolerable but more prosaic childhood trauma.

Creation of False Memories

The hypothesis that false memories could be created invites an inquiry into the important question of what is known about false memories. Since the mid-1970s at least, investigations have been done into the creation of false memories through exposure to misinformation. Now, nearly two decades later, there are hundreds of studies to support a high degree of memory distortion. People have recalled nonexistent broken glass and tape recorders, a cleanshaven man as having a mustache, straight hair as curly, and even something as large and conspicuous as a barn in a bucolic scene that contained no buildings at all (Loftus & Ketcham, 1991). This growing body of research shows that new, postevent information often becomes incorporated into memory, supplementing and altering a person's recollection. The new information invades us, like a Trojan horse, precisely because we do not detect its influence. Understanding how we can become tricked by revised data about our past is central to understanding the hypothesis that suggestions from popular writings and therapy sessions can affect autobiographical recall.

One frequently heard comment about the research on memory distortion is that all changes induced by misinformation are about trivial details (Darnton, 1991; Franklin & Wright, 1991). There is no evidence, the critics allege, that one can tinker with memories of real traumatic events or that one can inject into the human mind whole events that never happened.

CAN REAL TRAUMATIC MEMORIES BE CHANGED?

There are some who argue that traumatic events leave some sort of indelible fixation in the mind (e.g., "traumatic events create lasting visual images ... burned-in visual impressions," Terr, 1988, p. 103; "memory imprints are indelible, they do not erase—a therapy that tries to alter them will be uneconomical," Kantor, 1980, p. 163). These assertions fail to recognize known examples and evidence that memory is malleable even for life's most traumatic experiences. If Eileen Franklin's memory of witnessing her father murder her eight-year-old best friend is a real memory, then it too is a memory replete with changes over different tellings. However, there are clearer examples—anecdotal reports in which definite evidence exists that the traumatic event itself was actually experienced and yet the memory radically changed.

In the category of documented anecdotes there is the example of one of the worst public and personal tragedies in the history of baseball (Anderson, 1990; described in Loftus & Kaufman, 1992). Baseball aficionados may recall that Jack Hamilton, then a pitcher with the California Angels, crushed the outfielder, Tony Conigliaro, in the face with a first-pitch fastball. Although Hamilton thought he remembered this horrible event perfectly, he misremembered it as occurring during a day game, when it was actually at night, and misremembered it in other critical ways. Another example will be appreciated by history buffs, particularly those with an interest in the second world war. American Brigadier General Elliot Thorpe recalled the day after the bombing of Pearl Harbor one way in a memoir and completely differently in an oral history taken on his retirement. Both accounts, in fact, were riddled with errors (Weintraub, 1991).

Evidence of a less anecdotal, more experimental nature supports the imperfections of personally experienced traumatic memories. For example, one study examined people's recollections of how they heard the news of the 1986 explosion of the space shuttle *Challenger* (Harsch & Neisser, 1989; Neisser & Harsch, 1992). Subjects were questioned on the morning after the explosion and again nearly three years later. Most described their memories as vivid, but none of them were entirely correct, and more than one third were wildly inaccurate. One subject, for example, was on the telephone having a business discussion when her best friend interrupted the call with the news. Later she would remember that she heard the news in class and at first thought it was a joke, and that she later walked into a TV lounge and saw the news, and then reacted to the disaster.

Another study (Abhold, 1992) demonstrated the malleability of memory for a serious life-and-death situation. The subjects had attended an important high school football game at which a player on the field went into cardiac arrest. Paramedics tried to resuscitate the player and apparently failed. The audience reactions ranged from complete silence, to sobbing, to screaming. (Ultimately, fortunately, the player was revived at the hospital.) Six years later, many of these people were interviewed. Errors of recollection were common. Moreover, when exposed to misleading information about this life-and-death event, many individuals absorbed the misinformation into their recollections. For example, more than one fourth of the subjects were persuaded that they had seen blood on the player's jersey after receiving a false suggestion to this effect.

These anecdotes and experimental examples suggest that even details of genuinely experienced traumatic events are, as Christianson (1992) put it, "by no means, completely accurate" (p. 207).

Can One Inject a Complete Memory for Something That Never Happened?

It is one thing to discover that memory for an actual traumatic event is changed over time but quite another to show that one can inject a whole event into someone's mind for something that never happened. There are numerous anecdotes and experimental studies that show it is indeed possible to lead people to construct entire events.

Piaget's memory. Whole memories can be implanted into a person's real-life autobiography, as is best shown by Piaget's classic childhood memory of an attempted kidnapping (Piaget, 1962; described in Loftus & Ketcham, 1991, p. 19). The false memories were with him for at least a decade. The memory was of an attempted kidnapping that occurred when he was an infant. He found out it was false when his nanny confessed years later that she had made up the entire story and felt guilty about keeping the watch she had received as a reward. In explaining this false memory, Piaget assumed, "I, therefore, must have heard, as a child, the account of this story, which my parents believed, and projected into the past in the form of a visual memory."

Loud noises at night. Although widely disseminated and impressive at first glance, Piaget's false memory is still but a single anecdote and subject to other interpretations. Was this really a memory, or an interesting story? Could it be that the assault actually happened and the nurse, for some inexplicable reason, lied later? For these reasons it would be nice to find stronger evidence that a false memory for a complete event was genuinely implanted.

An apparently genuine 19th-century memory implantation was reported by Laurence and Perry (1983): Bernheim, during hypnosis, suggested to a female subject that she had awakened four times during the previous night to go to the toilet and had fallen on her nose on the fourth occasion. After hypnosis, the woman insisted that the suggested events had actually occurred, despite the hypnotist's insistence that she had dreamed them. Impressed by Bernheim's success, and by explorations by Orne (1979), Laurence and Perry asked 27 highly hypnotizable individuals during hypnosis to choose a night from the previous week and to describe their activities during the half hour before going to sleep. The subjects were then instructed to relive that night, and a suggestion was implanted that they had heard some loud noises and had awakened. Almost one half (13) of the 27 subjects accepted the suggestion and stated *after* hypnosis that the suggested event had actually taken place. Of the 13, 6 were unequivocal in their certainty. The remainder came to the conclusion on basis of reconstruction. Even when told that the hypnotist had actually suggested the noises, these subjects still maintained that the noises had occurred. One said "I'm pretty certain I heard them. As a matter of fact, I'm pretty damned certain. I'm positive I heard these noises" (Laurence & Perry, 1983, p. 524).

The paradigm of inducing pseudomemories of being awakened by loud noises has now been used extensively by other researchers who readily replicate the basic findings. Moreover, the pseudomemories are not limited to hypnotic conditions. Simply inducing subjects to imagine and describe the loud noises resulted in later "memories" for noises that had never occurred (Weekes, Lynn, Green, & Brentar, 1992).

Other false memories. Other evidence shows that people can be tricked into believing that they experienced an event even in the absence of specific hypnotic suggestions. For example, numerous studies have shown that people misremember that they voted in a particular election when they actually had not (Abelson, Loftus, & Greenwald, 1992). One interpretation of these findings is that people fill in the gaps in their memory with socially desirable constructions, thus creating for themselves a false memory of voting.

In other studies, people have been led to believe that they witnessed assaultive behavior when in fact they did not (e.g., Haugaard, Reppucci, Laurd, & Nauful, 1991). In this study, children aged four to seven years were led to believe that they saw a man hit a girl, when he had not, after hearing the girl lie about the assault. Not only did they misrecall the nonexistent hitting, but they added their own details: Of 41 false claims, 39 children said it happened near a pond, I said it was at the girl's house, and I could not specify exactly where the girl was when the man hit her.

Violent false memories. People can hold completely false memories for something far more traumatic than awakening at night, voting in a particular election, or a simulation involving a man and a girl. Pynoos and Nader (1989) studied children's recollections of a sniper attack at an elementary school playground. Some of the children who were interviewed were not at the school during the shooting, including some who were already on the way home or were on vacation. Yet, even the non-witnesses had memories:

One girl initially said that she was at the school gate nearest the sniper when the shooting began. In truth she was not only out of the line of fire, she was half a block away. A boy who had been away on vacation said that he had been on his way to the school, had seen someone lying on the ground, had heard the shots, and then turned back. In actuality, a police barricade prevented anyone from approaching the block around the school. (p. 238)

The memories apparently were created by exposure to the stories of those who truly experienced the trauma.

Memories of being lost. A question arises as to whether one could experimentally implant memories for nonexistent events that, if they had occurred, would have been traumatic. Given the need to protect human subjects, devising a means of accomplishing this was not an easy task. Loftus and Coan (in press), however, developed a paradigm for instilling a specific childhood memory for being lost on a particular occasion at the age of five. They chose getting lost because it is clearly a great fear of both parents and children. Their initial observations show how subjects can be readily induced to believe this kind of false memory. The technique involved a subject and a trusted family member who played a variation of "Remember the time that... .?" To appreciate the methodology, consider the implanted memory of 14-year-old Chris. Chris was convinced by his older brother, Jim, that he had been lost in a shopping mall when he was 5 years old. Jim told Chris this story as if it were the truth: "It was 1981 or 1982. I remember that Chris was 5. We had gone shopping at the University City shopping mall in Spokane. After some panic, we found Chris being led down the mall by a tall, oldish man (I think he was wearing a flannel shirt). Chris was crying and holding the man's hand. The man explained that he had found Chris walking around crying his eyes out just a few moments before and was trying to help him find his parents."

Just two days later, Chris recalled his feelings about being lost: "That day I was so scared that I would never see my family again. I knew that I was in trouble." On the third day, he recalled a conversation with his mother: "I remember mom telling me never to do that again." On the fourth day: "I also remember that old man's flannel shirt." On the fifth day, he started remembering the mall itself: "I sort of remember the stores." In his last recollection, he could even remember a conversation with the man who found him: "I remember the man asking me if I was lost."

It would be natural to wonder whether perhaps Chris had really gotten lost that day. Maybe it happened, but his brother forgot. But Chris's mother was subjected to the same procedure and was never able to remember the false event. After five days of trying, she said "I feel very badly about it, but I just cannot remember anything like this ever happening."

A couple of weeks later, Chris described his false memory and he greatly expanded on it.

I was with you guys for a second and I think I went over to look at the toy store, the Kay-bee toy and uh, we got lost and I was looking around and I thought, "Uh-oh. I'm in trouble now." You know. And then I … I thought I was never going to see my family again. I was really scared you know. And then this old man, I think he was wearing a blue flannel, came up to me … he was kind of old. He was kind of bald on top … he had like a ring of gray hair … and he had glasses.

Thus, in two short weeks, Chris now could even remember the balding head and the glasses worn by the man who rescued him. He characterized his memory as reasonably clear and vivid.

Finally, Chris was debriefed. He was told that one of the memories presented to him earlier had been false. When asked to guess, he guessed one of the genuine memories. When told that it was the getting-lost memory, he said, "Really? I thought I remembered being lost… and looking around for you guys. I do remember that. And then crying. And mom coming up and saying 'Where were you. Don't you … Don't you ever do that again.'"

A false memory of abuse. The lost-in-a-shopping-mall example shows that memory of an entire mildly traumatic event can be created. It is still natural to wonder whether

one could go even further and implant a memory of abuse. Ethically, of course, it would not be possible, but anecdotally, as it happens, it was done. It is one of the most dramatic cases of false memory of abuse ever to be documented—the case of Paul Ingram from Olympia, Washington (Ofshe, 1992; Watters, 1991). As described above, Ingram, was arrested for child abuse in 1988 at the time he was chair of the county Republican committee. At first Ingram denied everything, and detectives told him he was in denial. After five months of interrogation, suggestions from a psychologist, and continuing pressure from detectives and advisors, Ingram began to confess to rapes, assaults, child sexual abuse, and participation in a Satan-worshiping cult alleged to have murdered 25 babies (Ofshe, 1992). To elicit specific memories, the psychologist or detectives would suggest some act of abuse (e.g., that on one occasion, Ingram and several other men raped his daughter). Ingram would at first not remember these fragments, but after a concerted effort on his part, he would later come up with a detailed memory.

Richard Ofshe, a social psychologist hired by the prosecution to interview Ingram and his family members, decided to test Ingram's credibility. Ofshe had made up a completely fabricated scenario. He told Ingram that two of his children (a daughter and a son) had reported that Ingram had forced them to have sex in front of him. As with the earlier suggestions, Ingram at first could not remember this. But Ofshe urged Ingram to try to think about the scene and try to see it happening, just as the interrogators had done to him earlier. Ingram began to get some visual images. Ingram then followed Ofshe's instructions to "pray on" the scene and try to remember more over the next few hours. Several hours later, Ingram had developed detailed memories and wrote a three-page statement confessing in graphic detail to the scene that Ofshe had invented (Ofshe, 1992; Watters, 1991). Ofshe (1989, 1992) noted that this was not the first time that a vulnerable individual had been made to believe that he had committed a crime for which he originally had no memory and which evidence proved he could not have committed. What is crucial about the Ingram case is that some of the same methods that are used in repressed memory cases were used with Ingram. These include the use of protracted imagining of events and authority figures establishing the authenticity of these events.

These examples provide further insights into the malleable nature of memory. They suggest that memories for personally experience traumatic events can be altered by new experiences. Moreover, they reveal that entire events that never happened can be injected into memory. The false memories range from the relatively trivial (e.g., remembering voting) to the bizarre (e.g., remembering forcing one's daughter and son to have sex). These false memories, with more or less detail, of course do not prove that repressed memories of abuse that return are false. They do demonstrate a mechanism by which false memories can be created by a small suggestion from a trusted family member, by hearing someone lie, by suggestion from a psychologist, or by incorporation of the experiences of others into one's own autobiography. Of course, the fact that false memories can be planted tells nothing about whether a given memory of child sexual abuse is false or not; nor does it tell how one might distinguish the real cases from the false ones. These findings on the malleability of memory do, however, raise questions about the wisdom of certain recommendations being promoted in self-help workbooks, in handbooks for therapists, and by some therapists themselves. The false memories created in the examples above were accomplished with techniques that are not all that different from what some therapists regularly do—suggesting that the client was probably abused because of some vague symptoms, labeling a client's ambiguous recollections as evidence of abuse, and encouraging mental exercises that involve fantasy merging with reality.

FINAL REMARKS

The 1990s brought a blossoming of reports of awakenings of previously repressed memories of childhood abuse. One reason for the increase may be the widespread statistics on sex abuse percentages that are published almost daily: "By 1980... the government tallied almost 43,000 cases of child sex abuse annually" (Nathan, 1991, p. 154); "One in five women are 'incest victims,'" (p. 155); "6.8 million women nationwide would say they had been raped once, 4.7 million more than once" (Johnston, 1992, p. A9); "In 1972, 610,000 (child abuse cases) were reported nationally, and by 1985 the number had exceeded 1.7 million" (Baker, 1992, p. 37). "If it happens so often, did it happen to

me?" is a question many women and some men are asking themselves now more than ever before. The appearance of abuse statistics is one battle in the war waged against an earlier tendency on the part of society to disbelieve the abuse reports of women and children—a tendency that we should all deplore. The repressed memory cases are another outlet for women's rage over sexual violence. Although women's anger is certainly justified in many cases, and may be justified in some repressed memory cases too, it is time to stop and ask whether the net of rage has been cast too widely, creating a new collective nightmare.

Repressed memories of abuse often return in therapy, sometimes after suggestive probing. Today, popular writings have been so fully absorbed by the culture that these too can serve as a source of suggestion that can greatly influence what happens in therapy and outside of it (Guze, 1992). The result is memories that are often detailed and confidently held. Despite lack of corroboration, some of these recollections could be authentic. Others might not be.

Several implications of these observations follow. First, we need a renewed effort at research on the problem of repressed memories. This should encompass, in part, a reexamination of some of the widely cherished beliefs of psychotherapists. Is it true that repression of extremely traumatic experiences is common? Do these experiences invade us despite the fact that "all the good juice of consciousness has drained out" (Dennett, 1991, p. 325). It is common to see analogies drawn between Vietnam War veterans and the incest survivors (e.g., Herman, 1992; Rieker & Carmen, 1986). Do they share in common the use of "massive repression" (Wolf & Alpert, 1991, p. 314) as a mechanism for coping? If so, how do we explain findings obtained with children who witness parental murder and other atrocities? In one study (Malmquist, 1986), not a single child aged 5 to 10 years who had witnessed the murder of a parent repressed the memory. Rather, they were continually flooded with pangs of emotion about the murder and preoccupation with it.

Is it true that repressed material, like radioactive waste, "lies there in leaky canisters, never losing potency, eternally dangerous" (Hornstein, 1992, p. 260) and constantly threatens to erupt into consciousness? Psychotherapists have assumed for years that repressed memories are powerful influences because they are not accessible to consciousness (Bowers, 1992). Is there evidence for this assumption?

Is it necessarily true that all people who display symptoms of severe mental distress have had some early childhood trauma (probably abuse) that is responsible for the distress? With cutting-edge research now showing that mental distress involves neuronal and hormonal systems of a much wider scope than previously realized (Chrousos & Gold, 1992; Gershon & Rieder, 1992), should not other potential causes be at least considered?

Questions must also be examined about the well-intentioned treatment strategies of some clinicians. Is it possible that the therapist's interpretation is the cause of the patient's disorder rather than the effect of the disorder, to paraphrase Guze (1992, p. 78)? Is it necessarily true that people who cannot remember an abusive childhood are repressing the memory? Is it necessarily true that people who dream about or visualize abuse are actually getting in touch with true memories? Good scientific research needs to be done to support these assumptions, or they should be challenged. Challenging these core assumptions will not be an easy thing to do, anymore than it was for psychologists of the 1930s to challenge the radical subjectivity of psychoanalysis (Hornstein, 1992), or for psychologists of the 1980s to challenge the reliability of the clinical judgments made by psychologists and psychiatrists (Faust & Ziskin, 1988; Fowler & Matarazzo, 1988).[14] Nonetheless, when we move from the privacy of the therapy session, in which the client's reality may be the only reality that is important, into the courtroom, in which there can be but a single reality, then we as citizens in a democratic society are entitled to more solid evidence.

Until we have better empirical answers, therapists might consider whether it is wise to "suggest" that childhood trauma happened, to probe relentlessly for recalcitrant memories, and then to uncritically accept them as fact. Uncritical acceptance of uncorroborated trauma memories by therapists, social agencies, and law enforcement personal has been used to promote public accusations by alleged abuse survivors. If the memories are fabricated, this will of course lead to irreparable damage to the reputations of potentially innocent people, according to Ganaway (1989), who discussed the problem in the context of SRA memories.

Uncritical acceptance of uncorroborated trauma memories poses other potentially dangerous problems for society. According to Ganaway (1991), reinforcing the validity of unverifiable memories in the therapeutic setting may lead to diversionary paths in the patient's therapy away from actual childhood trauma. This could lead to interminable therapy and a total draining of the patient's financial resources as the therapist and patient collaborate in a mutual deception to pursue a bottomless pit of memories. Worse, the patients initial wonderings supported by therapist affirmations could then become fixed beliefs, precipitating suicidal thoughts and behaviors based on the new belief system, because the patient would no longer challenge the veracity of the new memories. Like Betsy Ross sewing the first American flag, the abuse becomes a myth that was never true but always will be (E. Frishholz, personal communication, May 1992). Patients who are reinforced into a new belief system could develop newer, larger problems. If actual childhood sexual abuse is associated with numerous negative long-term effects (e.g., severe sexual dysfunction; Ambrosoe-Bienkowski, Stahly, & Wideman, 1991), what might be the consequence of implanted childhood sexual abuse? If the memories are ultimately shown to be false, therapists may then become the targets of future ethics violations and lawsuits. They will be charged with a grave form of mind abuse—charges that have already been initiated in several states.

What should therapists do instead? As a first step, it is worth recognizing that we do not yet have the tools for reliably distinguishing the signal of true repressed memories from the noise of false ones. Until we gain these tools, it seems prudent to consider some combination of Herman's (1992) advice about probing for traumatic memories and Ganaway's (1991) advice about SRA memories. Zealous conviction is a dangerous substitute for an open mind. Psychotherapists, counselors, social service agencies, and law enforcement personnel would be wise to be careful how they probe for horrors on the other side of some presumed amnesic barrier. They need to be circumspect regarding uncorroborated repressed memories that return. Techniques that are less potentially dangerous would involve clarification, compassion, and gentle confrontation along with a demonstration of empathy for the painful struggles these patients must endure as they come to terms with their personal truths.

There is one last tragic risk of suggestive probing and uncritical acceptance of all allegations made by clients, no matter how dubious. These activities are bound to lead to an increased likelihood that society in general will disbelieve the genuine cases of childhood sexual abuse that truly deserve our sustained attention.

NOTES

1. Alaska, California, Colorado, Connecticut, Florida, Idaho, Illinois, Iowa, Maine, Minnesota, Missouri, Montana, Nevada, New Hampshire (revising an earlier law), Oregon, South Dakota, Vermont, and Virginia (see, for example, Napier, 1990).

2. In *Stubbings v. Webb and Another*, 1991, in which a British plaintiff claimed she was raped by her adoptive father and brother while she was a child. She sued 12 years after entering adulthood. The court permitted her suit, even though she knew she had been raped, arguing that she might not have associated the mental impairment that she was experiencing with the past rapes until she gained that knowledge as an adult.

3. One curiosity about this report is that the chief investigator published a landmark book on incest six years before this study (Herman, 1981). In the earlier book, the word *repression* did not even appear in the index. The 40, incest victims interviewed in depth appeared to have persisting, intrusive memories.

4. Many cognitive psychologists have argued that implicit theories about any topic (e.g., giftedness) guide a given society's thinking on that topic (e.g., Sternberg, 1992). More generally, intuitive theories are considered constructing working models of the world that people use in the service of understanding their world (Medin & Ross, 1992).

5. For those who think it is unlikely that one would ever borrow episodes from movies and popular literature and misremember them as actual events, one only has to examine Lou Cannon's (1991) biography of former President Reagan. A curious journalist who tried to verify Reagan's most famous mismemory of heroism found two that were suspiciously similar—one in the movie *A Wing and a Prayer*, and the other in a *Reader's Digest* story.

6. Since the publication of *Courage to Heal*, a number of cases have emerged in which women were led to believe they were abused, and later realized their memories were false (Watters, 1993). Lynn Gondolf

is a case in point. During more than a year of therapy she discovered repressed memories of her father raping her. After she stopped therapy, she realized that her therapist had "coerced her and the other members of her group into imagining memories of abuse" (Watters, 1993, p. 26).

7. Consider a brief sampling: From Poston and Lison (1990), "Women usually do not make an immediate incest connection. They may not recall for years that the incest occurred: memories have an uncanny way of coming only when the survivor can deal with them" (p. 193); and "Many women do not remember the incest; how are they then to connect adult problems with childhood pain?" (p. 196). From Farmer (1989): "You may have even repressed the memories of the abuse. The more severe the abuse, the more likely you were to repress any conscious recollection of it" (p. 52).

8. This book proudly displays an endorsement by Gloria Steinern: "This book, like the truth it helps uncover, can set millions free."

9. Popular writings might also be the source of some questionable lay beliefs about early memories. Bradshaw (1990, 1992), a leading figure in the field of recovery and dysfunctional families, invited readers to consult his "index of suspicion": Do you have trouble knowing what you want? Are you afraid to try new experiences? If someone gives you a suggestion, do you feel you ought to follow it? According to Bradshaw, if you answered even one of these questions "yes," then you "can count on some damage having been done to you ... between the 9th and 18th months of your life" (1992, p. 49). How many Bradshaw aficionados have struggled through their memories trying to find that childhood trauma?

10. *Dancing with Daddy* was reviewed in the *New York Times* by Culhane (1991). The reviewer called the book "as much a story about our desperate search for one dimensional solutions to multidimensional problems as it is a story about incest and its consequences" (p. 18).

11. The laws in Washington and other states were changed in part due to the efforts of Kelly Barton and Patti Barton of Seattle. Patti's allegations were described in Seattle newspapers, in *Newsweek* magazine (Darnton, 1991), and on the *Sally Jesse Raphael* show. According to the *Newsweek* account, Patti remembered the alleged

abuse when she was in her 30s—too late to sue under the old Washington law. So, with the help of a lawyer, she lobbied to extend the statute of limitations to allow victims to bring suit for up to three years after their memory returns. Patti's father, who denied all charges, moved to Alaska, where upon Patti turned her efforts on the Alaska legislature and introduced the same legislation there.

12. In the dream, there was "a fellow who was out to hurt and perhaps rape her. In the dream she could not get rid of him. In her primal, she fought him with words until I nudged her on the shoulder with a batacka (a padded bat), and what I did was, I nudged her on the shoulder and she was there. … She came unglued at that. She took the batacka, grabbed it, and began striking out. She worked and worked until she got rid of him at the door. She opened the door of the room and kicked him out and locked the door. The man looked like her manic-depressive brother but had mannerisms like Kelly (her husband)" (p. 43).

13. Here is one segment:

Son: "I would have dreams of uh little people …short people coming and walking on me … walking on my bed."

Psychologist: "What you saw was real."

Son: "Well, this is a different dream … everytime a train came by, a whistle would blow and … witch would come in my window … I would wake up, but I couldn't move. It was like the blankets were tucked under and … I couldn't move my arms."

Psychologist: "You were being restrained?"

Son: "Right and there was somebody on top of me."

Psychologist: "(Son's name) these things happened to you. … It's real. It's not an hallucination."

Before long, the dreams became the reality: The son soon remembered witches holding him down and joining his father in abuse.

REFERENCES

ABC News. (1992, April 2). *Primetime Live* (Transcript). Washington, DC: American Broadcasting Corporation.

Abelson, R. P., Loftus, E. F., & Greenwald, A. G. (1992). Attempts to improve the accuracy of self-reports of voting. In J. M. Tanur (Ed.), *Questions about survey questions: Meaning, memory, expression, and social interactions in surveys* (pp. 138–153). New York: Russell Sage Foundation.

Abhold, J. (1992). (Unpublished doctoral dissertation data.) University of Arkansas.

Ambroso-Bienkowski, M., Stahly, G. B., & Wideman, K. (1991, August). *Relationship of sexual fantasy and sexual dysfunction to childhood molestation.* Paper presented at the 99th Annual Convention of the American Psychological Association, San Francisco.

Anderson, D. (1990, February 27). Handcuffed in history to Tony C. *New York Times*, p. B9.

Baker, R. A. (1992). *Hidden memories*. Buffalo, NY: Prometheus Books.

Baron, J., Beattie, J., & Hershey, J. D. (1988). Heuristics and biases in diagnostic reasoning: Congruence, information, and certainty. *Organizational Behavior and Human Decision Processes*, 42, 88–110.

Barton v. Peters. (1990). Case No 4FA-90-0157, Superior Court for the State of Alaska, 4th Judicial District.

Bass, E., & Davis, L. (1988). *The courage to heal*. New York: Harper & Row.

Bass, E., & Thornton, L. (1991). *I never told anyone: Writings by women survivors of child sexual abuse*. New York: Harper Perennial.

Blume, E. S. (1990). *Secret survivors: Uncovering incest and its aftereffects in women*. New York: Ballantine.

Bottoms, B. L., Shaver, P. R., & Goodman, G. S. (1991, August). *Profile of ritualistic and religion-related abuse allegation reported to clinical psychologists in the United States.* Paper presented at the 99th Annual Convention of the American Psychological Association, San Francisco.

Bower, G. H. (1990). Awareness, the unconscious, and repression: An experimental psychologist's perspective. In J. Singer (Ed.), *Repression and dissociation: Implications for personality, theory, psychopathology, and health* (pp. 209–231). Chicago: University of Chicago Press.

Bowers, K. S. (1992, November 2). *Preconscious processes: How do we distinguish mental representations that correspond to perceived events from those that reflect imaginal processes?* Paper presented at National Institute of Mental Health workshop "Basic behavioral and psychological research: Building a bridge," Rockville, MD.

BRADSHAW, J. (1990). *HOMECOMING*. NEW YORK: BANTAM BOOKS.

BRADSHAW, J. (1992). DISCOVERING WHAT WE WANT. *LEAR'S*, 5, 49.

BRAUN, B. G., & SACHS, R. G. (1988, OCTOBER). *RECOGNITION OF POSSIBLE CULT INVOLVEMENT IN MPD PATIENTS*. PAPER PRESENTED AT THE FIFTH INTERNATIONAL CONFERENCE ON MULTIPLE PERSONALITY/DISSOCIATIVE STATES, CHICAGO.

BRIERE, J. (1992). STUDYING DELAYED MEMORIES OF CHILDHOOD SEXUAL ABUSE. *THE ADVISOR* (PUBLICATION OF THE AMERICAN PROFESSIONAL SOCIETY ON THE ABUSE OF CHILDREN), 5, 17–18.

BRIERE, J., & CONTE, J. (IN PRESS). SELF-REPORTED AMNESIA FOR ABUSE IN ADULTS MOLESTED AS CHILDREN. *JOURNAL OF TRAUMATIC STRESS*.

BRUHN, A. R. (1990). *EARLIEST CHILDHOOD MEMORIES: VOL. 1. THEORY AND APPLICATION TO CLINICAL PRACTICE*. NEW YORK: PRAEGER.

CANNON, L. (1991). *PRESIDENT REAGAN: THE ROLE OF A LIFETIME*. NEW YORK: SIMON & SHUSTER.

CHRISTIANSON, S.A. (1992). DO FLASHBULB MEMORIES DIFFER FROM OTHER TYPES OF EMOTIONAL MEMORIES? IN E. WINOGRAD & U. NEISSER (EDS.), *AFFECT AND ACCURACY IN RECALL: STUDIES OF "FLASHBULB" MEMORIES* (PP. 191–211). NEW YORK: CAMBRIDGE UNIVERSITY PRESS.

CHROUSOS, G. P., & GOLD, P. W. (1992). THE CONCEPT OF STRESS AND STRESS SYSTEM DISORDERS: OVERVIEW OF PHYSICAL AND BEHAVIORAL HOMEOSTASIS. *JAMA: JOURNAL OF THE AMERICAN MEDICAL ASSOCIATION*, 267, 1244–1252.

COLLIER, D. v. COLLIER, J. (1991, DECEMBER). DEPOSITION OF PLAINTIFF, CASE NO. 711752, SUPERIOR COURT, COUNTY OF SANTA CLARA, CALIFORNIA.

CULHANE, D. (1991, AUGUST 4). SINS OF THE FATHER (PETERSON, B. REVIEW OF DANCING WITH DADDY) *NEW YORK TIMES BOOK REVIEW*, P. 18.

THE DARKEST SECRET (1991, JUNE 10) *PEOPLE*, PP. 88–94.

DARO, D. (1988). *CONFRONTING CHILD ABUSE*. NEW YORK: FREE PRESS.

DARNTON, N. (1991, OCTOBER 7). THE PAIN OF THE LAST TABOO. *NEWSWEEK*, PP. 70–72.

DAVIS, L. (1991). MURDERED MEMORY. *IN HEALTH*, 5, 79–84.

DAWES, R. M. (1992). WHY BELIEVE THAT FOR WHICH THERE IS NO GOOD EVIDENCE? *ISSUES IN CHILD ABUSE ACCUSATIONS*, 4, 214–218.

DENNETT, D.C. (1991). *CONSCIOUSNESS EXPLAINED*. BOSTON: LITTLE, BROWN.

DOE, J. (1991). HOW COULD THIS HAPPEN? COPING WITH A FALSE ACCUSATION OF INCEST AND RAPE. *ISSUES IN CHILD ABUSE ACCUSATIONS*, 3, 154–165.

DORMEN, L. (1991, APRIL). A SECRET LIFE. *SEVENTEEN*, PP. 164–167.

DRISCOLL, L. N., & WRIGHT, C. (1991). SURVIVORS OF CHILDHOOD RITUAL ABUSE: MULTI-GENERATIONAL SATANIC CULT INVOLVEMENT. *TREATING ABUSE TODAY*, 1, 5–13.

EDMISTON, S. (1990, NOVEMBER). DADDY'S GIRL. *GLAMOUR*, PP. 228–231, 280–285.

ELLIS, B. (1992). SATANIC RITUAL ABUSE AND LEGEND OSTENSION. *JOURNAL OF PSYCHOLOGY AND THEOLOGY*, 20, 274–277.

ERDELYI, M.H. (1985). *PSYCHOANALYSIS: FREUD'S COGNITIVE PSYCHOLOGY*. NEW YORK: FREEMAN.

ERDELYI, M. H., & GOLDBERG, B. (1979). LET'S NOT SWEEP REPRESSION UNDER THE RUG: TOWARD A COGNITIVE PSYCHOLOGY OF REPRESSION. IN J. F. KIHLSTROM & F. J. EVANS (EDS.), *FUNCTIONAL DISORDERS OF MEMORY* (PP. 355–402). HILLSDALE, NJ: ERLBAUM.

FARMER, S. (1989). *ADULT CHILDREN OF ABUSIVE PARENTS*. NEW YORK: BALLANTINE.

FAUST, D., & ZISKIN, J. (1988). THE EXPERT WITNESS IN PSYCHOLOGY AND PSYCHIATRY. *SCIENCE*, 241, 31–35.

FIELDS, R. (1992, AUGUST 4). HOOD MUST PAY IN SEX-ABUSE CASE. *BEACON JOURNAL* (AKRON, OH), P. C5.

FORGETTING TO REMEMBER. (1991, FEBRUARY 11). *NEWSWEEK*, P. 58.

FORWARD, S., & BUCK, C. (1988). *BETRAYAL OF INNOCENCE: INCEST AND ITS DEVASTATION*. NEW YORK: PENGUIN BOOKS.

FOWLER, R. D., & MATARAZZO, J. D. (1988). PSYCHOLOGISTS AND PSYCHIATRISTS AS EXPERT WITNESSES. *SCIENCE*, 241, 1143–1144.

FRANKLIN, E., & WRIGHT, W. (1991). *SINS OF THE FATHER*. NEW YORK: CROWN.

FRAWLEY, M. G. (1990). FROM SECRECY TO SELF-DISCLOSURE: HEALING THE SCARS OF INCEST. IN G. STRICKER & M. FISHER (EDS.), *SELF-DISCLOSURE IN THE THERAPEUTIC RELATIONSHIP* (PP. 247–259). NEW YORK: PLENUM PRESS.

FREDRICKSON, R. (1992). *REPRESSED MEMORIES: A JOURNEY TO RECOVERY FROM SEXUAL ABUSE*. NEW YORK: SIMON & SHUSTER.

FREUD, S. (1953). THREE ESSAYS ON THE THEORY OF SEXUALITY. IN J. STRACHEY (ED.), *THE STANDARD EDITION OF THE COMPLETE PSYCHOLOGICAL WORKS OF SIGMUND FREUD* (VOL. 7, PP. 135–243). LONDON: HOGARTH PRESS. (ORIGINAL WORK PUBLISHED 1905)

FREYD, J. J. (1991, AUGUST 21). *MEMORY REPRESSION, DISSOCIATIVE STATES, AND OTHER COGNITIVE CONTROL PROCESSES INVOLVED IN ADULT SEQUELAE OF CHILDHOOD TRAUMA.* PAPER PRESENTED AT THE SECOND ANNUAL CONFERENCE ON PSYCHODYNAMICS-COGNITIVE SCIENCE INTERFACE, UNIVERSITY OF CALIFORNIA, SAN FRANCISCO.

GANAWAY, G. K. (1989). HISTORICAL VERSUS NARRATIVE TRUTH: CLARIFYING THE ROLE OF EXOGENOUS TRAUMA IN THE ETIOLOGY OF MPD AND ITS VARIANTS. *DISSOCIATION, 2,* 205–220.

GANAWAY, G. K. (1991, AUGUST). *ALTERNATIVE HYPOTHESES REGARDING SATANIC RITUAL ABUSE MEMORIES.* PAPER PRESENTED AT THE 99TH ANNUAL CONVENTION OF THE AMERICAN PSYCHOLOGICAL ASSOCIATION, SAN FRANCISCO.

GANAWAY, G. K. (1992). SOME ADDITIONAL QUESTIONS. *JOURNAL OF PSYCHOLOGY AND THEOLOGY, 20,* 201–205.

GARDNER, R. A. (1991). *SEX ABUSE HYSTERIA.* CRESSKILL, NJ: CREATIVE THERAPEUTICS.

GARDNER, R. A. (1992). *TRUE AND FALSE ACCUSATIONS OF CHILD SEX ABUSE.* CRESSKILL, NJ: CREATIVE THERAPEUTICS.

GERSHON, E. S., & RIEDER, R. O. (1992). MAJOR DISORDERS OF MIND AND BRAIN. *SCIENTIFIC AMERICAN, 267*(3), 127–133.

GORDON, J. S. (1991). THE UFO EXPERIENCE. *THE ATLANTIC MONTHLY, 268,* 82–92.

GUDJONSSON, G. (1992). *THE PSYCHOLOGY OF INTERROGATIONS, CONFESSIONS AND TESTIMONY.* CHICHESTER, ENGLAND: WILEY.

GUZE, S. B. (1992). *WHY PSYCHIATRY IS A BRANCH OF MEDICINE?* NEW YORK: OXFORD UNIVERSITY PRESS.

HARRIS, M. (1974). *COWS, PIGS, WARS, AND WITCHES: THE RIDDLES OF CULTURE.* NY: VINTAGE BOOKS.

HARSCH, N., & NEISSER, U. (1989, NOVEMBER). *SUBSTANTIAL AND IRREVERSIBLE ERRORS IN FLASHBULB MEMORIES OF THE CHALLENGER EXPLOSION.* POSTER PRESENTED AT THE ANNUAL MEETING OF THE PSYCHONOMIC SOCIETY, ATLANTA, GA.

HAUGAARD, J. J., REPPUCCI, N. D., LAURD, J., & NAUFUL, T. (1991). CHILDREN'S DEFINITIONS OF THE TRUTH AND THEIR COMPETENCY AS WITNESSES IN LEGAL PROCEEDINGS. *LAW AND HUMAN BEHAVIOR, 15,* 253–272.

HERMAN, J. L. (1981). *FATHER-DAUGHTER INCEST.* CAMBRIDGE, MA: HARVARD UNIVERSITY PRESS.

HERMAN, J. L. (1992). *TRAUMA AND RECOVERY.* NEW YORK: BASIC BOOKS.

HERMAN, J. L., & SCHATZOW, E. (1987). RECOVERY AND VERIFICATION OF MEMORIES OF CHILDHOOD SEXUAL TRAUMA. *PSYCHOANALYTIC PSYCHOLOGY, 4,* 1–14.

HOLMES, D. (1990). THE EVIDENCE FOR REPRESSION: AN EXAMINATION OF SIXTY YEARS OF RESEARCH. IN J. SINGER (ED.), *REPRESSION AND DISSOCIATION: IMPLICATIONS FOR PERSONALITY, THEORY, PSYCHOPATHOLOGY, AND HEALTH* (PP. 85–102). CHICAGO: UNIVERSITY OF CHICAGO PRESS.

HORNSTEIN, G. A. (1992). THE RETURN OF THE REPRESSED. *AMERICAN PSYCHOLOGIST, 47,* 254–263.

HOWE, M. L., & COURAGE, M. L. (1993). ON RESOLVING THE ENIGMA OF INFANTILE AMNESIA. *PSYCHOLOGICAL BULLETIN, 113,* 305–326.

JOHNSTON, D. (1992, APRIL 24). SURVEY SHOWS NUMBER OF RAPES FAR HIGHER THAN OFFICIAL FIGURES. *NEW YORK TIMES,* P. A9.

KANTOR, D. (1980). CRITICAL IDENTITY IMAGE. IN J. K. PEARCE & L. J. FRIEDMAN (EDS.), *FAMILY THERAPY: COMBINING PSYCHODYNAMIC AND FAMILY SYSTEMS APPROACHES* (PP. 137–167) NEW YORK: GRUNE & STRATTON.

KANTROWITZ, B. (1991, FEBRUARY 11). FORGETTING TO REMEMBER. *NEWSWEEK,* P. 58.

KIHLSTROM, J. F., & HARACKIEWICZ, J. (1982). THE EARLIEST RECOLLECTION: A NEW SURVEY. *JOURNAL OF PERSONALITY, 50,* 134–148.

KUTCHINSKY, B. (1992). THE CHILD SEXUAL ABUSE PANIC. *NORDISK SEXOLIGI, 10.* 30–42.

LAKER, B. (1992, APRIL 14). A NIGHTMARE OF MEMORIES. *SEATTLE POST-INTELLIGENCER,* P. C1.

LAMM, J. B. (1991). EASING ACCESS TO THE COURTS FOR INCEST VICTIMS: TOWARD AN EQUITABLE APPLICATION OF THE DELAYED DISCOVERY RULE. *THE YALE LAW JOURNAL, 100,* 2189–2208.

LAURENCE, J. R., & PERRY, C. (1983). HYPNOTICALLY CREATED MEMORY AMONG HIGHLY HYPNOTIZABLE SUBJECTS. *SCIENCE, 222,* 523–524.

LOFFT, K. V. LOFFT, D. (1989). COMPLAINT FOR DAMAGES. CASE NO. 617151, SUPERIOR COURT OF THE STATE OF CALIFORNIA FOR COUNTY OF SAN DIEGO.

LOFTUS, E. F. (1982). MEMORY AND ITS DISTORTIONS. IN A. G. KRAUT (ED.), *G. STANLEY HALL LECTURES* (PP. 119–154). WASHINGTON, DC: AMERICAN PSYCHOLOGICAL ASSOCIATION.

LOFTUS, E. F. (IN PRESS). DESPERATELY SEEKING MEMORIES OF THE FIRST FEW YEARS OF CHILDHOOD. *JOURNAL OF EXPERIMENTAL PSYCHOLOGY: GENERAL.*

LOFTUS, E. F., & COAN, D. (IN PRESS). THE CONSTRUCTION OF CHILDHOOD MEMORIES. IN D. PETERS (ED.), *THE CHILD WITNESS IN CONTEXT: COGNITIVE, SOCIAL AND LEGAL PERSPECTIVES.* NEW YORK: KLUWER.

Loftus, E. F., & Herzog, C. (1991). Unpublished data. University of Washington.

Loftus, E. F., & Kaufman, L. (1992). Why do traumatic experiences sometimes produce good memory (flashbulbs) and sometimes no memory (repression)? In E. Winograd & U. Neisser (Eds.), *Affect and accuracy in recall: Studies of "flashbulb" memories* (pp. 212–223). New York: Cambridge University Press.

Loftus, E. F., & Ketcham, K. (1991). *Witness for the defense.* New York: St. Martin's Press.

Loftus, E. F., Polonsky, S., & Fullilove, M. T. (1993). *Memories of childhood sexual abuse: Remembering and repressing.* Unpublished manuscript, University of Washington and Columbia University School of Public Health.

Loftus, E. F., Weingardt, K., & Hoffman, H. (1992). *Sleeping memories on trial: Reactions to memories that were previously repressed.* Unpublished manuscript, University of Washington.

Mack, J. E. (1980). Psychoanalysis and biography: Aspects of a developing affinity. *Journal of the American Psychoanalytic Association, 28,* 543–562.

Malmquist, C. P. (1986). Children who witness parental murder: Posttraumatic aspects. *Journal of the American Academy of Child Psychiatry, 25,* 320–325.

McMillan, P. (1992, April 28). Woman, 39, wins $500,000 in incest case. *Los Angeles Times,* p. B3.

Medin, D. L., & Ross, B. H. (1992). *Cognitive psychology.* Ft. Worth, TX: Harcourt Brace Jovanovich.

Monesi, L. (1992). (Reports of a private investigator, Falcon International Inc., Columbus, Ohio.)

Morton, J. (1990). The development of event memory. *The Psychologist, 1,* 3–10.

Mulhern, S. (1991). Satanism and psychotherapy: A rumor in search of an inquisition. In J. T. Richardson, J. Best, & D. Bromley (Eds.), *The satanism scare* (pp. 145–172). New York: Aldine de Gruyter.

Napier, C. W. (1990). Civil incest suits: Getting beyond the statute of limitations. *Washington University Law Quarterly, 68,* 995–1020.

Nash, M. (1987). What, if anything, is regressed about hypnotic age regression? A review of the empirical literature. *Psychological Bulletin. 102,* 42–52.

Nason girl fought. (1969, December 6). *San Jose Mercury.*

Nathan, D. (1991). *Women and other aliens.* El Paso, TX: Cinco Puntos Press.

Nathan, D. (1992, October). Cry incest. *Playboy* pp. 84–88, 162–164.

Neisser, U., & Harsch, N. (1992). Phantom flashbulbs: False recollections of hearing the news about *Challenger.* In E. Winograd & U. Neisser (Eds.), *Affect and accuracy in recall: Studies of "flashbulb" memories* (pp. 9–31). New York: Cambridge University Press.

Ofshe, R. (1989). Coerced confessions: The logic of seemingly irrational action. *Cultic Studies Journal, 6,* 1–15.

Ofshe, R. J. (1992). Inadvertent hypnosis during interrogation: False confession due to dissociative state, misidentified multiple personality and the satanic cult hypothesis. *International Journal of Clinical and Experimental Hypnosis, 40,* 125–156.

Oldenberg, D. (1991, June 20). Dark memories: Adults confront their childhood abuse. *Washington Post,* p. D1.

Olio, K. A. (1989). Memory retrieval in the treatment of adult survivors of sexual abuse. *Transactional Analysis Journal, 19,* 93–94.

Orne, M. T. (1979). The use and misuse of hypnosis in court. *International Journal of Clinical and Experimental Hypnosis, 27,* 311–341.

Petersen, B. (1991). *Dancing with daddy: A childhood lost and a life regained.* New York: Bantam.

Petersen v. Bruen (1990). 792 P.2d 18 (Nev. 1990).

Piaget, J. (1962). *Plays, dreams and imitation in childhood.* New York: Norton.

Pillemer, D. B., & White, S. H. (1989). Childhood events recalled by children and adults. In *Advances in child development and behavior* (Vol. 21). San Diego, CA: Academic Press.

Poston, C., & Lison, K. (1990). *Reclaiming our lives: Hope for adult survivors of incest.* New York: Bantam.

Pynoos, R. S., & Nader, K. (1989). Children's memory and proximity to violence. *Journal of the American Academy of Child and Adolescent Psychiatry, 28,* 236–241.

Rieker, P. P., & Carmen, E. H. (1986). The victim-to-patient process: The disconfirmation and transformation of abuse. *American Journal of Orthopsychiatry, 56,* 360–370.

Ritter, M. (1991, June 30). Sudden recall of forgotten crimes is a puzzler for juries, experts say. *Los Angeles Times,* p. A10.

Rogers, M. L. (1992a, March). A case of alleged satanic ritualistic abuse. Paper presented at the meeting of the American Psychology-Law Society, San Diego.

Rogers, M. L. (1992b). A call for discernment—natural and spiritual: Introductory editorial to a special issue on SRA. *Journal of Psychology and Theology, 20.* 175–186.

Schuker, E. (1979). Psychodynamics and treatment of sexual assault victims. *Journal of the American Academy of Psychoanalysis, 7,* 553–573.

Sgroi, S. M. (1989). Stages of recovery for adult survivors of child sex abuse. In S. M. Sgroi (Ed.), *Vulnerable populations: Sexual abuse treatment for children, adult survivors, offenders and persons with mental retardation* (Vol. 2, p. 112). Lexington, MA: Lexington Books.

Shaffer, R. E., & Cozolino, L. J. (1992). Adults who report childhood ritualistic abuse. *Journal of Psychology and Theology, 20,* 188–193.

Sherman, S. J., Cialdini, R. B., Schwartzman, D. F., & Reynolds, K. D. (1985). Imagining can heighten or lower the perceived likelihood of contracting a disease. *Personality and Social Psychology Bulletin. 11.* 118–127.

Smith, M. (1983). Hypnotic memory enhancement of witnesses: Does it work? *Psychological Bulletin, 94,* 387–407.

Smith, M., & Pazder, L. (1980). *Michelle remembers.* New York: Congdon & Lattes.

Snyder, M. (1984). When belief creates reality? In L. Berkowitz (Ed.). *Advances in experimental social psychology* (Vol. 18, pp. 247–305). San Diego, CA: Academic Press.

Snyder, M., & Swann, W. (1978). Hypothesis-testing processes in social interaction. *Journal of Personality and Social Psychology. 11.* 1202–1212.

"A star cries incest." (1991, October 7). *People,* pp. 84–88.

Sternberg, R. (1992). *Five-part theory of giftedness.* Paper presented at the Conference on Developmental Approaches to Identifying Exceptional Ability, Lawrence, K.S.

Stubbings v. Webb and Another (1991). 3 Weekly Law Reports 383. (Cited in Reports and Developments (1992). *Expert Evidence: The International Digest of Human Behaviour, Science, and Law,* 1, 26.)

Summit, R. (1992). Misplaced attention to delayed memory. *The Advisor* (published by the American Professional Society on the Abuse of Children), 5, 21–25.

Survivors of Incest Anonymous. (1985). *Is Survivors of Incest Anonymous for you?* Baltimore, MD: Author.

Survivors of Incest Anonymous. (1990). *Questions and answers.* (Distributed at Thursday night San Francisco SIA meeting, October 17).

Susan Nason body found in a dump. (1969, December 3). *San Francisco Chronicle,* p. 1.

Telegraphers v. Railway Express Agency. (1944). 321 U.S. 342, 348–349.

Terr, L. (1988). What happens to early memories of trauma? A study of 20 children under age five at the time of documented traumatic events. *Journal of the American Academy of Child and Adolescent Psychiatry,* 27, 96–104.

Trevor-Roper, H. R. (1967). *Religion, the Reformation, and social change.* London: Macmillan.

Trott, J. (1991a). The grade five syndrome. *Cornerstone,* 20, 16–18.

Trott, J. (1991b). Satanic panic. *Cornerstone,* 20, 9–12.

Toufexis, A. (1991, October 28). When can memories be trusted? *Time,* pp. 86–88.

Usher, J. A., & Neisser, U. (in press). Childhood amnesia and the beginnings of memory for four early life events. *Journal of Experimental Psychology: General.*

Van Benschoten, S. C. (1990). Multiple personality disorder and satanic ritual abuse: The issue of credibility. *Dissociation,* 3, 22–30.

Wakefield, H., & Underwager, R. (1992). Recovered memories of alleged sexual abuse: Lawsuits against parents. *Behavioral Sciences and the Law,* 10, 483–507.

Washington. (1989). Rev. Code Ann. Sec. 4.16.340 (1989 Supp).

Watson, B. (1992). Salem's dark hour: Did the devil make them do it? *Smithsonian,* 23, 117–131.

Watters, E. (1991). The devil in Mr. Ingram. *Mother Jones,* July–August, pp. 30–33, 65–68.

Watters, E. (1993). Doors of memory. *Mother Jones,* January–February, pp. 24–29, 76–77.

Weekes, J. R., Lynn, S. J., Green, J. P., & Brentar, J. T. (1992). Pseudo-memory in hypnotized and task-motivated subjects. *Journal of Abnormal Psychology,* 101, 356–360.

Weintraub, S. (1991, December 4). Three myths about Pearl Harbor. *New York Times,* p. A27.

Williams, L. M. (1992). Adult memories of childhood abuse: Preliminary findings from a longitudinal study. *The Advisor,* 5, 19–20.

WILLIAMS, M. (1987). RECONSTRUCTION OF AN EARLY SEDUCTION AND ITS AFTEREFFECTS. *JOURNAL OF THE AMERICAN PSYCHOANALYTIC ASSOCIATION*, 15, 145–163.

WINOGRAD, E., & KILLINGER, W. A., JR. (1983). RELATING AGE AT ENCODING IN EARLY CHILDHOOD TO ADULT RECALL: DEVELOPMENT OF FLASHBULB MEMORIES. *JOURNAL OF EXPERIMENTAL PSYCHOLOGY: GENERAL*, 112, 413–422.

WOLF, E. K., & ALPERT, J. L. (1991). PSYCHOANALYSIS AND CHILD SEXUAL ABUSE: A REVIEW OF THE POST-FREUDIAN LITERATURE. *PSYCHOANALYTIC PSYCHOLOGY*, 8, 305–327.

YOUNG, W. C, SACHS, R. G., BRAUN, B. G., & WATKINS, R. T. (1991). PATIENTS REPORTING RITUAL ABUSE IN CHILDHOOD: A CLINICAL SYNDROME REPORT OF 37 CASES. *INTERNATIONAL JOURNAL OF CHILD ABUSE AND NEGLECT*, 15, 181–189.

Stanley L. Brodsky served as action editor for this article.

This article is an expanded version of an invited address, the Psi Chi/Frederick Howell Lewis Distinguished Lecture, presented at the 100th Annual Convention of the American Psychological Association, Washington DC, August 1992. I thank Geoffrey Loftus, llene Bernstein, Lucy Berliner, Robert Koscielny, and Richard Ofshe for very helpful comments on earlier drafts. I thank many others, especially Ellen Bass, Mark Demos, Judie Alpert, Marsha Linehan, and Denise Park for illuminating discussion of the issues. My gratitude for the vast efforts of the members of the Repressed Memory Research Group at the University of Washington is beyond measure. The National Institute of Mental Health and the National Science Foundation have generously supported the underlying research on memory.

CHAPTER 9
Cognitive Development

The Development of Memory

USHA GOSWAMI

Adults have surprisingly few memories of the period before the age of around 3 years. This is surprising given that the first three years are an active period for conceptual development, which involves semantic memory about how the world is, and also for the development of physical knowledge and causal reasoning, which depend on a stable and efficient memory for events and their outcomes. The absence of early memories is often referred to as *infantile amnesia*. One explanation for this phenomenon has been that there is an age-related reorganisation or structural change in the memory system, with the system that supports conscious memories being late developing (e.g. Schacter & Moscovitch, 1984). We will discuss this view in the next section. However, the infancy research discussed in Chapters 1 and 2 suggests that it is unlikely that infants and young children represent and remember events in substantially different ways to adults. As learning, reasoning, and problem solving are all functioning effectively during the period of assumed infantile amnesia, and as these processes rely on memory, the notion of a structural change in the memory system with age is not persuasive.

One important factor that may need to be considered when thinking about the development of memory is that children (and adults) do not record events into their memories verbatim. Even though it may feel as though you can remember "exactly what happened" when you went to visit your friend, your friend is bound to have a somewhat different recollection of events to you. As

originally demonstrated by Bartlett (1932), children and adults *construct* memories, and the process of construction depends on prior knowledge and personal interpretation. It also depends on how much sense the memoriser can make of the temporal structure of their experiences. In other words, the development of memory cannot be isolated from the development of other cognitive processes, because remembering is embedded in larger social and cognitive activities. Thus the knowledge structures that young children bring to their experiences may be critical in explaining memory development.

Despite the importance of the larger social and cognitive context in explaining memory processes, it is the usual practice in cognitive psychology to discuss memory as a modular system. Emphasis is placed on the *fractionation* of the developed system, and different types of memory are considered independently of each other. Many studies of these different memory "modules" use tasks that are purposely disembedded from larger social/cognitive activities. The aim is to provide a "pure" measure of the memory system of interest. However, an unintended result may be that the applicability of the research findings from such tasks is limited. According to Neisser (1987, p.1) "Students of human memory ... (ignored) almost everything that people ordinarily remember. Their research did not deal with places or stories or friends or life experiences, but with lists of syllables and words ...(leading) to a preference for meaningless materials and unnatural learning tasks ..."

Wherever possible in this chapter, we will focus on studies of memory development that use more familiar, less artificial memory situations and that are based on memory tasks that have some meaning and relevance to the child—in other words, tasks with greater "ecological validity".

The different sub-types of memory that have been identified by researchers who study the developed adult system include semantic memory, recognition memory, working memory, implicit memory, episodic memory, and procedural memory. We have already discussed the development and organisation of semantic memory in the chapter on conceptual development (Chapter 3), and seen procedural memory at work in the infancy studies discussed in Chapter 1. Studies of the other memory systems identified by adult researchers have also been carried out with children, and following a brief review of early memory development, these studies will be considered in this chapter. In Chapter 6, we will discuss the development of mnemonic strategies, and will consider some recent theories of cognitive development that have been based on the development of processing capacity and representation in memory.

EARLY MEMORY DEVELOPMENT
Infantile amnesia: A real phenomenon?

The general absence of memories before the age of about 3 years is a genuine phenomenon (e.g. Howe & Courage, 1993). Even when we feel convinced that we can recall events from our own infancy, these events often turn out to have happened to someone else. For example, the memory researcher David Bjorklund (Bjorklund & Bjorklund, 1992, p.207) reports a vivid memory of having croup (bronchitis) as an infant.

> My crib was covered by a sheet, but I remember looking past the bars into the living room. I can hear the whir of the vaporiser, feel the constriction in my chest, and smell the Vicks Vaporub. To this day the smell of Vicks makes my chest tighten …

However, when he reminded his mother about this memory, it turned out that he had never had croup. She told him "You were such a healthy baby … That was your brother, Dick. You were about 3 years old then …"

The interesting question is why we have so few memories of the earliest period of our lives. One of the first explanations for infantile amnesia came from Freud (1938), who argued that early amnesia was caused by the repression of the emotionally traumatic events of early childhood. Although this idea can account for the active rejection of emotionally troublesome material from consciousness, it does not explain why memories for pleasant events are also later inaccessible. Another possibility is that early memories are coded in terms of physical action or pure sensation. Early memories are thus irretrievable, as they are stored in a different format to later memories, which depend on linguistically based encoding and storage. The finding that females tend to have earlier memories than males appears to be consistent with this explanation, as language development is usually more advanced in girls than in boys. According to this idea, early memories survive intact, but the context in which these memories were laid down is so discrepant from the one in which we seek to retrieve them (during later childhood or adulthood) that it is impossible to make contact with the relevant memory traces (Howe & Courage, 1993).

Alternatively, as noted earlier, it may be the case that the memory systems that support the formation of conscious memories are late developing, because the brain structures that underlie these systems are not functional at birth (e.g. Schacter & Moscovitch, 1984). One speculation is that the subcortical limbic-diencephalic structures are essential for the formation of conscious memories, and that this brain system only begins to function properly at around 2–3 years of age. However, such arguments depend largely on drawing parallels between infant humans and infant monkeys (infant monkeys perform poorly on tasks thought to depend on the limbic-diencephalic system until the age of around 2 years). McKee and Squire (1993) reject this view on the grounds that the limbic-diencephalic structures underlie visual recognition memory, which appears to be functional early in life (see Chapter 1). They argue instead that immaturities in the neocortical areas *served* by the limbic-diencephalic structures (e.g. inferotemporal cortex) may explain the phenomenon of infantile amnesia.

Finally, the development of knowledge structures may be important in explaining infantile amnesia. Fivush and Hammond (1990) argue that infantile amnesia may be due to a combination of the absence of distinctive memory cues and the fact that young children have yet to learn a *framework* for recounting and storing events. Because young children are in the process of trying to understand the world around them, they focus on what is similar about events, namely routines. The *routine* aspects of novel events do not make good retrieval cues for future recall. Similarly, because young children do not possess their own frameworks for constructing memories, early memories are fragmented, also making them more difficult to recall. Childhood amnesia is thus explained as a natural by-product of the development of the constructive process of memory itself.

Fivush and Hammond's argument is appealing, because it places infantile amnesia firmly within the context of memory development in general. According to their argument, the lack of early memories is not the result of basic structural changes in the memory system with development. Instead, it is a result of the absence of abstract knowledge structures for describing the temporal and causal sequences of events. We discuss the development of these abstract knowledge structures in the next section. By adulthood, the routine events that young children prefer to recall have merged into *scripts* (or generic knowledge structures) about specific events like "what happens when we go to a restaurant". Childhood amnesia is therefore due to a combination of script formation and the forgetting of novel events (see also Nelson, 1993).

Understanding symbolic representation as an aid to memory

The development of abstract knowledge structures for describing the temporal and causal sequences of events depends in part on linguistic coding. Language is a symbolic system. Words stand for or represent concepts and events in the everyday world, and we use them as symbols to encode our experiences. However, words are not the only symbols that we use. Children use a number of symbolic systems in addition to language at a young age. For example, they make gestures, they point to things, and they engage in symbolic (pretend) play. These symbolic systems seem to be innately specified in the same way as language (although some children, such as autistic children, may lack innate specification of gestures, pointing, and pretend play).

Other symbols are culturally determined. These include symbols such as maps and models. These symbols also represent or stand for objects or events, and include drawings, photographs, and sculptures. All of these symbols bring to mind something other than themselves. The use of many of these forms of symbolic coding enables children to represent information in memory in a form that will be accessible later on. As symbolic understanding *itself* develops, this may be another factor that helps us to understand why early memories are less accessible than later memories. One of the most intriguing sets of experiments investigating the development of symbolic understanding comes from work on young children's understanding of models (e.g. DeLoache, 1987, 1989, 1991).

The basic paradigm used in DeLoache's model studies is always the same. A 2½-or 3-year-old child is shown a scale model of a room, containing various pieces of furniture such as a couch, a dresser, a chair, and some pillows. The child is then introduced to two central characters, the stuffed toy animals Little Snoopy and Big Snoopy, who both like hiding. The scale model is introduced as Little Snoopy's room, and an adjacent room, which contains the same furniture as the model in the same spatial layout, is introduced as Big Snoopy's room. The child is told "Look, their rooms are just alike. They both have all the same things in their rooms!" Each correspondence is demonstrated "Look—this is Big Snoopy's big couch, and this is Little Snoopy's little couch. They're just the same".

Following this "orientation phase", the child watches as the experimenter hides one of the Snoopy toys in the appropriate room. For example, Little Snoopy might be hidden under the little couch in the model room. The child is then asked to find Big Snoopy in the real room. The child is told "Remember, Big Snoopy is hiding in the same place as Little Snoopy". Children of 3 go straight to the big couch and find Big Snoopy; 2½-year-old children do not. They search around the big room at random, even though a memory post-test shows that they can remember perfectly well where Little Snoopy is hiding. DeLoache argues that the problem for the younger children is that they do not understand the *correspondence* between the model room and the real room. They do not seem to appreciate that they have a basis for knowing where to search for Big Snoopy.

The most compelling reason for believing that the younger children's problem lies in their lack of awareness of the correspondence between the model and the room comes from DeLoache's "magical shrinking room" studies. In these studies, 2½-year-old children were persuaded that the experimenters had built a "shrinking machine" that could shrink a doll and a room (DeLoache, Miller, & Rosengren, 1996). They were then shown where Big Snoopy was hiding in the big room, and asked to find Little Snoopy in the model room. As the children believed that the model was the shrunken big room, there was no representational relationship between the model and the room to confuse them, and indeed the children were very successful at searching for Little Snoopy in this task. DeLoache has also shown that younger children can find Big Snoopy when they are shown Little Snoopy's hiding place in a picture, which implies that they do understand the representational relation between the *picture* and the room (DeLoache, 1991).

Furthermore, experience with the picture task transfers to the model task. Experience with a symbolic medium that is understood (or partially understood), as pictures are by the age of 2 years, seems to facilitate the use of an unfamiliar symbolic medium (the model). For example, Marzolf and DeLoache (1994) have shown that experience with a model-room relation can help 2½-year-old children to appreciate a map-room relation. DeLoache argues that early experience with symbolic relations helps the development of symbolic sensitivity, which is a basic readiness to recognise that one object or event can stand for another. Thus, in order to use these other symbols in memory and in learning, children may first have to learn what it is to *represent* something.

DeLoache's work shows clearly that symbol-referent relations are not always transparent to young children. However, the ability to represent the higher-order relation between symbol and referent (to adopt a "representational stance") appears to develop fairly rapidly during the first three years of life. As DeLoache has argued, the ability to *map* similarities between symbol and referent is an important component of the developing understanding of symbol-referent relations, and frequently depends on the ability to map *relational* similarities. The importance of relational mappings or analogies in cognitive development has been noted at a number of other points in this book. Given the centrality of symbol use in human cognition, it is interesting to note that DeLoache attributes a key role

to the ability to make relational mappings in her model of the development of early symbolic understanding (see DeLoache, in press, for a discussion). The links between early symbolic understanding and memory development in general are not well understood, however.

THE DEVELOPMENT OF DIFFERENT MEMORY SYSTEMS

As noted earlier, a number of different memory systems have been identified by researchers in adult cognitive psychology. All of these memory systems can also be studied in children. A selection of developmental studies of recognition memory, implicit memory, episodic memory, eyewitness memory and working memory will now be considered.

Recognition memory

Recognition memory is the ability to recognise that something is familiar and has been experienced before. In psychology, *recognition* memory is usually contrasted with *recall* memory, which is the retrieval of a conscious memory of what has been experienced in the past. We have already seen that infants have good visual recognition memories, and that individual differences in visual recognition memory in infancy are a reliable predictor of later individual differences in intelligence (see Chapter 1). It can also be argued that most of the other studies of memory in infancy that were discussed in Chapters 1 and 2 concern recognition memory rather than recall. Habituation, which is a key measure of information processing in infancy, is a recognition measure, and paradigms that use conditioned responses are also based on recognition (such as Rovee-Collier's kick-to-work-a-mobile paradigm, or de Caspar and Fifer's suck-to-hear-your-mother paradigm).

Recognition memory seems to be fairly ubiquitous in animals as well as in humans, and so this early developing memory system is far from unique. For example, pigeons can "remember" 320 pictures for 700 days when tested in a recognition memory paradigm (Vaughan & Greene, 1984). Given its ubiquity, the status of recognition memory as a *cognitive* skill can be questioned. For example, Fagan has argued that recognition memory may actually be a measure of *processing* rather than a measure of cognitive ability *per* se (see Fagan, 1992). It thus seems likely that psychologists will find little development in recognition memory with age. This is in fact the case.

The traditional way of examining recognition memory in young children is to show them a series of pictures, and then to measure the number of pictures that they recognise as familiar after a certain period of time. In a classic study of this type, Brown and Scott (1971) showed children aged from 3–5 years a set of 60 pictures drawn from four familiar categories: people, animals, outdoor scenes/objects, and household scenes/objects. Of the set of pictures, 44 recurred and 12 were seen only once, making a series of 100 pictures in all. The pictures that recurred were seen after a lag of either 0, 5, 10, 25, or 50 items. The children's task was to say "yes" if they had seen a picture before, and "no" if the picture was novel.

Brown and Scott found that the children showed accurate recognition memory on 98% of trials. There was also little difference in recognition accuracy depending on the lag between the items. In fact, the children were equally accurate for lags of 0 and 50 pictures, showing 100% recognition accuracy for each. Accuracy levels for lags of 5 and 25 pictures were around 95%, and for a lag of 10 pictures, 98%. These remarkable levels of performance fell slightly on a long-term retention test which was given after 1, 2, 7, or 28 days. In the long-term retention test, the children were shown the 12 pictures that had been seen only once, 24 of the 44 pictures that had been seen twice, and 36 new pictures. For intervals of up to seven days, recognition memory levels were above 94% for pictures that had been seen twice. The level was somewhat lower for pictures that had been seen only once, falling from 84% after one day to around 70% after seven days. After 28 days, recognition accuracy for pictures that had been seen twice was 78%, and for pictures that had been seen only once, 56%. In a subsequent study, Brown and Scott showed that the superior memory for items seen twice was due to *both* the extra exposure to the items and to the need to make a judgement in the recognition task given in the first phase of the study. The previous requirement of a "yes" judgement seemed *in itself to* act as a retrieval cue for the twice-seen items.

The excellent levels of recognition memory found in young children suggest that there is little for the developmental psychologist of memory to study here. However,

interest in children's memory for what is familiar has revived recently through the study of the development of implicit memory.

Implicit memory

Implicit memory is "memory without awareness". In implicit memory tasks, children and adults behave in ways that demonstrate that they have memory for information that they are not consciously aware of having. Although most of us would measure our memories in terms of what we can recall rather than in terms of what we can recognise, the possibility that previous experiences can facilitate performance on a particular memory task even though the subject has no conscious recollection of these previous experiences is a very intriguing one. Implicit memory has also been called "unintentional memory", or "perceptual learning".

Perceptual Learning Tasks. One of the first studies of implicit memory in children was carried out by Carroll, Byrne, and Kirsner (1985). They measured "perceptual learning" in 5-, 7-, and 10-year-old children using a picture recognition task. In the first phase of the experiment, the children were shown some pictures and either had to say whether each picture contained a cross (crosses had been drawn at random on 33% of the pictures), or to say whether the picture was of something portable. The "cross detection" task was intended to induce "shallow processing" of the pictures at a perceptual level only, and the "portability detection" task was intended to induce "deep processing" at the level of meaning.

Memory for the previously experienced pictures was then studied in an unexpected recognition task. In this task, the children were asked to name a mixture of the pictures that they had already seen along with some new ones. Implicit memory was measured by the difference in the children's reaction times to name the old vs. the new pictures. Half of the children received this *implicit* memory task, and the other half were asked to say whether the old and the new pictures were familiar or not. The latter was the measure of *explicit* memory.

Carroll et al. predicted that implicit memory for the pictures would not vary with depth of encoding, whereas explicit memory would. In other words, deep processing should lead to better explicit memory for the previously experienced pictures than shallow processing, whereas implicit memory levels should be identical for both processing manipulations. This was essentially what they found. Carroll et al. concluded that perceptual learning (implicit memory) does not develop with age.

Fragment-completion tasks. Another way of measuring whether implicit memory develops or not is to use a fragment completion task based on either words or pictures. For example, Naito (1990) devised a word-fragment completion task to measure implicit memory in children aged 5, 8, and 11 years. The children were given some of the letters in a target word, and were asked to complete each fragment into the first meaningful word that came to mind. Although Naito used words written in Japanese characters, her task was equivalent to presenting a fragment like CH——Y for the target word CHERRY. This is the example given in Naito's paper, and actually the fragment CH——Y could also be CHEERY or CHUNKY. However, each Japanese fragment was chosen to have only *one* legitimate completion.

Prior to receiving the fragment completion task, the children were given two other tasks based on 67% of the target words. For half of these words, the children were asked to make a *category* judgement in a forced choice task ("Is this a kind of fruit/clothes?"), intended to induce "deep" processing. For the other half of the words, they were asked to judge whether the target word contained a certain letter ("shallow" processing). Naito then measured whether more word fragments were completed correctly for the 32 previously experienced target words than for the 16 novel items. She found that the "old" items were completed correctly significantly more frequently than the "new" items at all ages, and that implicit memory did not vary with depth of processing (deep vs. shallow). She also found that implicit memory levels were invariant across age group (even though a group of adults were also included in the study). In a related experiment in which children were asked to recall the target words explicitly, Naito found a strong improvement in recall with age and an effect of depth of processing. Taken together, her results suggest that implicit memory does not develop, but that explicit memory does. Naito argued that her results showed that the two types of memory were developmentally dissociable.

In *picture*-fragment completion tasks, the child is shown an increasing number of fragments of a picture of a familiar object, such as a saucepan or a telephone, until the object is recognised. If the complete object has been presented in a prior task, such as a picture naming task, then implicit learning should result in faster recognition for fragments of previously experienced objects than for fragments of completely novel objects.

Russo, Nichelli, Gibertoni, and Cornia (1995) used a picture completion paradigm of this type to measure implicit memory in 4-and 6-year-old children. The children were first shown a series of 12 pictures for three seconds each, and were required to name each in turn. After a 10-minute break spent playing with blocks, the children were shown the fragmented versions of the familiar pictures along with fragmented versions of 12 new pictures, in random order. For each set of fragments, they were asked to say as quickly as possible what they thought the fragments were a picture of. The number of fragments that were presented was increased until the child recognised the picture. Performance in this implicit memory condition was contrasted with performance in an explicit version of the task, which was presented without time constraints. In the explicit memory task, the children were asked to use the fragments as cues to try and recall the pictures presented during the naming phase of the experiment.

Russo et al. found that children of both ages recognised the familiar pictures from fewer fragments than the novel pictures, showing implicit memory. A group of young adults who were given the same picture completion task performed at similar levels to the children. Significant age differences were found in the explicit memory task, however, with the 6-year-olds showing better recall than the 4-year-olds. Russo et al. concluded that implicit memory as measured by fragment completion tasks is equivalent in children and in adults, and that the memory processes supporting implicit memory are fully developed by 4 years of age.

A similar study carried out by Bullock Drummey and Newcombe (1995) suggested that even 3-year-olds may have fully fledged implicit memory processes. Their measure of implicit memory was the recognition of blurred pictures after long delays. Bullock Drummey and Newcombe showed 3-year-olds, 5-year-olds, and adults blurred versions of pictures that they had seen three months previously in a reading book. They found that all groups showed comparable levels of implicit memory for the pictures. However, the adults had better *explicit* memory of the pictures than the children.

Memory for faces. A third measure that can be used to study implicit memory in children is memory for faces. Faces have the advantage of being salient and important stimuli that are not dependent on verbal recall. For example, if the same face is presented to adult subjects on two occasions, the reaction time to recognise the face as familiar on the second occasion is dramatically reduced. This is known as a "priming" effect. Ellis, Ellis, and Hosie (1993) investigated whether young children would also show "priming" effects for faces.

In their experiment, children aged 5, 8, and 11 years were shown pictures of both their classmates and unfamiliar children, and were asked to judge whether the children were smiling or not (half were smiling) and whether the picture was of a boy or of a girl. Following this "priming" stage, the pictures of the children's classmates were presented for a second time, mixed in with previously unseen pictures of other classmates and with pictures of other unfamiliar children. On this second showing, the children were asked to judge whether the children depicted were familiar. Ellis et al. found that children of all ages were quicker to make judgements about the familiarity of the classmates that they had just seen in the priming phase of the experiment than about the familiarity of their non-primed classmates. The amount of implicit memory, as measured by the proportional differences in primed and unprimed reaction times, was the same for the 5-and 8-year-olds, and was slightly *less* for the 11-year-olds, again suggesting that the memory processes supporting implicit memory are fully developed early in childhood.

A different way to measure memory for faces is to study children's implicit memory of their classmates over time. Newcombe and Fox (1994) showed a group of 10-year-old children slides of 3-and 4-year-old children who had been their classmates in pre-school. These slides were intermixed with slides of other children from the same preschool who had attended the school five years later. In order to see whether the children had implicit memories of their familiar classmates, galvanic skin response measures were recorded, a measure of autonomic nervous system

arousal. The children were then shown the slides again, and were asked to say whether the depicted children were familiar and how much they liked them. The liking measure was included to see whether the children would show a preference for their previous classmates, even if they could not remember them.

Newcombe and Fox found that the children showed recognition of their former classmates according to *both* the implicit and the explicit measures. Overall recognition rates were fairly low (26% on the implicit measure and 21% on the explicit measure), but there were large individual differences in recognition rates. When the experimenters divided the children into two groups—a "high explicit recognition" group and a "low explicit recognition" group—they found that performance on the *implicit* recognition measure was equivalent in both groups. This is a very interesting result, as it implies that implicit memory for pre-school experiences can be maintained even when explicit memories are lacking. Newcombe and Fox's data thus support Naito's (1990) suggestion that implicit and explicit memories may be developmentally dissociable.

These studies demonstrate that "memory without awareness" is present in children as young as 3–4 years of age. Young children retain sufficient unconscious memories of previously presented pictures or words to facilitate later recognition on the basis of fragments, and their reaction time when judging previously experienced pictures (or children!) is significantly enhanced. However, it is worth noting that the idea that there are two dissociable memory systems in human cognition is currently the subject of dispute (e.g. Shanks & St. John, 1994). Two dissociable memory systems would require two dissociable learning systems, an implicit system that operates independently of awareness and an explicit system that cannot function without a concurrent awareness of what is being learned. Shanks and St. John have argued that most of the implicit learning and memory data do not require learning without awareness at all. Instead, they can be explained on the basis of memorising the instances or fragments of pictures or words that are presented during the training phase that is usual in implicit memory experiments. Whether their argument turns out to be correct or not, however, does not affect the fact that such memory processes are well-established in young children.

Episodic memory

There is no comparable debate concerning episodic memory, which all psychologists assume to be a memory system that involves awareness. Episodic memory usually refers to memory for episodes or events in one's life, and as such involves conscious or explicit recall. In adults, episodic memory tends to be organised around "schemas", or scripts, for routine events. Each script is a generic or abstract knowledge structure that represents the temporal and causal sequences of events in very specific contexts. For example, adults have a "restaurant schema" for representing the usual sequence of events when eating in a restaurant, and a "laundry schema" for representing the usual sequence of events when doing one's laundry. In order to study the development of episodic memory, we need to find out whether children organise episodic information in similar ways to adults. One way to do so is to model familiar event sequences to children, such as "having a bath". To see whether they have represented the temporal and causal sequences of events in this specific context, the children can then be asked to reproduce the modelled event.

Temporal order as an organising principle in children's episodic memories. Bauer and Shore (1987) modelled "having a bath" to young children aged from 17 to 23 months by demonstrating giving a teddy bear a bath. The sequence of events was that the teddy bear's t-shirt was removed, he was put in a toy tub, and he was washed and then dried by the experimenter (in pretend mode!). The teddy bear was then handed to the child, who was asked "Can you give the dirty bear a bath?". The children proved quite capable of reproducing the modelled event sequence when tested for immediate recall. They also remembered the correct sequence of events six weeks later, when they returned to the laboratory and were simply handed the teddy without prior modelling (delayed recall). These data suggest that very young children's representations of events are similar in structure to those of adults. Their event memory is not composed of a series of disorganised snapshots of individual components of the event. Instead, like adults, their representations display temporal ordering and are arranged around a goal.

Event sequences like "having a bath" are very familiar to young children, however, and this familiarity may aid

temporally ordered recall. An important question is whether the experimenters would have found similar effects if the temporally ordered events had been novel instead of familiar. To find out, Bauer and Shore invented a novel causal event sequence called "building a rattle".

During this event the experimenter modelled putting a plastic ball into a stacking cup, covering it with a slightly smaller stacking cup, and shaking the "rattle" near her ear. The children again showed both immediate and delayed recall for the elements of the sequence, and for their temporal order. Bauer and her colleagues argued that even very young children were sensitive to the causal relations underlying event sequences from their very first experience of them, and that this early causal sensitivity meant that very young children's representations displayed goal-oriented temporal ordering, just like those of adults.

Causal relations as an organising principle in children's episodic memories. To test the idea that causal relations play a special role in organising the temporal order of events for young children, Bauer and Mandler (1989b) carried out a study that used two novel causal event sequences and two familiar sequences. Their subjects were younger children aged either 16 or 20 months. The novel causal event sequences were "build a rattle" and "make the frog jump". "Make the frog jump" involved building a see-saw by putting a wooden board onto a wedge-shaped block, putting a toy frog at one end of the board, and making him "jump" by hitting the other end of the board. The familiar event sequences were "give teddy a bath", and "clean the table". For the "clean the table" event, a wastebasket, paper towel, and empty spray bottle were used. The experimenter mimed spraying the table, wiping it with the towel, and then throwing the towel away. In order to separate temporal from causal information, Bauer and Mandler also included "novel arbitrary" event sequences. An example of a novel event whose temporal ordering was arbitrary was the "train ride" event sequence. For this event, two toy train cars were linked together. A toy driver was then put into one of the cars, and a piece of track was produced for the train to sit on. Although the events were modelled in this order, there was no causal necessity in this ordering, and so these components could be reproduced in any order without affecting the final event.

Bauer and Mandler found that immediate recall for the temporal order of events was indeed significantly lower for the novel arbitrary events than for the novel causal events, even though recall levels for the former were still significant. Furthermore, they found that when an irrelevant component was inserted into each kind of novel event sequence (such as attaching a sticker either to one of the cups making up the rattle or to the toy train driver), then this irrelevant component was far more likely to be displaced in the causal event sequences. Attaching the sticker to the cup was frequently displaced to another position in the "building a rattle" sequence, or was even left out entirely. In contrast, attaching the sticker to the train driver was treated no differently from any of the other components in the "train ride" sequence. This finding suggests that causally related pairs of elements enjoy a privileged organisational status. Bauer and Mandler concluded that causal relations were an important organising principle both for constructing event memories and for aiding recall. The importance of causal relations in structuring *episodic* memory complements the data discussed in Chapter 3, in which we saw the importance of causal information for developing and organising *semantic* memory (e.g. Pauen, 1996b).

The work of Bauer and her colleagues has shown convincingly that even very young children show long-term ordered recall for novel events. Another way to find out whether children organise episodic information in similar ways to adults is to ask them about very familiar events. Bauer's work suggests that, if children are asked questions about familiar routines, then evidence for scriptlike information should be found.

The use of scripts to organise episodic memories.
Asking questions about familiar routines was exactly the method used by Nelson and her colleagues in their pioneering developmental work on scripts. They examined the episodic memories of 3-to 5-year-old children for events like going grocery shopping, attending birthday parties, and baking cookies. The children were simply asked to tell the experimenters "what happens" during such events. A series of ordered prompts was then used as necessary to encourage elaboration: "I know you know a lot about grocery shopping. Can you tell me what happens when you go grocery shopping? … Can you tell me anything else about grocery shopping? … What's the first thing that happens? What happens next?".

Even the youngest children gave ordered and conventionalised reports of what typically occurred during these events. For example, here is a 5-year-old telling the experimenters about going grocery shopping (Nelson, 1986, p. ix):

> Um, we get a cart, uh, and we look for some onions and plums and cookies and tomato sauce, onions and all that kind of stuff, and when we're finished we go to the paying booth, and um, then we, um, then the lady puts all our food in a bag, then we put it in the cart, walk out to our car, put the bags in our trunk, then leave.

Research such as this shows that episodic memory is organised around general event representations from a very early age. Nelson (1993) argues that the basic ways of structuring, representing and interpreting reality are consistent from early childhood into adulthood.

Because of this, as she points out, scripts for routine events may play a very salient role in memory development. Nelson (1988) has suggested that younger children *concentrate* on remembering routines, as routine events such as going to the babysitter are what makes their world a predictable place. The importance of this predictability means that routine events are focused on at the expense of novel and unusual events, which are forgotten.

The relationship between scripts and novel events.
However, more recent studies have shown that younger children can also remember novel and unusual events over long periods of time. In a study by Fivush and Hamond (1990), a 4-year-old recalled that, when he was 2½, "I fed my fish too much food and then it died and my mum dumped him in the toilet". Another 4-year-old told the experimenters that when he was 2½ "Mummy gave me Jonathan's milk and I threw up" (this child was lactose-intolerant). Both of these events were genuine memories. These novel events had obviously made a big impression on the children concerned, as they could remember them accurately 18 months later! Fivush and Hamond agree with Nelson's idea that young children focus largely on routines, but suggest that children's understanding of routine events

also helps them to understand novel events, events that differ from how the world usually works.

Fivush and Hamond's suggestion that the development of scripts enables the development of memories for novel events is at first sight inconsistent with other evidence showing that young children have a tendency to *include* novel events in their scripts, however. Whereas older children can separate novel events from the routine, tagging them separately in memory as atypical, younger children display a tendency to blur the routine with the unusual. For example, Farrar and Goodman (1990) compared 4-and 7-year-old children's ability to recall novel and repeated ("script") events. In their study, the children visited the laboratory five times during a two-week period in order to play "animal games". These games included making bunny and frog puppets jump fences, and having bears and squirrels hide from each other. Each game took place at a special table, and the games occurred in the same order on each visit. However, during one visit a novel event was inserted into the familiar routine (the event was two new puppets crawling under a bridge).

A week later, the children were interviewed about their experiences using both free recall techniques and specific questions such as "What happens when you play at this table with the puppets?". The younger children frequently reported that the novel event had occurred during the script visits as well as during the single deviational visit. They appeared to be unable to differentiate between a typical "animal game" visit and the novel event that had occurred only once. The older children did not report that the novel event had occurred during both the script visits and the deviational visit. They were more likely to have formed separate and distinct memories for the two types of visit, tagging the novel event as separate and as a departure from the typical script.

Farrar and Goodman suggested that younger children relied on their general event memory when recalling events, and that this general memory had absorbed information from *both* the script visits and the novel visit. They concluded that the ability to establish separate memories of unusual episodes may still be developing at age 4. However, it is also possible that both groups of researchers are correct. Younger children's tendency to merge novel events with their general event memories may depend on the *salience* of the novel event *to the child*. Highly salient novel events such as those documented by Fivush and Hamond (which may be frequently "refreshed" in family contexts) may be accorded a special status in younger children's memories, while less salient events such as the deviation from the game played in Goodman's laboratory may be merged with their scripts.

Parental interaction style and the development of episodic memories. There is also growing evidence that the ways in which parents interact with their children influences the development of event memories. Parents tend to ask young children fairly specific questions about shared past events, such as "Where did we go yesterday?", "Who did we see?", and "Who was there with us?" (Hudson, 1990). Repeated experience of such questions may help young children to organise events into the correct temporal and causal order, and to learn which aspects of events are the most important to recall. If this is so, then parents who ask more of these specific questions should have children with better memories. This seems to be the case. For example, in a longitudinal study of mother–child conversations about the past, Reese, Haden, and Fivush (1993) observed mother-child dyads talking about the past when the children were aged 40, 46, 58, and 70 months. The mothers were asked to talk about singular events from the past, like a special visit to a baseball game or a trip to Florida. They were asked to avoid routine events like birthday parties or Christmas, which could invoke a familiar script.

Reese et al. found that there were two distinct maternal narrative styles, which were related to the ways in which the children became able to recall their own past experiences. Some mothers consistently elaborated on the information that their child recalled and then evaluated it. Other mothers tended to switch topics and to provide less narrative structure, and seldom used elaboration and evaluation. For example, an elaborative mother who was helping her child to remember a trip to the theatre included questions like "Where were our seats?" and "What was the stage set up like?". A non-elaborative mother who was helping her child to recall a trip to Florida asked the same question repeatedly ("What kinds of animals did you see? And what else? And what else?"). The children of the elaborative mothers tended to remember more material at 58 and 70 months. Reese et al. suggested that maternal elaborativeness was a key factor in children's developing memory abilities.

Eye-witness memory

A rather different kind of recall memory is memory for events that may not have appeared significant at the time that they were experienced. This is eye-witness memory. Studies of eye-witness memory in adults have shown that they have remarkably poor memories for the specifics of events that they have seen. For example, adults who have witnessed a car accident in a video film can be misled into "remembering" false details such as a broken headlight simply by the experimenter asking them leading questions like "Did you see the broken headlight?" (Loftus, 1979). If the eye-witness memory of adults is faulty, then presumably the eye-witness memory of *children* is even worse. This is an interesting research question in its own right, but it is also becoming an important legal issue. As more and more children are being called as witnesses in investigations concerning physical and sexual abuse, the status of their testimony has become of paramount importance. In such cases, it is critical to know whether the abuse really occurred, or whether "memories" of abuse have been created as a result of repeated suggestive questioning by adults.

The accuracy of children's eye-witness testimony. Imagine that an experimenter comes to your school, takes you off to a quiet room to do a puzzle with two friends, and leaves you on your own. While you are working on the puzzle, a strange man comes into the room and messes around, dropping a pencil and fumbling with objects. He claims to be looking for the headmaster. He then steals a handbag and walks out. How much do you remember about these events? Ochsner and Zaragoza (1988, cited in Goodman, Rudy, Bottoms, & Aman, 1990) showed that 6-year-old children remembered quite a lot. The children produced more accurate statements about the other events that they had witnessed in the room and fewer incorrect statements than a group of control children who had experienced the same events except that the man had left the room without stealing the bag. The experimental group were also less suggestible, for example being less willing to select suggested misleading alternative events during a forced-choice test. This study suggests that the eye-witness testimony of young children may be no less accurate than that of adults.

The role of leading questions. Other studies, however, have found that although young children's memory for centrally important events is equivalent to that of adults, younger children are more suggestible than adults. For example, Cassel, Roebers, and Bjorklund (1996) reported a study in which 6-and 8-year-old children and adults watched a video about the theft of a bike. A week later the subjects were asked to recall the events in the video, and were asked a series of increasingly suggestive questions. Cassel et al. found that children and adults showed equivalent levels of recall for items central to the event (e.g. Whose bike was it?). However, when Cassel et al. compared the effect of repeated suggestive questioning on the 6-and 8-year-old children and the adults, they found a greater incidence of false memories in the children. Interestingly, they also found that *unbiased* leading questions such as "Did the bicycle belong to (a) the mother, (b) the boy, or (c) the girl?" were as likely to produce false memories as biased (misleading questions such as "The mother owned the bike, didn't she?". This is an important result, as it suggests that the mechanisms that result in false memories may be *general* ones to do with the way that the developing memory system functions, rather than *specific* ones related to false memories of negative events.

As Cassel et al.'s study relied on watching a video, we can hypothesise that leading questions may have an even *greater* effect on the recall of younger children when they actually experience an event themselves. Goodman and her colleagues devised a paradigm based on a visit to a trailer (caravan) to investigate this question (Rudy & Goodman, 1991, see also Goodman et al., 1990). In the "trailer experiment", children aged 4 and 7 years were taken out of their classrooms to a dilapidated old trailer, chosen to be a memorable location. The children went in pairs, and once inside the trailer they played games with a strange man. One child in each pair had the important task of watching (the bystander), and the other child (the participant) played games. This enabled the experimenters to see whether the children would show similar levels of suggestibility when they were participants or bystanders at real events. The games included "Simon Says", dressing up, having your photograph taken, and tickling. During the "Simon Says" game, the children had to perform various actions including touching the experimenter's knees. These games were chosen because child sexual abuse cases frequently involve reports of being photographed, of "tickling", and of other touching.

The children were later interviewed about what had taken place in the trailer. The interview began with the interviewer asking the child to tell him or her about everything that had happened in the trailer. The interview then continued with misleading questions like "He took your clothes off, didn't he?", "How many times did he spank you?", and "He had a beard and a moustache, right?". In fact, the dressing up game did not involve removing the children's clothes, no child was spanked, and the man was clean-shaven. Goodman et al. found that children of both ages recalled largely *correct* information about the games that they had played in the trailer. Neither participants nor bystanders invented information. The children were also largely accurate in their responses to specific questions about abuse, like "How many times did he spank you?", and "Did he put anything in your mouth?". The 7-year-olds answered 93% of the abuse questions correctly, and the 4-year-olds answered 83% correctly.

A related study with 3-and 5-year-olds showed that false reports of abuse did not increase when anatomically detailed dolls were provided to enable the children to *show* as well as tell what had happened (Goodman & Aman, 1990). In this study, however, the younger children *were* more susceptible to leading questions than the older children. Under the influence of misleading questions about abuse, the 3-year-olds tended to make errors of *commission* (that is, they agreed to things that had not happened) 20% of the time. Embroidery of these events was rare. In fact, the majority of commission errors occurred with the leading question "Did he kiss you?", to which the children simply nodded their heads. The 5-year-olds only made commission errors on 2 out of 120 occasions, and both of these errors were on the question "Did he kiss you?". The younger children made very few errors on the potentially more worrying misleading abuse questions such as "He took your clothes off, didn't he?" and "How many times did he spank you?".

The striking thing about Goodman's findings in these very "ecologically valid" studies is that, in the main, children did *not* invent false reports of abuse. They were

also fairly resistant to misleading questioning by the adult, and this resistance remained robust in the face of anatomically detailed dolls, a factor that might have been expected to encourage invention. Nevertheless, as in Cassel et al.'s video study, the younger children in Goodman et al.'s studies were more susceptible to leading questions. Other studies of young children's eye-witness testimony have also found that levels of suggestibility are higher in younger children (see Ceci & Bruck, 1993, for a review). The levels of suggestibility in different studies appears to vary with factors such as the emotional tone of the interview itself, the child's desire to please the interviewer, and whether the child is a participant in the action or not, among others. All studies find *some* age differences in suggestibility, however.

Links between the development of episodic memory and the development of eye-witness memory. Ceci and Bruck (1993) have suggested that the greater susceptibility of younger children to repeated questioning by adults might be related to the findings of Nelson and others concerning event memory. Their idea is that the over-dependency of younger children on scripted knowledge could mean that suggestions made by the experimenter get included into the children's script for an event, and are thereafter reported as having actually taken place. This clearly fits with Farrar and Goodman's finding that, when a novel event occurs in a standard setting, younger children tend to incorporate it into their script rather than tagging it separately (Farrar & Goodman, 1990). As children get older, they seem to become better at establishing separate memories of suggested episodes, and at keeping these suggestions distinct from their scripts. As they get older, they also become less susceptible to leading questions.

Ornstein and his colleagues have made the related point that children cannot provide accurate testimony about events that they cannot remember. In order to examine how much children actually remember about salient, personally experienced events, Ornstein, Gordon, and Larus (1992) investigated 3-and 6-year-old children's memories of a visit to the doctor for a physical examination. Each physical examination lasted about 45 minutes, and included weighing and measuring the child, checking hearing and vision, drawing blood, checking genitalia, and listening to the heart and lungs. Ornstein et al. argued that such visits shared a number of features with instances of sexual abuse.

These included physical contact with the child's body by an adult and emotional arousal due to injections and other procedures. Memory for the events in the physical examination was measured immediately after the examination was over, and after intervals of one and three weeks.

Ornstein et al. measured the children's memories by first asking them open-ended questions such as "Tell me what happened during your check-up". More detailed questions were then asked, such as "Did the doctor check any parts of your face? and "Did he/she check your eyes?" Misleading questions were also asked, involving features of the physical examination that had not been included in an individual child's check-up. Ornstein et al. found that children in both age groups showed good recall of the physical examination immediately after it was over, recalling 82% (3-year-olds) and 92% (6-year-olds) of the features respectively. Both groups showed some forgetting of these features after three weeks had passed, but recall was still highly accurate, being around 71% in the 3-year-olds. Responses to misleading questions were also largely accurate. Children in both age groups were able to correctly reject misleading features most of the time. For the 3-year-olds after a three-week delay, correct denials were made to 60% of the misleading questions, and for the 6-year-olds, to 65% of the misleading questions. Intrusions ("remembering" features that had not in fact occurred) were also at similar levels in the two groups after the three-week delay, being 26% for the 3-year-olds and 32% for the 6-year-olds. Ornstein et al. concluded that young children's recall of a personally experienced event was surprisingly good, supporting the findings obtained by Goodman and her colleagues in their "trailer" paradigm.

A different way of looking at the link between children's knowledge of routine, script-like information and their eye-witness recall is to investigate whether children who have *more* episodic knowledge about a certain class of events are *less* likely to demonstrate susceptibility effects. According to this hypothesis, the possession of prior knowledge about a class of events should result in the formation of more stable memories, and these more stable memories should be less susceptible to the influence of leading questions. This hypothesis can be examined by studying the role of knowledge in children's memories, and the more recent work of Ornstein and his colleagues provides a good example of such research.

Clubb, Nida, Merritt, and Ornstein (1993) looked at whether children's memories of what happens when you visit the doctor were linked to their knowledge and understanding of what happens during routine pediatric examinations. The children, who were 5-year-olds, were interviewed about their knowledge of physical examinations using open-ended questions like "Tell me what happens when you go to the doctor". They were then asked a series of yes-no probe questions such as "Does the doctor check your heart?". Clubb et al. found that the majority of the children remembered highly salient features such as having an injection (64%), having the doctor listen to your heart (64%), and having your mouth checked (55%). Few children remembered features such as having a wrist check (5%). These percentages were then taken as an index of knowledge. A different group of 5-year-olds provided the eye-witness memory scores. This group of children had been interviewed previously about a real visit to the doctor as part of an earlier study. Clubb et al. checked the percentages of these children who had spontaneously recalled the same features (injection, heart check, mouth check etc.) either immediately or one, three, or six weeks following their real examination. These "eye-witness memory" numbers were then correlated with the corresponding knowledge scores obtained from the first group of children.

The researchers found that the correlations between knowledge and memory were highly significant at each delay interval. From this finding, they argued that variability in knowledge in a given domain is associated with corresponding variability in recall. However, the significant correlations obtained by Clubb et al. do not tell us about the *direction* of the relationship between knowledge and memory. It could be that variability in recall determines variability in knowledge, rather than vice versa. The relationship would also be more convincing if it were demonstrated in the *same* children. Nevertheless, the hypothesis that there should be a relationship between episodic knowledge and susceptibility to leading questions seems worth exploring further.

Working memory

Both episodic memory and eye-witness memory are aspects of long-term recall. We also have a memory system for short-term recall, which is called *working* memory.

Working memory is a "workspace" that maintains information temporarily, and at the same time processes this information for use in other cognitive tasks such as reasoning, comprehension, and learning (e.g. Baddeley & Hitch, 1974). The information that is being maintained in working memory may either be new information, or it may be information that has been retrieved from the long-term system.

Working memory has at least three sub-components. These are the central executive, the visuo-spatial sketchpad, and the phonological loop. The central executive is conceived of as a regulatory device which co-ordinates the different working memory activities and allocates resources. The visuo-spatial sketchpad is thought to process and retain visual and spatial information in a visuo-spatial code, and also to hold any verbal information that is being stored as an image. The phonological loop is thought to maintain and process verbal information in the form of speech sounds. It can be conceptualised as a kind of tape-loop lasting 1–2 seconds. Decay in the phonological loop is fairly rapid, and so this verbal information may need to be *refreshed* or *rehearsed* by sub-vocal articulation.

Developmental psychologists have mainly been concerned with the development of the two "slave systems" of the central executive, the visuo-spatial sketchpad and the phonological loop. One influential idea has been that children initially rely on visual codes in short-term memory, and then switch to phonological codes at the age of around 5 years (e.g. Conrad, 1971). The age of this switch has been seen as potentially very important, as it is similar to the age at which Piaget proposed that a fundamental shift occurred in children's logical reasoning abilities (see Chapter 8). In fact, a number of information-processing theories of cognitive development, sometimes called "neo-Piagetian" theories, are loosely based on this temporal co-occurrence. As working memory has a central role in reasoning, comprehension and learning, it seems plausible to argue that the development of working memory must somehow be important for cognitive development in general. However, it is also possible that the development of reasoning, comprehension, and learning *in themselves* lead to improvements and developments in working memory. We will explore these neo-Piagetian theories briefly in the next chapter.

The visuo-spatial sketchpad. Most of the evidence for the idea that children rely on visual memory codes prior to around 5 years of age is indirect. It depends largely on showing that younger children are not susceptible to effects that are related to the use of speech sounds for coding material in working memory. As the presence of these effects is usually taken as evidence for the operation of the phonological loop (see later), the absence of these speech-based effects has been taken to imply that working memory in young children relies on the visuo-spatial sketchpad.

The classic study in this tradition was performed by Conrad (1971). He gave children aged 3–11 years a series of pictures to remember. The pictures had names that either sounded similar (rat, cat, mat, hat, bat, man, bag, tap), or sounded different (girl, bus, train, spoon, fish, horse, clock, hand). The children first learned to play a "matching game" with the pictures. In the matching game, one complete set of pictures was presented face-up in front of the child, and then two or three pictures from a second, duplicate, set were presented for matching. After the children had grasped the idea of matching, the experimental trials began. The experimenter set out the eight cards in the full set (using either the "sounds similar" pictures or the "sounds different" pictures), and then concealed them from view. A sub-set of the duplicate pictures were then presented for matching. The experimenter named each card in the duplicate set, turned the cards face-down, and then re-exposed the full set. The children had to match the face-down cards to the correct pictures.

As adults find names that sound similar more difficult to remember over short periods of time than names that sound different, Conrad expected that the children would find the "sounds similar" picture cards more difficult to match than the "sounds different" picture cards. However, this "phonological confusability" effect in adults arises because adults tend, to code the picture names verbally and then to retain them in the phonological loop using rehearsal. Conrad's argument was that if a phonological confusability effect did not occur in children (i.e. if the children found the "sounds different" cards as difficult to remember as the "sounds similar" cards), then they were using a different memory code to support recall, presumably a pictorial one.

Conrad's results showed that only the younger children showed a "no difference" pattern between the two picture sets (the 3- to 5-year-olds). The memory spans of this age group for the phonologically confusable and non-confusable pictures (measured by the number of pictures correctly recalled) were equivalent. Children aged 6 years and above showed longer memory spans for the "sounds different" picture cards than for the "sounds similar" picture cards, suggesting that they were using rehearsal strategies as a basis for recall. The possibility that the youngest subjects were also rehearsing but were idiosyncratically renaming the pictures prior to recall (e.g. "cat" as "pussy" or "Tibby", thereby effectively converting the "sounds similar" set into a "sounds different" set) was ruled out by the children's spontaneous naming behaviour. The youngest children tended to speak aloud as they performed the task, and made comments like "cat goes with cat" or "cat here". This suggested that young, non-rehearsing children use some form of visual storage to remember visually presented materials.

If short-term storage in younger children is visually based, then visually similar objects should be easily confused in short-term memory, just as phonologically similar names are confused when short-term storage is phonological. This prediction is easily tested by using pictures of objects that look like each other in a memory span task, and then seeing whether visually similar objects are more difficult to remember than visually dissimilar objects. Hitch, Halliday, Schaafstal, and Schraagan (1988) devised a picture confusion memory task of this type. Their visually similar set of pictures consisted of pictures of a nail, bat, key, spade, comb, saw, fork, and pen. Their visually dissimilar set of control pictures consisted of pictures of a doll, bath, glove, spoon, belt, cake, leaf, and pig. An additional set of visually dissimilar pictures that had long names was also used in the task. This set comprised an elephant, kangaroo, aeroplane, banana, piano, policeman, butterfly, and umbrella. Hitch et al. then compared 5- and 10-year-old children's memory for these pictures of familiar objects.

Hitch et al.'s memory task was similar to Conrad's, except that no matching was required. Instead, the experimenters presented each picture face-up, and then turned it over, telling the child that they would have to repeat the names of the pictures in the order in which they were shown. The 5-year-olds were given sequences of three pictures, and the 10-year-olds were given sequences of five pictures. Hitch et al. argued that, if the children were using

rehearsal to remember the order of the pictures, then they should find the pictures with long names more difficult to recall than the visually similar pictures and the control pictures. On the other hand, if the children were using visual memory strategies, then they should find the visually similar pictures the most difficult set to recall. Hitch et al. found that, for the 10-year-olds, the pictures with long names were the most difficult to recall. For the 5-year-olds, the visually similar pictures were the most difficult to recall, although there was a small effect of word length. Hitch et al. concluded that the tendency to use visual working memory becomes less pervasive as memory development proceeds.

All of these experiments, however, have studied the retention of *visually presented* items. Rather than showing that children rely on visual memory codes prior to around 5 years of age, it may be that younger children tend to rely on visual codes in working memory *when they are given visual information to remember*. This means that experimenters may be documenting a tendency in younger children to attempt to retain information in the modality in which it is presented, rather than a tendency to rely on visual memory codes. Older children may translate visually presented material into a speech code. The visual working memory effects observed by Conrad and by Hitch et al. may thus be due to children's failure to select a particular mnemonic strategy, rather than to an early reliance on visuo-spatial memory codes. We will discuss this possibility further in the next section.

Meanwhile, it is interesting to note that deaf children continue to rely heavily on visuo-spatial codes in memory, even for material that hearing children code linguistically. O'Connor and Hermelin (1973) devised a spatial span task to measure short-term recall in the deaf. In this task, three digits were presented successively on a screen, appearing in three different windows in a horizontal visual array (e.g. 5, 2, 7). The left-right order did not always correspond to the temporal-sequential order of presentation. For example, the first digit to appear might be the one in the middle window, the second the one in the right-hand window, and the third the one in the left-hand window, giving a left-right order of 7, 5, 2. O'Connor and Hermelin found that whereas the hearing children tended to recall the digits in their *temporal* order of appearance (5, 2, 7), the deaf children recalled them in the *spatial* order of their (left–right) appearance (7, 5, 2). This suggests that the hearing children were rehearsing the digits verbally in order to remember them, while the deaf children were representing the digits as visual images.

The phonological loop. Activity in the phonological loop is usually measured by the presence of effects that are related to the use of speech sounds for coding material. For example, it is more difficult to remember words that sound similar over a short period of time (bat, cat, hat, rat, tap, mat) than words that do not. This is called the "phonological confusability" or "phonological similarity" effect. Similarly, long words like "bicycle, umbrella, banana, elephant" take longer to rehearse than short words like "egg, pig, car, boy", and so more short than long words can be retained in working memory. This is called the "word length" effect.

The number of items that can be retained in the phonological loop over a short period of time is used to provide a measure of an individual's "memory span". Memory span gives a measure of working memory capacity, and increases with age. As span length differs with different types of material, however, such as long vs. short words (and with background knowledge, see Schneider & Bjorklund, in press), most measures of memory span are based on the retention of items like digits which are assumed to be equally familiar to all subjects. However, number words vary in length in different languages. This can lead to different estimates of memory span in children of the same age who speak different languages. Chinese children have much longer digit spans than English children, because the Chinese number words are much shorter than the English number words (e.g. Chen & Stevenson, 1988). Welsh children have shorter digit spans than American children, as the Welsh number words are longer than the English number words. As memory span is usually one of the things that is measured in IQ tests, at one time it was wrongly thought that Welsh children had lower IQs than American children! Upon closer investigation, it was found that the IQ difference was an artifact of systematically lower Welsh scores on the digit span component of the test (Ellis & Hennelley 1980).

Another important component of working memory capacity is speech rate or articulation rate, which also affects memory span. Children who articulate slowly tend to have shorter memory spans than children who can articulate more quickly, presumably because it takes them longer to rehearse individual items. Speech rate also increases with age. Because of this, it has been proposed that the development of memory span with age is entirely accounted for by developmental increases in speech rate. As older children speak more quickly than younger children, they can rehearse more information during the 1–2 seconds available in the phonological loop, and can thus remember more items than the younger children, giving them longer memory spans.

As required by this proposal, speech rate and memory span are highly correlated. This connection was established in a series of studies by Hulme and his colleagues, using a word repetition task (e.g. Hulme, Thomson, Muir, & Lawrence, 1984; Hulme & Tordoff, 1989). For example, in Hulme et al. (1984), children aged 4, 7, and 10 years and adults were given a pair of words, such as "apple, tiger", to repeat as quickly as they could. The number of words produced per second provided the measure of speech rate. The results showed that speech rate was linearly related to memory span: increases in memory span were always accompanied by increases in speech rate across age. Furthermore, the relation between recall and speech rate was constant across different word lengths. When the children's memory spans for long (e.g. helicopter, kangaroo), short (e.g. egg, bus) and medium-length (e.g., rocket, monkey) words was compared, Hulme et al. found that the relationship between recall and speech rate was constant across age. This shows that, at any age, subjects can recall as much as they can say in a fixed time interval (about 1.5 seconds). Hulme et al. argued that individuals with higher speech rates could rehearse information more quickly, and could thus remember it better.

When Hitch, Halliday, Dodd, and Littler (1989) replicated Hulme et al.'s work using pictures instead of words, however, the results were rather different. With *visual* presentation of the names to be remembered, only the 10-year-olds showed a correlation between speech rate and memory span, as only this group appeared to spontaneously rehearse the visual inputs. With auditory presentation, all age groups showed the correlation. Thus speech rate *does* govern the number of items that can be retained in working memory, but only when the items to be remembered are presented in speech form. This is, of course, in keeping with the findings of Conrad (1971) and Hitch et al. (1988) that we discussed earlier. Younger children appear to prefer to maintain visually presented information by using a visuo-spatial code, whereas older children spontaneously translate visual inputs into a speech code.

Henry and Millar (1993) explain this developmental pattern by proposing that rehearsal develops out of naming behaviour. They point out that younger children are frequently called upon to use naming to translate visual or tactile material into a verbal form, particularly as they enter school and rely increasingly on verbal strategies for learning and retaining information. Henry and Millar suggest that children's increasing speed and facility with naming leads to the discovery of rehearsal, and that the development of rehearsal probably explains the development of memory span after the age of about 7 years. The development of memory span prior to this point depends both on naming and on the child's familiarity with the items to be remembered. Items that are highly familiar in long-term (semantic) memory are easier to store and to retrieve. Highly familiar items also have well-specified phonological representations in the mental lexicon, and as the speech output system is used in memory span tasks for both rehearsal and recall, words with better specified representations will require less processing and can be articulated faster (see also Roodenrys, Hulme, & Brown, 1993). According to this view, although speech rate is related to the development of memory span, speech rate is also determined by the quality of a child's phonological representations.

Henry and Millar's proposal is an interesting one, as it suggests that the *development* of working memory is intimately related to the development of long-term or semantic memory. According to their argument, the key variable that affects the capacity of working memory, speech rate, is dependent on the development of well specified phonological representations in semantic memory. As we saw earlier (Chapter 3), the development of semantic memory is linked to conceptual and linguistic development. Items that have well specified phonological representations are those that are highly familiar, easily accessed and often retrieved for speech. Thus Henry and Millar's view implies that the conventional conceptual distinctions between short-term and long-term memory may be only partially applicable as far as the *development* of memory is concerned. Although children do use the phonological loop

to maintain information over short periods of time, just like adults, its utilisation appears to be gradual, depending on task features (e.g. verbal vs. pictorial input) as well as the age of the child. Nevertheless, the concept of a short-term "workspace" that enables the active processing of material on a moment-to-moment basis has made an important contribution to recent theories of cognitive development based on the notion of processing capacity, as we will see in Chapter 6.

Executive processes. The third component of working memory hypothesised by Baddeley and Hitch is the central executive, which is said to play a central role in cognition via planning and monitoring cognitive activity. The central executive is said to control the transmission of information among different parts of the cognitive system, to monitor the functioning and co-ordination of the phonological loop and the visuo-spatial sketchpad, and to retrieve information from long-term memory. Although it is difficult to study the central executive directly, it has been suggested that central executive activities are located in the frontal cortex. Tasks that measure frontal cortex involvement may thus also provide an index of "executive function".

We already know from Chapter 2 that the frontal cortex contains primary motor cortex, which is involved in the planning and control of movement. As discussed in that chapter, some of the errors made by infants (such as the A-not-B search error) that were thought to show cognitive confusions actually derive from immaturities in this neural system. These frontal immaturities lead to inappropriate searching behaviour because the infants are unable to inhibit a predominant action tendency to search at A, and not because of any misconceptions about where to look for hidden objects (e.g. Diamond, 1991). Similar arguments can be made about apparent cognitive confusions in young children. As the frontal cortex is also the site of higher thought processes such as planning and monitoring cognitive activity and abstract reasoning, and as young children are not always very good at planning and monitoring their cognitive activities, some developmental psychologists have suggested that this developmental deficiency may reflect the fact that the frontal cortex is still maturing. The idea that young children may have "executive deficits" has been studied by examining whether children make the kind of "executive errors" that are characteristic of adults who have injuries to the frontal cortex.

A typical "executive error" seen in adults with frontal cortex damage is perseverative card sorting. As discussed earlier (Chapter 2), if a frontal patient has been sorting a pack of cards according to a particular rule (e.g. colour) and the sorting rule is changed (e.g. to shape), then the patient finds it very difficult to change his sorting rule, and continues to sort the cards according to colour. However, at the same time as making these consistent sorting errors, the patient tells the experimenter "this is wrong, and this is wrong ..." (Diamond, 1988). It is as though the patient's behaviour is under the control of his previous action (he is unable to inhibit the "prepotent" tendency to search by the old rule), rather than under the control of his conscious intent. Clinical measures of card sorting behaviour, such as the neuropsychological test called the Wisconsin Card Sorting Test, typically require the patients to participate in many sorting trials, with a shift in sorting principle after each block of 10 trials. Patients with frontal lesions are found to make significantly more sorting errors and to achieve significantly fewer shifts than control subjects on the card sorting task. Pennington (1994) has argued that "executive errors" occur when behaviour is controlled by salient features of the environment, including prior actions, rather than by an appropriate rule held in mind.

A growing number of developmental psychologists have argued that some of the logical errors made by children at 3–4 years and at 6–7 years of age may be explained as "executive failures" (e.g. Russell, 1996). The idea is that children have inadequate strategic control over their mental processes. For example, Russell argues that at 3–4 years this inadequate strategic control can lead to failure on "theory of mind" tasks, because children cannot think "explicitly and at will" about mental processes. Similarly, at 6–7 years, this inadequate strategic control can lead to failure on Piagetian "conservation" tasks, because children cannot think "explicitly and at will" about certain properties of the objects that are being conserved (Russell, 1996, pp. 215, 222).

Although there is relatively little direct evidence for an "executive deficit" in 3-to 4-year-old children, recent work by Frye and Zelazo and their colleagues has shown that children of this age do experience difficulty in rule shifting, just like frontal patients. For example, Frye, Zelazo, and Palfai (1995) asked children aged 3, 4, and 5 years to sort a set of cards into two trays on the basis of either shape or colour. Each card depicted a single shape, a red triangle, a blue triangle, a red circle or a blue circle. To play the "colour game", the children were told that all the red ones went into one tray, and all the blue ones went into the other. The instructions were quite explicit: "We don't put any red ones in that box. No way! We put all the red ones over here, and only blue ones go over there. This is the colour game ...". After training in *both* games (colour and shape), the children were tested for their ability to shift their sorting strategy (e.g. from colour *to* shape) over three sets of five trials. On the first set of five trials, the children were given test cards to sort according to colour. Having sorted this set, they were then told "Okay, now we're going to play a different game, the 'shape game'. You have to pay attention". Five .new test cards were then presented to sort by shape. Finally, five consecutive switching trials were administered, during which the children had to sort according to a new rule (shape or colour) on each trial. Again, the instructions were quite explicit: "Okay, now we're going to switch again and play a different game, the colour game. You have to pay attention".

Frye et al. found that the 3-and 4-year-olds in their study experienced great difficulty in shifting their sorting strategy on the second set of five trials despite the explicit instructions from the experimenter. They typically sorted the cards correctly for the first five trials, and then continued to sort by colour (or shape) for the second five trials, perse-veratively using the wrong rule. Performance on the final set of five trials, which required consecutive switching, was at chance level. In contrast, the older children (5-year-olds) were able to switch sorting rule in the second set of five trials, and were also able to switch sorting rule on a trial-by-trial basis during the last set of five trials. They did not show the "executive failures" characteristic of the younger children.

In order to make sure that the difficulties of the 3-and 4-year-olds were not due to the use of abstract and perhaps unfamiliar geometric shapes, Frye et al. carried out a similar card sorting experiment using pictures of red and blue boats and red and blue rabbits. The children were again required to sort the cards first according to one rule, then according to a second rule, and finally to alternate between the two rules on the last set of trials. Essentially the same results were found as with the geometric shapes, although the 4-year-olds proved to be better at switching their sorting rule with the more familiar dimensions of boats and rabbits. Frye et al. also checked that the children's difficulties were not due to the use of the dimensions of shape and colour *per se,* by devising card sorting tasks based on rules about number and size. Again, essentially the same results were found, with 3-and 4-year-olds showing difficulties when required to switch their sorting rule.

On the basis of these findings, Frye et al. argued that children become able to make a judgement on one dimension while ignoring another between 3 and 5 years of age. Frye et al.'s results can also be explained within the "executive failure" account, by arguing that children cannot inhibit a prepotent tendency to use the pre-switch rule at will, even though the post-switch rule is known to them. In order to test the "executive failure" interpretation of Frye et al.'s results, we need evidence that the post-switch rules are indeed available to the younger children.

This evidence has been provided in a replication of the original card sorting study using shape and colour rules with pictures of flowers and cars (Zelazo, Frye, & Rapus, 1996). In this replication, Zelazo et al. found that 89% of the 3-year-olds who failed to use the new rule on the post-switch trials could verbally report the new rule. For example, when asked "Where do the cars go in the shape game? Where do the flowers go?" the children would point to the correct boxes, and then immediately sort according to the colour rule when told "Play the shape game. Here's a flower. Where does it go?". Similar results were found even when the children received only one pre-switch trial. These findings suggest that 3-year-olds fail to use post-switch rules despite knowing these rules and despite having insufficient experience with pre-switch rules to build up a habit to sort on one dimension only.

A complementary view of the role of the frontal cortex in cognitive development has been put forward by Dempster (1991). Dempster argues that intelligence cannot be understood without reference to *inhibitory* processes in the frontal cortex, and that individual differences in inhibitory processes show how efficient the frontal cortex is in different individuals. He suggests that the critical aspect of many "frontal" tasks like card sorting is that these tasks require the suppression of task-*irrelevant* information for effective performance. In Frye et al.'s paradigm, this would mean suppressing the colour rule when asked to begin

sorting the cards on the basis of the shape rule. Impaired inhibitory functioning could thus be the explanation for the children's susceptibility to interference.

As the frontal cortex is still developing in young children, and as children find clinical versions of card sorting tasks very difficult until the age of around 12 years (with children suffering from attention deficit disorders with hyperactivity showing particular problems), Dempster argues that inhibitory processes are a neglected dimension of cognitive development. According to Dempster's views, individual differences in frontal inhibitory activity should be correlated with individual differences in cognitive development, and with performance on "executive" tasks. This suggestion is consistent with the evidence discussed at the end of Chapter 1 concerning the predictive power of infant habituation and recognition memory for later cognitive development. As noted, McCall and Carriger (1993) argued that this predictive relationship arose because infant habituation and recognition memory measures provided an index of individual differences in the ability to *inhibit* responding to familiar stimuli. Although no-one has yet linked this argument to performance on executive tasks, Dempster's suggestions would seem to be important research questions for future work on the development of "executive functions".

Dempster's views concerning the relative neglect of inhibitory processes are closely related to the views of those who argue that the mechanisms underlying the development of selective attention should also receive greater emphasis in studies of cognitive development (e.g. Lane & Pearson, 1982). The development of selective attention requires the active *inhibition* of irrelevant stimuli as well as habituation to them. Although the habituation mechanisms of attention appear to be functioning as well in children as in adults, the inhibition mechanisms do not (Tipper, Bourque, Anderson, & Brehaut, 1989). However, the remarkable paucity of studies on the development of attention means that it is too early to draw any useful conclusions about individual differences in selective attention and individual differences in cognitive development.

SUMMARY

This survey of some of the different types of memory that can be measured in children has shown that, while some memory systems develop with age, others do not. Little developmental change was found in recognition memory and in implicit memory, while large developmental changes were found to occur in episodic memory, working memory, and semantic memory (see also Chapter 3). The different developmental trajectories of these different memory systems can be explained by the fact that the development of memory cannot be isolated from the development of other cognitive processes. The knowledge structures that young children bring with them to memory tasks play an important role in determining what is remembered, and such knowledge structures are important for organising episodic memory and semantic memory, and for increasing the efficiency of working memory. The memory systems that *develop* are thus characterised by the fact that they benefit from the increasing sophistication of other cognitive processes. In contrast, recognition memory and implicit memory are more automatic perceptual learning systems, and are relatively unaffected by the development of other processes.

The developmental changes in episodic and semantic memory in turn seem to explain some of the developments seen in other memory systems, such as the decrease in suggestibility found in eye-witness memory and the decline in "infantile amnesia". Older children are less likely than younger children to be susceptible to leading questions that cause them to falsely recall events that never took place, and this decline in susceptibilty seems to be related to the development of scripts and to the degree of children's episodic knowledge about the events being remembered. Similarly, the absence of infantile amnesia after the age of around 3 years may be linked to the development of a framework for storing and recounting events. Once abstract knowledge structures are available for describing the causal and temporal sequences of the events that constitute episodic memory, amnesia is no longer found. We also saw that the increase in working memory capacity (memory span) found with age may result in part from the development of semantic memory. The availability of long-term memory representations of items seems to facilitate short-term memory performance. The *development* of short-term and long-term storage systems may thus be intimately linked, even though when measured in adults the two memory systems appear to be distinct. However, the development of the executive component of working memory may depend on quite different factors. Rather than being consequent on the development of other aspects of the memory system, the development of the central executive may depend on neural development and the maturation of the frontal cortex.

Desperately Seeking Memories of the First Few Years of Childhood

The Reality of Early Memories

ELIZABETH F. LOFTUS

How far back into their childhoods can people remember? Previous research suggests that people's earliest memories date back to the ages of 3 or 4 years. J. A. Usher and U. Neisser (1993, this issue) reported that some events, like the birth of a sibling and a planned hospitalization, can be readily remembered if they occurred at age 2. However, the bits and pieces of such memories that were obtained in their research may not be indicative of genuine episodic memory. An alternative hypothesis is that these apparent memories are the result of educated guesses, general knowledge of what must have been, or external information acquired after the age of 2.

In 1963, President Kennedy was assassinated and most of us who were older than 8 at the time remember something about where we were when we learned the news. Virtually none of us who were younger than 3 can remember (Winograd & Killinger, 1983). What if we had known him personally? Would memory be different? Kennedy's son, John, was not quite 3 when his father died, and his sister Caroline was 5. On the basis of current conceptions of childhood amnesia (the early period in our infancy from which nothing is remembered), Caroline might be expected to have some memories of her father whereas John might be expected not to. Yet John claims he remembers his father sneaking gum to the kids because their mother would not allow it. Does he truly remember? If he does remember, is there one occasion in particular that he remembers, or is it a generalized script that he recalls? Childhood amnesia, or the earliest age at which an event is recalled, is about the recollection of specific episodes from our past.

Usher and Neisser (1993, this issue) would like to revise the way we think about childhood amnesia. Instead of the current view that our earliest episodic memories date back to the age of 3 or 3.5 years, these investigators suggest that some specific events can be remembered by adults even if they were 2 years old at the time they happened. Already these results are being accepted at face value as mandating a change in the way we think about childhood amnesia. Citing the Usher and Neisser findings, one sure-to-be-widely-cited Psychological Bulletin article accepts them wholeheartedly: "The offset of infantile amnesia occurs consistently earlier than previously thought (i.e., 2 years instead of 3)" and "there does appear to be solid evidence … that memories are available for many individuals from the age of 2 years" (Howe & Courage, 1993, p. 315).

The Usher and Neisser (1993) research has many attractive features. But before psychologists rush too quickly to revise their thinking about childhood amnesia, not to mention their textbooks, it is worth critically examining their findings to determine whether such revision might not be premature.

THE CURRENT VIEW OF CHILDHOOD AMNESIA

It is well known that humans experience a poverty of recollections of their first several years in life. Freud (1905/1953) identified the phenomenon in some of his earliest writings: "What I have in mind is the peculiar amnesia which, ... hides the earliest beginnings of the childhood up to their sixth or eighth year" (p. 174). Subsequent investigators would say that Freud's suggestion about the 6th year misses the mark. Most studies of childhood amnesia suggest that people's earliest recollection does not date back before the age of about 3 or 4 (Kihlstrom & Harackiewicz, 1982; Pillemer & White, 1989). One study showed that few subjects who were younger than 3 recalled any information about where they were when they heard about the Kennedy assassination (Winograd & Killinger, 1983). These are the kinds of studies that support the offset of childhood amnesia as being about the age of 3 or 4.

Usher and Neisser (1993) reviewed the earlier research on childhood amnesia in ample detail. They devoted a good deal of attention to a study by Sheingold and Tenney (1982) on adults' recollections of the birth of a younger sibling, given that their own study used the same targeted recall procedure in an adapted and modified form. In the earlier study, adults who experienced the birth of a younger sibling when they were age 1 and older were questioned. The adults answered 20 questions (e.g., "Who took care of you when your mother was in the hospital?"). Later the mothers of the adults were contacted to "verify" the answers of the older sibling. The investigators concluded that virtually no births were remembered by subjects who were younger than 3 at the time. In the words of Sheingold and Tenney, "Our data point to the period between three and four as being critical for the ability to remember a sibling birth" (p. 211).

THE USHER AND NEISSER (1993) STUDY

On the basis of data collected using a procedure similar to that of Sheingold and Tenney (1982), Usher and Neisser (1993) would have us believe that some people have a memory for the birth of a sibling that occurred at age 2. People also allegedly have memories for a hospitalization that occurred at age 2. Why an estimate that is so much earlier than the one proffered by Sheingold and Tenney? Is the earlier estimate justified?

To answer these questions, we need to scrutinize the new data carefully. In this study, adults (college students) tried to remember one of four target events that occurred when they were young. The birth of a sibling and a family move were recalled by adults who would have been ages 1 thru 5 at the time they happened. A childhood hospitalization for a planned surgical procedure (e.g., tonsillectomy) and the death of a family member were recalled by adults who would have been ages 2 through 5 when they happened. Usher and Neisser (1993) claim that the offset of childhood amnesia is age 2 for the birth of a sibling and for the hospitalization and age 3 for a death in the family or a family move. In thinking about this conclusion, it is important to keep in mind that "age 2" means anywhere between 2.0 and 2.99 years. Thus the events being remembered by the fraction of adults who claim to remember could have been occurring much closer to age 3 than to age 2. Usher and Neisser make this point, but without emphasis it is likely to get lost in the secondary source reports of their results. Still, we can ask whether their data warrant the conclusion that people can remember a sibling birth that happened prior to the age of 3.

In the Usher and Neisser (1993) study subjects tried to answer 17 questions about a sibling birth. What criterion shall we use to say that someone remembers? The strict criterion used by Usher and Neisser is that subjects could answer at least three of the questions posed. Close to 60% of their adults who were age 2 at the time their sibling was born satisfied this criterion. The mean recall score was .30, or about five items.

We must now ask what it means to answer three questions of the 17 asked. The first issue likely to enter a critic's mind is whether the answers are accurate. To address this issue, the investigators contacted the subjects' mothers and two thirds of the mothers who were contacted replied. The mothers judged the accuracy of their child's answers by indicating for each answer whether the mother's memory matched the child's, whether the two memories involved different aspects of the event, whether the child's memory could have been accurate even if it differed from the mother's, or whether the child was definitely inaccurate. Unfortunately, the accuracy data are not broken down separately for the four events, they are aggregated. Collapsed across memories for the four target events, the most common response given by the mothers was that the memory matched (61%), and claims that the child was inaccurate were not that common (12%). Usher and Neisser want to conclude that "most responses were judged to be accurate" (p. 162).

There are problems with this conclusion. First, we do not know how accurate the responses are for the specific questions about sibling birth. There is at least one question that the mother could not have had first-hand knowledge of ("What did you do right after your mother left?") and so judgments about accuracy seem particularly suspicious.

Second, the mother's responses necessarily involve a retrospective account from an event that occurred two decades earlier. How reliable are these memories? Finally, where is consideration of the motivational characteristics of the response? How many mothers feel completely comfortable even thinking, let alone telling their child's professor, that their child is dead wrong?

Apart from whether the answers are correct, another critical issue is this: To what extent are these answers subjects gave genuine episodic memories? A close examination of the particular questions posed to subjects reveals that some of them can be answered with an educated guess, and some can be answered with general knowledge as opposed to memory. Can you guess the answer to the question "Where were you the first time you saw the baby?" (At home? At the hospital?) How about "What was the baby doing?" (Sleeping? Crying? Looking?). If the subject had a nanny during the early years of life, is "Nanny" not the likely answer to the questions "Who took care of you while your mother was in the hospital?" and "Who was at home with you when they came home (from the hospital)?" The subject could readily achieve a score of 2 or 3 from educated guesses and general-knowledge. In short, it would be relatively easy to answer correctly some of the questions posed without relying on actual memory.

But why then are so few questions answered by the subjects who were age 1 at the time of their sibling's birth? Whereas nearly 60% of adults who were 2 at the time satisfied the recall criterion, only one fourth of those who were 1 at the time satisfied this criterion. Does this mean, as Usher and Neisser (1993) suggest, that memory occurs for age-2 events but not for age-1 events? Certainly this conclusion is tempting, because if subjects are accurately guessing or using general knowledge for the age-2 event, why would they not also do it for the age-1 event? But perhaps the pressure to answer is somewhat different. If subjects who were 1 at the time have an intuition that they should not be able to remember anything ("How would anyone be expected to remember that?"), they may not feel any pressure to answer. On the other hand, some subjects who were 2 at the time might have an intuition that they should or might be able to answer, and thus they might feel some pressure to go ahead and attempt to answer some of the questions. Pressure can lead to answers that are plausible and that subsequently go unchallenged by motivated mothers, producing the appearance of memory.

This discussion also needs to at least touch on the role of postevent rehearsal. More than 90% of the subjects reported that they had some source of external information in forms such as photographs, slides, videos, or family stories. It is possible that photographs of the newborn sibling that were in the house throughout the subject's life provided the information for both subject and mother to answer the question "What was the baby wearing?" Perhaps family stories provided new information that affected the subsequent memory. Of 61 subjects who answered about a sibling birth, 49 (80%) reported hearing family stories, which was the most common source of external information. This is not surprising, and this makes us wonder what role these stories play in enhancing or creating memories at a time later than the sibling's birth. There is one puzzling finding about external information: Subjects who remember family stories or photographs about sibling births that occurred at ages 1 or 2 recalled less than subjects who did not remember this external information. The reverse was true for siblings born when the subject was age 4–5; in these cases those who remembered family stories or photographs remembered more than those who did not. There are so few subjects who report no external information at all that it is difficult to know what to make of these data. Usher and Neisser infer that external information is not responsible for the recall of early memories, but this has not been unequivocally shown. Perhaps subjects who clearly remember the photographs or family stories about age-1 or age-2 events attribute what memory they have to the external information rather than to being a genuine memory of their own. Put another way, they have "memories" of a sort, but attribute them to this other source so they do not label them as genuine memories.

Sheingold and Tenney (1982) claimed that subjects do not remember sibling births that occurred earlier than age 3. In their research, only 3 of the 22 births occurring before the age of 3 could allegedly be remembered. In two cases, the subject was in the last quarter of the 2nd year, which gives us another opportunity to emphasize that people will sometimes talk about age 2 when they mean "almost 3." (The third case was an individual who admitted she had been told rather than remembered much of what she reported.) The median recall score was 0, as compared with a recall score of .30 (five items) for the Usher and Neisser (1993) subjects who were 2 at the time. Why virtually no memories in the earlier study, but some memories in the present one? It is hard to know. The earlier study involved 20 questions compared with 17 in the later study. The scoring criteria for an adequate answer was different. For example, in the Sheingold and Tenney study subjects had to say something specific. The question "What presents did the baby get?" and "Did you get any presents at the time?" had to be answered with more than simply "toys" or "clothes." An answer provided by the subject any place in the questionnaire could count, even if not given to the immediate question. Usher and Neisser apparently did not use these criteria. Then there is the difference pointed out by Usher and Neisser that the earlier study did not confine data collection to subjects who were instructed to recall only the most recent sibling birth; their study did. This methodological feature ensured that the subject did not have more recent births that might interfere with the recall of earlier ones, thus avoiding a retroactive interference problem.

EARLY MEMORIES OF OTHER EVENTS

This discussion has deliberately focused on the sibling birth because this is an event about which the most complete data were collected, and the authors report memories for events occurring at age 2. The demonstration of memories at age 2, but not age 1, is important, although, as noted, it is open to additional interpretation. The planned hospitalization is the other event about which early memory was presumably found, but it too is open to many of the considerations raised. Why did these two events show early memory (before age 3) whereas death in the family and family move did not? Cross-event comparisons must be made with caution. One difference might lie in the preevent or postevent activity. The birth of a sibling and

a planned hospitalization might be something that the family would talk about a great deal. A death in the family might not receive such extensive discussion, particularly if the death were unexpected. Moreover, the questions that were asked of a subject about a death in the family were obviously different from the ones asked about a sibling birth. For one thing, there were only 9 questions about the death, as opposed to 17 about the sibling birth. In comparing recall scores, we may be comparing apples and oranges (or, more appropriately, comparing losses to gains). Were the questions about the loss harder to answer than the ones about the gain? Were they harder to guess? Were they harder to answer by reliance on general knowledge?

CONCLUSION

Usher and Neisser are to be congratulated for conducting research with many admirable attributes on the difficult topic of childhood amnesia. They have studied multiple childhood events, not just one. They attempted to verify the childhood memories through parental agreement, however imperfect this method may be. They obtained information about sources of external information that could have influenced their subjects' recollection. Unfortunately, these measures too depended on less-than-trustworthy retrospection. From the collected data, they infer that the offset of childhood amnesia depends on the type of event being recalled. They conclude that the birth of a younger sibling or a planned hospitalization can be recalled from age 2. However, they fail to fully appreciate the alternative hypotheses for their subjects' reports, namely that the apparent memories are the result of educated guesses, general knowledge of what must have been, or external information acquired after age 2 (that could have occurred despite subjects' admissions or denials). What about people who never had a younger sibling or a hospitalization? Do those individuals live their lives with an autobiographical memory that contains a year's fewer memories?

Childhood amnesia is a fact of life, whether its offset is age 3 or 4, or 2 or 5. Although demonstrated in a variety of ways, its theoretical explanation has eluded us. Is the impairment in recollection from the first few years retrieval based? That is, does the mind hold the information but the information is simply difficult to access? Or is the impairment storage based? That is, did the mind once hold the information but no longer holds it? If evidence is found for storage-based impairment, the next question to be answered is how this process should be characterized. Does it principally involve a mechanism of trace destruction, trace fading, reorganization, or what? (Brainerd & Ornstein, 1991; Brainerd, Reyna, Howe, & Kingma, 1990; Wetzler & Sweeney, 1986). These possible cognitive mechanisms need to be explored to determine to what degree each is important in understanding childhood amnesia.

REFERENCES

Brainerd, C., & Ornstein, P. A. (1991). Children's memory for witnessed events. In J. Doris (Ed.), *The suggestibility of children's recollections* (pp. 10–20). Washington, DC: American Psychological Association.

Brainerd, C. J., Reyna, V. E, Howe, M. L., & Kingma, J. (1990). The development of forgetting and reminiscence. *Monographs of the Society for Research in Child Development, 55*(3), Whole No. 222).

Freud, S. (1953). Three essays on the theory of sexuality. In J. Strachey (Ed. and Trans.) *The standard edition of the complete psychological works of Sigmund Freud* (Vol. 7, pp. 135–243). London: Hogarth Press. (Original work published 1905).

Howe, M. L., & Courage, M. L. (1993). On resolving the enigma of infantile amnesia. *Psychological Bulletin, 113*, 305–326.

Kihlstrom, J. F., & Harackiewicz, J. M. (1982). The earliest recollection: A new survey. *Journal of Personality, 50*(2), 134–138.

Pillemer, D. B., & White, S. H. (1989). Childhood events recalled by children and adults. In H. W. Reese (Ed.), *Advances in child development and behavior* (Vol. 21, pp. 297–340). San Diego, CA: Academic Press.

Sheingold, K., & Tenney, Y. J. (1982). Memory for a salient childhood event. In U. Neisser (Ed.), *Memory observed* (pp. 201–212). New York: Freeman.

Usher, J. A., & Neisser, U. (1993). Childhood amnesia and the beginnings of memory for four early life events. *Journal of Experimental Psychology: General, 122*, 155–165.

Wetzler, S. E., & Sweeney, J. A. (1986). Childhood amnesia: An empirical demonstration. In D. C. Rubin (Ed.), *Autobiographical memory* (pp. 191–201). Cambridge, England: Cambridge University Press.

Winograd, E., & Killinger, W. A., Jr. (1983). Relating age at encoding in early childhood to adult recall: Development of flashbulb memories. *Journal of Experimental Psychology: General, 112*, 413–122.

Long-Term Memory for a Single Infancy Experience

EVE E. PERRIS, NANCY A. MYERS, AND RACHEL K. CLIFTON

Children's memory of a single infant experience was evaluated. Children in the experimental groups ($N = 16$ for 2.5-year-olds; $N = 8$ for 1.5-year-olds) had participated at 6.5 months in a study of auditory localization where they reached in the light and dark for a sounding object. They were reintroduced to the laboratory and the dark procedure they had experienced on that one occasion either 1 or 2 years previously. The first 5 trials were uninstructed; for the remaining 5 trials, children were instructed to find the sounding object. For half of the older group, a potential reminder of the infant procedure was introduced. The original infant rattle was sounded for 3 sec out of reach in the dark one-half hour prior to test trials. Equal numbers of age-matched inexperienced control subjects were also tested. The older children with infant experience reached and grasped the sounding object significantly more overall, and on instructed trials, than age-matched control children. Experienced 2.5-year-olds were also more likely to remain in the testing situation than children in the control group. The reminder facilitated uninstructed performance of the experienced children. Instructions to reach were helpful to all subjects. We conclude that children remembered aspects of a single experience that occurred when they were 6.5 months of age.

Contemporary theorists view memory as a system consisting of at least two levels, differing in terms of time of establishment, organization, and access. Early memories have been described as unconscious sensorimotor routines or associative learnings, heavily dependent upon contextual or affective cues. Later memories are described as conscious or episodic, involving purposeful mental coordination (Schacter & Moscovitch, 1984; White & Pillemer, 1979). Even this sparse theoretical description begins to suggest the possible limits to infant memory.

Psychologists in many domains (e.g., clinical, cognitive, developmental) have long been intrigued by the inaccessibility of early memories. Freud (e.g., 1899/1962) attributed this phenomenon, which he called infantile amnesia, to repression. Another perspective has been that impoverished encoding may result in poorly established traces of earlier experiences that then are exceptionally vulnerable to fading (Brainerd, Kingma, & Howe, 1985; Howe & Hunter, 1986). Other investigators have emphasized neurological, physical, and cognitive growth, as well as changes in social and sensory environments, to explain the loss of these early memories. They hypothesize that older children and adults may be unable to retrieve early memories because of the mismatch between the information encoded during infancy and the current perceptions or strategies used by the individual to retrieve information.

Eve Emmanuel Perris, Nancy Angrist Myers, and Rachel Keen Clifton, "Long-term Memory for a Single Infancy Experience," *Child Development*, vol. 61, no. 6, pp. 1796-1807. Copyright © 1990 by John Wiley & Sons, Inc. Reprinted with permission.

Failure to retrieve early memories may also be due to the lack of original contextual or affective cues, upon which they are so dependent (Campbell & Spear, 1972; Rovee-Collier & Hayne, 1987; White & Pillemer, 1979). In addition, the expression of memory may be constrained by the measures utilized or responses required (Spear, 1984).

To date, little is known empirically about long-term memory for experiences during the first year of life. The evidence of early childhood memories that does exist has been derived primarily from adult self-reports (Dudycha & Dudycha, 1941; Waldfogel, 1948) and parental diaries of their infants' and young children's behavior (Ashmead & Perl-mutter, 1980; Nelson & Ross, 1980). Recently, Rovee-Collier and her colleagues have conducted a systematic series of studies examining the characteristics of long-term memory in 2-, 3-, and 6-month-old infants over delays of up to 1 month (for review, see Rovee-Collier & Hayne, 1987).

Rovee-Collier employs a free-operant conditioning paradigm ("mobile conjugate reinforcement") in which infants' own foot-kicks produce movement in an overhead crib mobile. All infants show retention 24 hours after training; however, 2-month-olds forget after a retention interval of greater than 3 days, 3-month-old infants display gradual forgetting over a 2-week period, and 6-month-olds do not show forgetting until after 14 days, but forgetting is complete by 21 days. Rovee-Collier interprets these differences in retention in terms of retrieval failures due to the changing context of experience attributed to real physical or perceptual changes (e.g., for review, see Rovee-Collier & Hayne, 1987).

To the best of our knowledge, only one study has examined the duration of memory for events during the first year of life over delays substantially greater than a month. Myers, Clifton, and Clarkson (1987) reported that almost-3-year-olds remembered a repeated event that occurred during the first year of life. Five children had participated in a longitudinal study of auditory localization when they were between 6 and 40 weeks of age (Clifton, Muir, Clarkson, Ashmead, & Sherriff, 1985). The same procedure was followed for 15–19 sessions. Two years later, these children, as well as age-matched controls, participated in the original experimental sequence, which involved reaching to sounding objects in the light and in the dark. Myers et al. (1987) reported that the children who had participated

as infants were more likely to interact with the stimulus objects, demonstrating that they retained memory for early action sequences.

There are a number of aspects of the Myers et al. (1987) study that may have been important for memory. First, reaching in the dark is an unusual event conducted in a unique setting. Myers et al. (1987) tested their children in a double-walled sound-deadened chamber that attenuated the background noise to 29 dB (A scale). The infant auditory localization testing was conducted in exactly the same setting. The apparatus, room furniture, and experimenter were also the same as during the previous infancy project. Thus, the entire visual, auditory, and social context was preserved and reinstated for the memory testing. The importance of reinstating the original context of an event has been noted in animal (Balsam & Tomie, 1985; Spear, 1978) and human (Rovee-Collier & Hayne, 1987; Tulving, 1983) research. Similarly, reinstating the unique context in the Myers et al. (1987) study may have been critical for the children's memory retrieval 2 years later.

Another aspect of the Myers et al. (1987) study that may have influenced the children's memory was the extent of their prior experience. The children had been exposed to the experimental procedure and setting 15–19 times as infants. Thus, the event and the action patterns involved became quite familiar to these infants. How important was the repeated exposure to context and procedures for long-term retrieval? Perhaps children remembered the action sequences 2 years later only because they were so well practiced in infancy. In the present study, therefore, we evaluated children's memory of a *single unique event* that was experienced during infancy 1 or 2 years earlier. If encoding in infancy is limited and incomplete, the record of the event might be expected to be weak and rapidly fading. Would the shorter time between event and memory probe then be critical? Even if the unique context of an unusual event is completely reinstated, can children remember an event experienced in infancy only once? If so, what is the nature of the memory of this single experience?

Recognizing the severity of our memory demands, we speculated that even if the original contextual cues were present during testing, children might not remember a single experience 2 years later without additional assistance. Consequently, we introduced two further conditions. Investigators have demonstrated with animals (e.g.,

Campbell & Jaynes, 1966; Spear, 1973), young children (Hoving & Choi, 1972), and infants (e.g., Rovee-Collier & Hayne, 1987) that forgetting can be alleviated if the subject is exposed to a brief reminder of the original context. For instance, Rovee-Collier and her colleagues demonstrated that 3-month-old infants display no signs of retention 2 weeks following training, unless they are exposed for 3 min to noncontingent movement of the original training mobile 24 hours prior to testing (e.g., Rovee-Collier & Hayne, 1987). Similarly, we provided a potential reminder to some of the older children. These children were exposed to the sounding target object in the dark for 3 sec a half hour prior to testing.

We also evaluated the effects of a second manipulation that involved giving instructions to all of the children following the initial memory trials. We encouraged children to try to obtain the sounding object, in order to determine whether explicit elicitation of the action pattern would facilitate memory retrieval. Even if children with prior experience failed to reach spontaneously, with encouragement to engage in the target response they might demonstrate more frequent and accurate behavior than inexperienced children.

METHOD

Subjects

Thirty-two older children (mean age: 2–6; range: 2–4 to 2–9) and 16 younger children (mean age: 1–6; range: 1–4 to 1–7) participated in this experiment. Half of the children in each age group comprised the experimental groups. These children had participated at 6.5 months of age in one of two studies of auditory localization (Clifton, Perris, & Bullinger, 1989; Perris & Clifton, 1988) where they reached in the light and dark for a sounding object. The children had been exposed at that time to the experimental setting and task on only one occasion for approximately 20 min. The remaining children in each age range comprised the control groups. These children were selected to match the experimental subjects in age but to be naive to the experimental procedure.

Children were recruited from published birth announcements via a letter and a follow-up telephone call. Parents were told the task involved auditory localization

and that sounds would be presented to their children in the dark. They were not told the specific procedure, nor what the child was expected to do. Parents of the experimental children were informed that this study was a follow-up of the infant study. They were asked not to discuss the earlier visit with the child and to tell the child only that they were coming to the university to play a game.

Eight younger and 11 older children were tested but failed to complete the session, and three additional children were also eliminated from the sample because of the mother holding the child improperly (2) and experimenter error (1).

Apparatus and Procedure

The apparatus and procedure were essentially those of the previous infant study with a few additional memory probes, as outlined below. Parents brought their children to a laboratory in the psychology building. The parent and child were greeted at the door of a two-room experimental suite by the female experimenter who had conducted the infant studies. The experimenter played with the child in the outer observation room until the child was visibly comfortable. During this warm-up period, parents were asked to sign a consent form allowing their child to participate. The experimenter then escorted the parent and child through the observation room to the inner chamber. The child sat on the parent's lap. The chamber itself was a visually and acoustically unique setting. Its double walls and sound-treated ceiling, wall, and floor surfaces deaden sound and attenuate background noise to 29 dB (A scale). The illumination in the room was dim.

The test session was divided into three separate tasks. Two discrimination tasks (memory probes) were conducted in the light to determine if children retained information about the visual and auditory details of the original target stimulus. The third task, conducted in the dark, replicated the auditory localization procedure used in the earlier infant study. The apparatus consisted of five identical rectangular rattles positioned in a semicircle. A plastic "Sesame Street" Big Bird finger puppet was backed with velcro and attached to the front of each rattle.

Memory probes.—The experimenter knelt on the floor facing the child. As she moved a table in front of the child, she asked first if the child remembered the room, and then, after a pause for any response, "Do you remember playing a game in this room?" Following a reply or short pause, the experimenter informed the child that "We are going to play the game today, but first I am going to show you some toys." The experimenter presented the child five plastic hand toys on a plastic tray. They included the original target object (Big Bird) and four novel toys about the same size (Mickey Mouse, cow, elephant, and cat). The order and position of toy placement on the tray were randomized for each subject. The child was given 20 sec to interact with the toys. The equipment operator in the outer room signaled the experimenter with a click over the intercom to indicate that 20 sec had elapsed. The experimenter then placed the five toys in their original starting positions, and asked the child which toy they thought would be part of the game. Regardless of choice, the experimenter told the child that he or she had "made a very good guess," then added "but (or yes), the Big Bird does something in this game. Can you guess what the Big Bird does in this game?"

After a pause for any response, the experimenter stated that "the Big Bird makes a sound. He makes a sound like one of these." The experimenter then presented three sound stimuli (the rattle used in the original studies and two novel sounds, a bell and a clicker) encased in identical sealed boxes. Each box was sounded once by the experimenter, with order and position of box placement randomized for each subject. When all three boxes had been presented, they were moved simultaneously within the child's reach. The child was given 20 sec to interact with the three boxes. The observer in the outer room timed the presentation and signaled termination. The experimenter then sounded each box again and asked the child to "give me the sound Big Bird makes." The experimenter displayed approval of the child's choice, and informed the child of the correct response. The child was asked to guess what happened next, and the experimenter then reported, "We are going to play the game in the dark."

Dark trials.—The apparatus was moved into view in front of the child, so that he or she was facing the display of five Brazelton-type rattles with the Big Bird finger puppets attached. The rattles were mounted on rods that were positioned at midline (0°) $\pm$ 30° and $\pm$ 60° in a semicircle concave to the child. Each rod was hinged to a vertical post attached to the base of the apparatus, so that movement up and down produced the sound of the rattle. When the rattles were not being activated, the rods were weighted so that they rested in an extreme upward position, putting the rattles out of reach. The base of the apparatus was divided into eight 15° sectors radiating out from the child's body. The boundaries of these sectors were marked off with black chartpak tape.

The rattle was activated in each position once in each of two blocks of five trials. The order of presentation was randomized for each subject. The first five trials were *uninstructed* trials and followed the procedure for dark trials in the original study. Before each trial, the experimenter centered the child's attention at midline by calling his or her name. Children were told that the lights were going to go out but were not told what to expect, and they were not given any type of instruction about what to do. Mothers were instructed to hold their children by the hips at all times to minimize physical contact. Before touching the rod attached to the rattle for that trial, the experimenter pressed a foot pedal switching the room light off and infrared light on. The testing chamber was completely dark, so that nothing in the surrounding environment could be seen. In addition to forcing reliance on the auditory cues, the total darkness also prevented both mother and experimenter from inadvertently guiding the child toward the target, as they could not determine the hand position.

The experimenter then lowered the target rattle to the child's chest level, shook it three times, paused for approximately 2 sec, and then shook it again. This procedure continued for a maximum of 15 sec or until the child grasped and removed the Big Bird from the rattle. At the end of the trial the observer signaled the experimenter, who then turned on the lights for the intertrial interval. If the child had grasped the sounding object in the dark, he or she was allowed to play with it for a few seconds in the light, If the child had not grasped the toy, the experimenter spoke to the child in a playful manner for a few seconds, then initiated the next trial. Following these first five trials, children were given instructions. They were asked to try to "catch the noisy Big Bird in the dark," and given one to three trials in the light to ensure that they understood. The five instructed dark trials, paralleling the uninstructed trials, followed. At the end of the session, each child received a picture book.

All the younger children and one-half of the experimental and control older subjects experienced the test procedure as soon as the apparatus was revealed. The remaining older subjects received a potential reminder: a single presentation of one rattle for 3 sec in the dark, at midline but out of reach. The parent and child were then escorted back out into the observation room, where the experimenter and the child played for 30 min. After this break period, the parent and child were led back into the inner room, and testing in the dark was initiated after the child had comfortably settled into the parent's lap.

A child was included in the sample if all uninstructed trials and at least one of the instructed trials were completed. Only four children (all 2.5-year-olds) failed to complete all of the instructed trials due to fussiness. Three of these children were in the control groups: one child in the reminder condition missed two trials; two children in the no-reminder condition missed one and four instructed trials, respectively. Only one child with previous experience failed to complete the instructed trials; he was in the no-reminder condition and missed three trials.

The entire session was videotaped with an infrared sensitive camera (Panasonic model WV-1850) positioned directly overhead, 130 cm from the top of the apparatus. An infrared light source, also positioned directly overhead, was the only source of light during the dark trials. The video camera signal was fed through a video timer (For. A model VTG-33), into a videocassette recorder (Panasonic VHS NV-8950) located in the outer room. A Sony PVM-122 video monitor in the antechamber enabled the equipment operator to observe the session.

Scoring

Memory probes.—The major function of the memory probes was to determine if the children showed any preference toward the target object and the sound stimulus used in the infant procedure. Measures included latencies to contact the first object and the first sound stimulus, the number of times each object and each sound stimulus were touched, and the cumulative duration of interaction with each object and each sound stimulus.

Dark trials.—Two major dependent variables were defined for the reaching-in-the-dark procedure. A *reach* was the extension of the forearm in a forward motion away from the body, in the direction of the apparatus. A reach may consist of multiple movements (von Hofsten, 1979).

On each trial, only the first arm movement after sound onset was scored. The first reach was considered to be the most important index of localization because it is uncontaminated by what the hand touched or did not touch on previous movements (Fetters & Todd, 1987; von Hofsten, 1979). The second measure defined was a *success*, consisting of the first movement with either hand entering the target area for the activated rattle, which included contacts with the rattle and removal of the Big Bird.

Each hand was scored separately to determine the first sector of 15° entered after trial onset. The rattles at midline and at ± 30° were positioned at the boundary of two adjoining sectors, while the ± 60° rattles were positioned at the outer boundaries of sectors 1 and 8. The sectors that flanked the activated rattle during a particular trial were designated as target sectors for that trial. The target area for a correct response consisted of the width of the rattle and the Big Bird (4 × 8 × 8 cm) plus 4 cm on all sides of the stimulus. Thus, the target area consisted of a total area of 12 x 16 × 16 cm.

The end of the first arm movement was defined as the hand pausing for 40 msec or reversing the direction of movement. Trial onset was defined as the moment the rattle began to sound. The time at which the first movement ended was subtracted from trial onset to determine the latency of the first movement for each arm. It should be noted that this end-point latency includes time to initiate and execute the first movement. The sector entered at the termination of this first movement was also scored. If the object was contacted, the latencies were obtained by subtracting the time of contact from the trial onset time. The end of the trial was defined by the removal of the toy from the rattle or when the room lights were turned on after 15 sec.

All of the data were scored from the videotapes. To determine reliabilities, two independent observers scored 100% of the reaching data and 70% of the latency data. Disagreements were settled by a third observer blind to group identification. Reliability, computed as the number of agreements divided by the sum of agreements and disagreements, was .95 for reaches, .96 for successes, .89 for the latency to initiate a reach, and .91 for the latency to contact. The time span allowed for latency reliability was .40 sec.

Behavior in the Dark

The number of reaches for the rattle in the dark, the number of accurate reaches (successes), and the latencies for initiating reaches and making contact with targets were measured, and two analyses of variance were carried out on each of these four measures. One analysis was conducted on only 2.5-year-olds' data, and measures were evaluated as a function of early experience (experimental vs. control), reminder treatment (reminder vs. no-reminder), and trial type (uninstructed vs. instructed). The second analysis was conducted on only the no-reminder treatment data as a function of early experience, age, and trial type. As indicated above, four of the older children were missing instructed trials. The two children who missed either one or two were assigned a score of zero for those particular trials. Both remaining children received the no-reminder treatment. One child was in the experimental group and missed three trials. The other child was in the control group and missed four trials. These two children were assigned scores equal to their respective group's average for the instructed trials.

Reaches.—The mean number of reaches of the 2.5-year-olds may be seen in Figure 1 as a function of early experience, reminder, and trial type. Overall, the experimental groups reached more than the controls, $F(1,28) = 12.74$, $p < .001$, children in the reminder condition reached more than those in the no-reminder condition, $F(1,28) = 5.50$, $p < .05$, and all children reached more on instructed than uninstructed trials, $F(1,28) = 69.69$, $p < .001$.

As is evident in the figure, however, the effects of a reminder on the experience groups differed on uninstructed and instructed trials (experience × reminder × instruction), $F(1,28) = 13.49$, $p < .001$. On uninstructed trials, children in the experimental group who were given a reminder reached for the rattle more than three times as often as their controls and twice as often as their experimental counterparts with no reminder. On the other hand, children in the control group showed little uninstructed reaching with or without the reminder (experience × reminder), $F(1,28) = 7.46$, $p < .01$.

Experimental and control groups also differed significantly on the number of reaches they produced on the instructed trials, $F(1,28) = 7.17$, $p < .01$. Yet, when the reminder treatment was combined with instructions to reach, the controls reached just as readily as the children in the experimental groups with or without the reminder and more than children in the no-reminder control condition, $F(1,28) = 5.13$, $p < .05$.

Figure 2 illustrates the mean number of reaches of the no-reminder treatment groups as a function of early experience, age, and trial type. Overall, the younger children reached more than the older children, $F(1,28) = 5.16$, $p < .05$, and instructions increased reaching, $F(1,28) = 37.25$, $p < .001$. Children in the experimental groups reached more, although the early experience effect was not significant, $F(1,28) = 2.90$, $p < .10$. On uninstructed trials, the 1.5-year-olds reached more than twice as often as the 2.5-year-olds, $F(1,28) = 8.09$, $p < .01$; thus, instructions increased reaching more for the older groups, age × instruction, $F(1,28) = 6.18$, $p < .05$. On instructed trials, there was no age effect, but the experimental groups reached more often than the control groups, $F(1,28) = 7.50$, $p < .01$.

Successes.—The mean number of successes (accurate reaches) of the 2.5-year-olds can be seen in Figure 3 as a function of early experience, reminder treatment, and trial type. Overall, the experimental groups were more accurate than the controls at a marginal level of significance, $F(1,28) = 3.76$, $p < .06$, children in the reminder condition were more accurate than those in the no-reminder condition, $F(1,28) = 4.51$, $p < .05$, and all children reached more successfully on instructed than uninstructed trials, $F(1,28) = 23.49$, $p < .001$.

Figure 4 illustrates the mean number of successes of the no-reminder treatment groups as a function of early experience, age, and trial type. The children in experimental groups were more successful than those in the control groups, $F(1,28) = 4.52$, $p < .05$. The 1.5-year-old children made more accurate reaches than the 2.5-year-old children, $F(1,28) = 7.60$, $p < .05$. This may be a consequence of their higher level of reaching behavior reported previously. Instructions to reach increased successes significantly and equivalentiy at both ages, $F(1,28) = 13.43$, $p < .001$.

Latencies.—The mean latency to initiate a reach ranged from .01 to 15 sec, $M = 3.97$ sec. The mean latency to make contact with the target object in the dark ranged from .01 to 15.94 sec, $M = 5.31$ sec. In general, latencies did not differ significantly for the two age groups or for experimental and control subjects, although the older experimental group did display a marginally shorter latency

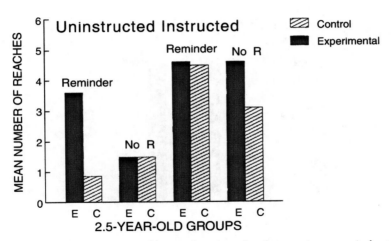

Fig. 1.—Mean number of reaches of the 2.5-year-olds as a function of early experience, reminder treatment, and trial type.

when initiating a successful reach than the older control group, $F(1,28) = 3.34$, $p < .08$.

Other indices.—The effect of prior experience is also evident in the children's response to being plunged into total darkness. While this procedure is not upsetting to 6.5-month-olds, it is to some 2.5-year-olds. However, children who had experienced the dark procedure as infants were more willing to remain in the experimental setting; only two, as compared to nine controls, asked to leave before completing the uninstructed trials, X^2 $(1, n = 32)$ $= 4.45$, $p < .05$. This phenomenon is further demonstrated in the small subset of children who met criterion to be included in the sample but did not remain in the setting for all five of the instructed trials. Three of these four children were control subjects.

In an attempt to detect any further relation between prior experience and current performance, Pearson correlation coefficients were calculated for reaches and successes at 6.5 months and 2.5 years only, because the behavior of the 1.5-year-olds was close to a ceiling level. The r & s were−.18 for the number of reaches and−.20 for the number of successes; clearly, no significant relation existed between performance levels at 6.5 months and at 2.5 years.

Behavior in the Light

Memory probes.—The verbal responses to the direct queries were basically equivalent across all groups. The majority of the children did not reply or gave "no" answers, although when asked whether they had been in the testing room on a previous occasion, many of the older children in both the experimental and control groups said "yes." The children were also asked to choose the target object and sound stimulus. The 2.5-year-old experimental groups selected Big Bird as the target equally as often as their control counterparts; six out of 16 children in each experience group made this choice. With the younger group, a similar pattern emerged; three out of eight experimental and two out of eight control group children chose the Big Bird. In selecting the target sound stimulus, again, 2.5-year-olds in both experience groups behaved similarly; only three experimental and two control children chose the rattle. The younger children in the experimental group, however, did show a preference for the target sound stimulus; five out of eight, in contrast to only one of the eight children in the control group, chose the rattle (Fisher exact test, $p < .06$).

Toy and sound interactions.—To evaluate interactions and any potential target preferences, the number of times each toy and sound stimulus were touched and the total interaction time with them were measured. For the no-reminder condition, the experimental groups touched the rattle more times than the controls, and the older children did so more than the younger children, F's$(1,28) = 5.20$, p's $< .05$. The total interaction time with all the toys for the 2.5-year-olds assigned to the reminder treatment was found to be higher than that of the children in the no-reminder groups, $F(1,28) = 11.53$, $p < .01$, and children in the reminder groups were also marginally more interactive

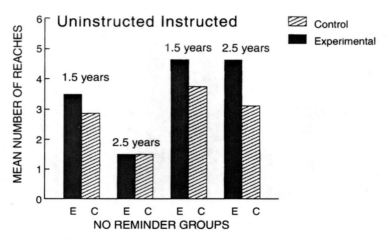

FIG. 2.—*Mean number of reaches of the no-reminder treatment groups as a function of early experience, age, and trial type.*

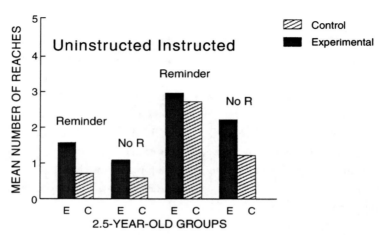

FIG. 3.—*Mean number of successes of the 2.5-year-olds as a function of early experience, reminder treatment, and trial type.*

with the Big Bird, $F(1,28) = 3.14$, $p < .07$. However, correlations between the total interaction time with the toys and the number of uninstructed reaches and uninstructed successes were not significant, r's $= +.19, -.05$, respectively.

DISCUSSION
Effects of Early Experience

Children who participated in the reaching-in-the-dark procedure as infants gave evidence of that experience in a number of ways. In virtually every comparison on trials in the dark, the experienced group performed differently than children in the control groups, although this was perhaps most evident for the older children on uninstructed

trials. Here, when first confronted with dark conditions, and given no verbal directions, the older children with infant experience in the situation clearly reached out toward the sound more than their inexperienced peers. This was especially true if they were given the opportunity to re-experience the dark and sound context for a brief period prior to testing. Children without infant experience, with or without the reminder treatment, did very little reaching without instructions at this age. This was not true of the 1.5-year-olds. Indeed, one major difference in behavior of the two age groups was the much higher level of reaching toward sound in darkness by the younger children. The 1.5-year-olds were more than twice as likely to reach without instructions in the dark than the older

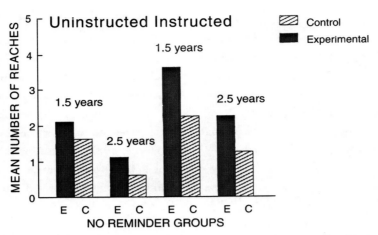

Fig. 4.—*Mean number of successes of the no-reminder treatment groups as a function of early experience, age, and trial type.*

group. The greater willingness of the younger children to reach in the dark made the effect of experience more difficult to demonstrate in this age group. Nonetheless, the children with infant experience 1 year earlier still showed marginally more reaching than those new to the task.

This differential behavior of experienced and inexperienced children was also evident with respect to accuracy of reach. With or without instructions to reach, with or without the dark-sound context reminder, both younger and older children who had participated as infants were more successful in directing their reaches and obtaining the sounding object than those children without the early experience. The older children in the experimental group even showed a slight tendency to begin reaching faster on these successful trials.

Further evidence of early experience was to be seen in the separable patterns of overall tolerance of the dark displayed by the older groups. Over a third of our full control sample of 2.5-year-old children without infant experience in the dark procedure evidenced discomfort in the task and, in fact, terminated the trials before instructions were instituted. This was more than four times the number of children in the full experimental sample who asked to stop, and was paralleled by a threefold ratio of control to experimental subjects leaving prior to the completion of subsequent instructed trials. There is little question that our dark trials were slightly aversive to the older group; there is equally clear indication that this was less true for

the children who 2 years earlier, at 6.5 months of age, had experienced the dark situation.

Finally, it is also interesting that early experimental participation was either not reflected or minimally reflected at either age on a number of other measures. For instance, the quality of early reaching was not shown to bear a relation to that done 2 years later; the best reachers at 6.5 months were not necessarily those with the highest incidence and accuracy at 2.5 years. Younger children in the experimental group did select the target sound more than younger control children, suggesting some memory for the rattle. Yet this was not true for the older age groups, when another year had elapsed. Early experience with the Big Bird and rattle did not affect verbal responses to memory probes, selection of or interaction with the original target toy, and total toy interactions. Thus, neither specific competence nor specific visual and auditory detail from the infant experience seems to have been readily accessible at the time of testing.

Two comments may temper these negative findings. First, the design was such that the memory probes for target details came first. As Rovee-Collier (e.g., Fagen & Rovee-Collier, 1983) has emphasized, there is a time-lagged character to infant memory retrieval, and the adult forgetting literature is also replete with examples of memory performance improving across test sequences. In future work, it would be interesting to determine if memory for specific detail could be demonstrated in infants if evaluated later in a long-term memory test sequence. A second potential consequence of the primary position of the target-recognition probes may have been to buttress the reminder treatment. Perhaps the target cues provided in these probes, even while not triggering immediate differential response, nonetheless served as effective supplements to the dark-sound reminder manipulation. Again, the components of the confound cannot be extricated here but pose questions for subsequent endeavors.

Influence of a Reminder and of Instructions

In general, the influence of the two manipulations introduced as potential retrieval aids facilitated responding. Only one-half of the older subjects were delivered a reminder of the early experience. The reminder treatment consisted of two parts: a single 3-sec presentation of one rattle out of reach in the dark, followed by a 30-min play period in an adjoining room. Two kinds of concomitant effects can be noted.

The more interesting memory effect is seen most clearly in the reaching behavior on uninstructed trials in the dark. The experienced 2-year-olds given a reminder of the rattle in the dark reached twice as often as their age-mates with similar infant experience but no reminder of it. For children in the control group, however, the reminder did not suffice to increase reaching behavior without explicit instructions to reach. With or without a reminder, these children reached very seldom on uninstructed trials.

Not very surprisingly, the suggestion to try and find the Big Bird on instructed trials increased reaching behavior and subsequent success. A major reason for introducing the instructions to reach, however, was to see if in combination with the reminder treatment, responding of experimental subjects might be cued more successfully than with the reminder alone, especially if the latter was not effective by itself. On instructed trials, however, both controls and experimental subjects given the reminder treatment reached equivalently, and no more than experimental subjects not given the reminder. All three groups responded significantly more than the control group with no reminder. Thus, with the encouragement of the experimenter on these instructed trials, either the memory or the familiarization component was sufficient to increase responding.

General Discussion and Conclusions

The results of this study are important to our knowledge of memory for events in the first year of life in several ways. First, they corroborate the general conceptualization of an early memory system that is functional in infancy (e.g., White & Pillemer, 1979) and can, at least by 6 months of age, mediate long-term memory (e.g., Rovee-Collier & Hayne, 1987). Moreover, they demonstrate memory after 2 years for one single experience in infancy. In so doing, these findings provide an important replication of the Myers et al. (1987) evidence that children almost 3 years of age retained memory of what they had done under identical laboratory conditions 2 years earlier. Under conditions preserving virtually every aspect of an unusual and distinctive laboratory environment and procedure, a much larger sample of children with only a single experience showed they remembered actions they had performed at approximately 6 months of age. Amid original contextual cues then, it appears that 2 years of physical, neurological, and cognitive changes do not prohibit retrieval based on the infant memory processes.

The current findings go well beyond just supporting the Myers et al. (1987) study, however. They also confirm the important role that a brief reminder of the original context plays in memory retrieval, as has been noted repeatedly in the animal and human infant literature (e.g., Rovee-Collier & Hayne, 1987; Spear, 1973). The only systematic work with children, however, conducted by Rovee-Collier and her colleagues, has reinstated conditions for 3 min several hours to a day earlier when testing memory over a matter of weeks (e.g., Rovee-Collier & Hayne, 1987). Fagen and Rovee-Collier (1983) described memory retrieval as a time-locked process. They found improved retention over a 24-hour period and hypothesized that aspects of the training context were slowly "dredged up" from memory (p. 222). In this case, we have seen that presenting the sounding object in the dark merely one-half hour before testing increased responding. As indicated earlier, it is possible that target cues from the immediately preceding memory probes contributed additional contextual support. Even so, it is notable that a minimal exposure to contextual cues, a brief interval prior to testing, facilitated performance of 2-year-olds 2 years after the event in question.

The major difference in early experience between the experimental subjects in this study and those in the Myers et al. (1987) investigation was one of extent. The five children in the longitudinal experiment had visited the laboratory and participated in the reaching procedure on at least 15 different occasions over several months of their first year. In this study, they had experienced the procedure on only a single occasion, at 6.5 months of age. Even if infant encoding processes were limited and the resultant memory traces fragile, forgetting was not complete. If the unique context of an unusual event is completely reinstated, then, and especially if a brief reminder of the event is introduced a short time beforehand, the memory system operational at 6 months and 2 years is powerful enough to facilitate performance of action sequences carried out during a single episode of infancy.

The one series of dark trials carried out in infancy was reflected not only in enhanced reaching action in the dark 2 years later, but also in an almost global emotional acceptance of an abrupt change from light to total and complete dark in initiating the dark procedure. The behavior of the experienced group of 2-year-olds was in notable contrast to the degree of discomfort displayed by the inexperienced control group, who clearly did not appreciate the conditions and asked to terminate them, or to leave. It could be argued that the mothers of experienced subjects were more relaxed during dark trials, and the children were somehow reacting to current cues rather than to memory cues in tolerating the procedure better. For several reasons, this seems unlikely. The upright seating with only hip-holding hand contact provided some protection from maternal postural cues, and the absolute dark prohibited visual expressive communication. Moreover, Perris (1989) reported a parallel finding with 14-month-olds whose mothers were not in the testing situation. Children who had play experience in a unique environmental context 4 months earlier were more willing to remain in this same context for a memory test than control children participating for the first time.

Thus, we believe that we are seeing here evidence of the kind of subjective, emotionally toned reactivity to events that first Freud (e.g., 1899/1962), and more recently, White and Pillemer (1979), argued is implicated in memory. The finding also supports Spear's (1984) general notion of differing levels of expression of memory. Children with the one early experience in reaching in the dark carry with them 2 years later not only a record of appropriate motor sequences but enough general emotional familiarity

to mediate acceptance of a second experience aversive to inexperienced peers. We conclude that the one unique experience at 6.5 months of age was sufficient to establish a memory of both action and meaning that became accessible upon reinstatement of the event in the third year of life.

REFERENCES

Ashmead, D. H., & Perlmutter, M. (1980). Infant memory in everyday life. *New Directions for Child Development*, **10**, 1–16.

Balsam, P. D., & Tomie, A. (Eds.). (1985). *Context and learning*. Hillsdale, NJ: Erlbaum.

Brainerd, C. J., Kingma, J., & Howe, M. L. (1985). On the development of forgetting. *Child Development*, **56**, 1103–1119.

Campbell, B. A., & Jaynes, J. (1966). Reinstatement. *Psychological Review*, **73**, 478–480.

Campbell, B. A., & Spear, N. E. (1972). Ontogeny of memory. *Psychological Review*, **79**, 215–236.

Clifton, R. K., Muir, D., Clarkson, M., Ashmead, D., & Sherriff, F. (1985, April). *Development of auditory localization in infants*. Paper presented at the meeting of the Society for Research in Child Development, Toronto.

Clifton, R. K., Perris, E. E., & Bullinger, A. (1989). *Infants' perception of auditory space*. Manuscript submitted for publication.

Dudycha, G. J., & Dudycha, M. M. (1941). Childhood memories: A review of the literature. *Psychological Bulletin*, **36**, 34–50.

Fagen, J. W., & Rovee-Collier, C. (1983). Memory retrieval: A time-locked process in infancy. *Science*, 222, 1349–1351.

Fetters, L., & Todd, J. (1987). Quantitative assessment of infant reaching movements. *Journal of Motor Behavior*, **19**, 147–166.

Freud, S. (1962). Screen memories. In J. Strachey (Ed. and Trans.), *The standard edition of the complete psychological works of Sigmund Freud* (Vol. 3, pp. 303–322). London: Hogarth. (Original work published 1899)

Hofsten, C. von. (1979). Development of visually directed reaching: The approach phase. *Journal of Human Movement Studies*, **5**, 160–178.

Hoving, K. L., & Choi, K. (1972). Some necessary conditions for producing reinstatement effects in children. *Developmental Psychology, 7,* 214–217.

Howe, M. L., & Hunter, M. A. (1986). Long-term memory in adulthood: An examination of the development of storage and retrieval processes at acquisition and retention. *Developmental Review, 6,* 334–364.

Myers, N. A., Clifton, R. K., & Clarkson, M. G. (1987). When they were very young: almost-threes remember two years ago. *Infant Behavior and Development, 10,* 123–132.

Nelson, K., & Ross, G. (1980). The generalities and specifics of long-term memory in infants and young children. *New Directions for Child Development, 10,* 87–102.

Perris, E. E. (1989). *Memory for events during the first year of life.* Unpublished doctoral dissertation, University of Massachusetts, Amherst.

Perris, E. E., & Clifton, R. K. (1988). Reaching in the dark toward sound as a measure of auditory localization in infants. *Infant Behavior and Development, 11,* 473–491.

Rovee-Collier, C. K., & Hayne, H. (1987). Reactivation of infant memory: Implications for cognitive development. In H. Reese (Ed.), *Advances in child development and behavior* (Vol. **20**, pp. 185–238). New York: Academic Press.

Schacter, D. L., & Moscovitch, M. (1984). Infants, amnesiacs, and dissociable memory systems. In M. Moscovitch (Ed.), *Infant memory: Advances in the study of communication and affect* (Vol. **9**, pp. 173–216). New York: Plenum.

Spear, N. E. (1973). Retrieval of memory in animals. *Psychological Review, 80,* 163–194.

Spear, N. E. (1978). *The processing of memories: Forgetting and retention.* Hillsdale, NJ: Erlbaum.

Spear, N. E. (1984). Behaviors that indicate memory: Levels of expression. *Canadian Journal of Psychology, 38,* 348–367.

Tulving, E. (1983). *Elements of episodic memory.* New York: Oxford University Press.

Waldfogel, S. (1948). The frequency and affective character of childhood memories. *Psychological Monographs, 62* (Whole No. 291).

White, S. H., & Pillemer, D. B. (1979). Childhood amnesia and the development of a socially accessible memory system. In J. F. Kihlstrom & F. J. Evans (Eds.), *Functional disorders of memory* (pp. 29–73). Hillsdale, NJ: Erlbaum.

CHAPTER 10
Language and Acquisition in Humans

Thought and Language

LESTER M. SDOROW AND CHERYL A. RICKABAUGH

In 1800 a boy who appeared to be about 12 years old emerged from a forest near Aveyron, France, apparently having survived for many years without human contact (Hunter, 1993). The boy, named Victor by physician Jared Itard, became known as the "Wild Boy of Aveyron." Victor learned to use gestures, comprehend speech, and read and write on a basic level. Though Itard made an intensive effort to teach him to speak French, the only word Victor learned to say was "lait" (milk). Similar reports have provided evidence of a **critical period** for language acquisition that extends from infancy to adolescence, during which language learning is optimal. If people are not exposed to a language until after childhood, they might never become proficient in speaking it (Grimshaw et al., 1998). There also seems to be a critical period for the acquisition of fluent sign language (Newman et al., 2002).

A more recent and well-documented case described an American girl, Genie, who had been raised in isolation. In 1970, 13-year-old Genie was discovered by welfare workers in a room in which her father had kept her restrained in a harness and away from social contact—and language—since infancy. He communicated with her by barking and growling and beat her whenever she made a sound. By 1981, more than a decade after returning to society and undergoing intensive language training, Genie had acquired a large vocabulary but only a limited ability to speak. Like Victor, Genie might have been past her

critical period for language acquisition when she returned to society (Pines, 1981).

Though the cases of Victor and Genie, as well as those of other children who have been reared in social isolation (Kenneally et al., 1998), support the view that there is a critical period for language acquisition, it is unwise to generalize too freely from case studies. For example, some children who have lived for years in social isolation, such as Kaspar Hauser, who was discovered in Nuremberg, Germany, in 1828 at age 17, have been able to learn language well even after reaching adolescence (Simon, 1979). Perhaps other factors could account for the findings in the cases of Victor and Genie. For example, suppose that Victor and Genie were born with brain disorders that interfered with their ability to acquire language. Even if they had been reared from birth in normal family settings, they still might have failed to acquire mature language.

LANGUAGE

Arguing about politics. Reading a newspaper. Using sign language. Each of these is made possible by **language**, a formal system of communication involving symbols—whether spoken, written, or gestured—and rules for combining them. In using language, we rely on spoken symbols to communicate through speech, written symbols to communicate through writing, and gestured symbols to communicate through sign language. We use language to communicate with other people, to store and retrieve memories, and to plan for the future.

But what makes a form of communication "language"? The world's several thousand languages share three characteristics: semanticity, generativity, and displacement. **Semanticity** is the conveying of the communicator's thoughts in a meaningful way to those who understand the language. For example, you know that *anti-* at the beginning of a word means being against something and *-ed* at the end of a word means past action. The language spoken by people with schizophrenia often lacks semanticity; it can be meaningless to other people.

Generativity is the combining of language symbols in novel ways, without being limited to a fixed number of combinations. In fact, each day you probably say or write things that have never been said or written by anyone before. This generativity of language accounts for baby talk, rap music, Brooklynese, and the works of Shakespeare.

Displacement is the use of language to refer to objects and events that are not present. The objects and events can be in another place or in the past or future. Thus, you can talk about someone in China, your fifth birthday party, or who will win the World Series next year.

Language is only one form of communication. Many animals, ourselves included, can communicate without using language. For example, researchers allowed dogs to witness a toy or treat being placed where the dogs could not access it. When their owners were present, the dogs would alternate their gaze between their owner and the unavailable object (Miklosi et al., 2000). But are dogs using language? No, because the only characteristic of language that dogs display is semanticity. Dogs do not exhibit generativity or displacement in their communications.

Other animals also communicate without using true language. A bee can communicate the location of nectar-containing flowers to residents of its hive. When a bee returns to its hive after finding nectar less than 50 yards away, it performs a "circle dance" on the wall of the hive. If the nectar is farther away, the bee does a "waggle dance," moving in a figure-eight pattern. The angle of the straight line in the figure-eight pattern relative to the sun indicates the direction of the nectar, and the duration of the dance indicates the distance of the nectar—the longer the duration, the farther away it is (Dyer, 2002). But these dances are merely a form of communication, not language. They

> **language** A formal system of communication involving symbols—whether spoken, written, or gestured—and rules for combining them.
>
> **semanticity** The characteristic of language marked by the use of symbols to convey thoughts in a meaningful way.
>
> **generativity** The characteristic of language marked by the ability to combine words in novel, meaningful ways.
>
> **displacement** The characteristic of language marked by the ability to refer to objects and events that are not present..

have semanticity and displacement, but they lack generativity—they are not used to indicate anything other than the location of nectar.

Consider also how monkeys use different alarm calls to signal the presence of particular kinds of predators. In one study, researchers presented Vervet monkeys with tape recordings of alarm calls that signified the presence of an eagle, a boa constrictor, or a leopard. The monkeys responded to eagle alarms by looking up, to boa constrictor alarms by looking down, and to leopard alarms by climbing up into trees (Seyfarth, Cheney, & Marler, 1980). Though monkeys use alarm calls to communicate, they do not use true language. Their calls have semanticity because they communicate the presence of a particular kind of predator, but they lack generativity and displacement. Monkeys neither combine their calls in novel ways nor use them to refer to animals that are not present.

In contrast to dogs, bees, and monkeys, human beings use true language. Without language, we would be severely limited in our ability to communicate with one another. You would not even be reading this book; books would not exist. Even the Old Testament book of Genesis recognizes the importance of language. In the story of the Tower of Babel, God punishes human beings for their pride by having them speak different languages—restricting their ability to communicate and to engage in cooperative projects, such as building a tower to heaven.

grammar The set of rules that governs the proper use and combination of language symbols.

phoneme The smallest unit of sound in a language.

phonology The study of the sounds that compose languages.

THE STRUCTURE OF LANGUAGE

English and all other languages have structures governed by rules known as grammar. The components of **grammar** include *phonology, syntax,* and *semantics.*

Phonology All spoken languages are composed of **phonemes**—the basic sounds of a language. The study of phonemes is called **phonology**. Languages use as few as 20 and as many as 80 phonemes. English contains about 40—the number varies with the dialect. Each phoneme is represented by either a letter (such as the *o* sound in *go*) or a combination of letters (such as the *sh* sound in *should).* Words are combinations of phonemes, and each language permits only certain combinations. A native speaker of English would realize that the combination of phonemes in *cogerite* forms an acceptable word in English even though there is no such word. That person also would realize that the combination of phonemes in *klputng* does not form an acceptable word in English. There is some evidence that women recognize and process phonemes faster than do men (Majeres, 1999).

One language might not include all the phonemes found in another language, and people learning to speak a foreign language might have more difficulty pronouncing the phonemes in the foreign language that are not in their native language. For example, native speakers of Japanese who learn English as adults have difficulty in distinguishing between *r* sounds, as in *rock,* and *l* sounds, as in *lock.* This difficulty may be due to differences in how phonemes are processed by the brain and early childhood experience with language— though providing training and feedback to native speakers of Japanese improves their ability to distinguish between the two sounds (McClelland, Fiez, & McCandliss, 2002). Catherine Best and Robert Avery investigated American and African adults' perception of *click consonants*—sounds produced by creating suction in the mouth and then releasing with the tongue, producing a sound that is similar to a "tsk" with an abrupt stop. English speakers process clicks acoustically, that is, as nonspeech sounds. In some African languages, clicks have linguistic significance and are perceived as consonants. Participants in the study were native speakers of English and Zulu and Xhosa, two African tone languages with click consonants. The experimental task involved identifying and matching click consonants and nonsense syllables. Results indicated that native Zulu and Xhosa speakers demonstrated more accurate performance on the experimental tasks, and the researchers attributed this finding to the fact that African tone language speakers processed the clicks linguistically rather than acoustically (Best & Avery, 2000).

Individual phonemes and combinations of phonemes form **morphemes**, the smallest meaningful units of language. Words are composed of one or more morphemes. For example, the word *book* is composed of a single morpheme. In contrast, the word *books* is composed of two morphemes: *book,* which refers to an object, and *-s,* which indicates the plural of a word. One of the common morphemes that affect the meaning of words is the *-ing* suffix, which indicates ongoing action. Note that the 40 or so phonemes in English build more than 100,000 morphemes, which in turn build almost 500,000 words. Using these words, we can create a virtually infinite number of sentences. One of the outstanding characteristics of language is, indeed, its generativity.

Websites You Can Use

Catherine Ball

www.georgetown.edu/faculty/ballc/

This is the home page of Catherine Ball, a linguist at Georgetown University. It contains a number of links related to language, most notably a comparison of animal sounds as spoken in many languages around the world.

Phonology: How to Pronounce Ghoti ... and Why

www.facstaff.bucknell.edu/rbeard/phono.html

This website was created by linguist Robert Beard at Bucknell University. It presents interesting information about phonology in regard to the pronunciation of words that do not sound like they are spelled.

Syntax In addition to rules that govern the acceptable combinations of sounds in words, languages have **syntax**—rules that govern the acceptable arrangement of words in phrases and sentences. Because you know English syntax, you would say "She ate the ice cream" but not "She the ice cream ate" (though poets do have a "license" to violate normal syntax). And syntax varies from one language to another. The English sentence *John hit Bill* would be translated into its Japanese equivalent as *John Bill hit*. The normal order of the verb and the object in Japanese is the opposite of their normal order in English (Gliedman, 1983). As for adjectives, in English they usually precede the nouns they modify, whereas in Spanish adjectives usually follow the nouns they modify. The English phrase *the red book* would be *el libro rojo* in Spanish. Therefore, a Spanish-speaker learning English might say "the book red," whereas an English-speaker learning Spanish might say "el rojo libro."

Semantics Not only must words be arranged appropriately in phrases and sentences, they must be meaningful. The study of how language conveys meaning is called **semantics**. Psycholinguist Noam Chomsky' has been intrigued by our ability to convey the same meaning through different phrases and sentences. Consider the sentences *The boy fed the horse* and *The horse was fed by the boy*. Both express the same meaning, but they use different syntax. Moreover, the meaning expressed by these sentences can be expressed in French, Chinese, Swahili, and so on, though the sentences used to express it in those languages would be different from the English sentences.

To explain this ability to express the same meaning using different phrases or different languages, Chomsky distinguishes between a language's deep structure and its surface structure. The **deep structure** is the underlying meaning of a statement; the **surface structure** is the word arrangements that express the underlying meaning. Our ability to discern the deep structure of literary works, for example, lets us appreciate the motives of the main characters. **Transformational grammar** is the term that Chomsky gives to the rules by which languages generate surface structures out of deep structures, and deep structures out of surface structures. Language comprehension involves transforming the surface structure, which is the verbal message, into its deep structure, which is its meaning. Thus, the sentences *The boy fed the horse* and *The horse was*

> **morpheme** The smallest meaningful units of language.
> **syntax** The rules that govern the acceptable arrangement of words in phrases and sentences.
> **deep structure** The underlying meaning of a statement.
> **surface structure** The word arrangements used to express meaning.
> **transformational grammar** The rules by which languages generate surface structures out of deep structures and deep structures out of surface structures.
> **displacement** The characteristic of language marked by the ability to refer to objects and events that are not present..
> **pragmatics** The relationship between language and its social context.

fed by the boy are transformed into the same deep structure, or meaning.

The meaning of a statement depends not only on its words and their arrangement but also on the social context in which the statement is made (Paradis, 1998). The branch of semantics that is concerned with the relationship between language and its social context is called **pragmatics**. To appreciate the relationship between language and its social context, consider the following statement made by a student about an upcoming meal in the cafeteria: "I can't wait to have dinner tonight." If spoken in an enthusiastic voice during Thanksgiving week, the statement might mean that the student expects to enjoy a delicious turkey dinner. Yet, if spoken in a sarcastic voice during a normal school week, the same statement might mean that the student expects to be confronted by the cafeteria's notorious "mystery meat."

Also consider the following embarrassing incident recounted by Elisabeth Kübler-Ross, the prominent death-and-dying researcher. She was reared in Switzerland but lived most of her adult life in the United States. "Last evening I spent 10 minutes trying to understand what a nurse was talking about when she invited me to attend a baby shower! Why should I want to look at a bathroom constructed for infants?" (Gill, 1980, p. 201). The incident is an example of the importance of a fund of cultural knowledge as a basis for language pragmatics (Reeder & Shapiro, 1993). Cross-cultural differences in the pragmatics that characterize Western and Asian languages include turn-taking (Lerner & Takagi, 1999) and directness of speech (Holtgraves, 1997).

The importance of pragmatics also is exemplified by the difficulty scientists have had in developing computer programs that can truly converse with human beings (Saygin & Cicekli, 2002). A program capable of comprehending speech would have to consider characteristics of the message, the speaker, and the situation. The difficulty in employing pragmatics in developing computer programs that can comprehend speech is illustrated in the following conversation (Gorman, 1985, p. 65) between a news reporter (R) and a computer "therapist" called Eliza (E):

R: Row, row, row your boat
E: What about your own boat?
R: Gently down the stream
E: Why do you say that?
R: Merrily, merrily, merrily, merrily
E: I am not sure I understand you fully
R: Life is but a dream
E: What does the dream suggest to you?

STAYING ON TRACK

The Structure of Language

1. What roles do semanticity, generativity, and displacement play in language?
2. What is the relationship between transformational grammar and the deep structure and surface structure of language?

THE ACQUISITION OF LANGUAGE

What accounts for a child's ability to progress from a crying, gurgling infant to a talkative 3-year-old? The process of language acquisition seems to be universal, with infants in all cultures acquiring language in similar ways as they pass through distinct stages (Rice, 1989). Though the timing of the stages can vary among infants, the order does not.

Language Milestones For the first few months after birth, infants are limited to communicating vocally through cooing, gurgling, and crying, which they use to indicate that they are content, happy, distressed, hungry, or in pain. Between 4 and 6 months of age, infants enter the babbling stage. When infants babble, they repeat sequences of phonemes, such as ba-ba-ba. Infants in all cultures begin babbling at about the same age and produce the same range of phonemes, including some that are not part of their parents' language (Roug, Landberg, & Lundberg, 1989). This similarity in phonemes might account for the prevalence of the words *mama, papa,* and *dada* to refer to parents in a variety of cultures. Even deaf infants begin babbling at the same age as infants who can hear, though their babbling is different from that of hearing infants (Oller & Eilers, 1988). The universality of the onset and initial content of babbling indicates that it is a product of the maturation of an inborn predisposition, rather than a product of experience. Nonetheless, by the age of 9 months, infants begin to show the influence of experience, as they limit their babbling to the phonemes of the language, or languages, in their social environment.

When infants are about 1 year old, they begin to say their first words. Their earliest words typically refer to objects that interest them. Thus, common early words include *milk* and *doggie.* In using words, older infants exhibit **overextension,** applying words too broadly (Behrend, 1988). Consider an infant who refers to her cat as "kitty." If she also refers to dogs, cows, horses, and other four-legged animals as "kitty," she would be exhibiting overextension. In contrast, if she refers to her cat, but to no other cats, as "kitty," she would be exhibiting **underextension**—applying words too narrowly (Caplan & Barr, 1989). As infants gain experience with objects and language, they rapidly learn to apply their words to the correct objects.

After learning to say single words, infants begin using them in **holophrastic speech,** which is the use of single words to represent whole phrases or sentences. For example, an infant might say "car" on one occasion to indicate that the family car has pulled into the driveway and on another occasion to indicate that he would like to go for a ride. Between the ages of 18 and 24 months, infants go beyond holophrastic speech by speaking two-word phrases, typically including a noun and a verb in a consistent order. The infant is now showing a rudimentary appreciation of proper syntax, as in "Baby drink" or "Mommy go." Because, in the two-word stage, infants rely on nouns and verbs and leave out other parts of speech (such as articles and prepositions), their utterances are called **telegraphic speech**. To save time and money, people who write telegrams leave out connecting parts of speech yet still communicate meaningful messages.

Until they are about 2 years old, infants use words to refer only to objects that are located in their immediate environment. At about age 2, children begin speaking sentences that include other parts of speech in addition to nouns and verbs. They also begin to exhibit displacement, as when a 2-year-old asks, "Grandma come tomorrow?" After age 2, children show a rapid increase in their vocabulary and in the length and complexity of their sentences. Psychologist Roger Brown (1973) invented a unit of measurement, the **mean length of utterance** (MLU), to assess children's level of language maturation. The MLU is calculated by taking samples of a child's statements and finding their average length in morphemes. The MLU increases rapidly in early childhood, though there is some variability from one child to another. The MLU is a better predictor of overall language ability at younger ages than in later childhood (Scarborough et al., 1991). The use of the MLU has proved useful in assessing language development with a variety of native languages, including Icelandic (Thordardottir & Weismer, 1998). The MLU also has been used to assess the language development of children with language disabilities (Parisse & Le Normand, 2002).

The increased sophistication that young children show in their use of language is partly attributable to their application of language rules, which they learn from listening to the speech of those around them. From the day of their birth, infants are exposed to sophisticated language. In fact, studies have found that, contrary to popular impressions, staff members in hospital nurseries do not rely solely on baby talk and soothing sounds when speaking to newborn infants. Instead, staff members spend much of the time speaking to the infants with normal, though perhaps simple, phrases and sentences (Rheingold & Adams, 1980). The language rules that children in European American cultures learn are strongly influenced by their parents'

> **overextension** The tendency to apply a word to more objects or actions than it actually represents.
>
> **underextension** The tendency to apply a word to fewer objects or actions than it actually represents.
>
> **holophrastic speech** The use of single words to represent whole phrases or sentences.
>
> **telegraphic speech** Speech marked by reliance on nouns and verbs while other parts of speech, including articles and prepositions, are omitted.
>
> **mean length of utterance** (MLU) A unit of measurement that assesses children's level of language maturation.
>
> **overregularization** The application of a grammatical rule without making necessary exceptions to it.

speech—especially mothers' (Leaper, Anderson, & Sanders, 1998). In most non-Western cultures, however, children acquire language through interacting with a number of adults and other children (Mohanty & Perregaux, 1997).

Many languages, like English, have exceptions to grammatical rules. This inconsistency might explain the phenomenon of **overregularization**—the application of grammatical rules without making necessary exceptions (Maratsos, 2000). For example, at first children using the past tense will, correctly, say words such as *did, went,* and *brought,* which violate the *-ed* rule for forming the past tense. They learn these words by hearing the speech of older children and adults. But as children learn the *-ed* rule, they say words such as *doed, goed,* or *bringed.* Later, when they realize that grammatical rules have exceptions, they learn not to apply the *-ed* rule to irregular verbs, and again say *did, went,* and *brought* (Kolata, 1987). Thus, children tend at first to use correct wording, then begin to over-regularize, and finally realize when to follow grammatical rules and when to break them (Marcus, 1995).

How do we know that infants learn rules rather than a series of specific instances of correct grammar? One source of evidence is a study by Jean Berko (1958), who reasoned that if children use correct grammar when confronted with words they have never heard, then they must be relying on rules, not rote memory. To test her assumption,

Berko developed the "Wug test," which included drawings of imaginary creatures called "wugs." Berko found that children would, indeed, apply grammatical rules to novel words. For example, when shown a picture identified as a "wug" and then a picture with two of them, children completed the statement "There are two ___" with the word *wugs*. This finding shows that they have learned to use the *-s* ending to indicate the plural.

Is There a Critical Period for Language Acquisition? As described at the beginning of the chapter, many language researchers believe that there is a critical period for the acquisition of language during childhood. Children who are kept isolated from contact with language and not intensively exposed to language until adolescence—typically because they live in an abusive household—usually have great difficulty becoming proficient in their use of language. But such case studies do not permit us to know for certain whether these children would have shown normal language development had they been exposed to language beginning in infancy in a nurturing household.

Another, perhaps stronger, line of research on critical periods is concerned with adults who learn second languages. Second languages become progressively more difficult to learn as we get older (Birdsong & Molis, 2001). Support for this finding came from a study in which older Korean and Chinese immigrants to the United States found it more difficult to learn English than did younger immigrants—even though the groups were intellectually equal (Johnson & Newport, 1989). Nonetheless, this finding must be viewed with caution in light of the many other factors that could account for differences in the ease with which younger and older immigrants learn a new language.

Websites You Can Use

Second Language Education on the Web
http://tortoise.oise.utoronto.ca/~aweinrib/sle/
This website is sponsored by Alice Adler of the University of Toronto. It includes links to sites concerned with second-language learning—particularly French and English.

Theories of Language Acquisition Language researchers debate this question: Is language acquired solely through learning, or is it strongly influenced by the maturation of an inherited predisposition to develop language? Those who favor the learning position assume that if it were possible to raise two infants together with no exposure to language, they would not develop true language. In contrast, those who favor the view that language emerges from an inherited predisposition assume that the two infants might develop a rudimentary form of language marked by semanticity, generativity, and displacement. According to this position, learning normally determines only which language an infant will speak, whether English, French, or Navajo.

Language as the Product of Learning B. F. Skinner (1957) claimed that language is acquired solely through learning, chiefly through the positive reinforcement of appropriate speech. For example, a 1-year-old child might learn to say "milk" because her parents give her milk and praise her when she says "milk." Similarly, a 2-year-old child named Jane might be given a cookie and praise for saying "Give Jane cookie" but not for saying "Jane cookie give." As you can see, Skinner assumed that vocabulary and grammar are learned through positive reinforcement. In a study supportive of Skinner's position, two groups of infants between 2 and 7 months old were positively reinforced for producing different phonemes. The infants were reinforced by smiles, *tsk* sounds, and light stroking of the abdomen. One group was reinforced for making vowel sounds, whereas the other group was reinforced for making consonant sounds. The infants responded by increasing their production of the phonemes that were reinforced. This study showed that positive reinforcement can affect language acquisition (Routh, 1969). Of course, it does not indicate that language is acquired *solely* through learning.

Albert Bandura (1977), the influential cognitive-behavioral psychologist, stresses the role of observational learning in language acquisition. He assumes that children develop language primarily by imitating the vocabulary and grammatical constructions used by their parents and others in their everyday lives. In a study that supported his position, adults replied to statements made by 2-year-old children by purposely using slightly more complex syntax than the children normally would. After 2 months, the children had developed more complex syntax than did children who had not been exposed to the adult models (Nelson, 1977). Additional support for the effect of modeling comes from findings that 2-year-olds whose parents read to them acquire language more rapidly than do 2-year-olds whose parents do not (Whitehurst et al., 1988). Yet, we cannot discount the possibility that other differences between the two groups of parents produced this effect.

Language as an Inherited Predisposition The assumption that language is acquired solely through learning has been challenged by Noam Chomsky and his followers (Rondall, 1994). Chomsky insists that infants are born with the predisposition to develop language. He believes they inherit a *language acquisition device*—a brain mechanism that makes them sensitive to phonemes, syntax, and semantics. In analyzing the interactions of parents and children, Chomsky has found that children in different cultures progress through similar stages and learn their native languages without formal parental instruction. Children say things that adults never say, and their parents do not positively reinforce proper grammar (or correct improper grammar) in any consistent manner. Modeling, too, cannot explain all language learning, because observations of children show that they vary greatly in the extent to which they imitate what their parents say (Snow, 1981).

What evidence is there to support Chomsky's position? One source of evidence comes from the Human Genome Project. In 2001 scientists discovered that the gene FOXP2 plays an important role in our ability to acquire spoken language (Marcus & Fisher, 2003). Another source of evidence is the universality in the basic features of language and the stages of language acquisition (Miller, 1990), which indicates that the tendency to develop language is inborn. Studies of deaf children and children of deaf parents support Chomsky's position. One study observed deaf children who were neither rewarded for using sign language nor exposed to a model who used it. Nonetheless, the children spontaneously developed their own gestural system in which they communicated by using signs with the characteristics of true language (Goldin-Meadow & Mylander, 1998). And infants born to deaf parents develop unique rhythmic hand movements that reflect the rhythmic patterns of language (Petitto et al., 2001).

Despite the evidence favoring language as innate and contradicting learning as an explanation for language

acquisition, research has provided some support for the learning position (Stemmer, 1990). One study tested the claim made by those who favor Chomsky's position that adults typically ignore children's speech errors and fail to correct their ungrammatical statements. The study found that language acquisition does depend in part on feedback provided by adults who correct specific instances of improper grammar. Adults do so by repeating a child's grammatically incorrect statements in grammatically correct form or by asking the child to clarify his or her statements (Bohannon & Stanowicz, 1988).

It seems that the positions of Chomsky, Skinner, and Bandura must be integrated to explain how language is acquired. We appear to be born with a predisposition to develop language, which provides us with an innate sensitivity to grammar. But we might learn our specific language, including its grammar, mainly through operant conditioning and observational learning.

Staying on Track
The Acquisition of Language
1. What are the main characteristics of the stages of language development during infancy?
2. How do the theories of Skinner and Chomsky differ in regard to language development?

The Relationship Between Language and Thought

In his novel *1984,* George Orwell (1949) envisioned a totalitarian government that controlled citizen's thoughts by regulating their language. By adding, removing, or redefining words, the government used *Newspeak* to ensure that citizens would not think rebellious thoughts against their leader, "Big Brother." For example, in Newspeak the word *joycamp* referred to a forced labor camp. And the word *free* was redefined to refer only to physical reality, as in *The dog is free from lice,* rather than to political freedom. Even democratic government officials will, at times, resort to euphemisms reminiscent of Newspeak. For example, to reduce public outrage about deceptive government practices, American officials coined the word *misinformation* to replace the word *lying.* Business people also understand the power of language to shape thought, as when used-car dealers refer to their vehicles as *previously owned* instead of *used*.

The Linguistic Relativity Hypothesis Orwell's view of the influence of language on thought was shared by the linguist-anthropologist Benjamin Lee Whorf (1897-1941), who expressed it in his **linguistic relativity hypothesis**, which assumes that our perception of the world is determined by the particular language we speak (Smith, 1996). Whorf (1956) pointed out that Inuit (once called "Eskimo") languages have several words for snow (such as words that distinguish between falling snow and fallen snow), whereas the English language has only one. According to the linguistic relativity hypothesis, the variety of words for snow in an Inuit language causes people who speak it to perceive differences in snow in that people who speak English do not.

Critics argue that, on the contrary, thought determines language. Perhaps the greater importance of snow in their culture led the Inuits to coin several words for snow, each referring to a different kind. Moreover, English speakers to whom snow is important, such as avid skiers, use different adjectives to describe different kinds of snow. Their ability to distinguish between crusty, powdery, and granular snow indicates that even English speakers can perceive wide variations in the quality of snow. And the number of words for snow in Inuit languages might have been exaggerated in the early reports that influenced Whorf and other linguistic relativity theorists (Pullum, 1991).

What does formal research have to say about the linguistic relativity hypothesis? In an early study bearing on Whorf's hypothesis (Carmichael, Hogan, & Walter, 1932), participants were presented with ambiguous drawings of objects that were given either of two labels. When later asked to draw the objects, participants drew pictures that looked more like the object that had been named than like the object they had seen. These results supported Whorf's hypothesis, at least in that language appeared to influence the participants' recall of objects.

Eleanor Rosch (1975) conducted a classic study to test whether language influences the perception of colors. She hypothesized that if the linguistic relativity hypothesis were correct, people who speak a language that has many color words would perceive colors differently than would people who speak a language with few color words.

linguistic relativity hypothesis Benjamin Whorf's hypothesis that one's perception of the world is molded by one's language.

When Rosch visited the Dani people of New Guinea, she found that the Dani language has two basic color words: *mili* for dark, cool colors, and *mola* for light, warm colors. In contrast, English has eleven basic color words: *black, white, red, green, yellow, blue, brown, purple, pink, orange,* and *gray*. To describe these colors, the Dani use relatively long phrases. Rosch wondered whether these differences in language would be associated with differences in the perception of colors. She decided to test this hypothesis by using "focal" colors, which are considered the best representatives of each of the colors (for example, "fire-engine red" for red), and nonfocal colors.

Dani and American participants were given a series of trials on which they were first shown a colored plastic chip for 5 seconds. After another 30 seconds, they were asked to select the chip from among 160 colored chips. Both the American participants and the Dani participants performed better when the chip to be recalled was a focal color than when it was a nonfocal color. These results contradicted Whorf's hypothesis, because though the Dani use only two color names, they are as capable as English-speaking people of perceiving all the focal colors in the English language. Perhaps we are genetically prepared to perceive these focal colors regardless of whether our language takes special note of them.

During the past decade, though, interest in the relationship between language and thought has been spurred by recent research in cognitive linguistics. Cognitive linguistics researchers have found that language may influence cross-cultural variation in a number of ways, including noun-verb relations, conversational and story-telling patterns, cultural scripts that encourage or discourage particular ways of thinking, encoding of the meaning of words, and theories of the self (Goddard, 2003). For example, one study investigated 39 languages spoken in 71 cultures. Cultures with "pronoun drop languages"—languages that omit personal pronouns (*I* and *you*) in conversation—are less individualistic than are cultures with languages that include personal pronouns (Kashima & Kashima, 1998).

Linguistic Relativity and Sexist Language Though language does not determine how we think about the world, it might influence how we think about the world (Hoffman, Lau, & Johnson, 1986). This presumption is the basis of the current concern about the traditional use of masculine pronouns, such as *his* and *him,* to refer to persons when no sexual identification is intended (Prentice, 1994). Critics of this practice claim that it makes people think that such statements refer primarily to men. Perhaps repeated exposure to such use of the male pronoun to refer to both women and men promotes the belief that certain gender-neutral activities are more suitable for men than for women, the topic of the following study.

ANATOMY OF A RESEARCH STUDY

Does Language Influence Children's Conceptions of Gender Roles?

Rationale

Janet Shibley Hyde (1984) conducted a classic study to test the effects of gendered pronouns on children's stereotypes about women and men.

Method

The participants in Hyde's study were 132 male and female third and fifth graders. All children read a story about a fictitious occupation: *wudgemaker.* Four versions of the story were prepared. In each version, the description of wudgemakers was identical; only the pronouns used in each story differed. One group read stories with *he* for the pronoun, the second read stories with *they,* the third read stories with *he* or *she,* and the fourth read stories with *she.* After reading the stories, the children were asked to provide two ratings: how well men could do the job and how well women could do the job.

Results and Discussion

Children's ratings of the male wudgemakers' competence were not affected by the pronouns they read in their stories. Male wudgemakers were seen as equally competent, regardless of the pronouns used in the stories. However, pronouns did have an effect on mean ratings of the female wudgemakers. The group who read stories with *he* as a pronoun rated female wudgemakers as "just O.K." In contrast, the other three groups rated female wudgemakers as significantly more competent. The highest rating was obtained for the group who read stories with *she* as a pronoun. Hyde concluded that pronoun use did have an influence on children's gender-role stereotypes.

These findings have been supported by more recent empirical research. Mykol Hamilton and her colleagues conducted three studies in which they asked children and adults to tell stories about sex-neutral stuffed animals (e.g., a dog, deer, or mouse). Most participants, regardless of age or sex, referred to the animals as "he" (Lambdin et al., 2003). Because our use of language can affect the way we think about gender roles as well as other aspects of everyday life, the linguistic relativity hypothesis might have some merit, as long as it is used to recognize that though language influences thought, it does not determine it (Davies, 1998).

The Relationship Between Language and Thought

1. How does Orwell's concept of Newspeak embody the belief that language affects thought?
2. How are concerns about sexist language related to the linguistic relativity hypothesis?

Language in Apes

In the early 17th century, the philosopher René Descartes argued that language was the critical feature that distinguished human beings from other animals. Interest in teaching animals cognitive skills, such as language, that normally are associated with human beings was stimulated by the case of "Clever Hans," a horse who impressed onlookers by solving arithmetic problems in Germany in the early 20th century. Hans was trained to count out the answers to arithmetic problems by tapping one of his hooves until he reached the correct answer. He counted anything present, including persons, hats, or umbrellas. But a psychologist named Oskar Pfungst showed that Hans stopped counting when he noticed tiny movements of his questioner's head, which cued the initiation and termination of counting. When the questioner knew the answer, Hans was correct almost all the time. But when the questioner did not know the answer, Hans was wrong all the time. So, Hans might have been clever, but he had no idea how to perform arithmetic (Davis & Memmott, 1982).

As interest waned in teaching animals to perform arithmetic, interest in teaching them language grew. As you read in the section, "Language," animals as diverse as bees, dogs, and monkeys can communicate in limited, stereotyped ways. But they do not use true language, which is characterized by semanticity, generativity, and displacement. Research on language learning in dolphins (Herman & Uyeyama, 1999) and sea lions (Gisiner & Schusterman, 1992) is promising but has yet to provide conclusive findings. A much larger body of research supports the belief that there is at least one kind of nonhuman animal capable of acquiring true language—the ape (Williams, Brakke, & Savage-Rumbaugh, 1997).

Teaching Chimpanzees to Use Language More than 50 years ago, Winthrop and Luella Kellogg (1933) published a book about their experiences raising a chimpanzee named Gua with their infant son, Donald. Even after being exposed to speech as a member of the family, Gua could not speak a single word. Another couple, Cathy and Keith Hayes (Hayes, 1951), had only slightly better results with Viki, a chimpanzee they too raised as a member of their family. Despite their intensive efforts over a period of several years, Viki learned to say only four words: *mama, papa, cup,* and *up.* The Hayeses concluded that the vocal anatomy of apes is not designed for producing speech.

In 1925 the primatologist Robert Yerkes, wondering whether apes have lots to say but no way of saying it, suggested teaching them to use sign language instead of speech. His suggestion was not carried out until 1966, when Allen and Beatrix Gardner (1969) of the University of Nevada began teaching American Sign Language (ASL) to a 1-year-old chimpanzee named Washoe. They raised Washoe in a trailer next to their house. To encourage her to use ASL, they never spoke in her presence; instead, they signed to each other and Washoe using simple words about various objects and everyday events (Dewsbury, 1996). They also asked Washoe simple questions, praised her correct signs, and tried to comply with her requests, just as parents do with young children. After 4 years of training, Washoe had a repertoire of 132 signs, which she used to name objects and to describe qualities of objects. The Gardners later replicated their work with four other apes, teaching each to use sign language (Gardner, Gardner, & Van Cantfort, 1989).

Washoe also displayed the ability to generalize her signs to refer to similar things. For example, she used the sign for *open* to refer to doors on a car, a house, and a refrigerator. Washoe even seemed to show an important characteristic of true language—generativity. On seeing a swan for the first time, Washoe made the signs for *water bird.* And in a chimpanzee colony in Washington State, Washoe taught ASL to a young chimpanzee named Loulis, whom she had "adopted" (Cunningham, 1981). After 5 years, Loulis had acquired a vocabulary of more than 50 signs, which he could have learned only from Washoe and other chimpanzees, since all human signing was forbidden when Loulis was present (Gardner, Gardner, & Van Cantfort, 1989).

During the past few decades, several other apes have been taught to use sign language or other forms of language. Ann and David Premack taught a laboratory chimpanzee named Sarah to use plastic chips of different shapes and colors to represent words (Premack, 1971).

Sarah learned to answer questions by arranging the chips in different sequences on a board to form sentences. Duane Rumbaugh taught a chimpanzee named Lana to use a computer to create sentences by pressing large keys marked by lexigrams—geometric shapes representing particular words (Rumbaugh, Gill, & von Glasersfeld, 1973). Lana formed sentences by pressing keys in a particular order. Lana's language was called "Yerkish," in honor of Robert Yerkes. When Lana made grammatically correct requests, she was rewarded with food, toys, music, or other things she enjoyed.

Controversy About Ape-Language Research Have Washoe, Sarah, and Lana learned to use true language? Do they exhibit semanticity, generativity, and displacement? That is, can they communicate meaningfully, create novel combinations of signs, and refer to objects that are not present? Columbia University psychologist Herbert Terrace, who once believed that apes can use language, says no (Terrace et al., 1979). Terrace taught a chimpanzee named Nim Chimpsky to use sign language. (Nim was named after Noam Chomsky, who believes that apes cannot learn true language.) After 5 years of training, Nim had mastered 125 signs. At first, Terrace assumed that Nim had learned true language. But after analyzing videotapes of conversations with Nim and videotapes of other apes that had been taught sign language, he concluded that Nim and the other apes did not display true language.

On what did Terrace base his conclusion? He found that apes merely learned to make signs, arrange forms, or press computer keys in a certain order to obtain rewards. In other words, their use of language was no different from that of a pigeon that learns to peck a sequence of keys to get food rewards. No researcher would claim that the pigeon is using language. So, the ability of an ape to produce a string of words does not indicate that the ape has learned to produce a sentence. Terrace also claims that the apparent generativity of ape language might be a misinterpretation of their actions. For example, Washoe's apparent reference to a swan as a "water bird" might have been a reference to two separate things—a body of water and a bird.

As additional evidence against ape language, Terrace claims that many instances of allegedly spontaneous signing by chimpanzees are actually responses to subtle cues from trainers. Terrace found that Nim communicated primarily in response to prompting by his trainer or by imitating signs recently made by his trainer. Thus, he did not use language in an original or spontaneous way, and his signs were simply gestures prompted by cues from his trainer that produced consequences he desired—a kind of operant conditioning (Terrace, 1985).

Terrace's attack has not gone unchallenged. Francine Patterson taught a gorilla named Koko to use more than 300 signs ("Ape Language," 1981). Koko even displays generativity, as in spontaneously referring to a zebra as a "white tiger." Patterson criticized Terrace for basing his conclusions on his work with Nim and on isolated-frames he has examined from films of other apes using ASL. She claimed that Nim's inadequate use of language might stem from his being confused by having 60 different trainers, which could account for Nim's failure to use sign language in a spontaneous way. In contrast, Patterson reported that Koko had only one primary trainer and used signs more spontaneously than Nim did. For example, Koko responded to a velvet hat by signing "that soft" (Patterson, Patterson, & Brentari, 1987).

In recent years, the strongest evidence in support of ape language comes from studies by Duane Rumbaugh and Sue Savage-Rumbaugh of the Language Research Center at Georgia State University. They trained two chimpanzees, Austin and Sherman, to communicate through Yerkish, the language used earlier by Lana. Austin and Sherman use language in a more sophisticated way than previous chimpanzees. In one study, Austin, Sherman, and Lana were taught to categorize three objects (an orange, a beancake, and a slice of bread) as "edible" and three objects (a key, a stick, and a pile of coins) as "inedible." When given other objects, Austin and Sherman, but not Lana, were able to categorize them as edible or inedible. Perhaps Lana could not learn this task because she had been trained to use language to associate labels with specific objects rather than to understand the concepts to which the labels referred (Savage-Rumbaugh et al., 1980).

Even when housed in different rooms, Austin and Sherman can request objects from each other. This ability was demonstrated when one of the chimpanzees was given a box from which he could obtain food or drink only by using a tool located in the other chimpanzee's room. The chimpanzee in the room with the food indicated the tool he needed by striking a specific series of keys on a computer keyboard. The chimpanzee in the room with the tools then passed that tool to the other chimpanzee (Marx, 1980).

More recently, Sue Savage-Rumbaugh and her colleagues (1986) described their work with two pygmy chimpanzees, Kanzi and Mulika, who have achieved language ability superior to that of previous apes. Savage-Rumbaugh and her researchers exposed the chimpanzees to human language during everyday activities rather than as part of an artificial training program (Menzel, Savage-Rumbaugh, & Menzel, 2002). Kanzi learned Yerkish spontaneously by observing people and other chimpanzees (including his mother) pressing appropriate lexigrams on a keyboard (Savage-Rumbaugh, 1990). He also can identify symbols referred to in human speech. Previous apes depended on their own particular language system to comprehend human communications. Kanzi can even form requests in which other individuals are either the agent or the recipient of action—which reflects his appreciation of syntax (Savage-Rumbaugh et al., 1993). Before, apes such as Nim made spontaneous requests only in which they were the targets of a suggested action. Moreover, Kanzi shows displacement, using lexigrams to refer to things that are not present (Savage-Rumbaugh, 1987).

Nonetheless, some critics insist that even Kanzi does not display all the characteristics of true language (Kako, 1999). Savage-Rumbaugh has responded to this criticism by asking critics to stress the important language skills that Kanzi has exhibited rather than continually seeking to identify the relatively minor aspects of language that he has failed to exhibit (Shanker, Savage-Rumbaugh, & Taylor, 1999). Moreover, Allen Gardner has reported that Washoe and other language-trained chimpanzees who are living together in retirement converse with one another and with human beings in a manner similar to that of human children (Jensvold & Gardner, 2000).

Perhaps future studies using pygmy chimpanzees will succeed where others have failed in demonstrating convincingly that apes are capable of using true language. But even if apes can use true language, no ape has gone beyond the language level of a 3-year-old child. Is that the upper limit of ape language ability, or is it just the upper limit using current training methods? Research soon might provide the answer. In any case, we do know that apes are capable of more complex communication than simply grunting to convey crude emotional states.

Staying on Track
Language in Apes
1. What evidence is there that apes such as Washoe demonstrate the characteristics of true language?
2. Why do critics doubt that these apes have acquired true language?

Will the Replication of a Classic Research Study on Mental Sets Produce Similar Findings Today?

In the section, "Problem Solving" you read about the cognitive impediment to problem solving called a mental set. A mental set is a predisposition to rely on an approach to solving a problem that has worked so well in the past that it blinds you to an effective solution to a current problem. The classic water-jar study supporting the negative effect of mental sets on problem solving was conducted more than 50 years ago (Luchins, 1946). In this exercise, you will conduct an approximate replication of the water-jar study to determine whether the original findings will hold up today.

Method
Participants

The participants will be 30 "naive" fellow male and female students, that is, students who have not taken introductory psychology. Using students who have taken introductory psychology might threaten the validity of your study by including some who have learned about mental sets, perhaps even reading about the classic water-jar study.

Materials

You will use three versions of the water-jar problem discussed earlier in the chapter. You will need to present these problems to the participants in a written format or on a computer screen.

Procedure

Create three versions of the water-jar problem. One version should be identical to that described earlier in the chapter: The first five problems will be solvable by the same approach and the sixth problem will not be solvable by that approach— though it will be solvable by a simpler approach. The second version should just present the sixth problem. The third version, added here to control for the possible effect of working on five problems before attempting the sixth, should present the same five problems as in the original study but the sixth problem should be solvable by the approach used in solving the first five.

Tell the participants that they will be participating in a study on problem solving, without revealing its exact purpose. Give 10 students the first version of the task, 10 students the second version, and 10 students the third version. To avoid biasing students who will be participating in the study later, ask your participants not to discuss the study with anyone else until it has been completed.

Results and Discussion

Count the number of correct responses to the problem in the second version and the sixth problem in the other two versions. Draw a bar graph (see Appendix C in the Online Edition) comparing the number of correct answers to those three problems.

Note how your results compare with those of Luchins (1946). Do the results appear to support the influence of a mental set? If not, try to explain why. Were there any confounding variables that might have adversely affected your study? Why would the use of an inferential statistic (see Chapter 2 and Appendix C in the Online Edition) have been preferable to subjectively judging the size of the differences between the three groups? Think of another study you could conduct to assess the effects of mental sets on problem solving.

CHAPTER SUMMARY

Thought

- The past few decades have seen a cognitive revolution in psychology, with increased interest in the study of thought.
- Thought is the purposeful mental manipulation of words and images.

Concept Formation

- Thought depends on concepts, which are categories of objects, events, qualities, or relations whose members share certain features.
- A logical concept is formed by identifying specific features possessed by all members of the concept.
- A natural concept is formed through everyday experiences and has fuzzy borders.
- The best representative of a concept is called a prototype.

Problem Solving

- One of the most important uses of concepts is in problem solving, the thought process that enables us to overcome obstacles to reach goals.
- A basic method of solving problems is trial and error, which involves trying one possible solution after another until finding one that works.
- The problem-solving strategy called insight depends on the mental manipulation of information.
- An algorithm is a rule that, when followed step by step, ensures that a solution to a problem will be found.
- A heuristic is a general principle that guides problem solving but does not guarantee the discovery of a solution.
- A mental set is a problem-solving strategy that has succeeded in the past but that can interfere with solving a problem that requires a new strategy.
- Our past experience also can impede problem solving through functional fixedness, the inability to realize that a problem can be solved by using a familiar object in an unusual way.

Creativity

- Creativity is a form of problem solving characterized by novel solutions that also are useful or socially valued.
- Creative people tend to have above-average intelligence and are able to integrate different kinds of thinking.
- Creative people are more motivated by their intrinsic interest in creative tasks than by extrinsic factors.
- Social-cultural factors also may influence the development and expression of creativity.
- Creativity also depends on divergent thinking, in which a person freely considers a variety of potential solutions to a problem.

Decision Making

- In decision making we try to make the best choice from among alternative courses of action.
- In using the representativeness heuristic, we assume that a small sample is representative of its population.
- In using the availability heuristic, we estimate the probability of an event by how easily instances of it come to mind.
- We are also subject to framing effects, which are biases introduced in the decision-making process by presenting a situation in a certain manner.

Artificial Intelligence

- Artificial intelligence is a field that integrates computer science and cognitive psychology to try to simulate or improve on human thought by using computer programs.
- Computer programs called expert systems display expertise in specific domains of knowledge.
- Computer scientists are studying human performance by creating robots that engage in problem solving while exploring and mapping the environment.

Language

- In using language, we rely on spoken symbols to communicate through speech, written symbols to communicate through writing, and gestured symbols to communicate through sign language.

- We use language to communicate with other people, to store and retrieve memories, and to plan for the future.

The Structure of Language

- True language is characterized by semanticity, generativity, and displacement.
- The rules of a language are its grammar.
- Phonemes are the basic sounds of a language, and morphemes are its smallest meaningful units.
- A language's syntax includes rules governing the acceptable arrangement of words and phrases.
- Semantics is the study of how language conveys meaning.
- Noam Chomsky calls the underlying meaning of a statement its deep structure and the words themselves its surface structure.
- We translate between the two structures by using transformational grammar.
- The branch of semantics concerned with the relationship between language and its social context is called pragmatics.

The Acquisition of Language

- Infants in all cultures progress through similar stages of language development.
- They begin babbling between 4 and 6 months of age and say their first words when they are about 1 year old.
- At first they use holophrastic speech, in which single words represent whole phrases or sentences.
- Between the ages of 18 and 24 months, infants begin speaking two-word sentences and use telegraphic speech.

- As infants learn their language's grammar, they may engage in overregularization, in which they apply grammatical rules without making necessary exceptions.
- There might be a critical period for language acquisition that extends from infancy to adolescence.
- B. F. Skinner and Albert Bandura believe that language is acquired solely through learning, whereas Noam Chomsky believes we have an innate predisposition to develop language.

The Relationship Between Language and Thought

- Benjamin Lee Whorf's linguistic relativity hypothesis assumes that our view of the world is determined by the particular language we speak.
- But research has shown that though language can influence thought, it does not determine it.

Language in Apes

- Researchers have taught apes to communicate by using sign language, form boards, and computers.
- The most well known of these apes include the gorilla Koko and the chimpanzees Washoe, Sarah, and Lana.
- Herbert Terrace, the trainer of Nim Chimpsky, claims that apes have not learned true language; instead, they have learned to give responses that lead to rewards, just as pigeons learn to peck at keys to obtain food.
- Francine Patterson, Duane Rumbaugh, and Sue Savage-Rumbaugh have countered by providing evidence that the apes have indeed learned true language characterized by semanticity, generativity, and displacement.

The Origin of Speech

CHARLES F. HOCKETT

Man is the only animal that can communicate by means of abstract symbols. Yet this ability shares many features with communication in other animals, and has arisen from these more primitive systems.

About 50 years ago the Linguistic Society of Paris established a standing rule barring from its sessions papers on the origin of language. This action was a symptom of the times. Speculation about the origin of language had been common throughout the 19th century, but had reached no conclusive results. The whole enterprise in consequence had come to be frowned upon—as futile or crackpot—in respectable linguistic and philological circles. Yet amidst the speculations there were two well-reasoned empirical plans that deserve mention even though their results were negative.

A century ago there were still many corners of the world that had not been visited by European travelers. It was reasonable for the European scholar to suspect that beyond the farthest frontiers there might lurk half-men or man-apes who would be "living fossils" attesting to earlier stages of human evolution. The speech (or quasi-speech) of these men (or quasi-men) might then similarly attest to earlier stages in the evolution of language. The search was vain. Nowhere in the world has there been discovered a language that can validly and meaningfully be called "primitive." Edward Sapir wrote in 1921: "There is no more striking general fact about language than its universality. One may argue as to whether a particular tribe engages in activities that are worthy of the name of religion or of art, but we know of no people that is not possessed of a fully developed language. The lowliest South African Bushman speaks in the forms of a rich symbolic system that is in essence perfectly comparable to the speech of the cultivated Frenchman."

The other empirical hope in the 19th century rested on the comparative method of historical linguistics, the discovery of which was one of the triumphs of the period. Between two languages the resemblances are sometimes so extensive and orderly that they cannot be attributed to chance or to parallel development. The alternative explanation is that the two are divergent descendants of a single earlier language. English, Dutch, German and the Scandinavian languages are related in just this way. The comparative method makes it possible to examine such a group of related languages and to construct, often in surprising detail, a portrayal of the common ancestor, in this case the proto-Germanic language. Direct documentary evidence of proto-Germanic does not exist, yet understanding of its workings exceeds that of many languages spoken today.

There was at first some hope that the comparative method might help determine the origin of language. This hope was rational in a day when it was thought that language might be only a few thousands or tens of thousands of years old, and when it was repeatedly being demonstrated that languages that had been thought to be unrelated were in fact related. By applying the comparative method to all the languages of the world, some earliest reconstructable horizon would be reached. This might not date back so early as the origin of language, but it might bear certain earmarks of primitiveness, and thus it would enable investigators to extrapolate toward the origin. This hope also proved vain. The earliest reconstructable stage for any language family shows all the complexities and flexibilities of the languages of today.

These points had become clear a half-century ago, by the time of the Paris ruling. Scholars cannot really approve of such a prohibition. But in this instance it had the useful result of channeling the energies of investigators toward the gathering of more and better information about languages as they are today. The subsequent progress in understanding the workings of language has been truly remarkable. Various related fields have also made vast strides in the last half-century: zoologists know more about the evolutionary process, anthropologists know more about the nature of culture, and so on. In the light of these developments there need be no apology-for reopening the issue of the origins of human speech.

Although the comparative method of linguistics, as has been shown, throws no light on the origin of language, the investigation may be furthered by a comparative method modeled on that of the zoologist. The frame of reference must be such that all languages look alike when viewed through it, but such that within it human language as a whole can be compared with the communicative systems of other animals, especially the other hominoids, man's closest living relatives, the gibbons and great apes. The useful items for this sort of comparison cannot be things such as the word for "sky"; languages have such words, but gibbon calls do not involve words at all. Nor can they be even the signal for "danger," which gibbons do have. Rather, they must be the basic features of design that can be present or absent in any communicative system, whether it be a communicative system of humans, of animals or of machines.

With this sort of comparative method it may be possible to reconstruct the communicative habits of the remote ancestors of the hominoid line, which may be called the protohominoids. The task, then, is to work out the sequence by which that ancestral system became language

as the hominids—the man-apes and ancient men—became man.

A set of 13 design-features is presented in the illustration on the opposite page. There is solid empirical justification for the belief that all the languages of the world share every one of them. At first sight some appear so trivial that no one looking just at language would bother to note them. They become worthy of mention only when it is realized that certain animal systems—and certain human systems other than language—lack them.

The first design-feature—the "vocal-auditory channel"—is perhaps the most obvious. There are systems of communication that use other channels; for example, gesture, the dancing of bees or the courtship ritual of the stickleback. The vocal-auditory channel has the advantage—at least for primates—that it leaves much of the body free for other activities that can be carried on at the same time.

The next two design-features—"rapid fading" and "broadcast transmission and directional reception," stemming from the physics of sound—are almost unavoidable consequences of the first. A linguistic signal can be heard by any auditory system within earshot, and the source can normally be localized by binaural direction-finding. The rapid fading of such a signal means that it does not linger for reception at the hearer's convenience. Animal tracks and spoors, on the other hand, persist for a while; so of course do written records, a product of man's extremely recent cultural evolution.

The significance of "interchangeability" and "total feedback" for language becomes clear upon comparison with other systems. In general a speaker of a language can reproduce any linguistic message he can understand, whereas the characteristic courtship motions of the male and female stickleback are different, and neither can act out those appropriate to the other. For that matter in the communication of a human mother and infant neither is apt to transmit the characteristic signals or to manifest the typical responses of the other. Again, the speaker of a language hears, by total feedback, everything of linguistic relevance in what he himself says. In contrast, the male stickleback does not see the colors of his own eye and belly that are crucial in stimulating the female. Feedback is important, since it makes possible the so-called internalization of communicative behavior that constitutes at least a major portion of "thinking."

The sixth design-feature, "specialization," refers to the fact that the bodily effort and spreading sound waves of speech serve no function except as signals. A dog, panting with his tongue hanging out, is performing a biologically essential activity, since this is how dogs cool themselves off and maintain the proper body temperature. The panting dog incidentally produces sound, and thereby may inform other dogs (or humans) as to where he is and how he feels. But this transmission of information is strictly a side effect. Nor does the dog's panting exhibit the design-feature of "semanticity." It is not a signal meaning that the dog is hot; it is part of being hot. In language, however, a message triggers the particular result it does because there are relatively fixed associations between elements in messages (e.g., words) and recurrent features or situations of the world around us. For example, the English word "salt" means salt, not sugar or pepper. The calls of gibbons also possess semanticity. The gibbon has a danger call, for example, and it does not in principle matter that the meaning of the call is a great deal broader and more vague than, say, the cry of "Fire!"

In a semantic communicative system the ties between meaningful message-elements and their meanings can be arbitrary or nonarbitrary. In language the ties are arbitrary. The word "salt" is not salty nor granular; "dog" is not "canine"; "whale" is a small word for a large object; "microorganism" is the reverse. A picture, on the other hand, looks like what it is a picture of. A bee dances faster if the source of nectar she is reporting is closer, and slower if it is farther away. The design-feature of "arbitrariness" has the disadvantage of being arbitrary, but the great advantage that there is no limit to what can be communicated about.

Human vocal organs can produce a huge variety of sound. But in any one language only a relatively small set of ranges of sound is used, and the differences between these ranges are functionally absolute. The English words "pin" and "bin" are different to the ear only at one point. If a speaker produces a syllable that deviates from the normal pronunciation of "pin" in the direction of that of "bin," he is not producing still a third word, but just saying "pin" (or perhaps "bin") in a noisy way. The hearer compensates if he can, on the basis of context, or else fails to understand. This feature of "discreteness" in the elementary signaling units of a language contrasts with the use of sound effects by way of vocal gesture. There is an effectively continuous scale of degrees to which one may raise his voice as in anger, or lower it to signal confidentiality. Bee-dancing also is continuous rather than discrete.

Man is apparently almost unique in being able to talk about things that are remote in space or time (or both) from where the talking goes on. This feature—"displacement"—seems to be definitely lacking in the vocal signaling of man's closest relatives, though it does occur in bee-dancing.

One of the most important design-features of language is "productivity"; that is, the capacity to say things that have never been said or heard before and yet to be understood by other speakers of the language. If a gibbon makes any vocal sound at all, it is one or another of a small finite repertory of familiar calls. The gibbon call system can be characterized as closed. Language is open, or "productive," in the sense that one can coin new utterances by putting together pieces familiar from old utterances, assembling them by patterns of arrangement also familiar in old utterances.

Human genes carry the capacity to acquire a language, and probably also a strong drive toward such acquisition, but the detailed conventions of any one language are transmitted extragenetically by learning and teaching. To what extent such "traditional transmission" plays a part in gibbon calls or for other mammalian systems of vocal signals is not known, though in some instances the uniformity of the sounds made by a species, wherever the species is found over the world, is so great that genetics must be responsible.

The meaningful elements in any language—"words" in everyday parlance, "morphemes" to the linguist—constitute an enormous stock. Yet they are represented by small arrangements of a relatively very small stock of distinguishable sounds which are in themselves wholly meaningless. This "duality of patterning" is illustrated by the English words

THIRTEEN DESIGN-FEATURES of animal communication, discussed in detail in the text of this article, are symbolized on opposite page. The patterns of the words "pin," "bin," "team" and "meat" were recorded at Bell Telephone Laboratories. They are totally distinct as to meaning, and yet are composed of just three basic meaningless sounds in different permutations. Few animal communicative systems share this design-feature of language—none among the other hominoids, and perhaps none at all.

It should be noted that some of these 13 design-features are not independent. In particular, a system cannot be either arbitrary or nonarbitrary unless it is semantic, and it cannot have duality of-patterning unless it is semantic. It should also be noted that the listing does not attempt to include all the features that might be discovered in the communicative behavior of this or that species, but only those that are clearly important for language.

It is probably safe to assume that nine of the 13 features were already present in the vocal-auditory communication of the protohominoids—just the nine that are securely attested for the gibbons and humans of today. That is, there were a dozen or so distinct calls, each the appropriate vocal response (or vocal part of the whole response) to a recurrent and biologically important type of situation: the discovery of food, the detection of a predator, sexual interest, need for maternal care, and so on. The problem of the origin of human speech, then, is that of trying to determine how such a system could have developed the four additional properties of displacement, productivity and full-blown traditional transmission. Of course the full story involves a great deal more than communicative behavior alone. The development must be visualized as occurring in the context of the evolution of the primate horde into the primitive society of food-gatherers and hunters, an integral part, but a part, of the total evolution of behavior.

It is possible to imagine a closed system developing some degree of productivity, even in the absence of the other three features. Human speech exhibits a phenomenon that could have this effect, the phenomenon of "blending." Sometimes a speaker will hesitate between two words or phrases, both reasonably appropriate for the situation in which he is speaking, and actually say something that is neither wholly one nor wholly the other, but a combination of parts of each. Hesitating between "Don't shout so loud" and "Don't yell so loud," he might come out with "Don't shell so loud." Blending is almost always involved in slips of the tongue, but it may also be the regular mechanism by which a speaker of a language says something that he has not said before. Anything a speaker says must be either an exact repetition of an utterance he has heard before, or else some blended product of two or more such

familiar utterances. Thus even such a smooth and normal sentence as "I tried to get there, but the car broke down" might be produced as a blend, say, of "I tried to get there but couldn't" and "While I was driving down Main Street the car broke down."

Children acquiring the language of their community pass through a stage that is closed in just the way gibbon calls are. A child may have a repertory of several dozen sentences, each of which, in adult terms, has an internal structure, and yet for the child each may be an indivisible whole. He may also learn new whole utterances from surrounding adults. The child takes the crucial step, however, when he first says something that he has not learned from others. The only way in which the child can possibly do this is by blending two of the whole utterances that he already knows.

In the case of the closed call-system of the gibbons or the protohominoids, there is no source for the addition of new unitary calls to the repertory except perhaps by occasional imitation of the calls and cries of other species. Even this would not render the system productive, but would merely enlarge it. But blending might occur. Let AB represent the food call and CD the danger call, each a fairly complex phonetic pattern. Suppose a protohominoid encountered food and caught sight of a predator at the same time. If the two stimuli were balanced just right, he might emit the calls ABCD or CDAB in quick sequence, or might even produce AD or CB. Any of these would be a blend. AD, for example, would mean "both food and danger." By virtue of this, AB and CD would acquire new meanings, respectively "food without danger" and "danger without food." And all three of these calls-AB, CD and AD—would now be composite rather than unitary, built out of smaller elements with their own individual meanings: A would mean "food"; B, "no danger"; C, "no food"; and D, "danger."

But this is only part of the story. The generation of a blend can have no effect unless it is understood. Human beings are so good at understanding blends that it is hard to tell a blend from a rote repetition, except in the case of slips of the tongue and some of the earliest and most tentative blends used by children. Such powers of understanding cannot be ascribed to man's prehuman ancestors. It must be supposed, therefore, that occasional blends occurred over many tens of thousands of years (perhaps, indeed, they still may occur from time to time among gibbons or the great apes), with rarely any appropriate communicative

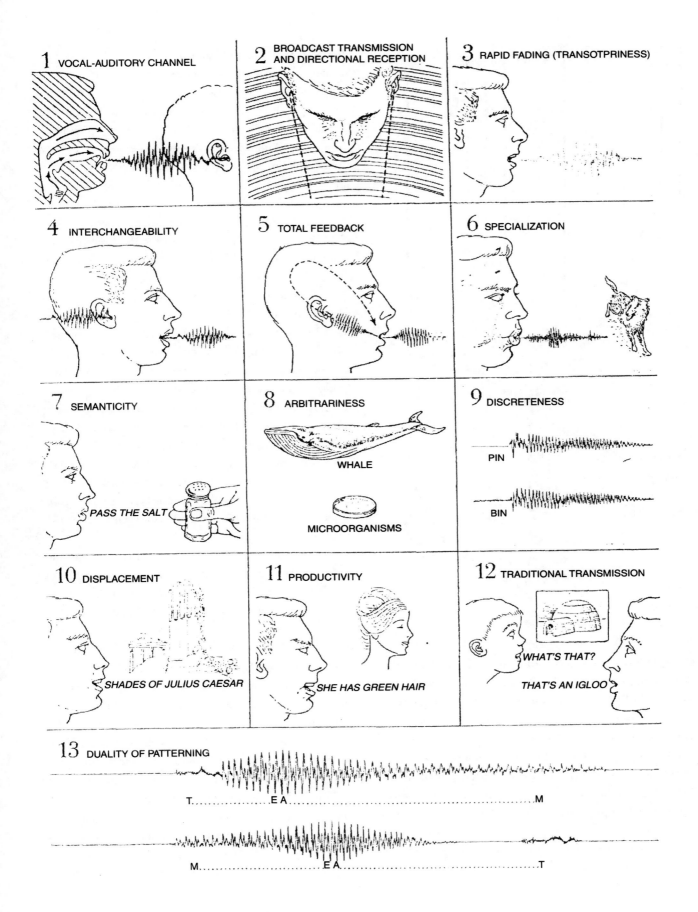

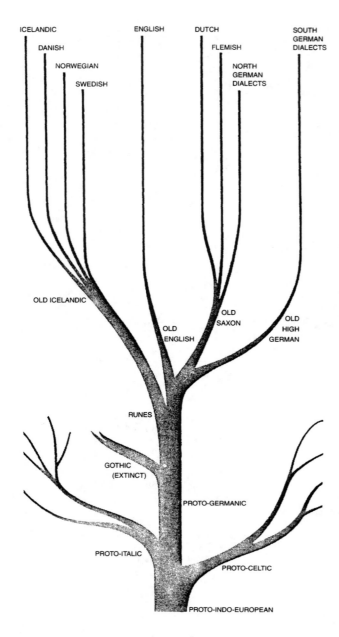

ORIGIN OF MODERN GERMANIC LANGUAGES, as indicated by this "family tree," was proto-Germanic, spoken some 2,700 years ago. Comparison of present-day languages has provided detailed knowledge of proto-Germanic, although no direct documentary evidence for the language exists. It grew, in turn, from the proto-Indo-European of 5000 B.C. Historical studies cannot, however, trace origins of language back much further in time.

impact on hearers, before the understanding of blends became speedy enough to reinforce their production.

However, once that did happen, the earlier closed system had become open and productive.

It is also possible to see how faint traces of displacement might develop in a call system even in the absence of productivity, duality and thoroughgoing traditional transmission, Suppose an early hominid, a man-ape say, caught sight of a predator without himself being seen. Suppose that for whatever reason-perhaps through fear-he sneaked silently back toward others of his band and only a bit later gave forth the danger call. This might give the whole band a better chance to escape the predator, thus bestowing at least slight survival value on whatever factor was responsible for the delay.

Something akin to communicative displacement is involved in lugging a stick or a stone around—it is like talking today about what one should do tomorrow. Of course it is not to be supposed that the first tool-carrying was purposeful, any more than that the first displaced communication was a discussion of plans. Caught in a cul-de-sac by a predator, however, the early hominid might strike out in terror with his stick or stone and by chance disable or drive off his enemy. In other words, the first tool-carrying had a consequence but not a purpose. Because the outcome was fortunate, it tended to reinforce whatever factor, genetic or traditional, prompted the behavior and made the outcome possible. In the end such events do lead to purpose behavior.

Although elements of displacement might arise in this fashion, on the whole it seems likely that some degree of productivity preceded any great proliferation of communicative displacement as well as any significant capacity for traditional transmission. A productive system requires the young to catch on to the ways in which whole signals are built out of smaller meaningful elements, some of which may never occur as whole signals in isolation. The young can do this only in the way that human children learn their language: by learning some utterances as whole units, in due time testing various blends based on that repertory, and finally adjusting their patterns of blending until the bulk of what they say matches what adults would say and is therefore understood. Part of this learning process is bound to take place away from the precise situations for which the responses are basically appropriate, and this means the promotion of displacement. Learning and teaching, moreover, call on any capacity for traditional transmission that the

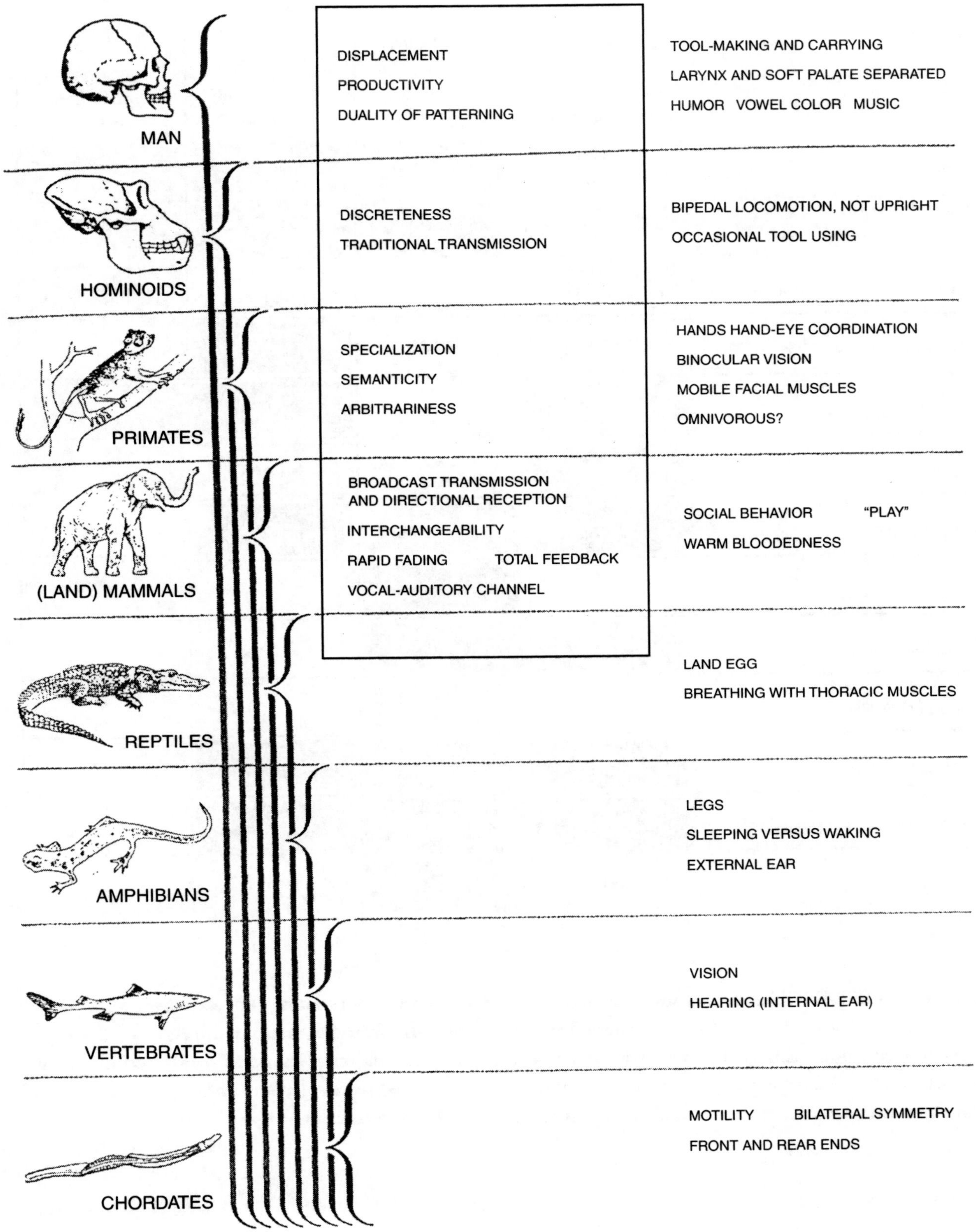

MAN

DISPLACEMENT

PRODUCTIVITY

DUALITY OF PATTERNING

TOOL-MAKING AND CARRYING

LARYNX AND SOFT PALATE SEPARATED

HUMOR   VOWEL COLOR   MUSIC

HOMINOIDS

DISCRETENESS

TRADITIONAL TRANSMISSION

BIPEDAL LOCOMOTION, NOT UPRIGHT

OCCASIONAL TOOL USING

PRIMATES

SPECIALIZATION

SEMANTICITY

ARBITRARINESS

HANDS HAND-EYE COORDINATION

BINOCULAR VISION

MOBILE FACIAL MUSCLES

OMNIVOROUS?

(LAND) MAMMALS

BROADCAST TRANSMISSION
AND DIRECTIONAL RECEPTION

INTERCHANGEABILITY

RAPID FADING   TOTAL FEEDBACK

VOCAL-AUDITORY CHANNEL

SOCIAL BEHAVIOR   "PLAY"

WARM BLOODEDNESS

REPTILES

LAND EGG

BREATHING WITH THORACIC MUSCLES

AMPHIBIANS

LEGS

SLEEPING VERSUS WAKING

EXTERNAL EAR

VERTEBRATES

VISION

HEARING (INTERNAL EAR)

CHORDATES

MOTILITY   BILATERAL SYMMETRY

FRONT AND REAR ENDS

	A	B	C	D
	SOME GRYLLIDAE AND TETTIGONIIDAE	BEE DANCING	STICKLEBACK COURTSHIP	WESTERN MEADOWLARK SONG
1 THE VOCAL-AUDITORY CHANNEL	AUDITORY, NOT VOCAL	NO	NO	YES
2 BROADCAST TRANSMISSION AND DIRECTIONAL RECEPTION	YES	YES		YES
3 RAPID FADING (TRANSITORINESS)	YES, REPEATED	?	?	YES
4 INTERCHANGEABILITY	LIMITED	LIMITED	NO	?
5 TOTAL FEEDBACK	YES	?	NO	YES
6 SPECIALIZATION	YES?	?	IN PART	YES?
7 SEMATICITY	NO?	YES		IN PART?
8 ARBITRATINESS	?	NO		IF SEMANTIC, YES
9 DISCRETENESS	YES?	NO	?	?
10 DISPLACEMENT		YES, ALWAYS		?
11 PRODUCTIVITY	NO	YES	NO	?
12 TRADITIONAL TRANSMISSION	NO?	PROBABLY NOT	NO?	?
13 DUALITY OF PATTERNING	? (TRIVIAL)	NO		?

EVOLUTION OF LANGUAGE and some related characteristics are suggested by this classification of chordates. The lowest form of animal in each classification exhibits the features listed at the right of the class. Brackets indicate that each group possesses or has evolved beyond the characteristics exhibited by all the groups below. The 13 design-features of language appear in the colored rectangle. Some but by no means all of the characteristics associated with communication are presented in the column at right.

band may have. Insofar as the communicative system itself has survival value, all this bestows survival value also on the capacity for traditional transmission and for displacement. But these in turn increase the survival value of the communicative system. A child can be taught how to avoid certain dangers before he actually encounters them.

These developments are also necessarily related to the appearance of large and convoluted brains, which are better

E	F	G	H
GIBBON CALLS	PARALINGUISTIC PHENOMENA	LANGUAGE	INSTRUMENTAL MUSIC AUDITORY, NOT VOCAL
YES	YES	YES	
YES	YES	YES	YES
YES, REPEATED	YES	YES	YES
YES	LARGELY YES	YES	?
YES	YES	YES	YES
YES	YES?	YES	YES
YES	YES?	YES	NO IN GENERAL
YES	IN PART	YES	
YES	LARGELY NO	YES	IN PART
NO	IN PART	YES, OFTEN	
NO	YES	YES	YES
?	YES	YES	YES
NO	NO	YES	

EIGHT SYSTEMS OF COMMUNICATION possess in varying degrees the 13 design-features of language. Column A refers to members of the cricket family. Column H concerns only Western music since the time of Bach. A question mark means that it is doubtful or not known if the system has the particular feature. A blank space indicates that feature cannot be determined because another feature is lacking or is indefinite.

storage units for the conventions of a complex communicative system and for other traditionally transmitted skills and practices. Hence the adaptative value of the behavior serves to select genetically for the change in structure. A lengthened period of childhood helplessness is also a longer period of plasticity for learning. There is therefore selection for prolonged childhood and, with it, later maturity and longer life. With more for the young to learn,

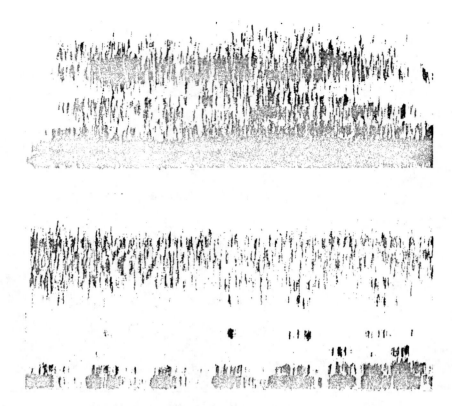

SUBHUMAN PRIMATE CALLS are represented here by sound spectrograms of the roar (top) and bark (bottom) of the howler monkey. Frequencies are shown vertically; time, horizontally. Roaring, the most prominent howler vocalization, regulates interactions and movements of groups of monkeys, and has both defensive and offensive functions. Barking has similar meanings but occurs when the monkeys are not quite so excited. Spectrograms were produced at Bell Telephone Laboratories from recordings made by Charles Southwick of the University of Southern Ohio during an expedition to Barro Colorado Island in the Canal Zone. The expedition was directed by C.R. Carpenter of Pennsylvania State University.

and with male as well as female tasks to be taught, fathers become more domesticated. The increase of displacement promotes retention and foresight; a male can protect his mate and guard her jealously from other males even when he does not at the moment hunger for her.

There is excellent reason to believe that duality of patterning was the last property to be developed, because one can find little if any reason why a communicative system should have this property unless it is highly complicated. If a vocal-auditory system comes to have a larger and larger number of distinct meaningful elements, those elements inevitably come to be more and more similar to one another in sound. There is a practical limit, for any species or any machine, to the number of distinct stimuli that can be discriminated, especially when the discriminations typically have to be made in noisy conditions. Suppose that

Samuel F. B. Morse, in devising his telegraph code, had proposed a signal .1 second long for "A," .2 second long for "B," and so on up to 2.6 seconds for "Z." Operators would have enormous difficulty learning and using any such system. What Morse actually did was to incorporate the principle of duality of patterning. The telegraph operator has to learn to discriminate, in the first instance, only two lengths of pulse and about three lengths of pause. Each letter is coded into a different arrangement of these elementary meaningless units. The arrangements are easily kept apart because the few meaningless units are plainly distinguishable.

The analogy explains why it was advantageous for the forerunner of language, as it was becoming increasingly-complex, to acquire duality of patterning. However it occurred, this was a major breakthrough; without it language could not possibly have achieved the efficiency and flexibility it has.

One of the basic principles of evolutionary theory holds that the initial survival value of any innovation is conservative in that it makes possible the maintenance of a largely traditional way of life in the face of changed circumstances. There was nothing in the makeup of the protohominoids that destined their descendants to become human. Some of them, indeed, did not. They made their way to ecological niches where food was plentiful and predators sufficiently avoidable, and where the development of primitive varieties of language and culture would have bestowed no advantage. They survive still, with various sorts of specialization, as the gibbons and the great apes.

Man's own remote ancestors, them, must have come to live in circumstances where a slightly more flexible system of communication, the incipient carrying and shaping of tools, and a slight increase in the capacity for traditional transmission made just the difference between surviving-largely, be it noted, by the good old protohominoid way of life—and dying out. There are various possibilities. If predators become more numerous and dangerous, any nonce use of a tool as a weapon, any co-operative mode of escape or attack might restore the balance. If food became scarcer, any technique for cracking harder nuts, for foraging over a wider territory, for sharing food so gathered or storing it when it was plentiful might promote survival of the band. Only after a very long period of such small adjustments to tiny changes of living conditions could the factors involved—incipient language, incipient culture—have started leading the way to a new pattern of life, of the kind called human.

Preference for Infant-Directed Speech in the First Month After Birth

ROBIN P. COOPER AND RICHARD N. ASLIN

2 experiments examined behavioral preferences for infant-directed (ID) speech over adult-directed (AD) speech in young infants. Using a modification of the visual-fixation-based auditory-preference procedure, Experiments 1 and 2 examined whether 12 1-month-old and 16 2-day-old infants looked longer at a visual stimulus when looking produced ID as opposed to AD speech. The results showed that both 1-month-olds and newborns preferred ID over AD speech. Although the absolute magnitude of the ID speech preference was significantly greater, with the older infants showing longer looking durations than the younger infants, subsequent analyses showed no significant difference in the relative magnitude of this effect. Differences in overall looking times between the 2 groups apparently reflect task variables rather than differences in speech processing. These results suggest that infants' preference for the exaggerated prosodie features of ID speech is present from birth and may not depend on any specific postnatal experience. However, the possible role of prenatal auditory experience with speech is considered.

It has commonly been noted in the language-learning literature that adults (particularly mothers) modify certain linguistic and paralinguistic (or prosodic) aspects of their speech when speaking to young children (Garnica, 1977; Newport, Gleitman, & Gleitman, 1977; Papousek, Papousek, & Bornstein, 1985). The linguistic features of child-directed speech include fewer words per utterance, more repetitions and expansion, better articulation, and decreased structural complexity. Prosodie modifications include higher overall pitch, wider pitch excursions, more distinctive pitch contours, slower tempo, longer pauses, and increased emphatic stress. Interest in the structure and function of this specialized form of child-directed speech (also known as "motherese") stems from the possibility that such speech may enhance the young child's language learning. Although some research has found no direct relation between mothers' usage of child-directed speech and objective measures of children's language development (e.g., Gleitman, Newport, & Gleitman, 1984), it is generally believed that successful language learning depends on a positive, interactive verbal environment between child and caretaker (Gottfried & Gottfried, 1984).

This possibility is supported by observations that adults also use motherese when speaking to younger infants who are not yet producing words or sentences. Since it is unlikely that infants under 6 months of age are processing speech semantically, the prosodie aspects of infant-directed speech have received more attention than the linguistic aspects. Such infant-directed (ID) speech has been observed in the interactions between 12-month-old infants and their parents in French, Italian, German, Japanese, British English, and American English homes (Fernald et al, 1989; see also Ferguson, 1977). Fernald and Simon (1984) found similar prosodic modifications in the ID speech of German mothers to their newborns. Grieser and Kuhl (1988) recently analyzed the speech of eight Mandarin Chinese mothers speaking to their 2-month-old infants and found that even in this tonal language (where pitch changes are used to signal phonemic distinctions) mothers alter their prosodic features when talking to infants. Using an American English sample, Stern, Spieker, Barnett, and MacKain (1983) recorded mothers' speech to their newborn, 4-, 12-, and 24-month-old infants and found that mothers modified the prosodie features of their speech to their infants at all ages, but particularly when the infants were about 4 months of age. Moreover, ID speech has been observed in the speech of males as well as females speaking to young infants (Fernald et al., 1989; Jacobson, Boersma, Fields, & Olson, 1983). Although some exceptions have been noted (e.g., Ratner & Pye, 1984), ID speech appears to be a prevalent form of language input to infants across a variety of ages and cultures.

Given that ID speech seems to be widely available for infant listening, it is important to ask whether experience with such speech induces or enhances some aspect(s) of the infant's development. Three broad functional categories for ID speech have been hypothesized: attentional, social/affective, and linguistic (Fernald, 1984; Grieser & Kuhl, 1988). The enhanced acoustic features of ID speech may differentially elicit and perhaps maintain infant attention. Using a conditioned head-turning procedure, Fernald (1985) showed that 4-month-old infants turned their heads more often in the direction necessary to activate a recording of female ID speech than female adult-directed (or AD) speech. Werker and McLeod (1989) measured the amount of time 4–5-month-old infants and 7–9-month-old infants viewed a television monitor that presented either a female or a male actor speaking ID or AD speech. They found that both groups of infants watched the monitor longer when ID speech was being presented, independent of the speaker's gender. Stern, Spieker, and MacKain (1982) noted that mothers often use characteristic, situationally specific pitch contours when speaking to their infants. For example, rising contours often occur when the mother is trying to elicit the infant's attention, but rising-falling contours are more common when the goal is to maintain the infant's interest (see also Sullivan & Horowitz, 1983). The specific effects that different contour shapes have on infant attention and whether these effects are consistent across different ages is currently unknown.

The possible affective role of ID speech was recently investigated by Werker and McLeod (1989). They reported that both 4–5-month-olds and 7–9-month-olds who were watching videotapes of a female talking to an infant and talking to an adult demonstrated more positive affect while watching the ID tape, and the magnitude of this effect was greater in the younger infants. This correlation between ID speech and positive affect may indicate that infants find ID speech less affectively ambiguous than AD speech. Some support for this decreased ambiguity comes from a recent study by Fernald (1989), who examined whether adults could categorize the meanings of naturally occurring pitch contours of adult speech samples that were gathered in both ID and AD contexts. Her results showed that adults could more easily and correctly categorize the ID pitch contours, suggesting that the speaker's affective and/or communicative intent may be more accessible in ID speech than in AD speech.

The potential linguistic benefit of ID speech may be that it facilitates the infant's detection and discrimination of segmental contrasts. Karzon (1985) reported that 1–4-month-olds could discriminate a change in the second syllable of a three-syllable word only if the phonetic contrast was accompanied by increases in fundamental frequency, intensity, and duration (the same prosodie features that co-occur in ID speech). Interestingly, Karzon also showed that it was not the general presence of these exaggerated prosodie cues that enhanced phonetic discrimination; when the same cues accompanied the initial (but not the target) syllable, no discriminative advantage was seen. Infant-directed speech has also been shown to affect linguistic perception at a more general level. Kemler-Nelson, Hirsh-Pasek, Jusczyk, and Wright-Cassidy (1989) found that 7–9-month-olds preferred to listen to speech that preserved natural clausal structure as long as the speech was ID; no preference for natural clausal structure was found with AD speech. In a nonspeech context, Aslin (1989) recently demonstrated that 8-month-old infants' ability to detect the presence of a frequency sweep (a phonetically relevant portion of the signal) was improved for long sweep durations. If the slower tempo of ID speech results in similar elongations, then ID speech may enhance a variety of phonetic discriminations.

Taken together, the available data indicate that ID speech is a prevalent form of language input to infants and that it may serve important social, attentional, and language-related functions in early development. Of course, not all of these functions are necessarily active at the same time. It is possible that the particular function such input serves changes with the developmental status of the infant, and we should not generalize these functions across developmental age without supporting evidence. Of particular interest is the possibility that infants are perceptually predisposed to attend to certain acoustic features of ID speech (Fernald, 1984, 1985). If such a perceptual predisposition exists, then infants of all ages should show a preference for ID over AD speech. However, since the youngest infants that have been tested were 4 months of age (Fernald, 1985; Fernald & Kuhl, 1987; Werker & McLeod, 1989), it is unknown to what extent this preference for ID speech generalizes to younger infants. Moreover, because longitudinal observations of mothers' speech to infants have shown that the prosodic features of mothers' speech to 4-month-old infants are even more exaggerated compared to their speech to both younger and older infants (Stern et al., 1983), it is possible that infant responsiveness to ID speech is the product of some emerging perceptual learning or familiarity process. The purpose of the following experiments was to determine whether infants much younger than those previously studied also prefer ID speech.

EXPERIMENT 1: PREFERENCE FOR ID SPEECH VERSUS AD SPEECH IN 1-MONTH-OLD INFANTS

This first experiment investigated whether 1-month-old infants prefer ID speech over AD speech. Preferences were assessed using a modification of a visual-fixation-based auditory-preference procedure (Colombo & Bundy, 1981) in which infants could activate either a recording of ID or AD speech by looking at a visual stimulus. The amount of time an infant spent looking at the visual stimulus while listening to different auditory stimuli was the dependent measure. In the following experiments, speech "preference"

was operationally defined as longer average looking times to the visual stimulus when looking was associated with a particular kind of speech.[1]

Method

Subjects.—Twelve 1-month-old infants comprised the final sample (*M* age = 34 days, SD = 5.29; seven females and five males). The mothers of these infants all reported having full-term, uncomplicated pregnancies. An additional six infants failed to complete testing due to excessive crying (5) or equipment failure (1). Infants were recruited for participation through the birth records of a local hospital and from local birth announcements by contacting their parents by letter and phone.

Speech stimuli.—Initially, speech samples were recorded from five adult females who were instructed to speak the following four sentences as if they were talking to an infant and then as if they were talking to another adult: "Good morning. How are you today? What are you doing? Let's go for a walk." These five different samples of the four ID and four AD sentences were recorded onto a Revox reel-to-reel tape recorder (Model B77) and then played back to 10 adults who judged the ID and AD recordings on a 5-point Likert-type scale for their appropriateness as speech directed to an infant or to an adult, respectively. The tape-recording of the female speaker whose ID and AD speech received the highest average ratings was then re-recorded onto a Uher reel-to-reel tape recorder (Model 4200) so that 30 min of continuous ID speech was on one channel and 30 min of continuous AD speech was on the other channel of the tape.

The ID and AD speech differed in several ways. Table 1 lists the following information for the four ID and four AD sentences: average fundamental frequency (F_0), F_0 range, sentence durations, and intersentence pause durations. In calculating average F_0s, only pitch values during voiced portions of the sentences were included (i.e., pitch readings of zero were excluded from the averages). This information was derived by analyzing all eight sentences with the Pitch Edit program from Micro Speech Lab software on a personal computer and by detailed inspection of the waveforms using a computer graphics program that allowed us to count individual pitch pulses per frame. When discrepant pitch values arose between these two techniques, we used the values from our visual inspection of the waveforms. Pitch tracings were then generated by plotting the successive fundamental frequencies. These pitch tracings for pairs of ID and AD sentences are presented in Figure 1a–d. As can be seen from both Table 1 and Figure 1a–d, the average F_0 and F_0 range of the four ID sentences is greater than the average F_0 and F_0 range of their AD counterparts. Moreover, the durations of all four ID sentences are longer than those of the four AD sentences, and the pause durations are slightly longer between ID than between AD sentences (see Table 1; the pause times are listed for all but ID1 and AD1 since these were the starting sentences in the original recording). Although these acoustic analyses revealed that the average F_0, F_0 variability and durational characteristics of the ID speech were different from those obtained from the AD speech, these results do not establish that these recordings *sound* like ID and AD speech. We also had 30 undergraduate students listen to these recordings after each had been low-pass filtered at 400 Hz and indicate whether the speech was ID or AD. Filtering speech in this way acts to remove higher-frequency information that is necessary for understanding semantic content, but preserves most of the prosodic information (e.g., F_0 contour, duration, amplitude modulation). The results showed that the students were between 87% and 100% accurate in correctly identifying the

sentences as being either ID or AD, with the distribution of errors being fairly equal across both ID and AD sentences.

Since the script used in the production of both speech tapes was identical, any preference shown by the infants in this experiment could not be the result of differences in the word content of the ID and AD recordings.[2] Thus, the experiment tested whether 1-month-old infants prefer the normally occurring prosodic features of ID speech over those of AD speech.

Apparatus and procedure.—Each infant was placed in an infant seat and positioned within a three-sided enclosure that was situated on top of a table, with the infant facing the front panel. All three panels (two sides and one front) were grey-colored. A 12.7-cm square black-and-white checkerboard (with 2.5-cm square checks) was located on the front panel, offset 7.6 cm from midline to the infant's right (or left). Infants were seated approximately 40.6 cm from this front panel so that the checkerboard subtended a visual angle of approximately 17°. A smaller grey panel blocked the checkerboard from the infant's view before testing began.

During testing, the room lights were turned off, and the testing enclosure was illuminated from behind the infant by a 40.6 cm long fluorescent light fixture. A small observation hole (1.3 cm) was located in the center of the front panel. One observer watched the infant through the

TABLE 1 PROSODIC FEATURES OF THE FOUR INFANT-DIRECTED (ID) AND THE FOUR ADULT-DIRECTED (AD) SENTENCES

	SENTENCES			
PROSODIC FEATURES	1	2	3	4
Average F_0 (Hz):				
ID................	376.6	280.9	340.6	265.4
AD	251.1	251.1	299.3	236.8
F_0 range (Hz):				
ID................	188–656	163–645	160–649	159–685
AD	210–354	167–400	161–372	181–302
Duration (sec):				
ID................	1.29	1.33	1.37	1.63
AD	.65	.74	.70	.94
Pause length (sec):				
ID................		.68	.91	.98
AD		.52	.73	.62

observation hole and recorded the duration of each look to the checkerboard by depressing a key on the keyboard of a Macintosh-Plus computer. This observer wore headphones and listened to uninterrupted female vocal music at a level that masked all extraneous sound. A second experimenter stood next to the apparatus and was responsible for uncovering and recovering the checkerboard at the beginning and end of each trial. The computer was connected to a custom-built interface that controlled independent access to the channels of the Uher tape recorder. The audio output from the interface was amplified (Realistic stereo amplifier Model SA-150) and presented via a loudspeaker (Realistic Model 40223, 8 ohms) located approximately 20.3 cm directly behind and slightly above the infant. The ID and AD recordings were presented at 63–65 dB SPL.

Once quiet and alert, the infant was placed in the infant seat and observed for about 30 sec to see if any side preference in looking pattern was obvious. Each infant was then tested on whichever side he or she tended to look toward most often. In both of the experiments to be reported here,

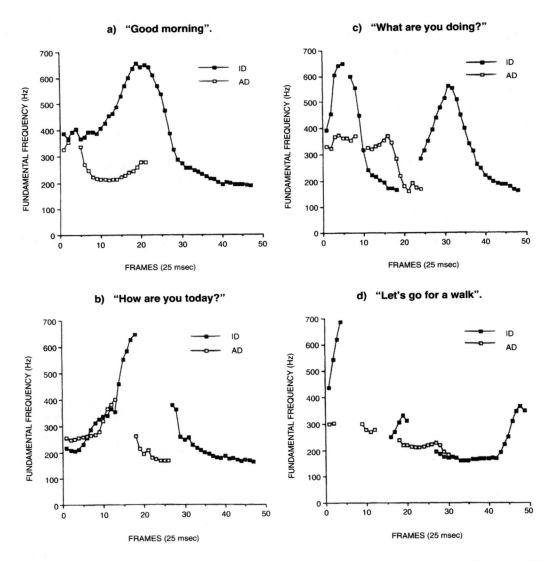

Fig. 1.—Fundamental frequency (F0) values plotted over successive 25-msec frames for four pairs of infant-directed (ID) and adult directed (AD) sentences: (*a*) Good morning. (*b*) How are you today? (*c*) What are you doing? and (*d*) Let's go for a walk. Frequency (in Hz) is represented on the vertical axes, whereas time (in msec) is represented on the horizontal axes.

over 90% of the infants initially looked more to the right than to the left, and so were tested on the right.

Prior to each trial, the second experimenter lifted the grey panel covering the checkerboard when the infant looked toward the midline of the front panel. The observer behind the front panel watched the infant's eye and head movements. When she judged that the infant was looking at the checkerboard, she depressed a key that activated channel 1 (or 2) of the tape recorder. The speech recording associated with that channel was played continuously through the loudspeaker until the observer judged that the infant had looked away from the checkerboard. As soon as the key was depressed, signaling the end of that look, the audio recording was gated off wherever the tape happened to be at that time. In order to prevent clicks at the onset and offset of the speech, the tape recording was ramped both on and off with a rise-fall time of 30 msec. Although the onset and offset of speech in midstream may have sounded unnatural to the infants, it presumably did so equally for each type of speech (given that the script was the same for ID and AD speech) and should not have affected responding to the two recordings differentially. At the end of each trial, the second experimenter re-covered the checkerboard with the grey panel and kept it covered until the infant looked toward the midline of the front panel. Once the infant looked toward midline, the checkerboard was again uncovered. During the next trial, the infant's look to the checkerboard activated channel 2 (or 1) of the tape recorder. Thus the ID and AD recordings alternated across trials, with trial duration determined by the length of the infant's look to the checkerboard. To control for any bias resulting from the order of presentation of the speech stimuli, six of the 12 infants heard the ID recording first, whereas the other six infants heard the AD recording first. Each session ended when the computer had accumulated 5 min of total looking time to the checkerboard. When this time limit was met, the trial in progress was truncated. Therefore, all final trials of the sessions were eliminated from the analyses.

Results and Discussion

To determine whether infants looked longer at the checkerboard when listening to ID speech than when listening to AD speech, each infant's looking time was separated into total ID and total AD durations and then divided by the number of ID and AD trials, respectively. The resultant group mean looking time to the checkerboard when the ID speech was presented ($M = 33.6$ sec) was significantly longer than the mean looking time when the AD speech was presented ($M = 21.4$ sec; see Fig. 2). A mixed 2 × 2 analysis of variance (ANOVA) was computed on the infants' mean looking times, with order (ID first vs. AD first) as the between-subjects factor and speech type (ID speech vs. AD speech) as the within-subjects factor. There was a significant main effect of speech type, $F(1,10) = 7.29, p < .02$, but no effect of order, $F(1,10) = .40$, and no order x speech type interaction, $F(1,10) = 1.55$. Eleven of the 12 infants tested had longer mean looking times to the ID speech ($p < .02$, two-tailed binomial test).

The average amount of time the infants spent looking at the checkerboard, regardless of which speech type was presented, was 268.7 sec (approximately 4.5 min), and the average number of looks to the checkerboard per session was 11.5 (range = 6–19). The average time the infants spent not looking at the checkerboard was 189.1 sec (approximately 3 min; M intertrial interval = 16.5 sec), resulting in an average session time (looking time + nonlooking time) of 447.8 sec (approximately 7.5 min). Although there

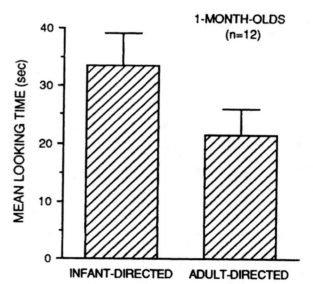

Fig. 2.—Mean looking times (in sec) of 1-month-old subjects from Experiment 1 (including standard errors); ID = infant-directed and AD = adult-directed.

was no effect of order in the ANOVA presented above, differences in the length of the first trial when looking produced ID speech compared to when looking produced AD speech were analyzed. The mean look duration on the first trial was longer when looking produced ID speech (ID M = 43.2 sec, SE = 15.9 vs. AD M = 20.9 sec, SE = 6.7), but this difference was not statistically significant, $t(10)$ = 1.12, p > .05. One final analysis examined whether the infants' preference for ID speech was more evident in one part of the session than another. Other researchers examining auditory preferences in young infants have shown that evidence for the predicted preference is typically seen late in the session (Fifer, 1987). Our data, however, showed no such effect: the mean looking times on ID trials and AD trials during the first half of the session (ID first = 32.4 sec, SE = 6.9 vs. AD first = 20.6 sec, SE = 3.8; $t(11)$ = 1.94, p < .04 (one-tailed)) and the last half of the session (ID last = 36.8 sec, SE = 7.4 vs. AD last = 21.6 sec, SE = 5.1; $t(11)$ = 1.83, p < .05 (one-tailed)) showed that the ID trials tended to be longer than AD trials during both the first and second half of the sessions.

The results of this first experiment showed that 1-month-old infants looked longer at a visual stimulus when looking produced a recording of ID speech than when looking produced a recording of AD speech. This finding extends the infant preference for ID speech previously shown in 4-month-olds to a much younger age. Although 1-month-old infants have certainly had less general experience listening to speech than 4-month-olds, it may be that early experience with ID speech within the first weeks after birth is sufficient to generate a preference for ID speech. If preference for ID speech is the result of this specific experience, then we might expect that the preference for ID speech would increase in magnitude as the infant gets older. One interesting finding that may be relevant to this hypothesis is that mothers have been found to use higher pitch, more pitch excursion, and shorter pauses in their speech to their 4-month-old infants compared to the same mothers' speech to their newborn infants (Stern et al., 1983). Apparently, mothers' exaggeration of some prosodic features of their speech increases with the age of the infant. In this regard, it would be interesting to examine whether the magnitude of the ID preferences previously seen in 4–5-month-old infants (Fernald, 1985; Werker & McLeod, 1989) is larger than the 1-month-old

infants' ID preferences from the present experiment. Unfortunately, several procedural differences make such cross-experimental comparisons untenable, although it may be possible to use the preference procedure from Experiment 1 to test 4-month-olds in order to facilitate cross-age comparisons.

Perhaps a more interesting way to address this issue is to test infants at an age when their prior experience with ID speech is minimal or absent. A likely candidate is the newborn infant. Although ID speech has been recorded in the speech of mothers to their newborns (Fernald & Simon, 1984), mothers do not exaggerate the prosodic features of their speech to newborns to the extent that they do when talking to older infants (Stern et al., 1983). Rheingold and Adams (1980) found that both male and female medical personnel talk to infants in newborn nurseries, but they do not use typical "baby talk" (the prosodie features of the speech, however, were not analyzed). Since newborn infants have shown preferences for other types of auditory events (e.g., DeCasper & Fifer, 1980; DeCasper & Sigafoos, 1984; DeCasper & Spence, 1986; Panneton, 1985), the purpose of our second experiment was to investigate whether newborn infants prefer ID over AD speech.

EXPERIMENT 2: PREFERENCE FOR ID SPEECH VERSUS AD SPEECH IN NEWBORN INFANTS

Method

Subjects.—Sixteen healthy, full-term newborns comprised the final sample (M age = 52 hours, SD = 13.7, range = 48–77; seven females and nine males). The average birthweight was 3,375 grams (range = 3,000–3,870), and the average gestational age was 40 weeks (range = 38–41). All newborns had an APGAR score of at least 8 at 1 and 5 min after birth. All of the mothers had uncomplicated vaginal deliveries with little or no obstetric medication. In addition to those infants included in the study, 24 other newborns did not complete testing due to excessive crying (7) or sleepiness (17). The mother of each infant was invited to come and watch the test session.

Speech stimuli.—The same ID and AD tapes from Experiment 1 were used in the present study.

Apparatus and procedure.—In general, the same apparatus and procedure front Experiment 1 were also used in this second experiment, with some minor changes. The newborns were situated slightly closer to the front panel (approximately 38 cm) than the 1-month-olds, and the loudspeaker was located directly in front of the newborns (rather than behind) and directly below the observation hole. As with the 1-month-olds, the sound level of the recordings was 63–65 dB SPL.

Testing typically took place directly after the newborns' 9:00–9:30 A.M. feeding in either an empty nursery or examination room. If the newborn was not in an awake and alert state when brought in for testing, one of the two experimenters present held and talked to the infant until he or she attained this state. The infant was then swaddled in an infant blanket and placed in the infant seat. Eight of the 16 infants heard the ID speech on the first trial, whereas the other eight infants heard AD speech first.

Results and Discussion

Each newborn's total looking time was separated into total ID and total AD durations and then divided by the number of ID and AD trials, respectively. In general, the newborns' eye movements were somewhat more difficult to observe and record' than those of the 1-month-old subjects. On some trials, the observer judged the infant to look at and then away from the checkerboard within 2 sec (this did not occur when testing the 1-month-old infants). On such trials, the speech recording was never heard, and so these trials were eliminated from all further analyses. A total of 17 trials that were less than 2 sec in duration was eliminated across all infants: nine ID trials and eight AD trials. The results showed that the group mean looking time across ID trials ($M = 18.3$ sec) was significantly longer than the mean looking time across AD trials ($M = 13.9$ sec; see Fig. 3). A mixed 2×2 ANOVA was computed on the infants' mean looking times, with order (ID first vs. AD first) as the between-subjects factor and speech type (ID vs. AD) as the within-subjects factor. A statistically significant main effect of speech type, $F(1,14) = 8.31$, $p < .02$, was found, but no effect of order, $F(1,14) = 1.51$, and no order x speech type interaction, $F(1,14) = 2.09$. Twelve of the 16 newborns tested had longer mean looking times to the ID speech ($p < .06$, two-tailed binomial test).

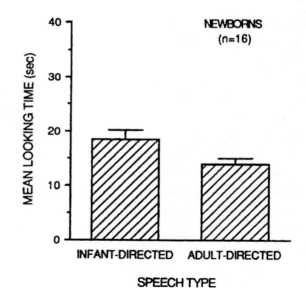

FIG. 3.—**Mean looking times (in sec) of newborn subjects from Experiment 2 (including standard errors); ID = infant-directed and AD = adult-directed.**

The average amount of time that these infants spent looking at the checkerboard across ID and AD trials was 276.7 sec (approximately 4.5 min), and the average amount of time they spent not looking at the checkerboard was 228.9 sec (M intertriai interval = 12.1 sec). The average total session time (looking time + nonlooking time) was 506 sec (approximately 8.5 min). These measures are all quite comparable to those obtained from the 1-month-old subjects in Experiment 1. However, the average number of looks per session for the newborns was 18.3 (range = 9–33, in contrast to the 1-month-olds' average of 11.5), which means that the newborns looked at the checkerboard considerably more often than the 1-month-olds but for much shorter durations (compare Fig. 2 with Fig. 3). Thus, although both groups of infants showed significant preferences for ID speech, the total amount of looking was much greater in the 1-month-olds.

In order to compare the two ages directly, an ANOVA was performed on mean looking times, with age (1-month-olds vs. newborns) and order (ID first vs. AD first) as between-subjects factors and speech type (ID vs. AD) as the within-subjects factor. The results showed significant main effects for age, $F(1,24) = 7.06$, $p < .02$, and speech type, $F(1,24) = 13.5$, $p < .01$. Examination of the mean looking times shows that: (*a*) the overall mean looking time across ID and AD trials of the 1-month-olds (M = 27.5 sec) was higher than that of the newborns (M = 16.1 sec), and (b) the overall mean looking time across ID trials (M = 24.9 sec) was higher than the mean looking time across AD trials (M = 17.1 sec). However, the interaction between age and speech type, $F(1,24)$ = 3.5, $p < .07$, was not statistically significant.

Although not significant, the 1-month-olds' mean looking time across ID trials was 33.6 sec, compared to the newborns' mean looking time of 18.3 sec, suggesting that a difference in the magnitude of the ID speech preference between the two groups may exist, with the newborns showing less of a preference than the older infants. In order to test this possibility, the ratios of looking times on ID trials to looking times on AD trials (i.e., M ID/(M ID + M AD)) were calculated so that the *relative* magnitude of the ID preference could be compared across groups. Although the average ratio from the 1-month-olds (M ratio = .61, SE = .04) was larger than that from the newborns (M ratio = .56, SE = .02), this difference was not statistically significant, $t(26)$ = 1.32, $p = .09$, one-tailed. Also, the average ratios for both groups were significantly higher than chance, or .50 (for 1-month-olds, $t(11)$ = 2.97, $p < .05$ (two-tailed); for newborns, $t(15)$ = 2.38, $p < .05$ (two-tailed)).

As with the 1-month-olds' data, we tested for a difference in the newborns' looking times on the first trial of the session as a function of hearing either ID or AD speech. Although the mean looking time on the first trial was longer when looking produced ID speech (ID M = 23.8 sec, SE = 7.5 vs. AD M = 10.4 sec, SE = 2.6), this difference was not statistically significant ($t(14)$ = 1.58, $p = .07$ (one-tailed)). One final analysis was performed on average ID and AD looking times occurring during the first half and last half of the session. Average looking times during the first half of the sessions were significantly longer during ID trials (ID first = 19.7 sec, SE = 1.5 vs. AD first = 14.6 sec, SE = 1.5; $t(15)$ = 3.45, $p < .02$, one-tailed). This trend was also seen during the last half of the sessions, although this result was not statistically significant (ID last = 17.1 sec, SE = 2.7 vs. AD last = 12.8 sec, SE = 1.1; $t(15)$ = 1.67, $p = .06$, one-tailed).

General Discussion

When the presentation of either ID or AD speech was contingent on looking at a visual target, both 1-month-old and newborn infants looked longer when looking produced the ID speech. These results support and extend other research demonstrating that older infants prefer ID over AD speech (Fernald, 1985; Werker & McLeod, 1989). In addition to this general preference for ID speech, we also found that the 1-month-old infants' ID looking times were slightly higher than the newborns' ID looking times. When comparing the proportion of looking on ID vs. AD trials, however, this difference between the two groups was not statistically significant, although the 1-month-olds did show a slightly higher proportion of looking on ID trials than the newborns. Hence, the difference in overall looking times between the older and younger infants most likely reflects attentional constraints on newborn visual and/or auditory behavior rather than an attenuated preference for ID speech in newborns. In fact, the average ratio of looking times on ID trials to AD trials for the newborn infants (.56) is quite consistent in magnitude with newborns' preference ratios obtained from other laboratories using different methodologies and different auditory stimuli (Fifer & Moon, in press; Moon & Fifer, in press; Spence & DeCasper, 1987).

Thus, infants are able to process the prosodic features of adult speech shortly after birth and seem to attend more to adult speech when its prosodic features are exaggerated.[3] Other studies examining early auditory preferences and discrimination support this finding that the young infant is sensitive to the prosodie features of speech. Newborn infants prefer their mother's voice to the voice of an unfamiliar female when both women are reading the same story (DeCasper & Fifer, 1980). In the DeCasper and Fifer study, the preference for the maternal voice cannot be attributed to linguistic idiosyncracies in the mother's speech since linguistic features were held constant across speakers. Also, it is unlikely that intonational contour differences produced the maternal voice preference since this prosodie feature was most likely constrained by the rhythmical structure of the story. Infants could, however, have responded to mother-specific fundamental frequency and/or temporal features. Interestingly, Mehler et al. (1988) have recently shown that newborn infants can discriminate two languages when one of the languages is native to their culture, but not when both languages are nonnative. This native language discrimination remains intact even when both languages are low-pass filtered so that only their intonational and temporal structures are maintained.

Since the infants in the studies discussed above were only a few days old, it appears that either postnatal experience with language does not have to be extensive for the infant to learn about the prosodic features of their native language, or that some of the required experience occurs prenatally. For example, newborn infants prefer to listen to a recording of their mothers reciting a story that the mothers previously recited during the last weeks of their pregnancy over a novel story (also recited by the mother; DeCasper & Spence, 1986). In the DeCasper and Spence study, mother-specific cues were held constant, but the linguistic, temporal, and intonational structure of the two stories varied. Thus, during the last weeks of gestation, the fetus apparently perceives and remembers such features of the mother's speech. In a subsequent study, Panneton (1985) showed that if linguistic structure is held constant, newborns still show a preference for the intonational contour and/or temporal patterning of a prenatally experienced melody. These results suggest that both prenatal and postnatal auditory experience affect the relative salience of prosodic cues for young infants (see Cooper & Aslin, 1989).

Taken together, the results of the studies discussed above suggest that newborns can recognize similarities between the prosodic features of auditory stimuli that were experienced prenatally and those heard postnatally (DeCasper & Fifer, 1980; DeCasper & Spence, 1986; Panneton, 1985). The exaggerated prosodic features of ID speech may be particularly interesting to the young infant because they deviate from those with which the newborn infant has the most experience. However, this hypothesis does not specify how the prosodic features of speech need to be exaggerated in order to capture infant attention, but only that they are exaggerated. We know from other studies that such prosodic changes cannot be arbitrary. For example, Mehler, Bertonicini, Barriere, and Jassik-Gerschenfeld (1978) showed that 1-month-old infants did not appear to recognize their mothers' voices when the mothers were talking in a monotone, although "monotone" can also be considered an exaggeration of prosodic features, albeit in the direction opposite to ID speech.

What is it about ID speech that seems to attract the attention of young infants? When compared to AD speech, ID speech typically has a slower tempo, is higher pitched, and is more modulated in both frequency and amplitude. Although it is possible that any of these features may act in isolation or in concert with other features to evoke the infant's attention, some recent evidence suggests that pitch and pitch modulation may be the most salient prosodic features of ID speech. Fernald and Kuhl (1987) tested 4-month-old infants in a preference procedure with sine-wave analogs of natural ID and AD speech in an attempt to isolate the prosodic feature(s) that are responsible for 4-month-olds' ID speech preferences. The infants heard synthesized ID and AD signals in which either: (a) frequency was modulated but amplitude was held constant, (b) amplitude was modulated but frequency was held constant, or (c) the durational characteristics were preserved but frequency and amplitude were held constant. The 4-month-old infants showed a preference only for the ID signals in which frequency and duration were allowed to vary, but amplitude was held constant; no preference was seen for the isolated amplitude envelopes or durational characteristics of ID speech. It is possible that younger infants also are attracted by the exaggerated pitch contours of ID speech, although the prosodic features of ID speech that differentially attract the infant could change during development. For example, the younger infant may require several exaggerated prosodic features of speech to co-occur in order for their attention to be differentially affected, whereas the older infant who may be more skilled at dissecting various aspects of speech may only require exaggerations in any one of several prosodic features. Future experiments are needed that investigate those specific features of ID speech that are necessary for affecting infant attention at various ages.

The results of the present experiments suggest that adults can influence infant attention by the nature of the speech they direct toward them. This enhanced attention may influence aspects of the social, affective, and language environment of the infant, although not necessarily at the same points in development. Although some research has begun to explore the possible functions of ID speech for infant development (e.g., Fernald, 1989; Karzon, 1985; Karzon & Nicholas, 1989; Werker & McLeod, 1989), new studies are needed that specifically address how such functions change over developmental age. Also, explorations into possible sources of natural variation in ID speech input would be particularly illuminating since they would provide the opportunity to examine whether diminished (or absent) input negatively affects certain aspects of infant development.

REFERENCES

Aslin, R. N. (1989). Discrimination of frequency transitions by human infants. *Journal of the Acoustical Society of America*, 86, 582–590.

Colombo, J., & Bundy, R. S. (1981). A method for the measurement of infant auditory selectivity. *Infant Behavior and Development*, 4, 219–223.

Cooper, R. P., & Aslin, R. N. (1989). The language environment of the young infant: Implications for early perceptual development. *Canadian Journal of Psychology*, 43, 247–265.

DeCasper, A. J., & Fifer, W. P. (1980). Of human bonding: Newborns prefer their mothers' voices. *Science*, 208, 1174–1176.

DeCasper, A. J., & Sigafoos, A. D. (1984). The intrauterine heartbeat: A potent reinforcer for newborns. *Infant Behavior and Development*, 6, 19–25.

DeCasper, A. J., & Spence, M. J. (1986). Newborns prefer a familiar story over an unfamiliar one. *Infant Behavior and Development*, 9, 133–150.

Ferguson, C. A. (1977). Baby talk as a simplified register. In C. E. Snow & C. A. Ferguson (Eds.), *Talking to children* (pp. 219–235), Cambridge: Cambridge University Press.

Fernald, A. (1984). The perceptual and affective salience of mothers' speech to infants. In L. Feagans, C. Garvey, & R. Golinkoff (Eds.), *The origins and growth of communication* (pp. 5–29). Norwood, NJ: Ablex.

Fernald, A. (1985). Four-month-old infants prefer to listen to motherese. *Infant Behavior and Development*, 8, 181–195.

Fernald, A. (1989). Intonation and communicative intent in mothers' speech to infants: Is the melody the message? *Child Development*, 60, 1497–1510.

Fernald, A., & Kuhl, P. (1987). Acoustic determinants of infant perception for motherese speech. *Infant Behavior and Development*, 10, 279–293.

Fernald, A., & Simon, T. (1984). Expanded intonation contours in mothers' speech to newborns. *Developmental Psychology*, 20, 104–113.

Fernald, A., Taeschner, T., Dunn, J., Papousek, M., de Boysson-Bardies, B., & Fukui, I. (1989). A cross-language study of prosodic modifications in mothers' and fathers' speech to preverbal infants. *Journal of Child Language*, 16, 477–501.

Fifer, W. P. (1987). Neonatal preference for mother's voice. In N. Krasnegor, E. Blass, M. Hofer, & W. Smotherman (Eds.), *Perinatal development: A psychobiological perspective* (pp. 111–124). New York: Academic Press.

Fifer, W. P., & Moon, C (in press). Early voice discrimination. In C. von Euler (Ed.), *The neurobiology of early infant behavior*. Wenner-Gren International Symposium Series (Vol. 45). New York: Stockton.

Garnica, O. K. (1977). Some prosodic and paralinguistic features of speech to young children. In C. E. Snow & C. A. Ferguson (Eds.), *Talking to children* (pp. 63–88). Cambridge: Cambridge University Press.

Gleitman, L. R., Newport, E. L., & Gleitman, H. (1984). The current status of the motherese hypothesis. *Journal of Child Language*, 11, 43–79.

Gottfried, H. W., & Gottfried, A. E. (1984). Home environment and cognitive development in young children of middle-socioeconomic-status families. In H. W. Gottfried (Ed.), *Home environment and early cognitive development: Longitudinal research* (pp. 329–342). Orlando, FL: Academic Press.

Grieser, D. L., & Kuhl, P. K. (1988). Maternal speech to infants in a tonal language: Support for universal prosodic features in motherese. *Developmental Psychology*, 24, 14–20.

Jacobson, J. L., Boersma, D. C. Fields, R. B., & Olson, K. L. (1983). Paralinguistic features of adult speech to infants and small children. *Child Development*, 54, 436–442.

Karzon, R. G. (1985). Discrimination of polysyllabic sequences by one-to four-month-old infants. *Journal of Experimental Child Psychology*, 39, 326–342.

Karzon, R. G., & Nicholas, J. G. (1989). Syllabic pitch perception in 2-to 3-month-old infants. *Perception and Psychophysics*, 45, 10–14.

Kemler-Nelson, D. G., Hirsh-Pasek, K., Jusczyk, P. W., & Wright-Cassidy, K. (1989). How the prosodic cues in motherese might assist language learning. Journal of Child Language, 16, 53–68.

Mehler, J., Bertoncini, J., Barriere, M., & Jassik-Gerschenfeld, D. (1978). Infant recognition of the mother's voice. Nature, 7, 491–497.

Mehler, J., Jusczyk, P. W., Lambertz, G., Halsted, N., Bertoncini, J., & Amiel-Tison, C. (1988). A precursor of language acquisition in young infants. Cognition, 29, 143–178.

Moon, C., & Fifer, W. P. (in press). Syllables as signals for 2-day-old infants. Infant Behavior and Development.

Newport, E. L., Gleitman, H., & Gleitman, L. R. (1977). Mother, I'd rather do it myself: Some effects and non-effects of maternal speech style. In C. E. Snow & C. A. Ferguson (Eds.), Talking to children (pp. 109–149). Cambridge: Cambridge University Press.

Panneton, R. K. (1985). Prenatal experience with melodies: Effect on postnatal auditory preference in human newborns. Unpublished doctoral dissertation, University of North Carolina at Greensboro.

Papousek, M., Papousek, H., & Bornstein, M. (1985). The naturalistic vocal environment of young infants: On the significance of homogeneity and variability in parental speech. In T. M. Field & N. A. Fox (Eds.), Social perception in infants (pp. 269–297). Norwood, NJ: Ablex.

Ratner, A. B., & Pye, C. (1984). Higher pitch in BT is not universal: Acoustic evidence from Quiche Mayan. Journal of Child Language, 11, 512–522.

Rheingold, H. L., & Adams, J. L. (1980). The significance of speech to newborns. Developmental Psychology, 16, 397–403.

Spence, M. J., & DeCasper, A. J. (1987). Prenatal experience with low-frequency maternal-voice sounds influence neonatal perception of maternal voice samples. Infant Behavior and Development, 10, 133–142.

Stern, D. N., Spieker, S., Barnett, R. K., & MacKain, K. (1983). The prosody of maternal speech: Infant age and context related changes. Journal of Child Language, 10, 1–15.

Stern, D. N., Spieker, S, & MacKain, K. (1982). Intonation contours as signals in maternal speech to prelinguistic infants. Developmental Psychology, 18, 727–735.

Sullivan, J. W., & Horowitz, F. D. (1983). The effects of intonation on infant attention: The role of the rising intonation contour. Journal of Child Language, 10, 521–534.

Werker, J. F., & McLeod, P. J. (1989). Infant preference for both male and female infant-directed-talk: A developmental study of attentional and affective responsiveness. Canadian Journal of Psychology, 43, 230–246.

NOTES

1. We are defining "preference" operationally and are not making any assumptions about the hedonic value that the infant may or may not associate with any particular auditory stimulus. "Preference" should also not be taken to mean that the infant attends to one stimulus to the exclusion of the other since preference data typically show that infants attend to both of the available stimuli, although attention to one may be greater than attention to the other.

2. Other researchers have shown that average F_0 and F_0 variability in adults' ID speech are greater under conditions where they are talking to actual infants than in a role-playing situation (Jacobson et al., 1983). However, these same authors also found a significant increase in F_0 and F_0 variability from a baseline to a role-playing situation. Although the ID and AD sentences used in the present study may have been more naturalistic had we recorded adult speech to an actual infant, the role-playing situation was sufficient to elicit the prosodic enhancements that we were interested in (see Table 1 and Fig. 1). In fact, a preference for ID speech generated under role-playing conditions suggests that more naturalistic ID speech may only increase the magnitude of the preference.

3. Although the results of these experiments show that young infants are sensitive to the prosodic features of adult speech, we are not suggesting that the basis of this perception is necessarily prosodic since it may well be that infants actually process acoustic cues that are correlated with prosodic features.

CHAPTER 11
Animal Communication and Language

Animal Language

Methodological and Interpretive Issues

SUE SAVAGE-RUMBAUGH AND KAREN E. BRAKKE

WHENCE THE NATURE AND ORIGINS OF LANGUAGE?

A sea lion takes a frisbee to a hoop after watching a person wave her hands in a certain way. A chimpanzee waves its hands and someone then unlocks a door for it. A parrot looks at a clothespin and says "pegwood." A dolphin touches a paddle after searching its tank when someone makes particular arm movements. Each of the behaviors performed by the animals above is in some way similar to the linguistic skills of the human child. Yet science has been reluctant to conclude that a sea mammal has syntax or that a parrot can name things or answer questions. The chimpanzee shares much of our phylogenetic history, but even its ability to grasp basic linguistic functions has repeatedly come under question (Savage-Rumbaugh et al. 1980; Terrace et al. 1979). Language, as opposed to most human characteristics, is believed by many to set us apart from the rest of the animal kingdom. Scientists and lay persons alike maintain that *Homo sapiens* is the only species capable of true language, in spite of increasingly convincing evidence that the bio-linguistic substratum for language exists in other primates.

There is, nonetheless, continuing interest in the nature and origins of language. The ontogeny of human language acquisition has been studied extensively and its course has been fairly well documented (e.g. Bates 1979; Dale 1976; Greenfield & Smith 1976; Lock 1980; Peters 1983). Still under debate, however, are issues concerning the relationship of language to other cognitive skills and the extent to which language is innate or learned (Moerk 1977; Waldron 1985). One approach to addressing these questions is to challenge the "linguistic uniqueness" perspective by attempting to establish linguistic skills in nonhuman species. This has been done in several research programs over the past few decades, yet the results of such studies have been mixed.

Some of the confusion has arisen because of logistical and technical concerns. Because nonhumans do not normally learn language, they must be taught the skills they acquire. And because they usually do not speak, they must be taught communication systems that do not utilize the primary channel of human language, speech. Methodological differences can make interspecific comparisons more difficult by shifting the focus away from the functional aspects of symbolic communication and toward the structure of the utterances themselves. In so doing, the adaptive and functional significance of language, which was undoubtedly crucial to its evolution, can become lost among concerns that have little to do with communication proper.

It would perhaps be productive at this juncture to return to some of the original issues which prompted the research: namely, the degree of analogy and homology between animal language skills and natural human language acquisition. But before it is possible to make fruitful comparisons between apes and other animals who have been taught language-like skills, it will be necessary to have a clearer understanding of what children do as they become competent language users. Most of the studies of single word utterances and the emergence of intentionality in children appeared after the initial reports of ape language. Consequently the early ape-language researchers worked without the benefit of the large body of data now available on early language processes in children. Needless to say, the paucity of such data at the time led to some confusions and misinterpretations of the relationships between ape and child symbol use.

LANGUAGE LEARNING IN CHILDREN

Language is, essentially, a form of intentional communication. As such, it functions to coordinate activity between individuals and to bring about change in one's environment (Bruner 1983). To use language is to engage in the adaptive behavior of altering one's social environment by talking to others. Consequently many investigators in the field of child language have recently begun to study it from a pragmatic rather than structural perspective (Bruner 1983; McShane 1980). Bates (1979: 366), in fact, defines functional communicative intent, which provides the basis for language acquisition, as "a social motivation to communicate, verbally or nonverbally, through shared reference to external objects." The earliest acts of the infant are not intentional, but by the end of the first year the child is clearly addressing its communications to adults; when it wants something, it will look at its intended audience as well as the desired object and will adjust its communicative actions in line with the caregiver's response. How does this change come about?

The development of intentional communication is an interpersonal process that is initiated by those who interact with the infant. That is, "meaning" is imparted to the infant's actions by a caregiver who is already familiar with the communicative and linguistic conventions of the culture. This caregiver will interpret, for example, a temporarily outstretched arm as meaning that the infant desires to be picked up, and will respond appropriately. Note that not only is the action interpreted by the adult but an intention is attributed to the infant by the adult, regardless of whether or not that intention is initially present in the mind of the infant.

As the infant matures and becomes familiar with common routines, it begins to associate certain acts with certain responses and starts to produce those acts in order to elicit the same responses. When the child recognizes and anticipates not only the desired outcome but also the role of the caregiver in fulfilling that outcome, then intentional communication can occur. For example, at this point the infant ceases to stretch its arm fully toward something it cannot reach. Instead, it partially reaches in the direction of the desired object then looks toward the adult and vocalizes. Clearly, the infant now expects the adult to execute the action for him or her and the reach has become a "signal" instead of an action intended to obtain a goal directly.

Behaviorally, an intention will be evidenced by the child's monitoring of the caregiver's responses and by making adjustments to its communicative acts until the interaction has been successfully negotiated and a satisfactory outcome produced (Bates 1979). At the same time that the child is learning how to communicate intentionally, it is also coming to recognize that other animate beings in the world act intentionally as well. Many of the daily routines of caregiver-infant interaction are repeated several times over the course of a week or even a day. They can be as simple as a peekaboo game or as elaborate as going to the grocery store. Each is characterized by a sequence of events that remains relatively invariant. By recognizing the events, or markers, that others use to announce or indicate each routine, the infant is able to predict and take part in that interaction (Bruner 1983). When an adult starts a simple peekaboo game by putting her hand over her eyes, for example, the infant anticipates the adult's next act of removing her hand and saying "Boo!," demonstrating this anticipation by smiling and vocalizing while the hand is still in place. An older infant may also say "Boo!" or reverse the roles entirely, hiding its own eyes.

Often, the behaviors that adults and older children use to mark their intentions are symbolic. For example, rather than putting her hand over her eyes to start a game, an adult may say "Shall we play peekaboo?" To the extent that the young child can extract information from what is said, it will become able to predict future events in its world and consequently to attempt to control them with its own actions. Eventually, the child will recognize that it too can use the same types of symbolic markers (i.e., words) to initiate routines and direct the attention of others.

At this point it is necessary to introduce the concept of "reference." When one says that someone is referring, one generally means that this person is using an intentional symbolic act to accomplish a specific goal (Gauker 1990; Savage-Rumbaugh 1990a). Reference is an inter-individual process in which a symbol (or group of symbols) is employed for the purpose of causing another party to think or behave in a specific way. Symbols used in such a way have the effect of causing the attention of the listener to become focused upon the topic of interest to the speaker. For example, an infant may point toward a toy outside its crib and look at an adult. Here, the direction of the outstretched arm indicates the toy and the desire is conveyed by facial expression and vocalization. No symbols are needed, because the toy is present. However, when the infant says "ball" and gestures toward the couch, the adult infers that the word "refers" to the ball which, among other toys, has been dropped behind the couch. A word is needed here, since the ball is not visually present and pointing would not convey which toy the infant desires. This view of "reference" is not a Lockean one. Rather, it stresses the inter-individual cause-effect nature of the development of the representational process. "Meaning" or "reference" is not seen as extant in the words themselves or even in the mind of the speaker (though it is partially determined by the expectancies the speaker brings to the outcome of his communications). Meaning exists in the interaction between speaker and listener. Words are used by the speaker, in the same way that a tool is employed to solve a physical task. That is, words are used to bring about an intended effect; however, they do not always accomplish this goal and often have unintended effects as well. Word meanings typically change dramatically with each usage. For example, the word "apple" refers to one thing in the context of conversation about fruit and quite another in the context of a conversation about cities. "Reference" is employed here as a descriptive term for the process of using words to achieve coordinated actions toward objects, locations, other persons, and so on. The type of "reference" that is of specific concern in the studies below is the process that occurs when one party, upon being asked, selects a specific object, or set of words, that "go with" a "label." However, the use of the term "reference" for this process is not intended to indicate a specific word-object relationship that exists apart from the process of using the word in an instrumental fashion (Gauker 1990).

The fact that human beings do associate classes of objects with words arises from interpretations of how these words are used in our presence. Cause-effect hypotheses are generated from analysis of word function and these hypotheses are used to generate an internalized language structure. For a thorough discussion of these complex philosophical issues of "reference," and its use by linguistically competent apes see Gauker (1990), Savage-Rumbaugh & Rumbaugh (1991), and Savage-Rumbaugh (1990a, 1990b, 1991, 1993). The perspective of reference expressed in these articles is very similar to that offered by Wells (1987: 20), which is summarized in this statement: "the problem of the origin of language is not, as has often been supposed, that of how sounds could become the signs of thoughts, but of how men discovered how to guide or influence the behavior of their neighbors by any means whatever, and later came to use arbitrary signs." The work with other species is helping to reveal the conditions under which this process does, and does not, come about.

IS LABELING THE LEARNING OF WORDS?

Consider, for example, the symbol-manipulation project undertaken with the chimpanzee (*Pan troglodytes*) Sarah (Premack 1970; Premack & Premack 1983). In this study, Sarah was trained to associate plastic chips with real objects. Her training began at age five with approximately an hour of drilled exercises per day in which she was required to put plastic chips ("words") on a magnetized board before receiving a piece of food. Eventually, Sarah was able to make same/ different judgements and complete analogies using the chips (Premack & Premack 1983). It was apparent that Sarah was, indeed, associating the plastic symbols with specific physical objects and attributes.

Yet what was Sarah communicating here? She did not share any new information; the trainer already knew the correct answer. Nor was she initiating the symbolic interactions in order to fulfill an intention. Symbol selection trials were set up by humans and Sarah merely solved the complex problems presented to her. In a statement that tells more about the limitations of this approach than about the limitations of the chimpanzee, Premack and Premack (1983: 34) express their view that, "Chimpanzees, we now know, are not initiators of language; they will, however, engage in dialogue once drawn into an exchange." Given that a primary use of language is the initiation of coordinated activity, however, there appears to be a critical difference between Sarah's symbol system and that of human children. Sarah had no opportunity nor reason to go beyond what she was trained to do and share new information with her experimenters.

A similar argument can be made about the data from Alex, an African Grey parrot (*Psittacus erithacus*) who has been taught via shaping of phonemic production to "label" objects held in front of it (Pepperberg 1981, 1983). For example, upon being shown a triangular piece of wood Alex will, when asked "What shape?," utter "three-corner." He then receives the item. If Alex makes an incorrect response, the trial is repeated until the correct utterance is emitted. Word acquisition is drilled in strict test situations consisting of problems to be solved before receipt of reward. Although Pepperberg is careful in her work not to make overt claims that language exists in the parrot, she insists that the vocal labels used by the parrot are "referential."

In the training paradigms employed by Premack (1970) and Pepperberg (1981, 1983) there is no opportunity for reference to occur, *even on the part of the experimenter*. That is, the experimenter does not use symbols the purpose of causing the animals to carry out a specific set of behaviors. In these paradigms, the experimenter holds up an object and requires the chimpanzee or parrot to produce the appropriate "label." The experimenter is not engaging in "reference" because the object does not indicate, or "refer to" anything. It is merely a stimulus for which one must produce the appropriate response. The subject, upon producing the appropriate label, also cannot be said to be employing that symbol for the purpose of "referring." Certainly, the only anticipated outcome from the subject's point of view is a reward, and selecting the symbol "hat" when shown a "hat" does not mean that the "hat symbol" refers to the reward. It is only selecting a response to receive a reward. Communication *per se* does not occur during such training, for there is nothing to be communicated.

IS "LEARNING TO DO AS YOU ARE TOLD" LANGUAGE?

In contrast to the symbol-production training with Sarah and Alex, some projects have undertaken study of animals' responses to utterances directed to them (Herman 1987,

1988; Herman et al. 1984; Schusterman & Krieger 1984, 1988). These studies have been conducted with two species of sea mammal: the dolphins Ake and Phoenix (*Tursiops truncatus*) and the sea lions Rocky and Gertie (*Zalophus californianus*). The receptive-language approach was taken with these subjects because of their apparent intelligence and their inability to make the manual or vocal responses conducive to producing signs or symbols. The focus of both studies has been on sensitivity to symbol relations whether, for example, the subjects will "flipper touch the ball" or "fetch the hoop to the frisbee" when instructed to do so, instead of performing some other action or relating the objects incorrectly.

Note that in this paradigm, the experimenter is the one producing the symbols and the subject responds differentially based on the specific instructions it is given. With this training technique, a message is given. The experimenter's signs communicate the behaviors that the person wants the dolphin or sea lion to perform. This context is somewhat more "language-like" than the productive one discussed above and may, in fact, be likened in some ways to the early interactions between human caregivers and infants who are beginning to respond to sentences within routines but cannot yet produce them. Critical differences remain, however, between this and the language learning of human children. Unlike the child, all of the actions carried out by Ake, Rocky, and the others in the test paradigm achieve a single goal—the receipt of a fish to eat (Herman et al. 1984; Herman 1987, 1988; Schusterman & Krieger 1984, 1988). In the routines of daily life, a child learns to carry out different actions for different ends and becomes a functional partner in the interactions. The correspondence between the communication and its result, that is natural for the child, is not present in the dolphin and sea lion studies. For the sea lions and dolphins, the important aspect of the interaction is the relationship between their actions and whether or not they receive food. For the child, the important relationship is between what is said and what is then done.

For example, a young child, upon hearing his friend say "would you like to play 'tagerm'" and then being shown the game, might find he would like to play again. He could initiate the game by asking to play "tagerm" even if he had never heard the word before. The dolphin, however, has little reason to learn in this way, since it a) cannot make the signs the experimenter makes, and b) probably does not particularly want to "take the frisbee to the hoop" in any case. It is more interested in reinstating the "effect" of receiving a fish than in the actions that were the result of the symbols "take the frisbee to the hoop."

In all of the studies described above, training and testing occur in a single context. The subjects are successful in making the responses that they have learned in order to obtain whatever reward is at hand. No data exist which suggest that their symbol use is intentionally communicative or referential. The study paradigms in which they participate do not foster the "social motivation to communicate intentions" that Bates (1979: 366) described. This is not to say that these animals lack intentionality and do not communicate to each other or to humans. Within the test situation, however, these capacities have no opportunity for expression. The utterances of children, by contrast, exhibit many different messages, even at the one word stage. Children learn many words that permit them to affect their world in many different ways. Dolphins learn many words that affect the world all in the same way (they produce a fish). Until training paradigms are utilized that permit the animal to do more than obtain one type of reward, the subjects cannot be expected to realize their potential for symbolic communication.

LANGUAGE AS IMMERSION IN SOCIAL ROUTINES

Recognizing the importance of social interaction and routines for the development of communicative intent, some investigators taught American Sign Language (ASL) signs to apes in "cross-fostering" studies (Gardner & Gardner 1969, 1975, 1984; Patterson 1978; Fouts et al. 1979; Terrace 1979).

These studies had several advantages over the "problem-oriented" paradigms reviewed earlier. Symbol use was integrated into routines involving food preparation, play, travel, and other activities which were relevant to the subjects. Experimenters used different symbols to announce different routines, and communication was not limited to one or two hours per day. As with human children, caretakers reacted to the behavior of the subjects as if it were intentional, even if it was not. Eventually, the subjects of each of these studies started producing symbols in ways that topically and structurally resembled those of young children (Gardner & Gardner 1975).

Despite the appearance of rearing environments that were similar to those of human children, there still existed fundamental differences in the teaching of symbols to these apes and what has been reported for normal children. Physical molding of the apes' hands, shaping of desired behaviors, and forced imitation were used as teaching techniques until they could make the signs without prompting. Once a sign was learned, they were required to produce it afterward within certain routines. For example, things to be opened could not be opened until the ape signed "open." Things to be eaten could not be eaten until the ape signed "food." Tickle games, once stopped by the experimenter, could not be continued until the ape signed "tickle." In such situations, the signs added no communicative information. They were merely used as a means of getting the ape or person to do something that was already understood by other means.

Such routines are analogous to the learning of a few words by human children, such as "please" or "thank you," but in most instances the motivation to use words comes from a desire to communicate novel information or information not otherwise apparent to the listener. The child's utterance may occur within a routine, it is true, but adults generally do not withhold items until the appropriate word is said. Rather, they tend to ask the child to talk only when it is otherwise not clear what the child wants. A further difference between early human communications and those of the ape sign projects is that the words or pseudo-words are selected and uttered by the infant. The infant also chooses the message it desires to convey. By contrast, when an experimenter takes a chimp's hands and molds them, even the act of communicating is originating within the mind of the experimenter, not that of the ape. The ape is a passive observer of its own sign. It does not select which sign is to be learned or which message to be expressed.

Nonetheless, if the ape begins to initiate or respond to communicative utterances in different contexts it can be said to be exhibiting language-like behavior, for at this point a process similar to early communications by humans begins. For example, Washoe first produced the sign "toothbrush" while looking at a group of toothbrushes in the bathroom. She had not been trained to use this sign and it was usually used by caretakers at the end of a meal. She had appeared to acquire the sign observationally (i.e.

through delayed imitation) and used it in an appropriate context other than that in which it had been learned (Gardner & Gardner 1969). Her behavior in this instance was quite similar to a child who names objects to himself or herself.

Unfortunately, the value of this behavior was not fully appreciated by Washoe's human companions. As soon as it occurred, the investigators required Washoe to produce the sign at the end of each meal, in effect reducing its value as a communicative event. Instead of letting the sign develop spontaneously, they forced it into a rote behavior to be produced in a specific situation before events could continue. Such procedures resemble those employed in the studies by Premack (1970) and Pepperberg (1981) and involve no referential communicative use of the symbols.

Washoe and other ape subjects in these studies have produced many different signs or symbols appropriately. Within context, they appear to act much like human children. However, most of their utterances have been limited to productive requests. Tests of receptive ability divorced from context (e.g. Fouts et al. 1976; Patterson 1978) are virtually nonexistent and thus it is gratuitous to inpute language understanding or comprehension to these animals. Also, many of the functions for which children use language, such as spontaneous naming or statements of intent, have not emerged in these apes, and thus some have concluded that nonhumans are incapable of moving beyond symbolic behaviors that reap immediate, primary rewards (Terrace 1985). Again, these conclusions may reflect limitations of the training paradigms as much or more than those of the animals involved.

THE LANGUAGE RESEARCH CENTER

Understanding the bio-linguistic substratum of language, particularly as it is manifested by apes, has been the focus of the research program at the Language Research Center since the early 1970s. Currently the center houses eleven apes, including five common chimpanzees, four bonobos or pygmy chimpanzees (*Pan paniscus*) and two orangutans (*Pongo pygmaeus*), all of whom are subjects in ongoing studies of bio-linguistic and higher cognitive processes.

The first ape subject at this laboratory, Lana, demonstrated that apes could readily discriminate among geometric symbols and could put symbols in a sequence

to form differentiated but structured symbol strings for the purposes of receiving various rewards (for example, "Please machine give juice" to receive a drink of grape juice.) (Rumbaugh 1977; Rumbaugh et al. 1973). By using geometric symbols located on contact-sensitive keys, Lana illustrated the value of providing an ape with a touch-sensitive communication system. The appearance of a system which made symbol production very simple (just press a key) resulted in a sharpening of the scientific focus upon the conceptual and procedural aspects of symbol use, rather than the productive aspects. Because it was now easy for a chimpanzee to produce symbols, and to combine them in the proper sequence, the fact that the ape could construct something that "looked like sentences" was quickly superseded by the questions of how one could legitimately draw parallels between human and ape communications. When, how, and under what conditions was it appropriate to equate symbol presses with words and sentences?

Clearly, as the earlier discussion reveals, questions of communicative competence could not be answered by determining whether or not chimpanzees could learn to answer questions or associate certain movements with different stimuli. The essence of human language lies in our ability to use symbols to tell others something that they do not already know. The more complex the message, the greater the need for structural rules regarding the units of which the message is composed. Did Lana understand the relationships between the symbols she used? Was she using key presses to convey messages or were these key presses simply conditioned responses performed for the purpose of obtaining food? Even more importantly, upon what basis could a legitimate determination of why and how Lana and other apes used symbols be made?

These questions were addressed with the addition of four more common chimpanzees (Ericka, Kenton, Sherman and Austin) to the Language Center's research program. They too learned to differentiate and use symbols. However, unlike Lana and other language-trained apes, they were not taught to label things upon demand but rather to ask for things of interest to them such as foods and tools. As with children, these skills were acquired through a process which stressed the development of communicative intentionality and joint regard (Savage-Rumbaugh 1986). The communications were negotiated first at the nonverbal level and secondarily at the verbal level. For example, when the chimpanzee needed a particular tool to solve a problem, it first expressed this desire nonverbally, by gesturing to the tool. Only later was a symbol learned as an alternate means of expressing which tool was needed. More importantly, a measure of concordance was employed to determine whether or not they knew which tool they had requested. By either replying inappropriately to their request (i.e. giving them the wrong tool) or by offering them the tool kit and allowing them to choose any tool, it was possible to determine whether what they said corresponded with what they then did.

These studies permitted "reference" to be objectified as a verifiable inter-individual process, rather than a postulate of internal mental structure. They put in place a behaviorally valid means of determining whether or not a chimpanzee knew what it said. This verbal-behavioral concordance also made it possible for the chimpanzee to make statements about intended future actions of its own. For example, the announcement of the intent to "tickle" followed by tickling, or the announcement of the intent to "go outdoors" followed by a trip outside, could occur. Previous symbol-using apes did not have announcement skills at their disposal. They had asked for things they wanted and had named things when told to do so, but they had not used symbols for the purpose of conveying their future actions.

This behavioral "legitimization" of the linguistic capacity of apes established that apes could use symbols in many of the same ways as human beings, and that they were not simply engaging in a series of tricks or conditioned routines lacking cognizance of the significance of their utterances. What this work did not do, however, was address one of the most significant aspects of differences between human and ape—the fact that nearly all children acquire language skills not only spontaneously but effortlessly. Adults do not have to teach them; indeed it is hardly possible to prevent children from learning language if they are reared in anything approaching a normal environment. Why did apes need tutoring, and fairly constant tutoring at that?

The addition of four new subjects of a different species, the bonobo, permitted studies at the Language Research Center to address this question (Savage-Rumbaugh et al. 1986; Savage-Rumbaush 1988; Savage-Rumbaugh et al. 1990). These subjects consisted of a wild caught adult bonobo female (Matata) and her offspring (one male, Kanzi, born in 1980; and two females, Mulika and Panbanisha, born in 1983 and 1985, respectively). A female common chimpanzee, Panzee, was born in 1985 and is being reared with the bonobos in a co-rearing study.

Studies with these subjects began with attempts to replicate the findings described above with common chimpanzees. The adult female, Matata, evidenced significantly greater difficulty discriminating symbols and sequencing them than previous subjects. Matata showed similar deficiencies in other areas such as match-to-sample, sorting, and tool use. More importantly, she did not display a stable concordance between her symbolic utterances and her nonverbal behaviors, suggesting that her lexigram usage could not accurately be characterized as "symbolic" or "referential," at least at the procedural level typified by the *Pan troglodytes* subjects Sherman and Austin (Savage-Rumbaugh et al. 1990).

By contrast, all of Matata's offspring (Kanzi, Mulika, and Panbanisha) acquired large symbol vocabularies. The most important finding with these additional ape subjects was that *it is not necessary to train language*. Simply by observing and listening to the caretakers' input, as a child observes and listens to those around it, they began to use symbols appropriately. Their acquisition of these skills has been described in detail elsewhere (Savage-Rumbaugh et al. 1986; Savage-Rumbaugh 1988); however, a brief summary is relevant here.

All of the young bonobos were exposed to caretakers who pointed to keyboard symbols as they spoke. Caretakers talked to them about daily routines, events, and about comings and goings of the laboratory. These events included trips to the woods to search for food, games of tickle and chase, trips to visit other primates at the laboratory, play with favorite toys such as balloons and balls, visits from friends, watching preferred TV shows, taking baths, helping pick up things, and other simple activities characteristic of daily life. They were not required to use the keyboard to get the caretaker to tickle, play, open doors, or give them food. Instead of requiring symbol production, caretakers talked to the apes about what they were doing and what was to be done next. These conversations were characterized by speaking while simultaneously pointing to symbols and were always contextually relevant. They were rarely, if ever, repetitive in the sense that the same word or sentence was uttered over and over. Nonetheless, across days, routines evidenced basic structures or schemata that tended to repeat themselves, just as do the routines of preschool children.

Unlike apes whose symbol vocabulary was assigned by the experimenter, the bonobos "selected" the symbols they were ready to acquire from the hundreds used around them each day. Like children, their first words were not all the same, though there was overlap. Also unlike other apes, the bonobos first learned to associate the spoken word with its real world referent, not the geometric symbol. Only after learning the relationship between a spoken word and its referent did they connect the word and the geometric symbol. Their initial acquisition was receptive, that is, they evidenced comprehension of things that were said to them and around them before they began to employ symbols to communicate their own desires.

DECODING SPEECH

When the input which the ape receives is spontaneous and context-appropriate natural language, each word is inevitably intermingled with others in many different types of sentences. For example, one might hear "balloon" in the sentences "Can you blow up the balloon?," "Can you find the balloon?," "Please don't swallow the balloon," "Would you put the balloon in the backpack?," and so on. From such complex input the ape must somehow abstract the phonemic combination of sounds that forms the word "balloon" and pair these sounds with the object. The ape's initial attempts to assign reference may differ from the accepted referent either by being too specific or too global. However, the constant attempts to interpret utterances produced by the models will eventually result in the appropriate delimiting of the referent for the word "balloon."

When symbols are acquired in this manner, the process of reference and the particular item of reference are comprehended for some time before the symbol is ever produced. Such comprehension is neither paced nor prodded by a teacher; indeed the caregiver may not be aware that comprehension is even occurring, since for the most part such comprehension is covert and self-reinforcing. The ape's motivation is to understand the message that is being directed toward it so that it can predict what will be happening in the social context, not to produce a motor act that will please the teacher and result in receipt of a banana or fish. When apes do begin to produce a symbol

which they have already learned to comprehend, they neither expect nor receive a reward for doing so. Instead, symbol production functions to provide information regarding their internal state.

SYNTAX

In the view of many linguists, language is defined largely by the existence of syntax (for a current review of this issue see Bates et al. 1990). Upon this perspective neither complex communications nor rational thought can take place as long as syntax is absent. It is assumed that all human communications involving more than a simple desire or alarm call need syntax as do all communications about the past and the future and all communications regarding relationships between agents, actions, objects, locations, and events.

The importance which linguists historically attributed to syntax caused these issues to supersede all others in the ape language debate. It was too quickly assumed that single word utterances produced by animals could be explained by the principles of conditioned discrimination learning, generalization, match-to-sample, and imitation (Brown 1973). For many scientists, the study by Terrace et al. (1979) was the final word on ape language. However, the premise upon which Terrace arrived at his negative conclusions was itself fatally flawed. This premise was that if an ape could use different symbols in different grammatical categories and if it could then sequence or properly arrange these categories, it must be said to posses a rudimentary syntax.

There are two reasons why the production of symbols ordered by category is not a sufficient demonstration of syntax. The first is that many words (for example, proper names) can function equally well in different syntactical categories. Thus the knowledge that "Kelly" goes in the agent position in an agent-action-object frame such as "Kelly throw ball" means little unless it can simultaneously be shown that "Kelly" is placed in a different category and different position in a sentence such as "Give the ball to Kelly."

It is noteworthy that Terrace did not search Nim's data for such differential syntactical categorization of common words. Rather, he attempted to determine which words, if any, tended to fall in a particular position such as first or last when they occurred conjointly. On the basis of this tally he concluded that lexical regularities existed in Nim's utterances. Nim's regularities were not positional and were, in some sense, rule based, though Terrace did not attempt to specify any rules that might account for the observed regularities. Terrace concluded that semantic categorical structure was not present because Nim used only a small number of words in most categories. For example, the only signs that served as "beneficiaries" were the synonymous signs "me" and "Nim." With only these signs as "beneficiaries" it is not reasonable to conclude that Nim had developed a functional semantically-based concept of the role of the "beneficiary" or that he could use a syntactically organized sentence.

It is possible to simultaneously accept Terrace's conclusions regarding Nim and question his premise that syntax can be demonstrated by looking at the order of Nim's signs. Simple action-agent-object ordering is not synonymous with syntactical structure. Syntactical structure can be demonstrated only by showing that the semantic relationship between words, which is encoded by order (or other syntactical devices) is understood.

More important, however, is the fact that the basic function of any sequence of words (with or without syntactical markers) is to convey specific novel meanings that cannot be expressed by the utterance of individual words. The communicative effect produced by a combination of a group of words is distinctively different from the production of individual words. The production of novel combinatorial utterances is an extremely powerful communicative process that characterizes all languages. It antedates the emergence of syntax proper, and because a new meaning is created which is not simply an additive result of the separate units, it cannot be satisfactorily reduced to the principles of conditioning, generalization, match-to-sample, or other similar psychological processes.

NOVEL AND CREATIVE COMBINATIONS WITHOUT SYNTAX

Terrace observed that "There is no evidence, however, that apes can combine such symbols in order to create new meanings." (Terrace et al. 1979: 900) In making such a statement, he assumed that syntax is a necessary condition for the generation of novel meanings, while overlooking the fact that word combinations themselves can be employed to create new meanings. For example, an utterance such as "Car trailer" or "Grouproom Matata," may well convey a novel meaning that its individual components, if uttered alone, could never generate.

The bonobo Kanzi regularly created combinations that differed from those of Washoe and Nim in substantive ways. For example, when Kanzi produced the combination "Car trailer" he was in the car and employed this utterance as a means of indicating that he wanted the car to be driven to the trailer rather than to walk. (The trailer is near the lab and Kanzi generally walked to the trailer when he wanted to go.) He followed the utterance with a gesture toward the trailer. When asked whether he wanted the car to go to the trailer, Kanzi produced a positive vocal response and again gestured to the trailer.

Had Kanzi said "car" alone, this single symbol utterance would have been interpreted as a comment about being in the car and would have simply been acknowledged. Had he said "trailer" alone, the caretaker would probably have simply gotten out of the car and walked with Kanzi to the trailer, since it was a very short distance to drive. However, by saying "car trailer" Kanzi produced a novel meaning and brought about a set of events that otherwise would not have been likely to occur (i.e., taking the car to the trailer).

Kanzi similarly produced the combination "Grouproom Matata" to convey something different than either symbol could convey alone. Kanzi was in the grouproom when he produced this combination and he had just heard Matata vocalize. Generally when he wanted to visit Matata, he would so indicate by simply saying "Matata" and gesturing "go" toward the colony room (where Matata was housed). However, on this occasion, by producing this combination he indicated that he wanted Matata to come to the group room. In response to his utterance he was asked, "Do you want Matata to come to the group room?" He immediately made loud positive vocal noises first to the experimenter, then to Matata, apparently announcing something about this to her. She responded with excited vocalizations also. Had Kanzi said only "grouproom," his utterance would have been interpreted as a comment on his location, just as "car" would have been in the preceding example. However, since one cannot take a room somewhere, the interpretation was that Kanzi wanted Matata to come into the grouproom. Kanzi's vocalization in response to the question and his ensuing behavior affirmed the correctness of this interpretation.

These utterances, which are characteristic of Kanzi, differ from Washoe's "water bird" in that they are not elicited by factors present in the environment and the experimenter's query. While it is not possible to know at any given moment why Kanzi said "Car trailer," "Matata grouproom," or any other of thousands of similar utterances, it is reasonable to conclude these utterances were provoked by an interaction between Kanzi's memory system and information that he was processing at the current time. Moreover, they reflected an attempt to communicate a specific message about his internal state to another party, rather than a simple naming of something pointed out by the experimenter. As such, these two-word messages were communicative and expressed things that the experimenter would not otherwise have known. The same cannot be said of the "water bird" response. (For additional examples of Kanzi's utterances.)

It is also possible to determine what Kanzi meant as a result of the utterance. One can simply agree with Kanzi and then look to see if his behavior corresponds to what has been agreed to. For example, does he head toward Matata's cage and unlock her door if given the opportunity? Does he sit down in the car and gesture toward the trailer? Since there are an unlimited number of other things he might do other than exhibit behaviors which correspond to his utterance, if he does do things which proceed along the lines of the utterances, it is reasonable to assume that he knows what he has said. It is not possible to use a similar approach with "water bird." This utterance is elicited by the experimenter's query and does not reflect Washoe's internal state in any sense. Whatever she does after the utterance is not relevant to her signing "water bird."

Multi-word utterances, then, can either represent strings of single signs or they can be attempts at the communication of complex messages that are not possible with signs or symbols used individually.

While all conditions do not need to be met for each utterance, it is essential that all of these conditions be satisfied in some sense by the total body of data available for the ape or other animal (see Savage-Rumbaugh 1990 for a more complete description of the need for each of these conditions). If the ape's multi-word utterances do not meet

these criteria, then the further search for syntactical structures in the utterances would not appear to be warranted. It is possible to evaluate and compare the multi-word utterances of different apes. For example, an utterance such as Washoe's "water-bird" meets only criteria 7 and 8, and fails all others. In some cases the failure to meet a criterion results from Washoe herself, but in other cases it results from a failure to report the behavior associated with the utterance.

Looking at Nim's combinations, we find that they fail into three classes of utterances, 1) those which contain a "wild card," 2) those which are ritualized and must be signed within a given routine, and 3) those in which a single sign is combined with a pointing gesture. It is even questionable whether two-word utterances such as "Food Nim," "Ice Nim," "Hungry me," etc. should be classified as two-word combinations since both the signs "Nim" and "me" are used as "wild cards" or signs that Nim added freely to any utterance.

These data suggest that it is not a tendency to imitate, nor a lack of syntactical competency, that is at the basis of Nim's failure to learn language, as Terrace's argues. Rather, his difficulty is more basic. It appears that Nim is unable to create truly novel two-word combinations regardless of order. Study of videotapes of Nim with his trainers reveals that they constantly addressed questions to Nim with the goal of producing more signs and sign combinations (Savage-Rumbaugh & Sevcik 1984). For example, if Nim wanted an apple that they held (which he indicated by reaching for the apple) he was asked "What this?" "What Nim want eat?" "Nim want eat apple?" "Who eat apple?" until he finally produced a combination such as "Me Nim apple eat." While Terrace maintains that Nim was not explicitly taught combinations, it is clear from these tapes that Nim was not permitted, most of the time, to use single signs to make his wants known. Moreover, the queries used by the trainers contained signs that they wanted Nim to make in order to expand upon the simple communication that he had already made. Consequently, the adoption of a strategy of imitating the teacher's utterance was the only means available to Nim of obtaining food, play, and other important things.

Are Nim's data indicative of the ultimate capacity of the ape? When Nim's data are contrasted with those of Kanzi, an ape who acquired symbols spontaneously without molding or other training, it is clear that Nim's limitations do not extend to all apes. A 5-month corpus of Kanzi's multi-word utterances (collected between April 1 and September 1, 1986) has been analyzed using the contextual data gathered on Kanzi's behavior at the time the utterance occurred (Greenfield & Savage-Rumbaugh 1991). In each case, the intent of the utterance was determined by Kanzi's behavior. This analysis indicates that Kanzi's combinations differ significantly from those of Washoe and Nim. None of the combinations used in this analysis were imitations (only 2.67% of Kanzi's combinations were either partial or full imitations of the preceding utterance; these were eliminated from analysis for the purposes of this data set). Both the context and Kanzi's ensuing behavior were recorded for each combination. This made it possible to determine whether or not Kanzi understood the utterance and what he intended that it mean.

The majority of Kanzi's utterances were novel and most of the messages could not have been conveyed by single words. Many of the utterances referred to events or objects which were absent at the time of the utterance. Kanzi employed a wide variety of semantic relations. Moreover, in the majority of his combinations, he tended to order symbols according to semantic function (see Greenfield & Savage-Rumbaugh 1990, 1991 for discussion). The variety of lexically distinct combinations was so great as to make it impossible for the combinations to have been formed on the basis of lexical position preference. Also, many items occurred in different positions in different combinations. For example, "Grab Matata" occurred as an action-object combination signalling Kanzi's desire to play a game of "grab" with Matata. However, the utterance "Matata bite" was not used to indicate a desire to playbite with Matata, but the fact that Matata had bitten Kanzi quite hard. Similarly, Kanzi used the combination "Hide peanut" to comment that he had just hidden some peanuts in the grass. However, he then formed the combination "Chase hide" to ask the caretaker to play a game of chase and hide with him.

CUING: HOW TO DRAW ACCURATE CONCLUSIONS

The issue of cuing is one that has been, and must continue to be, of concern in this field, as Wilder (chapter 3 of this reader) observes. However, in the past this issue has also been used unfairly to attack the entire field as a questionable one. The purpose of these one-sided attacks has not been to develop standardized methodologies to eliminate cuing, but rather simply to raise doubts as to whether it is possible ever to eliminate the scent of Clever Hans, and thus to argue that no animal studies can be valid under any circumstances. This is patently false. Indeed, it is possible to determine what animals can do using methodologies that control for cuing (Rumbaugh et al. 1990). There are many different ways of doing this, and the "correct" way at any given time depends upon that which one is trying to demonstrate. However, there are some very simple principles that apply to the majority of situations. The first is that it is important to distinguish between what the animal does in training situations or during daily conversation and what it does in testing formats. During training and/or conversation settings, it is to be expected that the experimenter will provide a model for the animal, much as a parent provides a model for its child and that the adult will try to help the animal to communicate. This is an essential process in language acquisition for the child and there is no reason to deny it to animals attempting to learn language. Similarly, some cuing or prompting may be done by parents during this period. The goal, however, is to understand what it is the child or chimpanzee is attempting to say, by whatever means is at hand. Data from such sessions *are not expected to be free of parental or experimental input*. Such data are however, important for revealing many facts regarding the learning process itself.

During *test settings*, all such input must be removed. Test settings must be designed to determine, in an explicit sense, the capacities that the animal (or child) has developed fully enough to be able to exhibit them out of the communicative context when queried under conditions that prevent contextual and/or experimenter input to the response. Wilder at times seems to confuse these two settings in his critique, taking pains to point out that cuing of different sorts can occur in daily conversations with Kanzi. Indeed, if no rapport were permitted between Kanzi and the experimenter in the daily context of language use, it is difficult to see how a functional symbolic communication system could ever develop.

However, Wilder overlooks some important aspects of the daily conversational setting with Kanzi which mitigate against the kind of cuing that is of concern to him. Certainly the experimenter could devise a means of cuing Kanzi in this setting, but the concern of the experimenter is not that of getting Kanzi to say what is "right" or "correct" or to answer a question. Rather, the experimenter is interested in whatever Kanzi has to say. It does not matter where Kanzi goes, what game he wants to play, what he would like to eat, or what he would like to do. There are no experimental constraints which determine this. It is up to Kanzi. Consequently, *there is no preprogrammed correct answer that the experimenter is waiting for or wanting Kanzi to produce.* If Clever Hans could have stomped his foot as many times as he wished, regardless of the question he was asked, it is not likely that he would have begun to look to the trainer for cues.

Blind tests have been a standard control in the field and fully adequate tests to eliminate cuing have been employed by Gardner and Gardner (1984), Herman (1987), Schusterman & Krieger (1984), Rumbaugh (1977), Savage-Rumbaugh (1986), and Savage-Rumbaugh et al. (1986). Fully adequate controls have not been employed by Patterson (1978), Terrace (1979), Miles (1978), or Pepperberg (1981), or by Boysen & Berntsen (1989) in tests of numerical ability. Fouts (1973) initially used adequate controls, but dropped them in some of his later research (Fouts et al. 1984). (It is this work which Wilder criticizes.) Adequate controls require that all potential means of indicating the correct response to the animal, prior to its occurrence be ruled out. This is most easily accomplished by having the experimenter who judges the animal's response be blind. This means that this experimenter either cannot see the animal (and the animal cannot see him/her) or that the experimenter does not know what response the animal is to make (such as left, right, or middle). Sufficient trials must be administered to rule out chance responding. When conceptual or novel responses are of interest, trial one data must be employed.

An ideal example of such a test is the use of headphones to determine comprehension of the English words (Savage-Rumbaugh, 1988). In this test, Kanzi wears headphones so that only he can hear the target word. The experimenter does not know what Kanzi heard, nor does he/she know what lexigrams are available for Kanzi to choose from until after his selection has already been made. Target words and alternatives are selected randomly from trial to trial. Additionally, Kanzi is given food for participating in the test, but food or other reward is never contingent upon a correct response. It is given as requested. The importance of being able to give tests without reward is often underestimated with regard to the issue of cuing (Wilder, chapter 3 of this reader). If the organism has nothing to gain by being correct and nothing to lose by being incorrect, it has no reason to search for cues, inadvertent or otherwise, and it does not do so.

Terrace (1979) and Miles (1978) report no blind tests. Pepperberg (1981) is the judge of whether or not the parrot answers correctly and she is present in the room and knows which item is shown to Alex. Boysen & Berntsen (1989) report too few blind trials to ascertain whether the novel behavior (adding) was chance or not.

CONCLUSION

Kanzi's ability to combine symbols without drill or withholding of preferred items implies that many fundamental aspects of language cannot be specific to *Homo*. While his capacity for extremely complex syntactical devices remains limited, it is still expanding. It also must be remembered that Kanzi's brain is one-third the size of our own. Given that he can, without training, decode speech into individual words, determine how those function in different and novel communicative settings (Savage-Rumbaugh 1988), use them spontaneously and appropriately in novel combinations (Greenfield & Savage-Rumbaugh 1990), and comprehend sentential relationships (Savage-Rumbaugh 1989), it is reasonable to conclude that the language gap between man and ape may result from a difference in information processing capacity and memory, rather than innate linguistic structures.

We find, then, that it is possible to tap, not train, abilities in other extant species that give evidence of a bio-linguistic substratum for language. Given an appropriate communicative environment and the opportunity to develop skills without rote, reward-based training or drilling, bonobos have developed symbol use that functions much like that of human children. They not only use the symbols to communicate requests, statements, and comments, but they also understand the utterances of others. Additionally, Kanzi, the oldest symbol-using bonobo, has spontaneously begun to use multisymbol utterances to encode information that cannot be expressed with a single symbol. The evidence from Kanzi and the other bonobos casts doubt on two widely-held beliefs in the scientific community: that language is possible because of unique structures in the human brain and that even complex skills are best taught to nonhumans through simplistic shaping and conditioning techniques.

At the moment, it is not known whether the bonobo alone can demonstrate these homologies to children's language, or whether the freedom from methodological constraints has allowed this capacity to develop naturally. There is evidence that some of the cognitive components of language are present in members of other species. Certainly, a correspondence of some kind between sign or symbol and its referent has been established in dolphins (Herman, et al. 1984), sea lions (Schusterman & Krieger 1984), parrot (Pepperberg 1981, 1983), chimpanzee (Gardner & Gardner 1969, 1984; Savage-Rumbaugh 1986; Savage-Rumbaugh et al. 1986, 1990), and gorilla (Patterson 1978). The nature of this correspondence may not be equivalent to that found in bonobos, but its presence suggests that further studies of these and other species is warranted. Future research should focus upon the animal's ability to comprehend symbolic communicative messages which are directed to it. These messages must be able to convey novel propositional information (such as "There is a snake hiding in the blanket") and the motivation to comprehend such messages must reside in their intrinsic worth and the appropriateness of their context. For it is from the comprehension of the novel messages of others that the capacity to produce novel messages of one's own must rise.

ACKNOWLEDGMENTS

The preparation of this chapter and research described herein were supported by National Institutes of Health grant NICHD-06016, which supports the Language Research Center, cooperatively operated by Georgia State University and the Yerkes Regional Primate Research Center of Emory University. In addition the research is supported in part by RR-00165 to the Yerkes Primate Research Center of Emory University. This research was also supported by the College of Arts and Sciences of Georgia State University. The authors wish to thank Kelly McDonald, Jeannine Murphy, Elizabeth Rubert, Rose Sevcik, and Philip Shaw for their work with the bonobos. The authors also appreciate the efforts of Robert Astur toward the preparation of this manuscript.

LITERATURE CITED

BATES, E. 1979. THE EMERGENCE OF SYMBOLS. NEW YORK: ACADEMIC PRESS.

BATES, E., THAL, D. & MARCHMAN, V. 1990. SYMBOLS AND SYNTAX: A DARWINIAN approach to language development. IN: THE BIOLOGICAL FOUNDATION OF LANGUAGE DEVELOPMENT (ED. BY N. KRASNEGOR, D. RUMBAUGH, M. STUDDERT-KENNEDY & R. SCHIEFELBUSCH). OXFORD: OXFORD UNIVERSITY PRESS.

BOYSEN, S. T. & BERNTSEN, G. G. 1989. NUMERICAL COMPETENCE IN A CHIMPANZEE (PAN TROGLODYTES). JOURNAL OF COMPARATIVE PSYCHOLOGY 103, 23–31.

BROWN, R. 1973. A FIRST LANGUAGE: THE EARLY STAGE. CAMBRIDGE, MASSACHUSETTS: HARVARD UNIVERSITY PRESS.

BRUNER, J. 1983. CHILD'S TALK. NEW YORK: NORTON.

DALE, P. S. 1976. LANGUAGE DEVELOPMENT: STRUCTURE AND FUNCTION. (2ND EDITION). NEW YORK: HOLT, REINHART AND WINSTON.

FOUTS, R. S. 1973. ACQUISITION AND TESTING OF GESTURAL SIGNS IN FOUR YOUNG CHIMPANZEES. SCIENCE 180, 978–980.

FOUTS, R. S., CHOWN, W. M. & GOODIN, L. 1976. TRANSFER OF SIGNED RESPONSES IN AMERICAN SIGN LANGUAGE FROM VOCAL ENGLISH STIMULI TO PHYSICAL OBJECT BY A CHIMPANZEE (PAN). LEARNING AND MOTIVATION, 7, 458–475.

FOUTS, R. S., COUCH, J. B. & O'NEAL, C. R. 1979. STRATEGIES FOR PRIMATE LANGUAGE TRAINING. IN: LANGUAGE INTERVENTION FROM APE TO CHILD (ED. BY R. L. SCHIEFELBUSCH & J. H. HOLLIS), PP. 295–323. BALTIMORE, MARYLAND: UNIVERSITY PARK PRESS.

FOUTS, R. S., FOUTS, D. H., & SCHOENFELD, D. 1984. SIGN LANGUAGE CONVERSATIONAL INTERACTION BETWEEN CHIMPANZEES. SIGN LANGUAGE STUDIES 42, 1–12.

GARDNER, R. A. & GARDNER, B. T. 1969. TEACHING SIGN LANGUAGE TO A CHIMPANZEE. SCIENCE 165, 664–672.

_____. 1975. EARLY SIGNS OF LANGUAGE IN CHILD AND CHIMPANZEE. SCIENCE 187, 752–753.

_____. 1984. A VOCABULARY TEST FOR CHIMPANZEES (PAN TROGLODYTES). JOURNAL OF COMPARATIVE PSYCHOLOGY 98, 381–404.

GAUKER, C. (1990). HOW TO LEARN A LANGUAGE LIKE A CHIMPANZEE. PHILOSOPHICAL PSYCHOLOGY 3, 31–53.

Gill, T. V. 1977. Conversations with Lana. In: *Language Learning by a Chimpanzee: The LANA Project* (ed. by D. M. Rumbaugh), pp. 225–246. New York: Academic Press.

Greenfield, P. M. & Savage-Rumbaugh, E. S. (1990). Grammatical combination in *Pan paniscus*: Learning and invention in the evolution and development of language. In: *Comparative Developmental Psychology of Language and Intelligence in Primates* (ed. by S. Parker & K. Gibson), New York: Cambridge University Press.

_____. (1991). Imitation, grammatical development, and the invention of protogrammar by an ape. In: *Biobehavioral Foundations of Language Development* (ed. by N. Krasnegor, D. Rumbaugh, M. Studdert-Kennedy & R. Schiefelbusch), pp. 235–258. Hillsdale, New Jersey: Lawrence Erlbaum Associates.

Greenfield, P. M., & Smith, H. 1976. *The Structure of Communication in Early Language Development*. New York: Academic Press.

Herman, L. M. 1987. Receptive competencies of language-trained animals. In: *Advances in the Study of Behavior* Vol. 17 (ed. by J. S. Rosenblatt, C. Beer, M.-C. Busnel, & P. J. B. Slater), pp. 1–60. Petaluma, California: Academic Press.

_____. 1988. The language of animal language research: Reply to Schusterman and Gisiner. *The Psychological Record* 38, 349–362.

Herman, L. M., Richards, D. G. & Wolz, J. P. 1984. Comprehension of sentences by bottlenosed dolphins. *Cognition* 16, 129–219.

Lock, A. 1980. *The Guided Reinvention of Language*. London: Academic Press.

McShane, J. 1980. *Learning to Talk*. Cambridge: Cambridge University Press.

Miles, H. L. 1978. Language acquisition in apes and children. In: *Sign Language Acquisition in Man and Ape: New Dimensions in Comparative Psycholinguistics* (ed. by F. C. C. Peng). Boulder, Colorado: Westview Press.

Moerk, E. L. 1977. *Pragmatic and Semantic Aspects of Early Language Development*. Baltimore, Maryland: University Park Press.

Patterson, F. 1978. Linguistic capabilities of a lowland gorilla. In: *Sign Language Acquisition in Man and Ape: New Dimensions in Comparative Psycholinguistics* (ed. by F. C. C. Peng), pp. 161–201. Boulder, Colorado: Westview Press.

Pepperberg, I. 1981. Functional vocalizations by an African Greyparrot(*Psittacuserithacus*)*ZeitschriftfürTieresychologie*55, 139–160.

_____. 1983. Cognition in the African Grey parrot: Preliminary evidence for auditory/vocal comprehension of the class concept. *Animal Learning and Behavior* 11(2), 179–185.

Peters, A. M. 1983. *The Units of Language Acquisition*. Cambridge: Cambridge University Press.

Premack, D. 1970. The education of Sarah: A chimp learns the language. *Science* 170, 54–58.

Premack, D. & Premack, A. 1983. *The Mind of an Ape*. New York: Norton.

Rumbaugh, D. M. 1977. *Language Learning by a Chimpanzee: The LANA Project*. New York: Academic Press.

Rumbaugh, D. M., Gill, T. V., & von Glasersfeld, E. C. 1973. Reading and sentence completion by a chimpanzee. *Science* 182, 731–733.

Rumbaugh, D. M., Washburn, D., Hopkins, W. D., & Savage-Rumbaugh, E. S. (1990). Chimpanzee competence for counting in a video-formatted task situation. In: *Proceedings of the Hawaii Conference on Animal Cognition* (ed. by H. Roitblat). Hillsdale, New Jersey: Lawrence Erlbaum Associates.

Savage-Rumbaugh, E. S. 1986. *Ape Language: From Conditioned Response to Symbol* New York: Columbia University Press.

_____. 1988. A new look at ape language: Comprehension of vocal speech and syntax. In: *Nebraska symposium on motivation*, 35 (ed. by D. Leger). Lincoln, NE: University of Nebraska Press.

_____. 1989. Language: Our erroneous but cherished preconceptions. Invited lecture, Animal Language Workshop, University of Hawaii at Manoa.

_____. 1990a. Language as a cause-effect communication system. *Philosophical psychology.* 3, 55–76.

_____. 1991. Language learning in the bonobo: How and why they learn. In: *Biobehavioral Foundations of Language Development* (ed. by N. Krasnegor, D. M. Rumbaugh, M. Studdert-Kerinedy & R. Schiefelbusch), pp. 209–233. Hillsdale, New Jersey: Lawrence Erlbaum.

_____. 1990b. Language acquisition in a nonhuman primate species: Implications for the innateness debate. *Developmental Psychobiology.* 23, 1–22.

_____. 1993. Language learnability in man, ape, and dolphin. In: *Proceedings of the Hawaii Conference on Animal Cognition* (ed. by H. Roitblatt, L. M. Herman, & P. E. Nachtigall), pp. 457–484. Hillsdale, New Jersey: Lawrence Erlbaum.

Savage-Rumbaugh, E. S., McDonald, K., Sevcik, R. A., Hopkins, W. D., & Rubert, E. 1986. Spontaneous symbol acquisition and communicative use by pygmy chimpanzees (*Pan paniscus*). *Journal of Experimental Psychology: General* 115, 211–235.

Savage-Rumbaugh, E. S., & Rumbaugh, D. M. 1988. A theory of language acquisition in apes. Paper presented at NICHD Conference, "Biobehavioral Foundations of Language Development." Leesburg, Virginia.

_____. 1991. A theory of language acquisition in apes. In: *Biobehavioral Foundations of Language Development* (ed. by N. Krasnegor, D. M. Rumbaugh, M. Studdert-Kennedy & D. Schiefelbusch). Hillsdale, New Jersey: Lawrence Erlbaum Associates.

Savage-Rumbaugh, E. S., Rumbaugh, D. M. & Boysen, S. 1980. Do apes use language? *American Scientist* 68, 49–61.

Savage-Rumbaugh, E. S. & Sevcik, R. A. 1984. Levels of communicative competency in the chimpanzee: Pre-representational and representational. In: Behavioral evolution and integrative levels (ed. by G. Greenberg & E. Tobach), pp. 197–219. Hillsdale, New Jersey: Lawrence Erlbaum.

Savage-Rumbaugh, E. S., Sevcik, R. A., Brakke, K. E., & Rumbaugh, D. M. 1990. Symbols: Their communicative use, combination, and comprehension by bonobos (*Pan paniscus*). In: *Advances in Infancy Research 6* (ed. by C. Rovee-Collier & L. P. Lipsitt), pp. 221–278. Norwood, New Jersey: Ablex.

Schusterman, R. L., & Krieger, K. 1984. California sea lions are capable of semantic comprehension. *The Psychological Record* 34, 3–23.

_____. 1988. Artificial language comprehension in dolphins and sea lions: The essential cognitive skills. *The Psychological Record* 38, 311–348.

Terrace, H. S. 1979. *Nim.* New York: Alfred A. Knopf.

_____. 1985. In the beginning was the "name." *American Psychologist* 40, 1011–1028.

Terrace, H. S., Pettito, L. A., Sanders, R. J. & Bever, T. G. 1979. Can an ape create a sentence? *Science* 206, 891–900.

Waldron, T. P. 1985. Principles of Language and Mind. London: Routledge & Kegan, Paul.

Wells, G. A. 1987. *The Origin of Language: Aspects of the Discussion from Condillac to Wundt.* La Salle, Illinois: Open Court.

The Flight Paths of Honeybees Recruited by the Waggle Dance

J.R. RILEY, U. GREGGERS, A.D. SMITH, D.R. REYNOLDS, AND R. MENZEL

In the 'dance language' of honeybees[1,2], the dancer generates a specific, coded message that describes the direction and distance from the hive of a new food source, and this message is displaced in both space and time from the dancer's discovery of that source. Karl von Frisch concluded that bees 'recruited' by this dance used the information encoded in it to guide them directly to the remote food source, and this Nobel Prize-winning discovery revealed the most sophisticated example of non-primate communication that we know of[3,4]. In spite of some initial scepticism[5–9], almost all biologists are now convinced that von Frisch was correct[3,4,10–14], but what has hitherto been lacking is a quantitative description of how effectively recruits translate the code in the dance into flight to their destinations. Using harmonic radar[15–17] to record the actual flight paths of recruited bees, we now provide that description.

There have been some important advances since von Frisch's original experiments, and it has been believed for some time that the honeybee communication system does not instantly specify a food location to the recruits, without any hesitancy and with pinpoint accuracy[18]. In fact, detailed observations have shown that recruits may go through several iterations of dance session and resultant search flight before they eventually arrive at the indicated food source, and some never find the food at all[3,19–21]. The current interpretation of the von Frisch hypothesis thus predicts that newly recruited bees should fly directly from the hive to the vicinity of a food source, and then proceed to search for its exact location using odour and other cues[2]. This searching period would neatly account for the fact that the arrival of recruits at the source is often very much later than would be expected for a direct flight between the hive and food source—the anomaly that caused the initial scepticism about the hypothesis.

We began our experiments by capturing recruited bees as they left our observation hive, attaching a harmonic transponder, and then releasing them. The hive was not equipped to make quantitative measurements of individual dance angles or frequencies, but we observed that, at any given time, the dances of bees that had been previously recorded at the feeder were almost all aligned about a common direction. At midday this direction was at about 90° to the vertical, and this confirmed our expectation that the bees were feeding exclusively at our artificial feeder that lay 200 m directly east of the hive, and that it was to this food source that the waggle dances referred. Neither the feed nor the feeder station itself carried any artificial scents at any time.

Most recruited bees released from the hive almost immediately undertook a straight flight of direction and length that brought them directly into the vicinity of the feeder demonstrates that the mean direction of these flights lay impressively close to the hive-to-feeder direction for the first 200 m or so but, in spite of this, only two of the recruits actually found and alighted on the feeder. This was not a surprising result, given that similar low rates of success in finding unscented feeders have been found in conventional studies of recruit flight[22]. At the end of their straight outward flights, some recruits promptly initiated fairly direct return flights to the hive, but more usually they engaged in what appeared to be local searching manoeuvres for several minutes. It was noticeable that searching bees occasionally passed within just a few metres of the feeder without finding it, and in a few cases, searches lasted as long as 20 min, taking recruits as far as 200 m from the feeder location. These bees often returned to the point at which they had begun their searching behaviour before flying back to the hive, but fairly direct homeward flights from other points were also seen.

In a parallel experiment, recruited bees captured leaving the hive were taken to three release points 200–250 m away, and then released. These bees did not fly towards the actual position of the feeder, but instead made straight flights on the vector that would have taken them to the feeder had they not been displaced. Their flights were thus exactly like those of recruits released at the hive, and similarly often extended to searching behaviour at the expected feeder position. Unable to locate the feeder, the bees then returned to their release site. The processes by which they eventually returned to their hive are described elsewhere[23].

The wind fields in which the bees were flying were almost always uniform, with no evidence of large-scale mixing eddies or back flow. The flow was predominantly from the west or southwest during our experiments, typically at 2–4 ms^{-1}, and this guaranteed that no odours from the feeder could possibly have been available to guide the recruits leaving the hive. As one would expect in these circumstances, the flight paths showed no evidence of the casting or upwind zigzagging that is known to characterize odour-following flight in other insects[24–26]. These two facts together carry the very convincing inference that recruits leave the hive with prior knowledge of the direction and distance of a food source that they have never previously visited. By themselves, these observations thus provide extremely strong, direct support for von Frisch's

hypothesis that recruited bees 'read' the waggle dance, but the most compelling evidence comes from the flights of displaced recruits. These bees made direct flights to where the feeder should have been, and did so without the aid of any landscape or odour cues that might have existed on the true hive-to-feeder route. There was also, of course, no possibility that they were following either regular foragers directly, or ephemeral odour trails left in the hive-to-feeder flight corridor by regular forager traffic.

It is important to note that, although the feeder was in the overall downwind direction from the hive, the recruits were not simply flying downwind. This ability to compensate for lateral wind drift appears to be common to both bumble bees[27] and honeybees[28] and it was clearly demonstrated in most of the recruits that we observed. In spite of wind compensation, the translation by individual recruits of information encoded in the waggle dance into flight to the intended destination was rarely perfect. While the diagram shows that the mean of the outward vector flights was impressively close to the target (within 6 m), most ended tens of metres from the feeder. Thus some form of terminal guidance would normally be essential for successful homing on the target and, in the case of natural food sources, this would usually be available in the form of visual and odour cues, and sometimes from experienced foragers manoeuvring over the source[22].

In summary, we have provided the first quantitative and direct description of the degree to which recruits translate information encoded in the waggle dance into flight to the vicinity of the designated destination. Our results have shown that although this process is highly effective, most recruits would not reach the intended food sources without the use of odour and visual cues in the final stages of their flight. We hope that together with earlier studies, particularly those of Gould[10], Srinivasan et al.[13] and Esch et al.[14], our results will also be accepted as a vindication of the von Frisch hypothesis.

METHODS
Harmonic radar

Most of our knowledge of insect flight behaviour at high altitudes has been derived from the use of radar modified for entomological observations[29]. More recently, it has become possible to apply this technique to low-flying insects by tagging them with tiny harmonic transponders, weighing only a few milligrams (6–20 mg, depending on the degree of mechanical robustness required). The transponders return signals to the radar at twice the original transmitted frequency, and because these signals can be distinguished from returns from ground features and other unwanted targets, the position of tagged insects can be determined while they are in flight[15–17]. In our experiments we caught bees as they exited their hive, attached transponders, and released them from the hive (or from remote release points), and recorded their subsequent flight trajectories. Nineteen of the 23 recruits (83%) released from the hive flew off satisfactorily, and produced good radar tracks, all to the east. Of the remaining four, three also went east, but were not detected by the radar enough times to produce a satisfactory track, probably because they were flying very low. Only one failed to leave the vicinity of the hive. Similar results were achieved for the remote releases, except during a period when the tubes in which the recruits were being transported became accidentally contaminated with sucrose solution, with the result that these bees did not fly away from the release point.

Experimental arena

The flight observations were made over a carefully selected[30], large area of mown pasture land, approximately 1×1.5 km, where the terrain was unusually flat and free from obstacles that would have obscured the radar's field of view[28]. The radar was positioned on the southern edge of the arena, so that it overlooked an observation hive and a feeding station 200 m to the east of the hive. Three release points were set 200 250 m in the sector to the southwest of the hive. There were very few natural sources of pollen and nectar present during our study period (late July/early August 2000).

Description of the wind field

Wind speed and direction were recorded at 10-s intervals at a height of 2.7m by anemometers and wind vanes placed at the corners of a 500m × 600m rectangle centred on the hive. We also setup a mast near to the centre of the rectangle, holding a nemometers at heights of 0.65, 1.3, 2.7 and 8.2m, and a wind vane at 2.7m. The clocks of the recording data loggers were synchronized each morning with a master clock at the radar to ensure that wind data were recoverable for the duration of each individual recorded flight. Using interpolation methods described else where[16,27] the data collected by these instruments were then combined to describe the mean wind field within which each of the flights recorded by the radar took place.

The observation hive

We used a two-frame colony, equipped with a transparent side panel that faced directly into a small, low tent attached to the hive. From within this darkened enclosure we could observe the dance behaviour of the bees, and their entry into and exit from the hive. Most of the bees in the small colony were marked with numbered tags. The entrance to the hive was in the form of clear plastic tube, so that observers stationed outside the tent could also observe entry and exit, and capture selected bees for tagging with transponders.

The flight experiments

We began our study by establishing in our experimental bees (European species *Apis mellifera carnica*)a route memory of the position of a feeding station relative to the hive. The feeder was placed directly to the east of the hive, and supplied with 0.2 1 M sucrose solution, and training to a distance of 200 m was accomplished over two days. No artificial odour cues were used in the procedure. From the start, observers at the feeder recorded the identification number of every marked bee that arrived there, and the hive was never opened unless an observer was at the feeder. Once foraging flights between hive and feeder were well established, observers in the tent watched the waggle dances. Whenever a numbered bee was seen to follow a dance and then move directly towards the exit, an observer outside the tent was alerted to catch the bee as it attempted to leave. If its identification number indicated that it had never previously visited the feeder, the bee was confirmed as a recruit, and a transponder attached. The bee was then either released directly from the hive exit, or taken in an opaque tube to one of three release points 200–250 m from the hive, and allowed to fly from there. Bees fitted with transponders could be detected while in flight within a 190° arc of radius 900 m, centred on the radar; their positions were shown once every 3 s on the screen of a desktop personal computer, and their coordinates recorded[17].

1. von Frisch, K. *The Dance Language and Orientation of Bees* (Harvard Univ. Press, Cambridge, Massachusetts, 1967).
2. Dyer, F. C. The biology of the dance language. *Annu. Rev. Entomol.* **47**, 917–949 (2002).
3. Gould, J. L. Honey bee recruitment: the dance-language controversy. *Science* **189**, 685–693 (1975).
4. Sherman, G. & Visscher, P. K. Honeybee colonies achieve fitness through dancing. *Nature* **419**, 920–922 (2002).
5. Wenner, A. M. & Johnson, D. L. Honeybees: do they use direction and distance information provided by their dancers? *Science* **158**, 1076–1077 (1967).
6. Wells, P. H. & Wenner, A. M. Do honey bees have a language? *Nature* **241**, 171–175 (1973).
7. Wenner, A. M. & Wells, P. H. *Anatomy of a Controversy: the Question of a "Language" Among Bees* (Columbia Univ. Press, New York, 1990).
8. Wenner, A. M., Meade, D. E. & Friesen, L. J. Recruitment, search behavior, and flight ranges of honey bees. *Am. Zool* **31**, 768–782 (1991).
9. Wenner, A. M. The elusive honey bee dance "language" hypothesis. *J. Insect Behav.* **15**, 859–878 (2002).
10. Gould, J. L. The dance-language controversy. *Q. Rev. Biol.* **51**, 211 244 (1976).
11. Dyer, F. C. & Smith, B. H. A review of "Anatomy of a Controversy: the Question of a 'Language' Among Bees" by A.M. Wenner & P.H. Wells. *Anim. Behav.* **47**, 1242–1244 (1994).
12. Seeley, T. D. Bee warned. *Nature* **349**, 114 (1991).
13. Srinivasan, M. V, Zhang, S. W., Altwein, M. & Tautz, J. Honeybee navigation: nature and calibration of the "odometer". *Science* **287**, 851 853 (2000).
14. Esch, H. E., Zhang, S. W., Srinivasan, M. V. & Tautz, J. Honeybee dances communicate distances measured by optic flow. *Nature* **411**, 581–583 (2001).
15. Riley, J. R. *et al.* Tracking bees with harmonic radar. *Nature* **379**, 29 30 (1996).
16. Riley, J. R. & Osborne, J. L. in *Insect Movement: Mechanisms and Consequences* (eds Woiwod, I. P.,

Reynolds, D. R. & Thomas, C. D.) 129 157 (CAB International, Wallingford, UK, 2001).
17. Riley, J. R. & Smith, A. D. Design considerations for an harmonic radar to investigate the flight of insects at low altitude. *Comput. Electron. Agric.* **35**, 151 169 (2002).
18. Towne, W. F. & Gould, J. L. The spatial precision of the honey bee's dance communication. *J. Insect Behav.* **1**, 129 155 (1988).
19. Esch, H. & Bastian, J. A. How do newly recruited honeybees approach a food site? *Z. Vergl. Physiol.* **68**, 175 181 (1970).
20. Mautz, D. Der Kommunikationseffekt der Schwänzeltänze bei Apis mellifica carnica (Pollm.). *Z. Vergl. Physiol.* **72**, 197 220 (1971).
21. Seeley, T. D. Division of labor between scouts and recruits in honeybee foraging. *Behav. Ecol. Sociobiol.* 12, 253 259 (1983).
22. Tautz, J. & Sandeman, D. C. Recruitment of honeybees to non-scented food sources. *J. Comp. Physiol. A* **189**, 293–300 (2003).
23. Menzel, R. *et al.* Honeybees navigate according to a map-like spatial memory. *Proc. Natl Acad. Sci. USA* **102**(8), 3040–3045 (2005).
24. Baker, T. C. & Haynes, K. F. Pheromone-mediated optomotor anemotaxis and altitude control exhibited by male oriental fruit moths in the field. *Physiol. Entomol.* **21**, 20–31 (1996).
25. Carde, R. T. & Mafra-Neto, A. in *Insect Pheromone Research: New Directions* (eds Cardé, R. T. & Minks, A. K.) 275 290 (Chapman & Hall, New York, 1997).
26. Riley, J. R. *et al.* Harmonic radar as a means of tracking the pheromone-finding and pheromone-following flight of male moths. *J. Insect Behav.* **11**, 287–296 (1998).
27. Riley, J. R. *et al.* Compensation for wind drift by bumble-bees. *Nature* **400**, 126 (1999).
28. Riley, J. R. *et al.* The automatic pilot of honeybees. *Proc. R. Soc. Lond. B* **270**, 2421 2424 (2003).
29. Reynolds, D. R. *et al.* in *Methods in Ecological and Agricultural Entomology* (eds Dent, D. R. & Walton, M. P.) 111 145 (CAB International, Wallingford, UK, 1997).
30. Chittka, L. & Geiger, K. Honeybee long-distance orientation in a controlled environment. *Ethology* **99**, 117 126 (1995).

Interactive Use of Sign Language by Cross-Fostered Chimpanzees (Pan Troglodytes)

MARY L. JENSVOLD AND R.A. GARDNER

Cross-fostered as infants in Reno, Nevada, chimpanzees (*Pan troglodytes*) Washoe, Moja, Tatu, and Dar freely converse in signs of American Sign Language with each other as well as with humans in Ellensburg, Washington. In this experiment, a human interlocutor waited for a chimpanzee to initiate conversations with her and then responded with 1 of 4 types of probes: general requests for more information, on-topic questions, off-topic questions, or negative statements. The responses of the chimpanzees to the probes depended on the type of probe and the particular signs in the probes. They reiterated, adjusted, and shifted the signs in their utterances in conversationally appropriate rejoinders. Their reactions to and interactions with a conversational partner resembled patterns of conversation found in similar studies of human children.

In cross-fostering, adults of one species rear the young of another species. Sign language studies of cross-fostered chimpanzees are a tool for studying the fuzzy overlap between human behavior and the behavior of other animals and between verbal behavior and other intelligent behavior (B. T. Gardner & Gardner, 1989, 1998; R. A. Gardner & Gardner, 1998; R. A. Gardner, Gardner, & Van Cantfort, 1989; Goodall, 1967, 1986; Hayes & Nissen, 1971; Plooij, 1984). The cross-fosterlings acquired and used the signs of American Sign Language (ASL), a naturally occurring human language, under nursery and conversational conditions. Comparable conditions and comparable measures reveal similar patterns of development in human infants and cross-fostered chimpanzees (Bloom, Rocissano, & Hood, 1976; Braine, 1976; Brown, 1968; De Villiers & De Villiers, 1986; Ervin-Tripp, 1970; D. H. Fouts, 1994; B. T. Gardner & Gardner, 1998; B. T. Gardner, Gardner, & Nichols, 1989; Krause & Fouts, 1997; Leonard, 1976; Nelson, 1973; Reich, 1986; Wells, 1974). This article reports an experimental study of patterns of conversational interaction between cross-fostered chimpanzees and a human interlocutor.

METHOD

Subjects

The 4 chimpanzee subjects (*Pan troglodytes*) of this experiment were Washoe, Moja, Tatu, and Dar. Washoe was captured wild in Africa. She arrived in the Gardner laboratory in Reno on June 21, 1966, when she was about 10 months old and lived as a cross-fosterling until October 1, 1970, when she left to become the first chimpanzee in the Fouts laboratory in Oklahoma. Moja, Pili, Tatu, and Dar were born in U.S. laboratories, and each arrived in Reno within a few days of birth. Moja was born at the Laboratory for Experimental Medicine and Surgery in Primates, New York, on November 18, 1972, and arrived

Mary Lee A. Jensvold and R. Allen Gardner, "Interactive Use of Sign Language by Cross-fostered Chimpanzees (Pan Troglodytes)," *Journal of Comparative Psychology*, vol. 114, no. 4, pp. 335-346. Copyright © 2000 by American Psychological Association. Reprinted with permission.

in Reno on the following day. Cross-fostering continued for Moja until winter 1979 when she left for the Fouts laboratory in Oklahoma. In 1980, Washoe and Moja moved to the Fouts laboratory in Ellensburg where the present study took place. Tatu was born at the Institute for Primate Studies, Oklahoma, on December 30, 1975, and arrived in Reno on January 2, 1976. Dar, a male, was born at Albany Medical College, Holloman Air Force Base, New Mexico, on August 2, 1976, and arrived in Reno on August 6, 1976. Cross-fostering continued for Tatu and Dar until May, 1981, when they left to join Washoe and Moja in Ellensburg.

The objective of the procedure was to sample conversational interactions between Washoe, Moja, Tatu, and Dar and a familiar human interlocutor under typical daily conditions in this laboratory (R. S. Fouts, Abshire, Bodamer, & Fouts, 1989). A video camera recorded the sign language responses of the chimpanzees to four distinct types of sign language probes presented by the human interlocutor.

Interlocutor

The first author of this article, Mary Lee A. Jensvold (MLJ), served as the interlocutor. At the time of data collection, she had 8 years of experience caring for and interacting with this group of chimpanzees and 10 years of experience communicating in ASL.

Procedure

When she arrived at the interaction area, MLJ either approached a chimpanzee or waited for a chimpanzee to approach her as she normally did in the course of a day. The interlocutor then attempted to engage the chimpanzee in a typical conversational interaction on a subject such as looking at a book, eating a meal, playing a game, or some other common activity (R. S. Fouts et al., 1989). The chimpanzees were free to interact with the interlocutor or to ignore her. As the participants settled down during this pretrial period, the camera operator positioned camera and started the tape record.

A second person operated a video camera to record each trial. At the beginning of a trial, the interlocutor stood or knelt to the right of the chimpanzee and positioned herself so that she and the chimpanzee were facing each other at an angle of about 90°. The operator positioned the camera so that the hands and faces of both interlocutor and chimpanzee appeared in the viewfinder of the camera. The camera operator used a list containing the sequence of conditions to prompt the interlocutor in English to present the correct condition on each trial.

Although ASL was virtually the only language that the human members of their foster families used in the Gardner laboratory, Moja, Tatu, and Dar often heard spoken English in the Fouts laboratory and understood spoken English to some extent (Bodamer, Fouts, & Fouts, 1987; Shaw, 1989). To avoid the possibility that the camera operator might prompt the chimpanzee as well as the interlocutor by announcing each upcoming condition, the operator used a numerical code rather than English words to specify conditions and changed the code three times during the course of the study. The prompting of the camera operator was the only English speech heard during these sessions, and this prompting always occurred before the beginning of any trial.

When ready, the camera operator signaled that the camera was ready and prompted the interlocutor by indicating which condition to present on that trial. The next time that the chimpanzee signed to the interlocutor, she replied with the first probe in the series specified by the condition for that trial. When the chimpanzee signed in response to the first probe, the interlocutor probed again, and so on until the interlocutor completed the series of three planned probes specified for that trial.

The interlocutor waited for the end of each chimpanzee turn before presenting the next probe. Signers normally end an utterance by dropping their hands or holding their hands without movement (Covington, 1973; Grosjean & Lane, 1977; Stokoe, 1972). The chimpanzees also use these behaviors at the end of an utterance. In the last third of the film, *Teaching Sign Language to the Chimpanzee, Washoe* (R. A. Gardner & Gardner, 1973, 1974), there are several examples of extended utterances. In one example, Washoe signs the following to Susan Nichols:

Washoe: YOU (HOLD) ME/ YOU ME WASHOE ME (HOLD) GO/

Between the phrases YOU ME/ AND YOU ME WASHOE ME GO/, Washoe holds her hands in the signing space, but they are relaxed. After the final go, Washoe drops her hands. These utterance boundary markers are different from the hesitation pauses after the first you and the last me. The hesitation pauses are typical of the halting signing and speech of young children (Stokoe, 1978, pp. 83–85). Utterance boundaries of this type are clear, and judgments yield independent interobserver agreement of 81% to 95% (R. A. Gardner & Gardner, 1998, pp. 194–195; Rimpau, Gardner, & Gardner, 1989, pp. 245–250).[1]

Transcriptions of signs in this article indicate three types of modulation. An "x" following a gloss indicates immediate reiteration of that sign. A question mark (?) following a gloss indicates a questioning inflection. A slash (/) indicates an utterance boundary (see B. T. Gardner & Gardner, 1998, p. 167). B. T. Gardner and Gardner (1998) and Rimpau et al. (1989) describe how cross-fosterlings inflected signs and phrases in the Gardner laboratory.

After each probe, the chimpanzee was free to answer with any signs or phrases in his or her vocabulary, to continue to face the interlocutor, to look away, or to leave the scene entirely. If the chimpanzee ended the interaction by leaving the scene, the response to that probe and all remaining probes of that trial were scored as no response. Because the interlocutor never signed to a chimpanzee unless the chimpanzee was facing her, all cases in which she failed to regain the attention of the chimpanzee within 5 s of the last probe or the last chimpanzee response had to be scored as if the chimpanzee had left the scene.

When the chimpanzee failed to respond to a probe in signs within 5 s but continued to face the interlocutor, the interlocutor presented the next probe in the series. Failures to regain attention appeared in two forms. First, when the chimpanzee signed and then looked away, the interlocutor attempted to regain the attention of the chimpanzee by waving her arms or by making a noise such as tongue-clicking noise or kissing noise. If the chimpanzee faced the interlocutor again within 5 s, the interlocutor presented the next probe in the series. If the chimpanzee failed to face the interlocutor for 5 s, the trial ended and the response to the next and to all the remaining probes of that trial were scored as no response. Second, when the chimpanzee looked away before responding to a probe in signs, the interlocutor also attempted to regain the attention of the chimpanzee by waving her arms or by making a noise such as tongue-clicking noise or kissing noise. If the chimpanzee faced the interlocutor again within 5 s without signing, this was scored as a failure to respond, and the interlocutor presented the next probe. If the chimpanzee failed to face the interlocutor for 5 s without responding in signs, the trial ended and the response to that probe and all remaining probes of that trial were scored as no response.

Other chimpanzees near the interaction area were free to observe or to participate in the interactions at any time as usual in daily interactions. If a 2nd chimpanzee interfered with the interaction, then the interlocutor aborted that trial and discarded it from the record. If the 2nd chimpanzee approached without interfering, the interlocutor ignored the 2nd chimpanzee until the end of the trial with the 1st chimpanzee. At the end of the trial with the 1st chimpanzee, the interlocutor was free to begin a new trial with the 2nd chimpanzee.

Conditions

There were four conditions in this experiment. The probes in the general condition consisted of a series of three general questions. The probes in the on-topic condition consisted of a series of three on-topic questions. The probes in the off-topic condition consisted of a series of three off-topic questions. Finally, the probes in the can't condition consisted of a series of three negative statements.

General trials. For each general trial, the interlocutor asked three general question probes that indicated failure to understand the chimpanzee. The interlocutor always presented the same three general probes in this order: (a) a questioning facial expression without any signs, (b) the sign WHAT?/, and (c) I NOT UNDERSTAND?/ or NOT UNDERSTAND?/, often signed with a negative head shake, which is common usage in ASL (Baker-Shenk, 1985, p. 299; Humphries, Padden, & O'Rourke, 1980). In her questioning facial expressions, the interlocutor pulled her eyebrows together, leaned forward, and held her eye gaze on the chimpanzee. Baker-Shenk describes this as the typical interrogative facial expression of ASL. The only condition in which the sign WHAT?/ appeared alone in a probe was the general condition. An example of a general trial is the following:

Trial #3/1:04:40
1:04:35 Washoe: ME OIMMEX/
1:04:40 Probe 1: questioning expression
1:04:41 Washoe: GIMME/
1:04:49 Probe 2: WHAT?/

1:04:51 Washoe: MEX GIMMEX/
1:04:54 Probe 3: NOT UNDERSTAND?/
1:04:56 Washoe: FOOD GIMME/

Here and throughout this article, each videotaped dialogue between a chimpanzee and a human interlocutor begins with the address of the observation in the videotaped record of this study. In this case, the address "Trial #3/1:04:40" indicates that this dialogue is a transcription from the third videotape and that the interlocutor's first probe began at 1 hr 4 min 40 s from the beginning of the videotape. Note that the address of a trial is the address of Probe 1. Some examples contain a whole trial, and it is easy to see that the address is the address of Probe 1. Other examples only contain part of a trial. These partial cases sometimes include Probe 1 and sometimes begin later, but the address on the tape remains the address of Probe 1.

On-topic trials. In each on-topic trial, the interlocutor asked three Wh-questions that incorporated a relevant sign from the chimpanzee utterance that started the trial and were also appropriate to the context of the interaction. The on-topic condition contained probes such as, WHO WANT FLOWER?/ if the chimpanzee utterance had included FLOWER; WHO EAT?/ if the chimpanzee utterance had included eat; and WHERE CHASE?/ if the chimpanzee utterance had included CHASE. These were typical questions that human familiars asked the chimpanzees in daily signed interactions. If the chimpanzee's reply to an on-topic probe contained an appropriate sentence constituent (Brown, 1968; B. T. Gardner & Gardner, 1975), then the interlocutor probed again with a different on-topic Wh-question. If the chimpanzee's utterance failed to include an appropriate sentence constituent, then the next probe repeated the previous probe. As is normal in signed interactions of human and nonhuman primates, a questioning facial expression accompanied signed questions.

In the cross-fostering laboratory in Reno, B. T. Gardner and Gardner (1975) and Van Cantfort, Gardner, and Gardner (1989) showed that Washoe, Moja, Tatu, and Dar responded to Wh-questions with appropriate sentence constituents (e.g., names or pronouns in response to WHO?/ questions, names of objects in response to WHAT THAT?/ questions, and so on). In their replies to Wh-questions, the cross-fosterlings developed in patterns that resembled the patterns of human children (Bloom

et al., 1976; Brown, 1968; Clancy, 1989; Ervin-Tripp, 1970; Parnell, Patterson, & Harding, 1984; Tyack & Ingram, 1977). An example of on-topic trial is the following:

Trial #2/0:07:51
0:07:47 Dar: GUMX GOODX GUMX THERE/
0:07:51 Probe 1: WHO WANT GUM?/
0:07:52 Dar: DARX HEIDI DAR THERE/
0:07:56 Probe 2: WHERE GUM?/
0:07:56 Dar: DARX GUM/
0:07:59 Probe 3: WHERE GUM?/
0:08:00 Dar: DARX THERE/

Off-topic trials. For each off-topic trial, the interlocutor asked a series of three Wh-questions that were unrelated to the chimpanzee's first utterance in the trial and inappropriate to the context, as in the following:

Trial #2/0:15:12
0:15:08 Washoe: SHOEX GIMMEX/
0:15:12 Probe: WHERE ROGER?/

Trial #3/0:56:08
0:56:04 Washoe: RED THERE/
0:56:08 Probe: WHO FUNNY?/

As in the on-topic condition, the interlocutor made the characteristic interrogative facial expression, and probes were typical questions that human familiars asked the chimpanzees in daily signed interactions. Indeed, off-topic probes were often identical to probes that the interlocutor presented in the on-topic condition. If the chimpanzee's reply to an off-topic probe contained a sentence constituent that was appropriate to the question, then the next probe contained a different off-topic Wh-question. If the chimpanzee's reply failed to include a sentence constituent that was appropriate to the question, then the next probe repeated the previous probe. An example of an off-topic trial is the following:

Trial #5/0:08:49
0:08 46 Washoe: FRUIT GIMMEX/
0:08:49 Probe 1: WHO FUNNY?/
0:08:51 Washoe: ROGER/
0:08:54 Probe 2: WHERE CAT?/

0:08:56 Washoe: ROGER GIMMEX/
0:09:03 Probe 3: WHERE CAT?/
0:09:05 Washoe: GIMMEX/

Can't trials. For each can't trial, the interlocutor replied with a series of three negative statements indicating that the interlocutor would not or could not comply with the chimpanzee's request or continue the interaction. Typical examples of can't probes were CAN'T/, SORRY CAN'T/, and I MUST GO/. An example of a can't trial is the following:

Trial #1/1:26:13
1:26:06 Tatu: YOUX SMELL YOUX SMELL YOU/
1:26:13 Probe 1: CAN'T/
1:26:14 Tatu: YOU SMELL/
1:26:17 Probe 2: CAN'T NOW/
1:26:18 Tatu: THAT (towards floor)/
1:26:20 Probe 3: CAN'T/ Tatu: No signed response

Design

Each chimpanzee received 20 trials under each of the four conditions, yielding a total of 80 trials for each chimpanzee. The maximum number of trials for 1 chimpanzee in 1 day was three trials. The sequence of conditions was random without replacement, except that the same condition never appeared on two consecutive trials in the same day.

Videotape Transcription

During all trials in this experiment, the interlocutor appeared on the right and the chimpanzee appeared on the left of the television screen. When transcribing the signs of the interlocutor, transcribers occluded the chimpanzee, and when transcribing the signs of the chimpanzee, transcribers occluded the interlocutor.

All of the signs that appeared in the transcription of this experiment appear in Table 3.2 of B. T. Gardner et al. (1989) and in R. S. Fouts (1993). With the exception of a few "home" signs, such as POTTY and PEEKABOO, all of these signs also appear in standard dictionaries of ASL as described and explained in B. T. Gardner et al. We created name signs by the normal procedures for creating name signs in the deaf community. The only pointing sign on

this list is the indexical, THAT/THERE, which is also a pointing sign in ASL (see also the sequential analysis of THAT and THERE in B. T. Gardner & Gardner. 1998, pp. 182–184). Two other signs, ME and YOU, are made by pointing to oneself or to an interlocutor in dictionaries of ASL as well as in the vocabularies of Washoe, Moja, Tatu, and Dar. In the published film (R. A. Gardner & Gardner, 1973), Washoe names her image in a mirror signing both ME and ME WASHOE in response to the question WHO THAT? When she points to herself the gloss is ME; when she makes the name sign WASHOE, the gloss is WASHOE. Only when she makes both signs in the same utterance is the gloss ME WASHOE. In any phrase glossed as THAT APPLE or THERE DOG, both the indexical and the object sign must appear.

There were approximately 75 trials on each 120-min videotape. It took approximately 10 weeks to fill a videotape with trials.

Interlocutor. After a videotape was filled, MLJ assigned glosses to each sign in each probe on the entire videotape using the place, configuration, and movement (PCM) system. The PCM system (R. S. Fouts, 1993; B. T. Gardner et al., 1989) is a description of how the sign is formed using the place where the sign is made, the configuration of the hand, and the movement of the hand.

Chimpanzee. Next, MLJ assigned glosses to each sign in each chimpanzee utterance on the entire videotape using the PCM system.

Reliability. A second observer independently scored a randomly selected sample of 20% of the videotapes for interlocutor and chimpanzee glosses using the same PCM system (R. S. Fouts, 1993; B. T. Gardner et al., 1989) as MLJ. These comparisons yielded agreements ranging from 87% to 95%.

Modulation. B. Gardner and Gardner (1998) describe modulation as follows:

> Dictionaries of ASL, like dictionaries of spoken languages, show signs in citation form—the form that is seen when an informant responds to the question "What is the sign for X?" In normal conversation, fluent signers inflect their signs in a variety of ways. The sign, GIVE, for example, may start near the signer's body and move out toward the addressee to indicate, "I give you". The same sign with the direction of

the movement reversed, indicates, "You give me". Inflection makes signs more versatile and more expressive; a single lexical item can become several different signs. Typical inflections have parallel effects on many different signs. At least 20 different types of inflection appear in the field records (of the Reno laboratory). Each type can be characterized by an aspect of sign form—e.g., Place or Movement—and by the way in which this aspect differs from citation form. (p. 167)

In this study, the cross-fosterlings modulated their signs as they did in most casual interchanges. As she glossed each utterance, MLJ also reported two prominent types of modulation: reiteration, in which the signer repeats a sign one or more times, and placement, in which the signer forms a sign on a place that differs from the citation form (Rimpau et al., 1989).

A chimpanzee could reiterate the sign APPLE by signing APPLE APPLE APPLE APPLE instead of a single APPLE. Both human children (Hoffmeister, Moores, & Ellenberger, 1975, p. 123; Keenan, 1977; Keenan & Klein, 1975; Nelson, 1980; Scollon, 1979) and cross-fostered chimpanzees (B. T. Gardner & Gardner. 1998, p. 168; R. A. Gardner, Gardner, & Drumm, 1989, p. 47; Rimpau et al., 1989, p. 249; Van Cantfort et al., 1989, pp. 210–211) commonly reiterate words or signs within an utterance. R. A. Gardner, Gardner, and Drumm found that Tatu and Dar, like the human children studied by Keenan and Keenan and Klein, were likely to reiterate signs in their response to positive announcements and unlikely to reiterate signs in responding to neutral or negative announcements. This indicates that reiteration within an utterance serves as a pragmatic device expressing emphasis or assent. We use reiteration here rather than repetition following R. A. Gardner, Gardner, and Drumm:

When used in this context, the term repetition leads to confusion since confusion is compounded by the practice of classifying some incorporations as repetitions and some as imitations, depending upon adult inferences about the intention of the child. Terminological confusion is still further compounded by the widespread disagreement as to the criteria that might distinguish repetition from imitation in human children's replies (Keenan, 1977, pp. 125–129). It is for this reason that we recommend the terms incorporation, for items also found in the preceding utterance of an interlocutor, and reiteration, for items mat recurred within a single utterance. (p. 47)

Both human signers (Wilbur, 1980) and cross-fostered chimpanzees vary the place of a sign to express person, place, and instrument (Rimpau et al., 1989). For example, in its citation form, the place for TICKLE is the back of the hand. In the Gardner laboratory, Rimpau et al. found that Dar also signed TICKLE on the addressee to indicate that the addressee should tickle him and on objects to indicate that the addressee should tickle Dar with the object (p. 257).

RESULTS

Sign language studies of cross-fostered chimpanzees simulate the natural conditions in which human children engage in interactive conversations. This must be distinguished from laboratory experiments that measure success and failure on arbitrary tests. Typically, such experiments present subjects with a series of forced-choice tests, sometimes with as many as four alternatives, but usually with only two alternatives. When the proportion of correct choices exceeds chance estimates in such studies, the result is interpreted as confirming a particular theoretical hypothesis about the cognition of a particular species.

By contrast, sign language studies of cross-fostered chimpanzees, like developmental studies of human children, typically use productive tests in which subjects are free to use any word or sign in their vocabulary and any number of words or signs in any given utterance. Moreover, as in studies of human subjects, utterances are relatively appropriate or inappropriate rather than precisely correct or incorrect. Many different utterances can be appropriate in any given conversational context, and different utterances are appropriate in different conversational contexts. Appropriateness is judged by patterns of responses rather than by high or low scores.

Before we could analyze appropriateness in an objective fashion, we first transcribed the utterances of the chimpanzees and the probes of the interlocutor separately and independently according to the procedures described in the Method section of this article. Next, we classified the utterances into a fixed number of categories to analyze the distribution of the categories in response to the four different types of probes.

Because the appropriate data of this experiment consist of patterns of frequency distributions, the appropriate statistic is chi-square. With the chi-square, we could evaluate the most important contrasts that normally appear in an analysis of variance (ANOVA). We could compare different patterns evoked by different probes within chimpanzees, and we could compare common patterns and individual differences among chimpanzees (Wickens, 1989). Finding both common patterns and individual differences is important for two reasons. First, cross-fostered chimpanzees are like human children in that they exhibit both commonalities and individual differences. Second, demonstrable individual differences show that the patterns originate with the individual chimpanzees rather than from artificial experimental constraints.

This section presents the scheme of classification followed by analyses of the distribution of the classified responses to the four types of probe. Later sections present the distributions and their analysis.

For convenience, this analysis designates each chimpanzee utterance as C_n, where the chimpanzee utterance that initiated each trial is C_0, and the sequence of replies to the interlocutor is C_1, C_2, and C_3. Similarly, this analysis designates each interlocutor probe as P_n, where the sequence of three probes is P_1, P_2, and P_3. The first analysis measures the reaction of the chimpanzees to each probe by comparing the signs in each chimpanzee utterance with the signs in the immediately preceding chimpanzee utterance, that is, $C_1:C_0$, $C_2:C_1$, and $C_3:C_2$. The second analysis measures the interaction of the chimpanzees with each probe of the interlocutor by comparing the signs in each reply with the signs in the immediately preceding probe, that is, $C_1:P_1$, $C_2:P_2$, and $C_3:P_3$.

Classification Into Categories

Using the gloss transcriptions, MLJ classified the reaction of each chimpanzee utterance, $C_1:C_0$, $C_2:C_1$, and $C_3:C_2$ and the interaction of each chimpanzee utterance, $C_1:P_1$, $C_2:P_2$, and $C_3:P_3$.

Reaction categories ($C_n:C_{n-1}$). 1. S (same): The signs in C_n were the same as the signs in C_{n-1} in both gloss and modulation. An example of S is the following:

> Trial #3/0:26:03
> 0:26:07 Moja: CLOTHESX/
> 0:26:09 Probe: NOT UNDERSTAND?/
> 0:26:11 Moja: CLOTHESX/

2. S–: The signs in C_n contained some but not all of the same signs in C_{n-1} without additional signs or changes in modulation. An example of S– is the following:

> Trial #3/1:39:45
> 1:39:42 Moja: YOU SHOEX/
> 1:39:45 Probe: SHOE CAN'T HAVE/
> 1:38:48 Moja: YOU/

3. S★: The signs in C_n were the same as the signs in C_{n-1} except that the modulation changed either in reiteration or in place. Reiteration changes consisted of a shift from a single iteration to one or more reiterations or from one or more reiterations to a single iteration. An example of change in reiteration is the following:

> Trial #1/0:47:53
> 0:47:49 Moja: FLOWER/
> 0:47:53 Probe: WHAT?/
> 0:47:54 Moja: FLOWERX/

Place changes consisted of a shift in place modulation. An example of place is the following:

> Trial #2/1:12:49
> 1:12:50 Moja: YOU (toward MLJ's chest)/
> 1:12:52 Probe: CAN'T/
> 1:12:52 Moja: YOU (toward MLJ's head)/

Although the configuration and movement were the same, Moja changed the referent by changing the place of the sign.

4. S+: All of the signs in C_{n-1} appeared in Cn together with new signs. An example of S+ is the following:

Trial #3/0:21:29
0:21:23 Washoe: GIMMEX/
0:21:29 Probe: QUESTIONING EXPRESSION
0:21:30 Washoe: FOOD GIMMEX/

5. S+/−: Some but not all of the signs in C_{n-1} appeared in Cn together with new signs. An example of S+/−is the following:

Trial #5/0:07:30
0:07:28 Washoe: HURRYX GIMMEX/
0:07:30 Probe: WHO STUPID?/
0:07:32 Washoe: PERSONX GIMME/

In cases of S+ and S+/-, the chimpanzees expanded on their previous utterances (Bloom et al., 1976; B. T. Gardner & Gardner, 1998, p. 168; Keenan, 1977).

6. Dc: All the signs in C_{n-1} were different from the signs in Cn. An example of Dc is the following:

Trial #5/0:08:24
0:08:33 Washoe: GRASSX GIMME/
0:08:34 Probe: WHO WANT GRASS?/
0:08:35 Washoe: PERSONX HURRYX/

7. NR (no response): The chimpanzee failed to respond within 5 s after the probe (Brinton, Fujiki, Loeb, & Winkler, 1986, p. 77). If the chimpanzee looked away or moved away before the interlocutor could present the next probe, the response was classified as NR.

Interaction categories $(C_n{:}P_n)$. 1. I (incorporation): All of the signs in C_n appeared in P_n (R. A. Gardner, Gardner, & Drumm, 1989, p. 47). An example of incorporation is the following:

Trial #1/0:15:56
0:16:08–11 Probe: WHOSE BERRY?/
0:16:14 Tatu: BERRYX/

2. I+ (expansion): All of the signs in C_n appeared in P_n together with new signs. In cases of I+, the chimpanzees expanded on the probes of the interlocutor (Bloom et al., 1976; Bohannon & Stanowicz, 1989; B. T. Gardner & Gardner, 1998, p. 168; Keenan, 1977). An example of I+ is the following:

Trial #3/0:49:58
0:49:58 Probe: WHO WANT FLOWER?/
0:49:59 Washoe: FLOWER ME/

3. Dp: All the signs in C_n were different from the signs in P_n. An example of Dp is the following:

Trial #1/0:38:09
0:38:09 Probe: CAN'T/
0:38:09 Moja: YOU BUG/

4. NR (no response): The chimpanzee failed to respond within 5 s after the probe (Brinton, Fujiki, Loeb, & Winkler, 1986, p. 77). If the chimpanzee looked away or moved away before the interlocutor could present the next probe, the response was classified as NR.

Reliability. A second observer independently scored a randomly selected sample of 20% of the videotapes for reiteration and place modulation, and the transcriptions for interaction and reaction categories. These comparisons yielded agreements ranging from 93% to 96%.

Reaction Results

Although MLJ and the second observer agreed on more than 96% of their assignments of reactions to the seven categories, we combined S★, S+, and S+/−into a single category, Sc, for statistical analyses.

The effect of each of the three successive probes in each of the 20 trials on the distribution of reactions to each probe condition yielded 16 chi-squares with five categories of reaction versus three probes. Of these 16 chi-squares, 12 probabilities were greater than .50, and the lowest probability was greater than .08. On the basis of this insignificant difference between successive probes within a trial, we treated each probe within a trial as independent. This yielded three times 20, or 60 independent probes for each probe condition in all further analyses of reaction to probe type.

A one-way chi-square for each distribution is significant with $p < .006$; there were two exceptions that were significant with $p < .05$. The distribution of reactions among categories was significantly different from chance equality for each chimpanzee and for each condition.

Condition versus condition. The effect of conditions on the pattern of reaction yielded four chi-squares, one for each chimpanzee. With four conditions and five categories of reaction, each test had 12 degrees of freedom. For Washoe, the chi-square for conditions was significant: $\chi^2(12, N = 240) = 55.90, p < .0001$. Pairwise comparisons showed significant differences ($p < .02$) between each pair of conditions except the general versus off-topic conditions ($p < .16$). For Par also, the chi-square between conditions was significant: $\chi^2(12, N = 240) = 55.85, p < .0001$. Pairwise comparisons showed significant differences ($p < .005$) between all of the pairs except the general versus on-topic conditions ($p < .30$) and the general versus off-topic conditions ($p < .16$), which only approached significance. The chi-squares for conditions were for Moja, $\chi^2(12, N = 240) = 13.98, p < .3$; and for Tatu, $\chi^2(12, N = 240) = 17.70. p < .125$.

General condition. The Dc and Sc categories were the most frequent reactions to the general probes. The chi-square for 4 chimpanzees by five categories of reaction was insignificant, $\chi^2(12, N = 240) = 8.22, p = .7679$, indicating that all 4 chimpanzees had a similar distribution of reactions to general probes. Anselmi, Tomasello, and Acunzo (1986); Brinton, Fujiki, Loeb, and Winkler (1986); Brinton, Fujiki, Winkler, and Loeb (1986); and Wilcox and Webster (1980) found that human children often incorporate and expand across turns when asked questions.

On-topic condition. Washoe's and Dar's distributions peaked in the Sc category. Tatu's and Moja's distributions peaked in the Dc and Sc categories. The chi-square for 4 chimpanzees by five categories of reaction was significant, $\chi^2(12, N = 240) = 31.35, p = .0017$, indicating significant individual differences.

Off-topic condition. The chi-square for 4 chimpanzees by five categories of reaction was insignificant, $\chi^2(12, N = 240) = 16.5, p = .169$, indicating that all 4 chimpanzees had a similar distribution of reactions to off-topic probes. The chimpanzees' reactions often fell into the Dc and NR categories and rarely fell into the S and S–categories.

Can't condition. The chi-square for 4 chimpanzees by five categories of reaction was significant, $\chi^2(12, N = 240) = 57.3, p < .0001$, indicating significant individual differences. Washoe and Dar rarely used S, S–, or Sc in this condition. Instead they used a different sign (Dc) or failed to respond (NR). Moja and Tatu had more Sc responses and more total responses than Dar and Washoe. In the can't condition, Moja and Tatu were more persistent than Washoe and Dar. In the following example, before having a meal, Tatu first had to enter another area:

Trial #1/0:56:18
0:56:14 Tatu: EATX?/
0:56:18 Probe: CAN'T/
0:56:20 Tatu: IN/

Another example of persistence occurred while Moja was outside; she was referring to flowers that were beyond her reach:

Trial #3/0:24:59
0:25:00 Moja: FLOWERX THERE FLOWER THERE/
0:25:09 Probe: FLOWER CAN'TX/
0:25:10 Moja: FLOWERX YOU/

Moja persisted in the topic she initiated in spite of the negative response of the interlocutor. In contrast, Washoe and Dar usually failed to respond to can't probes, and when they did respond, they mostly reacted with different (Dc) or modified (Sc) utterances.

In summary, in the general condition, all 4 chimpanzees reacted with a similar pattern; their reactions most often fell into the Sc and Dc categories. In the on-topic condition, Washoe and Dar had one pattern of reaction, and Moja and Tatu had a different pattern of reaction. Washoe's and Dar's reactions often fell into the Sc category, whereas Moja's and Tatu's often fell into both the Sc and Dc categories. In the off-topic condition, all 4 chimpanzees reacted similarly; their reactions most often fell into the Dc and NR categories. In the can't condition, as in the on-topic condition, Washoe and Dar had one pattern of reaction, whereas Moja and Tatu had a different pattern. Washoe and Dar often refused to respond, and when they did respond, their responses often fell into the Dc category. Moja and Tatu responded more often to the can't condition, and their responses fell into the Sc and Dc categories.

Interaction Results

As in the case of reaction, the effect of each of the three successive probes in each of the 20 trials on the distribution of interactions with each probe condition yielded 16 chi-squares with four categories of reaction versus three probes. Of these 16 chi-squares, nine probabilities were greater than .50, and the lowest probability was greater than .09. On the basis of this insignificant difference between successive probes within a trial, we treated each probe within a trial as independent. This yielded three times 20, or 60 independent probes for each probe condition in all further analyses of interaction with probe type.

As in the case of reaction, the effect of repeated probes on the interaction of each utterance with the previous probe yielded 16 chi-squares with four categories of interaction. This indicates that the distribution of interactions among categories was significantly different from chance equality for each chimpanzee and for each condition in all but two cases. The exceptions were the interactions with the on-topic probes for Tatu and Dar, which yielded chi-squares of 1.7, $p > .63$ for Tatu, and 0.7, $p > .87$ for Dar. As Consequently, the chi-squares for this condition omitted these columns of response and had fewer degrees of freedom.

Condition versus condition. The effect of conditions on the pattern of interaction yielded four chi-squares, one for each chimpanzee. With four conditions and four categories of interaction, each test had nine degrees of freedom. These tests yielded chi-squares of 115.55 for Washoe, 80.13 for Moja, 67.44 for Tatu, and 104.26 for Dar. All four were significant with $p < .0001$. Of the 24 possible pairwise chi-squares, 22 were significant with $p < .05$. The pairwise comparisons between can't and off-topic for both Moja and Tatu were insignificant with $p < .21$ and .75, respectively. In the pairwise comparisons, there were three degrees of freedom for two conditions and four categories of interaction. In pairwise comparisons between the can't and general conditions for Washoe and Dar, however, the I and I+ columns had frequencies of less than three, and these chi-squares were computed as 2×2 contingency tables with one degree of freedom. In the pairwise comparison between the general and off-topic conditions for Moja, the I column had a frequency of zero, and this chi-square was computed as a 2×3 contingency table with two degrees of freedom.

General condition. All 4 chimpanzees often responded with different (Dp) signs and never responded with incorporations (I) or expansions (I+). Since there were no responses in the I or I+ categories, the chi-squares for

this condition omitted these columns of response and had fewer degrees of interaction was insignificant, $\chi^2(3, N = 240) = 2.73, p = .4354$, indicating that all chimpanzees had a similar distribution of reactions to the general probes. Different signs were the most appropriate response in this condition because incorporations and expansions would be like answering a question with a question and would end the conversation.

On-topic condition. All 4 chimpanzees used incorporations (I) and expansions (I+) more in the on-topic condition than in the other conditions. The chi-square for 4 chimpanzees by four categories of interaction was significant, $\chi^2(9, N = 240) = 18.05, p = .0346$, indicating significant individual differences. In the following example, Washoe responded with the I category and incorporated the sign of the interlocutor into her utterance without adding any new signs:

Trial #3/0:49:58
0:49:58 Probe: WHO WANT FLOWER?/
0:49:59 Washoe: FLOWER/

In the following example, Tatu responded with the I+ category and incorporated the sign smell into an expanded utterance:

Trial #2/0:19:23
0:19:26 Probe: WHO SMELL?/
0:19:27 Tatu: TATU SMELL YOU/

Off-topic condition. Off-topic probes also depressed responses but less than can't probes. When the chimpanzees did respond to off-topic probes, most of their utterances contained different (Dp) or added new signs to incorporations (I+). The chi-square for 4 chimpanzees by four categories of interaction was insignificant, $\chi^2(9, N = 240) = 11.81, p = .2244$, indicating that all chimpanzees had a similar distribution of reactions to the off-topic probes.

In this condition, the probes were neither contingent on the chimpanzee's previous utterance nor contingent on the context of the interaction. The interactive effect of off-topic probes on the chimpanzees was to evoke different signs from them. For example, note the following interaction:

Trial #1/0:19:26
0:19:15 Tatu: CRACKERX/
0:19:26 Probe: WHERE DOG?/
0:19:31 Tatu: EATX TIMEX EATX/

Can't condition. Can't probes depressed responses; the NR category appeared in this condition more often than in other conditions. Because there were few responses in the I or I+ categories, the chi-squares for this condition omitted these columns of response and had fewer degrees of freedom. The chi-square for 4 chimpanzees by four categories of interaction was significant, $\chi^2(9, N = 240) = 44.86$, $p < .0001$, indicating significant individual differences. There were two patterns of response: one common to Washoe and Dar and another common to Moja and Tatu. Most of Washoe's and Dar's responses to can't probes fell into the NR category, whereas the remainder fell mostly into the Dp category. Most of Moja's and Tatu's responses to can't probes fell into the Dp category, but most of the rest of their responses to can't probes fell into the no response (NR) category. Incorporations (I) and expansions (I+) did appear in responses to can't probes, but they were rare. Instead, the chimpanzees usually signed something different from the probe (Dp) or failed to respond (NR).

In summary, Washoe's, Moja's, Tatu's, and Dar's responses depended on the probes of their conversational partner. When the interlocutor asked general probes, the chimpanzees responded with different signs. When the interlocutor asked on-topic probes, the chimpanzees responded with incorporations and expansions more than in the other conditions. When the interlocutor asked off-topic probes, the chimpanzees used fewer incorporations and expansions and often refused to respond. In the can't condition, the chimpanzees rarely used incorporations and expansions; instead, they used different signs or failed to respond.

DISCUSSION

Except, perhaps, for the word salad of schizophrenia and the speaking in tongues of religious ecstasy, verbal behavior depends on context. Conversations between two speakers or signers depend on the verbal give-and-take between conversational partners. Conversational contingency appears in utterances of children as young as 2 years old (Anselmi et al., 1986; Bloom et al., 1976; Gallagher, 1977;

Marcos & Bernicot, 1994; Wilcox & Webster, 1980). In this experiment, Washoe, Moja, Tatu, and Dar signed to a human familiar whose rejoinders varied according to a systematic experimental design.

The responses of the cross-fosterlings were contingent on the rejoinders of the human interlocutor. The chimpanzees reacted to probes appropriately by maintaining or altering the signs in their previous utterance. They *interacted* with probes appropriately by adjusting their signs in relation to the probes.

This experiment varied the conversational input to chimpanzees and showed that systematic variations in input from a familiar conversational partner resulted in systematic variations in the contents and the quality of the responses of 4 cross-fostered chimpanzees. The responses of the chimpanzees were conversational responses that were contingent on the conversational probes of the interlocutor. The responsive, conversational responses of the chimpanzees resembled the conversational responses of human children in similar studies and resembled older children more than very young children. The chimpanzees reacted to general probes by expanding like older hearing children and deaf children (Brinton, Fujiki, Loeb, & Winkler, 1986; Ciocci & Baran, 1998). Like older hearing children, the chimpanzees expanded across turns and were responsive to facial expressions without any signs (Anselmi et al., 1986; Brinton, Fujiki, Loeb, & Winkler, 1986; Pearl, Donahue, & Bryan, 1981). Incorporation and expansion are ways that adult humans and children maintain topic in a conversation (Brinton & Fujiki, 1984; Garvey, 1977; Halliday & Hasan, 1976, p. 278; Wilcox & Webster, 1980), and the chimpanzees incorporated and expanded as well. The effect of on-topic and off-topic probes on the children in Dunham and Dunham's (1995) study was similar to the effects found in the chimpanzees in the present study. In both cases, on-topic probes evoked more incorporations and expansions and fewer failures to respond than did off-topic probes. Marcos and Bernicot (1994) examined reactions of 18-to 30-month-old human children to an interlocutor who refused to cooperate with requests for objects. Like the chimpanzees in this experiment, the children sometimes persisted in their original request, and sometimes they switched to a different topic, but more often they failed to respond. Also, like human children, Washoe, Moja, Tatu, and Dar varied among themselves.

They showed patterns of individual differences in their conversational styles.

The cross-fosterlings developed into conversational partners because interlocutors had always treated them as conversational partners. Interactive sign language had always been an integral part of their daily lives, beginning at an infantile level and rising to gradually more sophisticated levels as they matured. The development of human children into conversational partners also depends on their treatment as conversational partners (Singleton, Morford, & Goldin-Meadow, 1993).

The chimpanzee-human dialogues in this experiment were embedded in the casual interactions of daily life in the Ellensburg laboratory. For experimental purposes, the interlocutor always waited for the chimpanzee to initiate a dialogue, but Washoe, Moja, Tatu, and Dar normally took the lead in chimpanzee-human dialogues in Reno (B. T. Gardner et al., 1989, p. 63) and Ellensburg. In this formal experiment, the interlocutor varied her input according to a systematic experimental design, but this experimental testing blended seamlessly into the social world of the cross-fosterlings. The resulting dialogues have the quality of human conversations because they took place in an appropriate environment. They are comparable to dialogues in similar research with human children because cross-fostered chimpanzees and human children carry on conversations under similar conditions.

In this experiment, the cross-fosterlings showed their conversational skills. When appropriate, they incorporated signs from the interlocutor's responses into their own turns in the conversation and expanded on the signs they incorporated. When appropriate, they also clarified and amplified their own previous responses with suitable expansions. They responded contingently to maintain the interaction and the topic of the interaction. They could keep the conversational ball in the air. They acquired these conversational skills in a conversational environment.

REFERENCES

ANSELMI, D., TOMASELLO, M., & ACUNZO, M. (1986). YOUNG CHILDREN'S RESPONSES TO NEUTRAL AND SPECIFIC CONTINGENT QUERIES. *JOURNAL OF CHILD LANGUAGE, 13*, 135–144.

BAKER-SHENK, C. (1985). THE FACIAL BEHAVIOR OF DEAF SIGNERS: EVIDENCE OF A COMPLEX LANGUAGE. *AMERICAN ANNALS OF THE DEAF, 130*, 297–304.

BLOOM, L., ROCISSANO, L., & HOOD, L. (1976). ADULT–CHILD DISCOURSE: DEVELOPMENTAL INTERACTION BETWEEN INFORMATION PROCESSING AND LINGUISTIC KNOWLEDGE. *COGNITIVE PSYCHOLOGY, 8*, 521–552.

BODAMER, M., FOUTS, R., & FOUTS, D. (1987, APRIL). *COMPREHENSION OF VOCAL ENGLISH AND ASL TRANSLATION BY A CHIMPANZEE.* PAPER PRESENTED AT THE MEETING OF THE WESTERN PSYCHOLOGICAL ASSOCIATION, LONG BEACH, CA.

BOHANNON, J. N., & STANOWICZ, L. (1989). BIDIRECTIONAL EFFECTS OF IMITATION AND REPETITION IN CONVERSATION: A SYNTHESIS WITHIN A COGNITIVE MODEL. IN G. E. SPEIDEL & K. E. NELSON (EDS.), *THE MANY FACES OF IMITATION IN LANGUAGE LEARNING* (PP. 121–150). NEW YORK: SPRINGER-VERLAG.

BRAINE, M. D. (1976). CHILDREN'S FIRST WORD COMBINATIONS. *MONOGRAPHS OF THE SOCIETY FOR RESEARCH IN CHILD DEVELOPMENT, 11(1*, SERIAL NO. 164).

BRINTON, B., & FUJIKI, M. (1984). DEVELOPMENT OF TOPIC MANIPULATION SKILLS IN DISCOURSE. *JOURNAL OF SPEECH AND HEARING RESEARCH, 27*, 350–358.

BRINTON, B., FUJIKI, M., LOEB, D. F., & WINKLER, E. (1986). DEVELOPMENT OF CONVERSATIONAL REPAIR STRATEGIES IN RESPONSE TO REQUESTS FOR CLARIFICATION. *JOURNAL OF SPEECH AND HEARING RESEARCH, 29*, 75–81.

BRINTON, B., FUJIKI, M., WINKLER, E., & LOEB, D. (1986). RESPONSES TO REQUESTS FOR CLARIFICATION IN LINGUISTICALLY NORMAL AND LANGUAGE-IMPAIRED CHILDREN. *JOURNAL OF SPEECH AND HEARING DISORDERS, 51*, 370–378.

BROWN, R. (1968). THE DEVELOPMENT OF WH QUESTIONS IN CHILD SPEECH. *JOURNAL OF VERBAL LEARNING AND VERBAL BEHAVIOR, 7*, 277–290.

CIOCCI, S. R., & BARAN, J. A. (1998). THE USE OF CONVERSATIONAL REPAIR STRATEGIES BY CHILDREN WHO ARE DEAF. *AMERICAN ANNALS OF THE DEAF, 143*, 235–245.

CLANCY, P. M. (1989). FORM AND FUNCTION IN THE ACQUISITION OF KOREAN WH-QUESTIONS. *JOURNAL OF CHILD LANGUAGE, 16*, 323–347.

COVINGTON, V. (1973). JUNCTURE IN AMERICAN SIGN LANGUAGE. *SIGN LANGUAGE STUDIES, 2*, 29–38.

DE VILLIERS, J. G., & DE VILLIERS, P. A. (1986). THE ACQUISITION OF ENGLISH. IN D. I. SLOBIN (ED.), *THE*

CROSSLINGUISTIC STUDY OF LANGUAGE ACQUISITION (VOL. 1, PP. 27–139). HILLSDALE, NJ: ERLBAUM.

DUNHAM, P. J., & DUNHAM, F. (1995). OPTIMAL SOCIAL STRUCTURES AND ADAPTIVE INFANT DEVELOPMENT. IN C. MOORE & P. J. DUNHAM (EDS.). JOINT ATTENTION: ITS ORIGINS AND ROLE IN DEVELOPMENT (PP. 159–188). HILLSDALE, NJ: ERLBAUM.

ERVIN-TRIPP. S. (1970). DISCOURSE AGREEMENT: HOW CHILDREN ANSWER QUESTIONS. IN J. HAYES (ED.), COGNITION AND THE DEVELOPMENT OF LANGUAGE (PP. 79–107). NEW YORK: WILEY.

FOUTS, D. H. (1994). THE USE OF REMOTE VIDEO RECORDINGS TO STUDY THE USE OF AMERICAN SIGN LANGUAGE BY CHIMPANZEES WHEN NO HUMANS ARE PRESENT. IN R. A. GARDNER, B. T. GARDNER. B. CHIARELLI, & F. X. PLOOIJ (EDS.), THE ETIOLOGICAL ROOTS OF CULTURE (PP. 271–284), DORDRECHT, THE NETHERLANDS: KLUWER ACADEMIC.

FOUTS, R. S. (1993). THE SHAPES OF THE SIGNS IN THE VOCABULARY OF THE CROSS-FOSTERED CHIMPANZEES AT CHCI. UNPUBLISHED MANUSCRIPT. CENTRAL WASHINGTON UNIVERSITY, ELLENSBURG.

FOUTS, R. S., ABSHTRE, M. L., BODAMER, M. D., & FOUTS, D. H. (1989), SIGNS OF ENRICHMENT: TOWARD THE PSYCHOLOGICAL WELL-BEING OF CHIMPANZEES. IN E. SEGAL (ED.), HOUSING, CARE AND PSYCHOLOGICAL WELLBEING OF CAPTIVE AND LABORATORY PRIMATES (PP. 376–388). PARK RIDGE, NJ: NOYES.

GALLAGHER, T. M. (1977). REVISION BEHAVIORS IN THE SPEECH OF NORMAL CHILDREN DEVELOPING LANGUAGE. JOURNAL OF SPEECH AND HEARING RESEARCH, 20, 293–302.

GARDNER, B. T., & GARDNER, R. A. (1975). EVIDENCE FOR SENTENCE CONSTITUENTS IN THE EARLY UTTERANCES OF CHILD AND CHIMPANZEE. JOURNAL OF EXPERIMENTAL PSYCHOLOGY. 104, 244–267.

GARDNER, B. T., & GARDNER. R. A. (1989), PRELINGUISTIC DEVELOPMENT OF CHILDREN AND CHIMPANZEES. JOURNAL OF HUMAN EVOLUTION, 4, 433–460.

GARDNER, B. T., & GARDNER, R. A. (1998). DEVELOPMENT OF PHRASES IN THE UTTERANCES OF CHILDREN AND CROSS-FOSTERED CHIMPANZEES. HUMAN EVOLUTION, 13, 161–188.

GARDNER, B, T., GARDNER, R. A., & NICHOLS, S. G. (1989). THE SHAPES AND USES OF SIGNS IN A CROSS-FOSTERING LABORATORY. IN R. A. GARDNER, B. T. GARDNER, & T. E. VAN CANTFORT (EDS.), TEACHING SIGN LANGUAGE TO CHIMPANZEES (PP. 55–180). ALBANY, NY: STATE UNIVERSITY OF NEW YORK PRESS.

GARDNER, R. A., & GARDNER, B, T. (1973). TEACHING SIGN LANGUAGE TO THE CHIMPANZEE, WASHOE (FILM). (AVAILABLE FROM PENN STATE MEDIA SERVICES, UNIVERSITY PARK, PA)

GARDNER, R. A., & GARDNER, B. T. (1974), TEACHING SIGN LANGUAGE TO THE CHIMPANZEE, WASHOE. BULLETIN D'AUDIO PHONOLOGIE, 4(5). 145–173.

GARDNER, R. A., & GARDNER, B. T. (1998). ETHNOLOGICAL ROOTS OF CULTURE. HUMAN EVOLUTION. 13. 189–207.

GARDNER, R. A., GARDNER, B. T., & DRUMM, P. (1989). VOICED AND SIGNED RESPONSES IN CROSS-FOSTERED CHIMPANZEES. IN R. A. GARDNER, B. T. GARDNER, & T. E. VAN CANTFORT (EDS.), TEACHING SIGN LANGUAGE TO CHIMPANZEES (PP. 29–54). ALBANY, NY: STATE UNIVERSITY OF NEW YORK PRESS.

GARDNER, R. A., GARDNER. B. T., & VAN CANTFORT. T. E. (EDS.). (1989). TEACHING SIGN LANGUAGE TO CHIMPANZEES. ALBANY, NY: STATE UNIVERSITY OF NEW YORK PRESS.

GARVEY, C. (1977). CONTINGENT QUERIES AND THEIR RELATIONS IN DISCOURSE. IN E. OCHS & B. SCHIEFFELIN (EDS.), DEVELOPMENTAL PRAGMATICS (PP. 363–372). NEW YORK: ACADEMIC PRESS.

GOODALL, J. (1967). MOTHER-OFFSPRING RELATIONSHIPS IN FREE-RANGING CHIMPANZEES. IN D. MORRIS (ED.), PRIMATE ETHOLOGY (PP. 287–346). LONDON: WEIDENFELD & NICOLSON.

GOODALL, J. (1986). THE CHIMPANZEES OF GOMBE. CAMBRIDGE, MA: HARVARD UNIVERSITY PRESS.

GROSJEAN, F., & LANE, H. (1977), PAUSES AND SYNTAX IN AMERICAN SIGN LANGUAGE. COGNITION, 5. 101–117.

HALLIDAY, M. A. K., & HASAN, R. (1976). COHESION IN ENGLISH. LONDON: LONGMAN.

HAYES, K. J., & NISSEN, C. H. (1971). HIGHER MENTAL FUNCTIONS OF A HOME-RAISED CHIMPANZEE. IN A. M. SCHRIER & F. STOLLNITZ (EDS.), BEHAVIOR OF NONHUMAN PRIMATES (VOL. 4, PP. 59–115). NEW YORK: ACADEMIC PRESS.

HUFFMEISTER, R. J., MOORES D F., & ELLENBERGER R. L. (1975). SOME PROCEDURAL GUIDELINES LOR THE STUDY OF THE ACQUISITION OF SIGN LANGUAGES. SIGN LANGUAGE STUDIES. 7. 121–137.

HUMPHRIES, T., PADDEN, C., & O'ROURKE, T. J. (1980). A BASIC COURSE IN AMERICAN SIGN LANGUAGE. SILVER SPRING, MD: T. J. PUBLISHERS.

KEENAN, E. O. (1977). MAKING IT REPETITION IN CHILDREN'S DISCOURSE. IN S. ERVIN-TRIPP & C. MITCHELL-KERNAN (EDS.), CHILD DISCOURSE (PP. 125–138). NEW YORK: ACADEMIC PRESS.

KEENAN, E. O., & KLEIN, E. (1975). COHERENCY IN CHILDREN'S DISCOURSE. *JOURNAL OF PSYCHOLINGUISTIC RESEARCH* 4, 365–380.

KRAUSE, M. A., & FOUTS, R. S. (1997) CHIMPANZEE (PAN TROGLODYTES) POINTING: HAND SHAPES, ACCURACY, AND THE ROLE OF EYE GAZE. *JOURNAL OF COMPARATIVE PSYCHOLOGY, 111,* 330–336.

LEONARD, L. B. (1976). *MEANING IN CHILD LANGUAGE.* NEW YORK: GRUNE & STRATTON.

MARCOS, H., & BERNICOT, J. (1994) ADDRESSEE TO OPERATION AND REQUEST REFORMULATION IN YOUNG CHILDREN. *JOURNAL OF CHILD LANGUAGE, 21,* 677–692.

NELSON, K. (1973). STRUCTURE AND STRATEGY IN LEARNING TO TALK. *MONOGRAPHS OF THE SOCIETY FOR RESEARCH IN CHILD DEVELOPMENT, 38* (1–2, SERIAL NO. 149).

NELSON, K. (1980 MARCH) *FIRST WORDS OF THE DUMP AND CHILD.* PAPER PRESENTED AT THE SOUTHEASTERN PSYCHOLOGICAL ASSOCIATION SYMPOSIUM ON APES AND LANGUAGE. WASHINGTON. DC.

PARNELL, M. M., PATTERSON. S. S., & HARDING. M. A. (1984). ANSWERS TO WH-QUESTIONS: A DEVELOPMENTAL STUDY. *JOURNAL OF SPEECH AND HEARING RESEARCH, 27,* 297–305.

PEARL, R., DONAHUE D. M., & BRYAN, T. (1981) CHILDREN'S RESPONSES TO NONEXPLICIT REQUESTS FOR CLARIFICATION *PERCEPTUAL AND MOTOR SKILLS, 55,* 919–925.

PLOOIJ, F. X. (1984). *THE BEHAVIORAL DEVELOPMENT OF FREE-LIVING CHIMPANZEE BABIES AND INFANTS.* NORWOOD, NJ: ABLEX.

REICH, P. A. (1986) LANGUAGE DEVELOPMENT. ENGLEWOOD CLIFFS, NJ: PRENTICE HALL.

RIMPAU, J. B., GARDNER, R. A., GARDNER, B. T. (1989). EXPRESSION OF PERSON, PLACE, AND INSTRUMENT IN ASL UTTERANCES OF CHILDREN AND CHIMPANZEES. IN R. A. GARDNER. B. T. GARDNER, & T. E. VAN CANFORT (EDS.), *TEACHING SIGN LANGUAGE TO CHIMPANZEES* (PP. 240–268). ALBANY, NY: STATE UNIVERSITY OF NEW YORK PRESS.

SCOLLON, R. (1979). A REAL EARLY STAGE: AN UNZIPPERED CONDENSATION OF A DISSERTATION ON CHILD LANGUAGE. IN E. OCHS & B. SCHIEFFELIN (EDS.), *DEVELOPMENTAL PRAGMATICS* (PP. 215–227). NEW YORK: ACADEMIC PRESS.

SHAW, H. L. (1989). *COMPREHENSION OF THE SPOKEN WORD AND ASL TRANSLATION BY CHIMPANZEES.* UNPUBLISHED MASTER'S THESIS, CENTRAL WASHINGTON UNIVERSITY, ELLENSBURG.

SINGLETON, J. L., MORFORD, J. P., & GOLDIN-MEADOW, S. (1993). ONCE IS NOT ENOUGH: STANDARDS OF WELL-FORMEDNESS IN MANUAL COMMUNICATION CREATED OVER THREE DIFFERENT TIMESPANS. *LANGUAGE, 69,* 683–715.

STOKOE, W. C. (1972). *SEMIOTICS AND HUMAN SIGN LANGUAGES.* THE HAGUE, THE NETHERLANDS: MOUTON.

STOKOE, W. C. (1978). SIGN LANGUAGE VERSUS SPOKEN LANGUAGE. *SIGN LANGUAGE STUDIES, 18,* 69–90.

TYACK, D., & INGRAM, D. (1977). CHILDREN'S PRODUCTION AND COMPREHENSION OF QUESTIONS. *JOURNAL OF CHILD LANGUAGE, 4,* 211–224.

VAN CANTFORT, T. E., GARDNER, B. T., & GARDNER, R. A. (1989). DEVELOPMENTAL TRENDS IN REPLIES TO WH-QUESTIONS BY CHILDREN AND CHIMPANZEES. IN R. A. GARDNER, B. T. GARDNER, & T. E. VAN CANTFORT (EDS.), *TEACHING SIGN LANGUAGE TO CHIMPANZEES* (PP. 198–239). ALBANY, NY: STATE UNIVERSITY OF NEW YORK PRESS.

WELLS, G. (1974). LEARNING TO CODE EXPERIENCE THROUGH LANGUAGE. *JOURNAL OF CHILD LANGUAGE, 1,* 243–269.

WICKENS, T. D. (1989). *MULTIWAY CONTINGENCY TABLES ANALYSIS FOR THE SOCIAL SCIENCES.* HILLSDALE, NJ: ERLBAUM.

WILBUR, R. (1980). THE LINGUISTIC DESCRIPTION OF AMERICAN SIGN LANGUAGE, IN H. LANE & F. GROSJEAN (EDS.), *RECENT PERSPECTIVES ON AMERICAN SIGN LANGUAGE* (PP. 7–31). HILLSDALE, NJ: ERLBAUM.

WILCOX, M. J., & WEBSTER, E. J. (1980). EARLY DISCOURSE BEHAVIOR: AN ANALYSIS OF CHILDREN'S RESPONSES TO LISTENER FEEDBACK. *CHILD DEVELOPMENT, 51,* 1120–1125.

NOTE

1. Here and throughout this report, transcriptions of signs appear in all capital letters. Signed utterances are transcribed into word-for-sign English because more literal translations would add words and word endings that lack signed equivalents either in the vocabularies of the chimpanzees or in ASL. This mode of transcription makes the utterances appear to be in a crude or pidgin dialect, but the reader should keep in mind the fact that equally literal word for word transcriptions between English and say, Russian or Japanese, appear equally crude.

CHAPTER 12
Imagery

Spatial Knowledge, Imagery and Visual Memory

DOUGLAS L. MEDIN, BRIAN H. ROSS, AND ARTHUR B. MARKMAN

One picture is worth more than ten thousand words.
                                    —*Chinese proverb*

INTRODUCTION

Suppose you are sitting in your living room at night and all of a sudden the power goes out. You could probably navigate around furniture or other obstacles that are in their usual places. The ability to mentally keep track of the environment and spatial relations among objects is necessary for any sort of navigation in the world. You could probably also describe what your furniture looks like. In both of these cases, you are accessing knowledge that you learned from visual experience in the world. Memory is clearly essential for many tasks, and much of what we learn is from our visual experience. The purpose of this chapter is to explore how spatial and visual knowledge is represented and the different ways in which we can use this knowledge.

In our discussion of perception in Chapter 3, we noted that organisms must develop representations of the three-dimensional world from two-dimensional projections on the retina. That is, organisms do not perceive the world directly but rather must figure out the connection between events associated with their perceptual system and events in the world. Informally, we could say that people construct an internal model of the world.

Our mental representations of our environment are typically so good that we are not even aware that they are representations—under "normal" conditions our representations mirror the world quite closely. But try a simple experiment (which you very likely performed in childhood) that creates "abnormal" conditions. Press on the corner of your eyeball with your eyes open. The scene in front of you seems to move (this is easiest to do with one eye closed), even though you "know" that it did not. But if you just move your eyes back and forth normally, the scene does not shift. The brain is able to take active movement into account in developing a representation but has no mechanism for dealing with the passive movement associated with pressure on the eyeball.

The point of this example is that we *represent* our environment, and when we successfully make our way around a darkened room, we are relying on previously stored representations of the layout of the room. A fundamental question concerns the form of mental representations of the environment and objects in it. A good deal of the research associated with this question has focused on imagery or mental images. Are images "pictures in the head" and, if so, what properties do they have? What is the relation between imagery and perception? Finally, are images fundamentally different from the mental representations of abstract propositions expressed through language?

Chapters 5 and 6 focused on basic ideas concerning memory for new simple events and for factual knowledge. However, most of the work in those chapters examined knowledge that was gained from reading or verbal communication. Our evolutionary history suggests that we had to learn how to successfully move about in the world long before we developed any language skills. Therefore, it seems likely that understanding how we develop and use knowledge about our environment provides basic clues into the nature of human intelligence. Although the information-processing tradition has found computers to be a useful metaphor for understanding intelligence, that metaphor may pay insufficient attention to the close link between organisms and their environment. Computers don't have to worry about the environment—the programmer puts information directly into the machine. Researchers in artificial intelligence are still in the very early stages of interfacing computers with an environment as they attempt to build robots capable of moving about in the world. As we shall see, useful representations are a crucial prerequisite for intelligent action.

In this chapter, we describe work on spatial and visual knowledge from the perspective of asking questions about mental representations. We first take a closer look at the notion of a mental representation and then provide a sampling of ongoing research on spatial knowledge, imagery, and visual memory.

REPRESENTATIONS

Relations Between Representations and Referents

We have already suggested that an internal model of the three-dimensional environment makes it easier to move and act appropriately than does a two-dimensional retinal pattern. A **representation** of the outside world is an internal model that is linked to external objects and events and that preserves information that is important for the organism. Representations are analogous to the data structures used by computers to store information that is used by programs. What form do these representations take? Some motion pictures about the nervous system, for example, seem to suggest that the internal representation is essentially a tiny replica of the item in the outside world being represented (the *external referent*). In many cases, the films also include a tiny person (a *homunculus*) whose function is to perceive the internal representation! Of course, the films do not indicate how the perceptual system of the tiny person works, though perhaps the homunculus also

has representations (in which case we really need to study the psychology of homunculi).

Roger Shepard (1981, p. 290) has argued that a representation need not be literally similar to its referent, any more than a lock must resemble a key. In his words,

> Just as the essential thing about a lock and its key is the unique functional relation between them whereby the lock is normally (i.e., from the outside) operated only by its corresponding key, the essential thing about a perceptual representation and its object is the unique functional relation between them whereby the percept is normally (except while dreaming or hallucinating) elicited only by its corresponding object.

To use another example, we often use a map to navigate between one part of the country and another. The fact that major highways are colored red while minor roads are black or gray tells us nothing about the color of the actual roads. Major highways with many lanes are drawn thicker on maps than two-lane highways. Representing more lanes with thicker lines is a natural convention, but we recognize that it is simply a convention. One could use the opposite coding scheme, and people could adjust accordingly. Whatever the coding scheme, certain crucial information such as spatial relationships and type of roads must be preserved. But the map is not literally a likeness of the country. The two keys to representation are that the information important to the organism is preserved and that the cognitive system have some mechanism for extracting the information in the representation and using it (Markman, 1999; Palmer, 1978).

Analog Representations

To say that representations of referents must preserve relevant information does little to restrict the form that representations must take. Researchers such as Roger Shepard and Stephen Kosslyn, have argued that mental representations of objects and spatial relationships are *analog* in character. An **analog representation** mimics the structure of the referent in a more or less direct manner. Immediately, this definition runs into difficulty because we have not said what we mean by structure or a direct manner. In the case of space, one can propose that two relevant structural properties are that space is continuous and that spatial relationships are salient (e.g., that the nose is above the mouth on a face).

But what do we mean by "more or less direct manner"? We mean that the representation has properties that bear the same relationships as the properties of the external referent. In the external referent for this map, city A is closer to city B than it is to city C. Because a two-dimensional map is being used for this representation, it is a natural property of distances that once points A, B, and C are placed on the map that point A is closer to point B than it is to point C. Because distances in a two-dimensional map must have the same relationships as the distances between cities, the map is an analog representation. Of course, this map has a lot of information that corresponds to the external referent in an analog fashion. The map is probably drawn to scale (e.g., 1 inch on the map may correspond to 100 miles). Also, the relative directions are preserved by the map. City F is directly north of city E, and on the map F is directly above E, and so on.

This same information could be represented as a series of languagelike propositions, as discussed in presenting the ACT model in Chapter 6. **Prepositional representations** are assertions that have a truth value (e.g., city F is north of city E)—they are abstract and not tied to any particular sensory modality. The representation form on the left encodes city locations relative to some reference point, in this case city F (any reference point would do). This representation makes some information easy to determine. For example, one can directly look up (retrieve) the fact that A is 30 miles south and 10 miles west of F. Other information is less easy to come by. For example, what are the relative positions of C and D? To answer this question, one would need to retrieve the facts that D is 10 miles south and 10 miles west of F and that C is 30 miles south and 10 miles east of F and then combine these facts with some rules (e.g., if D is X miles south of F and C is Y miles south of F, then C is Y minus X miles south of D) to come up with the answer.

The cost is that many propositions have to be encoded. For six cities, we require 30 propositions; for seven cities, 42 propositions; and for only 40 cities, 1,560 propositions. And even with all these propositions, we have not exhausted all the information about spatial relationships. For example, the route information does not tell us that the most direct route from A to C requires that we pass

through B. Again, we could develop a procedure for deriving this information.

The general point is that particular types of representations allow us to access some types of information easily and other types of information with greater difficulty. Analog representations are good for configurai (spatial relationship) information, and they allow for easy integration of new information. Adding a new city is simple and does not require that a large set of new propositions be encoded (as does a route representation).

Propositions *can* represent spatial relations, so there has been much debate on the need for analog representations (J. R. Anderson, 1978; Kosslyn & Pomerantz, 1977; Minsky, 1975; Palmer, 1978; Pylyshyn, 1981; Shepard, 1981; see Barsalou, 1994, for an overview). Our reading is that most researchers now agree that people have both analog and propositional representations. For example, the ACT model described in Chapter 6 that encodes much information as propositions also contains analog representations for capturing visuospatial information. The argument as to why general purpose representations, such as propositions, may be poor choices for biological organisms is best summarized by Shepard (1981, p. 288):

> Such a general purpose system will not be suited to the rapid prediction of and preparation for external developments in a three-dimensional, Euclidean world. (...) The more nearly the constraints prevailing in the world have been "hard-wired" into the system, the greater will be the effectiveness of the system in that particular world.

Summary

In this section, we have distinguished between analog representations (such as maps) and propositional representations. Each type of representation has advantages for some types of processing. Although there has been much debate over whether analog representations are needed to account for human abilities, most researchers accept the need for such representations. (See Barsalou, 1999, for a strong argument for the primacy of such representations.) We have belabored the subject of representation because it is crucial to understanding the basis of much of the ongoing research on spatial knowledge and imagery. The issue of representation sounds a bit esoteric, but it is central to the problem of how organisms are able to act intelligently in their environment. We turn now to related empirical work, beginning with spatial knowledge.

SPATIAL KNOWLEDGE

Maps and Navigation

Our mental representations include information about spatial relationships and about how to navigate in our environment. Let us begin with two simple examples from Thorndyke and Hayes-Roth (1982): "Point to the Statue of Liberty from where you are sitting. Now point to your favorite local restaurant from where you are sitting." These two cases are accomplished by most people in very different ways. For the first case, we remember that the Statue of Liberty is in New York City, where New York City is relative to our town, and what direction we are facing. For the local restaurant case, we may simply remember how we get there and point in that direction. These examples illustrate two of the main types of knowledge we have about space: **survey knowledge**, a bird's-eye view often learned from maps, and **route knowledge**, gained from navigating through the environment. Researchers are interested in characterizing these types of knowledge and in understanding when and how they might be learned. What sorts of experiences lead to survey as opposed to route knowledge? We can begin by noting that the different types of knowledge are useful for different spatial tasks.

Survey knowledge is very useful for making judgments involving global spatial relations, such as distance judgments between two points. Survey knowledge allows fast scanning and measuring. It can often be acquired quite easily. However, if knowledge is acquired from maps, some judgments, such as those involving orientation, may be difficult. For example, Thorndyke and Hayes-Roth (1982) tested people on their spatial knowledge of the floor of a large, irregularly-shaped office building. Simplifying the results, subjects just shown the floor plan were able to perform many tasks quite well, such as estimating distances, but had great difficulty with orientation tasks, such as pointing to one location while standing in another.

Route knowledge may require more time to learn but does allow people to perform well on tasks that are difficult if the knowledge is learned only from maps. Direct experience with the routes appears to lead to a more orientation-free representation, so that people can use their knowledge of the route very flexibly (see, e.g., Presson, DeLange, & Hazelrigg, 1989). If the environment is irregular (e.g., the streets are winding and cross at unusual angles), the knowledge acquired through navigation may distort the overall view (Byrne, 1982; B. Tversky, 1981). However, if the environment is regular (i.e., a city with a grid of streets, a building with a simple layout), experience in navigation is often sufficient for learning survey knowledge as well. An interesting proposal is that this greater navigational experience may lead to a different type of survey knowledge than that acquired from maps in which the full layout may be seen from a navigational perspective (Thorndyke & Hayes-Roth, 1982) or in a more integrated model-like way (Presson et al., 1989).

For both theoretical and practical reasons, how navigational experience affects the representation of space is of great interest and is under much current investigation. Recent theoretical work has examined learning differences that arise not just from different experiences but from different goals of the learner (e.g., Taylor, Naylor, & Chechile, 1999). They explored the differences in the spatial representations people formed depending on whether they had the goal of learning the overall layout of a building or routes between different locations. As active processors of information, the particular goals people have in learning spatial knowledge can have large effects on the representation. For example, people were much more accurate at estimating distances between points in a building when they started with the goal of developing a layout representation than when they started with the goal of learning routes. Applied research has also focused on the role of experience in learning spatial representations. As one example, an important area of research builds upon the great improvements in virtual-reality environments to address how people may navigate and explore such spaces (e.g., Ruddle, Payne, & Jones, 1999).

Spatial Representations From Descriptions

Although much of our spatial knowledge derives from our experiences in the environment, we also receive spatial information via descriptions. Spatial representations are often important in text comprehension. Readers do not simply remember descriptive sentences but rather spontaneously construct spatial mental models of scenes being described (e.g., B. Tversky, 1991). For example, suppose you are on a street corner and you walk north one block, turn left and walk a block, turn left again and walk one block, and then turn left one final time and walk a block. If you developed a spatial representation as you were reading, you should know that you are back at your original starting point.

Further research suggests that spatial representations are organized around landmarks (important locations) and are independent of the perspective from which a text is written (e.g., Ferguson & Hegarty, 1994; Taylor & Tversky, 1992). How was this generalization established? Let's take a closer look at one of the Taylor and Tversky experiments. In their first study, people were given either survey or route descriptions of four different settings.. The descriptions were fairly lengthy, and we'll give you only enough to illustrate the difference:

> *Survey Description of Resort Area.* The resort area is bordered by four major landmarks: the National Forest, Matilda Bay, Bay Rd., and the Forest Highway. The eastern border is made up of the National Forest. The National Forest has facilities for camping, hiking, and rock climbing. The southern border is made up of Matilda Bay. …

> *Route Description of Resort Area.* To reach the Pigeon Lake region, drive south along Bay Rd. until you reach, on your left, the point where Forest Highway dead-ends into Bay Rd. From this intersection you can see in the distance that Bay Rd. continues to Matilda Bay and its many recreational areas. You turn left and travel about 40 miles. …

It is important to remember that at no point did the people reading the descriptions see any map. For each of the descriptions, a series of tests was given to assess comprehension. The test questions were verbatim, paraphrased, or required an inference from the spatial information given in the text. For example, a verbatim, nonspatial test probe might be: "The National Forest has facilities for camping,

hiking, and rock climbing," a statement that appeared in both the survey and route descriptions. The key questions concerned location inferences. An example of a survey inference is: "Horseshoe Dr. runs along the southern shore of Pigeon Lake," which did not appear in either description. A corresponding route inference might be: "Driving from the boat launch up toward Madison, you see Pigeon Lake on your right." Of course, there were also statements that were false.

The first thing to note is that people were pretty accurate. Error rates never exceeded 20% in any condition. Second, people were fastest and most accurate for verbatim (and paraphrase) statements that did not involve any spatial information. Third, for verbatim items that did involve spatial information, each group was faster and more accurate in responding to the exact information they had read (types 5 and 6). This result is not very surprising, since the verbatim route statements were actually inferences for people who read the survey descriptions and vice versa. Fourth, and the most important result, is what happens when subjects have to respond to inference questions, that is questions that ask about information that was not directly provided in the text. Here, there was no interaction between how the group learned the information and how it was tested (route versus survey)—there were no reliable differences in reaction time or errors. If the route and survey groups had different forms of spatial knowledge, one would have expected that the survey group would be faster than the route group on survey inference questions and that the route group would be faster than the survey group on route inference questions (just as they were for the verbatim route and survey information). But there is no evidence for such an interaction. These and other studies support the idea that spatial representations of the reader can be independent of the perspective given in the text. Often people construct an integrated mental model of the space whether given route or survey knowledge. (See Bryant & Tversky, 1999, for some further ideas of what can influence the perspectives taken.)

Hierarchical Representations of Space

It is tempting to view our representations of spatial layouts like maps. However, there is evidence that our representations of space are influenced by nonspatial knowledge.

Answer the following question: Is Seattle north or south of Montreal? Most people believe Seattle is south of Montreal, although in fact it is north of it. In this case, most of us do not know the latitudes of both cities or their relative latitudes, but we do know that Canada is generally north of the United States, that Seattle is in the United States (i.e., that the United States is *superordinate* to Seattle), and that Montreal is in Canada (i.e., that Canada is *superordinate* to Montreal). We then make the reasonable inference that Montreal is north of Seattle. This type of plausible reasoning will usually lead to the right answer, but not always, especially given irregular boundary lines. (Try your friends on "Which is farther east: Reno or Los Angeles?" Again, Nevada is east of California, but L.A. is east of Reno.) These errors suggest that people use hierarchically organized information (Reno is in Nevada, Nevada is east of California) to answer questions about spatial relationships.

Stevens and Coupe (1978) provide further experimental evidence of the use of superordinates (Nevada is superordinate to Reno) in making spatial judgments by showing systematic distortions with this type of material. In addition, they found that even after learning from simple new maps such distortions occur. For example, in one study subjects learned a map, then had to judge, from memory, the relative positions of x and y. Performance was much better when superordinate information was congruent with the question. For example, subjects were more accurate at saying that x was west of y when the superordinate was east-west and more accurate at saying that x was south of y when the superordinate was north-south. Thus, it appears that the superordinate units are used to make spatial judgments.

A number of other studies show that such nonspatial influences do not depend on having some unambiguous hierarchical structure. For example, Hirtle and Jonides (1985) conducted some studies on residents of Ann Arbor, Michigan, involving various locations in Ann Arbor. They found that each of the residents had a hierarchical representation that was used for making spatial judgments, though the particular hierarchy differed from person to person. McNamara (1986), using a layout of objects in a simple rectangular space, found that people tend to organize such a layout hierarchically and that the organization is evidenced in spatial judgments about the layout. For example, if they thought of two buildings as being in the

downtown area, they might underestimate the distance between the two buildings and overestimate the distance between one of these buildings and a building not in the downtown area. (For further reading, a very interesting paper by B. Tversky, 1981, provides some demonstrations of heuristics that people employ in remembering maps that lead to other types of systematic distortions, such as misremembering that two streets cross at right angles when they do not.)

Thus, evidence suggests that a simple spatial map view of spatial knowledge is not correct. Rather, learners organize the spatial information to include nonspatial knowledge as well. Note that this effect occurs for knowledge learned both by survey and routes. Clearly people do have extensive knowledge about the spatial layout of an area, which may be stored in an analog fashion. However, additional knowledge about relations, such as hierarchies of locations, is also used in making spatial judgments. Thus, many researchers believe people may have a dual representation of spatial knowledge, including both distance (analog) and nondistance (often propositional) information (e.g., Curiel & Radvansky, 1998; McNamara. Halpin, & Hardy, 1992).

The Brain and Spatial Cognition

This dual representation idea also has some support from cognitive neuroscience. For example, Stephen Kosslyn (1987) suggests that the human brain has at least two distinct kinds of representations for spatial relations. One type is categorical in nature and determines relations such as "inside of" or "above." The second form of representation specifies distances in a continuous or analog form. In support of Kosslyn's theory, Hellige and Michimata (1989) report evidence that the left hemisphere of the brain is specialized for categorical information and the right for metric information concerning space (see Kosslyn, 1994, for other arguments and evidence on this point, and Ivry & Robertson, 1998, for an alternative interpretation of this evidence). In addition to the behavioral and neuropsychological evidence for this dual representation, computational models of spatial cognition that use the dual representations are able to simulate a variety of findings in this area (e.g., Baker, Chabris, & Kosslyn, 1999).

The importance of spatial cognition to our normal lives is underlined by studies of people who have suffered brain injury and have impaired spatial cognition. A particularly striking phenomenon is **spatial neglect**, which we described in Chapter 3. Patients appear behaviorally unaware of objects or events on the neglected side—as if part of their world effectively ceased to exist (see, e.g., Chedru, 1976). In some patients, unilateral neglect includes or may be confined to their own limbs and body surface (Bisiach, Perani, Vallar, & Berti 1986). For example, in putting on a shirt, such a patient may not put the arm on the neglected side through the shirt sleeve. Even more striking, when their attention is called to a neglected limb, such patients may deny that it is theirs and express puzzlement concerning how it got there. The study of such patients has provided some important clues to how space is normally represented (see Bisiach, 1996, for an overview).

Summary

Our spatial knowledge is crucial for our navigation in the world. In this section, we have examined how people represent and use spatial knowledge in a variety of tasks. We began by distinguishing between survey and route knowledge, and the different tasks for which each might be most useful. The work on spatial descriptions from texts suggests that people often represent the space being described in an internal model and use the model to both understand and reason about further information in the text. The knowledge gained from maps and surveys, however, is not just metric, distance information, but also knowledge of other relationships (such as hierarchies). Both types of knowledge are used in making spatial judgments, and the work in cognitive neuroscience supports such a distinction. In addition, spatial representations play a crucial role in a variety of more abstract tasks such as understanding of graphs and diagrams (e.g., Novick, Hurley, & Francis, 1999; Tversky, 1995).

IMAGERY

Try these three examples. First, imagine a capital letter *F*, and then imagine it rotated clockwise 90 degrees (quarterturn). Next, picture what your high school looked like, or picture the face of a good friend or the Statue of Liberty. Finally, imagine yourself walking from one friend's house to another's, or imagine giving someone directions for getting from the grocery store to your school. Almost all people experience visual images in performing these, and many other, tasks. In this section, we examine various results and ideas about how such images occur and are used. In addition, we examine the relation between imagery and perception.

As we just described in the last section, our knowledge about space is used in accomplishing many goals. However, this knowledge can be used even when we are not in the space or when we do not have a map available. Imagine being in a room with objects. Shut your eyes and take two steps forward. You are easily able to compute where you now are in relation to many of the objects. As in all memory tasks, you are augmenting the incomplete information available by bringing relevant knowledge to bear. Furthermore, what knowledge you bring to bear and how it is represented will have a large impact on the complexity of processing and your ability to accomplish your goals. Images are one form of representation that appears to preserve much about the spatial relations among objects, making it easy to know the relative positions of the objects even as we move.

By its nature, imagery is a totally internal event. As discussed in Chapter 1, psychology went through a long period in which internal events were not studied. No one doubted that people could have mental images, but there was much doubt about whether these images were psychologically relevant. For example, imagine a robin. Do robins have beaks? Do robins lay eggs? It may seem that you answer the first question by inspecting your image and that you answer the second by the use of some other knowledge in your memory. Nonetheless, it is possible that even the first question was answered by your use of other knowledge. You presumably know either that robins have beaks or that robins are birds and birds have beaks. If you are able to answer the question without the image, what is the evidence that you in fact used the image to answer it? Let's take a closer look at this question.

Evidence for Use of Visual Imagery

A great deal of evidence exists for the importance of images in performing various tasks. A full discussion of such evidence and its implications would be a book in itself (see, e.g., Kosslyn, 1983, 1994; Richardson, 1980). A brief discussion of several different types of evidence may provide you with an appreciation of the case for visual imagery.

Selective Interference

The earliest pieces of evidence in the modern work on imagery relied on the idea of *selective interference.* In these studies (see, e.g., Brooks, 1968), subjects would be asked to perform some task while imaging or not imaging. If imaging led to a decrease in task performance, the argument goes, there is evidence that imagery is using related processes. Most important, however, is the idea that the influences would be selective. That is, interference should be greater between tasks using the hypothesized same processes than on tasks thought to use different processes. The work by S. J. Segal and Fusella (1970) provides a clear example. Before each trial, the subject was asked either to form a visual image of a common object (e.g., a tree), to form an auditory image of a common sound (e.g., a typewriter sound), or to form no image. Then the subject was presented with a very weak visual signal (a small blue arrow), a very weak auditory signal (a chord from a harmonica), or no signal. The subject's task was to say whether there had been a visual signal, an auditory signal, or no signal. The results were quite clear. First, imaging led to worse detection performance than not imaging. Second, and most important, the two types of imagery selectively interfered with detection of their corresponding signals. That is, visual imaging led to worse performance on detecting visual signals, and auditory imaging led to worse performance on detecting auditory signals. Not only were subjects less likely to detect a signal in these cases but also, when no signal was presented, they were more likely to report a signal of the type they had been imaging (i.e., a false alarm). Thus, these results show that imagery can selectively interfere with the detection of signals.

Manipulation of Mental Images

Some of the best known evidence for the use of visual images are the studies of **mental rotation** conducted by Shepard and his associates (see, e.g., L. A. Cooper & Shepard, 1973, 1978; Shepard & Cooper, 1982; Shepard & Metzler, 1971). In these studies, subjects are presented with an object and asked whether another object is merely a rotation of the first. The forms in A and B can be rotated into correspondence, but the forms in C cannot be aligned through rotation. Therefore, the correct answer would be "yes" for A and B and "no" for C. Most people are able to do this task accurately, but the time to make the decision can be taken as an indication of the difficulty of the task. The larger the required rotation, the longer it took to answer the question. In fact, the increase in time was extremely systematic; the increase from 0 to 60 degrees was the same as between 60 and 120 degrees, which in turn was the same as between 120 and 180 degrees.

These results were interpreted as strong support for an analog representation underlying visual imagery. If the representation were analog, then one would expect these results, just as it would take longer to rotate the actual object for larger angles. However, if the underlying image were propositional, there is no reason why such a systematic relation between angle and reaction time would occur. The findings led to a number of challenges (see Anderson, 1978, and Kosslyn, 1994, for discussions). For example, Just and Carpenter (1976) suggested that the linear reaction time effects are artifacts of eye movements, not due to the use of images. In particular, they found that when patterns in a mental rotation task are presented simultaneously, participants move their eyes back and forth between the patterns and do so more with increasing angular disparity. How could one test their suggestion? One possibility is to present the two objects one after the other, instead of simultaneously. Even under these circumstances, reaction time continues to be a linear function of degree of rotation (e.g., L. A. Cooper, 1975, 1976; Cooper & Shepard, 1973). Thus, the mental rotation results do not appear to be due to eye movements.

Although there is still some controversy, many researchers believe that the mental rotation findings provide good evidence for the use of imagery. This linear function suggests that mental rotation takes place at a fixed rate, like the movement of the hands on a clock. These results are consistent with the idea of an analog internal representation—to see if the objects are the same, the image of one is rotated in a rigid way at a fixed rate, just as you might do with real objects.

Pictorial Properties of Mental Images

A variety of other results show that mental processing of images is very similar to what would happen with physical objects. Stephen Kosslyn has demonstrated that people's scanning of mental images shows effects similar to scanning physical scenes or maps (Kosslyn, 1973; Kosslyn, Ball, & Reiser, 1978). For example, in one study (Kosslyn et al., 1978) subjects learned a simple map in which seven locations were marked by objects. The test trials began with the naming of one of the objects. Subjects were asked to image the entire map and focus on the location of the named object. Another object was then named. If the object was not on the map, subjects pressed one button. If the object was one of those marking a location on the map, subjects scanned to it and pressed another button when they reached it. (The instructions were to image a black speck moving in the shortest straight line from the first object to the second.) The results showed that longer distances took longer to scan, just as it might be if one moved one's eyes across a scene or map from one location to the next.

Further parallels between images and the manipulation of physical objects come from another clever set of studies by Kosslyn (1975, 1976) examining the effect of image size. This research begins with the observation that the smaller an object, the harder it is to see any attribute of it. Is the same true of images? In these studies, subjects were told to image objects at different sizes. After they had an image, subjects were asked whether the object had some physical attribute (e.g., ears, a beak). Kosslyn found that the smaller the image, the longer it took to verify that this attribute was present (when it was) and to decide that it was not present (when it was not).

These and other studies providing support for imagery have received some sound methodological criticisms (Intons-Peterson, 1983; Intons-Peterson & White, 1981; Mitchell & Richman, 1980). For example, these critics have argued that subjects might well have figured out what effect the experiment was examining, which may have influenced the results. (It is standard practice in experiments to not let the subjects know the exact issues being examined so that such knowledge will not affect their performance.) Although some studies did suffer from methodological problems, on the whole, the main findings appear to survive (see Finke, 1985, for a balanced review, and Barsalou, Solomon, & Wu, 1999, for some recent results and discussion).

Representation of Images
How Equivalent Are Imagery and Perception?

The findings just reviewed make a good case that images are analog representations and that they can interfere with perception. However, it is not clear how these images correspond to the representation one has of visually perceived objects. Some researchers believe that there are major differences between our representations from imaging and from perception. Chambers and Reisberg (1985) argued that perceptual stimuli must be interpreted, but images are already interpretations. In support of their position, they produced strong evidence that visual stimuli and images behave differently. In one experiment, they presented participants with ambiguous stimuli. Chambers and Reisberg showed a figure for 5 seconds, asked people to form a clear mental image of it, and then removed it. This brief presentation did not give people time to reinterpret the figure. None of the 15 participants was able to come up with a second interpretation by using just their mental image of the figure. When, however, the participants were asked to draw the figure (from memory) and then reinterpret it, all 15 were able to see the second interpretation! (If you have not yet seen both possibilities, it may help to know that one interpretation is a rabbit—the left side is its ears—and the other a duck—the left side is its bill.)

Finke, Pinker, and Farah (1989), however, were able to demonstrate some ability of people to reinterpret visual images. For example, participants asked to imagine the letter *D* on its side and placed on top of the letter *J* spontaneously report "seeing" an umbrella. Therefore, mental images can, under some circumstances, be given new interpretations; reinterpretation does not constitute a qualitative difference between imagery and perception.

M. A. Peterson, Kihlstrom, Rose, and Glisky (1992) conducted a systematic series of studies on reinterpretations of mental images. They find a consistent pattern of reversals (even for the duck-rabbit figure) that suggests that mental images can indeed be ambiguous. Peterson et al. distinguish between reversals that involve feature reinterpretations (e.g., thinking of the curve in a *J* as the handle of an umbrella) and those that require a shift in reference frame (e.g. the front of the rabbit figure as the back of the duck figure). Although they observed both types of reversal, changes in reference frame were harder than feature reinterpretations. This difference may explain why Finke et al.

(1989) were more successful than Chambers and Reisberg in observing reversals (though the debate continues; see Rouw, Kosslyn, & Hamel, 1997, and Reisberg, 1998).

Are Visual Images Visual?

It seems clear from the studies we have reviewed that images encode analog spatial information. The results are consistent with either of two very different ideas about the nature of this representation. One possibility is that these visual images are really spatial representations. On this view, the knowledge we use to generate and use images is abstract and not tied to any specific modality. It is more like knowledge about the general layout of an object or scene, rather than just the type of information we could get by looking at the scene. The contrasting idea is that these visual images are truly visual representations; that is, the visual images are tied to the visual modality, and we have encoded knowledge about the literal appearance of the objects or scenes. On this view, a visual image requires some of the same representations and brain systems usually engaged when that same object is seen.

This distinction addresses the question of whether visual imaging involves the visual system. In addition to its centrality in research on visual imagery, the question has important implications for a number of theories of cognition (see Farah, 1988, for some examples). The results from research on this issue have been somewhat mixed. In favor of spatial representation, one impressive argument is that congenitally blind subjects show a number of imagery effects. For example, Kerr (1983) conducted research patterned after Kosslyn's scanning and size experiments just discussed. In one study, similar to the Kosslyn, Ball, and Reiser (1978) scanning study, she had blind and sighted subjects learn a simple layout of seven different geometric figures on a board. Following learning (the figures were raised so that blind subjects could learn by feeling them), subjects were read the name of an object and asked to imagine the board and "focus" on the named object. They were then given the name of another object and asked to imagine a raised dot going from the first to the second object. When the dot reached the second object, they were to push a button. The results revealed that both blind and sighted subjects showed the usual increase in response time with distance.

Because the blind subjects have been blind from birth, it is assumed that they do not have visually based representations (though they can encode spatial information). Thus, finding that the scanning effects are similar for blind and sighted subjects suggests that there is no reason to believe a visual representation is necessary for imagery.

Although these findings seem problematic for the idea of visual representations, other results provide strong support for such an idea. Martha Farah has marshaled several strong arguments in favor of visual representations (see also Finke, 1985). First, relying on neuropsychological studies of brain-damaged patients, she notes that when cortical lesions from brain damage lead to selective visual deficits, there are often parallel imagery deficits (Farah, 1988). For example, if cortical damage leads to central color blindness, the patients lose their ability to image in color. Second, she provides some interesting data combining reaction times and brain potential recordings that are consistent with visual representations (Farah, Peronnet, Gonon, & Giard, 1988). This study used a procedure similar to the selective interference paradigm but looked for facilitation of imaging and detecting the same content. In particular, subjects were asked to form an image of a capital H or a capital T or not to form an image. They were then given a very brief (20 milliseconds) presentation of one of these letters or nothing, followed by a masking stimulus. The subjects' task was to report whether they had seen a letter or not. These researchers found that people were better at detecting a letter if they had been imaging the same letter; that is, if they were imaging H, they were more likely to detect H than T. Thus, the facilitation was specific to the content of the image, suggesting that at some point the visual and imaginal representations joined (or fed into the same process). In addition, event-related potentials were recorded by putting electrodes on various scalp areas of the subjects: These recordings from the visual cortex showed systematic effects of this match between the image and the stimulus (i.e., whether they were the same, H-H or T-T, or were different, H-T or T-H) less than 200 milliseconds after the stimulus was presented. This finding provides strong support for the idea that the representation of the image involves the visual cortex and is truly visual.

Converging support for visual rather than abstract imagery comes from a study using the positron emission tomography (PET) recording procedure described in

Chapter 1. Roland and Friberg (1985) measured blood flow while people performed either an auditory (imagining a tune) or a visual (walking through one's neighborhood) imagery task. They found an increase in blood flow to the visual cortex during visual imagery but not during auditory imagery, and the reverse pattern for blood flow in the auditory cortex.

Summing up, we have evidence for both spatial and visual representation of images. Farah, Hammond, Levine, and Calvanio (1988) suggest that the evidence is mixed because the representation is neither entirely visual nor entirely spatial. Rather, both spatial and visual representations of images exist, but which is used depends on the task. In addition to accounting for the number of mixed findings and some other general arguments, they describe two further pieces of relevant evidence. First, they note that there may well be two anatomically distinct cortical systems for dealing with visual representations. One system is involved in representing the appearance of objects, and the other with the location of the objects in space (the what and where systems discussed in Chapter 3).

A second piece of evidence in favor of this compromise solution comes from neuropsychology. Of most relevance, Farah, Hammond, et al. (1988) present results from a patient who suffered brain damage from an automobile accident. Although the patient does well in intelligence and simple visual acuity tests, he suffers from severe deficits in visual recognition. Not only is he unable to recognize a number of common objects and animals but also he often has trouble recognizing his wife and children. In various imagery tasks, he sometimes performed at normal levels and sometimes at far below normal levels. Most interesting, normal performance was found on all seven of the spatial imagery tasks for which he was tested. These tasks, such as the scanning and mental rotation tasks, clearly require spatial information but have sometimes been shown not to require visual representations (such as from the work with congenitally blind subjects). In contrast, on the four visual imagery tasks that require specifically visual representations (that is, asking about a visual property such as the color of objects), the patient performed much below normal. In summary, the evidence appears to favor the compromise view in which both spatial and visual representations exist, as also suggested for working memory models (as mentioned in Chapter 5, Smith & Jonides, 1997). This is not, however, an uninteresting compromise, and it may serve as inspiration for integrative models of visuospatial representation.

Summary

This section has reviewed the evidence for mental imagery and examined the nature of the representation. Most researchers believe that people use mental imagery for a wide variety of tasks. The evidence from paradigms, such as mental rotation, selective interference, and scanning, suggests that the images are analog representations. There is still considerable debate about further details of these representations. We reviewed an ongoing controversy about whether the images could be reinterpreted, as one could reinterpret the representation of a visually perceived object. In addition, we examined evidence for whether these representations are visual or spatial. This latter controversy seems to have been settled by compromise—there is evidence for both visual and spatial representations.

VISUAL MEMORY

Many people feel that their memory for visually perceived objects, scenes, and faces is quite good. We can remember what our cars look like, the inside of a restaurant, and the faces of friends and acquaintances. We may not be able to remember the name of someone with whom we have been only briefly acquainted, but we are confident that we would at least know we had seen the person somewhere before. In this section, we examine some research on memory for visual stimuli.

Remembering Details

Our confidence in our visual memory abilities is generally not misplaced. Before examining the impressive memory we have, however, let us consider a potential problem illustrated by the following two examples. First, picture the front of a very familiar public building. How many windows does it have on the front? Many people are able to picture the building but, when trying to answer this question, find that their image of the building does not include any definite number of windows.

For the second example, draw the front of a penny. Most people find this hard to do but still might feel that they know what it looks like. Nickerson and Adams (1979) asked subjects (all American citizens.) to perform this task. When asked to draw a penny, they omitted far more than half the features or located them in the wrong place. When asked to choose a drawing of the real penny from 15 possibilities, fewer than half the subjects picked the correct one. G. V. Jones (1990) performed some related experiments with British coins (and British subjects) and found similar results. In fact, slightly fewer than half the subjects even knew the number of edges on a 50-pence coin (seven).

These results are quite surprising. Think of the number of times most people have seen a penny—how can they not remember what it looks like? As Nickerson and Adams note, however, the details that are not remembered are almost always irrelevant to one's use of a penny. People don't mistake a penny for a quarter or a button because they cannot remember where the date is on the penny. Memory is being used to accomplish goals; details that are without function with respect to these goals often may not be remembered as well as goal-relevant details. Again, we are active processors of information—we cannot encode all the information about every object, so we tend to encode information that is relevant to our goals.

Memory for Pictures

Suppose that you are allowed to look through 612 color pictures of common settings. When you finish, after about an hour (averaging about 6 seconds per picture), you are then shown two pictures at a time and asked to pick out which of the two were in the 612 pictures you had already seen. One picture is one of the 612, and the other picture is selected from the same general pool (i.e., it is of the same type). How well do you think you would be able to do this?

Shepard (1967) conducted this experiment and found that people were correct about 97% of the time. If they were not tested for 3 days, they were still 92% correct. In fact, 120 days later, they were still 58% correct.

Realize that we are not claiming that subjects are remembering all the details of these pictures. As we just saw from the study on pennies, memory for details is not always good. Many different types of knowledge could allow subjects to perform well in this picture memory experiment. For instance, they might remember one unusual detail from a picture. However, to do this well on recognition, they clearly are making use of some memory for the pictures seen. It is important to realize that these are distinctive real scenes, not abstract pictures of similar items, such as snowflakes. Even so, when we remember that they saw more than 600, one after the other, and for a very brief time each, such memory seems quite impressive.

The results of Standing (1973) show an even more impressive memory for pictures. He presented up to 10,000 pictures for 5 seconds each over several days. Two days later, he tested for memory by presenting two pictures and asking subjects to pick the old one. The correct picture was chosen 83% of the time. Clearly, much can be remembered from very short exposures to visual stimuli.

Performance on picture memory tasks changes in an interesting way as we age. Koustaal and Schacter (1997) tested college students and older adults (around 60–75 years old) for their memory of photographs. Older adults were more likely to say they recognize a new photograph that was similar to one of the photographs presented for study (for example, one boat when the earlier photograph was of a different boat). In one experiment, when they had been shown 18 objects from the same category (for example, 18 boats), both groups were good at positively recognizing the ones they had seen—81% accuracy for the younger subjects and 83% for the older subjects. Taken alone, this finding might suggest that both groups were equally good at recognizing pictures they had seen. However, when subjects were shown new examples from the same category (a new boat), the younger subjects incorrectly said they had seen these boats 35% of the time, but older adults claimed to have seen them 70% of the time. That now changes our interpretation of the earlier finding. Younger subjects seem to have enough information in their visual memories to adopt a pretty stringent criterion for saying the pictures were ones they had seen. That allowed them to distinguish reasonably accurately between pictures they had seen before and those they had not. In contrast, older adults appear to have less information about the pictures. Thus, they tend to say that many pictures of items from the same class they saw at study had been seen before. This strategy makes the older adults appear accurate when we look only at their performance on the studied pictures. However, when we take into account their performance on the new pictures from the same category, we can see that older people are setting a criterion for saying that a picture is old that also lets through a lot of pictures that were not shown at the study phase.

Younger adults can rely on their visual memory to help distinguish photographs, but the older adults appear to process the photographs less fully, relying on the gist of what was presented.

The Picture-Superiority Effect

A common intuition is that pictures are better remembered than words. This intuition is generally correct. As one example, in the Shepard (1967) study just mentioned. Another group of subjects looked at words rather than pictures. Even though there were fewer words than pictures (540 vs. 612), words were not recognized as well (88% vs. 97%). Many studies in the last 25 years have carefully controlled various factors and still found better memory for pictures, using a variety of picture types and testing conditions. This memory advantage for pictures over words is called the **picture-superiority effect**. This difference is found even if the memory test involves simply the names of the pictures rather than the pictures themselves.

Suppose you were giving directions to someone who stopped you on the street and had something block your view of the person for a second. When you can see the person again, it is a different person. Would you notice? Most people are sure they would. The correct answer is "maybe."

In the An Enigma box in Chapter 3, we discussed *change blindness,* the work showing that people are not good at detecting changes. Researchers have suggested that these failures show that the visual representations are quite impoverished and contain few details (see Irwin, 1996, and Simons & Levin, 1997, for reviews). However, all of this work has been done with photographs or videos. Would the failures occur if the change was made in the real world where the visual information is so rich and the person is actively engaged in processing the world? Although we have discussed a simpler case earlier, we felt the possibility that people might be insensitive to real world changes merited another examination.

Simons and Levin (1998) tested this possibility, essentially by conducting the study described in the first paragraph. More specifically, they had an experimenter (let's call him Experimenter 1) stop a pedestrian on the Cornell University campus and ask for directions to a nearby building (see panel a on page 318). After 10 to 15 seconds, two people came by carrying a door and rudely walked right between the pedestrian and Experimenter 1. As they did, Experimenter 1 quickly changed places with one of the door carriers, Experimenter 2 (see panel b), so that when the door was past the pedestrian, Experimenter 2 was now standing there asking for directions (see panel c). (The change took about one second.) The pedestrian and Experimenter 2 conversed for a few minutes more. The pedestrian was then told this was a Psychology experiment about the "things people pay attention to in the real world. Did you notice anything unusual at all when that door passed by a minute ago?" Only about half the people did. So even though the change was central to the scene, occurred instantaneously (was not gradual), and was in the middle of an ongoing event, people often did not notice. Why?

One clue as to the difficulty can be seen with a further breakdown of the data. The younger subjects (20–30), who were about the same age as the experimenters, tended to notice much more often than the older (35–65) subjects. Simons and Levin suggested that this difference could be due to a well-known effect in which people pay more attention to people of their own group, in order to discriminate them, whereas they pay less attention to people out of their group, because they are satisfied just to categorize them (for example, "college student"). This idea is similar to the finding by Nickerson and Adams that we described earlier in which people do not remember the visual details of pennies, because they focus primarily on information needed to categorize the coins. They tested this idea by redoing the experiment with both experimenters dressed as construction workers (though dressed with different-colored clothes). The prediction was that these workers were now a different group than the younger subjects, so the subjects might now simply note that the person asking for directions was in a different group (e.g., construction worker) and therefore would not show a high rate of change detection.... The prediction was confirmed—younger subjects detected the difference only 33% of the time.

So, people do not appear to store detailed visual representations of these events—rather they may categorize some of the people and objects and store those categorizations (such as construction worker). If the change involves a change in category, then it is likely to be detected. For example, people are often categorized by age, race, gender, and profession (if obvious), so that if the change was from male to female or construction worker to police officer, then it would be detected. A second important predictor of whether the change will be detected is whether there are any consequences for the goal of the perceiver. If the change has no effect on what the person is trying to do then it is much less likely to be detected (similar to the reason why the penny details are not noticed). If however, the change caused a change in what the person was trying to do, then it is likely to be detected. The main idea, however, is that we do not appear to store detailed visual representations of much of what we perceive.

Much of the research has been connected to the ideas of Allan Paivio, which are reviewed in Paivio (1971). He proposed a **dual-coding hypothesis** that predated many of the arguments about propositional and analog representations—items could be stored in either a verbal code (similar to the propositional view), an imaginal code (similar to the analog view), or both. This dual-coding hypothesis helped to make sense of many earlier results and gave explanations for later findings. For example, he suggested that pictures are better remembered because they are more likely to be stored in two independent codes than are words. As a further indication of distinct codes, Schooler and Engstler-Schooler (1990) found that verbally describing pictures of faces can *interfere* with memory for them. If there were only a single code, then verbal descriptions should only help memory. Instead, it appears that there are two codes and that the more attention paid to one type of code (e.g., verbal) the less time available for the other (imaginal) code. Although other hypotheses have been suggested for this effect as well, a common assumption is that picture superiority is caused by a richer, more distinctive coding for pictures than for words (e.g., Weldon & Coyote, 1996).

Memory for Faces

Despite the fact that most faces have the same set of features (nose, eyes, etc.), our memory for faces is excellent. In one fascinating study, Bahrick, Bahrick, and Wittlinger (1975) tested the memory of people for their high school classmates. For all 392 subjects, the experimenters obtained their high school yearbooks. These subjects ranged in age from 17 (newly graduated) to 74 (not so newly graduated). Of interest here is the face recognition test. Ten pictures were randomly chosen from each yearbook and photocopied. Each picture was put on a card with four other pictures taken from other yearbooks (but chosen so that fashion changes over the years and differences in picture type could not be used as a clue). Subjects were then asked to pick the face of their classmate from the set of five. The correct choice was made 90% of the time, and this accuracy persisted even in groups that had graduated about 35 years earlier. The group that had graduated nearly 48 years earlier still chose the correct face 71% of the time. Our memory for faces is quite incredible, making prosopagnosia, the lost ability to recognize faces that is associated with certain types of brain damage, even more dramatic (see the discussion in Chapter 3 on Face Recognition).

Although this excellent memory for faces may seem to contradict the findings that people do not remember details, the two findings are really quite consistent. In particular, the details not remembered are those that are not relevant for the goal (e.g., of recognizing a penny). For faces, however, the goal is not to recognize that it is a face (as opposed to, for example, a car), but rather to recognize whose face it is. Thus, the goal in face recognition forces one to consider at least some details to distinguish all the different faces one knows.

Summary

Much of our knowledge of the world derives from our visual experience, so our memory for visually experienced environments and objects is an important part of what we know. We have only been able to give a brief overview of the wide variety of results on visual memory. At the risk of oversimplification, we mention two conclusions that we think are particularly important for understanding visual memory. First, the great detail and complexity of visually perceived environments and objects leads to very rich representations. Think of comparing what you might encode from hearing the word *airplane* versus seeing an airplane. Second, although we have rich encodings of visual stimuli, we do not store everything. We lose much of the detail and actively encode the information that is most relevant to our goals.

SUMMARY

We have argued that spatial knowledge and mental representations of visual information are fundamental to cognition. We have further suggested that, despite the controversy between analog and propositional theories of representation, the evidence favors the idea that human cognition uses both analog and propositional representations. Our definition of an analog representation was that it mimics or parallels the structure of what is being represented in a more or less direct manner. Both the notion of structure and "more or less direct manner" allow for considerable leeway in how literally imagery mirrors perception. Any particular representation scheme allows a system to access some forms of knowledge easily and other forms of knowledge only with difficulty. Studies of visuospatial cognition suggest that what the human conceptual system accomplishes easily is consistent with representations having many analoglike properties.

We began the chapter by examining spatial representations, which are crucial for navigation in space. Different types of spatial knowledge were distinguished, survey versus route knowledge, and the types of tasks that each allowed easier performance on were discussed. Spatial knowledge is important not just in navigating, but also in understanding descriptions of space, such as might occur in text. Interestingly, both behavioral and neuroscience results indicate that many of our spatial judgments do not rely solely on analog representations of the space, but make use of other, more categorical knowledge as well.

Visual imagery is an experience people commonly report, but there has been much debate about whether it influences performance. The evidence for the use of imagery that has been amassed over the last 30 years is very compelling. The debate is now over how visual images are represented. One issue is whether visual images contain enough detailed information so that they can be reinterpreted. The results seem to indicate that they sometimes do, but there is still a question as to how the images differ from the representations of visually perceived objects. A second debate has centered on the question as to whether visual images are really visual or might be spatial. Here, the evidence suggests that both representations occur.

The final section examined a variety of results in visual memory. Rather than repeat them here, we repeat the conclusions. First, visual experience provides a richness of representation beyond what one might usually get from verbal communication. Second, despite this richness, many details are not represented, though in many cases that is not obvious to the person unless they are queried directly about it. Much of the information not represented is not central to our goals, so we may often not notice that it is missing.

On a broader level, the study of visuospatial cognition is important because other cognitive mechanisms may have evolved by modifying existing systems. Given that the spatial representation system is probably one of the oldest, one might expect that other cognitive systems show a "spatial bias." The representation of spatial relations does appear to be fairly ubiquitous in human thought. Many of the

metaphors that we use to describe how we think and feel rely on spatial relations (feeling up, feeling down, feeling close to another person, "higher"-level thinking, placing a plan on the back burner, and so on; see Lakoff & Johnson, 1980). We also find it natural to discuss the similarity of entities such as color in terms of being "close to" or "far from" each other.

Finally, in our discussions of comprehension and reasoning, we will make frequent reference to "mental models," which centrally employ spatial representations. To close our argument that spatial cognition may bias other forms of cognition, we offer another spatial metaphor: The apple may not fall far from the tree.

KEY TERMS

analog representation	representation
dual-coding hypothesis	route knowledge
mental rotation	spatial neglect
picture-superiority effect	survey knowledge
propositional representation	

RECOMMENDED READINGS

THERE IS A LARGE LITERATURE ON THE DEBATE CONCERNING ANALOG VERSUS PROPOSITIONAL REPRESENTATIONS. FOR FURTHER DISCUSSION, SEE ARTICLES BY KOSSLYN AND SHWARTZ (1977), PYLYSHYN (1979, 1981), ANDERSON (1978), SHEPARD (1981), AND BARSALOU (1994). KOSSLYN'S (1983, 1994) BOOKS OFFER EXTENSIVE OVERVIEWS OF THE STRUCTURE AND FUNCTION OF IMAGES. MARKMAN (1999) PROVIDES AN OVERVIEW OF APPROACHES TO MENTAL REPRESENTATION.

SPATIAL COGNITION IS A TOPIC THAT IS RECEIVING INCREASING ATTENTION. B. TVERSKY (1981) AND BYRNE (1982) REPORT INTERESTING LIMITATIONS IN MEMORY FOR SPATIAL INFORMATION. H. A. TAYLOR ET AL. (1999) PROVIDE A RECENT ANALYSIS OF WHAT MIGHT LEAD TO ROUTE VERSUS SURVEY KNOWLEDGE. THE PHENOMENON OF SPATIAL NEGLECT IS AS INTRIGUING AS IT IS DISTURBING. DESCRIPTIONS OF NEGLECT CAN BE FOUND IN CHEDRU (1976) AND BISIACH ET AL. (1986), AND A BRIEF REVIEW IS GIVEN IN BISIACH (1996).

PARALLELS BETWEEN IMAGERY AND PERCEPTION FROM A NEUROSCIENCE PERSPECTIVE CAN BE READ ABOUT IN FARAH (1988) AND KOSSLYN AND KOENIG (1992), PLUS IT IS DISCUSSED IN A GENERAL TREATMENT OF MEMORY BY SCHACTER (1996).

A DEBATE
Are Faces Special?

Faces are important visual stimuli—accurate recognition of faces allows us to differentiate our mate from our nonmates, our friends from our enemies. This importance has led to suggestions that we may have evolved with special mechanisms for face recognition. Do we recognize faces in the same way as we do other objects, or are they special? This issue has been the source of some debate.

There are several pieces of evidence that strongly support a faces-are-special position (see Farah, Wilson, Drain, & Tanaka, 1998, for an excellent overview and discussion). First, there is evidence that the brain regions involved in face recognition are not the same as those involved in object recognition. For example, some patients with brain injuries show impairment of face recognition, but not impairment of recognizing objects of equal visual difficulty. Second, there are recordings from single brain cells in monkeys that respond to faces and not to other visual stimuli. Third, infants' preferences for faces can be seen very soon after birth, suggesting some innate mechanism. For example, when they are 30 minutes old, infants will watch a moving face longer than they will other equivalent objects. Fourth, changes in the orientation of faces interferes with recognition much more than it does for other visual stimuli. Try taking a photograph of someone you know well and turning it upside down—it is much harder to recognize. This change in usual orientation affects the recognition of most kinds of objects, but much more so for faces. This greater impairment for faces when the objects are inverted is called the *inversion effect*.

Although most researchers agree on the effects, there is debate about how to interpret them. We concentrate here on one argument concerning how to interpret the first and last point above to give a flavor for the controversy. Gauthier and Tarr (1997) suggest that the different data for faces may not be due to their being innately special, but rather to their being treated differently than many other objects in two ways. First, we simply have much more experience with faces than with other objects, so part of the specialness may be due to this much greater experience. Second, when recognizing faces we need to know exactly which face it is, whereas when recognizing many other objects we only need to know the category, such as whether it is a cup, not exactly which cup it is. Because we often do not need to distinguish objects at much more specific levels, we may not develop the detailed processing and representations for them that we do for faces. As evidence for their claim, Gauthier and Tarr constructed some new nonface objects, which they called *greebles*. They found that when subjects learned to discriminate very similar greebles over a large number of trials, they showed an inversion effect on the greebles. Thus, they argue that some of the evidence for faces may be due to extended experience discriminating similar stimuli.

Our reading of this literature is that although the debate is not over, faces do appear to be special. Our best guess at this time is that some of this specialness may indeed be due to our great deal of experience at distinguishing individual faces, but some is also likely to be due to mechanisms that have evolved because of our special need to be able to expertly recognize faces.

Rouw et al. (1997) and Reisberg (1998) contain recent discussions of whether images are reinterpreted. Schooler, Ohlsson, and Brooks (1993) provide intriguing evidence that verbalization can interfere with solving insight problems.

The three boxes (mental rehearsal, change detection, and face recognition) each contains mention of a review article that can be used for gaining access to the relevant literature. There is also a journal, *Visual Cognition*, that often has articles addressing topics in this chapter.

Acute Effects of Stress-Reduction Interactive Guided Imagery on Salivary Cortisol in Overweight Latino Adolescents

MARC J. WEIGENSBERG, CHRISTIANNE JOY LANE, OSCAR WINNERS,
THOMAS WRIGHT, SELENA NGUYEN-RODRIGUEZ,
MICHAEL I. GORAN, AND DONNA SPRUIJT-METZ

INTRODUCTION

The prevalence of obesity is increasing dramatically in children, particularly among Latino youth.[1] This is associated with a high prevalence of obesity-related morbidities such as type 2 diabetes, pre-diabetes, and metabolic syndrome in this population.[2,3] Specifically, we have previously shown that ~32% of overweight Latino children and adolescents with a family history of type 2 diabetes have pre-diabetes,[4,5] while ~30% have metabolic syndrome (a cluster of cardiovascular disease risk factors related to insulin resistance).[6]

Chronic stress may increase obesity-related disease risk through hyperactivity of the hypothalamic-pituitary-adrenal axis (HPA).[7,8] Evidence supporting this hypothesis includes the findings that increased stress-related cortisol secretion is associated with features of the metabolic syndrome in both men,[9] and women,[10,11] and men with metabolic syndrome have increased urinary cortisol metabolite secretion.[12] We have recently reported that among overweight Latino teenagers, those with metabolic syndrome have higher concentrations of morning serum cortisol than those without metabolic syndrome.[13]

There is evidence that adolescents of today may have significantly elevated chronic life stress. Twenge has shown that today's adolescents suffer from increased anxiety relative to those of the past.[14] The transition into high school may be a time of particularly higher risk for emotional distress and disordered eating.[15] Inner-city Latino adolescents are frequently exposed to specific environmental factors that have been linked to chronic stress, including crime, disturbed family and social connections,[14] racial discrimination,[15] and lower socioeconomic status.[16] The increasing environmental stress upon today's urban, minority adolescents may, in the setting of increased availability of inexpensive, high caloric food and diminished physical activity, promote both general obesity (through lifestyle behaviors such as emotional overeating) and visceral obesity (through HPA axis activation and increased cortisol secretion). This suggests overweight Latino teens as an ideal population to study the relationships between chronic stress and obesity-related metabolic complications.

Insofar as chronic stress with increased cortisol levels may be associated with metabolic disease risk, stress-reduction interventions may hold promise for reducing such chronic disease risk in obese youth. Stress reduction mind-body modalities such as meditation, guided imagery, and hypnotherapy have been shown to reduce stress and affect other health outcomes favorably.[17–19] For example, Pawlow and Jones showed acute reductions of salivary cortisol in response to brief progressive muscle relaxation.[20] However, most reports of the benefits of mind-body stress reduction interventions have centered on adult, primarily white, populations. The use of such interventions in an inner-city teenage minority population naïve to mind-body modalities has not been previously investigated. Furthermore, the effectiveness of guided imagery in general, and Interactive Guided Imagery[SM] (IGI) in particular, on lowering salivary cortisol levels has not been previously assessed.

Therefore, the purpose of this study was to conduct a 4-week pilot intervention to determine whether stress-reduction IGI could serve as an acceptable and effective stress-reduction modality in overweight, Latino adolescents. Our primary hypotheses were that stress-reduction IGI would (1) be acceptable to this population, and (2) result in acute decreases in salivary cortisol levels.

MATERIALS AND METHODS

Participants were boys and girls aged 14–16 years, who were in the 9th grade or higher. All were of Latino heritage per parental self-report of all four biological grandparents being Latino, similar to entry criteria of other studies by our research group relating to chronic metabolic disease risk in overweight Latino adolescents.[4,21,22] Other entry criteria included overweight status, defined as body mass index (BMI) percentile greater than the 95th percentile for age and sex using CDC 2000 criteria.[23] Participants were excluded if they had participated in any weight loss program within the previous 6 months, had a serious chronic illness, had a medical condition or were taking medication that would affect body composition or insulin sensitivity/secretion, had participated regularly in any mind-body stress reduction or related practices in the past, had a clinically diagnosed psychiatric or eating disorder, or were cognitively or language/hearing impaired.

Weight and height were measured in triplicate using a beam medical scale and wall-mounted stadiometer, to the nearest 0.1 kg and 0.1 cm, respectively. BMI percentile was calculated using software EpiInfo, Version 3.3.2 (Centers for Disease Control and Prevention, Atlanta, GA). Tanner pubertal stage was assigned based on breast stage for girls and pubic hair stage for boys by a licensed pediatric care provider.[24,25] This study was approved by the Institutional Review Board of the University of Southern California (USC). Written parental consent and youth assent were obtained prior to initiation of any study procedures.

Interactive Guided Imagery intervention

Subjects were randomly assigned using a random number table to either IGI (Experimental Group) or nonintervention (Control Group). Participants in the experimental group received a weekly 45-minute IGI session for 4 consecutive weeks, conducted after school on weekdays, generally beginning between 4 and 5:30 PM. Imagery sessions were conducted individually for each participant by a single certified Interactive Guided Imagery[SM] practitioner (MW) (Academy for Guided Imagery, Malibu, CA).

The IGI method utilizes the subject's personalized images to promote health through several standardized, yet adaptable, techniques including, for the purposes of this study, relaxation/stress reduction. The IGI facilitator's goal is to enable the subject to engage his/her own images that are symbolic of his/her specific health or life issues, in order to develop health-directed insights, health-promoting behavior changes, or direct physiologic changes.[26] For this study, the four 45-minute IGI sessions utilized standard stress-reduction techniques of IGI, with each session building successively on the previous sessions. Session 1 included focused relaxation breathing and an explanation of the basic mind-body principles underlying guided imagery. In Session 2, head-to-toe progressive muscle relaxation was added, characterized by focused attention and subsequent relaxation of each successive muscle group, synchronized to the focused relaxation breathing. In Session 3, relaxed-place imagery was added, which involves a facilitated exploration of an image of a safe, comfortable place specific to the participant. For this exercise, following an induction of relaxed breathing and muscle relaxation, the subject invites an image of a place that represents just relaxation and freedom from stress. The facilitator then guides the subject through an exploration of this image through dialogue with the subject who is continually engaged with the image. Exploration of the image includes sensory recruitment (visual, auditory, olfactory, tactile, and kinesthetic), particularly focusing on linking elements of relaxation in the image to the physiologically relaxed state simultaneously being experienced by the subject. In the final weekly session, conditioned relaxation was added, a technique in which participants access their relaxed-placed image more quickly by linking the appearance of the image with a single deep "signal" breath, rather than with an extended breathing-muscle relaxation induction.[27]

Participants were instructed to practice at home the stress-reduction techniques they had learned in each IGI session for 10 minutes, twice a day, in between weekly sessions. Practice logs were given to participants to record the times of their practice as well as a qualitative description of their imagery practice experience.

SALIVARY CORTISOL

At the beginning and end of each 45-minute session, experimental subjects provided a salivary cortisol sample. Research staff phoned control group subjects to ensure collection of salivary cortisol samples at home at the same time of day as those collected from the IGI group. Control samples were successfully obtained on 92% of occasions. Salivary cortisol level reflects circulating free (unbound) plasma cortisol and is thus a good indicator of the physiologically active form of the hormone.[28] Saliva was obtained using the Salivette® system (Sarstedt, Newton, NC). A dry cotton swab was placed in the mouth for 2 minutes, yielding approximately 1 mL of passively absorbed saliva. Wet swabs were kept at room temperature, typically for 1–2 hours, until transferred to the laboratory the same evening of collection, then stored overnight at 4°C. Control subjects immediately placed collected samples in their home refrigerator until retrieved that same evening by study staff, and then processed as per the experimental group samples. The morning following collection, Salivettes were centrifuged at 2500 revolutions per minute for 10 minutes, and saliva supernatant was then frozen at–70°C until assayed. Cortisol in saliva is very stable *in vitro*,[29] and prior validation studies in our laboratory had shown salivary cortisol levels are stable through at least two freeze-thaw cycles (correlation of fresh versus twice-frozen/thawed samples = 0.97, $p < 0.001$). Samples were assayed for cortisol using an automated enzyme immunoassay (Tosoh AIA 600 II analyzer, Tosoh Bioscience, Inc., South San Francisco, CA) in the General Clinical Research Center Core Laboratory. The assay sensitivity was 0.02 μg/dL, interassay coefficient of variation (CV) was 7.8%, and intra-assay CV was 3.4%.

Other measures

Baseline outcome measures were obtained during an outpatient visit in the USC General Clinical Research Center (GCRC). Perceived Stress was assessed using a 17-item version of the Perceived Stress Scale.[30] Stressful life-events over the past year were measured using a 65-item checklist developed and validated in a mostly Latino population of middle school students.[31] Fasting serum cortisol was measured using an automated enzyme-linked immunoassay (Tosoh AIA 600 II analyzer). Acceptability of the guided imagery intervention to this study population was assessed by compliance with imagery session visits, home practice logbook records, and qualitative questioning of individual subjects at the beginning and completion of each session.

Data analysis

Comparison of age, Tanner stage, and BMI percentile in controls and IGI groups were performed to assure that randomization to experimental group was effective. Any notable differences ($p < 0.10$, due to small sample sizes) were controlled for in further group comparative analyses. Within-group acute changes in salivary cortisol were compared pre-and postsession using paired t tests for each of the individual sessions. Between-group comparisons of acute change in salivary cortisol were made using multiple linear regression analysis, controlling for any sample differences in demographics and pre-session salivary cortisol level. A p value <0.05 was taken to indicate statistical significance. Because making statistical inferences with small sample sizes is challenging, emphasis was also placed on quantifying clinical relevance with the use of effect sizes. Effect sizes were calculated as the ratio of the difference in the group means to the pooled standard deviation; they provide an indication of the strength of a difference between groups. The following standard guidelines suggested by Cohen (1988)[32] were used to determine the strength of effects: <0.4 = "small," 0.4–0.7 = "moderate," 0.7–1.0 = "high" (or "large"), and > 1.0 = "very high" (or "very large"). All statistical tests were performed using SPSS (Version 11.0; SPSS Inc., Chicago, IL).[33]

RESULTS
Comparison of group characteristics

According to Table 1, there were no significant differences in age, gender, BMI, or BMI percentile between the two randomized groups. The experimental group had slightly less advanced pubertal stage ($p < 0.1$). There were no significant differences between groups in baseline levels of stress as assessed by either perceived stress or life events scales. Morning serum cortisol did not differ between the groups.

Table 1. *Baseline Subject Characteristics*

	IGI (n = 6)	*Control* (n = 6)
Age (yrs)	16.1 ± 0.6	15.8 ± 1.1
Gender (F/M)	3/3	3/3
Tanner stage	4.0 ± 0.9	4.8 ± 0.4[a]
BMI (kg/m²)	36.2 ± 6.3	33.2 ± 6.4
BMI percentile	98.5 ± 1.1	97.1 ± 2.2
Perceived stress	14.7 ± 7.2	21.0 ± 5.5
Stressful life events	17.2 ± 10.1	16.2 ± 6.9
Fasting serum cortisol (μg/dL)	7.3 ± 2.4	6.8 ± 2.1

[a]Between-group comparisons by independent t test: $p = 0.07$. IGI, Interactive guided Imagery[SM]; BMI, body-mass index.

Acceptance of intervention

All subjects in the experimental group completed the 4-week intervention, with 100% compliance in attendance of all weekly imagery sessions (i.e., there were no missed sessions). In general, the imagery sessions were subjectively well received by all 6 subjects in the experimental group, as indicated by qualitative postintervention evaluations. Specific characteristic statements when asked their experience of the IGI stress-reduction sessions included: "cool"; "It was really relaxing"; "It felt good—took the tension away"; and, "I was able to concentrate on my math test better." Despite their enthusiasm for the IGI sessions, compliance with recommended twice-daily home imagery practice was poor. Review of home practice log entries showed that most participants reported practicing only a few times a week. Most practiced only once a day at most, typically for 5–10 minutes per practice session.

Within-group comparisons

Table 2 reports the salivary cortisol levels for the two groups before and after each weekly session, as well as the change in salivary cortisol across each individual session. Within the IGI group, there were significant declines in

salivary cortisol across sessions 2, 3, and 4. The magnitude of the change remained fairly consistent across the 4 weeks, with no significant differences in the magnitude of decline between any two individual sessions and no general trend in degree of change in salivary cortisol across the 4 weeks ($p = 0.33$). There were no significant changes in salivary cortisol within the Control group across any of the sessions.

Between-group comparisons

When comparing the degree of decline in acute salivary cortisol across individual sessions between the experimental and control group, there was a trend toward a treatment group effect seen in Session 4 ($p = 0.099$). When the changes in salivary cortisol for all four sessions were combined, there was a significant between-group effect for the change in salivary cortisol in IGI versus Controls, controlling for Tanner stage and repeated measures within individuals (Fig. 1, $p = 0.007$).

Effect sizes

Measures of effect size of change within each session were high to very high in the experimental group, ranging from−0.72 to−1.4 (Fig. 2). In all but one session (Session 2), there was a mean decrease of 1 standard deviation or more in salivary cortisol from pre-to post-IGI session. Effect sizes were small to moderate within the control group (ranging from−0.04 to−0.69). There was a moderate effect (−0.54) between groups in the pre-post change when all sessions were combined (adjusted for repeated measures).

Discussion

We sought in this pilot study to demonstrate the acceptability and effectiveness of acutely lowering salivary cortisol levels of stress-reduction IGI in an overweight Latino adolescent subject population. Our results demonstrate that the guided imagery was generally acceptable as well as enjoyed by this group of youth, and that it resulted in moderate to large acute decreases in salivary cortisol. High to very high effect sizes were seen in each of the four imagery sessions, and were reasonably consistent across sessions. To our knowledge, these results are the first to suggest that IGI can acutely lower salivary cortisol, and that IGI may be an acceptable and effective stress-reduction intervention in this adolescent population.

Prior work in adults suggests that chronic stress resulting in increased activity of the HPA axis may play an important role in obesity-related disease risk. The HPA axis is a prime mediator of the physiologic stress response, and chronic stress, via neuroendocrine mechanisms producing subtle hypercortisolism, may result in a "pseudo-Cushingoid" obesity phenotype characterized by visceral adiposity, insulin resistance, and metabolic syndrome.[8,34,35] Supporting this hypothesis, it has been shown that cynomolgus monkeys subjected to chronic social stress over 2 years demonstrated hypercortisolism.[36] Among obese identical twins, high visceral fat was associated with increased urine cortisol and increased psychosocial stress.[37] Obese women with abdominal obesity show higher urinary free cortisol excretion, along with other markers of hypercortisolism, compared to both controls and women with peripheral, nonabdominal obesity.[38,39] Finally, adults with abdominal obesity and/or metabolic syndrome have been shown to have increased stress-related salivary cortisol secretion,[9,10] increased excretion of urinary cortisol metabolites,[12] and other measures of HPA hyperactivity.[40]

There are far fewer pediatric data relating cortisol to obesity or obesity-related complications. Reinehr has shown that obese, insulin-resistant youth have higher morning cortisol levels, and cortisol decreases with weight-reduction and improved insulin sensitivity.[41] We have recently shown that overweight Latino youth with metabolic syndrome have higher morning serum cortisol levels than those without metabolic syndrome.[13] Our findings of a significant acute decrease in salivary cortisol with a biologically large effect size suggest that IGI may represent a promising mind-body therapy for reducing exposure to the relatively higher cortisol levels that may contribute to obesity-related disease risk in chronically stressed individuals. It remains an area for future investigation to determine whether the acute reductions in cortisol occasioned by IGI in this study would, over time, also be reflected in changes in other measures of cortisol that have been linked to obesity-related diseases, such as morning cortisol,[13] stress-related cortisol secretion,[9] or urinary cortisol levels.[12]

The fact that IGI was successful in acutely reducing salivary cortisol is consistent with similar effects by other related mind-body interventions. Progressive muscle relaxation, music therapy, and mindful meditation have all been shown to produce significant reductions in measures of cortisol and/or stress.[18-20] Thus, the effect of IGI may not be specific to this form of mind-body therapy, but may reflect the similarity of relaxation methodologies utilized by all of these mind-body therapies. Nonetheless, our findings of acceptability of the IGI intervention in this population are encouraging that IGI could be utilized effectively as a stress-reduction treatment in these youth.

Our first objective of this pilot study was to demonstrate the acceptability of the use of IGI in a group of inner-city youth at high risk for obesity-related complications. We could find nothing in the literature to guide us in this direction. In our extensive clinical experience, this population is generally not aware of, and does not utilize,

Table 2. *Change in Salivary Cortisol Following Stress-Reduction Guided Imagery*

| Session number | Guided Imagery group | | | Control group | | |
| | Salivary cortisol (µg/dL) | | | Salivary cortisol (µg/dL) | | |
	Pre-session	Post-session	Change	Pre-session	Post-session	Change
1	0.83 ± 0.17	0.64 ± 0.19	−0.19 ± 0.30	0.56 ± 0.29	0.52 ± 0.25	−0.04 ± 0.25
2	0.66 ± 0.26	0.52 ± 0.12	−0.14 ± 0.15**	0.68 ± 0.25	0.55 ± 0.20	−0.12 ± 0.17
3	0.66 ± 0.16	0.48 ± 0.10	−0.18 ± 0.09*	0.50 ± 0.16	0.40 ± 0.14	−0.10 ± 0.14
4	0.61 ± 0.19	0.44 ± 0.16	−0.18 ± 0.08*ᵃ	0.52 ± 0.31	0.50 ± 0.28	−0.01 ± 0.28ᵃ

Between-group comparisons: $^a p < 0.10$.

Data reported are unadjusted means ± standard deviation for salivary cortisol.

Within-group comparisons: $*p < 0.01$; $**p < 0.10$.

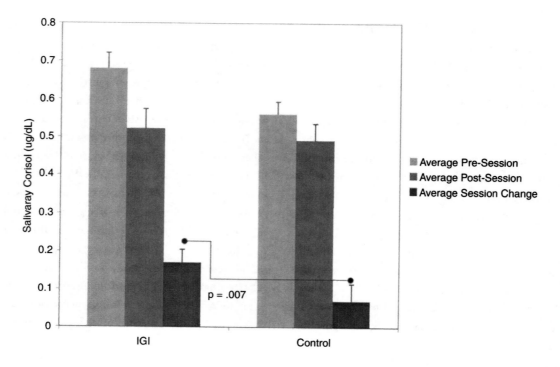

FIG. 1. *Average pre-and postsession salivary cortisol for control and Interactive Guided Imagery^SM (IGI) groups (four sessions combined). N = 24 observations for IGI group; N = 22 observations for the Control Group. Post-pre difference was–0.17 ± 0.17 for IGI and–0.07 ± 0.21 for controls. Group comparison of difference was p = 0.007, using repeated-measures analysis of covariance adjusting for Tanner stage.*

mind-body stress-reduction methodologies. However, our anecdotal use of these techniques with adolescents in our clinics suggested to us that these youth would be responsive to an IGI intervention. In addition, we have carried out preliminary focus-group qualitative studies, which strongly suggested that these youth would respond well to stress-reduction IGI (data not shown). On the whole, our results indicate that the 4-week intervention was quite well accepted and even enjoyed by the imagery study group. The 100% compliance for the guided imagery sessions, in which no participant missed any of the sessions, and very positive qualitative participant evaluations, support this conclusion. Besides enjoyment of the novel intervention, attendance compliance was aided by our use of friendly, bilingual research staff, and by providing transportation to the sessions when needed. Despite their enthusiasm for the IGI sessions, compliance with the home imagery practice portion of the intervention was poor. Thus, in the future, focusing more efforts on increasing compliance with stress-reduction imagery practice at home should be a major

goal of any intervention hoping to effect physiologically significant long-term reductions in cortisol levels.

The strengths of this novel study relate primarily to its demonstrated effects in providing a physiologically effective and well accepted stress-reduction intervention in a chronically understudied group that is at very high risk of obesity-related complications, and for whom there is a paucity of information regarding effective interventions. The results thus suggest that guided imagery may hold promise as an effective mode of therapeutic intervention in this population. The treatment was relaxing, enjoyable, and non-invasive, and the physiological response was immediate and reproducible week to week. Our current groups of subjects were equivalent in levels of baseline stress, so that these variables were unlikely to confound our results regarding salivary cortisol changes in response to guided imagery. Statistically and biologically (effect size) significant reductions in salivary cortisol were demonstrated in the imagery group despite the small numbers of subjects,

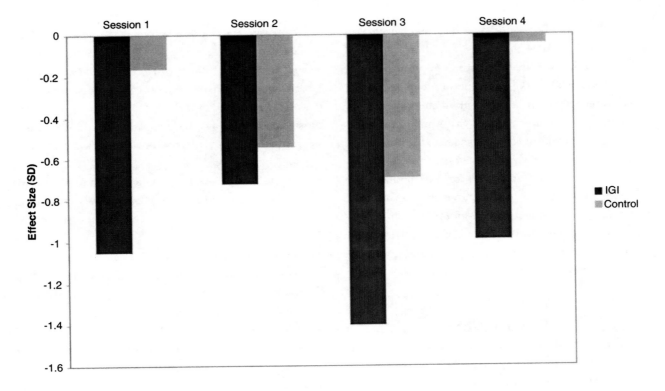

FIG. 2. *Effect size of salivary cortisol change across individual sessions. Bars represent effect sizes ((M_{post}–M_{pre})/SD_{pooled}) for change in salivary cortisol at each session. IGI, Interactive Guided Imagery,[SM]; SD, standard deviation.*

indicating it is a potentially powerful modality that can produce physiologically significant results.

The main limitation of this study is the small sample size. However, this project was designed as a pilot study with the aim of determining feasibility and effect sizes. Both of these goals were realized, in addition to the significant within-group effect on salivary cortisol in the imagery group. Although there were suggestions of between-group differences in salivary cortisol, the small sample size undoubtedly prevented statistically significant between-group differences to be demonstrated, other than the trend seen in Session 4 (IGI versus Control difference in salivary cortisol change < 0.1), and when all session cortisol values were combined (Fig. 1, $p = 0.001$). Another weakness was that salivary cortisol was obtained from the control group in their home environment, not entirely identical to that of the imagery study group. It is likely that the drop in salivary cortisol in control subjects across session time, more modest than in the imagery group, was related to the normal diurnal decline of cortisol in the late afternoon, plus a possible decrease in psychological stress

as the participants came home from school and relaxed in their home environment. The different environments between groups may also partly explain the appearance of lower presession cortisol values in the control group compared to the imagery group, in that it is conceivable the imagery group experienced higher presession cortisols due to transient anticipatory stress as they entered a new, unfamiliar experience: the imagery sessions. We also cannot exclude a "floor effect" in the control group, whereby starting from a relatively lower baseline cortisol, significant further reductions were unlikely. However, these factors seem unlikely to have accounted for our results, since much lower salivary cortisol levels at 10 PM (averaging 0.22 ± 0.05 µg/dL; data from ongoing studies in this population) argue against the "floor effect," the presession cortisols were not statistically different between the groups (reaching a trend only in Session 3, $p < 0.1$), and because our analyses of cortisol change were adjusted for baseline (i.e., presession) cortisol. It is also unlikely that the Tanner stage differences between the groups accounted for these differences, because for the group as a whole (n = 12) there was no relationship between Tanner stage and salivary cortisol measured at 6 PM (bivariate correlation $r = -0.08$, $p = 0.8$). Another way that the control group may not be directly comparable to the intervention group is that they did not receive the same individualized attention that the IGI group did. It could be argued that some of the effectiveness of IGI in this study could be due to the nonspecific effect of participants receiving special attention by friendly and caring research staff. To correct for these limitations, it will be important for future studies to include an adequate sample size to determine between-group effects of IGI, as well as ensure more equal treatment of control and study groups in terms of environmental exposure and study team contact variables.

CONCLUSIONS

In conclusion, IGI shows promise as a feasible and effective modality in acutely reducing salivary cortisol levels in overweight Latino adolescents. Future studies will need to extend these results to determine whether stress-reduction IGI can result in more long-term reductions in chronic stress and measures of HPA activity. The long-term effectiveness of IGI as an effective intervention for obesity-related disease risk in this population remains to be demonstrated.

ACKNOWLEDGMENTS

This study was supported by grant 5 M01 RR00043–46 from National Center for Research Resources/National Institutes for Health (NCRR/NIH). NCRR had no further role in study design, execution of study, analyses, or manuscript preparation. We would like to thank the GCRC nursing staff for their help. Finally, we would like to acknowledge and thank the study subjects and their families for their participation.

DISCLOSURE STATEMENT

The authors have no conflicts of interest to declare.

REFERENCES

HEDLEY AA, OGDEN CL, JOHNSON CL, ET AL. Prevalence of overweight and obesity among US children, adolescents, and adults, 1999–2002. *JAMA* 2004;291:2847.

WEISS R, DZIURA J, BURGERT TS, ET AL. Obesity and the metabolic syndrome in children and adolescents. *NEJM* 2004;350: 2362.

ROSENBLOOM AL, JOE JR, YOUNG RS, WINTER WE. Emerging epidemic of type 2 diabetes in youth. *Diabetes Care* 1999; 22:345–354.

WEIGENSBERG MJ, BALL GD, SHAIBI GQ, ET AL. Decreased beta-cell function in overweight Latino children with impaired fasting glucose. *Diabetes Care* 2005;28:2519–2524.

GORAN MI, BERGMAN RN, AVILA Q, ET AL. Impaired glucose tolerance and reduced beta-cell function in overweight Latino children with a positive family history for type 2 diabetes. 2004;89:207.

CRUZ ML, WEIGENSBERG MJ, HUANG TT, ET AL. The metabolic syndrome in overweight Hispanic youth and the role of insulin sensitivity. 2004;89:108.

BJORNTORP P, ROSMOND R. Hypothalamic origin of the metabolic syndrome X. *Ann NY Acad Sci* 1999;892:297–307.

CHROUSOS GP. The role of stress and the hypothalamic-pituitary-adrenal axis in the pathogenesis of the metabolic syndrome: Neuro-endocrine and target tissue-related causes. *Int J Obes Relat Metab Disord* 2000;24(suppl 2):S50.

ROSMOND R, DALLMAN MF, BJORNTORP P. Stress-related cortisol secretion in men: Relationships with abdominal obesity and endocrine, metabolic and hemodynamic abnormalities. *J Clin Endocrinol Metab* 1998;83:1853–1859.

EPEL ES, MCEWEN B, SEEMAN T, ET AL. Stress and body shape: Stress-induced cortisol secretion is consistently greater among women with central fat. *Psychosom Med* 2000;62:623.

PASQUALI R, VICENNATI V. Activity of the hypothalamic-pituitary-adrenal axis in different obesity phenotypes. *Int J Obes Relat Metab Disord* 2000;24 (suppl 2):S47.

BRUNNER EJ, HEMINGWAY H, WALKER BR, ET AL. Adrenocortical, autonomic, and inflammatory causes of the metabolic syndrome: Nested case-control study (see comment). *Circulation* 2002;106:2659–2665.

WEIGENSBERG M. Relationship between metabolic syndrome and morning serum cortisol in overweight Latino youth. *J Clin Endocrinol Metab* 2008;93:1372–1378.

Twenge JM. The age of anxiety? Birth cohort change in anxiety and neuroticism, 1952–1993. *J Pers Soc Psychol* 2000;79: 1007.

Stein KF, Hedger KM. Body weight and shape self-cognitions, emotional distress, and disordered eating in middle adolescent girls. *Arch Psychiatr Nurs* 1997;11:264.

Williams DR. Race, socioeconomic status, and health: The added effects of racism and discrimination. *Ann N Y Acad Sci* 1999;896:173.

Gruzelier JH. A review of the impact of hypnosis, relaxation, guided imagery and individual differences on aspects of immunity and health. *Stress* 2002;5:147.

Schneider N, Schedlowski M, Schurmeyer TH, Becker H. Stress reduction through music in patients undergoing cerebral angiography. *Neuroradiology* 2001;43:472.

Speca M, Carlson LE, Goodey E, Angen M. A randomized, waitlist controlled clinical trial: The effect of a mindfulness meditation-based stress reduction program on mood and symptoms of stress in cancer outpatients. *Psychosom Med* 2000;62:613.

Pawlow LA, Jones GE. The impact of abbreviated progressive muscle relaxation on salivary cortisol. *Biol Psychol* 2002;60:1.

Cruz ML, Weigensberg MJ, Huang TT, et al. The metabolic syndrome in overweight Hispanic youth and the role of insulin sensitivity. *J Clin Endocrinol Metab* 2004;89:108–113.

Goran MI, Bergman RN, Avila Q, et al. Impaired glucose tolerance and reduced beta-cell function in overweight Latino children with a positive family history for type 2 diabetes. *J Clin Endocrinol Metab* 2004;89:207–212.

Charts CfDCaPCg. Centers for Disease Control and Prevention: CDC Growth Charts. Online document at: www. cdc.gov/nchs/about/major/nhanes/growthcharts.

Marshall WA, Tanner JM. Variations in the pattern of pubertal changes in boys. *Arch Dis Child* 1970;45:13–23.

Marshall WA, Tanner JM. Variations in pattern of pubertal changes in girls. *Arch Dis Child* 1969;44:291–303.

Rossman ML. *Guided Imagery for Self-Healing.* Tiburon, CA: HJ Kramer, New World Library, 2000.

Bresler D. Conditioned Relaxation. In: *Free Yourself from Pain Series, DB101.* New York: Alpha Books, 2003.

Laudat MH, Cerdas S, Fournier C, et al. Salivary cortisol measurement: A practical approach to assess pituitary-adrenal function. *J Clin Endocrinol Metab* 1988;66:343–348.

Clow A, Thorn L, Evans P, Hucklebridge F. The awakening cortisol response: Methodological issues and significance. *Stress* 2004;7:29.

Cohen S, Kamarck T, Mermelstein R. A global measure of perceived stress. *J Health Soc Behav* 1983;24:385.

Booker CL, Gallagher P, Unger JB, Ritt-Olson A, Johnson CA. Stressful life events, smoking behavior, and intentions to smoke among a multiethnic sample of sixth grader. *Ethn Health* 2004;9:369–397.

Cohen J. *Statistical Power Analysis for the Behavioral Sciences. 2nd ed.* Hillsdale, NJ: Lawrence Erlbaum Associates, 1988.

SPSS *Mac OS X Version. 11.0 ed.* Chicago: SPSS Inc., 2005.

Bjorntorp P, Rosmond R. Neuroendocrine abnormalities in visceral obesity. *Int J Obes Rel Metab Disord* 2000;24(suppl 2):S80.

Charmandari E, Kino T, Souvatzoglou E, Chrousos GP. Pediatric stress: Hormonal mediators and human development. *Horm Res* 2003;59:161.

Shively CA, Laber-Laird K, Anton RF. Behavior and physiology of social stress and depression in female cynomolgus monkeys. *Biol Psychiatry* 1997;41:871.

Marniemi J, Kronholm E, Aunola S, et al. Visceral fat and psychosocial stress in identical twins discordant for obesity. *J Intern Med* 2002;251:35.

Marin P, Darin N, Amemiya T, et al. Cortisol secretion in relation to body fat distribution in obese premenopausal women. *Metabolism* 1992;41:882.

Pasquali R, Cantobelli S, Casimirri F, et al. The hypothalamic-pituitary-adrenal axis in obese women with different patterns of body fat distribution. *J Clin Endocrinol Metab* 1993;77:341–346.

Pasquali R, Vicennati V, Cacciari M, Pagotto U. The hypothalamic-pituitary-adrenal axis activity in obesity and the metabolic syndrome. *Ann NY Acad Sci* 2006;1083:111–128.

Reinehr T, Andler W. Cortisol and its relation to insulin resistance before and after weight loss in obese children. *Horm Res* 2004;62:107–112.

Guided Imagery and Recovered Memory Therapy

Considerations and Cautions

AMANDA THAYER AND STEVEN JAY LYNN

In the last half century, one of the most contentious issues that has emerged in the field of psychology is whether psychotherapists create rather then simply "recover" ostensibly repressed or dissociated memories of traumatic experiences, including early childhood sexual abuse. Numerous researchers and practitioners (e.g., Lindsay & Read, 1994; Loftus & Ketcham, 1994; Ofshe & Watters, 1994; Lynn, Lock, Loftus, Krackow, & Lilienfeld, 2003) have articulated manifold risks inherent in the proliferation of memory recovery techniques. However, proponents of the use of such techniques have marshalled a vigorous defense based on three contentions. First, the mere fact that a patient fails to recall sexual abuse should not deter a therapist from implementing memory recovery techniques insofar as traumatic memories are commonly represssed (e.g., see Williams, 1994). Second, memory research does not, in the main, apply to traumatic memories because there are salient differences in the recall of traumatic and mundane events (Alpert, Brown, & Courtois, 1998a, b; van der Kolk, 1994). Finally, therapists are duty-bound to help their clients, which necessitates taking a non-judgmental stance toward remembrances that arise in treatment (Fredrickson, 1992; Herman, 1992).

Given that the general topic of memory recovery techniques has been debated in multiple forums, we will limit our discussion to four points: (1) memory work in general, and guided imagery in particular, is by no means a rare event; (2) extant research has failed to document any therapeutic benefit for revisiting early memories of traumatic events; (3) attempts to help clients recall early abuse, including the use of guided imagery, can engender false memories; and (4) studies of source monitoring and imagination inflation provide compelling reasons to be wary of the use of guided imagery techniques. We will address each of these issues in turn.

GUIDED IMAGERY AS "MEMORY WORK" IN THE TREATMENT OF CHILDHOOD ABUSE SURVIVORS

Memory work refers to a constellation of techniques that are designed to help clients recover memories in psychotherapy (Shobe & Kihlstrom, 2002). These techniques include hypnosis and hypnotic age regression, bibliotherapy, dream interpretation, and guided imagery (e.g., Lindsay & Read, 1994). The risks associated with hypnosis in creating false memories are legion and have been well documented (e.g., Laurence & Perry, 1983; Lynn, Weekes, & Milano, 1989; Spanos & McLean, 1986), although controversy persists regarding the use of hypnosis for memory recovery (e.g., Brown, Scheflin, & Hammond, 1998). Furthermore, problems of false memories in conjunction with biblio-therapy and dream interpretation have been discussed elsewhere (e.g., Lynn, Lock, Loftus, Krackow, & Lilienfeld, 2003; Mazzoni, Loftus, & Kirsch, 2001; Mazzoni, Loftus, Seitz, & Lynn, 1999; Mazzoni, Lombardo, Malvagia, & Loftus, 1997). Accordingly, we will focus our commentary on the

Amanda Thayer and Steven Jay Lynn, "Guided Imagery and Recovered Memory Therapy: Considerations and Cautions," *Journal of Forensic Psychology Practice,* vol. 6, pp. 63-73. Copyright © 2006 by Taylor & Francis Group LLC. Reprinted with permission.

problems associated with the use of guided imagery for enhancing memory retrieval.

In guided imagery, a person imagines scenarios that are suggested or described by another person (Lindsay & Read, 1994). In psychotherapy, the individual is often relaxed and invited to close his or eyes in order to facilitate imagination. When memory accuracy is not a concern, guided imagery techniques are arguably useful (e.g., treatment of phobias, see Kazdin, 1994). However, we will contend that there is no empirical warrant for the use of guided imagery for memory recovery.

Our concerns about the use of guided imagery emanates, in part, from the visibility and popularity of these techniques. Not only is an extensive literature regarding childhood sexual abuse and memory recovery available to mental health consumers (e.g., Bass & Davis, 1988, 1993; Frederickson, 1992), but therapists frequently employ memory recovery techniques. For example, Poole and her colleagues' (1995) national survey of doctoral-level psychotherapists reported that 71% of the respondents used one of a number of different memory recovery techniques, and 32% of respondents used guided imagery specifically. Similarly, Polusny and Follete's (1996) national survey of psychologists found that more than a quarter of the sample used guided imagery, dream interpretation, and referral to a sexual abuse survivor's group with clients failing to report childhood sexual abuse. Finally, Maki and Syman's (1997) survey of clinical and counseling psychology programs revealed that many of these methods were routinely taught to graduate students. In short, there is ample reason for concern about guided imagery and memory recovery techniques, in general, given their ubiquity and widespread acceptance in the professional community.

QUESTIONABLE "BENEFITS" OF MEMORY RECOVERY

"Recovered memory therapy ... is predicated on the trauma-memory argument-that memories of traumatic events have special properties that distinguish them from ordinary memories of the sort usually studied in the laboratory (p. 70) ... Nothing about the clinical evidence suggests that traumatic memories are special, or that special techniques are required to recover them" (Shobe & Kihlstrom, 1997, p.74). Nevertheless, the claim persists that traumatic

memories are not only different than ordinary memories, but that research on false memories has done little to advance our understanding of the application of clinical procedures, which are far removed from emotionally sterile laboratory conditions (e.g., Alpert et al., 1998a,b). It follows then, that retiring these potentially beneficial techniques on the basis of infrequent instances of false recollections, and research constrained by limited generalizability to the real world is, in effect, throwing the baby out with the bathwater.

However, contrary to this viewpoint, the assumption that the recovery of repressed material is an ingredient of effective psychotherapy is dubious and has precious little empirical support. In fact, Littrell (1998) has argued that re-experiencing painful memories and emotions can have many negative consequences. When treatment gains are achieved in psychotherapy, they are not the result of simple catharsis. Rather, optimal treatment effects are associated with new learning and enhanced emotional self-regulation. Moreover, as Lindsay (1998) has explained, there is little to be gained by searching for lost memories, as there is no empirical evidence to suggest a causal relation between psychopathology and forgotten abuse. Even if such a causal link were established, Ornstein, Ceci, and Loftus (1998) point out that it is a logical fallacy to assume that if a certain manifestation of psychopathology follows sexual abuse, then a history of sexual abuse must exist when this particular symptom is present. This error in logic is what is commonly referred to as "affirming the consequent." As Ornstein et al. (1998) have noted, "we cannot argue from current symptoms back to a history of presumed abuse"(p. 1008).

GUIDED IMAGERY AND FALSE MEMORY CREATION

Guided imagery and related memory recovery methods are commonly used by professionals—but are they risky, and perhaps even "dangerous" procedures? We canted that research implies that the answer is "yes." Hyman and Pentland (1996) examined the effects of guided imagery on college students' false memory reports for early childhood events. To verify that the suggested events did not in fact occur, they contacted participants' parents. Participants were then brought to the laboratory and asked to recall an event that was ostensibly verified by their parents to have occurred when they were very young (e.g., knocking over a punchbowl at a wedding). Participants assigned to the control group were encouraged to recall the event, whereas those assigned to a guided imagery condition imagined the event taking place. After three recall trials, 25% of participants in the guided imagery condition recalled the false event, whereas only 9% of the control subjects did so. In a similar study, Hyman and Billings (1998) found that false memory reports correlate with imaginative ability as measured by the Creative Imagination Scale (CIS: Wilson & Barber, 1978). Moreover, measures of vividness of visualization have been found to be related to the production of memory errors across a variety of other suggestibility paradigms (Dobson & Markham, 1993; Tousignant, 1984; Winograd, Peluso, & Glover, 1998). Although not all measures of imagination consistently reveal increased false memory risk across studies, we know of no study that shows that imagination can reduce false memory risk.

It is also worth emphasizing that false memory reports in the laboratory are not limited to minor yet plausible early childhood experiences. Porter, Yuille, and Lehman (1999) asked college students to recall *highly emotional* (e.g., serious animal attack, serious medical procedure) early childhood events over three sessions using guided imagery techniques. Contrary to the notion that false memories rarely emerge for traumatic experiences, Porter et al. found that over repeated interviews, more than 25% of participants reported experiencing a stressful emotional event that was false.

IMAGINATION INFLATION AND GUIDED IMAGERY

Why does guided imagery increase the likelihood of false memory reports? Part of the answer undoubtedly lies in people's difficulties in monitoring the source of information (e.g., memory vs. imagination), and in distinguishing imagination and reality. Adequate source monitoring requires that we are not only able to retrieve a particular memory, but also to locate the source of the memory as well (Johnson, Hashtroudi, & Lindsay, 1993). Since Johnson and Raye's (1981) early research in reality monitoring (i.e., deciding whether a memory originated from our perceptions or only our imagination), substantial evidence has emerged that breakdowns in source monitoring can account for decision-making errors across a variety

of domains such as adult (e.g., Lindsay, 1993) and child (e.g., Ceci, Loftus, Leichtman, & Bruck, 1995) eyewitness testimony. Indeed, the mere act of imagining events that have never occurred can engender what is known as "imagination inflation"—enhanced confidence that the imagined events occurred in reality (Garry, Manning, Loftus, & Sherman, 1996).

Early studies demonstrated that some participants display considerable difficulties in distinguishing real versus imagined events. For example, Anderson (1984) asked subjects to trace line drawings or only imagine tracing line drawings. Later, these subjects were asked if they traced the drawings or only imagined doing so. Of those who reported tracing the drawings, 39% had, in fact, only imagined tracing. In their initial investigation of imagination inflation, Garry et al. (1996) developed a three-step procedure, which has become the conventional paradigm for investigating imagination inflation. Subjects were first asked about childhood events, as measured by the Life Events Inventory (LEI), which consists of 40 childhood events (e.g., "broke a window with your hand"), and asked to rate the likelihood of the event on an 8-point scale. The researchers then selected 8 events that all participants were least likely to have experienced. Two weeks later, participants returned to the laboratory and were assigned 4 of the 8 items and were given an imagination procedure for each of the 4 items. The imagination task involved participants reading a brief description of the event and then imagining the experience, with encouragement to include familiar places, people, and things in the imagined event. After completing the imagination task, participants were told that their original responses to the LEI had been misplaced and they were asked to complete the scale a second time. The researchers found that for the majority of items, there was no change in confidence between time 1 and time 2. They also found a small percentage of items decreased in confidence from time 1 to time 2. However, for those items where confidence increased from time 1 to time 2, it was more likely that it was an imagined item (34%) than a not-imagined item (25%). This imagination inflation effect has been demonstrated in numerous other instances (e.g., Horselenberg, Merkelbach, Muris, Rassin, Sijsenaar, & Spaan, 2000; Paddock, Joseph, Chan, Terranova, Manning, & Loftus, 1998; Paddock, Noel, Terranova, Eber, Manning, & Loftus, 1999).

Relatedly, Goff and Roediger (1998) examined whether repeatedly imagining an event increases the likelihood that it is judged to be a real event. For the first session, participants enacted, imagined, or only heard about action events. For the second session a day later, individuals were asked to imagine these events 0, 1, 3, or 5 times. For session three, two weeks after session 1, participants were given a recognition test and were asked to judge whether (for the first session) they had enacted the action, imagined the action, or only heard about the action (i.e., made a source monitoring judgment). As the number of imagining trials increased, so did the likelihood that a participant incorrectly reported they enacted an event. Moreover, source monitoring judgments fell to chance levels when subjects imagined events five times.

The findings reviewed raise the index of suspicion that source monitoring errors can play a role in false memories of childhood events. In the course of therapy, clients may be repeatedly asked to imagine abuse events, which, over time, prove increasingly difficult to disentangle what is real from what is only imagined. As the perceptual clarity of the imagined event increases, misattributing it to an actual experience becomes all the more likely (Johnson, Foley, Suengas, & Raye, 1989).

FINAL CONSIDERATIONS

In closing, we return to the claims of the defenders of the use of guided imagery and other memory recovery techniques in psychotherapy that we mentioned at the outset. If there were benefits associated with excavating and working with "repressed memories" in psychotherapy, then the use of techniques such as guided imagery might be justified for this purpose. However, to date, no such benefits have been documented.

It is true that generalizability of results from the laboratory to the clinic is an important issue. However, it seems plausible, if not likely, that expectancies, suggestive procedures, demand characteristics, and imagination inflation play a far more significant role in the consulting room than the laboratory. The therapists's potential to exert influence on a help-seeking, eager to please, vulnerable patient is likely much greater than the experimenter's influence on a subject participating in a "one shot" experiment for money or course credit (Lynn et al., 2003). Even if some laboratory-based findings fail to generalize to clinical practice, it does not provide an affirmative justification for the use of guided imagery for memory recovery.

The argument that therapists are duty-bound to take a nonjudgmental stance toward memories that surface in treatment is a completely separate issue from the advisability of using such techniques in treatment. Moreover, given that false memories can wreak havoc on individuals and families, therapists should make every effort to evaluate the role of suggestion, suggestibility, and imagination inflation in their treatment. That said, the questionable status of guided imagery procedures as memory recovery techniques has no direct bearing on the therapeutic efficacy of specific techniques such as hypnosis, which must ultimately be investigated and judged on their own merit.

REFERENCES

ALPERT, J.L., BROWN, L.S., & COURTOIS, C.A. (1998A). SYMPTOMATIC CLIENTS AND MEMORIES OF CHILDHOOD ABUSE: WHAT THE TRAUMA AND CHILD SEXUAL ABUSE LITERATURE TELLS US. PSYCHOLOGY, PUBLIC POLICY, AND LAW, 4, 941–995.

ALPERT, J.L., BROWN, L.S., & COURTOIS, C.A. (1998B). COMMENT ON ORNSTEIN, CECI, AND LOFTUS (1998): ADULT RECOLLECTIONS OF CHILDHOOD ABUSE. PSYCHOLOGY, PUBLIC POLICY, AND LAW, 4, 1052–1067.

ANDERSON, R.E. (1984). DID I DO IT OR DID I ONLY IMAGINE DOING IT? JOURNAL OF EXPERIMENTAL PSYCHOLOGY: GENERAL, 113, 594–613.

BASS, E., & DAVIS, L. (1988). THE COURAGE TO HEAL. NEW YORK: HARPER & ROW.

BASS, E., & DAVIS L. (1993). BEGINNING TO HEAL: A FIRST BOOK FOR SURVIVORS OF CHILDHOOD SEXUAL ABUSE. NEW YORK: HARPER COLLINS.

BROWN, D., SCHEFLIN, A.W., & HAMMOND, D.C. (1998). MEMORY, TRAUMA TREATMENT, AND THE LAW. NEW YORK, NY: NORTON & CO., INC.

CECI, S.J., LOFTUS, E.F., LEICHTMAN, M.D., & BRUCK, M. (1995). THE POSSIBLE ROLE OF SOURCE MISATTRIBUTIONS IN THE CREATION OF FALSE BELIEFS AMONG PRESCHOOLERS. INTERNATIONAL JOURNAL OF CLINICAL & EXPERIMENTAL HYPNOSIS, 42, 304–320.

DOBSON, M., & MARKHAM, R. (1993). IMAGERY ABILITY AND SOURCE MONITORING: IMPLICATIONS FOR EYEWITNESS MEMORY. BRITISH JOURNAL OF PSYCHOLOGY, 84(1), 111–118.

Frederickson, R. (1992). *Repressed memories*. New York: Fireside/Parkside.

Garry, M., Manning, C.G., Loftus, E.F., & Sherman, S.J. (1996). Imagination inflation: Imagining a childhood event inflates confidence that it occurred. *Psychonomic Bulletin & Review, 3*, 208–214.

Goff, L.M.,& Roediger, H.L. (1998). Imagination inflation for action events: Repeated imaginings lead to illusory recollections. *Memory & Cognition, 26*, 20–33.

Herman, J.L. (1992). *Trauma and recovery: The aftermath of violence*. New York: Basic Books.

Horselenberg, R., Merkelbach, H., Muris, P., Rassin, E., Sijsenaar, M., & Spaan, V. (2000). Imagining hypothetical childhood events: The role of individual differences in imagination inflation. *Clinical Psychology and Psychotherapy, 7*, 128–137.

Hyman, I., & Billings, F. (1998). Individual differences and the creation of false childhood memories. *Memory, 6(1)*, 1–20.

Hyman, I., & Pentland, J. (1996). The role of mental imagery in the creation of false childhood memories. *Journal of Memory & Language, 35*, 101–117.

Johnson, M.K., Foley, M.A., Suengas, A.G., & Raye, C.L. (1989). Pnenomenal characteristics of memories for perceived and imagined autobiographical events. *Journal of Experimental Psychology: General, 117*, 371–376.

Johnson, M.K., Hashtroudi, S., & Lindsay, D.S. (1993). Source Monitoring. *Psychological Bulletin, 114*, 3–28.

Johnson, M.K., & Raye, C.L. (1981). Reality monitoring. *Psychological Review, 88*, 67–85.

Kazdin, A.E. (1994). *Behavior modification in applied settings*. PacificGrove, CA: Brooks Cole.

Laurence, J.R., & Perry, C. (1983). Hypnotically created memory among highly hypnotizable subjects. *Science, 222*, 523–524.

Lindsay, D.S. (1998). Depolarizing views on recovered memory experiences. In S.J. Lynn & K. McConkey (Eds.), *Truth in memory* (pp. 481–494). New York: Guilford.

Lindsay, D. (1993). Eyewitness suggestibility. *Current Directions in Psychological Science, 2*, 86–89.

Lindsay, D., & Read, J. (1994). Psychotherapy and memories of childhood sexual abuse: A cognitive perspective. *Applied Cognitive Psychology, 8*, 281–338.

Littrell, J. (1998). Is the experience of painful emotion therapeutic? *Clinical Psychology Review, 18*, 71–102.

Loftus, E.F., & Ketcham, K. (1994). *The myth of repressed memory*. NewYork: St. Martin's Press.

Lynn, S.J., Lock, T., Loftus, E.F., Krackow, E., & Lilienfeld, S.O. (2003). The remembrance of things past: Problematic memory recovery techniques in psychotherapy. In S.O. Lilienfeld, S.J. Lynn, & J.M. Lohr (Eds.), *Science and pseudoscience in clinical psychology*. New York: The Guilford Press.

Lynn, S.J., Weekes, J.R., & Milano, M.J. (1989). Reality versus suggestion: Pseudo-memory in hypnotizable and simulating subjects. *Journal of Abnormal Psychology, 98*, 137–144.

Maki, R.H., & Syman, E.M. (1997). Teaching of controversial and empirically validated treatments in APA-accredited clinical and counseling psychology programs. *Psychotherapy, 34*, 44–57.

Mazzoni, G.A., Loftus, E.F., & Kirsch, I. (2001). Changing beliefs about implausible autobiographical events: A little plausibility goes a long way. *Journal of Experimental Psychology: Applied, 7*, 51–59.

Mazzoni, G.A., Loftus, E.F., Seitz, A., & Lynn, S.J. (1999). Creating a new childhood: Changing beliefs and memories through dream interpretation. *Applied Cognitive Psychology, 13*, 125–144.

Mazzoni, G.A., Lombardo, P., Malvagia, S., & Loftus, E.F. (1997). *Dream interpretation and false beliefs*. Unpublished manuscript, University of Florence and University of Washington.

Ofshe, R., & Watters, E. (1994). *Making monsters: False memories, psychotherapy, and sexual hysteria*. New York: Scribner's.

Ornstein, P.A., Ceci, S.J., & Loftus, E.F. (1998). Comment on Alpert, Brown, and Courtois (1998): The science of memory and the practice of psychotherapy. *Psychology, Public Policy, and Law, 4*, 996–1010.

Paddock, J.R., Joseph, A.L., Chan, F.M., Terranova, S., Manning, C., & Loftus, E.F. (1998). When guided visualization procedures may backfire: Imagination inflation and predicting individual differences in suggestibility. *Applied Cognitive Psychology, 12*, 63–75.

Paddock, J.R., Noel, M., Terranova, S., Eber, H.W., Manning, C., & Loftus, E.F. (1999). Imagination inflation and the perils of guided visualization. *The Journal of Psychology, 133*, 581–595.

Polusny, M.A., & Follete, V.M. (1996). Remembering childhood sexual abuse: A national survey of psychologists' clinical practices, beliefs, and personal experiences. *Professional Psychology: Research and Practice, 27,* 41–52.

Poole, D.A., Lindsay, D.S., Memon, A., & Bull, R. (1995). Psychotherapy and the recovery of memories of childhood sexual abuse: U.S. and British practitioner's opinions, practices, and experiences. *Journal of Consulting & Clinical Psychology, 63,* 426–437.

Porter, S., Yuille, J.C., & Lehman, D.R. (1999). The nature of real, implanted, and fabricated memories for emotional childhood events: implications for the recovered memory debate. *Law and Human Behavior, 23*(5), 517–537.

Shobe, K.S., & Kihlstrom, J.F. (1997). Is traumatic memory special? *Current Directions in Psychological Science, 6,* 70–74.

Shobe, K.K., & Kihlstrom, J.F. (2002). Interrogative suggestibility and "memory work." In M.L. Eisen (Ed.), *Memory and suggestibility in the forensic interview* (pp. 309–327). Mahwah, NJ: Lawrence Erlbaum Associates.

Spanos, N.P., & McLean, J. (1986). Hypnotically created pseudomemories: Memory distortions or reporting biases? *British Journal of Experimental Hypnosis, 3,*155–159.

Tousignant, J.P. (1984). Individual differences in response bias and recall: A characterization of the effects of misleading postevent information. *Dissertation Abstracts International, 48* (5–B), 1069.

van der Kolk, B.A. (1994). The body keeps the score: Memory and the evolving psychobiology of posttraumatic stress. *Harvard Review of Psychiatry, 1,* 253–265.

Williams, L.M. (1994). Recall of childhood trauma: A prospective study of women's memories of child sexual abuse. *Journal of Consulting & Clinical Psychology, 62,* 1167–1176.

Wilson, S.C., & Barber, T.X. (1978). The creative imagination scale as a measure of hypnotic responsiveness: Applications to experimental and clinical hypnosis. *The American Journal of Clinical Hypnosis, 20*(4), 235–253.

Winograd, E., Deluso, J.P., & Glover, T.A. (1998). Individual differences in susceptibility to memory illusions. *Applied Cognitive Psychology, 12,* 5–27.

The Effects of Cognitive and Motivational Imagery on Acquisition, Retention and Transfer of the Basketball Free Throw

S.M. VAEZ MOUSAVI AND R. ROSTAMI

ABSTRACT

The present study was designed to compare the effects of physical practice, cognitive imagery accompanied with physical practice and motivational imagery accompanied with physical practice on acquisition, retention and transfer of the basketball free throw. Seventy-eight female students with no prior experience in the task participated in the study in partial fulfillment of the requirements for their P.E. course. They were assigned in three groups according to the results of Motor Imagery Ability questionnaire, Sport Imagery Questionnaire and pretest scores. All groups participated in eighteen sessions of practices and acquisition, retention and transfer tests. The results of one way ANOVA indicated that physical practice group was better in acquisition phase, but cognitive imagery group produced better results in retention and transfer tests. These results pointed out that the cognitive functions of the mental imagery, not the motivational functions, may improve the processes of learning a new motor skill.

Key words: Motivational Imagery, Cognitive Imagery, Basketball Free Throw, Retention, Transfer, Performance

INTRODUCTION

Basketball is an exciting game and has many fans all around the world. Free throw is one of the important basketball skills and most coaches believe that it is one of the main factors for a team to succeed. To successfully perform this skill, not only physical abilities but also mental skills are important.

Mental imagery is defined by Richardson (1963) as a Para-perceptual experience or a Para-sensory awareness while lacking of factual stimulus causing these. It is a mental skill which plays an important role in learning motor skills, rehearsing special skills, improving self-confidence, controlling stress, excitement … (1). Schmidt (2005) stated that mental imagery is an effective method to rehearse skills. It can be always performed and need no assets (2). Magil (2002) confirmed the advantages of mental imagery in learning skills, healing injuries and preparing to perform efficiently (3). McMorris (2004) asserted that mental imagery, similar to physical practice, creates a skill model in the central nervous system; therefore, when we imagine performing a skill, the central nervous system learns as much as when we really perform that skill (4).

Wulf *et al.* (1995) considered the reduction of the relative frequency of the feedback during physical practice as useful. They believed that mental imagery, due to lack of feedback, operates similar to physical practice without feedback; therefore, they stressed the physical practice accompanied by imagery (5). In his theoretical framework, Paivio (1985) emphasized the role cognitive imagery and motivational imagery play in performing and learning motor skills (17). In their conceptual model, Martin *et al.* (1998) divided the cognitive and motivational functions of the imagery into several categories.

S. M. VaezMousavi and R. Rostami, "The Effects of Cognitive and Motivational Imagery on Acquisition, Retention and Transfer of the Basketball Free Throw," *World Journal of Sport Sciences*, vol. 2, no. 2, pp. 129-135. Copyright © 2009 by International Digital Organization for Scientific Information. Reprinted with permission.

Motivational specific imagery is used to imagine special goals and goals-oriented behaviors such as the victory in a competition or the joy after a successful performance. Motivational general imagery is used to psych-up generally and to improve self-confidence. Cognitive specific imagery is used to improve the skill level. Finally, cognitive general imagery is used to imagine training and competition strategies. Compared to cognitive imagery, it seems that limited researches investigated the effects of motivational imagery on novice and elite players' performance and learning; mainly these researches were not conclusive (6–10).

Murphy (1992) asserted that novices rarely use mental imagery (11). Feltz and Landers (1983) and Rayn and Simon (1983) stated that mental imagery more affects delicate skills with more cognitive aspects (12, 13). Hall (1998) stated that mental imagery significantly affected novice and professional players' performance although it more affected professional players' performance (14). In contrast, researchers such as Mulder (2004) and Overdorf (2004) did not believe in the effect of mental imagery on novices' performance (15, 16). Different theories of mental imagery attempted to explain the effectiveness of mental imagery. In his psycho-neuromuscular theory, Carpenter (1993) stated that as mental imagery activates neural-muscular patterns, it facilitates learning motor skills. In his symbolic learning theory, Saket (1934) indicated that mental imagery provides an opportunity for the performer to practice motor sequences as the symbolic aspects of a skill. This speculation suggests the learning resulted from mental imagery and the cognitive learning as related and points to the perception of motor patterns. In fact, mental imagery codifies the movements necessary to perform the skill and creates the motor program in the central nervous system. The codification of the movements in the brain facilitates the performance of motor skills (1). Magil (1976) believes that mental imagery is more effective in the early stages of learning a skill as cognitive processes are dominant; therefore, mental imagery is more effective for those learning a new or reviving an old skill. Mental imagery can help the individuals to perform more ideally in the absence of physical pressure (3). Schmidt (1975) suggested mental imagery as effective in the early stages of learning a skill as well. This suggestion is contrary to Richardson (1979) as he suggests the effectiveness of mental imagery and familiarity with the skill as directly related (2). Feltz

and Posner (1976) believed that mental imagery in the early stages of learning leads to learning a motor skill more ideally (3). As there are controversies over the effectiveness of imagery in the early stages of learning a skill, it seems that more researches on mental imagery and its functions should be carried out to reach more subtle grounds.

Researchers studied the effectiveness of cognitive functions as well as motivational functions of imagery. Burhans et al. (1988) used the cognitive functions of imagery and increased their subjects' speed after four weeks (18). Lee et al. (1990) and Murphy et al. (1998) stated that both cognitive and motivational imageries promote the performance of skills (14, 23). Blair, Hall and Leyshon (1993) found a 6-week regular physical practice accompanied with cognitive imagery as advantageous to perform fundamental football movements (19). Hall et al. (1998) and Cumming et al. (2001) asserted that novice players use the cognitive functions of imagery more (20, 21). Short et al. (2002) suggested the cognitive and motivational functions of imagery as effective to perform golf putting task (22).

On the other hand, the evidence for motivational imagery does not present consistant results. Burhans et al. (1988) suggested the motivational imagery as advantageous at the end of a series of practices (18). Feltz and Riessinger (1990) indicated that motivational imagery group performed a muscular endurance task more ideally than the control group (13). Lee et al. (1990) reported that motivational imagery group enjoyed more self-confidence and performed more ideally than the control group (7). Hall, Toews and Rodgers (1990) reported that motivational imagery encouraged the subjects to practice and participate more in the training (21). Murphy et al. (1998) indicated that motivational imagery alone was not better than concurrent cognitive and motivational imageries in improving a strength skill (11). Callow and Hardy (2001) stated that motivational imagery increases incentive and lead to reach the goal (23). On the contrary, Jones et al. (2002) concluded that novice mountain climbers who used motivational imagery did not perform differently from the control group (6).

Above mentioned researches generally show that the elites use motivational imagery for efficient performance, more ideal arousal level and better goal setting; but it is still unknown how novices qualitatively and quantitatively use motivational functions.

It is also vague how beginners in basketball use imagery to improve their free throw skills, since most researches were carried out on elite subjects. For example, Clooney (1977), Lane (1980), Wrisberg and Anshel (1989) stated that mental imagery improved basketball penalty throw (24, 8, 25). Ross (1985) observed that basketball free throw improved when mental imagery and physical practice were used together (26). However, Kearnes and Crossman (1992), Lerner *et al.* (1996) and Meyers and Schleser (1980) stated that mental imagery weakened university basketball players' free throw (27, 28).

Briefly, the existing results lack universality because: first, the advantages of cognitive and motivational imagery are not separated as several researches suggested cognitive imagery as useful (18–21, 29) and some other researches motivational imagery (13, 21, 23). Second, the effectiveness of these two kinds of imagery is not clear in novices learning motor skills as most researchers confined the effectiveness of mental imagery to elites (13, 30, 6, 23, 21, 7,31). Third, the effectiveness of cognitive and motivational imagery when learning basketball free throw is vague. On the one hand, researches focus on the promotion of elite basketball players' performance (20, 32, 33, 27, 26, 25, 8, 24). On the other hand, some researchers rejected the effectiveness of mental imagery on this skill (15, 16); therefore, conducting an investigation to meet the vague points seems necessary. The present study tends to investigate the effectiveness of cognitive and motivational imagery plus physical practice on the performance and learning of basketball free throw. We hypothesized that both cognitive and motivational imagery increase the novice learners' scores in acquisition, retention and transfer phases compared to the control group. We also hypothesized that novices will benefit more from cognitive imagery, as they perform in the early stage of learning.

MATERIALS AN METHODS

Subjects: 78 female university students at Shiraz Medical Sciences University, with no prior experience in participating in basketball training and competitions, participated in this study. We used stratified blocking randomization, based on the results from Hall and Martin's MIQ-R (Movement Imagery Questionnaire), Hall and Martin's (1998) SIQ (Sport Imagery Questionnaire) and pretest scores, to divide the subjects into three levels: high, medium and low (each group=26 members) and three groups: physical practice, cognitive imagery+physical practice and motivational imagery+physical practice.

Instruments: The Following Instruments Were Used to Gather Data:

- Hall and Martin's (1997) Movement Imagery Questionnaire: 8 questions in two subscales (visual and sensory-motor)
- Hall and Martin's (1998) Sport Imagery Questionnaire: 30 questions in five subscales of cognitive (general and specific) and motivational (general and specific at expertise and motivation levels)
- Free throw test: throws were scored based on AAPEHRD's[1] basketball test: 3 point to hit the ball into the basket without hitting the hoop or the board, 2 scores to hit the ball into the basket while hitting the board or the hoop, 1 score to hit the ball to the board or the hoop, 0 score to not to hit the ball to the board or the hoop.
- A registration form to keep the subjects' scores in practices and phases.

Procedures: After filling out their general data form and consent form, the subjects' height and weight were measured. Then, they filled out the MIQ-R and SIQ questionnaires. Next, the subjects were instructed with basketball free throw and participated in the pretest. Based on the pretest scores and questionnaire results, the three groups practiced basketball free throw for 18 sessions. The practice was carried out by a special protocol designed by Paivio (1985), Martin *et al.* (1998) and Munroe *et al.* (2000).

Cognitive imagery group imagined the details of the skill performance plus performing physical practice. They performed 640 physical throws and 270 mental throws. Motivational imagery group performed physical practice and they imagined the motivation and excitement during the successful performance of the movement. They performed 640 physical throws and 270 mental throws. The audio tape of imagery groups consisted of mental warm-up (Hickman) as well as the instructions on cognitive or motivational imagery. The warm-up took 10 minutes and when subjects improved their imagery to clear, controllable and real movement imagination, 10 minutes was reduced to 7 minutes. Physical practice group performed only 640 physical practices.

The subjects' performances in the acquisition phase were registered. Of course, they were not aware of the registration. The acquisition test was held 24 hours after the last acquisition session, the retention test was held 24 hours after the acquisition test and the transfer test 24 hours after the retention test from an angle 45 minutes to the side of the hoop. The degree of difficulty to reach the goal was determined considering the highest score gained in practice sessions so that the required score was 10% higher than the ideal performance. If the subjects gained the required scores in retention and transfer tests, they were awarded the complete score in physical education course.

Data Analysis: Descriptive statistics were used to achieve median, mean and standard deviation. One-way ANOVA and multiple comparisons Tukey test were used to compare the results among the groups.

RESULTS

Table 1 indicates the subjects' general data in the three groups.

One-way ANOVA results showed no significant difference in height ($p=0.636$ and $F_{(2 \text{ and } 75)} = 1.39$), weight $p=0.63$ and $F_{(2 \text{ and } 75)} = 0.46$) and age $p=0.86$ and $F_{(2 \text{ and } 75)} = 0.14$) among the three groups.

A) the Comparison of Pretest Scores: The means of randomly divided subjects scores in the pretest were compared (Table 2).

One-way ANOVA results showed no significant difference in the means of the scores among the three groups. This finding supports the subjects' random division.

B) Acquisition Test: One-way ANOVA in the acquisition test showed a significant difference in the means of the scores among the three groups (Table 3).

As you can see in the above table, one-way ANOVA results showed the superiority of physical practice group over the other groups in the acquisition test. Next, cognitive imagery+physical practice group performance better than motivational imagery+physical practice group.

C) Retention Test: One-way ANOVA in the retention test showed a significant difference among the three groups (Table 4).

As it can be seen in the above table, one-way ANOVA results in the retention test showed the superiority of cognitive imagery+physical practice group over the other groups. Next, the mean score of physical practice group was higher than that of motivational imagery+physical practice group.

D) Transfer Test: One-way ANOVA in the transfer test showed a significant difference among the three groups (Table 5).

As you can see in the above table, one-way ANOVA results in the transfer test showed the superiority of cognitive

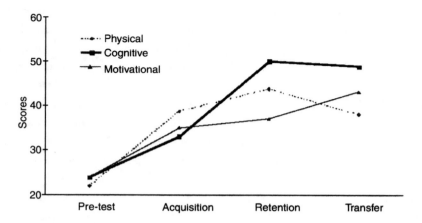

Fig. *1: Improvements of the three groups*

Table 1: The mean and standard deviation of the subjects' general characteristics

	Cognitive imagery + physical practice	Physical practice	Motivational imagery + physical practice
Mean Age	20.92	21.34	21.03
SD	2.46	3.21	3.03
Mean Weight	56.07	55.15	56.80
SD	5.05	7.88	5.29
Mean Height	162.46	161.58	164.15
SD	4.54	6.17	6.11

Table 2: One-way ANOVA findings to compare the means of the scores in the pretest

Index Group	Mean	SD	F	P
Cognitive imagery+physical practice	24.46	10.67		
Physical practice	23.15	9.63	0.24	0.781
Motivational imagery+physical practice	25.19	11.34		

Table 3: One-way ANOVA findings in the acquisition test

Index Group	Mean	SD	F	P
Cognitive imagery+physical practice	35.3	10.15		
Physical practice	42.15	10.91	4.02	0.022
Motivational imagery+physical practice	35.15	9.72		

Table 4: One-way ANOVA findings in the retention test

Index Group	Mean	SD	F	P
Cognitive imagery+physical practice	53.12	10.28		
Physical practice	46.85	9.55	15.11	0
Motivational imagery+physical practice	39.85	5.49		

imagery+physical practice group over the other groups. Next, the mean score of motivational imagery+physical

Table 5: One-way ANOVA findings in the transfer test

Index Group	Mean	SD	F P
Cognitive imagery+physical practice	52.62	7.57	
Physical practice	40.15	7.68	15.27 0
Motivational imagery+physical practice	46.69	9.05	

practice group was higher than that of physical practice group.

Figure 1 shows the improvement of the three groups during the pretest, acquisition test, retention test and transfer test.

While all groups seem equivalent in pre-test, they started to differ in the acquisition test in which physical practice group showed more improvement. This improvement did not last to the retention test in which the cognitive group performed better. Cognitive group also performed better in transfer test.

The above figure indicates that cognitive imagery group performed better than the other groups in retention and transfer tests. It means that these subjects learned free throw skill better than the other subjects did.

DISCUSSION AND CONCLUSION

The results of the present study showed the superiority of physical practice group in the acquisition test. It means that physical practice group acquired the skill better than the other groups, but they did not performed well in the retention and transfer phases. This finding supports previous findings which attributed the profitability of contextual interference to the test phase, not to the acquisition phase; for example, Hird et al. (1991) in the pegging board task, Kohl et al. (1992) in the pursuit rotor skill and Wright and Smith (2007) in a computer game (14, 34, 35). However, it should be considered that the cognitive and motivational groups participated in mental practice as well as physical practice. As all groups performed 640 physical throws, lower scores of the two mental imagery groups in the acquisition test may be attributed to the temporary and negative effects of contextual interference.

The present findings also indicated the superiority of cognitive imagery group over other groups in retention and transfer tests. These findings support Kolonay (1977), Lane et al. (1980), Ross (1985), Burhans et al. (1988), Weisberg and Anshel (1989), Lee et al. (1990), Hall

(1990,1998), Cumming *et al.* (2001) and Short *et al.* (2002) (25, 24, 26,18, 8, 36, 7, 21, 20,15). Therefore the following results should be confirmed: cognitive imagery group improved more than motivational imagery group. If the profitability of imagery to learn a motor skill can be attributed to psychological readiness aspects such as motivation, goal-orientation and self-confidence, as Hall, Toews and Rodgers (1990), Munroe *et al.* (2000) and Callow, Hardy and Hall (2001) confirmed (21,10, 37), it is expected that motivational imagery group will perform better. However, it was observed that cognitive imagery group learned best of all; therefore, it seems that cognitive aspects are more effective in learning basketball free throw than motivational ones. It seems that conceptual/cognitive characteristics of basketball free throw support the above suggestion. This finding partially supports Burhans *et al.* (1998) who found that cognitive imagery group performed their best on the fourth week while motivational imagery group on the twelfth week (18). Cognitive researchers state that mental imagery help the individual to respond to the problems on performing a movement in early perplexing stages of motor skill learning. In this stage, the individual tries to respond to the questions such as "what should I do?", "how should I perform the skill?" and "what should I do next?"; therefore, mental imagery helps to review of symbolic aspects, to the perception of motor pattern, to the codification of movements necessary to perform the skill in the brain and the creation of a motor program in central nervous system (13, 3, 1). Cognitive imagery can involve the individual more effectively in practice strategies. It seems that as it emphasizes the movement aspects, the cognitive imagery directs the individual's attention to most superior aspects of the skill and consequently enhances learning.

To support this finding, it seems that we can use McMorris's (2005) explanation. He believed that the effectiveness of imagery results from creating a model in the central nervous system. Learning when we imagine a skill is the same as learning when we really perform the skill; therefore, when an individual imagines, he will benefit from an extra practice.

Briefly, mental imagery is not effective on the skill acquisition; cognitive imagery is more effective than motivational imagery and physical practice in skill retention. However, the effectiveness of motivational imagery should not be neglected. Although motivational imagery was not as effective as cognitive imagery when learning a skill, results from previous researches on the profitability of motivational imagery and the effectiveness of motivational imagery in competition indicates that motivational imagery might result in a better performing a skill in emotional situations (for example, a competition). Therefore, the future direction of the present study will compare the effectiveness of the two types of imagery on these types of performance.

REFERENCES

MARTIN, K. A., S.E. MONTZ and C.R. HALL, 1999. IMAGERY USE IN SPORT: A LITERATURE REVIEW AND APPLIED MODEL. *JOURNAL THE SPORT PSYCHOLOGIST*, 13: 245–268.

SCHMIDT, R.A. and T.D. LEE, 2005. *MOTOR CONTROL AND LEARNING, HUMAN PERFORMANCE RESEARCH*, FOURTH EDITION, E-BOOK.

MAGIL, R.A., 2004. *MOTOR LEARNING AND CONTROL. CONCEPTS AND APPLICATIONS (7 TH ED)*. BOSTON, MA: MC GRAW HILL.

McMORRIS, T., 2004. *ACQUISITION AND PERFORMANCE OF SPORTS SKILLS. (1ST ED)*. JOHN WILLY AND SONS, LTD.

WULF, G., G. HORSTMANN and B. CHOI, 1995. DOES MENTAL PRACTICE WORK LIKE PHYSICAL PRACTICE WITHOUT INFORMATION FEEDBACK? *JOURNAL RESEARCH QUARTERLY FOR EXERCISE AND SPORT*. 66, 3: 262–267.

JONES, M.V., S.R. BRAY, RD. MACE, A.E. MAC RACE and STOCKBRIDGE, 2002. THE IMPACT OF MOTIVATIONAL IMAGERY ON THE EMOTIONAL STATE AND SELF-EFFICACY LEVEL OF NOVICE CLIMBERS. *JOURNAL OF SPORT BEHAVIOR*. 25: 57–73.

LEE, C., 1990. PSYCHING UP FOR MUSCULAR ENDURANCE TASK: EFFECTS OF CONTENT ON PERFORMANCE AND MOOD STATE, *JOURNAL OF SPORT AND EXERCISE PSYCHOLOGY*, 12: 66–73.

WEISBERG, C. AND M. ANSHEL, 1989. THE EFFECT OF COGNITIVE STRATEGIES ON THE FREE THROW SHOOTING PERFORMANCE OF YOUNG ATHLETES. *THE SPORT PSYCHOLOGIST*, 3: 95–104.

SINGER, H., 2000. *AN EXAMINATION OF DATA SUPPORTING HYPOTHESIZED MEDIATION PATHWAYS UNDERLYING. THE RELATIONSHIP BETWEEN MENTAL IMAGERY AND MOTOR SKILL PERFORMANCE. A META-ANALYSIS*. UNPUBLISHED DOCTORAL DISSERTATION.

MUNROE, K.J., P.R GIACOBBI, C. HALL AND R. WEINBERG, 2000. THE FOUR Ws OF IMAGERY USE: WHERE, WHY, WHEN, AND WHAT. *THE SPORT PSYCHOLOGIST* 14: 119–137.

Murphy, S.M., R.L. Woolfolk and A.J. Budney, 1998. The effect of emotive imagery on strength performance. *Journal Sport and Exercise Psychology*, 10: 334–345.

Ryan, E.D. and J. Simons, 1982. Efficacy of mental imagery in enhancing mental rehearsal of motor skills, *Journal of Sport Psychology*, 4: 4–51.

Feltz, D.L. and L.A. Riessinger, 1990. Effects of in vivo emotion imagery and performance feedback on self-efficacy and muscular endurance. *Journal of Sport and Exercise Psychology*, 12: 132–140.

Hird, J.S., D.M. Landers, J.R. Thomas and J.J. Horan, 1991. Physical Practice is superior to mental practice in enhancing cognitive and motor task performance. *Journal of Sport and Exercise Psychology*, 8: 293.

Mulder, T., S. Zijlstar, W. Zijlstra and J. Hochstenbach, 2004. The role of motor imagery in learning a totally novel movement, *Exp. Brain Research*, 154(2): 211–217.

Overdorf, Virginia, 2004. Mental and physical practice schedules in acquisition and retention of novel timing skills: *Perceptual and Motor Skills*, 1,12: 51–62.

Paivio, A., 1985. Cognitive and motivational functions of imagery in human performance. *Canadian Journal of Applied Sciences*, 10: 225–228.

Burhans, III, R.S., C.L. Richman and D.B. Bergey, 1998. Mental training: Effect on running speed performance. *International J. Sport Psychology*, 19: 26–37.

Blair, A., C. Hall and G. Leyshon, 1993. Imagery effects on the performance of skill and novice soccer players, *Journal Sport Sci.*, 11(2): 95–101.

Cumming, J. and D.M. Ste-Marie, 2001. The cognitive and motivational effects of imagery training: A matter of perspective. *The Sport Psychologist*, 15: 276–278.

Hall, C., J. Toews and W. Rodgers, 1990. Les aspects motivationnels de l'imagerie en activities motrices. *Revue des Sciences et Techniques des Activités Physiques et Sportives*, 11: 27–32.

Short, S.E., J.M. Bruggrman, S.G. Engel, T.L. Marback, L.J. Wang, A. Willadsen and M.W. Short, 2002. The effect of imagery function and imagery direction on self-efficacy and performance on a golf putting task. *The Sport Psychologist*, 16: 48–61.

Callow, N., L. Hardy and C. Hall, 2001. The effect of a motivational general-mastery imagery intervention on the sport confidence of high-level badminton players. *Research Quarterly For Exercise And Sport*, 72: 389–400.

Lane, J.F., 1980. Improving athletic performance through visuo-motor behavior rehearsal. INR. Suinn (Ed). *Psychology In Sports: Methods and Applications* (pp. 316–320,). Minneapolis, MN: Burgess.

Kolonay, B.J., 1997. The effects of visuo-motor behavior rehersal on athletic performance. Unpublished Masters Thesis, City University Of New York, Hunter College, NY.

Ross, S.L., 1985. The effectiveness of mental practice in improving the performance of college trombonists, *Journal of Research In Music Education*, 33: 221–230.

Lerner and Ostrow, 1996. The effect of goal-setting and imagery training programs on the free throw performance of female collegiate basketball players, *Journal The Sport Psychologist*.

Meyers, A.W. and R. Schleser, 1980. A cognitive behavioral intervention for improving basketball performance. *Journal of Sport Psychology*, 2: 69–73.

Martin, K.A. and C. Hall, 1995. Using mental imagery to enhance intrinsic motivation. *Journal Of Sport and Exercise Psychology*, 17: 54–69.

Hall, C.R., D.M. Mack, A. Paivio and H.A. Hausenblas, 1998. Imagery use by athletes: Development of the sport imagery questionnaire. *International Journal Of Sport Psychology*, 29: 73–89.

Shelton, T.O. and M.J. Mahoney, 1978. The content and effect of psyching-up strategies in weight lifters. *Cognitive Theory and Research*, 2: 275–284.

Onestak and Pittsburgh, 1997. The effect of visio-motor behavior rehearsal (VMBR) and videotape modeling (VM) on the free throw performance of inter collegiate athletes. *Journal of Sport Behavior*.

Weinberg, Hanks and Jackson, 1991. Effect of the length and temporal location of the mental preparation interval on basketball shooting performance. INT. *Journal of Sport Psychology*.

Kohl, R.M., S.D. Ellis and D.L. Roenker, 1992. Alternating actual and imagery practice: preliminary theoretical consideration. *Research Quarterly for Exercise and Sport*, 63: 162–70.

Wright C.J. and D.K. Smith, 2007. The effect of short-term PETTLEP imagery international a cognitive

TASK. *JOURNAL OF IMAGERY RESEARCH IN SPORT AND PHYSICAL ACTIVITY*, PP: 2–10.

HALL, C.R., W.M. RODGERS AND K.A. BARR, 1990. THE USE OF IMAGERY BY ATHLETES IN SELECTED SPORTS. *THE SPORTS PSYCHOLOGIST*, 4: 1–10.

CALLOW, N., L. HARDY AND C. HALL, 1998. THE EFFECTS OF A MOTIVATIONAL-MASTERY IMAGERY INTERVENTION OF THE SPORT CONFIDENCE OF THREE ELITE BADMINTON PLAYERS. MANUSCRIPT SUBMITTED FOR PUBLICATION.

CHAPTER 13
General Knowledge Representation

What Predicts the Own-Age Bias in Face Recognition Memory?

YI HE, NATALIE C. EBNER, AND MARCIA K. JOHNSON

Younger and older adults' visual scan patterns were examined as they passively viewed younger and older neutral faces. Both participant age groups tended to look longer at their own-age as compared to other-age faces. In addition, both age groups reported more exposure to own-age than other-age individuals. Importantly, the own-age bias in visual inspection of faces and the own-age bias in self-reported amount of exposure to young and older individuals in everyday life, but not explicit age stereotypes and implicit age associations, significantly and independently predicted the own-age bias in later old/new face recognition. We suggest these findings reflect increased personal and social relevance of, and more accessible and elaborated schemas for, own-age than other-age faces.

Human faces provide information critical for social interactions. Some of the information extracted from faces (e.g., expression, race, or age) affects how faces are encoded and remembered (Bäckman, 1991; Ebner & Johnson, 2009; Meissner & Brigham, 2001). For instance, people of different ages are more likely to attend to, and are faster and more accurate in recognizing, faces of their own than another age group (Anastasi & Rhodes, 2005; Ebner & Johnson, 2010; Lamont, Stewart-Williams, & Podd, 2005; see Harrison & Hole, 2009, for an overview).

There are several factors that may predict the own-age bias in face recognition as discussed below.

VISUAL INSPECTION OF OWN-AGE AND OTHER-AGE FACES

Differential attention can be reflected in patterns of looking at faces (Buswell, 1935; Isaacowitz, Wadlinger, Goren, & Wilson, 2006; Knight, Seymour, Gaunt, Baker, Nesmith et al., 2007), and visual scan pattern can affect encoding and recognition of faces (Henderson, Williams, & Falk, 2005). For example, face recognition is impaired when eye movements during face encoding are restricted to the center of a face instead of allowing for free sampling of facial features and their interrelations (Henderson et al., 2005).

Younger and older adults differ in how they visually scan faces: Whereas younger adults look more at eyes than mouths, older adults show the reverse pattern on an emotional expression identification task (Murphy & Isaacowitz, 2010; Sullivan, Ruffman, & Hutton, 2007; Wong, Cronin-Golomb, & Neargarder, 2005, but see Ebner, He, & Johnson, in press). But do younger and older adults differently scan faces of their own age group as opposed to faces of the other age group, and if so, do differences in scan pattern predict the own-age bias in later face recognition? To our knowledge, the only study that addressed these questions asked younger and older adults to rate the quality of pictures of younger and older faces and to evaluate the age of

Yi He, Natalie C. Ebner, and Marcia K. Johnson, "What Predicts the Own-age Bias in Face Recognition Memory?" *Social Cognition*, vol. 29, no. 1, pp. 97-109. Copyright © 2011 by Guilford Publications, Inc. Reprinted with permission.

the faces (Firestone, Turk-Browne, & Ryan, 2007). Under these conditions, there was no indication of an own-age bias in visual inspection of faces. Rather, overall looking time, number of fixations, and number of transitions between facial features were greater for younger than older faces in both age groups and visual scan pattern did not correlate with old/new face recognition. However, the particular rating tasks used may have increased similarity among participants in how they scanned faces. It may be that under more natural, passive free viewing conditions, scan patterns would show an own-age bias in attention which would be related to memory.

AMOUNT OF EXPOSURE TO OWN-AGE AND OTHER-AGE PERSONS

Both younger and older adults report a greater amount of exposure to individuals of their own as compared to another age group in their daily lives. In addition, the more contact younger adults report to have with older adults the better they are able to later correctly recognize older faces, but no such effect is observed for older adults (Ebner & Johnson, 2009). It seems reasonable to suppose that, as a consequence of more frequent encounters with persons of their own age, individuals develop and/or maintain better schemas supporting own age face recognition. However, older adults may engage a less than optimal scan pattern when inspecting faces, offsetting a potential benefit from available schemas. Further examination of age differences in both scan patterns and amount of exposure to individuals of different ages, and the independent contributions of these factors to predicting own-age bias in face recognition should be informative.

EXPLICIT AGE STEREOTYPES AND IMPLICIT AGE ASSOCIATIONS ABOUT OWN-AGE AND OTHER-AGE PERSONS

In the context of artificially assigned minimal group membership, individuals evaluate in-group members more positively than out-group members (Brewer, 1979), and recognize in-group faces more accurately than out-group faces (Bernstein, Young, & Hugenberg, 2007). If age operates like an in-group, then younger and older adults should show age-related stereotypes that favor their own

age group. These stereotypes may guide attention to, and potentially enhance memory for, individuals of different ages (as shown in the context of the own-race bias, see Meissner & Brigham, 2001). However, studies of age-related stereotyping indicate that younger and older individuals view older persons more negatively than younger persons (Ebner, 2008; Gluth, Ebner, & Schmiedek, 2010; Kite, Stockdale, Whitley, & Johnson, 2005) and both age groups have more negative implicit associations toward older targets (Hummert, Garstka, O'Brien, Greenwald, & Mellott, 2002). These findings suggest that both younger and older adults should be influenced in the same direction by explicit and implicit age associations and should show more attention to, and better memory for, the more positively viewed (i.e., the younger, not older) individuals.

PURPOSE OF THE STUDY

The aim of this study was to examine whether visual inspection, amount of exposure, explicit age stereotypes, and/or implicit age associations independently predicted the own-age bias in face recognition memory in younger and older adults. We recorded eye movements of younger and older adults during passive free viewing of younger and older neutral faces. This was followed by a surprise old/new face recognition memory task, a questionnaire assessing exposure to younger and older persons in daily life, and assessment of explicit age stereotypes and implicit age associations. We hypothesized that younger and older participants would (1) look longer at own-age than other-age faces, and (2) report more exposure to individuals of their own than the other age group. Furthermore, we expected that (3) differences in looking time at younger and older faces and differences in the amount of exposure to younger and older individuals would independently contribute to the own-age bias in old/new face recognition memory. Given the two, somewhat contradictory, lines of evidence in the literature, we did not have predictions regarding own-age bias in explicit age stereotypes and implicit age associations and their relations to face recognition memory.

METHODS

PARTICIPANTS

Forty-seven younger adults (age range 18-30 years, $M = 22.2$, $SD = 2.9$, 57% women) were recruited through flyers on campus, and 33 older adults (age range 63-92 years, $M = 74.9$, $SD = 7.8$, 70% women) from the community through flyers posted in, or mailing to, community or senior citizen centers. Only participants who had more than 67% trials with valid gazing information (defined as gazes focused within 1° of visual angle for at least 0.1 seconds) were included in the analyses, resulting in a final sample of 25 younger participants (age range 19-29 years, $M = 22.2$, $SD = 2.9$, 60% women) and 24 older participants (age range 63-92 years, $M = 73.9$, $SD = 7.8$, 71% women). All participants were compensated for participation. The majority of the younger participants were Yale University undergraduates (varying majors). Older participants reported a mean of 16.7 years of education $(SD = 1.6)$. Younger and older participants did not differ in self-reported health, but they differed in near vision, contrast sensitivity, and visual-motor processing speed (Table 1).[1]

STIMULI AND EQUIPMENT

Stimuli were taken from the FACES database, a standardized set of color photographs of naturalistic Caucasian (frontal view) faces of different ages (Ebner, Riediger, & Lindenberger, 2010). Equal numbers of faces from younger (18-31 years) and older individuals (69-80 years), half male and half female, were presented on a 17-inch display (1024 x 768 pixels) at a distance of 24 inches (face stimuli: 623 x 768 pixels). Stimulus presentation was controlled using Gaze Tracker (Eye Response Technologies, Inc., Charlottesville, VA) for the eye tracking task and E- Prime (Schneider, Eschman, & Zuccolotto, 2002) for the other computer tasks. An Applied Science Laboratories (Bedford, MA) Model 504 Eye Tracker recorded eye movements at a rate of 60 Hz.

PROCEDURE

After giving consent, participants rested their head on a chinrest to minimize head movement. The eye tracking camera was adjusted to locate the corneal reflection and pupil of participants' left eye, followed by an individual 9-point calibration covering the area of stimulus presentation. Participants first worked on the *Passive Face Viewing Task* (described below) for about 10 minutes. They then filled in a short demographic and physical health questionnaire on paper and worked on the Digit-Symbol-Substitution Test as a measure of processing speed (Table 1). After 10 minutes, participants performed the (surprise) *Old/New Face Recognition Task* (described below), followed by the Rosenbaum Pocket Vision Screener and the MARS Letter Contrast Sensitivity Test (Table 1).

Participants then took the *Older-Younger Implicit Association Task* (Age IAT; Hummert et al., 2002), as a measure of implicit age associations. In this task participants responded to either younger or older faces using the same key as responding to positive or negative words and response times were measured. Higher positive IAT scores indicate more positive associations for younger than older targets (for calculation of this difference score, see Greenwald, Nosek, & Banaji, 2003).

Participants indicated the amount of social exposure to persons of their own and the other age group using the same 8-point scale for each question where 1 = *less than once per year*, and 8 = *daily* (Media exposure: *"How often are you exposed to younger [approx. between 18-30 years of age]/ older [approx. 65 years of age and older] adults on television or in other media?"*; Personal exposure: *"How often do you have personal contact with younger/older adults?"*; Other types of exposure: *"How often do you have other types of contact with younger/older adults?"*).

Finally, they responded to the AGED Inventory (Knox, Gekoski, & Kelly, 1995), as a measure of explicit age stereotypes, comprising 28 adjective pairs, with respect to younger *(approx. between 18-30 years of age)* and older *(approx. 65 years of age and older)* adults. Only the subscale of *"positiveness"* (including seven adjective pairs, e.g., 1 = *pessimistic*, 7 = *optimistic*; 1 = *unproductive*, 7 = *productive)* was used in the final analysis.

---

1 Entering near vision, contrast sensitivity, and visual-motor processing into the model did not change the results.

TABLE 1. Means/percentages (Standard deviations) and Significance Tests for Health, Cognition, and Vision Measures for Younger and Older Participants

Measures	Younger Participants M/% (SD)	Older Participants M/% (SD)	Age Group Differences
Self-Reported Health	4.36 (0.70)	4.21 (0.72)	$F(1, 48) = 0.56, p = .46, \eta_p^2 = .01$
Hearing Difficulties	0.0%	58.3%	$\chi^2(1, N = 49) = 20.42, p < .001$
Near Vision (binocular)	22.40 (5.02)	52.08 (50.43)	$F(1, 48) = 8.58, p < .001, \eta_p^2 = .15$
Contrast Sensitivity (binocular)	1.72 (0.09)	1.54 (0.19)	$F(1, 48) = 18.82, p < .001, \eta_p^2 = .29$
Visual-Motor Processing Speed	67.48 (1 1.96)	45.46 (7.86)	$F(1, 48) = 57.50, p < .001, \eta_p^2 = .55$

Note. Self-reported health: *"In general (i.e., over the past year), how would you rate your health and physical well-being?"* (1 = poor, 5 = excellent); hearing difficulties: *"Do you have any hearing difficulties?"* (yes, no); near vision: Rosenbaum Pocket Vision Screener (Rosenbaum, Granham-Field Surgical Co Inc, New York, NY; lower scores indicate better vision); contrast sensitivity: MARS Letter Contrast Sensitivity Test (Arditi, 2005; higher scores indicate better sensitivity); Visual-motor processing speed: Digit-Symbol-Substitution Test (Wechsler, 1981; higher scores indicate higher speed in performance).

(A) Passive Face Viewing (Eye Tracking)

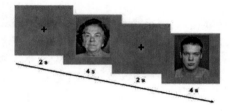

(B) Old/New Face Recognition (No Eye Tracking)

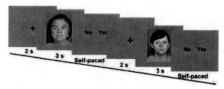

FIGURE 1. *Experimental Tasks: (A) Passive Face Viewing During Which Eye Movements Were Recorded; (B) Old/New Face Recognition Task During Which No Eye Movements Were Recorded.*

EXPERIMENTAL TASKS: PASSIVE FACE VIEWING AND OLD/NEW FACE RECOGNITION

As shown in Figure 1, the experiment consisted of two tasks: (A) a *Passive Face Viewing Task* during which eye movements were recorded; and (B) an *Old/New Face Recognition Task* during which key press responses and response times, but no eye tracking, were recorded. For both tasks, the experimenter gave verbal instructions and a computer program provided additional written instructions and practice runs.

During the *Passive Face Viewing Task,* participants saw 24 younger and 24 older faces, one face at a time, for a fixed presentation time of 4 seconds. Participants were instructed to *"Look naturally at whatever is interesting to you in the images as if you were at home watching TV,"* while blinking naturally. A black cross on a grey background appeared for 2 seconds between trials. No more than two faces of the same age or gender repeated in a row. Overall gaze time and number of gazes (defined as amount of time, and number of times, participants' pupil and corneal reflection were recorded during face presentation) were extracted. In addition, each face was divided into an upper (covering the area around the eyes) and a lower (covering the area around the mouth) half, without overlap or gap, and gaze time of these two areas of interest was extracted.

During the *Old/New Face Recognition Task* participants were shown 48 (24 younger and 24 older) target faces from the passive viewing phase and 48 (24 younger and 24 older) new, distracter faces, again one face at a time, for a fixed interval of 3 seconds. After the face disappeared, the computer prompted participants to make an old/new judgment for the face, before the next face presentation. Again a black cross on a grey background appeared for 2 seconds between trials. No more than two faces of the same age or gender and no more than three target or distracter faces repeated in a row. Target and distracter faces were counterbalanced across participants.

RESULTS

OWN-AGE BIAS IN OLD/NEW FACE RECOGNITION MEMORY

We conducted a mixed-model analysis of variance (ANOVA) on old/new face recognition memory (indexed by d'; Green & Swets, 1966) with *Age of Participants (younger, older)* as a between-subjects factor and *Age of Faces (younger, older)* as a within-subject factor. The main effects of *Age of Participants*, $F(1, 47) = 10.60$, $p < .01$, $\eta_p^2 = .18$, *Age of Faces*, $F(1, 47) = 4.32$, $p < .05$, $\eta_p^2 = .08$) and the *Age of Participants x Age of Faces* interaction, $F(1, 47) = 14.79$, $p < .001$, $\eta_p^2 = .24$) were significant (Figure 2A): Both younger and, marginally significant, older participants recognized own-age faces better than other-age faces[2]

(Younger participants: $M(d')_{\text{Younger faces}} = 1.99$, $SD = 0.84$, $M(d')_{\text{Older faces}} = 1.42$, $SD = 0.67$; $t(24) = 3.53$, $p < .01$; $M(hits)_{\text{Younger faces}} = 17.2$, $SD = 3.30$, $M(hits)_{\text{Older faces}} = 16.32$, $SD = 3.00$; $M(FA)_{\text{Younger faces}} = 6.75$, $SD = 4.92$, $M(FA)_{\text{Older faces}} = 8.25$, $SD = 4.05$; Older participants: $M(d')_{\text{Younger faces}} = 1.07$, $SD = 0.63$, $M(d')_{\text{Older faces}} = 1.24$, $SD = 0.54$; $t(23) = 1.67$, $p = .11$; $M(hits)_{\text{Younger faces}} = 15.42$, $SD = 4.2$, $M(hits)_{\text{Older faces}} = 19.08$, $SD = 3.84$; $M(FA)_{\text{Younger faces}} = 8.05$, $SD = 5.93$, $M(FA)_{\text{Older faces}} = 10.48$, $SD = 4.80$).

PREDICTORS OF OWN-AGE BIAS IN OLD/NEW FACE RECOGNITION MEMORY

Next, we addressed the questions of whether either overall gaze time at younger and older faces, self-reported amount of exposure to younger and older persons, explicit age stereotypes, and/or implicit age associations predicted the observed own-age bias in old/new face recognition memory. We first tested for an own-age bias in each of these variables.

Overall Gaze Time. We conducted a mixed-model ANOVA on overall gaze time (in seconds) with *Age of Participants (younger, older)* as a between-subjects factor and *Age of Faces (younger, older)* and *Target Face Recognition (correct recognition, missed recognition)* as within-subject factors. None of the main effects were significant but the *Age of Participants* by *Age of Faces* interaction was significant, $F(1, 43) = 4.66$, $p < .05$, $\eta_p^2 = 10$; Figure 2B). The interaction resulted because both age groups tended to look longer at own-age than other-age faces, although neither comparison was independently significant (Younger participants: $M_{\text{Younger faces}} = 3.74$, $SD = 0.29$, $M_{\text{Older faces}} = 3.71$, $SD = 0.28$; $t(23) = 1.40$, $p = .17$; Older participants: $M_{\text{Younger faces}} = 3.65$, $SD = 0.29$, $M_{\text{Older faces}} = 3.68$, $SD = 0.29$; $t(20) = -1.73$, $p = .10$). This pattern of results was similar in the number of gazes on younger and older faces.

Gaze Time at Upper and Lower Half of Faces. To explore gaze time differences in upper versus lower half of faces, respectively, we conducted separate mixed-model ANOVAs with *Age of Participants* as a between-subjects factor and

---

2 In the total sample ($N = 80$; including participants without valid gazing information), the effect was significant in both participant age groups, $F(1, 77) = 16.88$, $p < .001$, $\eta_p^2 = .18$; Younger participants: $M(d')_{\text{Younger faces}} = 1.95$, $SD = 0.80$,

$M(d')_{\text{Older faces}} = 1.47$, $SD = 0.66$; $t(46) = 4.07$, $p < .001$; Older participants: $M(d')_{\text{Younger faces}} = 1.02$, $SD = 0.73$, $M(d')_{\text{Older faces}} = 1.22$, $SD = 0.62$; $t(31) = 1.97$, $p = .05$.

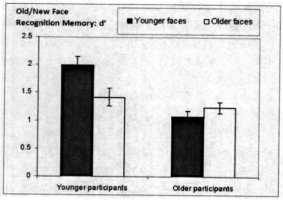

FIGURE 2A.

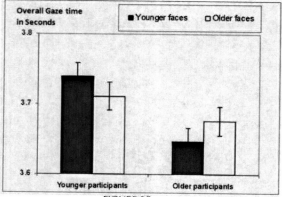

FIGURE 2B.

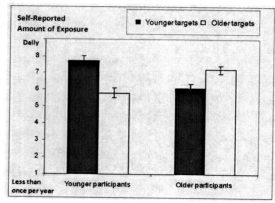

FIGURE 2C.

FIGURE 2A. Significant interaction between *Age of Participants* and *Age of Faces* Observed in Old/New Face Recognition Memory *(d')*. **FIGURE 2B.** Significant interaction between *Age of Participants* and *Age of Faces* Observed in Overall Gaze Time (in Seconds). **FIGURE 2C**. Significant interaction between *Age of Participants* and *Age of Targets* Observed in Self-Reported Amount of Exposure to Younger and Older Persons. *Note.* Error bars represent standard errors of condition mean differences.

Age of Faces and *Target Face Recognition* as within-subject factors. For looking time at lower half of faces there was a significant main effect for *Old Face Recognition* $F(1,43) = 5.22$, $p < .05$, $\eta_p^2 = 11$, with longer gaze time at correctly remembered ($M = 1.00$, $SD = 0.60$) than missed (M = 0.93, $SD = 0.65$) faces. No other effect was significant. In addition, for older, but not younger, participants longer gaze time at the upper half of older faces predicted more accurate recognition of older faces *(r = .42, p < .05)*, while longer gaze time at the lower half of older faces predicted worse recognition of older faces *(r = -.45, p < .05)*.

Self-Reported Amount of Exposure. We then conducted a mixed-model ANOVA on amount of exposure to younger and older persons (composite score [max: 8, indicating daily contact] of media, personal, and other types of exposure) with *Age of Participants (younger, older)* as a between-subjects factor and *Age of Targets (younger, older)* as a within-subject factor. There were no significant main effects, but the interaction between *Age of Participants* and *Age of Targets* was significant, $F(1, 46) = 55.98$, $p < .001$, $\eta_p^2 = 55$). As shown in Figure 2C, both participant groups had more contact with persons of their own than the other age group (Younger participants: $M_{\text{Younger targets}} = 7.72$, $SD = 0.69$, $M_{\text{Older targets}} = 5.80$, $SD = 1.62$, $t(24) = 6.11$, $p < .001$; Older participants: $M_{\text{Younger targets}} = 6.06$, $SD = 1.39$, $M_{\text{Older targets}} = 7.20$, $SD = 0.76$; $t(22) = 4.46$, $p < .001$).

Explicit Age Stereotype. A mixed-model ANOVA of explicit age stereotype scores (composite score [max = 7] of items from the *positiveness* subscale) with *Age of Participants (younger, older)* as a between-subjects factor and *Age of Targets (younger, older)* as a within-subject factor showed a main effect for *Age of Targets*, $F(1,46) = 34.05$, $p < .001$, $\eta_p^2 = 43$): Participants rated younger targets as more positive ($M = 4.98$, $SD = 0.74$) than older targets ($M = 4.17$, $SD = 0.86$). No other effect was significant.

Implicit Age Associations. Conducted separately within younger and older participants, one-sample t-tests (test against 0, which indicates no difference in response time between associating younger faces with positive words as compared to older faces) showed that both age groups had more positive implicit associations for younger than older faces (Younger participants: $M = 0.41$, $SD = 0.30$, $t(24) = 6.99$, $p < .001$; Older participants: $M = 0.55$, $SD = 0.27$, $t(23) = 10.01$, $p < .001$). The difference between younger and older participants was not significant.

Testing Independent Predictors of Own-Age Bias in Old/ New Face Recognition Memory. We then conducted a multiple linear regression analysis to examine whether overall gaze time, self-reported amount of exposure, explicit age stereotypes, and implicit age associations (independently) predicted old/new face recognition memory for younger and older faces in younger and older participants. As presented in Table 2, in a first step we entered the difference between overall gaze time at younger as compared to older faces as predictor of the difference between remembering younger as compared to older faces. Overall gaze time significantly predicted old/new face recognition memory. In a second step, we introduced the difference between self-reported amount of exposure to younger as compared to older persons as additional predictor into the model. This variable significantly predicted old/new face recognition memory, over and above overall gaze time. In a third step, we entered the difference between ratings for younger and older persons in terms of positiveness (explicit age stereotypes) and implicit age associations toward younger over older persons as additional predictors. In this model, overall gaze time remained a significant predictor, self-reported amount of exposure became marginally significant, while neither explicit age stereotypes nor implicit age associations significantly predicted the own-age bias in face recognition memory (Table 2).

DISCUSSION

The present study is largely in line with previous findings of an own-age bias in old/new face recognition memory[3]

---

3 Whereas young adults were better at remembering own-age than other-age faces, this effect was only marginally significant in older adults. This is consistent with several studies suggesting a more reliable own-age bias in old/new face recognition in younger than older adults (Bartlett & Leslie, 1986; Fulton & Bartlett, 1991; but see Anastasi & Rhodes, 2006; Ebner, Riediger, & Lindenberger, 2009). It is possible that the slightly greater exposure of older adults to younger individuals as compared to younger adults to older individuals as self-reported by participants (see also Ebner & Johnson, 2009) makes the own-age bias less prominent in older adults. In addition, or alternatively, in the present study the age range of older participants (age range: 63–92 years) was much larger than that of younger participants (age range: 18–30 years). This greater age heterogeneity in older participants and the fact

(see Harrison & Hole, 2009). Furthermore, it provides evidence of an own-age bias in visual inspection of younger and older faces (see also Ebner, He, & Johnson, in press), and in the self-reported amount of exposure to younger and older persons in everyday life in younger and older adults. Most importantly, it shows that own-age biases in visual inspection and in self-reported amount of exposure, but neither explicit age stereotypes nor implicit age associations, constitute independent predictors of the own-age bias in face recognition memory. In addition, looking at upper half of older faces was beneficial for old/new face recognition memory in older, but not younger, adults. Below we discuss possible interpretations of these findings.

GREATER PERSONAL AND SOCIAL RELEVANCE OF OWN-AGE THAN OTHER-AGE FACES

It seems likely that greater personal and social relevance for own-age than other-age faces plays an important role in generating the own-age bias in attention and memory observed in the present study (see also Harrison & Hole, 2009). The self-reference effect (Rogers, Kuiper, & Kirker, 1977) suggests that information related to the self is encoded more elaborately and retrieved more accurately than non–self-referential information (Symons & Johnson, 1997). Participants in the present study may have used more self-referential encoding for own-age than other-age faces, as own-age persons are more likely to be similar to the self and to be personally relevant as potential social partners. This greater personal and social relevance may affect individuals' interest in, and their motivation to, carefully scan own-age as compared to other-age faces as reflected in longer overall gaze time and consequently better recognition memory.

---

that some of the presented older (age range: 69–80 years) but not younger (age range: 18–31 years) faces were not overlapping with the age range of the older participants may have contributed to a less pronounced/homogenous own-age bias in this group.

TABLE 2. Results of Multiple Linear Regression Analysis: Predictors of Old/New Face Recognition Memory (Younger Faces/Targets Minus Older Faces/Targets)

Variables	B	SE B	β
Step 1			
Overall Gaze Time (YF - OF)	3.67	1.26	.40★
Step 2			
Overall Gaze Time (YF - OF)	3.46	1.21	.38★
Self-Reported Amount of Exposure (YT - OT)	0.11	0.05	.30★
Step 3			
Overall Gaze Time (YF - OF)	3.40	1.23	.37★
Self-Reported Amount of Exposure (YT - OT)	0.09	0.05	.25+
Explicit Age Stereotypes (YT - OT)	0.02	0.11	.02
Implicit Age Associations	-0.36	0.28	-.17

Note. $R^2 = .28$, and $\Delta R^2_{Step1} = .16$, $\Delta R^2_{Step2} = .09$, $\Delta R^2_{Step3} = .03$; YF = Younger faces, OF = Older faces; YT = Younger Targets, OT = Older Targets. ★$p < .05$, +$p < .10$.

MORE ACCESSIBLE AND ELABORATED SCHEMAS FOR OWN-AGE THAN OTHER-AGE FACES

Both younger and older adults reported more everyday contact with own-age than other-age persons (see also Ebner & Johnson, 2009). This is likely to result in more accessible and elaborated schemas—general knowledge structures or set of beliefs that guide perception, organize information, and reconstruct memory (Bartlett, 1932; Bransford & Johnson, 1973)—for own-age than other-age faces. This interpretation is in line with *Face Space Theory* (Valentine, 1991) suggesting that representations of social in-group (e.g., own-age or own-race) faces are stored along dimensions optimized for individuation of those faces. In contrast, representations of social out-group (e.g., other-age) faces, according to this theory, are stored closer to each other and thus are more difficult to differentiate from one another.

EXPLICIT AND IMPLICIT MEASURES OF POSITIVE/NEGATIVE AGE ASSOCIATIONS

In line with the literature on the negative aging stereotype (Gluth et al., 2010; Hummert et al., 2002; Kite et al., 2005), both younger and older participants showed more positive explicit stereotypes and implicit associations for younger than older persons. Furthermore, in line with indications

of no direct influence of racial attitudes and preferences on the own-race bias in face recognition memory (Meissner & Brigham, 2001), neither explicit age stereotypes nor implicit age associations were related to overall looking time, or predicted the own-age bias in face recognition memory. This finding is particularly intriguing, in that it suggests that personal and social relevance and appropriate schemas based on experience, rather than age-related stereotypes, affect how younger and older adults visually inspect and later remember faces of their own as opposed to another age group. If so, there are important practical implications for face recognition contexts, such as eye-witness testimony, or screening for individuals at airports. Stereotypes may affect accuracy at face recognition less than perceived social relevance and available schemas for face processing.

IN-GROUP/OUT-GROUP DIFFERENTIATION

The present findings for age of face are similar to those obtained in studies on race of face. There is an "own-race bias" (Meissner & Brigham, 2001) reflected in more fixations on own-race than other-race faces with differences in visual scan patterns predicting better recognition of own-race than other-race faces (Goldinger, He, & Papesh, 2009). These similarities in the pattern of results pertaining to age and race of faces suggest general in-group/out-group processing differences at encoding and/or retrieval of faces (Ebner, He, Fichtenholtz, McCarthy, & Johnson, 2010; Symons & Johnson, 1997).

WHAT PREDICTS THE OWN-AGE BIAS IN FACE RECOGNITION MEMORY?

To conclude, during passive free viewing, younger and older adults tended to spend more time looking at own-age than other-age faces, which is possibly related to greater self-relevance of, and social motivation for, faces of their own age group. Furthermore, both age groups reported more frequent exposure to own-age than other-age persons in their daily routines, which likely leads to a more available repertoire of exemplars/associations ("that person looks like Joe") or better schemas for configural encoding of features of own-age individuals. Importantly, both these effects (longer looking time and greater self-reported amount of exposure for own-age faces), but not age-related attitudes and associations, made unique contributions to explaining better recognition memory for own-age than other-age faces.

REFERENCES

ANASTASI, J. S., & RHODES, M. G. (2005). AN OWN-AGE BIAS IN FACE RECOGNITION FOR CHILDREN AND OLDER ADULTS. *PSYCHONOMIC BULLETIN & REVIEW, 12*(6), 1043-1047.

ANASTASI, J. S., & RHODES, M. G. (2006). EVIDENCE FOR AN OWN-AGE BIAS IN FACE RECOGNITION. *NORTH AMERICAN JOURNAL OF PSYCHOLOGY, 8*, 237-253.

ARDITI, A. (2005). IMPROVING THE DESIGN OF THE LETTER CONTRAST SENSITIVITY TEST. *INVESTIGATIVE OPHTHALMOLOGY AND VISUAL SCIENCE, 46*, 2225-2229.

BACKMAN, L. (1991). RECOGNITION MEMORY ACROSS THE ADULT LIFE SPAN: THE ROLE OF PRIOR KNOWLEDGE. *MEMORY & COGNITION, 19*, 63-71.

BARTLETT, F. C. (1932). *REMEMBERING: A STUDY IN EXPERIMENTAL AND SOCIAL PSYCHOLOGY.* CAMBRIDGE, UK: CAMBRIDGE UNIVERSITY PRESS.

BARTLETT, J. C., & LESLIE, J. E. (1986). AGING AND MEMORY FOR FACES VERSUS SINGLE VIEWS OF FACES. *MEMORY & COGNITION, 14*, 371-381.

BERNSTEIN, M. J., YOUNG, S. G., & HUGENBERG, K. (2007). THE CROSS CATEGORY EFFECT: MERE SOCIAL CATEGORIZATION IS SUFFICIENT TO ELICIT AN OWN-GROUP BIAS IN FACE RECOGNITION. *PSYCHOLOGICAL SCIENCE, 18*, 706-712.

BRANSFORD, J. D., & JOHNSON M. K. (1973). CONSIDERATION OF SOME PROBLEMS OF COMPREHENSION. IN W. G. CHASE (ED.), *VISUAL INFORMATION PROCESSING.* NEW YORK: ACADEMIC PRESS.

BREWER, M. B. (1979). IN-GROUP BIAS IN THE MINIMAL INTERGROUP SITUATION: A COGNITIVE- MOTIVATIONAL ANALYSIS. *PSYCHOLOGICAL BULLETIN, 86*, 307-324.

BUSWELL, G. T. (1935). *HOW PEOPLE LOOK AT PICTURES.* CHICAGO: UNIVERSITY OF CHICAGO PRESS.

EBNER, N. C. (2008). AGE OF FACE MATTERS: AGE- GROUP DIFFERENCES IN RATINGS OF YOUNG AND OLD FACES. *BEHAVIOR RESEARCH METHODS, 40*, 130-136.

EBNER, N. C., HE, Y., FICHTENHOLTZ, H. M., MCCARTHY, G., & JOHNSON, M. K. (IN PRESS). ELECTROPHYSIOLOGICAL CORRELATES OF PROCESSING FACES OF YOUNGER AND OLDER INDIVIDUALS. *SOCIAL COGNITIVE AND AFFECTIVE NEUROSCIENCE.*

EBNER, N. C., HE, Y., & JOHNSON, M. K. (IN PRESS). AGE AND EMOTION AFFECT HOW WE LOOK AT A FACE: VISUAL SCAN PATTERNS DIFFER FOR OWN-AGE VERSUS OTHER-AGE EMOTIONAL FACES. *COGNITION AND EMOTION.*

EBNER, N. C., & JOHNSON, M. K. (2010). AGE- GROUP DIFFERENCES IN INTERFERENCE FROM YOUNG AND OLDER EMOTIONAL FACES. *COGNITION AND EMOTION, 24*(7), 1095-1116.

EBNER, N. C., & JOHNSON, M. K. (2009). YOUNG AND OLDER EMOTIONAL FACES: ARE THERE AGE-GROUP DIFFERENCES IN EXPRESSION IDENTIFICATION AND MEMORY? *EMOTION, 9*, 329-339.

EBNER, N. C., RIEDIGER, M., & LINDENBERGER, U. (2010). FACES—A DATABASE OF FACIAL EXPRESSIONS IN YOUNG, MIDDLE-AGED, AND OLDER WOMEN AND MEN: DEVELOPMENT AND VALIDATION. *BEHAVIORAL RESEARCH METHODS, 42*, 351-362.

EBNER, N. C., RIEDIGER, M., & LINDENBERGER, U. (2009). SCHEMA RELIANCE FOR DEVELOPMENTAL GOALS INCREASES FROM EARLY TO LATE ADULTHOOD: IMPROVEMENT FOR THE YOUNG, LOSS PREVENTION FOR THE OLD. *PSYCHOLOGY AND AGING, 24*, 310-323.

FIRESTONE, A., TURK-BROWNE, N., & RYAN, J. (2007). AGE-RELATED DEFICITS IN FACE RECOGNITION ARE RELATED TO UNDERLYING CHANGES IN SCANNING BEHAVIOR. *AGING, NEUROPSYCHOLOGY, AND COGNITION, 14, 594-607.*

Fulton, A., & Bartlett, J. C. (1991). Young and old faces in young and old heads: The factor of age in face recognition. *Psychology and Aging*, 6, 623-630.

Gluth, S., Ebner, N. C., & Schmiedek, F. (2010). Attitudes toward younger and older adults: The German Aging Semantic Differential. *International Journal of Behavioral Development*, 34, 147-158.

Goldinger, S. D., He, Y., & Papesh, M. H. (2009). Deficits in cross-race face learning: Insights from eye movements and pupillometry. *Journal of Experimental Psychology: Learning, Memory, and Cognition*, 35, 1105-1122.

Green, D., & Swets, J. (1966). *Signal detection theory and psychophysics*. New York: Wiley.

Greenwald, A. G., Nosek, B. A., & Banaji, M. R. (2003). Understanding and using the Implicit Association Test: I. An improved scoring algorithm. *Journal of Personality and Social Psychology*, 85, 197-216.

Harrison, V., & Hole, G. J. (2009). Evidence for a contact-based explanation of the own-age bias in face recognition. *Psychonomic Bulletin & Review*, 16, 264-269.

Henderson, J.M., & Williams, C. C., & Falk, R. J. (2005). Eye movements are functional during face learning. *Memory & Cognition*, 33, 98-106.

Hummert, M. L., Garstka, T. A., O'Brien, L. T., Greenwald, A. G., & Mellott, D. S. (2002). Using the implicit association test to measure age differences in implicit social cognitions. *Psychology and Aging*, 17, 482-495.

Isaacowitz, D. M., Wadlinger, H. A., Goren, D., & Wilson, H. R. (2006). Is there an age-related positivity effect in visual attention? A comparison of two methodologies. *Emotion*, 6, 511-516.

Kite, M. E., Stockdale, G. D., Whitley, B. E., & Johnson, B. T. (2005). Attitudes toward younger and older adults: An updated meta-analytic review. *Journal of Social Issues*, 61, 241-266.

Knight, M., Seymour, T. L., Gaunt, J. T., Baker, C., Nesmith, K., & Mather, M. (2007). Aging and goal-directed emotional attention: Distraction reverses emotional biases. *Emotion*, 7, 705-714.

Knox, V. J., Gekoski, W. L., & Kelly, L. E. (1995). The Age Group Evaluation and Description (AGED) Inventory: A new instrument for assessing stereotypes of and attitudes toward age groups. *International Journal of Aging and Human Development*, 40, 31-55.

Lamont, A. C., Stewart-Williams, S., & Podd, J. (2005). Face recognition and aging: Effects of target age and memory load. *Memory and Cognition*, 33, 1017-1024.

Meissner, C. A., & Brigham, J. C. (2001). Thirty years of investigating the own-race bias in memory for faces: A meta-analytic review. *Psychology, Public Policy, & Law*, 7, 3-35.

Murphy, N. A., & Isaacowitz, D. M. (2010). Age effects and gaze patterns in recognizing emotional expressions: An in-depth look at gaze measures and covariates. *Cognition & Emotion*, 24, 436-452.

Rogers, T. B., Kuiper, N. A., & Kirker, W. S. (1977). Self-reference and the encoding of personal information. *Journal of Personality and Social Psychology*, 35, 677-688.

Schneider, W., Eschman A., & Zuccolotto, A. (2002). *E-Prime reference guide*. Psychology Software Tools Inc, Pittsburgh, PA.

Sullivan S., Ruffman T., & Hutton S. (2007). Age differences in emotion recognition skills and the visual scanning of emotion faces. *Journal of Gerontology: Psychological Sciences*, 62B, P53-P60.

Symons, C. S., & Johnson, B. T. (1997). The self-reference effect in memory: A meta-analysis, *Psychological Bulletin*, 121, 371-394.

Valentine. T. (1991). A unified account of the effects of distinctiveness, inversion, and race in face recognition. *Quarterly Journal of Experimental Psychology*, 43A, 161-204.

Wechsler, D. (1981). *Manual for the Wechsler Adult Intelligence Scale-Revised (WAIS-R)*. New York: Psychological Corporation.

Wong, B., Cronin-Golomb, A., & Neargarder, S. A. (2005). Patterns of visual scanning as predictors of emotion identification in normal aging. *Neuropsychology*, 19, 739-749.

Examining Differences in the Levels of False Memories in Children and Adults Using Child-Normed Lists

BY JEFFREY S. ANASTASI AND MATTHEW G. RHODES

Several previous studies have demonstrated that children, when compared with adults, exhibit both lower levels of veridical memory and fewer intrusions when given semantically associated lists. However, researchers have drawn these conclusions using semantically associated word lists that were normed with adults, which may not lead to the same level of activation or gist generation in children. In the current study, the authors used similar associative word lists normed with children and then evaluated the memory of children and adults using these newly normed lists as well as the typical adult-normed lists. Results indicate that children showed lower true and false memories with both the child-normed and adult-normed lists. Thus, these data suggest that the negative relationship between age and false memories in the Deese-Roediger-McDermott (DRM; J. Deese, 1959; H. L. Roediger & K. B. McDermott, 1995) paradigm is not an artifact of the age group used to construct the lists.

Well over the past decade of memory research has seen a substantial increase in work aimed at documenting errors in memory accuracy (for reviews, see Jacoby & Rhodes, 2006; Koriat, Goldsmith, & Pansky, 2000; Roediger, 1996). A great deal of this research has utilized the Deese-Roediger-McDermott (DRM; Deese, 1959; Roediger & McDermott, 1995) paradigm as a method for reliably eliciting memory errors. In the DRM paradigm, participants are presented with a list of words (e.g., *door, glass, pane, shade, ledge, glass, house*) that converge on a central theme word (e.g., *window*), the critical lure, that is not presented. The consistent finding across a number of studies (e.g., Anastasi, Rhodes, & Burns, 2000; Rhodes & Anastasi, 2000; Roediger & McDermott, 1995) is that participants frequently recognize or recall the critical lure, often at levels comparable with presented list items. However, the developmental literature has revealed a significant exception to this pattern: Children, particularly young children, are generally less susceptible to the DRM illusion than adults (e.g., Brainerd, Forrest, Karibian, & Reyna, 2006; Brainerd & Reyna, 1996; Brainerd, Reyna, & Forrest, 2002; Dewhurst & Robinson, 2004; Holliday & Weekes, 2006; Howe, 2005; but see Ghetti, Qin, & Goodman, 2002). That is, memory errors in the DRM paradigm appear to be negatively correlated with age, such that children are less likely to recall or recognize critical lures than are adults or adolescents.

These conclusions have primarily been drawn by researchers using lists developed with adults (Roediger

Jeffrey S. Anastasi and Matthew G. Rhodes, "Examining Differences in the Levels of False Memories in Children and Adults Using Child-Normed Lists," *Developmental Psychology*, vol. 44, no. 3, pp. 889-894. Copyright © 2008 by American Psychological Association. Reprinted with permission.

& McDermott, 1995; Stadler, Roediger, & McDermott, 1999), leaving open the possibility that the negative relationship between age and the probability of errors in the DRM paradigm is due to the use of adult-normed lists. That is, younger children may be more likely to exhibit false memories if they were exposed to lists developed with children. Several prior studies have demonstrated changes in children's memory performance when child-appropriate materials are employed. For example, Lindberg (1980) examined adults' and third graders' recall of two types of categorized lists. One list was developed on the basis of interviews with third graders and included categories such as their favorite books and movies, whereas another list was developed with adult category norms. Whereas adults recalled more items from the adult-normed lists than did children, the opposite pattern was apparent for third-grade lists, as children's recall was superior to that of adults. Bjorklund and Thompson (1983) reported similar findings. They observed that children recalled more exemplars from categorized lists that had been normed with children than a similar list that had been normed with adults, leading them to conclude that "...the degree of knowledge children possess with respect to the to-be-remembered items can have important consequences for performance on memory tasks" (p. 341). Other work demonstrating enhancements in memory performance when to-be-remembered items are consistent with children's expertise further support this claim (e.g., Chi, 1978; Schneider & Bjorklund, 1992).

We know of only two studies in which researchers have examined this issue with respect to the DRM paradigm by using age-appropriate lists. Metzger et al. (2008) had third graders and college students engage in a free association task to several words (e.g., *sleep, foot*). The most common associates reported by third graders were then used as stimuli in a subsequent experiment that tested memory across a range of age groups (second graders, third graders, fifth graders, eighth graders, and college students). Results showed that the youngest age group, second graders, was less likely to recall or recognize the critical lure than older age groups, replicating prior findings (e.g., Brainerd et al., 2002, 2006; Dewhurst & Robinson, 2004). However, participants were only tested on lists created on the basis of child norms,[1] making it impossible to directly compare performance on child-and adult-normed lists.

In a second study, Carneiro, Albuquerque, Fernandez, and Esteves (2007; Experiment 2) evaluated preschoolers and preadolescents using Portuguese free association norms from these age groups. They found that preschoolers were more likely to recall critical lures with preschool-normed lists, whereas preadolescents recalled more critical lures with preadolescent-normed lists. However, it is unclear whether this pattern of findings will extend to the more typical DRM lists used in most investigations of false memories and whether this pattern will likewise extend to comparisons between adults and children.

In the current study, we attempted a more stringent test of developmental increases in false memory production by using age-appropriate, DRM-type lists. Specifically, we tested children and adults using lists normed with adult populations and lists that were normed with children. A repeated measures design was used, with all participants exposed to both child-and adult-normed lists, permitting us to make direct comparisons of performance. If the negative relationship between age and the probability of errors in the DRM paradigm in past studies is due to the use of adult-normed lists, then employing lists developed with children should increase false memories in children, thus minimizing age differences in false memories between children and adults. However, if false memories do not differ between the adult-and child-normed DRM lists, this would provide strong support for the generality of the negative relation between age and false memories in the DRM paradigm. We examine the implications of our findings for developmental theories of false memories in the Discussion section.

METHOD

Participants

Sixty-two individuals participated in the current study, including 30 children between the ages of 5 and 8 years (mean age = 6.6 years, SD = 0.7) and 32 young adults (mean age = 24.7 years, SD = 5.8) enrolled at Arizona State University West. Children were tested at local elementary schools and after-school programs from a predominately middle-class suburban setting in the Phoenix (Arizona) area and received small toys or stickers for their participation. Both the children (53% male) and young adults (46% male) had a nearly equal mix of male and female participants. All participants reported being native English speakers.

Materials and Procedure

The lists used in the current study were 12 lists taken from Roediger and McDermott (1995) that were developed and normed with adult participants, and 12 additional lists that were developed and normed by Anastasi, Lewis, and Quinlan (2007) with children using the same critical lures used by Roediger and McDermott. Specifically, Anastasi et al. gave 5- to 8-year-old children (mean age = 6.4 years, SD = 1.1) each of the 24 critical lures and asked them to say aloud the first three words that came to mind. Similar to the adult DRM lists, the 15 most common associates generated made up the child-normed lists (see the Appendix). In the current study, we used the Roediger-McDermott and Anastasi-Lewis-Quinlan lists that were based on the *Window, Smell, Rough, Sleep, Music, River, Rubber, City, Fruit, Car, Lion,* and *King* critical lures. Overall, 26% of the words on the child-normed lists are also included on the adult-normed lists.

Each participant was tested individually and received a total of 12 lists. Half of the participants were given 6 adult-normed lists followed by 6 child-normed lists, whereas the remaining participants received the opposite order. Participants were instructed to pay attention to each of the list items as they were read aloud at approximately a 2-s rate. Following each list, participants were told to say aloud as many words from the list as they could remember.[2] Each of the items recalled was checked off on a pre-prepared testing sheet, whereas any extralist items were written down. After participants indicated that they could not remember any additional list items, they were given the next list in the same manner. This process was continued for each of the 6 initial lists. Immediately after the sixth recall test, participants were given a 36-item yes/no recognition test (18 list items, 6 critical lures, and 12 nonlist items) for all of the previous 6 lists. Participants were instructed to indicate whether they remembered each of the items said aloud by the experimenter. Participants' answers were recorded on a pre-prepared testing sheet. After a short break, participants were given the remaining 6 lists and were tested in an identical manner.

RESULTS
Recall Data

The proportion of list items and critical lures recalled by children and adults was analyzed with a 2 (Age: children, adults) × 2 (List Norm: child-normed, adult-normed) × 2 (Item Type: list, critical lure) mixed-factor analysis of variance. (The alpha level for all statistical tests was set to .05.) Results show that adults (M = 0.38) recalled reliably more items than children (M = 0.24), $F(1, 62) = 39.63$, $\eta_p^2 = .35$. Participants also exhibited higher levels of recall for adult- (M = 0.33) compared with child-normed (M = 0.29) lists, $F(1, 62) = 8.35$, $\eta_p^2 = .12$. Furthermore, list items (M = 0.39) were recalled more frequently than critical lures (M = 0.23), $F(1, 62) = 67.52$, $\eta_p^2 = .52$. An Age × Item Type interaction, $F(1, 62) = 4.06$, $\eta_p^2 = .06$, was also present. In particular, adults (M = 0.28) recalled reliably more critical lures than children (M = 0.18), $F(1, 62) = 7.49$, $\eta_p^2 = .11$. Furthermore, adults (M = 0.48) recalled substantially more list items than children (M = 0.30), $F(1, 62) = 93.52$, $\eta_p^2 = .60$. Finally, List Norm interacted with Item Type, $F(1, 62) = 21.57$, $\eta_p^2 = .26$. Specifically, the difference in recall of list items and critical lures was greater for the child-normed lists, $F(1, 62) = 100.10$, $\eta_p^2 = .62$, than for the adult-normed lists, $F(1, 62) = 13.15$, $\eta_p^2 = .18$. No other interactions were reliable ($ps > .50$).

Planned comparisons showed that adults recalled the same proportion of list items from the child- and adult-normed lists, $F(1, 33) = 1.27$, $p = .27$, $\eta_p^2 = .04$, but fewer critical lures from the child- than adult-normed lists, $F(1, 33) = 6.64$, $\eta_p^2 = .17$. However, children recalled more list items from the child- than adult-normed lists, $F(1, 29) = 19.62$, $\eta_p^2 = .40$, but, like adults, they recalled more critical lures from the adult- than child-normed lists, $F(1, 29) = 10.00$, $\eta_p^2 = .26$. These data indicate that although the child-normed lists increased children's veridical recall, they did not result in elevated levels of false recall.

Recognition Data

We calculated A' scores (see Snodgrass & Corwin, 1988) for each participant, and we analyzed them using the same factors described for the analysis of the recall data.[3] Results show that adults' discriminability (M = 0.88) exceeded that of children (M = 0.80), $F(1, 62) = 17.20$, $\eta_p^2 = .22$.

Discriminability was reliably better for list items (M = 0.86) than for critical lures (M = 0.82), $F(1, 62) = 25.80$, $\eta_p^2 = .29$, but it did not differ between adult-normed (M = 0.85) and child-normed (M = 0.83) lists, $F(1, 62) = 2.85$, $p = .10$, $\eta_p^2 = .04$. However, a significant List Norm × Item Type interaction was present, $F(1, 62) = 7.56$, $\eta_p^2 = .11$. In particular, whereas list item discriminability was virtually identical for child-and adult-normed lists (M = 0.86), $F < 1$, critical lure recognition was significantly greater for adult-normed (M = 0.84) compared with child-normed (M = 0.79) lists, $F(1, 62) = 6.29$, $\eta_p^2 = .09$.

Planned comparisons showed that adults' list item recognition did not differ between adult-normed and child-normed lists, $F(1, 33) = 2.72$, $p = .11$, $\eta_p^2 = .08$. However, adults' critical lure recognition was greater for adult-normed than child-normed lists, $F(1, 33) = 4.38$, $\eta_p^2 = .12$. Neither children's list item recognition, $F(1, 29) = 1.44$, $p = .24$, $\eta_p^2 = .05$, nor their critical lure recognition, $F(1, 33) = 2.15$, $p = .15$, $\eta_p^2 = .07$, differed between adult-normed and child-normed lists. Thus, only adults' false recognition was sensitive to the type of list studied.

Child Subgroup Analyses

The children tested in the current study came from a broader age range (5- to 8-year-olds) than that typically used in investigations of developmental trends in false memories. To further examine possible differences between children of different ages, we divided children into two age groups (5- to 6-year-olds, $n = 14$; and 7- to 8-year-olds, $n = 16$) and examined recall and recognition performance. In the interest of brevity, we report only those results that pertain to Child Age Group.[4] First, recall data for children were analyzed in a 2 (List Norm: child-normed, adult-normed) × 2 (Item Type: list, critical lure) × 2 (Child Age Group: 5–6, 7–8) mixed-factor analysis of variance. Results show that Child Age Group did not interact with any variables ($ps > .20$). An analysis that used the same factors for A' scores revealed a marginally reliable Child Age Group × Item Type interaction, $F(1, 28) = 3.76$, $p = .06$, $\eta_p^2 = .12$. In particular, for the 5- to 6-year-olds, list item recognition (M = 0.82) exceeded critical lure recognition (M = 0.75), $F(1, 13) = 6.17$, $\eta_p^2 = .32$. In contrast, for 7- to 8-year-olds, list item recognition (M = 0.82) did not differ reliably from critical

lure recognition (M = 0.80), $F(1, 15) = 1.46$, $p = .25$, $\eta_p^2 = .25$. Thus, whereas 5- to 6-year-olds recognized the same proportion of list items as 7- to 8-year-olds, they exhibited lower levels of false recognition.

Table 1
Proportion of List Items and Critical Lures Recalled

Participant	Adult-normed lists		Child-normed lists	
age	List items	Critical lures	List items	Critical lures
Children	.27 (.08)	.23 (.20)	.32 (.08)	.12 (.14)
Adults	.48 (.09)	.33 (.21)	.49 (.08)	.23 (.20)

Note. Standard deviations are in parentheses. The average number of nonlist intrusions recalled by children was .36 and .31 for each adult- normed and child-normed list, respectively. Adults recalled an average number of .36 and .34 nonlist intrusions for each adult-normed and child- normed list, respectively.

Table 2
Proportion of List Items and Critical Lures Recognized

Participant	Adult-normed lists		Child-normed lists	
age	List items	Critical lures	List items	Critical lures
Children	.57 (.21)	.54 (.27)	.63 (.19)	.46 (.25)
Adults	.82 (.11)	.74 (.25)	.79 (.14)	.63 (.22)

Note. Standard deviations are in parentheses. The proportion of nonlist items children recognized was .14 and .18 for the adult-normed and child-normed lists, respectively. Adults recognized .16 and .22 nonlist items for the adult- normed and child-normed lists, respectively.

Table 3
A' Values for List Items and Critical Lures for Adult- and Child-Normed Lists

Participant	Adult-normed lists		Child-normed lists	
age	List items	Critical lures	List items	Critical lures
Children	.81 (.13)	.80 (.12)	.83 (.11)	.76 (.13)
Adults	.91 (.05)	.88 (.08)	.89 (.06)	.83 (.11)

Note. Standard deviations are in parentheses.

DISCUSSION

Children in the current study exhibited lower levels of false memories than adults on both recall and recognition measures, consistent with a number of other studies (e.g., Brainerd et al., 2002, 2006; Brainerd & Reyna, 1996; Dewhurst & Robinson, 2004; Holliday & Weekes, 2006; Howe, 2005). Of greater importance, the negative relation between age and false memories was evident for both adult-normed and child-normed lists. Thus, the finding that children are less likely than adults to falsely recall or recognize the critical lure in the DRM paradigm is not an artifact of the specific type of lists used in previous studies and generalizes to lists that were developed with children. However, it should be noted that these data are inconsistent with Carneiro et al. (2007), who reported that false recall was dependent on the specific list norms used. It is unclear whether this difference is due to the use of different lists, different languages, different age groups, or some other potential factor. Thus, more research investigating these developmental trends in false memories is warranted.

How do the current findings fit within the primary theories—fuzzy-trace theory (Brainerd & Reyna, 1996, 1998; Reyna & Brainerd, 1995) and activation-monitoring theory (AMT; Gallo, Roediger, & McDermott, 2001; McDermott & Watson, 2001; Roediger & McDermott, 1995; Roediger, Watson, McDermott, & Gallo, 2001)—used to explain false memories? On the surface, both may provide equally plausible explanations of the current findings. Fuzzy trace theory suggests that encoding results in a verbatim and gist representation of the original experience. Verbatim representations refer to the specific details of an experience, whereas gist representations correspond to the general content or meaning of an experience. In the context of the DRM paradigm, verbatim representations would comprise the actual items presented (e.g., *sill, pane, door*), whereas a gist representation would comprise the central theme word that is not presented (e.g., *window*). Thus, memory for list items reflects the strength of the verbatim (and potentially gist) representation, whereas false memories for the critical lure are supported by a gist representation. Accordingly, developmental increases in false memories occur because the ability to extract the gist increases with age (Brainerd & Reyna, 1996, 1998). Consistent with this, several studies have reported that young children exhibit less category clustering in free recall than do older children and adults (e.g., Bjorklund & Hock, 1982; Bjorklund & Jacobs, 1985), likely because they are less sensitive to the general thematic content of lists. By extension, the lower levels of false memories exhibited by children in the current study for both types of lists may have occurred because the young children were less likely to extract the gist of the presented lists. Thus, fuzzy-trace theory provides a good explanation for lower levels of false memory production for children compared with adults.

AMT accounts for false memories as the product of implicit activation of related associates during the list presentation (cf. Underwood, 1965). In particular, viewing a list of associates of a central theme word increases the probability of activating that central theme word (e.g., *window*) as each list item is presented. This frequent activation makes it highly likely that the central theme will be misattributed to the presented study list. Later instantiations of AMT proposed that false memories were the product of a tradeoff between such activation and the efficiency with which the rememberer monitors items during retrieval (Gallo et al., 2001; McDermott & Watson, 2001; Roediger et al., 2001), with proficient monitoring reducing the probability of exhibiting false memories. Thus, AMT suggests that false memories result from mistakenly reporting or endorsing a critical lure that has been activated during study or retrieval and when participants are unable to counter activation of the critical lure with proficient monitoring.

On the basis of AMT, one might presume there would be developmental decreases in false memories if they were the product of monitoring deficiencies, rather than the developmental increases in false memories that are observed. However, with the addition of one assumption that is not explicitly stated by the AMT theory, AMT also provides a relatively simple explanation of this counterintuitive finding (Carneiro et al., 2007). Several researchers have posited that children are less likely to activate critical lures than adults because of a potentially less developed associative network than adults (see Bjorklund, 1987; Carneiro et al., 2007; Howe, 2006). This activation mechanism alone would predict fewer false memories in children compared with adults. However, monitoring should lead to an age-related decline in false memories because of the fact that children are less adept at source monitoring than adults (Foley & Johnson, 1985; Foley, Johnson, & Raye, 1983).

Thus, source monitoring deficiencies in children may be masked by having to judge less frequently whether an activated critical lure was presented during study. One potential weakness of AMT is the vagueness of these mechanisms. For example, it is unclear whether activation or monitoring is the more important mechanism at any given time, what the contribution of each would be, and when the balance between the two would change.

Nevertheless, an important feature of AMT is that it suggests that false memories result from associative activation and not the development of a gist representation. One form of evidence for this are studies demonstrating that the best predictor of false recall is the probability that a list item activates the critical lure (i.e., backward associative strength; BAS). For example, across 55 lists examined by Roediger et al. (2001), BAS was the single best predictor of false recall (r = .73) and, to a lesser extent, false recognition (r = .43). In the current study, BAS was likewise a strong predictor of false recall for both adults (r = .50) and children (r = .75) for adult-normed lists. BAS also predicted children's false recognition (r = .48) with adult-normed lists but was not a strong predictor of adult false recognition (r = −.07). However, comparable child norms providing BAS data are not currently available, making it impossible to evaluate how well BAS predicts performance on child-normed lists.[5] This is a critical issue, as children's associative networks are not identical to those of adults (cf. Howe, 2006). For example, Bjorklund (1987) noted that the strength and number of links to particular items increase with age, likely as the product of greater exposure to particular items. Thus, BAS measures derived from adults may not adequately reflect the associative networks of younger children.

Given that BAS was a strong predictor of false memories, the evidence would seem to favor such an interpretation of the results of the current study. However, associative strength may be confounded with thematic activation, making it difficult to tease the two apart. For example, the sleep list produces false recall at a very high level (M = 0.61) and likewise has a high mean BAS value (M = 0.43). However, this list would also be expected to result in high levels of false recall on the basis of strong levels of thematic activation resulting from its constituent list items (e.g., bed, rest, awake, tired, dream, etc.). Hutchison and Balota (2005) have reported a potential solution to this problem.

Specifically, participants in several experiments studied lists that all converged on a single meaning, akin to the typical DRM lists used, and they also studied lists that converged on two different meanings (homographie lists). For example, the homographic lists for the critical lure fall consisted of items related to the "stumble" meaning (stumble, slip, trip, etc.) and items related to the "autumn" meaning (autumn, season, spring, etc.). If false memories are the result of thematic activation, one would expect false memories to be more prevalent for lists that converge on a single meaning (DRM lists) than lists that converge on multiple meanings (homographic lists). However, if false memories are the result of associative activation, then the number of associates and not singularity of meaning should be the crucial factor. Results are consistent with the latter prediction. In particular, false recall and recognition did not differ between DRM and homographic lists, whereas veridical recall was sensitive to thematic organization, with recall superior for lists that converged on a single meaning (see Howe, 2006, for a similar pattern with children). Thus, the evidence seems to suggest that associative activation is the primary causal factor in false memories. By this account, the lower probability of exhibiting false memories for child-normed lists in the current study may be the product of weaker associative relations between the critical lure and list items for such lists.

In summary, the current study, like many previous studies, has demonstrated that children display fewer false memories in the DRM paradigm compared with adults. This lower level of false memories was found even when we used word lists developed and normed with other similarly aged children. Thus, the typical finding of lower rates of false memories in children does not appear to be a product of the type of list used to evaluate their memory in the DRM paradigm.

REFERENCES

Anastasi, J. S., Lewis, S., & Quinlan, F. (2007). *Normative data for semantically associated word lists that create false memories in children.* Unpublished manuscript.

Anastasi, J. S., Rhodes, M. G., & Burns, M. C. (2000). Distinguishing between memory illusions and actual memories utilizing phenomenological measurements and explicit warnings. *American Journal of Psychology, 113,* 1–26.

Bjorklund, D. F. (1987). How age changes in knowledge base contribute to the development of children's memory: An interpretive review. *Developmental Review, 7,* 93–130.

Bjorklund, D. F., & Hock, H. S. (1982). Age differences in the temporal locus of memory organization in children's recall. *Journal of Experimental Child Psychology, 32,* 347–362.

Bjorklund, D. F., & Jacobs, J. W. (1985). Associative and categorical processes in children's memory: The role of automaticity in the development of organization in free recall. *Journal of Experimental Child Psychology, 39,* 599–617.

Bjorklund, D. F., & Thompson, B. E. (1983). Category typicality effects in children's memory performance: Qualitative and quantitative differences in the processing of category information. *Journal of Experimental Child Psychology, 35,* 329–344.

Brainerd, C. J., Forrest, T. J., Karibian, D., & Reyna, V. F. (2006). Development of the false-memory illusion. *Developmental Psychology, 42,* 962–979.

Brainerd, C. J., & Reyna, V. F. (1996). Mere memory testing creates false memories in children. *Developmental Psychology, 32,* 467–476.

Brainerd, C. J., & Reyna, V. F. (1998). Fuzzy-trace theory and children's false memories. *Journal of Experimental Child Psychology, 71,* 81–129.

Brainerd, C. J., Reyna, V. F., & Forrest, T. J. (2002). Are young children susceptible to the false-memory illusion? *Child Development, 73,* 1363–1377.

Carneiro, P., Albuquerque, P., Fernandez, A., & Esteves, F. (2007). Analyzing false memories in children with associative lists specific for their age. *Child Development, 78,* 1171–1185.

Chi, M. T. H. (1978). Knowledge structures and memory development. In R. Siegler (Ed.), *Children's thinking: What develops?* (pp. 73–96). Hillsdale, NJ: Erlbaum.

Deese, J. (1959). On the prediction of occurrence of particular verbal intrusions in immediate recall. *Journal of Experimental Psychology, 58,* 17–22.

Dewhurst, S. A., & Robinson, C. A. (2004). False memories in children: Evidence for a shift from phonological to semantic associations. *Psychological Science, 15,* 782–786.

Foley, M. A., & Johnson, M. K. (1985). Confusions between memories for performed and imagined actions: A developmental comparison. *Child Development, 56,* 1145–1155.

Foley, M. A., Johnson, M. K., & Raye, C. L. (1983). Age-related changes in confusion between memories for thoughts and memories for speech. *Child Development, 54,* 51–60.

Gallo, D. A., Roediger, H. L., & McDermott, K. B. (2001). Associative false recognition occurs without strategic criterion shifts. *Psychonomic Bulletin and Review, 8,* 579–586.

Ghetti, S., Qin, J. J., & Goodman, G. S. (2002). False memories in children and adults: Age, distinctiveness, and subjective experience. *Developmental Psychology, 38,* 705–718.

Holliday, R. E., & Weekes, B. S. (2006). Dissociated developmental trajectories for semantic and phonological false memories. *Memory, 14,* 624–636.

Howe, M. L. (2005). Children (but not adults) can inhibit false memories. *Psychological Science, 16,* 927–931.

Howe, M. L. (2006). Developmentally invariant dissociations in children's true and false memories: Not all relatedness is created equal. *Child Development, 77,* 1112–1123.

Hutchison, K. A., & Balota, D. A. (2005). Decoupling semantic and associative information in false memories: Explorations with semantically ambiguous and unambiguous critical lures. *Journal of Memory and Language, 52,* 1–28.

Jacoby, L. L., & Rhodes, M. G. (2006). False remembering in the aged. *Current Directions in Psychological Science, 15,* 49-53.

Koriat, A., Goldsmith, M., & Pansky, A. (2000). Toward a psychology of memory accuracy. *Annual Review of Psychology, 51,* 481–537.

Lindberg, M. A. (1980). Is knowledge base development a necessary and sufficient condition for memory development? *Journal of Experimental Child Psychology, 30,* 401–410.

McDermott, K. B., & Watson, J. M. (2001). The rise and fall of false recall: The impact of presentation duration. *Journal of Memory and Language, 45,* 160–176.

Metzger, R. L., Warren, A. R., Shelton, J. T., Price, J. D., Reed, A. W., & Williams, D. (2008). Do children "DRM" like adults? False memory production in children. *Developmental Psychology, 44,* 169–181.

Nelson, D. L., McEvoy, C. L., & Schreiber, T. A. (1998). The University of South Florida word association,

RHYME, AND WORD FRAGMENT NORMS. RETRIEVED FROM
HTTP://W3.USF.EDU/FREEASSOCIATION/

REYNA, V. F., & BRAINERD, C. J. (1995). FUZZY-TRACE THEORY:
AN INTERIM SYNTHESIS. *LEARNING AND INDIVIDUAL DIFFER-
ENCES, 7,* 1–75.

RHODES, M. G., & ANASTASI, J. S. (2000). THE EFFECTS OF A
LEVELS-OF-PROCESSING MANIPULATION ON FALSE RECALL.
PSYCHONOMIC BULLETIN AND REVIEW, 7, 158–162.

ROEDIGER, H. L. (1996). MEMORY ILLUSIONS. *JOURNAL OF
MEMORY AND LANGUAGE, 35,* 76–100.

ROEDIGER, H. L., & MCDERMOTT, K. B. (1995). CREATING
FALSE MEMORIES: REMEMBERING WORDS NOT PRESENTED
IN LISTS. *JOURNAL OF EXPERIMENTAL PSYCHOLOGY: LEARNING,
MEMORY, AND COGNITION, 21,* 803–814.

ROEDIGER, H. L., WATSON, J. M., MCDERMOTT, K. B., & GAL-
LO, D. A. (2001). FACTORS THAT DETERMINE FALSE RECALL:
A MULTIPLE REGRESSION ANALYSIS. *PSYCHONOMIC BULLETIN
AND REVIEW, 8,* 385–407.

SCHNEIDER, W., & BJORKLUND, D. F. (1992). EXPERTISE, APTI-
TUDE, AND STRATEGIC REMEMBERING. *CHILD DEVELOPMENT,
63,* 461–473.

SNODGRASS, J. G., & CORWIN, J. (1988). PRAGMATICS OF MEA-
SURING RECOGNITION MEMORY: APPLICATION TO DEMENTIA
AND AMNESIA. *JOURNAL OF EXPERIMENTAL PSYCHOLOGY: GEN-
ERAL, 117,* 34–50.

STADLER, M. A., ROEDIGER, H. L., & MCDERMOTT, K. B.
(1999). NORMS FOR WORD LISTS THAT CREATE FALSE MEMO-
RIES. *MEMORY & COGNITION, 27,* 494–500.

UNDERWOOD, B. J. (1965). FALSE RECOGNITION PRODUCED BY
IMPLICIT VERBAL RESPONSES. *JOURNAL OF EXPERIMENTAL PSY-
CHOLOGY, 70,* 122–129.

NOTES

1. A group of college students also provided free association data. However, all lists were created in descending order of associative strength on the basis of third graders' norms.

2. Because many of the children were not adept at reading and writing, the list items and memory tests were administered orally to both children and adults to ensure that any differences between children and adults were not due to encoding and output methods.

3. The manner of calculation renders it such that list item performance is calculated with recognition of nonlist items as false alarms. Likewise, performance for the critical lure was assessed by first entering critical lure recognition as "hits" in the formula and recognition of nonlist items as "false alarms." Thus, high values of A' for critical lures are indicative of high levels of false memories for the critical lure.

4. The full set of data and analyses are available upon request from Jeffrey S. Anastasi.

5. Using the adult *BAS* norms from Roediger et al. (2001) and Nelson, McEvoy, and Schreiber (1998), we found that the average *BAS* values for the adult-normed lists in the current study were .26, whereas average *BAS* values for child-normed lists were .20. However, it should be noted that *BAS* values were available for 80% of the items on the adult lists but only 46% of the items from the child lists. Thus, there may be some bias in these estimates because these data are based only on adult *BAS* norms.

Twelve Child-Normed Lists Used in the Current Study in Descending Order of Associative Strength

Window	River	Car	Sleep	Rubber	Lion
glass (2)	*water* (1)	wheel	*bed* (1)	*stretchy* (15)	*roar* (11)
see	*fish* (13)	*drive* (6)	pillow	band	fur
house (7)	*swim* (7)	seat	*blanket* (8)	*bounce* (2)	teeth
open (8)	*stream* (2)	fast	*tired* (4)	plastic	meat
blinds	*lake* (3)	steering	*dream* (5)	squishy	eat
outside	ocean	engine	*snore* (11)	toys	scary
tree	*flow* (8)	gas	*nap* (12)	duck	tail
doors (1)	frog	school	*rest* (2)	goo	zoo
metal	beach	doors	awake	hard	hair
air	wet	radio	comfortable	smooth	growl
clear	*bridge* (14)	tires	covers	weird	loud
square	clear	horn	lay	wheels	*mane* (8)
wood	drown	light	quiet	*ball* (5)	big
curtains (9)	land	motorcycle	room	pop	cat
breakable	long	people	afternoon	break	*jungle* (3)

Smell	City	Fruit	Rough	Music	King
good	buildings	*apple* (1)	hurt	dance	*crown* (3)
stink	people	eat	*smooth* (1)	*sing* (4)	*queen* (1)
nose (1)	houses	*banana* (8)	*bumpy* (2)	loud	castle
food	skyscrapers	healthy	wall	*sound* (2)	*royal* (13)
flowers	*town* (1)	*orange* (3)	fight	drum	boss
scent (9)	*state* (3)	grape	scratch	guitar	princess
sneeze	work	sweet	hit	nice	ruler
taste	hotels	watermelon	mad	play	*throne* (8)
allergies	store	seeds	wrestling	*instrument* (10)	*prince* (4)
body	animals	taste	argument	listen	cape
breathe	lights	*vegetable* (2)	boys	quiet	*leader* (14)
candle	small	food	brother	*radio* (5)	rich
cookie	loud	hungry	houses	*piano* (3)	sword
diaper	parks	*juice* (12)	kick	relaxing	clothes
oven	*street* (5)	peach	nice	songs	suit

Note. Items in bold font indicate the critical lures for each 15-item list. Items in italics indicate those words that are also included in Stadler, Roediger, and McDermott's (1999) adult norms. The number in parentheses indicates that item's rank within Stadler et al.'s lists.

Concepts and Categories

Representation and Use

DOUGLAS L. MEDIN, BRIAN H. ROSS AND ARTHUR B. MARKMAN

Mind and world in short have evolved together, and in consequence are something of a mutual fit.

—*William James*

INTRODUCTION

Why Categorize?

A basic cognitive function is to categorize. We have names for groups of things such as dogs, cats, cars, computers, birds, birthdays, and balloons. Likewise, we have names for properties (tall, tepid, tense) as well as actions (walk, waver, wallow). Furthermore, we can combine single words to create an unlimited number of new categories, like green-garbed grumpy golfers and camel-carted carpets. But why do we need categories?

The answer is that without categories we would be unable to make any sense of our experience or to profit from it. If each thing we encountered was unique and totally unlike anything else we had ever known, we would not know how to react to it or make any useful predictions about its properties. We would be literally lost in a sea of new experiences, helpless to employ any of our prior knowledge to navigate it. Imagine a clinical psychologist unwilling to form or use any diagnostic categories, who argues that every individual is unique and requires a totally individualized plan of treatment. The concept of unique treatments for every individual seems reasonable, even

commendable, but when implemented it is completely-self-defeating. Following Kendall (1975), suppose we have available treatment A and treatment B (and presumably more). What is our rationale for selecting which treatment to give? We are trying to predict which treatment will be more effective, but if each individual is unique, we have no basis whatsoever for making predictions! If we knew only that a patient seemed to be more similar to people who had responded well to treatment A than to those who had responded well to treatment B, we would have some rationale for thinking that treatment A would be more effective. Of course, to draw on our experience in this way is to categorize. Even before medicine had any sort of effective set of treatments, a major conceptual advance was made when people began to reject the idea that every instance of illness was unique. It seems inevitable, then, that to have any basis for providing (and even tailoring) a treatment, we need to categorize, even if we do not necessarily use formal diagnostic categories.

The need to categorize is not specific to clinical diagnosis but rather applies wherever relevant knowledge might be brought to bear. When we recognize some entity as a dog, our knowledge about dogs (e.g., that they sometimes bark, usually like to be petted, and so on) allows us to make predictions about and understand their actions. Categorization is pervasive.

Computational Complexity

It is easy to show that categorization quickly runs into problems of computational complexity. That is, we could categorize things in an unlimited number of ways, and we necessarily employ a minuscule subset of these possibilities. Suppose we have a set of n things (where n stands for some number). We can determine that the number of ways of assigning those things to categories increases very rapidly with n. With two objects a and b, we can set up two categorization schemes: (a) (b) and (ab), where the parentheses define category boundaries. If we double the number of objects, we can have 15 distinct category structures: (a)(b)(c)(d), (ab)(c)(d), (a)(bc)(d), (a)(b)(cd), (ac)(b)(d), (ad)(b)(c), (a)(bd)(c), (abc)(d), (a)(bcd), (acd)(b), (abd)(c), (ab)(cd), (ad)(bc), (ac)(bd), and (abcd). By the time we get up to 10 objects, there are more than 100,000 possibilities!

The fact that there are so many possibilities makes it natural to ask why we have the categories we have rather than others. One possible answer is that our categories mirror the structure of the world. Perhaps the world comes organized into natural "clusters," and our concepts mirror those natural groupings or categories. An alternative possibility is that we have the categories we have because we are the sort of creatures we are. Another way of putting it is that the categories we have represent a solution for a set of problems (e.g., coping with ignorance, making predictions) and that perhaps we can better understand human concepts by asking what problems they address and what functions they serve (see Malt, 1995, for a cross-cultural perspective on these questions). In the following sections, we will review these functions, describe a body of research on category learning, and then return to the question of why we have the categories we have.

Functions of Concepts

So far, we have described concepts at a relatively informal level. When we try to be more precise, we see that concepts serve a number of distinct roles. In this discussion, we will often mention both *concepts* and *categories*. These terms have sometimes been used interchangeably in the literature on categorization. In this chapter, we use concept to refer to a mental representation and category to refer to the set of entities or examples picked out by the **concept**. Some researchers suggest that **categories** have independent existence in the world (independent of the organisms that conceive of them). We do not endorse this view because we believe that in many cases (if not all) categories are constructed by the human mind as it relates to the world. As we'll see, our categories have to be linked to the world if they are to prove useful.

Classification

A central function of concepts is to allow us to treat discriminably different things as equivalent. We use the word *things* here, because category members may be physical objects, living things, properties, actions, or even abstract ideas such as "democracy." Deciding that two (or more) items are members of the same category is the process of *classification*. As we will see, classification is one of the most widely studied functions of categories in psychology.

Understanding and Explanation

Classification allows intelligent organisms to break apart their experience into meaningful chunks and to construct an interpretation of it. A major facet of this understanding is bringing old knowledge to bear on the current situation. For example, a person on a hike in the mountains who recognizes an animal as a rattlesnake will interpret the situation as dangerous. Concepts also support *explanations*; understanding why a friend reacted to a stick with alarm is explained with the knowledge that he or she initially classified it as a rattlesnake.

Prediction

A key aspect of classification is that it allows one to make *predictions* concerning the future, predictions that can be used to select plans and actions. For example, after we identify an animal as a rattlesnake, we can act to avoid it.

Reasoning

Concepts support *reasoning*. One does not need to store every fact and possibility if inferences can be derived from information that is stored. From the knowledge that all animals breathe, that reptiles are animals, and rattlesnakes are reptiles, one may reason (deductively) that rattlesnakes must also breathe, even though one may never have directly stored that fact. Furthermore, people can combine concepts to describe novel situations and to envision future states of affairs. You probably have never thought about or seen a *paper bee*. We asked a few people about this novel concept, and most of them came up with the idea that a paper bee is a bee made out of paper. Furthermore, everyone who arrives at this interpretation also envisions that such a bee would not be alive and could not breathe. To get an idea of how complex conceptual combination is, try to figure out the concept *paper committee*. Though it was natural to interpret paper bee as a bee *made* of paper, it seems more natural to interpret paper committee as a committee *concerned with* paper (or perhaps one that *exists* on paper, but not in reality) and certainly not one made out of paper.

Communication

To the extent that people share knowledge and index it in terms of the same categories, they will be able to communicate with each other. Communication allows learning on the basis of indirect experience. When an expert tells us to avoid sudden movements in the presence of rattlesnakes, we can follow this advice the very first time we are confronted with a rattlesnake.

Summary

One can readily see that concepts function in multiple ways and are essential to mental life. Understanding, explanation, and prediction are at the core of intelligent behavior. As we shall see, there is also a moral for researchers: the various conceptual functions may interact with and influence each other. For example, the reasoning and communication functions may affect categorization (e.g. Ross, 1997; Markman & Makin. 1998). Before turning to the question of how categories are structured, we focus on an important consequence of categorization.

Concepts and Misconceptions

While categories are clearly crucial for human cognitive activity, our ability to use categories sometimes causes problems. We may form the wrong categories or categories that are too broad for our purposes. Furthermore, the very nature of our categories virtually ensures that important information may be lost or that inappropriate inferences will be made. On the one hand, our categories are a sign that some set of items should be treated equivalently in some way. On the other hand, we cannot treat the items from a common category exactly the same in every way. After all, both pit bulls and poodles are dogs, but one might not want to interact with them identically. Nonetheless, we may end up treating members of a category as being very similar simply because of their common category membership.

As an example, Tajfel and Wilkes (1963) showed people four short lines labeled "A" and four long lines labeled "B" and asked them to estimate the lengths of the lines. A control group was given the same task without the category labels. Relative to the control group, people given labels rated the short lines as more similar in length than did people in the control group and they also rated the short lines as more different from the long lines than people in the control group. In other words the labels made the examples within a category more similar and the differences across categories more distinctive.

Consequences of categorization are also evident in the important domain of social categorization. When people are brought into laboratories and divided into groups based on an arbitrary dimension (e.g., whether they overestimated or underestimated the number of dots in a picture), in-group favoritism results. What do we mean by in-group favoritism? It is easiest to answer this by looking at an experiment, such as the one reported by Howard and Rothbart (1980). They created an arbitrary method for dividing people into groups. Howard and Rothbart showed people a page full of dots, and asked them to estimate how many dots were there. Then, they arbitrarily told people that they had overestimated or underestimated the number of dots. Further, they told people that there were groups of people who tended to overestimate and underestimate dots and that these people often had other characteristics in common. Then, each person was told favorable and unfavorable information about members of their group (the *in-group*) and the other group (the *out-group*). Despite the fact that this division into groups was arbitrary, people showed significantly better memory for negative behaviors of the out-group than for negative behaviors of the in-group.

Thus, these categories influenced people's perceptions in a way that favored the in-group.

What about more socially relevant categories? Hirschfeld (1994, 1996) has shown that the development of children's understanding of race involves much more than a passive accumulation of information in the environment. Instead, it appears their thinking about race is organized by theories and beliefs about innate potential. For example, in one of his studies, Hirschfeld asked children to judge what the offspring of racially mixed couples would look like. Two groups of children (7-to 8-year-olds and 11-to 12-year-olds) from a suburban middle-class school (where there were few minority children) were shown pictures one at a time of four couples, consisting of a black male and a black female, a white male and a white female, a black male and a white female, or a white male and a black female. Each child then was shown pictures of three infants representing a white infant, a black infant, and an infant intermediate between the white and black infants in terms of skin color, hair color, and hair texture. Finally, each child was asked which of the infants was the child of the couple. The normatively correct answer for the mixed race couple is the infant depicted as intermediate.

All children judged that the black couple would have a black infant and the white couple a white infant. Of greatest interest are the judgments for the racially mixed couples. Younger children showed no clear preference among the three choices. Strikingly, however, older children overwhelmingly chose the black baby for both mixed race pairs. Furthermore, in a comparison condition involving skin and hair color of animals, older children make the normatively correct choice of intermediate color. These results suggest that by early adolescence children have learned the culturally dominant model of social potential—in our culture, children of black-white mixed couples are treated as black. (Regardless of whether one thinks this is sensible, it appears to be a fact.) Interestingly, when Hirschfeld gave the same task to children from an integrated inner-city school, both younger and older children tended to pick the infant depicted as intermediate. This pattern held for both children who identify as white and as black, suggesting that the results are driven by cultural environment rather than the children's racial status per se. In short, race is a salient social category that is susceptible to systematic misperceptions and cultural influences.

The results just described are somewhat sobering and certainly do not leave the impression that categorization is necessarily a good thing. The process of categorization leads only too naturally to stereotypes and misperceptions of other groups (see Devine, 1989; Tajfel, 1981, for examples). Perhaps knowledge of the fact of the human propensity for forming stereotypes can moderate or weaken our reliance on them. On a more optimistic note, there is evidence that stereotypes may yield to more concrete, specific information. Locksley, Borgida, Brekke, and Hepburn (1980) asked people to rate the assertiveness of target individuals who were described in one of three ways: (1) name only (conveying gender information), (2) name plus a descriptive paragraph irrelevant to assertiveness, or (3) name plus a descriptive paragraph relevant to assertiveness. In the first two conditions, male targets were rated as more assertive than female targets, but in the third females were rated as being as assertive as males; that is, when relevant information was provided, it was used and gender information was not used. In some cases, it seems, stereotypes are treated as default values that are employed only when no other information is available. Of course, what would be most helpful is a general theory about the conditions under which perceivers attend to and process information at the level of individuals versus categories. Both social psychologists and cognitive psychologists are keenly interested in this issue (e.g. Barsalou, Huttenlocher & Lamberts, 1998; Fiske, Neuberg, Beattie, & Milberg, 1987; Fiske, Lin, & Neuberg, 1999).

In short, categorization is necessary for all the reasons listed at the beginning of this chapter. But the benefits of categorization may come at some cost. Specifically, categorizing a set of objects can lead us to treat the members of the category as more similar to each other than they really are. In the case of social categories the result may be stereotyping.

Summary

In this section we noted that it is necessary to categorize in order to access relevant knowledge and make appropriate predictions and inferences. There are virtually an unlimited number of different ways in which we may categorize things and an important question is why we have the categories we have and not other ones. Part of the answer to that question is likely to be based on the different functions that categories serve (i.e. classification, understanding and explanation, prediction, reasoning, and communication). Finally we noted that for all of its benefits, categorization can both exaggerate (between category) differences and inappropriately minimize (within category) differences. We now turn our attention to the structural underpinnings of categories, beginning with natural object categories such as bird, fish, and tree.

STRUCTURE OF NATURAL OBJECT CATEGORIES

Almost all theories about the structure of categories assume that, roughly speaking, similar things tend to belong to the same category and that dissimilar things tend to be in different categories. For example, robins and sparrows both belong to the category *bird* and are more similar to each other than they are to squirrels or pumpkins. *Similarity* is a pretty vague term, but most commonly it is defined in terms of shared properties or attributes. If you are asked to justify why you think robins and sparrows are more similar to each other than either is to squirrels you are likely to appeal to specific attributes or properties. For example, you might note that robins and sparrows are similar in that they are living, animate, have feathers, wings, and hollow bones, and can sing, fly, build nests, and lay eggs. Squirrels have only some of these properties, and pumpkins have fewer still. Although alternative theories assume concepts are structured in terms of shared properties, theories differ greatly in their organizational principles. Let's take a look at the main views concerning category structure.

The Classical View

The **classical view** assumes that concepts have defining features that act like criteria for determining category membership. For example, a triangle is a closed geometric form of three sides with the sum of the interior angles equaling 180 degrees. Each of these properties is necessary for an entity to be a triangle, and together these properties are sufficient to define *triangle*. According to the classical view, concepts have rigid boundaries in that a given example either does or does not meet the definition. All members of a category are equally good examples of it, and learning involves discovering these defining features.

Most of us have the initial intuition that our concepts conform to the classical view and have defining features. But think a bit more about a concept like chair or furniture. What makes a chair a chair? We might start by saying that a chair is something an individual can sit on, but that definition does not exclude sofas, benches, or even rocks. Next one might add the proviso that chairs must have four legs, but that would exclude beanbag chairs. The more we think about it, the trickier it becomes. For example, we might start to worry about the difference between stools and chairs and ultimately decide either that we do not know exactly what a chair is or that we may be unable to describe it.

There has, in fact, been a fair amount of research done on people's knowledge about object categories like bird, chair, and furniture. Not only do people fail to come up with defining features but also they do not necessarily agree with each other (or even with themselves when asked at different times) on whether something is an example of a category (Bellezza, 1984; McCloskey & Glucksberg, 1978). For example, is a rug considered furniture? A parquet floor? A telephone?

Philosophers and scientists also have worried about whether naturally occurring things like plants and animals (so-called natural lands) have defining features. And the current consensus is that most natural concepts do not fit the classical view. Even the concept of species is not well defined (see Sokal, 1974). For example, a species might be defined as an interbreeding population. But in some species, the males of one group are fertile with the females of the other, but the females of the first group are not fertile with the males of the other. Although some concepts like triangle may be well defined, many concepts do not appear to be, and for this reason cognitive psychologists have pretty much abandoned the classical view.

The Probabilistic View

The major alternative to the classical view is the probabilistic view. It argues that concepts are organized around properties that may be typical or characteristic of category members. For example, most people's concept of bird may include the properties of building nests, flying, and having hollow bones, even though not all birds have these properties (e.g., ostriches, penguins).

The probabilistic view has major implications for how we think about categories. First, if categories are organized around characteristic properties, some members may have more of these properties than other members. In this sense, some members may be better examples or more typical of a concept than others, as we noted in Chapter 6. For example, people judge a robin to be a better example of a bird than an ostrich is and can answer category membership questions more rapidly for good examples than for poor examples (see, e.g., E. E. Smith, Shoben, & Rips, 1974; Rips, 1989; Medin & Heit, 1999, for reviews). A second implication is that, category boundaries may be fuzzy. Nonmembers of a category may have almost as many characteristic properties of a category as do certain members. For example, whales have a lot of the characteristic properties of fish, and yet they are mammals. Third, learning about a category cannot be equated with determining what the defining features are because there may not be any.

Features and Typicality

In some pioneering work aimed at clarifying the structural basis of fuzzy categories, Rosch and Mervis (1975) had subjects list properties of exemplars for a variety of concepts such as bird, fruit, and tool. They found that the listed properties for some category members occurred frequently in other members, whereas other members had properties that occurred less frequently. Most importantly, the more frequently a category member's properties appeared within a category, the higher was its rated **typicality** for that category. Typicality is a measure of how good or common an item is as a member of a given category. The correlation between number of characteristic properties possessed and typicality rating was very high and positive. For example, robins have characteristic bird properties of flying, singing, eating worms, and building nests in trees, and they are rated to be very typical birds. Penguins have none of these properties, and they are rated as very atypical birds. In short, the Rosch and Mervis work relating typicality to number of characteristic properties put the probabilistic view on fairly firm footing.

Although typicality effects are robust and problematic for the classical view, the underlying basis for typicality effects may vary with both the kind of category being studied and with the population being studied. Barsalou

(1985) showed that the internal structure of taxonomic categories is based primarily on the central tendency (or the average member) of a category. In contrast, the internal structure of goal-derived categories such as "things to wear in the snow" is determined by some ideal (or the best possible member) associated with the category. The best example of snow clothing, a down jacket, was not the example that was most like other category members; instead it was the example with the maximum value of the goal-related dimension of providing warmth.

One might hypothesize that ideals will only come into play when the category of interest lacks the natural similarity structure that characterizes common taxonomic categories such as bird, fish, and tree. However, recent evidence undermines this conjecture. Lynch, Coley, and Medin (2000) found that, for tree experts, the internal structure of the category *tree* was organized around the ideals of weediness and height. The best examples of *tree* were not trees of average height but trees of extraordinary height (and free of "weedy" characteristics like having weak limbs, growing where they aren't wanted, and being susceptible to disease).

It might occur to you that "best example" isn't the same thing as "most typical." However, Lynch et al. used exactly the same instructions employed by Rosch and Mervis (1975) in their original investigation of typicality effects. Moreover, Lynch et al. also ran undergraduate participants, and they showed no effects of ideals (their responses were mainly based on familiarity). In short, the differences in goodness of example effects appear to depend on expertise, not the wording of the instructions.

Atran (1998) reports a similar finding in studies comparing goodness of example effects for the category *bird* among University of Michigan undergraduates and Itzá Maya adults living in the rainforests of Guatemala. Undergraduates based typicality on overall similarity (central tendency) just as Rosch and Mervis (1975) had observed. The Itzá Maya, in contrast, based typicality on ideals—the best example of bird was the wild turkey which is culturally significant, prized for its meat, and strikingly beautiful. In short, ideals may play an important role in the internal organization of categories. There remains the question of why undergraduates differed from the Itzá Maya in the basis for their judgments. The fact that Lynch et al. (2000) found that U.S. tree experts based typicality on ideals suggests that it's not just that the

Itzá have a different notion of what typicality means. One speculation is that the internal structure of categories is determined not only by classification processes but also by other conceptual functions (e.g., those mentioned at the beginning of this chapter). Undergraduates may know little about birds or trees and their interactions with them may not go beyond categorization (if that). Tree experts and Itzá Maya presumably have extended and complex interactions with trees and birds, respectively, and ideals have more opportunity to come into play. Perhaps similarity is a useful way to structure concepts used primarily for classification whereas ideals may be better for concepts used for a broader range of conceptual functions. (See Ross, 1997: Markman, Yamauchi, & Makin, 1997; and Solomon, Medin, & Lynch, 1999, for different ways of developing this argument.)

Mental Representations of Fuzzy Categories

If categories are not represented in terms of definitions, what form do our mental representations take? The term *probabilistic view* seems to imply that people organize categories via statistical reasoning. Actually, there is a more natural interpretation of fuzzy categories that has been referred to as a family resemblance principle. Many people in an extended family might share features such as a distinctive chin, certain expressions, or a high forehead. For example, the faces might all share many properties, though no two faces are identical. The general idea is that category members resemble each other in the way that family members do.

A simple summary representation for such a family resemblance structure would be an example that possessed all the characteristic features of a category. The best example is referred to as the prototype.

In a prototype model of categorization, classifying a new example is done by comparing the new item to the prototype. If the candidate example is similar enough to the prototype for a category, it is classified as a member of that category. The general notion is that, based on experience with examples of a category, people abstract out the central tendency or prototype that becomes the summary mental representation for the category. Note that no individual category member need have all the properties that are represented in the prototype. In that sense, a prototype is like a stereotype, which also may be true of no individual.

Laboratory studies of categorization using artificially constructed categories have been used to evaluate prototype theory. In these studies the experimenter creates the stimuli using salient properties and then assigns the stimuli to categories to create different kinds of category structures. For example, the stimuli might be geometric shapes varying in shape, size, and color, and fuzzy categories can be constructed by making sure that there is no simple rule that determines category membership. For example, one category might have examples that are usually large, usually red, and usually circular but there would be exceptions to each of these generalizations.

Normally many variables relevant to human category learning tend to be correlated with each other, and it is hard to determine which variables really are important. For instance, typical examples tend to be more frequent, and people's ability to classify typical examples quickly may be related to typicality, frequency, or both factors. The general rationale for laboratory studies with artificially created categories is that one can isolate some variable or set of variables of interest by breaking these natural correlations. Experiments with artificial categories reveal a number of salient phenomena associated with fuzzy categories, and several of these are consistent with prototype theories. For example, one observes typicality effects in learning and on transfer tests using both correctness and reaction time as the dependent measure (see, e.g., Rosch & Mervis, 1975). A striking result, readily obtained, is that the prototype for a category may be classified more accurately during transfer tests than are the previously seen examples that were used during original category learning (see, e.g., Homa & Vosburgh, 1976; Medin & Schaffer, 1978; Peterson, Meagher, Chait, & Gillie, 1973).

Typicality effects and excellent classification of prototypes are consistent with the idea that people are learning these fuzzy categories by forming prototypes. More detailed analyses, however, show problems with prototypes as mental representations. As we noted earlier, prototype theory implies that the only information abstracted from categories is the central tendency. A prototype representation discards information concerning category size, the variability of the examples, and correlations of attributes. The evidence suggests that people can use all three of these types of information (Estes, 1986; Flannagan, Fried, & Holyoak, 1986; Fried &

Holyoak, 1984; Medin, Altom, Edelson, & Freko, 1982; Medin & Schaffer, 1978).

These same issues arise for real-world categories. For example, people seem to know that small birds are more likely to sing than large birds—a prototype does not capture this awareness of correlational information (Malt & Smith, 1983). In addition, how well an item belongs to a concept depends on the context in which it is presented (Roth & Shoben, 1983). For example, a harmonica is a typical musical instrument in the context of a campfire but atypical in the context of a concert hall. People seem to adjust their expectations in a manner sensitive to different settings. In short, prototype representations seem to discard too much information that can be shown to be relevant to human categorization.

Let's look at one further problem of prototype models in detail: predictions concerning category learning. To our knowledge, every model for category learning has some constraints or biases associated with it in the sense of predicting that some kinds of classification problems should be easier to master than others. One way to evaluate alternative learning models is to see if the problems they predict should be easy or difficult to acquire are, in fact, easier or more difficult for people to learn.

One constraint of interest is known as **linear separability**. Categories are linearly separable if one can categorize the examples perfectly by adding up the evidence from individual features. It is easiest to see what this means with a concrete example. Prototype models imply that categories must be linearly separable to be learnable. One way to conceptualize the process of classifying examples on the basis of similarity to prototype is that it involves a summing of evidence against a criterion. For example, if an instance has enough features characteristic of birds, it will be classified as a bird. More technically, there must be some weighted, additive combination of properties (some similarity function) that will be higher for all category members than for any nonmembers. If this is true, then the categories are linearly separable. All bird examples must be more similar to the bird prototype than to alternative prototypes, and all non-birds must be more similar to their respective prototypes than to the bird prototype. If a bat were more similar to the bird prototype than to the mammal prototype, it would be incorrectly classified and the categories would not be linearly separable.

Figure 10.4 gives a more intuitive description of linear separability for examples that have values on two dimensions. In each graph category, members in categories A and B are denoted respectively by the letters A and B. The position of each letter corresponds to its value on the X and Y dimensions (if it helps to be more concrete, think of these dimensions as the size and ferocity of animals). The categories are linearly separable if there is a straight line that perfectly partitions the categories (Figure 10.4a). If no straight line will partition the categories (Figure 10.4b), there is no way to construct prototypes such that all examples are closer to their own category prototype than to the prototype for the contrasting category. A number of neural network learning models favor categories that are linearly separable because, in effect, they add up the evidence favoring a classification decision (Minsky & Papert, 1988).

If linear separability acts as a constraint on human categorization, people should find it easier to learn categories that are linearly separable than categories that are not linearly separable. Studies employing a variety of stimulus materials, categories, subject populations, and instructions have failed to find any evidence that whether the categories are linearly separable influences the ease with which people learn categories (see, e.g., Kemler-Nelson, 1984; Medin & Schwanenflugel, 1981; see Smith, Murray, & Minda, 1997, for a dissenting opinion). This generalization has one striking exception: For social categories, there is strong evidence that linear separability does matter (Wattenmaker, 1995).

Wattenmaker suggests that social categories may be more compatible with a summing of evidence because (1) people may have a set of schemas or thematic structures that facilitate the integration of information across dimensions (e.g., the characteristic features knowledgeable, competent, hard working, and composed can readily be integrated if the category *scientist* is activated), and (2) people show considerable flexibility in relating features of examples to more abstract underlying properties (e.g., the characteristic features relaxed, thoughtful, and friendly could be seen as consistent with the abstract trait *intelligent,* but they may also be seen as consistent with the trait *kind*). Even with this salient exception of social categories, the sort of domain-general linear separability constraint implied by prototype models does not appear to hold. Overall, then, prototype models appear to have a number of serious limitations. An alternative approach, which is also consistent with the probabilistic view, assumes that much more information about specific examples is preserved. This approach appropriately falls under the general heading of exemplar theories.

Exemplar Theories

Exemplar theories provide an alternative way of representing probabilistic or fuzzy categories. Exemplar models assume that people initially learn some examples of different concepts and then classify a new instance on the basis of how similar it is to the previously learned examples. The idea is that a new example reminds the person of similar old examples and that people assume that similar items will belong to the same category. For example, you might classify one animal as a rodent because it reminds you of a mouse (which you know is a rodent) but classify some other animal as a rodent because it reminds you of a squirrel (which you also know is a rodent). As another example, suppose you are asked whether large birds are more or less likely to fly than small birds. You probably will answer "less likely," based on retrieving examples from memory and noting that the only nonflying birds you can think of are large (e.g., penguin, ostrich).

The exemplar models that have received the most attention (Brooks, 1978; Hintzman, 1986; Medin & Schaffer, 1978: Nosofsky, 1986) assume that examples that are most similar to the item to be classified have the greatest influence on categorization. This could arise because the likelihood of retrieving an example from memory depends on its similarity to the item. The idea that retrieval is similarity-based and context-sensitive is in accord with much of the memory literature (see, e.g., Tulving, 1983; Chapter 5). Surprisingly, exemplar models can even account for the observation that the prototype may be more accurately classified on a transfer test than examples seen during original learning. The reason is as follows: The prototype will tend to be similar to many examples from its own category and not very similar to examples from alternative categories. Therefore, the prototype should reliably remind the learner of examples from the correct category. In contrast, some of the examples seen during training may not be highly similar to some of the other examples from their own category and may actually be similar to examples from other categories. In this case, the example may remind the learner of examples from alternative categories. It is important to bear in mind that exemplar models do not assume that people are necessarily able to retrieve individual examples one at a time without confusing them. Instead, the idea is that a test example will tend to activate a number of similar stored representations.

Quite a few experiments have contrasted the predictions of exemplar and prototype models. In head-to-head competition, exemplar models have been substantially more successful than prototype models (Barsalou & Medin, 1986; Estes, 1986, 1994; Lamberts, 1995; Medin & Coley, 1998; Nosofsky, 1988a, 1988b, 1991; Nosofsky & Palmeri, 1997) even for natural language categories (Storms, De Boeck, & Ruts, 2000). See Homa, 1984, and Smith & Minda, 1998, for opposing views.

Why should exemplar models fare better than prototype models? One of the main functions of classification is to allow one to make inferences and predictions on the basis of partial information (see J. R. Anderson, 1990a, 1990b). Here we are using classification loosely to refer to any means by which prior (relevant) knowledge is brought to bear, ranging from a formal classification rule to an idiosyncratic reminding of a previous case (which, of course, is in the spirit of exemplar models; see also Kolodner, 1993). Relative to prototype models, exemplar models tend to be conservative about discarding information that facilitates predictions. For instance, sensitivity to correlations of properties within a category enables finer predictions: From noting that a bird is large, one can predict that it cannot sing. In short, exemplar models better allow predictions and inferences than prototype models.

Exemplar models do seem to preserve more information than prototype models. Because the prototype is an average exemplar, it loses information about the specific category members that were seen. Although the exemplar model stores the category members, that does not mean that it will ever be possible to retrieve that single exemplar, because activating one exemplar is likely to activate others that are similar to it. Generally speaking, however, exemplar models preserve more information than prototype models—information that people seem to be able to use. This does not prove that exemplar models are correct, but it suggests that learning depends more on examples than proto-type models have assumed (Medin & Ross, 1989).

In short, exemplar models appear to have a number of effective characteristics, and future generations of models will likely embody these characteristics, directly or indirectly. For example, recent models of category learning that combine searching for rules with memory for examples have proven successful, at least for artificial categories (e.g. Nosofsky, Palmeri, & McKinley, 1994; Erickson & Kruschke, 1998; see also Ashby, Alfonso-Reese, Turken, & Waldron, 1998, for another dual-process approach to categorization). Instance-based ideas have also been incorporated into artificial intelligence categorization models (see, e.g., Kibler & Aha, 1987; Stanfill & Waltz, 1986). Finally, we note that there have been formal proofs that classifying on the basis of the single most similar example (a "nearest neighbor" principle) is not far from the optimal classification (Cover & Hart, 1967).

Although exemplar models have the virtue that they discard very little information that is potentially relevant to later judgments, the exemplar notion is incomplete as a theory of categories. Items are assumed to be placed in the category with the exemplars they are most similar to, but exemplar theories do not explain how concepts are created in the first place; that is, there are no constraints on what can be a concept. Furthermore, the only explanation for why a new example should be placed into a category is "because it is similar to an old example"—a very limited form of explanation. In addition, these models focus on how people learn to classify objects to the exclusion of other functions like prediction, reasoning, or communication. As we shall see, these three problems are also true for probabilistic view theories.

Summary

The proposals about types of category representations are summarized in Figure 10.5. Despite the strong intuition that categories are organized around defining features, the classical view of concepts does not account for a variety of observations (e.g., fuzzy categories, typicality effects) and the consensus favors the idea that concepts are structured more probabilistically. For this reason, various probabilistic views of categorization have been developed. The two most prominent theories of this type are the prototype

and exemplar models. The prototype model assumes that category representations consist of a central tendency or average member of a category. The exemplar model assumes that people store individual exemplars of categories, and then classify new instances with respect to their similarity to these stored exemplars. In general, it appears that people's categorization shows a context-sensitivity that is better described by exemplar models than prototype models. So far, however, we have focused mainly on the categorization functions of concepts. It is not clear how probabilistic view models will address other conceptual functions such as conceptual combination (see Kamp & Partee, 1995; Osherson & Smith, 1982, 1997; Fodor & Lepore, 1996, for discussion).

The discussion to this point has focused exclusively on the way information about individual categories is represented (or *within-category structure*). It is almost meaningless to talk about within-category structure without also worrying about how different categories are organized with respect to each other (or *between-category structure*). For example, when we say that examples within a category tend to be similar to each other we mean that they are more similar than pairs of examples that come from different categories. We turn now to some ideas concerning between-category structure before worrying again about why we have the categories we have and not others.

Between-Category Structure

Most things have membership in numerous categories. In this section we consider two types of between-category structure: a hierarchical, taxonomic structure and structures such as social categories that provide multiple, overlapping contrasts with, at best, a weak hierarchical structure.

Hierarchical Structure and the Basic Level

Often categories are organized *taxonomically* at different levels of abstraction. At each level, an example belongs to one of a set of mutually exclusive categories (as we saw in our discussion of models of semantic knowledge in Chapter 6). A poodle is also a canine, a mammal, an animal, a living thing, and an object (Figure 10.6). A poodle is a mammal and not a reptile, an animal and not a plant, and so on.

An important observation about categories is that people are not "confused about which label to use when asked about an object. For example, if you were looking at a four-legged furry animal that had just fetched a ball, you would be more likely to call it a *dog* than an *animal* or a *golden retriever*. This middle level of abstraction, which seems to provide the label that we would use as a default is called the basic level, and it appears to be psychologically privileged. For example, basic level concepts are the first to be learned, the natural level at which objects are named, and the highest level in which the instances all share the same parts and overall shape (Rosch, Mervis, Gray, Johnson, & Bayes Braem, 1976). The **basic level**, resides at a middle level of abstraction. More abstract categories (like animal) are called *super-ordinates,* and more specific categories (like golden retriever) are called *subordinates.* There is some evidence that as one becomes more expert in an area, what was previously the subordinate level becomes the basic level. For example, dog might be a basic-level category for most people, but poodle might be at the basic-level for dog

trainers (Tanaka & Taylor, 1991; see also Johnson & Mervis, 1997, 1998).

If we could understand just why the basic level is basic, we might gain further insight into what types of categories are natural or cohesive. One possibility is that the basic level is the highest level at which entities tend to share parts (B. Tversky & Hemenway, 1984; see Markman & Wisniewski, 1997, for a related idea). Another idea is that levels higher than the basic level have different purposes. For example, super-ordinate categories may serve to organize scenes (Murphy & Wisniewski, 1989; see also Wisniewski, Imai, & Casey, 1996), and superordinate category members may tend to share common functions more than perceptual similarities (see, e.g., Rosch et al, 1976; Murphy & Smith, 1982).

Nonhierarchical Categories

Many of the categories that we use do not fit into a taxonomic hierarchy. This is particularly true in the domain

---

AN APPLICATION
Exemplar Similarity in Medical Diagnosis

Medical diagnosis is an important categorization task. Therefore, one ought to expect that models of categorization would be relevant to medicine and that questions about prototypes versus exemplars might apply to medicine. Brooks, Norman, and Allen (1991) demonstrated that exemplar similarity influences medical diagnosis and not just performance on tasks set up in psychology laboratories. They ran experiments with medical residents and general practitioners involving diagnoses of dermatological (skin) problems. The materials they used were color slides of dermatological lesions from the slide libraries of two practicing and teaching dermatologists. Slides were selected from a range of diagnostic categories to construct examples for a study phase (30 slides) and a test phase (60 slides). The test phase slides included some examples from the study phase, some selected to be very similar to a study example, and some that were not very similar but involved the same category. Not surprisingly, the physicians were more accurate on old examples that they had studied than for new examples. Of greatest interest is the fact that physicians were more accurate on a new example highly similar to an old example than they were on a new, less similar example involving the same category.

This finding is surprising because both the residents and the general practitioners had considerable prior experience with dermatological diagnosis. One estimate is that about 6% of the cases general practitioners see involve dermatology. The physicians in the study by Brooks et al. had between 5 and 49 years of postgraduate experience. Nonetheless, the effect of specific example similarity did not diminish as a function of experience. It also appeared on both an immediate test and after a two-week delay between the study phase and the test phase. The effect was on the order of 10% to 20%, which is not only statistically reliable but clinically significant. This result is important because it suggests that if you need to see a doctor, the diagnosis may depend partially on the sorts of cases the doctor has seen recently. In summary, categorization processes studied in the laboratory are relevant to real world applications and a better understanding of these processes may have important application to medical diagnosis and training.

of socially-relevant concepts. One can be a mother, a psychologist, a Democrat, a golf player, and a Mexican-American all at the same time, and no single category is either superordinate or subordinate with respect to the others. If there is no clear hierarchy, then by definition there is no basic level. Given that people tend to use categories to understand their experience, one can think of the various categorization schemes as competing for attention. We already know from the memory literature that it is implausible to think that to understand some behavior, people access all the potentially relevant categories they have and reason with them. So what does determine which categories people access and use? Two factors that influence category access are the frequency and recency with which a category has been used. For example, in one study (Srull & Wyer, 1979, Experiment 1), people first performed a sentence construction task that was designed to activate concepts associated with hostility. Then, in an ostensibly separate experiment, the participants were asked to form impressions of people based on reading a description of behaviors. The behaviors were ambiguous with respect to hostility. Ratings of the descriptions with respect to hostility increased directly with the number of times hostility-related concepts had been activated on the presumably unrelated sentence construction task. The Srull and Wyer study illustrates the point that category accessibility has an important influence on how social information is encoded and interpreted (see also Smith, Fazio, & Cejka, 1996).

Is there a notion of privilege for nonhierarchical categories? Some social categories, such as those marking race, age, and gender, may be accessed automatically (e.g. Bargh, 1994; Greenwald & Banaji, 1995) independent of any intentions on the part of people. There is even some intriguing evidence that the activation of one social category leads to the inhibition of competing social categories (Macrae, Bodenhausen, & Milne, 1995). Although the structural differences between hierarchical and nonhierarchical categories are important, there is little or no work that has directly compared them.

Summary

The idea of a privileged or basic level is a very important principle of categorization. Originally it was interpreted as indicating that the world is organized into natural chunks that more or less impose themselves on minds. Evidence

that the basic level changes with expertise suggests that privilege depends on the interaction of goals, activities, and experience with objects and events in the world.

So far all of our discussion of within-and between-category structure has explicitly or implicitly assumed that similarity relations determine categorization (the classical view can be seen as a special case where only defining features contribute to similarity). We turn now to a closer examination of similarity. As we shall see, the notion of similarity can be a bit slippery. It is a very important construct but one must be very careful about how it is used.

Does Similarity Explain Categorization?

Similarity is a very intuitive explanation for how people categorize—we put things into the same category because they are similar. But similarity is very difficult to pin down. One problem with using similarity to define categories is that similarity is too variable. An example of the context-dependent nature of similarity is shown in Figure 10.7 (taken from Medin, Goldstone, & Gentner, 1993). People were either shown stimulus A and B together or stimulus B and C from sets of three like those shown in the figure. For each pair, people were asked to list common (shared) and distinctive features. Medin et al. (1993) found that the properties ascribed to stimulus B depended on whether it was paired with A or C. For example, for the top set, B was described as having three prongs when it was paired with A but four prongs when it was paired with C. For the bottom set, B was seen as three-dimensional when paired with A but two-dimensional when paired with C. Such observations suggest that similarity is heavily influenced by context.

Formal models of similarity allow similarity to be quite flexible. For example, Tversky's (1977) influential contrast model defines similarity as depending on common and distinctive features weighted for salience or importance. According to this model, similarity relationships depend heavily on the particular weights given to individual properties or features. A zebra and a barber pole could be seen as more similar than a zebra and a horse if the feature striped is given sufficient weight. This would not necessarily be a problem if the weights were stable. However, Tversky and others have convincingly shown that the relative weighting of a feature (as well as the relative importance of matching and mismatching features) varies with the stimulus context, experimental task (Gati & Tversky, 1984; Tversky, 1977), and probably even the concept under consideration (Ortony, Vondruska, Foss, & Jones, 1985). For example, a person from Maine and a person from Florida will seem less similar when they meet in Washington, DC, than when they meet in Tokyo.

Once we recognize that similarity is dynamic and depends on some (not well understood) processing principles, earlier work on the structure of fuzzy categories can be seen in a somewhat different light. Recall that the Rosch and Mervis (1975) studies asked subjects to list attributes or properties of examples and categories. It would be a mistake to assume that people had the ability to read and report their mental representations of concepts in a perfectly accurate manner. Indeed, Keil (1979, 1981) pointed out that examples like robin and squirrel share many important properties that almost never show up in attribute listings (e.g., has a heart, breathes, sleeps, is an organism, is an object with boundaries, is a physical object, is a thing, can be thought about, and so on). In fact, Keil argued that knowledge about just these sorts of properties serves to organize children's conceptual and semantic development. For present purposes, the point is that attribute listings provide a biased sample of people's conceptual knowledge.

To take things a step further, one could argue that without constraints on what is to count as a feature, any two things may be arbitrarily similar or dissimilar. Thus, as Murphy and Medin (1985) suggested, the number of properties that plums and lawn mowers have in common could be infinite: Both weigh less than 1,000 kg, both are found on the earth, both are found in our solar system, both cannot hear well, both have parts, both are not worn by elephants, both are used by people, both can be dropped, and so on (see also Goodman, 1972; Watanabe, 1969). Now consider again the status of attribute listings. They represent a biased subset of stored or readily inferred knowledge. The correlation of attribute listings with typicality judgments is a product of such knowledge and a variety of processes that operate on it. Without a theory of that knowledge and those processes that use it, it simply is not clear what these correlations indicate about mental representations.

If similarity is so flexible, how can it provide the basis for determining categories? One possibility is that children are not as flexible about similarity as adults. Linda Smith (1989) has proposed that there is a developmental increase in the tendency of children to weight dimensions differentially, with the youngest children biased toward responding in terms of overall similarity. If flexibility arises only after most perceptual categories are learned, then similarity might be stable enough to support the initial development of many categories. A closely related idea is that children rapidly learn what types of similarity matter in particular contexts.

In part, the question may be just how flexible similarity is. For example, the object recognition theories reviewed in Chapter 4 certainly assume that similarity is stable enough to be useful. In particular, structural approaches to similarity such as geon theory may be more constrained than featural approaches (because it is the combination of geons and their relations that is important rather than some flexible weighting of individual features) and consequently may provide more stability (e.g., Medin et al., 1993; Goldstone, 1994a).

Even if similarity can be constrained, it still may not explain categorization. We believe that similarity is properly viewed as a general guideline or heuristic for categorization but that it does not provide, the backbone of conceptual structure. Things that look alike do tend to belong to the same category. (But there are exceptions: Mannequins may look enough like people for us to confuse them with the real thing, but only briefly.) Furthermore, things that look alike superficially often tend to be alike in other, deeper ways (e.g., structure and function tend to be correlated). Overall similarity is a good but fallible guideline to category membership. When additional information (or a closer look) suggests that overall similarity is misleading, it is readily abandoned.

A nice illustration of the fact that even young children are not strongly constrained by overall similarity comes from a set of experiments by Gelman and Markman (1986). They pitted category membership against perceptual similarity in an inductive reasoning task (an example is shown in Figure 10.8). Young children were first shown pictures of two animals and taught that different novel properties were true of them. Then they were asked which property was also true of a new (pictured) example that was perceptually similar to one alternative but belonged to the category of the other alternative, from which it differed perceptually. For example, children might be taught that a flamingo feeds its baby mashed-up food and that a bat feeds its baby milk, and then asked what a blackbird feeds its baby (see Figure 10.8). The blackbird was perceptually more similar

AN ENIGMA
Will the True Basic Level Please Stand Up?

The idea of a basic level did not originate in cognitive psychology—it began with anthropological studies examining categorization in different cultures. The lion's share of this work was done in enthnobiology. The general question was whether people in different cultures organize biological categories in similar ways (that is, whether there are universal principles of biological categorization). The general answer proved to be "yes" but cross-cultural agreement in people's categorization of plants and animals appears to especially strong at one level in taxonomic hierarchies, the basic level (Atran, 1990; Berlin, 1992; Berlin, Breedlove, & Raven, 1973; see Malt, 1995, for a review). But herein lies a yet-unresolved puzzle. The level that the cross-cultural studies of biological categorization suggest is basic corresponds more or less to the genus level (e.g., maple) in scientific taxonomy. Rosch et al., however, found that, for Berkeley undergraduates, examples of this level acted like subordinates. Rather than maple, oak, trout, and cardinal being basic, Rosch et al. (1976) found that tree, fish, and bird met their criteria for basicness.

Why do ethnobiological and psychological measures of the basic level disagree? One possibility is that the Berkeley undergraduates in Rosch's studies knew little about biological categories, especially relative to the people studied in cross-cultural investigations, in other words, maybe the difference is a difference in expertise (as in the findings of Tanaka and Taylor described earlier which suggest that the basic level may become more specific with expertise). A second possibility grows out of the fact that exactly comparable measures of basicness were not used; different measures may pick out different levels as privileged. Ethnobiological studies tend to use naming or linguistic criteria for basicness., whereas Rosch et al. relied more heavily on feature listings and perceptual tests. Interestingly, the clearest changes with expertise in the Tanaka and Taylor studies involved naming preferences. Until this puzzle is resolved we have to admit that we do not know exactly what makes the basic level basic.

More recently some direct cross-cultural comparisons have been done using comparable measures. Coley, Medin, and Atran, 1997 (see also Atran, Estin. Coley, & Medin, 1997), compared U.S. undergraduates and Itzá Maya adults of Guatemala using *inductive confidence* (reasoning from being told that one member has some novel property to all members having that property) as a measure of basicness. They assumed that if the basic level is the most abstract level at which category members share many properties, then inductive confidence should drop abruptly for categories above the basic level. For example, if U.S. undergraduates know that birds share many properties, then they might be confident that a property true of robins will be true of all birds. But since there are many fewer properties that all members of the category animals share, they presumably would not be at all confident that a property true of robins would be true of all animals. The Itzá Maya are members of a more traditional society and they rely on the rainforest for their livelihood. They might show a greater differentiation of the category bird (see larger differences among birds), and they might believe that a property true of a specific bird would not necessarily be true of all birds. This is the prediction one would make from the point of view that people in traditional societies tend to be biological experts, relative to U.S. undergraduates. Surprisingly, both the Itzá Maya and U.S. undergraduates consistently privileged the same level and this corresponded to the level of genus (robin, trout, and oak rather than bird, fish, and tree), consistent with expectations derived from anthropology.

These results raise a number of new puzzles that can only be answered by future research. Why do undergraduates show a different privileged level for induction versus other tasks such as speeded categorization or feature listing? One possibility draws on the distinction between knowledge and expectations. Undergraduates might be hard-pressed to list features that distinguish elms from oaks but they might nonetheless expect them to have lots of differences. It may be that the inductive confidence task gets at expectations rather than knowledge. Another question is how people from traditional cultures would perform on Rosch's perceptual tasks. Would they be fastest at the level of categorizing examples into bird, fish and tree or robin, trout, and oak? The Tanaka and Taylor studies with bird and dog experts suggest that the Itzá Maya might be fastest at the genus level, because the Itzá are almost certainly biological experts. Cross-cultural comparisons are needed to address this question.

to the bat than to the flamingo, but even 4-year-olds made inferences on the basis of category membership rather than similarity. That is, they thought that the blackbird would feed its baby mashed-up food. Therefore, even for young children, similarity acts as a general guideline that can be overridden by other forms of knowledge.

But similarity is not a notion to be lightly dismissed. Even if similarity is not some bedrock principle for *explaining* categorization it may nonetheless play an extremely important role. One way to summarize the upshot of current research is to say that similarity affects categorization *and* categorization affects similarity as well. There is increasing evidence that the features or building blocks of categories are not hard-wired into the nervous system but rather can be modified by experience (e.g. Gauthier & Tarr, 1997; Goldstone, 1994b; Oliva & Schyns, 1997; Schyns & Rodet, 1997; Schyns, Goldstone, & Thibaut, 1998). There is also abundant evidence that the relative weight given to different kinds of features varies with their relevance to a given categorization task. For example, in Chapter 4, we discussed that people can attend either to fine-detail information or coarse information when processing an image. Schyns and Oliva (1999) extended this finding by demonstrating that people could learn to preferentially attend to either a coarse spatial scale or a fine spatial scale in a speeded categorization task. These results suggest that categorization and (perceptual) similarity are closely intertwined, so much so that one could as well say that categorization causes similarity as the converse.

Summary

It does not seem that similarity, at least in the form that it takes in current theories, is going to be adequate to explain categorization. As we have seen, similarity may be the outcome or by-product rather than the cause of categorization. To use a rough analogy, winning basketball teams have in common scoring more points than their opponents, but one must turn to more basic principles to explain why they score more points. Similar things may share properties and be in the same category, but similarity may not explain *why* they are in the same category. We will explore the process by which similarity is determined in Chapter 11. Now, we will focus on the idea that concepts are organized around theories. In the next section, we will

briefly summarize some of the current work on the role of knowledge structures and theories in categorization and then turn to a way of relating similarity and knowledge-based categorization principles.

Concepts as Organized by Theories

A number of researchers have argued that the organization of concepts is knowledge-based (rather than similarity-based) and driven by intuitive theories about the world (see, e.g., Carey, 1985; Gopnik & Meltzoff, 1997; Keil, 1986, 1989, 1995; Murphy & Medin, 1985; Rips & Collins, 1993; Schank, Collins, & Hunter, 1986; Waldmann, Holyoak, & Fratianne, 1995; Wattenmaker, 1995; see Komatsu, 1992; Murphy, 1993; Medin & Heit, 1999, for general reviews). Murphy and Medin suggested that the relation between a concept and an example is analogous to the relation between theory and data; that is, classification is not based simply on a direct matching of properties of the concept with those in the example, but rather requires that the example have the right "explanatory relationship" to the theory organizing the concept. Classification may be more like an inference process than like a similarity judgment. We may induce that a man is drank because we see him jump into a pool fully clothed. If so, our determination is probably not because the property "jumps into pools while clothed" is directly listed with the concept *drunk*. Rather, it is because part of our concept of drunk involves a theory of impaired judgment that serves to explain the man's behavior.

One of the more promising aspects of the theory-based approach is that it begins to address the question of why we have the categories we have or why categories are sensible. In fact, coherence may be achieved in the absence of any obvious source of similarity among examples. Consider the category comprised of children, money, photo albums, and pets. Out of context, the category seems odd. But if we are told that the category represents "things to take out of one's house in case of a fire," the category becomes sensible (Barsalou, 1983). In addition, one could readily make judgments about whether new examples (e.g., personal papers, magazines) belonged to the category, judgments that would not be based on overall similarity to category members.

Susan Carey (1982, 1985) has shown that children's biological theories guide their conceptual development.

In one study, 6-year-old children rated a toy monkey to be more similar to people than is a worm, but they also judged that the worm was more likely to have a spleen than was the toy monkey (a spleen was described as "a green thing inside people"). Although worms may be less similar to people than are toy monkeys, they are more similar in some respects, namely, common biological functions. And Carey's work shows that children's biological theories help them determine which respects are relevant. Thus, the 6-year-old children's rudimentary biological knowledge influences the structure of their concept of animal (see also Au & Romo, 1999; Coley, 1995; Gelman, 1996; Hatano & Inagaki, 1994; Inagaki, 1997; Keil, 1989; Simons & Keil, 1995, for other studies on the development of biological knowledge).

The idea that concepts might be knowledge-based rather than similarity-based suggests a natural way in which concepts may change—namely, through the addition of new knowledge and theoretical principles. We have a different set of categories for mental disorders now than we had 100 years ago, in part because our knowledge base has become more refined. Often knowledge of diseases develops from information about patterns of symptoms to a specification of underlying causes. For example, the advanced stages of syphilis were treated as a mental disorder until the causes and consequences of this venereal disease were better understood.

Putting Similarity in Its Place

How are theories and similarity related? Clearly, theories may affect similarity (Wisniewski & Medin, 1994). For example, people can now recognize that the fact that the planets revolve around the sun is similar to the fact that when something is dropped it falls down and not up, because both involve gravity. Interestingly, similarity may also act as a constraint on theories. The impact of perceptual similarity on the development of causal explanations is evident in the structure of people's everyday theories. Frazer's (1959) cross-cultural analysis of belief systems pointed to the widespread character of two principles; homeopathy and contagion. The principle of **homeopathy** is that causes and effects tend to be similar. One manifestation of this principle is homeopathic medicine, in which the cure (and the cause) are seen to resemble the symptoms. In the

Azande culture, for example, the cure for ringworm is to apply fowl's excrement because the excrement looks like the ringworm. Shweder (1977) has provided strong support for the claim that resemblance is a fundamental conceptual tool of everyday thinking in all cultures, not just so-called primitive cultures. In our culture, people reject acceptable foods just because they are shaped into a form that represents a disgusting object (Rozin, Millman, & Nemeroff, 1986). We will spare you a concrete example.

Contagion is the principle that a cause must have some form of contact to transmit its effect. In general, the nearer two events are in time and space, the more likely they are to be perceived as causally related (see, e.g., Dickinson, Shanks, & Evenden, 1984; Michotte, 1963). Of course, even children recognize that the timing relations may be rather subtle. If children are exposed to a ball that hits a second ball and there is a delay before the second ball moves away, then they will not interpret the collision of the balls as causing the movement (Leslie, 1988), though the collision will be seen as causing the second ball to move if it starts to move right after the collision. People also tend to assume that causes and effects should be of similar magnitude. Einhorn and Hogarth (1986) pointed out that the germ theory of disease initially met with great resistance because people could not imagine how such tiny organisms could have such devastating effects.

It is important to recognize that homeopathy and contagion often point us in the right direction. Immunization can be seen as a form of homeopathic medicine that has an underlying theoretical principle supporting it. Our reading of these observations, however, is not that specific theoretical (causal) principles are constraining similarity but rather that similarity (homeopathy and contagion) acts as a constraint on the search for causal explanations. Even in classical conditioning studies, the similarity of the conditioned stimulus and the unconditioned stimulus can have a major influence on the rate of conditioning (Testa, 1974).

One way of integrating similarity and explanation is in terms of a notion of **psychological essentialism** (Gelman, Coley, & Gottfried, 1994; Keil, 1989; Medin & Ortony, 1989; Wattenmaker, Nakamura, & Medin, 1988). The main ideas are as follows: People act as if things (e.g., objects) have essences or underlying natures that make them the thing that they are. Essentialism seems to be an idea present in many cultures (e.g. Atran, 1990; Walker.

1992). For biological categories in our culture, people might identify essence with genetic structure. The essence constrains or generates (often external) properties that may vary in their centrality. For example, people in our culture believe that the categories male and female are genetically determined, but to pick someone out as male or female we rely on characteristics such as hair length, height, facial hair, and clothing that represent a mixture of secondary sexual characteristics and cultural conventions. Although these characteristics are less reliable than genetic evidence, they are far from arbitrary. Not only do they have some validity in a statistical sense but also they are tied to our biological and cultural conceptions of male and female.

Note that psychological essentialism refers not to how the world really is but rather to how people approach the world. Wastebaskets presumably have no true essence, although we may act as if they do. Both social and psycho-diagnostic categories are at least partially culture-specific and, therefore, may represent constructions rather than discoveries about the world (see also Morey & McNamara, 1987).

Why should people act as if things had essences? Possibly the reason is that it may be a good strategy for learning about the world. Recall that categorization faces computational complexity problems and that organisms face a strong need to make correct and useful predictions and inferences on the basis of their categorization schemes. One could say that people adopt an essentialist strategy or heuristic, namely, the generalization that things that look alike tend to share deeper properties (similarities) because it's typically an effective strategy. That is, our perceptual and conceptual systems appear to have evolved such that the essentialist heuristic is very often correct (Atran, 1990; Medin & Wattenmaker, 1987; Shepard, 1987). This is true even for human artifacts such as cars, computers, and camping stoves because structure and function tend to be correlated. Surface characteristics that are perceptually obvious or readily produced on feature-listing tasks may not so much constitute the core of a concept as point toward it. This observation suggests that classifying on the basis of similarity will be relatively effective much of the time, but that similarity will yield to knowledge of deeper principles. Thus, in the work of Gelman and Markman (1986) discussed earlier (Figure 10.8), category membership was more important than perceptual similarity in determining

inductive inferences. Gelman and Wellman (1991) showed that even young children seem to use notions of essence in reasoning about biological kinds (see also Gelman & Hirschfeld, 1999). Susan Gelman has systematically traced the development of essentialism and its role in conceptual and linguistic development (see Gelman, 1998, for a review).

We have presented one way of relating similarity to knowledge structures and theories. Still, it would be misleading to state that there is any strong consensus on this general issue. Indeed, in the area of machine learning, a great deal of attention has been directed at the question of how to integrate similarity-based and explanation-based learning (see, e.g., Ellman, 1989; Flann & Dietterich, 1989; Rajamoney & DeJong, 1987; Wisniewski & Medin, 1994). Note that research on theories shares with the work on perceptual learning the idea that similarity has an important role to play but that role is governed by the consequences of other processes that work to constrain similarity.

Are There Kinds of Categories?

Almost all of our discussion has been focused on object concepts and their structure. But what about abstract concepts such as *democracy* or *dilemma,* adjective concepts such as *daring,* or verb concepts such as *dance?* Do the generalizations concerning object concepts apply equally to these other kinds of concepts or are there different principles involved when one moves beyond object concepts? One motivation for an interest in kinds of categories is that a number of researchers, especially in the area of cognitive development have suggested that cognition is organized in terms of distinct domains, each characterized by (usually) innate constraints or skeletal principles of development. For example, naive psychology (theories about people), naïve biology (theories about livings things), and naive physics (theories about the physical world) may constitute distinct domains with somewhat different principles of conceptual development (see Hirschfeld & Gelman, 1994, for examples).

It is transparently obvious that there are different kinds of categories, at least in the everyday sense of *different* and *kinds.* But to answer the sorts of questions we have raised, one must have some specific criteria in mind for what counts as a different kind. One might imagine that categories might differ in structure (as in our distinction between hierarchical and nonhierarchical categories), in the processing principles associated with them, or in principles that are tied to specific contents. The latter idea is tied to the notion of domain-specificity; the idea is that by looking only at principles that apply to all categories, we may be missing important principles that apply only to an important subset of categories (e.g., psychology vs. biology vs. physics).

Some of the candidate distinctions among kinds of categories, such as Barsalou's contrast between taxonomic and goal-derived categories have already been mentioned. We have space only to give a few examples of other contrasts. One distinction receiving increasing research interest is that between nouns and verbs, which may differ in structure (e.g., Macnamara, 1972; Gentner, 1981). One proposal is that nouns refer to clusters of correlated properties that create bounded chunks of perceptual experience. Verbs generally focus on relations among these entities involving things such as causal relations, activity, or change of state. Since relations require objects, nouns may be conceptually simpler than verbs and more constrained by perceptual experience. If so, then we might expect more cross-linguistic variability in verbs than nouns and that syntactic structure should play a greater role in verb learning than in noun learning. There is evidence for both of these claims (e.g., Bowerman, 1996; Choi & Bowerman, 1991; Levinson, 1994; Naigles, 1990; Pinker, 1994). Be aware, however, that the distinction between nouns and verbs is more subtle than we have implied. For example, motion may be associated with both nouns and verbs (e.g., runner); nonetheless, there is a bias for nouns to be associated with motion intrinsic to an object and verbs to be associated with motions involving relations between objects (Kersten, 1998a, 1998b).

Even more attention has been directed at the idea of domain-specificity. Much of the work on essentialism has been conducted in the context of exploring children's naive biology (see also Au, 1994; Carey, 1995; Gopnik & Wellman, 1994; Spelke, Phillips, & Woodward, 1995). Although is it difficult to give a precise definition of a domain, the notion of domain-specificity has served to organize a great deal of research on conceptual development. For example, there has been a strong focus on the question of whether and when young children distinguish between psychology and biology. Carey (1985) argues that young children understand biological concepts in terms of a naïve psychology where human beings are the prototypical psychological entity. Only later on do they reorganize their knowledge into a less humanocentric, biological form where human beings are simply one animal among many. Others (e.g., Keil, 1989) have argued that young children do have biologically specific theories, though not as elaborate as those of adults. The issue is not a matter of idle debate because understanding how children's biological knowledge develops is highly relevant to science education as well as children's health-related behaviors (e.g., Au & Romo, 1996).

Summary

Research on object concepts has received disproportionate attention in the psychology of concepts. This work suggests that people may use similarity and theories as organizing principles for their categories, though neither type of information is sufficient by itself to account for people's behavior with concepts. Indeed, in many cases, both similarity and theories are related, as theories may help determine what people consider similar, and physical similarity may influence the development of theories.

Other kinds of concepts (besides object concepts) may have different structure and different processing principles (e.g., mechanisms by which they are learned). In addition, it appears to be a useful research strategy to analyze conceptual development in terms of different domains. Overall, then, there is a trend to organize categorization principles in terms of specific kinds of concepts (see Medin, Lynch, & Solomon, 2000, for a general review).

USE OF CATEGORIES IN REASONING

So much attention has been paid to structural aspects of categories that only modest attention has been given to the question of how categories may be used in reasoning. The promising results from the few studies that have been done suggest that this question is worthy of much more attention.

Goals and Ad Hoc Categories

Earlier we mentioned Barsalou's work on goal-derived categories (1985, 1987, 1989). In particular he has studied the organization of categories constructed in the service of goals, which we will refer to as **ad hoc categories**. "Things to take on a camping trip" and "foods to eat while on a diet" are two such ad hoc categories. Barsalou has found that ad hoc categories show the same typicality or goodness-of-example effects that are seen with more established categories. As we noted before, however, the basis for these effects is not overall similarity of examples to each other or to a prototype, but rather similarity to an ideal. For example, typicality ratings for the category of things to eat on a diet is determined by how closely examples conform to the ideal of zero calories. If goal-dervied categories are used repeatedly and consistently, they may become more stable in memory. In short Barsalou's work suggests that goals and the reasoning processes associated with them can affect category structure.

Conceptual Combination

As we mentioned at the beginning of this chapter, concepts provide "building blocks" or "mental tokens" that enable the construction of new concepts from old ones. For example, people use their knowledge of chocolate and rash to interpret *chocolate rash* as a rash caused by chocolate, even though they may never have seen the term chocolate rash before. **Conceptual combination** allows us to produce a virtually unlimited set of new concepts. Given that we hear novel combinations of concepts all the time, an important question is how people are able to understand them.

To our knowledge, a complete theory of how people combine concepts does not exist. Basically, we know that the most straightforward ideas are incomplete. One idea is that adjective-noun combinations are understood by constructing modified prototypes, the selective modification model of Smith & Osherson (1984). For example, according to their model, to understand the term *brown apple,* the apple prototype would be retrieved, the dimension of color would receive extra attention, and the prototypical value of red would be replaced with brown. In effect, one would be constructing a new prototype, brown apple, and the typicality of examples could be judged with respect to this constructed prototype. This modification model accounts for a number of phenomena associated with typicality judgments for combined

adjective-noun concepts (Smith, Osherson, Rips, & Keane, 1988).

But conceptual combination is more complex than the modification model (or any other current model) implies. One problem is that the typicality of combined concepts cannot be predicted from the typicality of constituents. As an illustrative example, consider the concept *spoon.* People rate small spoons as more typical spoons than large spoons, and metal spoons as more typical spoons than wooden spoons. If the concept spoon is represented by a prototypic spoon, then a small metal spoon should be the most typical spoon, followed by small wooden and large metal spoons, and large wooden spoons should be the least typical. Instead, people find large wooden spoons to be more typical spoons than either small wooden spoons or large metal spoons (Medin & Shoben, 1988). One way for a prototype model to handle these results is to argue that people have separate prototypes for small spoons and large spoons. But this strategy creates new problems. Obviously one cannot have a separate prototype for every adjective-noun combination, because there are simply too many possible combinations. One might suggest that there are distinct subtypes for concepts like spoon, but one would need a theory describing how and when subtypes are created.

Another problem is that combined concepts may have properties that do not appear as properties of either constituent concept (Hampton, 1987, 1996; Murphy, 1988; see also Storms, De Boeck, Van Mechelen, & Ruts, 1998). For example, a salient property of the concept *pet bird* is that they live in cages, but this property is very atypical of either pets or birds by themselves.

A third problem is that people may complicate analyses by using a variety of strategies for comprehending combined concepts (Wisniewski, 1996, 1997; Wisniewski & Gentner. 1991). Consider, for example novel noun-noun combinations. When the two nouns are easily compared (because they have similar kinds of properties and are said to be "alignable") the combination is typically interpreted by extending a salient property of the modifying noun to the main noun. For example, a "zebra horse" might be understood as a horse with stripes. When the nouns are less comparable the most likely result is an integration where some relationship is found that meaningfully links the two concepts. For example, a "zebra house" typically is understood as a house for zebras rather than as a house

Studies of patients with brain damage often provide clues to normal brain functioning. One striking observation is that patients may show selective, **category-specific deficits** where they lose their ability to recognize and name category members from a particular domain of concepts. Nelson (1946) reported a patient who was unable to recognize a telephone, a hat, or a car but could identify people and other living things. Other researchers have noted the opposite deficit where people lose their ability to identify living kinds but retain the ability to categorize nonliving kinds.

Category-specific deficits seem consistent with ideas about domain-specific cognition but their interpretation has proven to be a matter of some controversy. On one side is the idea that living kinds and nonliving kinds are represented in anatomically and functionally distinct systems (Sartori & Job, 1988). An alternative view is that these deficit patterns can be accounted for by the fact that different kinds of information are needed to identify different kinds of objects (Warrington & Shallice, 1984). For example, sensory information may be relatively more important for recognizing living kinds and functional information more important for identifying nonliving kinds (e.g., artifacts). Although the evidence appear to be more consistent with the kinds of information view (see Damasio, Grabowski, Tranel, & Hichwa, 1996; Forde & Humpheys, 1999, for reviews), the issue continues to be hotly debated (see Caramazza & Shelton, 1998, for a vigorous defense of the domain specificity view of category specific deficits).

with stripes. Models of conceptual combination that rely on a single process cannot account for these results (see Wisniewski & Love, 1998). So far, it seems that conceptual combination is as difficult as it is important (see Gagné & Shoben, 1997; Gerrig & Murphy, 1992; and Hampton, 1993, for other approaches to conceptual combination).

Categories and Induction

Finally, we note that categories play an important role in inductive reasoning. **Induction**, the use of some knowledge to draw inferences or expectations about other, more general situations, will be an important part of Chapter 11, but we include a sample here to illustrate the combined influence of similarity to examples and category membership in reasoning. Osherson, Smith, Wilkie, Lopez, and Shafir (1990) developed a formal model of category-based induction (see also Rips, 1975). The main idea is that judgments are based on both similarity to examples and knowledge of category membership. The model is formulated in terms of "argument strength," going from a premise or premises to the conclusion (candidate inference). For example, a premise might be "robins have property x" and the conclusion "sparrows also have property x" or "all birds have property x." We are using "have property x" to illustrate that properties were chosen so that participants in experiments would have no knowledge of whether these

properties are true (e.g., "birds have sesamoid bones"). The task of the participants was to judge which argument form is stronger. For example, from the premise that robins have some property, people judge the argument with the conclusion that sparrows also have the property to be stronger than the argument with the conclusion that all birds have the property.

Argument strength is assumed to depend on two factors: the similarity of premise categories to the conclusion category and the similarity of the premise categories to examples of the lowest level category that the premise and conclusion categories share. For example, the strength of "robins have x" for the conclusion, "all birds have x," is based on the similarity of robins to bird (assumed to be perfect, because robins are birds) and the similarity of robins to other birds. The net confidence is assumed to be based on some weighting of these two factors. Similarly, the strength of "ostriches have x" for the conclusion, "all birds have x," is a function of the similarity of ostriches to bird (again, assumed to be perfect) and the similarity of ostriches to other birds. It follows directly that "robins have x" should be stronger than "ostriches have x" for the conclusion that all birds have x, because ostriches are less similar to other birds than are robins. In short, the model predicts typicality effects in reasoning (robins are more typical than ostriches).

Many of the predictions of the Osherson et al. model make intuitive sense, but a few predictions are quite surprising. The model predicts that going from the premise "bears have x" to the conclusion that "all mammals have x" will be stronger than going from "bears have x" to the conclusion "rabbits have x," even though rabbits are mammals. Note that whatever is true of all mammals must also be true of rabbits. The reason for this prediction by the model is that going from bears to rabbits involves weighting separately the similarity of bears to rabbits (which may be low), whereas going from bears to mammals is based on the overall similarity of bears to other mammals (which should be fairly high because bears are typical mammals). The results agree with this counterintuitive prediction.

Another prediction of the model makes intuitive sense but the associated results depend very much on who the research participants are. The prediction concerns premise *diversity*. Consider the following arguments: "Suppose we discover two new diseases, A and B. So far we know that Disease A affects the white pine and the weeping willow and that Disease B affects the paper birch and the river birch. Which disease is more likely to affect all trees, A or B? The Osherson et al. model predicts that people will say A for the same reasons it predicts typicality effects. The two trees associated with Disease A are very different from each other and together they represent the category "tree" better (trees that the white pine isn't similar to the weeping willow may be similar to). You, the reader, probably would make the same judgment, perhaps because you think that Disease B might be specific to birches. Surprisingly, however, when items like this (the items are different, because the plants and animals are different in Guatemala) are given to Itzá Maya adults, they do *not* pick the more diverse premises (Atran, 1998). And, in case you were starting to wonder about the reasoning processes of people in traditional societies, it also is the case that U.S. adults who know a lot about trees do not choose the disease associated with the more diverse pair consistently either (Coley, Medin, Proffitt. Lynch, & Atran, 1999). In fact, on the particular example given above tree maintenance workers overwhelming picked Disease B as more likely to affect all trees!

What accounts for these surprising results? The answer seems to be that both tree experts and Itzá Maya are reasoning about ecological relations and potential causal mechanisms. For example, a typical justification for choosing Disease B on the above item was that birches are very susceptible to disease and are very widely planted so there would be many opportunities for the disease to spread. Aside from suggesting that models of category-based reasoning need to make provision for people reasoning about potential mechanisms, these results point out that categorization and reasoning by novices in a domain may differ substantially from that of experts. If nothing else it should make cognitive psychologists more cautious about generalizing from results with undergraduate populations to all people.

Overall, the category-based induction model is quite successful. As we said at the beginning of this section, psychologists are just starting to explore the use of categories in reasoning (for extensions to nonblank properties, see Sloman, 1994; Smith, Shark, & Osherson, 1993). The work on reasoning is part of a general trend to study how concepts are used and we can already see that this approach is delivering new insights into the nature of concepts.

SUMMARY

Concepts serve to organize our mental life. Analyses of conceptual structure provide some important conclusions for our understanding of human cognition. Contrary to one's initial impression, many categories do not have defining properties but rather are fuzzy or probabilistic. These probabilistic categories may be organized around an average example (a prototype) or around specific examples seen during learning. The research we reviewed also suggests that things that are superficially similar tend to be similar in deeper ways, but similarity does not provide the basis for conceptual coherence. Concepts are often organized around theories and are knowledge-based rather than similarity-based.

Another important issue is that categories have many different functions. Much research on categorization has focused on how people learn to classify a set of items. However, people also use their categories to communicate, to reason, and to make predictions. Psychologists are now working on how category representations are used to serve these functions and also what people learn about categories in the process of using them.

What about the questions and problems with which we began this chapter? Why do we have the particular categories we have, out of the virtually unlimited number of possibilities? Are categories in the world to be discovered, or are they imposed on the world by our minds? We have suggested that perceptual similarity may serve as an initial classification strategy that is refined, deepened, and itself modified by knowledge and developing theories about the world. If our perceptual and conceptual systems suggested to us categorization schemes that did not serve our goals and did not allow for predictions and explanations, we would be poorly adapted. Therefore, it is tempting to say that categories are organized around our goals and that different organisms with different goals would have very different categorization schemes. Although this may be true, it is equally important to recognize the importance of our environment. If we lived in a very different world, we would need a different perceptual and conceptual system to pick out categories that would be useful in that world. As indicated in our opening quotation, we believe that William James was correct when he suggested that mind and world "are something of a mutual fit."

KEY TERMS

ad hoc categories	family resemblance
basic level	homeopathy
category	induction
category-specific deficits	linear separability
classical view	probabilistic view
concept	prototype
conceptual combination	psychological essentialism
contagion	typicality
exemplar models	

RECOMMENDED READINGS

Because all three authors do research on categorization, we are tempted to say, "Read everything!" Fortunately, a number of reviews of the literature exist. For basic historical background, the edited volume by Rosch and Lloyd (1978)

and the book by Smith and Medin (1981) are recommended. More recent analyses and overviews are provided by Estes (1994), Medin and Heit (1999), and the edited volumes by Hirschfeld and Gelman (1994), Lamberts and Shanks (1997), and Van Mechelen. Hampton, and Michalski (1993). A nice review of cross-cultural research on biological categorization is provided by Malt (1995) and the edited volume by Medin and Atran (1999) covers both cross-cultural and developmental research. Lillard (1998) argues that adult folk psychology differs across cultures—such a fact would have important implications for understanding the development of naïve or folk psychology. For analyses that focus on tests of or contrasts between particular models of categorization, see Anderson (1990a, 1990b), Erickson and Kruschke (1998), Estes (1994), Heit (1994), Hintzman (1986), Maddox and Ashby (1993), Murphy and Ross (1994), Nosofsky et al. (1994), Nosofsky and Palmeri (1997), Storms, De Boeck, and Ruts (2000), and Wisniewski and Medin (1994). A special issue of the journal *Cognition,* edited by Sloman and Rips (1998), is devoted to the topic of the role of similarity in cognition. Malt, Sloman, Gennari, Shi, and Wang (1999) offer a nice cross-cultural analysis of the relation between perceived similarity of containers and how they are named.

Finally, there is increasing interest in the use of categories in reasoning. A good place to start is Rips (1975), Osherson et al. (1990), Smith et al. (1993), and Sloman (1993, 1994, 1998); for developmental work, see Gelman and Markman (1986), Gelman and Wellman (1991), Gutheil and Gelman (1997), Keil (1989), and Lopez, Gelman, Gutheil, and Smith (1992); for cross-cultural work see Atran (1998), Choi, Nisbett, and Smith (1997), and Lopez, Atran, Coley, Medin, and Smith (1997).

CHAPTER 14
Thinking and Problem Solving

Problem Solving and Creativity

ARNOLD L. GLASS AND KEITH J. HOLYOAK

INTRODUCTION

Problem Solving: Basic Definitions

In many ways this chapter is the culmination of those that have come before it. All the basic cognitive processes we have explored in earlier chapters—perceiving, categorizing, remembering, and reasoning—are used in dealing with problems. Problem-solving skills hinge on the way information can be represented in memory and later retrieved and applied in novel situations. The ability to formulate creative solutions to problems is what most people consider the most central aspect of thinking.

At an intuitive level everyone knows what a problem is; we all have them from time to time. Consider a few examples:

Deciding how to lose weight	Designing a house
Solving a crossword puzzle	Building a spaceship
Selecting a good chess move	Writing a play

Basically, a person has a problem when he or she wants something that is not immediately attainable. The goal of the problem may be quite specific (solve today's crossword puzzle) or more general (write a story good enough to win an award). The actions involved in obtaining the goal may range from physical activities (e.g., walking) to acts of the imagination (e.g., visualizing the problem). While problems can be extremely diverse, all have four basic components:

1. A *goal,* or a description of what would constitute a solution to the problem.
2. A description of *objects* relevant to achieving a solution, such as resources that can be used, the problem solver, and any allies or opponents that may be involved.
3. A set of *operations,* or actions that can be taken to help achieve a solution.
4. A set of *constraints* that must not be violated in the course of solving the problem.

For example, consider the problem of solving a crossword puzzle. The object description would include the pattern of blank spaces on the puzzle, a specification of where each word has to fit in, and a set of clues for what each word means. The operations that a person might employ include searching semantic memory, counting the number of letters in a word, and assigning possible words to spaces. The goal state is a complete set of assignments of words to spaces, with all words correctly spelled and appropriate in meaning. Constraints might include strictures against cheating in getting the solution (e.g., getting a friend who is an expert at crossword puzzles to do it for you).

The term *problem* is typically reserved for situations in which the goal is not achieved by an automatic process of perception or recognition. Rather, problems are cases in which some obstacle initially blocks achievement of the goal. In a complex problem there may be many false starts, dead ends, and intervening steps before a solution is achieved. Problems such as the examples listed earlier will usually require a substantial amount of time to reach the goal—at least several seconds, often minutes or hours, sometimes years.

Problem-Solving Process: Overview

Just as a problem has basic components, the process of solving one can be described in terms of several major steps. While the schemas for solving different kinds of problems are somewhat different, they all have some general steps in common. A general problem-solving schema: The four major steps in the process are (1) forming an initial representation of the problem (in terms of goal, objects, operations, and constraints); (2) using problem-solving methods to plan a potential solution; (3) if necessary, reformulating the problem; and (4) executing a procedure to carry out a plan and checking the results.

To take a relatively simple example, consider the problem of proving a geometry theorem of the sort you probably encountered in high school. Step 1 in the solution process might involve listing the information given and drawing a diagram. Step 2 would involve applying operations (e.g., relevant theorems) to construct a sequence of steps that actually yield a proof. If step 2 cannot be done on the first attempt, you might have to try to reformulate the problem in some way (step 3). For example, you might try reducing a problem given in three dimensions to a similar one that you know how to solve in two dimensions; then you use the result to help develop a plan for the more complex problem. If attempts to reformulate a problem initially fail and you are stuck, taking a break and returning to the problem later may be helpful. (We will consider the possible benefits of such incubation later when we discuss creative thinking.)

Once a potential plan has been generated, step 4 would involve actually giving an explicit step-by-step statement of the proof. In addition, you might then check the results by using a different method, or by trying the same method on a similar problem, to make sure that the solution is correct.

We will discuss the process of solving problems in more detail later, but a few points deserve emphasis at the outset. A major point concerns the concept of a *plan*. A plan is a procedure for a sequence of actions that implicitly makes a prediction: "If I take the following actions, then I will achieve a solution." One of the most basic aspects of problem solving is that a plan is often created and then mentally tested *before* overt actions are taken. This step is extremely important, because many problems are unforgiving of errors. For example, suppose the police are trying to rescue hostages being held by a gunman. If the police attempt to solve this problem by a sudden raid on the building and something goes wrong, the hostages may be killed. In such a situation the police must plan with great care in advance, since there will probably be no second chance. One criterion for evaluating plans, in fact, involves anticipating the consequences of failure. For example, negotiation is often preferable to attack in a hostage situation, because the police can explore different approaches to negotiation, whereas they can usually expect to attack only once.

Well-Defined vs. Ill-Defined Problems

A major dimension along which problems vary is the extent to which they are *well defined* (Newell 1969; Reitman 1964; Simon 1973). In a well-defined problem the components are all completely specified. A good example is an algebra problem (e.g., solve the equation $ax - b = x$ for x). The objects involved (the algebraic symbols) are clear to any algebra student; the operations are the rules of algebra (e.g., add a constant to both sides of the equation); the goal state is to have only x on the left side of the equal sign and everything else on the right; and the main constraint is to use legal algebraic manipulations.

Ill-defined problems, on the other hand, are those for which the problem solver has more uncertainty concerning the given information and starting materials, the operations that can be used, and the final product that must be achieved. Unfortunately, the term *ill-defined problem* has a slightly negative ring to it. In fact, however, many ill-defined problems are very creative tasks. When people decide to paint pictures, write books, or perform experiments, they are all undertaking ill-defined but creative tasks.

Virtually all real-life problems are actually ill defined in one way or another. Take an apparently simple problem like cooking dinner. The available objects may not be precisely determined (Shall I use whatever is in the house or go shopping in a gourmet food store?), nor the possible operations (Shall I fry hamburgers or use a recipe in my Tibetan cookbook?), nor the goal state (Do I really need dessert?). Most problems are even less well defined than this one. For example, consider the problem of writing a novel. How would we define the initial-knowledge state of the author? Not only do writers use a vast store of information based on knowledge of other novels, but they also often base the content of the book on some real-life experiences. So at first glance the initial-knowledge state seems virtually unlimited. Similarly, the rules of composition, which are the operations used in writing a novel, are not clearly specified.

The goal state is particularly critical in ill-defined problems, because to specify what will count as a successful problem solution is difficult. Many problems like this one are so open-ended that finding a "perfect" solution, or even recognizing one should you stumble upon it, is virtually impossible. In the case of the novelist, how would he or she decide that the story is finished? Usually, one must stop after achieving a solution that is good enough by some criterion. For example, a student may adopt a certain satisfaction criterion in writing a term paper and may decide to turn in a paper that he or she expects will receive a B grade, because to produce an A paper would require more time than the student is willing to put into if. In general, a problem solver needs to be able to evaluate progress toward a solution and also to be able to decide when an acceptable solution has been reached.

Because of the uncertainties involved in ill-defined problems, the problem solver must often devote a great deal of time to both the step of forming an initial representation of the problem and the step of reformulating it. Often a more specific reformulation will go a long way toward solving the problem; e.g., in the dinner problem, deciding on the meal one wants to cook constrains the choice of grocery stores. In some ill-defined problems the plan that is first generated does not remain fixed. For example, writers often get an idea and then let the plot and characters unfold as the story progresses, without having a clear conception of how the story will end. In other words, the planned solution may actually evolve during the course of writing. This idea is expressed very clearly by the novelist John Fowles (1969, pp. 81–82):

You may think novelists always have fixed plans to which they work, so that the future predicted by Chapter One is always inexorably the actuality of Chapter Thirteen. But novelists write for countless different reasons.... Only one same reason is shared by all of us: we wish *to create worlds as real as,* but other than *the* world *that* is. Or was. That is why we cannot plan. We know a world is an organism, not a machine. We also know that a genuinely created world must be independent of its creator; a planned world (a world that fully reveals its planning) is a dead world. It is only that when our characters and events begin to disobey us that they begin to live.

For ill-defined problems the first step in problem solving, forming an initial representation, deserves special emphasis. This step actually includes the process of *finding* a problem in the first place. The ability to create problems appears to be a peculiarly human ability. People not only bring images of things they have seen into consciousness but also manipulate them and so imagine a green horse or a mouse flying through the air. We call this ability to create new representations *imagination,* and at its core is the ability to manipulate perceptual representations through imagery. But humans can also manipulate conceptual representations and hence imagine machines that turn lead into gold and sunlight into power. A great deal of what we call creative thinking occurs in finding a problem that is worth solving. A writer must find a story worth telling, a painter an idea worth capturing on canvas, a scientist a question about nature that needs to be answered.

Finding a problem to solve is as important, and often as difficult, as solving it. Many students working on a Ph.D. dissertation find that getting a good idea is harder than doing the actual research. For any creative problem solver, such as an artist, writer, or scientist, few experiences are more painful than a dry period without a project worth pursuing.

Problem Representations in Chimpanzees and Humans

Problem-solving behavior requires such extensive conscious manipulation of representations that we would not expect to find much evidence of it in nonhuman species. In fact, only a few animals engage in anything that closely resembles human problem-solving behavior. In particular, the classic studies of the Gestalt psychologist Wolfgang Kohler (1925) demonstrated that chimpanzees can sometimes overcome functional fixedness. In one sequence the chimp Sultan was in a cage and noticed a banana lying outside out of reach. In the cage was a bushy tree. Sultan suddenly went to the tree, broke off a branch, ran back to the bars and used the branch to bring the banana into reach. What was at first not even a separate object was suddenly recognized as a potential tool.

More recently, David Premack and his colleagues have conducted an extensive investigation of problem solving by chimpanzees (Premack and Woodruff 1978). Rather than have chimps actually execute problem solutions, they tested the chimps on their ability to comprehend solutions. In a typical experiment a chimpanzee was shown a videotape of a human actor struggling to obtain bananas that were attached to the ceiling out of reach. Then the animal was shown a pair of still photographs, one illustrating a solution to the problem and the other a nonsolution. For example, the solution scene might show the actor stepping onto a box, while the nonsolution scene might show him moving a box aside. The two alternatives were placed in a cardboard box, and the experimenter then left the room. The chimp had to pick up the correct picture, place it in a designated location, and ring a bell to recall the experimenter. The experimenter would then say either "Good, that's right" or "No, that's wrong."

Such problems were presented to Sarah, a chimp who became famous for her performance in studies of "language" training (see Chapter 14). When tested at the age of fourteen years (about eight years after the studies of language training had ended), Sarah was able to reliably choose the correct alternative in tasks such as that just described (Premack and Woodruff 1978). Moreover, Sarah's choices were influenced by some very humanlike motives. In one experiment the actor in the videotape of the problem situation was varied. When the actor was Sarah's favorite trainer, she invariably selected the correct-solution photograph. But when the actor was a man who Sarah was known to dislike, Sarah was likely to pick out a photograph of a bad outcome, such as the actor stepping right through the box. Seemingly, Sarah not only knew how to solve problems but also knew when she would just as soon see the problem solver fail.

An intriguing observation that Premack has made is that chimps like Sarah, who have received language training, seem to be especially adept at complex problem-solving tasks. Although it remains a speculative possibility, such training may serve to develop internal representations that facilitate problem solving. In any case, humans clearly have a unique ability to manipulate representations and to transfer information between various codes, and this ability allows them to solve a wide variety of problems. Foremost among those codes used to solve problems are the visuo-spatial representation and those codes involved in language, which will be collectively referred to as the verbal representation.

PROCESS OF PROBLEM SOLVING

We will now examine each of the four basic steps of problem solving in more detail.

Forming an Initial Representation

Problem representation. A key to understanding the first step of problem solving is to gain some insight into how the problem solver arrives at an initial problem representation. For example, consider the following problem:

> The price of a notebook is four times that of a pencil. The pencil costs 30¢ less than the notebook. What is the price of each?

This problem is presented in a purely verbal form. However, this form is not a very good representation for solving if. If you are like most people who have learned algebra, you will probably translate the problem into a different representation, perhaps as follows:

Let n = notebook and let p = pencil.
Initial state: $n = 4p$. and $p = n-30$.
Substitute for n: $p = 4p-30$.

Subtract 4p from both sides:−3 p =−30.
Therefore p = 10 and n = 40.

An algebraic representation makes use of both the verbal and the visuospatial representations to bring into play a set of operations for manipulating equations, making the problem quite simple to solve. Algebra makes use of the name relation in the semantic code (Chapter 5) to identify variables, but it also makes use of the visuospatial code in substituting variables and moving them from one side of the equation to the other.

However, one can also translate the verbal representation directly into the visuospatial code. When this problem was given to S., the remarkable mnemonist studied by Luria (see Chapter 10), S. reported imagining a series of visual equations. In Figure 12.2(a) he imagined a notebook beside four pencils. Then in Figure 12.2(b) he mentally pushed three pencils aside and replaced them with 30¢, since one pencil plus 30¢ equals the value of the notebook. Since 30¢ therefore is equivalent to three pencils, S. immediately realized (presumably by simple arithmetic) that one pencil was worth 10¢ and the notebook was worth 40¢. Some of S.'s major problem-solving operations were thus manipulations of visual images.

Importance of task analysis. The example of the algebra problem illustrates the fact that a problem can have more than one representation, because the person often defines the problem in his or her own way. The question is, What is the best way to think of a problem in order to solve it more easily? Here we find some individual differences; e.g., some people claim they usually think visually. However, some problems can be solved much more easily with one form of representation than another.

One common example of a dramatic shift in representation is the game of number scrabble (Newell and Simon 1972), which can be described as follows:

Each of the digits 1 through 9 is written on a separate piece of paper. Two players draw digits alternately. As soon as either player gets any three digits that sum to 15, that player wins. If all nine digits are drawn without a win, then the game is a draw.

Most people who play this verbally encoded game a few times are still surprised when told that it is actually equivalent to the visuospatially encoded game tic-tac-toe. Figure 12.3 illustrates why they are equivalent. The nine digits can be placed on the squares in such a way that each horizontal, vertical, or diagonal row sums to 15. As a result, the rule for winning number scrabble (select three digits that add to 15) is equivalent to the rule for winning tic-tac-toe (occupy three squares in a row).

Even though the two games are equivalent, so that we can represent one in terms of the other, most people find tic-tac-toe easier. For one thing, the digits disappear; we no longer have to compute sums of numbers, as in number scrabble. Also, in tic-tac-toe scanning all possible solutions is easier. If players actually discover that number scrabble can be represented as tic-tac-toe, this insight may substantially alter the way they play the game. For example, many people know that a good strategy in tic-tac-toe is to occupy the corner squares. The equivalent strategy in number scrabble is to select even digits. This strategy might not occur to you unless you thought about it in terms of tic-tac-toe. This point is a general point about problem-solving strategies: the kind of representation will affect the strategies chosen.

Another example of how problem representation can affect the ease of solution is the Buddhist monk problem. This problem, like many of those commonly dicussed by psychologists, originated with the Gestalt psychologists of the early twentieth century (in this case, Karl Duncker). The problem is as follows:

One morning, exactly at sunrise, a Buddhist monk began to climb a tall mountain. A narrow path, no more than a foot or two wide, spiraled around the mountain to a glittering temple at the summit. The monk ascended at varying rates of speed, stopping many times along the way to rest and eat dried fruit he carried with him. He reached the temple shortly before sunset. After several days of fasting and meditation he began his journey back along the same path, starting at sunrise and again walking at variable speeds, with many pauses along the way. His average speed descending was, of course, greater than his average climbing speed. Show that there is a spot along the path that the monk will occupy on both trips at precisely the same time of day.

People who think about this problem verbally or algebraically are unlikely to solve it. They may conclude that it would be an improbable coincidence for the monk to find himself at the same spot at the same time on two different days. But one can actually visualize the solution, as the following report by a young woman suggests (Koestler 1964, p. 184):

I tried this and that, until I got fed up with the whole thing, but the image of the monk in his saffron robe walking up the hill kept persisting in my mind. Then a moment came when, superimposed on this image, I saw another, more transparent one, of the monk walking down the hill, and I realized in a flash that the two figures must meet at some point in time—regardless of what speed they walk and how often each of them stops. Then I reasoned out what I already knew: whether the monk descends two days or three days later comes to the same; so I was quite justified in letting him descend on the same day, in duplicate so to speak.

Figure 12.4 provides a somewhat more abstract, visual solution to the problem. This graph plots the altitude of the monk on the mountain as a function of time of day, for both his ascent and his descent. We see that the two paths must cross, regardless of the monk's variable rates of progress. The point of intersection is the point on the path that the monk will occupy at the same time of day on both trips.

In the report quoted above the problem solver experiences a flash of *insight* when she visualizes the solution. Insight, a concept stressed by Gestalt psychologists who investigated problem solving, seems to involve a rapid reorganization of a problem representation that proceeds finding a solution. We will encounter other illustrations of insight as our discussion proceeds.

The successful visual solution to the Buddhist monk problem can be contrasted with the solution to the following mental paper-folding problem (from Adams 1974, p. 63):

Picture a large piece of paper. 1/100 of an inch thick. In your imagination, fold it once (now having two layers), fold it once more (now having four layers), and continue folding it over on itself 50 times. It is true that it is impossible to fold any actual piece of paper 50 times. But for the sake of the problem, imagine that you can. About how thick would the 50-times-folded paper be?

At first glance this problem might seem like another problem requiring a visual solution. But in fact a visual solution is impossible. Note that the first fold will result in 2 times the original thickness, while the second fold will result in $2 \times 2 = 4$ times the original thickness. In fact, each fold increases the thickness by a factor of 2. So 50 folds will increase the paper's thickness by a factor of 2 multiplied by 2 exactly 50 times, or 2^{50}. This number works out to about 1,100,000,000.000,000, a number so large that the resulting thickness of the folded paper would approximate the distance from the earth to the sun.

Obviously, visual imagery cannot produce this result. People who try to visualize a few folds and then extrapolate to estimate the thickness resulting from fifty folds (a kind of visual application of the availability heuristic) invariably wildly underestimate the correct answer. In this case only a mathematical representation can easily produce an accurate solution.

The contrast between the Buddhist monk problem and the mental paper-folding problem highlights the importance of *task analysis*. Understanding the nature of the task and defining what is necessary for a solution is usually a major step toward finding a representation that can be used effectively to solve the problem. This principle is a useful one to remember when you are studying problem solving. Often by thinking about how a problem could be solved, one can get a good idea of how an intelligent problem solver actually would solve the problem.

We see, then, that a major part of forming an initial problem representation is selecting the best code to represent it in. This selection process requires making implicit information explicit, weeding out irrelevant information, and noting what is forbidden and what is permitted by the problem. We will see shortly that if the initial problem representation proves inadequate, these same considerations arise again in the step of reformulation.

Planning a Potential Solution

As the flowchart in Figure 12.1 indicates, the three final steps of the problem-solving process do not follow each other in a fixed order. Rather, the problem solver is basically trying to plan a potential solution (step 2). However, if no plan can be constructed (perhaps because the representation is ill defined in some way), an attempt will be made to reformulate the problem (step 3), after which step 2 will be repeated. Once a plan is actually constructed, it can be tested (step 4); if the plan fails, the process cycles back to step 2 to generate a new plan. In this section we will consider how a solution plan can be generated (step 2) if the problem representation is adequate. However, you should keep in mind that in actual problem solving steps 3 and 4 may intervene many times before an adequate representation is achieved.

In order to create a plan, one must use problem-solving methods. Let us examine some of the most important such methods.

General methods for problem solving. The process of generating a problem solution can be viewed as a search through a space of *possible* solutions (Newell and Simon 1972). In many problems a major difficulty is that the space to be searched is potentially enormous. A good example is the problem of winning a game of chess.

The course of a chess game can be represented as a tree similar to the one shown in Figure 12.5. The top node in the tree represents the initial position on the chessboard. Each of the possible alternative moves will lead to a different new position. At an average choice point a chess player may have twenty or thirty possible alternatives; for simplicity only three alternatives are shown at each choice point in the figure. At the second level in the tree the opponent will select a move, again changing the board position. The first player then chooses one of the next set of possible moves, etc. As Figure 12.5 illustrates, the final positions at the bottom of the tree determine how the game ends—whether the first player wins, ties, or loses. The dark line in the figure shows a path through the tree (i.e., a sequence of moves) that leads to a win. Only a few of the possible paths are shown in

Figure 12.5, and all the paths are just four moves long. An actual chess game will often be fifty or more moves long.

There is a clear way to win a game that can be represented as a decision tree, as in Figure 12.5. This method is to explore every possible path in the tree to determine its final outcome and then to always select a move that sends the game along a path that cannot end in a win for the opponent. The problem with this approach is that the number of paths that would have to be considered at each choice point may be astronomical. An astronomical number will certainly arise in a complex game like chess, in which the tree of possible moves is both very wide (many alternatives at each choice point) and very deep (many moves to complete a game). As a result, the only effective way to play a good chess game—even for a computer—is to use intelligent problem-solving methods that sharply restrict the search space.

As Newell (1969) pointed out, problem-solving methods range from those that are very general (applicable to almost any problem) to those that are very specialized (applicable to only a small class of problems). An example of a specialized method is a procedure for solving quadratic equations; it works very well on quadratic equations, but it is no use at all for playing chess. If a suitable specialized method is available, it will make it far easier to solve the kind of problem for which the method is tailored. As we will see shortly, expertise in a problem domain is based in part on knowledge of specialized methods.

The number of specialized methods is, of course, extremely large, since many vastly different types of problems present themselves. In contrast, there seem to be only a handful of truly general methods. Here we will discuss two representative examples.

Generate-test method. The most basic general method is the *generate-test method* (Newell and Simon 1972). This method is extremely similar to the generate-recognize process of recall that was described in Chapter 7. In fact, we can illustrate the generate-test method with a simple memory search problem: Produce the name of a fruit that has a vowel as its fourth letter.

As its name implies, the generate-test method has two steps:

1. Generate a candidate for a solution.

2. Test to see whether it is actually a solution.

If the candidate fails the test, another candidate is generated, and the cycle repeats until a solution is found. For the fruit-letter task a person might generate a series of fruits and test each one to see whether it has a vowel as its fourth letter, e.g., apple (no), orange (no), peach (no), banana (yes!).

Newell and Simon (1972) discuss four potential sources of difficulty for the generate-test method:

1. Generating each candidate may be hard. For the fruit-letter problem, generating the first few candidates is usually easy, but then thinking of new possibilities may become quite difficult.

2. Testing whether the candidate is actually the solution may be hard. The test is simple for the fruit-letter problem (check the fourth letter), but in many problems testing is the hardest part. For example, generating a possible chess move is easy, but testing whether it is the best move possible is very difficult.

3. The size of the search space may be very large. This feature is the principle behind the use of combination locks. If a lock on a bank vault has ten dials, each of which can be set at any number from 00 to 99 then there are 100^{10} or 100 billion billion, combinations. Since only one randomly chosen combination will open the lock, the sheer size of the search space will protect the bank vault from a thief who tries to use the generate-test method to discover the correct combination.

4. The correct solution may be low in the sequence of candidates that will be generated. This feature also provides the effectiveness of the combination lock; the correct solution will, on average, be found after one tests half the possibilities (i.e., after 50 billion billion tries). Compare this difficulty with the problem of naming a fruit that begins with an *a*. Even though you know many fruits, and almost none of them start with a, it is quite likely that *apple* will be the first possibility that you generate, since it is a highly typical fruit. No matter how big the search space is, the problem will be easy if the correct solution is generated early in the sequence.

The generate-test method thus has two major drawbacks as an approach to problems. First, it does not provide a mechanism for selecting good candidate solutions to be tested. If the search space is large, preselecting candidate solutions becomes critical so that one does not waste time testing candidates that are obviously wrong. A good problem solver will tend to select candidate solutions that are increasingly close to the desired goal. The name "heuristic search" is usually reserved for "intelligent" methods of selecting possible solutions to a problem. (The term heuristic, as we saw in Chapter 11, refers to a procedure that tends to produce successful solutions, even though success is not guaranteed.)

Second, the simple generate-test method involves generating a complete possible solution before testing it to see whether it is correct. For many problems this procedure is clearly very inefficient. For example, you would not try to solve a crossword puzzle by filling in all the spaces and only then checking to see whether you had a correct solution. Rather, you would work on the problem one word at a time. Finding even one correct word is clearly a partial solution that brings you closer to a full solution to the problem. This example illustrates the general usefulness of breaking down a problem into parts, sometimes called the problem reduction *approach* (Nilsson 1971). In this approach the original problem is broken down into subproblems, or subgoals, so that a solution to all the subproblems implies a solution to the overall problem. In the example of the crossword puzzle, if we set up subgoals of solving each word, the crossword puzzle will be solved once all the words have been found. A set of subgoals constitutes a plan for finding a problem solution.

One way the generate-test method could be elaborated to solve a crossword problem is to generate words of the specific lengths given in the puzzle and then to test whether the words match at intersections (Newell and Simon 1972). Note that the problem reduction approach does not eliminate search from the problem-solving process. The person now has to search for good subproblems to solve.

Means-ends analysis. A heuristic strategy for finding subgoals is *means-ends analysis*. This procedure requires problem solvers to determine the ends they are trying to achieve and the means that will serve to reach these ends. In doing so, problem solvers set up subgoals. Means-ends analysis is used frequently in everyday life. Consider the problem of cooking a Chinese dinner. You might work through this problem by using means-ends analysis and by thinking approximately as follows: "What's the difference between what I have now (my initial state) and dinner (the goal state)? A cooked meal. What is needed to cook a meal? Food, an oven. I have an oven. I also have some food, but not Chinese food. What do I do to get Chinese food? Go to the grocery store. The grocery store is down the street, but I haven't any money. What can I do to get some money? Go to the bank, which is beside the grocery store. How can I get there? Walk." And so on.

As you can see from this example, a major component of means-ends analysis consists of two steps applied repeatedly: (1) identifying the differences between the current state and the desired goal, and (2) applying an operation to reduce one of these differences. This two-step procedure is often called difference reduction. The method can be illustrated by using the simple algebra problem mentioned earlier: Solve the equation ax $-b = x$ for x. The goal state for this problem can be described as "term x on the left-hand side of the equation; all other terms on the right." At each step the current known version of the equation is compared with the goal state and differences are noted. Then an algebraic operation (e.g., "add a term to both sides of the equation"), which will eliminate one of the differences, is selected and applied. The process is then repeated until no differences remain.

Note that a major difference between the algebra problem and the dinner problem is that the algebra problem does not require subgoals. Everything needed to solve the algebra problem is available from the start, which was not the case in the example of cooking dinner. Since the required food was not immediately available, we had to set up a subgoal of getting food, and then a subgoal of getting money, etc. Problems that require subgoals are often difficult because they require extra information to be stored in memory. The person has to remember what the subgoals are and the reasons for achieving them. If we didn't remember why the subgoals were established in the first place, we might find ourselves in the position of going to the bank and then forgetting why we went there.

A more complex problem that illustrates the importance of planning and setting up subgoals in the strategy of means-ends analysis is the well-known Tower of Hanoi puzzle depicted in Figure 12.6. A number of disks (three in Figure 12.6)

must be moved from peg A to peg G. Only one disk (the top disk on a peg) can be moved at a time, and no disk can ever be placed on top of a disk smaller than itself. This puzzle derives its name from a legend that a group of monks near Hanoi are working on a version of the puzzle that uses sixty-four disks. The legend says that the world will end when they finish the puzzle, which at the rate of one perfect move every second, will take them about a trillion years (Raphael 1976).

The three-disk version of the puzzle is considerably more tractable, but it still requires a degree of planning in selecting moves and generating subgoals that will bring the problem closer to a solution. For example, clearly the solution to the puzzle in Figure 12.6 requires that the largest disk (disk 3) be placed on peg C first. (This approach is an illustration of working backward from the goal to solve a problem.) Therefore we begin by setting up a subgoal of getting disk 3 to peg C. Also clear is that disks 1 and 2 have to be moved from disk 3 before the latter can be moved. This step results in a further subgoal of moving disks 1 and 2, which in turn sets up a subgoal of first moving disk 1.

But should disk 1 go to peg B or peg C? Here looking ahead a few moves will help. For if we move disk 1 to peg B, then disk 2 will have to go on peg G. But then disk 3 won't be able to go on peg C. On the other hand, if we begin by moving disk 1 to peg C, the following sequence will accomplish the subgoal of moving disk 3 to peg C:

Disk 1 to peg C;
Disk 2 to peg B;
Disk 1 to peg B;
Disk 3 to peg C.

Having completed the initial subgoal, we can set up the next subgoal, getting disk 2 onto peg C. This step is easily accomplished:

Disk 1 to peg A;
Disk 2 to peg C.

Then a final move (disk 1 to peg C) completes the puzzle.

Note that this approach to the Tower of Hanoi puzzle involves formulating a hierarchy of subgoals (e.g., the subgoal "move disk 3 to peg C" generates the subgoal "move disk 2 off disk 3," which in turn generates the subgoal "move disk 1 off disk 2"). This puzzle becomes increasingly difficult when more disks are used, because the subgoal hierarchies get deeper. Thinking far enough ahead in planning moves and remembering how all the subgoals that are generated relate to each other becomes difficult. Egan and Greeno (1974) observed subjects as they worked on a six-disk, Tower of Hanoi problem, and they found that the probability of a subject's making an error on a move increased with the number of subgoals that had to be set up between the preceding move and the current one.

Note that means-ends analysis solves the first problem for the generate-test method that we noted earlier. Each new knowledge state is closer to the desired goal than was the previous one. Whereas each test in the generate-test method gave very little information—just "yes, it's a solution" or "no, it's not"—each test in means-end analysis provides information about how the current state differs from the goal state and how this difference can be reduced.

Reformulating Problem Representations

As noted earlier, the initial problem representation may not be adequate for the task of planning a solution. In such cases the representation must be somehow reformulated (step 3 in the overall problem-solving process depicted in Figure 12.1). In many ways the reformulation process resembles the process of forming an initial representation; in fact, in extreme cases the problem solver may essentially discard the initial representation and construct a new one.

Removing unnecessary constraints. In other cases, however, the initial representation may undergo much more subtle changes. An example is provided by the well-known nine-dot problem. The problem is to draw four straight lines through all the nine dots depicted in Figure 12.7(a) without lifting the pencil from the paper. The Gestalt psychologists noticed that people see a square boundary around the nine dots, owing to the perceptual principle of closure (see Chapter 4). As a result, when most people are given this problem, they tend to assume that the four lines can't go outside the imaginary boundary. But, in fact, the problem can be solved only by extending some of the lines beyond the boundary, as in Figure 12.7(b).

Adams (1974) calls this difficulty a "conceptual block"; problem solvers impose an unnecessary constraint on the problem that actually blocks its solution. If problem solvers can modify their internal representation of the problem by eliminating this constraint, they may be able to develop a solution. Weisberg and Alba (1981) tested this possibility by instructing some subjects, after they had made several unsuccessful attempts, that it was necessary to draw lines outside the boundary to solve the problem. Although the problem still proved far from easy, about 25 percent of these subjects eventually solved the problem, whereas subjects in a control condition that did not receive such a hint invariably failed.

Noticing and applying analogies. Often a problem must be reformulated in order to define it more clearly. This type of reformulation seems to be especially important in relatively creative types of problem solving. One method that can be used to reformulate a problem is to model its representation after that of some structurally similar or *analogous* problem. An analogy can result in the reformulation of a problem such that the solution to a known problem can be used to plan a solution to the new one. Analogies are important in developing new scientific theories. For example, the wave theory of light was based on an analogy with sound waves (Oppenheimer 1956).

As this example suggests, useful analogies can sometimes be found between concepts that are superficially very different. Gick and Holyoak (1980, 1983) have investigated the use of such analogies in solving relatively ill-defined problems. Their results indicate that analogies are indeed useful in reformulating problems, at least once their relevance is noticed by the problem solver. The problem they studied most extensively was the radiation problem made famous by the Gestalt psychologist Karl Duncker (1945). The problem runs as follows:

> Suppose you are a doctor faced with a patient who has a malignant tumor in his stomach. To operate on the patient is impossible, but unless the tumor is destroyed, the patient will die. A kind of ray, at a sufficiently high intensity, can destroy the tumor. Unfortunately, at this intensity the healthy tissue that the rays pass through on the way to the tumor will also be destroyed. At lower intensities the rays are harmless to healthy tissue but will not affect the tumor, either. How can

the rays be used to destroy the tumor without injuring the healthy tissue?

This problem is reasonably realistic, since it describes a situation similar to what actually arises in radiation therapy. Most of the problem components are reasonably well specified; however, the operations are extremely vague. The problem solver might imagine the possibilities of altering the effects of the rays or of avoiding contact between the rays and the healthy tissue. However, none of these operations immediately specify realizable actions; they remain at the level of wishful thinking.

Gick and Holyoak (1980) wanted to find out whether college students could use a remote analogy to develop a clearer problem representation and hence solve the problem. To provide the students with a potential analogy, the experimenters first had them read a story about the predicament of a general who wished to capture a fortress located in the center of a country. Many roads radiated outward from the fortress, but these roads were mined so that although small groups could pass over them safely, any large group would detonate the mines. Yet the general needed to get his entire large army to the fortress in order to launch a successful attack. Thus the general's situation was analogous to that of the doctor in the radiation problem.

Different versions of the story described different solutions to the military problem. For example, in one version the general divided his men into small groups and dispatched them simultaneously down multiple roads to converge on the fortress. All subjects were then asked to suggest solutions to the radiation problem, using the military story to help them. Subjects who received the multiple-road version were especially likely to suggest a convergence solution—directing multiple weak rays at the tumor from different directions. This solution is in fact similar to actual medical procedures for radiation therapy. About 75 percent of the subjects who received the relevant story generated this solution, compared with fewer than 10 percent of control subjects who did not receive an analogy.

Even though the particular objects involved (e.g., army and rays, fortress and tumor) are very different, the basic relations that make the convergence solution possible are present in both. The goal, resources (and other objects), operations, and constraints are structurally similar, and they can be matched, or "mapped," from one problem to the other. Because the military story provides clear operations (e.g., "divide the army"), subjects are able to use the mapping to construct corresponding operators (e.g., "reduce ray intensity") that can be used to solve the ray problem. The abstract structure common to the two problems can be viewed as a schema for convergence problems.

Other experiments by Gick and Holyoak (1980. 1983) revealed that subjects often fail to make use of a potentially helpful analogy unless its relevance is pointed out to them. The difficulty of noticing distant analogies is perhaps not surprising, since the underlying schema is quite abstract, whereas the many superficial differences between the two cases are very obvious.

Sometimes, people are explicitly taught to think about one domain in terms of a very different one so that the problem of noticing the analogy is avoided. For example, students are often told that electricity behaves like a hydraulic system. As depicted in Figure 12.8, electricity is analogous to water flowing through a pipe; batteries act like reservoirs, and resistors act like constrictions in the pipe. Centner and Centner (1983) have demonstrated that the ease with which high school and college students solve particular types of electricity problems depends on the degree to which the analogy they have been taught generates correct inferences about the relevant electrical concepts.

Another way in which the difficulty of noticing distant analogies can be overcome is by encouraging abstraction of the underlying schema. Notice that the schema captures the commonalities among different examples of a type of problem while deleting the differences among them. As a result, a novel example will be more similar to the schema than to another example (Tversky 1977). If retrieval depends on similarity, then a novel problem is more likely to cue recall of a schema than of a stored problem.

Gick and Holyoak (1983) tested this hypothesis by having subjects first read *two* convergence stories, such as the military story and a story about fire fighting (e.g., a story in which the hero extinguished an oil well fire by using multiple small hoses). The subjects were asked to describe ways in which the stories were similar, thus encouraging them to map the two stories with each other and hence to potentially abstract the shared convergence schema. When such subjects subsequently attempted to solve the radiation problem, they were much more likely to generate the parallel solution (either with or without a hint to use the stories) than were subjects who received just one prior story.

These results suggest that analogical mapping is used not only to reformulate novel problems but also to learn more abstract problem schemas that can be stored in memory and later retrieved and applied. As we will see shortly, the acquisition of problem schemas seems to be a key factor in the development of expertise in problem solving.

Executing a Solution Plan

Once a solution plan has been developed, the problem solver can actually execute and test it. This final step in problem solving often lacks the excitement that can be generated by a creative reformulation of the problem, but it is nonetheless essential. Often enough, the initial plan will prove inadequate when it is actually tried. Information about *why* the plan fell short may be used in cycling back to generate a modified plan. For example, if an analogy was used to construct the initial plan, the shortcomings of the plan may lead to a critical evaluation of the analogy. The plan may then be altered slightly or abandoned in favor of an entirely different approach.

EXPERTISE IN PROBLEM SOLVING

One of the most intriguing issues involving problem solving concerns the differences between novices and experts. Obviously, training and practice are important, but what is if that experts learn that makes it relatively easy for them to solve new problems in their knowledge domain? We will look at two domains in which a great deal of research has addressed this question: playing complex board games, such as chess, and solving problems in physics.

Expertise in Chess

Memory and perception. The pioneering work on chess skills was done by De Groot (1965). His basic question was simple: What makes a master chess player better than a weaker player? To investigate this question, he collected protocols from some of the best chess players in the world as they selected chess moves.

De Groot's findings were quite different from what most people might expect. The master chess players did not seem to reason in any unusual ways. Nor did the masters search through more possible moves before selecting one. In fact, if anything, the masters considered fewer alternatives than did ordinary players. The difference was that the masters explored particularly good moves, whereas weaker players spent more time considering bad moves. Somehow, the good moves seemed to be immediately apparent to the master players.

The most striking difference between masters and weaker players emerged in a test of perceptual and memory abilities. In this test a chess position, such as the middle game (board position in the middle of an actual game) shown in Figure 12.9(a), was displayed for 5 seconds and then removed. The player then had to reconstruct the board position from memory. Chase and Simon (1973) performed this experiment with a master player (an expert), a class A player (a very good player), and a beginning (B) player. As shown, memory performance is ordered in the same way as the level of chess skill: the master recalled the most pieces, followed by the class A player and the beginner.

This result might suggest that master players simply have the best memories. But this conclusion is not quite right. Chase and Simon also performed the memory test with positions in which the pieces were arranged randomly. With these random games the superiority of the master player completely disappeared. In fact, the master actually tended to recall fewer correct pieces than the weaker players.

Apparently, then, the master players are especially good at a very specialized task—encoding actual chess positions. If you recall our discussion of perceptual learning in Chapter 9, you might wonder whether the master players perform so well because they can recognize large meaningful chunks in board positions. Chase and Simon (1973) found evidence that this recognition is indeed the case. They timed how long the subjects paused between each placement of a piece as they recalled the positions on the first trial. If the pause was less than 2 seconds long, the two successive pieces were defined as belonging to the same chunk. If the pause was longer than 2 seconds, the two pieces were defined as belonging to different chunks. Chase and Simon found that pieces belonging to the same chunk tended to be recalled together on both the first and second trials, even though the order of recall within a cluster varied. This result suggests that each chunk is stored in memory as a single compound representation.

If the unitization hypothesis is correct, the master should have recalled larger chunks than the weaker players. The master did. In addition to recalling larger chunks, the master also recalled more chunks. This result suggests that the master is able to establish more associations in memory between chunks, so that one chunk can serve as a retrieval cue for another.

Recall that only a limited number of representations can be maintained in awareness. Britton and Tesser (1982) hypothesized that if experts activated more knowledge when performing a problem-solving task, they would be slower to detect a target that was part of a secondary task. Both expert and novice chess players were given chess problems to solve, but they were also told to press a telegraph key when they heard a click. The expert took longer than the novices to respond to the clicks.

Related evidence has been found with another complex board game, the oriental game of go. The game involves placing black and white stones on a grid and fighting for territory on the board. A player can capture an enemy stone by surrounding if with his or her own pieces. Judith Reitman (1976) studied a go master and a beginner, using the kinds of memory tests used earlier with chess players. As in chess, the go master player showed superior memory for real go positions but not for random positions.

The go master also tended to recall pieces in clusters. Figure 12.11 shows several examples of board positions (labeled A through D) that were presented to the master. The circles show how the master himself partitioned the pieces into chunks. Note that the go master saw the chunks as overlapping in many different ways. That is, the same piece was often included in several different clusters. The numbers on the pieces in Figure 12.11 give the order in which the pieces were recalled on that trial (if there is no number, the piece was not recalled). As shown, pieces that were part of the same pattern had a very strong tendency to be recalled together.

What is the basis for the perception of a chunk? One might expect that two pieces would be united together if they were related in some way that was important to the game. Chase and Simon (1973) examined five relations between two pieces that are important in chess:

1. One piece can attack another.
2. One piece can defend another.
3. Two pieces can be on adjacent squares.
4. Two pieces can have the same color.
5. Two pieces can be of the same type (e.g., both pawns).

Figure 12.12 plots the length of the pause between the recall of one piece and the next as a function of the number of relations between them. As the figure shows, the more relations there were between the two pieces, the shorter was the pause. This result suggests that the more ways two pieces are related, the more likely they are to be coded into a single chunk. Similarly, in go, chunks seem to be defined by attack-defense relationships, groups of stones of the same color, and other meaningful configurations. Chunks therefore contain information about important relations between pieces that will make th'; information readily available to help plan the next move.

Simon and Gilmartin (1973) developed a computer program that simulates the way chess players store board positions in memory. The program contains information about many familiar patterns of pieces. Simon and Gilmartin used the performance of their program to estimate how many patterns a master chess player has stored in memory. Their estimate was 30,000. This estimate may seem like a very large number of patterns, but it is no larger than the number of words (another type of meaningful pattern) that a good reader can recognize. And a master chess player will have spent as much time studying chess positions as a good reader will have spent reading. In fact, the most basic requirement for becoming a master player appears to be an incredible amount of practice: as many as 50,000 hours spent working with chess positions. As a result of this practice, the master is able to recognize complex chess patterns as chunks, just as a skilled reader recognizes words as chunks.

Perception and thought. The fact that skilled chess and go players seem to have their knowledge of board positions organized into large perceptual chunks has important consequences for how they select moves. Good players often seem to know immediately after looking at a board what the best move is. Simon (1973) suggests that the selection of chess moves is partly based on a set of rules, built up through years of experience. These rules can be stated in an if-then form (see Chapter 3): "If a particular board configuration is present, then a particular move should be taken." In other words, perception of a familiar perceptual chunk leads directly to an appropriate action.

This human style of play is very different from that of computer programs, such as the many programs that have been developed to play chess, which operate by searching through game trees of the sort depicted in Figure 12.5. Most chess programs do have heuristics to restrict the number of possible moves they consider, but these heuristics don't involve incorporating chunks into the knowledge available to the program. Part of the reason that existing chess programs can be beaten by good human players may be that current programs do not use chunks. Some chess enthusiasts such as Hearst (1977) have advised programmers to model their programs more closely on human characteristics, such as the use of perceptual chunks.

Expertise in Other Domains

Problem schemas in physics. Recent work on differences between novices and experts in domains such as physics problem solving has largely confirmed the major conclusions derived from work on board games (Larkin, McDermott, Simon, and Simon 1980). In domains such as physics, in which knowledge is highly systematized, the role of specialized problem schemas is especially apparent. A major factor differentiating experts from novices is that experts have both more and better problem schemas, which allow them to rapidly classify problems and retrieve relevant solution procedures.

A study of experts and novices in the domain of physics problems by Chi, Feltovich, and Glaser (1981) is especially illuminating. When subjects were asked to sort problems into clusters on the basis of similarity, novices tended to form categories based on relatively surface features of the problem statements (e.g., inclined-plane problems). In contrast, experts sorted the problems with respect to applicable physical laws (e.g., problems solvable by the principle of conservation of energy). If you compare the problem pairs depicted in Figure 12.13, which were grouped together by

novices, with those depicted in Figure 12.14, which were grouped by experts, you will get a sense of the greater degree of abstraction involved in the experts' problem categories. Further differences were apparent in protocols in which subjects described their problem categories. The experts were able to articulate the equivalent of rules for realizable actions—i.e., explicit solution procedures for problems of a given type. The novices' protocols, on the other hand, even when they mentioned abstract problem features, usually did not reveal such rules for action. Rather, their rules seemed to set further abstract subgoals that lacked specific solution procedures.

Expertise and problem definition. The richer problem schemas of the expert can account for the observation that the degree to which a problem is ill defined depends on the knowledge of the problem solver. To use an example discussed by Simon (1973). most of us would find the problem of designing a house quite ill defined. The list of alternative styles (ranch, colonial, neo-Gothic) and materials (wood, brick, Plexiglas, camel's hide) could go on indefinitely. An architect, however, can quickly call up a hierarchy of relevant schemas that effectively decompose the problem, providing clear solution procedures.

The first step is to determine some general constraints: What basic design is desired? How much money is available? The architect knows that a home consists of a general floor plan plus structure; a structure consists of roofing plus siding plus utilities; utilities consist of plumbing plus heating system plus electrical system; etc. Once the problem is broken down in this hierarchical way, the number of reasonable alternatives at each choice point will usually be fairly limited. The heating system, for instance, may reduce to a choice between a gas or an electric furnace. For the expert with specialized problem schemas, this ill-defined problem eventually becomes a series of well-structured problems. If this process of problem reformulation proceeds rapidly enough, the expert may scarcely notice that the original problem statement was vague.

BLOCKS THAT HINDER PROBLEM SOLVING

So far we have been discussing ways in which prior knowledge stored in memory is helpful in solving problems. But in some cases the problem solver's knowledge actually hinders the ability to achieve a solution. Let's examine some of these blocks to effective problem solving in the light of what we know about memory and problem solving.

Problem-Solving Set

As we saw in earlier chapters, a very general principle of behavior is that activities, both physical and mental, tend to be strengthened by repetition. In the case of problem solving people often exhibit a *problem-solving set*—a tendency to repeat a solution process that has been previously successful.

The classic demonstration of a problem-solving set (*einstellung* in German) was a series of experiments by Luchins (1942; Luchins and Luchins 1950). Luchins tested over nine thousand subjects, ranging in age from elementary school children to adults, on water jar problems. The subject is asked to imagine three jars of various specified capacities and told to find a way to get a required amount of water. For the first problem the solution is to fill jar *B,* then to take out the volume of jar *A,* and then to take out the volume of jar C twice. The series of problems is set up so that this same general solution (B–A–2C) works for the first five problems. This series is designed to establish a problem-solving set.

On trials 6 and 7 there are two possible solutions; the previously successful formula and also a simpler one. One measure of the effect of a set is how often people discover the simpler solution. Finally, trial 8 is a problem for which the earlier formula won't work but a simpler one (A–C) will. Luchins found that subjects very often failed to notice the simpler solutions to problems 6 and 7 and sometimes failed to solve problem 8 at all. Seemingly, an initially successful solution procedure tends to be repeated, blocking discovery of alternative solutions.

The set effect is hardly surprising given what we know about learning and memory. Attempting to apply previously successful solution procedures to similar new problems is only reasonable. Educators can minimize the negative aspects of set by carefully selecting the examples used to teach skills in solving a particular type of problem. To begin by exposing the students to only a narrow range of examples is unwise. Although the students may learn how to solve the initial examples, the limited problem-solving rules that they acquire may actually interfere with their ability to solve a wider range of problems.

Functional Fixedness

Another kind of negative influence of memory on problem solving is illustrated by the following experiment. Duncker (1945) presented subjects with several objects lying on a table and asked them to find a way to use them to support a board. The available objects included two iron joints and a pair of pliers. The solution to the problem was to use the iron joints to support one end of the board and the pliers to support the other. In one condition the subject first had to use the pliers to free the board.

Duncker found that subjects who began the experiment by using the pliers to free the board were less likely to find the solution of using the pliers as a support. He called this phenomenon *functional fixedness:* If an object has one established use in a situation, subjects have difficulty in using the object in another way.

Functional fixedness, like set, is a block to effective problem solving resulting from prior experience. But whereas set is a tendency to repeat previously successful problem-solving operations, functional fixedness is a tendency to think of past uses of an object to the exclusion of novel potential uses. Functional fixedness can also be understood in terms of memory processes. The most familiar functions of objects are likely to be directly stored with the concept in the semantic network (e.g., the concept pliers might be associated with the function "used for grasping objects"). These familiar uses will be the most available ones, especially if they have already been activated in the current context (as occurred when the pliers were used to free the board). But the perceptual attributes of an object (e.g., its shape, size, or weight) may be compatible with other potential uses, sometimes called *affordances* (J. J. Gibson 1966). A pair of pliers can therefore be used as a support. However, these potential uses are usually harder to think of than functions that have already been stored in memory.

As is the case for the set effect, functional fixedness can be viewed as a negative side effect of a generally useful property of memory organization, which is also reflected in the availability heuristic (Chapter 11). Whatever functions of objects are activated in a given context will be most readily available for generation of a solution to a problem. Indeed, Per Saugstad showed that success in generating a problem solution can be predicted by measures of the availability to the problem solver of the functions required for a solution.

Saugstad (1955) showed 57 college students objects to be used later in a problem in which some hollow tubes and putty had to be used to blow out a candle 6 feet away. Nothing was mentioned of the problem itself. Subjects were simply instructed to list all the possible functions that the objects might serve. All 13 subjects who listed functions for the objects that were later necessary to solve the problem did, in fact, solve the problem. In contrast, only 58% of the remaining subjects solved the problem. In another experiment, Saugstad and Raaheim (1960) demonstrated the functions of some objects, which turned out to be critical to the solution of a problem, to 20 male high school students. Nineteen of the boys later solved the problem. In contrast, only 10 of 45 boys who had not seen the demonstration were able to solve the problem.

Another task that illustrates functional fixedness is the so-called candle problem (Duncker 1945). In this problem subjects are given the task of affixing a candle to a wall and lighting it. The objects available for use are some matches, a candle, and a matchbox filled with thumbtacks. The optimal solution, as defined by Duncker, is to use the tacks to fix the matchbox to the wall, put the candle on the box, and then light it with the matches. Duncker found that more subjects used the box as a candle holder when it was presented empty than when if was full of tacks. He considered functional fixedness to be a perceptual problem. Seeing the box as a container for tacks makes if difficult for subjects to see it also as a platform. Presenting it empty makes it easier for them to perceive the box as a candle holder.

Samuel Glucksberg, Robert Weisberg, and their colleagues (Glucksberg and Banks 1968; Glucksberg and Weisberg 1966; Weisberg and Suls 1973) performed several experiments that illustrate how subtle changes in the experimental situation can affect how the candle problem is solved. For example, sometimes the experimenter would name the box while giving instructions to the subject, while sometimes he only named the tacks. More subjects solved the problem by using the box as a platform (the box solution) when the box itself was labeled. One way to interpret this result is to suppose that when only the tacks

are labeled, the box that holds them is not really "seen" as a separate object. But once the name box is heard, the subjects become aware not only of the box as an object but also of the various familiar uses of boxes that are stored in the conceptual network. Since these familiar uses are likely to include the use of boxes to support other objects, hearing the name box makes it easier *to* find the solution.

Glucksberg and Danks (1968) also found cases where hearing the name of an object actually hindered problem solving. In this experiment the subject's task was to complete an electric circuit. The objects provided were batteries, a bulb, a switch, and a wrench. The solution was to use the wrench to complete the circuit. In this case subjects were more likely to find the solution when they were required to refer to the wrench by a nonsense name such as vorpin rather than by the familiar name wrench.

Why did the name wrench interfere with solving this problem, whereas the name box facilitated the process in our previous example? The critical difference is that the box had to be used in a relatively familiar way (as a support), whereas the wrench had to be used in a more novel way (to conduct electricity). The name wrench therefore activated known uses stored in memory that actually conflicted with the critical potential use, which could be discovered by exploring the perceptual properties of the object.

However, Weisberg and Suls (1973) offer a different interpretation of the functional fixedness observed in the candle problem. They point out that the experimenter decides in advance that the box solution is the "best." Perhaps if subjects do not realize that there is a best solution, they may simply attempt to produce a solution in the most obvious way, which is probably to try to tack the candle directly to the wall. However, if the experimenter gives a clue about what solution is desired (by leaving the box empty or by labeling it), the subject may catch on that the experimenter wants him or her to use the box. According to this interpretation, then, subjects may not be inhibited from using objects in a novel way. That is, unless the experimenter somehow indicates that he or she is looking for a novel solution, subjects will solve the problem in the most straightforward way.

But while the experimenter's expectations may play a role in producing the functional fixedness phenomenon, those expectations are probably not the whole story. Sometimes, there is simply no way to solve a problem without putting some object to a novel use. For example, if you forget your frying pan on a camping trip, you might end up cooking pancakes on a flattened tin can.

Productive Thinking

What is learned from experience with examples of a type of problem can differ with respect to later transfer to novel cases. One can learn a procedure by rote, which Max Wertheimer (1959) termed *reproductive thinking*, or one can learn it in a way that makes it easy to generalize to new situations. Wer-theimer termed this second, more flexible type of problem-solving procedure productive *thinking*. An example that illustrates the contrast between reproductive and productive thinking is Wertheimer's parallelogram problem, illustrated in Figure 12.15(a).

Consider the problem of finding the area of this parallelogram. One method taught in a class observed by Wertheimer was to draw two perpendicular lines, one from each upper corner, as shown by the dotted lines in Figure 12.15(a). Students are then told to prove that the area of the parallelogram is the product of the length of the base times the altitude by using the fact that the two triangles formed by the perpendicular are equivalent. However, as shown in Figure 12.15(b), some of the students blindly drew perpendiculars from the upper corners and then became confused, since the resulting figure didn't resemble the parallelogram they had been trained on. That is, the students were unable to form two triangles, one inside and one outside the parallelogram. These students had been thinking reproductively.

Another group of students, however, drew the dotted lines as in Figure 12.15(c). These students were think-ing productively. They had grasped the critical relations between the parts of the figure (the triangles) and the whole (the parallelogram). These students realized that the essential principle underlying the method is that the parallelogram is really like a rectangle. That is, removing the inner triangle from the parallelogram and adding on the outer triangle produces a rectangle. Since the triangle removed and the triangle added have the same area, the original parallelogram must have the same area as the re-sulting rectangle. However, merely drawing perpendiculars from the upper corners of all parallelograms will not form the necessary triangles. The student who understands the

underlying principle can search for alternate ways to draw the perpendiculars such that the necessary triangles will be formed. The ability to think productively seems to depend on learning the kinds of abstract problem categories that, as we saw earlier, distinguish expert from novice problem solvers.

ANALYZING PROBLEM-SOLVING BEHAVIOR

One of the most important aspects of the study of problem solving is the methods that are used. How can we tell what representations and strategies are being used in particular problem-solving tasks? We have already mentioned a few possible methods, such as observing the frequencies of certain specific types of solutions or errors. In the case of problems that require explicit moves, one can also time how long it takes a person to make each move. However, most problems do not have such a rigid format. Clearly, the most interesting aspects of problem solving take place in the person's head. Given that we can't read minds, is there any way to observe this internal problem-solving behavior?

Protocol Analysis

One important technique, used extensively by Newell and Simon (1972), is *protocol analysis*. This technique involves asking a subject to think out loud while solving a problem, with the experimenter recording the resulting protocol (a verbatim transcript of the session) for later analysis. Newell and Simon used this technique to study the ways in which people solve "cryptarithmetic" problems. In these puzzles the problem solver must substitute digits for letters to represent an arithmetic problem. Each letter represents a distinct digit, and each assignment is unique. The following is a simple example and its solution:

$$
\begin{array}{rr}
AA & 22 \\
+BB & +99 \\
\hline
CAC & 121
\end{array}
$$

Some more complex puzzles include the following:

SEND	DONALD	(*Hint*: D = 5)	CROSS
+MORE	+GERALD		+ROADS
MONEY	ROBERT		DANGER

You might like to try solving one or more of these brainteasers to get a feeling for what cryptarithmetic puzzles are like. The answers are given at the end of this chapter.

In one technique for doing a protocol analysis, the first step is to break up the transcript into fragments that correspond to different states of the subject's knowledge or mental activity. This division is done intuitively by the experimenter.

The next step is to identify the general approach to the task that the subject is using. The protocol from the subject reveals that he is working on the problem in a way typical of most college students. He realizes that the task involves a relationship between numbers and letters and that his task is to discover that relationship. In working on the problem, he assigns numbers to letters and makes inferences by using his knowledge of arithmetic to check that each number assignment is consistent with the rest of the letters.

...

Problem behavior graphs. The results of the protocol analysis with the operations that have been identified can be summarized in a problem *behavior graph*. Each box represents a new knowledge state, and the arrows represent operators that change one knowledge state into another. The numbers in the upper left corner of each box refer to the first line in the protocol that appears to correspond to that knowledge state. For example, at line 4 the subject states that D is 1, and the next few lines simply expand on why he has reached that conclusion. The vertical lines on the graph mark places at which the subject returns to an earlier knowledge state. For example, at line 10 the subject once again notes that the two S's must be equal, and he starts to process that piece of information for a second time. Note that to read the graph in the order in which the subject's knowledge states occurred in time, you read across the top row to the far right, then go down to the next row, across to the right again, etc.

The problem behavior graph makes a notable feature of problem-solving behavior very explicit. The subject's line of thought does not move in a direct line to the solution. Rather, he explores one line of thought as far as he can, and then he returns to an earlier state and starts out again. Sometimes, he finds an important piece of information before reaching a dead end (e.g., his first attack leads to the conclusion that D is 1). But other times, an approach will end up with an error, and everything will have to be undone back to an earlier point. This feature is shown at line 16, where the subject decides to tentatively assume that S is 8. As it turns out, this assumption is wrong (S is really 3). About fifty lines later in the protocol the subject finds himself trapped in a contradiction and has to return to the same knowledge state as line 14.

Limitations of protocol analysis. Protocol analysis is often a useful technique for analyzing problem-solving behavior, especially when it can be complemented by nonverbal measures, such as recordings of eye movements (Ericsson and Simon 1980). However, the technique has its limitations. Often a protocol will seem to have gaps in which the subject forgets to speak or takes a "mental leap," reaching some conclusion without mentioning any intermediate steps. Sometimes, the protocol will be ambiguous or difficult to interpret. Protocol analysis is always a cumbersome method, requiring painstaking and tedious work.

There are also other, more serious limitations. These limitations relate to the fact that protocols are obviously verbal. It is virtually impossible to get a useful protocol from a young child, and it is difficult with many subjects other than highly verbal college students. There are probably restrictions on the problems that can be studied as well as on the subjects. It may be difficult to provide a detailed verbal description of what you are thinking if you are using visual imagery or some other nonverbal representation. Also, if there are important unconscious components to problem solving, they will, of course, not be reported in a protocol. Furthermore, since subjects are being watched, they may use a more systematic method than usual, because they are aware that the protocol is being carefully recorded. As a result, the strategies inferred from the protocol may not tell you what subjects normally do in private. But despite these limitations, protocol analysis is currently an important technique for studying problem-solving behavior.

Computer Simulation of Problem Solving

GPS. One of the most important tools for developing theories of problem solving is simulation by computer programs. An early example of this approach, which has greatly influenced more recent computer models, is the General Problem Solver, or GPS (Ernst and Newell 1969).

The GPS is a kind of theory of how humans might do various tasks, against which human performance can be compared.

The general strategy that GPS uses is means-ends analysis. The program operates by breaking a problem into subgoals and then attacking each subgoal in turn by using a difference reduction strategy. The GPS requires a variety of information in order to tackle a new problem. The most important information includes the following:

> (1) A description of the initial state, goal state, and operations. (2) A description of the possible differences among states. (3) A specification of which operations can be used to reduce each possible difference.

How does the performance of GPS compare with that of human problem solvers? In many cases, such as the Tower of Hanoi puzzle and logic problems, the performance of GPS bears a close resemblance to human performance. For example, in the Tower of Hanoi problem people take the most time and make the most errors on moves on which GPS would have to set up a series of subgoals (e.g. an and Greeno 1974). Such similarities are not surprising, given that people, like GPS, tend to use the strategy of means-ends analysis.

There are some problems, however, that people tend to solve somewhat differently from GPS. One example that has been studied extensively is the missionaries and cannibals problem (sometimes known as the hobbits and orcs problem), which can be stated as follows:

> Three missionaries and three cannibals are on one side of a river, and all of them must get to the other side. They can row themselves across with a rowboat that can hold two people. There is one important thing to remember: The cannibals must never outnumber the missionaries on either side of the river. Find a sequence of river crossings that will get all six people safely to the other side. Remember that someone will have to row the boat back after each trip across.

Try your hand at solving the missionaries and cannibals problem for a few minutes, and then work through the solution path shown in Figure 12.17. Each box shows where the missionaries, cannibals, and boat are located at each state on the way to the solution. The arrows show which people cross the river on a particular trip. Note that the trips following even-numbered states are always to return the boat.

The interesting thing about this problem is that the correct sequence is almost completely determined by the rules. Only the trips following the first and tenth states involve a choice (more than one path leading from a given state). In all other cases there is only one legal move (this solution ignores such dead ends as taking the same people back and forth repeatedly).

Nevertheless, many people find this problem quite difficult. Much of the difficulty for people occurs at the sixth state, which is usually the key to the solution (shown as boldface type in Figure 12.17). This return trip must send across a missionary and a cannibal. There is no other way to avoid having the cannibals outnumber the missionaries on one side or the other. People usually pause for a long time before making this move and are especially likely to make an error at this point (Thomas 1974).

Since there is no other legal move available, why do people find this step in the problem so difficult? The reason is that it appears to lead away from the final goal state. People naturally try to maximize the number of people on the other side of the river after each trip. Thus they prefer to send two people across and just one back. The critical sixth trip is a kind of detour—the difference between the current state and the goal state has to be temporarily increased in order to solve the problem.

The missionaries and cannibals problem is one in which people usually consider just one move at a time. There is little or no choice at each decision point once the illegal moves have been eliminated. As a result, people appear to use a difference reduction strategy, but without setting up subgoals (Jeffries, Poison, Razran, and Atwood 1977; Simon and Reed 1976). The performance of GPS on the problem differs in some ways from that of human problem solvers (Greeno 1974). For example, people run into trouble at state 6 because they are always comparing the current state directly with the final goal state. Since GPS solves the problem by generating subgoals and executing each in turn, it avoids this difficulty. However, the human strategy affords an advantage at state 11, where people immediately bring back both the rower and the cannibal to achieve the final goal. In contrast, GPS at this point is working on the subgoal of bringing back the one cannibal that was on the left side at state 10. As a result, at state 11 the program first considers sending only the one cannibal back to the other side. In this instance GPS has a tendency to be trapped by its rigid adherence to subgoals.

There are other, more fundamental limitations to GPS and similar programs as models of human problem solving. One is that GPS can only operate on well-defined problems. Without a clear description of the goal state, for example, the program cannot compute the difference between the goal state and the current state; as a result, GPS cannot apply means-ends analysis. More generally, GPS is unable to reformulate a problem representation in any way. A second severe limitation is that GPS learns nothing at all from its problem-solving experiences. Solving a problem does not help in solving the same problem again, far less in solving a different one. No matter how many problems it is given, GPS will remain a novice.

Expert systems. As the name *General Problem Solver* implies, GPS uses general methods to solve problems. But as we saw in our discussion of expertise, experts appear to use solution methods that are specialized for particular categories of problems. Many problem-solving programs developed by researchers in artificial intelligence have, in fact, taken what is called an "expert systems" approach (Davis, Buchanan, and Shortliffe 1977; Feigenbaum, Buchanan, and Lederberg 1971). The programmer builds in a tremendous amount of specialized knowledge that the program can use, consulting extensively with human experts in the process. Such programs can contribute to complex problem-solving tasks such as medical diagnosis and chemical analyses. Nonetheless, current expert systems are also severely limited in their ability to learn from experience, and for this reason they fall far short of human flexibility (for a review, see Duda and Shortliffe 1983).

Machine learning. Some progress is now being made in developing computer programs that can learn from experience in problem-solving tasks. For example, Lenat (1979) incorporated a variety of heuristic strategies in a computer program called AM that searches for interesting concepts in elementary mathematics. He has a list of 250 heuristics for searching for interesting new concepts. Some of the heuristics are used to select problems that are likely to yield interesting concepts. For example, one heuristic is to explore more general concepts, like number, before more specific ones, like even number. Other heuristics are used to decide what to do once a concept has been selected for study, such as to examine extreme examples. A person might investigate the concept set and find that some sets have no members. Since such extreme examples of a concept are likely to be interesting, the person might create the new concept empty set.

Another heuristic is to find examples of a concept for which no examples are yet known. For instance, suppose you start with the concept divisor of number but have no examples of the concept. You might begin by simply producing examples; e.g., the divisors of 6 are 1, 2, 3, and 6. Then you might decide to look at extreme examples, like numbers with small sets of divisors. This step might cause you to find examples of numbers with only two divisors, e.g., 2(1, 2), 3(1, 3), 5(1, 5), 7(1, 7), 11 (1,11). You might then notice that for all such numbers one divisor is 1 and the other is the number itself. Since this result is an unexpected and therefore interesting regularity, you would store in memory a new concept that we call *prime* number. Some of these heuristics are similar to those discussed by Polya (1973).

A major limitation of the AM program is that it does not learn any new heuristics for investigating mathematics. In more recent work Lenat (1983) is developing a program called Eurisko that uses heuristics to modify its own set of heuristics. Eurisko has been used to generate the design for a novel and potentially useful type of computer chip. Nonetheless, the development of automated learning systems is still in its infancy. Human beings, despite their propensities to be trapped by set effects and functional fixedness, remain the most flexible and adaptive of all known intelligent systems.

CREATIVE THINKING

A work of art, whether a painting or piece of music, appears creative if it is both good (i.e., emotionally moving or intellectually stimulating) and looks or sounds like nothing the observer or listener has ever seen before. Similarly, a scientific theory is viewed as creative if it makes use of some new assumption about the world to generate interesting predictions and explanations.

Where do good new ideas come from? Is it a matter of luck? Studies of creative individuals and acts of creation indicate that there is more to creativity than just chance. Some individuals appear more likely to come up with creative solutions than others.

Talent

Talent must stand as the most obvious, least understood, and least studied factor in creativity. Clearly, some people are born with extraordinary abilities to draw lifelike pictures, remember musical compositions, solve mathematical problems, etc. Many outstanding figures in these areas were child prodigies who exhibited their talent at an early age before they had received much formal training. Furthermore, talent in one area does not guarantee ability in other areas. On the one hand, Leonardo Da Vinci coupled an extraordinary drawing ability with a variety of superior skills. But in stark contrast, some children are *idiot savants* who combine an extraordinary drawing, musical, or mnemonic ability with a profound retardation in language and reasoning. Unfortunately, there have been few detailed studies of idiot savants published, which is why Selfe's (1977) study of Nadia, an autistic child with extraordinary drawing ability, is so important.

Nadia was born in Nottingham, England, in 1967. From the first her development was slow. As an infant she was unresponsive and would not turn at her mother's approach. Her first words appeared at nine months; but at eighteen months, two-word utterances, which normally appear, did not develop, and she used the single-word utterances she had acquired less and less frequently. During this time she became increasingly isolated emotionally, and her family began to worry that her development was not proceeding normally.

Nadia entered a special school for severely subnormal children in 1972. She was physically large for her age, but she was slow and lethargic in her movements. Her typical behavior exhibited passivity and excessive slowness, and she was mute and inactive. She had an effective vocabulary of less than ten words. She could not dress herself without assistance.

When she was 3 1/2 years old, Nadia suddenly displayed an extraordinary drawing ability. Over the next three years she created many striking drawings. From the beginning her drawings were three-dimensional, lifelike, and quite beautiful. Nadia drew pictures of horses, with and without riders, of birds, of other animals, of trains, and of people. Her drawings were based on both pictures she had seen and solid objects, but her drawings were not copies. Rather, elements of what she had seen appeared in drawings done weeks later in new and original perspectives. Her drawings were not wooden portraits but contained scenes of vigorous action, sometimes containing strange, new creatures. For example, one of her animals looks part giraffe and part donkey. A comparison of Nadia's drawings with 24,000 "pictures of mommy" from a local newspaper contest made it clear how unique Nadia was. A further search of the psychological literature revealed no documented case of such exquisite drawing ability emerging at such an early age.

Nadia was left-handed and drew with a ballpoint pen, which she held firmly and comfortably. She rapidly executed strokes with the kind of command that suggests years of training. She could stop a line exactly where it met another even while drawing quite rapidly. She could change the direction of a line and draw lines at any angle toward or away from the body. She could draw a small but perfect circle in one movement and place a dot in the center.

Nadia drew intensively for varying intervals of time up to a minute and then usually sat back to survey the effect, moving her head perhaps to vary the viewing angle. This study usually gave her great pleasure, and after surveying intently what she had drawn, she often smiled, babbled, and shook her head and knees in glee. During her most productive period she drew four or five times a week.

Nadia entered a school for autistic children when she was seven, and in the next two years her sociability and language improved greatly. However, she virtually stopped drawing spontaneously, though she would produce a recognizable sketch of a classmate upon request.

Nadia's remarkable talent emphasizes that we still know very little about the sources of individual differences in creative potential. Let us now examine the general nature of the creative process in more detail.

Creative Process

In an early analysis Wallas (1926) proposed that the creative process has four steps:

1. *Preparation*: Formulating the problem and making preliminary attempts to solve it.
2. *Incubation*: Leaving the problem to work on other things.
3. *Illumination:* Achieving insight into the solution.
4. *Verification:* Making sure that the solution really works.

Certainly, not every example of creative problem solving shows all these separate phases, and Wallas's framework has been criticized for this reason and others (Perkins 1981). However, one famous example that apparently illustrates the four phases is an introspective report by the French mathematician Henri Poincaré (1913). He was attempting to develop a theory of Fuchsian functions (what these are is not important to understanding how Poincaré discovered them). He reports that he began by working on the problem almost constantly for fifteen days, until one sleepless night when "ideas rose in crowds; I felt them collide until pairs interlocked, so to speak, making a stable combination." Poincaré continues (1913, pp. 387–388):

> I wanted to represent these functions by the quotient of two series; this idea was perfectly conscious and deliberate; the analogy with elliptic functions guided me. I asked myself what properties these series must have if they existed, and succeeded without difficulty in forming the series I have called theta-Fuchsian.

> Just at this time I left Caen, where I was living, to go on a geologic excursion under the auspices of the school of mines. The changes of travel made me forget my mathematical work. Having reached Coutances, we entered an omnibus to go some place or other. At the moment when I put my foot on the step the idea came to me. without anything in my former thoughts seeming to have paved the way for it, that the transformations I had used to define the Fuchsian functions were identical to those of non-Euclidean geometry. I did not

verify the idea; I should not have had time, as, upon taking my seat in the omnibus, I went on with a conversation already commenced, but I felt a perfect certainty. On my return to Caen, for conscience's sake, I verified the result at my leisure.

Here we see that the preparatory period for Poincaré consisted of fifteen days of intense work, culminating in some new ideas that arose one restless night and formed a "stable combination." Poincaré then wished to define the class of functions he had discovered more clearly. In doing so, he developed an analogy with another class of functions. Then followed a period of incubation during his travel, leading to his experience of illumination. Later he verified his results.

Preparation. Where did Poincaré's "stable combinations" come from? What kind of mental activity was occurring during those fifteen days of intensive preparation? This period seemed to involve the generation of many combinations of ideas and then the discarding of some and the selection of some to pursue further. Actually, to say that the preparation period for Poincaré lasted fifteen days is a bit misleading. Although this intensive two-week period was important, Poincaré's preparation really consisted of his entire mathematical education up to that point. Without his vast stock of acquired mathematical knowledge, he could not have made his discovery. For example, this knowledge was necessary to develop the analogy with elliptic functions, which played an important role in the development of Poincaré's ideas about Fuchsian functions. In general, without thorough training and an intense initial period of work on a problem, it is unlikely that an incubation period will be fruitful. Successful incubation requires an intense dedication to finding a solution, a motivation to acquire as much relevant knowledge as possible, and a willingness to return to the problem over periods of perhaps years.

In fact, if we look at other areas of discovery, we find that the period of preparation plays an even more fundamental role: It influences the selection of the problem in the first place. There is a saying in science, "Chance favors the prepared mind." What this saying means is that no discoveries are made simply by accident. For example, a well-known story of an "accidental" discovery is Alexander Fleming's discovery of penicillin, when he noticed that a culture of staphylococcus did not grow near a contaminant that had literally dropped out of the air onto the culture dish. However, such contamination was routine in every laboratory in the world. Only Fleming realized its significance and did not simply wash the contaminant away. The large body of knowledge provided by an intense period of preparation makes it more likely that creative individuals will recognize an important problem when they see it.

The importance of preparation to problem selection becomes even more significant when we turn from science to art and music. The composer Arnold Schönberg turned away students who had come to learn his twelve-tone system, saying that they could not learn the new music until they had mastered the old. Schönberg's point was that first people must thoroughly master the art of their times, so creating a work in the contemporary style is no longer a novel and creative act for them personally. Only then are they in a position to take the next step forward and create something that no one else has done before.

Incubation. Perhaps the most fascinating aspect of the creative process is the incubation phenomenon. Why should an interruption of problem solving help one to reach a solution? There are several possible explanations (Posner 1973):

1. Interruption permits one to recover *from fatigue.* Problem solvers may simply tire of working on the problem and will work harder again after a rest. The few experimental demonstrations of improved performance on a problem-solving task after a break (Fulgosi and Guilford 1968; Murray and Denny 1969; Silveira 1971) can largely be explained on this basis alone.

2. Interruption allows one to *forget inappropriate approaches.* Over time, problem solvers may forget what they were doing when they last worked on the problem. If what they were doing was exploring a dead end, an interruption may make it more likely that they will take a more fruitful approach when they tackle the problem again. This explanation is supported by evidence that the effect of functional fixedness can be diminished by increasing the delay between the initial use of an object and presentation of the new problem (Adamson and Taylor 1954).

3. Interruption may promote *conscious problem solving.* Problem solvers may actually work on the problem from time to time during the break. Many people commonly find themselves thinking about an important problem in the middle of doing something else. Problem solvers may often forget about having returned to the problem, so later they are unaware of having worked on the problem during the interlude.

4. Interruption permits one to reorganize. We saw in Chapters 8 and 9 that after a retention interval when a person attempts to recall, various facts that were learned at different times about a common topic are recalled together. This grouping leads to a novel organization in memory. Such novel organizations may make fresh approaches to a problem possible.

Illumination. The essence of creative thought is the synthesis of new concepts. In the moment of illumination there is a *juxtaposition of ideas,* ideas that until then were only thought of separately are brought together. Creative thought is therefore closely tied to reasoning by analogy.

As we saw, Poincaré felt he was aware of his own unconscious processes at work during the sleepless night that led to his initial progress. In another famous incident the chemist Kekulé describes the origin of his idea of the benzene ring (from Koestler 1964, p. 118):

> I turned my chair to the fire and dozed…Again the atoms were gamboling before my eyes… My mental eye…could now distinguish larger structures, of manifold conformation; long rows, sometimes more closely fitted together; all twinning and twisting in snakelike motion. But look!…One of the snakes had seized hold of its own tail, and the form whirled mockingly before my eyes. As if by a flash of lightning I awoke.

Kekulé realized that the structure of certain organic compounds is like that of the snake biting its own tail—a closed chain or ring. This case provides a striking example of a visual analogy. Other statements by creative individuals also indicate that the period preceding illumination is often occupied by sleep or dreaming.

Conceptual synthesis is apparent in the development of other scientific theories, as reconstructed in historical case studies. Gruber's (1974) analysis of the origin of Charles Darwin's theory of natural selection illustrates how multiple analogies can contribute to a new conceptual structure. Darwin was aware of *artificial* selection—the procedures by which breeders mold varieties of animals and plants by selecting specimens with desirable traits for reproductive use. He therefore considered the hypothesis that species are molded by some type of *natural* selection analogous to artificial selection. However, this analogy was clearly imperfect. For one thing, the criterion for selection had to be different: Forms were not adapted to serve human purposes but to fit natural environments. For another, and most critically, it was not clear what constituted the agent of natural selection, since it obviously was not human breeders.

Darwin used a very different analogy to solve this central problem. He learned of Malthus's theory of population, according to which human populations will inevitably outstrip their food supply, because human reproduction will outstrip agricultural production. Darwin generalized this idea beyond just human populations to an incessant "struggle for existence" everywhere in nature. As a result of this struggle, only the fittest would survive and reproduce. In this way Darwin arrived at a causal mechanism that could drive natural selection. Thus the overall theory was a conceptual synthesis based on two previously unrelated analogies.

Imagination—i.e., the ability to take things from different domains and put them together—is a fundamental human ability. As a simple example, Figure 12.18 presents a child's solution to the problem of improving the design of the human body. The child who drew this picture thought that an aerial could be added to detect attackers and that springs would make useful legs (at least for a person who wants to be a good goalie in soccer). The recommendations of three noses to improve smell and three eyes to see with seem to be based on a time-honored heuristic: "More is better." The resulting design is an amalgam of various ideas intended to upgrade certain functions of the human body.

Real inventions sometimes have a similar origin. For example, at one time television aerials came in pieces and had to be assembled on the rooftop—not an easy job, especially in bad weather. More recently, the design was improved by constructing aerials that fold up like umbrellas, so they can simply be opened up on the roof, with minimal assembly. Just as in the child's drawing, the improved design depended on the import of an idea from a different problem domain.

Analogies may be verbal as well as visual. Metaphors, for example, have the creative element of pointing out a hidden analogy. Geoffrey Leech (1974, p. 44) gives the example of the Anglo-Saxon expression mere-hengest ("sea-steed"), which is used in a poem as a metaphor for ship. The meanings of ship and steed are connected by their shared properties. Both ships and horses carry men from one place to another, with an up-and-down movement. In the context of the heroic poem both are associated with journeys for adventure and warfare. When the meanings of the two words are combined in a metaphor, the similarities are emphasized, while the obvious dissimilarities (horses are animate, ships are not; horses move on land, ships on the sea) are pushed into the background. The result is a new concept that focuses on the analogy between ships and horses.

Thus Koestler (1964) argues that the diverse forms of creativity that can be found in literature, art, and science are basically similar. All have the fundamental property of synthesizing novel combinations of ideas. According to Koestler, even a good joke has this property of juxtaposing ideas, as well as the critical element of surprise. Here is a "Freudian joke" paraphrased from Koestler (1964, pp. 32–33):

> Two women meet while shopping at a supermarket in the Bronx.
> One looks cheerful, the other depressed. The cheerful one inquires:
> "What's eating you?"
> "Nothing's eating me."
> "Death in the family?"
> "No, God forbid!"
> "Worried about money?"
> "No…nothing like that."
> "Trouble with the kids?"
> "Well, if you must know, it's my little Jimmy."
> "What's wrong with him then?"
> "Nothing is wrong. His teacher said he must see a psychiatrist." Pause. "Well, well, what's wrong with seeing a psychiatrist?"

"Nothing's wrong. The psychiatrist said he's got an Oedipus complex." Pause. "Oedipus-Schmoedipus! I wouldn't worry so long as he's a good boy and loves his mama."

If you missed the punch line, your Freudian psychology is rusty—an Oedipus complex is the sexual desire of a boy for his mother. The humor is generated by the conflict between two notions of what "loves his mama" means: the duty of a child to treat his mother with affection, and the Freudian view that the son-mother relationship can involve frustrated sexual attraction. One is good, the other is bad; and the humor is increased by the fact that the speaker is obviously unaware of the contradiction in what she is saying.

Verification. One can become so bedazzled by the drama of the moment of illumination that the importance of verification to the creative process may be overlooked. Verification is important because there may be false moments of illumination whose flaws appear only when a systematic attempt at verification is made. In addition, often the only way a person who has attained a moment of illumination can share it with others is by taking them through the process of verification.

In the history of science we find, paradoxically, that some of the most original scientific discoveries occur as ideas to several different people at different places and times. But only when one of those individuals has the ability, persistence, and courage to verify the idea does it become accepted by the entire scientific community. For example, the theory of evolution was worked out independently by Charles Darwin and Alfred Wallace, but Darwin spent twenty years gathering data that supported the theory before he published it. As another example, you might think that the importance of such a useful substance as penicillin would be obvious. However, years before Fleming's fateful ruined culture, penicillin had been discovered, presented in a scientific paper, given no interest, and completely forgotten. Fleming's own original report was also ignored, but Fleming had the confidence in his own insight to continue to work with penicillin until its importance was verified.

Painters, musicians, and other artists have even more difficulty than scientists in sharing their insights with others. They must validate their visions by creating original works that will have sufficient dramatic appeal to attract attention.

Problem Solving and the Creative Process

The steps involved in the creative process can be related to the general problem-solving steps we discussed earlier (see Figure 12.1). The preparation step in creative thinking is simply an extended case of forming an initial problem representation. Incubation, as we saw, is poorly understood; however, it can be viewed as a means of overcoming difficulties in reformulating a problem (i.e., getting stuck in the flowchart of Figure 12.1). For example, if incubation serves to allow inappropriate approaches to be forgotten, thus reducing initial difficulties due to set and functional fixedness, the problem solver may then achieve a new reformulation. Illumination may simply correspond to the result of achieving such a reformulation. Finally, verification appears to correspond to the problem-solving steps of planning a concrete solution and then executing and testing it. An act is recognized as creative when it is a new solution to an old problem and when it is a solution to a problem that has never been solved before.

SUMMARY

Our discussion in this chapter has dealt with human performance in complex problem-solving tasks, ranging from well-defined puzzle problems (e.g., the Tower of Hanoi) to such *ill-defined,* creative problems as invention and scientific discovery. Although these tasks seem very different, certain global similarities in the problem-solving process can be identified. Problem solving involves the steps of forming an initial problem representation, trying to plan a potential solution, reformulating the problem if necessary, and executing and testing the solution plan. The planning step usually requires heuristics such as means-ends analysis. Problem reformulation, which is often critical in solving ill-defined, creative problems, often involves noticing and applying an analogy. The skill of experts on many types of problems, including complex board games and physics, can be largely attributed to knowledge and perceptual abilities specifically related to the expert's task domain. In some cases, however, problem-solving experience can have deleterious effects, as evidenced by the phenomena of *functional fixedness* and set.

Some useful tools for studying problem solving and creative thinking are *protocol analysis* (theorizing from verbal reports) and computer simulation. The GPS is a simulation model based on means-ends analysis. Recent work in artificial intelligence has been directed toward the development of expert systems based on specialized, prestored knowledge. Some work is being done on the development of computer programs that can learn in a problem-solving environment. Experimental techniques have also been developed for studying complex problem solving by nonhuman primates, especially chimpanzees.

Creative thinking can be viewed as a type of problem solving in which reformulation based on conceptual synthesis is often critical. A period of incubation in which the problem is set aside is often important in achieving a successful reformulation. Conceptual synthesis is exhibited in such diverse phenomena as humor, literature, invention, and generation of scientific theories.

RECOMMENDED READINGS

There are many good sources for further reading about problem solving. Three important works in the Gestalt tradition are Kohler's *Mentality of Apes* (1925), Wertheimer's *Productive Thinking* (1945), and Duncker's monograph *On Problem-Solving* (1945). An important book in the information-processing tradition is *Human Problem Solving* (1972) by Newell and Simon. This book remains influential, but it is also extremely long (over nine hundred pages) and difficult to read. *Cognitive Skills and Their Acquisition* (1981), edited by Anderson, contains a number of papers on learning and problem solving. A good introduction to artificial-intelligence models of problem solving is provided in textbooks by Winston (1984) and Rich (1983). The collection of papers in *Machine Learning* (1983), edited by Michalski, Garbonell, and Mitchell, gives a state-of-the-art treatment of computer programs that learn.

There are a number of good how-to books on problem solving. Two of the best are Polya's *How to Solve It* (1957) and Wickelgren's *How to Solve Problems* (1974). *Conceptual Blockbusting* (1974) by Adams is easy and fun. Koestler provides an interesting discussion of creativity in *The Act of Creation* (1964). This book is very long, and the first part (Book One) is the best. *The Mind's Best Work* (1981) by Perkins is an engaging discussion of the creative process.

Solutions to Cryptarithmetic Problems

SEND	9,567	DONALD	526,485	CROSS	96,233
+MORE	+1,085	+GERALD	+197,485	+ROADS	+62,513
MONEY	10,652	ROBERT	723,970	DANGER	158,746

Clinical Versus Actuarial Judgment

ROBYN M. DAWES, DAVID FAUST, AND PAUL E. MEEHL

Professionals are frequently consulted to diagnose and predict human behavior; optimal treatment and planning often hinge on the consultant's judgmental accuracy. The consultant may rely on one of two contrasting approaches to decision-making—the clinical and actuarial methods. Research comparing these two approaches shows the actuarial method to be superior. Factors underlying the greater accuracy of actuarial methods, sources of resistance to the scientific findings, and the benefits of increased reliance on actuarial approaches are discussed.

A PSYCHIATRIC PATIENT DISPLAYS AMBIGUOUS SYMPTOMS. Is this a condition best treated by psychotherapy alone or might it also require an antipsychotic medication with occasionally dangerous side effects? An elderly patient complains of memory loss but neurologic examination and diagnostic studies are equivocal. The neuropsychologist is asked to administer tests to help rule out progressive brain disease. A medical work-up confirms a patient's worst fears: he has terminal cancer. He asks the doctor how long he has to put his life in order.

These three brief scenarios illustrate a few of the many situations in which experts are consulted to diagnose conditions or to predict human outcomes. Optimal planning and care often hinge on the consultant's judgmental accuracy. Whether as physicians, psychiatrists, or psychologists, consultants perform two basic functions in decision-making: they collect and interpret data. Our interest here is in the interpretive function, specifically the relative merits of clinical versus actuarial methods.

METHODS OF JUDGMENT AND MEANS OF COMPARISON

In the clinical method the decision-maker combines or processes information in his or her head. In the actuarial or statistical method the human judge is eliminated and conclusions rest solely on empirically established relations between data and the condition or event of interest. A life insurance agent uses the clinical method if data on risk factors are combined through personal judgment. The agent uses the actuarial method if data are entered into a formula, or tables and charts that contain empirical information relating these background data to life expectancy.

Clinical judgment should not be equated with a clinical setting or a clinical practitioner. A clinician in psychiatry or medicine may use the clinical or actuarial method. Conversely, the actuarial method should not be equated with automated decision rules alone. For example, computers can automate clinical judgments. The computer can be programmed to yield the description "dependency traits," just as the clinical judge would, whenever a certain response appears on a psychological test. To be truly actuarial, interpretations must be both automatic (that is, prespecified or routinized) and based on empirically established relations.

Virtually any type of data is amenable to actuarial interpretation. For example, interview observations can be coded quantitatively (patient appears withdrawn: (1) yes, (2) no). It is thereby possible to incorporate qualitative observations and quantitative data into the predictive mix. Actuarial output statements, or conclusions, can address virtually any type of diagnosis, description, or prediction of human interest.

The combination of clinical and actuarial methods offers a third potential judgment strategy, one for which certain viable approaches have been proposed. However, most proposals for clinical-actuarial combination presume that the two judgment methods work together harmoniously and overlook the many situations that require dichotomous choices, for example, whether or not to use an antipsychotic medication, grant parole, or hospitalize. If clinical and actuarial interpretations agree, there is no need to combine them. If they disagree, one must choose one or the other. If clinical interpretation suggests brain damage but the actuarial method indicates otherwise, one does not conclude that the patient is and is not brain damaged.

Although some research appeared on clinical and actuarial judgment before the mid-fifties, Meehl (1) introduced the issue to a broad range of social scientists in 1954 and stimulated a flurry of studies. Meehl specified conditions for a fair comparison of the two methods.

First, both methods should base judgments on the same data. This condition docs not require that clinical judge and statistical method, before comparison, use the same data to derive decision strategies or rules. The clinician's development of interpretive strategies depends on prior experience and knowledge. The development of actuarial methods requires cases with known outcome. The clinical and actuarial strategies may thus be derived from separate or overlapping data bases, and one or the other may be based on more or fewer cases or more or less outcome information. For example, the clinician may have interpreted 1000 intelligence tests for indications of brain dysfunction and may know the outcome for some of these cases based on radiologic examination. The actuarial method may have been developed on the subset of these 1000 cases for which outcome is known.

Second, one must avoid conditions that can artificially inflate the accuracy of actuarial methods. For example, the mathematical procedures (such as regression analysis or discriminant analysis) used to develop statistical actuarial decision rules may capitalize on chance (nonrepeating) relations among variables. Thus, derivation typically should be followed by cross-validation, that is, application of the decision rule to new or fresh cases, or by a standard statistical estimate of the probable outcome of cross-validation. Cross-validation counters artificial inflation in accuracy rates and allows one to determine, realistically, how the method performs. Such application is essential because a procedure should be shown to work where it is needed, that is, in cases in which outcome is unknown. If the method is only intended for local use or in the setting in which it was developed, the investigator may partition a representative sample from that setting into derivation and cross-validation groups. If broader application is intended, then new cases should be representative of the potential settings and populations of interest.

RESULTS OF COMPARATIVE STUDIES

The three initial scenarios provide examples of comparative studies. Goldberg studied the distinction between neurosis and psychosis based on the Minnesota Multiphasic Personality Inventory (MMPI), a personality test commonly used for such purposes (2, 3). This differential diagnosis is of practical importance. For example, the diagnosis of psychosis may lead to needed but riskier treatments or to denial of future insurance applications. Goldberg derived various decision rules through statistical analysis of scores on 11 MMPI scales and psychiatric patients' discharge diagnoses. The single most effective rule for distinguishing the two conditions was quite simple: add scores from three scales and then subtract scores from two other scales. If the sum falls below 45, the patient is diagnosed neurotic; if it equals or exceeds 45, the patient is diagnosed psychotic. This has come to be known as the "Goldberg Rule."

Goldberg next obtained a total of 861 new MMPIs from seven different settings, including inpatient and outpatient services from cither medical school, private, or Veterans Administration hospital systems in California, Minnesota, and Ohio. The accuracy of the decision rules when applied to these new cases was compared with that of 29 judges who analyzed the same material and attempted the same distinction. Some of the judges had little or no prior experience with the MMPI and others were Ph.D. psychologists with extensive MMPI experience.

Across the seven settings, the judges achieved mean validity coefficients ranging from $r = 0.15$ to 0.43, with a total figure of 0.28 for all cases, or 62% correct decisions. The single best judge achieved an overall coefficient of 0.39, or 67% correct decisions. In each of the seven settings, various decision rules exceeded the judges' mean accuracy level. The Goldberg Rule performed similarly to the judges in three of the settings and demonstrated a modest to substantial advantage in four of the settings (where the rule's validity coefficient exceeded that of the judges by 0.16 to 0.31). For the total sample, the Goldberg Rule achieved a validity coefficient of 0.45, or 70% correct decisions, thereby exceeding both the mean accuracy of the 29 judges and that of the single best judge.

Rorer and Goldberg then examined whether additional practice might alter results. Judges were given MMPI training packets consisting of 300 new MMPI profiles with the criterion diagnosis on the back, thus providing immediate and concrete feedback on judgmental accuracy. However, even after repeated sessions with these training protocols culminating in 4000 practice judgments, none of the judges equaled the Goldberg Rule's 70% accuracy rate with these test cases. Rorer and Goldberg finally tried giving a subset of judges, including all of the experts, the outcome of the Goldberg Rule for each MMPI. The judges were free to use the rule when they wished and knew its overall effectiveness. Judges generally made modest gains in performance but none could match the rule's accuracy; every judge would have done better by always following the rule.

In another study using the same 861 MMPI protocols, Goldberg constructed mathematical (linear) models of each of the 29 judges that reproduced their decisions as closely as possible (4). Modeling judges' decisions requires no access to outcome information. Rather, one analyzes relations between the information available to the judge and the judge's decisions. In principle, if a judge weights variables with perfect consistency or reliability (that is, the same data always lead to the same decision), the model will always reproduce that judge's decisions. In practice, human decision-makers are not perfectly reliable and thus judge and model will sometimes disagree. Goldberg found that in cases of disagreement, the models were more often correct than the very judges on whom they were based. The perfect reliability of the models likely explains their superior performance in this and related studies (5).

Leli and Filskov studied the diagnosis of progressive brain dysfunction based on intellectual testing (6). A decision rule derived from one set of cases and then applied to a new sample correctly identified 83% of the new cases. Groups of inexperienced and experienced clinicians working from the same data correctly identified 63% and 58% of the new cases, respectively. In another condition, clinicians were also given the results of the actuarial analysis. Both the inexperienced and experienced clinicians showed improvement (68% and 75% correct identifications, respectively), but neither group matched the decision rule's 83% accuracy. The clinicians' improvement appeared to depend on the extent to which they used the rule.

Einhorn (7) studied the prediction of survival time following the initial diagnosis of Hodgkin's disease as established by biopsy. At the time of the study, survival time was negatively correlated with disease severity (Hodgkin's is now controllable). All of the 193 patients in the study subsequently died, thus tragically providing objective outcome information.

Three pathologists, one an internationally recognized authority, rated the patients' initial biopsy slides along nine histological dimensions they identified as relevant in determining disease severity and also provided a global raring of severity. Actuarial formulas were developed by examining relations between the pathologists' ratings and actual survival time on the first 100 cases, with the remaining 93 cases used for cross-validation and comparison. The pathologists' own judgments showed virtually no relation to survival time; cross-validated actuarial formulas achieved modest but significant relations. The study revealed more than an actuarial advantage. It also showed that the pathologists' ratings produced potentially useful information but that only the actuarial method, which was based on these ratings, tapped their predictive value.

Additional research. These three studies illustrate key features of a much larger literature on clinical versus actuarial judgment. First, the studies, like many others, met the previously specified conditions for a fair comparison.

Second, the three studies are representative of research outcomes. Eliminating research that did not protect sufficiently against inflated results for actuarial methods, there remain nearly 100 comparative studies in the social sciences. In virtually every one of these studies, the actuarial method has equaled or surpassed the clinical method, sometimes slightly and sometimes substantially (8–10). For example, in Watley and Vance's study on the prediction of college grades the methods tied (11); in Carroll et al.'s study on the prediction of parole violation, the actuarial method showed a slight to modest advantage (12); and in Wittman's study on the prediction of response to electroshock therapy, the actuarial method was correct almost twice as often as the clinical method (13).

The earlier comparative studies were often met with doubts aboutvalidity and generalization. It was claimed, for example, that the studies misrepresented the clinical method either by denying judges access to crucial data sources such as interviews, by using artificial tasks that failed to tap their areas of expertise, or by including clinicians of questionable experience or expertise.

The evidence that has accumulated over the years meets these challenges. First, numerous studies have examined judgments that are not artificial but common to everyday practice and for which special expertise is claimed. Examples include the three studies described above, which involved the differential between less serious and major psychiatric disorder, the detection of brain damage, and the prediction of survival time. Other studies have examined the diagnosis of medical versus psychiatric disorder (14); the description or characterization of personality (15); and the prediction of treatment outcome (16), length of psychiatric hospitalization (17), and violent behavior (18). These are decisions that general practitioners or specialists often address, and in a number of studies investigators did not introduce judgment tasks that clinicians then performed, but rather examined decisions already made in the course of everyday practice.

Other studies have provided clinicians or judges with access to preferred sources of information. Even in 1966, Sawyer was able to locate 17 comparisons between actuarial and clinical judgment based on the results of psychological testing and interview (8). Other investigators have allowed judges to collect whatever data they preferred in whatever manner they preferred. In Carroll et al.'s naturalistic study on the prediction of parolees' behavior after release, the parole board did not alter the data collection procedures (12). In Dawes's study on the prediction of graduate student performance, the admissions committee relied on the same data normally used to reach decisions (19). None of the 17 comparisons reviewed by Sawyer and neither the study by Carroll et al. nor Dawes favored clinical over actuarial judgment.

Nor has the outcome varied within or across studies involving judges at various levels of experience or expertise. In Goldberg's study novice and experienced MMPI interpreters performed similarly when using the clinical method and neither group surpassed the actuarial method, results parallel to those of Leli and Filskov in their Study on the detection of brain damage (2, 6). Other studies on the detection and localization of brain damage have yielded similar results (20, 21). For example, Wedding found that neither clinicians with extensive experience interpreting the tests under study nor a nationally prominent neuropsychologist surpassed the overall accuracy of actuarial methods in determining the presence, location, and cause of brain damage (20).

The comparative studies often do not permit general conclusions about the superiority of one or another specific actuarial decision rule. Some studies, such as Goldberg's, do show application across settings, but much of the research has involved restricted samples. Investigators have been less interested in a specific procedure's range of application than in performing an additional test of the two methods and thereby extending the range of comparative studies.

The various studies can thus be viewed as repeated sampling from a universe of judgment tasks involving the diagnosis and prediction of human behavior. Lacking complete knowledge of the elements that constitute this universe, representativeness cannot be determined precisely. However, with a sample of about 100 studies and the same outcome obtained in almost every case, it is reasonable to conclude that the actuarial advantage is not exceptional but general and likely encompasses many of the unstudied judgment tasks. Stated differently, if one poses the query: "Would an actuarial procedure developed for a particular judgment task (say, predicting academic success at my institution) equal or exceed the clinical method?", the available research places the odds solidly in favor of an affirmative reply. "There is no controversy in social science that shows such a large body of qualitatively diverse studies coming out so uniformly … as this one" (*9*, p. 373).

Possible exceptions. If fair comparisons consistently favor the actuarial method, one may then reverse the impetus of inquiry and ask whether there are certain circumstances in which the clinical judge might beat the actuary. Might the clinician attain superiority if given an informational edge? For example, suppose the clinician lacks an actuarial formula for interpreting certain interview results and must choose between an impression based on both interview and test scores and a contrary actuarial interpretation based on only the test scores. The research addressing this question has yielded consistent results (*8, 10, 22*). Even when given an information edge, the clinical judge still fails to surpass the actuarial method; in fact, access to additional information often does nothing to close the gap between the two methods.

It is not difficult to hypothesize other circumstances in which the clinical judge might improve on the actuarial method: (i) judgments mediated by theories and hence difficult or impossible to duplicate by statistical frequencies alone, (ii) select reversal of actuarial conclusions based on the consideration of rare events or utility functions that are not incorporated into statistical methods, and (iii) complex configurai relations between predictive variables and outcome (*23–25*).

The potential superiority of theory-mediated judgments over conclusions reached solely on the basis of empirical frequencies may seem obvious to those in the "hard" sciences. Prediction mediated by theory is successful when the scientist has access to the major causal influences, possesses accurate measuring instruments to assess them, and uses a well-corroborated theory to make the transition from theory to fact (that is, when the expert has access to a specific model). Thus, although most comparative research in medicine favors the actuarial method overall, the studies that suggest a slight clinical advantage seem to involve circumstances in which judgments rest on firm theoretical grounds (*26*).

The typical theory that underlies prediction in the social sciences, however, satisfies none of the needed conditions. Prediction of treatment response or violent behavior may rest on psychodynamic theory that permits directly contradictory conclusions and lacks formal measurement techniques. Theory-mediated judgments may eventually provide an advantage within psychology and other social sciences, but the conditions needed to realize this possibility are currently but a distant prospect or hope.

Clinicians might be able to gain an advantage by recognizing rare events that are not included in the actuarial formula (due to their infrequency) and that countervail the actuarial conclusion. This possibility represents a variation of the clinical-actuarial approach, in which one considers the outcome of both methods and decides when to supersede the actuarial conclusion. In psychology this circumstance has come to be known as the "broken leg" problem, on the basis of on an illustration in which an actuarial formula is highly successful in predicting an individual's weekly attendance at a movie but should be discarded upon discovering that the subject is in a cast with a fractured femur (*1, 25*). The clinician may beat the actuarial method if able to detect the rare fact and decide accordingly. In theory, actuarial methods can accommodate rare occurrences, but the practical obstacles are daunting. For example, the possible range of intervening events is infinite.

The broken leg possibility is easily studied by providing clinicians with both the available data and the actuarial conclusion and allowing them to use or countervail the latter at their discretion. The limited research examining this possibility, however, all shows that greater overall accuracy is achieved when clinicians rely uniformly on actuarial conclusions and avoid discretionary judgments (*3, 8*). When operating freely, clinicians apparently identify too many "exceptions," that is, the actuarial conclusions correctly modified are outnumbered by those incorrectly modified. If clinicians were more conservative in overriding actuarial conclusions they might gain an advantage, but this conjecture remains to be studied adequately.

Consideration of utilities raises a related possibility. Depending on the task, certain judgment errors may be more serious than others. For example, failure to detect a condition that usually remits spontaneously may be of less consequence than false identification of a condition for which risky treatment is prescribed. The adjustment of decision rules or cutting scores to reduce either false-negative or false-positive errors can decrease the procedure's overall accuracy but may still be justified if the consequences of these opposing forms of error are unequal. As such, if the clinician's counter-actuarial judgments, although less likely than the actuarial to be correa, were shown empirically to lower the probability of the rule's deliverances being correct (say, from 0.8 to 0.6), then in some contexts consideration of the joint probability-utility function might rationally reverse the action suggested by reliance on the formula alone. This procedure is formally equivalent to putting the clinician's judgment (as a new variable) into the actuarial equation, and more evidence on this process is needed to adequately appraise its impact. Here again, one cannot assume that the clinician's input helps. The available research suggests that formal inclusion of the clinician's input does not enhance the accuracy, nor necessarily the utility, of the actuarial formula and that informal or subjective attempts at adjustment can easily do more harm than good (8).

The clinician's potential capacity to capitalize on configurai patterns or relations among predictive cues raises two related but separable issues that we will examine in order: the capacity to recognize configurai relations and the capacity to use these observations to diagnose and predict. Certain forms of human pattern recognition still cannot be duplicated or equaled by artificial means. The recognition of visual patterns has challenged a generation of researchers in the field of artificial intelligence. Humans maintain a distinct advantage, for example, in the recognition of facial expressions. Human superiority also exists for language translation and for the invention of complex, deep-structure theories. Thus, for example, only the human observer may recognize a particular facial expression or mannerism (the float-like walk of certain schizophrenic patients) that has true predictive value. These observational abilities provide the potential for gathering useful (predictive) information that would otherwise be missed.

The possession of unique observational capacities clearly implies that human input or interaction is often needed to achieve maximal predictive accuracy (or to uncover potentially useful variables) but tempts us to draw an additional, dubious inference. A unique capacity to observe is not the same as a unique capacity to predict on the basis of integration of observations. As noted earlier, virtually any observation can be coded quantitatively and thus subjected to actuarial analysis. As Einhorn's study with pathologists and other research shows, greater accuracy may be achieved if the skilled observer performs this function and then steps aside, leaving the interpretation of observational and other data to the actuarial method (7).

FACTORS UNDERLYING THE SUPERIORITY OF ACTUARIAL METHODS

Contrasts between the properties of actuarial procedures and clinical judgment help to explain their differing success (27). First, actuarial procedures, unlike the human judge, always lead to the same conclusion for a given data set. In one study rheumatologists's and radiologists's reappraisals of cases they themselves had evaluated previously often resulted in different opinions (28). Such factors as fatigue, recent experience, or seemingly minor changes in the ordering of information or in the conceptualization of the case or task can produce random fluctuations in judgment (29). Random fluctuation decreases judgmental reliability and hence accuracy. For example, if the same data lead to the correct decision in one case but to a different, incorrect decision in the second case, overall accuracy will obviously suffer.

Perhaps more importantly, when properly derived, the mathematical features of actuarial methods ensure that variables contribute to conclusions based on their actual predictive power and relation to the criterion of interest. For example, decision rules based on multiple regression techniques include only the predictive variables and eliminate the nonpredictive ones, and they weight variables in accordance with their independent contribution to accurate conclusions. These achievements are essentially automatic with actuarial prediction but present formidable obstacles for human judges.

Research shows that individuals have considerable difficulty distinguishing valid and invalid variables and commonly develop false beliefs in associations between variables (30). In psychology and psychiatry, clinicians often obtain little or no information about the accuracy of their diagnoses and predictions. Consultants asked to predict violence may never learn whether their predictions were correct. Furthermore, clinicians rarely receive immediate feedback about criterion judgments (for example, diagnoses) of comparable validity to that physicians obtain when the pathologist reports at the end of a clinico-pathological conference (31). Lacking sufficient or clear information about judgmental accuracy, it is problematic to determine the actual validity, if any, of the variables on which one relies. The same problem may occur if actuarial methods are applied blindly to new situations or settings without any performance checks.

In other circumstances, clinical judgments produce "self-fulfilling prophecies." Prediction of an outcome often leads to decisions that influence or bias that outcome (32). An anecdote illustrates this problem. A psychiatrist in a murder trial predicted future dangerousness, and the defendant was sentenced to death. While on death row the defendant acted violently, which appeared to support the psychiatrist's predictive powers. However, once sentenced to death this individual had little to lose; he may have acted differently had the psychiatrist's appraisal, and in turn the sentence, been different.

Additionally, known outcomes seem more predictable than they are in advance (33), and past predictions are mistakenly recalled as overly consistent with actual outcomes (34, 35). For example, Arkes *et al.* presented the same case materials to groups of physicians and asked them to assign probabilities to alternate diagnoses. When probabilities were assigned in foresight, each diagnosis was considered about equally likely. However, when the physicians were informed that one or another diagnosis had been established previously and they were then asked to state what initial diagnosis they likely would have made, they assigned the highest probability to whatever diagnosis they were told had been established (36). If one's view or recall of initial judgments is inadvertently shaped to fit whatever happens to occur, outcome information will have little or no corrective value.

The clinician is also exposed to a skewed sample of humanity and, short of exposure to truly representative samples, it may be difficult, if not impossible, to determine relations among variables. For example, suppose that about half of the adolescents appraised for a history of juvenile delinquency show subtle electroencephalographic (EEG) abnormalities. Based on these co-occurrences, the clinician may come to consider EEG abnormality a sign of delinquency or may conclude that delinquency is associated with brain dysfunction. In fact, clinicians have often postulated these relations (37).

One cannot determine, however, whether a relation exists unless one also knows whether the sign occurs more frequently among those with, versus those without, the condition. For example, to determine whether EEG abnormality is associated with delinquency, one must also know the frequency with which delinquents do not obtain EEG abnormalities and the frequencies with which nondelinquents do and do not obtain EEG abnormalities.

Further, even should a valid relation exist, one cannot determine the sign's actual utility unless one knows: (i) how much more frequently it occurs when the condition is present than when it is absent and (ii) the frequency of the condition. For example, a sign that is slightly more common among those with the condition may be of little diagnostic utility. If the condition is infrequent, then positive identifications based on the sign's presence can even be wrong in most cases, for most individuals who display the sign will not have the condition. If 10% of brain-damaged individuals make a particular response on a psychological test and only 5% of normals, but nine of ten clinic patients are not brain-damaged, most patients who show the feature will not be brain-damaged.

In practice, the clinician is far more likely to evaluate individuals with significant problems than those without them, and this skewed exposure hinders attempts to make all of the needed comparisons. In fact, empirical study shows that EEG "abnormalities" are common among normal children and further suggests that the incidence of delinquency is no greater among those with than without neurological disorder (37, 38). The formation of such false beliefs is further compounded by a decided human tendency to over-attend to information consistent with one's hypotheses and to under-attend to contradictory information (39). The result is that mistaken beliefs or conclusions, once formed, resist counterevidence. Error is also fostered by a tendency to disregard frequency data and instead to form diagnostic judgments based on the perceived match between one or more of the presenting symptoms (for example, EEG abnormality) and some prototype or instance of the diagnostic category (delinquency) stored in memory (40, 41).

The same factors that hinder the discovery of valid relations also promote overconfidence in clinical judgment. When the clinician misinterprets contrary evidence as indicative of judgmental accuracy, confidence will obviously be inflated. Research shows that judges are typically more confident than their accuracy warrants (42). In one study demonstrating the upper range of misappraisal, most clinicians were quite confident in their diagnosis although not one was correct (43).

The difficulty in separating valid and invalid variables on the basis of clinical experience or judgment is demonstrated in many studies examining diagnostic or predictive accuracy (44). Research shows that clinical judgments based on interviews achieve, at best, negligible accuracy or validity (*12*). Other studies show that clinical judgments based on psychological test results may be of low absolute validity (*6, 18, 20, 21*). Although clinical interviews or psychological tests can produce useful information, the clinical judge often cannot distinguish what is useful from what is useless. In all studies cited immediately above, statistical analysis of the same data uncovered useful variables or enhanced predictive accuracy.

The optimal weighting of variables is a less important advantage of the statistical method than is commonly assumed. In fact, unit (equal) weights yield predictions that correlate highly with those derived from optimally weighted composites, the only provisos being that the direction in which each predictor is related to the criterion can be specified beforehand and the predictors not be negatively correlated with each other (*J, 45–47*). Further, optimal weights are specific to the population in which they were derived, and any advantage gained in one setting may be lost when the same method is applied in another setting. However, when optimal weighting-adds meaningfully to predictive accuracy, the human judge is at a decided disadvantage. As Meehl (*9*, p. 372) has stated:

Surely we all know that the human brain is poor at weighting and computing. When you check out at a supermarket, you don't eyeball the heap of purchases and say to the clerk, "Well it looks to me as if it's about $17.00 worth; what do you think?" The clerk adds it up. There are no strong arguments … from empirical studies … for believing that human beings can assign optimal weights in equations subjectively or that they apply their own weights consistently.

It might be objected that this analogy, offered not probatively but pedagogically, presupposes an additive model that a proponent of configural judgment will not accept. Suppose instead that the supermarket pricing rule were, "Whenever both beef and fresh vegetables are involved, multiply the logarithm of 0.78 of the meat price by the square root of twice the vegetable price"; would the clerk and customer eyeball that any better? Worse, almost certainly. When human judges perform poorly at estimating and applying the parameters of a simple or component mathematical function, they should not be expected to do better when required to weight a complex composite of these variables.

LACK OF IMPACT AND SOURCES OF RESISTANCE

Research on clinical versus statistical judgment has had little impact on everyday decision making, particularly within its field of origin, clinical psychology. Guilmette *et al.*'s survey showed that most psychologists specializing in brain damage assessment prefer procedures for which actuarial methods are lacking over those for which actuarial formulas are available (*48*). The interview remains the sine qua non of entrance into mental health training programs and is required in most states to obtain a license to practice (*49*). Despite the studies that show that clinical interpretation of interviews may have little or no predictive utility, actuarial interpretation of interviews is rarely if ever used, although it is of demonstrated value.

Lack of impact is sometimes due to lack of familiarity with the scientific evidence. Some clinicians are unaware of the comparative research and do not even realize an issue exists. Others still refer to earlier studies and claim that the clinician was handicapped, unaware of the subsequent research that has rendered these arguments counterfactual.

Others who know the evidence may still dismiss it based on tendentiousness or misconception. Mental health professionals' education, training, theoretical orientations and identifications, and personal values may dictate against recognition of the actuarial advantage. Some psychologists, for example, believe that the use of a predictive equation dehumanizes their clients. The position overlooks the human costs of increased error that may result.

A common anti-actuarial argument, or misconception, is that group statistics do not apply to single individuals or events. The argument abuses basic principles of probability. Although individuals and events may exhibit unique features, they typically share common features with other persons or events that permit tallied observations or generalizations to achieve predictive power. An advocate of this anti-actuarial position would have to maintain, for the sake of logical consistency, that if one is forced to play Russian roulette a single time and is allowed to select a gun with one or five bullets in the chamber, the uniqueness of the event makes the choice arbitrary.

Finally, subjective appraisal may lead to inflated confidence in the accuracy of clinical judgment and the false impression that the actuarial method is inferior. Derivation and cross-validation of an actuarial method yields objective information on how well it does and does not perform

(50). When the clinician reviews research that shows, for example, that the Goldberg Rule for the MMPI achieved 70% accuracy in a comparable setting and exceeded the performance of all 29 judges in the study, this may still seem to compare unfavorably to self-perceived judgmental powers. The immediacy and salience of clinical experience fosters the misappraisal. The clinician may recall dramatic instances in which his interpretations proved correct or in which he avoided error by countervailing an actuarial conclusion, failing to recognize or correctly tally counter instances.

Ultimately, then, clinicians must choose between their own observations or impressions and the scientific evidence on the relative efficacy of the clinical and actuarial methods. The factors that create difficulty in self-appraisal of judgmental accuracy are exactly those that scientific procedures, such as unbiased sampling, experimental manipulation of variables, and blind assessment of outcome, are designed to counter. Failure to accept a large and consistent body of scientific evidence over unvalidated personal observation may be described as a normal human failing or, in the case of professionals who identify themselves as scientific, plainly irrational.

APPLICATION OF ACTUARIAL METHODS: LIMITS, BENEFITS, AND IMPLICATIONS

The research reviewed in this article indicates that a properly developed and applied actuarial method is likely to help in diagnosing and predicting human behavior as well or better than the clinical method, even when the clinical judge has access to equal or greater amounts of information. Research demonstrating the general superiority of actuarial approaches, however, should be tempered by an awareness of limitations and needed quality controls.

First, although surpassing clinical methods, actuarial procedures are far from infallible, sometimes achieving only modest results. Second, even a specific procedure that proves successful in one setting should be periodically reevaluated within that setting and should not be applied to new settings mindlessly. Although theory and research suggest that the choice of predictive variables is often more important than their weighting, statistical techniques can be used to yield weights that optimize a procedure's accuracy when it is applied to new cases drawn from the same population. Moreover, accuracy can be easily monitored as predictions are made, and methods modified or improved to meet changes in settings and populations. Finally, efforts can be made to test whether new variables enhance accuracy.

When developed and used appropriately, actuarial procedures can provide various benefits. Even when actuarial methods merely equal the accuracy of clinical methods, they may save considerable time and expense. For example, each year millions of dollars and many hours of clinicians' valuable time are spent attempting to predict violent behavior. Actuarial prediction of violence is far less expensive and would free time for more productive activities, such as meeting unfulfilled therapeutic needs. When actuarial methods are not used as the sole basis for decisions, they can still serve to screen out candidates or options that would never be chosen after more prolonged consideration.

When actuarial methods prove more accurate than clinical judgment the benefits to individuals and society are apparent. Much would be gained, for example, by increased accuracy in the prediction of violent behavior and parole violation, the diagnosis of disorder, and the identification of effective treatment. Additionally, more objective determination of limits in knowledge or predictive power can prevent inadvertent harm. Should a confident but incorrect clinical diagnosis of Alzheimer's disease be replaced by a far more cautious statement, or even better by the correct conclusion, we would avoid much unnecessary human misery.

Actuarial methods are explicit, in contrast to clinical judgment, which rests on mental processes that are often difficult to specify. Explicit procedures facilitate informed criticism and are freely available to other members of the scientific community who might wish to replicate or extend research.

Finally, actuarial methods—at least within the domains discussed in this article—reveal the upper bounds in our current capacities to predict human behavior. An awareness of the modest results that are often achieved by even the best available methods can help to counter unrealistic faith in our predictive powers and our understanding of human behavior. It may well be worth exchanging inflated beliefs for an unsettling sobriety, if the result is an openness to new approaches and variables that ultimately increase our explanatory and predictive powers.

The argument that actuarial procedures are not available for many important clinical decisions does not explain failure to use existent methods and overlooks the case with which such procedures can be developed for use in special settings. Even lacking any outcome information, it is possible to construct models of judges that will likely surpass their accuracy (4, 5). What is needed is the development of actuarial methods and a measurement assurance program that maintains control over both judgment strategies so that their operating characteristics in the field are known and an informed choice of procedure is possible. Dismissing the scientific evidence or lamenting the lack of available methods will prove much less productive than taking on the needed work.

REFERENCES AND NOTES

1. P. E. Meehl, *Clinical Versus Statistical Prediction* (Univ. of Minnesota Press, Minneapolis, MN, 1954).

2. L. R. Goldberg, *Psychol. Monogr.*, 79 (no. 9) (1965).

3. _____, *Am. Psychol.* 23, 483 (1968).

4. _____, *Psychol. Bull.* 73, 422 (1970).

5. R. M. Dawes and B. Corrigan, *ibid.* 81, 95 (1974).

6. D. A. Leli and S. B. Filskov, *J. Clin. Psychol.* 40, 1435 (1984).

7. H. J. Einhorn, *Organ. Behav. Human Perform.* 7, 86 (1972).

8. J. Sawyer, *Psychol. Bull.* 66, 178 (1966).

9. P. E. Meehl, *J. Personal. Assess.* 50, 370 (1986).

10. W. M. Grove, who is conducting the first formal meta-analysis of studies in the social sciences and medicine (and a few other areas) that compared clinical and actuarial judgement, has reported a preliminary analysis in simple "box score" terms (paper presented at the Annual Meeting of the Minnesota Psychological Association, Minneapolis, 8 May 1986). The clinical method showed an advantage in only 6 of 117 studies. These exceptions mainly involved the medical field. The clinical advantage was generally slight and the rarity of this outcome across so many comparisons raises the possibility that some or most of these exceptions were statistical artifacts.

11. D. J. Watley and F. L. Vance, U.S. Office of Education Cooperative Research Project No. 2022 (University of Minnesota, Minneapolis, MN 1974).

12. J. S. Carroll *et al.*, *Law Society* Rev. 17, 199 (1982).

13. M. P. Wittman, *Elgin Pap.* 4, 20 (1941).

14. S. Oskamp, *Psychol. Monogr.* 76 (no. 28) (1962).

15. C. C. Halbower, thesis, University of Minnesota, Minneapolis, MN (1955).

16. F. Barron, *J. Consult. Clin. Psychol.* 17, 233 (1953).

17. H. W. Dunham and B. M. Meitzer, *Am. J. Sociology* 52, 123 (1946).

18. P. D. Werner, T. L. Rose, J. A. Yesavage, *J. Consult. Clin. Psychol.* 51, 815 (1983).

19. R. M. Dawes, *Am. Psychol.* 26, 180 (1971).

20. D. Wedding, *Clin. Neuropsychol.* V, 49 (1983).

21. D. A. Leli and S. B. Filskov, *J. Clin Psychol.* 37, 623 (1981).

22. J. S. Wiggins, *Clin. Psychol. Rev.* 1, 3 (1981).

23. P. E. Meehl. *J. Counseling Psychol.* 6, 102 (1959).

24. _____, *Problems in Human Assessment*, D. N. Jackson and S. Messick, Eds. (McGraw-Hill, New York, 1976), pp. 594–599.

25. _____, *J. Counseling Psychol.* 4, 268 (1957).

26. W. B. Martin, P. C. Apostolakos, H. Roazen, *Am. J. Med. Sci.* 240, 571 (1960).

27. L. R. Goldberg, in preparation.

28. J. F. Fries et al., *Arthritis Rheum.* 29, 1 (1986).

29. D. Kahneman and A. Tversky, *Am. Psychol.* 39, 341 (1984); K. R. Hammond and D. A. Summers, *Psychol. Rev.* 72, 215 (1965).

30. L. J. Chapman and J. P. Chapman, *J. Abnorm. Psychol.* 72 193 (1967); *ibid.* 74, 271 (1969).

31. P. E. Meehl, *Psychodiagnosis:* Selected Papers (Univ. of Minnesota Press, Minneapolis, MN 1973).

32. H. J. Einhorn and R. M. Hogarth, *Psychol.* Rev. 85, 395 (1978).

33. B. Fischhoff, *J. Exper. Psychol. Human Percep. Perform.* 1, 288 (1975).

34. _____, *New Directions for Methodology of Social and Behavioral Science*, R. A. Schweder and D. W. Fiske, Eds. (Jossey-Bass, San Francisco, CA, 1980), pp. 79–93.

35. B. Fischhoff and R. Beyth-Marom, *Organ. Behav. Human Perform.* 13, 1 (1975).

36. H. R. Arkes *et al.*, *J. Appl. Psychol.* 66, 252 (1981).

37. O. Spreen, *J. Nerv. Ment. Dis.* 169, 791 (1981).

38. A. J. Capute, E. F. L. Neidermeyer, F. Richardson, *Pediatrics* 41, 1104 (1968).

39. A G. Greenwald, A. R. Pratkanis, M. R. Leippe, M. H. Baumgardner, *Psychol. Rev.* 93, 216 (1986).

40. A Tversky and D. Kahneman, *Cognit. Psychol.* 5, 207 (1973).

41. R. M. Dawes, *Clin. Psychol. Rev.* 6, 425 (1986).

42. B. Fischhoff, *in Judgment Under Uncertainty*, D. Kahneman, P. Slovic, A. Tversky, Eds. (Cambridge Univ. Press, New York, 1982), pp. 424–444.

43. D. Faust, K. Hart, T. J. Guilmette, *J. Consul. Clin. Psychol.* 56, 578 (1988).

44. D. Faust, *The Limits of scientific Reasoning* (Univ. of Minnesota Press, Minneapoli MN, 1984).

45. H. J. Einhorn and R. M. Hogarth, *Organ. Behav. Human Perform* 13 171

46. H. Wainer, *Psychol. Bull.* 8S, 267(1978).

47. S. S. Wilks, *Psychometrika* 8, 23 (1938).

48. T. J. Guilmette, D. Faust, K. Hart, H. R. Arkes, Arch. Clin. Neuropsychol. in press

49. Handbook of Licensing and Certification Requirements for Psychologists in North America (American Association of Sute Psychology Boards, Washington, DC, America 1987). Augus

50. R. M. Dawes, *Am. Psychol.* 34, 571 (1979).

51. We would like to thank S. Fienberg, B. Fischhoff, L. Furby, L. Goldberg W Grove, J. Kadane, and L. Yonce for their helpful comments and suggestions.

Emotion Regulation and Memory

The Cognitive Costs of Keeping One's Cool

JANE M. RICHARDS AND JAMES J. GROSS

An emerging literature has begun to document the affective consequences of emotion regulation. Little is known, however, about whether emotion regulation, also has cognitive consequences. A process model of emotion suggests that *expressive suppression* should reduce memory for emotional events but that *reappraisal* should not. Three studies tested this hypothesis. Study 1 experimentally manipulated expressive suppression during film viewing, showing that suppression led to poorer memory for the details of the film. Study 2 manipulated expressive suppression and reappraisal during slide viewing. Only suppression led to poorer slide memory. Study 3 examined individual differences in typical expressive suppression and reappraisal and found that suppression was associated with poorer self-reported and objective memory but that reappraisal was not. Together, these studies suggest that the cognitive costs of keeping one's cool may vary according to how this is done.

Western culture is decidedly ambivalent about emotions. On the one hand, emotions are seen as wanton marauders that supplant good judgment with primitive, immature, and destructive thoughts and impulses (Young, 1943). On the other hand, emotions are seen as indispensable guardians of our well-being that direct our responses to life's challenges (Leeper, 1948).

As is so often the case with intractable ambivalence, each side of the "emotions are harmful-emotions are helpful" divide captures part of the truth. Recognizing this fact, emotion researchers have begun to examine how individuals go about regulating their emotions and have begun to document what consequences such attempts at emotion regulation have (Gross, 1998b). There are countless ways of regulating emotions (Parrott, 1993), but one particularly common form of emotion regulation is down-regulating negative emotions. Examples include construing a critical remark as helpful rather than hurtful or simply maintaining the appearance of having taken no offense (DePaulo, Kashy, Kirkendol, Wyer, & Epstein, 1996; Gross & Richards, 2000).

Despite the fact that researchers, philosophers, and laypersons alike have had an age-old fascination with emotional control, empirical data regarding the consequences of emotion down-regulation are of relatively recent vintage (e.g., Eisenberg, Fabes, & Losoya, 1997; Gross, 1998a; Thayer, Newman, & McClain, 1994). Most of these data concern the affective consequences of emotion regulation. This is natural enough. Feeling bad and looking worse are no fun, and it stands to good reason that we would often want to soften these negative feelings and expressions. If one major aim of emotion regulation is to influence emotions, then the first order of business certainly should be to figure out whether emotion regulation actually alters the

Jane M. Richards and James Jay Gross, "Emotion Regulation and Memory: The Cognitive Costs of Keeping One's Cool," *Journal of Personality and Social Psychology*, vol. 79, no. 3, pp. 410-424. Copyright © 2000 by American Psychological Association. Reprinted with permission.

experiential, behavioral, and physiological components of the emotional response.

However, feeling good and looking better are not one's only priorities during emotionally trying times. People also wish to function at their best cognitively. This comes as no surprise when one considers that emotions frequently arise when important goals are at stake—and, thus, when peak cognitive performance is critical. In light of mounting evidence that emotional and cognitive processes are tightly interwoven in everyday life (Damasio, 1994) and that people often regulate their emotions to preserve cognitive functioning (Gross & Richards, 2000), we sought to extend the boundaries of emotion regulation research by asking two related questions. First, does emotion regulation lead people to remember events differently then they would have absent these processes, or are emotion regulatory processes so overlearned that they unfold with no cognitive cost? Second, if emotion regulation does have discernible cognitive consequences, are these consequences the same for all forms of emotion regulation, or do they vary according to how the emotion is regulated?

In the following sections, we first define what we mean by emotion regulation. We then consider whether emotion regulation might influence one's memory for the events that transpire while one is regulating emotion, and if so, whether there is reason to believe that different forms of emotion regulation should have different cognitive consequences.

EMOTION REGULATION

Emotion regulation refers to the evocation of thoughts or behaviors that influence which emotions people have, when people have them, and how people experience or express these emotions. Because emotions may be regulated in almost limitless ways, we have found it helpful to adopt a consensual model of emotion to provide an overarching framework for studying emotion regulation (Gross, 1998b, 1999). This model focuses on the processes by which emotion is generated and makes a distinction between two broad classes of emotion regulation. According to this model, emotion regulatory efforts may be directed at two different points in the emotion generative process. *Antecedent-focused emotion regulation* is evoked at the front-end, or very early on in the emotion-generative process,

whereas *response-focused emotion regulation* occurs at the back-end, or after emotion response tendencies have been triggered. Thus, response-focused regulation mops up one's emotions; antecedent-focused regulation keeps them from spilling in the first place.

In the context of a potentially stressful situation, antecedent-focused emotion regulation might take the form of construing a potentially emotional situation in a way that decreases its emotional relevance (e.g., Beck, 1991; Lazarus, 1991; Scherer, 1984), a process that has been called reappraisal (Gross, 1998a). For example, appraising an upcoming task as a challenge rather than a threat (e.g., Tomaka, Blascovich, Kibler, & Ernst, 1997), construing an upcoming medical procedure as beneficial rather than painful (e.g., Lazarus & Alfert, 1964), and believing gory photographs of dead people to be pulled from a fictitious movie rather than police files (Kramer, Buckhout, Fox, Widman, & Tusche, 1991) can drastically reduce subjective emotion experience and concomitant emotion-expressive behavior. In other words, because reappraisal is antecedent to a potentially upsetting event, if effective, it actually preempts full-blown emotional responses.

By contrast, response-focused emotion regulation occurs much later in the emotion generative process. In the case of this back-ended form of emotion regulation, individuals do not nip emotion in the bud by virtue of construing an event up front in less emotional terms. Rather, response-focused emotion regulation is evoked after an event already has been appraised in emotional terms and thus has triggered emotional response tendencies. Frequently, this kind of emotion regulation takes the form of inhibiting the urge to act on emotional impulses that continually press for expression, as when one bites his or her lip to keep from crying or maintains a poker face despite having been dealt a great hand of cards. This process, which we term expressive suppression, has affective consequences that differ from reappraisal.[1] Whereas reappraisal leads to global reductions in emotional responding, expressive suppression appears to selectively decrease emotion-expressive behavior (Gross, 1998a; Gross & Levenson, 1993).

EMOTION REGULATION AND MEMORY

What effects—if any—might emotion regulation have for cognitive processes? In the following section, we describe two quite different possibilities.

Emotion Regulation Is Effortless

One possibility is that emotion regulation allows one to look and feel better during emotional circumstances without any discernable cognitive costs. Emotion theorists have long emphasized that emotion regulation is widespread among adults in Western cultures, and some theorists have gone so far as to argue that it is rare to see adult emotion that is not regulated (Tomkins, 1962). Frontal brain structures that allow for emotion regulation are evident in infants as young as 9 months (Fox, 1994), and by age 6, children have developed a sophisticated arsenal of emotion regulatory strategies (e.g., Cummings, 1987; Harris, 1989; Saarni, 1984). By adulthood, managing how one looks and feels would seem a natural candidate for the growing list of automatic responses one draws upon in everyday life (Bargh, 1997; Greenwald & Banaji, 1995) and would seem so overlearned that it would have no impact on cognitive activities such as attending to information for later recall.

Emotion Regulation Is Effortful

A quite different possibility is suggested by Baumeister and colleagues' ego-depletion model (Baumeister, Bratslavsky, Muraven, & Tice, 1998; Muraven, Tice, & Baumeister, 1998), which holds that any sort of self-regulation depletes mental resources. Linking this model to emotion regulation in particular, Muraven, Tice, and Baumeister (1998) conducted an emotional-film-viewing study in which an experimenter told some participants to "try to deny any emotions you may feel.... When I look over the videotape of your facial expressions, I don't want to be able to tell which videotape you are watching" (M. Muraven, personal communication, September 16, 1997). Results revealed that regulation participants (relative to no-regulation controls) persevered for a shorter period of time on a subsequent hand grip task. In a similar study testing the effects of this emotion-regulation manipulation on a subsequent anagram task, regulation participants were found to solve fewer problems than no-regulation participants (Baumeister et al., 1998).

Although these studies do not show that emotion regulation impairs performance on tasks coincident with emotion regulatory efforts, attentional models of self-regulation suggest that this should be the case (e.g., Carver & Scheier, 1981). Such models portray attention as a finite resource. Efforts to maintain or change behaviors evoke a negative feedback loop whereby an existing condition of a system is compared with some salient standard. If a discrepancy between the two is detected, an operating process is evoked to lessen this discrepancy and achieve the desired state or behavior (Macrae, Bodenhausen, & Milne, 1998). These self-monitoring processes serve important self-regulatory functions. However, they may do so at a cost. Strategically evaluating and modifying one's thoughts, feelings, or behaviors may have the effect of decreasing attentional resources available for other tasks (Ellis & Ashbrook, 1989). Much of the support for the idea that emotion regulation consumes cognitive resources derives from studies in which emotion regulation is the dependent variable (DePaulo, Blank, Swaim, & Hairfield, 1992; Wegner, 1994; Wegner, Erber, & Zanakos, 1993). For example, Wegner et al. (1993) found that mood regulation success was reduced by cognitive load. This research suggests that emotion regulation consumes cognitive resources, but it does not show that it does so at the expense of other concurrent tasks. Indeed, we are aware of only one report that has tested whether emotion regulation influences memory. This research, which examined women only, found that expressive suppression reduced memory for orally presented information accompanying emotion-eliciting slides (Richards & Gross, 1999).

Integration

Although the automaticity, ego-depletion, and attentional views differ in a number of ways, each offers a blanket prediction that lumps together different forms of emotion regulation. On the automaticity view, emotion regulation is overlearned and is thus cognitively inexpensive. On the ego-depletion and attentional views, emotion regulation is consumptive of finite self-regulatory energy or attentional resources. However, is it really reasonable to assume that all forms of emotion regulation are going to be either cognitively inexpensive or cognitively costly?

To address this question, we drew upon the consensual model of emotion discussed earlier, which makes a distinction between antecedent-focused emotion regulation and response-focused emotion regulation (Gross, 1998b, 1999). This distinction between emotion regulatory efforts that occur before (e.g., reappraisal) and those that occur after (e.g., expressive suppression) an event unfolds suggests that these forms of emotion regulation might have different cognitive costs due to differing self-regulatory demands. Emotion regulation that requires continual self-monitoring and ongoing self-corrective action during an emotional event, such as expressive suppression, should require a continual outlay of cognitive resources and thus should decrease the fidelity of memory. By contrast, emotion regulation that is evoked early on in the emotion generative process, such as reappraisal, should not require continual self-regulatory effort during an emotional event. Entering into a situation after having construed it in less emotional terms should preempt a full-blown emotional response and thus obviate the need for continual self-regulatory effort, leaving memory for the details of the events that transpire intact.

THE PRESENT RESEARCH

Typically, people form memories by simply experiencing events as they unfold around them and not by actively memorizing or rehearsing their details. For this reason, we tested our prediction that expressive suppression should lead to poorer memory for details of emotional events, whereas reappraisal should not, by conducting three studies in which incidental memory was assessed. In the first study, we experimentally manipulated expressive suppression in a controlled laboratory setting to test whether this specific form of emotion regulation had any discernible effects on memory for visual and auditory material presented during the suppression period. Once we were convinced that expressive suppression impaired memory, we conducted a second study in which we manipulated both expressive suppression and reappraisal and administered two different types of memory tests to explore the roles of self-focus and self-monitoring in producing any memory decrements. Finally, in a third study, we tested whether naturally occurring individual differences in suppression and reappraisal were associated with memory in everyday life.

STUDY 1: DOES EXPRESSIVE SUPPRESSION IMPAIR MEMORY?

Three criteria must be met to test whether expressive suppression impairs memory: (a) Emotion must be elicited in a controlled situation, (b) participants' expressive behavior must be manipulated, and (c) convergent memory measures must be obtained. To meet these criteria, we used a short film clip known to elicit negative emotion. This permitted us to control the information presented during the emotion induction period. We manipulated emotion-expressive behavior by randomly assigning participants to one of two instructional conditions (Gross & Levenson, 1993, 1997). Half of the participants were given instructions to inhibit emotion-expressive behavior during the film clip (expressive suppression condition). The rest of the participants received no regulation instructions (watch condition). To assess the effects of suppression on memory, we used a verbal cued-recognition test for auditory and visual details contained within the film clip. We chose this type of test over a nonverbal recognition test involving photo spreads—a favorite of traditional emotion and memory research (e.g., Christianson & Loftus, 1987; Christianson, Loftus, Hoffman, & Loftus, 1991)—because we questioned whether a nonverbal test would be sensitive to memory differences resulting from decreases in depth of processing and verbal encoding (Craik & Lockhart, 1972) that should derive from the self-monitoring processes associated with expressive suppression.

Method

Participants

Fifty-three participants (45% men, 55% women) who had not seen our stimulus film before participated to fulfill a course requirement or to receive monetary compensation. On average, participants were 19.8 years old ($SD = 1.7$ years). The ethnic composition of this sample was 4% African American, 26% Asian American, 62% Caucasian, and 8% Hispanic.

Procedure

Participants were run in mixed-gender group sessions by a female experimenter (mean number of participants per group = 4.7; range = 1 to 8). After signing a consent form, participants completed a baseline self-report measure of emotion experience so that we could assess whether our subsequent emotion induction increased negative emotion levels above preinduction levels. Then, participants were told that they would view a brief film clip (described below). Immediately before viewing this clip, the entire group of participants was randomly assigned to one of two experimental conditions. Participants in the watch condition ($N = 28$) were told the following: "I will show you the film clip in just a moment. Please watch and listen to it carefully." Participants in the expressive suppression condition ($N = 25$) were told the following:

> I will show you the film clip in just a moment. Please watch and listen to it carefully. In addition, it is extremely important for the sake of this study that if you have any feelings as you watch the film clip, please try your best not to let those feelings show. In other words, as you watch the film clip, please try to behave in such a way that a person watching you would not know you are feeling anything at all. So, watch the film clip carefully, but please try to behave so that someone watching you would not know you are feeling anything at all.

Because we were interested in incidental memory, no mention was made of any forthcoming memory tests. After viewing the film clip, participants answered questions about their emotion experience and expression during the film clip. Participants then worked on a distractor task (verbal and math problems) for 10 min before taking a paper-and-pencil cued-recognition test of visual and auditory details contained in the film clip. Participants were allowed to take this test at their own pace; those who finished early filled out additional questionnaires until the last participant had finished. (These data were not analyzed.) Finally, participants were debriefed and thanked for their participation.

Film Stimulus

To elicit negative emotion, we showed a 140-s film clip in which a husband confesses to his wife that he has had an extramarital affair and that the other woman is pregnant as a result. Clearly heartbroken, the wife becomes agitated and upset. A shouting match and physical scuffle ensue. The couple's fight is witnessed by their young child, who begins to sob. Pretesting revealed that this clip reliably induces a negative affective state in both men and women, characterized by sadness, anxiety, and anger.

Measures

Emotion experience and expression. Participants used a 7-point Likert scale (0 = not at all; 6 = a great deal) to rate the extent to which they experienced negative emotion at two time points. Participants made their first (i.e., baseline) rating after signing the consent form; they made their second rating after viewing the film. The expressive suppression instructions used here have been shown to reduce emotion-expressive behavior in several studies that unobtrusively videotaped and coded participants' behaviors (e.g., Gross, 1998a; Gross & Levenson 1993, 1997). Logistics of the group viewing sessions did not allow us to obtain the close-up video recordings of each participant that would be necessary for behavioral coding. However, because it was important to confirm that participants in this experiment understood the suppression instructions, we had participants use a 7-point Likert scale (0 = *not at all*; 6 = *a great deal*) to rate the extent to which they showed negative emotion-expressive behavior during the film clip.

Memory. After viewing the film clip, participants answered 24 five-alternative, forced-choice memory questions that covered the entire duration of the film clip. Twelve of these items tapped into visual detail information (e.g., objects in the room, attire worn by the characters); the remaining items tapped into auditory detail information (e.g., what the characters said). Although we did not expect modality differences, we included equal numbers of visual and auditory items so that this possibility could be explored with separate objective memory scores. We also computed memory confidence scores for visual and auditory information by having participants rate how confident they felt about each of their 24 answers (0 = not at all confident; 5 = very confident) on the objective memory test.

Results

We present our analyses in two steps. First, we examine the affective consequences of expressive suppression. On the basis of our prior research in this area (Gross, 1998a; Gross & Levenson 1993, 1997), we expected that compared with watch participants, suppression participants would evidence decreased emotion-expressive behavior but comparable negative-emotion experience. Next, we examine the cognitive consequences of expressive suppression. As described above, we hypothesized that expressive suppression should impair memory for information concerning the film.[2]

Affective Consequences of Expressive Suppression

Emotion experience. We computed a repeated measures analysis of variance (ANOVA) on the negative-emotion-experience reports obtained before and after the film clip, with time as a within-participants factor and instructional condition (watch, expressive suppression) as a between-participants factor. The main effect for time indicated that negative-emotion experience reported for the film period ($M = 3.9$, $SD = 1.3$) increased significantly from prefilm levels, $M = 1.3$, $SD = 1.3$, $F(1, 50) = 123.00$, $p < .001$. This main effect for time showed that the film succeeded in eliciting negative-emotion experience. As expected, neither the main effect for instructional condition, $F(1, 50) = 0.18$, *ns*, nor the interaction term, $F(1, 50) = 0.19$, *ns*, attained significance, indicating that suppression did not influence negative-emotion experience.

Emotion expression. We computed a one-way ANOVA on participants' reports of their own negative-emotion-expressive behavior, with instructional condition (watch, expressive suppression) treated as a between-participants factor. As expected, expressive suppression participants ($M = 1.0$, $SD = 1.0$) reported less negative-emotion-expressive behavior during the film period than did watch participants, $M = 1.9$, $SD = 1.5$, $F(1, 51) = 7.28$, $p = .009$.

Cognitive Consequences of Expressive Suppression

Objective memory scores. We computed an ANOVA on participants' memory scores (i.e., proportion correct), treating information type (visual, auditory) as a within-participants factor and instructional condition (watch, expressive suppression)

as a between-participants factor.[3] As predicted, results revealed a main effect for instructional condition, $F(1,51) = 8.98$, $p = ,004$. There also was an information type effect, $F(1,51) = 7.31$, $p = .009$, but the Instructional Condition $\times$ Information Type interaction did not attain significance, $F(1, 51) = 1.00$, *ns*. Suppression participants remembered the emotion-eliciting film less well than watch participants, regardless of information type (visual, auditory). Additionally, regardless of instructional condition, participants recalled auditory information better than visual information.

Memory confidence ratings. We conducted a similarly structured ANOVA on auditory and visual memory confidence ratings. Results paralleled the pattern of relations found for objective memory scores. Suppression participants reported less confidence in their memory than watch participants, $F(1, 51) = 14.58$, $p < .001$, and regardless of instructional condition, participants reported less confidence in their memory for visual information than in their memory for auditory information, $F(1, 51) = 9.62$, $p = ,003$. Once again, the Instructional Condition x Information Type interaction did not attain significance, $F(1, 51) = 0.02$, *ns*.

Summary and Limitations

Compared with participants who simply watched a negative-emotion-eliciting film, those randomly assigned to hide their feelings during the film showed poorer memory for its auditory and visual details. This study extends the memory effects of suppression reported previously (Richards & Gross, 1999) from women to a mixed-gender sample, from emotional slides to a dynamic film-viewing context, from a solitary to a social experimental setting, and from memory for words to memory for visual and auditory (i.e., conversational) details. Moreover, this study shows that the memory deficit associated with suppression was pronounced enough to be evident to suppression participants themselves, who reported less confidence in their memory than participants who simply watched the film.

These findings are encouraging, but several limitations of Study 1 should be noted. First, this study did not manipulate reappraisal. We are, therefore, unable to draw any support for our specificity prediction that suppression should impair memory but that reappraisal should not. Second, Study 1 made use of group-viewing sessions. We have no reason to believe that the group format influenced our findings, but because we did not systematically vary group size, we cannot directly test any impact of viewing format. Third, measures of emotion experience and expressive behavior were single-item self-report measures. A more robust approach would be to use multiple measures of emotion experience and to directly record participants' ongoing expressive behavior for the purposes of objective behavioral coding. Fourth, Study 1 elicited emotion at one intensity level, which precluded an assessment of the boundary conditions of the cognitive consequences of expressive suppression. Fifth, Study 1 did not address the question of how expressive suppression led to poorer memory. One possibility is that suppression leads to active avoidance of emotion-eliciting events, which could be tested by measuring whether suppression participants, relative to no-suppression participants, are more likely to look away from ongoing emotional stimuli. Another possibility stems from self-regulation theory (Carver & Scheier, 1981; Duval & Wicklund, 1972), which suggests that suppression should not lead to complete disengagement from ongoing events but rather evokes subvocal self-monitoring processes or heightened self-focus. Could one or more of these processes be linked to the effects of suppression on memory?

To address these issues, we conducted a second experiment. In this study, we (a) explicitly manipulated expressive suppression and reappraisal, (b) used single-subject sessions, (c) obtained multiple measures of emotion experience and videotaped expressive behavior, (d) used slides to elicit high and low levels of emotion, and (e) used memory measures expected to be differentially sensitive to the operation of self-monitoring and self-focus processes.

STUDY 2: COGNITIVE COSTS FOR EXPRESSIVE SUPPRESSION BUT NOT REAPPRAISAL?

We had three primary goals in Study 2. Our first goal was to show that experimentally manipulating reappraisal and expressive suppression in a controlled laboratory setting would differentially influence memory for information presented during the induction period. To this end, participants watched emotion-eliciting slides under one of three instructional conditions: watch, suppress, or reappraise. In

this study, we refined the Study 1 expressive suppression instructions by more explicitly directing participants to engage in ongoing, response-focused emotion regulation. Our reappraisal instructions, by contrast, explicitly directed participants to engage in antecedent-focused—or front-ended—reconstrual of the upcoming event.

Our second goal was to determine whether suppression would lead to poorer memory even when low levels of emotion were elicited. To this end, participants viewed slides that elicited either high or low levels of emotion. If the cognitive consequences of expressive suppression are proportional to the magnitude of to-be-suppressed emotional impulses, we might expect suppression to affect memory only for the high-emotion slide set. However, if—as we expected—expressive suppression takes its cognitive toll through continual monitoring of ongoing expressive behavior, cognitive impairments should be evident whenever participants try to suppress emotion-expressive behavior, whether under conditions of high or low emotion.

Our third goal was to examine mechanisms by which expressive suppression might affect memory. One mechanism was active avoidance, or looking away from the emotion-eliciting stimuli. A second mechanism was self-focus, which might decrease attention to external events while increasing attention to internally generated stimuli, such as sensations (e.g., emotional experience, physiological changes). To the extent that increased self-focus diverted attentional resources away from the environment (Ellis & Ash-brook, 1989), it should impair memory. A third mechanism was subvocalization, engendered by an internal self-regulatory dialogue. (e.g., "Am I showing emotion? I don't want to show emotion. Uh oh, I might be showing emotion. There, I just held back an impulse.") To the extent that subvocal self-monitoring decreased verbal elaboration of incoming information (Craik & Lockhart, 1972), it should hamper the refreshing of decaying representations of auditory information in the phonological store, limit the conversion of visual information into phonological representations (Gathercole & Baddeley, 1993), and thereby weaken memory.

Because participants were asked to attend to the stimuli, we did not expect active avoidance to be responsible for the memory effects. We tested this hypothesis by examining whether suppression participants were more likely to look away from the emotional stimuli than other participants. We thought it possible that self-focus might play a role, but because we had not seen any heightening of emotional response in suppression (which might be expected if self-focus led to increased awareness of sensations), we did not think that self-focus would play a decisive role. We did think it likely, however, that subvocal self-monitoring processes might be involved. To test the role of self-focus and subvocalization, we administered memory measures that would be differentially sensitive to these processes. We reasoned that if increased subvocal self-monitoring was responsible for the memory effects of suppression, much like articulatory suppression (e.g., Brandimonte et al., 1992; Macken & Jones, 1995), expressive suppression should lead to poorer performance on memory tests for information encoded verbally (Bartlett, Till, & Levy, 1980; Daniel & Ellis, 1972) but should not influence performance on memory tests for which verbal encoding is irrelevant or harmful (e.g., photo spread visual recognition; Schooler & Engstler-Schooler, 1990). On the other hand, if heightened levels of self-focus were responsible for the effects of expressive suppression on memory, we should see poorer performance not only on verbally based tests but even on tests for which verbal encoding is irrelevant. This is because self-focus should not selectively decrease verbal encoding but rather should impair all encoding, reducing performance on any kind of memory test. Our expectation was that suppression should impair verbal memory but should have little effect on nonverbal memory.

Method

Participants

Eighty-three female participants enrolled in this study to fulfill a course requirement or to receive monetary compensation.[4] On average, participants were 19.7 years old ($SD = 1.3$ years). The ethnic composition of this sample was 16% African American, 24% Asian American, 48% Caucasian, 7% Hispanic, 3% Native American, and 2% other.

Procedure

Participants were run in individual sessions by a female experimenter. After signing a consent form, participants were informed that the study was designed to understand how people use visual and biographical information when "forming impressions of people who have been injured." Specifically, participants were told that they would see several slides of people who had all been severely injured at one time or another and that they would hear each person's name, occupation, and type of accident. Some of the slides would show people who appeared healthy because their injuries had happened a long time ago (low-emotion slide set), but other slides would show people who appeared gravely injured because they had been photographed shortly after sustaining their injuries (high-emotion slide set). This cover story was used to allay any suspicions participants might have had regarding the real purpose of the study and to thereby decrease the likelihood that participants would attempt to strategically memorize information presented with each slide.

Just before viewing a set of nine individually presented slides, each of which was accompanied by orally presented biographical information, participants randomly assigned to the watch condition were instructed as follows ($N = 41$): "We will show you the slides in just a moment. Please view them carefully and listen to the accompanying background information."[5]

Participants randomly assigned to the expressive suppression condition ($N-20$) were instructed as follows:

> We will show you the slides in just a moment. Please view them carefully and listen to the accompanying background information. In addition, we would like to see how well you can control your facial expressions. Therefore, it is very important to us that you try your best to adopt a neutral facial expression as you watch the slides. To do this, we would like for you to keep your facial muscles from moving. In other words, as you watch the slides, try to keep a straight face by keeping the muscles around your neck, your chin, your lips, your cheeks, your eyes, and your forehead very still. So, watch the slides carefully, but please try to keep your

facial muscles still so that you don't make any expressions at all.

Participants randomly assigned to the reappraisal condition ($N = 22$) were instructed as follows:

> We will show you the slides in just a moment. Please view them carefully and listen to the accompanying background information. In addition, we would like to see how well you can control the way you view things. Therefore, it is very important to us that you try your best to adopt a neutral attitude as you watch the slides. To do this, we would like for you to view these slides with the detached interest of a medical professional. In other words, as you watch the slides, try to think about them objectively and analytically rather than as personally, or in any way, emotionally relevant to you. So, watch the slides carefully, but please try to think about what you are seeing in such a way that you don't feel anything at all.

After viewing the first set of slides, participants completed a self-report emotion experience measure. Participants were then reminded of their instructions and shown the second set of slides. Participants who viewed the low-emotion slides first viewed the high-emotion slides second, whereas participants who viewed the high-emotion slides first viewed the low-emotion slides second.[6] After the second slide set, all participants completed another emotion experience measure. A distractor task (solving anagrams) was then administered for 10 min, followed by a cued-recognition test of the slides and a cued-recall test of the orally presented biographical information (described below). Finally, participants were debriefed and thanked for their participation.

Slide Stimuli

Eighteen slides were presented in two sets of nine slides each on a 20-in. (50.8-cm) television monitor placed at a distance of 1.75 m from each participant (Richards & Gross, 1999).[7] One set of slides was composed of color photographic images of average-looking men who supposedly had been injured at an earlier point in time. These slides

were intended to call forth low levels of negative emotion. Another set of slides was composed of color images of badly wounded men who supposedly had been injured shortly before they were photographed. These slides were intended to call forth high levels of negative emotion. As slides were presented, three bits of information—a name, an occupation, and a cause of injury—were presented using an audio recording. Injury information was presented to help focus participants' attention on the terrible things said to have happened to the people shown in the slides. Name and occupation were presented to heighten the emotionality of the slides by personalizing them. Slides were presented individually for 10 s; slides within each set were separated by 4 s.

Measures

Emotion experience. Participants used a 7-point Likert scale ($0 = not\ at\ all$; $6 = extremely$) to rate the extent to which they felt each of four negative emotions (i.e., sadness, anger, revulsion, distress) during the low-and high-emotion slide sets. These ratings were used to create a four-item negative-emotion composite for each slide set. The alpha was 80 for the low-emotion slide set and .81 for the high-emotion slide set.

Emotion expression. Participants' behavioral responses to the slides were recorded unobtrusively by a remotely controlled, high-resolution video camera placed behind darkened glass on a bookshelf. After the experimental session, participants' behaviors were coded from videotape by two female coders who were blind to the slides participants were watching and to their experimental conditions. To assess negative-emotionexpressive behavior, coders used a 5-point (0–4) global coding system derived from (a) Ekman and Friesen's (1975) description of specific behavioral expressions of discrete negative emotions and (b) a specific coding strategy that takes into account expressive duration and intensity (Gross & Levenson, 1993). To assess participants' active efforts to withdraw their attention from the stimuli, coders counted the number of times each participant broke her line of vision from the television monitor during the slide-viewing period (e.g., shielding face with hands, looking away from the television, closing eyes for more than 1 s). Coding reliabilities were good (mean interrater reliability = .80). Final values for each of the codes were determined by averaging each of the coder's ratings for a given participant's expressive behavior. Composites were created to represent overall negative-emotion-expressive behavior and obscuring vision during the low-emotion slide set and the high-emotion slide set.

Nonverbal memory. Participants were shown 18 photo spreads, one corresponding to each of the 18 slides they saw in the first phase of the experiment. For each photo spread, participants were asked to identify which of four alternatives moat closely resembled the slide they had seen earlier. The correct alternative was the same image participants had seen earlier, with the only difference being that it was reduced in size. Incorrect alternatives were generated by (a) horizontally rotating the original image so that elements on the left-hand side of the slide would appear on the right-hand side, (b) slightly modifying the original image in Adobe Photoshop (1996; e.g., removing a pair of glasses, moving the location of a scar, changing the shape of a nose), and (c) horizontally rotating the slightly modified image. The presentation order of the photo spreads matched that of the original slides. Participants had 8 s to view each photo spread and to give their answer. All answers were then transcribed from videotape. Two nonverbal memory scores were derived: mean proportion of correctly chosen alternatives for the low-and high-emotion slide sets.

Verbal memory: After viewing the photo spreads, participants viewed the original slides one more time. This time, they were asked to write down the information that had been paired with each slide during the initial slide-viewing phase (i.e., name, occupation, injury). Two verbal memory scores were derived: mean proportion correct for information presented with the low-and high-emotion slides. Participants were allowed to take this cued-recall memory test at their own pace.

Results

Our analyses were designed to address six questions. First, did our low-and high-emotion slide sets successfully elicit two levels of negative-emotion experience? Second, did expressive suppression produce selective decreases in behavior, and did reappraisal produce decreases in behavior and emotion experience? Third, did expressive suppression lead to active efforts to withdraw attention from the emotion-eliciting stimuli? Fourth, did expressive suppression

(but not reappraisal) impair memory? Fifth, were the effects of expressive suppression specific to verbal memory? Sixth, were the effects of expressive suppression evident in both low-and high-emotion contexts?

Manipulation Check

We computed a repeated measures ANOVA on the negative-emotion-experience composite scores for the low-and high-emotion slide sets, treating instructional condition (watch, expressive suppression, reappraisal) as a between-participants factor. As expected, a main effect of slide set was revealed, $F(1, 80) = 134.88$, $p < .001$, indicating that across all three instructional conditions, negative-emotion experience was greater for the high-emotion slide set ($M = 2.4$, $SD = 1.4$) than for the low-emotion slide set ($M = 0.9$, $SD = 1.1$). The negative-emotion experience for the low-emotion slide set, averaged over watch ($M = 0.9$, $SD = 1.2$), expressive suppression ($M = 0.9$, $SD = 0.9$), and reappraisal ($M = 1.0$, $SD = 1.1$) instructional conditions, was significantly greater than zero, $t(82) = 7.85$, $p < .001$, indicating that the low-emotion slide set reliably elicited low levels of negative emotion.

Affective Consequences of Emotion Regulation

Consistent with prior research (Gross, 1998a) and the process conception of emotion described in the introduction to this article, we expected that reappraisal (i.e., construing a potentially upsetting event in less emotional terms) would decrease both emotion experience and behavior, whereas expressive suppression would decrease behavior only. In view of the low means and variability in negative emotion during the low-emotion slides, we expected that the affective consequences would be evident during the high-emotion slides only.

To examine the effects of emotion regulation on emotion experience for the high-emotion slides, we referred to the ANOVA described in the manipulation check section above. As predicted, we found a significant interaction of Instructional Condition × Slide Set, $F(2, 80) = 7.01$, $p = .002$. To trace the source or sources of this interaction, we conducted follow-up t tests. As expected, compared with watch participants ($M = 2.8$, $SD = 1.4$), reappraisal participants ($M = 1.9$, $SD = 1.5$) reported less negative-emotion experience in response to the high-emotion slides, $t(61) = 2.48$, $p < .05$. Importantly, this was not the case for expressive suppression participants, whose negative-emotion experience in response to the high-emotion slides ($M = 2.3$, $SD = 1.2$) did not differ from that of watch participants, $M = 2.8$, $SD = 1.4$, $t(59) = 1.56$, ns. Our finding that expressive suppression neither increased nor decreased negative-emotion experience is consistent with prior research (Gross & Levenson, 1993, 1997).

To confirm that the expressive suppression instructions diminished emotion expressive-behavior, we computed a similarly structured repeated measures ANOVA on our negative-emotion-expression measure with slide set (low emotion, high emotion) treated as a within-participants factor and instructional condition (watch, expressive suppression, reappraisal) treated as a between-participants factor. Consistent with the emotion experience findings, a significant interaction emerged, $F(2, 75) = 6.1$, $p = .004$.[8] To trace the source or sources of this effect, we computed follow-up t tests. As expected, expressive suppression participants, $M = 0.2$, $SD = 0.6$, $t(55) = 2.86$, $p = .006$, and reappraisal participants, $M = 0.4$, $SD = 0.7$, $t(58) = 2.49$, $p = .02$, showed reliably less negative-emotion-expressive behavior than watch participants ($M = 0.9$, $SD = 1.0$) during the high-emotion slides, and negative-emotion-expressive behavior did not differ significantly between reappraisal participants and suppression participants, $t(37) = 0.93$, ns. For the low-emotion slides, expressive suppression participants ($M = 0.01$, $SD = 0.03$) showed reliably less negative-emotion-expressive behavior than watch participants, $M = 0.14$, $SD = 0.38$, $t(55) = 2.06$, $p = .05$, and reappraisal participants, $M = 0.18$, $SD = 0.35$, $t(37) = 2.19$, $p = .04$; watch and reappraisal participants' mean levels did not differ significantly for the low-emotion slides.

To examine whether expressive suppression led to active avoidance behaviors, we computed a similarly structured repeated measures ANOVA on our behavioral avoidance measure with slide set (low emotion, high emotion) treated as a within-participants factor and instructional condition (watch, expressive suppression, reappraisal) treated as a between-participants factor. Results revealed a significant main effect for slide set, $F(1, 75) = 5.59$, $p = .02$. Not surprisingly, participants were more likely to look away from the high-emotion slide set, which was significantly more upsetting and graphic. However, the Instructional Condition × Slide Set interaction term did not attain significance, $F(2, 75) = 2.82$, ns, indicating that this effect did not vary as a function of instructional condition. Thus, suppression participants were no more likely to look away from the slides than watch participants. In fact, if anything, watch participants ($M = 0.32$, $SD = 0.49$) looked away from the high-emotion slides more frequently than did suppression participants ($M = 0.11$, $SD = 0.25$) or reappraisal participants ($M = 0.09$, $SD = 0.25$).

Cognitive Consequences of Emotion Regulation

We predicted that expressive suppression should be associated with ongoing, language-based self-monitoring whereas reappraisal should not and that this monitoring should lead to poorer memory during expressive suppression but not during reappraisal. We expected to find these cognitive costs of suppression under conditions of high and low emotion but only for verbal memory tests.

Verbal memory. To test whether reappraisal and expressive suppression influenced verbal memory, we conducted a repeated measures ANOVA on cued-recall test scores, with slide set (low emotion, high emotion) treated as a within-participants factor and instructional condition (watch, expressive suppression, reappraisal) as a between-participants factor. Results revealed significant main effects of slide set, $F(1, 80) = 14.46$, $p < .001$, and instructional condition, $F(2, 80) = 3.26$, $p = .04$, but no Instructional Condition × Slide Set interaction, $F(2, 80) = 0.20$, ns. The main effect for slide set indicates that, overall, verbal information was remembered less well if it accompanied high-emotion slides. To decompose the main effect of instructional condition, we conducted a one-way ANOVA, collapsing over slide set, and used follow-up t tests to test pairwise differences between means. As predicted, only suppression participants showed a reliable decrease in memory. Specifically, suppression participants performed less well on the memory test than watch participants, $t(59) = 2.47$, $p < .05$. No other significant pairwise differences emerged.

Nonverbal memory. To test whether reappraisal and expressive suppression influenced nonverbal memory, we conducted a similarly structured ANOVA with nonverbal memory scores. Results revealed a near significant Instructional Condition × Slide Set interaction, $F(2, 75)$

= 2.93, p = .056. To trace the source or sources of this interaction, we conducted follow-up t tests. Unexpectedly, reappraisal participants were more likely to correctly identify high-emotion slides they had seen earlier than watch participants, $t(59)$ = 2.11, p < .05. As expected, expressive suppression participants' nonverbal memory was not reliably different from watch participants for either high-emotion, $t(54)$ = 0.49, ns, or low-emotion, $t(54)$ = 1.38, ns, slide sets. No other significant differences emerged.

Summary

These findings permit three major conclusions. First, different forms of emotion down-regulation have different cognitive consequences. Compared with controls, participants who suppressed ongoing emotion-expressive behavior showed poorer memory for verbally encoded information presented during emotion-eliciting slides. By contrast, we found no evidence that reappraisal diminished memory. In fact, reappraisal actually enhanced nonverbal memory. One explanation for this unpredicted effect, albeit speculative, is that assuming the perspective of a medical professional activates a "doctor script" that directs attention to medically relevant (i.e., visual) aspects of the slides showing injuries. It is unclear, however, whether this reappraisal-induced memory enhancement will generalize to other contexts in which one's reconstrual of an event does not lead so naturally to preferential processing of a specific type of information. Second, changes in emotion experience and behavior do not seem to mediate the effects of expressive suppression. Suppression impaired verbally encoded memory without affecting emotion experience (Studies 1 and 2) or active attentional withdrawal (Study 2). Moreover, memory impairment was evident for both the low-emotion and high-emotion conditions, even though expressive suppression participants differed in their expressive behavior from the watch participants during only the high-emotion slide sets. Third, the cognitive consequences of expressive suppression appear to be specific to memory that is verbally encoded. Whereas we found that expressive suppression led to poorer verbal memory performance, it had no impact on nonverbal memory performance. This pattern of findings suggests that subvocal self-monitoring may play an important role in accounting for the effects of suppression on memory.

STUDY 3: EXPRESSIVE SUPPRESSION AND REAPPRAISAL IN EVERYDAY LIFE

Studies 1 and 2 tested predictions about the cognitive consequences of emotion regulation under controlled laboratory conditions. For the cognitive consequences of emotion regulation to matter, however, they must be evident in everyday life. To examine the impact of emotion regulation on cognitive functioning in everyday life, we conducted a third study in which we used questionnaire and daily diary methodology to assess individual variation in the tendency to engage in expressive suppression or reappraisal and in the memory for contexts in which these forms of emotion regulation should manifest themselves.

We assessed the degree to which people engage in expressive suppression and reappraisal by administering self-report measures of emotion regulation. We assessed memory using two measures designed to tap contexts in which individual differences in emotion regulation tendencies might be evident. The first is a self-report measure that assesses how well one remembers conversations, a social context in which emotion regulation is common (Gross & Richards, 2000). The second is an objectively scored free-recall test for spontaneous emotion regulation episodes that occurred over a 2-week period (and that were recorded daily). We reasoned that participants would report episodes in which they engaged in their preferred form of emotion regulation. By asking them to later recall these episodes, we could derive an objective measure of memory for these episodes and thus assess the memory consequences of spontaneous emotion regulation. On the basis of Studies 1 and 2, we predicted that compared with individuals who typically express their emotions, those who suppress their emotion-expressive behavior would report poorer memory for conversations and be less likely to remember their own emotion-regulation episodes. By contrast, we expected that tendencies to engage in reappraisal would be uncorrelated with self-reported or objective memory.

Method

Participants

Eighty-six participants (31% men, 69% women) took part in this study to receive course credit. On average, participants were 19.8 years old (*SD* = 1.1 years). The ethnic composition of this sample was 6% African American, 32% Asian American, 45% Caucasian, 14% Hispanic, and 3% other.

Procedure

Participants completed a packet that included two measures of expressive suppression, one measure of reappraisal, and one measure of memory for conversations. One month later, participants kept a 2-week diary in which they described one situation per day during which they attempted to regulate their emotions. Finally, a week after the last diary entry, participants took a free-recall test of their memory for the emotion regulatory experiences they reported in their diaries.

Measures

Expressive suppression. Two measures were administered to assess expressive suppression. The four-item expressive suppression scale of the Emotion Regulation Questionnaire (ERQ-S; Gross & John, 2000) asks participants to rate the extent to which they typically try to inhibit their emotion-expressive behavior (1 = *strongly disagree*; 7 = *strongly agree*). The ERQ-S includes items such as "I keep my emotions to myself" and "I control my emotions by not expressing them." The four ERQ-S items (α = .77) were averaged to form a composite score. The short form of the Ambivalence Over Emotional Expression Questionnaire (AEQ; King & Emmons, 1990) consists of the 12 highest loading items on the full AEQ. This scale asks participants to rate how conflicted they feel about showing their emotions (1 = *I have never felt like this*; 5 = *I frequently feel like this*). The AEQ includes items such as "I try to suppress my negative feelings around others, even though I am not being fair to those close to me" and "I would like to be more spontaneous in my emotional reactions but I just can't seem to do

it." The 12 AEQ items (α = .88) were averaged to form a composite score.

Reappraisal. One measure was administered to assess reappraisal. The six-item reappraisal scale of the Emotion Regulation Questionnaire (ERQ-R; Gross & John, 2000) asks participants to rate the extent to which they typically try to think about situations differently in order to change how they feel (1 = *strongly disagree*; 7 = *strongly agree*). The ERQ-R includes items such as "When I'm faced with a stressful situation, I make myself *think about it* in a way that helps me stay calm" and "I control my emotions by *changing the way I think.*" The six ERQ-R items (α = .75) were averaged to form a composite score.

Self-reported memory. One measure was administered to assess conversational memory. Participants completed the 11-item conversation scale of the Inventory of Memory Experiences (IME-C; Herrmann & Neisser, 1978), which asks participants to rate how frequently they forget what they have told other people or what other people have told them (1 = *once in a while*; 6 = *always*). The following is an example item from the inventory: "When someone says he has told you something already, how often do you find that you have no recollection of his telling you any such thing?" The 11 IME-C items (α = .82) were averaged to form a composite score. For ease of interpretability, reverse scoring was used.

Objective memory. At the end of each day over a 14-day period, participants were asked to "take a few minutes to think of a time today when you tried to influence your emotional experience and/or expression" and to "describe the situation so that someone who was not there could picture what the situation was like for you." Participants were given three fourths of an 8.5-× 11-in. (25.6-× 27.9-cm) page to describe this emotion regulatory episode, and pages were collected twice each week. Finally, a week after the last diary entry, participants came to our laboratory to take an unanticipated free-recall test of their memory for the emotion regulation episodes they reported in their diaries. Participants were asked to try to remember each of the episodes they had described over the reporting period and then to write down a brief description as each episode came to mind. Participants were given 20 min to complete the free-recall test. Their descriptions of each event typically were two sentences in length.

Our objective memory measure was derived by coding participants' recall protocols. A trained coder cross-referenced each participant's recall protocol against the original descriptions he or she provided during the daily reporting period. The coder then made a dichotomous decision as to whether or not an episode described during the reporting period was mentioned on the recall protocol. A second coder applied the same scoring procedure for 20% of participants. Coders were blind to all participant information. The kappa coefficient computed on coders' overlapping scoring revealed adequate agreement (k = .76, p < .001). For subsequent analyses, the first coder's scoring was used to compute a proportion of original descriptions recalled correctly by each participant. We interpret this score as an aggregated measure of participants' typical ability to remember events during which they regulate their emotions and during which they would be expected to rely on their preferred form of emotion regulation.

Control Measures

The correlational approach taken in this study meant that any observed association between emotion regulation and memory might be attributable to some third variable. Two individual difference variables seemed particularly likely candidates in this regard. First, neuroticism is related to complaints about physical and mental functioning (Watson & Pennebaker, 1989). Neuroticism also is related to increased levels of negative emotion (Gross, Sutton, & Ketelaar, 1998), which might trigger increased attempts at emotion suppression. Conceivably, therefore, neuroticism could be responsible for any observed association between worse memory and expressive suppression. Second, social desirability is negatively related to reports of poor cognitive functioning (Bell, Gardner, & Woltz, 1997). Social, desirability also might be negatively related to statements concerning the habitual control of powerful emotional impulses. If so, this pattern of hypothesized relations suggests that social desirability, too, might be responsible for any observed relation between memory and suppression.

We administered two control measures. First, we administered the neuroticism subscale of the Big Five Inventory (BFI; John, Donahue, & Kentle, 1991), which asks participants to use a 5-point scale (1 = *very slightly or not at all*; 5 = *extremely*) to rate the extent to which they see

themselves as someone who is "moody," "depressed, blue," "can be tense," and "worries a lot." Scores used in subsequent analyses were computed by averaging participants' responses to all eight items (α = .84). We also administered the Marlowe-Crowne Social Desirability Scale (MCSD; Crowne & Marlowe, 1960), which is a 33-item true-false questionnaire that measures participants' tendencies to respond in a socially desirable manner. Alpha was .74 in the present sample.

Results and Discussion

We first examined convergent (within-domain) and divergent relations among measures. Next, we tested the association between our three measures of emotion regulation and our two measures of memory. Finally, we introduced our two control measures to assess whether the obtained pattern of correlations could be explained by either neuroticism or social desirability.

Convergent Relations Among Measures

As expected, the AEQ and ERQ-S scales correlated positively with each other (r = 65, p < .001), indicating that people who report greater conflict over their tendency to inhibit emotion-expressive behavior also report that they try not to express their emotions. The AEQ (r = -.06, ns) and ERQ-S (r = .09, ns) did not correlate with the ERQ-R, providing evidence of discriminant validity. The cross-method correlation between the IME-C and the objective memory measure was modest but nonetheless positive and significant (r = .25, p = .02), indicating that people who report more frequent lapses in memory for conversations show poorer memory for their own emotion regulatory experiences as well. In each case, the correlations are not so large as to suggest that our measures of expressive suppression and memory are redundant; however, they do suggest that these measures are internally consistent to some degree and thus tap into common underlying constructs.

Expressive Suppression and Memory

The crucial question, of course, was whether self-ratings of typical expressive suppression and reappraisal would correlate with either self-reported or objective memory measures. On the basis of our two prior laboratory studies, we predicted that expressive suppression should be negatively correlated with both memory measures (indicating that greater suppression is associated with worse memory), whereas reappraisal should be unrelated to both memory measures.

As shown in Table 1, these predictions were entirely born out. Beginning first with self-reported memory, one can see that the IME-C is negatively related to both the AEQ and the ERQ-S but unrelated to the ERQ-R. Similarly, if one turns to objective memory, it can be seen that the objective diary measure is negatively related to both the AEQ and the ERQ-S but not to the ERQ-R. Although the magnitude of mese findings is modest, the fact that expressive suppression is associated with worse self-reported and objective memory performance strongly suggests that the laboratory findings from Studies 1 and 2 do in fact generalize to expressive suppression in everyday life. Likewise, the finding that reappraisal is unrelated to either memory measure confirms that the cognitive costs of emotion regulation vary according to precisely how one goes about regulating one's emotions.

Control Analyses

To test the plausibility of neuroticism and social-desirability accounts of the correlations presented in Table 1, we first computed correlations between these two variables and our measures of expressive suppression and memory. As expected, neuroticism correlated positively with the AEQ ($r = .43$, $p < .001$) and negatively with the IME-C ($r = -.28$, $p = .01$). Social desirability correlated negatively with the AEQ ($r = -.25$, $p = .02$). No other significant relations emerged. This pattern of correlations does not provide strong grounds for the view that neuroticism or social desirability mediated the association between expressive suppression and memory. Nonetheless, we computed partial correlations, entering neuroticism and social desirability as covariates. As shown in the right half of Table 1, partialing for neuroticism and social desirability leaves the pattern of findings unchanged. This finding suggests that the obtained association between expressive suppression and memory cannot be accounted for by these potentially confounding individual difference variables.

Summary

Study 3 extended the laboratory findings from Studies 1 and 2 to everyday life. Compared with individuals who were low in expressive suppression, individuals who were high in expressive suppression (a) were more likely to report lapses in memory for the conversations they had and (b) were less likely to remember emotion regulation episodes that they had kept track of over a 2-week period. Neuroticism and social desirability could not account for these findings, and individual differences in reappraisal showed no such associations with memory. The fact that multiple measures of suppression and memory showed similar associations gives us confidence in the robustness of our findings.

GENERAL DISCUSSION

The human capacity to self-regulate provides the cornerstone for adaptive success. One critical manifestation of this self-regulatory capacity is the ability to regulate emotional responses. Given how widespread emotion regulation is among adults in Western cultures, it might seem unlikely that it should interfere with cognitive funtioning. After all, it would be poor design indeed if humans' ubiquitous emotion-regulatory processes degraded ongoing and vital cognitive processes. This, however, seems to be just what happens, at least for certain forms of emotion regulation.

Cognitive Consequences of Emotion Regulation

The notion that there might be cognitive consequences of emotion regulation has been anticipated by several prior researchers. Baumeister's ego-depletion model (Baumeister et al., 1998; Mu-raven et al., 1998), in fact, makes the argument that any form of self-regulation is cognitively costly. This prediction meshes well with the tenets of self-regulation theory (Carver & Scheier, 1981; Duval & Wicklund, 1972), which suggests that self-monitoring requires an ongoing expenditure of cognitive resources as one compares the current state of a system (e.g., one's facial expression of anger) with a desired state of that system (e.g., a facial expression of calm concern) and then takes action to narrow the gap between the actual and the ideal.

On the basis of a process conception of emotion regulation, we offered a more specific prediction regarding the cognitive consequences of emotion regulation, namely, that reappraisal should have few if any cognitive costs but that expressive suppression should have clear costs. We made this differential prediction on the basis of a self-regulatory analysis of the demands of these two particular forms of emotion regulation. We expected that reappraisal, an antecedent-focused form of emotion regulation, should occur relatively early in the emotion generative process and should require relatively few cognitive resources. Once a situation is successfully reconstrued, its emotional "reality" is changed, and no further cognitive work should be necessary. By contrast, we expected that expressive suppression, a form of response-focused emotion regulation, should occur relatively late in the emotion-generative process and should require not only more resources but a chronic expenditure of these resources in order to monitor and successfully down-regulate ongoing emotion-expressive behavior throughout the course of an emotion-eliciting situation.

We tested these predictions in three studies that differed in induction procedure (films, slides), method (experimental, correlational), setting (laboratory, field), information modality (auditory, visual), and type of memory test (verbal, nonverbal). In Study 1, participants viewed a negative emotion-eliciting film either with instructions to hide their ongoing emotion-expressive behavior or with instructions to simply watch the film. Participants who were asked to suppress ongoing emotion-expressive behavior during the film had worse memory for the details of the film than participants who simply watched the film. In Study 2, participants viewed high-and low-negative-emotion slides under one of three instructional sets: suppression, reappraisal, or a just-watch control. As expected, expressive suppression led to worse performance on a verbal, cued-recall memory test, whereas reappraisal did not. These memory effects were evident in high-and low-emotion contexts but were specific to information that required verbal encoding; there were no suppression effects for a nonverbal memory test. In Study 3, we found evidence that our laboratory findings generalized to everyday life, a finding consistent with the growing evidence that laboratory and field estimates of effect sizes across a broad range of tasks converge to a greater degree than commonly thought (Anderson, Lindsay, & Bushman, 1999). Compared with individuals who were low in expressive suppression, individuals who were high in expressive suppression had worse self-reported memory and worse performance on an objective memory test for their own emotional experiences. Reappraisal had no effects on either self-reported or objective memory performance. Together, these replicated findings suggest that some forms of emotion regulation may be cognitively costly, whereas others are not.

Implications for Personality Processes, Individual Differences, and Social Functioning

Any self-regulating system—people included—must monitor ongoing processes in order to adjust them. Our findings suggest that the active self-regulation required by expressive suppression comes at a higher price than might be expected given the ubiquity of this form of emotion regulation. Drawing on the self-regulation literature (Carver & Scheier, 1981; Duval & Wicklund, 1972), we interpret these findings as supportive of the view that upon making the decision to hide their feelings, individuals instigate on-line comparisons between how they think they are behaving on the one hand and some salient standard on the other, such as a mental representation of an unemotional facial expression or the way the face feels when it is not expressing emotion. To make these comparisons, individuals need to monitor for lapses and correct them by dynamically adjusting ongoing behavior. Doing so apparently places special demands on language centers needed to verbally encode information, and we speculate that this competition may be responsible for the compromised verbal memory performance associated with expressive suppression. Interestingly, we are aware of relatively few studies carried out within the self-regulation tradition that have tested the tenets of self-regulation models by manipulating self-regulation directly. Typically, self-focus—not self-regulation—is manipulated, and the presence of self-regulatory activity is then inferred from increases in attention that is directed inward (Carver & Scheier, 1981). By taking a closer look at expressive suppression and other forms of ongoing emotion regulation, researchers might better delineate the precise workings of these and other basic forms of self-regulation.

Emotion regulation constitutes a basic personality process. There are, however, robust individual differences in preferred modes of emotion regulation. These differences are of great interest to anyone who wants to predict the behavior of another person. It should therefore come as no surprise that such differences are reflected in the language people use to describe other people. Thus, it is sometimes said that one person is "hot headed" and prone to "flying off the handle" while it is said of another person that she is "cool as a cucumber" and "keeps a lid on her emotions." These differences in emotion regulation have long been thought to have affective consequences both for the individual doing the regulating (or failing to do so) and for others with whom that individual is interacting. The present research shows that these individual differences in emotion regulation also have cognitive consequences. This suggests that we might want to add memory problems to the growing list of negative consequences associated with chronic efforts to inhibit emotional impulses, such as poorer health, adjustment, and coping responses (Pennebaker, 1990). Although the research presented here cannot speak directly to the broader implications of regulating emotions in ways that compromise memory, it encourages speculation about how the suppression-memory relation might influence personality organization. Could it be that habitual reliance on expressive suppression leaves individuals with incomplete, impoverished memories of emotional events, which in turn increase reliance on such cognitive shortcuts as confabulation, scripts, biases, and schemas when forming judgments about themselves, other people, and the world? Might individual variation in expressive suppression help to explain why some people have differentiated, complex conceptions of the self, based on a rich store of memories, whereas other people have more simplistic, "gist-like" conceptions of the self? Previous research has linked individual differences in emotionality (e.g., depressive tendencies) to variation in "self-defining" autobiographical memories (Singer & Salovey, 1993). The present research suggests that certain emotion regulation tendencies may shape memory as well. An important next step is to understand whether these effects are specific to memories of emotional events or whether they generalize to nonemotional memories as well (e.g., grocery lists, mundane conversations).

Emotion regulation often occurs in social interactions, and these social interactions require memory processes to initiate and guide their successful execution. The finding that emotion regulation affects memory therefore suggests that emotion regulation might also have consequences for social functioning. We might speculate, for example, that the impoverished, incomplete memories stemming from cognitively costly emotion regulation could negatively affect relationships. Overreliance on expressive suppression during an argument could reduce memory for who said what and when they said it. Unfortunately, misunderstandings and ill feelings can be perpetuated when this happens and can aggregate over time to erode relationship satisfaction. Albeit speculative, this intersection between emotion regulation and memory also might shed light on gender differences in close relationships. For example, researchers have shown that men tend to be less expressive than women (Kring & Gordon, 1998) and that, more specifically, men are more likely to engage in expressive suppression during heated interchanges than women, a process referred to as *stonewalling* (Gottman & Levenson, 1988). On the basis of our findings, we might predict that men should remember the details of their conversations less well than women. This difference, in turn, might lead to very different memories of important conversations, and, potentially, to difficulty and frustration at the apparent mismatch between perceptions of these interactions.

Limitations and Future Directions

In three interlocking studies, we have demonstrated that expressive suppression impairs memory and that reappraisal does not. These studies break exciting new ground in the study of emotion regulation. They also provide tantalizing hints regarding the nature of the mechanisms underlying these effects. At this point, alterations in emotion experience do not seem likely mediators of the cognitive consequences. Reappraisal affected emotion experience but had no effect on memory, whereas expressive suppression had no effect on emotion experience but did impair memory. We find it more useful to interpret these findings using a cognitive resource allocation perspective, which asserts that expressive suppression impairs memory because it consumes cognitive resources that are necessary for verbal encoding of memories. We recognize, however, that much more must be done to fully understand the mechanisms by which this form of self-regulation affects memory. In the following paragraphs, we consider several limitations of the present studies and describe three directions for future research, including (a) assessing other forms of emotion regulation, (b) studying other emotions, and (c) examining richer social contexts.

Adults regulate their emotions and moods with a dizzying array of emotion regulatory strategies (e.g., Lyubomirsky & Tucker, 1998; Morris & Reilly, 1987; Thayer et al., 1994). In view of the potentially overwhelming number of forms of emotion regulation (Gross & Richards, 2000) and the limitless supply of possible control tasks (e.g., finger tapping, counting the number of times someone says "the" while talking), our strategy was to identify two theoretically defined forms of emotion regulation that we regarded as viable response options in situations that individuals face in everyday life. This comparison afforded the possibility of showing that certain forms of emotion regulation had cognitive consequences, and that not all self-regulatory tasks involving emotion down-regulation had such consequences. Although we can now be certain that it is not just any task that impairs memory, with just two regulation conditions, we are unable to comment on the cognitive effects of emotion regulation in general. Furthermore, we are unable to discern which of the many differences between reappraisal and suppression were responsible for the observed memory effects. To address these questions, future research will be necessary in which other forms of emotion regulation, such as thought suppression (Wegner, 1994), rumination (Lyubomirsky & Nolen-Hoeksema, 1995), and ingratiation (Gilbert, Krull, & Pel-ham, 1988) are measured and manipulated. Although we used explicit instructions to isolate the effects of two specific forms of emotion regulation, a complementary approach would be to manipulate emotion regulation indirectly by introducing or removing critical situational factors (e.g., the presence of others, norms, goals) that prompt spontaneous efforts to alter emotional responding.

Adults are more likely to regulate negative emotions than positive emotions, and the down-regulation of negative emotion through reappraisal and expressive suppression is common (Gross & Richards, 2000). For this reason, we chose to focus our two experimental studies on emotion down-regulation in the context of negative emotion. In Study 1, the target emotional state was mixed and included sadness, anger, and anxiety. In Study 2, we elicited two levels of negative emotion, which in the high-emotion condition is probably best characterized as disgust.

The effects of expressive suppression were consistent across each of these negative emotional states. However, these studies do not permit us to comment on the effects of emotion regulation in other emotional contexts. Despite a long history of interest in the relation between emotion and memory (for reviews, see Christianson, 1992; Deffenbacher, 1994; Easterbrook, 1959), too little is currently known about the effects of emotion on cognitive processes to make confident predictions. It seems possible, however, that at intense levels, negative emotions such as anger might in and of themselves impair cognitive performance (Bushman, 1998). This suggests the prediction that although reappraisal had no detectable effects in the present studies (with the exception of the unpredicted enhancement of memory in Study 2), reappraisal might have salutary consequences in the context of high levels of anger if this reappraisal were effective in producing decreases in negative emotion. One important research direction, therefore, is to systematically assess the effects that emotion per se—as well as other forms of emotion regulation—may have on memory processes.

Any study that attempts to bring complex, multiply determined phenomena under experimental control requires decisions about the kinds of contexts on which to focus. We thought it prudent to build on the methodology of previous experimental investigations of emotion regulation (Baumeister et al., 1998; Gross & Levenson, 1997) and memory (Christianson, 1992) that have used standardized emotion-eliciting stimuli such as films and slides. Now that we have demonstrated cognitive consequences of emotion regulation in passive-viewing paradigms, it will be important to determine whether emotion regulation has cognitive costs during social interactions. In this context, the regulatory demands of bidirectional interactions might be even less predictable for the regulator than they were in our studies, requiring greater flexibility and quicker reactions in order to successfully manage emotional responding. This leads to the prediction that the costs of response-focused emotion regulation such as expressive suppression might be even greater when evoked during conversations than when evoked in the more passive and solitary contexts studied experimentally here. Future studies that take complex social contexts into account will permit a more complete analysis of the consequences of emotion regulation for different forms of memory, as well, perhaps, for other forms of cognitive activity, such as decision making, social perception, and speech. Such research will provide valuable insights into the mechanisms by which self-regulation affects cognitive functioning.

Concluding Comment

Emotions arise when something important is at stake. At these critical junctures, emotions occasionally generate thoughts, feelings, behaviors, and sensations that one would rather not have. One can decrease the unwelcome signs of negative emotions in many ways, and can do so regularly. However, if it is important to someone to preserve the fidelity of cognitive functioning during emotionally trying times, some emotion regulatory strategies appear to have more to recommend them than others. Keeping a still face and stiff upper lip decreases one's memory for the details of the unfolding emotion-eliciting situation, whereas cognitively transforming the situation by changing one's thinking does not appear to exact such a cognitive cost. An old adage reminds us that an ounce of prevention is worth a pound of cure; so, too, it seems that it is more efficient to construe events in unemotional terms than to try to hold back emotional impulses that already have arisen.

NOTES

1. The term suppression has been used to describe the inhibition of feelings (Freud, 1915/1957), emotion-expressive behavior (Gross & Lev-enson, 1993), vocalizations (Brandimonte, Hitch, & Bishop, 1992), and thoughts (Wegner, 1994). To avoid confusion, we use the term expressive suppression to refer to conscious efforts to inhibit overt emotion-expressive behavior.

2. All analyses were first computed including gender as a factor. Because gender did not interact with any of our other factors, we conducted our primary analyses without including this factor.

3. We conducted secondary analyses using aresine transformed proportions. Results were identical to those based on raw proportions.

4. Two additional participants enrolled in the study but withdrew their participation during the experiment because they did not wish to see the high-emotion slides. Because Study 1 showed no reliable differences between male and female participants, we elected to enroll only women in Study 2 to decrease within-cell variance in expressive behavior.

5. We included twice as many participants in the watch condition than were in each of the other two conditions for a companion study concerned with the effects of emotion on memory.

6. We had no grounds for predicting that slide set order (low emotion first, high emotion first) should interact with instructional condition and thus counterbalanced across conditions. To confirm that order did not interact with our predicted instructional condition effect, we conducted a repeated measures ANOVA on the cued-recognition scores, with slide set (low emotion, high emotion) treated as a within-participants factor and instructional condition (watch, expressive suppression, reappraisal) and slide set order (high emotion first, low emotion first) treated as between-paiticipants factors. Slide set order did not interact with instructional condition either for verbal memory, $F(2, 77) = 0.86$, *ns*, or for nonverbal memory, $F(2, 72) = 0.46$, *ns*.

7. The first three and last three slides were used to absorb any possible primacy and recency effects and therefore were not included in the analyses. Slides were drawn from the International Affective Picture System (IAPS; Lang & Greenwald, 1988) and supplemented by other slides drawn from obscure sources.

8. Complete video records were available for 78 participants.

REFERENCES

ANDERSON, C. A., LINDSAY, J. J., & BUSHMAN, B. J. (1999). RESEARCH IN THE PSYCHOLOGICAL LABORATORY: TRUTH OR TRIVIALITY? *CURRENT DIRECTIONS IN PSYCHOLOGICAL SCIENCE, 8*, 3–9.

BARGH, J. A. (1997). THE AUTOMATICITY OF EVERYDAY LIFE. IN R. S. WYER (ED.), *ADVANCES IN SOCIAL COGNITION* (VOL. 10. PP. 1–61). MAHWAH, NJ: ERLBAUM.

BARTLETT, J. C, TILT, R. E., & LEVY, J. C. (1980). RETRIEVAL CHARACTERISTICS OF COMPLEX PICTURES. EFFECTS OF VERBAL ENCODING. *JOURNAL OF VERBAL LEARNING AND VERBAL BEHAVIOR, 19*, 430–449.

BAUMEISTER, R. F., BRATSLAVSKY, E., MURAVEN, M. & TICE, D. M. (1998). EGO DEPLETION: IS THE SELF A LIMITED

RESOURCE? *JOURNAL OF PERSONALITY AND SOCIAL PSYCHOLOGY, 74,* 1252–1265.

BECK, A. T. (1991). COGNITIVE THERAPY: A 30-YEAR RETRO-SPECTIVE. *AMERICAN PSYCHOLOGIST, 46,* 368–375.

BELL, B. G., GARDNER, M. K., & WOLTZ, D. J. (1997). INDI-VIDUAL DIFFERENCES IN UNDETECTED ERRORS IN SKILLED COGNITIVE PERFORMANCE. *LEARNING AND INDIVIDUAL DIFFER-ENCES, 9,* 43–61.

BRANDIMONTE, M. A., HITCH, G. I., & BISHOP, D. V. M. (1992). VERBAL RECODING OF VISUAL STIMULI IMPAIRS MEN-TAL IMAGE TRANSFORMATION. *MEMORY AND COGNITION, 20,* 449–455.

BUSHMAN, B. J. (1998). EFFECTS OF TELEVISION VIOLENCE ON MEMORY FOR COMMERCIAL MESSAGES. *JOURNAL OF EXPERIMEN-TAL PSYCHOLOGY: APPLIED, 4,* 291–307.

CARVER, C. S., & SCHEIER, M. F. (1981). *ATTENTION AND SELF-REG-ULATION: A CONTROL-THEORY APPROACH TO HUMAN BEHAVIOR.* NEW YORK: SPRINGER-VERLAG.

CHRISTIANSON, S. -A. (1992). EMOTIONAL STRESS AND EYEWIT-NESS MEMORY: A CRITICAL REVIEW. *PSYCHOLOGICAL BULLETIN, 112,* 284–309.

CHRISTIANSON, S. -A., & LOFTUS, E. F. (1987). MEMORY FOR TRAUMATIC EVENTS. *APPLIED COGNITIVE PSYCHOLOGY. 1,* 225–239.

CHRISTIANSON, S. -A., LOFTUS, E., HOFFMAN, H., & LOF-TUS, G. R. (1991). EYE FIXATION AND ACCURACY IN DETAIL MEMORY OF EMOTIONAL VERSUS NEUTRAL EVENTS. *JOURNAL OF EXPERIMENTAL PSYCHOLOGY: LEARNING, MEMORY, AND. COGNITION, 17,* 693–701.

CRAIK, F. I. M., & LOCKHART, R. S. (1972). LEVELS OF PRO-CESSING: A FRAMEWORK FOR MEMORY RESEARCH. *JOURNAL OF VERBAL LEARNING AND VERBAL BEHAVIOR, 11,* 671–684.

CROWNE, D. P., & MARLOWE, D. A. (1960). A NEW SCALE OF SOCIAL DESIRABILITY INDEPENDENT OF PSYCHOPATHOLOGY. *JOURNAL OF CONSULTING PSYCHOLOGY, 24,* 349–354.

CUMMINGS, M. E. (1987). COPING WITH BACKGROUND ANGER IN EARLY CHILDHOOD. *CHILD DEVELOPMENT, 58,* 976–984.

DAMASIO. A. R. (1994). *DESCARTES' ERROR: EMOTION, REASON, AND THE HUMAN BRAIN.* NEW YORK: GROSSERT/PUTNAM.

DANIEL, T. C., & ELLIS, H. C. (1972). STIMULUS CODABILITY AND LONG-TERM RECOGNITION MEMORY FOR VISUAL FORM. *JOURNAL OF EXPERIMENTAL PSYCHOLOGY, 93,* 83–89.

DEFFENBACHER, K. (1994). EFFECTS OF AROUSAL ON EVERYDAY MEMORY. *HUMAN PERFORMANCE, 7,* 141–161.

DEPAULO, B. M., BLANK, A. L., SWAIM, G. W., & HAIRFIELD, J. G. (1992). EXPRESSIVENESS AND EXPRESSIVE CONTROL. *PER-SONALITY AND SOCIAL PSYCHOLOGY BULLETIN, 18,* 276–285.

DEPAULO, B. M., KASHY, D. A., KIRKENDOL, S. E., WYER, M. M., & EPSTEIN, J. A. (1996). LYING IN EVERYDAY LIFE. *JOUR-NAL OF PERSONALITY AND SOCIAL PSYCHOLOGY, 70,* 979–995.

DUVAL, S., & WICKLUND. R. A. (1972). *A THEORY OF OBJECTIVE SELF-AWARENESS.* SAN DIEGO, CA: ACADEMIC PRESS.

EASTERBROOK, J. A. (1959). THE EFFECT OF EMOTION ON CUE UTILIZATION AND THE ORGANIZATION OF BEHAVIOR. *PSYCHO-LOGICAL REVIEW, 66,* 183–201.

EISENBERG, N., FABES, R. A., & LOSOYA, S. (1997). EMOTIONAL RESPONDING: REGULATION, SOCIAL CORRELATES, AND SO-CIALIZATION. IN *EMOTIONAL DEVELOPMENT AND EMOTIONAL INTEL-LIGENCE: EDUCATIONAL IMPLICATIONS* (PP. 129–167). NEW YORK: BASIC BOOKS.

EKMAN, P., & FRIESEN, W. V. (1975). *UNMASKING THE FACE: A GUIDE TO RECOGNIZING EMOTIONS FROM FACIAL CLUES.* ENGLEWOOD CLIFFS, NJ: PRENTICE HALL.

ELLIS, H. C., & ASHBROOK, P. W. (1989). THE "STATE" OF MOOD AND MEMORY RESEARCH: A SELECTIVE REVIEW. *JOURNAL OF SO-CIAL BEHAVIOR AND PERSONALITY, 4,* 1–21.

FOX, N. A. (1994). DYNAMIC CEREBRAL PROCESSES UNDERLYING EMOTION REGULATION. *MONOGRAPHS OF THE SOCIETY FOR RESEARCH IN CHILD DEVELOPMENT, 59* (2–3, SERIAL NO. 240) 152–186.

FREUD, S. (1957). A SHORT ACCOUNT OF PSYCHOANALYSIS. IN J. STRACHEY (ED. AND TRANS.), *THE STANDARD EDITION OF THE COMPLETE PSYCHOLOGICAL WORKS OF SIGMUND FREUD* (VOL. 14, PP. 191–209). LONDON: HOGARTH PRESS. (ORIGINAL WORK PUBLISHED 1924)

GATHERCOLE, S. E. & BADDELEY, A. D. (1993). *WORKING MEMO-RY AND LANGUAGE.* LONDON: ERLBAUM.

GILBERT, D. T., KNILL, D. S., & PELHAM, B. W. (1988). OF THOUGHTS UNSPOKEN: SOCIAL INFERENCE AND THE SELF-REGU-LATION OF BEHAVIOR. *JOURNAL OF PERSONALITY AND SOCIAL PSYCHOL-OGY, 55,* 685–694.

GOTTMAN, J. M., & LEVENSON, R. W. (1988). THE SOCIAL PSYCHO-PHYSIOLOGY OF MARRIAGE. IN P. NOLLER & M. A. FITZPATRICK (EDS.), *PERSPECTIVES ON MARTIAL INTERACTION* (PP. 182–200). CLEV-EDON, ENGLAND: MULTILINGUAL MATTERS.

GREENWALD, A. G., & BANAJI, M. R. (1995). IMPLICIT SOCIAL COGNITION: ATTITUDES, SELF-ESTEEM, AND STEREOTYPES. *PSYCHOLOGICAL REVIEW, 102,* 4–27.

GROSS, J. J. (1998A). ANTECEDENT- AND RESPONSE-FOCUSED EMOTION REGULATION: DIVERGENT CONSEQUENCES FOR

EXPERIENCE, EXPRESSION, AND PHYSIOLOGY. *JOURNAL OF PERSONALITY AND SOCIAL PSYCHOLOGY, 74,* 224–237.

GROSS, J. J. (1998B). THE EMERGING FIELD OF EMOTION REGULATION: AN INTEGRATIVE REVIEW. *REVIEW OF GENERAL PSYCHOLOGY, 2,* 271–299.

GROSS, J. J. (1999). EMOTION AND EMOTION REGULATION. IN L. A. PERVIN & O. P. JOHN (EDS.), *HANDBOOK OF PERSONALITY: THEORY AND RESEARCH* (2ND ED., PP. 525–552). NEW YORK: GUILFORD PRESS.

GROSS, J. J., & JOHN, O. P. (2000). *MEASURING INDIVIDUAL DIFFERENCES IN EMOTION REGULATION: THE EMOTION REGULATION QUESTIONNAIRE.* MANUSCRIPT IN PREPARATION.

GROSS, J. J., & LEVENSON, R., W. (1993), EMOTIONAL SUPPRESSION: PHYSIOLOGY, SELF-REPORT, AND EXPRESSIVE BEHAVIOR. *JOURNAL OF PERSONALITY AND SOCIAL PSYCHOLOGY, 64,* 970–986.

GROSS, J. J., & LEVENSON, R. W. (1997). HIDING FEELINGS: THE ACUTE EFFECTS OF INHIBITING NEGATIVE AND POSITIVE EMOTION. *JOURNAL OF ABNORMAL PSYCHOLOGY, 106,* 95–103.

GROSS, J. J., & RICHARDS, J. M. (2000). *EMOTION REGULATION IN EVERYDAY LIFE: SEX, ETHNICITY, AND SOCIAL CONTEXT.* MANUSCRIPT IN PREPARATION.

GROSS, J. J., SUTTON, S. K., & KETELAAR, T. V. (1998). RELATIONS BETWEEN AFFECT AND PERSONALITY: SUPPORT FOR THE AFFECT-LEVEL AND AFFECTIVE-REACTIVITY VIEWS. *PERSONALITY AND SOCIAL PSYCHOLOGY BULLETIN, 24,* 279–288.

HARRIS, P. L. (1989). *CHILDREN AND EMOTION.* NEW YORK: BLACKWELL.

HERRMANN, D., & NEISSER, U. (1978). AN INVENTORY OF EVERYDAY MEMORY EXPERIENCES. IN M. M. GRUNEBERG, P. E. MORRIS, & R. N. SYKES (EDS.), *PRACTICAL ASPECTS OF MEMORY* (PP. 35–51). LONDON: ACADEMIC PRESS.

JOHN, O. P., DONAHUE, E. M., & KENTIE, R. L. (1991). *THE BIG FIVE INVENTORY: VERSIONS 4A AND 54* (TECH. REP.). BERKELEY, CA: INSTITUTE OF PERSONALITY AND SOCIAL RESEARCH, UNIVERSITY OF CALIFORNIA, BERKELEY.

KING, L. A., & EMMONS, R. A. (1990). CONFLICT OVER EMOTIONAL EXPRESSION: PSYCHOLOGICAL AND PHYSICAL CORRELATES. *JOURNAL OF PERSONALITY AND SOCIAL PSYCHOLOGY. 58,* 864–877.

KRAMER, T. H., BUCKHOUT, R., FOX, P., WIDMAN, E., & TUSCHE, B. (1991). EFFECTS OF STRESS ON RECALL. *APPLIED COGNITIVE PSYCHOLOGY, 5,* 483–488.

KRING, A. M." & GORDON, A. H. (1998). SEX DIFFERENCES IN EMOTION: EXPRESSION, EXPERIENCE, AND PHYSIOLOGY. *JOURNAL OF PERSONALITY AND SOCIAL PSYCHOLOGY, 74,* 686–703.

LANG, P. J., & GREENWALD, M. K. (1988). *THE INTERNATIONAL AFFECTIVE PICTURE SYSTEM STANDARDIZATION PROCEDURE AND INITIAL GROUP RESULTS FOR AFFECTIVE JUDGMENTS* (*TECH. REP. NOS. IA & IB*). GAINESVILLE, FL: CENTER FOR RESEARCH IN PSYCHOPHYSIOLOGY, UNIVERSITY OF FLORIDA.

LAZARUS, R. S. (1991). *EMOTION AND ADAPTATION.* NEW YORK: OXFORD UNIVERSITY PRESS.

LAZARUS, R. S., & ALFERT, E. (1964). SHORT-CIRCUITING OF THREAT BY EXPERIMENTALLY ALTERING COGNITIVE APPRAISAL. *JOURNAL OF ABNORMAL AND SOCIAL PSYCHOLOGY, 69,* 195–205.

LEEPER, R. W. (1948). A MOTIVATIONAL THEORY OF EMOTION TO REPLACE 'EMOTION AS DISORGANIZED RESPONSE.' *PSYCHOLOGICAL REVIEW, 55,* 5–21.

LYNBOMIRSKY, S., & NOTEN HOEKSEMA. S. (1995). EFFECTS OF SELF-FOCUSED RUMINATION ON NEGATIVE THINKING AND INTERPERSONAL PROBLEM SOLVING. *JOURNAL OF PERSONALITY AND SOCIAL PSYCHOLOGY, 69,* 176–190.

LYNBOMIRSKY, S., & TUCKER, K. L. (1998). IMPLICATIONS OF INDIVIDUAL DIFFERENCES IN SUBJECTIVE HAPPINESS FOR PERCEIVING, INTERPRETING, AND THINKING ABOUT LIFE EVENTS. *MOTIVATION AND EMOTION, 22,* 155–186.

MACKEN, W. J., & JONES, D. M. (1995). FUNCTIONAL CHARACTERISTICS OF THE INNER VOICE AND THE INNER EAR. SINGLE OR DOUBLE AGENCY? *JOURNAL OF EXPERIMENTAL PSYCHOLOGY: LEARNING, MEMORY, AND COGNITION, 21,* 436–448.

MACRAE, C. N., BODENHAUSEN, G. V., & MILNE, A. B. (1998). SAYING NO TO UNWANTED THOUGHTS: SELF-FOCUS AND THE REGULATION OF MENTAL LIFE. *JOURNAL OF PERSONALITY AND SOCIAL PSYCHOLOGY, 74,* 578–589.

MORRIS, W. N., & REILLY, N. P. (1987). TOWARD THE SELF-REGULATION OF MOOD: THEORY AND RESEARCH. *MOTIVATION AND EMOTION, 11,* 215–249.

MURAVEN, M., TICE, D. M., & BAUMEISTER, R. F. (1998). SELF-CONTROL AS A LIMITED RESOURCE: REGULATORY DEPLETION PATTERNS. *JOURNAL OF PERSONALITY AND SOCIAL PSYCHOLOGY, 74,* 774–789.

PARROTT, W. G. (1993). BEYOND HEDONISM: MOTIVES FOR INHIBITING GOOD MOODS AND FOR MAINTAINING BAD MOODS. IN J. W. PENNEBAKER & D. M. WEGNER (EDS.), *HANDBOOK OF MENTAL CONTROL* (PP. 278–305), ENGLEWOOD CLIFFS, NJ: PRENTICE HALL.

PENNEBAKER, J. W. (1990). *OPENING UP: THE HEALING POWER OF CONFIDING IN OTHERS.* NEW YORK: MORROW.

RICHARDS, J. M., & GROSS, J. J. (1999). COMPOSURE AT ANY COST? THE COGNITIVE CONSEQUENCES OF EMOTION

SUPPRESSION. *PERSONALITY AND SOCIAL PSYCHOLOGY BULLETIN, 25,* 1033–1044.

SAARNI, C. (1984). AN OBSERVATIONAL STUDY OF CHILDREN'S ATTEMPTS TO MONITOR THEIR EXPRESSIVE BEHAVIOR. *CHILD DEVELOPMENT, 55,* 1504–1513.

SCHERER, K. R. (1984). ON THE NATURE AND FUNCTION OF EMOTION: A COMPONENT PROCESS APPROACH. IN K. R. SCHERER & P. EKMAN (EDS.), *APPROACHES TO EMOTION* (PP. 293–318). HILLSDALE, NJ: ERLBAUM.

SCHOOLER, J. W." & ENGSTLER-SCHOOLER, T. Y. (1990). VERBAL OVERSHADOWING OF VISUAL MEMORIES: SOME THINGS ARE BETTER LEFT UNSAID. *COGNITIVE PSYCHOLOGY, 22,* 36–71.

SINGER, J. A., & SALOVEY, P. (1993). THE *REMEMBERED SELF: EMOTION AND MEMORY IN PERSONALITY.* NEW YORK: FREE PRESS.

THAYER, R. E., NEWMAN, J. R., & MCCLAIN, T. M. (1994). SELF-REGULATION OF MOOD: STRATEGIES FOR CHANGING A BAD MOOD, RAISING ENERGY, AND REDUCING TENSION. *JOURNAL OF PERSONALITY AND SOCIAL PSYCHOLOGY, 67,* 910–925.

TOMAKA, J., BLASCOVICH, J., KIBLER, J., & EMST, J. M. (1997). COGNITIVE AND PHYSIOLOGICAL ANTECEDENTS OF THREAT AND CHALLENGE APPRAISAL. *JOURNAL OF PERSONALITY AND SOCIAL PSYCHOLOGY, 73,* 63–72.

TOMKINS, S. S. (1962). *AFFECT, IMAGERY, CONSCIOUSNESS: THE POSITIVE AFFECTS.* (VOL. 1). NEW YORK: SPRINGER.

WATSON, D., & PENNEBAKER, J. W. (1989). HEALTH COMPLAINTS, STRESS, AND DISTRESS: EXPLORING THE CENTRAL ROLE OF NEGATIVE AFFECTIVITY. *PSYCHOLOGICAL REVIEW, 96,* 234–254.

WEGNER, D. M. (1994). IRONIC PROCESSES OF MENTAL CONTROL. *PSYCHOLOGICAL REVIEW, 101,* 34–52.

WEGNER, D. M., ERBER, R., & ZANAKOS, S. (1993). IRONIC PROCESSES IN THE MENTAL CONTROL OF MOOD AND MOOD RELATED THOUGHT. *JOURNAL OF PERSONALITY AND SOCIAL PSYCHOLOGY, 58,* 409–418.

YOUNG, P. T. (1943). *EMOTION IN MAN AND ANIMAL: ITS NATURE AND RELATION TO ATTITUDE AND MOTIVE.* NEW YORK: WILEY.

The Heat of the Moment

The Effect of Sexual Arousal on Sexual Decision Making

DAN ARIELY AND GEORGE LOEWENSTEIN

INTRODUCTION

The sex drive is a vitally important motivational force in human behavior, from the perspective of both the individual and the society. Sexual motivation plays a direct role in considerable economic activity, including pornography and prostitution, and a less direct role in diverse industries and activities such as night-time entertainment, advertising, and fashion. Sexual motivation and behavior also underlies numerous social ills, including sexually transmitted disease, unwanted pregnancies, and sex-related crimes.

Despite the importance of the topic, most of the information we have about the effect of sexual arousal on judgment, choice, and behavior more generally, comes from personal or vicarious experience. Unlike the extensive research on, for example fear (e.g., LeDoux, 1996; Lerner & Keltner, 2001; Panksepp, 1998), there has been very little research tracing out the diverse effects of sexual arousal on judgment and decision making. In this paper, we examine the effect of sexual arousal in young male adults on three aspects of judgment and choice: (1) their preferences for a wide range of sexual stimuli and activities, (2) their willingness to engage in morally questionable behaviors in order to obtain sexual gratification, and (3) their willingness to engage in unsafe sex when sexually aroused.

There are good reasons, beyond introspection and casual empiricism, to suspect that sexual arousal will affect these dimensions of judgment and choice. The sexual circuitry of men and women evolved not only to orchestrate sexual behavior but also to motivate it in suitable situations (Buss, 2003; Rolls, 1999). By exogenously arousing male subjects we are, in effect, parasitizing men's evolved psychological mechanisms, providing internal and external cues that would ordinarily be associated with increased odds of gaining access to what Buss and Schmitt (1993) refer to as "short-term opportunistic copulation."

Most appetitive systems in the brain, including hunger and thirst, are designed to increase motivation during times of opportunity (Rolls, 1999), and there is no reason to expect sex to be an exception to the rule. When the brain receives cues that are commonly associated with opportunities for copulation, which would include experiencing a state of high sexual arousal, we should expect to observe an increase in motivation to have sex.[1] This increase in motivation should, in turn, have diverse consequences for judgments and decisions. Consistent with such a prediction, prior research has shown that sexual motivation can distort judgments of the risk of contracting sexually transmitted disease (Blanton & Gerrard, 1997; Ditto, Pizarro, Epstein, Jacobson, & MacDonald, 2005), and that it leads to steeper time discounting in males (Wilson & Daly, 2004).

The next question is whether individuals can correctly estimate the effects of high sexual arousal states on their preferences and behavior. Based on prior research on "hot-cold empathy gaps" (Loewenstein, 1996; Loewenstein, O'Donoghue, & Rabin, 2003; Van Boven & Loewenstein,

Dan Ariely and George Loewenstein, "The Heat of the Moment: The Effect of Sexual Arousal on Sexual Decision Making," *Journal of Behavioral Decision Making*, vol. 19, no. 2, pp. 87-98. Copyright © 2006 by John Wiley & Sons, Inc. Reprinted with permission.

2003), we anticipated that people who were not aroused would underestimate the influence of emotional arousal on their preferences and decisions. Previous research has demonstrated hot-cold empathy gaps across several emotional states. For example, people who do not own an object underestimate how attached they would be to it and how much money they would require to part with the object if they owned it (Loewenstein & Adler, 1995; Van Boven, Dunning, & Loewenstein, 2000). People who are about to exercise predict they would be less bothered by thirst if they were lost without food or water than do people who have just exercised and are thirsty and warm (Van Boven & Loewenstein, 2003). People who are sated because they have just eaten are less likely to choose a high-calorie snack to consume at a well-defined time in the future than hungry people who have not eaten (Read & van Leeuwen, 1998), and people who are hungry because they have not eaten expect to be more interested in eating a plate of spaghetti for breakfast than people who are sated (Gilbert, Gill, & Wilson, 2002). Heroin addicts who are not currently craving because they just received a "maintenance" dose of opioid agonist, value getting an extra dose a week later about half as highly as those asked to value the extra dose an hour earlier, before they have received their maintenance dose (Giordano et al., 2002). And, in the prior research most obviously relevant to the research reported here, men who are not sexually aroused predicted they would be less likely to engage in sexually aggressive behavior than men who are sexually aroused as a result of viewing photographs of nude women (Loewenstein, Nagin, & Paternoster, 1997).

A finding that sexual arousal affects predictions of the individual's own judgments and behavior would not only support the idea that arousal influences decision making, but also suggest that people have little insight into these effects. If people were aware of how their judgments and (hypothetical) decisions were being influenced by their own state of arousal then they could compensate for such influences in their judgments and decisions. When not aroused, if they appreciated how being aroused would influence their responses and expected to be aroused in the situation asked about in the question, they could adjust their answers accordingly. The same logic would apply to those who were aroused if they fully appreciated how the arousal was influencing their responses.

The experiment presented below was designed to jointly test if a state of sexual arousal influences these three aspects of judgment and choice (preferences for a wide range of sexual stimuli; willingness to engage in morally questionable behavior; and their willingness to engage in unprotected sex), and whether our participants can accurately predict these influences.

THE STUDY
Method

Research participants were given a laptop computer and were asked to answer a series of questions using a small handheld keypad. The keypad and the program that administered the questions were designed to be operated easily using only the non-dominant hand. In the control (non-aroused) treatment, subjects answered the questions while in their natural, presumably not highly aroused, state. In the arousal treatment, subjects were first asked to self-stimulate themselves (masturbate), and were presented with the same questions only after they had achieved a high but sub-orgasmic level of arousal.

The screen of the computer, as it appeared in the arousal treatment, was divided into three panels, each with a different function (see Figure 1). Three keys on the top left corner of the keypad switched between these three panels, with the activated panel indicated on the screen by a bright red border. The panels on the right and on the top left part of the screen were displayed only in the arousal treatment. The panel on the right, when activated, displayed an "arousal thermometer" with regions colored from blue to red representing increasing levels of arousal. Two keys on the keypad allowed the user to move the probe on the arousal meter to indicate their momentary level of arousal. The panel on the top left occupied the largest part of the screen, displaying diverse erotic photographs. When this panel was activated, the same two keys used to move the probe on the arousal thermometer allowed the subject to scroll forward and backward through the photographs. The panel at the bottom of the screen presented the series of questions that the subjects answered. This panel was visible in both treatments, but, in the arousal treatment, the questions could be answered only when the self-declared level of arousal was 75% or higher on the arousal thermometer. (This criteria was set to create high level of arousal but at the same time not too high in order to avoid ejaculation.) The same two keys used to move the probe on the arousal thermometer, and to scroll forward and backward through the photographs, allowed the subject to move a probe to indicate their answers to the questions presented in this panel. A different key was used to submit the answer and progress to the next question.

The questions took the form of statements, which participants could react to on a visual-analog scale that stretched between "no" on the left to "possibly" in the middle to "yes" on the right. Because the movement of the probe on the visual-analog scale was carried out by repeatedly pressing keys, we used a discrete scale with twenty-six steps along the visual-analog scale. Responses were converted to a 0–100 scale, where 0 is the most extreme negative response and 100 is the most extreme positive response.

The questions were presented in three modules, each designed to address one of the issues mentioned earlier: the attractiveness of different sexual activities to the respondent, the lengths the respondent would go to in order to obtain sexual gratification, and their attitude toward sexual risks in the heat of passion.

The set of questions that asked subjects to evaluate the attractiveness of different sexual stimuli and activities included questions about the attractiveness of women's shoes, a 12-year-old girl, an animal, a 40-, 50-, and 60-year-old-woman, a man, an extremely fat person, a hated person, a threesome including a man, a woman who was sweating, cigarette smoke, getting tied up by their sexual partner, tying up their sexual partner, a woman urinating, getting spanked by a woman, spanking a woman, anal sex, contacts with animals, having sex with the lights on, and reactions to "just" kissing.

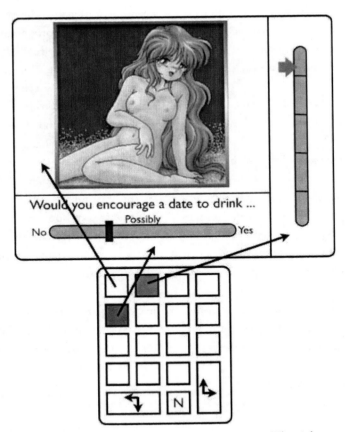

Figure 1. *An illustration of the screen with a non-representative cartoon image. The right panel and the top left panel were only available in the arousal condition. The keypad below illustrates the controls of the interface.*

The set of questions that asked subjects to assess the lengths they would go to procure sex included questions about whether they would encourage a date to drink, slip her a drug, take her to a fancy restaurant or tell her they loved her (when they in fact did not), in all cases with the goal of having sex, and also whether they would try to have sex even after the person they were dating said "no."

The items dealing with sexual risk-taking elicited the respondent's self-reported likelihood of using birth control and the likelihood of negative consequences if one failed to do so. Still other items, not discussed in this paper, asked subjects to make a series of hypothetical intertemporal and risky choices for monetary out-comes.[2]

Subjects

Research participants were 35 University of California, Berkeley male undergraduates recruited with ads placed around campus, who received $10 per session in exchange for participating. Before the experimental session subjects were informed about the experiment, including the fact that it would involve masturbation,[3] signed a consent form, and were randomly assigned to one of the three order-conditions.

Design

The experimental design was a mixed within-and between-subjects design (as described in Table 1). In the N condition, subjects answered the questions in the non-aroused treatment, returned the laptop to the experimenter on the following day, and were paid $10. In the AN condition, subjects first participated in the arousal treatment; then, when they returned the laptop the following day, they were informed about the second session and were asked to participate in the non-aroused treatment. After completing the non-aroused treatment, the subjects returned the laptop to the experimenter and were paid $20. In the

NAN condition, the subjects first answered the questions in the non-aroused treatment; then, when they returned the laptop, they were asked to participate in the aroused treatment. When they returned the laptop again, they were asked to participate in another non-aroused session. After completing this second non-aroused treatment subjects returned the laptop to the experimenter and were paid $30. In all cases there was at least a one-day delay between participation in the different sessions.

Results

First, we examined the impact of the arousal treatment on the reported levels of online arousal. Figure 2 presents the mean reported level of arousal in the arousal treatment as a function of the session's duration. Note that the range of the scale in Figure 2 is from 75 to 100, since participants were not permitted to answer questions until their self-reported arousal level, as indicated on the arousal thermometer, reached the required level of 75%. As can be seen in Figure 2, reported momentary arousal kept increasing during the experiment. It is important to note that all the subjects completed the sessions, and no one reported that they accidentally ejaculated during the session (subjects were instructed to press the tab key if they ejaculated, which would have ended the session).

The experimental design included some comparisons between, and some within, the subjects (see Table 1). The minimum delay of one day between the experimental sessions was designed to minimize contamination effects of repeated exposure to the questions. To test whether repeated exposure to the questions in fact had any impact on the responses, three tests were conducted.

In the first-order test all four non-aroused treatments were compared in a two-factor mixed ANOVA, with all the different responses by the same subject (all the questions) as a within-subject factor, and the four types of non-aroused treatments as a between-subject factor. We

Table 1. *The three experimental order-conditions*

Condition	Treatment 1	Treatment 2	Treatment 3	Analysis
N (*n* = 11)	Non-aroused 1			—
AN (*n* = 12)	Aroused 2	Non-aroused 3		2 versus 3
NAN (*n* = 12)	Non-aroused 4	Aroused 5	Non-aroused 6	5 versus (4 + 6)/2

used this model to examine the effect of the different non-aroused treatments controlling for the different questions and for individual subjects effects. This analysis revealed that none of the non-aroused treatments were statistically different from the others ($F(3,43) = 0.17, p = 0.92$), that the questions were statistically different from each other ($F(32,1376) = 60.88, p < 0.001$), and that the interaction between them was not significant ($F(96,1376) = 0.65, p = 1$).

A second-order test focused on the comparison of the first and second non-aroused treatments in the NAN condition. If being aroused made subjects permanently aware of the effect of arousal on their attitudes and behaviors, we would expect a difference between the two non-aroused treatments—running in the same direction as the difference between the aroused and the first non-aroused treatment. This test was a two factorial within ANOVA with the first and second non-aroused treatments as one repeated factor, and all the different responses by the same subject (all the questions) as a second within-subject factor. The analysis revealed that the two non-aroused treatments were statistically indistinguishable from each other ($F(1,11) = 0.1, p = 0.76$), that the questions were statistically different from each other ($F(32,352) = 19.53, p < 0.001$), and that the interaction between them was not significant ($F(32,352) = 0.91, p = 0.61$). The third-and final-order test compared responses for the arousal treatment when it was first (AN) to when it followed the non-aroused treatment (NAN). These two arousal treatments were compared in a two-factor mixed ANOVA, with all the different responses by the same subject (all the questions) as a within-subject factor, and the two order-conditions as a between-subject factor. This analysis revealed that the two arousal treatments were statistically indistinguishable from each other ($F(1,22) = 0.50, p = 0.49$), that the questions were statistically different from each other ($F(32,704) = 24.78, p < 0.001$), and that the interaction between them was not significant ($F(32,704) = 0.69, p = 0.90$). Overall these results suggest that while there were systematic differences between the different questions (which is somewhat obvious given the different nature of the questions), there were no systematic order effects for either the non-aroused or the aroused treatments. Moreover, there were no interactions between the order and the type of question—indicating that it is

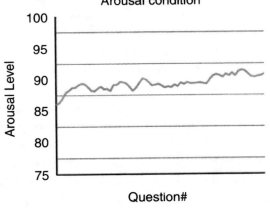

Figure 2. *Momentary self-reported arousal in the arousal condition. Note that the abscissa is in terms of questions, and that in this condition, subjects could not answer any questions until their arousal was at least 75.*

not the case that the order of the treatments systematically influenced the responses for some questions but not others.

Based on this lack of order effects, and for simplicity of presentation, we present the main results as a within-subjects ANOVA, focusing on the comparison between the aroused and non-aroused treatments. For this analysis the N condition was eliminated from the analysis (since it has no within subjects comparison), and the responses of each subject in the two non-aroused treatments in the NAN condition were averaged, resulting in a within-subject comparison across the arousal and non-aroused conditions for each of the questions (see last column of Table 1).

The task included 20 different items that elicited subjects' preferences for sexual stimuli and activities. To examine the effect of the state of arousal on these items, we analyzed them with a 20 (questions) × 2 (state of arousal) fully within ANOVA. The overall model revealed a significant main effect for the arousal state ($F(1,23) = 53.81, p < 0.001$), an overall significant main effect for the questions factor ($F(19,437) = 43.31, p < 0.001$), and an overall significant interaction between arousal state and the questions factor ($F(19,437) = 1.98, p = 0.009$). These results suggest that that the arousal state had a significant effect on the responses to the different questions, that the questions were not all the same, and that the arousal state had a differential effect on the different questions. Therefore, we followed these analyses with a set of 20 independent paired *t*-tests for each of the questions. As can be seen in Table 2, subjects found a variety of potential sexual activities to be more attractive under high arousal than they did under low arousal. From the 20 questions of this type only one activity (Do you prefer to have sex with the light on?) was viewed as less appealing by those in the arousal condition than by those in the non-aroused condition, though not significantly so ($p = 0.46$). One activity (Can you imagine having sex with a man?) was viewed as more appealing, but not significantly so ($p = 0.14$) by those who were aroused, and one question was only marginally significant (Would you find it exciting to spank your sexual partner? $p = 0.1$). The remaining 16 questions were all significantly different in the predicted direction. A one-sample sign test over all 20 items revealed a highly significant effect ($p < 0.001$), indicating that, overall, arousal fundamentally increases predicted enjoyment and liking for the diverse activities that we queried subjects about.

Five other questions asked subjects about their willingness to engage in morally questionable behavior to procure sex. To examine the effect of the state of arousal on these items, we analyzed them with a 5 (questions) × 2 (state of arousal) fully within ANOVA. The overall model revealed a significant main effect for arousal state ($F(1,23) = 26.40$, $p < 0.001$), an overall significant main effect for the questions factor ($F(4,92) = 55.70$, $p < 0.001$), and an overall non-significant interaction between arousal state and the questions factor ($F(4,92) = 0.41$, $p = 0.8$). These results suggest that the arousal state had significant effect on the responses to the different questions, that the questions were not all the same, but that the arousal state had a similar effect on the different questions. To examine these effects in more detail, we followed these analyses with a set of five independent paired t-tests for each of the questions. As can be seen in Table 3, arousal had a strong influence on participants' self-reported likelihood of engaging in a set of morally questionable behaviors to increase the likelihood of obtaining sex. In this set of questions, all five individual questions were statistically significant in the expected direction.

Finally, the survey included eight questions that elicited subjects' willingness to engage in risky sexual practices. To examine the effect of arousal on these items, we analyzed them with an 8 (questions) × 2 (state of arousal) fully within ANOVA. The overall model revealed a non-significant

main effect for the arousal state ($F(1,23) = 0.05$, $p = 0.82$), an overall significant main effect for the questions factor ($F(7,161) = 47.6$, $p < 0.001$), and an overall significant interaction between arousal state and the questions factor ($F(7,161) = 5.90$, $p = 0.009$). These results suggest that the arousal state did not have a significant main effect on the responses to the different questions, that the questions were not all the same, and that the arousal state had a differential effect on the different questions. We followed these analyses with a set of eight independent paired *t*-tests for each of the questions. As can be seen in Table 4, the results for these questions are not as clear-cut as the other two sets of questions. There were no differences between the aroused and non-aroused treatments for the four questions dealing with the perceived efficacy of coitus-interruptus, acknowledgment that a friend can transmit STDs, trusting someone they have just met, and assigning responsibility for birth control to women (which was marginally significant). Answers to all four questions dealing with condoms were, however, strongly influenced by sexual arousal. For all four condom-related questions, subjects in the aroused treatment indicated a lower likelihood of using a condom compared with subjects in the non-aroused treatment. This difference between the two types of questions might suggest that arousal does not change the general knowledge of individuals about the risks of unprotected sex, but when it comes to concrete steps involving condoms, sexual arousal changes one's perceptions of the tradeoffs between benefits and disadvantages in a fashion that decreases the tendency to use them.

GENERAL DISCUSSION

This study examined the effect of high levels of sexual arousal on the subjective attractiveness of different activities, on self-reported willingness to take various morally dubious measures to procure sex, and on willingness to engage in risky sexual activities. Our results on attractiveness of activities suggest that sexual arousal acts as an amplifier of sorts. Activities that are not perceived as arousing when young males are not sexually aroused become sexually charged and attractive when they are, and those activities that are attractive even when not aroused, become more attractive under the influence of arousal. By showing that, when aroused, the same individual will find a much wider range of activities sexually

Table 2. *Mean response, standard deviations, and differences for the different questions on the attractiveness of different activities*

Question	Non-aroused	Aroused	Difference	p (t (23))
Are women's shoes erotic?	42 (5.9)	65 (4.06)	23	<0.001
Can you imagine being attracted to a 12-year-old girl?	23 (4.11)	46 (6.08)	23	<0.001
Can you imagine having sex with a 40-year-old woman?	58 (3.32)	77 (2.07)	19	<0.001
Can you imagine having sex with a 50-year-old woman?	28 (4.80)	55 (4.69)	27	<0.001
Can you imagine having sex with a 60-year-old woman?	7 (2.55)	23 (4.61)	16	<0.001
Can you imagine having sex with a man?	8 (2.47)	14 (3.78)	6	= 0.14 (ns)
Could it be fun to have sex with someone who was extremely fat?	13 (4.30)	24 (5.29)	11	<0.05
Could you enjoy having sex with someone you hated?	53 (6.04)	77 (3.59)	24	<0.001
If you were attracted to a woman and she proposed a threesome with a man, would you do it?	19 (4.97)	34 (7.10)	25	<0.005
Is a woman sexy when she's sweating?	56 (3.1)	72 (5.62)	16	<0.01
Is the smell of cigarette smoke arousing?	13 (3.88)	22 (6.00)	9	<0.03
Would it be fun to get tied up by your sexual partner?	63 (5.09)	81 (4.49)	18	<0.005
Would it be fun to tie up your sexual partner?	47 (3.22)	75 (3.89)	28	<0.001
Would it be fun to watch an attractive woman urinating?	25 (5.57)	32 (5.53)	7	<0.03
Would you find it exciting to spank your sexual partner?	61 (5.35)	72 (4.70)	11	<0.1
Would you find it exciting to get spanked by an attractive woman?	50 (3.40)	68 (5.29)	18	<0.003
Would you find it exciting to have anal sex?	46 (4.91)	77 (3.58)	31	<0.001
Can you imagine getting sexually excited by contact with an animal?	6 (2.55)	16 (4.19)	10	<0.02
Do you prefer to have sex with the light on?	52 (5.84)	50	–2	= 0.46 (ns)
Is just kissing frustrating?	41 (4.43)	69	28	<0.001

Note: Each question was presented on a visual-analog scale that stretched between "no" on the left (0) to "possibly" in the middle (50) to "yes" on the right (100).

appealing than when not aroused, these findings weigh in against the view of sexual preferences as being purely an individual difference variable—i.e., as dispositionally rather than situationally determined. Certainly, there are robust individual differences in sexual preferences and in the likelihood of engaging in various behaviors, but there also seem to be striking intra-individual differences caused, in our study, by externally caused variations in arousal level.

Our results further suggest that the change in attractiveness influences the intensity of motivation to have sex relative to other goals. Specifically, the increase in motivation to have sex produced by sexual arousal seems to decrease the relative importance of other considerations such as behaving ethically toward a potential sexual partner or protecting oneself against unwanted pregnancy or sexually transmitted disease. Like other drive-states (Loewenstein, 1996), and also somewhat analogous to the effects of alcohol (Ditto et al., 2005; Steele & Josephs, 1990), sexual arousal seems to narrow the focus of motivation, creating a kind of tunnel-vision where goals other than sexual fulfilment become eclipsed by the motivation to have sex (c.f., Blanton & Gerrard, 1997).

As noted in the introduction, a secondary implication of our findings is that people seem to have only limited insight into the impact of sexual arousal on their own judgments and behavior. Such an under-appreciation

Table 3. *Mean response, standard deviations, and differences for the different questions on the likelihood to engage in immoral "date-rape" like behaviors (a strict order of severity is not implied)*

Question	Non-aroused	Aroused	Difference	p (t (23))
Would you take a date to a fancy restaurant to increase your chance of having sex with her?	55 (5.86)	70 (3.83)	15	0.01
Would you tell a woman that you loved her to increase the chance that she would have sex with you?	30 (5.40)	51 (4.54)	21	0.001
Would you encourage your date to drink to increase the chance that she would have sex with you?	46 (5.80)	63 (2.87)	17	<0.005
Would you keep trying to have sex after your date says "no."	20 (4.32)	45 (3.44)	25	<0.001
Would you slip a woman a drug to increase the chance that she would have sex with you?	5 (2.51)	26 (3.65)	21	<0.001

Note: Each question was presented on a visual-analog scale that stretched between "no" on the left (0) to "possibly" in the middle (50) to "yes" on the right (100).

could be important for both individual and societal decision making.

At the individual level, there is a considerable research showing that one's meta-understanding of one's own preferences can in many situations be almost as important as the preferences themselves. For example, as O'Donoghue and Rabin (2003) show, the impact of hyperbolic time discounting on actual intertemporal choice behavior depends critically on whether one is naïve or sophisticated about the fact that one will face self-control problems in the future. Ariely and Wertenbroch (2002) likewise found, in a study of students taking a class, that those who were aware of their own tendency to procrastinate, and hence voluntarily set deadlines for themselves, got higher course grades than those who did not. Self-insight when it comes to sexual arousal and sexual behavior is similarly likely to be important for decision making. For example, the most effective means of self-control is probably not willpower (which has been shown to be of limited efficacy), but rather avoiding situations in which one will become aroused and lose control. Any failure to appreciate the impact of sexual arousal on one's own behavior is likely to lead to inadequate measures to avoid such situations. Similarly, if people under-appreciate their own likelihood of having sex, they are likely to fail to take precautions to limit the potential damage from such encounters. A teenager who embraces "just say no," for example, may feel it unnecessary to bring a condom on a date, thus greatly increasing the

likelihood of pregnancy or transmission of STDs if he/she ends up getting caught up in the heat of the moment.

The same logic applies interpersonally. If people judge others' likely behavior based on observing them when they are not sexually aroused, and fail to appreciate the impact of sexual arousal, then they are likely to be caught by surprise by the other's behavior when aroused. Such a pattern could easily contribute to date-rape. Indeed, it can create the perverse situation in which people who are the least attracted to their dates are most likely to experience date-rape because being unaroused themselves they completely fail to understand or predict the other (aroused) person's behavior.

At a social level the failure to appreciate the influence of sexual arousal when one is unaroused can have diverse consequences. For example, judges and jurors, who are generally unaroused when making decisions of guilt and punishment, may be excessively condemnatory and punitive toward sexual offenders because they make their decisions in a sexually unaroused state and fail to appreciate how intense sexual arousal would alter even their own decision making in potentially compromising circumstances. The result is that decisions will be stigmatized as immoral misbehavior even by people who would themselves make the same choice when in an aroused state. It should be clear that such effects of arousal cannot justify any sexual exploitation, but they can make such behaviors somewhat more understandable. From the perspective of the legal system it is possible that sexual

Table 4. *Mean response, standard deviations, and differences for the different questions on willingness to engage in, and outcomes of, sexually unsafe behaviours*

Question	Non-aroused	Aroused	Difference	p (t (23))
If you pull out before you ejaculate, a woman can still get pregnant (N)	92 (2.95)	92 (4.55)	0	= 0.97 (ns)
A woman who is a good friend can give you a sexually transmitted disease (N)	86 (4.44)	89 (4.89)	−3	= 0.21 (ns)
Would you trust a woman you've just met who says she is using birth control? (A)	29 (5.14)	25 (5.51)	−4	= 0.47 (ns)
Birth control is the woman's responsibility (A)	34 (5.41)	44 (5.69)	10	= 0.051
A condom decreases sexual pleasure (A)	66 (3.88)	78 (3.73)	12	<0.002
A condom interferes with sexual spontaneity (A)	58 (5.21)	73 (4.45)	15	<0.01
Would you always use a condom if you didn't know the sexual history of a new sexual partner? (N)	88 (2.66)	69 (6.33)	19	<0.003
Would you use a condom even if you were afraid that a woman might change her mind while you went to get it? (N)	86 (3.04)	60 (4.32)	26	<0.001

Note: Each question was presented on a visual–analog scale that stretched between "no" on the left (0) to "possibly" in the middle (50) to "yes" on the right (100).

The expected higher response is marked with A for aroused or N for non-aroused.

arousal should be given more credit as a partially mitigating factor than it would normally receive. Moreover, understanding these effects can help guide individuals (sex offenders for example) such that they will be less likely to sexually exploit or re-exploit. Finally, as alluded to in the discussion of individual decision making, the failure to appreciate sexual arousal by those who are not themselves immediately aroused can also help to explain the enactment of misguided and ineffective policies such as "just say no", leaving young adults unprepared to limit the potential damage from their own behavior in the heat of the moment.

Limitations

As an initial investigation into the effect of sexual arousal on judgment and decision making, our study inevitably suffers from serious limitations. For example, it is important to note that we did not observe actual behavior. It is therefore possible that the effect of sexual arousal was not to change the desirability of different actions and activities, but to make respondents more willing to *admit* to their feelings. If this were the case, however, we should expect to see a stronger effect for items that people are embarrassed about (e.g., finding a 12-year-old girl attractive, or

being excited by animals), but the effects were fairly similar across these types of items and those that were unlikely to draw much shame (e.g., being attracted to a 40-year-old).

A second limitation incumbent in not observing actual behavior is that we have no way to ascertain whether respondents' predictions of their own behaviors are more accurate when subjects respond under treatments of arousal or non-arousal. Based on previous research on hot-cold empathy gaps (Bouffard, 2002; Loewenstein, Nagin, & Paternoster, 1997), which shows that people often mispredict how they would behave in an affective state different from the one they are in, we suspect that behavioral predictions made under states of arousal more accurately predict behavior in the heat of the moment than do predictions made when respondents are not aroused. However, without observing actual behavior in the situations we ask about, we have no ability to ascertain whether this is in fact the case.

A third limitation concerns the lack of control that we had over the experimental setting. We had subjects conduct the experiment in the privacy of their own residence so as to provide privacy and reduce inhibitions, but this limited our ability to ensure that they carefully and conscientiously carried out the instructions. Indeed, our initial expectations were that at least some of the subjects in the arousal condition would indicate by pressing the tab key that they had accidentally ejaculated, but none did. Finally, our experimental setup did not allow us to measure subjects' arousal using physiological methods, so we instead relied on self-reports of arousal, which have been shown to be fallible (Janssen, 2002). However, since we manipulated sexual arousal experimentally, the validity of our results do not hinge upon the accuracy of our measures of arousal.

Yet a fourth limitation is that the study focused only on men, so it is possible that the observed effects do not generalize to women. Baumeister, Catanese, and Vohs (2001) concluded from multiple sources of evidence that the male sex drive is more intense and uncompromising than the female, and it is at least, in principle, possible that the lesser intensity of the female sex drive entails that women would not be (or not as much) affected by sexual arousal in their decisions. The present work shows that sexual arousal changes the way males would make sexual decisions, but without further data it is not safe to assume that women would show the same pattern.

Clearly, there are many ways in which the experimental design could be improved, though we suspect that design changes intended to eliminate existing shortcomings would inevitably introduce new ones. For example, better monitoring of subjects' sexual arousal by conducting the study in the laboratory and taking physiological measures of arousal could induce greater inhibition on the part of subjects and decrease truthful responding. Given the politically and socially charged nature of sex, research on the topic is inherently difficult, so compromises are unavoidable.

In sum, the current study shows that sexual arousal influences people in profound ways. This should come as no surprise to most people who have personal experience with sexual arousal, but the magnitude of the effects is nevertheless striking. At a practical level, our results suggest that efforts to promote safe, ethical sex should concentrate on preparing people to deal with the "heat of the moment" or to avoid it when it is likely to lead to self-destructive behavior. Efforts at self-control that involve raw *willpower* (Baumeister & Vohs, 2003) are likely to be ineffective in the face of the dramatic cognitive and motivational changes caused by arousal.

ACKNOWLEDGMENT

We thank Tamar Krishnamurti for comments.

REFERENCES

ARIELY, D., & WERTENBROCH, K. (2002). PROCRASTINATION, DEADLINES, AND PERFORMANCE: SELF-CONTROL BY PRECOMMITMENT. *PSYCHOLOGICAL SCIENCE, 13,* 219–224.

BAUMEISTER, R. F., CATANESE, K. R., & VOHS, K. D. (2001). IS THERE A GENDER DIFFERENCE IN STRENGTH OF SEX DRIVE? THEORETICAL VIEWS, CONCEPTUAL DISTINCTIONS, AND A REVIEW OF RELEVENT EVIDENCE. *PERSONALITY & SOCIAL PSYCHOLOGY REVIEW, 5,* 242–273.

BAUMEISTER, R. F., & VOHS, K. D. (2003). WILLPOWER, CHOICE AND SELF-CONTROL. IN G. LOEWENSTEIN, D. READ, & R. BAUMEISTER (EDS.), *TIME AND DECISION: ECONOMIC AND PSYCHOLOGICAL PERSPECTIVES ON INTERTEMPORAL CHOICE* (PP. 201–216). NEW YORK: RUSSELL SAGE FOUNDATION PRESS.

BLANTON, H., & GERRARD, M. (1997). EFFECT OF SEXUAL MOTIVATION ON MEN'S RISK PERCEPTION FOR SEXUALLY TRANSMITTED DISEASE: THERE MUST BE 50 WAYS TO JUSTIFY A LOVER. *HEALTH PSYCHOLOGY, 16,* 374–379.

BOUFFARD, J. A. (2002). THE INFLUENCE OF EMOTION ON RATIONAL DECISION MAKING IN SEXUAL AGGRESSION. *JOURNAL OF CRIMINAL JUSTICE, 30,* 121–134.

BRENDL, C. M., MARKMAN, A. B., & MESSNER, C. (2003). THE DEVALUATION EFFECT: ACTIVATING A NEED DEVALUES UNRELATED CHOICE OPTIONS. *JOURNAL OF CONSUMER RESEARCH, 29,* 463–473.

BUSS, D. M., & SCHMITT, D. P. (1993). SEXUAL STRATEGIES THEORY: AN EVOLUTIONARY PERSPECTIVE ON HUMAN MATING. *PSYCHOLOGICAL REVIEW, 100,* 204–232.

BUSS, D. M. (2003). *THE EVOLUTION OF DESIRE: STRATEGIES OF HUMAN MATING* (REVISED ED.). NEW YORK: BASIC BOOKS.

DITTO, P. H., PIZARRO, D. A., EPSTEIN, E. B., JACOBSON, J. A., & MACDONALD, T. K. (2005). *MOTIVATIONAL MYOPIA: VISCERAL INFLUENCES ON RISK TAKING BEHAVIOR* (SUBMITTED FOR PUBLICATION).

GILBERT, D. T., GILL, M. J., & WILSON, T. D. (2002). THE FUTURE IS NOW: TEMPORAL CORRECTION IN AFFECTIVE FORECASTING. *ORGANIZATIONAL BEHAVIOR AND HUMAN DECISION PROCESSES, 88,* 430–444.

GIORDANO, L. A., BICKEL, W. K., LOEWENSTEIN, G., JACOBS, E. A., MARSCH, L., & BADGER, G. J. (2002). MILD OPIOD DEPRIVATION INCREASES THE DEGREE THAT OPIOD-DEPENDENT

OUTPATIENTS DISCOUNT DELAYED HEROIN AND MONEY. *PSY-CHOPHARMACOLOGY, 163*, 174–182.

JANSSEN, E. (2002). PSYCHOPHYSIOLOGICAL MEASUREMENT OF SEXUAL AROUSAL. IN M. W. WIEDERMAN, & B. E. WHITLEY, (EDS.), *HANDBOOK FOR CONDUCTING RESEARCH ON HUMAN SEXUALITY* (PP. 139–171).

MAHWAH, LEDOUX, J. (1996). THE EMOTIONAL BRAIN. NEW YORK: SIMON & SCHUSTER.

LERNER, J., & KELTNER, D. (2001). FEAR, ANGER, AND RISK. *JOURNAL OF PERSONALITY AND SOCIAL PSYCHOLOGY, 81*, 146–159.

LOEWENSTEIN, G. (1996). OUT OF CONTROL: VISCERAL INFLUENCES ON BEHAVIOR. *ORGANIZATIONAL BEHAVIOR AND HUMAN DECISION PROCESSES, 65*, 272–292.

LOEWENSTEIN, G., & ADLER, D. (1995). A BIAS IN THE PREDICTION OF TASTES. *THE ECONOMIC JOURNAL, 105*, 929–937.

LOEWENSTEIN, G., NAGIN, D., & PATERNOSTER, R. (1997). THE EFFECT OF SEXUAL AROUSAL ON PREDICTIONS OF SEXUAL FORCEFULNESS. *JOURNAL OF CRIME AND DELINQUENCY, 32*, 443–473.

LOEWENSTEIN, G., O'DONOGHUE, T., & RABIN, M. (2003). PROJECTION BIAS IN PREDICTING FUTURE UTILITY. *QUARTERLY JOURNAL OF ECONOMICS, 118*, 1209–1248.

O'DONOGHUE, T., & RABIN, M. (2003). SELF-AWARENESS AND SELF-CONTROL. IN G. LOEWENSTEIN, D. READ, & R. BAUMEISTER (EDS.), *TIME AND DECISION: ECONOMIC AND PSYCHOLOGICAL PERSPECTIVES ON INTERTEMPORAL CHOICE* (PP. 201–216). NEW YORK: RUSSELL SAGE FOUNDATION PRESS.

PANKSEPP, J. (1998). *AFFECTIVE NEUROSCIENCE.* NEW YORK: OXFORD UNIVERSITY PRESS.

READ, D., & VAN LEEUWEN, B. (1998). TIME AND DESIRE: THE EFFECTS OF ANTICIPATED AND EXPERIENCED HUNGER AND DELAY TO CONSUMPTION ON THE CHOICE BETWEEN HEALTHY AND UNHEALTHY SNACK FOOD. *ORGANIZATIONAL BEHAVIOR AND HUMAN DECISION PROCESSES, 76*, 189–205.

ROLLS, E. T. (1999). *THE BRAIN AND EMOTION* (PP. 218–243). OXFORD: OXFORD UNIVERSITY PRESS.

STEELE, C. M., & JOSEPHS, R. A. (1990). ALCOHOL MYOPIA: ITS PRIZED AND DANGEROUS EFFECTS. *AMERICAN PSYCHOLOGIST, 45*, 921–933.

VAN BOVEN, L., DUNNING, D., & LOEWENSTEIN, G. (2000). EGOCENTRIC EMPATHY GAPS BETWEEN OWNERS AND BUYERS: MISPERCEPTIONS OF THE ENDOWMENT EFFECT. *JOURNAL OF PERSONALITY AND SOCIAL PSYCHOLOGY, 79*, 66–76.

VAN BOVEN, L., & LOEWENSTEIN, G. (2003). SOCIAL PROJECTION OF TRANSIENT DRIVE STATES. *PERSONALITY AND SOCIAL PSYCHOLOGY BULLETIN, 29*, 1159–1168.

WILSON, M., & DALY, M. (2004). DO PRETTY WOMEN INSPIRE MEN TO DISCOUNT THE FUTURE? *BIOLOGY LETTERS, 271*, S177–S179.

Authors' biographies:

Dan Ariely is the Luis Alvarez Renta Professor at the Sloan School of Management and at the Media Laboratory, both at MIT. He received a PhD from the University of North Carolina in 1995, and a PhD from Duke University in 1998. Professor Ariely directs the Center for Advanced Hindsight. For more information see http://web.mit.edu/ariely/www

George Loewenstein is Professor of Economics and Psychology at Carnegie Mellon University. He received his PhD from Yale University in 1985 and has held positions at the University of Chicago, the Center for Advanced Study in the Behavioral Sciences, Institute for Advanced Study in Princeton, Russell Sage Foundation, and Institute for Advanced Study in Berlin.

Authors' addresses:

Dan Ariely, Massachusetts Institute of Technology, 77 Massachusetts Avenue, Cambridge, MA 02139, USA.

George Loewenstein, Carnegie Mellon University, 5000 Forbes Avenue, Pittsburgh, PA 15213, USA.

NOTES

1. We might also expect to observe a commensurate decrease in other dimensions of motivation (see, Brendl, Markman, & Messner, 2003).

2. The general finding from these items was that aroused subjects tended to be more risk-seeking and more short-sighted. We are currently following up this part of the study by presenting aroused and non-aroused subjects with choices involving real consequences.

3. This, and the within-subject nature of the experiment, avoided the problem of differential dropout between conditions.

CHAPTER 15
Judgment and Reasoning

Judgment

Drawing Conclusions From Evidence

DANIEL REISBERG

Imagine that you want to cheer up your friend Allen and so you need to figure out what will do the trick, based on things you have seen Allen do or heard him say. How will you proceed? Or, as a different example, should you buy a European car or one from Japan? In this case, you have seen ads telling you something like "Buy a VW!" You'll probably try to ignore those instructions, though, in making your choice. Instead, you'll try to recall what you have heard about different car types, and draw your conclusions based on these remembered facts.

As these examples suggest, we often take actions based on knowledge that we have, in effect, created for ourselves—by drawing inferences based on things we have seen or heard. In short, we draw conclusions from our experiences, and so we need to ask: How and how well do we draw these conclusions? If we draw lessons from our experience, do we draw the *right* lessons?

In this chapter, our focus will be on induction, typically described as a process in which you try to go beyond the available information—drawing inferences about a pattern, based on a few examples, or making projections about novel cases, based on what you've seen so far. Inductive conclusions are never guaranteed to be true. (What if the examples you've seen so far are just atypical?) Nonetheless, if induction is done properly, the conclusions are likely to be true, and so we'll want to ask whether the ordinary use of induction is done properly or not. Thus, we'll want to compare a **descriptive account** of human induction,

telling us how the process ordinarily proceeds, with a **normative account**, telling us how things *ought to go*. In this way, we'll be able to ask whether our day-to-day judgments are foolish or sensible, and whether our commonsense conclusions are justified or not.

JUDGMENT HEURISTICS

Experience can be an extraordinary teacher; indeed, we sometimes say things like, "There's no substitute for experience." With that, we put considerable faith in the judgments that a physician makes, based on her years of experience, or the advice we hear from a car mechanic, based on the many cars he's worked on, or the suggestions of a police officer, based on what he's seen "on the streets."

But, of course, the process of education doesn't depend just on the "teacher"—it also depends on the student! If a student pays no attention in class or remembers only a few bits of what the teacher said, then it won't matter if the teacher was talented or not. Likewise for learning from daily experience: Here, too, the capacity to learn depends on the person who has that experience and (among other concerns) depends on the person's *memory*: In order to draw a conclusion based on previous observations and experiences, the person needs to recall those experiences. As a result, virtually any factor that influences memory will, sooner or later, influence the pattern of our conclusions and the quality of our judgments.

PREVIEW OF CHAPTER THEMES

- In a wide range of circumstances, people use cognitive shortcuts, or "heuristics," to make judgments. These heuristics tend to be relatively efficient, and they often lead to sensible conclusions. However, heuristic use can lead to error.

- People use these heuristics even when they are trying to be careful in their judgment, and even when they are highly motivated to be accurate. The heuristics are used both by experts and by ordinary people, and so expert judgments, too, are vulnerable to error.

- However, heuristic use is far from inevitable, and we can easily identify circumstances in which people rely on more sophisticated forms of reasoning—and so they judge covariation accurately, are sensitive to base rates, are alert to the problems of drawing a conclusion from a small sample of evidence, and so on.

- We will consider when people use their more sophisticated ("System 2") reasoning and when they rely on the heuristics ("System 1"). Evidence suggests that System 2 comes into play only if the circumstances are right and only if the case being judged contains the appropriate triggers for this form of reasoning.

This point provides an immediate basis for caution in evaluating human judgment. Often we draw conclusions based on experiences gathered over months and even years ("I can always tell when someone is lying"; "Have you noticed that creative people are usually a little bit crazy?"; "This year's freshmen seem more mature than last year's"), and so these conclusions rest on memories stretching back across a considerable time period. If these memories are selective (how many juvenile freshmen have you overlooked?), or incomplete, or somehow distorted, then the validity of these conclusions is questionable. In fact, Chapter 7 reviewed evidence that our memories often are selective, or incomplete, or distorted, raising a question right at the start about whether we really can rely on "learning from experience."

Attribute Substitution

If judgments often depend on remembered evidence, is there anything you can do to help yourself, so that memory problems are less likely to pull you off track? One option is attribute substitution: You use this strategy when you're trying to evaluate some point but don't have easy access to the target information. You therefore rely instead on some other aspect of experience that's more accessible and that is (you hope) a plausible substitute for the information you seek.

For example, imagine that you're trying to predict whether you'll do well in Organic Chemistry next semester. To figure this out, you might ask yourself, "How well have my friends done in this course? How many have gotten good grades, and how many have done poorly?" In this case, you're seeking information about *frequencies*—assessments

of how often various events have happened in the past. However, these frequency counts may not be easily accessible for you: Surely, you've not kept a tally, in the past, of friends' Chemistry grades. Likewise, you may not be able, right now, to recall a dozen friends who've taken this course and the grade for each friend. Therefore, you may have trouble estimating the relevant frequencies.

What can you do instead? One option is that you might do a quick scan through memory, seeking relevant cases. If you easily can think of four friends who got good grades in Organic Chemistry, you'll probably conclude that this is a relatively frequent occurrence. If you can think of few friends with good grades, or if the relevant memories come to mind only slowly, you'll probably draw the opposite conclusion: This must be a rare occurrence. In this fashion, you are relying on *availability*—the ease with which things come to mind—as an index *for frequency,* Tversky and Kahneman (1973) referred to this substitution—the reliance on availability as a substitute for frequency—as the **availability heuristic**.

As a different example, imagine that you're trying to judge whether David is lying to you or not. You could, as one option, try to remember everything you know about David and everything you know about liars, asking whether David truly fits into the category "liar." However, this makes considerable demands on memory. It may be easier, therefore, to rely on attribute substitution: Rather than trying to judge David's *category membership,* you could instead think about whether David *resembles* your notion of a typical liar. If he does, you could judge him to be a liar; if not, then you count him as honest. This substitution—using resemblance in place of information about category membership—is called the **representativeness heuristic**.

The Availability Heuristic

We introduced the idea of *heuristics* in Chapter 9. Heuristics are defined as reasonably efficient strategies that usually lead us to the right answers. The key word, however, is "usually." Heuristics do allow errors, but that is simply the price one pays in order to gain efficiency. To avoid the errors, you would need a strategy that would be much slower and much more effortful.

The availability and representativeness heuristics both fit this profile. In both cases, the attribute being used (availability or resemblance) is easy to assess. In both cases, the attribute being relied on is correlated with the target dimension, so that it can serve as a proxy for the target. Events or objects that are frequent are, in fact, likely to be easily available in memory, and so usually we can rely on availability as an index for frequency. And many categories are homogeneous enough so that members of the category do resemble each other; that's why we can often rely on resemblance as a way of judging category membership. (Indeed, this was crucial for us in Chapter 9.)

Nonetheless, it is easy to find cases in which these strategies lead to error. To take a simple case, ask yourself, "Are there more words in the dictionary beginning with the letter *R* ('rose,' 'rock,' 'rabbit') or more words with an *R* in the third position ('tarp,' 'bare,' 'throw')?" Most people assert that there are more words beginning with *R* (Tversky & Kahneman, 1973, 1974), but the reverse is true—by a margin of at least two to one.

Why do people get this wrong—and by so much? The answer lies in availability. If you search your memory for words starting with *R,* many will come to mind. (Try it: How many *R*-words can you name in 10 seconds?) But if you search your memory for words with an *R* in the third position, fewer will emerge. (Again, try this for 10 seconds.) This difference, favoring the words beginning with *R,* arises simply because your memory is organized roughly like a dictionary is, with the words sharing a starting sound all grouped together. As a consequence, it's easy to search memory using "starting letter" as your cue; a search based on "*R* in third position" is much more difficult. In this way, the organization of memory creates a bias in what's easily

available, and this bias in availability leads to an error in frequency judgment.

The Wide Range of Availability Effects

Use of the availability heuristic seems sensible in the question about "R-words." After all, the question isn't very interesting, and so you probably don't want to spend much effort or time in choosing a response. But evidence suggests that people use strategies like availability in a wide range of other cases, including cases in which they're making judgments of some importance.

For example, consider the fact that people regularly overestimate the frequency of events that are, in actuality, quite rare (Attneave, 1953; Liclitenstein, Slovic, Fischhoff, Layman, & Combs, 1978). This probably plays a part in people's willingness to buy lottery tickets; they overestimate the likelihood of winning! Sadly, it also can play a role in more important domains. For example, there is evidence that physicians may, in many circumstances, overestimate the likelihood of a rare disease and, in the process, fail to pursue other, perhaps more appropriate, diagnoses. (For an example, see Elstein et al., 1986.)

What causes this pattern? Events that are unusual or peculiar are, by their nature, likely to catch your attention. You will therefore notice these events and think about them, ensuring that these events are well recorded in memory. This will, in turn, make these events easily available to you. As a consequence, if you rely on the availability heuristic, you will overestimate the frequency of these unusual events and, correspondingly, will overestimate the likelihood of similar events happening in the future.

As a different example, participants in one study were asked to recall a number of examples in their lives in which they had acted in an assertive fashion (N. Schwarz et al., 1991; also see Raghubir & Menon, 2005). Half of the participants were asked to recall 6 examples; half were asked to recall 12 examples. Then all the participants were asked some more general questions, including how assertive, overall, they thought they were.

What should we expect here? Participants will probably have an easy time coming up with 6 examples, and so, using the availability heuristic, they are likely to conclude, "Those examples came easily to mind; therefore, there must be a large number of these examples; therefore, I must be an assertive person." In contrast, participants asked for 12 examples are likely to have more difficulty generating this longer list, and so they will conclude. "If these examples are so difficult to recall, I guess the examples can't be typical for how I act."

Consistent with these suggestions, participants who recalled fewer examples judged themselves to be more assertive. Notice, ironically, that the participants who recalled *more* examples actually had more evidence in their view for their own assertiveness. But it's not the quantity of evidence that matters. Instead, what matters is the ease of coming up with the examples. Participants who were asked for a dozen examples had a hard time with the task *because they had been asked to do something difficult*. But participants seemed not to realize this. They reacted only to the fact that the examples were difficult to generate and, using the availability heuristic, concluded that being assertive was relatively infrequent in their past.

In this example, availability is being influenced by the experimenters request (for 6 examples or 12). But availability can also be influenced by many other factors. Imagine that you have been asked to vote on how much money the government should spend on various research projects, all aimed at saving lives. It seems sensible that you would choose to spend your resources on the more frequent causes of death, rather than investigating rare problems, and that leads to our questions: Should we spend more on preventing death from motor vehicle accidents or death from stomach cancer? Which is more common? Should we spend more on preventing homicides or diabetes? People reliably assert that motor vehicle accidents and homicide are the more frequent in each pair, although the opposite is true in both cases—by a substantial margin (Combs & Slovic, 1979; Slovic, Fischhoff, & Lichtenstein, 1982).

What produces this error? In estimating the likelihood of these events, people are heavily influenced by the pattern of media coverage. Homicide makes the front page, while diabetes does not; and this is reflected in participants' estimates of frequency. Indeed, their estimates for each of the causes of death correspond rather closely to frequency of report in the media, rather than to actual frequency of occurrence. Thus, once again, we find an influence of availability, just as some information is less available to us via the selectivity of memory, some information is less available via the selectivity of the media. And it is the available data

that people use, making the media bias as important as the memory bias.

The Representativeness Heuristic

Similar points can be made about a different form of attribute substitution—namely, the representativeness heuristic, the strategy of relying on resemblance when what you're really after is a judgment of category membership. At its essence, this heuristic amounts to an assumption that the categories we encounter are relatively homogeneous. It's this assumption that leads us to act as if each member of a category is "representative" of the category—that is, each member has all of the traits that we associate with the category overall. Thus, if someone is a lawyer, we give in to the stereotype and expect her to have the traits we associate with lawyers. Conversely, if someone looks like (our idea of) a typical lawyer—that is, has "lawyer traits"—we conclude she is a lawyer.

This assumption of homogeneity leaves us quite willing to draw conclusions from a relatively small sample: If each member of a group is representative of the group, then it's fair to draw conclusions about the whole after one or two observations, and thus we agree to statements such as, "If you've seen one lawyer, you've seen em all."

Of course, these reasoning patterns often lead us to the correct conclusions, because many categories we encounter are homogeneous. If after one or two nights at a Marriott you conclude that most hotel rooms have Bibles in them, your conclusion is warranted. If you conclude that Sue probably is comfortable with math because she is, after all, an engineer, this conclusion, too, is probably correct; engineers are likely to be reasonably homogeneous in this particular dimension. But as with all heuristics, it is easy to find cases in which this sort of reasoning can lead to error.

Reasoning from the Population to an Instance

Imagine tossing a coin over and over, and let's say that the coin has landed heads up six times in a row. Many people (and many gamblers) believe that in this situation the coin is more likely to come up tails than heads on the next toss. But this conclusion is wrong, and this belief is commonly referred to as the "gambler's fallacy." The "logic" leading to this fallacy seems to be that if the coin is fair, then a series of tosses should contain equal numbers of heads and tails. If no tails have appeared for a while, then some are "overdue" to bring about this balance.

But how could this be? The coin has no "memory," so it has no way of knowing how long it has been since the last tails. More generally, there simply is no mechanism through which the history of the previous tosses could influence the current one. Therefore, the likelihood of a tail on toss number 7 is 50–50 (i.e., .50), just as it was on the first toss, and just as it is on every toss.

Where, then, does our (mistaken) belief come from? The explanation lies in our assumption of category homogeneity. We know that over the long haul a fair coin will produce equal numbers of heads and tails. Thus, the category of "all tosses" has this property. Our assumption of homogeneity, though, leads us to expect that any "representative" of the category will also have this property—that is, any sequence of tosses will also show the 50–50 split. But this isn't true: Some sequences of tosses are 75% heads, some are 5% heads, some are 100% heads. It is only when we combine all these sequences that the 50–50 split emerges.

A different way to say this appeals to the notion of sample size. If we examine a large number of cases (i.e., a large sample), we will find patterns close to those in the overall population. This is what statisticians refer to as the "law of large numbers," a law that states (roughly) that the larger the sample you consider is, the greater the resemblance will be between the properties of the sample and the properties of the population at large. There is, however, no "law of small numbers": There is no tendency for small samples to approximate the pattern of the population. Indeed, small samples can often stray rather far from the population values. But people seem not to appreciate this, and they act as though they expect small samples to show the pattern of the whole. (For a different perspective on the gambler's fallacy, though, see Ayton & Fischer, 2004.)

Reasoning From a Single Case to the Entire Population

If people believe categories are homogeneous, then they will expect each subset of the category, and each individual within the category, to have the properties of the category overall; this is the error we were just discussing. But if people believe

categories to be homogeneous, they'll also make the opposite error: They will expect the overall category to have the properties of the individuals, and so they will be quite willing to extrapolate from a few instances to the entire set. And this error, too, is easy to document, even when people are explicitly told that the instance they are considering is not representative of the larger group.

Hamill, Wilson, and Nisbett (1980) showed their participants a videotaped interview in which a person identified as a prison guard discussed his job. In one condition, the guard was compassionate and kind, and he expressed great concern for rehabilitation. In the other condition, the guard expressed contempt for the prison inmates, and he scoffed at the idea of rehabilitation. Before seeing either of these videotapes, some participants were told that this guard was quite typical of those at the prison; other participants were told that he was quite *atypical,* chosen for the interview precisely because of his extreme views. Still other participants were given no information about whether the interviewed guard was typical or not.

Participants were later questioned about their views of the criminal justice system, and the data show that they were clearly influenced by the interview they had seen: Those who had seen the humane guard indicated that they were now more likely to believe that prison guards in general are decent people; those who had seen the inhumane guard reported more negative views of guards. What is remarkable, though, is that participants seemed largely to ignore the information about whether the interviewed guard was typical or not. Those who were explicitly told the guard was atypical were influenced by the interview just as much, and in the same way, as those who were told chat the guard was typical.

Similar data are easily observed outside of the laboratory. Consider what Nisbett and Ross (1980) have referred to as "man who" arguments. Imagine that you are shopping for a new car. You have read various consumer magazines and decided, on the basis of their reports of test data and repair records, that you will buy a Smackobrand car. You report this to your father, who is aghast. "Smacko?! You must be crazy. Why, I know a man who bought a Smacko, and the transmission fell out 2 weeks after he got it. Then the alternator went. Then the brakes. How could you possibly buy a Smacko?"

What should you make of this argument? The consumer magazines tested many cars and reported that 2% of all Smackos break down. In your father's "data," 100% of the Smackos (one out of one) break down. Should this "sample of one" outweigh the much larger sample tested by the magazine? Your father presumably believes he is offering a persuasive argument, but what is the basis for this? The only basis we can see is the presumption that the category will resemble the instance; only if that were true would reasoning from a single instance be appropriate.

If you listen to conversations around you, you will regularly hear "man who" (or "woman who") arguments. "What do you mean cigarette smoking causes cancer?! I have an aunt who smoked for 50 years, and she runs in marathons!" Often these arguments seem persuasive. But these arguments have force only by virtue of the representativeness heuristic—our assumption that categories are homogeneous, and therefore our peculiar willingness to take a small sample of data as seriously as a larger sample.

ANCHORING

In sum, we often rely on shortcuts that involve one form or another of attribute substitution. Thus, we rely on availability to judge frequency; we rely on resemblance as an indicator of category membership (and also rely on category membership as a basis for expecting resemblance!). We also use other substitutes—for example, using our emotional responses to a stimulus as a basis for judging danger (Slovic & Peters, 2006), and in other cases, using the *length* of an essay as a basis for judging *how persuasive it is* (Josephs, Giesler, & Silvera, 1994).

In all cases, it's reasonable to employ these shortcuts: Yes, the shortcuts can lead to error, but they lead to the right answer more often than not, and using the shortcuts surely is easy. What's troubling, though, is that we use the shortcuts in such a wide range of settings—including cases (like medical diagnosis or making important consumer choices) in which important issues are at stake.

Perhaps, though, these shortcuts provide only a person's initial view of an issue, something like a "rough draft" of his or her ultimate conclusion. Perhaps people then revise and refine their beliefs, based on other considerations. In this case, they could enjoy the benefits of the shortcuts, but without the cost. Unfortunately, though, this optimistic view is *wrong,* thanks in part to a tendency known as anchoring (Tversky & Kahneman, 1974; for more recent work, see Epley & Gilovich, 2001, 2006; Janiszewski & Uy, 2008; Krosnick, Miller, & Tichy, 2004).

In many situations, we don't know the answer to a particular question, but we do have an idea about what "ballpark" the answer is in. What we can therefore do is use that initial idea as an "anchor" and then reach our answer by making some suitable adjustment to that anchor. The problem, though, is that we usually adjust too little, and so we are more influenced by the initial anchor than we should be.

In one study, participants had to estimate how old Mahatma Gandhi was when he died. Some participants were first asked the absurdly easy question of whether Gandhi lived to the age of 140; after they'd responded, they were asked how long he actually did live. Their estimate, on average, was that he lived to be 67 years old. Other participants were first asked whether Gandhi lived past the age of 9; then they, too, had to estimate how long he lived. Given this much lower anchor, they gave appreciably lower estimates, judging on average that he lived to age 50 (Strack & Mussweiler, 1997; it turns out, by the way, that all of these estimates were off target: Gandhi was 78 when he died).

A reliance on anchors is widespread, and so this becomes an important part of our theorizing about how people make judgments. But, in addition, anchoring has another consequence: When judgment errors arise for *other* reasons, anchoring serves to cement them in place. Imagine, for example, that you're trying to judge which is more frequent in the United States—death by homicide or death by diabetes (see p. 380). You know perfectly well that homicides tend to be front-page news; diabetes, on the other hand, is rarely reported unless the victim happens to be someone famous. Because you are aware of this bias and aware of how it might have shaped your initial estimate, you might seek to adjust that estimate, and it is here that anchoring plays its role. The initial response, even though misguided, will influence subsequent judgments, making it difficult to undo the error. (For related claims, see Wilson & Brekke, 1994.)

DETECTING COVARIATION

It cannot be surprising that we often rely on shortcuts in our thinking. After all, many judgments we need to make in life are relatively trivial, and we are often pressed for time by some aspect of the circumstances. And, as we have noted, the shortcuts usually serve us well—providing the correct answer with very little effort.

It is unsettling, though, that people use these shortcuts even when making consequential judgments and even when making judgments about familiar domains. It is also worrisome that (thanks to anchoring) the errors produced by the shortcuts can be long-lasting. As a consequence of these points, people are sometimes influenced by availability even when there's an obvious bias in what's available. Likewise, they take small samples of evidence too seriously and treat evidence as though it were representative even if told explicitly that it is not.

The impact of these shortcuts can also be seen when people are trying to make judgments about **covariation**. This term has a technical meaning, but for our purposes we can define it this way: X and Y "covary" if X tends to be on the scene whenever Y is, and if X tends to be absent whenever Y is absent. For example, exercise and stamina covary: People who do the first tend to have a lot of the second. Owning audio CDs and going to concerts also covary, although less strongly than exercise and stamina. (Some people own many CDs but rarely go to concerts.) Note, then, that covariation is a matter of degree: Covariation can be strong or weak. Covariation can also be either negative or positive. Exercise and stamina, for example, covary positively (as exercise increases, so does stamina). Exercise and body fat, in contrast, covary negatively (as exercise increases, body fat decreases).

Covariation is important for many reasons—including the fact that it's what we need to consider whenever we are checking on a belief about cause and effect. For example, does education lead to a higher-paying job? If so, then degree of education and salary should covary. Likewise, do you feel better on days in which you eat a good breakfast? If so, then the presence or absence of breakfast in a day should covary with how you feel as the day wears on. Similarly for many other cause-effect questions: Are you more likely to fall in love with someone tall? Do vertical stripes make you look thinner? Does your car start more easily if you pump the gas? These are all questions that can be addressed by asking how things covary, and they are the sorts of questions people frequently ask. So how well do we do when we think about covariation?

Illusions of Covariation

Psychologists have developed a wide variety of tests to measure personality characteristics or behavioral inclinations. One well-known example is the Rorschach test, in which participants are shown inkblots and asked to describe them. Psychologists then examine the descriptions, looking for certain patterns. A mention of humans in motion is said to indicate imagination and a rich inner life; responses that describe the white spaces around the inkblot are taken as indications of rebelliousness.

Is this valid? Do specific responses really covary with certain personality traits? And how astutely do people detect this covariation? To attack these questions, Chapman and Chapman (1971) created a number of Rorschach protocols—that is, written transcripts of a person's responses. The protocols were actually fictional, made up for this study, but they were designed to resemble real Rorschach responses. The Chapmans also made up fictional descriptions of the people who had supposedly offered these responses: One protocol was attributed to someone who "believes other people are plotting against him"; another protocol was attributed to someone who "has sexual feelings toward other men."

The Chapmans randomly paired the protocols and the personality descriptions—one protocol and one description, the next protocol and a different description. These randomly assembled protocol—profile pairs were then shown to a group of undergraduates, students who had no prior experience with the Rorschach test and who did not know the theory behind the test. These students were asked to examine the pairs and to determine what responses covaried with what traits. In particular, the students were asked which responses covaried with homosexuality.

Before pressing on, we should emphasize that the Chapmans' research was done more than three decades ago, at a time when many psychiatrists viewed homosexuality as a "disorder" to be diagnosed. Psychiatry has long since abandoned this utterly indefensible view, and so we discuss the Chapmans' research because it is a classic study of covariation, and not because it tells us anything about homosexuality.

Returning to the study itself, we know that thanks to the random pairing, there was no covariation in this set of "data" between protocols and descriptions. Nonetheless, the students reported seeing a pattern of covariation.

Certain responses, they reported, seemed consistently good indicators that the respondent was a homosexual. For example, they reported that homosexual respondents were particularly likely to perceive buttocks in the inkblots. Therefore, mention of buttocks was a reasonable indicator, they claimed, of homosexuality.

Of course, there was no pattern in these (randomly assembled) data, and therefore the covariation the students were perceiving was illusory—"observed" in the data even though it was plainly not there. And oddly enough, the covariation "perceived" by these students was identical to that alleged at the time by professional clinicians. On the basis of their extensive experience with patients, clinicians were convinced that certain Rorschach responses were valid indicators of homosexuality, and the responses they mentioned were exactly the ones nominated by the participants in the laboratory study. The clinicians, like the Chapmans' participants, reported that use of the "buttocks" response did covary with sexual orientation, with homosexuals being much more likely to use this response.

Is it just a coincidence that the **illusory covariation** detected" by the laboratory participants matches the pattern observed by the clinicians? It turns out to be no coincidence at all, because the pattern observed by the clinicians *is also illusory.* We know this because researchers have examined the Rorschach responses from homosexuals and heterosexuals and asked statistically whether the "buttocks" responses are more likely from one group than the other. It turns out that the two groups do not differ at all in the likelihood of this response, and so there is no covariation between sexual orientation and the use of the response. Thus, the clinicians are seeing a "pattern" that really isn't there. With all of their training, with their years of experience, and when they are making consequential professional judgments, the clinicians are caught by the same illusion that the lab participants are. (For related evidence, see Arkes & Harkness, 1983; Schustack & Sternberg, 1981; Shaklee & Mims, 1982; Smedslund, 1963.)

Theory-Driven and Data-Drivers Detection of Covariation

In day-to-day work, a professional can accumulate great quantities of experience. A physician sees many cases of the flu; a salesperson sees many customers; a teacher sees many students. Each of these individuals, therefore, has a great opportunity to accumulate "professional wisdom" within his or her area of special expertise. The clear message of the Chapmans' data, though, is that we might be wary of this "professional wisdom." Their data remind us that professional training does not make someone immune to illusions. Professionals, just like everyone else, are capable of projecting their beliefs onto the evidence and perceiving patterns that aren't there. (For more on how expertise influences judgment, see Phillips, Klein & Sieck, 2004.)

What about nonexperts? Do we generally fall into the pattern indicated by the Chapmans' data—projecting our own biases onto the evidence we observe, and seeing only the patterns of covariation we expect to see? It's surely true that people have many false beliefs about covariation. For example, many people are convinced that there is a relationship between a persons handwriting and personality, yet no serious study has documented this covariation. Apparently, therefore, this is another example of illusory covariation (King & Koehler, 2000). Likewise, many people believe they can predict the weather by paying attention to their arthritis pain ("My knee always acts up when a storm is coming"). This, too, turns out to be groundless, and so it is another example that people are prone to perceive covariation when in truth there is none (Redelmeier & Tversky, 1996).

But what exactly causes these illusions? In a study by Jennings, Amabile, and Ross (1982), college students were asked to make covariation judgments in two types of situations: situations in which they had no prior expectations or biases, and situations in which they did. For example, in the "prior belief" (or "theory-based") case, the participants were asked to estimate how strong the covariation is between (a) children's dishonesty as measured by false report of athletic performance, and (b) children's dishonesty as measured by the amount of cheating in solving a puzzle. If a child is dishonest according to one of these indices, is she also dishonest according to the other? Or, as a different example, participants estimated the covariation between (a) how highly a student rated U.S. presidents' performance in the last decade, and (b) how highly the student rated business leaders' performance in the last decade. If you think highly of our presidents, do you also think highly of leaders in the business community?

The participants presumably made these judgments by reflecting on their prior experience and their intuitions; no new data were presented in the experimental procedure. Participants expressed these judgments by selecting a number between 0 and 100, where 0 indicated that the two traits were unrelated (i.e., did not covary) and 100 indicated that the traits covaried perfectly. Participants could also use negative values (to–100) to indicate the belief that the two traits covary, but with the presence of one indicating the absence of the other.

The participants were also asked to make a comparable judgment in a "no prior belief" (or "data-based") case—that is, with variables they had never met or considered before. For example, they were presented with ten pictures, each showing a man holding a walking stick. The heights of the men varied in the pictures, as did the length of the walking stick, and participants had to judge whether the two variables covaried, again choosing a value between–100 and +100.

Figure 12.1 shows the results from the data-based cases—that is, the cases in which participants had no prior beliefs. Here the estimates of covariation were reasonably regular: The stronger the covariation, the stronger the estimate. The judgments also tended to be rather conservative: Estimates exceeded +30 only when the objective correlation was very strong.

Figure 12.2 shows a very different picture for the theory-based cases. The participants tended to be far more extravagant in these estimates, with estimates as high as + 60 and +80, They were also far less regular in the theory-based cases, with only a weak relation between the magnitude of the estimated covariation and the magnitude of the actual covariation. For example, the "children's dishonesty" pair, mentioned earlier, is shown as the green square in the figure. In this case, the objective correlation, statistically measured, is fairly small: that is, children who are dishonest in one context are, in truth, often honest in other contexts. Participants estimated this covariation to be quite large, though, with an average estimate of almost +60. For the "presidents and business leaders" case (the green star in the figure), the objective correlation is much stronger than in the "dishonesty" pair, but participants estimated it to be much weaker.

At the very least, then, participants are performing differently in the theory-based and data-based judgments. The former judgments are often extravagant; the latter tend to be conservative. The data-based judgments track the objective facts fairly well; the theory-based judgments do not. Given these results, it is difficult to avoid the conclusion that theory biased what the participants "saw" in the data and that it led them to see much stronger (or weaker) covariation than was there. (Other relevant data are reviewed by Allan, 1993; Alloy & Tabachnik, 1984; Baron, 1988.)

What Causes Illusory Covariation?

Plainly, people *can* judge covariation in the absence of prior beliefs; we see that in Figure 12.1. Why, therefore, do they perform so poorly when judging covariation about familiar cases—cases for which they do have beliefs or expectations? One proposal focuses on the *evidence* people consider, rather than the process itself (Baron, 1988; Evans, 1989; Gilovich, 1991; Jennings, Amabile, & Ross, 1982). Specifically, the claim is that in making these judgments people consider only a subset of the evidence, and it's a subset that's shaped by their prior expectations. This virtually guarantees mistaken judgments, since even if the judgment process were 100% fair, a biased input would lead to a biased output.

This proposal rests on a tendency known as **confirmation bias**, a tendency to be more alert and more responsive to evidence that *confirms* one's beliefs, rather than to evidence that might *challenge* one's beliefs (Nisbett & Ross, 1980; Tweney, Doherty, & Mynatt, 1981). We will have more to say about confirmation bias in Chapter 13, and there we will consider some of the data documenting the breadth and power of this bias. For now, though, let's think through how confirmation bias applies to the assessment of covariation. Let us say, for the sake of discussion, that you have the belief that big dogs tend to be vicious. As a result of this belief, whenever you are thinking about dogs or looking at dogs, confirmation bias will lead you to notice the big dogs that are, in fact, vicious and the little dogs that are friendly. Your memory schemata will also help you to remember episodes that fit with this belief and will work against your remembering counterexamples. (Recall that one effect of memory schemata is to "regularize" our past experiences, bringing our recollections into line with our schema-based expectations; see Chapter 7.)

Thanks to these mechanisms, a biased sample of dogs is available to you—both in the dogs you perceive (because of a bias in attention) and in the dogs you remember (because of the bias in attention plus the effects of memory schemata). Therefore, if you are asked to estimate covariation between dog size and temperament, you will probably overestimate the covariation. This isn't because you are ignoring the facts, nor is it because you're incompetent in thinking about covariation. The problem instead lies in your "data"; and if the data are biased, so will be your judgment.

How alarmed should we be by these observations? It's worth bearing in mind that many social stereotypes are based on illusory covariation (e.g., the anti-Semitic illusion that being overly concerned with money "covaries" with being Jewish, or the racist illusion that being lazy "covaries" with being black). In cases like these, the perception of illusory covariation obviously has ugly consequences. Likewise, if you're convinced that money makes people happy, and so you design your life in hopes of maximizing your wealth, then here, too, an illusion of covariation is having powerful effects. (For a glimpse of the data on the actual relationship between having money and being happy, see Myers, 2000.) Thus, the stakes are often high in judgments involving covariation, making our errors in this domain rather troubling.

Base Rates

Our assessment of covariation can also be pulled off track by another problem: our neglect of *base-rate* information. As a way of entering this issue, consider the following problem (Kahneman & Tversky, 1973; Nisbett & Ross, 1980):

> I have a friend who is a professor. He likes to write poetry, is rather shy, and is small in stature. Which of the following is his field: (a) Chinese studies or (b) psychology?

In response to this question, most people conclude that the friend is in Chinese studies, and presumably this judgment is based on something like the representativeness heuristic: The example describes someone close to many people's stereotype of a Chinese scholar, and so they draw the appropriate conclusion.

However, this judgment overlooks an important bit of information. As you can probably guess, the number of psychologists in the world is much greater than the number

of scholars in Chinese studies. To see how this matters, let us assume, just for the sake of argument, that virtually all Chinese scholars—say, 90%—fit the stereotype. Let us assume further that only 5% of the psychologists fit the stereotype. In this case, "fitting the stereotype" would be high-quality diagnostic information—information that does indeed indicate that a person is in one category rather than another.

But now let's factor in how many psychologists there are in total, and how many Chinese scholars. We've already suggested that there are relatively few Chinese scholars in the world; even if 90% of these fit the description, this is still 90% of a small number. In contrast, merely 5% of the psychologists fit the description, but this will be 5% of a much larger number. To make this concrete, let's say there are 10,000 Chinese scholars in the United States, and 200,000 psychologists. In this case, 9,000 Chinese scholars fit the description (90% of 10,000), but 10,000 psychologists do as well (5% of 200,000). Therefore, even though the *proportion* of Chinese scholars fitting the description is larger than the proportion of psychologists (90% vs. 5%), the *number* of psychologists who fit the description is greater than the number of Chinese scholars fitting the description (10,000 vs. 9,000). As a result, chances are that the friend is a psychologist, because the description is compatible with more psychologists than Chinese scholars.

To put this point more generally, you need two types of information in order to make judgments like this one: both the diagnostic information and also the base rate—the overall likelihood that a particular case will be in this category or that one, independent of the diagnostic information. Often the base rate is expressed as a probability or as a percentage, and so, in our example, the base rate for "being a Chinese scholar," from the total group being considered, is 4.8%.[1]

Base rates are always important to consider, and in some cases they can overturn a conclusion suggested by the diagnostic information. This is evident in out "Chinese studies" example and is true in many other cases as well. Imagine that we are testing a new drug and discover that 70% of the patients who take this drug recover from the malady being treated. Does that mean the drug is effective? The answer depends on the base rate. In general, how many patients recover? If the answer is 70%, then the drug is having no effect whatsoever. Likewise, do good-luck charms help?

Let's say that you wear your lucky socks whenever your favorite team plays, and the team has won 85% of its games. We again need to ask about base rates: How many games has your team won over the last few years? Perhaps the team has won 90% overall but only 85% when you are wearing your lucky socks; in that case, your socks are actually a jinx.

Base-Rate Neglect

In a classic study, Kahneman and Tversky (1973) asked participants this question: If someone is chosen at random from a group of 70 lawyers and 30 engineers, what is his profession likely to be? Participants understood perfectly well that the person is likely to be a lawyer. When asked to estimate the probability of this outcome, they sensibly responded .70. Thus, in this setting, participants made full and accurate use of the base-rate information.

Other participants were given a similar task, but with no base-rate information. They were instead given diagnostic information—brief descriptions of certain individuals—and asked, based on these descriptions, whether each individual was more likely to be a lawyer or an engineer. Some of the descriptions had, in fact, been crafted to suggest that the person was a lawyer; some suggested engineer; some were relatively neutral. For example, a description favoring the engineer stereotype described a man whose hobbies include home carpentry, sailing, and mathematical puzzles and who has no interest in political or social issues.

Not surprisingly, participants were easily able to use these descriptions, and their judgments sensibly reflected the content of the thumbnail sketches. Thus, it appears that participants are responsive to base rates if this is the only information they have, indicating that they know the base rates are relevant to this judgment. Likewise, they make appropriate use of diagnostic information if this is all they have. But now let's ask: What happens if we provide participants with both sorts of information—the base rates and the diagnostic information?

Participants in a third group were again provided with the thumbnail descriptions, but they were told, in addition, that the individuals being described had been selected at random from a group of 30 engineers and 70 lawyers. We have just seen evidence that participants understand the value of both pieces of information: the thumbnail sketch and the overall composition of the group. Therefore, we should

expect the participants, when given both, to consider both and to combine these two sources of information as well as they can. If the base rate and the diagnostic information both favor the lawyer response, participants should offer this response with some confidence. If the base rate indicates one response and the diagnostic information the other response, then participants should temper their estimates accordingly.

However, this is not what the participants do. When they are provided with both types of information, participants ignore the base rate and rely only on the diagnostic information. Thus, in the lawyer/engineer problem, participants' responses were completely determined by the degree of resemblance between the individual described and their stereotype of a lawyer or an engineer. Indeed, they responded the same way if the base rates were as already described (70 lawyers, 30 engineers) or if the base rates were reversed (30 lawyers, 70 engineers). This reversal had no impact whatsoever on participants' judgments, confirming that they were indeed ignoring the base rates.

What produces this neglect of base rate? The answer, in part, is attribute substitution: When asked whether a particular person—Tom, let's say—is a lawyer or an engineer, people seem to turn this question about category membership into a question about resemblance. (In other words, they rely on the representativeness heuristic.) Thus, to ask whether Tom *is* a lawyer, they ask themselves how much Tom *resembles* (their idea of) a lawyer. This substitution is in many circumstances sensible. (Again, attribute substitution is efficient and often provides us with the right answer.) But the substitution can also cause problems: We earlier saw that the representativeness heuristic leads us to ignore sample size (pp. 383–384); we now add that the heuristic also leads us to ignore base rates.

The neglect of base rates, in turn, causes other problems, For example, someone who is insensitive to base rates will be inept in judging covariation, which means that he will be inaccurate whenever he tries to figure out cause-and-effect relationships. Likewise, base rates are crucial for questions of categorization (lawyer or engineer; Chinese scholar or psychologist), and some types of categorization are deeply consequential. For example, is a particular tumor malignant or benign? Is a patient truly suicidal or not? It turns out that experts making these decisions (physicians, psychotherapists) also show the pattern of base rate neglect

(Dawes, 1988; Eddy, 1982; Klayman & Brown, 1993), high-lighting just how important (and just how worrisome) this pattern can be.

ASSESSING THE DAMAGE

We seem to be painting a grim portrait of human judgment. We have discussed several sources of error, and we have suggested that these errors are rather widespread. Most of the studies we have cited have been run at prestigious universities, and so the participants (students at those universities) are, presumably, intelligent and motivated. The errors occur nonetheless. (For reviews, see Arkes, 1991; Einhorn & Hogarth, 1981; Gilovich. 1991.)

Even experts make these errors. We have mentioned poor diagnostic reasoning in physicians and illusory correlations in experienced therapists. Likewise, if we add just a little subtlety to our problems, analogous errors can be observed even among people with considerable training in statistics and methodology (Kahneman & Tversky, 1982a; Tversky & Kahneman, 1971, 1983; also see Mahoney & DeMonbreun, 1978; Shanteau, 1992). And as we've seen, people make these errors even when the stakes are high. In a number of studies, participants have been offered cash bonuses if they perform accurately. These incentives do have an impact on performance (Arkes, 1991; Gilovich, 1991; Hertwig & Ortmann, 2003), but even so, many errors remain. In addition, we have discussed errors in the context of medical diagnosis; other studies have documented similar errors in the professional work of highly motivated financial managers (e.g., Hilton, 2003). In these cases, the stakes are high indeed, yet the errors can still be documented.

More-Sophisticated Judgment Strategies

Could it be that human judgment is so fundamentally flawed? If so, this might help explain why warfare, racism, neglect of poverty, and environmental destruction are widespread; perhaps these consequences are the inevitable outcome of our inability to understand the facts and to draw decent conclusions. Likewise, it's no wonder that people are so ready to believe in telepathy, astrology, and a variety of bogus cures (Gilovich, 1991; King & Koehler, 2000).

Before we make these claims, however, we need to acknowledge that there is another side to our story and, with that, evidence showing that people can rise above the simple strategies we have described and avoid the errors we have catalogued. This will in turn demand a new line of questioning—asking why people sometimes rely on judgment short-cuts (with the attendant risk of error), and why people sometimes use more-sophisticated strategies.

Let's start, though, by documenting the simple but crucial fact that sometimes human judgment does rise above the heuristics we have described so far. For example, we argued earlier that people often rely on availability when they are trying to judge frequency, asking themselves, "How easily can I think of cases of type X?" in order to decide, "How common is type X?" But people don't always do this. Sometimes people are alert to the fact that they don't know much about a category, and this dissuades them from relying on the availability heuristic. For example, how many sumo wrestlers are there in your state? If you relied on availability in answering this question, you might answer "zero" (assuming that none of your friends or relatives are sumo wrestlers). But in this situation you are probably alert to your own lack of expertise, and so you will seek some other basis for making this judgment. (For experimental demonstrations of this, see Oppenheimer, 2004; N. Schwarz, 1998; Winkielman & Schwarz, 2001.)

Similarly, consider the common reliance on the representativeness heuristic. This reliance is evident in many ways, including the fact that people are far too willing to draw conclusions from a small sample of evidence (we saw this in the power of "man who" arguments). This (and other findings) seems to suggest that people do not understand the importance of *sample size* when evaluating a pattern of evidence. Other evidence, however, makes it clear that people *do* understand sample size. As an illustration, imagine the following dialogue:

> Bart: I've got a great system for choosing lottery
> numbers! I chose a number yesterday, and I won!
> Lisa: Come on—that doesn't mean your system's
> great; maybe you just got lucky.

In this setting, Lisa's response sounds perfectly fine; we all know that lucky accidents do happen, and so Bart's boast does sound unjustified. But now consider this bit of dialogue:

> Marge: I've got a great system for choosing lottery numbers! I've tried it 11 times, and I won every time!
>
> Homer: Come on—that doesn't mean your system's great; maybe you just got lucky each time.

This time, Homer's response sounds odd, and Marge's boast does seem sensible. Yes, lucky accidents do happen, but they don't keep happening over and over. If something does happen over and over, therefore, it's probably not an accident.

These are easy points to grasp, and it's precisely this ease of understanding that's important here, because it reveals a comprehension of some crucial facts about sample size. Specifically, you understand these bits of dialogue only because you already know that it's dangerous to draw conclusions from a small sample of evidence. This is why you side with Lisa, not Bart. Likewise, you side with Marge because you understand that it's legitimate to draw conclusions from a larger sample; you know that a pattern in a larger set is less likely to be the result of accident.

Experimental data also make it clear that in some circumstances people are alert to the size of the data set they are considering. For example, Nisbett, Krantz, Jepson, and Kunda (1983) asked participants in one study to imagine that they had encountered a new bird, the "shreeble." The one shreeble observed so far was blue, and on this basis participants were asked how likely they thought it was that all shreebles were blue. These participants were also asked to imagine that they had encountered a new element, "floridium." Only one sample of floridium had been examined, and when heated, it burned with a blue flame. Given this evidence, the participants were asked how likely they thought it was that all floridium, when heated, burns with a blue flame. Finally, in still other trials, the same participants were told about a previously unknown tribe living on a Pacific island. One member of the tribe had been observed and was obese. With this information, the participants were asked how likely they thought it was that all members of this tribe were obese.

In each of these judgments, the research participants seemed to draw on their prior knowledge about how homogeneous these categories (heated elements, bird colors, and body sizes) are likely to be. As a result, for floridium, participants were quite willing to believe that a single instance allows generalization to the whole set, and so they asserted that all floridium would burn blue when heated. Participants were less willing to extrapolate from a single case when thinking about shreebles, and even less willing when thinking about obese islanders. For these categories, the participants were willing to draw conclusions only after they were told about several observations (several shreebles or several tribespeople) in addition to the initial case.

Clearly, therefore, people sometimes *are* sensitive to sample size, and so, apparently, they do not always use the representativeness heuristic. People could, in principle, have made their judgment about shreebles by relying on a "man who" argument (or, more precisely, "bird who"): "I know a shreeble that is blue; therefore all shreebles… " But instead, people sensibly realize that shreebles may vary, and so they draw no conclusion until they have more evidence. Obviously, then, use of the heuristic is not inevitable.

CHAPTER SUMMARY

- Induction often relies on attribute substitution, so that (for example) people estimate frequency by relying on availability, and so they judge an observation to be frequent if they can easily think of many examples of that observation. The more available an observation is, the greater the frequency is judged to be.

- Judgments based on the availability heuristic are often accurate, but they do risk error. This is because many factors influence availability, including the pattern of what is easily retrievable from memory, bias in what we notice in our experiences, and also bias in what the media report. Even if people detect these biases, they often fail to adjust for them, because of anchoring.

- People also rely on the representativeness heuristic when they extrapolate from observations they have made. This heuristic rests on the assumption that categories are relatively homogeneous, so that any case drawn from the category will be representative of the entire group. Because of this assumption, people expect a relatively small sample of evidence to have all the properties that are associated with the entire category; one example of this is the gambler's fallacy. Similarly, people seem insensitive to the importance of sample size, and so they believe that a small sample of observations is just as informative as a large sample. In the extreme, people are willing to draw conclusions from just a single observation, as in "man who" arguments.

- People are also likely to make errors in judging co-variation. In particular, their beliefs and expectations sometimes lead them to perceive illusory covariations. These errors have been demonstrated not just in novices working with unfamiliar materials but also in experts dealing with the sorts of highly familiar materials they encounter in their professional work.

- People are accurate in assessing covariation if they have no prior beliefs or expectations about the data. This suggests that people do understand the concept of covariation and understand (roughly) how to assess covariation. When people have prior beliefs, though, their judgments of covariation are sometimes extreme and often erratic. This may be attributable to the fact that confirmation bias causes people to notice and remember a biased sample of the evidence, which leads to bad covariation judgments.

- People also seem insensitive to base rates, and again, this can be demonstrated both in novices evaluating unfamiliar materials and in experts making judgments in their professional domains.

- Use of heuristics is widespread, and so are the cor-responding errors. However, we can also find cases in which people rely on more-sophisticated judgment strategies, and so are alert to sample size and sample bias, and do consider base rates. This has led many theorists to propose dual-process models of thinking. One process (often called System 1) relies on fast, ef-fortless short-cuts; another process (System 2) is slower and more effortful, but less likely to lead to error.

- System 1 thinking is more likely when people are pressed for time or distracted. System 1 thinking also seems more likely in people with lower working-memory capacity. However, System 1 thinking can be observed even in high-intelligence individuals and even in the absence of time pressure or distraction. System 1 thinking can be observed even when the matter being judged is both familiar and highly consequential.

- System 2 thinking seems more likely "when the data are described in terms of frequencies rather than prob-abilities and also when the data are easily coded in statistical terms (as a *sample* of data, with *chance* playing a role in shaping the sample). System 2 thinking is also more likely if people bring to a situation background knowledge that helps them to code the data and to understand the cause-and-effect role of sample bias or base rates. Training in statistics also makes System 2 thinking more likely, leading us to the optimistic view that judging is a *skill* that can be improved through suitable education.

The Workbook Connection

See the *Cognition Workbook* for further exploration of judgment:

- Demonstration 12.1: Sample Size
- Demonstration 12.2: Relying on the Representative Heuristic
- Demonstration 12.3: Applying Base Rates
- Research Methods: Systematic Data Collection
- Cognitive Psychology and Education: Making People Smarter
- Cognitive Psychology and the Law: Juries' Judgment

NOTES

1. In our example, we said that there were 10,000 Chinese scholars in the country, and 200,000 psychologists. That means the *proportion* of Chinese scholars, out of all the people we're considering, is 10,000 out of 210,000. Expressed as a decimal, that fraction equals 0.0476, or roughly 4.8%.

The Hot Hand in Basketball

On the Misperception of Random Sequences

THOMAS GILOVICH, ROBERT VALLONE AND AMOS TVERSKY

We investigate the origin and the validity of common beliefs regarding "the hot hand" and "streak shooting" in the game of basketball. Basketball players and fans alike tend to believe that a player's chance of hitting a shot are greater following a hit than following a miss on the previous shot. However, detailed analyses of the shooting records of the Philadelphia 76ers provided no evidence for a positive correlation between the outcomes of successive shots. The same conclusions emerged from free-throw records of the Boston Celtics and from a controlled shooting experiment with the men and women of Cornell's varsity teams. The outcomes of previous shots influenced Cornell players' predictions but not their performance. The belief in the hot hand and the "detection" of streaks in random sequences is attributed to a general misconception of chance according to which even short random sequences are thought to be highly representative of their generating process.

In describing an outstanding performance by a basketball player, reporters and spectators commonly use expressions such as "Larry Bird has the hot hand" or "Andrew Toney is a streak shooter." These phrases express a belief that the performance of a player during a particular period is significantly better than expected on the basis of the player's overall record. The belief in "the hot hand" and in "streak shooting" is shared by basketball players, coaches, and fans, and it appears to affect the selection of plays and the choice of players. In this paper we investigate the origin and the validity of these beliefs.

People's intuitive conceptions of randomness depart systematically from the laws of chance.[1] It appears that people expect the essential characteristics of a chance process to be represented not only globally in the entire sequence, but also locally, in each of its parts. For instance, people expect even short sequences of heads and tails to reflect the fairness of a coin and contain roughly 50% heads and 50% tails. This conception of chance has been described as a "belief in the law of small numbers" according to which the law of large numbers applies to small samples as well (Tversky & Kahneman, 1971). A locally representative sequence, however, deviates systematically from chance expectation: It contains too many alternations and not enough long runs.

A conception of chance based on representativeness, therefore, produces two related biases. First, it induces a belief that the probability of heads is greater after a long sequence of tails than after a long sequence of heads—this is the notorious gambler's fallacy (see, e.g., Tversky & Kahneman, 1974). Second, it leads people to reject the randomness of sequences that contain the expected number of runs because even the occurrence of, say, four heads in a row—which is quite likely in a sequence of 20 tosses—makes the sequence appear nonrepresentative (Falk, 1981; Wagenaar, 1972).

Thomas Gilovich, Robert Vallone, and Amos Tversky, "The Hot Hand in Basketball: On the Misperception of Random Sequences," *Cognitive Psychology*, vol. 17, no. 3, pp. 295-314. Copyright © 1985 by Elsevier Science and Technology. Reprinted with permission.

Sequences of hits and misses in a basketball game offer an interesting context for investigating the perception of randomness outside the psychological laboratory. Consider a professional basketball player who makes 50% of his shots. This player will occasionally hit four or more shots in a row. Such runs can be properly called streak shooting, however, only if their length or frequency exceeds what is expected on the basis of chance alone. The player's performance, then, can be compared to a sequence of hits and misses generated by tossing a coin. A player who produces longer sequences of hits than those produced by tossing a coin can be said to have a "hot hand" or be described as a "streak shooter." Similarly, these terms can be applied to a player who has a better chance of hitting a basket after one or more successful shots than after one or more misses.

This analysis does not attempt to capture all that people might mean by "the hot hand" or "streak shooting." Nevertheless, we argue that the common use of these notions—however vague or complex—implies that players' performance records should differ from sequences of heads and tails produced by coin tossing in two essential respects. First, these terms imply that the probability of a hit should be greater following a hit than following a miss (i.e., positive association). Second, they imply that the number of streaks of successive hits or misses should exceed the number produced by a chance process with a constant hit rate (i.e., non-stationarity).

It may seem unreasonable to compare basketball shooting to coin tossing because a player's chances of hitting a basket are not the same on every shot. Lay-ups are easier

than 3-point field goals and slam dunks have a higher hit rate than turnaround jumpers. Nevertheless, the simple binomial model is equivalent to a more complicated process with the following characteristics: Each player has an ensemble of shots that vary in difficulty (depending, for example, on the distance from the basket and on defensive pressure), and each shot is randomly selected from this ensemble. This process provides a more compelling account of the performance of a basketball player, although it produces a shooting record that is indistinguishable from that produced by a simple binomial model in which the probability of a hit is the same on every trial.

We begin with a survey that explores the beliefs of basketball fans regarding streak shooting and related phenomena. We then turn to an analysis of field goal and free-throw data from the NBA. Finally, we report a controlled experiment performed by the men and women of Cornell's varsity teams that investigates players' ability to predict their performance.

STUDY 1: SURVEY OF BASKETBALL FANS

One hundred basketball fans were recruited from the student bodies of Cornell and Stanford University. All participants play basketball at least "occasionally" (65% play "regularly"). They all watch at least 5 games per year (73% watch over 15 games per year). The sample included 50 captains of intramural basketball teams.

The questionnaire examined basketball fans' beliefs regarding sequential dependence among shots. Their responses revealed considerable agreement: 91% of the fans believed

Table 1. *Probability of Making a Shot Conditioned on the Outcome of Previous Shots for Nine Members of the Philadelphia 76ers*

Player	P (hit/3 misses)	P (hit/2 missed)	P (hit/1 miss)	P (hit)	P (hit/1 hit)	P (hit/2 hits)	P (hit/3 hits)	Serial Correlation r
Clint Richardson	.50 (12)	.47 (32)	.56 (101)	.50 (248)	.49 (105)	.50 (46)	.48 (21)	−.020
Julius Erving	.52 (90)	.51 (191)	.51 (408)	.52 (884)	.53 (428)	.52 (211)	.48 (97)	0.016
Lionel Hollins	.50 (40)	.49 (92)	.46 (200)	.46 (419)	.46 (171)	.46 (65)	.32 (25)	−.004
Maurice Cheeks	.77 (13)	.60 (38)	.60 (126)	.56 (339)	.55 (166)	.54 (76)	.59 (32)	−.038
Caldwell Jones	.50 (20)	.48 (48)	.47 (117)	.47 (272)	.45 (108)	.43 (37)	.27 (11)	−.016
Andrew Toney	.52 (33)	.53 (90)	.51 (216)	.46 (451)	.43 (190)	.40 (77)	.34 (29)	−.083
Bobby Jones	.61 (23)	.58 (66)	.58 (179)	.54 (433)	.53 (207)	.47 (96)	.53 (36)	−.049
Steve Mix	.70 (20)	.56 (54)	.52 (147)	.52 (351)	.51 (163)	.48 (77)	.36 (33)	−.015
Daryl Dawkins	.88 (8)	.73 (33)	.71 (136)	.62 (403)	.57 (222)	.58 (111)	.51 (55)	−.142**
Weighted means	**.56**	**.53**	**.54**	**.52**	**.51**	**.50**	**.46**	**−.039**

Note: Since the first shot of each game cannot be conditioned, the parenthetical values in columns 4 and 6 do not sum to the parenthetical value in column 5. The number of shots upon which each probability is based is given in parentheses.

* *p* < .05
**p < .01

that a player has "a better chance of making a shot after having just *made* his last two or three shots than he does after having just *missed* his last two or three shots"; 68% of the fans expressed essentially the same belief for free throws, claiming that a player has "a better chance of making his second shot after *making* his first shot than after *missing* his first shot"; 96% of the fans thought that "after having made a series of shots in a row … players tend to take more shots than they normally would"; 84% of the fans believed that "it is important to pass the ball to someone who has just made several (two, three, or four) shots in a row."

The belief in a positive dependence between successive shots was reflected in numerical estimates as well. The fans were asked to consider a hypothetical player who shoots 50% from the field. Their average estimate of his field goal percentage was 61% "after having just made a shot," and 42% "after having just missed a shot." Moreover, the former estimate was greater than or equal to the latter for every respondent. When asked to consider a hypothetical player who shoots 70% from the free-throw line, the average estimate of his free-throw percentage was 74% "for second free throws after having made the first," and 66% "for second free throws after having missed the first."

Thus, our survey revealed that basketball fans believe in "streak shooting." It remains to be seen whether basketball players actually shoot in streaks.

STUDY 2: PROFESSIONAL BASKETBALL FIELD GOAL DATA

Field goal records of individual players were obtained for 48 home games of the Philadelphia 76ers and their opponents during the 1980–1981 season. These data were recorded by the team's statistician. Records of consecutive shots for individual players were not available for other teams in the NBA. Our analysis of these data divides into three parts. First we examine the probability of a hit conditioned on players' recent histories of hits and misses, second we investigate the frequency of different sequences of hits and misses in players' shooting records, and third we analyze the stability of players' performance records across games.

Analysis of Conditional Probabilities

Do players hit a higher percentage of their shots after having just *made* their last shot (or last several shots), than after having just *missed* their last shot (or last several shots)? Table 1 displays these conditional probabilities for the nine major players of the Philadelphia 76ers during the 1980–1981 seasons. Column 5 presents the overall shooting percentage for each player ranging from 46% for Hollins and Toney to 62% for Dawkins. Columns 6 through 8 present the players' shooting percentages conditioned on having *hit* their last shot, their last two shots, and their last three shots, respectively. Columns 2 through 4 present the players' shooting percentages conditioned on having *missed* their last shot, their last two shots, and their last three shots, respectively. Column 9 presents the (serial) correlation between the outcomes of successive shots.

A comparison of columns 4 and 6 indicates that for eight of the nine players the probability of a hit is actually lower following a hit (weighted mean: 51%) than following a miss (weighted mean: 54%), contrary to the hot-hand hypothesis. Consequently, the serial correlations in column 9 are negative for eight of the nine players, but the coefficients are not significantly different from zero except for one player (Dawkins). Comparisons of column 7, P (hit/2 hits), with column 3, P (hit/2 misses), and of column 8, P (hit/3 hits), with column 2, P (hit/3 misses), provide additional evidence against streak-shooting; the only trend in these data runs counter to the hot-hand hypothesis (paired $t = -2.79$, $p < .05$ for columns 6 and 4, $t = -3.14$, $p < .05$ for columns 7 and 3, $t = -4.42$, $p < .01$ for columns 8 and 2). Additional analyses show that the probability of a hit following a "hot" period (three or four hits in the last four shots) was lower (weighted mean: 50%) than the probability of a hit (weighted mean: 57%) following a "cold" period (zero or one hit in the last four shots).

Analysis of Runs

Table 2 displays the results of the Wald-Wolfowitz run test for each player (Siegel, 1956). For this test, each sequence of consecutive hits or misses is counted as a "run." Thus, a series of hits and misses such as X000XX0 contains four runs. The more a player's hits (and misses) cluster together, the fewer runs there are in his record. Column 4 presents the observed number of runs in each player's record (across all 48 games),

Table 2. *Runs Test—Philadelphia 76ers*

Players	Hits	Misses	Number of runs	Expected number of runs	z
Clint Richardson	124	124	128	125.0	−0.38
Julius Erving	459	425	431	442.4	0.76
Lionel Hollins	194	225	203	209.4	0.62
Maurice Cheeks	189	150	172	168.3	−0.41
Caldwell Jones	129	143	134	136.6	0.32
Andrew Toney	208	243	245	225.1	−1.88
Bobby Jones	233	200	227	216.2	−1.04
Steve Mix	181	170	176	176.3	0.04
Daryl Dawkins	250	153	220	190.8	−3.09**
M =	**218.6**	**203.7**	**215.1**	**210.0**	**−0.56**

* $p < .05$
** $p < .01$

and column 5 presents the expected number of runs if the outcomes of all shots were independent of one another. A comparison of columns 4 and 5 indicates that for five of the nine players the observed number of runs is actually greater than the expected number of runs, contrary to the streak-shooting hypothesis. The z statistic reported in column 6 tests the significance of the difference between the observed and the expected number of runs. A significant difference between these values exists for only one player (Dawkins), whose record includes significantly *more* runs than expected under independence, again, contrary to streak shooting.

Run tests were also performed on each player's records within individual games. Considering both the 76ers and their opponents together, we obtained 727 individual player game records that included more than two runs. A comparison of the observed and expected number of runs did not provide any basis for rejecting the null hypothesis (t (726) < 1).

Test of Stationarity

The notions of "the hot hand" and "streak shooting" entail temporary elevations of performance—i.e., periods during which the player's hit rate is substantially higher than his overall average. Although such changes in performance would produce a positive dependence between the outcomes of successive shots, it could be argued that neither the runs test nor the test of the serial correlation are sufficiently powerful to detect occasional "hot" stretches embedded in longer stretches of "normal" performance. To obtain a more

sensitive test of stationarity, or a constant hit rate, we partitioned the entire record of each player into nonoverlapping sets of four consecutive shots. We then counted the number of sets in which the player's performance was high (three or four hits), moderate (two hits), or low (zero or one hit). If a player is occasionally hot, then his record must include more high-performance sets than expected by chance.

The number of high, moderate, and low sets for each of the nine players were compared to the values expected by chance, assuming independent shots with a constant hit rate (derived from column 5 of Table 1). For example, the expected proportions of high-, moderate-, and low-performance sets for a player with a hit rate of 0.5 are 5/16, 6/16, and 5/16, respectively. The results provided no evidence for nonstationarity, or streak shooting, as none of the nine χ^2 values approached statistical significance. This analysis was repeated four times, starting the partition into consecutive quadruples at the first, second, third, and fourth shot of each player's shooting record. All of these analyses failed to support the nonstationarity hypothesis.

Analysis of Stability across Games—Hot and Cold Nights

To determine whether players have more "hot" and "cold" nights than expected by chance, we compared the observed variability in their per game shooting percentages with the variability expected on the basis of their overall record. Specifically, we compared two estimates of the standard error of each players' per game shooting percentages: one based on the standard deviation of the player's shooting percentages for each game, and one derived from the player's overall shooting percentage across all games. If players' shooting percentages in individual games fluctuate more than would be expected under the hypothesis of independence, then the (Lexis) ratio of these standard errors (*SE* observed/*SE* expected) should be significantly greater than 1 (David, 1949). Seven 76ers played at least 10 games in which they took at least 10 shots per game, and thus could be included in this analysis (Richardson and C. Jones did not meet this criterion). The Lexis ratios for these seven players ranged from 0.56 (Dawkins) to 1.03 (Erving), with a mean of 0.84. No player's Lexis ratio was significantly greater than 1, indicating that variations in shooting percentages across games do not deviate from their overall shooting percentage enough to produce significantly more hot (or cold) nights than expected by chance.

Discussion

Before discussing these results, it is instructive to consider the beliefs of the Philadelphia 76ers themselves regarding streak shooting and the hot hand. Following a team practice session, we interviewed seven players and the coach who were asked questions similar to those asked of the basketball fans in Study 1.

Most of the players (six out of eight) reported that they have on occasion felt that after having made a few shots in a row they "know" they are going to make their next shot—that they "almost can't miss." Five players believed that a player "has a better chance of making a shot after having just made his last two or three shots than he does after having just missed his last two or three shots." (Two players did not endorse this statement and one did not answer this question.) Seven of the eight players reported that after having made a series of shots in a row, they "tend to take more shots than they normally would." All of the players believed that it is important "for the players on a team to pass the ball to someone who has just made several (two, three, or four) shots in a row." Five players and the coach also made numerical estimates. Five of these six respondents estimated their field goal percentage for shots taken after a hit (mean: 62.5%) to be higher than their percentage for shots taken after a miss (mean: 49.5%).

It is evident from our interview that the Philadelphia 76ers—like our sample of basketball fans, and probably like most players, spectators, and students of the game—believe in the hot hand, although our statistical analyses provide no evidence to support this belief.

It could be argued that streak shooting exists but it is not common and we failed to include a "real" streak shooter in our sample of players. However, there is a general consensus among basketball fans that Andrew Toney is a streak shooter.

In an informal poll of 18 recreational basketball players who were asked to name five streak shooters in the NBA, only two respondents failed to include Andrew Toney, and he was the first player mentioned by half the respondents. Despite this widespread belief that Toney runs hot and cold, his runs of hits and misses did not depart from chance expectations.[2] We have also analyzed the field goal records of two other NBA teams: the New Jersey Nets (13 games) and the New York Knicks (22 games). These data were recorded from live television broadcasts. A parallel analysis of these records provides evidence consistent with the findings reported above. Of seven New York Knicks and seven New Jersey Nets, only one player exhibited a significant positive correlation between successive shots (Bill Cartwright of the Knicks). Thus, only two of the 23 major players on three NBA teams produced significant serial correlations, one of which was positive, and the other negative.

The failure to detect evidence of streak shooting might also be attributed to the selection of shots by individual players and the defensive strategy of opposing teams. After making one or two shots, a player may become more confident and attempt more difficult shots; after missing a shot, a player may get conservative and take only high-percentage shots. This would obscure any evidence of streak shooting in players' performance records. The same effect may be produced by the opposing team's defense. Once a player has made one or two shots, the opposing team may intensify their defensive pressure on that player and "take away" his good shots. Both of these factors may operate in the game and they are probably responsible for the (small) negative correlation between successive shots. However, it remains to be seen whether the elimination of these factors would yield data that are more compatible with people's expectations. The next two studies examine two different types of shooting are uncontaminated by shot selection or defensive data that pressure.

STUDY 3: PROFESSIONAL BASKETBALL FREE-THROW DATA

Free-throw data permit a test of the dependence between successive shots that is free from the contaminating effects of shot selection and opposing defense. Free throws, or foul shots, are commonly shot in pairs, and they are always shot from the same location without defensive pressure. If there is a positive correlation between successive shots, we would expect players to hit a higher percentage of their second free throws after having made their first free throw than after having missed their first free throw. Recall that our survey of basketball fans found that most fans believe there is positive dependency between successive free throws, though this belief was not as strong as the corresponding belief about field goals. The average estimate of the chances that a 70% free-throw shooter would make his second free throw was 74% after making the first shot and 66% after missing the first shot.

Do players actually hit a higher percentage of their second free throws after having just *made* their first free throw than after having just *missed* their first free throw? Table 3 presents these data for all pairs of free throws by Boston Celtics players during the 1980–1981 and the 1981–1982 seasons. These data were obtained from the Celtics' statistician. Column 2 presents the probability of a hit on the second free throw given a *miss* on the first free throw, and column 3 presents the probability of a hit on the second free throw given a *hit* on the first free throw. The correlations between the first and the second shot are presented in column 4. These data provide no evidence that the outcome of the second free throw is influenced by the outcome of the first free throw. The correlations are positive for four players, negative for the other five, and none of them are significantly different from zero.[3]

STUDY 4: CONTROLLED SHOOTING EXPERIMENT

As an alternative method for eliminating the effects of shot selection and defensive pressure, we recruited members of Cornell's intercollegiate basketball teams to participate in a controlled shooting study. This experiment also allowed us to investigate the ability of players to predict their performance.

The players were 14 members of the men's varsity and junior varsity basketball teams at Cornell and 12 members of the women's varsity team. For each player we determined a distance from which his or her shooting percentage was roughly 50%. At this distance we then drew two 15-ft arcs on the floor from which each player took all of his or her shots. The centers of the arcs were located 60° out from the left and right sides of the basket. When shooting baskets, the players were required to move along the are between shots so that consecutive shots were never taken from exactly the same spot. Each player was to take 100 shots, 50 from each arc.[4]

Table 3. *Probability of Making a Second Free Throw Conditioned on the Outcome of the First Free Throw for Nine Members of the Boston Celtics during the 1980–1981 and 1981–1982 Seasons*

Players	$P(H_2/M_1)$	$P(H_2/H_1)$	Serial correlation r
Larry Bird	.91 (53)	.88 (285)	−.032
Cedric Maxwell	.76 (128)	.81 (302)	.061
Robert Parish	.72 (105)	.77 (213)	.056
Nate Archibald	.82 (76)	.83 (245)	.014
Chris Ford	.77 (22)	.71 (51)	−.069
Kevin McHale	.59 (49)	.73 (128)	.130
M.L. Carr	.81 (26)	.68 (57)	−.128
Rick Robey	.61 (80)	.59 (91)	−.019
Gerald Henderson	.78 (37)	.76 (101)	−.022

Note: The number of shots upon which each probability is based is given in parentheses.

The players were paid for their participation. The amount of money they received was determined by how accurately they shot and how accurately they predicted their hits and misses. This payoff procedure is described below. The initial analyses of the Cornell data parallel those of the 76ers.

Analysis of Conditional Probabilities

Do Cornell players hit a higher percentage of their shots after having just *made* their last shot (or last several shots), than after having just *missed* their last shot (or last several shots)? Table 4 displays these conditional probabilities for all players in the study. Column 5 presents the overall shooting percentage for each player ranging from 25 to 61% (mean: 47%). Columns 6 through 8 present the players' shooting percentages conditioned on having *hit* their last shot, their last two shots, and their last three shots, respectively. Columns 2 through 4 present the players' shooting percentages conditioned on having *missed* their last shot, their last two shots, and their last three shots, respectively. Column 9 presents the serial correlation for each player.

A comparison of players' shooting percentages after hitting the previous shot (column 6, mean: 48%) with their shooting percentages after missing the previous shot (column 4, mean: 47%) indicates that for most players P (Hit/Hit) is less than P (Hit/Miss), contrary to the hot hand hypothesis. Indeed the serial correlations were negative for 14 out of the 26 players and only one player (9) exhibited a significant positive correlation. Comparisons of column 7, P (hit/2 hits), with column 3, P (hit/2 misses), and column 8, P (hit/3 hits), with column 2, P (hit/3 misses), lead to the same conclusion (paired t's < 1 for all three comparisons). Additional analyses show that the probability of a hit following a "hot" period (three or four hits in the last four shots) was not higher (mean: 46%) than the probability of a hit (mean: 47%) following a "cold" period (zero or one hit in the last four shots).

Analysis of Runs

Table 5 displays the results of the Wald-Wolfowitz run test for each player (Siegel, 1956). Recall that for this test, each streak of consecutive hits or misses is counted as a run. Column 4 presents the observed number of runs in each player's performance record, and column 5 presents the number of runs expected by chance. A comparison of these two columns reveals 14 players with slightly more runs than expected and 12 players with slightly fewer than expected. The z statistic reported in column 6 shows that only the

ble 4. *Probability of Making a Shot Conditioned on the Outcome of Previous Shots for All Cornell Players*

ayer	P (hit/3 misses)	P (hit/2 missed)	P (hit/1 miss)	P (hit)	P (hit/1 hit)	P (hit/2 hits)	P (hit/3 hits)	Serial Correlation r
ales								
	.44 (9)	.50 (18)	.61 (46)	.54 (100)	.49 (53)	.48 (25)	.50 (12)	−.118
	.43 (28)	.33 (42)	.35 (65)	.35 (100)	.35 (34)	.25 (12)	.00 (3)	−.001
	.67 (6)	.68 (19)	.49 (39)	.60 (100)	.67 (60)	.62 (40)	.60 (25)	.179
	.47 (15)	.45 (29)	.43 (53)	.40 (90)	.36 (36)	.23 (13)	.33 (3)	−.073
	.75 (12)	.60 (30)	.47 (57)	.42 (100)	.36 (42)	.40 (15)	.33 (6)	−.117
	.25 (12)	.38 (21)	.48 (42)	.57 (100)	.65 (57)	.62 (37)	.65 (23)	.173
	.29 (7)	.50 (16)	.47 (32)	.56 (75)	.64 (42)	.63 (27)	.65 (17)	.174
	.50 (6)	.50 (12)	.52 (25)	.50 (50)	.46 (24)	.64 (11)	.57 (7)	−.062
	.35 (20)	.33 (30)	.35 (46)	.54 (100)	.72 (53)	.79 (38)	.83 (30)	.370**
	.57 (7)	.50 (14)	.64 (39)	.59 (100)	.79 (38)	.60 (35)	.57 (21)	−.058
	.57 (7)	.61 (18)	.56 (41)	.58 (100)	.59 (58)	.62 (34)	.62 (21)	.025
	.41 (17)	.43 (30)	.46 (56)	.44 (100)	.42 (43)	.39 (18)	.43 (7)	−.046
	.40 (5)	.32 (13)	.67 (39)	.61 (100)	.58 (60)	.56 (60)	.50 (18)	−.084
	.50 (6)	.62 (16)	.60 (40)	.59 (100)	.58 (59)	.58 (59)	.60 (20)	−.031
males								
	.67 (9)	.61 (23)	.55 (51)	.48 (100)	.42 (48)	.45 (20)	.33 (9)	−.132
	.43 (28)	.36 (44)	.31 (65)	.34 (100)	.41 (34)	.36 (14)	.40 (5)	.104
	.36 (25)	.38 (40)	.33 (60)	.39 (100)	.49 (39)	.42 (19)	.50 (8)	.154
	.27 (30)	.33 (45)	.34 (68)	.33 (100)	.29 (31)	.33 (9)	.33 (3)	−.048
	.22 (27)	.36 (42)	.34 (64)	.35 (100)	.37 (35)	.50 (12)	.20 (5)	.028
	.54 (11)	.58 (26)	.52 (54)	.46 (100)	.38 (45)	.41 (17)	.29 (7)	−.141
	.32 (25)	.28 (36)	.36 (58)	.41 (100)	.49 (41)	.65 (20)	.62 (13)	.126
	.67 (9)	.55 (20)	.57 (47)	.53 (100)	.50 (52)	.58 (26)	.73 (15)	−.075
	.46 (13)	.55 (29)	.47 (55)	.45 (100)	.41 (44)	.47 (17)	.50 (8)	−.064
	.32 (19)	.34 (29)	.46 (54)	.47 (100)	.47 (45)	.67 (21)	.71 (14)	.004
	.50 (10)	.56 (23)	.51 (47)	.53 (100)	.56 (52)	.50 (28)	.39 (13)	.047
	.32 (37)	.32 (54)	.27 (74)	.25 (100)	.20 (25)	.00 (5)	— (0)	.036
$=$	**.45**	**.47**	**.47**	**.47**	**.48**	**.49**	**.49**	**.015**

te: Since the first shot cannot be conditioned, the parenthetical values in columns 4 and 6 sum one less than to the parenthetical value in column 5. The mber of shots upon which each probability is based is given in parentheses.

$p < .05$
$p < .01$

Table 5. *Runs Test—Cornell Players*

Player	Hits	Misses	Number of runs	Expected number of runs	z
Males					
1	54	46	56	50.7	−1.08
2	35	65	46	46.5	0.11
3	60	40	40	49.0	1.89
4	36	54	47	44.2	−0.62
5	42	58	55	49.7	−1.09
6	57	43	41	50.0	1.85
7	42	33	31	38.0	1.64
8	25	25	27	26.0	−0.29
9	54	46	32	50.7	3.78**
10	60	40	51	49.0	−0.42
11	58	42	48	49.7	0.35
12	44	56	52	50.3	−0.35
13	61	39	52	48.6	−0.72
14	59	41	50	49.4	−0.13
Females					
1	48	52	57	50.9	−1.22
2	34	66	41	45.9	1.09
3	39	61	41	48.6	1.60
4	32	68	46	44.5	−0.34
5	36	64	45	47.1	0.45
6	46	54	57	50.7	−1.28
7	41	59	43	49.4	1.33
8	53	47	54	50.8	−0.64
9	45	55	53	50.5	−0.51
10	46	54	50	50.7	0.14
11	53	47	48	50.8	0.57
12	25	75	41	38.5	−0.67
M =	*45.6*	*51.2*	*46.3*	*47.3*	*.21*

* $p < .05$
** $p < .01$

record of player 9 contained significantly more clustering (fewer runs) of hits and misses than expected by chance.

Test of Stationarity

As in Study 2, we divided the 100 shots taken by each player into nonoverlapping sets of four consecutive shots and counted the number of sets in which the player's performance was high (three or four hits), moderate (two hits), or low (zero or one hit). If a player is sometimes hot, the number of sets of high performance must exceed the number expected by chance, assuming a constant hit rate and independent shots. A χ^2 test for goodness of fit was used

to compare the observed and the expected number of high, moderate, and low sets for each player. As before, we repeated this analysis four times for each player, starting at the first, second, third, and fourth shots in each player's record. The results provided no evidence for departures from stationarity for any player but 9.

Test of Predictability

There is another cluster of intuitions about "being hot" that involves predictability rather than sequential dependency. If, on certain occasions, a player can predict a "hit" before taking a shot, he or she may have a justified sense of being "hot" even when the pattern of hits and misses does not stray from chance expectation. We tested players' ability to predict hits and misses by having them bet on the outcome of each upcoming shot. Before every shot, each player chose whether to bet high in which case he or she would win 5¢ for a hit and lose 4¢ for a miss; or bet *low,* in which case he or she would win 2¢ for a hit and lose 1¢ for a miss. The players were advised to bet high when they felt confident in their shooting ability, and to bet low when they did not.

We also obtained betting data from another player who observed the shooter. The players were run in pairs, alternating between the roles of "shooter" and "observer." On each trial, the observer also bet high or low on the outcome of the upcoming shot. The shooter and observer did not know each other's bets. Each player was paid $2, plus or minus the amount of money won or lost on the bets made as a shooter and observer.

If players can predict their hits and misses, their bets should correlate with their performance. The correlations between the shooters' performance and the bets made by the shooters and observers are presented in Table 6. These data reveal that the players were generally unsuccessful in predicting hits and misses. The average correlation between the shooters' bets and their performance, presented in column 2, was .02. Only 5 of the 26 individual correlations were statistically significant, of which 4 were quite low (.20 to .22), and the 5th was negative (−.51). The four small but significant positive correlations may reflect either a limited ability to predict the outcome of an upcoming shot, or a tendency to try harder following a high bet.

As one might expect, the observers were also unsuccessful in predicting the shooters' performance. The average correlation between the observers' bets and the shooters' performance, presented in column 3, was .04. On the other hand, the bets of both shooters and observers *were* correlated with the outcome of the shooter's *previous* shot as shown in columns 4 and 5 (mean $r = .40$ for the shooters and .42 for the observers). It appears that both the shooter and observer anticipated a hit if the shooter had made the last shot. This betting strategy, which reflects a belief in the hot hand, produced chance performance because of the absence of a positive serial correlation. It also produced agreement between shooters' and observers' bets (column 6, mean $r = .22$) that vanishes when the effect of the previous shot is partialed out (column 7, mean $r = .05$).

DISCUSSION

This article investigated beliefs and facts concerning the sequential characteristics of hits and misses in basketball. Our survey shows that basketball fans believe that a player's chances of hitting a basket are greater following a hit than following a miss. Similar beliefs were expressed by professional basketball players. However, the outcomes of both field goal and free throw attempts were largely independent of the outcome of the previous attempt. Moreover, the frequency of streaks in players' records did not exceed the frequency predicted by a binomial model that assumes a constant hit rate. A controlled experiment, with the varsity players of Cornell University, led to the same conclusions. With the exception of one player, no significant correlation between shots was found. Players' predictions of their own performance, expressed in the form of a betting game, revealed a consistent belief in the hot hand, although their actual performance did not support this belief. Evidently, the sense of being "hot" does not predict hits or misses.

How can we account for the prevalent belief in streak shooting despite the absence of sequential dependencies? This phenomenon could be due to a memory bias. If long sequences of hits (or misses) are more memorable than alternating sequences, the observer is likely to overestimate the correlation between successive shots. Alternatively, the belief in the hot hand may be caused by a misperception of chance that operates even when the data are in front of the subject rather than retrieved from memory.

The misperception hypothesis received support from our study of 100 basketball fans (Experiment 1). Following the survey, we presented each fan with six different sequences of hits (indicated by X's) and misses (indicated by O's). Subjects were asked to classify each sequence as "chance shooting," "streak shooting," or "alternate shooting." Chance shooting was defined as sequences of hits and misses that are just like the sequences of heads and tails usually found when flipping coins. Streak shooting and alternate shooting were defined as clusters of hits and misses that are longer or shorter, respectively, than the clusters of heads and tails usually found in coin tossing.

All six sequences included 11 hits and 10 misses. They differed in the number of runs (9, 11, ..., 19), and thus the probability of alternation (0.4, 0.5, ..., 0.9, respectively), or the probability that the outcome of a given shot will be different from the outcome of the previous shot. In coin

Table 6. *Correlations between Bets and Performance for all Cornell Players*

Player	Shooter's bets with shooter's hits	Observer's bets with shooter's hits	Shooter's bets with previous shot	Observer's bets with previous shot	Observer's bets with shooter's bets	Observer's bets with shooter's bets, partialling out previous shot
Males						
1	.06	−.06	.44**	.76**	.25*	−.14
2	−.01	−.06	.94**	.35**	.32**	−.03
3	−.07	.01	.35**	.38**	.37**	.27**
4	−.16	−.20*	.20	.75**	.24*	.14
5	−.03	.01	.38**	−.13	−.12	−.08
6	.22*	.24*	.36**	.72**	.27**	.02
7	.18	.24*	.17	.66**	−.03	−.19
8	.04	.21	.33**	.13	.21	.18
9	.05	.21*	.47**	.55**	.12	−.19
10	.00	−.19	.31**	.09	.27**	.26*
11	−.51*	.03	.15	.12	.07	.05
12	.20*	.00	.37**	.36**	.31**	.20*
13	.00	−.11	.23*	.42**	.19	.11
14	.20*	−.05	.21*	.59**	.27**	.19
Females						
1	−.04	−.09	.52**	.37**	.24*	.06
2	.17	.05	.39**	.72**	.40**	.13
3	.05	.16	.40**	.72**	.24*	−.08
4	−.05	−.03	.49**	.12	.18	.14
5	.03	.14	.43**	.42**	.43**	.30**
6	.03	.05	.31**	.53**	.02	−.18
7	.22*	.20*	.65**	.71**	.53**	.13
8	.07	.13	.50**	−.05	.35**	.43**
9	.11	−.01	.49**	.39**	.23*	.05
10	−.01	.11	.62**	.63**	.10	−.48**
11	.11	.18	.33**	.18	.22*	.17
12	.02	−.07	.35**	.42**	−.03	−.21*
M =	**.02**	**.04**	**.40**	**.42**	**.22**	**.05**

★ $p < .05$
★★ $p < .01$

tossing, the probability of alternation is 0.5—the outcome of a given trial is independent of the outcome of the previous trial. Streaks are produced when the probability of alternation is less than 0.5, and alternating sequences are produced when the probability of alternation is greater than 0.5. For example, the sequence X0X0X000XX0X0X00XXX0X, and its mirror image, which consist of 15 runs, were used for the probability of alternation of 0.7.

The percentage of "streak," and "chance" responses for each sequence is presented in Fig. 1. The percentage of "alternate" responses is the complement of these values. As expected, the tendency to perceive a sequence as streak shooting decreases with the probability of alternation. The

most significant feature of Fig. 1, however, is the respondents' perception of chance shooting. The sequences selected as best examples of chance shooting had probabilities of alternation of 0.7 and 0.8 rather than 0.5. Furthermore, the sequence with the probability of alternation of 0.5 (the proper example of chance shooting) was classified as chance shooting only by 32% of subjects, whereas 62% identified it as an example of streak shooting.

Evidently, people tend to perceive chance shooting as streak shooting, and they expect sequences exemplifying chance shooting to contain many more alternations than would actually be produced by a random (chance) process. Thus, people "see" a positive serial correlation in

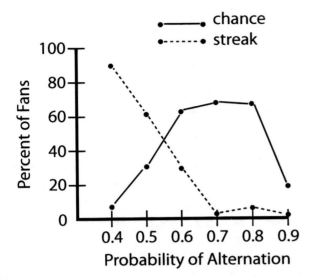

Figure 1. *Percentage of basketball fans classifying sequences of hits and misses as examples of streak shooting or chance shooting, as a function of the probability of alternation within the sequences.*

independent sequences, and they fail to detect a negative serial correlation in alternating sequences. Hence, people not only perceive random sequences as positively correlated, they also perceive negatively correlated sequences as random. These phenomena are very much in evidence even when the sequences are displayed to the subject rather than retrieved from memory. Selective coding or biased retrieval, therefore, are not necessary for generating an erroneous belief in streak shooting, although they may enhance the effect. We attribute this phenomenon to a general misconception of the laws of chance associated with the belief that small as well as large sequences are representative of their generating process (Tversky & Kahneman, 1974). This belief induces the expectation that random sequences should be far more balanced than they are, and the erroneous perception of a positive correlation between successive shots. These observations are highly consistent with earlier work on the perception of randomness in other contexts. Specifically, the "chance" curve in Fig. 1 closely resembles Falk's (1981) data on the judged randomness of sequences of 21 yellow and green cards.

This account explains both the formation and maintenance of the erroneous belief in the hot hand: If random sequences are perceived as streak shooting, then no amount of exposure to such sequences will convince the player, the coach, or the fan that the sequences are in fact random. The

more basketball one watches and plays, the more opportunities one has to observe what appears to be streak shooting. In order to appreciate the sequential properties of basketball data, one has to realize that coin tossing produces just as many runs. If people's perceptions of coin tossing are biased, it should not be surprising that they perceive sequential dependencies in basketball when none exist.

The independence between successive shots, of course, does not mean that basketball is a game of chance rather than of skill, nor should it render the game less exciting to play, watch, or analyze. It merely indicates that the probability of a hit is largely independent of the outcome of previous shots, although it surely depends on other parameters such as skill, distance to the basket, and defensive pressure. This situation is analogous to coin tossing where the outcomes of successive tosses are independent but the probability of heads depends on measurable factors such as the initial position of the coin, and its angular and vertical momentum (see Keller, 1985). Neither coin tossing nor basketball are inherently random, once all the relevant parameters are specified. In the absence of this information, however, both processes may be adequately described by a simple binomial model. A major difference between the two processes is that it is hard to think of a credible mechanism that would create a correlation between successive coin tosses, but there are many factors (e.g., confidence, fatigue) that could produce positive dependence in basketball. The availability of plausible explanations may contribute to the erroneous belief that the probability of a hit is greater following a hit than following a miss.

The preceding discussion applies to the perception of randomness in general with no special reference to sports events or basketball. However, there are several specific factors linked to basketball that might enhance the effect. First, the intuition that a player is "hot" may stem from observations of his defense, hustling, and passing, which may be overgeneralized to shooting as well. Second, the coding of events may also help support the belief in sequential dependency. The common occurrence of a shot that pops out of the rim of the basket after having seemingly been made may be interpreted as continued evidence of being "hot" if the player had made the previous shot and as evidence of being "cold" if the player missed the previous shot (cf. Gilovich, 1983).

The present data demonstrate the operation of a powerful and widely shared cognitive illusion. Such illusions or biases have been observed in the judgments of both laypeople and experts in several fields (see, e.g., Fischhoff, Slovic, & Lichtenstein, 1981; Kahneman, Slovic, & Tversky, 1982; Nisbett & Ross, 1980; Tversky & Kahneman, 1983). If the present results are surprising, it is because of the robustness with which the erroneous belief in the "hot hand" is held by experienced and knowledgeable observers. This belief is particularly intriguing because it has consequences for the conduct of the game. Passing the ball to the player who is "hot" is a common strategy endorsed by basketball players. It is also anticipated by the opposing team who can concentrate on guarding the "hot" player. If another player, who is less "hot" on that particular day, is equally skilled, then the less guarded player would have a better chance of scoring. Thus the belief in the "hot hand" is not just erroneous, it could also be costly.

NOTES

1. Feller (1968) describes some striking examples of the nonintuitive character of chance processes (e.g., matching birthdates or the change of sign in a random walk), which he attributes to "faulty intuitions" about chance and common misconceptions of "the law of averages."

2. Why do people share the belief that Toney, for example, is a streak shooter if his record does not support this claim? We conjecture that the players who are perceived as "streak shooters" are the good shooters who often take long (and difficult) shots. Making a few such shots in a row is indeed a memorable event, the availability of which may bias one's recollection of such players' performance records (Tversky & Kahneman, 1973). The finding that 77% of the players identified as "streak shooters" in our survey play the guard position provides some support for our conjecture because long shots are usually taken by guards more frequently than by other players.

3. Aggregating data across players is inappropriate in this case because good shooters are more likely to make their first shot than poor shooters. Consequently, the good shooters contribute more observations to P (hit/hit) than to P (hit/miss) while the poor shooters do the opposite, thereby biasing the pooled estimates.

4. Three of the players were not able to complete all 100 shots.

REFERENCES

David, F. N. (1949). *Probability theory for statistical methods.* Cambridge: Cambridge Univ. Press.

Falk, R. (1981). The perception of randomness. In *Proceedings, Fifth International Conference for the Psychology of Mathematics Education.* Grenoble, France.

Feller, W. (1968). *An introduction to probability theory and its applications* (Vol. 1, 3rd ed). New York: Wiley.

Fischhoff, B., Slovic, P., & Lichtenstein, S. (1981). Lay foibles and expert fables in judgments about risk. In T. O'Riordan & R. K. Turner (Eds.), *Progress in resource management and environmental planning* (Vol. 3). Chichester: Wiley.

Gilovich, T. (1983). Biased evaluation and persistence in gambling. *Journal of Personality and Social Psychology,* 40, 797–808.

Kahneman, D., Slovic, P., & Tversky, A., (Eds.). (1982). *Judgment under uncertainty: Heuristics and biases.* New York: Cambridge Univ. Press.

Keller, J. B. (1985). The probability of heads. *American Mathematical Monthly.*

Nisbett, R., & Ross, L. (1980). *Human inference: Strategies and shortcomings of social judgment.* New Jersey: Prentice-Hall.

Siegel, S. (1956). *Nonparametric statistics.* New York: McGraw-Hill.

Tversky, A., & Kahneman, D. (1971). Belief in the law of small numbers. *Psychological Bulletin,* 76, 105–110.

Tversky, A., & Kahneman, D. (1973). Availability: A heuristic for judging frequency and probability. *Cognitive Psychology,* 5, 207–232.

Tversky, A., & Kahneman, D. (1974). Judgment under uncertainty: Heuristics and biases. *Science (Washington, D.C.),* 185, 1124–1131.

Tversky, A., & Kahneman, D. (1983). Extensional vs. intuitive reasoning: The conjunction fallacy in probability judgment. *Psychological Review,* 91, 293–315.

Wagenaar, W. A. (1972). Generation of random sequences by human subjects. A critical survey of literature. *Psychological Bulletin,* 77, 65–72. (Accepted March 15, 1985)

Try It, You'll Like It

The Influence of Expectation, Consumption, and Revelation on Preferences for Beer

LEONARD LEE, SHANE FREDERICK, AND DAN ARIELY

The quality of an experience is jointly determined by bottom-up processes, which reflect character-istics of the stimulus impinging on the perceiver's sensory organs, and top-down processes, which reflect the perceiver's beliefs, desires, and expectations. The role of each kind of process can be illustrated by the perception of ambiguous figures, such as Jastrow's famous rabbit-duck illusion. Visual experience surely depends on what is in the image, but may also be affected by what one expects to see. Although Jastrow's figure is never interpreted as a giraffe or a scorpion, it might look like either a rabbit or a duck depending on which concept has been primed.

The influence of top-down and bottom-up processes has been a central theme across many domains of psychology. Visual perception is affected by prior conceptual structures, as well as by characteristics of the visual stimulus itself (Biederman, 1972; Palmer, 1975); assessments of a person's ability are influenced by expectations of his or her ability, as well as by objective performance measures (Darley & Gross, 1983; Jones, Rock, Shaver, Goethals, & Ward, 1968); judgments of extended events are driven by the quality of one's experiences and the interpretation one imposes on them (Brief, Butcher, George, & Link 1993; David, Green, Martin, & Suls, 1997); the enjoyment of a film is influenced by expectations of its quality, as well as by its true quality and the conditions under which it is viewed (Klaaren, Hodges, & Wilson, 1994); and even memories can be colored by one's theories of what should

have occurred, rather than what did occur (Cohen, 1981; Stangor & McMillan, 1992).

The domain of food and drinks provides a particu-larly fertile testing ground for researching the influence of conceptual information on subjective experiences: Coke is rated higher when consumed from a cup bearing the brand logo rather than from an unmarked cup (McClure et al., 2004); a slice of turkey is rated higher if thought to come from a popular brand rather than an unpopular one (Makens, 1965); Perrier is preferred to Old Fashioned Seltzer when the beverages are consumed with the labels showing, but not otherwise (Nevid, 1981); preference for one's favorite beer vanishes if the labels on the beers being compared are removed (Allison & Uhl, 1964); describing the protein of nutrition bars as "soy protein" causes them to be rated as more grainy and less flavorful than when the word "soy" is not included (Wansink, Park, Sonka, & Morganosky, 2000); bitter coffee seems less so if consumers are repeatedly misinformed that it is not bitter (Olson & Dover, 1978); strawberry yogurt and cheese spreads are liked more if labeled "full-fat" than if labeled "low-fat" (Wardle & Solomons, 1994); and, intriguingly, people eat more vanilla ice cream if it is accurately labeled "high fat" than if it is labeled "low fat" (Bowen, Tomoyasu, Anderson, Carney, & Kristal, 1992).

Besides documenting the separate influences of top-down and bottom-up processes, some researchers have examined how they interact by manipulating when conceptual information is presented relative to the experience. For example, Hoch and Ha (1986) showed respondents ads exaggerating the qualities of a J.C. Penney shirt either before or after the respondents examined it and found that they spent more time examining the fabric and evaluated the shirt more favorably if the information was provided before the examination (see also Levin & Gaeth, 1988). This suggests that prior knowledge can affect the allocation of attention or use of information (such as the time spent examining the stitching). However, it remains unclear whether knowledge can also change the experience itself (e.g., the tactile quality of the material), just as it remains unclear in most taste-test studies whether brand identity is just another input to respondents' overall evaluation (a valued attribute in its own right, like temperature or sweetness) or whether it modifies the actual gustatory experience (by affecting the tongue's chemoreceptors or the part of the brain that interprets the gustatory signal).

In the current research, we examined whether information affects perception by comparing people's preference for unadulterated beer versus beer mixed with a small amount of balsamic vinegar—an additive that most people find conceptually offensive.[1] We compared preferences across three conditions: a blind condition, in which the additive was not mentioned, and two disclosure conditions, in which the identity of the secret ingredient was revealed either before tasting or after tasting. The latter (after) condition allowed us to diagnose whether conceptual information affects only preferences or whether it changes one's experience of the stimulus. To understand how the after condition could shed light on the interaction of top-down and bottom-up processes, suppose Allison and Uhl (1964) had included a third condition in which participants received brand information after they sampled the five beers. If this group had rated the beers similarly to the before group (the ordinary, or control, condition in which participants knew which brand they were consuming), this would suggest that brand information is a distinct, separate input to evaluations—an expression of support for one's preferred brand. If, however, the ratings of the after group had resembled the ratings of the blind group, this would suggest that brand information affects the taste experience itself, but that once the taste is established, brand information has no further influence and does not alter the way in which people characterize their consumption experience.

A similar design could be used in studies investigating the role of affective expectations. For example, in a study by Wilson, Lisle, Kraft, and Wetzel (1989), all participants saw three truly funny cartoons, followed by three not-so-funny ones. Half of the participants were told nothing about the contents of the cartoons, whereas the other half were led to expect that all the cartoons would be funny. The misinformed group rated the less funny cartoons to be just as funny as the truly funny ones. A videotape of their facial expressions suggested that positive expectations improved their cartoon-viewing experience, that the ratings were not just an experimental demand effect reflecting respondents' reluctance to admit that they did not "get" the cartoons that were allegedly found funny by other people. Nevertheless, it would have been instructive to know how respondents would have rated the cartoons if they had received the bogus information about other people's ratings *after* seeing the cartoons. Would their prior "unbiased" experience govern their ultimate evaluation, or would they also be affected by this delayed (mis)information?

EXPERIMENTAL APPROACH

In the first three experiments of the present study, respondents consumed two beer samples: one unadulterated sample and one sample of "MIT brew," which contained several drops of balsamic vinegar—a beer flavoring that most participants find conceptually offensive, but that does not, at this concentration, degrade the beer's flavor (in fact, it slightly improves it). Respondents were randomly assigned to one of three conditions. In the *blind* condition, they tasted the two samples without any information about the contents. In the *before* condition, they were told which beer contained balsamic vinegar, prior to tasting either. In the *after* condition, they first tasted the beers and were then told which beer contained balsamic vinegar (see Fig. 1).

If top-down processes play no role in taste preferences, preferences in the three conditions should not differ (blind ≈ before ≈ after). However, if knowledge does influence preferences, as our intuition and prior research suggest, preference for the MIT brew should be lower in both disclosure conditions than in the blind condition. Of greatest interest were the results of the after condition. If the presence of a conceptually aversive additive is an independent input to evaluations, the timing of the information should not matter, and preferences for the MIT brew should be reduced equally in the two disclosure conditions (blind > before ≈ after). However, if expectations influence the consumption experience itself, preference for the MIT brew should be markedly lower in the before condition than in the after condition (blind ≥ after > before).

EXPERIMENTS 1–3: PREFERENCES

Our first three experiments were conducted at two local pubs: The Muddy Charles and The Thirsty Ear. Patrons were approached and asked to participate in a short study involving free beer. Those who agreed (nearly everyone) tasted two 2-oz. samples of beer: "regular" beer (Budweiser or Samuel Adams) and the MIT brew, which included several drops of balsamic vinegar.[2]

There were 388 participants in total (90 in Experiment 1, 139 in Experiment 2, and 159 in Experiment 3). In each experiment, participants were randomly assigned to one of the three experimental conditions (blind, before, and after). After tasting the two samples, respondents indicated their preference between them. In Experiment 1, participants simply indicated which of the two samples they liked more. In Experiment 2, they also received a full (10-oz.) serving of the sample they preferred. In Experiment 3, the blind condition was the same as in Experiment 2, but in the before and after conditions, participants received a full (10-oz.) glass of regular beer, some balsamic vinegar, a dropper, and the "secret recipe" ("add three drops of balsamic vinegar per ounce and stir"). We monitored how much balsamic vinegar participants actually added to their beer, and used this information to code their degree of preference for one beer over the other. It turned out that all participants added either the exact amount of balsamic vinegar specified by the recipe or none at all, creating a binary dependent measure.

As can be seen in Figure 2, preference for the MIT brew was higher in the blind condition (59%) than in the before condition (30%). This difference was significant overall, $F(1, 385) = 23.15, p_{rep} > .99, \eta^2 = .057$, and for each of the three experiments individually (all p_{rep}s > .95). More important, the preference for the MIT brew was significantly lower in the before condition than in the after condition, both overall (30% vs. 52%), $F(1,385) = 13.86, prep > .99, \eta^2 = .035$, and for each of the experiments individually (all p_{rep}s > .90). By contrast,

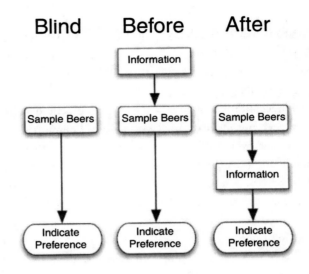

Blind   Before   After

Fig. 1. Illustration of the three experimental conditions, in which we manipulated whether information about the presence of balsamic vinegar in one of the samples was disclosed and if so, when it was disclosed relative to tasting and evaluation.

the after condition did not differ significantly from the blind condition, either overall (52% vs. 59%), $F(1, 385) = 1.17, p_{rep} = .66, \eta^2 = .003$, or for any of the individual experiments (all p_{rep}s < .56).

Together, the results show that preference for the MIT brew was affected by disclosure of its contents, but only if disclosure preceded tasting, which suggests that preferences are influenced primarily through the effect of expectations on the taste experience itself. Respondents in the after condition appeared content to let their experience dictate their preferences, and apparently did not reinterpret their experience to align with the mildly unsettling news about what they had just consumed. These results are compatible with those of Levin and Gaeth (1988), who found that hamburger falsely labeled as "25% fat" received slightly lower taste ratings if that fat content was reported before tasting than if it was reported after tasting, although the difference in their study was not significant (perhaps because people do not regard beef fat as tasting bad, even if they have health concerns about eating it).

EXPERIMENT 4: ARE THESE RESULTS OBVIOUS?

Our mothers often used creative labeling to trick us into eating something they knew we would otherwise oppose (e.g., by calling crab cakes "sea hamburgers"). They knew such deception was required to gain our consent, but that they need not maintain the lie *after* we had consumed the foods, and would often debrief us afterward, with smug satisfaction ("By the way, son, in case you were wondering, "sea" means "crab."). They suspected (correctly in most cases) that we could not "handle the truth" before eating, but could handle it after our senses had signaled that this was good stuff.

Were our mothers using an obvious strategy, or were they especially clever? To test whether the results we obtained are obvious, we presented Experiment 2 to 68 MIT students. After describing the procedure, we told them, truthfully, that the MIT brew had been chosen over regular beer by 70% of participants in the blind condition and by 41% in the before condition, and asked them to predict the percentage who chose it in the after condition, offering $50 for the most accurate prediction.

As can be seen from Figure 3, respondents could not generally predict the results. Predictions were uniformly spread between 41% and 70% (with some even falling

outside this interval). They were not clustered near the upper range of this interval, as would be predicted if our results could be foreseen. Thus, our results are not obvious—at least not to MIT students.

GENERAL DISCUSSION

Our study focused on the relative importance of, and interaction between, two different bases for preferences: knowledge (top down) and experience (bottom up). The results across three experiments suggest that information (about the presence of a conceptually offensive ingredient) influences preferences more when received before consumption than when received after consumption. The MIT brew was liked much less when disclosure preceded sampling than when respondents learned about the balsamic vinegar after they had tasted both samples. Indeed, disclosure of the secret ingredient after consumption did not significantly reduce preferences for our MIT brew (there were no significant differences between the blind

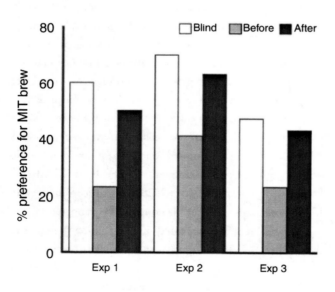

Fig. 2. Percentage of respondents preferring the MIT brew across the three conditions in Experiments 1 through 3.

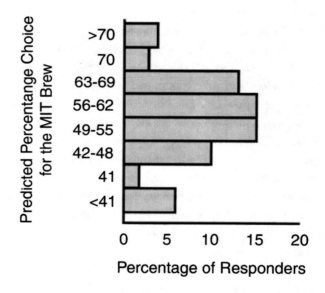

Fig. 3. Results from Experiment 4: distribution of respondents' predictions of the percentage of Experiment 2 participants in the after condition who preferred the MIT brew. The instructions gave the real preferences in the blind and before conditions: 70% and 41%, respectively.

and after conditions). Together, these results suggest that expectations affected real-time experience itself, not just people's post hoc characterization of the experience.

Our results raise several additional questions. First, how important are the temporal intervals between sensory experience, the receipt of other information, and the evaluative judgment? In our experiments, negative information received after consumption did not markedly reduce evaluations of the MIT brew. By contrast, Braun (1999) found that respondents who consumed diluted orange juice tainted with vinegar evaluated the juice markedly more favorably if they were later told that it was "sweet, pulpy, and pure." Her results may differ from ours because that misleading information was presented 30 min after respondents drank the orange juice, and during this time they may have partially forgotten the experience, which would have diminished its weight relative to the misinformation.

A second question raised by these experiments concerns the speed with which conceptual attitudes align with experiences. If people are coerced or tricked into discovering that they actually enjoy some unusual food (sea urchin roe), food additive (balsamic vinegar), or sexual practice (fill in the blank), do they eagerly consume it at the next opportunity, or do their prior expectations linger, despite the disconfirmation? In our experiments, preferences converged with experiences after only a single trial (recall that only 20% of participants thought balsamic vinegar would improve a beer's flavor, yet 52% in the after condition preferred the MIT brew). However, it remains unclear whether those respondents in the after condition who preferred the MIT brew would continue to prefer it on subsequent visits to the pub. Sometimes a single positive taste experience may extinguish preconceptions, but in other cases, the original negative conception may linger and gradually regain ascendance over fading taste memories. Tuorila, Cardello, and Lesher (1994) found that expectations quickly return, even after being dis-confirmed. In their study, respondents tasted normal and fat-free versions of saltine crackers and pound cake. Although a blind taste test disconfirmed respondents' expectations that fat-free products would taste worse, when the respondents came back to the lab a month later, they retained their original negative impressions of those products. A study by Klaaren et al. (1994) suggests that positive expectations may also linger. In that study, students who were told they would enjoy *The Immigrant* (a silent film starring Charlie Chaplin) not only reported greater enjoyment of the film than those who were not told this, but were also more likely to participate in a subsequent study involving a different Chaplin film. Moreover, their willingness to participate correlated only with their original affective expectation, and not with manipulations of their real-time experience (the comfort of the chair and the angle at which they were forced to view the film). These results suggest that hedonic theories (expectations) may sometimes outweigh hedonic experience as determinants of remembered and predicted utility.

A third question concerns how specific perceptual, attentional, and cognitive mechanisms mediate the effect of expectations on experience (or reported experience). One interpretation of our results is that people (reasonably) anticipated disliking the MIT brew, and this negative anticipatory emotion lingered to degrade their subsequent consumption experience (see Wilson & Klaaren, 1992). Another possibility, advanced by Hoch and Ha (1986), is that expectations bias informational search. They found that evaluations of J.C. Penney polo shirts were more favorable if participants were first told that the shirts were made with "great craftsmanship, styling and meticulous quality control" than if those claims were presented after participants had examined the shirts (and shirts of competing brands). Hoch and Ha proposed that the brand-specific claims induced respondents to devote more time to inspecting the J.C. Penney shirts, searching for information that confirmed the claims. It seems unlikely that participants in our before condition spent extra time consuming the MIT brew, searching for negative aspects of the experience. However, prior knowledge of the additive may have changed the way they interpreted their ambiguous beer experience (some combination of wet, bitter, sweet, sour, carbonated, and malty). When the secret ingredient was disclosed before consumption, they may have focused on the negative aspects of that multidimensional experience, and falsely attributed those negative elements to the vinegar rather than the beer. However, when the information was disclosed following the experience, they did not appear to attribute negative aspects of their ambiguous consumption experience to the presence of the balsamic vinegar. Thus, the malleability of one's tastes is likely influenced by the timing of attitude-discrepant information.

In a review of the influence of sensory expectation on sensory perception, Deliza and MacFie (1996) concluded that "it is an immensely complex topic which has had very little research attention" (p. 122). We agree. As emphasized by our discussion, the relative influence of perceptual and conceptual inputs on overall evaluations likely depends on the timing of the information, the timing of the judgment, the particular domain, and the range of sensory and cognitive processes engaged by the particular task instructions. We are therefore not confident that we could train pub goers to be willing to pay extra for the MIT brew. However, we are confident that our experimental approach will prove intellectually profitable to researchers interested in the relations among conceptual knowledge, experience, and the construction of preference.

Acknowledgments—We thank Stephen Garcia, Reid Hastie, Nathan Novemsky, Jonathan Schooler, and Timothy Wilson for their thoughtful comments and suggestions; the Muddy Charles and Thirsty Ear for letting us peddle our MIT brew; and Trader Joe's for making a balsamic vinegar that so nicely complements the subtle notes of light beers.

END NOTES

1. To verify our assumption that people would be averse to the idea of balsamic vinegar in beer, we asked 121 patrons of The Muddy Charles, a local pub, to rate how beer would taste if balsamic vinegar were added, using a scale ranging from 1 (*much worse*) to 10 (*much better*). Eighty percent of the respondents expected that balsamic vinegar would make the beer taste worse. The mean rating was 4.03, which was significantly below 0, $F(1, 119) = 22.45, p < .01$.

2. When the control beer was Samuel Adams, we added six drops. When it was the lighter Budweiser, we added four drops. Budweiser was used in the first two experiments, and Sam Adams in the third. We switched after discovering that Budweiser is not a very popular beer among our participants, many of whom even disputed whether it deserves to be called a "beer."

REFERENCES

ALLISON, R.I., & UHL, K.P. (1964). Influence of beer brand identification on taste perception. *Journal of Marketing Research, 1,* 36–39.

BIEDERMAN, I. (1972). Perceiving real-world scenes. *Science, 177,* 77–80.

BOWEN, D.J., TOMOYASU, N., ANDERSON, M., CARNEY, M., & KRISTAL, A. (1992). Effects of expectancies and personalized feedback on fat consumption, taste, and preference. *Journal of Applied Social Psychology, 22,* 1061–1079.

BRAUN, K.A. (1999). Postexperience advertising effects on consumer memory. *Journal of Consumer Research, 25,* 319–334.

BRIEF, A.P., BUTCHER, A.H., GEORGE, J.M., & LINK, K.E. (1993). Integrating bottom-up and top-down theories of subjective well-being: The case of health. *Journal of Personality and Social Psychology, 64,* 646–653.

COHEN, C.E. (1981). Person categories and social perception: Testing some boundaries of the processing effect of prior knowledge. *Journal of Personality and Social Psychology, 40,* 441–452.

DARLEY, J.M., & GROSS, P.H. (1983). A hypothesis-confirming bias in labeling effects. *Journal of Personality and Social Psychology, 44,* 20–33.

DAVID, J.P., GREEN, P.J., MARTIN, R., & SULS, J. (1997). Differential roles of neuroticism, extraversion, and event desirability for mood in daily life: An integrative model of top-down and bottom-up influences. *Journal of Personality and Social Psychology, 73,* 149–159.

DELIZA, R., & MACFIE, H.J.H. (1996). The generation of sensory expectation by external cues and its effect on sensory perception and he-donic ratings: A review. *Journal of Sensory Studies, 11,* 103–128.

HOCH, S.J., & HA, Y. (1986). Consumer learning: Advertising and the ambiguity of product experience. *Journal of Consumer Research, 13,* 221–233.

JONES, E.E., ROCK, L., SHAVER, K.G., GOETHALS, G.R., & WARD, L.M. (1968). Pattern of performance and ability attribution: An unexpected primacy effect. *Journal of Personality and Social Psychology, 10,* 317–340.

KLAAREN, K.J., HODGES, S.D., & WILSON, T.D. (1994). The role of affective expectations in subjective experience and decision-making. *Social Cognition, 12,* 77–101.

Levin, I., & Gaeth, G.J. (1988). How consumers are affected by the framing of attribute information before and after consuming the product. *Journal of Consumer Research, 15,* 374–378.

Makens, J.C. (1965). Effect of brand preference upon consumers' perceived taste of turkey meat. *Journal of Applied Psychology, 49,* 261–263.

McClure, S.M., Li, J., Tomlin, D., Cypert, K.S., Montague, L.M., & Montague, P.R. (2004). Neural correlates of behavioral preference for culturally familiar drinks. *Neuron, 44,* 379–387.

Nevid, J.S. (1981). Effects of brand labeling on ratings of product quality. *Perceptual and Motor Skills, 53,* 407–410.

Olson, J.C., & Dover, P.A. (1978). Cognitive effects of deceptive advertising. *Journal of Marketing Research, 15,* 29–38.

Palmer, S.E. (1975). The effects of contextual scenes on the identification of objects. *Memory & Cognition, 3,* 519–526.

Stangor, C., & McMillan, D. (1992). Memory for expectancy-congruent and expectancy-incongruent social information: A meta-analytic review of the social psychological and social developmental literatures. *Psychological Bulletin, 111,* 42–61.

Tuorila, H., Cardello, A.V., & Lesher, L.L. (1994). Antecedents and consequences of expectations related to fat-free and regular-fat foods. *Appetite, 23,* 247–263.

Wansink, B., Park, S.B., Sonka, S., & Morganosky, M. (2000). How soy labeling influences preference and taste. *International Food and Agribusiness Management Review, 3,* 85–94.

Wardle, J., & Solomons, W. (1994). Naughty but nice: A laboratory study of health information and food preferences in a community sample. *Health Psychology, 13,* 180–183.

Wilson, T.D., & Klaaren, K.J. (1992). Expectation whirls me round: The role of affective expectations on affective experiences. In M.S. Clark (Ed.), *Review of personality and social psychology: Vol. 14. Emotion and social behavior* (pp. 1–31). Newbury Park, CA: Sage.

Wilson, T.D., Lisle, D.J., Kraft, D., & Wetzel, C.G. (1989). Preferences as expectation-driven inferences: Effects of affective expectations on affective experience. *Journal of Personality and Social Psychology, 56,* 519–530.

The MPG Illusion

RICHARD P. LARRICK AND JACK B. SOLL

Many people consider fuel efficiency when purchasing a car, hoping to reduce gas consumption and carbon emissions. However, an accurate understanding of fuel efficiency is critical to making an informed decision. We will show that there is a systematic misperception in judging fuel efficiency when it is expressed as miles per gallon (MPG), which is the measure used in the United States. People falsely believe that the amount of gas consumed by an automobile decreases as a linear function of a car's MPG. The actual relationship is curvilinear. Consequently, people underestimate the value of removing the most fuel-inefficient vehicles. We argue that removing the most inefficient vehicles is where policy and popular opinion should be focused and that representing fuel efficiency in terms of amount of gas consumed for a given distance—which is the common representation outside of the United States (e.g., liters per 100 kilometers)—would make the benefits of greater fuel efficiency more transparent (1–3).

To illustrate these issues, consider the criticism that has been directed at adding hybrid engines to sport utility vehicles (SUVs). In a *New York Times* Op-Ed column, an automotive expert (4) has said that hybrid cars are like "fat-free desserts"—they "can make people feel as if they're doing something good, even when they're doing nothing special at all." The writer questions the logic of granting tax incentives to buyers of "a hypothetical hybrid Dodge Durango that gets 14 miles per gallon instead of 12 thanks to its second, electric power source" but not to a "buyer of a conventional,

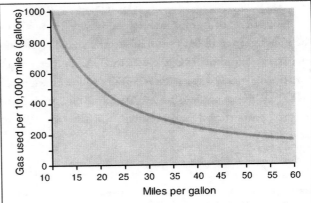

Gas consumed driving 10,000 miles. Gallons of gas used per 10,000 miles driven as a function of fuel efficiency of car (expressed in MPG).

gasoline-powered Honda Civic that gets 40 miles per gallon." The basic argument is correct: The environment would benefit most if all consumers purchased highly efficient cars that get 40 MPG, not 14, and incentives should be tied to achieving such efficiency. An implicit premise in the example, however, is that an improvement from 12 to 14 MPG is negligible. However, the 2 MPG improvement is actually a significant one in terms of reduction in gas consumption. The amount of gas used by a vehicle to drive 10,000 miles at different levels of MPG is shown in the graph above. A car that gets 12 MPG consumes 833 gallons to cover that distance (10,000/12); a car that gets 14 MPG consumes 714 gallons (10,000/14). The roughly 120-gallon reduction in fuel used is larger than the reduction achieved by replacing

Richard P. Larrick and Jack B. Soll, "Economics: The MPG Illusion," *Science*, vol. 320, no. 5883, pp. 1593-1594. Copyright © 2008 by American Association for the Advancement of Science. Reprinted with permission.

a car that gets 28 MPG with a car that gets 40 MPG over that distance.

We conducted three experiments to test whether people reason in a linear, but incorrect, fashion about gas mileage. In study 1 (5), 77 college students were asked to "assume that a person drives 10,000 miles per year and is contemplating changing from a current vehicle to a new one." They were asked to rank-order five pairs of old and new vehicles in order of "their benefit to the environment (i.e., which new car would reduce gas consumption the most compared to the original car)" using 1 for the most beneficial change and 5 for the least beneficial change.

Perceptions of improvement corresponded directly to the linear change in MPG and not to the actual reduction in gas consumption (see table below). Sixty percent of participants ordered the pairs according to linear improvement and 1% according to actual improvement. A third strategy, proportional improvement, was used by 10% of participants (5).

Using "miles per gallon" as a measure of fuel efficiency leads people to undervalue the benefits of replacing the most inefficient automobiles.

Study 2 tested whether the price that people would pay for more efficient vehicles would also show a linear relationship to MPG. College participants (n = 74) were told they had several vehicles from which to choose that were identical except for the efficiency of the engine (5). Participants were told to assume "you drive 10,000 miles per year for work, and this total amount cannot be changed. The baseline model gets 15 miles per gallon and costs $20,000."

Participants were then asked to state the highest price they would be willing to pay for five vehicles that varied only in the MPG of their engines. Mean willingness to pay (WTP) showed a clear linear relationship with MPG improvement. The best-fitting strategy for the majority of participants was a linear strategy (62%) followed by a proportional strategy (18%); the actual savings was the best-fitting strategy for only 15% of participants. Participants gave mean WTP values that, compared with expected gas savings, significantly undervalued the improvements to 19 and 25 MPG and overvalued the improvement to 55 MPG (6).

Study 3 was designed to test whether the MPG illusion could be decreased if fuel efficiency were framed in terms of gallons per 100 miles (GPM) instead of MPG. The study was presented in an online survey to 171 participants who were drawn from a national subject pool. Participants ranged in age from 18 to 75, with a median age of 35. All participants were given the following scenario (5): "A town maintains a fleet of vehicles for town employee use. It has two types of vehicles. Type A gets 15 miles per gallon. Type B gets 34 miles per gallon. The town has 100 Type A vehicles and 100 Type B vehicles. Each car in the fleet is driven 10,000 miles per year." They were then asked to choose a plan for replacing the original vehicles with corresponding hybrid models if the "overriding goal is to reduce gas consumption of the fleet and thereby reduce harmful environmental consequences."

Perceived and actual benefits of improving gas mileage

Change in vehicle pairs* (old vehicle to new vehicle)	Perceived rank in gas savings (mean)	Actual rank in gas savings	Actual reduction in gas consumption per 10,000 miles
34 MPG to 50 MPG	1.18	3	94.1
18 MPG to 28 MPG	1.95	1	198.4
42 MPG to 48 MPG	3.29	5	29.8
16 MPG to 20 MPG	3.73	2	125.0
22 MPG to 24 MPG	4.86	4	37.9

*Vehicle pairs are listed in order from largest linear change (34 to 50) to smallest linear change (22 to 24). Participants did not see the actual rank in gas savings or the actual reduction in gas consumption when they gave their answers.

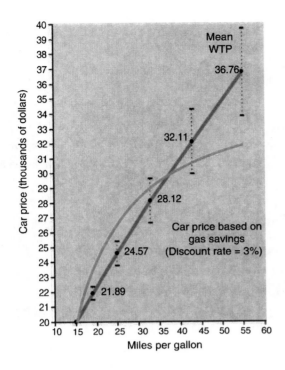

How much will you pay for gas savings? The straight blue line plots the mean willingness to pay for the different engines (95% confidence intervals are plotted for each mean). The curved orange line plots the value of the car, based on future gas savings (calculated using a 3% real discount rate, a 10-year life of the car, and a Spring 2007 gas price of $2.80 per gallon (5)).

One group of 78 participants was randomly assigned to a policy choice framed in terms of MPG. They were asked to choose between two options: (option 1) replace the 100 vehicles that get 15 MPG with vehicles that get 19 MPG and (option 2) replace the 100 vehicles that get 34 MPG with vehicles that get 44 MPG. Note that town fuel efficiency is improved more in option 1 (by 14,035 gallons) than in option 2 (by 6,684 gallons). As expected, the majority (75%) of participants in the MPG condition chose option 2, which offers a large gain in MPG but less fuel savings (95% confidence interval (CI) = 65 to 85%).

Participants in the GPM condition (n = 93) were given the same instructions as those in the MPG condition. In addition, they were told that the town "translates miles per gallon into how many gallons are used per 100 miles. Type

A vehicles use 6.67 gallons per 100 miles. Type B vehicles use 2.94 gallons per 100 miles." They read the same choice options as used in the MPG condition, including the MPG information, but with an additional stem that translated outcomes into GPM for the hybrid vehicles ((option 1) replace the 100 vehicles that get 6.67 gallons per 100 miles with vehicles that get 5.26 GPM and (option 2) replace the 100 vehicles that get 2.94 gallons per 100 miles with vehicles that get 2.27 GPM). As expected, the majority of participants (64%) in the GPM frame chose option 1, which offers a small gain in MPG but more fuel savings (CI = 54 to 74%). Overall, the percentage choosing the more fuel-efficient option increased from 25% in the MPG frame to 64% in the GPM frame (P < 0.01).

These studies have demonstrated a systematic misunderstanding of MPG as a measure of fuel efficiency. Relying on linear reasoning about MPG leads people to undervalue small improvements on inefficient vehicles. We believe this general misunderstanding of MPG has implications for both public policy and research on environmental decision-making (7–9). From a policy perspective, these results imply that the United States should express fuel efficiency as a ratio of volume of consumption to a unit of distance. Although MPG is useful for estimating the range of a car's gas tank, GPM allows consumers to understand exactly how much gas they are using on a given car trip or in a given year (10–14) and, with additional information, how much carbon they are releasing. GPM also makes cost savings from reduced gas consumption easier to calculate.

Although the current work has focused on misunderstanding the curvilinear relationship between MPG and fuel efficiency, other cognitive processes may also lead people to undervalue small improvements for inefficient cars. For example, if the 50 MPG fuel efficiency of popular small hybrids is used as a standard of comparison, small improvements on inefficient cars (e.g., a 5 MPG improvement from 15 to 20) look like "a drop in the bucket" (15,16).

The issue of translating car efficiency to gas consumption and carbon emissions is a special case of a general policy problem: People need a common metric to compare the consequences of their activities across a range of daily actions (14, 17). Choosing a more efficient car is just one means to reduce greenhouse gas emissions. Arming consumers with information about the relative greenhouse gas emissions of various activities expressed in a common metric can allow concerned consumers to make beneficial trade-offs in their daily decisions.

REFERENCES AND NOTES

1. Decision-makers often focus on the surface attributes of a decision problem and fail to recognize the more fundamental structure (2, 3).

2. C. K. Hsee, F. Yu, J. Zhang, Y. Zhang, *J. Consum. Res.* 30, 1 (2003).

3. D. Kahneman, S. Frederick, in *Heuristics and Biases: The Psychology of Intuitive Judgment,* T. Gilovich, D. Griffin, D. Kahneman, Eds. (Cambridge Univ. Press, New York, 2002), pp. 49–81.

4. J. L. Kitman, *New York Times,* 16 April 2006, §4, p. 12.

5. Materials, methods, and additional examples and analyses are available as supporting online material (SOM) on *Science* Online.

6. Section IV of the SOM provides additional analyses of WTP versus expected gas savings.

7. J. D. Sterman, L. B. Sweeney, *Clim. Change* 80, 213 (2007).

8. A. E. Tenbrunsel, K. A. Wade-Benzoni, D. M. Messick, M. H. Bazerman, *Acad. Manag. J.* 43, 854 (2000).

9. E. U. Weber, *Clim. Change,* 77, 103 (2006).

10. Section I of the SOM discusses possible GPM measures.

11. Decisions are often improved more by changing the decision context than by trying to improve individual reasoning (*12–14*).

12. J. Klayman, K. Brown, *Cognition* 49, 97 (1993).

13. J. W. Payne, J. R. Bettman, D. A. Schkade, *J. Risk Uncertain.* 19, 243 (1999).

14. R. H. Thaler, C. R. Sunstein, *Nudge* (Yale Univ. Press, New Haven, CT, 2008).

15. J. Baron, *J. Risk Uncertain.* 14, 301 (1997).

16. C. Heath, R. P. Larrick, G. Wu, *Cognit. Psychol.* 38, 79 (1999).

17. J. Baron, *J. Public Policy Market.* 23, 7 (2004).

18. The authors thank D. T. Robinson for advice on discount rate assumptions in study 3.

CHAPTER 16
Intelligence

The Brief and Sometimes Dirty History of Intelligence and IQ Tests

JOHN HATTIE AND RICHARD FLETCHER

For many a scientific discipline it would be uncommon to claim that its history has been plain sailing and that its evolution has been uncontroversial. It is because science advances in a cannibalistic manner, devouring old theories for new theories, that anything that challenges the status quo is often met with disdain or disbelief and then the debate becomes embroiled in controversy. A combination of time and evidence, however, often results in new theories taking hold and, like the old ways before them, they become the accepted doctrine—until, that is, another challenger arrives on the scene.

Intelligence testing and its history are no exception and, like most branches of science, it has been built on the strengths and weaknesses of previous theory and research. Thus, the present-day notions of intelligence and its measurement stand on diverse theoretical foundations. We should be pleased that there is a diversity in views, as this makes for spirited debate and serves to advance our understanding of this often-misunderstood and controversial concept. Indeed, if the history of IQ and its measurement were not without controversy, this would make for a boring chapter. For the most part, we say the debate is healthy, and long may it continue,

As with most historical events, the social norms and ideologies of the day played a significant role in the development of intelligence and IQ testing. These concepts did not develop in a social vacuum and the developers, as well as their practices and outcomes, were very much bound up in the context of the times. We would be the first to admit that there *is* a tarnished history that sits behind IQ testing, but such a history is what it is—a history—and thus it should not be used to prejudge the current debates on definitions and measurement. Most people today operate in a world of political, social and cultural diversity, as well as equity, which was not the case in the not-too-distant history when IQ testing was emerging. Suffice to say times have changed, and we should be thankful for that; scientists today are more aware of the socio-political climate and are more constrained by the ethical, moral and consequential outcomes of their research. There certainly has been a tendency to 'politicize the debate on intelligence, or even regard certain issues (pertaining to it) as taboo' (Howe, 1997: 13). We were also well aware of these reactions throughout the development of the *Test the Nation: The New Zealand IQ Test* programmes, as were the Television New Zealand producers and staff. It is important not to be put off because IQ has been misused and abused in the past, but rather to look at where it is now and judge for oneself the merits or demerits of such a concept and also to take comfort in the fact that we have learned from the mistakes and successes of others.

At the centre of the historical debate on IQ and its testing are arguments such as intelligence is immutable and intelligence testing is merely a sorting device for placing people into neat, identifiable categories from which they cannot escape. Antagonists such as Stephen Jay Gould

(1981) have argued that the perniciousness of the IQ testing process means that a single score does not take into account the complexity of the individual and context in which they exist. Above all, Gould argued that IQ tests are simply a tool to maintain the social order by confirming a person's societal position. After all, there are divisions in society and what better way to highlight these by using a seemingly 'objective' measure of ability. In other words, he argued IQ tests are blunt instruments with which to maintain societal order while at the same time allowing one to passively ignore the complex issues and problems that underlie differential levels of ability.

If only the debate were so simple. Sure, it is easy to debunk the whole notion of intelligence and the associated methods of assessing it. It is easy to claim that 'intelligence is what the intelligence test measures' but that because measurement definitions are so narrow and culturally specific we should ban all intelligence testing. But such an argument is akin to throwing the baby out with the bath water. Most psychologists and psychometricians would agree that intelligence testing has its limitations, but most would also support the notion of intelligence as being a major dimension in an individual's overall psychological make-up and, therefore, something that should not be ignored (as Wittgenstein commented, 'The strength of the rope lies not in any one thread but in the overlapping of many fibres'—intelligence is but one thread). Indeed, measures of intelligence can be important in many ways. Yes, IQ has had some bad press, and yes, it has not always been used in the most ethical or defensible ways, but the same could be said about personality and many other forms of testing. In today's highly competitive workforce the preponderance of personality tests and their use when making important employment decisions about people is on the rise, yet there is too little criticism of these methods. This lack of critique could be because there have been fewer 'dirty' stories about the misuse of these methods, less connection in the past between personality and race issues and because the scientific community has been less rigorous in its attention to the measurement and use of these methods. So let us take a look at the history of this controversial concept of intelligence and its measurement—but please keep in mind our earlier comment that the history of IQ, like so many other controversial topics, is located within a much larger social debate that reflects the beliefs, biases and prejudices of the prevailing views of the time. While it is easy to ridicule IQ based on its history, it is harder to refute the notion of individual differences in ability, be they intellectual or physical, especially when one can see such variation in everyday things.

> There are three kinds of intelligence: one kind understands things for itself, the other appreciates what others can understand, the third understands neither for itself nor through others. This first kind is excellent, the second good, and the third kind useless.
>
> Niccolò Machiavelli

THE EARLIEST ABILITY TESTING

From a historical perspective, ability testing can be traced back to ancient China in 2200 BC. For anyone wanting to work in the public office, the Chinese Emperor initiated a series of tests designed to find the most proficient candidates in areas such as law, agriculture, military affairs, finance and geography. The testing process was gruelling and often took many days to complete. The selection process began with preliminary examinations to identify the top 7 per cent, who then progressed to the district assessment. From here, between 1 per cent and 10 per cent moved to Peking for the final examinations, of which about 3 per cent would pass and become members of the Mandarin class of bureaucrats. The process was very much in the spirit of ranking individuals by merit and one can well imagine the stress and competitiveness of the candidates throughout the process. It was only as recently as 1906 that the exam was abolished. Such was the influence of the Chinese examination system that some European countries fashioned their civil service examinations in a similar manner and many continue it to this day.

FRANCIS GALTON

It was not until the nineteenth century, when the Industrial Revolution took hold and capitalism swung into full gear, that people began to show an interest in human capacity. Chiefly, it was the scientist Francis Galton (half-cousin of Charles Darwin) who began to develop methods for measuring many people's skills, and thus set his legacy as the doyen of measurement of individual differences. His incursions into the field of experimental psychology, as well as his immense contribution to statistics, marked Galton as a significant pioneer of the then developing area of psychological measurement.

Central to Galton's views on psychology was the influence of evolutionary theory. What intrigued him most was the notion of heredity—in particular, mental inheritance. In essence, he believed that reputation was a good measure of a person's mental ability and that genius was something passed on to the next generation. That is, prominent people tended to produce prominent children. The problem with his line of thinking was that it did not include the vitally important social factors affecting different groups. The son or daughter of a king and queen will one day be a king or queen, but to say this has anything to do with intelligence is hard to defend. While Galton's theory might suggest sons become as prominent as their fathers, this was, and perhaps still is (as in the case of George W. Bush), very much a function of social standing and privilege and not intelligence. Indeed, for many years (until the 1960s) some of the finest universities in the United States favoured admitting sons of alumni and aimed for graduates who would have the most influence on leadership in government and business—and thus had very small quotas on those who could enter on ability (Karabel, 2005).

There is no doubting Galton's influence on psychology and particularly his work on measuring individual differences. His main books, *Hereditary Genius* (1869), and *Inquiries into Human Faculty and its Development* (1907) were serious academic works that aimed at shedding light on the mental inheritance and the improvement of races. These books laid the foundation of the eugenics movement, which was later taken up with great zeal by the intelligence testers in the United States at the beginning of the twentieth century. What the eugenics movement sought was to regulate marriage and family size according to hereditary parental capacity and (in Galton's case) this was defined as mental capacity. The argument was that if your parents were bright then you should be allowed to marry and produce offspring. The opposite was also the case and was, by and large, the controversial dimension—dull people should not be allowed to procreate and produce more dull kids. In developing a method for measuring mental ability, Galton mainly used sensory motor tasks such as reaction times.

Hence, those with faster reaction times were by Galton's calculations the most intellectually adept. Galton's use of sensory motor tasks, along with the tests of the American James McKeen Cattell (who coined the term 'mental test' and whose work paralleled Galton's), was discredited as being too simplistic to capture the complexity of intellectual functioning and was, not surprisingly, abandoned, but their logic, as we will see, remained chillingly intact.

Undernourished, intelligence becomes like the bloated belly of a starving child: swollen, filled with nothing the body can use.

Andrea Dworkin

CHARLES SPEARMAN

Charles Spearman was the person who was the most responsible for setting the foundations for our current views on intelligence. He noticed that when a series of ability tests were administered there was much overlap in the skills required to perform these tests. He introduced the notion of 'g' or general intelligence to explain the common attribute that seemed to underlie the many achievement tasks (Spearman, 1904; Jensen, 1998); 'g' has become a major, albeit controversial, psychological construct in the history of education and psychology. This has become one of the most replicated findings in psychology; while some may not wish to explain the overlap as 'g' or intelligence, some explanation for the commonality is needed. Regardless of whether one agrees or disagrees with his notions, it is extremely difficult to ignore Spearman's contributions to the field of intelligence and its measurement.

ALFRED BINET

At the same time as Spearman was driving the theoretical debate, the French psychologist Alfred Binet, along with Theodore Simon, picked up the measurement baton where Galtonian science left off. Binet's approach to understanding intelligence, however, was radically different from that of Galton and Cattell in that he believed individual differences in intelligence were much more complex than just assessing sensory acuity and response times. Binet argued that higher-order thinking processes, such as memory, attention and imagination, were most critical and that these were the key dimensions to measure.

The original motive for the intelligence scale that Binet and Simon developed in 1905 was to identify children within the Parisian school system who were not benefiting from regular forms of instruction. The implication was that intelligence was not fixed or necessarily due to any single cause, but that appropriate schooling could modify intelligence—this was in stark contrast to his predecessors. Binet's work, in effect, signalled the beginning of the special education programmes and the assessment of students most likely to benefit from these programmes (and those likely to receive benefit in the 'regular' or sometimes 'gifted' classrooms), which still exists in some form in modern-day schools. Binet and Simon's measure was aimed at assessing a child's general intellectual development and was composed of 30 tests, arranged in ascending order of difficulty. The tests ranged from vocabulary to physical performance tasks. It is important to understand that the motive for Binet and Simon in their testing of intelligence was not for comparative purposes but rather for identifying or classifying which children would be better educated in special classrooms.

The Binet-Simon scale was revised in 1908 to include the concept of mental level, which was simply the ordering of the test by the age level at which typically they were passed. So if 80 to 90 per cent of children aged five, say, passed certain questions then these were classified at the five-year-old level. So, for example, a nine-year-old child operating at a five-year-old mental age would be classified as being 'retarded' by four years and therefore a likely candidate for special education. The subsequent 1911 revision resulted in each age level having five tests as well as the age range being extended to adulthood.

THE AMERICAN ADOPTION OF IQ

It was, in many ways, the introduction of the concept 'mental age' that influenced much of the subsequent practices of the intelligence testing movement in the United States. Indeed, in 1912 the German psychologist William Stern, unhappy with the notion of mental age, suggested dividing the mental age by the actual age to get the 'mental quotient', which American psychologist Lewis Terman

later multiplied by 100 to make it more understandable and thus called it the 'intelligence quotient' or 'IQ'.

The birth of this concept of IQ (as the psychometric measurement of 'intelligence') is a critical historical development that has shaped the debate regarding intellectual functioning and its associated uses. Once IQ had been defined and methods for measurement were established, it was then put to work in many different contexts. In general the argument ran along the lines of 'If you can measure IQ then you can rank people and if you can rank people then there is great utility in testing IQ'. Thus, as Stephen Jay Gould (1981) and others have suggested, began the mass-marketing of IQ, especially in the United States.

It has yet to be proven that intelligence has any survival value.

Arthur C. Clarke

HENRY HERBERT GODDARD

One of the first people to see the potential use of IQ testing was Henry Herbert Goddard, who translated the Binet-Simon scale for use in the United States. Goddard was hired by the Vineland Training School for Feeble-Minded Boys and Girls in New Jersey to understand more about the education and identification of categories of 'feeble-minded' students (today we call 'feeble-mindedness' developmental disability). Using his translated Binet-Simon scale, Goddard classified students using diagnostic criteria and mental age into categories he called idiots, imbeciles or feeble-minded persons.

Goddard's work soon found him sitting comfortably in the hereditarian camp, as his work reflected the same logic and sentiment as Galton's earlier work. What underpinned his work was the belief that intelligence was genetically derived and that 'feeble-mindedness' was the result of a single recessive gene. Later studies by Goddard provided data indicating that about 3 per cent of children could be classified as 'feeble-minded'. Goddard became concerned about the effects the 'feeble-minded' might have on society, and espoused views that children with such classifications should be segregated from society and even sterilised to prevent them from breeding. Such was the concern that 33 states in the United States of America passed laws permitting the sterilisation of 'feeble-minded' individuals, and more than 60,000 men and women housed in mental institutions were sterilised, with many not knowing what was happening to them.

Armed with his new hammer (mental testing), Goddard set out on a crusade to try to fix what he saw as a serious adjunct to 'feeble-mindedness'—notably, the influx of poorer southern and eastern European immigrants to the United States. What concerned Goddard most was their potential to compound the 'menace of feeble-mindedness' even more by their breeding with other 'feeble-minded' mates. Thus, the answer to this problem was simple: test all new immigrants arriving at Ellis Island and determine their 'mental' level and send back those with low scores. As we noted earlier, science often walks hand in hand with the dominant social ideology of the day; thus, Goddard's work at Ellis Island was, at that time, complementary to a view that immigration needed to be more tightly restricted and those with low scores on his test should be deported to their country of origin. What better way to justify such actions than by using the latest scientific tool!

The backbone of Goddard's operation at Ellis Island was a two-stage approach. First, an assistant would wander through the halls and visually identify people thought to be mentally defective (subjective bias as well as informed consent was yet to emerge as a debate in psychological enquiry). Once identified, the potential candidate, often confused and frightened, was taken to another location where the revised Binet-Simon scale, along with some other performance measures, was administered. If the person was found to be mentally defective they were often deported. How awful it must have been for those people denied entry to the 'land of opportunity' because they had the unfortunate opportunity to meet Henry H. Goddard and his troupe of testers.

Ethical issues aside, it is worth dwelling on the notion that Goddard translated the scale from French to English and then retranslated it into various other languages; therefore, the accuracy of these tests was likely compromised, given that French norms were used in the classification. Even today, translating a test into another language is a controversial and difficult process. This combined with the poor reliability and validity of the translated measures, as well as the huge cultural issues involved in testing people from such varied backgrounds and especially in these tense situations of border and customs checks, creates a grossly unfair testing process. The widespread use of Goddard's procedures at Ellis Island saw the numbers of immigrants deported grow exponentially.

Although Goddard initially held staunch hereditarian views, he later recanted his opinion in favour of the nurture over nature argument. In essence, he acknowledged that 'feeble-mindedness' was something that could be treated, and that institutionalising people on the basis of IQ scores was not necessary. One positive thing in Goddard's favour was that he helped draft one of the first state laws mandating that special provisions be made for special education classes. Obviously Goddard was a complex and contradictory man of his day (see Zenderland, 1998).

Low is the triumph of imagination over intelligence.

Henry Louis Mencken

LEWIS TERMAN

The next major event in the IQ testing movement came in 1916 when Lewis Terman revised the Binet-Simon scale and renamed it the Stanford-Binet scale (Terman was a professor at Stanford University and named his test after the university and in honour of Binet). Terman's contribution to IQ testing was enormous and the new Stanford-Binet scale set a benchmark by which all other tests came to be evaluated. Not only was the new scale increased in length but also it could be used with 'retarded' and normal children as well as normal and superior adults. One of the most radical aspects of the overhaul was setting the average IQ to 100 and the average variability around that score to 15. The Stanford-Binet scale is in its fifth revision; its scaled scoring system has been adopted by many other IQ measures and it remains one of the more widely used.

One of Terman's lasting legacies was his use of the Stanford-Binet scale in his study of gifted children and their life trajectories. Originally started in 1922 and designed to run for 10 years, the study aimed to shed light on how 'intellectually gifted' children, if selected early enough and cultivated in the right manner, would eventually take their rightful place at the top of society. Such was Terman's interest in the intellectual development of these children that this continues to the present day. Of the 1,528 original recruits—856 males and 672 females, nearly all white and living in California—some 200 (as of July 2000) 'Termites', as they are called, were still alive, some of them quite famous; for example, the famous educationalist Lee Cronbach and the physiologist Ancel Keys (he discovered the link between cholesterol and heart disease). Although the sampling of subjects was haphazard and subjective, some interesting facts have emerged. For example, more than two-thirds went on to higher education, 97 gained doctorates, 57 became medical doctors and 83 became lawyers.

THE ROLE OF THE UNITED STATES ARMY

The First World War provided the catalyst for the development and mass use of IQ tests. Both Goddard's and Terman's influence on IQ testing meant that they were often invited to work with some of the most prominent psychologists of the day. As a member of Robert Yerkes' testing team at Yale University, Goddard was involved in the development and administration of the United States Army Alpha and Beta tests, which differed markedly from earlier IQ tests. Whereas the Binet-Simon scale, and its translated versions, was individually administered, the army Alpha and Beta tests were developed for group testing. The advantage of this approach was that recruits could be tested and scored quicker. Thus, IQ testing developed into an efficient, scientifically-based industry, which over the years has grown in importance (examples include the Educational Testing Service and the Law School Admission Test). IQ testing had truly come of age.

The Alpha and Beta tests were administered to identify those recruits with low intelligence as well as those suited to certain jobs or officer training. The Alpha test was used with recruits who could read and write, whereas the Beta test was used for illiterate recruits or those who could not speak English. Like most of the early IQ tests, little was known about their psychometric properties. For example, the Beta test was usually administered to large groups by the examiner, who used pictorial cues as well as hand signals and facial expressions when reading each question aloud. One of the main criticisms of the Army Alpha and Beta tests was the lack of uniformity of the conditions forgiving the test, as well as the variability of the examiners, both of which can dramatically affect the validity of the scores. Although the tests were given to more than 1.75 million soldiers, it is unclear whether the testing programme made any difference to military functioning or efficiency. Indeed, many higher-ranking military officers were sceptical about the uses of psychological testing and, thus, much of the data went unused. After the war, it was found that while the Alpha test had high reliability, it had lower validity for predicting 'officer material'—indeed, the Alpha tests were better predictors of truck driving, which would surprise few who have watched movie footage of the US troops in battle.

One person who did use the army Alpha tests was Carl Brigham, who in 1923 analysed the racial differences between recruits. He concluded that African Americans and Mediterranean and Alpine recruits were 'intellectually inferior', and so continued the many debates on IQ and ethnicity. Like his colleague Goddard, Brigham later recanted and attributed these differences to language and cultural differences.

> Anyone who conducts an argument by appealing to authority is not using his intelligence; he is just using his memory.
>
> Leonardo da Vinci

SIR CYRIL BURT

With the rise of Nazism and its beliefs about racial superiority, it is not surprising that the eugenics movement lost favour and momentum in the West. That is not to say that IQ disappeared from view; it merely meant that other means of showing the link between IQ and hereditary needed to be found, and thus entered the first knight of psychology: Sir Cyril Burt. There is no denying Cyril Burt's influence on psychology, especially his development of educational psychology. He was also instrumental in refining the statistical technique of factor analysis, which is still at the forefront of most psychological research today. Factor analysis is a complex correlational technique that is used to detect if groups of questions or tests share a common underlying theme. It is the critical method used in determining if measures can be compartmentalised into smaller units. Thus, it can test if overall IQ has subdimensions, such as numerical reasoning, verbal analogy and so on, and whether these subdimensions can be meaningfully weighted to form a single (unidimensional) score.

Cyril Burt was a staunch hereditarian who undertook his pioneering work on special education in Britain throughout the twentieth century, and has been (falsely) attributed as the father of the eleven-plus examination, whereby children sit tests at age 11 to decide on the nature of the high school they attend (academic, vocational and so on). Indeed, Burt argued that IQ tests, like the 11-plus examination, could be used to identity children from the lower classes who could profit from a more academic schooling (he was certain that intelligence genes were not confined to the British upper class). He also started the largest study of identical twins who had been separated at birth and reared in different families.

Burt, like many researchers in the area of intelligence, was subjected to many personal barbs and the greatest was the accusation of fraud, published after he died in 1976. A front-page news item in a British newspaper claimed that Burt was a fraud because he invented crucial data. His biographer, Hearnshaw (1979), also made various claims against Burt; he could not have possibly collected some of his post-war data and thus he fabricated them by inventing data to fit his theories; his work was an 'elaborately constructed piece of work' based on invented data; some of his co-workers were fictitious; he used his position to change other researchers' papers to reflect better his views and contributions; and he altered the history of his area to claim priority over some contributors.

> He falsified history in the interest of self-aggrandizement. That he was guilty of malfeasance there can be no reasonable doubt. The only question at issue can be, was he guilty simpliciter or guilty with diminished responsibility as a result of pathological influences?
>
> (p. 180)

Hearnshaw answered the question by supporting the latter argument.

The reason why Burt undertook these actions was, claimed his biographer, because he had Ménière's disease, which is typical of obsessive-compulsive types—the connection is abject nonsense. During his childhood, claimed Hearnshaw, he was forced to survive by observing his peers and enemies closely, 'to keep his feelings to himself, to bluff it out, and to outmanoeuvre those who tried to molest

him' (Hearnshaw, 1979: 273). Hearnshaw's claim is that Burt learned his deviousness because he studied Greek and Latin for ten years as a student—as, in preparation of producing pieces of Greek and Latin prose, the perfect copy or fake achieves the highest mark—hence he was trained in copying and faking! 'In the lost boyhood of Cyril Burt psychology was betrayed'. Worse, in his adulthood he was not a 'sociable or clubbable man' (p. 291).

None of these accusations have withstood critique—although Burt may have been careless and not always clear in his methods—but his reputation has been sullied. His work, however, has been replicated so many times that it almost does not matter whether he was a fraud or not (Joynson, 1989; Hattie, 1991). But the claims are not uncommon for researchers studying this topic; there are many critics. Recently, as another example, a noted American scholar, Linda Gottfredson, has spoken about the accusations, deceit and harassment she has experienced because of her work on intelligence (Wainer and Robinson, 2009). The most famous case of death threats, rioting and ugly critique relates to Arthur Jensen (see next section). Since the 1970s, intelligence and IQ testing has lost its aura of mainstream respectability: in many places IQ tests have been banned, research on the topic has diminished, new names are being invented to test developers and users do not have to use 'IQ' for things such as problem-solving and differential abilities. One of the now more popular IQ measures is called the 'assessment battery for children.'

> Great spirits have always found violent opposition from mediocrities. The latter cannot understand it when a man does not thoughtlessly submit to hereditary prejudices but honestly and courageously uses his intelligence.
>
> Albert Einstein

ARTHUR R. JENSEN

In 1969, Arthur R. Jensen, a Berkeley psychologist, published a controversial paper in the *Harvard Educational Review*. In his paper, Jensen approached the now taboo subject of race and IQ by highlighting the interplay between nature (genetics) and nurture (environment) in explaining differences between African Americans and Caucasians. Jensen's paper was primarily an attack on the utility of compensatory education—that is, education designed to lessen the gap in achievement between those from minority backgrounds compared with those from the majority. In particular, Jensen argued that environment alone was not the sole cause for any disparity between certain groups, and factors such as genetics may explain some of the achievement score differences, thus compensatory education was not the means to close the gap. But it was one sentence that caused an uproar: 'The preponderance of the evidence is, in my opinion, less consistent with a strictly environmental hypothesis than with a genetic hypothesis, which, of course, does not exclude the influence of environment or its interaction with genetic factors' (p. 82). This claim that there may be innate differences between blacks and whites on IQ prompted a torrent of abuse, and Jensen was heckled, threatened, abused and generally vilified. Jensen went on to become one of the most eminent scholars in the field of intelligence and continued his research on the differences between the IQ of various groups, although this is not as well known. It is not the fact that there are differences in IQ scores across groups that is contentious: it is the claimed reasons for this difference.

THE FLYNN EFFECT

We also know, thanks to New Zealand scholar James Flynn, that there has been an increase in the average IQ over the generations. For example, it is now well documented that *both* African-American and Caucasians gained 15 IQ points during the past 30 years. So in one sense, the African-American community has closed the entire 'gap', which certainly demonstrates the power of environment (the problem is that the Caucasian IQ has also increased 12 to 15 IQ points during this same period).

Indeed, this effect, now called the 'Flynn effect', is well established. Nations, almost without exception, have shown gains of about 20 IQ points per generation (30 years). These gains are highest for IQ tests that are most related to reasoning and the capacity to figure out novel problems (this is often called 'fluid intelligence'); and least related to knowledge, which arises from better educational opportunity, a history of persistence and good motivation for learning (this is often called 'crystallised intelligence'). It is, therefore, important to note that these gains in IQ across decades and generations is *not* related to the type of knowledge gained from increased schooling, increased test-taking sophistication, increased nutrition, greater urbanisation, eradication of childhood diseases, upgrading of early childhood or preschool programmes or education in general.

HERRNSTEIN AND MURRAY

Perhaps the best instance of extreme argument about IQ and race differences is Richard Herrnstein and Charles Murray's now-infamous 1994 book *The Bell Curve*. The book includes reports of many research studies, but it was the authors' interpretations of the research that caused an outcry. For example, when citing research on the relation between IQ and illegitimacy, they noted that

> the smarter a woman is, the more likely that she deliberately decides to have a child and calculates the best time to do it. The less intelligent the woman is, the more likely that she does not think ahead from sex to procreation, does not remember to use birth control, does not carefully consider when and under what circumstances she should have a child. How intelligent a woman is may interact with her impulsiveness, and hence her ability to exert self-discipline and restraint on her partner in order to avoid pregnancy.
>
> (p. 179)

They go on to conclude that 'low intelligence is an important independent cause of illegitimacy' (p. 189). Such (il)logic and the assumption that having a baby is entirely up to one sex, the omission of mentioning the father, and the conclusion of 'welfare being the prime suspect' is more rhetoric than research.

They also used other studies on intelligence to stretch claims so that they could make particular public policy statements. For example, Herrnstein and Murray argued that the United States is run by rules congenial to people with high IQs and that makes life more difficult for everyone else. Herrnstein and Murray argue that this has led to the creation of complicated, sophisticated systems of fairness, justice and right and wrong that those creating such systems claim are ethically superior to simple, black-and-white versions. Hence the recommendation from Herrnstein and Murray to have less government, let business be business—unhampered by complicated rules—let communities make their own decisions, have less welfare and centralised handouts, and so forth.

The Bell Curve was a reawakening of the Jensen debates, although it did not last as long as or have the same depth of scholarly analysis associated with Jensen's works. There were reactions in newspapers and popular journals, books attacking the claims and spurious logic, but the overwhelming reaction was 'Sigh, here we go again'. Both the more outlandish claims and scholarly debate is likely to continue on the topic of IQ differences between race and cultural groups, and we could be optimistic if we could discover ways to reduce these gaps.

> Military intelligence is a contradiction in terms.
> Groucho Marx

IQ RESEARCH TODAY

The debates about IQ today are rarely mainstream for psychologists. Instead, research is more related to the notions of 'cognitive functioning', developed during the 1970s and 1980s, whereby there is a search for the various strategies and manners in which we process information. This has led to the identification of many strategies, and some researchers seem to be concerned that some of us have more versatility and expertise in the use of these strategies and that this seems to relate to the notion of general intelligence, or 'g'. In many ways, researchers of today rarely refer to the notion of 'g'. This makes life easier as it avoids the debates about race, heredity and "designer genes'; but one does not need to scratch too far beyond the surface to note that the issues of IQ are still present.

The small number of researchers who are still publishing on intelligence today are more focused on the nature of 'g' and the many dimensions of intelligence. It seems that older rejected theories (such as faculty psychology, which assumed that there were various bumps on the head that could be traced to different thinking patterns) have been reinvented in the name of multiple intelligences and dimension theories of intelligence—that is, there is a denial of the notion of 'g' and a denial that whenever tests of cognitive abilities are related to each other there is a source

of commonality that can explain these relations. These newer 'g'-denial theories have not influenced the work of psychologists very much (as these theories have limited support for them), but they are sufficiently seductive to be very evident and are present in some educational claims.

There is a large amount of research seeking alternative measures of 'g' using brain functioning, blood flow and other physiological cues. This may be fascinating but is unlikely to lead to much change in the debate if the major impact is to replace IQ tests with neurological-based measures. We may have a semblance of more pure, or cultural-free, measures, but any new physiologically based test will still only be as important as its capacity to predict and explain our thinking—and we have already rehearsed these debates over the past century with psychologically based tests.

The concept of IQ has an enduring appeal, although for the past 40 years its popularity has been waning. Despite this waxing and waning, IQ has emerged in many different forms and has found its rank among the plethora of theoretically and empirically based psychological constructs. Indeed, it stands out as being one of the most well-supported notions in educational and mainstream psychology, with many uses in education, industry and health, to name but a few.

> Neither a lofty degree of intelligence nor imagination nor both together go to the making of genius. Love, love, love, that is the soul of genius,
> Wolfgang Amadeus Mozart

Researchers and practitioners most certainly have learned from the mistakes and abuses of the past, and contemporary IQ tests reflect the advances made in test construction, scoring and analysis. Although the criticisms of IQ from people such as Stephen Jay Gould (1981), the accusations of fraud about Burt and the tensions raised concerning Jensen's research have not benefited the reputation of IQ, there is much that is good in the modern research literature; for example, the use of IQ tests in identifying patients with Alzheimer's or Parkinson's disease, identification of children who have not had opportunities to learn but have remarkable cognitive thinking skills, and ensuring that students with some physical disadvantages are not then considered to be unable to think and not derive benefit from schooling—to name a few.

As with many research areas where controversy abounds, this provides a healthy forum to check the positives and negatives of each argument. This, indeed, is the manner in which science advances. The net result is that the theory with the most evidence will likely gain the foreground (or the one without damning evidence against it) and must then be prepared to take on new challengers. IQ and intelligence have done this in the form of 'g' and, whether you agree or disagree with it, its ability to withstand the many attacks says much about its staying power. Ignoring it ignores scientific evidence and we do this for many cultural and social reasons, but it rarely leads to advances in our understanding.

Truly great madness cannot be achieved without significant intelligence.

Henrik Tikkanen

WHERE TO FROM HERE?

For more than a century scientists have had an enduring fascination with IQ and its correlates. Stating that there are differences between groups has proven a highly controversial topic. It is worth remembering that IQ, as envisaged by Binet and many since, was about individual differences and not group differences. This is where the research baton needs to be redirected. It is important to recognise and understand why such differences exist. Any psychological construct is only as important as its value, consequences and predictive powers. So how useful is intelligence?

Skin Color and Intelligence in African Americans

RICHARD LYNN

The relation between skin color and intelligence was examined in a representative sample of 430 adult African Americans. A statistically significant positive correlation of 0.17 was obtained between light skin color and intelligence. It is proposed that the result supports the hypothesis that the level of intelligence in African Americans is significantly determined by the proportion of Caucasian genes.

A general theory of human population differences in terms of r-K reproductive strategy has been advanced by Rushton (2000). The concept of r-K reproductive strategy is taken from evolutionary biology to describe the alternatives of producing large numbers of offspring of which few survive and designated the r strategy, and producing only a few offspring of which many more survive. Fish, amphibians and reptiles adopt the r strategy, while mammals adopt the K strategy. Species adopting the r strategy let their offspring fend for themselves while species adopting the K strategy look after their offspring during infancy and childhood. In general species adopting the K strategy have longer lives, larger brains and are more intelligent than species adopting the r strategy. In his application of this concept to humans, Rushton has proposed that Mongoloids have evolved the strongest K strategy, Negroids are stronger r strategists, while Caucasoids fall intermediate but are closer to Mongoloids. Rushton uses this general theory to explain a large number of differences between the three races including brain size, intelligence, sexuality and numbers of children. Race differences within the context of r/K theory are thus of great relevance to population issues generally.

In regard to intelligence, there is considerable evidence that there are race differences consistent with Rushton's theory such that Mongoloids have the highest average IQs of about 105, Caucasoids have average IQs of around 100 and Negroids have average IQs of around 70. The world wide evidence for this generalization is presented in Lynn (1997) and Rush-ton (2000). In the United States it has been found in numerous studies that the average IQ of African Americans is around 85 (Jensen, 1998; Mackintosh, 1998). This is consistent with the world wide evidence because many African Americans have mixed Negroid and Causasoid ancestry and consequently fall intermediate between the two parent races. Despite these well established racial differences in average IQs, there is no consensus on whether they have a genetic basis, as demanded by Rushton's theory, or whether they are wholly environmentally determined. The case for a genetic basis has been presented by Jensen (1998) and Rushton (2000), while the case for environmental determination has been presented by Brody (1992) and Mackintosh (1998).

It has long been believed that it would be possible to resolve the disputed issue of whether genetic factors are involved in the black-white difference in intelligence by an examination of the relationship between intelligence and

Richard Lynn, "Skin Color and Intelligence in African Americans," *Population and Environment*, vol. 23, no. 4, pp. 365–375. Copyright © 2002 by Springer Science+Business Media. Reprinted with permission.

the amount of white ancestry among African Americans and other black and colored populations with significant amounts of white ancestry. If genetic factors are partly responsible for the black-white difference, there should be a positive association between the proportion of white ancestry and intelligence.

The first attempts to test this hypothesis consisted of taking skin color as a measure of the amount of white ancestry on the assumption that the lighter the skin the greater the proportion of white ancestors and hence of white genes. The hypothesis that genetic factors are involved in the black-white difference in intelligence predicts that there should be a positive association between light skin and intelligence. The examination of whether such an association exists would be a test of the genetic theory in so far as that the absence of an association would disconfirm the theory.

The early research on the relation between skin color and intelligence among black populations was reviewed by Shuey (1966). She summarised 18 studies of which 15 were carried out in the United States, two in Jamaica and one in Canada. Some association between lightness of skin and intelligence was found in 16 of the studies. However, the magnitude of the association between skin color and intelligence was quite low. Only four of the studies expressed the relationship in terms of correlations. These were carried out by Herskovits (1926) on college students (N = 115, r = .17, NS); by Klineberg (1928) on 7–16 year olds (N = 139, r = .12, NS); and by Peterson and Lanier (1929) on two samples of 12 year olds (N = 83, r = .18, NS; N = 75, r = .30, $p < .01$). The results of the four studies are open to two interpretations. On the one hand, it could be argued that three of the four correlations are not statistically significant and the overall pattern is one of no significant association between skin color and intelligence. On the other hand, it could be argued that all four correlations show a positive association between light skin color and intelligence and that taken together they indicate a real association. The average of the four correlations is .09, so if a real association exists, the four studies show that it is weak. All of the four studies were carried out in the 1920's and the remaining studies reviewed by Shuey were quite early. All except one were carried out in the first half of the twentieth century.

Since Shuey's review, it is believed that only one study has examined the relation between skin color and intelligence among African Americans. This is the investigation by Scarr, Pakstis, Katz and Barker (1977) of 288 twins aged 10–16 years. Five intelligence tests were given and yielded the following correlations with skin color with intelligence. Progressive Matrices: .13; Peabody Picture Vocabulary Scale: .00; Columbia Test of Mental Maturity: .04; Revised Test of Figural Memory: .10; and a paired associate test: -.12 (the minus sign indicates that dark skinned blacks performed better on this test). Scarr et al. conclude that none of these correlations is statistically significant assuming a sample size of 144 because the subjects were twins. They also calculated the first principal component of their five tests and report that the correlation of this with light skin color is .05 and not statistically significant. They conclude that the results show that there is no association between skin color and intelligence. Nevertheless, a different interpretation of the results is possible. It is arguable that the paired associate test is a measure of rote learning ability and not of intelligence and should be excluded. It is also arguable that of the four remaining tests the Progressive Matrices is widely regarded as the best measure of g (Jensen, 1998; Mackintosh,1998) and the correlation of .13 between the Progressive Matrices and light skin color is statistically significant if the number of subjects is taken as 288 and not halved to 144 because they were twins. An alternative treatment of the results would be to discard the paired associates test and average the results of the four intelligence tests to give a correlation of .07 between light skin color and intelligence. This interpretation would make the results of the study consistent with the four earlier studies reviewed by Shuey finding a small positive relation between light skin and intelligence.

In addition to the studies of skin color and intelligence, there were three early studies—Bean (1906), Vint (1934), and Pearl (1934)—that found that brain size is positively associated with degree of white admixture. Because brain size is positively associated with intelligence, these results strengthen the case for an association between light skin color and intelligence.

INTERPRETING THE EVIDENCE ON SKIN COLOR AND INTELLIGENCE

Those who have discussed this issue have drawn different conclusions from the existing evidence. Three positions can be identified. First, some scholars have concluded that there is no association between intelligence and skin color or other indices of the amount of white ancestry. Thus, Flynn (1980, p. 78) writes that "the results seem to show that white ancestry confers neither an advantage nor a disadvantage within the American black population".

Brody (1992, p. 309) writes that "there is no relationship between the degree of white ancestry and intelligence in black samples"; Howe (1997, p. 73) writes that "the evidence clearly indicates the absence of a relationship between the degree of white ancestry and intellectual skills"; and Hill (2000, p. 1456) writes that "research has failed to uncover any association between white ancestry and intellectual ability among African Americans." This conclusion is also drawn by Scarr et al. (1977), although they consider only their own data and not the other studies.

A second position is that the evidence indicates the existence of a true positive association between light skin color and intelligence but that the correlation is so low that it suggests hardly any genetic difference between blacks and whites. This position is adopted by Nisbett (1998, p. 89) who concludes that the research suggests a correlation of around .15 between light skin color and intelligence and that this "does not suggest that European ancestry strongly affects IQ." The use of the word "strongly" seems to imply that this correlation suggests that the proportion of European ancestry has a weak effect on IQ.

The third position is taken by Jensen (1973, p. 223) who concludes that "these studies leave little doubt of a true relationship between skin color (and other visible features ranged along a Negroid-Caucasoid continuum) and scores on intelligence tests." Jensen is not concerned that the correlations between skin color and intelligence are low. He argues that the measure of skin color as an index of white ancestry has such low reliability that a correlation of about .20 is the highest that could be expected on the basis of the genetic hypothesis. He argues that the existence of a correlation of around this figure, or not significantly different from it, is consistent with the genetic theory although "the fact that a correlation this high or higher could arise for quite other reasons make it a weak and inconclusive

type of evidence with respect to the central thesis" (p. 223). Rushton (2000) also concludes that there is a true relation between light skin color and intelligence.

One of the major problems with the existing evidence on this issue is that it is not sufficiently extensive to show conclusively whether or not a positive association is present between light skin color and intelligence. The existing studies show low positive but preponderantly non-statistically significant correlations. This allows some scholars such as Flynn, Brody, Howe, Hill and Scarr et al. to conclude that no association is present, while others such as Nisbett, Jensen and Rushton to draw the opposite conclusion that there is a true association. The problem is that the sample sizes in the studies have been too small to determine whether the predominantly low positive correlations are statistically significant. While most of the correlations are not significantly different from zero, they are also not significantly different from significant correlations. Most of the correlations lie in the limbo between zero and statistical significance. The solution to this problem is to test the hypothesis on a sufficiently large sample to determine whether a significant relation between skin color and intelligence exists. This is the principal objective of the present paper.

Before presenting new data on this issue, it should be noted that skin color is not the only index of the amount of white ancestry that has been studied in relation to intelligence in African American populations. Two studies have analysed blood groups as indices of the amount of white ancestry. In the first of these, Loehlin, Vandenberg and Osborne (1973) obtained no significant association between intelligence and 16 blood groups used to estimate the amount of white ancestry in a sample of 84 blacks. However, the average correlations between the blood group indices was –.03, indicating very low reliability of the measure. The second of these studies by Scarr et al. (1977) found correlations between the blood group index of the amount of white ancestry and intelligence closely similar to those obtained from skin color. The average of the correlations for the four intelligence tests was .06 for blood groups and .07 for skin color. This study also found very low reliability of blood groups as an index of the amount of white ancestry. Scarr et al. calculated the amount of white ancestry from three blood groups and from 9 blood groups and found that the correlation between the two indices was .11 and not statistically significant. A final study of the relation between the amount of white ancestry and intelligence among African Americans was carried out by Witty and Jenkins (1936). They obtained a sample of 63 black children from Chicago schools with IQs over 120 and had their parents report their proportion of white ancestry. They found the reported proportion of white ancestors was no different from that in the African American population as a whole. However, it is questionable whether the parents would be able to assess accurately the proportion of their white ancestors, many of whom would have been acquired in the seventeenth, eighteenth and early nineteenth centuries and of which the they would have had no knowledge. For this reason, it is doubtful whether any weight can be placed on this study.

METHOD

The data for this study come from the Chicago based National Opinion Research Center's (NORC) opinion poll survey of 1982. The NORC surveys are based on representative samples of the adult population of the continental United States, excluding non-English speakers and those in institutions. The sampling procedures are described by Davis and Smith (1996). The NORC survey of 1982 collected information on a large number of subjects, of which the relevant ones for our present purposes are race, skin color and vocabulary size. The 1982 survey is the only one in which African Americans have been asked to assess their skin color. The racial identify questions are of two kinds. First, the respondents were asked if they would describe themselves as white, black or other. Second, if they described themselves as black they were asked whether they would describe themselves as very dark, dark brown, medium brown, light brown or very light. On the basis of their replies they were placed into one of these categories.

The vocabulary test consisted of 10 words whose meaning has to be given and each correct answer is scored one point. Vocabulary size is a good measure of intelligence and has a high correlation with the general factor, the first principal component or (see, e.g. Jensen and Reynolds, 1982).

RESULTS

Table 1 shows the numbers of respondents in each group, their mean vocabulary scores and standard deviations. The salient features of this table are as follows. Whites score significantly higher than the blacks ($t = 11,92, p < .001$). In standard deviation units, whites score .66 sd above blacks, equivalent to 10 IQ points. Among the five subgroups of blacks, light skin is significantly correlated with light skin ($r = .17, p < .01$); tested by analysis of variance, ($F = 5.29, p = < .001$). The number of blacks in the table (442) is greater than the total number of those analyzed by skin color (430) because 14 of the those who identified them selves as black did not answer the question on shade of black.

DISCUSSION

The results raise six points of interest. First, they go a considerable way to establishing that there is a significant association between light skin color and intelligence among African Americans. The previous research on this question is inconclusive because the studies have found low positive but for the most part statistically non-significant correlations. This is attributable to the small sample sizes in these studies. The present study has produced much the same sized correlation as those found in previous studies, viz. .17 as compared with .17 (Herskovits, 1926), .12 (Klineberg, 1928), .18 and .30 (Peterson and Lanier, 1929) and .07 (Scarr et al., 1977). But because the sample size in the present study is several times greater than in any of the previous studies, the obtained correlation of .17 is statistically significant at the 1 percent level.

2. We consider now the totality of the research literature on the correlations between skin color and intelligence. The five previous studies summarized in the introduction can be summed, weighted by sample size, to give a mean correlation of .13 ($N = 556, p < .05$). This can be combined (weighting by sample size) with the sample reported in the present study to give a correlation of .15 ($N = 996, p < .001$). This should be regarded as the best estimate from the data currently available of the magnitude of the correlation between light skin color and intelligence. This highly significant correlation is corroborated by the 14 studies reviewed by Shuey (1966) that did not report correlations but of which 12 found some association between

light skin and IQ. This evidence taken as a whole adds up to a fairly strong case that there is a true association between light skin color and IQ. It is therefore considered that the conclusion advanced by Scarr et al. (1977), Flynn (1980), Brody (1992), Howe (1997) and Hill (2000) cited in the introduction that there is no association between skin color and IQ is incorrect.

3. The conclusion that there is a true association between skin color and IQ is consistent with the hypothesis that genetic factors are partly responsible for the black-white difference in intelligence. The genetic hypothesis predicts that such an association should exist, so the evidence that a statistically significant correlation is present confirms the genetic hypothesis. Conversely, if the evidence showed that there is no association between light skin color and IQ, the genetic hypothesis would be disconfirmed. In terms of Popper's falsification theory of the logic of scientific explanation, the genetic hypothesis has survived an attempt at falsification and is to some degree strengthened.

4. Shuey (1996) and Nisbett (1998) have argued that while a true relation between light skin color and intelligence appears to be present, the correlation is so low that genetic factors can only make a very small contribution to the black-white intelligence difference. A contrary position is adopted by Jensen (1973, p. 222) who cites evidence that skin color is not a highly reliable index of the amount of Caucasian ancestry in African American populations and that the correlation of skin color with amount of Caucasian ancestry is about .3 to .4. The reason for this low correlation is that in hybrid populations the genes inherited from the two parent populations tend to segregate independently, in accordance with Mendel's second law. Jensen estimates that if the correlation between IQ and the amount of Caucasian ancestry is .5 and skin color is assumed to correlate at .4 with the amount of Caucasian ancestry, the highest correlation that could be found between IQ and skin color would be about .2. Scarr (1981, p. 521) using the same assumptions, estimates the highest correlation at .245. If these estimates are accepted, the obtained correlation of .15 indicates that around half to three quarters of the black-white intelligence difference can be attributed to genetic factors, as proposed by Jensen (1973).

5. While the significant correlation between skin color and intelligence is predictable from the theory that genetic factors are partly responsible for the black-white difference

in intelligence, we need to consider how far a wholly environmental theory of the black-white intelligence difference could explain this association. Environmental theorists would likely advance selective discrimination by whites against darker skinned blacks as responsible factor. Environmental theorists have proposed that discrimination by whites could be responsible for impairing the intelligence of blacks. For instance, Scarr (1995) accepts that her study of black babies adopted by white parents showed no gains in IQ and have average IQs the same as those of blacks reared by blacks (Weinberg, Scarr & Waldman, 1992). To explain this she writes that "the results of the transracial adoption study allow either a social discrimination hypothesis or a racial genetic hypothesis because the low scores of the black adoptees could be due primarily to either" (p. 7). The theory is that social discrimination by whites could impair the IQs of blacks. By extension this hypothesis might propose that whites discriminate against dark skinned blacks more than against light skinned blacks, and this reduces their intelligence more.

The hypothesis that discrimination by whites is wholly or partly responsible for the low IQs obtained by blacks and for the lower IQs obtained by dark skinned as compared with light skinned blacks, is implausible on three grounds. First, it is doubtful whether there is any known mechanism by which discrimination by whites could impair the IQs obtained by blacks, particularly in the conditions studied by Weinberg, Scarr and Waldman (1992) in which black infants were adopted and reared in white middle class homes. Second, Krieger, Sidney and Coakley (1998) have studied the question of whether dark skinned blacks experience more discrimination than light skinned blacks. Their sample consisted of 1844 black men and women aged 22 to 44 divided into four categories of skin color by a Photo-volt reflectance meter and asked in a questionnaire whether they had experienced racial discrimination. There was no association between skin color and self-reported experience of discrimination for getting a job, at work, getting housing, getting medical care or in public places. Among men there was a significant association between light skin color and reporting having experienced discrimination at school (contrary to the prediction from environmentalist theory, which would predict an association between dark skin and experience of discrimination). Among working class respondents, but not among middle class, there was a significant association between dark skin color and perceived racial discrimination from the police or in the courts. It does not seem plausible that this sole item of reported discrimination could have an adverse impact on the IQs of dark skinned blacks. The findings of this study that dark skinned blacks do not report greater experience of discrimination than that reported by light skinned blacks, with the one exception noted above, appears to disconfirm the theory that discrimination by whites can explain the correlation between skin color and IQ. A third problem with the discrimination theory is that the white majority in the United States has discriminated against Jews and Asians, yet Jews have average IQs above that of whites (MacDonald, 1994) and Asians have average IQs that are either about the same as that of whites (Flynn, 1991) or higher (Lynn, 1996). Taking this evidence as a whole, it is proposed that the higher IQs obtained by light skinned blacks cannot be plausibly explained in terms of a social discrimination or by any other environmental theory. For these reasons it is proposed that the most straightforward interpretation of the significant association between light skin color and intelligence is that it confirms the hypothesis that genetic factors are partly responsible for the black-white difference in intelligence.

6. The difference in intelligence between light and dark skinned African Americans is probably a significant factor in the difference in socioeconomic status documented by Hill (2000), because intelligence is a significant determinant of socio-economic status (Herrnstein and Murray, 1994).

REFERENCES

BEAN, R. B. (1906). SOME RACIAL PECULIARITIES OF THE NEGRO BRAIN. *AMERICAN JOURNAL OF ANATOMY*, 5, 353–432.

BRODY, N. (1992). *INTELLIGENCE*. SAN DIEGO: ACADEMIC.

DAVIS, J. A., & SMITH, T. W. (1996). *GENERAL SOCIAL SURVEYS; CUMULATIVE CODEBOOK*. CHICAGO: NATIONAL OPINION RESEARCH CENTER.

FLYNN, J. R. (1980). *RACE, IQ AND JENSEN*. LONDON: ROUTLEDGE AND KEGAN PAUL.

FLYNN, J. R. (1991). *ASIAN AMERICANS: ACHIEVEMENT BEYOND IQ*. HILLSDALE, NJ: LAWRENCE ERLBAUM.

HERRNSTEIN, R. J., & MURRAY, C. (1994). *THE BELL CURVE*. NEW YORK: FREE PRESS.

HERSKOVITS, M. J. (1926). ON THE RELATION BETWEEN NEGRO-WHITE MIXTURE AND STANDING IN INTELLIGENCE TESTS. *PEDOLOGICAL SEMINARY*, 33, 30–42.

HILL, M. E. (2000). COLOR DIFFERENCES IN THE SOCIO-ECONOMIC STATUS OF AFRICAN AMERICAN MEN: RESULTS OF A LONGITUDINAL STUDY. *SOCIAL FORCES*, 78, 1473–1460.

HOWE, M. J. (1997). *IQ IN QUESTION*. LONDON: SAGE.

JENSEN, A. R. (1973). *EDUCABILITY AND GROUP DIFFERENCES*. LONDON: METHUEN.

JENSEN, A. R. (1981). OBSTACLES, PROBLEMS AND PITFALLS IN DIFFERENTIAL PSYCHOLOGY. IN S. SCARR (ED), *RACE, SOCIAL CLASS AND INDIVIDUAL DIFFERENCES IN IQ*. HILLSDALE, NJ: LAWRENCE ERLBAUM.

JENSEN, A. R., & REYNOLDS, C. R. (1982). RACE, SOCIAL CLASS AND ABILITY PATTERNS ON THE WISC-R. *PERSONALITY AND INDIVIDUAL DIFFERENCES*, 3, 423–438.

KLINEBERG, O. (1928). AN EXPERIMENTAL STUDY OF SPEED AND OTHER FACTORS IN RACIAL DIFFERENCES. *ARCHIVES OF PSYCHOLOGY*, 15, No. 93.

KRIEGER, N., SIDNEY, S., & COAKLEY, E. (1998). RACIAL DISCRIMINATION AND SKIN COLOR IN THE CARDIA STUDY: IMPLICATIONS FOR PUBLIC HEALTH RESEARCH. *AMERICAN JOURNAL OF PUBLIC HEALTH*, 88, 1308–1313.

LOEHLIN, J. C., VANDENBERG, S. G., & OSBORNE, R. T. (1973). BLOOD GROUP GENES AND NEGRO-WHITE ABILITY DIFFERENCES IN ABILITY. *BEHAVIOR GENETICS*, 3, 263–270.

LYNN, R. (1996). RACIAL AND ETHNIC DIFFERENCES IN INTELLIGENCE IN THE UNITED STATES ON THE DIFFERENTIAL ABILITY SCALE. *PERSONALITY AND INDIVIDUAL DIFFERENCES*, 20, 271–273.

LYNN, R. (1997). GEOGRAPHICAL VARIATION IN INTELLIGENCE, IN H. NYBORG (ED.), *THE SCIENTIFIC STUDY OF HUMAN NATURE*, OXFORD: PERGAMON.

MACDONALD, K. (1994). *A PEOPLE THAT SHALL DWELL ALONE: JUDAISM AS A GROUP EVOLUTIONARY STRATEGY*. WESTPORT, CT: PRAEGER.

MACKINTOSH, N. J. (1998). *IQ AND HUMAN INTELLIGENCE*. OXFORD, UK: UNIVERSITY PRESS.

NISBETT, R. E. (1998). RACE, GENETICS AND IQ. IN C. JENCKS & M. PHILLIPS (EDS.), *THE BLACK-WHITE TEST SCORE GAP*. WASHINGTON, DC: BROOKINGS INSTITUTION.

PEARL, R. (1934). THE WEIGHT OF THE NEGRO BRAIN. *SCIENCE*, 80, 431–434.

PETERSON, J., & LANIER, L. L. (1929). STUDIES IN THE COMPARATIVE ABILITIES OF WHITES AND NEGROES. *COMPARATIVE PSYCHOLOGY MONOGRAPHS*, No. 5.

RUSHTON, J. P. (2000). *RACE, EVOLUTION AND BEHAVIOR*. PORT HURON, MI: CHARLES DARWIN RESEARCH INSTITUTE.

SCARR, S. (1981). COMMENTS AND REPLIES. IN S. SCARR *RACE, SOCIAL CLASS, AND INDIVIDUAL DIFFERENCES IN IQ*. HILLSDALE, NJ: LAWRENCE ERLBAUM.

SCARR, S. (1995). INHERITANCE, INTELLIGENCE AND ACHIEVEMENT. *PLANNING FOR HIGHER EDUCATION*, 23, 1–9.

SCARR, S., PAKSTIS, A. J., KATZ, S. H., & BARKER, W. B. (1977). ABSENCE OF A RELATIONSHIP BETWEEN DEGREE OF WHITE ANCESTRY AND INTELLECTUAL SKILLS WITHIN A BLACK POPULATION. *BEHAVIOR GENETICS*, 39, 68–86.

SHOCKLEY, W. (1971). HARDY-WEINBERG LAW GENERALIZED TO ESTIMATE HYBRID VARIANCE FOR NEGRO POPULATIONS AND REDUCE RACIAL ASPECTS OF THE ENVIRONMENT-HEREDITY UNCERTAINTY. *PROCEEDINGS OF THE NATIONAL ACADEMY OF SCIENCES*, 68, 1390.

SHUEY, A. (1966). *THE TESTING OF NEGRO INTELLIGENCE*. NEW YORK: SOCIAL SCIENCE PRESS.

VINT, F. W. (1934). THE BRAIN OF THE KENYAN NATIVE. *JOURNAL OF ANATOMY*, 48, 216–223.

WEINBERG, R. S., SCARR, S., & WALDMAN, I. R. (1992). THE MINNESOTA TRANSRACIAL ADOPTION STUDY: A FOLLOW-UP OF IQ TEST PERFORMANCE AT ADOLESCENCE. *INTELLIGENCE*, 16, 117–135.

WITTY, P. A., & JENKINS, M. D. (1936). INTRA-RACE TESTING AND NEGRO INTELLIGENCE. *JOURNAL OF PSYCHOLOGY*, 1, 179–192.

Ethnic Differences in Children's Intelligence Test Scores

Role of Economic Deprivation, Home Environment and Maternal Characteristics

JEANNE BROOKS-GUNN, PAMELA K. KLEBANOV, AND GREG J. DUNCAN

We examine differences in intelligence test scores of black and white 5-year-olds. The Infant Health and Development Program data set includes 483 low birthweight premature children who were assessed with the Wechsler Preschool and Primary Scale of Intelligence. These children had been followed from birth, with data on neighborhood and family poverty, family structure, family resources, maternal characteristics, and home environment collected over the first 5 years of life. Black children's IQ scores were 1 SD lower than those of white children. Adjustments for ethnic differences in poverty reduced the ethnic differential by 52%. Adjustments for maternal education and whether the head of household was female did not reduce the ethnic difference further. However, differences in home environment reduced the ethnic differential by an additional 28%. Adjustments for economic and social differences in the lives of black and white children all but eliminate differences in the IQ scores between these two groups.

Black children do less well on cognitive tests such as intelligence and ability tests and preschool readiness tests than do white children (Loehlin, Lindzey, & Spuhler, 1975; Scarr, 1981; Scarr-Salapatek, 1971; Weinberg, 1989). Later on, they are also more likely to repeat a grade and to drop out of school (Haveman, Wolfe, & Spaulding,

1991; Mare, 1980; Natriello, 1987; Rumberger, 1983). Test-score differences are usually in the range of three-quarters to one standard deviation. A variety of explanations have been offered for these ethnic differences, including variations in innate abilities, family structure and poverty, family socialization and learning-oriented practices, the quality of schools attended, residential segregation and the socioeconomic composition of neighborhoods, access to and treatment in schools, and access to the job market, as well as the cultural equivalence of and biases in tests.

Perhaps the most striking difference between children from ethnic minority backgrounds and those from nonminority families is that minority children are far more likely to be poor (Bane & Ellwood, 1989). Three times as many black (and Hispanic) children as white children live in families below the official U.S. poverty line. The Census Bureau-based measure of poverty, which focuses on children living below the poverty line in any one year, underestimates income disparities between black and white children. Since income is quite volatile (Duncan, 1988; Duncan, Smeeding, & Rodgers, in press), many children, especially in nonminority families, who are classified as not poor in a given year would be classified as poor in another year. Using the nationally representative Panel Study of Income Dynamics (PSID, an ongoing longitudinal survey of U.S. households begun in 1968 by the Survey Research Center of the University of Michigan; Hill, 1992) to estimate the percentages of children (initially birth to age 3)

Jeanne Brooks-Gunn, Pamela K. Klebanov, and Greg J. Duncan, "Ethnic Differences in Children's Intelligence Test Scores: Role of Economic Deprivation, Home Environment, and Maternal Characteristics," *Child Development*, vol. 67, no. 2, pp. 396–408. Copyright © 1996 by John Wiley & Sons, Inc. Reprinted with permission.

living in families below the poverty line over a 6-year period, 66.4% of the black and 25.8% of the white children's families were found to be below the poverty line in at least 1 of the 6 years (Duncan, Brooks-Gunn, & Klebanov, 1994). Persistent poverty (in this analysis defined as family income below the poverty line for 5–6 years of the 6-year period) was a characteristic of 40% of black but only 5% of white children. Thus ethnic disparities in family poverty increase substantially as the accounting period over which income is measured lengthens.

Family income data do not take into account another possibly critical dimension of poverty—namely, the income distribution in the neighborhood in which a child lives. Neighborhoods vary widely with respect to the affluence of their residents (Jencks & Peterson, 1991; Wilson, 1987). Black families are more likely to live in poor neighborhoods, whether or not they are poor themselves (Duncan et al., 1994; Kasarda, 1990; Wilson, 1987). Using the PSID sample of young children again, neighborhood poverty was determined by matching census tract information from the decennial census to the children's addresses and defined as the average fraction of nonelderly neighbors with incomes below the poverty line. About 57% of the black children lived in poor neighborhoods (defined as having 20% or more neighbors living in poverty) as compared with 7.5% of the white children. Taking into account family and neighborhood poverty, almost one-half of all black children whose families were not poor resided in poor neighborhoods compared with less than 10% of the comparable white children (Duncan et al., 1994).

Other factors associated with poverty (often termed poverty co-factors) are more common in minority than nonminority children. These include characteristics related to family structure and resources: single parents, parents with low educational levels and low literacy scores, unemployed parents, and young parents are more likely to be found in poor households (Featherman & Hauser, 1978; Hernandez, 1993; McLoyd & Wilson, 1990; Parker, Greer, & Zuckerman, 1988; Sandefur, McLanahan, & Wojtkiewicz, 1992; Wilson, 1987).

These poverty co-factors and the various dimensions of poverty have been linked to childhood and adolescent outcomes. Persistent family poverty and neighborhood poverty contribute to high school drop-out rates and teenage motherhood over and above other indicators of the socioeconomic status of the family (Brooks-Gunn, Duncan, Klebanov, & Sealand, 1993; Corcoran, Gordon, Laren, & Solon, 1992; Haveman et al., 1991). Living in single-parent households and having parents with low educational levels also contribute to less positive adolescent outcomes, when one controls for family income levels (Garfinkel & McLanahan, 1986; Hauser & Featherman, 1977; McLanahan, Astone, & Marks, 1991; Sandefur et al., 1992). While most studies have not focused on young children, poverty and its co-factors have been associated with lower cognitive test scores and school achievement among such children as well (Bradley et al., 1989; Duncan et al., 1994; McLoyd, 1990; Sameroff, Seifer, Baldwin, & Baldwin, 1993; Sameroff, Seifer, Barocas, Zax, & Greenspan, 1987). Few of these studies consider neighborhood poverty, persistent poverty, family structure, and parental education simultaneously, nor do they consider their effect on the ethnic differences seen in these childhood and adolescent outcomes.

In this article, we examine differences in intelligence test scores of black and white 5-year-olds. Our focus on young children enables us to concentrate on the role of family and neighborhood factors rather than factors that more directly influence older children, such as treatment in the schools and job markets and access to schools, jobs, and housing. Our analytic strategy is a straightforward application of multiple regression techniques to estimate the extent to which environmental differences between black and white children account for differences in the IQ scores of 5-year-olds. New in what we do is the use of an exceptionally rich set of data containing high-quality longitudinal measures of childhood poverty, family structure, and other important components of family socioeconomic status; maternal verbal ability; the home learning environment; and IQ at age 5.

It is expected that a substantial portion of the ethnic difference in IQ (estimated in our data to be about 1 SD, consistent with earlier work) will be accounted for by the large differences in family and neighborhood poverty, maternal education, and rates of single parenthood. In contrast to previous research, our data set contains information on persistent family poverty and neighborhood poverty, which are likely to account in large measure for ethnic differences in intelligence test scores. We are also able to adjust for the effects of maternal verbal ability, which is shaped by innate as well as environmental factors (i.e., the education of the mother, the verbal stimulation provided to her as a child, the poverty and resources of her family, her access to schools, jobs, and housing as a child, and so on), on ethnic differences in child's test scores (Angoff, 1988; Weinberg, 1989). Variations in family socialization practices, specifically the types of learning experiences provided, also are expected to be associated with ethnic differences in intelligence tests (Berlin, Brooks-Gunn, Spicer, & Zaslow, 1995; Bradley et al., 1989; Gottfried, 1984; Sugland et al, 1995; Wachs & Gruen, 1982).

METHOD

Infant Health and Development Program Data Set Design.— We use data from the Infant Health and Development Program (IHDP). The IHDP is an eight-site randomized clinical trial to test the efficacy of educational and family-support services and high-quality pediatric follow-up offered in the first 3 years of life in reducing the incidence of developmental delay in low birthweight (LBW), preterm infants (Infant Health and Development Program Staff, 1990). Infants weighing no more than 2,500 grams at birth and 37 weeks or less gestational age were screened for eligibility if they were 40 weeks postconceptional age between January 7, 1985, and October 9, 1985, and were born in one of eight participating medical institutions (University of Arkansas for Medical Sciences, Little Rock; Albert Einstein College of Medicine, Bronx; Harvard Medical School; University of Miami School of Medicine; University of Pennsylvania School of Medicine, Philadelphia; University of Texas Health Science Center at Dallas; University of Washington School of Medicine, Seattle; and Yale University School of Medicine). Of the 1,302 infants who met enrollment criteria, 274 (21.0%) were eliminated because consent was refused, and 43 were withdrawn before entry into their assigned group. The IHDP research design included stratification by clinical site and into birthweight groups. One-third of the infants were randomized to the intervention group, and two-thirds to the follow-up only group. All of our empirical work uses the follow-up only group. The intervention program was initiated on discharge from the neonatal nursery and continued until 36 months. The services for infants in the intervention group consisted of home visits over the 3 years,

an educational child-care program at a child-development center in the second and third years, and bimonthly parent-group meetings in the child's second and third years of life (Brooks-Gunn, Klebanov, Liaw, & Spiker, 1993; Ramey et al., 1992). Pediatric surveillance was provided seven times over the first 3 years of life for both groups. The IHDP was designed to show whether the children in the intervention group differed from those in the follow-up only group in cognitive functioning, behavioral competence, and/or health status (Brooks-Gunn et al., 1994; Infant Health and Development Program Staff, 1990; McCormick et al., 1991). Children with birth weights of 1,000 grams or less are omitted from these analysis (N = 61 at age 5). Extremely low birthweight children are very likely to have low cognitive functioning because of biological insults (McCormick, Brooks-Gunn, Workman-Daniels, Turner, & Peckham, 1992). Informed consent was obtained from the mothers of the children.

*Cognitive outcome.—*The analyses reported in this article are based on the black and white children in the follow-up only group (N = 483). The small sample of Hispanic children was excluded from these analyses since the number of these children was small (N = 105 in the sample at the time of recruitment and 90 with IQ data at age 5). Also, Hispanic children were concentrated in three of the eight sites rather than being distributed among the eight sites, as was the case for black and white children (McCarton, Brooks-Gunn, & Tonascia, 1994). Children's cognitive functioning was assessed when the children were 3 and 5 years of age (corrected for gestational age). At age 3, 93% of the children were assessed and at age 5, 82% were assessed. At age 5, 90% of the original 985 families were interviewed (Brooks-Gunn et al., 1994). The Stanford-Binet Intelligence Scale Form L-M, third edition (Terman & Merrill, 1973) was given at age 3. The Wechsler Preschool and Primary Scale of Intelligence (WPPSI; Wechsler, 1989), a test developed for use with children between the ages of 4 and 6 1/2 years, was used at age 5. The Binet IQ scale is normed so that the mean score is 100 and the standard deviation is 16, while the WPPSI is normed with a mean of a 100 and a standard deviation of 15 (WPPSI Manual, 1989). Results are presented in this article for age 5 (similar results were obtained from the age 3 test and are available from the authors).

Initial status and control variables.—To control for differences across the eight study sites, dummy variables were created for seven of the sites and included in our regression analyses. The following initial status variables also were controlled for: birthweight (in grams), length of neonatal health index (a measure that standardized the length of stay for the neonatal hospitalization by birthweight (standardized to a mean of 100, with higher values signifying better neonatal health), Scott, Bauer, Kraemer, & Tyson, 1989), sex of the child (coded male = 1, female = 0), completed schooling of the mother (in years), whether the family was headed by the mother (two dummy variables: female headship at 24 or 36 months = 1, other = 0; female headship at 24 and 36 months = 1, other = 0, with female headship at neither 24 nor 36 months omitted as a control), and whether the mother was black (black = 1, white = 0). The child's birthweight, gender, maternal age, maternal education, and maternal ethnicity were recorded at birth, neonatal stay was recorded based on hospital discharge records, and female headship was measured when the child was 2 and 3 years old.

Neighborhood conditions.—Neighborhood conditions were constructed by matching family addresses to a 1980 census tract neighborhood identifier ($N = 483$). Census tracts usually consist of between 4,000 and 6,000 individuals and are defined with the advice of local committees to approximate "real" neighborhoods. Details are available from the authors upon request. The relevant address was taken at the time of randomization. Six of the centers were located in major metropolitan areas with large populations of poor families, and two in metropolitan areas serving both urban and rural communities. Because concentrations of poor and affluent neighbors may each have distinct influences on developmental outcomes (Mayer & Jencks, 1989; Wilson, 1991a, 1991b), the neighborhood's income distribution for the nonelderly population was used to construct three indicators: the fraction of families in the tract with incomes under $10,000, the fraction of families with incomes over $30,000, and the fraction of families with incomes between $10,000 and $30,000. 1980 census data show that about one-quarter of families had incomes above $30,000, while about one-fifth had incomes below $10,000.

Family-level poverty.—The measurement of "official" U.S. poverty is based on a set of income thresholds that were developed in the 1960s and are adjusted each year for changes in the cost of living, using the Consumer Price Index. The poverty thresholds are *not* adjusted for real (i.e., above inflation) improvements in living standards, so the poverty line is a smaller fraction of median income now than it was 20 years ago. In 1991, U.S. poverty thresholds for families of three, four, and five persons were $10,860, $13,924 and $16,460, respectively. Families with annual cash incomes, before taxes, that exceed these thresholds are considered "not poor," while families with income falling below them are "poor." Respondents were asked to provide an estimate of total family income in a series of categories. The categorical responses were converted into a continuous measure by assigning the midpoints of each interval. A family income-to-needs ratio was computed by dividing each household's income by its corresponding poverty threshold. Then, income to needs was averaged across a 3-year period (i.e., when the child was 1, 2, and 3 years old). In 1991, children (as well as other family members) living in a four-person household whose income totaled $41,772 would have income-to-needs ratios of 3.0 (= $41,772/$13,924) and be considered nonpoor in that year; members of four-person households with a total household income of only $6,962 would each have an income-to-needs ratio of 0.5 and be designated as poor. By definition, an income-to-needs ratio of 1.0 indicates that a family income is equal to the poverty threshold.

Home environment.—We used both the infant-toddler (birth to age 3) and early childhood (ages 3–6) versions of the *Home Observation for Measurement of the Environment* (HOME; Bradley & Caldwell, 1984). The HOME was administered when the child was 1 year and 3 years of age as a measure of the child's level of stimulation in the home environment (Bradley et al., 1994). One subscale of the infant version was used here: Provision of learning stimulation, which is a composite of the learning materials, parental involvement, and variety of stimulation subscales (e.g., child has complex eye-hand coordination toys, parent provides toys that challenge child to develop new skills, and parent reads stories to child at least three times weekly); alpha = 0.80 for 20 items. Maternal acceptance at 12 months of age is not included in the regression analyses due to a low alpha coefficient. Two subscales of the early childhood version were used: Provision of learning stimulation, which is a composite of the learning, academic, and language stimulation and variety in experience subscales (e.g., child has toys that teach color, size, shape, child is encouraged to learn the alphabet and numbers); alpha = .87 for 32 items; and warmth (parent caresses, kisses, or cuddles child during visit); alpha = .64 for seven items.

Maternal characteristics.—Three maternal characteristics were examined: maternal depressive symptoms, social support, and maternal verbal ability. Maternal depressive symptoms were measured at 1, 2, and 3 years of age by the General Health Questionnaire (Goldberg, 1978), which consists of 12 items and taps depression, somatization, and anxiety dimensions. Respondents provide reports as to how they have been feeling over the past few weeks, from better than usual (0) to much less than usual (3) with scores ranging from 0 to 36. Social support was measured using six vignettes adapted from Cohen and Lazarus (1977) by the National Study Office of the IHDP (Gross and Spiker) and are designed to tap characteristics of the mother's support network within the household and out of the household when the child was 1 and 3 years of age. Mothers responded yes (1) or no (0) to whether support was present within the household or outside of the household. An overall measure of support was obtained by summing all six items, with higher scores indicative of more support (scores range from 0 to 12). These vignettes have good discriminant validity (McCormick, Brooks–Gunn, Shorter, Holmes, & Heagarty, 1989; McCormick et al., 1987). Maternal verbal ability was assessed using the Peabody Picture Vocabulary Test—Revised (Dunn & Dunn, 1981) when the child was 1 1/2 years old. Only the later measure significantly contributed to IQ scores at age 5 and is included in our analysis.

Analytic Plan

Four sets of Ordinary Least Square (OLS) multiple linear regressions were conducted to examine the mean difference in IQ scores at age 5 for black and white children. Because the reduction in ethnic differences as environmental controls are introduced is of primary interest, regressions first control for site and child characteristics; then economic status variables are entered, given the central hypotheses. Maternal characteristics are entered next, given maternal education and verbal ability are associated with IQ scores. Home environment measures are entered in the last regression.

Descriptive Characteristics

The mean IQ scores at both ages, and the familial and neighborhood variables for black and white children: The white children had a mean IQ that was over 1 SD higher than that of the black children. The white children were also more advantaged—they were less likely to be poor in any one year (not shown; for example, 57% of the black children vs. 14% of the white children resided in families with an average income below the poverty line when they were 3 years of age), had higher income-to-needs ratios across the first years of life, were less likely to live in poor neighborhoods (i.e., 34% of the white children vs. 86% of the black children lived in neighborhoods in which 20% or more of the neighbors had family incomes of $10,000 or less), and were more likely to live in affluent neighborhoods (i.e., 64% of the white children vs. 11% of the black children lived in neighborhoods in which 20% or more of the neighbors had family incomes of more than $30,000). Black children were more likely to live in single-parent households and to have mothers without college-level schooling. Mothers of black children had lower PPVT-R scores and provided fewer learning experiences in the home.

Leading Predictors of Ethnic Difference

The first estimated difference in IQ controls for study site and for child's gender, birthweight, and length of neonatal stay; the last three variables were not significantly associated with IQ scores at either age). Ethnic-differences are 17.8 IQ points. The standard error of the difference is 1.9 IQ points. The second set of regressions then adds controls for the family and neighborhood poverty measures which reduce the ethnic differences in IQ by 52% (to 8.5 IQ points). Only the family measure of poverty significantly contributed to the equation. The fraction of neighbors who are affluent did not significantly contribute to IQ scores at age 5, ps > .12, although it did contribute to IQ scores at age 3. In the third regression, female headship, maternal education, maternal age, and maternal verbal score (PPVT-R) are added. These variables do not reduce the IQ differential over and above what was found for the poverty measures (ethnic difference is 7.8 points). However, maternal education and verbal ability contribute to the equation (standardized coefficients are each .19; not shown). Finally, measures of home environment were then added. Variations in the provision of learning experiences at both ages and maternal warmth at 36 months reduce the ethnic differences in IQ by an additional 28% of the original difference. The difference is now 3.4 points, and the 95% confidence interval includes zero. A regression that had also included maternal depressive symptoms and social support did not alter the ethnic IQ difference further, as maternal depressive symptoms and social support were not associated with children's IQ scores.

We also examined the relative effects of income, maternal characteristics, and home environment using a backward elimination procedure. The first variables to be eliminated are site, gender, birthweight, and neonatal health. Then neighborhood income and ethnicity are eliminated, followed by female headship, maternal age, and maternal education. Family income, home environmental scores, and maternal verbal ability are left in the equation. These analyses demonstrate that the effects of income and home environment are predictive, while ethnicity is not a predictor of IQ in this sample, with the set of SES and home variables available.

DISCUSSION

In this sample, young black children's IQ scores are about 1 SD lower than those of white children, as other studies of both low birthweight and normal birthweight children have consistently found. When we used IHDP data, adjustments for ethnic differences in family and neighborhood poverty measures reduced the ethnic differential by 52%. Adding other family structural and resource measures (maternal age, marital status, education, and verbal ability) does not result in further reductions. Regressions were conducted where the family structural and resource variables were entered before poverty measures; the reductions in ethnic differences in IQ were much less substantial (i.e., 20% rather than 52% at the second step). In part, this is because poor black families are more likely to have lower levels of family resources than poor white families (i.e., analyses not shown here). Most developmental studies do not take into account ethnic differences in poverty rates

or in persistent poverty, which may have resulted in an overestimation of ethnic differences in IQ. Considering maternal education differentials alone, or in conjunction with household structure, does not account for as much of the variance between ethnic groups as does poverty.

The other major contributor to ethnic differences in IQ was home environment. Provision of learning experiences is not only significantly associated with IQ, as many other studies have shown (Bradley, Caldwell, & Elardo, 1979; Bradley et al., 1989), but reduced the ethnic gap in IQ by an additional 28% of the original difference. Provision of learning experiences, as measured at both 12 and 36 months, affects child IQ over and above its correlation with the poverty indices measured here. Differences in female headship did not affect the ethnic differences in IQ scores, in part because female headship is more likely to occur in poor families and is a cause of poverty (McLanahan et al., 1991). It also is associated with low maternal education.

While maternal verbal ability was associated with child IQ, as expected, this variable did not add a great deal to the regression, once differences in maternal education were taken into account. However, since maternal education and verbal ability are highly correlated themselves, it is difficult to ascertain the contribution of each separately.

The IHDP sample consists of LBW, premature infants from eight sites across the United States. Whether similar results would be found for a national sample of normal birthweight children is not known. We suspect that the findings would be similar, based on results from a large study of low and normal birthweight children at the age of 8. These results suggest that education, ethnicity, and female headship are similarly associated across the birthweight distribution (McCormick et al., 1992). The unique aspect of the IHDP is that it is the only developmental data set that combines high-quality measurement of developmental outcomes (i.e., full-scale IQ tests) with longitudinal data on family economic status, neighborhood conditions, family structure variables, and home environment.

That these results may have relevance for normal birthweight children is suggested by two studies of school achievement rather than IQ. In two analyses of older children's school achievement test scores (not IQ scores), family poverty and a measure of home environment reduced differences in IQ scores among three ethnic groups (Crane, 1993; Mercer & Brown, 1973).

The IHDP study was not designed to address directly the debate over possible genetic contributions to IQ as an explanation of ethnic differences nor to estimate the unique and interactive contributions of nature to children's intelligence test scores (Bouchard & McGuire, 1981). Estimates of heritability for IQ cannot be made without a design comparing twins, adopted children with their birth and adoptive parents, or siblings with the same two (genetic) parents, one parent in common, or no parents in common. In any case, such studies yield estimates of heritability within ethnic groups and do not speak to variation across ethnic groups (Chipuer, Rovine, & Plomin, 1990; Lewontin, 1976; Loehlin et al., 1975; Scarr-Salapatek, 1971; Schiff & Lewontin, 1986).

However, our approach should not be used to argue that genetic effects do not contribute to variation within ethnic groups. Maternal verbal ability test scores probably reflect genetics, environment, the interaction between the two, and the covariation between the two (Jencks, 1992; Plomin, 1989; Scarr & McCartney, 1983; Weinberg, 1989). The same may be true for the home environment scores as well (Plomin & Bergmann, 1991).

The analyses also do not address the possible differences in the strength of potential predictors within each ethnic group separately. Supplemental analyses show that more variance is explained for the white children's intelligence test scores than for those of the black children, probably because of the distributional differences between groups. (These analyses are available from the authors upon request. For example, $R2$ estimates in regression 4 are 63% for the former and 27% for the latter; see also Jensen, 1980). When these analyses also were run for poor (income-to-needs ratio < 1.5) and nonpoor (income-to-needs ratio > 1.5) subgroups, similar patterns of results were found—more variance is explained for nonpoor families than for poor families (the $R2$ estimates in regression 4 are 49% and 23%, respectively). Thus, the finding of more variance explained in the white sample suggests that there is a greater range in the independent and dependent variables than in the black sample. Moreover, the effect of ethnicity was nonsignificant for both poor and for nonpoor families in regression 4. These supplemental analyses reinforce the other regression results that poverty significantly reduces the difference between black and white children's test scores.

This study only addresses the links between poverty, ethnicity, and intelligence test scores during the late 1980s and early 1990s. The proportions of black and white children whose families are poor or who reside in poor neighborhoods have changed over time. Family poverty rates may be charted easily from 1959 onward, since the current poverty threshold was developed at that time (Orshansky, 1965). Estimates of relative poverty rates for black and white children from 1939 to 1988 are available in Hernandez (1993, Table 9.3). Actual poverty rates for blacks dropped from 76% in 1939 (census data) to 53% in 1988 (Current Population Survey data) and from 33% to 22% for whites. For example, a little over half of blacks and a little under one in five whites were below the poverty threshold in 1959 (Axelson, 1985). By the end of the 1960s, these rates have dropped to about one-third of blacks and one in ten of whites, with these rates remaining relatively stable through the late 1980s or rising somewhat (Hernandez, 1993, in press; Ruiz, 1990). At the same time, residence in neighborhoods with high concentrations of poor people may have intensified for blacks between 1970 and 1980, given the increase in such neighborhoods in urban metropolitan areas, with these neighborhoods being home to primarily blacks and Hispanics (Bane & Ellwood, 1989). In any case, changes in the relative proportions over time may influence the pattern of results seen (Helms, 1992).

It is often assumed that intelligence tests, and cognitive tests more generally, have cultural biases and may not be equivalent across cultures. Tests (both the items and the testing situation) may have different meaning for subgroups who are not white and who are not middle class. In these analyses, including an adequate range of SES in both black and white sub samples rectifies part of the problem, as does including a measure of persistent family poverty as well as neighborhood poverty. However, controlling for these differences is not the same as seeing whether intelligence tests have the same meaning across subgroups (Helms, 1992).

At the same time, these analyses may overestimate the differences between black and white children, given that cultural equivalence and bias are likely to play more of a role in the performance of black children than white children, even controlling for SES (Helms, 1992). Discrimination limits opportunities of black families in housing, work, and education. Consequently, black families have less access to high quality education and housing than white families across the SES spectrum. How discrimination and unequal treatment influence performance on cognitive tests is not addressed here nor has it been given much psychometric consideration (Helms, 1992; Landrum-Brown, 1990). Culture also may influence values and beliefs in ways that might influence test performance. Helms (1992) persuasively argues that cognitive ability tests have been constructed based on Eurocentric values, which are different than Afrocentric values (as well as other cultural values). Consequently, children brought up in families and neighborhoods that espouse a different cultural belief system may not respond the same to tests constructed with specific types of cognitive strategies being represented and other strategies not being represented (Heath, 1989). The fact that the provision of learning experiences in the home, as assessed using the HOME scale, reduces the black-white differences over and above the large effects of poverty, may be associated with Eurocentric and Acrocentric differences in child-rearing strategies (although we do not have data to test this hypothesis directly).

What our analyses do show is that age-5 IQ differences between black and white children are almost completely eliminated by adjusting for differences in neighborhood economic conditions, family poverty, maternal education, and learning experiences. Differences in maternal verbal ability do not add significantly to the explanation of ethnic differences, once the effects of these other environmental differences are taken into account.

What are the implications of these findings? First, the differential rates of persistent family and neighborhood poverty for black and white children are significantly associated with the ethnic differences in IQ scores. Policies designed to reduce the number of children living in poverty, if applied equitably, could reduce this income differential. Policies such as the Earned Income Tax Credit and increased efforts to enforce child support payments from absent fathers could alter the differential. Possible policy initiatives such as increases in the minimum wage and changes in public housing policy (i.e., increases in scattered site housing and Section 8 vouchers for rentals in the private housing market) could also affect relatively more black than white poor children. However, little evidence is available on the effects of such policies, or changes in policies, on child outcomes, let alone family outcomes

(Duncan & Brooks-Gunn, in press). Second, policies and programs have been developed with a focus on providing low income mothers with the skills to enter the job market and to move into higher skilled positions, in order to move families out of poverty. These job training and work programs have typically been evaluated with respect to effects in the employment arena, not in the parenting or child outcome domains (Chase-Lansdale & Brooks-Gunn, 1995; Smith, 1995). Third, programs focus on family support via home visiting programs, literacy programs, and community resource centers. Such programs have been found to influence parenting and, to a much lesser extent, child outcomes (Benasich, Brooks-Gunn, & Clewell, 1992; Futures of Children, 1992; Olds & Kitzman, 1993). Fourth, providing high quality preschool education programs to poor children is a strategy that has been shown to enhance children's developmental outcomes (Haskins, 1989; Lazar, Darlington, Murray, Royce, & Snipper, 1982; Ramey, Bryant, Sparling, & Wasik, 1985; Zigler, 1992). Fifth, enhancing the quality of elementary school education, providing continuity between preschool and kindergarten experiences, and strengthening the links between family and school all are being tested in poor neighborhoods. Our data do not suggest which of these interventions for poor families, or what combination of them, might be most effective. They do suggest that a focus on poor families is critical to altering the life chances of black children.

REFERENCES

ANGOFF, W. (1988). THE NATURE-NURTURE DEBATE, APTITUDES, AND GROUP DIFFERENCES. *AMERICAN PSYCHOLOGIST*, 43, 713–720.

AXELSON, J. A. (1985). *COUNSELING AND DEVELOPMENT IN A MULTICULTURAL SOCIETY*. MONTEREY, CA: BROOKS/COLE.

BANE, M. J., & ELLWOOD, D. T. (1989). ONE FIFTH OF THE NATION'S CHILDREN: WHY ARE THEY POOR? *SCIENCE*, 245, 1047–1053.

BENASICH, A. A., BROOKS-GUNN, J., CLEWELL, B. C. (1992). HOW DO MOTHERS BENEFIT FROM EARLY INTERVENTION PROGRAMS. *JOURNAL OF APPLIED DEVELOPMENTAL PSYCHOLOGY*, 13, 311–362.

BERLIN, L. J., BROOKS-GUNN, J., SPIKER, D., & ZASLOW, M. J. (1995). EXAMINING OBSERVATIONAL MEASURES OF EMOTIONAL SUPPORT AND COGNITIVE STIMULATION IN BLACK

AND WHITE MOTHERS OF PRESCHOOLERS. *JOURNAL OF FAMILY ISSUES*, 16, 664–686.

BOUCHARD, T. J., & McGUIRE, M. (1981). FAMILIAL STUDIES OF INTELLIGENCE: A REVIEW. *SCIENCE*, 212, 1055–1058.

BRADLEY, R. H., & CALDWELL, B. M. (1984). THE HOME INVENTORY AND FAMILY DEMOGRAPHICS. *DEVELOPMENTAL PSYCHOLOGY*, 20, 315–320.

BRADLEY, R. H., CALDWELL, B. M., & ELARDO, R. (1979). HOME ENVIRONMENT AND COGNITIVE DEVELOPMENT IN THE FIRST TWO YEARS: A CROSSED-LAGGED PANEL ANALYSIS. *DEVELOPMENTAL PSYCHOLOGY*, 15, 246–250.

BRADLEY, R. H., CALDWELL, B. M., ROCK, S. L., RAMEY, C. T., BARNARD, K. E., GRAY, C., HAMMOND, M. A., MITCHELL, S., GOTTFRIED, A. W., SIEGEL, L., & JOHNSON, D. L. (1989). HOME ENVIRONMENT AND COGNITIVE DEVELOPMENT IN THE FIRST THREE YEARS OF LIFE: A COLLABORATIVE STUDY INCLUDING SIX SITES AND THREE ETHNIC GROUPS IN NORTH AMERICA. *DEVELOPMENTAL PSYCHOLOGY*, 25, 217–235.

BRADLEY, R. H., WHITESIDE, L., MUNDFROM, D. J., CASEY, P. H., KELLEHER, K. J., & POPE, S. K. (1994). EARLY INDICATIONS OF RESILIENCE AND THEIR RELATION TO EXPERIENCES IN THE HOME ENVIRONMENTS OF LOW BIRTHWEIGHT, PREMATURE CHILDREN LIVING IN POVERTY. *CHILD DEVELOPMENT*, 65, 346–360.

BROOKS-GUNN, J., DUNCAN, G. J., KLEBANOV, P. K., & SEALAND, N. (1993). DO NEIGHBORHOODS INFLUENCE CHILD AND ADOLESCENT BEHAVIOR? *AMERICAN JOURNAL OF SOCIOLOGY*, 99, 353–395.

BROOKS-GUNN, J., KLEBANOV, P. K., LIAW, F., & SPIKER, D. (1993). ENHANCING THE DEVELOPMENT ON LOW-BIRTHWEIGHT, PREMATURE INFANTS: CHANGES IN COGNITION AND BEHAVIOR OVER THE FIRST THREE YEARS. *CHILD DEVELOPMENT*, 63, 736–753.

BROOKS-GUNN, J., McCARTON, C., ET AL. (1994). EARLY INTERVENTION IN LOW BIRTH-WEIGHT, PREMATURE INFANTS: RESULTS THROUGH AGE 5 YEARS FROM THE INFANT HEALTH AND DEVELOPMENT PROGRAM. *JOURNAL OF THE AMERICAN MEDICAL ASSOCIATION*, 272, 1257–1262.

CHASE-LANSDALE, P. L., & BROOKS-GUNN, J. (EDS.). (1995). *ESCAPE FROM POVERTY: WHAT MAKES A DIFFERENCE FOR CHILDREN?* NEW YORK: CAMBRIDGE UNIVERSITY PRESS.

CHIPUER, H. M., ROVINE, M. J., & PLOMIN, R. (1990). LISREL MODELING: GENETIC AND ENVIRONMENTAL INFLUENCES ON IQ REVISITED. *INTELLIGENCE*, 14, 11–19.

COHEN, J. B., & LAZARUS, R. S. (1977). *SOCIAL SUPPORT QUESTIONNAIRE*. BERKELEY: UNIVERSITY OF CALIFORNIA.

CORCORAN, M., GORDON, R., LAREN, D., & SOLON, G. (1992). THE ASSOCIATION BETWEEN MEN'S ECONOMIC STATUS AND THEIR FAMILY AND COMMUNITY ORIGINS. *JOURNAL OF HUMAN RESOURCES*, 27, 575–600.

CRANE, J. (1993). *RACE AND COGNITIVE SKILLS: STRONG EVIDENCE AGAINST GENETIC EFFECTS*. MANUSCRIPT SUBMITTED FOR PUBLICATION.

DUNCAN, G. J. (1988). VOLATILITY OF FAMILY INCOME OVER THE LIFE COURSE. IN P. BALTES, D. FEATHERMAN, & R. M. LERNER (EDS.), *LIFE-SPAN DEVELOPMENT AND BEHAVIOR* (VOL. 9, PP. 317358). HILLSDALE, NJ: ERLBAUM.

DUNCAN, G. J., & BROOKS-GUNN, J. (EDS.) (IN PRESS). *GROWING UP POOR: CONSEQUENCES ACROSS THE LIFE SPAN*. NEW YORK: RUSSELL SAGE FOUNDATION PRESS.

DUNCAN, G. J., BROOKS-GUNN, J., & KLEBANOV, P. K. (1994). ECONOMIC DEPRIVATION AND EARLY CHILDHOOD DEVELOPMENT. *CHILD DEVELOPMENT*, 65, 296–318.

DUNCAN, G. J., SMEEDING, T., & ROGERS, W. (IN PRESS). W(H)ITHER THE MIDDLE CLASS? A DYNAMIC VIEW. IN E. WOLFF (ED.), *INEQUALITY AT THE END OF THE TWENTIETH CENTURY*.

DUNN, L. M., & DUNN L. M. (1981). *PEABODY PICTURE VOCABULARY TEST-REVISED*. CIRCLE PINES, MN: AMERICAN GUIDANCE SERVICE.

FEATHERMAN, D. L., & HAUSER, R. M. (1978). *OPPORTUNITY AND CHANGE*. NEW YORK: ACADEMIC.

FUTURE OF CHILDREN. (1995). *THE FUTURE OF CHILDREN: CRITICAL ISSUES FOR CHILDREN AND YOUTH*, 5(2).

GARFINKEL, I., & McLANAHAN, S. (1986). *SINGLE MOTHERS AND THEIR CHILDREN: A NEW AMERICAN DILEMMA*. WASHINGTON, DC: URBAN INSTITUTE PRESS.

GOLDBERG, D. (1978). *MANUAL OF THE GENERAL HEALTH QUESTIONNAIRE*. LONDON: NFER PUBLISHING CO.

GOTTFRIED, A. W. (ED.). (1984). *HOME ENVIRONMENT AND EARLY COGNITIVE DEVELOPMENT*. NEW YORK: ACADEMIC.

HASKINS, R. (1989). BEYOND METAPHOR: EFFICACY OF EARLY CHILDHOOD EDUCATION. *AMERICAN PSYCHOLOGIST*, 44, 274–282.

HAUSER, R. M., & FEATHERMAN, D. L. (1977). *OPPORTUNITY AND CHANGE*. NEW YORK: ACADEMIC.

HAVEMAN, R., WOLFE, B., & SPAULDING, J. (1991). CHILDHOOD EVENTS AND CIRCUMSTANCES INFLUENCING HIGH SCHOOL COMPLETION. *DEMOGRAPHY*, 28, 133–157.

HEATH, S. B. (1989). ORAL AND LITERATE TRADITIONS AMONG BLACK AMERICANS LIVING IN POVERTY. *AMERICAN PSYCHOLOGIST, 44*, 367–373.

HELMS, J. E. (1992). WHY IS THERE NO STUDY OF CULTURAL EQUIVALENCE IN STANDARDIZED COGNITIVE ABILITY TESTING? *AMERICAN PSYCHOLOGIST, 47*, 1083–1101.

HERNANDEZ, D. J. (1993). *AMERICAN'S CHILDREN: RESOURCES FROM FAMILY, GOVERNMENT AND THE ECONOMY.* NEW YORK: RUSSELL SAGE.

HERNANDEZ, D. J. (IN PRESS). POVERTY IN AMERICA. IN G. J. DUNCAN & J. BROOKS-GUNN (EDS.), *GROWING UP POOR: CONSEQUENCES ACROSS THE LIFE SPAN.* NEW YORK: RUSSELL SAGE FOUNDATION PRESS.

HILL, M. (1992). THE PANEL STUDY OF INCOME DYNAMICS. *THE SAGE SERIES GUIDES TO MAJOR SOCIAL SCIENCE DATA BASES* (VOL. 2). NEWBURY PARK, CA: SAGE PUBLICATIONS.

INFANT HEALTH AND DEVELOPMENT PROGRAM STAFF. (1990). ENHANCING THE OUTCOMES OF LOW BIRTHWEIGHT, PREMATURE INFANTS: A MULTISITE RANDOMIZED TRIAL. *JOURNAL OF THE AMERICAN MEDICAL ASSOCIATION, 263*, 3035–3042.

JENCKS, C. (1992). *RETHINKING SOCIAL POLICY: RACE, POVERTY AND THE UNDERCLASS.* CAMBRIDGE, MA: HARVARD UNIVERSITY PRESS.

JENCKS, C., & PETERSON, P. E. (EDS.). (1991). *THE URBAN UNDERCLASS.* WASHINGTON, DC: BROOKINGS.

JENSEN, A. R. (1980). *BIAS IN MENTAL TESTING.* NEW YORK: FREE PRESS.

KASARDA, J. D. (1990). CITY JOBS AND RESIDENTS ON A COLLISION COURSE: THE URBAN UNDERCLASS DILEMMA. *ECONOMIC DEVELOPMENT QUARTERLY, 4*, 313–319.

LANDRUM-BROWN, J. (1990). BLACK MENTAL HEALTH AND RACIAL OPPRESSION. IN D. S. RUIZ (ED.), *HANDBOOK OF MENTAL HEALTH AND MENTAL DISORDER AMONG BLACK AMERICANS* (PP. 113–132). NEW YORK: GREENWOOD.

LAZAR, I., DARLINGTON, R., MURRAY, H., ROYCE, J., & SNIPPER, A. (1982). LASTING EFFECTS OF EARLY EDUCATION: A REPORT FROM THE CONSORTIUM FOR LONGITUDINAL STUDIES. *MONOGRAPHS OF THE SOCIETY FOR RESEARCH IN CHILD DEVELOPMENT, 47*(2–3, SERIAL NO. 195).

LEWONTIN, R. (1976). THE FALLACY OF BIOLOGICAL DETERMINISM. *SCIENCES, 16*, 6–10.

LOEHLIN, J. C., LINDZEY, G., & SPUHLER, J. N. (1975). *RACE DIFFERENCES IN INTELLIGENCE.* SAN FRANCISCO: W. H. FREEMAN.

MARE, R. D. (1980). SOCIAL BACKGROUND AND SCHOOL CONTINUATION DECISIONS. *JOURNAL OF THE AMERICAN STATISTICAL ASSOCIATION, 74*(370), 295305.

MAYER, S. E., & JENCKS, C. C. (1989). GROWING UP IN POOR NEIGHBORHOODS: HOW MUCH DOES IT MATTER? *SCIENCE, 243*, 1441–1445.

MCCARTON, M. C., BROOKS-GUNN, J., & TONASCIA, J. (IN PRESS). THE COGNITIVE, BEHAVIORAL AND HEALTH STATUS OF MAINLAND PUERTO RICAN CHILDREN IN THE INFANT HEALTH AND DEVELOPMENT PROGRAM. IN C. GARCIA COLL & G. LAMBERT (EDS.), *HEALTH AND DEVELOPMENT OF PUERTO RICAN MOTHERS AND CHILDREN IN THE MAINLAND.* NEW YORK: PLENUM.

MCCORMICK, M. C., BROOKS-GUNN, J., SHAPIRO, S., BENASICH, A. A., BLACK, G., & GROSS, R. T. (1991). HEALTH CARE USE AMONG YOUNG CHILDREN IN DAY-CARE: RESULTS SEEN IN A RANDOMIZED TRIAL OF EARLY INTERVENTION. *JOURNAL OF THE AMERICAN MEDICAL ASSOCIATION, 265*, 22122217.

MCCORMICK, M. C., BROOKS-GUNN, J., SHORTER, T., HOLMES, J. H., & HEAGARTY, M. C. (1989). FACTORS ASSOCIATED WITH MATERNAL RATING OF INFANT HEALTH IN CENTRAL HARLEM. *JOURNAL OF DEVELOPMENTAL AND BEHAVIORAL PEDIATRICS, 10*, 139–144.

MCCORMICK, M. C., BROOKS-GUNN, J., SHORTER, T., WALLACE, C. Y., HOLMES, J. H., & HEAGARTY, M. C., (1987). THE PLANNING OF PREGNANCY AMONG LOW INCOME WOMEN IN CENTRAL HARLEM. *AMERICAN JOURNAL OF OBSTETRICS AND GYNECOLOGY, 156*, 145–149.

MCCORMICK, M. C., BROOKS-GUNN, J., WORKMAN-DANIELS, K., TURNER, J., & PECKHAM, G. (1992). THE HEALTH AND DEVELOPMENTAL STATUS OF VERY LOW BIRTH WEIGHT CHILDREN AT SCHOOL AGE. *JOURNAL OF AMERICAN MEDICAL ASSOCIATION, 267*, 2240–2280.

MCLANAHAN, S., ASTONE, N. M., & MARKS, N. F. (1991). THE ROLE OF MOTHER-ONLY FAMILIES IN REDUCING POVERTY. IN A. C. HUSTON (ED.), *CHILDREN IN POVERTY: CHILD DEVELOPMENT AND PUBLIC POLICY* (PP. 51–78). CAMBRIDGE, MA: CAMBRIDGE UNIVERSITY PRESS.

MCLOYD, V. C. (1990). THE IMPACT OF ECONOMIC HARDSHIP ON BLACK FAMILIES AND CHILDREN: PSYCHOLOGICAL DISTRESS, PARENTING, AND SOCIOEMO-TIONAL DEVELOPMENT. *CHILD DEVELOPMENT, 61*, 311–346.

MCLOYD, V. C., & WILSON, L. (1990). MATERNAL BEHAVIOR, SOCIAL SUPPORT, AND ECONOMIC CONDITIONS AS PREDICTORS OF DISTRESS IN CHILDREN. IN V. MCLOYD & C. A. FLANAGAN (EDS.), *ECONOMIC STRESS: EFFECTS ON FAMILY LIFE AND CHILD DEVELOPMENT* (PP. 50–67). SAN FRANCISCO: JOSSEY-BASS.

Mercer, J. R, & Brown, W. C. (1973). Racial differences in IQ: Fact or artifact? In C. Senna (Ed.), *The fallacy of IQ* (pp. 56–113). New York: Third Press.

Natriello, G. (Ed.). (1987). *School dropouts: Patterns and policies.* New York: Teachers College Press.

Olds, D. L., & Kitzman, H. (1993). Review of research on home visiting for pregnant women and parents of young children. *Future of Children* (Special issue on home visiting), 3, 53–92.

Orshansky, M. (1965). Counting the poor: Another look at the poverty profile. *Social Security Bulletin, 26*, 3–29.

Parker, L., Greer, S., & Zuckerman, B. (1988). Double jeopardy: The impact of poverty on early child development. *Pediatric Clinics of North America, 35*, 1227–1240.

Plomin, R. (1989). Environment and genes: Determinants of behavior. *American Psychologist, 44*, 105–111.

Plomin, R., & Bergmann, C. S. (1991). The nature of nurture: Genetic influence on "environmental" measures. *Behavioral and Brain Sciences, 14*, 373–427.

Ramey, C. T., Bryant, D. M., Sparling, J. J., & Wasik, B. H. (1985). Educational interventions to enhance intellectual development: Comprehensive day care versus family education. In S. Harel & N. J. Anastasiow (Eds.), *The at-risk infant: Psycho/socio/medical aspects* (pp. 75–85). Baltimore: Paul H. Brookes.

Ramey, C. T., Bryant, D. M., Wasik, B. H., Sparling, J. J., Fendt, K. H., & LaVange, L. M. (1992). The Infant Health and Development Program for low birthweight, premature infants: Program elements, family participation, and child intelligence. *Pediatrics, 3*, 454–465.

Ruiz, D. S. (1990). Social and economic profile of Black Americans, 1989. In D. S. Ruiz (Ed.), *Handbook of mental health and mental disorder among Black Americans* (pp. 1–52). New York: Greenwood.

Rumberger, R. W. (1983). Dropping out of high school: The influence of race, sex, and family background. *American Educational Research Journal, 20*, 199–220.

Sameroff, A. J., Seifer, R., Baldwin, A., & Baldwin, C. (1993). Stability of intelligence from preschool to adolescence: The influence of social and family risk factors. *Child Development, 64*, 80–97.

Sameroff, A. J., Seifer, R., Barocas, R., Zax, M., & Greenspan, S. (1987). Intelligence quotient scores of 4-year-old children: Social environment risk factors. *Pediatrics, 79*, 343–350.

Sandefur, G. D., McLanahan, S., & Wojtkiewicz, R. A. (1992). The effects of parental marital status during adolescence on high school graduation. *Social Forces, 71*, 103–121.

Scarr, S. (1981). *Race, social class, and individual differences in I.Q.* Hillsdale, NJ: Erlbaum.

Scarr, S., & McCartney, K. (1983). How people make their own environment: A theory of genotype → environment effect. *Child Development, 54*, 424–435.

Scarr-Salapatek, S. (1971). Race, social class, and IQ. *Science, 74*, 1285–1295.

Schiff, M., & Lewontin, R. (1986). *Education and class: The irrelevance of IQ genetic studies.* Oxford: Clarendon Press.

Scott, D. T., Bauer, C. R., Kraemer, H. C, & Tyson, J. (1989). Neonatal health index for preterm infants. *Pediatrics Research, 25*, 263a.

Smith, S. (1995). Two-generation program models: A new intervention strategy. In P. L. Chase-Lansdale & J. Brooks-Gunn (Eds.), *Escape from poverty: What makes a difference for children?* New York: Cambridge University Press.

Sugland, B. W., et al. (1995). The Early Childhood HOME Inventory and Home-Short Form in differing racial/ethnic groups: Are there differences in underlying structure, internal consistency of subscales, and patterns of prediction? *Journal of Family Issues, 16*, 632663.

Terman, L. M., & Merrill, M. A. (1973). *Stanford-Binet intelligence scale: Manual for the third revision, form L-M.* Boston: Houghton Mifflin.

Wachs, T. D., & Gruen, G. E. (1982). *Early experiences and human development.* New York: Plenum.

Wechsler, D. (1989). *Wechsler preschool and primary scale of intelligence.* San Antonio, TX: Psychological Corp.

Weinberg, R. A. (1989). Intelligence and IQ: Landmark issues and great debate. *American Psychologist, 44*, 98–104.

Wilson, W. J. (1987). *The truly disadvantaged: The innercity, the innerclass, and public policy.* Chicago: University of Chicago Press.

Wilson, W. J. (1991a). Studying inner-city social dislocations: The challenge of public agenda research. *American Sociology Review, 56*, 1–14.

WILSON, W. J. (1991B). PUBLIC POLICY RESEARCH AND "THE TRULY DISADVANTAGED." IN C. JENCKS & P. E. PETERSON (EDS.), *THE URBAN UNDERCLASS* (PP. 460–481). WASHINGTON, DC: BROOKINGS.

ZIGLER, E. (1992). EARLY CHILDHOOD INTERVENTION: A PROMISING PREVENTATIVE FOR JUVENILE DELINQUENCY. *AMERICAN PSYCHOLOGIST, 47*, 9971006.

Motivational Processes Affecting Learning

CAROL S. DWECK

ost research on effective learning and performance of cognitive tasks analyzes the particular cognitive skills required to succeed at those tasks. In contrast, the focus here is on motivational processes that affect success on cognitive tasks. That is, the focus is on psychological factors, other than ability, that determine how effectively the individual acquires and uses skills.

It has long been known that factors other than ability influence whether children seek or avoid challenges, whether they persist or withdraw in the face of difficulty, and whether they use and develop their skills effectively. However, the components and bases of adaptive motivational patterns have been poorly understood. As a result, commonsense analyses have been limited and have not provided a basis for effective practices. Indeed, many "commonsense" beliefs have been called into question or seriously qualified by recent research—for example, the belief that large amounts of praise and success will establish, maintain, or reinstate adaptive patterns, or that "brighter" children have more adaptive patterns and thus are more likely to choose personally challenging tasks or to persist in the face of difficulty.

In the past 10 to 15 years a dramatic change has taken place in the study of motivation. This change has resulted in a coherent, replicable, and educationally relevant body of findings—and in a clearer understanding of motivational phenomena. During this time, the emphasis has shifted to a social-cognitive approach—away from external contingencies, on the one hand, and global, internal states on the other. It has shifted to an emphasis on cognitive mediators, that is, to how children construe the situation, interpret events in the situation, and process information about the situation. Although external contingencies and internal affective states are by no means ignored, they are seen as part of a process whose workings are best penetrated by focusing on organizing cognitive variables.

Specifically, the social-cognitive approach has allowed us to (a) characterize adaptive and maladaptive patterns, (b) explain them in terms of specific underlying processes, and thus (c) begin to provide a rigorous conceptual and empirical basis for intervention and practice.

ADAPTIVE AND MALADAPTIVE MOTIVATIONAL PATTERNS

The study of motivation deals with the causes of goal-oriented activity (Atkinson, 1964; Beck, 1983; Dollard & Miller, 1950; Hull, 1943; Veroff, 1969). Achievement motivation involves a particular class of goals—those involving competence—and these goals appear to fall into two classes: (a) *learning goals,* in which individuals seek to increase their competence, to understand or master something new, and (b) *performance goals,* in which individuals seek to gain favorable judgments of their competence or avoid negative judgments of their competence (Dweck & Elliott, 1983; Nicholls, 1984; Nicholls & Dweck, 1979).[1]

Adaptive motivational patterns are those that promote the establishment, maintenance, and attainment of personally challenging and personally valued achievement goals. Maladaptive patterns, then, are associated with a failure to establish reasonable, valued goals, to maintain effective striving toward those goals, or, ultimately, to attain valued goals that are potentially within one's reach.

Research has clearly documented adaptive and maladaptive patterns of achievement behavior. The adaptive ("mastery-oriented") pattern is characterized by challenge seeking and high, effective persistence in the face of obstacles. Children displaying this pattern appear to enjoy exerting effort in the pursuit of task mastery. In contrast, the maladaptive ("helpless") pattern is characterized by challenge avoidance and low persistence in the face of difficulty. Children displaying this pattern tend to evidence negative affect (such as anxiety) and negative self-cognitions when they confront obstacles (e.g., Ames, 1984; C. Diener & Dweck, 1978, 1980; Dweck & Reppucci, 1973; Nicholls, 1975).

Although children displaying the different patterns do not differ in intellectual ability, these patterns can have profound effects on cognitive performance. In experiments conducted in both laboratory and classroom settings, it has been shown that children with the maladaptive pattern are seriously hampered in the acquisition and display of cognitive skills when they meet obstacles. Children with the adaptive pattern, by contrast, seem undaunted or even seem to have their performance facilitated by the increased challenge.

If not ability, then what are the bases of these patterns? Most recently, research has suggested that children's goals in achievement situations differentially foster the two patterns. That is, achievement situations afford a choice of goals, and the one the child preferentially adopts predicts the achievement pattern that child will display.

Basically, children's theories of intelligence appear to orient them toward different goals: Children who believe intelligence is a fixed trait tend to orient toward gaining favorable judgments of that trait (performance goals), whereas children who believe intelligence is a malleable quality tend to orient toward developing that quality (learning goals). The goals then appear to set up the different behavior patterns.[2]

LEARNING AND PERFORMANCE GOALS CONTRASTED

How and why do the different goals foster the different patterns? How do they shape task choice and task pursuit to facilitate or impede cognitive performance? The research reviewed below indicates that with performance goals, the entire task choice and pursuit process is built around children's concerns about their ability level. In contrast, with learning goals the choice and pursuit processes involve a focus on progress and mastery through effort. Further, this research shows how a focus on ability judgments can result in a tendency to avoid and withdraw from challenge, whereas a focus on progress through effort creates a tendency to seek and be energized by challenge.

Although relatively few studies as yet have explicitly induced and compared (or measured and compared) learning versus performance goals (see M. Bandura & Dweck, 1985; Elliott & Dweck, 1985; Farrell & Dweck, 1985; Leggett, 1985, 1986), many have manipulated the salience and value of performance goals, and hence the relative value of the two types of goals. This has been done, for example, by instituting a competitive versus individual reward structure (e.g., Ames, 1984; Ames, Ames, & Felker, 1977), by varying the alleged diagnosticity of the task vis à vis important abilities (e.g., Nicholls, 1975), by introducing an audience or evaluator versus allowing the individual to perform privately or focusing his or her attention on the task (e.g., Brockner & Hulton, 1978; Carver & Scheier, 1981; E. Diener & Srull, 1979), and by presenting the task with "test" instructions versus "game" or neutral instructions (e.g., Entin & Raynor, 1973; Lekarczyk & Hill, 1969; McCoy, 1965; Sarason, 1972).

Taken together, the results suggest that highlighting performance goals relative to learning goals can have the following effects on achievement behavior.

Goals and Task Choice

Appropriately challenging tasks are often the ones that are best for utilizing and increasing one's abilities. Recent research has shown that performance goals work against the pursuit of challenge by requiring that children's perceptions of their ability be high (and remain high) before the children will desire a challenging task (M. Bandura & Dweck, 1985; Elliott & Dweck, 1985). That is, if the goal is to obtain a favorable judgment of ability, then children need to be certain their ability is high before displaying it for judgment. Otherwise, they will choose tasks that conceal their ability or protect it from negative evaluation. For example, when oriented toward performance goals, individuals with low assessments of their ability are often found to choose personally easy tasks on which success is ensured or excessively difficult ones on which failure does not signify low ability (M. Bandura & Dweck, 1985; Elliott & Dweck, 1985; see also deCharms & Carpenter, 1968; Moulton, 1965; Nicholls, 1984; Raynor & Smith, 1966). Even individuals with high assessments of their ability may sacrifice learning opportunities (that involve risk of errors) for opportunities to look smart (Elliott & Dweck, 1985; see Covington, 1983). Thus, performance goals appear to promote defensive strategies that can interfere with challenge seeking.

With learning goals, however, even if children's assessment of their present ability is low, they will tend to choose challenging tasks that foster learning (M. Bandura & Dweck, 1985; Elliott & Dweck, 1985), Specifically, in studies by Elliott and Dweck (1985), in which learning and performance goals were experimentally manipulated, and by M. Bandura and Dweck (1985), in which learning and performance goals were assessed, children with learning goals chose challenging tasks regardless of whether they believed themselves to have high or low ability (see also Meyer, Folkes, & Weiner, 1976; Nicholls, 1984). Thus with a learning goal, children are willing to risk displays of ignorance in order to acquire skills and knowledge. Instead of calculating their exact ability level and how it will be judged, they can think more about the value of the skill to be developed or their interest in the task to be undertaken.

Goals and Task Pursuit

Outcome interpretation and impact. Although within a performance goal children's confidence in their ability needs to remain high to sustain task involvement, that confidence is difficult to maintain. Research shows that children with performance goals are more likely to interpret negative outcomes in terms of their ability. That is, they attribute errors or failures to a lack of ability (Ames, 1984; Ames et al., 1977; Elliott & Dweck, 1985) and view them as predictive of continued failure (Anderson & Jennings,

1980). This in turn tends to result in defensive withdrawal of effort or debilitation in the face of obstacles (Covington & Omelich, 1979; Elliott & Dweck, 1985; Frankl & Snyder, 1978; Nicholls, 1976, 1984; see also Berglas & Jones, 1970; Weiner, 1972, 1974).

In contrast, children with learning goals tend to use obstacles as a cue to increase their effort or to analyze and vary their strategies (Ames, 1984; Ames et al., 1977; Elliott & Dweck, 1985; Leggett, 1986; Nicholls, 1984), which often results in *improved* performance in the face of obstacles. That is, the more children focus on learning or progress, the greater the likelihood of maintaining effective strategies (or improving their strategies) under difficulty or failure (A. Bandura & Schunk, 1981; Elliott & Dweck, 1985; Farrell & Dweck, 1985; see also Anderson & Jennings, 1980; C. Diener & Dweck, 1978).

Satisfaction with outcomes. Once again, within the performance goal versus learning goal framework, the focus is on ability versus effort. For performance-goal children, satisfaction with outcomes is based on the ability they believe they have displayed, whereas for learning-goal children, satisfaction with outcomes is based on the effort they have exerted in pursuit of the goal. Ames et al. (1977), for example, found that with an autonomous reward structure (learning goal), children's pride in their performance in both the success and the failure conditions was related to the degree of effort they perceived themselves to have exerted. However, within the competitive reward structure (performance goal), pride in performance was related to the degree of ability (and luck) they believed themselves to have. Thus, failure within a performance goal, because it signifies low ability, yields little basis for personal pride or satisfaction.

Indeed, within a performance goal, high effort may be *negatively* related to satisfaction: Leggett (1986) showed that children with performance goals are significantly more likely than children with learning goals to view effort per se as indicative of low ability (see also Jagacinski & Nicholls, 1982; Surber, 1984).

Findings by M. Bandura and Dweck (1985) also support the differential emphasis on effort versus ability as the basis for satisfaction within learning and performance goals. When asked to indicate their affective reactions to low-effort mastery, children with learning goals were more likely than children with performance goals to choose "bored" or "disappointed" as opposed to "proud" or "relieved."

Finally, within a performance framework, childrens' own outcome satisfaction and that of their peers may be in conflict. Results from the Ames et al. (1977) study are consonant with this view. Children's own satisfaction and perceived other's satisfaction with performance were negatively correlated under the competitive reward structure (−.70) but not in the autonomous reward structure (.06), even though their relative outcomes were identical in the two conditions. In addition, in rating how deserving of rewards (stars) both persons were, given their level of performance, children were more magnanimous toward the poorer performer (whether it was self or other) in the noncompetitive condition than they were in the competitive one. Indeed, in the noncompetitive condition, they even awarded the losing other slightly more stars than they awarded themselves.

Intrinsic motivation. It has been noted that persistence in the face of obstacles is made more difficult within a performance goal because obstacles tend to cast doubt on the child's ability and hence to call into question goal attainment (favorable ability judgments). Persistence is also made more difficult by the fact that "intrinsic" motivational factors—such as task interest or the enjoyment of effort—may be more difficult to access within a performance goal. That is, effort in the face of uncertainty appears to be experienced as aversive for children with performance goals, and worry about goal attainment may well overwhelm any intrinsic interest the task may hold for the child (Ames et al., 1977; M. Bandura & Dweck, 1985; Elliott & Dweck, 1985). Indeed, performance goals may well create the very conditions that have been found to undermine intrinsic interest (Deci & Ryan, 1980; Lepper, 1980; Lepper & Greene, 1978; Maehr & Stallings, 1972; Ryan, Mims, & Koestner, 1983).

In concluding this section on goal orientation and task pursuit, we might ask: Do children's goal orientations play a role in what and how they actually learn in classroom settings? One of the hallmarks of effective learning (and of intelligent thinking) is the tendency to apply or transfer what one has learned to novel tasks that embody similar underlying principles.

In a recent study, Farrell and Dweck (1985) examined the relationship between children's goal orientations and transfer of learning. As a week-long unit in their regular science classes, eighth-grade children were taught one of three scientific principles by means of self-instructional booklets. They were then tested for their generalization of this learning to tasks involving the two (conceptually related) principles that had not been taught. The results showed that children who had learning goals for the unit, compared to those who had performance goals, (a) attained significantly higher scores on the transfer test (and this was true for children who had high *and* low pretest scores); (b) produced about 50% more work on their transfer tests, suggesting that they were more active in the transfer process; and (c) produced more rule-generated answers on the test even when they failed to reach the transfer criterion, again suggesting more active attempts to apply what they had learned to the solution of novel problems.

To summarize, a performance goal focuses children on issues of ability. Within this goal, children's confidence in their current ability must be high and must remain high if they are to choose appropriately challenging tasks and pursue them in effective ways. Yet the same focus on ability makes their confidence in their ability fragile—even the mere exertion of effort calls ability into question. A strong orientation toward this goal can thus create a tendency to avoid challenge, to withdraw from challenge, or to show impaired performance in the face of challenge. Ironically, then, an overconcern with ability may lead children to shun the very tasks that foster its growth.

In contrast, a learning goal focuses children on effort—effort as a means of utilizing or activating their ability, of surmounting obstacles, and of increasing their ability. Not only is effort perceived as the means to accomplishment, it is also the factor that engenders pride and satisfaction with performance. The adoption of learning goals thus encourages children to explore, initiate, and pursue tasks that promote intellectual growth.

THE RELATION OF ABILITY AND MOTIVATION

Does Ability Predict Motivational Patterns?

One might suppose that children who had the highest IQ scores, achievement test scores, and grades would be the ones who had by far the highest expectancies for future test scores and grades, as well as for performance on novel experimental tasks. Surprisingly often, this is not the case. In fact, one of the things that makes the study of motivation particularly intriguing is that measures of children's actual competence do not strongly predict their confidence of future attainment (M. Bandura & Dweck, 1985; Crandall, 1969; Stipek & Hoffman, 1980; see also Phillips, 1984). Indeed, M. Bandura and Dweck found that their low-confidence children tended to have somewhat higher achievement test scores than their high-confidence group. Interestingly, the low-confidence children did not have poorer opinions of their past attainment or abilities but faced the upcoming task with low expectancies of absolute and relative performance.

One might also suppose that high-achieving children would be much less likely than low achievers, when encountering an obstacle, to attribute their difficulty to a lack of ability and to show deteriorated performance. But this supposition, too, is often contradicted by the evidence (e.g., Licht & Dweck, 1984; Stipek & Hoffman, 1980; see also C. Diener & Dweck, 1978, 1980).

A tendency toward unduly low expectancies (Crandall, 1969; Stipek & Hoffman, 1980), challenge avoidance (Licht, Linden, Brown, & Sexton, 1984; see also Leggett, 1985), ability attributions for failure (Licht & Shapiro, 1982; Nicholls, 1979), and debilitation under failure (Licht et al., 1984; Licht & Dweck, 1984) has been especially noted in girls, particularly bright girls.[3] Indeed, some researchers have found a negative correlation for girls between their actual ability and these maladaptive patterns (Crandall, 1969; Licht et al., 1984; Licht & Dweck, 1984; Licht & Shapiro, 1982; Stipek & Hoffman, 1980).

An extensive study of sex differences in achievement cognitions and responses to failure recently completed by Licht et al.(1984) yields illustrative evidence. On the basis of their grades, Licht divided her subjects into A, B, C, and D students and, among other measures, administered a novel concept formation task. A significant sex difference was found among the A students (and only among the A students) in their response to failure, with the A girls showing the greatest debilitation of the eight groups and the A boys being the only group to show any facilitation. In addition, Licht found a strong sex difference in task preferences between A girls and A boys: The A girls much preferred tasks they knew they were good at, whereas A boys preferred ones they would have to work harder to master.

It is also interesting to note that in Leggett's (1985) study of bright junior high school students, there was a greater tendency for girls than boys to subscribe to an "entity" theory of intelligence (smartness as a fixed trait, a static entity) and for those who did to choose a performance goal that avoided challenge.

Again, it is not the case that these girls are unaware of their attainments (Licht & Dweck, 1984; Nicholls, 1979; Parsons, Meece, Adler, & Kaczala, 1982), but knowledge of past successes does not appear to arm them for confrontations with future challenges. For example, in a study by Licht and Dweck (1984) that examined the impact of initial confusion (vs. no confusion) on subsequent learning, high-achieving girls rated themselves as being bright but still showed greater debilitation than low-achieving girls. Whereas in the no-confusion condition, the brighter the girl (by her own self-rating and by IQ score), the more likely she was to master the new material ($r = .47$), in the confusion condition, the brighter the girl, the less likely she was to reach the mastery criterion ($r = -.38$, pdiff < .02). (For boys in this study the correlation between self-rated ability and task performance tended to increase from the no-confusion to the confusion condition: $rs = .15$ and .34, respectively.)

In short, being a high achiever and knowing one has done well in the past does not appear to translate directly into high confidence in one's abilities when faced with future challenges or current difficulties. Nor does it clearly predict the maintenance of one's ability to perform or learn under these conditions. It is apparent, then, that a maladaptive motivational pattern is not the sole province of the low-achieving, "failure-prone" child.

Does Motivational Pattern Predict Ability Over Time?

If there is a sizable proportion of high achievers with maladaptive motivational patterns (see Phillips, 1984), and if these patterns are important to achievement, then why are these children still high achievers? Drops in achievement can result from performance debilitation or task avoidance. That is, both the presence of failure or the opportunity to avoid challenging subject areas may lead to cumulative skill deficits in children with maladaptive patterns. For good students, grade school may not provide either of these. It may present neither tasks that are difficult enough to create failure and debilitation nor the choice of not pursuing a given subject area. For these reasons, maladaptive patterns may not yet typically come into play. Licht and Dweck (1984) showed, however, in an experiment conducted in classrooms, that when confusion does accompany the initial attempt to learn new material, mastery of the material is seriously impaired for these children.

It may be that only in subsequent school years will these maladaptive tendencies have their impact on achievement, when children with these patterns may elect to avoid challenging courses of study, drop out of courses that pose a threat of failure, or show impairment of performance under real difficulty. Thus, our experimental studies may create conditions that good students will encounter fully only in later years but that reveal underlying patterns already in place in the grade school years.

In the following section, sex differences in motivational patterns and achievement are used as a means of exploring the ways in which motivational patterns can affect achievement, and ability, over time.

The Case of Sex Differences in Mathematical Versus Verbal Achievement

Discrepancies between males and females in mathematical and verbal achievement have long been a source of puzzlement and concern. Although in the grade school years girls equal boys in mathematical achievement (and surpass them in verbal achievement), during the junior high and high school years, boys pull ahead and remain ahead in mathematical achievement (Donlon, Ekstrom & Lockheed, 1976; Fennema & Sherman, 1977; Hilton & Berglund, 1974; Maccoby & Jacklin, 1974). A wide assortment of explanations has been advanced, ranging from claims about the nature of the genetic equipment (Benbow & Stanley, 1980) to arguments about the impact of sex role stereotypes (Sherman & Fennema, 1977). Without ruling out other explanations, one can add a motivational explanation based on the research findings reviewed above. Specifically, the fact that the two sexes often display different motivational patterns and the fact that the academic subject areas in question differ in major ways aside from

the skills they require suggest that perhaps motivational patterns contribute to these achievement discrepancies.

This suggestion is made even more plausible when one considers that (a) sex differences in mathematical achievement are greatest among the brightest students (Astin, 1974; Fox, 1976) and (b) sex differences in motivational patterns and associated behavior appear to be greatest among the brightest students. As noted above, bright girls compared to bright boys (and compared to less bright girls) seem to display shakier expectancies, lower preference for novel or challenging tasks, more frequent failure attributions to lack of ability, and more frequent debilitation in the face of failure or confusion (Licht et al., 1984; Licht & Dweck, 1984; Stipek & Hoffman, 1980). Moreover, some characteristics of mathematical versus verbal areas are precisely those that would work against individuals with this pattern but that would favor individuals with the more confident, challenge-seeking pattern (see Licht & Dweck, 1984, for a more detailed discussion of these characteristics).

Specifically, new units and courses in mathematics, particularly after the grade school years, tend to involve new skills, new concepts, or even entirely new conceptual frameworks (for example, algebra, geometry, calculus). These new skills and concepts are not only different from but are often more difficult than those the child has mastered in the past. In the verbal areas, however, once the basic skills of reading and writing are mastered, one does not as typically encounter leaps to qualitatively different tasks, tasks requiring mastery of completely unfamiliar verbal skills. Increments in difficulty appear to be more gradual, and new units or courses often simply ask the student to bring existing skills to bear on new material.

This general difference between mathematical and verbal areas may have several important psychological consequences. For one thing, as children ponder future math courses, the greater novelty and difficulty of the future courses compared to present ones would be expected to precipitate declines in confidence for bright girls, but not for bright boys. Indeed, in the study cited above, Parsons et al. (1982) found significant sex differences in expectancies for future math courses even when females and males were equivalent in their perceptions of their present mathematical ability and in their expectancies for their present math courses.

Task preference data as well suggest that a greater discrepancy between present and future tasks in mathematical versus verbal areas may render math less appealing to bright girls, but perhaps more appealing to bright boys. Bright girls, it will be recalled, tend to prefer tasks they are fairly certain they are good at and can do well on, whereas bright boys are more attracted to tasks that pose some challenge to mastery (Licht et al., 1984; see also Leggett, 1985).

Yet another consequence of this proposed math-verbal difference is that in math, children are more likely to experience failure or confusion at the beginning of a new unit or course. This might be expected to produce debilitation (or escape attempts, such as course-dropping) in bright girls but perseverance in bright boys. And, indeed, support for this prediction of differential debilitation comes from the Licht and Dweck (1984) study, described earlier, in which confusion (or no confusion) attended the introduction of new subject matter, and from the Licht et al. (1984) study in which obstacles were encountered in the acquisition of a new skill. In both cases, bright girls showed the most impairment and bright boys the most facilitation.

In short, mathematics appears to differ from verbal areas in ways that would make it more compatible with the motivational patterns of bright boys and less compatible with those of bright girls. Thus, given two children with equal mathematical aptitude and mathematical achievement in the grade school years, but with differing motivational patterns, we would predict precisely the sex differences in course taking and long-term achievement that are found to occur (Donlon et al., 1976; Fennema & Sherman, 1977; Hilton & Berglund, 1974).

With increasing age, children make increasingly consequential decisions, and maladaptive patterns may begin to impair their achievement and constrict their future choices. Maladaptive patterns such as those displayed by bright girls may even fail to foster intellectual growth in general. In a 38-year longitudinal study of IQ change (measured at mean ages of 4.1, 13.8, 29.7, and 41.6), Kangas and Bradway (1971) found that for males the higher the preadult level, the more they gained in later years, whereas for females the higher the preadult level, the less they gained in later years. In fact, of the six groups in the study (males and females with high, medium, and low preadult IQs), all showed surprisingly large gains over the years (between 15 and 30 points) except the high-IQ

females, who showed little gain (about 5 points). Although there are many possible interpretations of these results, the general picture suggests that bright females, compared to bright males, are not thriving. Our analysis suggests that appropriate motivational interventions may help prevent some of the achievement discrepancies between the sexes. Let us turn, then, to the experiences or interventions that appear to foster adaptive motivational patterns.

EXPERIENCES THAT FOSTER ADAPTIVE PATTERNS

The question for motivational interventions is: What are we aiming for and how do we get there? When one considers the necessity for, but the vulnerability of, confidence within a performance goal framework, one is led to the position that challenge seeking and persistence are better facilitated by attempts to foster a learning goal orientation than by attempts to instill confidence within a performance framework.

Nonetheless, much current educational practice aims at creating high-confidence performers and attempts to do so by programming frequent success and praise. (See Brown, Palincsar, & Purcell, 1984, for a discussion of this issue.) How did this situation arise? I propose that misreadings of two popular phenomena may have merged to produce this approach. First was the growing belief in "positive reinforcement" (interpreted as frequent praise for small units of behavior) as the way to promote desirable behavior. Yet a deeper understanding of the principles of reinforcement would not lead one to expect that frequent praise for short, easy tasks would create a desire for long, challenging ones or promote persistence in the face of failure. On the contrary, continuous reinforcement schedules are associated with poor resistance to extinction, and errorless learning, as evidenced by Terrace's (1969) renowned pigeons, has been found to produce bizarre emotional responses following nonreinforcement.

Second was a growing awareness of teacher expectancy effects. As is well known, the teacher expectancy effect refers to the phenomenon whereby teachers' impressions about students' ability (e.g., manipulated via test information) actually affect students' performance, such that the students' performance falls more in line with the teachers' expectancies (Rosenthal & Jacobson, 1968). The research on this "self-fulfilling prophecy" raised serious concerns that teachers were hampering the intellectual achievement of children they labeled as having low ability. One remedy was thought to lie in making low-ability children feel like high-ability children by means of a high success rate.

In light of the implications that were drawn from teacher expectancy effects, it is interesting to contrast them with the views of the original researchers (see, e.g., Rosenthal, 1971, 1974; Rosenthal & Jacobson, 1968). Unlike many of their followers, they appeared to frame their work within (and provide teachers with) an incremental theory of intelligence. Specifically, in the Rosenthal and Jacobson (1968) study, teachers were told that the "test for intellectual blooming" indicated that the target children would show remarkable gains in intellectual competence during the school year. Moreover, when hypothesizing possible mechanisms through which gains were produced, the original researchers thought in terms of teachers' having stimulated intellectual growth through challenge. And, in reviewing work on undesirable expectancy effects, they lamented that "lows" seemed to be given too little work, and work that was too easy, to spur cognitive gains (Rosenthal, 1971). (See also, Brown et al., 1984, who argued cogently that it is not ill treatment, but a failure to teach the necessary high-level skills, that accounts for much of the achievement deficit of low-reading groups.) Thus, these original researchers were oriented toward producing intellectual growth in children rather than simply giving children an illusion of intelligence.

The motivational research is clear in indicating that continued success on personally easy tasks (or even on difficult tasks within a performance framework) is ineffective in producing stable confidence, challenge seeking, and persistence (Dweck, 1975; Relich 1983). Indeed, such procedures have sometimes been found to backfire by producing lower confidence in ability (Meyer, 1982; Meyer et al., 1979). Rather, the procedures that bring about more adaptive motivational patterns are the ones that incorporate challenge, and even failure, within a learning-oriented context and that explicitly address underlying motivational mediators (Andrews & Debus, 1978; A. Bandura & Schunk, 1981; Covington, 1983; Dweck, 1975; Fowler & Peterson, 1981; Relich, 1983; Rhodes, 1977; Schunk, 1982). For example, retraining children's attributions for failure (teaching them to attribute their failures to effort or strategy instead of ability) has been shown to produce sizable changes in persistence in the face of failure, changes that persist over time and generalize across tasks (Andrews & Debus, 1978; Dweck, 1975; Fowler & Peterson, 1981; Relich, 1983; Rhodes, 1977).

Thus far, only short-term experimental manipulations of children's goal orientations have been attempted (Ames, 1984; Ames et al., 1977; Elliott & Dweck, 1985). Although these goal manipulations have been successful in producing the associated motivational patterns, much research remains to be conducted on how best to produce lasting changes in goal orientation.

To date, motivational interventions, such as attribution retraining, have been conducted primarily with less successful students (those who display both a lag in skill level *and* a maladaptive response to difficulty). Yet, the earlier discussion suggests that some of the brightest students, who in grade school as yet show little or no obvious impairment in the school environment, may be prime candidates for such motivational interventions. Among these are children (e.g., bright girls) who have had early, consistent, and abundant success yet, despite this (or perhaps even because of this), do not relish the presence or the prospect of challenge.

SUMMARY AND CONCLUSION

Motivational processes have been shown to affect (a) how well children can deploy their existing skills and knowledge, (b) how well they acquire new skills and knowledge, and (c) how well they transfer these new skills and knowledge to novel situations. This approach does not deny individual differences in present skills and knowledge or in "native" ability or aptitude. It does suggest, however, that the use and growth of that ability can be appreciably influenced by motivational factors.

The social-cognitive approach, with its emphasis on specific mediating processes, has generated important implications for practice and ameliorative interventions. Indeed, ways of appropriately incorporating issues of "self-concept" into education have long been sought. The social-cognitive approach, by identifying particular self-conceptions (e.g., children's theories of their intelligence) and by detailing their relationship to behavior, may well provide the means.

In addition, there is growing evidence that the conceptualization presented here is relevant not only to effectiveness on cognitive tasks but also to effectiveness in social arenas. For example, children's attributions for social outcomes predict whether they respond adaptively to rejection (Goetz & Dweck, 1980), and children's social goals are related to their popularity among their classmates (Taylor & Asher, 1985). Thus the present approach may illuminate adaptive and maladaptive patterns in diverse areas of children's lives and may thereby provide a basis for increasingly effective socialization and instructional practices across these areas.

NOTES

1. The word *performance* will be used in several ways, not only in connection with performance goals. It will also be used to refer to the child's task activity (performance of a task) and to the product of that activity (level of performance). The meaning should be clear from the context.

2. See M. Bandura and Dweck (1985), Dweck and Elliott (1983), and Leggett (1985) for a more extensive treatment of children's theories of intelligence. The present article will focus on achievement goals and their allied behavior patterns.

3. It is important to note that sex differences, like most individual differences, are by no means found in every study. However, when sex differences are found, the same ones are typically found. Thus, the pattern described is a recurrent one that has been found in many studies from many different laboratories.

REFERENCES

Ames, C. (1984). Achievement attributions and self-instructions under competitive and individualistic goal structures. *Journal of Educational Psychology, 76,* 478–487.

Ames, C., Ames, R., &Felker, D. W. (1977). Effects of competitive reward structure and valence of outcome on children's achievement attributions. *Journal of Educational Psychology, 69,* 1–8.

Anderson, C. A., & Jennings, D. L.(1980). When experiences of failure promote expectations of success: The impact of attributing failure to ineffective strategies. *Journal of Personality, 48,* 393–407.

Andrews, G. R., & Debus, R. L. (1978). Persistence and the causal perceptions of failure: Modifying cognitive attributions. *Journal of Educational Psychology, 70,* 154–166.

Astin, H. (1974). Sex differences in scientific and mathematical precocity. In J. C. Stanley, D. P. Keating, & L. H. Fox (Eds.), *Mathematical talent: Discovery, description and development.* Baltimore, MD: Johns Hopkins University Press.

Atkinson, J. W. (1964). *An introduction to motivation.* Princeton, NJ: Van Nostrand.

Bandura, A., & Schunk, D. H. (1981). Cultivating competence, self-efficacy, and intrinsic interest through proximal self-motivation. *Journal of Personality and Social Psychology, 41.* 586–598.

Bandura, M., & Dweck, C. S. (1985). *Self-conceptions and motivation: Conceptions of intelligence, choice of achievement goals, and patterns of cognition, affect, and behavior.* Manuscript submitted for publication.

Beck, R. C. (1983). *Motivation: Theories and principles.* Englewood Cliffs, NJ: Prentice-Hall.

Benbow, C. P., & Stanley, J. C. (1980). Sex differences in mathematics ability: Fact or artifact. *Science, 10,* 1262–1264.

Berglas, S., & Jones, E. E. (1970). Drug choice as a self-handicapping strategy in response to noncontingent success. *Journal of Personality and Social Psychology, 36,* 405–417.

Brockner, J., & Hulton, A. J. B. (1978). How to reverse the vicious cycle of low self-esteem: The importance of attentional focus. *Journal of Experimental Psychology 14,* 564–578.

Brown, A. L., Palincsar, A. S., & Purcell, L. (1984). Poor readers: Teach don't label. In Neisser, (Ed.), *The academic performance of minority children: A new perspective.* Hillsdale, NJ: Erlbaum.

Carver, C. S., & Scheier, M. F. (1981). *Attention and self-regulation: A control-theory approach to human behavior.* New York: Springer-Verlag.

Covington, M. V. (1983). Strategic thinking and the fear of failure. In S. F. Chipman, J. Segal, & R. Glaser (Eds.), *Thinking and learning skills: Current research and open questions* (Vol. 2). Hillsdale, NJ: Erlbaum,

COVINGTON, M. V., & OMELICH, C. L. (1979). EFFORT: THE DOUBLE-EDGED SWORD IN SCHOOL ACHIEVEMENT. *JOURNAL OF EDUCATIONAL PSYCHOLOGY, 71,* 169–182.

CRANDALL, V. C. (1969). SEX DIFFERENCES IN EXPECTANCY OF INTELLECTUAL AND ACADEMIC REINFORCEMENT. IN C. P. SMITH (ED.), *ACHIEVEMENT-RELATED MOTIVES IN CHILDREN.* NEW YORK: RUSSELL SAGE.

deCHARMS, R., & CARPENTER, V. (1968). MEASURING MOTIVATION IN CULTURALLY DISADVANTAGED SCHOOL CHILDREN. IN H. J. KLAUSMEIER, & G. T. O'HEARN (EDS.), *RESEARCH AND DEVELOPMENT TOWARD THE IMPROVEMENT OF EDUCATION.* MADISON, WI: DEMBAR EDUCATIONAL SERVICES.

DECI, E. L., & RYAN, R. M. (1980). THE EMPIRICAL EXPLORATION OF INTRINSIC MOTIVATIONAL PROCESSES. IN L. BERKOWITZ (ED.), *ADVANCES IN EXPERIMENTAL SOCIAL PSYCHOLOGY* (VOL. 13). NEW YORK: ACADEMIC PRESS.

DIENER, C. L, & DWECK, C. S. (1978). AN ANALYSIS OF LEARNED HELPLESSNESS: CONTINUOUS CHANGES IN PERFORMANCE, STRATEGY, AND ACHIEVEMENT COGNITIONS FOLLOWING FAILURE. *JOURNAL OF PERSONALITY AND SOCIAL PSYCHOLOGY, 56,* 451–462.

DIENER, C. I., & DWECK, C. S. (1980). AN ANALYSIS OF LEARNED HELPLESSNESS; II. THE PROCESSING OF SUCCESS. *JOURNAL OF PERSONALITY AND SOCIAL PSYCHOLOGY, 39,* 940–952.

DIENER, E., & SRULL, T. K. (1979). SELF-AWARENESS, PSYCHOLOGICAL PERSPECTIVE, AND SELF-REINFORCEMENT IN RELATION TO PERSONAL AND SOCIAL STANDARDS. *JOURNAL OF PERSONALITY AND SOCIAL PSYCHOLOGY, 37,* 413–423.

DOLLARD, J., & MILLER, N. E. (1950). *PERSONALITY AND PSYCHOTHERAPY.* NEW YORK: MCGRAW-HILL.

DONLON, T., EKSTROM, R., & LOCKHEED, M. (1976, SEPTEMBER). *COMPARING THE SEXES ON ACHIEVEMENT ITEMS OF VARYING CONTENT.* PAPER PRESENTED AT THE MEETING OF THE AMERICAN PSYCHOLOGICAL ASSOCIATION, WASHINGTON, DC.

DWECK, C. S. (1975). THE ROLE OF EXPECTATIONS AND ATTRIBUTIONS IN THE ALLEVIATION OF LEARNED HELPLESSNESS. *JOURNAL OF PERSONALITY AND SOCIAL PSYCHOLOGY, 31,* 674–685.

DWECK, C. S., & ELLIOTT, E. S. (1983). ACHIEVEMENT MOTIVATION. IN E. M. HETHERINGTON (ED.), *SOCIALIZATION, PERSONALITY, AND SOCIAL DEVELOPMENT.* NEW YORK: WILEY.

DWECK, C. S., & REPPUCCI, N. D. (1973). LEARNED HELPLESSNESS AND REINFORCEMENT RESPONSIBILITY IN CHILDREN. *JOURNAL OF PERSONALITY AND SOCIAL PSYCHOLOGY, 25,* 109–116.

ELLIOTT, E., & DWECK, C. S. (1985). *GOALS: AN APPROACH TO MOTIVATION AND ACHIEVEMENT.* MANUSCRIPT SUBMITTED FOR PUBLICATION.

ENTIN, E. E., & RAYNOR, J. O. (1973). EFFECTS OF CONTINGENT FUTURE ORIENTATION AND ACHIEVEMENT MOTIVATION ON PERFORMANCE IN TWO KINDS OF TASKS. *JOURNAL OF EXPERIMENTAL RESEARCH IN PERSONALITY, 6,* 320–341.

FARRELL, E., & DWECK, C. (1985). *THE ROLE OF MOTIVATIONAL PROCESSES IN TRANSFER OF LEARNING.* MANUSCRIPT SUBMITTED FOR PUBLICATION.

FENNEMA, E., & SHERMAN, J. (1977). SEX-RELATED DIFFERENCES IN MATHEMATICS ACHIEVEMENT, SPATIAL VISUALIZATION, AND AFFECTIVE FACTORS. *AMERICAN EDUCATIONAL RESEARCH JOURNAL, 14,* 51–71.

FOWLER, J. W., & PETERSON, P. L. (1981). INCREASING READING PERSISTENCE AND ALTERING ATTRIBUTIONAL STYLE OF LEARNED HELPLESS CHILDREN. *JOURNAL OF EDUCATIONAL PSYCHOLOGY, 73,* 251–260.

FOX, L. (1976). SEX DIFFERENCES IN MATHEMATICAL PRECOCITY: BRIDGING THE GAP. IN D. P. KEATING (ED.), *INTELLECTUAL TALENT: RESEARCH AND DEVELOPMENT.* BALTIMORE, MD: JOHNS HOPKINS UNIVERSITY PRESS.

FRANKL, A., & SNYDER, M. L. (1978). POOR PERFORMANCE FOLLOWING UN-SOLVABLE PROBLEMS: LEARNED HELPLESSNESS OR EGOTISM? *JOURNAL OF PERSONALITY AND SOCIAL PSYCHOLOGY, 36,* 1415–1423.

GOETZ, T., & DWECK, C. (1980). LEARNED HELPLESSNESS IN SOCIAL SITUATIONS. *JOURNAL OF PERSONALITY AND SOCIAL PSYCHOLOGY, 39,* 246–255.

HILTON, T., & BERGLUND, G. (1974). SEX DIFFERENCES IN MATHEMATICS ACHIEVEMENT—A LONGITUDINAL STUDY. *JOURNAL OF EDUCATION RESEARCH, 67,* 231–237.

HULL, C. L. (1943). *PRINCIPLES OF BEHAVIOR.* NEW YORK: APPLETON-CENTURY-CROFTS.

JAGACINSKI, C. M., & NICHOLLS, J. G. (1982, MARCH). *CONCEPTS OF ABILITY.* PAPER PRESENTED AT THE MEETING OF THE AMERICAN EDUCATIONAL RESEARCH ASSOCIATION, NEW YORK.

KANGAS, J., & BRADWAY, K. (1971). INTELLIGENCE AT MIDDLE AGE: A THIRTY-EIGHT YEAR FOLLOW-UP. *DEVELOPMENTAL PSYCHOLOGY, 5,* 333–337.

LEGGETT, E. (1985, MARCH). *CHILDREN'S ENTITY AND INCREMENTAL THEORIES OF INTELLIGENCE: RELATIONSHIPS TO ACHIEVEMENT BEHAVIOR.* PAPER PRESENTED AT THE MEETING OF THE EASTERN PSYCHOLOGICAL ASSOCIATION, BOSTON.

Leggett, E. (1986, April). *Individual differences in effort-ability inference rules: Implications for causal judgments.* Paper presented at the meeting of the Eastern Psychological Association, New York.

Lekarczyk, D. T., & Hill, D. T. (1969). Self-esteem, test anxiety, stress and verbal learning. *Developmental Psychology, 1,* 147–154.

Lepper, M. R. (1980). Intrinsic and extrinsic motivation in children: Detrimental effects of superfluous social controls. In W. A. Collins (Ed.), *Minnesota Symposium on Child Psychology* (Vol. 14). Hillsdale, NJ: Erlbaum.

Lepper, M. R., & Greene, D. (Eds.) (1978). *The hidden costs of reward: New perspectives on the psychology of human motivation.* Hillsdale, NJ: Erlbaum.

Licht, B. G., & Dweck, C. S. (1983). Sex differences in achievement orientations: Consequences for academic choices and attainments. In M. Marland (Ed.), *Sex differentiation and schooling,* London: Heinemann.

Licht, B. G., & Dweck, C. S. (1984). Determinants of academic achievement: The interaction of children's achievement orientations with skill area. *Developmental Psychology, 20,* 628–636.

Licht, B. G., Linden, T. A., Brown, D. A., & Sexton, M. A. (1984, August). *Sex differences in achievement orientation: An "A" student phenomenon?* Paper presented at the meeting of the American Psychological Association, Toronto, Canada.

Licht, B. G., & Shapiro, S. H. (1982, August). *Sex differences in attributions among high achievers.* Paper presented at the meeting of the American Psychological Association, Washington, DC.

Maccoby, E. E., & Jacklin, C. N. (1974). *The psychology of sex differences.* Stanford, CA: Stanford University Press.

Maehr, M. L., & Stallings, W. M. (1972). Freedom from external evaluation. *Child Development, 43,* 177–185.

McCoy, N. (1965). Effects of test anxiety on children's performance as a function of instructions and type of task. *Journal of Personality and Social Psychology, 2,* 634–641.

Meyer, W. U. (1982). Indirect communications about perceived ability estimates. *Journal of Educational Psychology, 74,* 888–897.

Meyer, W., Bachman, M., Biermann, U., Hempelmann, M., Ploger, F., & Spiller, H. (1979). The informational value of evaluative behavior: Influences of praise and blame on perceptions of ability. *Journal of Educational Psychology, 71,* 259–268.

Meyer, W. W., Folkes, V., & Weiner, B. (1976). The perceived informational value and affective consequences of choice behavior and intermediate difficulty task selection. *Journal of Research in Personality, 10,* 410–423.

Moulton, R. W. (1965). Effects of success and failure on level of aspiration as related to achievement motives. *Journal of Personality and Social Psychology, 1,* 399–406.

Nicholls, J. G. (1975). Causal attributions and other achievement related cognitions: Effects of task outcome, attainment value, and sex. *Journal of Personality and Social Psychology, 31,* 379–389.

Nicholls, J. G. (1976). Effort is virtuous but it's better to have ability: Evaluative responses to perceptions of effort and ability. *Journal of Research in Personality, 10,* 306–315.

Nicholls, J. G. (1979). Development of perception of own attainment and causal attributions for success and failure in reading. *Journal of Educational Psychology, 71,* 94–99.

Nicholls, J. G. (1984). Conceptions of ability and achievement motivation. In R. Ames & C. Ames (Eds.), *Research on motivation in education* (Vol. 1). New York: Academic Press.

Nicholls, J. G., & Dweck, C. S. (1979). *A definition of achievement motivation.* Unpublished manuscript, University of Illinois.

Parsons, J. E., Meece, J. L., Adler, T. F., & Kaczala, C. M. (1982). Sex differences in attributions and learned helplessness. *Sex Roles, 8,* 421–432.

Phillips, D. (1984). The illusion of incompetence among high-achieving children. *Child Development, 55,* 2000–2016.

Raynor, J. O., & Smith, C. P. (1966). Achievement related motives and risk-taking in games of skill and chance. *Journal of Personality, 34,* 176–198.

Relich, J. D. (1983). *Attribution and its relation to other affective variables in predicting and inducing arithmetic achievement.* Unpublished doctoral dissertation, University of Sydney, Sydney, Australia.

RHODES, W. A. (1977). *GENERALIZATION OF ATTRIBUTION RETRAINING*. UNPUBLISHED DOCTORAL DISSERTATION, UNIVERSITY OF ILLINOIS, CHAMPAIGN, IL.

ROSENTHAL, R. (1971). TEACHER EXPECTATIONS AND THEIR EFFECTS UPON CHILDREN. IN G. S. LESSER (ED.), *PSYCHOLOGY AND EDUCATIONAL PRACTICE*. GLENVIEW, IL: SCOTT, FORESMAN.

ROSENTHAL, R. (1974). *ON THE SOCIAL PSYCHOLOGY OF THE SELF-FULFILLING PROPHECY: FURTHER EVIDENCE FOR PYGMALION EFFECTS AND THEIR MEDIATING MECHANISMS*. NEW YORK: MSS MODULAR PUBLICATIONS.

ROSENTHAL, R., & JACOBSON, L. (1968). *PYGMALION IN THE CLASSROOM*. NEW YORK: HOLT, RINEHART & WINSTON.

RYAN, R. M., MIMS, V., & KOESTNER, R. (1983). THE RELATIONSHIP OF REWARD CONTINGENCY AND INTERPERSONAL CONTEXT TO INTRINSIC MOTIVATION: A REVIEW AND TEST USING COGNITIVE EVALUATION THEORY. *JOURNAL OF PERSONALITY AND SOCIAL PSYCHOLOGY, 45,* 736–750.

SARASON, I. G. (1972). EXPERIMENTAL APPROACHES TO TEST ANXIETY: ATTENTION AND THE USES OF INFORMATION. IN C. D. SPIELBERGER (ED.), *ANXIETY AND BEHAVIOR: CURRENT TRENDS IN THEORY AND RESEARCH* (VOL. 2). NEW YORK: ACADEMIC PRESS.

SCHUNK, D. H. (1982). EFFECTS OF EFFORT ATTRIBUTIONAL FEEDBACK ON CHILDREN'S PERCEIVED SELF-EFFICACY AND ACHIEVEMENT. *JOURNAL OF EDUCATIONAL PSYCHOLOGY, 74,* 548–556.

SHERMAN, J., & FENNEMA, F. (1977). THE STUDY OF MATHEMATICS BY HIGH SCHOOL GIRLS AND BOYS: RELATED VARIABLES? *AMERICAN EDUCATIONAL RESEARCH JOURNAL, 14,* 159–168.

STIPEK, D. J., & HOFFMAN, J. (1980). DEVELOPMENT OF CHILDREN'S PERFORMANCE-RELATED JUDGMENTS. *CHILD DEVELOPMENT 51,* 912–914.

SURBER, C. (1984). INFERENCES OF ABILITY AND EFFORT: EVIDENCE FOR TWO DIFFERENT PROCESSES. *JOURNAL OF PERSONALITY AND SOCIAL PSYCHOLOGY, 46(2),* 249–268.

TAYLOR, A., & ASHER, S. (1985, APRIL). *GOALS, GAMES AND SOCIAL COMPETENCE: EFFECTS OF SEX, GRADE LEVEL, AND SOCIOMETRIC STATUS*. PAPER PRESENTED AT THE BIENNIAL MEETING OF THE SOCIETY FOR RESEARCH IN CHILD DEVELOPMENT, TORONTO, CANADA.

TERRACE, H. S. (1969). EXTINCTION OF A DISCRIMINATIVE OPERANT FOLLOWING DISCRIMINATION LEARNING WITH AND WITHOUT ERRORS. *JOURNAL OF THE EXPERIMENTAL ANALYSIS OF BEHAVIOR, 12,* 571–582.

VEROFF, J. (1969). SOCIAL COMPARISON AND THE DEVELOPMENT OF ACHIEVEMENT MOTIVATION. IN C. P. SMITH (ED.), *ACHIEVEMENT-RELATED MOTIVES IN CHILDREN*. NEW YORK: RUSSELL SAGE.

WEINER, B. (1972). *THEORIES OF MOTIVATION: FROM MECHANISM TO COGNITION*. CHICAGO: MARKHAM.

WEINER, B. (ED.). (1974). *ACHIEVEMENT MOTIVATION AND ATTRIBUTION THEORY*. MORRISTOWN, NJ: GENERAL LEARNING CORPORATION.

CHAPTER 17
Human Factors

Human Factors Psychology

H.L. ROEDIGER, E.D. CAPALDI, S.G. PARIS, J. POLIVY, AND C. P. HERMAN

The tools and environment provided are a critical aspect of work. Ideally, a worker's environment and facilities make that worker's tasks efficient, safe, and pleasurable. Human factors psychology is concerned with designing machines and equipment for human use and training humans in the proper operation of machines. The field, so named because the "human factor" is taken into account, is sometimes called *human engineering psychology*. The same field in England is called *ergonomics* (from the Greek *ergon* for "work" and *nomos* for "natural laws"; hence, the laws of work). As engineers provide complex systems with increasing technological sophistication, the challenge for human factors psychologists is to help design systems that can be easily used by workers or consumers. Human factors psychologists are employed by virtually all large companies concerned with complex technological systems—computers, telephones, automobiles, aircraft—because the success of the systems will depend on their "user friendliness." They are also employed by the military and other government agencies.

Until the 1940s, engineers designed machinery, tools, equipment, and even entire industrial complexes with little or no regard for the workers who would eventually use them (Schultz & Schultz, 1990). They made decisions about the way machines should be designed based on "engineering considerations" only—the mechanics, the electrical needs, and requirements of size and space. Thus, workers (or consumers) simply had to adapt to the machinery, no matter how unsafe, uncomfortable, or difficult to operate. Efforts were occasionally made to train workers as well as possible or to select workers likely to succeed, but few attempts were made to bring in the "human factor from the very start in designing machines. Eventually, this situation had to come to an end, because equipment was becoming too complex. The advent of World War II helped usher in human factors psychology—new military equipment such as radar, complex aircraft, and submarines were being plagued by "human error." (It should be noted, however, that the errors blamed on humans are often the result of poorly designed systems.) Pilots during World War II were often switched from one aircraft to another. Controls with similar-looking knobs had completely different functions on two types of aircraft, yet the pilots received no retraining. Pilots used to operating by touch were no longer able to do so and had to pay more attention to the controls instead of the situation. Many pilots died because of "human error."

Since World War II, human factors psychologists have been employed by the military in great numbers, as well as in industry; however, problems still exist. For example, in the mid-1980s, at great expense the army built a new tank called the M-1 Abrams. Engineering psychologists were not involved in the design, which may explain some of the surprises that awaited army personnel when the tank was put into use (Cordes, 1985). The interior work space was so poorly designed that 27 of the 29 test drivers developed neck and back problems requiring medical attention. Further, the

PSYCHOLOGY IN OUR TIMES
GENDER DISCRIMINATION IN THE WORKPLACE

In the United States, Under Title VII of the 1964 Civil Rights Act prohibits private employers, unions, employment agenties, joint labor-management committees, and local, state, and federal governments from discriminating on the basis of gender, race, color, religion, or national origin. More recently, legislation has been enacted to protect the rights of individuals with disabilities. The crafters of these various piece's of legislation sought to end the practice of denying employment or promotion to an otherwise qualified individual because of his or her "membership" in one of these protected groups or classes.

Although the enactment of Title VII has resulted in marked improvements in the hiring and promotion practices of U.S. employers, glaring acts of discrimination still occur. One example of gender discrimination involves the case of Ann Hopkins, an accountant with the big-six firm of Price Waterhouse. In 1982, Ann Hopkins was the only woman of 88 candidates proposed for partnership. Despite stellar performance in terms of billable hours, account revenue, and client satisfaction, she was denied partnership that year and was not even nominated for partnership the following year. When Hopkins claimed that she had been denied partnership because she was a woman, Price Waterhouse responded that she was "macho," "overcompensated for being a woman," and needed a "course at charm school." Instead of taking this "advice" to heart, Hopkins took Price Waterhouse to court. In 1982, she filed a complaint in the federal district court of the District of Columbia, alleging a violation of Title VII of the Civil Rights Act of 1964. Hopkins won the initial round at the district court level. Price Waterhouse appealed to an appellate court, where, again, the judge ordered in favor of Hopkins. As a last-ditch effort, Price Waterhouse appealed to the justices of the U.S. Supreme Court, who agreed to review the case.

During the initial district court trial, Hopkins's attorneys, Douglas Huron and James Heller, asked Susan T. Fiske, a social psychologist, to testify about the psychology of gender stereotyping. Gender stereotyping is the act of ascribing a role or placing certain expectations or prescriptions on an individual's behavior based on gender. (We offered a brief discussion of gender stereotyping in Chapter 17.) In the case of *Hopkins v. Price Waterhouse,* it became clear to Fiske and, eventually, the majority of the U.S. Supreme Court justices, that Hopkins was placed in a "no-win" dilemma in her pursuit of partnership at Price Waterhouse. The Supreme Court justices wrote:

> In the specific context of (gender) stereotyping, an employer who acts on the basis of a belief that a woman cannot be aggressive, or that she must not be, has acted on the basis of gender…We are beyond the day when an employer could evaluate employees by assuming or insisting that they matched the stereotype associated with their group. … An employer who objects to aggressiveness in women but whose positions require this trait places women in an intolerable Catch 22: out of a job if they behave aggressively and out of a job if they don't. Title VII lifts women out of this bind. (*Price Waterhouse v. Hopkins,* 1989, pp. 1790–1791)

This case set a precedent not only within legal circles, but within the ranks of psychology. When it became apparent that *Hopkins v. Price Waterhouse* would be reviewed by the highest court in the land, the American Psychological Association (APA) decided to enter the case for two reasons: First, the district and appellate courts grounded their findings of discrimination largely on Fiske's testimony regarding the stereotypical attitudes that permeated Price Waterhouse's promotion process and second, Price Waterhouse had "consistently disparaged Fiske's testimony by criticizing the methodology and the concepts she used in arriving at her expert opinion that (Price Waterhouse) discriminated against Hopkins on the basis of (gender)" (Fiske, Bersoff, Borgida, Deaux, & Heilman, 1991, p.1053). A panel of social and industrial/organizational psychologists—Susan T. Fiske, Eugene Borgida, Kay Deaux, and Madeline

E. Heilman—prepared and submitted a brief on behalf of APA to attest to the scientific merits of the research on gender stereotyping. The brief also explained how stereotyping can result in discriminatory decisions, especially under such conditions as prevailed at Price Waterhouse. In reading the opinion filed by the Supreme Court, it is clear that the justices were convinced by the arguments outlined in APA's brief. More importantly, the work of the psychologists representing APA helped to make explicit, for the first time, that gender ; stereotyping is a form of gender discrimination and, as such, is prohibited under Title VII of the 1964 Civil Rights Act.

The role of the applied psychologist as advisor to the court is not always an easy one. Psychologists who offer expert testimony and draft APA briefs are often subject to harsh criticism from their colleagues. Some of the criticism is justified; some is undeserved. If you are interested in issues of gender discrimination and find this particular case interesting, you might want to follow the "paper trail" of Fiske's and APA's involvement in Hopkins v. Price Waterhouse. A good place to begin is with Fiske's (1993) article on the issue of control in gender stereotyping. In this, article, you will also find more detail regarding the experiences of Lois Robinson, the welder described in the opening paragraphs of this chapter, and Ann Hopkins of Price Waterhouse. Finally, Fiske's article will provide not only interesting reading, but insight into the debate concerning the standards to be placed on the "giving away of psychology" to society.

visibility from the tank was so poor that drivers were unable to see the ground for 9 yards in front of the tank and unable to avoid objects as well. Meanwhile, the noise level inside prevented good communication among crew members, and the interior work stations were so poorly designed that the crew reported severe problems in seeing what they were doing.

Nuclear power plants have also been plagued, on occasion, with poor human factors engineering (Kantowitz & Sorkin, 1986). In the disaster at Three Mile Island in 1979, the control instruments and the warning dials of the control room were too far apart. When operators detected problems by examining one set of dials, they lost precious seconds in running across the room to operate the controls that would rectify the problem. In 1983, the Nuclear Regulatory Commission required that all control rooms for nuclear power plants be evaluated and modified to take human engineering considerations into account.

These examples illustrate the importance of human factored psychology in large organizations, but you can also see the importance of human factors engineering, or the lack thereof, in everyday life. For example, if you have ever scalded yourself trying to work one of those fancy shower controls in which heat and volume of water are controlled by a single knob, you have experienced poor human factors design. In *The Psychology of Everyday Things,* Donald Norman (1988) exhibits a whole collection of items—doors, computer displays, faucets, cars, typewriters—that do not operate easily, or as they should, because of poor design. Everyday objects should be easy to use, but often they are not. Consider the door, a simple device.

If the door has a horizontal bar in the middle, you push it; you do the same if there is a plate on it about two-thirds of the way to the top. A door that should be pulled requires appropriate hardware, such as a knob or a vertical bar. But sometimes the signals are mixed up. For example, a door at the registrar's office at Rice University. This door exemplifies bad design from the viewpoint of human factors psychology. The door has vertical "pull" bars, but in actuality, it must be pushed to be opened. Because of problems with the door, the registrar's office found it necessary to add a "Push" sign. As Norman says in his book, "When a device as simple as a door has to come with an instruction manual—even a one-word manual—then it is a failure, poorly designed" (1988, p. 87).

The job of the human factors psychologist is to create a harmonious relationship between human beings and the myriad material objects that surround them. Next we give some typical examples of human factors research and applications.

TRAFFIC SAFETY

Traffic safety is a major area of study in human factors psychology, and one that affects nearly all of us. Since the introduction of the first automobile in the early part of the twentieth century, the number of automobiles on the road has increased steadily, with a corresponding increase in traffic accidents. America's love affair with the automobile shows no signs of abating despite rising operation costs, air pollution, and the increasing frequency and severity of traffic jams in many of our major cities. Traffic accidents pose a serious threat to the young in our society, as automobile crashes represent the single leading cause of death among Americans aged 4 to 35 (McGnnis, 1984). If your car was manufactured after 1986, then you are a direct beneficiary of one of human factors psychology's greatest success stories—the *centered high-mounted brake light*. The impetus for the development of this light was the finding that 25 percent of all multivehicle accidents and 7.4 percent of fatal accidents involve rear-end collisions. In early 1977, Malone and Kirkpatrick conducted a large-scale field study involving 2,100 taxicabs in the Washington, D.C., area. The cabs were equally divided into four experimental groups with different brake light configurations: centered high-mounted brake light; dual separated high-mounted brake lights; a separated function condition that separated the taillight function from the stop/turn functions; and the typical, or existing configuration. The centered high-mounted brake light resulted in an accident rate that was 54 percent lower than for cabs with the existing configuration in which brake lights and turn signal lights were combined on the sides of the cars. When accidents did occur, the centered high-mounted brake light was found to reduce the extent of damage to vehicles by 38 percent. Malone and Kirkpatrick concluded that the centered high-mounted brake light resulted in faster brake application in the following vehicle because it is close to the normal line of regard—where we normally look when driving (McGinnis, 1984).

Decreasing the risk for older drivers poses a special challenge for human factors psychologists who work in the area of traffic safety. Older drivers constitute the most rapidly growing segment of the driving population (Waller, 1991). Furthermore, they experience accidents, many fatal, at a higher rate than all other age-groups except those aged 16 to 25 (Laux &. Brelsford, 1990). The need for solutions in this area is so great that the foremost journal in human factors psychology, *Human Factors,* devotes one issue each year exclusively to investigating ways to improve the design of automobiles, road signs, and roadways in an attempt to prolong the period of autonomy for the older driver and to reduce the associated level of risk.

The results from one study suggest that older drivers are aware that the task of driving imposes greater demands on them than on younger drivers and that they take steps to reduce those demands (Laux & Brelsford, 1990). This study examined whether age alone was a good predictor of driving problems or whether individuals' cognitive and physical abilities were more appropriate for determining who might be at risk in driving an automobile. Older drivers (age 50 to 92) and younger drivers (age 40 to 49) kept a driver checklist every day for three months on which they recorded how many times they drove, the weather conditions, and the number of "near misses" (e.g., failing to see another car and almost hitting it or turning the wrong way on a one-way street). The drivers also participated in a number of tasks designed to measure cognitive, sensory, psychomotor, and physical functioning. Overall, there were significant age-related changes on the various tasks, indicating that the older drivers were experiencing decrements in such areas as vision and short-term memory. However, age was not significantly correlated with driving performance. Why was this the case? Older drivers reported taking steps to reduce driving demands (e.g., avoiding rush-hour traffic and nighttime driving). This action, most likely, allowed them to keep the number of difficulties or "near misses" from increasing despite decrements in sensory, cognitive, psychomotor, and physical functioning. Studies like Laux and Brelsford's (1990) aid researchers in better understanding the problems faced by our aging driving population. As evidenced here, the primary goal in this area should be to reduce the demands placed on older drivers so that they are able to drive safely and maintain the autonomy that is so critical to them and their families.

Rather than focusing on environmental factors (e.g., centered high-mounted brake lights and road signs) or personal factors (e.g., age-related deficits), some human factors psychologists try to improve traffic safety by focusing on behavioral factors. A classification model developed by Scott Geller and his colleagues (1990) represents the three contributing factors: environment, person, and behavior. They are currently working to develop and evaluate interventions that can change people's behavior and minimize injuries in automobile accidents. In one study, Ludwig and Geller (1990) implemented a safety belt program for pizza deliverers that included group discussions, pledge cards to obtain individual commitments to buckle up, buckle-up signs, and verbal buckle-up reminders among employees. In addition to increasing shoulder belt use by 143 percent over baseline, the program resulted in a 25 percent increase in the use of turn signals among the deliverers. Geller and his colleagues attribute these findings to a response generalization. That is, voluntarily performing one behavior in the interest of personal safety or health may increase the probability that the individual will perform other similar behaviors. Seat belt use is but one of the many behaviors that human factors psychologists hope to influence through theory-based interventions.

The research we have covered in this section was chosen to illustrate the broad range of interventions that human factors psychologists pursue in their efforts to reduce the incidence of automobile accidents. These interventions range from improving the design of automobiles (environmental factors), to identifying decrements in cognitive and physical ability that contribute to traffic accidents (personal factors), to discovering ways to motivate individuals to assume responsibility for their health and well-being through the use of safety restraints (behavioral factors). By all accounts, human factors psychologists are enjoying great success in the area of traffic safety.

CONCEPT SUMMARY
APPROACHES TO THE STUDY OF TRAFFIC SAFETY

APPROACH	EXAMPLE
Environmental factors	Centered high-mounted brake light (McGinnis, 1984)
Personal factors	Older drivers (Laux & Brelsford, 1990)
Behavioral factors	Seat belt use (Ludwig & Geller, 1990)

INFORMATION DISPLAYS

How should machines display information to their human operators? Should there be a visual display? an auditory display? a tactile display? The kind of display that is chosen will depend on the task requirements. For example, if a person needs to monitor a piece of equipment to get an exact numerical reading, then a machine should feature a digital visual display (Chapanis, 1965). Quantitative readings demand exact numbers, so it is easy to see why digital displays are preferred. Three different types of visual displays—a moving pointer on a fixed scale, a moving scale with a fixed pointer, and a digital readout—can

be imagined, along with four monitoring functions that might be required. A plus sign in the grid indicates the type of display recommended, a minus sign indicates the type not recommended, and a zero signals neutrality. The digital counter is good for determining precise numerical values and settings but is poor for quick check readings and tracking (because a user must do much more mental work to interpret the numbers as falling in an acceptable range or to track their rate of change). The moving pointer is good for check readings (seeing if the equipment is functioning in an acceptable range), for determining a specific setting of the equipment, and for tracking changes over time in the readings. The worst type of display is the moving scale, which is the hardest to track. People expect to see increases with movement in a clockwise direction—and to see higher numbers on the left side of the display, both expectations deriving from their experience with clocks. These expectations can be violated by the moving scale, however, resulting in confusion and errors.

There are many types of visual displays. The appropriate choice is not always obvious without research (Martin, 1989). Digital displays may not be necessary if precise quantitative information is not needed. For example, you do not need to know the precise temperature of your engine when driving a car. You merely need to know if it is operating in a normal range. Thus, a scale indicates that the car is operating in the normal range. Such a display is good for a quick check reading. A designer might argue that even this display provides more information than you really need and suggest an even simpler display—a go-no go display—so called because it tells whether operating a machine is safe (and should go). Perhaps the simplest visual display is the warning light. When it is off, the system is operating normally. When it is lit, a problem exists and the system should be shut down until it is corrected.

Despite its simplicity, the warning light remains an important design issue for human factors psychologists. To detect safety problems, operators must remain vigilant and alert over long periods of time. This is a difficult task, as evidenced by the fact that performance invariably declines over time. In a recent study, Galinsky, Warm, Dember, and Weeler (1990) compared displays that alternated between sensory modalities—auditory and visual—essentially a multi-sensory display. They contrasted this display that alternated between modalities with traditional displays that presented information to one sense, either the eyes or the ears. The results from this study were encouraging, as the multisensory display produced modest improvements in participants' ability to detect critical fluctuations in the display. The design for this display was based on the theory that providing variety might sustain participants' attention. Such research has direct applications for traffic safety. No doubt you have been warned not to gaze in any one direction for too long while driving at night. Like the vigilance task in the Galinsky and colleagues (1990) study, driving long distances requires vigilant attention over long periods of time. With this in mind, realize that you are more likely to fall asleep at the wheel if you gaze at lane-dividing lines for extended periods of time than if you periodically monitor your car gauges, glance in your rearview and side mirrors, and check out billboards in addition to monitoring the road ahead.

The design of display and warning systems affects human performance in a wide variety of activities: industrial quality control, airplane navigation, nuclear power plant operations, monitoring of vital signs in medical settings, traffic safety, and air-traffic control, to name just a few. Given the consequences of failure in these areas, it is no wonder that this remains a critical area of study in human factors psychology.

CONTROL OPERATIONS

Another critical aspect of human performance in person-machine interactions is control. A person must be able to control a machine. Do you remember the first time you tried to operate a car or a personal computer? If you do, you understand the importance of control. Human factors psychologists endeavor to design situations so that people can learn to operate a system easily, effectively, and accurately.

As in the case of displays, there are many different types of controls. Their appropriate selection may require considerable research. First, controls can be either discrete (having a few distinct positions) or continuous (having many possible positions). A light switch typically has two positions (on and off), whereas the volume control on a stereo has many possible positions. Second, controls can be rotary (turned like a knob) or linear (pushed like a button or a lever). Third, controls can have just one spatial dimension (as in the previous examples) or two (like a joystick on a computer game or on an airplane).

In selecting various controls, human factors psychologists need to be sensitive to people's beliefs about the way controls ought to operate. For example, panels indicate the typical ways to turn on machines with the five devices shown. Generally, toggles and levers are pushed up, and buttons and pedals down. Although these ways seem natural to us, they are not universal. For example, although North Americans push the top of a rocker assembly (like a wall light switch) to turn lights on, Australians push the bottom (Martin, 1989).

As mentioned previously, in the early days of aviation, the cockpit controls of different aircraft were not standardized. Controls that looked and felt the same performed entirely different functions on different aircraft, resulting in massive amounts of negative transfer (or interference) for pilots when they switched airplanes. (Imagine suddenly trying to drive a car in which the accelerator was placed to the left of the brake pedal, rather than to its right.) Today, human factors psychologists working for the air force have developed a standard series of shape-coded knobs for use in aircraft (Schultz 6k Schultz, 1990). The shape of the knob signals its function, so that, for example, the knob to control the landing flaps looks, to some extent, like a landing flap. Each knob has a distinctive shape so that pilots can transfer more easily from one airplane to another and reduce errors.

We all use control knobs and buttons every day, although we rarely pause to notice them unless they malfunction or seem inappropriate. We have all searched for light switches in the wrong place, cursed appliances with confusing controls, and wished a particular handle could have been larger or smaller. All these problems could be avoided through appropriate human engineering research. To take but one example, George Kohl, a human factors psychologist working for the American Telephone & Telegraph Company, wanted to know the optimal size and shape of knobs for workers who performed in dangerous conditions (high up on telephone poles or on transmission towers). Kohl (1983) tested four sizes of five different shapes (e.g., circular, square, triangular). The results showed that a triangular knob about 3 inches in diameter was generally easiest to operate, although larger triangular and square knobs were better when great force was required to turn them.

Many other issues must be faced in designing control panels, such as the proper positioning of the controls and their relation to the displays of information. (Recall the control room of the Three Mile Island nuclear power plant, where controls were on the other side of the room from the warning displays.) Often, arrangements of controls and displays cannot be decided a priori (although a designer can try to use principles of good design), but rather must be tested on human users by experimentally varying the conditions of use.

HUMAN-COMPUTER INTERACTION

In the past 20 years, the increasingly common use of computers in the workplace has raised a host of interesting human factors problems. How can people more easily learn about and use computers? How can physical problems associated with sitting before computer displays (eyestrain, backaches) be ameliorated? How can people be taught to program computers and to debug programs more efficiently?

Because computers are generally designed by engineers who worry more about the technical expertise of the system than about the more naive humans who will eventually operate the equipment, human factors psychologists are needed to design the interface. How can the system be designed to be more transparent and readily usable? Norman (1988) cites several general principles applicable in designing computers and other everyday objects. First, the way a machine operates should rely on natural mappings based on past experience. Mapping refers to the relation between two things—in this case between the means of control and the performance of the machine. For example, turning a steering wheel clockwise ("to the right") results in a car turning to the right; the opposite turns the car to the left. Second, operation of the controls should be visible to the user. Third, a machine should also provide feedback when operated, so that a person can know if the actions taken are correct. In the case of the steering wheel, the mapping seems natural, the operation is visible, and feedback about the correctness of the action is provided immediately.

A large part of the problem with modern computers, even ones touted as "user-friendly," is that the relation between the controls (the keys and command functions) and the resulting performance is arbitrary. Little attempt has been made to incorporate into computer design the knowledge that humans bring to a computer. In fairness, operating a piece of equipment as complicated as a computer probably cannot be made completely transparent to a user—some learning must take place—but most human factors psychologists agree that much better designs can be achieved. In addition, for operations that can only be accomplished by relatively arbitrary mappings of controls to functions, standardization across the computer industry would greatly benefit the user. At the moment, various computer systems accomplish similar functions in strikingly different ways, so that the controls must be learned anew for each system. This lack of standardization makes it quite difficult to switch from one system to another. Because of these design problems, workers often require much training in learning to use a computer system.

Human factors considerations also come into play in the long-term life of computers. Many users complain that the video display terminal (VDTs) cause vision problems. The general conclusion of much research is that extended use of VDTs does not cause permanent visual disorders. Workers complain nevertheless that the terminals cause eyestrain, making their jobs less pleasant and probably reducing productivity (Howarth & Istance, 1986). Human factors psychologists have conducted a number of studies to determine the causes of such complaints and these studies have created a number of changes in computer technology. For example, computer screens are now frequently coated with material to reduce the amount of glare they reflect. In addition, indirect lighting (rather than harsh fluorescent light) is typically recommended in rooms with VDTs (Marriott 6k Stuchly, 1986).

Reading from VDTs is generally slower than reading from paper, although why this should be is still not well understood. Part of the difficulty may be that the image quality of characters in VDTs is not as good as in text materials (Gould et al., 1987). Other problems, such as backaches and wrist problems, can be traced to inappropriate chairs. The best chairs for computer use are adjustable so that they can be fitted to the human user and have good back support.

SPACE EXPLORATION

Nearly three decades have passed since the first astronauts walked on the moon. Since that time, space exploration has evolved rapidly with extravehicular activity (EVA) playing an ever-increasing role. It is no wonder, then, that many human factors psychologists devote their life's work to the unique problems posed by EVA. According to Cohen and Bussolari (1987), "The current space station operations baseline will require an estimated 2,000 to 3,000 hours of EVA per year. ... Each EVA shift will last approximately 9 hours, including suit checking, donning, doffing, and any post-EVA cleaning and servicing that is necessary" (p. 2). Imagine yourself spending 9 hours outside a space vehicle! No doubt, one of your major concerns would involve the safety and comfort of your space suit. Also, you would want a suit and a servicing system that was easy to operate in order to devote your energies to the various complex tasks involved in the actual EVA. Fortunately, there are individuals like Cohen and Bussolari who share these same concerns. In fact, the goal of their study was to outline and compare four concepts for the servicing of EVA suits on board the future space station.

Basically, the various concepts they developed all share a common feature called an "airlock." The airlock is an airtight chamber with carefully regulated pressure. This is the chamber from which astronauts exit to engage in EVA. When they have finished a shift, they reenter the space station via this same airlock. Where the four concepts differ is in the actual design and size of the airlock. For example, one concept features an all-encompassing airlock that can support everything from the stowage and servicing of suits to room for two astronauts, one to don or doff a space suit and the other to assist. In another design, the airlock is much smaller and suitable only for transit (i.e., exiting and entering). So, donning, doffing, and the servicing of the space suit must take place outside the airlock. According to Cohen and Bussolari (1987), NASA must strike a balance between human factors and technological concerns. For example, astronauts might find it easier to cope with the first, all-encompassing airlock design. However, this design is the most costly in terms of loss of air pressure per EVA shift because it is the largest in size. Work on the problem of support for EVA is ongoing. This work will proceed from work like Cohen and Bussolari's in concept development and discussion to the design and testing of prototype models. We have provided this example to give you a sense of the challenges faced by human factors psychologist working for NASA in the area of space exploration.

To summarize this section, human factors psychologists are concerned with human/machine systems that can be operated safely and efficiently. In addition, human factors psychologists are often concerned about the total work environment, which leads to the next topic—environmental psychology.

Cell-Phone–Induced Driver Distraction

DAVID L. STRAYER AND FRANK A. DREWS

This article focuses on a dual-task activity that over 100 million drivers in the United States currently engage in: the concurrent use of a cell phone while operating a motor vehicle. It is now well established that cell-phone use significantly impairs driving performance (e.g., McEvoy et al., 2005; Redelmeier & Tibshirani, 1997; Strayer, Drews, & Johnston, 2003; Strayer & Johnston, 2001). For example, our earlier research found that cell-phone conversations made drivers more likely to miss traffic signals and react more slowly to the signals that they did detect (Strayer & Johnston, 2001). Moreover, equivalent deficits in driving performance were obtained for users of both hand-held and hands-free cell phones (see also Strayer, Drews, & Crouch, 2006). By contrast, listening to radio broadcasts or books on tape did not impair driving. These findings are important because they demonstrate that listening to verbal material, by itself, is not sufficient to produce the dual-task interference associated with using a cell phone while driving. The data indicate that when a driver becomes involved in a cell-phone conversation, attention is withdrawn from the processing of the information in the driving environment necessary for safe operation of the motor vehicle.

EVIDENCE OF INATTENTION BLINDNESS

The objective of this article is to muster evidence in support of the hypothesis that cell-phone conversations impair driving by inducing a form of inattention blindness in which drivers fail to see objects in their driving environment when they are talking on a cell phone. Our first study examined how cell-phone conversations affect drivers' attention to objects they encounter while driving. We contrasted performance when participants were driving but not conversing (i.e., single-task conditions) with that when participants were driving and conversing on a hands-free cell phone (i.e., dual-task conditions). We used an incidental-recognition-memory paradigm to assess what information in the driving scene participants attended to while driving. The procedure required participants to perform a simulated driving task without the foreknowledge that their memory for objects in the driving scene would be subsequently tested. Later, participants were given a surprise recognition-memory test in which they were shown objects that had been presented while they were driving and were asked to discriminate these objects from foils that had not been in the driving scene. Differences in incidental recognition memory between single-and dual-task conditions provide an estimate of the degree to which attention to visual information in the driving environment is distracted by cellphone conversations.

Each of the four studies we report here used a computerized driving simulator (made by I-SIM; shown in Fig. 1) with high-resolution displays providing a 180-degree field of view. (The dashboard instrumentation, steering wheel, gas, and brake pedal are from a Ford Crown Victoria sedan

David L. Strayer and Frank A. Drews, "Cellphone-induced Driver Distraction," *Current Directions in Psychological Science*, vol. 16, no. 3, pp. 128-131. Copyright © 2007 by Sage Publications. Reprinted with permission.

with an automatic transmission.) The simulator incorporates vehicle-dynamics, traffic-scenario, and road-surface software to provide realistic scenes and traffic conditions. We monitored the eye fixations of participants using a video-based eye-tracker (Applied Science Laboratories Model 501) that allows a free range of head and eye movements, thereby affording naturalistic viewing conditions for participants as they negotiated the driving environment.

The dual-task conditions in our studies involved naturalistic conversations with a confederate on a cell phone. To avoid any possible interference from manual components of cell-phone use, participants used a hands-free cell phone that was positioned and adjusted before driving began (see Fig. 1). Additionally, the call was begun before participants began the dual-task scenarios. Thus, any dual-task interference that we observed had to be due to the cell-phone conversation itself, as there was no manual manipulation of the cell phone during the dual-task portions of the study.

Our first study focused on the conditional probability of participants recognizing objects that they had fixated on while driving. This analysis specifically tested for memory of objects presented where a given driver's eyes had been directed. The conditional probability analysis revealed that participants were more than twice as likely to recognize roadway signs encountered in the single-task condition than in the dual-task condition. That is, when we focused our analysis on objects in the driving scene on which participants had fixated, we found significant differences in recognition memory between single-and dual-task conditions. Moreover, our analysis found that even when participants' eyes were directed at objects in the driving environment for the same duration, they were less likely to remember them if they were conversing on a cellular phone. The data are consistent with the inattention-blindness hypothesis: The cell-phone conversation disrupts performance by diverting attention from the external environment associated with the driving task to an engaging context associated with the cellphone conversation.

Our second study examined the extent to which drivers who engage in cell-phone conversations strategically reallocate attention from the processing of less-relevant information in the driving scene to the cell-phone conversation while continuing to give highest priority to the processing of task-relevant information in the driving scene. If such a reallocation policy were observed, it would suggest that

Fig. 1. *A participant talking on a hands-free cell phone while driving in the simulator.*

drivers might be able to learn how to safely use cell phones while driving. The procedure was similar to that of the first study except that we used a two-alternative forced-choice recognition-memory paradigm to determine what information in the driving scene participants attended to while driving. We placed 30 objects varying in relevance to safe driving (e.g., pedestrians, cars, trucks, signs, billboards, etc.) along the roadway in the driving scene; another 30 objects were not presented in the driving scene and served as foils in the recognition-memory task. There were different driving scenarios for different participants and target objects for some participants were foil objects for others. Objects in the driving scene were positioned so that they were clearly in view as participants drove past them, and the target and foils were counterbalanced across participants. Here again, participants were not informed about the memory test until after they had completed the driving portions of the study.

As in the first study, we computed the conditional probability of recognizing an object given that participants fixated on it while driving. Like the first study, this analysis specifically tested for memory of objects that were located where the driver's eyes had been directed. We found that participants were more likely to recognize objects encountered in the single-task condition than in the dual-task condition and that this difference was not affected by how long they had fixated on the objects. Thus, when we ensured that participants looked at an object for the same amount of time, we found significant differences in recognition memory between single-and dual-task conditions.

After each forced-choice judgment, participants were also asked to rate the objects in terms of their relevance to safe driving, using a 10-point scale (participants were initially given an example in which a child playing near the road might receive a rating of 9 or 10, whereas a sign documenting that a volunteer group cleans a particular section of the highway might receive a rating of 1). Participants' safety-relevance ratings ranged from 1.5 to 8, with an average of 4.1. A series of regression analyses revealed that there was no association between recognition memory and traffic relevance. In fact, traffic relevance had absolutely no effect on the difference in recognition memory between single-and dual-task conditions, suggesting that the contribution of an object's perceived relevance to recognition-memory performance is negligible. This analysis is important because it indicates that drivers do not strategically reallocate attention from the processing of less-relevant information in the driving scene to the cell-phone conversation while continuing to give highest priority to the processing of task-relevant information in the driving scene.

The studies discussed thus far have relied on explicit-memory measures taken after the driving session to test the hypothesis that cell-phone conversations interfere with the initial encoding of information in the driving scene. However, an alternative possibility is that there are no differences in the initial encoding but rather differences in the retrieval of the information during subsequent memory tests. This distinction is more than academic, because the former has direct implications for traffic safety whereas the latter does not (i.e., failing to recognize an item at a later point in time does not necessarily imply an impairment in encoding and reaction to an object in the driving environment).

Our third study tested the inattention-blindness hypothesis by recording on-line measures of brain activity elicited by events in the driving environment. Prior research has found that the amplitude of the P300 component of the event-related brain potential (ERP) is sensitive to the attention allocated to a task (e.g., Sirevaag, Kramer, Coles, & Donchin, 1989; Wickens, Kramer, Vanasse, & Donchin, 1983) and, further, that memory performance is superior for objects eliciting larger-amplitude P300s during encoding (e.g., Fabiani, Karis, & Donchin, 1986; Otton & Donchin, 2000). Moreover, ERPs recorded in flight simulation revealed that the P300 component discriminates between different levels of task difficulty, decreasing as the task demands increased (e.g., Kramer, Sirevaag, & Braun, 1987; Sirevaag et al., 1993).

In this study, we used a car-following paradigm in which participants drove on a simulated multilane freeway. Participants followed a pace car that would brake at random intervals and ERPs were time-locked to the onset of the pace-car brake lights in both single-and dual-task conditions. If the impairments in memory performance are due to differences in the initial encoding of objects in the driving scene, then P300 amplitude should be smaller in dual-task conditions than in single-task conditions. By contrast, if the memory differences are due to impaired retrieval of information at the time of the recognition-memory test but not at the time of encoding, then we would not expect to find differences in P300 amplitude between single-and dual-task conditions.

The average ERPs are presented in Figure 2. Visual inspection reveals a large positive potential between 250 and 750 milliseconds (the P300 component of the ERP). Our analysis indicated that the amplitude of the P300 component of the ERPs was reduced by 50% when the drivers were talking on the cell phone. Thus, drivers using a cell phone fail to see information in the driving scene because they do not encode it as well as they do when they are not distracted by the cell-phone conversation. These data suggest that drivers using a cell phone will be less able to react with alacrity in situations that demand it because of the diversion of attention from driving to the phone conversation (see also Strayer, Drews, & Johnston, 2003).

Our fourth study contrasted two modes of conversation commonly engaged in while driving: Conversation with a friend via a hands-free cell phone versus conversation with a friend seated in the passenger seat located next to the driver in the vehicle. We hypothesized that these two conversations would differ because passengers tend to adjust their conversation based on driving difficulty; often helping the driver to navigate and identify hazards on the roadway and pausing the conversations during difficult sections of the drive. By contrast, this real-time adjustment based upon traffic demands is not possible with cellphone conversations.

Participants were instructed to drive on a multilane freeway and exit at a rest stop approximately 8 miles down the road. We found that the majority of drivers (88%) who were conversing with a passenger successfully completed the task of navigating to the rest area, whereas 50% of the drivers talking on a cell phone failed to navigate to the rest area. Analysis of the video recordings indicated that a primary difference between these two modes of communication was that the passenger helped the driver in the navigation task by reminding them to exit at the rest stop. Moreover, our analysis of the content of the conversation indicated that references to traffic conditions were more likely with passenger conversations than they were with cell-phone conversations.

THEORETICAL CONSIDERATIONS AND FUTURE DIRECTIONS

What are the implications of these findings for the architecture of cognition? Multiple-resource models of dual-task performance (e.g., Wickens, 1984) have been interpreted as suggesting that an auditory/verbal/vocal cell-phone conversation may be performed concurrently with little

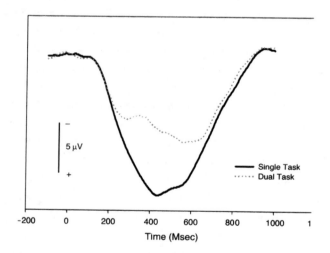

Fig. 2. *Event-related potentials (ERPs) elicited by the onset of a pace car's brake light when talking on a cell phone (dual-task condition) and when not talking on a cell phone (single-task condition). The amplitude of the P300 component of the ERP (which is a manifestation of higher cognitive processing such as memory encoding) was reduced by 50% when participants were conversing on a hands-free cell phone.*

or no cost to a visual/spatial/manual driving task. That is, given the apparent lack of overlap in processing resources, the cell phone and driving dual-task combination should be performed with little degradation in performance. However, given the clear and consistent interference between cell-phone and driving tasks, it would appear that multiple-resource models do not apply well to this dual-task combination.

One alternative possibility that we are currently exploring is that the dual-task interference stems from a central-processing bottleneck, wherein attending to the cell-phone conversation temporarily blocks or impedes the processing of information in the driving environment (cf. Levy, Pashler, & Boer, 2006). We hypothesize that the central-processing bottleneck forces serial processing of these two sources of information (i.e., the information necessary for the safe operation of a motor vehicle and the cell-phone conversation) and that the cell-phone conversation may not lend itself to parsing in ways that are compatible with driving (cf. Strayer & Johnston, 2001). That is, a conversation on the phone cannot be successfully broken into arbitrary units, but instead is composed of "turns" that engage the central-processing bottleneck for prolonged periods of time (e.g., pausing in mid-sentence/thought impedes the flow of the conversation); moreover, this turn-taking is often asynchronous with the processing demands of driving. Supporting this idea is the observation that in-vehicle conversations do not interfere with driving as much as cell-phone conversations do because there is a greater ability to synchronize an in-vehicle conversation with the processing demands of driving than there is with a cell-phone conversation.

The findings reported here highlight the need for sharpening our theoretical understanding of multitasking in complex naturalistic environments. The usefulness of such theory increases with the ever-increasing prevalence of new technologies allowing people to engage in concurrent activities. Theory development will improve our ability to determine why some tasks are successfully performed in combination whereas others are incompatible.

In sum, the data indicate that cell-phone conversations place demands upon the driver that differ qualitatively from those of other auditory/verbal/vocal tasks commonly performed while operating a motor vehicle. Even when cell-phone drivers direct their gaze at objects in the driving environment, they often fail to "see" them because attention has been diverted to the cellphone conversation.

RECOMMENDED READING

Redelmeier, D.A., & Tibshirani, R.J. (1997). (See References)

Strayer, D.L., & Johnston, W.A. (2001). (See References)

REFERENCES

Fabiani, M., Karis, D., & Donchin, E. (1986). P300 and re-call in an incidental memory paradigm. *Psychophysiology, 23*, 298–308.

Kramer, A.F., Sirevaag, E.J., & Braun, R. (1987). A psychophysiological assessment of operator workload during simulated flight missions. *Human Factors, 29*, 145–160.

Levy, J., Pashler, H., & Boer, E. (2006). Central interference in driving: Is there any stopping the psychological refractory period? *Psychological Sciences, 17*, 228–235.

McEvoy, S.P., Stevenson, M.R., McCartt, A.T., Woodward, M., Haworth, C., Palamara, P., & Cercarelli, R. (2005). Role of mobile phones in motor vehicle crashes resulting in hospital attendance: A case-crossover study. *British Medical Journal, 331*, 428–433.

Otton, L.J., & Donchin, E. (2000). Relationship between P300 amplitude and subsequent recall for distinctive events: Dependence on type of distinctiveness attribute. *Psychophysiology, 37*, 644–661.

Redelmeier, D.A., & Tibshirani, R.J. (1997). Association between cellular-telephone calls and motor vehicle collisions. *The New England Journal of Medicine, 336*, 453–458.

Sirevaag, E.J., Kramer, A.F., Coles, M.G.H., & Donchin, E. (1989). Recourse reciprocity: An event-related brain potential analysis. *Acta Psychologia, 70*, 77–97.

Sirevaag, E.J., Kramer, A.F., Wickens, C.D., Reisweber, M., Strayer, D.L., & Grenell, J.H. (1993). Assessment of pilot performance and mental workload in rotary wing aircraft. *Ergonomics, 9*, 1121–1140.

Strayer, D.L., Drews, F.A., & Crouch, D.J. (2006). Comparing the cellphone driver and the drunk driver. *Human Factors, 48*, 381–391.

Strayer, D.L., Drews, F.A., & Johnston, W.A. (2003). Cell phone induced failures of visual attention during simulated driving. *Journal of Experimental Psychology: Applied, 9*, 23–52.

Strayer, D.L., & Johnston, W.A. (2001). Driven to distraction: Dual-task studies of simulated driving and conversing on a cellular phone. *Psychological Science, 12*, 462–466.

Wickens, C.D. (1984). Processing resources in attention. In R. Parasuraman & R. Davies (Eds.), *Varieties of Attention*. (pp. 63–101). New York: Academic Press.

Wickens, C.D., Kramer, A.F., Vanasse, L., & Donchin, E. (1983). Performance of concurrent tasks: A psychophysiological assessment of the reciprocity of information-processing resources. *Science, 221*, 1080–1082.

Many to One

Using the Mobile Phone to Interact with Large Classes

STEPHEN KINSELLA

The perennial problem of communicating with large classes of over 100 students can be resolved using students' mobile phones and a piece of software written to take advantage of the ubiquity of the mobile phone.[1] This paper describes the first steps towards one possible resolution. Several methods exist which allow students to communicate with lecturers in large groups (See Aronson, 1987; Davis, 1993; Guthrie & Carlin, 2004; Hall, Collier, Thomas & Hilgers, 2005; Judson, 2002), but none, to my knowledge, combine ease of use, speed of transmission and student feedback in as cost-effective a manner as the one described below.

In lectures which use this application, students can send anonymous text messages to the phone number displayed in the application, and each student in the class can see the results of the communication, because the results of the text message output on the screen behind the lecturer when the lecturer chooses to release the messages on to the screen. This represents a new communication channel between the Many (students) and the One (lecturer). The application facilitates student interaction within the class and with the lecturer, and allows the lecturer to respond to student observations, questions and comments in a controlled manner within a large class.

The lecturer must therefore adapt his or her lecture to take advantage of the ability of students to communicate anonymously, and in real time with them. The main area examined in the pilot module within which the application was introduced for the first time consisted of multiple choice questions at the end of each lecture, designed to give students the experience of the type of questions they might see in a final exam. This incentivised students to answer questions using their mobile phones, both to see the answers and to see how the answers were arrived at in class.

Another area in which lectures have been adapted previously is mini-summaries. Through an hour-long class, the results and derivations of one 20-minute segment would be summarised and elaborated upon, before moving to a successive topic or example. In this 'break' period, students were encouraged to send in questions, comments, or observations through text. Some of these texts were revealing, insightful and often funny, which lightened the atmosphere in class and made it more interesting and interactive for the lecturer at the same time.

INSTANT FEEDBACK IN LARGE LECTURES

Communication with large groups is a persistent issue in university teaching. It is difficult to judge whether students are learning within the lecture format, and if they do not, no immediate student feedback is forthcoming.

Though several technical solutions also exist to communicate with students (for example, eInstruction, 2006; Quizdom, 2006; Texas Instruments, 2007), they are in general costly, proprietary and force the students to learn a new interface.

The application described here simply allows the student to interact with the lecturer through a mobile phone, which every modern student has, and knows how to use so no learning barrier exists with this technology. No costly hardware is required, because the interface is the student's phone. The only barrier to communication between the lecturer and the student is the negligible mobile phone tariff, which can be alleviated using a free phone number if desired.

Pedagogically, the interface allows lecturers access to instant feedback on their material and gives the students some purchase over the direction of the lecture.

CHANGING THE LECTURE FORMAT TO ACCOMMODATE THE SOFTWARE

At first, students were quite sceptical about using their phones to send messages to a lecturer, but this changed once they realised all their comments would be responded to in an open-minded way.

The issue of control of the flow of messages became apparent early on in the lectures, so a 'process' button was added to stop a free-for-all of texting in the lecture and allow the class to focus on lecture content.

Feedback generally fell into two categories. Firstly, procedural or definitional queries such as 'can you write more clearly' or 'will there be negative marking on the exam?' Secondly, students sent texts with questions of economic theory or policy, which changed the direction of the lecture. For example, when talking about money demand, a student sent a question about Zimbabwean inflation, then soaring at 160, 000%, and asked how to stop it. This derailed the lecture, but it encouraged students to think about the problem, and later that day, a post on the class weblog allowed students to visit websites giving them more information on the phenomenon of hyperinflation.

Negative aspects of the process were the long set-up times in each lecture actually getting the application to work with the phone and overcoming student reticence to communicate in lectures. Most of the time, once the students were aware that their comments would be shown and responded to without judgment, the comments were germane, thoughtful and informative.

NOTE

1. Available from the author's homepage www.stephen-kinsella.net as open source software.

REFERENCES

Aronson, R. J. (1987). Six keys to effective instruction in large classes: advice from a practitioner. In Maryellen Gleason Weimer (Ed.), *Teaching Large Classes Well* (pp. 31–37). New Directions for Teaching and Learning, No. 32. San Francisco, CA: Jossey-Bass.

Davis, B. G. (1993). *Tools for teaching*. San Francisco, CA: Jossey-Bass.

eInstruction (2006) Retrieved July 2, 2008, from http://www.einstruction.com/ and http://www.educue.com/

Guthrie, R. & Carlin, A. (2004). Waking the dead: using interactive technology to engage passive listeners in the classroom. *Proceedings of the Tenth Americas Conference on Information systems*, New York, NY, 1–8.

Hall, R. H., Collier, H. L., Thomas, M. L. & Hilgers, M. G. (2005). A student response system for increasing engagement, motivation, and learning in high enrollment lectures. *Proceedings of the Americas Conference on Information Systems*, 621–626.

Judson, E. & Sawada, D. (2002). Learning from past and present: electronic response systems in college lecture halls. *Journal of Computers in Mathematics and Science Teaching*, 21, 2, 167–181.

Quizdom (2006) Retrieved from July 2, 2008 from http://www.qwizdom.com/

Texas Instruments (2007) *TI-Navigator*. Retrieved from July 2, 2008 from http://education.ti.com/educationportal/sites/US/productDetail/us_ti_navigator.html

Designing a Licence Plate for Memorability

JAN M. SCHRAAGEN AND KEES VAN DONGEN

Good memorability of licence plates is important in those cases where licence plates are viewed for a brief period of time and the information is essential for police investigations. The purpose of the current study was to design a new Dutch licence plate that could be remembered well. A memory experiment was conducted, in which 16 different character arrangements were presented for both 450 and 550 ms to 48 participants with ages varying between 20 and 57 years. Participants had to rehearse the stimuli for 6 s, after which they had to be written down. Based on literature on short-term memory for serial order, character arrangements differed on three dimensions: 1) number of alternations between letters and digits; 2) letter to digit ratio; and 3) equality of group size. Results showed that number of alternations between characters of different categories affected memory performance the most. Letter to digit ratio and equality of group size affected memory performance to a lesser, but still significant, extent. A significant interaction between the latter two factors indicates that equal groups only lead to fewer memory errors when more than three letters are used. With three or fewer letters, group size is not a significant factor any more. Based on these results, a new licence plate for Dutch vehicles was recommended, which was subsequently adopted.

1. INTRODUCTION

The primary function of licence plates, according to a survey among law enforcement officers and motor vehicle administrators, is to display the information necessary for fast and accurate identification of automobiles (Karmeier *et al.* 1960). In case of hit-and-run accidents or criminals fleeing by vehicle, eyewitness reports form an important part of police investigations. Eyewitnesses may be able to provide information on the licence plate, next to the colour, year and make of the vehicle. The more characters are remembered and reported to the police, the smaller the search space for the police. This puts a premium on the optimal design of licence plates, both in terms of legibility and memorability.

This article is not concerned with the issue of legibility, but solely with memorability. The customer, the Centre for Transport Technology and Information in The Netherlands, wanted to know, within the constraints of the current physical layout of Dutch licence plates, what alternative character arrangements would be optimal from a memorability point of view. This question arose from the expectation that the combinatorial possibilities of the current type of licence plates run out in 2004. Therefore, a

Jan Maarten Schraagen and Kees Van Dongen, "Designing a Licence Plate for Memorability," *Ergonomics*, vol. 48, no. 7, pp. 796–806. Copyright © 2005 by Taylor & Francis Group LLC. Reprinted with permission.

new arrangement of digits and letters had to be developed, preferably one that would be remembered easily. Character height and width, distance between characters, colour of characters and background, etc. would all remain the same as they are now, and were therefore not subject to human factors research. The total number of characters would also remain as six, due to IT-data structure constraints. However, within these constraints, TNO Human Factors were at liberty to experiment with varying combinations of digits and letters, and with different groupings.

Human factors research on memory for licence plates should take advantage of the large literature on short-term memory for serial order. Based on this literature, the following general principles were formulated for the design of novel licence plates.

1.1. Avoid many alternations between letters and digits

Broadbent and Gregory (1964), Sanders and Schroots (1968a, b) and Hull (1976) all found that as the number of alternations between letters and digits increases, lists are remembered less well. Either straight digit or letter numbering systems can accomplish avoiding alternations. As long as it does not become necessary to use more than six characters, straight numerical systems will be better remembered than straight letter systems (following well-established differences between recall of letters and digits in memory span experiments, e.g. Brener 1940, Crannell and Parrish 1957). However, for practical purposes of obtaining a sufficient number of combinatorial possibilities for licence plates, straight numerical systems will often yield too few combinations to accommodate the foreseen demand for licence plates. In practice, therefore, some combination of letters and digits always needs to be used. Given that constraint, using a predictable grouping of letters and digits may minimize alternations. The number of alternations is defined as the number of changes between characters of different categories (e.g. letters and digits) within spatially separated groups. Hull (1976) found that regular patterns of alternation (e.g. TBD328 or WF93RD) were better remembered than irregular patterns of alternation (e.g. V1TG15 or P3B6DC). Regular patterns have fewer alternations than irregular patterns.

1.2. Use more digits than letters

Both Aldrich (1937) and Karmeier et al. (1960) found that with the introduction of more letters, the percentage of memory errors also increased. For instance, Karmeier et al. (1960) found that licence plates of the 123 456 type yielded 75% correct reproduction, whereas licence plates of the ABC 123 type yielded only 53% correct reproduction. However, the type AB 1234 did not significantly differ in the percentage correct reproduction from the all-numeric type 123 456 (70 vs. 75%, respectively). And AB 1234 was recalled significantly better than the seven-digit type 1234 567 (70 vs. 28%, respectively; 28% may seem an unusually small number for remembering seven digits. One has to remember, however, that Karmeier et al. (1960) used simultaneous visual presentation at 0.5 s rates; typical digit span studies employ auditory presentation with 1.0 s presentation rates). These results suggest that the number of digits should not exceed six, which is not surprising in light of classic findings on average digit span (e.g. Miller 1956). Even more so, the number of characters as a whole should not exceed six, given that memory span for letters is somewhat below digit span. More important, the results suggest that combinations of two letters and four digits are easier to remember than combinations of three letters and three digits. This principle only holds as long as the letters and digits are combined into same-category groups, thus minimizing alternations between letters and digits (see section 1.1 above). Four digits and two letters are less easy to remember than three letters and three digits when the four digits are split into groups of two, yielding the type 12AB34. Hull (1976), for instance, found that the 12AB34 type was less well remembered than the 123ABC type.

However, for practical purposes, two letters may yield too few combinatorial possibilities. Karmeier et al. (1960) calculated that two letters and four digits would give up to 6000 000 possibilities. This is true if one can use the entire alphabet of 26 letters. In The Netherlands, however, certain letters are reserved for certain special classes of vehicles (military, royal family, diplomatic corps), vowels are excluded, as well as visually similar letters (Q and O). This leaves 17 letters in total to choose from. The general principle to use more digits than letters, therefore, is at conflict with the desire to have a sufficient number of combinations. For instance, if one wants to be able to use a specific system of numbering for at least 5 years, and each year 1000 000 licence plates are issued, one needs at least 5000 000 combinations. With 17 letters, this can only be achieved with at least three letters and three digits, not with two letters and four digits, even though the latter system is desirable from a human factors point of view.

1.3. Use grouping by spatial separation

Short-term storage of material is usually facilitated when the entire material is sliced up into groups. For digits, chunk sizes of three to four are best (Murdock 1974). A telephone number of seven digits may therefore best be split up into groups of three and four (Severin and Rigby 1963, Klemmer and Stocker 1974). These studies employed experimenter-imposed groupings. Thorpe and Rowland (1965) investigated 'natural' groupings spontaneously employed by their participants in verbally recalling visually presented sequences of digits. For seven-digit sequences and 1 s/digit presentation time, the three to four grouping pattern was most often employed (with the more atypical unlimited time to memorize, the three–three–one grouping pattern was most often used).

For combinations of digits and letters, fewer studies have systematically investigated the effects of grouping. Two issues should be distinguished here. First, as digits and letters constitute different categories, they are grouped naturally as long as they remain together in subcategories. For instance, AB1234 constitutes the most extreme form of grouping; 12AB34 also provides some grouping, but the digits are now split into two subgroups; finally, 1A23B4 provides very little grouping. Framed this way, the issue becomes one of alternations between different categories, and research pertaining to this issue was discussed above. The second issue is grouping by spatial separation. For instance, is the format AB 1234 better remembered than AB1234? Kahneman and Henik (1977) found strong effects of spatial separation on immediate recall. Recall probabilities were similar within each group and varied sharply between spatially separated groups. An even more extreme form of spatial separation would be to place the letters above the digits. Biegel (1938) found better memory after tachistoscopic (0.5 s) presentation of licence plates where the letters were put above the digits, as compared with licence plates where letters and digits were placed on a single line (96 vs. 77%, respectively).

Although it is known that memory performance can be facilitated by spatially separating groups of characters, it is not known whether it matters how groups of characters are spatially separated. Does it, for instance, matter whether characters are arranged in groups of unequal sizes (e.g. ABC-D-EF, A-12-BCD, 12-ABC-3) or whether characters are arranged in groups of equal sizes (e.g. AB-CD-EF, AB-12-CD, ABC-123)?

1.4. Research question

In this experiment the effects that the factors 1) alternations, 2) letter to digit ratio and 3) equality of group size have on memory performance were tested and the relative contribution of these factors for memory performance were also tested.

2. METHOD
2.1. Participants

Forty-eight participants (24 males and 24 females) with an age ranging between 20 and 57 years, with an average of 41 years, were randomly selected from a database with a pool of drivers. The average driving experience of this group ranged between 1000 and 60000 km per year, with an average experience of 17260 km per year. For participation each participant received a reward of €40.

2.2. Design

A $5 \times 3 \times 2$ incomplete factorial design was used to test the effects of alternations, letter:digit ratio and equality of group size on memory performance (see table 1). The factor alternations had five levels ranging from no alternations between letters and digits within the spatially separated groups to four alternations. The factor letter:digit ratio had four levels ranging from character arrangements with three letters and three digits to character arrangements with six letters and zero digits. The factor equality of group size had two levels, that is, character arrangements either consisted of groups of equal or unequal size. Because the levels of the factors alternations and letter:digit ratio were not completely independent, in that the possible number of alternations was limited when the letter:digit ratio reaches extremes, only the first three levels of the factor letter:digit ratio were used in the analysis. For economic reasons it was not possible to test all variants indicated in table 1; therefore, a full factorial experimental design was not possible.

The mean number of wrongly reported characters has been used as an indication of memory performance and was used as the dependent variable. The number of errors was calculated by comparing participant's responses with the actual presented character arrangements, including the placement of the dashes between the letters and digits. The first two responses to each sequence of ten licence plates were not used in the analysis since subjects had to adjust to the new character arrangement.

In addition to the objective assessment of memorability, a subjective measure was used. After the experiments, participants were asked to indicate which three of the new licence plate designs were most easy to remember and which three licence plate designs were most difficult to remember. Memorability for each licence plate design was determined by subtracting the number of indications for difficult memorability from the number of indications of easy memorability.

2.3. Stimulus materials

For each of the 16 types of character arrangements 20 variants were randomly generated for each participant using digits and letters with the exclusion of the letters: A, C, E, I, M, O, Q, U and W (these are not used in current Dutch licence plates). The character arrangements had the form of official Dutch licence plates. The presented licence plates had an onscreen size of 6.0 x 1.3 cm and were perceived from a distance of 85 cm on a computer screen with a size of 33.8 x 27.1 cm. With a horizontal and vertical visual angle of 4.04° x 0.86° in the experimental setting this corresponded to a viewing distance of a real licence plate from a distance of 7.4 m.

2.4. Procedure

The participants received written instructions, a demonstration of the task and a training session before the experiment.

Participants were instructed to remember the order of consonants and digits for the licence plates for 6 s, after which the remembered character arrangement had to be written down and subsequently entered into the computer. Participants were able to correct typing errors as they

Table 1. *Experimental design*

Letter-digit ratio	Equality of group size	Number of alternations				
		0	1	2	3	4
3:3	Yes	ABC-123★	AB-C1–23	AB1–23C	A1-B2-C3★	A1B-2C3
	No	12-ABC-3★	12–3AB-C	A1-BC2–3★	1A-B2C-3	–
4:2	Yes	AB-12-CD★	A12-BCD★	A1-BC-3D★	A1B-2CD	A1B-C2D★
		AB-CD-12★				
		12-AB-CD★				
	No	A-12-BCD★	1–2A-BCD	A-1B-2CD	A-1B-C2D	–
5:1	Yes	AB-C1-DE	ABC-1DE★	ABC-D1E	–	–
	No	ABC-1-DE★	ABC-D-1E	A1B-C-DE	–	–
6:0	Yes	AB-CD-EF★	–	–	–	–
		ABC-DEF★				
	No	ABC-D-EF★	–	–	–	–

★ Character arrangements that were used in the experiment.
–indicates impossible combinations of the factors.
For further details of design, see p. 00.

entered the numbers and letters into the computer. The rationale behind this procedure was to reproduce the real-life phenomenon in which witnesses frequently have to engage in some form of verbal rehearsal before they are able to write down or report the licence plate they have seen. Furthermore, by first asking participants to write down the character arrangement, it was hoped to minimize the memory decay that could occur when participants have to search for keys on their keyboard. The participants were instructed to press the 'enter' button when they completed their response to a licence plate for the next presentation. They were told that ten licence plates of a certain type would be presented before a new sequence of ten would start. After the first block of 16 types there was a break of 10 min, after the break the second block started.

After the instructions were read individually, the experimenter demonstrated to the groups of four participants how the task was performed. In the training session participants were given the opportunity to individually familiarize themselves with the memory task. In the training session 20 licence plates of the variants 12–3 4-AB and AB-12–3 4 were presented for 550 ms and 450 ms respectively (these types of licence plates were not used in the experiment). After the training the participants had the opportunity to ask questions and it was ensured that all participants were able to perform the task

In two experimental blocks, with stimulus presentation times of 450 and 550 ms, the 16 types of character arrangements were randomly presented to the participants in two series of ten. Pilot studies had indicated that these presentation times yielded a sufficient number of errors. However, individual participants differed in their error rate, depending on the exact presentation time. It was therefore decided to use both presentation times. Each participant participated in both blocks and the order of the blocks was balanced between participants. So as to avoid repetition effects it was ensured that no character occurred in the same serial position as the preceding presentation. The experiment, including training, demonstration and instructions took, in total, 3 h.

3. RESULTS

The results of an ANOVA using a General Linear Motor type III procedure, in which the effect of individual

differences was filtered from the error term, pointed out that the effects on memory performance of the number of alternations, the letter:digit ratio, the equality of group size and presentation time were statistically significant (see table 2). Further, a significant interaction between the effect of letter:digit ratio and equality of group size was found. Since interaction effects with presentation time were not statistically significant all further analyses were conducted on the pooled presentation times.

3.1. Effect of alternations

The number of errors in memory performance was higher for character arrangements with more alternations between letters and digits, $F(4, 9919) = 475.15, p < 0.001$. For variants with no alternations between letters and digits within the spatially separated groups, the mean number of errors was 1.14 characters; for variants with one alternation, the mean number of errors increased to 1.43 characters. For variants with two, three or four alternations the mean number of errors increased further to respectively 2.29, 1.96 and 2.44 characters. Unexpectedly, fewer errors were made for character arrangements with three compared to two alternations ($M = 1.96$ vs. $M = 2.29$). However, character arrangements with two (for instance, A1-BC2–3) and three alternations (A1-B2-C3) differed in that in the latter a letter in a group is always followed by a number. This replicates Hull's (1976) result that regular patterns of alternation are better remembered than irregular patterns of alternation.

For the variants in which the levels of the factors letter:digit ratio (4:2) and equality of group size (equal) were held constant, the number of errors systematically increased with increasing alternations. For the variants with zero (AB-12-CD), one (A12-BCD), two (A1-BC-3D) and four (A1B-C2D) alternations the mean number of errors increased respectively from 0.92, 1.19, 2.27 to 2.44. Pairwise comparisons showed that all variants differed significantly from each other (Tukey Honestly Significantly Different, $p < 0.05$).

3.2. Effect of letter:digit ratio

The number of errors in memory performance was higher for character arrangements with more letters and correspondingly fewer digits, $F(2, 9919) = 104.81, p < 0.001$. For variants with three or four letters, the mean number of errors was 1.51 and 1.48, respectively. The mean number of errors increased to 1.74 characters for variants with five letters, and 1.87 characters for variants with six letters. Unexpectedly, the number of errors for character arrangements with three letters did not significantly differ from the number of errors for character arrangements with four letters, $F(1, 47) < 1$. However, when the effect of letter:digit ratio was isolated from the other factors, that is, when the number of alternations (none) and equality of group size (unequal) were held constant, the number of errors systematically increased with an increasing number of letters. For the variants with a letter:digit ratio of 3:3 (12-ABC-3), 4:2 (A-12-BCD), 5:1 (ABC-12-D) and 6:1 (ABC-D-EF) the mean number of errors increased respectively from 0.82, 1.44, 1.80 to 2.20. Pairwise comparisons showed that all variants differed significantly from each other (Tukey HSD, $p < 0.05$).

3.3. Effect of equal group size

The number of errors in memory performance was on average higher for character arrangements with unequal group sizes compared to character arrangements with equal group sizes, $F(2, 9919) = 39.53, p < 0.001$. For variants in which the groups were of equal size, the mean number of errors was 1.50 characters compared to 1.59 characters for arrangements with unequal group sizes. However, the effect of equal group size is not independent of the factor letter:digit ratio as is indicated by the significant letter:digit ratio x equality of group size interaction effect, $F(2, 9919) = 20.39, p < 0.001$.

The difference in the number of errors between character arrangements with equal and unequal group size disappears when the number of letters in character arrangements decreases. When the number of alternations in variants was held constant (no alternations), the results showed that the number of errors for character arrangements with equal and unequal group size significantly differed for variants with a letter:digit ratio of 6:0 and 4:2, respectively $F(1,47) = 11.10, p < 0.01$ and $F(1,47) = 15.21, p < 0.01$. The respective means for variants with a 6:0 ratio were $M = 1.75$ (AB-CD-EF) and $M = 2.20$ (ABC-D-EF); for variants with a 4:2 ratio, the means were $M = 0.92$ (AB-12-CD) and $M = 1.44$ (A-12-BCD) (see figure 1). For variants with a 3:3 letter:digit ratio, however, the mean number of errors between variants with unequal and equal group sizes did not differ significantly,

Table 2. ANOVA *for the effects of alternations, letter:digit ratio, equality of group size, participant and presentation time†*

Source	df	F
Alternations (A)	4	475.15*
Letter–digit ratio (L)	2	104.81*
Group size equality (E)	1	39.85*
Participant (P)	47	94.45*
Presentation time (T)	1	35.94*
A*T	4	2.74
L*T	2	.58
E*T	1	2.50
L*E	2	20.39*
Error	9919	

*Statistical significance at $p < 0.01$.

†Variants with a letter:digit ratio of 6:0 were left out of the ANOVA because for these variants the factors letter:digit ratio and alternations were confounded.

F (1,47) = 2.51, p = 0.12, with M = 0.94 (ABC-123) compared to M= 0.82 (12-ABC-3).

3.4. Correlation objective and subjective measurements

Table 3 lists the character arrangements according to their objective ranking and, in the third column, according to their subjective judgement of memorability. Note that subjective judgements were not asked on existing arrangements, in order to avoid biased judgements due to familiarity with the existing types. The fifth column in table 3 shows the difference between the number of participants who indicated that a particular licence plate was 'easy to remember' and the number of participants who indicated

that a particular licence plate was 'difficult to remember.' For instance, with the licence plate arrangement 12-ABC-3, 23 participants indicated they found this 'easy to remember', and five indicated they found this 'difficult to remember.' The difference score of 18 appears in column 5 of table 3.

The correlation between objective (number of errors) and subjective measures (number of judgements easy minus difficult) of memorability was high, r_p = 0.95, $p < 0.001$. The rank order correlation, Spearman's *rho,* based on objective and subjective ranking of the same measures, was r_s = 0.90, $p < 0.001$.

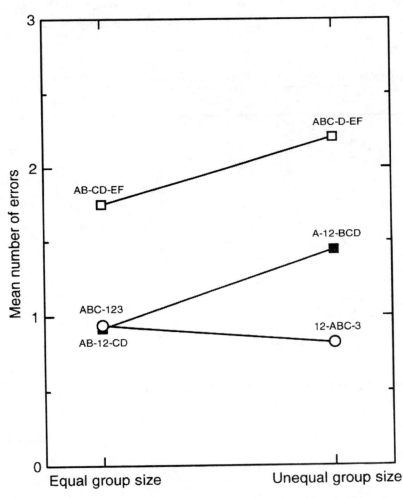

Figure 1. *Main and interaction effects of the factors equality of group size and letter-digit ratio on memory performance.*

3.5. Relative importance of factors

The relative importance of the factors alternations, letter:digit ratio and equality of group size was assessed by calculating the standardized coefficients of the regression equation. The weak and non-significant intercorrelations between the factors ($r < 0.28$, $p =$ NS) and low variance inflation factors (< 1.12) indicated that there was no problem with multicollinearity. This suggests that the standardized coefficient for the factors can be reliably interpreted as the degree to which the factors contributed to memory performance. Using a stepwise, forward and backward regression analysis it was found that the factor alternations had the highest standardized coefficient ($\beta_a = 0.34$, $p < 0.001$), followed by the factors equality of group size ($\beta_e = 0.12$, $p < 0.001$) and letter:digit ratio ($\beta_r = 0.11$, $p < 0.001$), which did not differ in the degree to which they contributed to memory performance.

4. DISCUSSION

It has been shown that memory performance is better: 1) when character arrangements have fewer alternations between characters of different categories; 2) when character arrangements have a lower letter:digit ratio, that is, consist of fewer letters and more digits; and 3) when character arrangements consist of groups of equal sizes, except in cases when the letter:digit ratio is low, in which case it does not seem to matter whether groups have equal sizes. It has been shown that objective measures of memorability correlate highly with subjective measures, confirming the validity of the measures. This is not to say that, in the future, researchers can do away with objective measures and use subjective measures instead. In some cases, for instance, with the types AB-CD-EF and A12-BCD, relatively large discrepancies occurred between subjective and objective measures. If the difference among the various alternative character arrangements is small,

Table 3. *Comparison of objective and subjective indications of memorability*

Character arrangement	Objective rank*	Subjective rank*	Average number of errors**	Number judgements easy minus difficult**
12-ABC-3	1	2	0.82	18
AB-12-CD	2	–	0.92	–
ABC-123	3	1	0.94	37
AB-CD-12	4	–	1.03	–
12-AB-CD	5	–	1.06	–
A12-BCD	6	6	1.19	4
A-12-BCD	7	4	1.44	7
ABC-DEF	8	5	1.67	6
ABC-1DE	9	8	1.68	–3
AB-CD-EF	10	3	1.75	11
ABC-1-DE	11	7	1.80	–1
A1-B2-C3	12	10	1.96	–9
ABC-D-EF	13	11	2.20	–13
A1-BC-2D	14	9	2.27	–3
A1-BC2-D	15	12	2.31	–24
A1B-C2D	16	13	2.44	–31

Existing designs of type AB-12-CD, AB-CD-12, and 12-AB-CD were not included in the subjective judgements.
*Spearman's *rho*: $r_s = 0.90$, $p < 0.001$.
**Pearson's *rho*: $r_p = 0.95$, $p < 0.001$.

in terms of mean number of errors, and the ergonomics practitioner needs to be accurate, the best measure is still the objective one.

In comparing the degree to which each factor influences memory performance it can be concluded that the number of alternations between characters of different categories affects memory performance the most. The letter:digit ratio and equality of group size affect memory performance to a lesser degree and do not seem to differ in the degree to which they contribute to memory performance. As has already been stated, the primary function of licence plates is to display the information necessary for fast and accurate identification of automobiles. When designing character arrangements for licence plates for memorability it seems to be most important to avoid alternations between characters from different categories within the spatially separated groups. Given that the set size for the letters for any given position is much larger than for numbers, one might have expected *a priori* the letter:digit ratio to be a more important factor. If this had been the case, then all six-letter combinations would have been the worst to recall. This was clearly not the case, as can be seen in table 3. In fact, the three arrangements that were the most difficult to recall all contained a large number of alternations between letters and digits, with no more than four letters.

The results of the current study may have a wider applicability than licence plates. Postal or zip codes would be one obvious example that comes to mind. Codes with a large number of alternations between letters and digits, such as in the Canadian system (A1B 2C3) or to lesser extent in the British system (AB1 2CD), are less optimal, from a memorability point of view, than the Dutch system (1234 AB) (Ten Hoopen 1978).

Given the findings above, the customer, the Centre for Transport Technology and Information in The Netherlands, has been advised, given the constraints of the current physical layout of Dutch licence plates, that licence plates of the type 12-ABC-3 or 123-ABC would be optimal from a memorability point of view (AB-12-CD and AB-CD-12 also yielded very few errors but had to be excluded as these are the types that are currently in use and need to be replaced). Based on these recommendations, the Centre has selected the type 12-ABC-3 as the future character arrangement for Dutch vehicles.

REFERENCES

ALDRICH, M. H., 1937, PERCEPTION AND VISIBILITY OF AUTOMOBILE LICENCE PLATES. *HIGHWAY RESEARCH BOARD PROCEEDINGS*, 17, 393–412.

BIEGEL, R. A., 1938, REPORT CONCERNING AN INVESTIGATION ON COLOUR COMBINATIONS AND ARRANGEMENT OF LICENSE PLATES (IN DUTCH: RAPPORT BETREFFENDE EEN ONDERZOEK OVER KLEURENCOMBINATIES EN INDEELING VAN NUMMERBORDEN). *WEGEN*, 14, 1–19.

BRENER, R., 1940, AN EXPERIMENTAL INVESTIGATION OF MEMORY SPAN. *JOURNAL OF EXPERIMENTAL PSYCHOLOGY*, 26, 467–482.

BROADBENT, D. E., AND GREGORY, M., 1964, STIMULUS SET AND RESPONSE SET: THE ALTERNATION OF ATTENTION. *QUARTERLY JOURNAL OF EXPERIMENTAL PSYCHOLOGY*, 16, 307–317.

CRANNELL, C. W. AND PARRISH, J. M., 1957, A COMPARISON OF IMMEDIATE MEMORY SPAN FOR DIGITS, LETTERS, AND WORDS. *JOURNAL OF PSYCHOLOGY*, 44, 319–327.

HULL, A. J., 1976, HUMAN PERFORMANCE WITH HOMOGENEOUS, PATTERNED, AND RANDOM ALPHANUMERIC DISPLAYS. *ERGONOMICS*, 6, 741–750.

KAHNEMAN, D., AND HENIK, A., 1977, EFFECTS OF VISUAL GROUPING ON IMMEDIATE RECALL AND SELECTIVE ATTENTION. IN *ATTENTION AND PERFORMANCE VI*, S. DORNIČ (ED.), PP. 307–332 (HILLSDALE, NJ: LAWRENCE ERLBAUM ASSOCIATES).

KARMEIER, D. F., HERRINGTON, C. G., AND BAERWALD, J.E., 1960, A COMPREHENSIVE ANALYSIS OF MOTOR VEHICLE LICENSE PLATES. IN *HIGHWAY RESEARCH BOARD, PROCEEDINGS OF THE THIRTY-NINTH ANNUAL MEETING*, NAS-NRC PUBLICATIONS 773, 39, H.P. ORLAND (ED.), (WASHINGTON, DC: NATIONAL ACADEMY OF SCIENCES) PP. 416–440.

KLEMMER, E. T., AND STOCKER, L.P., 1974, EFFECTS OF GROUPING OF PRINTED DIGITS ON FORCED-PACED MANUAL ENTRY PERFORMANCE. *JOURNAL OF APPLIED PSYCHOLOGY*, 59, 675–678.

MILLER, G. A., 1956, THE MAGICAL NUMBER SEVEN, PLUS OR MINUS TWO: SOME LIMITS ON OUR CAPACITY FOR PROCESSING INFORMATION. *PSYCHOLOGICAL REVIEW*, 63, 81–96.

MURDOCK, B. B., 1974, *HUMAN MEMORY: THEORY AND DATA*. (NEW YORK: LAWRENCE ERLBAUM).

SANDERS, A. F., AND SCHROOTS, J. J. F., 1968A, COGNITIVE CATEGORIES AND MEMORY SPAN: SHIFTING BETWEEN CATEGORIES. *QUARTERLY JOURNAL OF EXPERIMENTAL PSYCHOLOGY*, 4, 370–372.

SANDERS, A. F., AND SCHROOTS, J. J. F., 1968B, COGNITIVE CATEGORIES AND MEMORY SPAN: THE EFFECT OF TEMPORAL vs. categorical recall. *Quarterly Journal of Experimental Psychology*, 4, 373–379.

Severin, F. T., and Rigby, M. K., 1963, Influence of digit grouping on memory for telephone numbers. *Journal of Applied Psychology*, 47, 117–119.

Ten Hoopen, G., 1978, To remember: postal codes (in Dutch: Om te onthouden: postcodes). In *Proeven op de Som: Psychonomie in het Dagelijks Leven*, W.A. Wagenaar, P. A. Vroon, and W. H. Janssen (Eds.), pp. 26–32 (Deventer: van Loghum Slaterus B.V.).

Thorpe, C. E., and Rowland, G. E., 1965, The effect of "natural" grouping of numerals on short term memory. *Human Factors*, 7, 38–44.

CPSIA information can be obtained at www.ICGtesting.com
Printed in the USA
LVOW09s2109190815

450643LV00012B/55/P